THE ∞ INFINITY WATCH

WRITER:
Jim Starlin

PENCILERS:
Angel Medina, Rick Leonardi, Tom Raney & Tom Grindberg
with **Steve Carr** & **Deryl Skelton**

INKERS:
Terry Austin, Bob Almond & Keith Williams

COLORISTS:
Ian Laughlin
with **Renée Witterstaetter**

LETTERERS:
Jack Morelli, Janice Chiang, Ken Lopez & Jon Babcock

ASSISTANT EDITORS:
John Lewandowski & Lynaire Brust

EDITOR:
Craig Anderson

FRONT COVER ARTISTS: Angel Medina, **Terry Austin** & **Tom Smith**
BACK COVER ARTISTS: Tom Raney & **Terry Austin**

COLLECTION EDITOR: Mark D. Beazley
ASSOCIATE EDITOR: Sarah Brunstad
ASSOCIATE MANAGER, DIGITAL ASSETS: Joe Hochstein
ASSOCIATE MANAGING EDITOR: Alex Starbuck
EDITOR, SPECIAL PROJECTS: Jennifer Grünwald
VP, PRODUCTION & SPECIAL PROJECTS: Jeff Youngquist
RESEARCH: Mike Hansen & Jeph York
LAYOUT: Jeph York
PRODUCTION: Jerron Quality Color,
ColorTek & Joe Frontirre
BOOK DESIGNER: Jay Bowen

SVP PRINT, SALES & MARKETING: David Gabriel
EDITOR IN CHIEF: Axel Alonso
CHIEF CREATIVE OFFICER: Joe Quesada
PUBLISHER: Dan Buckley
EXECUTIVE PRODUCER: Alan Fine

INFINITY WATCH VOL. 1. Contains material originally published in magazine form as WARLOCK AND THE INFINITY WATCH #1-22. First printing 2016. ISBN# 978-0-7851-9527-6. Published by MARVEL WORLDWIDE, INC., a subsidiary of MARVEL ENTERTAINMENT, LLC. OFFICE OF PUBLICATION: 135 West 50th Street, New York, NY 10020. Copyright © 2016 MARVEL No similarity between any of the names, characters, persons, and/or institutions in this magazine with those of any living or dead person or institution is intended, and any such similarity which may exist is purely coincidental. Printed in the U.S.A. ALAN FINE, President, Marvel Entertainment; DAN BUCKLEY, President, TV, Publishing & Brand Management; JOE QUESADA, Chief Creative Officer; TOM BREVOORT, SVP of Publishing; DAVID BOGART, SVP of Business Affairs & Operations, Publishing & Partnership; C.B. CEBULSKI, VP of Brand Management & Development, Asia; DAVID GABRIEL, SVP of Sales & Marketing, Publishing; JEFF YOUNGQUIST, VP of Production & Special Projects; DAN CARR, Executive Director of Publishing Technology; ALEX MORALES, Director of Publishing Operations; SUSAN CRESPI, Production Manager; STAN LEE, Chairman Emeritus. For information regarding advertising in Marvel Comics or on Marvel.com, please contact Vit DeBellis, Integrated Sales Manager, at vdebellis@marvel.com. For Marvel subscription inquiries, please call 888-511-5480. Manufactured between 2/3/2016 and 3/7/2016 by R.R. DONNELLEY, INC., SALEM, VA, USA.
10 9 8 7 6 5 4 3 2 1

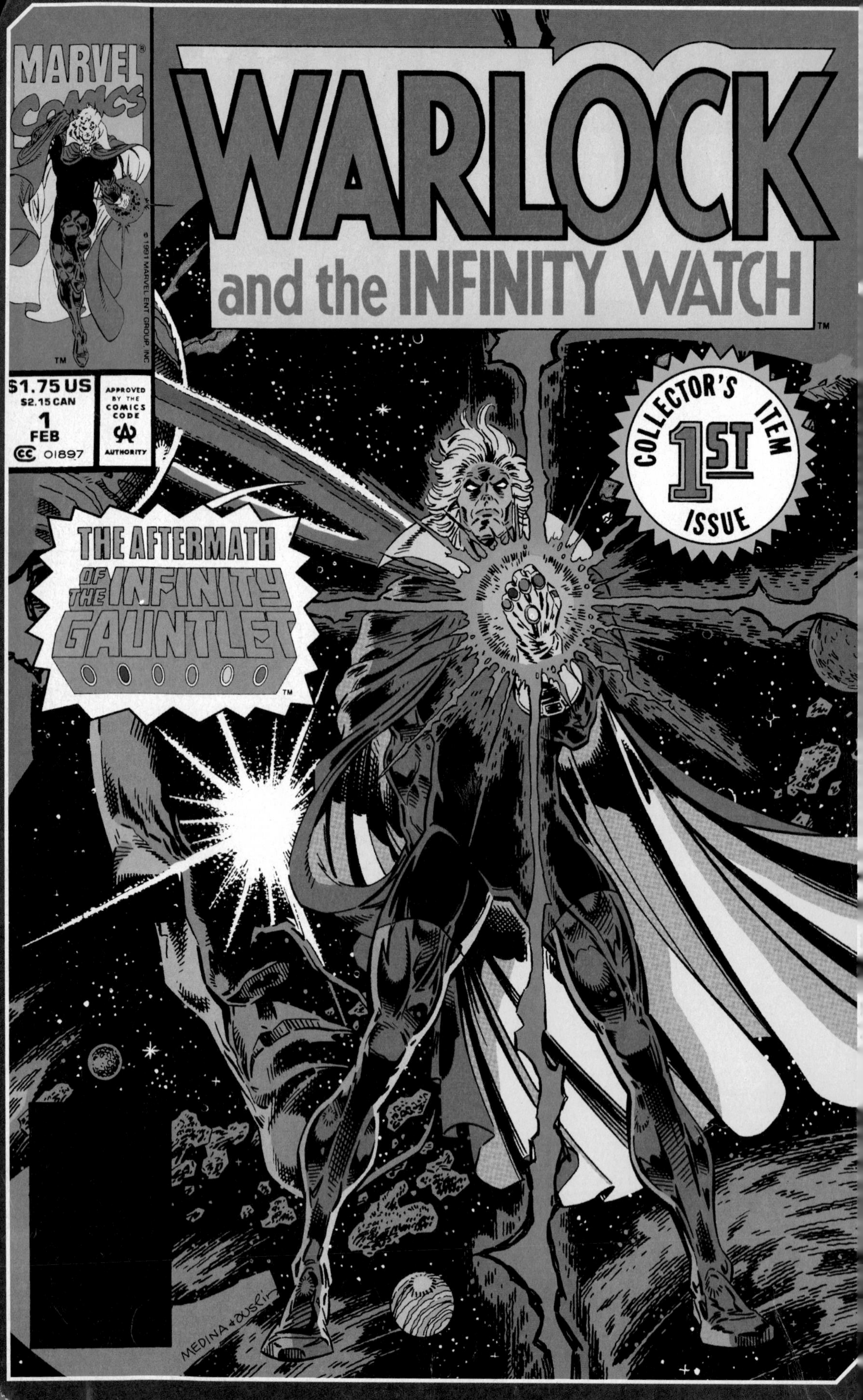

MARVEL COMICS
WARLOCK
and the INFINITY WATCH
© 1991 MARVEL ENT. GROUP, INC.
$1.75 US
$2.15 CAN
1
FEB
01897
APPROVED BY THE COMICS CODE AUTHORITY
COLLECTOR'S ITEM
1ST
ISSUE
THE AFTERMATH OF THE INFINITY GAUNTLET

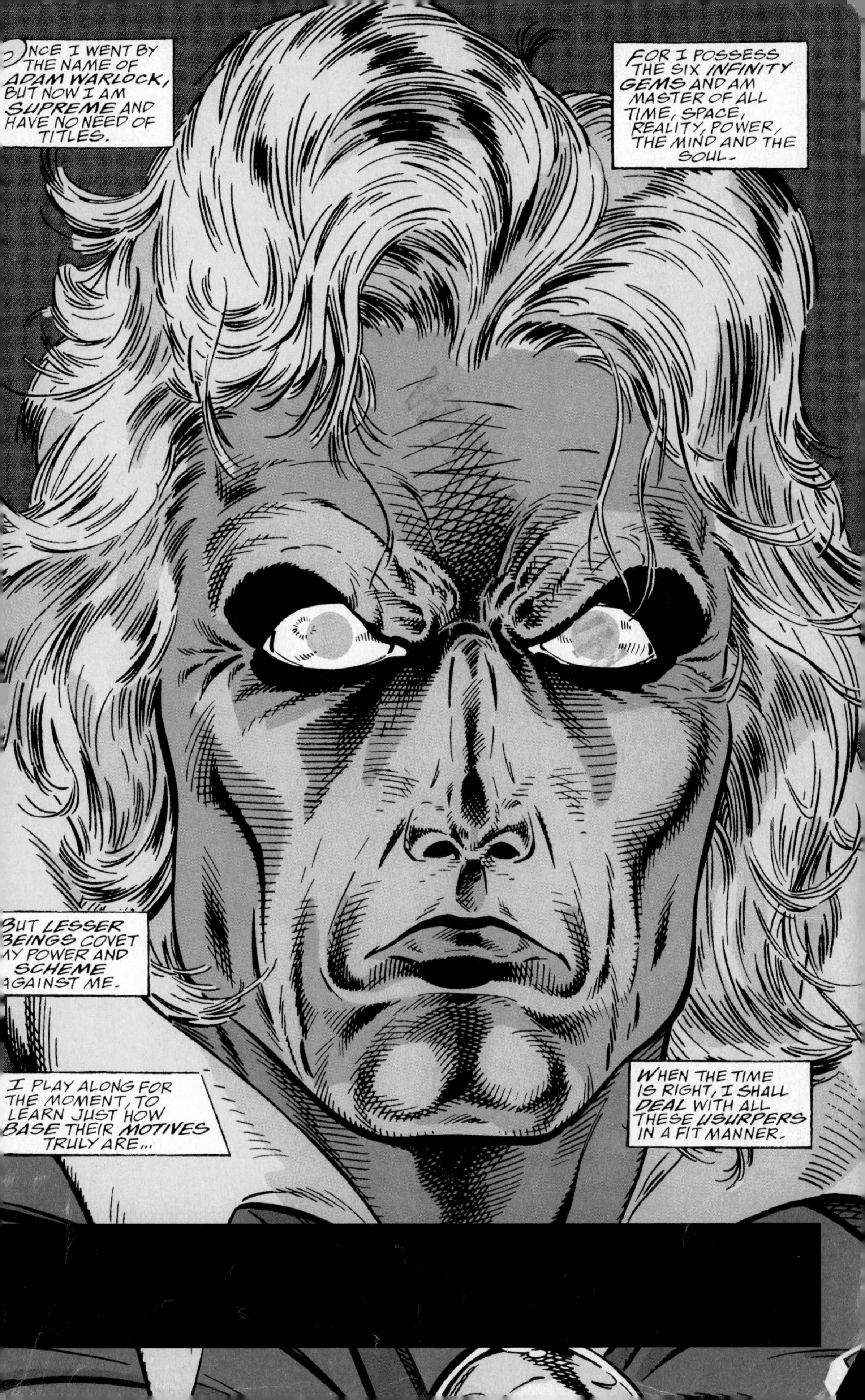
ONCE I WENT BY THE NAME OF ADAM WARLOCK, BUT NOW I AM SUPREME AND HAVE NO NEED OF TITLES.
FOR I POSSESS THE SIX INFINITY GEMS AND AM MASTER OF ALL TIME, SPACE, REALITY, POWER, THE MIND AND THE SOUL.
BUT LESSER BEINGS COVET MY POWER AND SCHEME AGAINST ME.
I PLAY ALONG FOR THE MOMENT, TO LEARN JUST HOW BASE THEIR MOTIVES TRULY ARE...
WHEN THE TIME IS RIGHT, I SHALL DEAL WITH ALL THESE USURPERS IN A FIT MANNER.
[redacted]

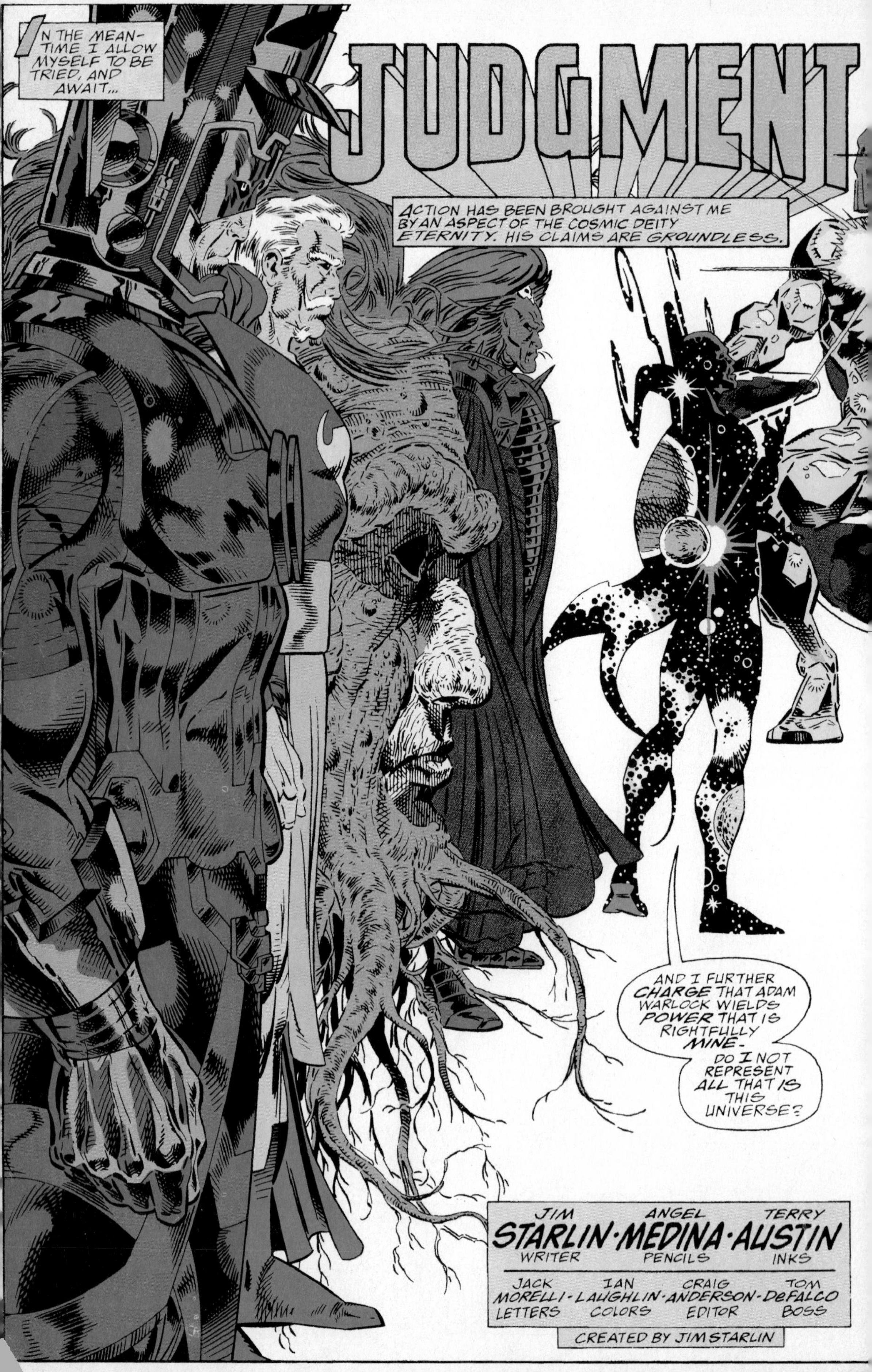
In the mean-time I allow myself to be tried, and await...
JUDGMENT
ACTION HAS BEEN BROUGHT AGAINST ME BY AN ASPECT OF THE COSMIC DEITY ETERNITY. HIS CLAIMS ARE GROUNDLESS.
AND I FURTHER CHARGE THAT ADAM WARLOCK WIELDS POWER THAT IS RIGHTFULLY MINE-
DO I NOT REPRESENT ALL THAT IS THIS UNIVERSE?
JIM STARLIN · ANGEL MEDINA · TERRY AUSTIN
WRITER PENCILS INKS
JACK MORELLI - IAN LAUGHLIN - CRAIG ANDERSON - TOM DeFALCO
LETTERS COLORS EDITOR BOSS
CREATED BY JIM STARLIN

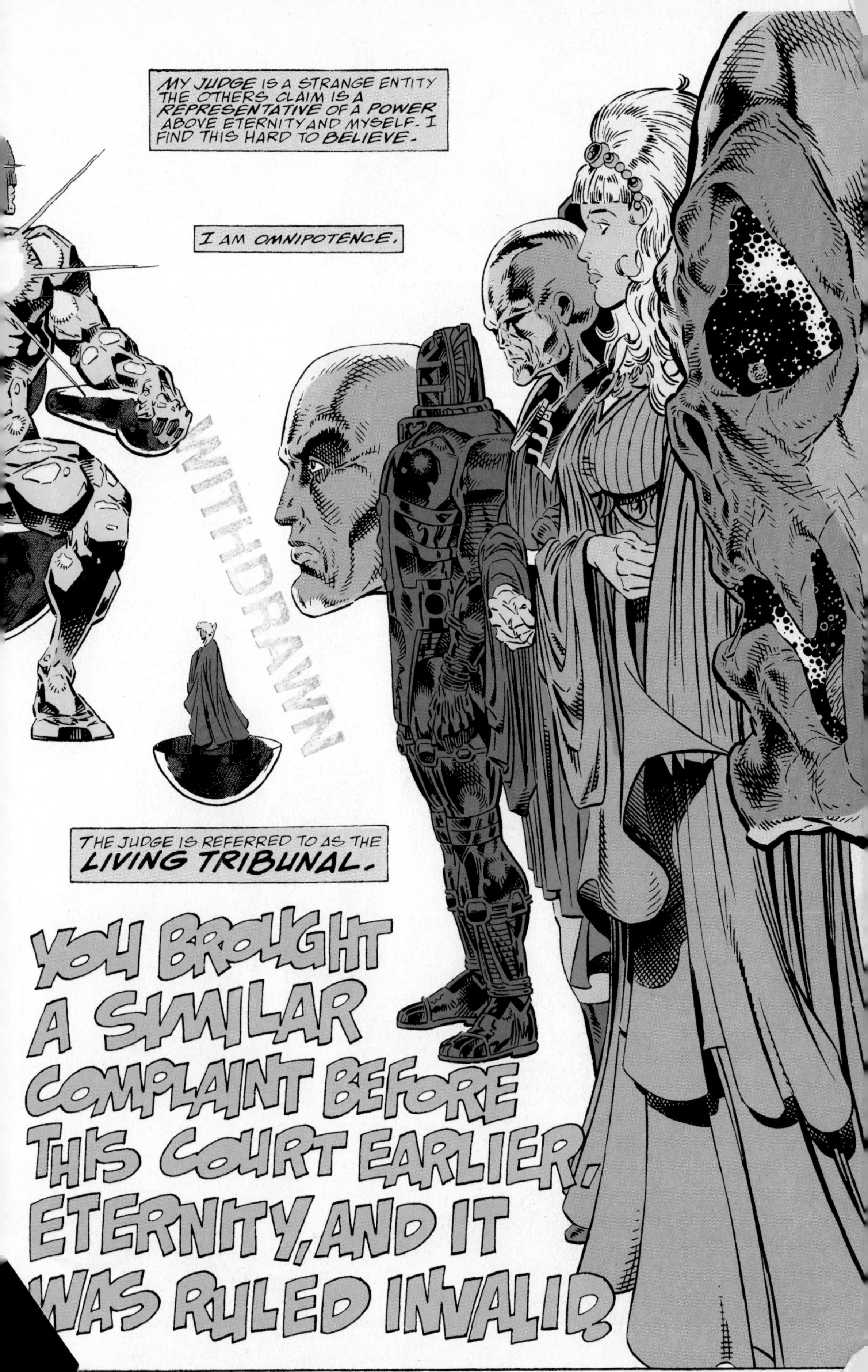
MY JUDGE IS A STRANGE ENTITY THE OTHERS CLAIM IS A REPRESENTATIVE OF A POWER ABOVE ETERNITY AND MYSELF. I FIND THIS HARD TO BELIEVE.
I AM OMNIPOTENCE.
THE JUDGE IS REFERRED TO AS THE LIVING TRIBUNAL.
YOU BROUGHT A SIMILAR COMPLAINT BEFORE THIS COURT EARLIER, ETERNITY, AND IT WAS RULED INVALID.

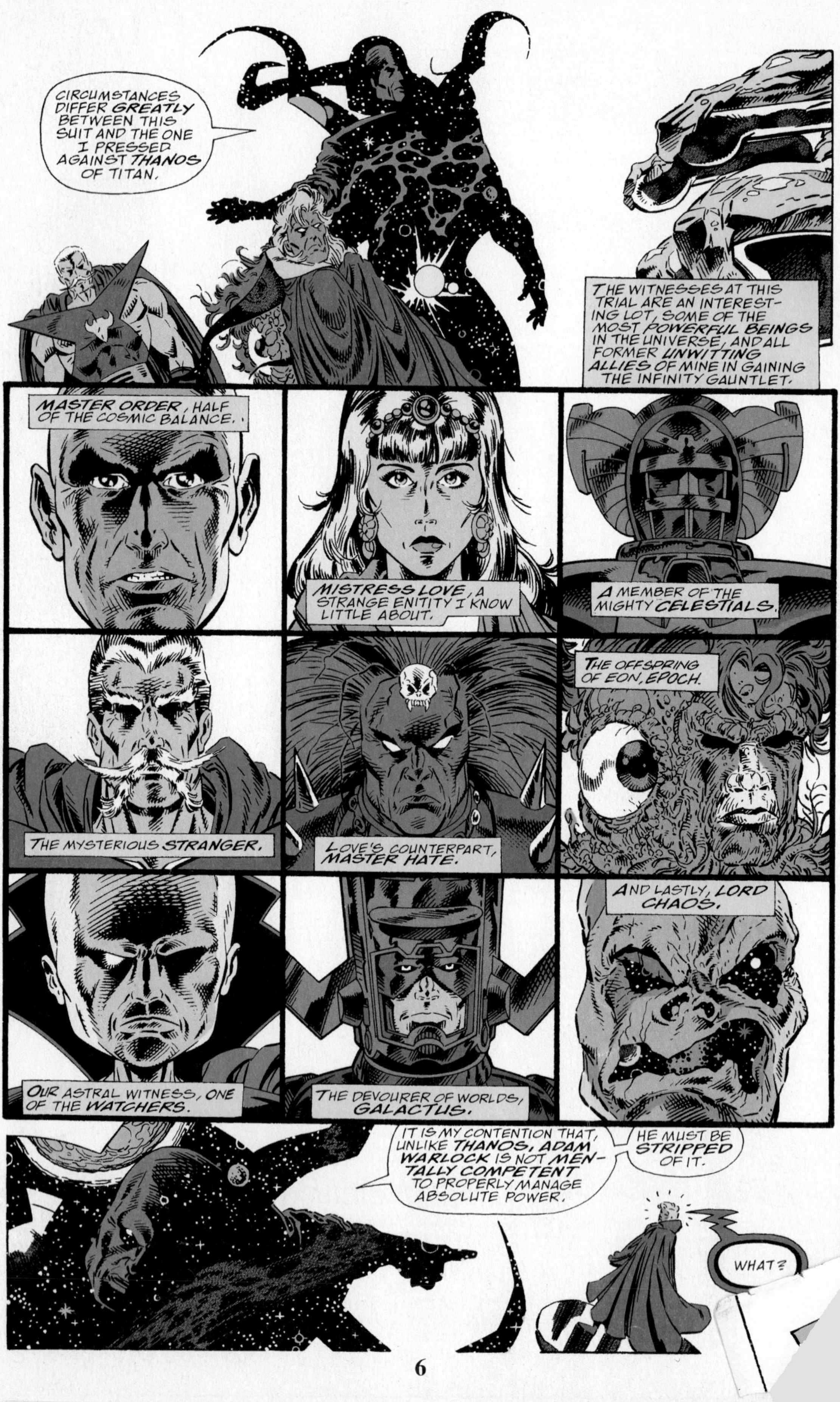

CIRCUMSTANCES DIFFER GREATLY BETWEEN THIS SUIT AND THE ONE I PRESSED AGAINST THANOS OF TITAN.
THE WITNESSES AT THIS TRIAL ARE AN INTERESTING LOT, SOME OF THE MOST POWERFUL BEINGS IN THE UNIVERSE, AND ALL FORMER UNWITTING ALLIES OF MINE IN GAINING THE INFINITY GAUNTLET.
MASTER ORDER, HALF OF THE COSMIC BALANCE.
MISTRESS LOVE, A STRANGE ENITITY I KNOW LITTLE ABOUT.
A MEMBER OF THE MIGHTY CELESTIALS.
THE MYSTERIOUS STRANGER.
LOVE'S COUNTERPART, MASTER HATE.
THE OFFSPRING OF EON, EPOCH.
OUR ASTRAL WITNESS, ONE OF THE WATCHERS.
THE DEVOURER OF WORLDS, GALACTUS.
AND LASTLY, LORD CHAOS.
IT IS MY CONTENTION THAT, UNLIKE THANOS, ADAM WARLOCK IS NOT MENTALLY COMPETENT TO PROPERLY MANAGE ABSOLUTE POWER.
HE MUST BE STRIPPED OF IT.
WHAT?

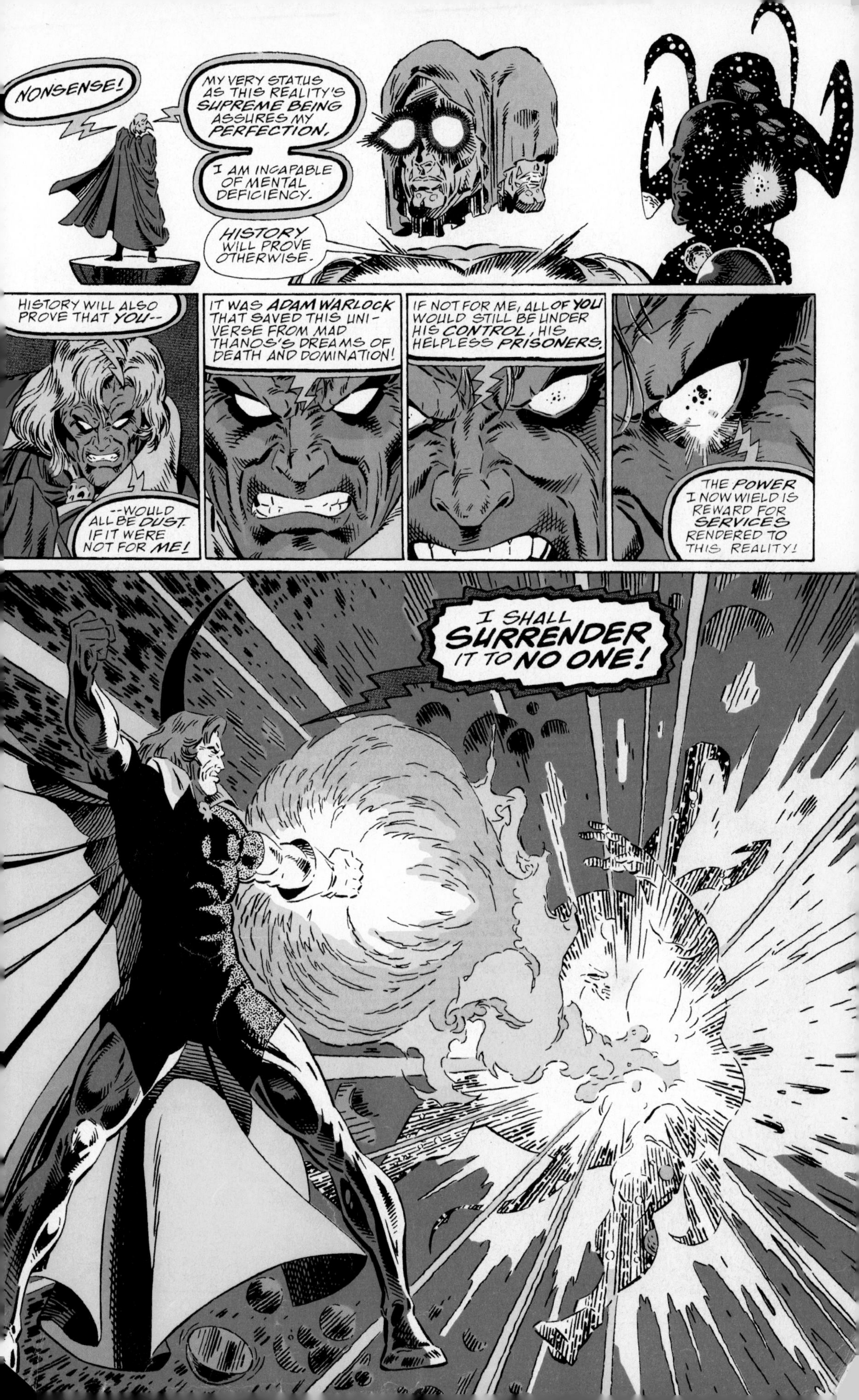
NONSENSE!
MY VERY STATUS AS THIS REALITY'S SUPREME BEING ASSURES MY PERFECTION.
I AM INCAPABLE OF MENTAL DEFICIENCY.
HISTORY WILL PROVE OTHERWISE.
HISTORY WILL ALSO PROVE THAT YOU--
--WOULD ALL BE DUST. IF IT WERE NOT FOR ME!
IT WAS ADAM WARLOCK THAT SAVED THIS UNI-VERSE FROM MAD THANOS'S DREAMS OF DEATH AND DOMINATION!
IF NOT FOR ME, ALL OF YOU WOULD STILL BE UNDER HIS CONTROL, HIS HELPLESS PRISONERS.
THE POWER I NOW WIELD IS REWARD FOR SERVICES RENDERED TO THIS REALITY!
I SHALL SURRENDER IT TO NO ONE!

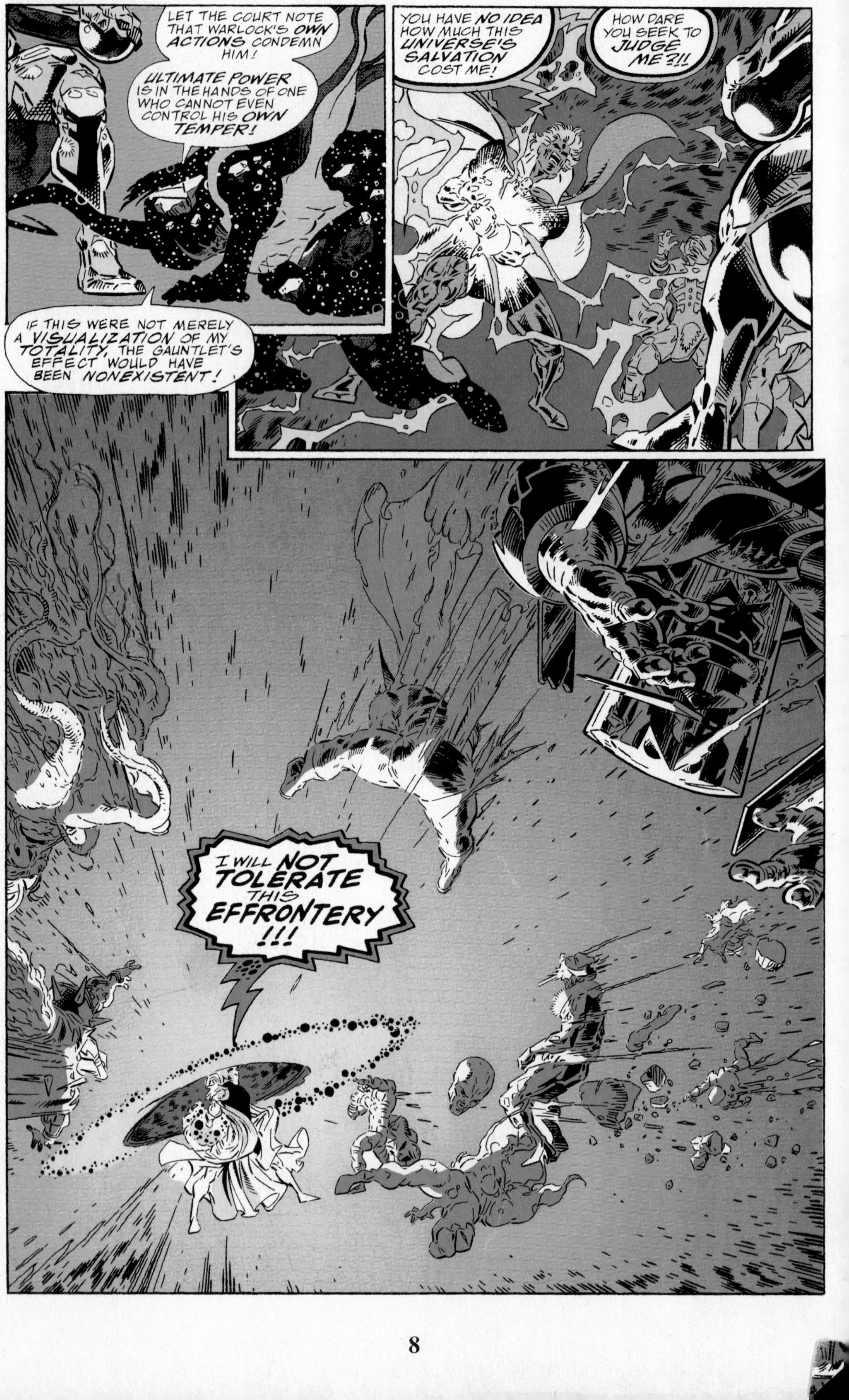
LET THE COURT NOTE THAT WARLOCK'S OWN ACTIONS CONDEMN HIM!
ULTIMATE POWER IS IN THE HANDS OF ONE WHO CANNOT EVEN CONTROL HIS OWN TEMPER!
IF THIS WERE NOT MERELY A VISUALIZATION OF MY TOTALITY, THE GAUNTLET'S EFFECT WOULD HAVE BEEN NONEXISTENT!
YOU HAVE NO IDEA HOW MUCH THIS UNIVERSE'S SALVATION COST ME!
HOW DARE YOU SEEK TO JUDGE ME?!!
I WILL NOT TOLERATE THIS EFFRONTERY!!!

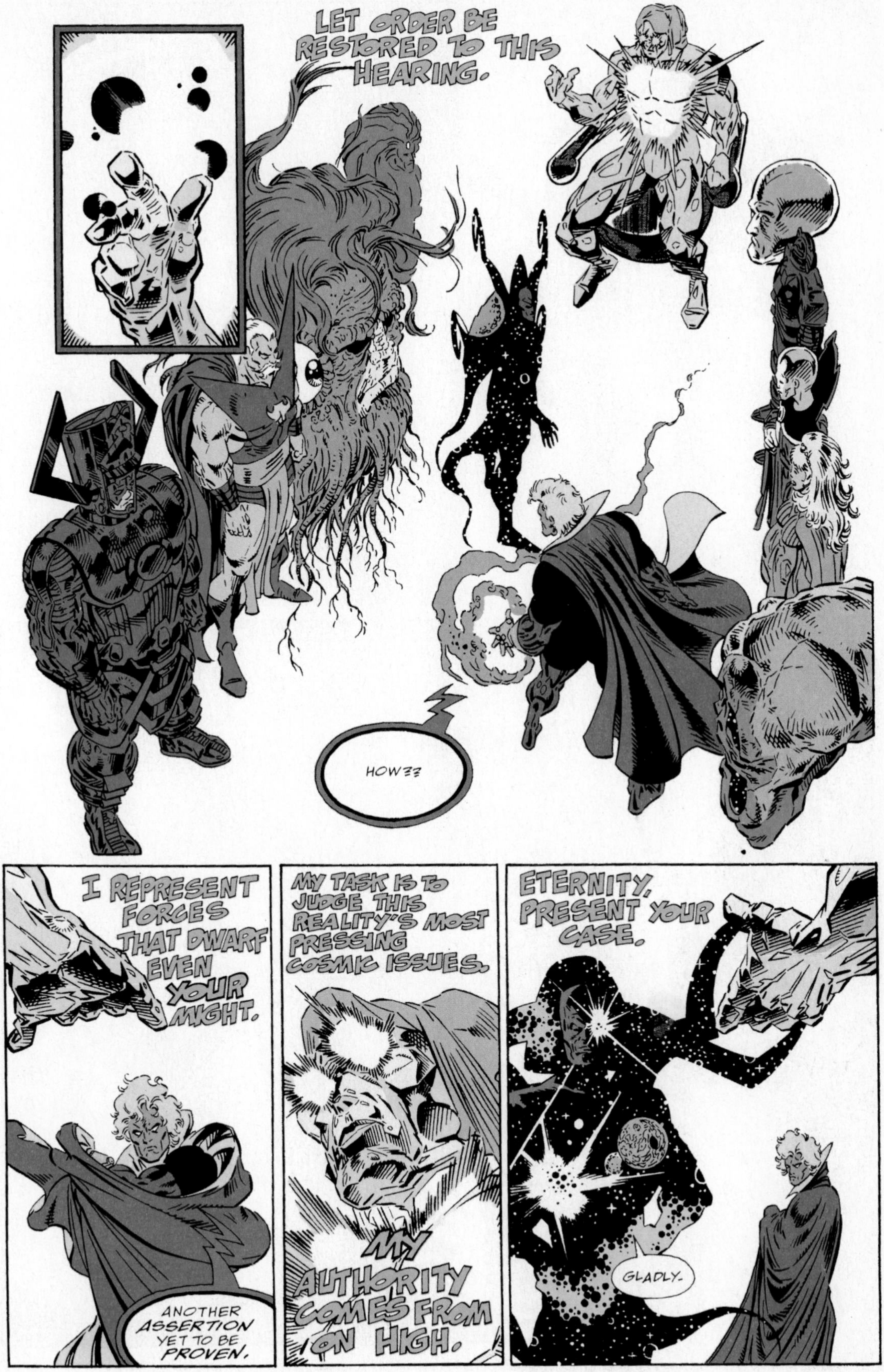
LET ORDER BE RESTORED TO THIS HEARING.
HOW??
I REPRESENT FORCES THAT DWARF EVEN YOUR MIGHT.
ANOTHER ASSERTION YET TO BE PROVEN.
MY TASK IS TO JUDGE THIS REALITY'S MOST PRESSING COSMIC ISSUES.
MY AUTHORITY COMES FROM ON HIGH.
ETERNITY, PRESENT YOUR CASE.
GLADLY.

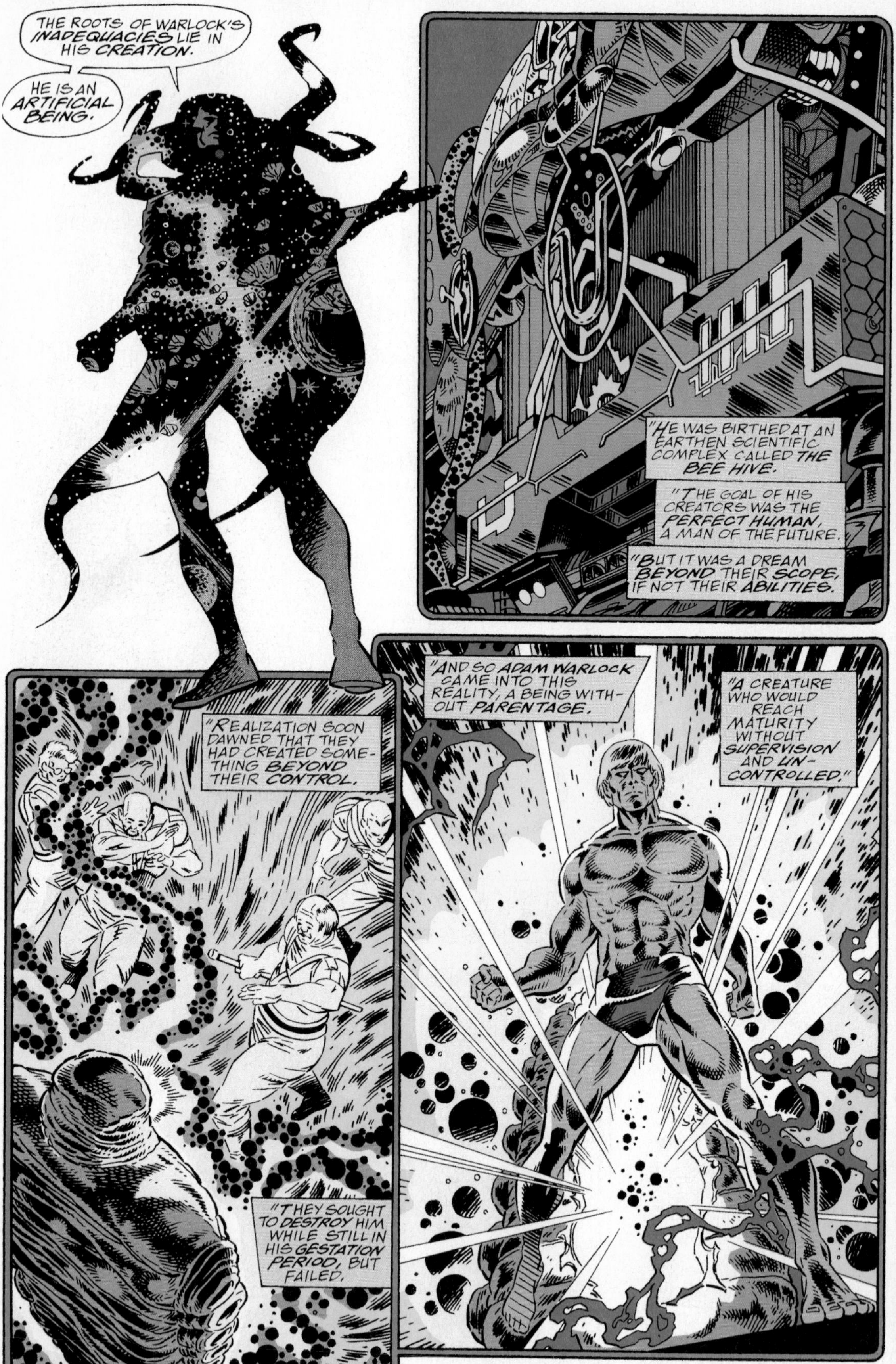
THE ROOTS OF WARLOCK'S INADEQUACIES LIE IN HIS CREATION.
HE IS AN ARTIFICIAL BEING.
"HE WAS BIRTHED AT AN EARTHEN SCIENTIFIC COMPLEX CALLED THE BEE HIVE.
"THE GOAL OF HIS CREATORS WAS THE PERFECT HUMAN, A MAN OF THE FUTURE.
"BUT IT WAS A DREAM BEYOND THEIR SCOPE, IF NOT THEIR ABILITIES.
"REALIZATION SOON DAWNED THAT THEY HAD CREATED SOMETHING BEYOND THEIR CONTROL.
"THEY SOUGHT TO DESTROY HIM WHILE STILL IN HIS GESTATION PERIOD, BUT FAILED.
"AND SO ADAM WARLOCK CAME INTO THIS REALITY, A BEING WITHOUT PARENTAGE.
"A CREATURE WHO WOULD REACH MATURITY WITHOUT SUPERVISION AND UNCONTROLLED."

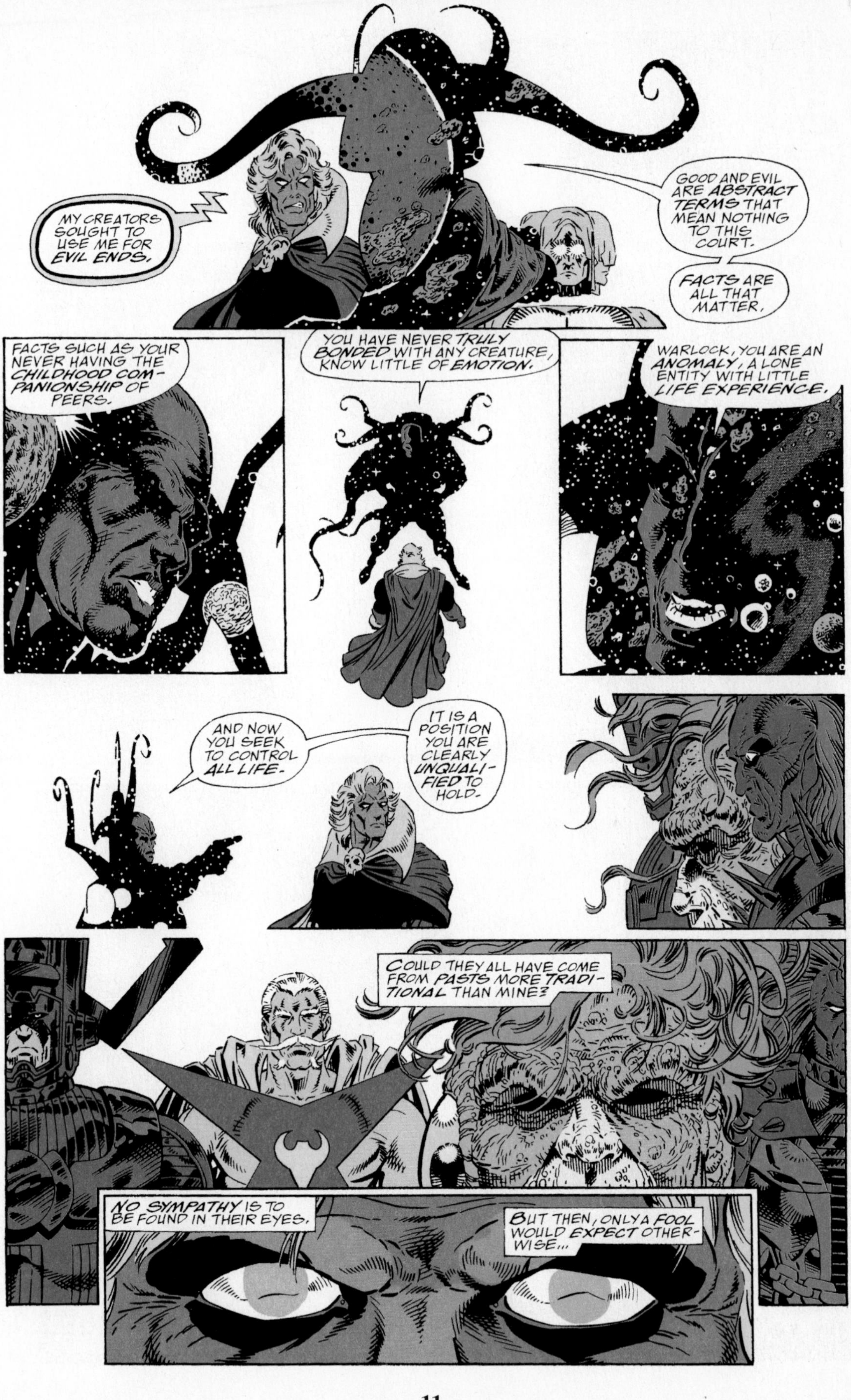
MY CREATORS SOUGHT TO USE ME FOR EVIL ENDS.
GOOD AND EVIL ARE ABSTRACT TERMS THAT MEAN NOTHING TO THIS COURT.
FACTS ARE ALL THAT MATTER.
FACTS SUCH AS YOUR NEVER HAVING THE CHILDHOOD COMPANIONSHIP OF PEERS.
YOU HAVE NEVER TRULY BONDED WITH ANY CREATURE, KNOW LITTLE OF EMOTION.
WARLOCK, YOU ARE AN ANOMALY, A LONE ENTITY WITH LITTLE LIFE EXPERIENCE.
AND NOW YOU SEEK TO CONTROL ALL LIFE.
IT IS A POSITION YOU ARE CLEARLY UNQUALIFIED TO HOLD.
COULD THEY ALL HAVE COME FROM PASTS MORE TRADITIONAL THAN MINE?
NO SYMPATHY IS TO BE FOUND IN THEIR EYES.
BUT THEN, ONLY A FOOL WOULD EXPECT OTHERWISE...

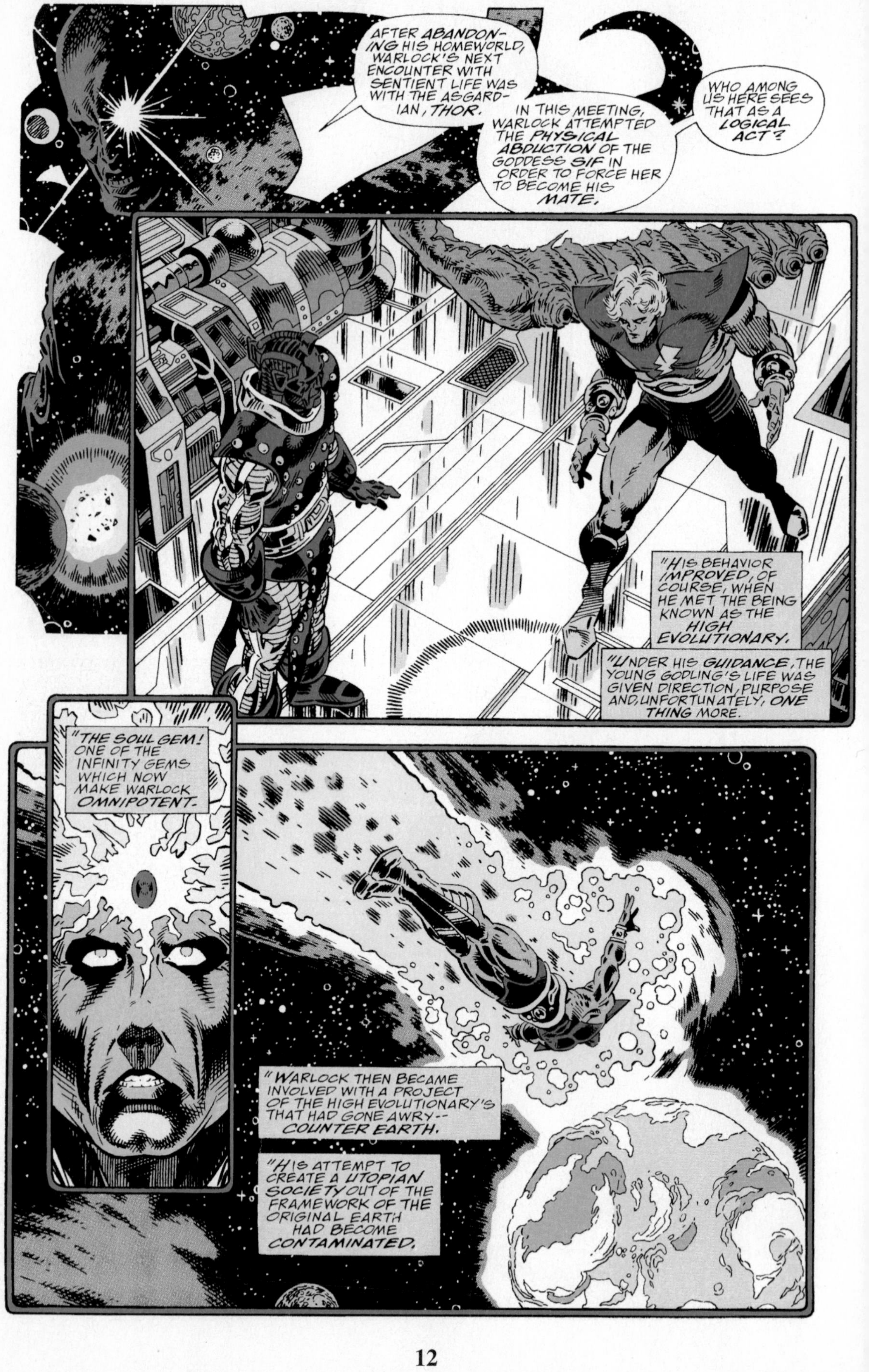
AFTER ABANDONING HIS HOMEWORLD, WARLOCK'S NEXT ENCOUNTER WITH SENTIENT LIFE WAS WITH THE ASGARDIAN, THOR.
IN THIS MEETING, WARLOCK ATTEMPTED THE PHYSICAL ABDUCTION OF THE GODDESS SIF IN ORDER TO FORCE HER TO BECOME HIS MATE.
WHO AMONG US HERE SEES THAT AS A LOGICAL ACT?
"HIS BEHAVIOR IMPROVED, OF COURSE, WHEN HE MET THE BEING KNOWN AS THE HIGH EVOLUTIONARY.
"UNDER HIS GUIDANCE, THE YOUNG GODLING'S LIFE WAS GIVEN DIRECTION, PURPOSE AND, UNFORTUNATELY, ONE THING MORE.
"THE SOUL GEM! ONE OF THE INFINITY GEMS WHICH NOW MAKE WARLOCK OMNIPOTENT.
"WARLOCK THEN BECAME INVOLVED WITH A PROJECT OF THE HIGH EVOLUTIONARY'S THAT HAD GONE AWRY-- COUNTER EARTH.
"HIS ATTEMPT TO CREATE A UTOPIAN SOCIETY OUT OF THE FRAMEWORK OF THE ORIGINAL EARTH HAD BECOME CONTAMINATED.

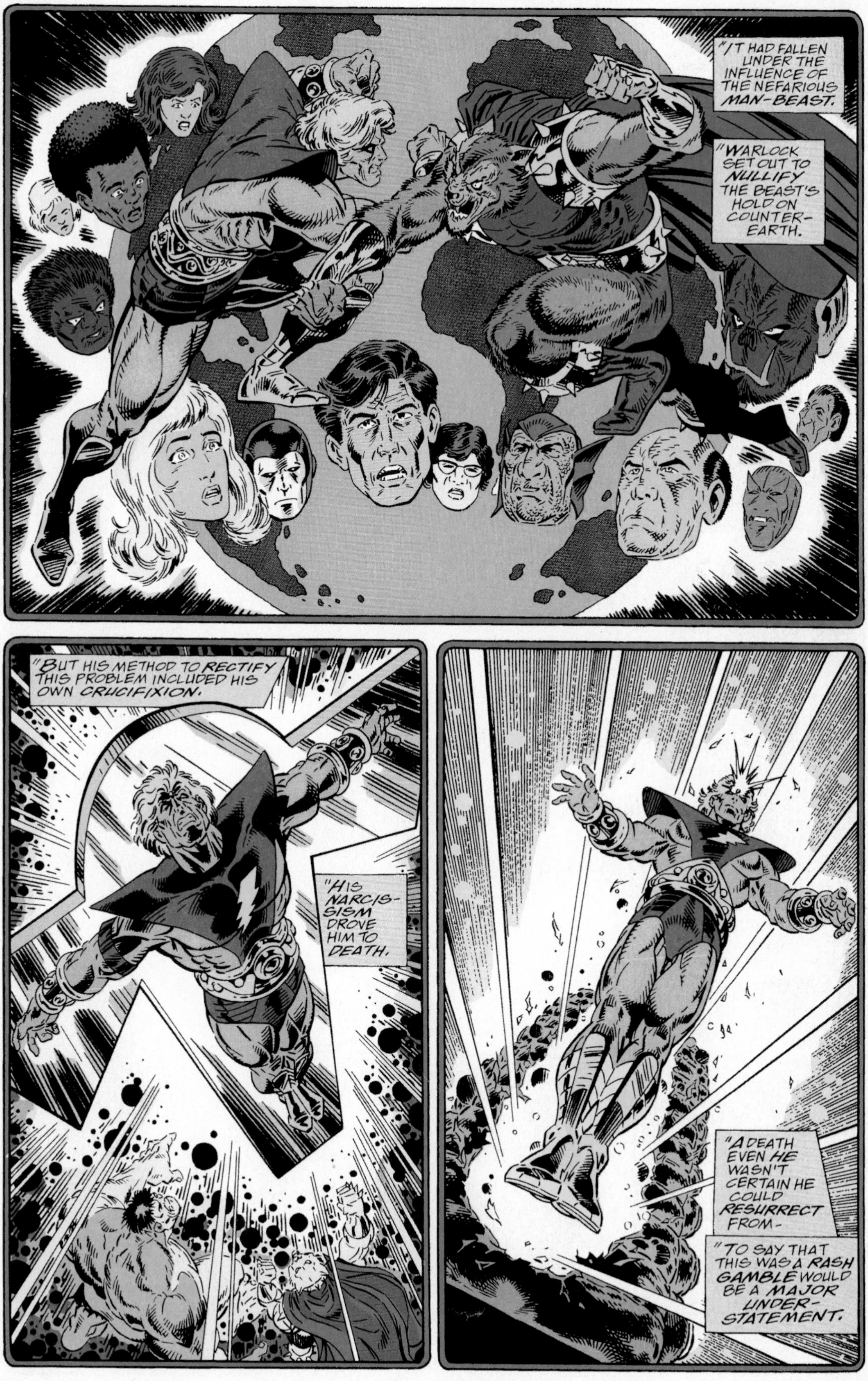
"IT HAD FALLEN UNDER THE INFLUENCE OF THE NEFARIOUS MAN-BEAST.
"WARLOCK SET OUT TO NULLIFY THE BEAST'S HOLD ON COUNTER-EARTH.
"BUT HIS METHOD TO RECTIFY THIS PROBLEM INCLUDED HIS OWN CRUCIFIXION.
"HIS NARCISSISM DROVE HIM TO DEATH.
"A DEATH EVEN HE WASN'T CERTAIN HE COULD RESURRECT FROM--
"TO SAY THAT THIS WAS A RASH GAMBLE WOULD BE A MAJOR UNDER-STATEMENT.

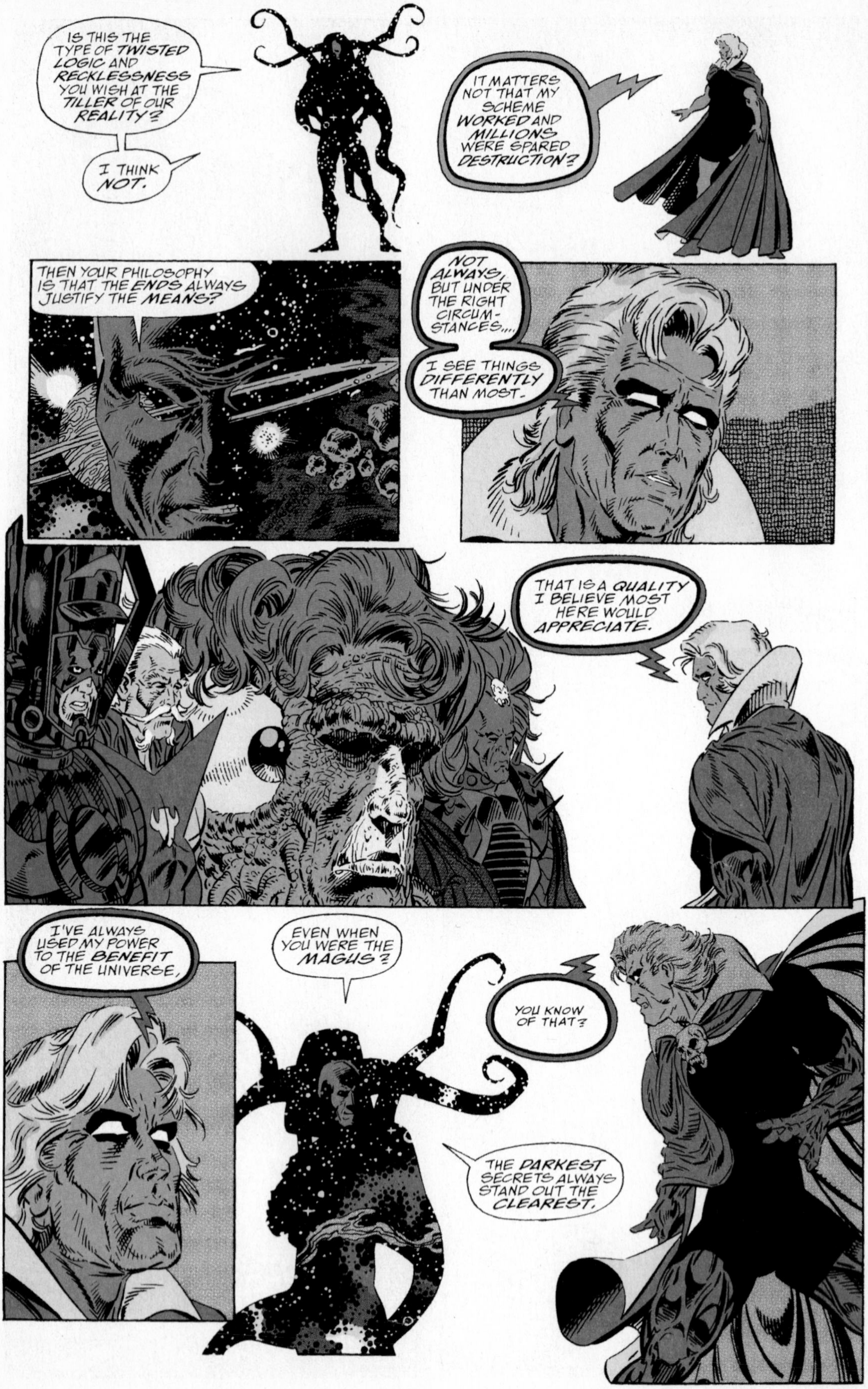
IS THIS THE TYPE OF TWISTED LOGIC AND RECKLESSNESS YOU WISH AT THE TILLER OF OUR REALITY?
I THINK NOT.
IT MATTERS NOT THAT MY SCHEME WORKED AND MILLIONS WERE SPARED DESTRUCTION?
THEN YOUR PHILOSOPHY IS THAT THE ENDS ALWAYS JUSTIFY THE MEANS?
NOT ALWAYS, BUT UNDER THE RIGHT CIRCUM-STANCES....
I SEE THINGS DIFFERENTLY THAN MOST.
THAT IS A QUALITY I BELIEVE MOST HERE WOULD APPRECIATE.
I'VE ALWAYS USED MY POWER TO THE BENEFIT OF THE UNIVERSE.
EVEN WHEN YOU WERE THE MAGUS?
YOU KNOW OF THAT?
THE DARKEST SECRETS ALWAYS STAND OUT THE CLEAREST.

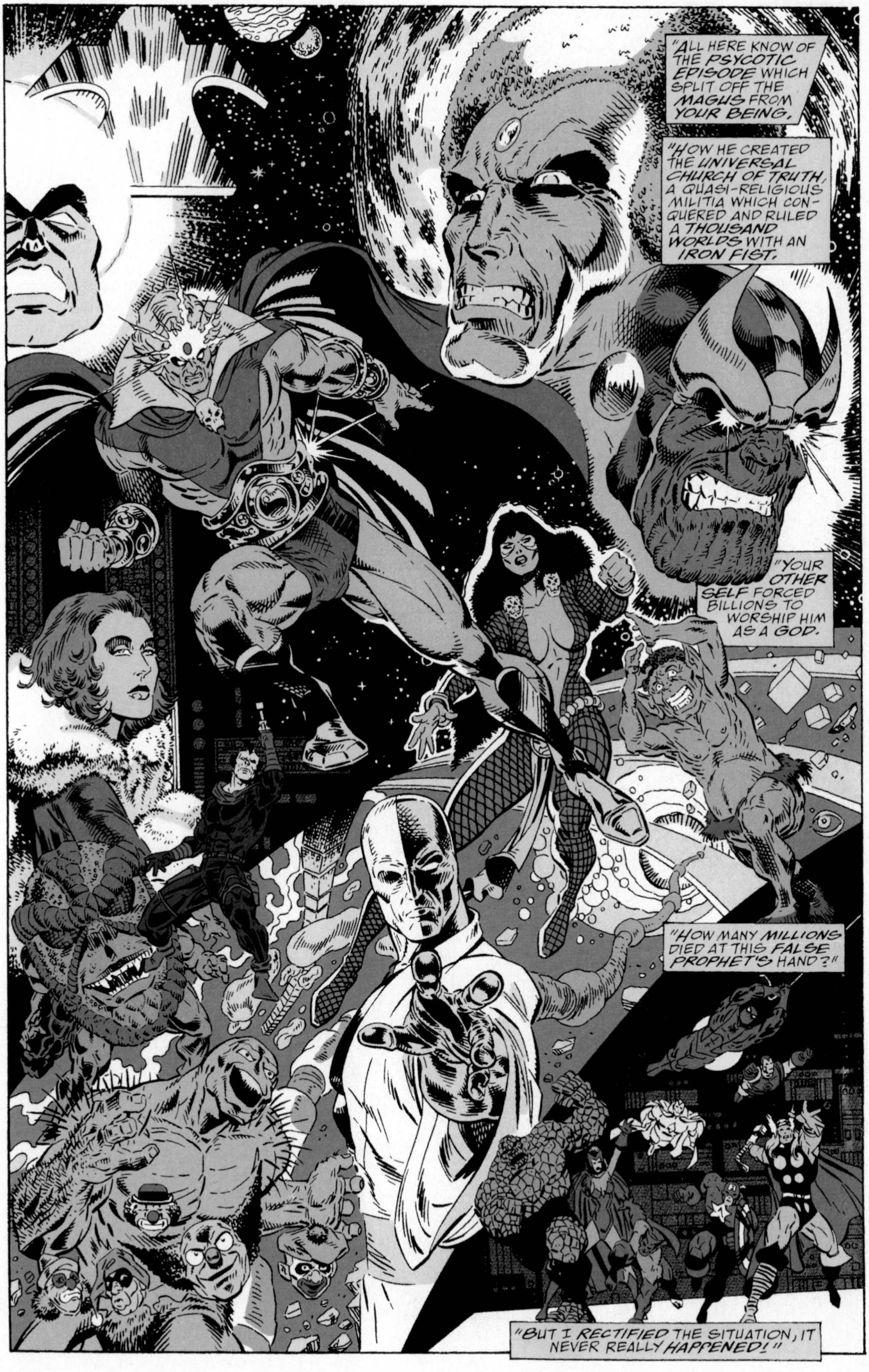
"ALL HERE KNOW OF THE PSYCOTIC EPISODE WHICH SPLIT OFF THE MAGUS FROM YOUR BEING.
"HOW HE CREATED THE UNIVERSAL CHURCH OF TRUTH, A QUASI-RELIGIOUS MILITIA WHICH CONQUERED AND RULED A THOUSAND WORLDS WITH AN IRON FIST.
"YOUR OTHER SELF FORCED BILLIONS TO WORSHIP HIM AS A GOD.
"HOW MANY MILLIONS DIED AT THIS FALSE PROPHET'S HAND?"
"BUT I RECTIFIED THE SITUATION, IT NEVER REALLY HAPPENED!"

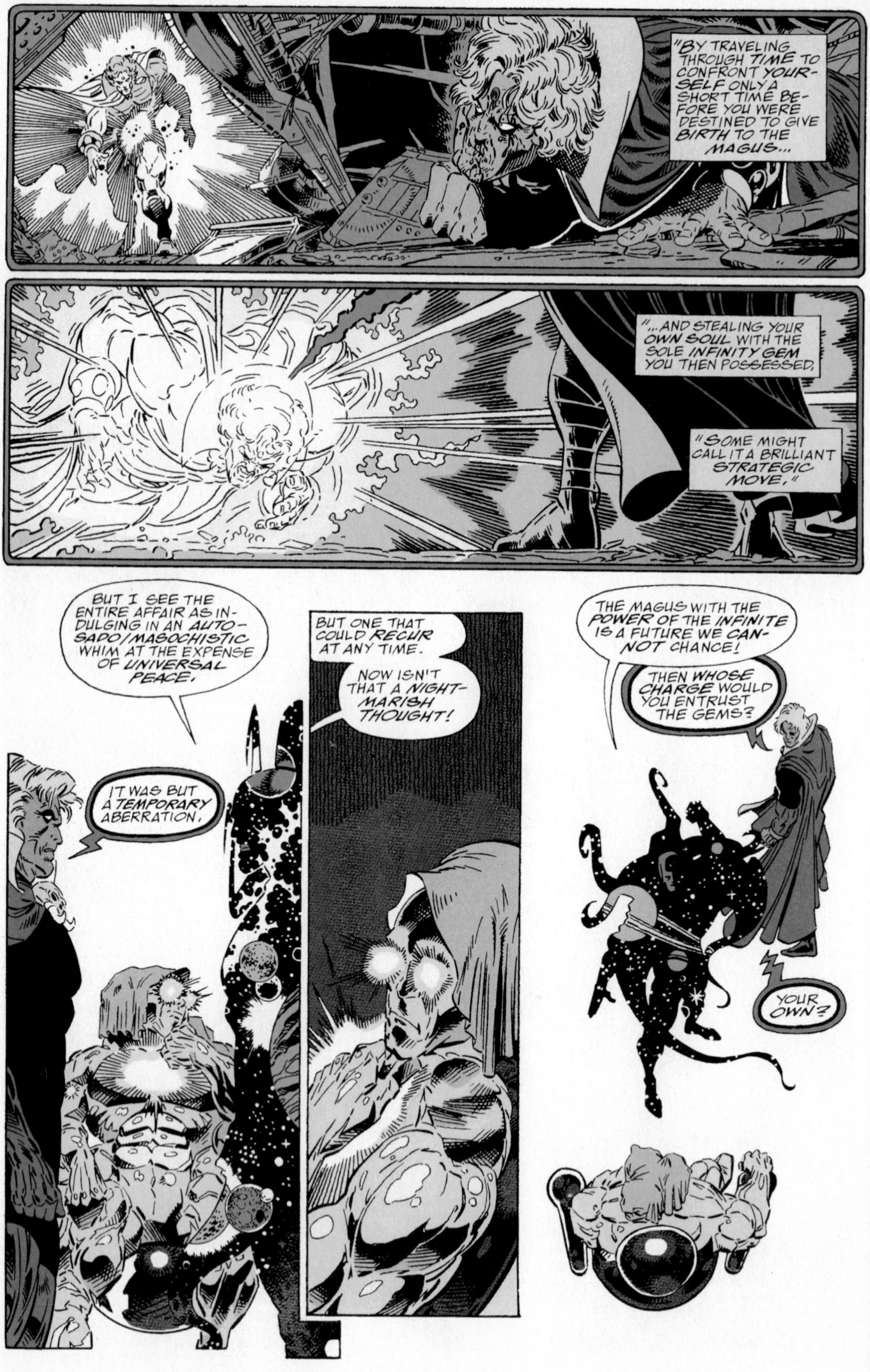
"BY TRAVELING THROUGH TIME TO CONFRONT YOURSELF ONLY A SHORT TIME BEFORE YOU WERE DESTINED TO GIVE BIRTH TO THE MAGUS...
"...AND STEALING YOUR OWN SOUL WITH THE SOLE INFINITY GEM YOU THEN POSSESSED,
"SOME MIGHT CALL IT A BRILLIANT STRATEGIC MOVE."
BUT I SEE THE ENTIRE AFFAIR AS INDULGING IN AN AUTO-SADO/MASOCHISTIC WHIM AT THE EXPENSE OF UNIVERSAL PEACE.
IT WAS BUT A TEMPORARY ABERRATION.
BUT ONE THAT COULD RECUR AT ANY TIME.
NOW ISN'T THAT A NIGHTMARISH THOUGHT!
THE MAGUS WITH THE POWER OF THE INFINITE IS A FUTURE WE CANNOT CHANCE!
THEN WHOSE CHARGE WOULD YOU ENTRUST THE GEMS?
YOUR OWN?

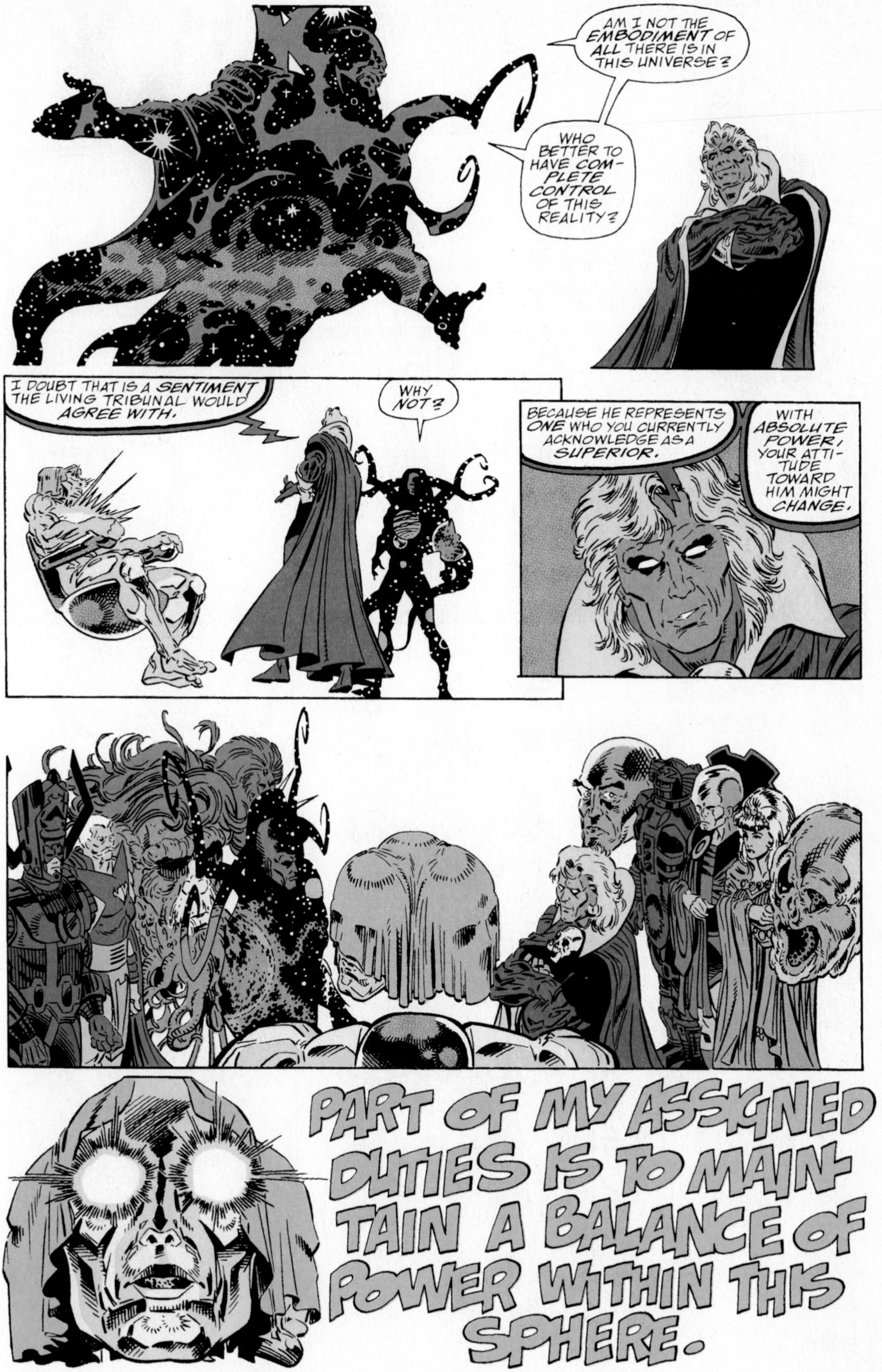
AM I NOT THE EMBODIMENT OF ALL THERE IS IN THIS UNIVERSE?
WHO BETTER TO HAVE COMPLETE CONTROL OF THIS REALITY?
I DOUBT THAT IS A SENTIMENT THE LIVING TRIBUNAL WOULD AGREE WITH.
WHY NOT?
BECAUSE HE REPRESENTS ONE WHO YOU CURRENTLY ACKNOWLEDGE AS A SUPERIOR.
WITH ABSOLUTE POWER, YOUR ATTITUDE TOWARD HIM MIGHT CHANGE.
PART OF MY ASSIGNED DUTIES IS TO MAINTAIN A BALANCE OF POWER WITHIN THIS SPHERE.

SO IN OTHER WORDS, IT ALL COMES DOWN TO YOU DECIDING IF I SHOULD RETAIN CONTROL OF THE *INFINITY GEMS*.

AND DETERMINING IF I HAVE THE POWER TO...

...WREST THE *GAUNTLET* FROM ME-

LIVING TRIBUNAL, WE AWAIT THE *WISDOM* OF YOUR *JUDGMENT*.

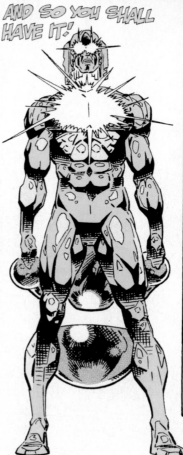

AND SO YOU SHALL HAVE IT!

REMEMBER, YOU ARE ABOUT TO HAND DOWN A *VERDICT* ON ONE WHO IS THE *MASTER* OF POWER, SPACE, REALITY, THE SOUL, THE MIND, AND TIME.

18

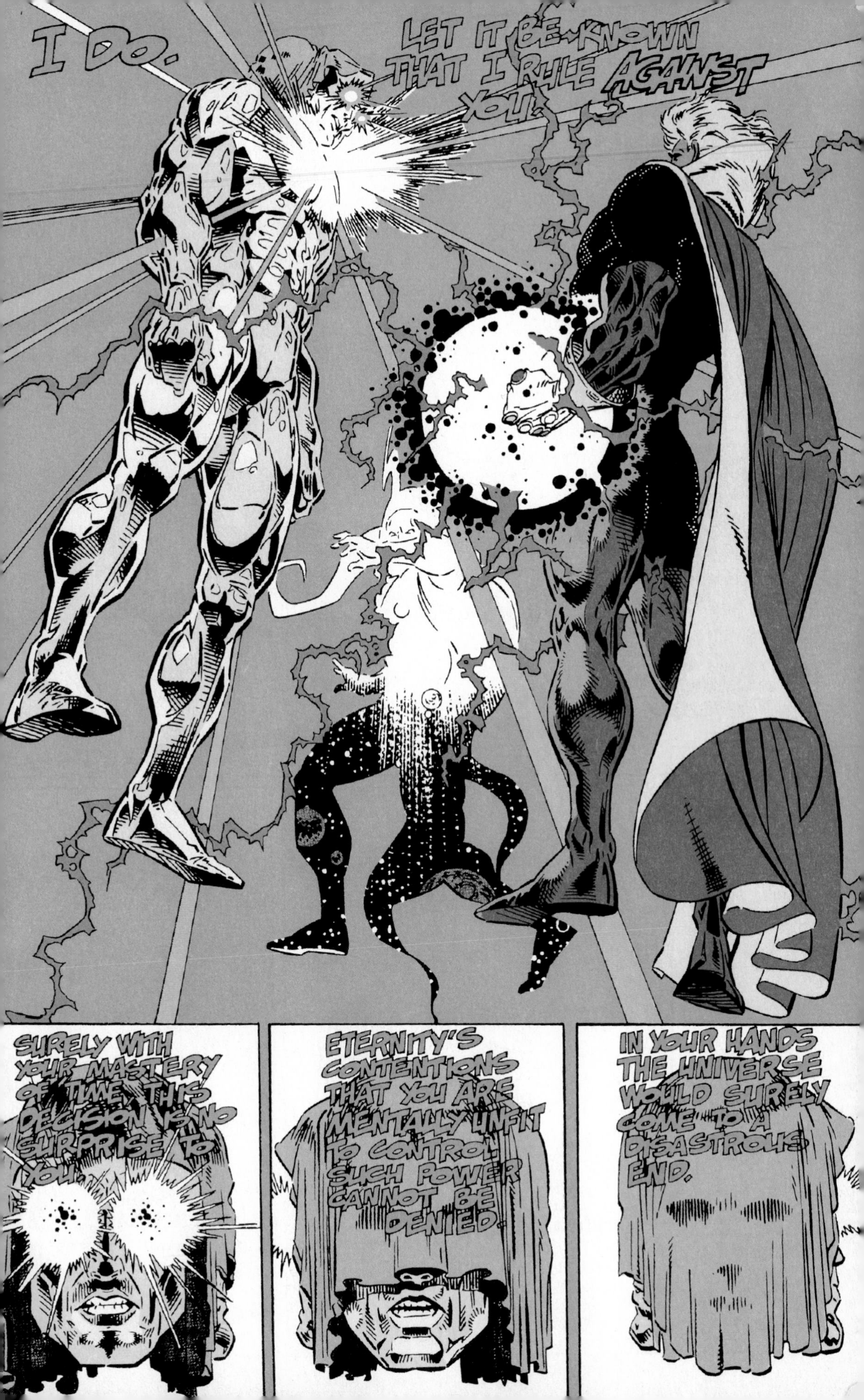

I DO.
LET IT BE KNOWN THAT I RULE AGAINST YOU.
SURELY WITH YOUR MASTERY OF TIME THIS DECISION IS NO SURPRISE TO YOU.
ETERNITY'S CONTENTIONS THAT YOU ARE MENTALLY UNFIT TO CONTROL SUCH POWER CANNOT BE DENIED.
IN YOUR HANDS THE UNIVERSE WOULD SURELY COME TO A DISASTROUS END.

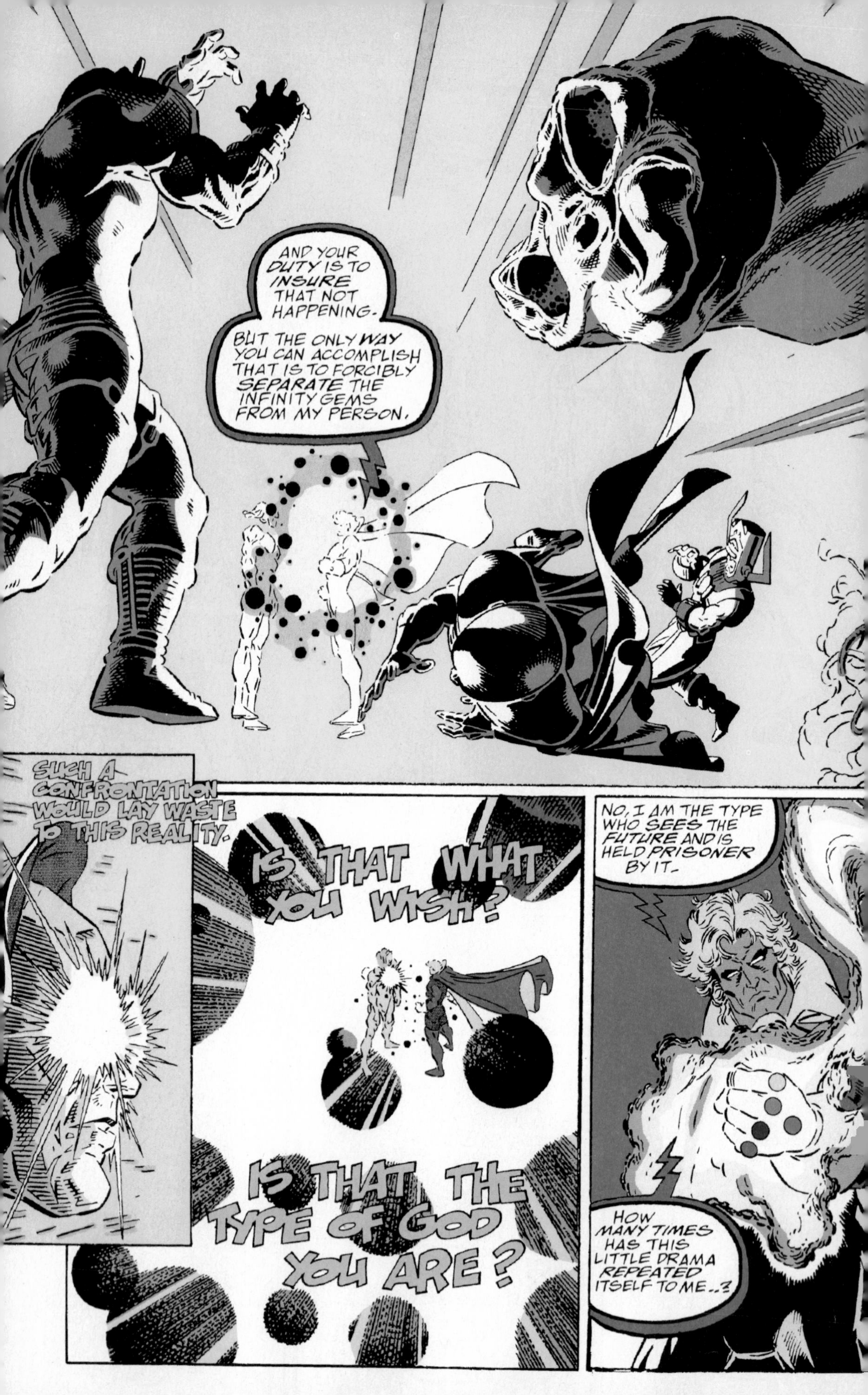
AND YOUR DUTY IS TO INSURE THAT NOT HAPPENING.
BUT THE ONLY WAY YOU CAN ACCOMPLISH THAT IS TO FORCIBLY SEPARATE THE INFINITY GEMS FROM MY PERSON.
SUCH A CONFRONTATION WOULD LAY WASTE TO THIS REALITY.
IS THAT WHAT YOU WISH?
IS THAT THE TYPE OF GOD YOU ARE?
NO, I AM THE TYPE WHO SEES THE FUTURE AND IS HELD PRISONER BY IT.
HOW MANY TIMES HAS THIS LITTLE DRAMA REPEATED ITSELF TO ME..?

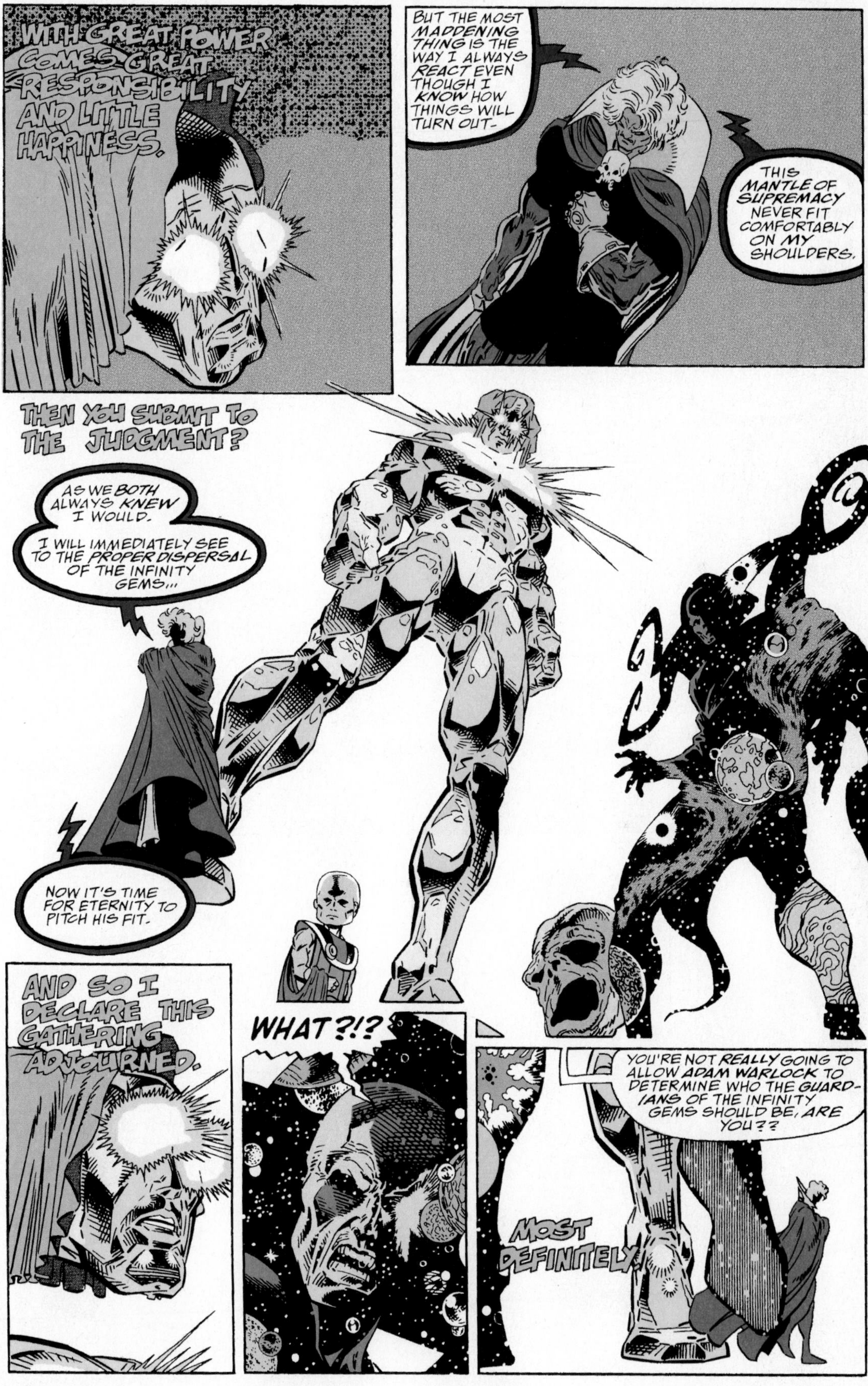
WITH GREAT POWER COMES GREAT RESPONSIBILITY AND LITTLE HAPPINESS.
BUT THE MOST MADDENING THING IS THE WAY I ALWAYS REACT EVEN THOUGH I KNOW HOW THINGS WILL TURN OUT-
THIS MANTLE OF SUPREMACY NEVER FIT COMFORTABLY ON MY SHOULDERS.
THEN YOU SUBMIT TO THE JUDGMENT?
AS WE BOTH ALWAYS KNEW I WOULD.
I WILL IMMEDIATELY SEE TO THE PROPER DISPERSAL OF THE INFINITY GEMS...
NOW IT'S TIME FOR ETERNITY TO PITCH HIS FIT.
AND SO I DECLARE THIS GATHERING ADJOURNED.
WHAT?!?
YOU'RE NOT REALLY GOING TO ALLOW ADAM WARLOCK TO DETERMINE WHO THE GUARDIANS OF THE INFINITY GEMS SHOULD BE, ARE YOU??
MOST DEFINITELY.

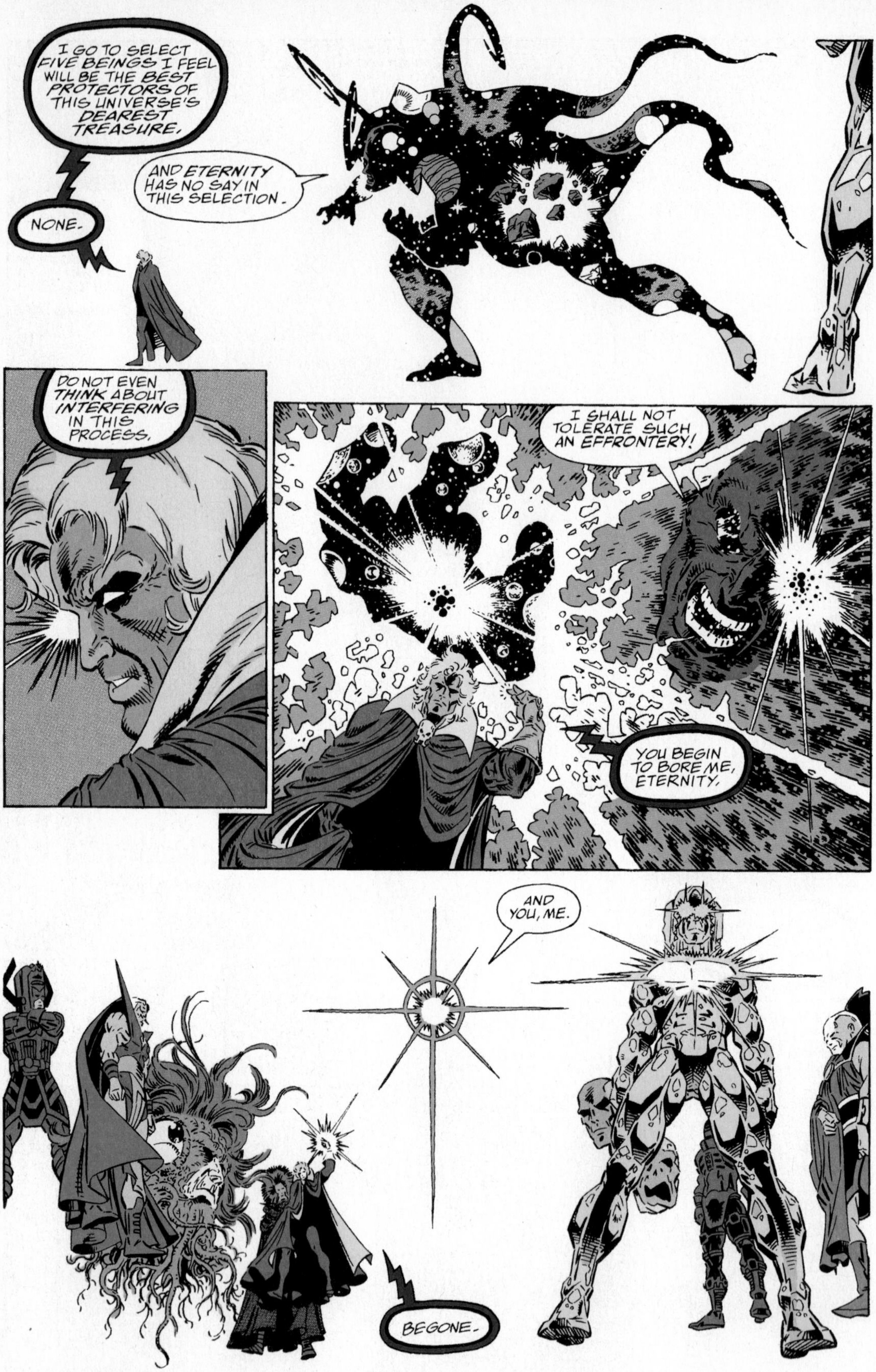

I GO TO SELECT FIVE BEINGS I FEEL WILL BE THE BEST PROTECTORS OF THIS UNIVERSE'S DEAREST TREASURE.
AND ETERNITY HAS NO SAY IN THIS SELECTION.
NONE.
DO NOT EVEN THINK ABOUT INTERFERING IN THIS PROCESS.
I SHALL NOT TOLERATE SUCH AN EFFRONTERY!
YOU BEGIN TO BORE ME, ETERNITY.
AND YOU, ME.
BEGONE.

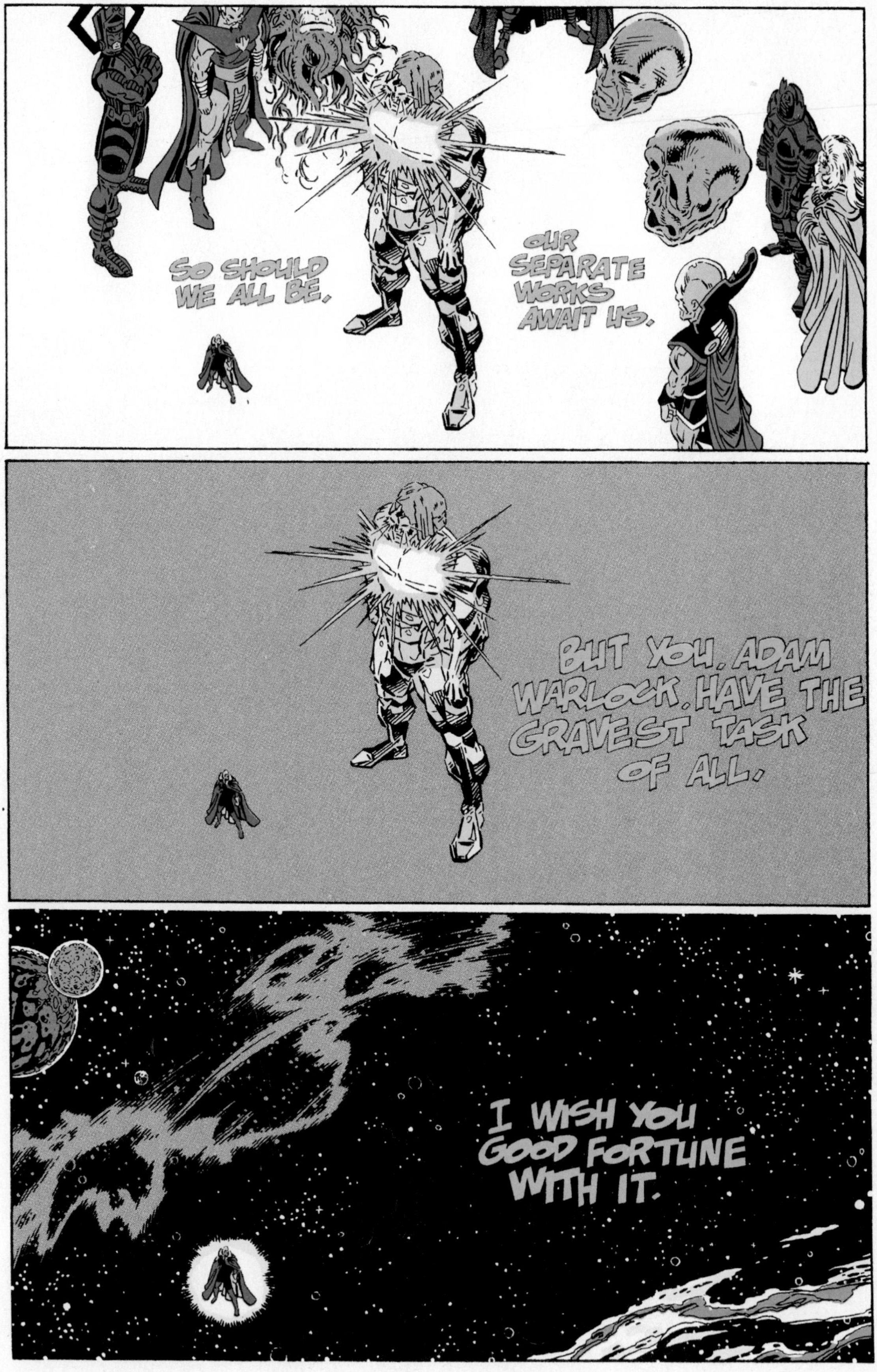
SO SHOULD WE ALL BE.
OUR SEPARATE WORKS AWAIT US.
BUT YOU, ADAM WARLOCK, HAVE THE GRAVEST TASK OF ALL.
I WISH YOU GOOD FORTUNE WITH IT.

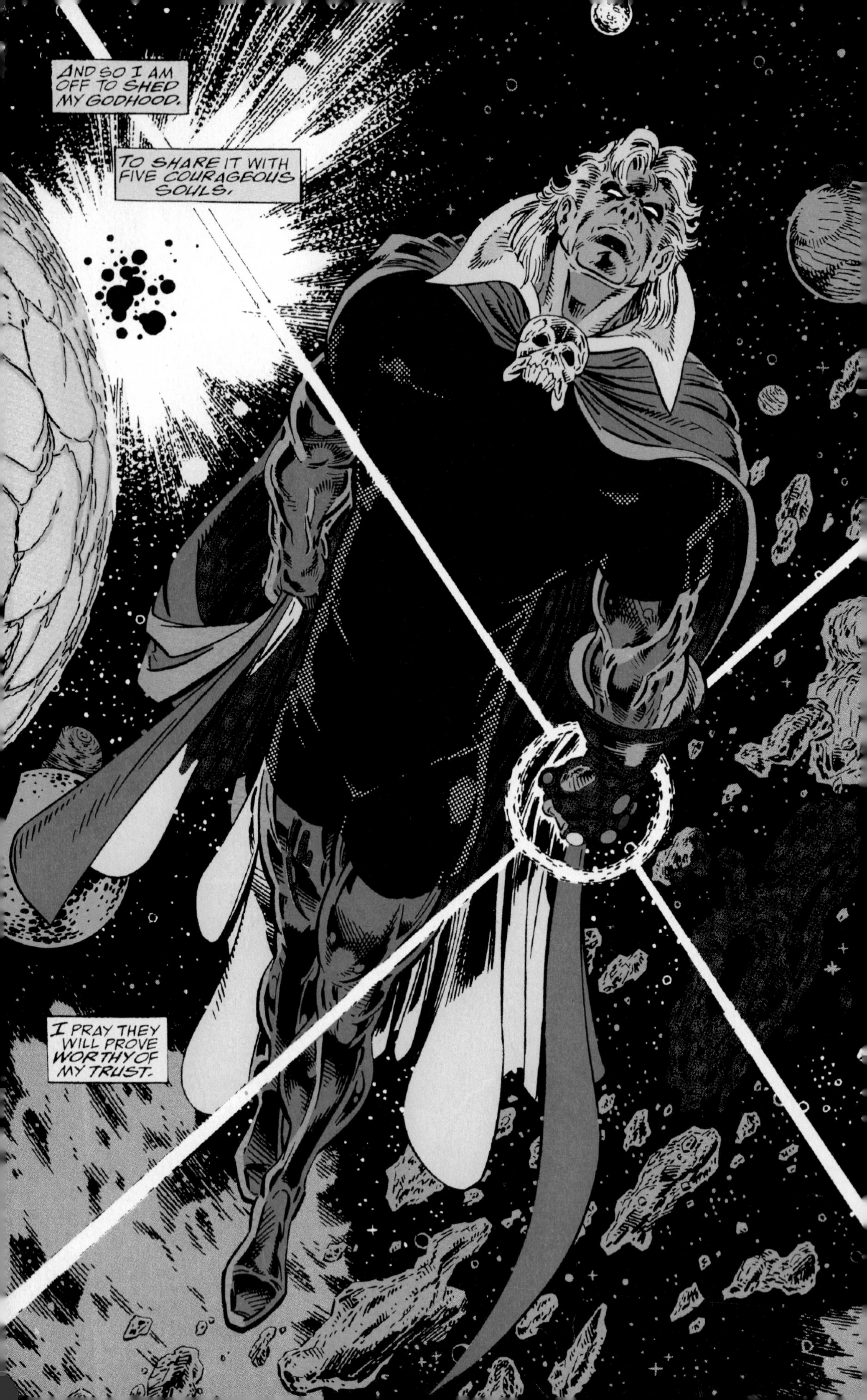
AND SO I AM OFF TO SHED MY GODHOOD.
TO SHARE IT WITH FIVE COURAGEOUS SOULS.
I PRAY THEY WILL PROVE WORTHY OF MY TRUST.

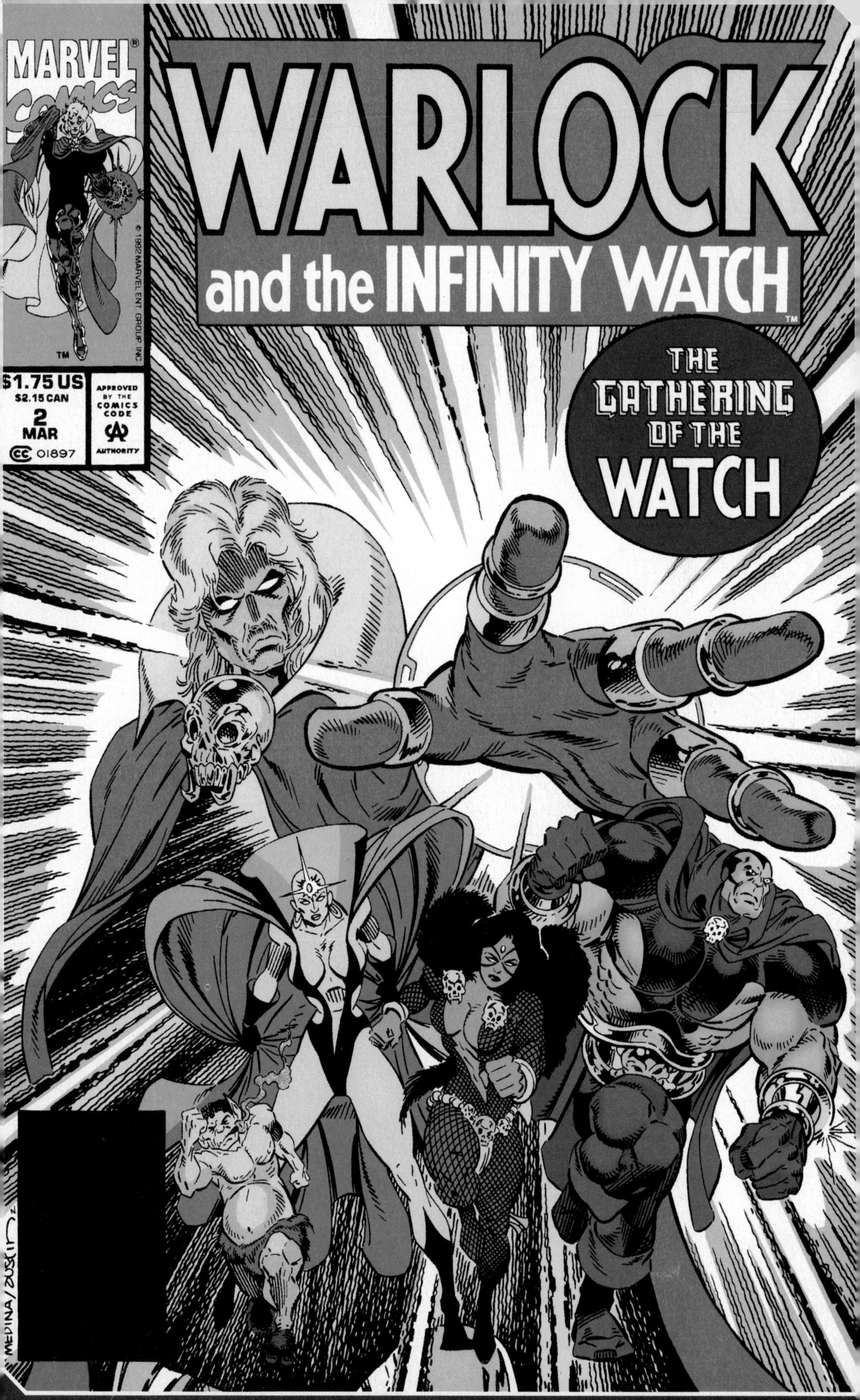

MARVEL® COMICS
WARLOCK
and the INFINITY WATCH™
$1.75 US
$2.15 CAN
2
MAR
CC 01897
APPROVED BY THE COMICS CODE CA AUTHORITY
© 1992 MARVEL ENT. GROUP INC
THE GATHERING OF THE WATCH

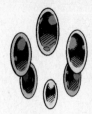

JIM
STARLIN
WRITER
ANGEL
MEDINA
PENCILS
TERRY
AUSTIN
INKS
JACK
MORELLI
LETTERS
IAN
LAUGHLIN
COLORS
CRAIG
ANDERSON
EDITOR
TOM
DeFALCO
CHIEFTAN

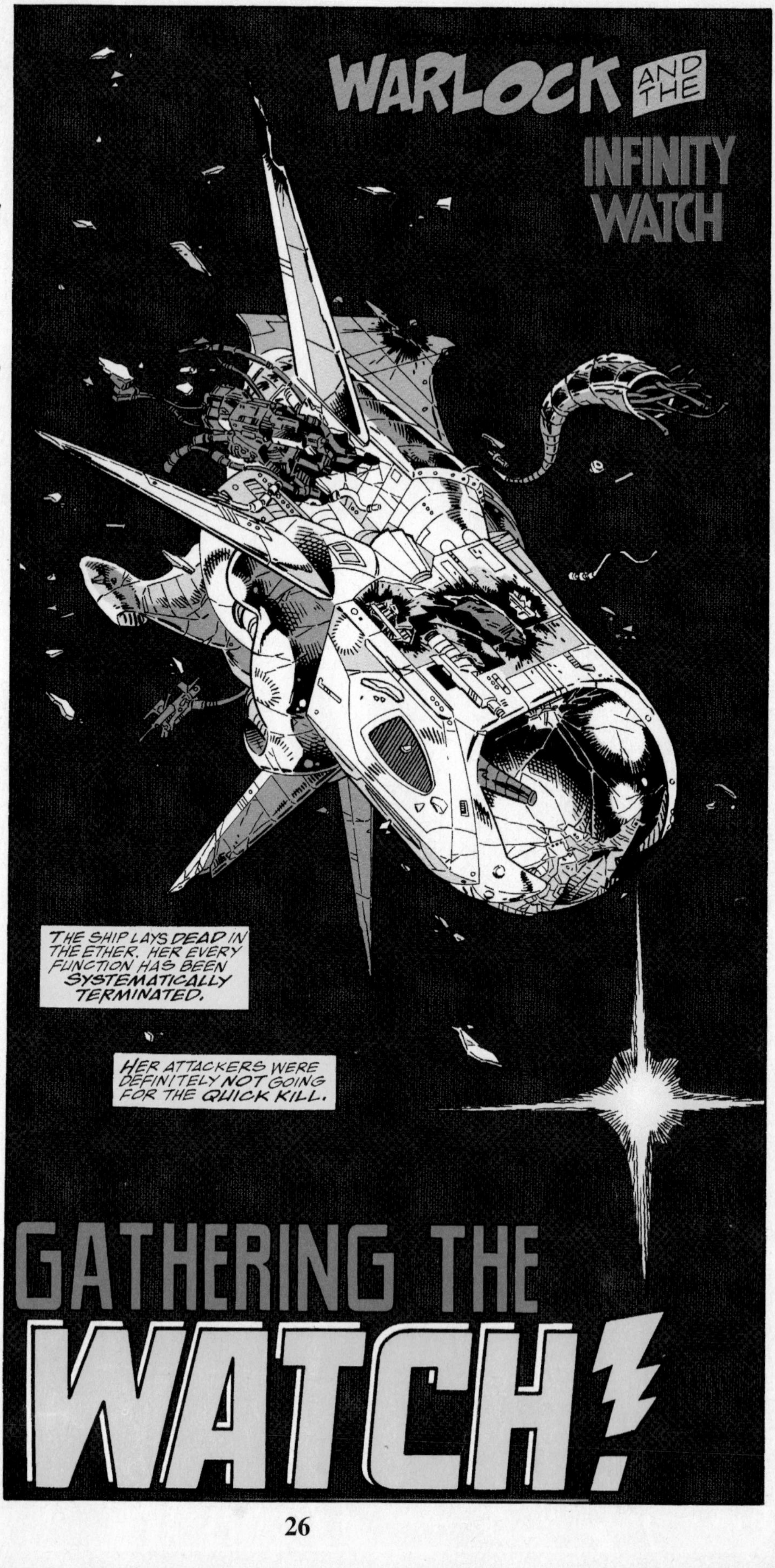

WARLOCK AND THE
INFINITY WATCH
THE SHIP LAYS DEAD IN THE ETHER. HER EVERY FUNCTION HAS BEEN SYSTEMATICALLY TERMINATED.
HER ATTACKERS WERE DEFINITELY NOT GOING FOR THE QUICK KILL.
GATHERING THE
WATCH!

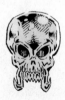

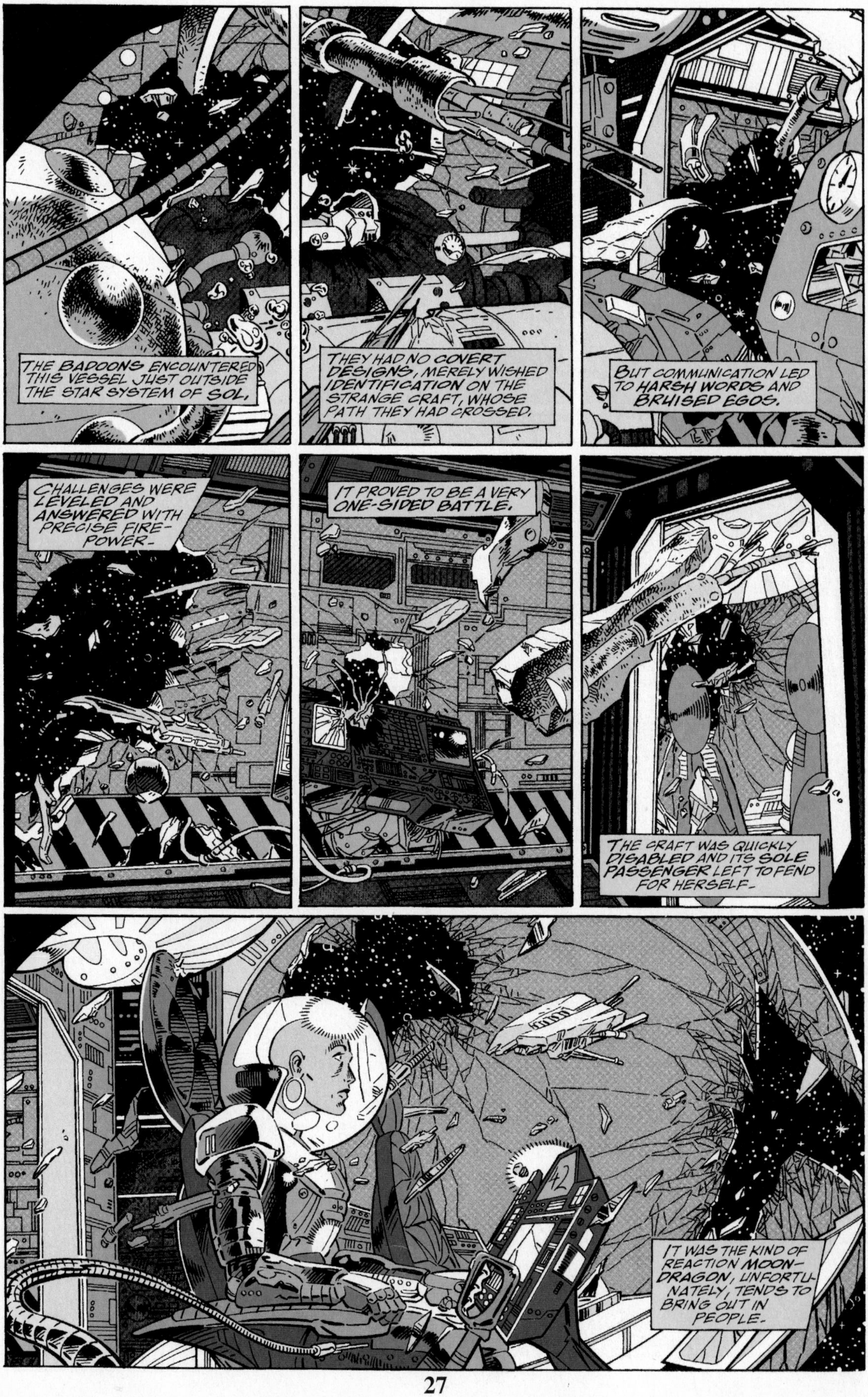
THE BADOONS ENCOUNTERED THIS VESSEL JUST OUTSIDE THE STAR SYSTEM OF SOL,
THEY HAD NO COVERT DESIGNS, MERELY WISHED IDENTIFICATION ON THE STRANGE CRAFT, WHOSE PATH THEY HAD CROSSED.
BUT COMMUNICATION LED TO HARSH WORDS AND BRUISED EGOS.
CHALLENGES WERE LEVELED AND ANSWERED WITH PRECISE FIRE-POWER-
IT PROVED TO BE A VERY ONE-SIDED BATTLE.
THE CRAFT WAS QUICKLY DISABLED AND ITS SOLE PASSENGER LEFT TO FEND FOR HERSELF-
IT WAS THE KIND OF REACTION MOON-DRAGON, UNFORTU-NATELY, TENDS TO BRING OUT IN PEOPLE.

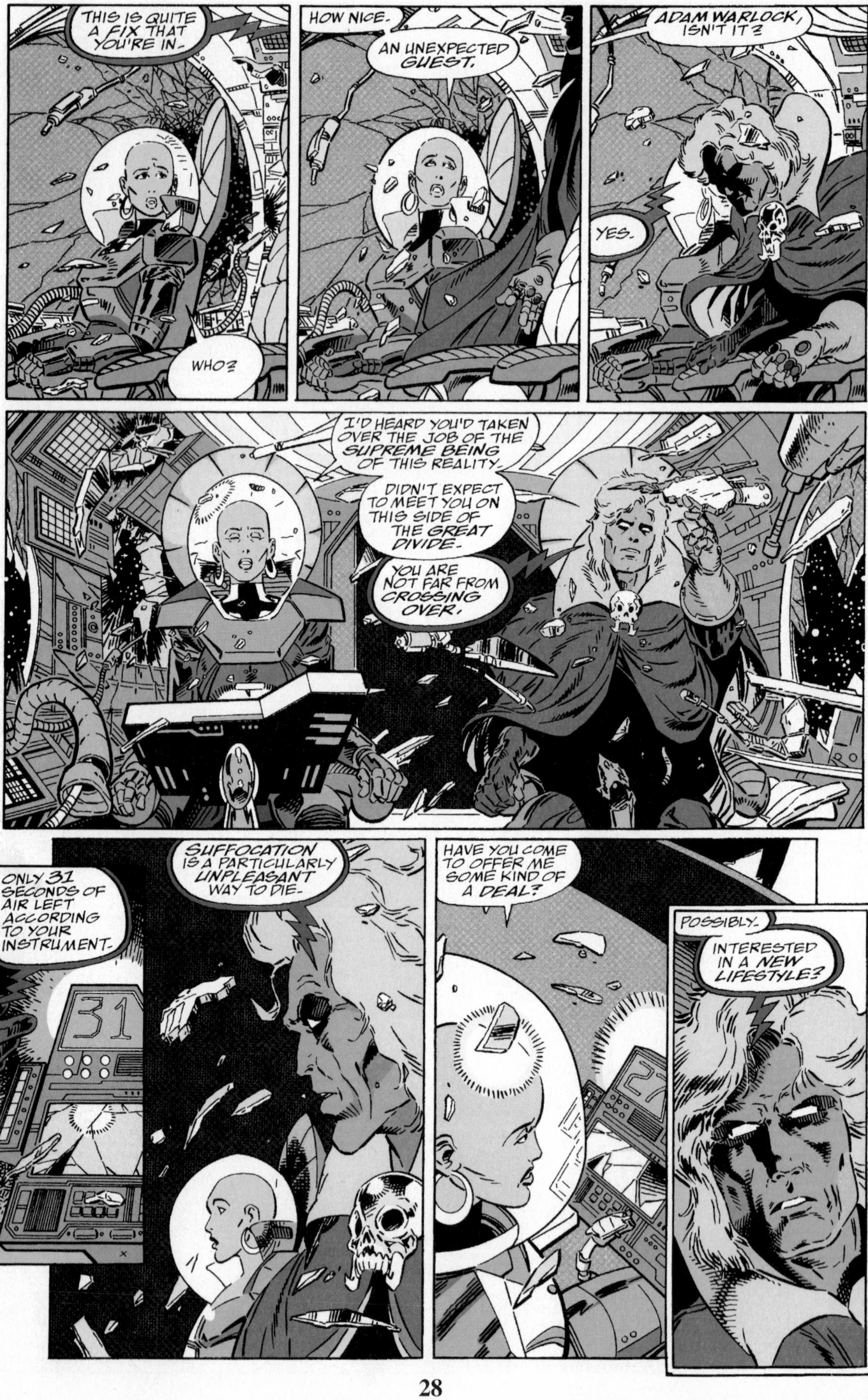

THIS IS QUITE A FIX THAT YOU'RE IN.
WHO?
HOW NICE.
AN UNEXPECTED GUEST.
ADAM WARLOCK, ISN'T IT?
YES.
I'D HEARD YOU'D TAKEN OVER THE JOB OF THE SUPREME BEING OF THIS REALITY.
DIDN'T EXPECT TO MEET YOU ON THIS SIDE OF THE GREAT DIVIDE.
YOU ARE NOT FAR FROM CROSSING OVER.
ONLY 31 SECONDS OF AIR LEFT ACCORDING TO YOUR INSTRUMENT.
SUFFOCATION IS A PARTICULARLY UNPLEASANT WAY TO DIE.
HAVE YOU COME TO OFFER ME SOME KIND OF A DEAL?
POSSIBLY.
INTERESTED IN A NEW LIFESTYLE?

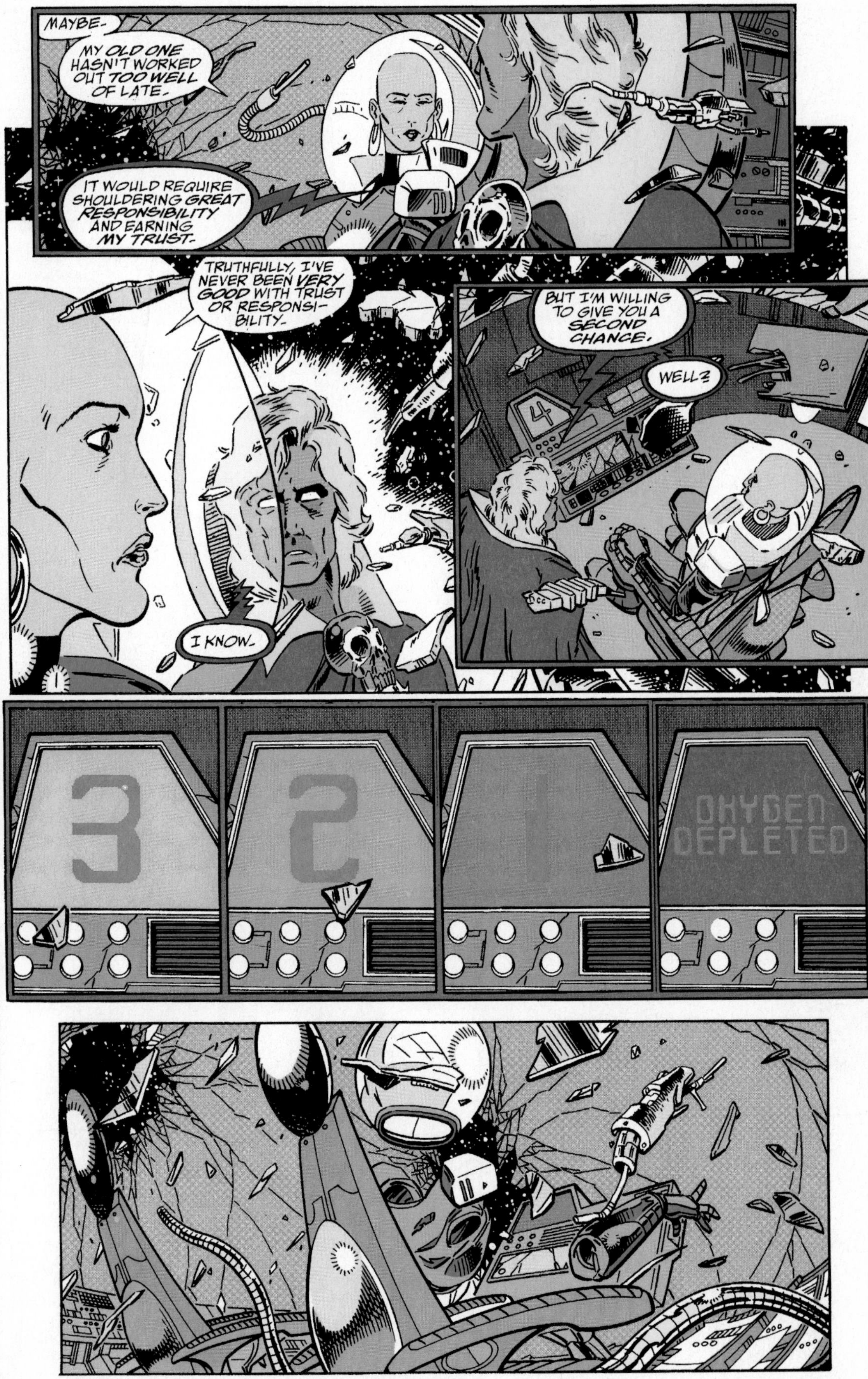
MAYBE-
MY OLD ONE HASN'T WORKED OUT TOO WELL OF LATE-
IT WOULD REQUIRE SHOULDERING GREAT RESPONSIBILITY AND EARNING MY TRUST-
TRUTHFULLY, I'VE NEVER BEEN VERY GOOD WITH TRUST OR RESPONSI-BILITY-
I KNOW-
BUT I'M WILLING TO GIVE YOU A SECOND CHANCE.
WELL?
4
3
2
1
OXYGEN DEPLETED

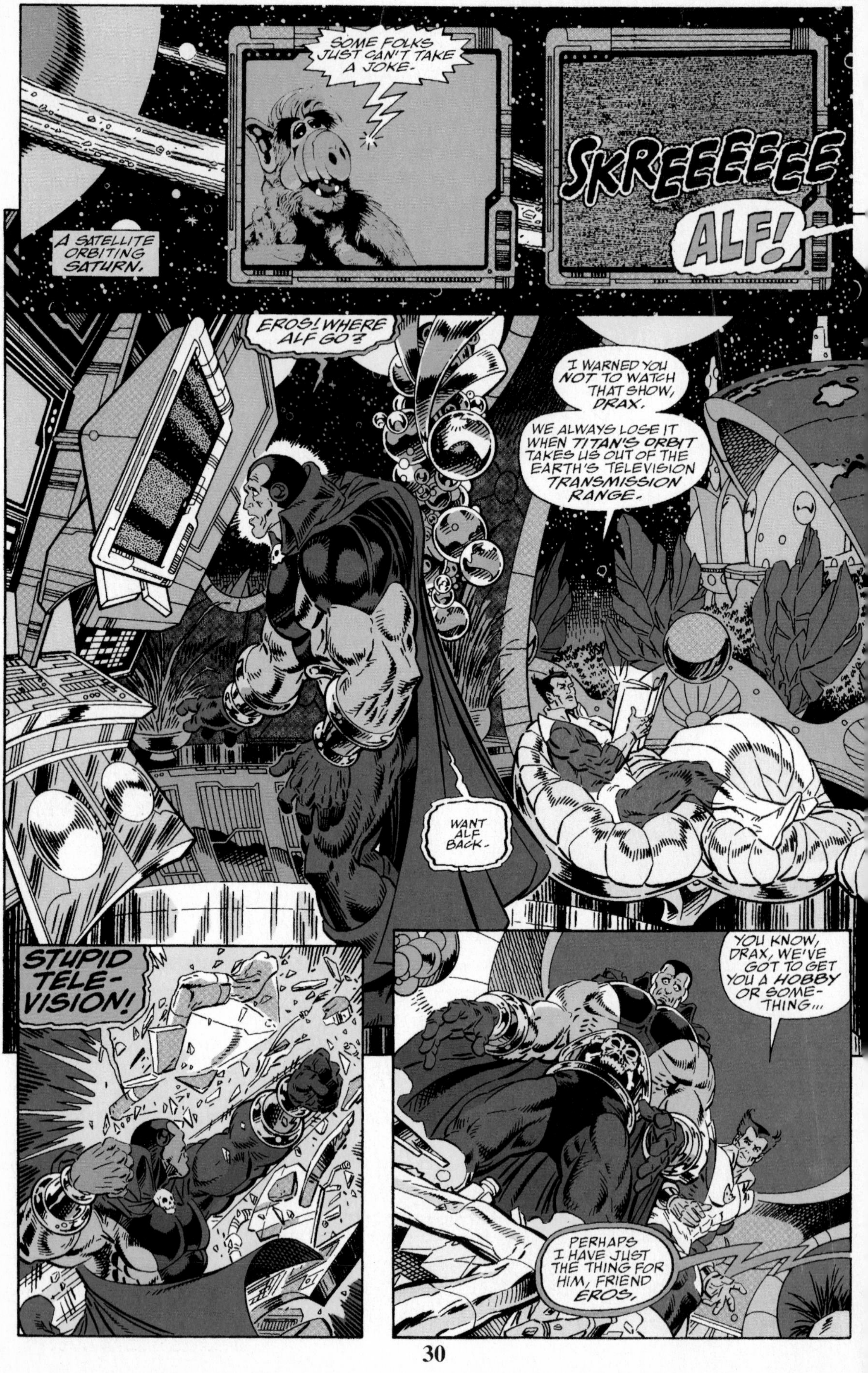
SOME FOLKS JUST CAN'T TAKE A JOKE.
A SATELLITE ORBITING SATURN.
SKREEEEEEE
ALF!
EROS! WHERE ALF GO?
I WARNED YOU NOT TO WATCH THAT SHOW, DRAX.
WE ALWAYS LOSE IT WHEN TITAN'S ORBIT TAKES US OUT OF THE EARTH'S TELEVISION TRANSMISSION RANGE.
WANT ALF BACK.
STUPID TELE-VISION!
YOU KNOW, DRAX, WE'VE GOT TO GET YOU A HOBBY OR SOME-THING...
PERHAPS I HAVE JUST THE THING FOR HIM, FRIEND EROS.

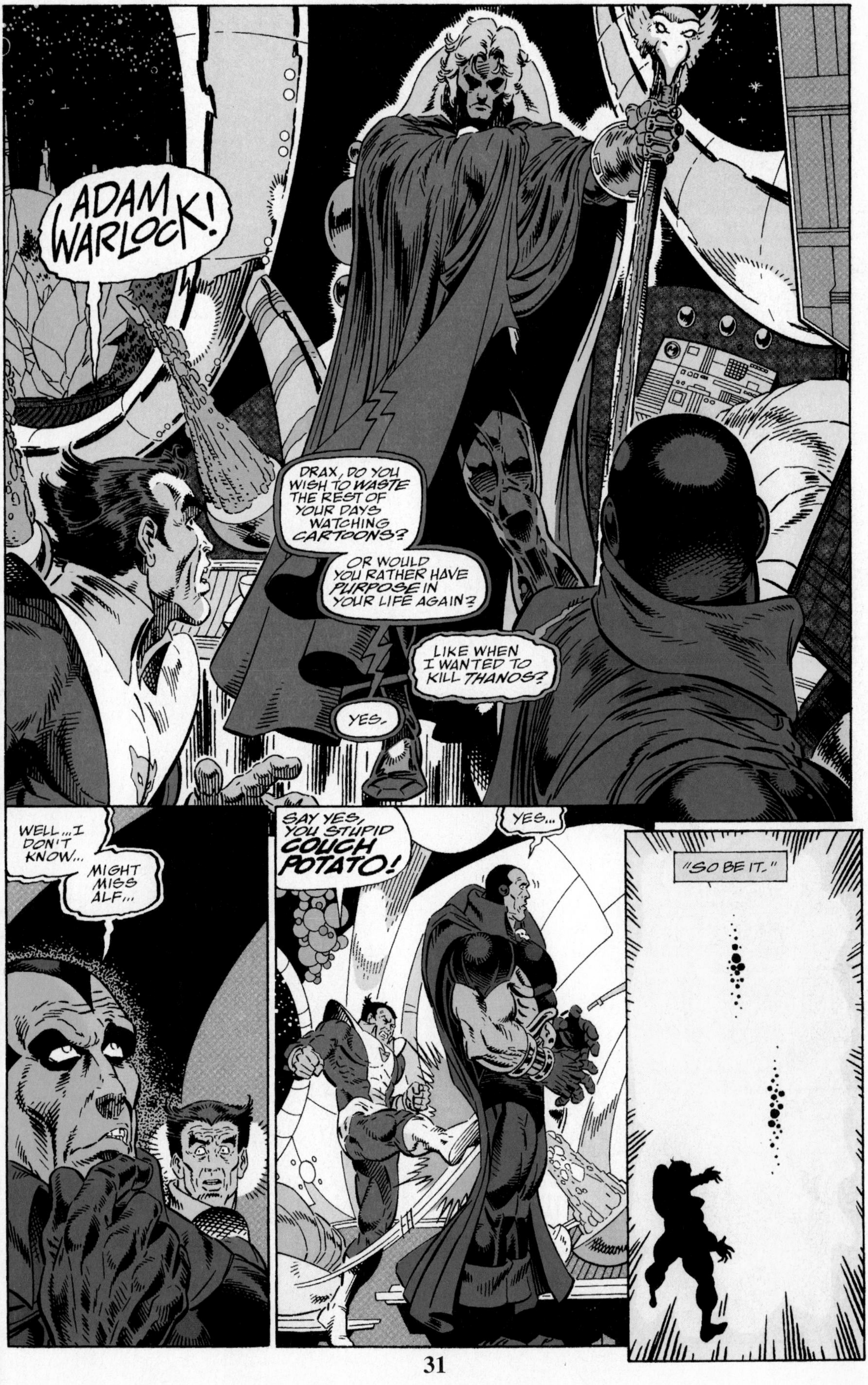
ADAM WARLOCK!
DRAX, DO YOU WISH TO WASTE THE REST OF YOUR DAYS WATCHING CARTOONS?
OR WOULD YOU RATHER HAVE PURPOSE IN YOUR LIFE AGAIN?
LIKE WHEN I WANTED TO KILL THANOS?
YES.
WELL...I DON'T KNOW...
MIGHT MISS ALF...
SAY YES, YOU STUPID COUCH POTATO!
YES...
"SO BE IT."

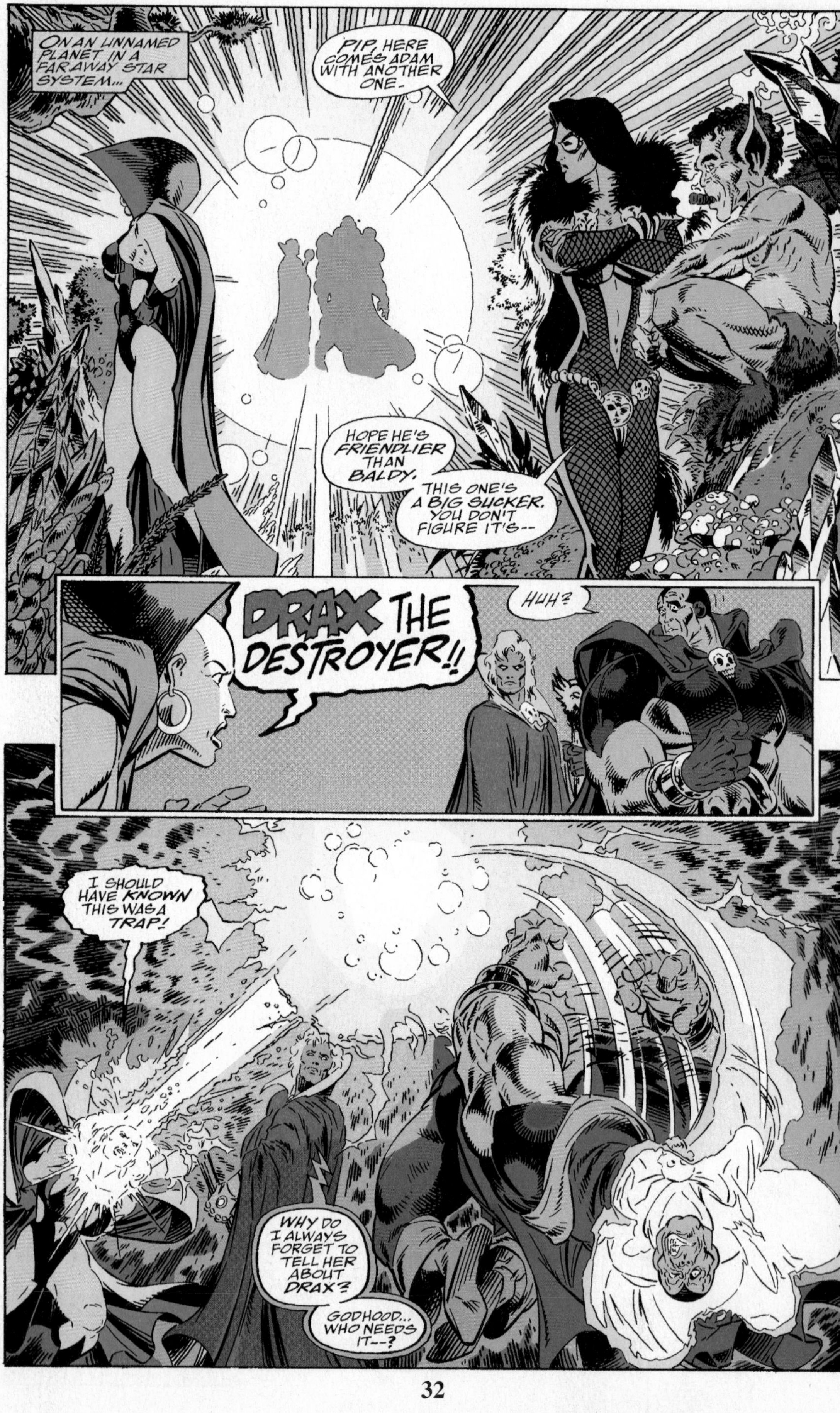
ON AN UNNAMED PLANET IN A FARAWAY STAR SYSTEM...
PIP, HERE COMES ADAM WITH ANOTHER ONE.
HOPE HE'S FRIENDLIER THAN BALDY.
THIS ONE'S A BIG SUCKER. YOU DON'T FIGURE IT'S--
DRAX THE DESTROYER!!
HUH?
I SHOULD HAVE KNOWN THIS WAS A TRAP!
WHY DO I ALWAYS FORGET TO TELL HER ABOUT DRAX?
GODHOOD... WHO NEEDS IT--?

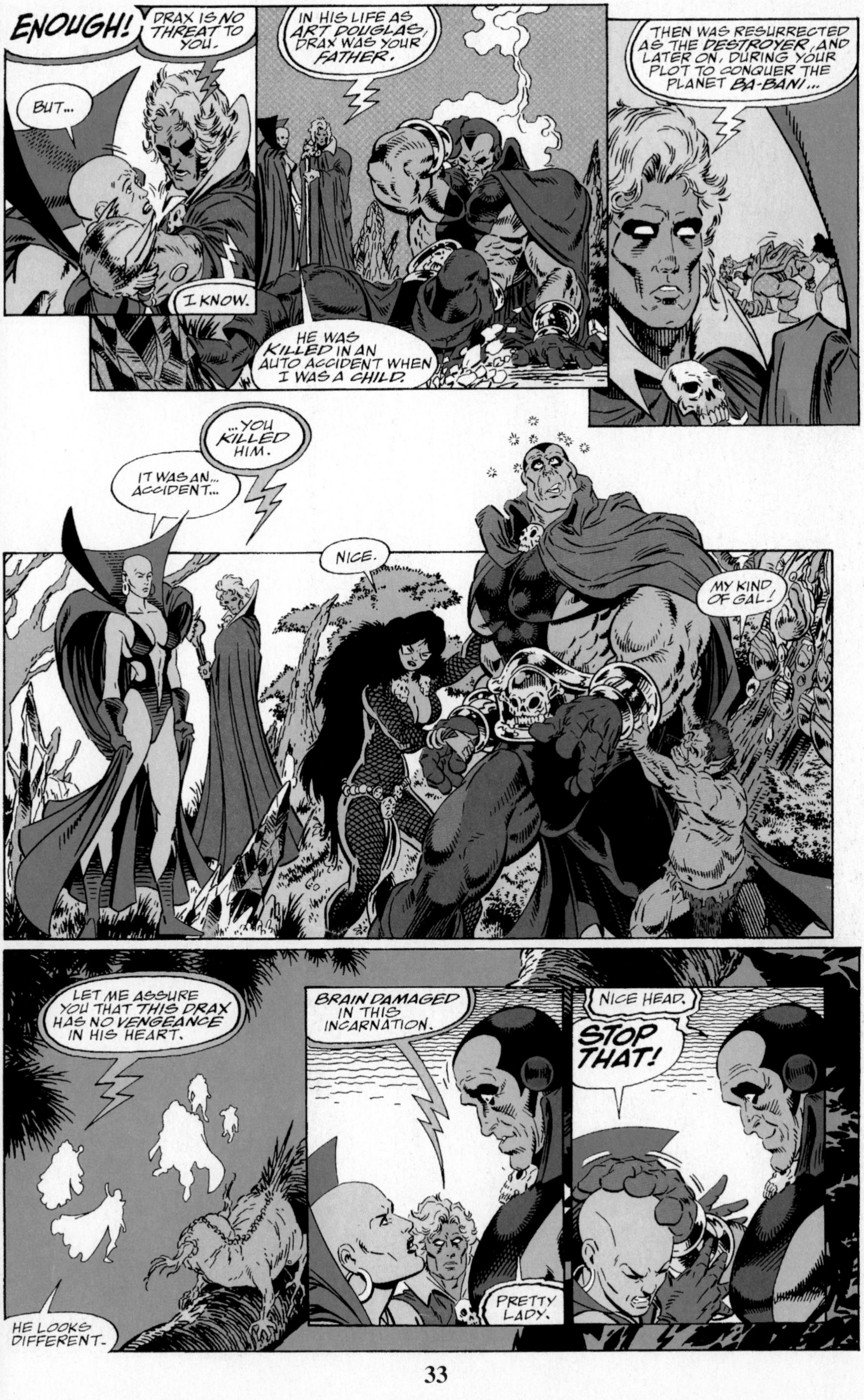
ENOUGH!
DRAX IS NO THREAT TO YOU.
BUT...
I KNOW.
IN HIS LIFE AS ART DOUGLAS, DRAX WAS YOUR FATHER.
HE WAS KILLED IN AN AUTO ACCIDENT WHEN I WAS A CHILD.
THEN WAS RESURRECTED AS THE DESTROYER, AND LATER ON, DURING YOUR PLOT TO CONQUER THE PLANET BA-BANI...
IT WAS AN... ACCIDENT...
...YOU KILLED HIM.
NICE.
MY KIND OF GAL!
LET ME ASSURE YOU THAT THIS DRAX HAS NO VENGEANCE IN HIS HEART.
HE LOOKS DIFFERENT-
BRAIN DAMAGED IN THIS INCARNATION.
PRETTY LADY.
NICE HEAD.
STOP THAT!

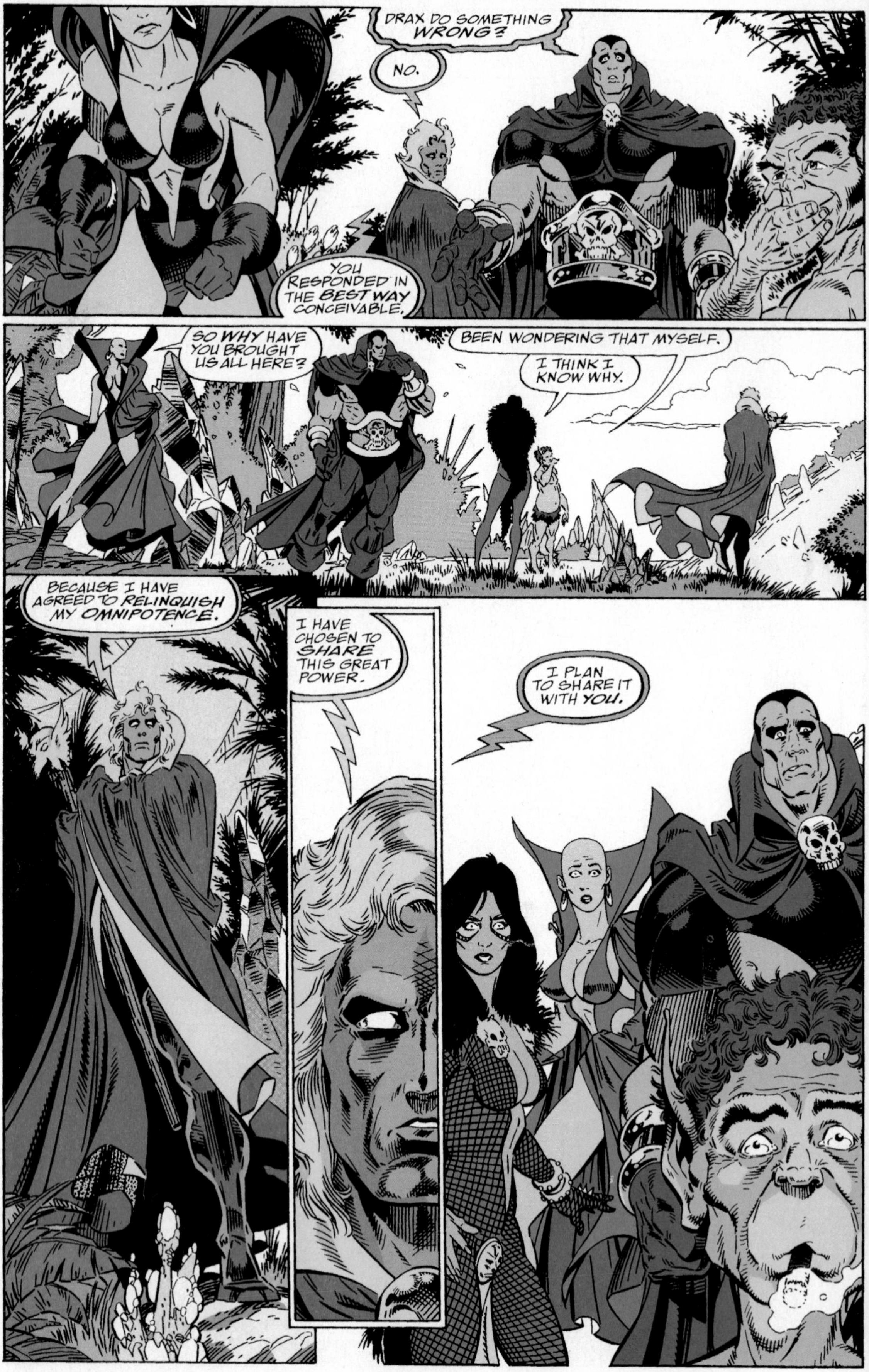
DRAX DO SOMETHING WRONG?
NO.
YOU RESPONDED IN THE BEST WAY CONCEIVABLE.
SO WHY HAVE YOU BROUGHT US ALL HERE?
BEEN WONDERING THAT MYSELF.
I THINK I KNOW WHY.
BECAUSE I HAVE AGREED TO RELINQUISH MY OMNIPOTENCE.
I HAVE CHOSEN TO SHARE THIS GREAT POWER.
I PLAN TO SHARE IT WITH YOU.

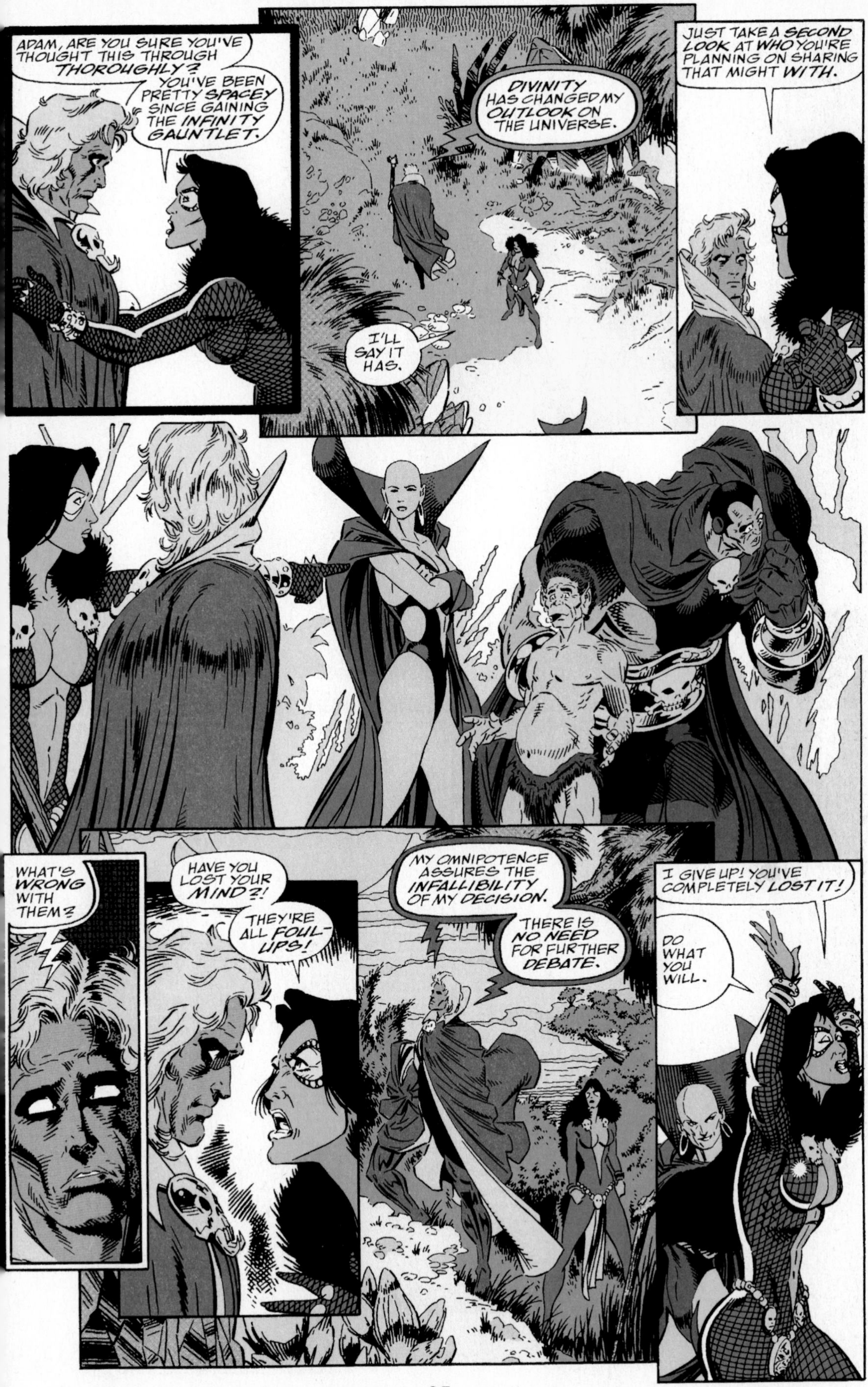
ADAM, ARE YOU SURE YOU'VE THOUGHT THIS THROUGH THOROUGHLY?
YOU'VE BEEN PRETTY SPACEY SINCE GAINING THE INFINITY GAUNTLET.
DIVINITY HAS CHANGED MY OUTLOOK ON THE UNIVERSE.
I'LL SAY IT HAS.
JUST TAKE A SECOND LOOK AT WHO YOU'RE PLANNING ON SHARING THAT MIGHT WITH.
WHAT'S WRONG WITH THEM?
HAVE YOU LOST YOUR MIND?!
THEY'RE ALL FOUL-UPS!
MY OMNIPOTENCE ASSURES THE INFALLIBILITY OF MY DECISION.
THERE IS NO NEED FOR FURTHER DEBATE.
I GIVE UP! YOU'VE COMPLETELY LOST IT!
DO WHAT YOU WILL.

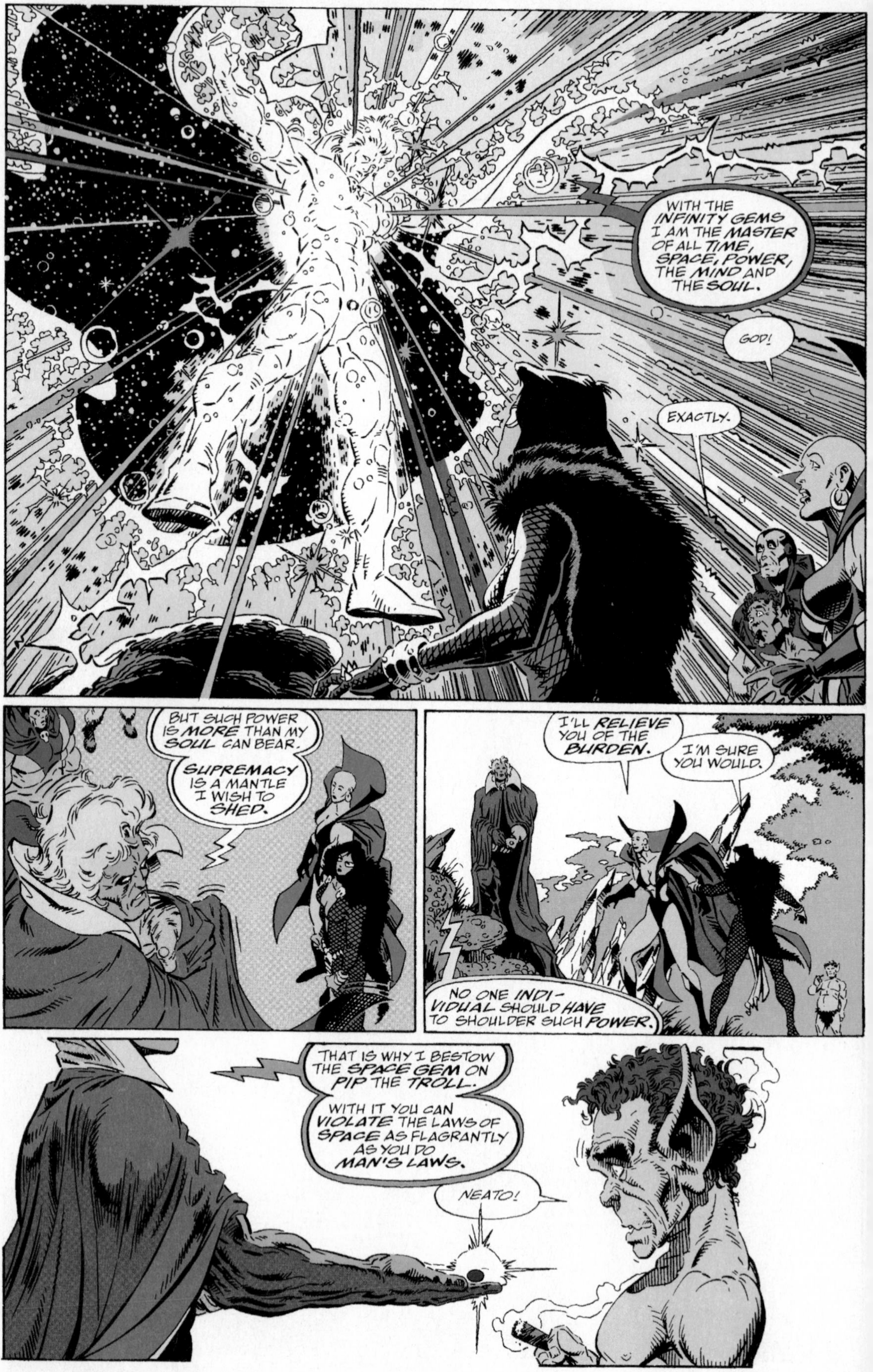
WITH THE INFINITY GEMS I AM THE MASTER OF ALL TIME, SPACE, POWER, THE MIND AND THE SOUL.
GOD!
EXACTLY.
BUT SUCH POWER IS MORE THAN MY SOUL CAN BEAR.
SUPREMACY IS A MANTLE I WISH TO SHED.
I'LL RELIEVE YOU OF THE BURDEN.
I'M SURE YOU WOULD.
NO ONE INDI-VIDUAL SHOULD HAVE TO SHOULDER SUCH POWER.
THAT IS WHY I BESTOW THE SPACE GEM ON PIP THE TROLL.
WITH IT YOU CAN VIOLATE THE LAWS OF SPACE AS FLAGRANTLY AS YOU DO MAN'S LAWS.
NEATO!

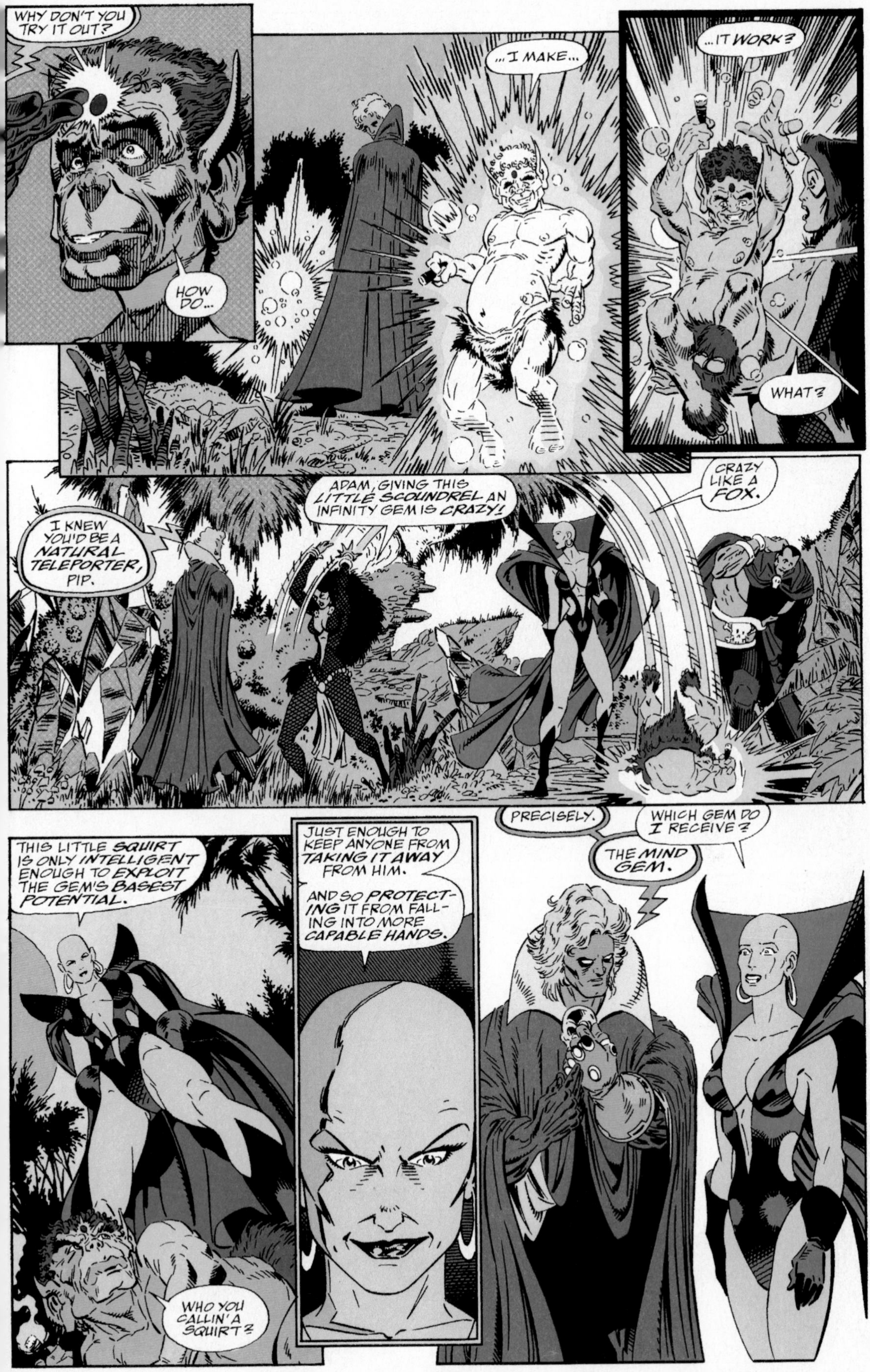
WHY DON'T YOU TRY IT OUT?
HOW DO...
...I MAKE...
...IT WORK?
WHAT?
I KNEW YOU'D BE A NATURAL TELEPORTER, PIP.
ADAM, GIVING THIS LITTLE SCOUNDREL AN INFINITY GEM IS CRAZY!
CRAZY LIKE A FOX.
THIS LITTLE SQUIRT IS ONLY INTELLIGENT ENOUGH TO EXPLOIT THE GEM'S BASEST POTENTIAL.
WHO YOU CALLIN' A SQUIRT?
JUST ENOUGH TO KEEP ANYONE FROM TAKING IT AWAY FROM HIM.
AND SO PROTECTING IT FROM FALLING INTO MORE CAPABLE HANDS.
PRECISELY.
WHICH GEM DO I RECEIVE?
THE MIND GEM.

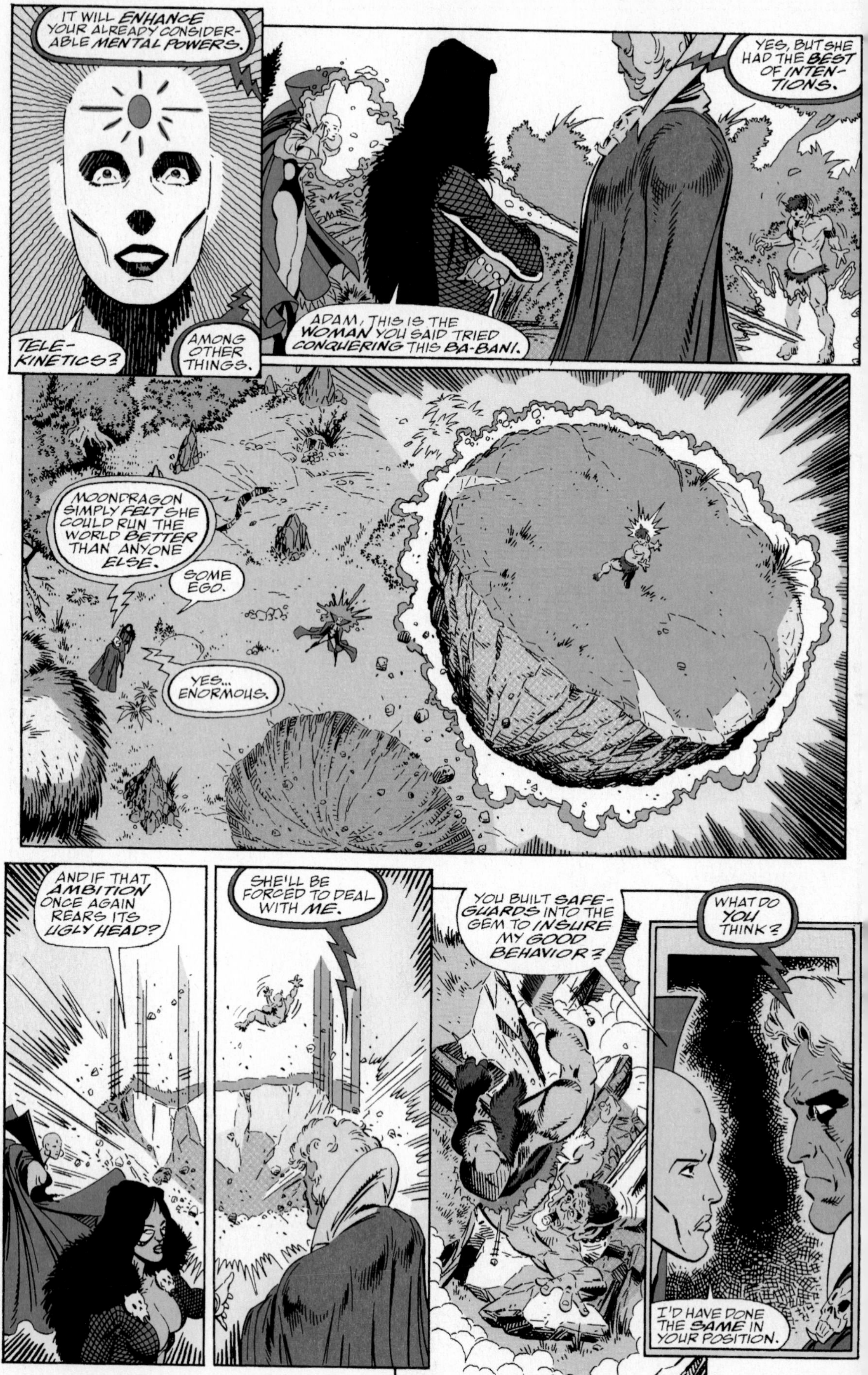

IT WILL ENHANCE YOUR ALREADY CONSIDERABLE MENTAL POWERS.
TELE-KINETICS?
AMONG OTHER THINGS.
YES, BUT SHE HAD THE BEST OF INTENTIONS.
ADAM, THIS IS THE WOMAN YOU SAID TRIED CONQUERING THIS BA-BANI.
MOONDRAGON SIMPLY FELT SHE COULD RUN THE WORLD BETTER THAN ANYONE ELSE.
SOME EGO.
YES... ENORMOUS.
AND IF THAT AMBITION ONCE AGAIN REARS ITS UGLY HEAD?
SHE'LL BE FORCED TO DEAL WITH ME.
YOU BUILT SAFEGUARDS INTO THE GEM TO INSURE MY GOOD BEHAVIOR?
WHAT DO YOU THINK?
I'D HAVE DONE THE SAME IN YOUR POSITION.

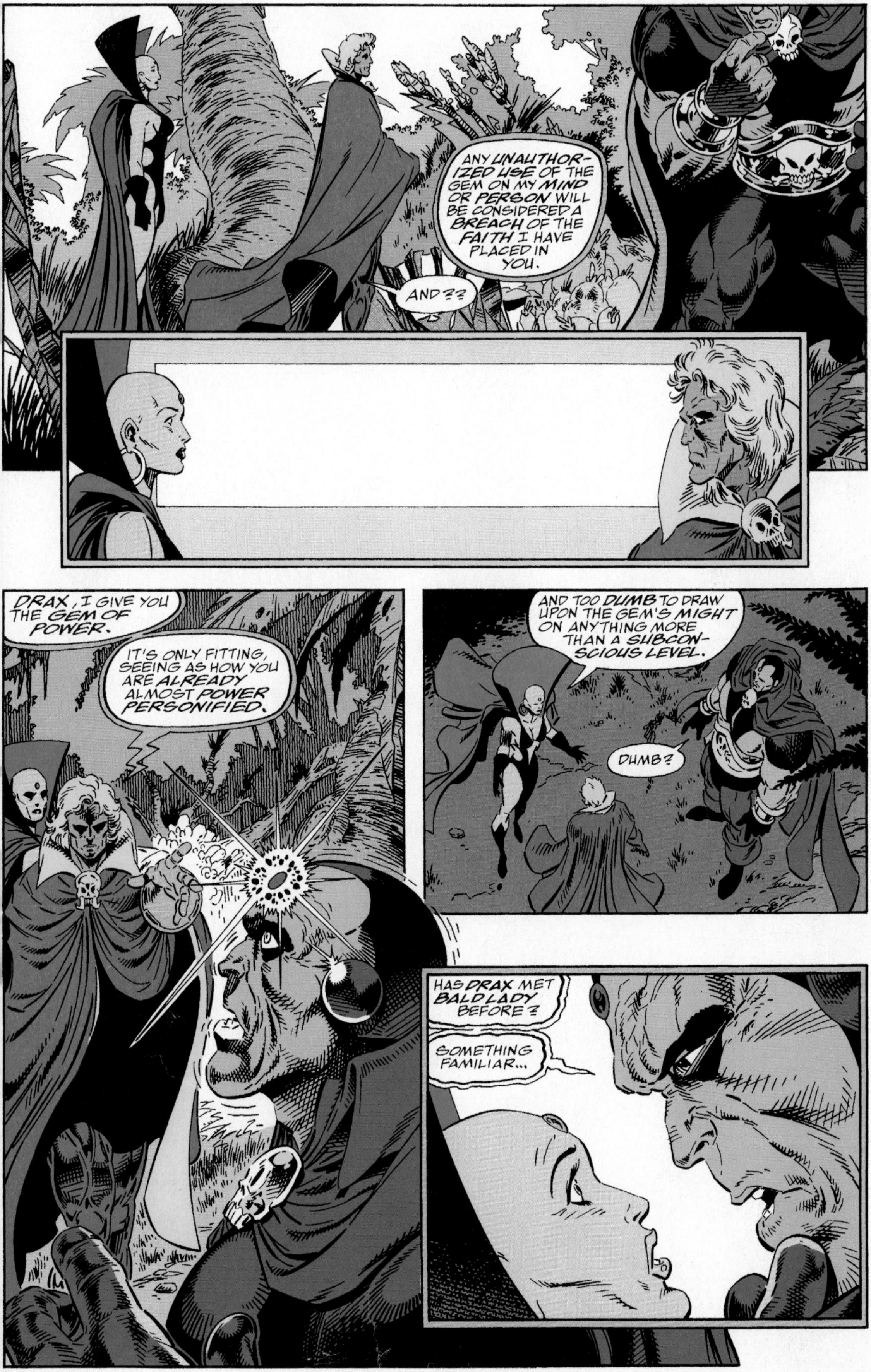
ANY UNAUTHORIZED USE OF THE GEM ON MY MIND OR PERSON WILL BE CONSIDERED A BREACH OF THE FAITH I HAVE PLACED IN YOU.
AND??
DRAX, I GIVE YOU THE GEM OF POWER.
IT'S ONLY FITTING, SEEING AS HOW YOU ARE ALREADY ALMOST POWER PERSONIFIED.
AND TOO DUMB TO DRAW UPON THE GEM'S MIGHT ON ANYTHING MORE THAN A SUBCONSCIOUS LEVEL.
DUMB?
HAS DRAX MET BALD LADY BEFORE?
SOMETHING FAMILIAR...

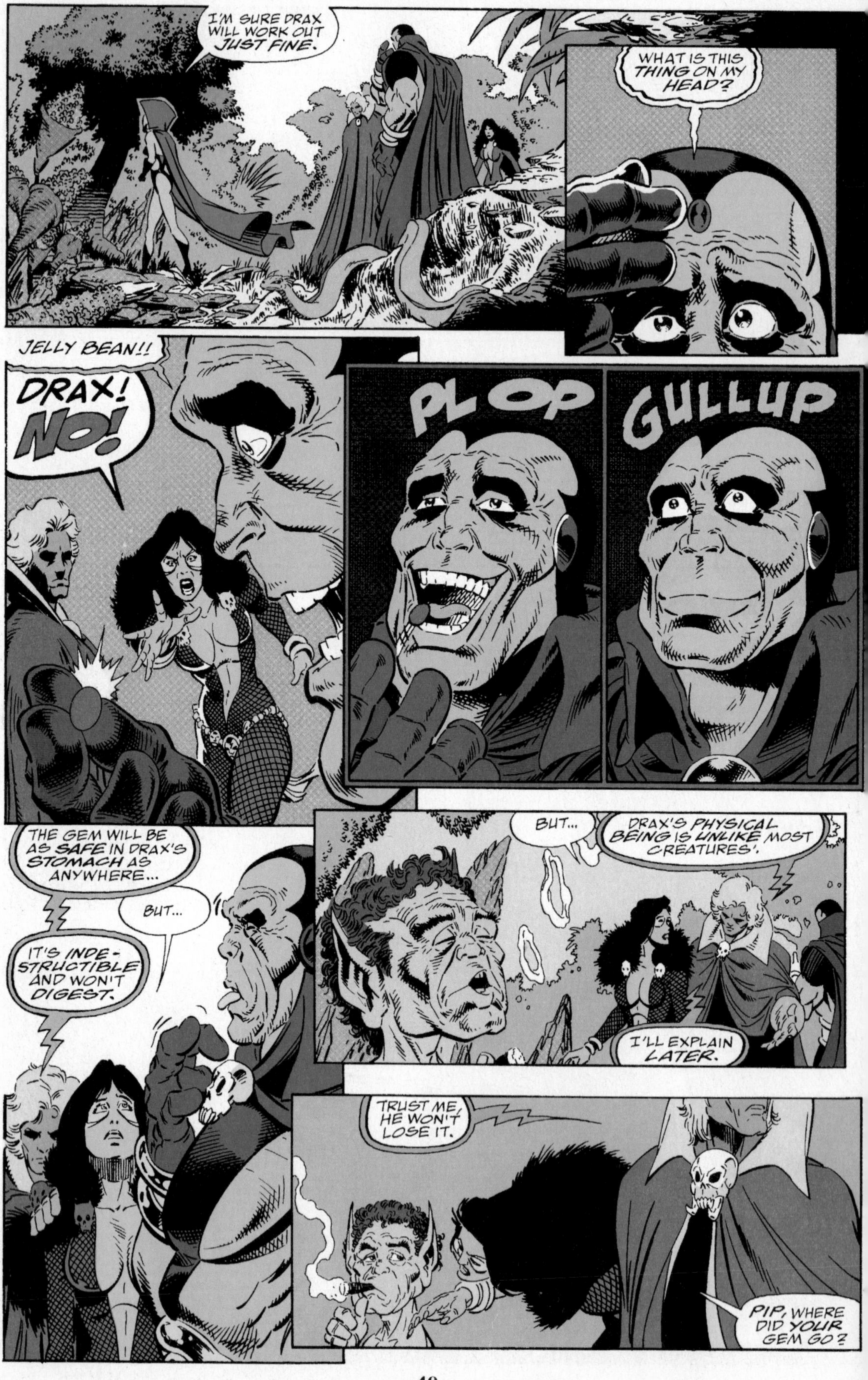

I'M SURE DRAX WILL WORK OUT JUST FINE.
WHAT IS THIS THING ON MY HEAD?
JELLY BEAN!!
DRAX! NO!
PLOP
GULLUP
THE GEM WILL BE AS SAFE IN DRAX'S STOMACH AS ANYWHERE...
BUT...
IT'S INDE-STRUCTIBLE AND WON'T DIGEST.
BUT...
DRAX'S PHYSICAL BEING IS UNLIKE MOST CREATURES'.
I'LL EXPLAIN LATER.
TRUST ME, HE WON'T LOSE IT.
PIP, WHERE DID YOUR GEM GO?

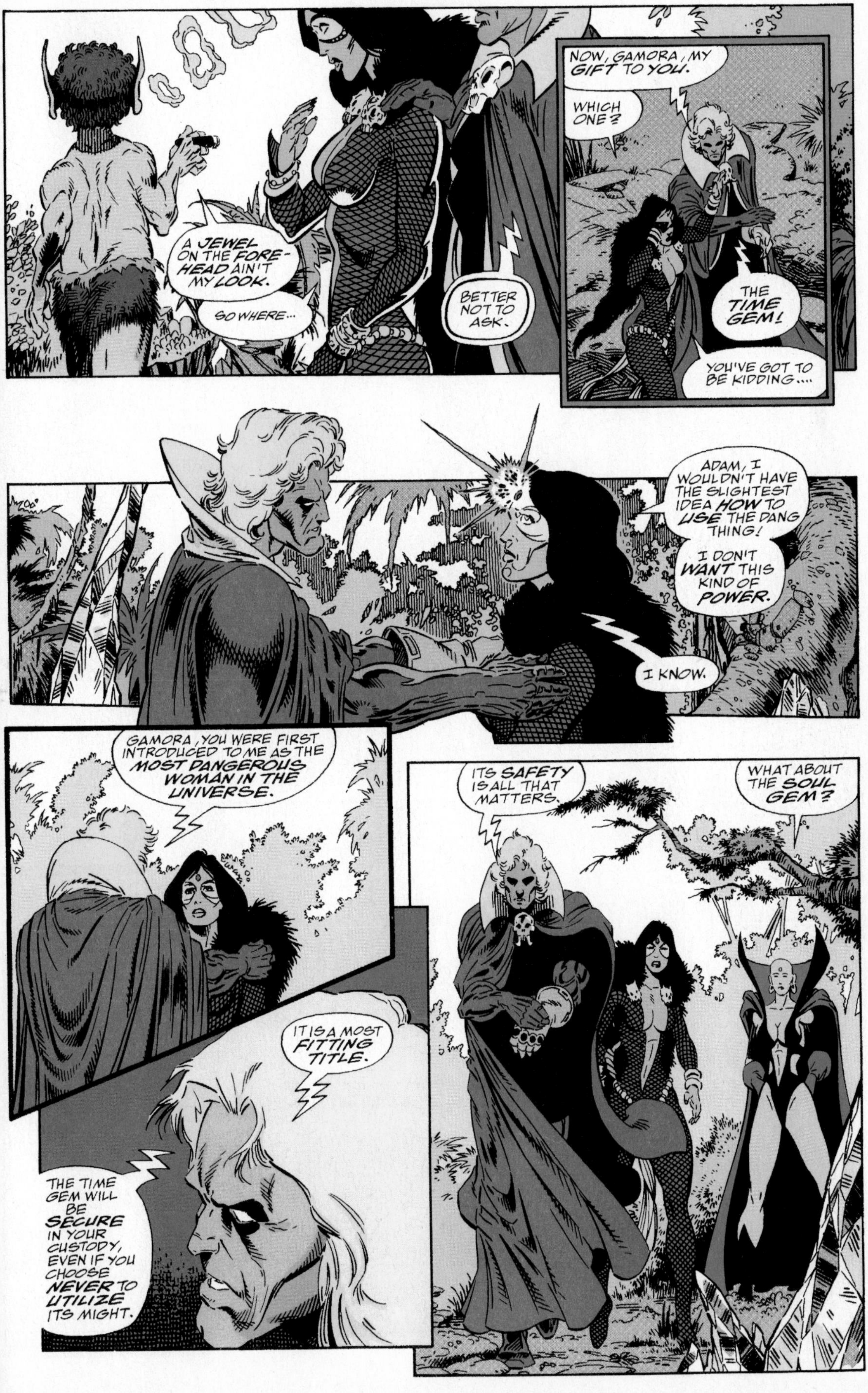
A JEWEL ON THE FORE-HEAD AIN'T MY LOOK.
SO WHERE...
BETTER NOT TO ASK.
NOW, GAMORA, MY GIFT TO YOU.
WHICH ONE?
THE TIME GEM!
YOU'VE GOT TO BE KIDDING....
ADAM, I WOULDN'T HAVE THE SLIGHTEST IDEA HOW TO USE THE DANG THING!
I DON'T WANT THIS KIND OF POWER.
I KNOW.
GAMORA, YOU WERE FIRST INTRODUCED TO ME AS THE MOST DANGEROUS WOMAN IN THE UNIVERSE.
IT IS A MOST FITTING TITLE.
THE TIME GEM WILL BE SECURE IN YOUR CUSTODY, EVEN IF YOU CHOOSE NEVER TO UTILIZE ITS MIGHT.
ITS SAFETY IS ALL THAT MATTERS.
WHAT ABOUT THE SOUL GEM?

THIS BAUBLE AND I ARE OLD FRIENDS.

FOR BETTER OR WORSE IT STAYS WITH ME.

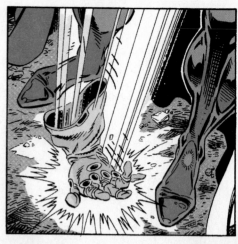

THERE WERE SIX INFINITY GEMS, WEREN'T THERE?

THE REALITY GEM!

WHERE'D IT GO?

TO A CARETAKER WHOSE IDENTITY WILL REMAIN UN-KNOWN TO ALL BUT ME.

YOUR NAMELESS ENFORCER?

SOMEONE WHO'D FROWN UPON ANYONE ATTEMPTING TO GATHER ALL THE JEWELS FOR THEIR PERSONAL AGGRAN-DIZEMENT.

I CAN'T IMAGINE WHO...

42

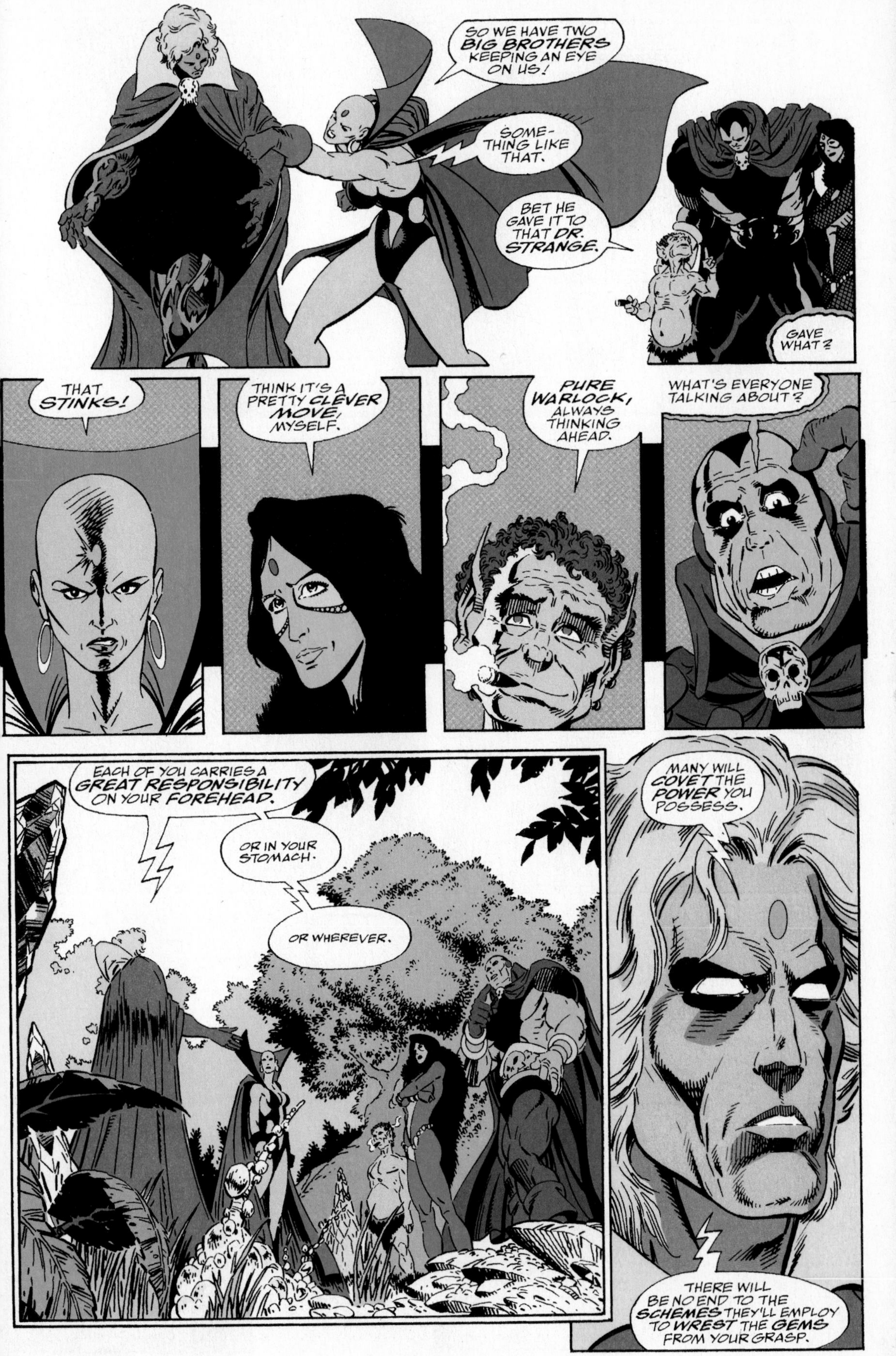
SO WE HAVE TWO BIG BROTHERS KEEPING AN EYE ON US!
SOME-THING LIKE THAT.
BET HE GAVE IT TO THAT DR. STRANGE.
GAVE WHAT?
THAT STINKS!
THINK IT'S A PRETTY CLEVER MOVE, MYSELF.
PURE WARLOCK, ALWAYS THINKING AHEAD.
WHAT'S EVERYONE TALKING ABOUT?
EACH OF YOU CARRIES A GREAT RESPONSIBILITY ON YOUR FOREHEAD.
OR IN YOUR STOMACH.
OR WHEREVER.
MANY WILL COVET THE POWER YOU POSSESS.
THERE WILL BE NO END TO THE SCHEMES THEY'LL EMPLOY TO WREST THE GEMS FROM YOUR GRASP.

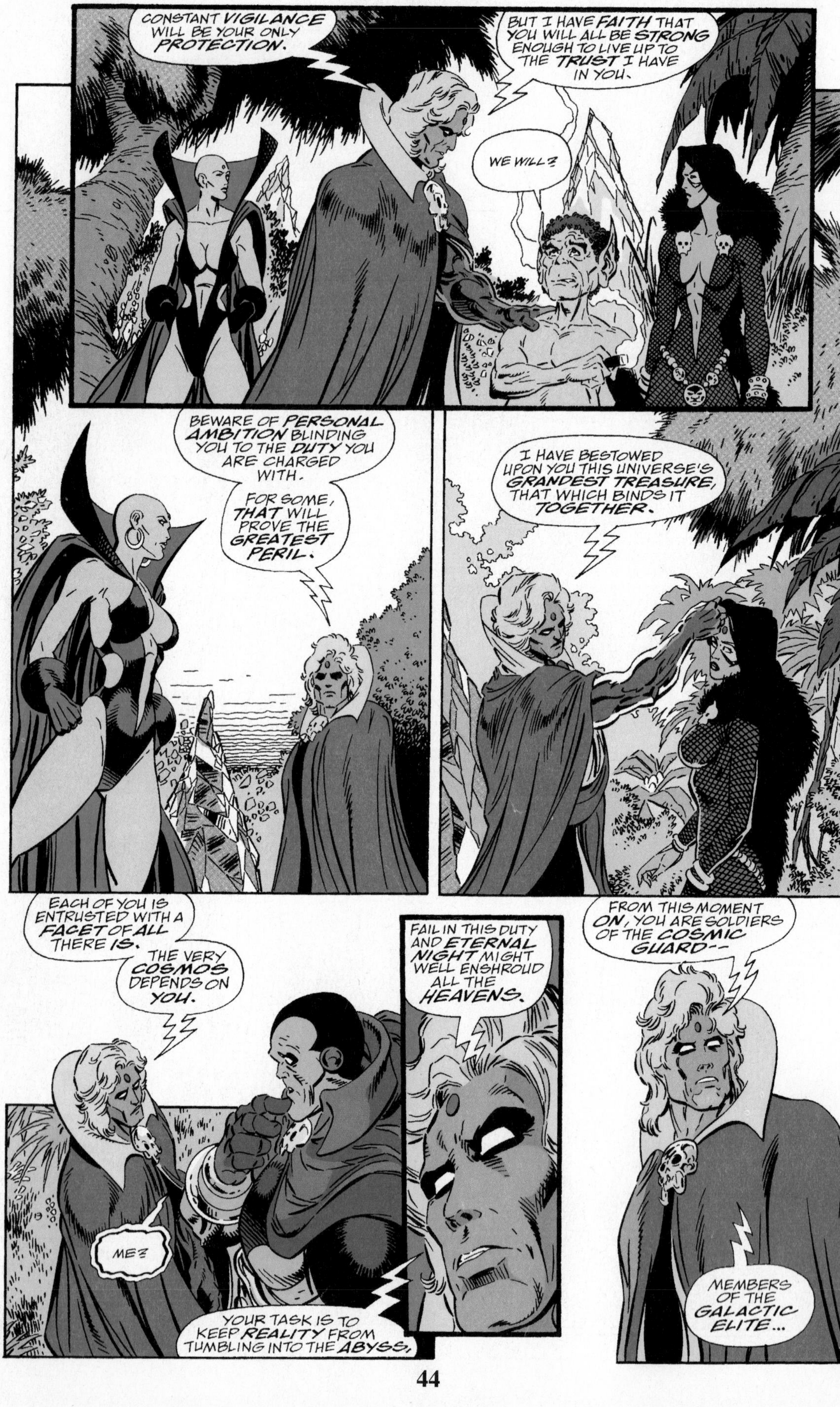
CONSTANT VIGILANCE WILL BE YOUR ONLY PROTECTION.
BUT I HAVE FAITH THAT YOU WILL ALL BE STRONG ENOUGH TO LIVE UP TO THE TRUST I HAVE IN YOU.
WE WILL?
BEWARE OF PERSONAL AMBITION BLINDING YOU TO THE DUTY YOU ARE CHARGED WITH.
FOR SOME, THAT WILL PROVE THE GREATEST PERIL.
I HAVE BESTOWED UPON YOU THIS UNIVERSE'S GRANDEST TREASURE, THAT WHICH BINDS IT TOGETHER.
EACH OF YOU IS ENTRUSTED WITH A FACET OF ALL THERE IS.
THE VERY COSMOS DEPENDS ON YOU.
ME?
FAIL IN THIS DUTY AND ETERNAL NIGHT MIGHT WELL ENSHROUD ALL THE HEAVENS.
YOUR TASK IS TO KEEP REALITY FROM TUMBLING INTO THE ABYSS.
FROM THIS MOMENT ON, YOU ARE SOLDIERS OF THE COSMIC GUARD--
MEMBERS OF THE GALACTIC ELITE...

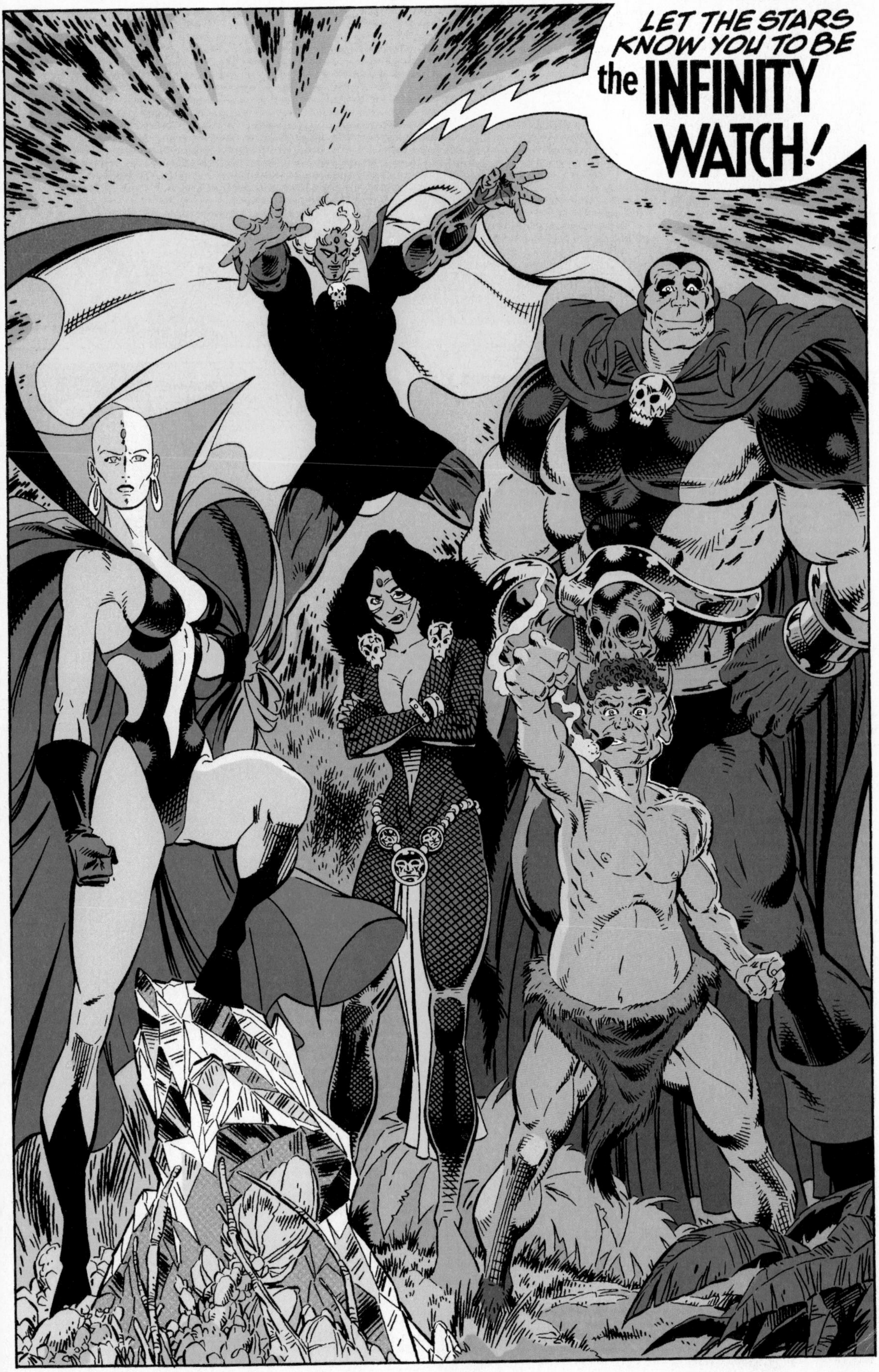
LET THE STARS KNOW YOU TO BE the INFINITY WATCH!

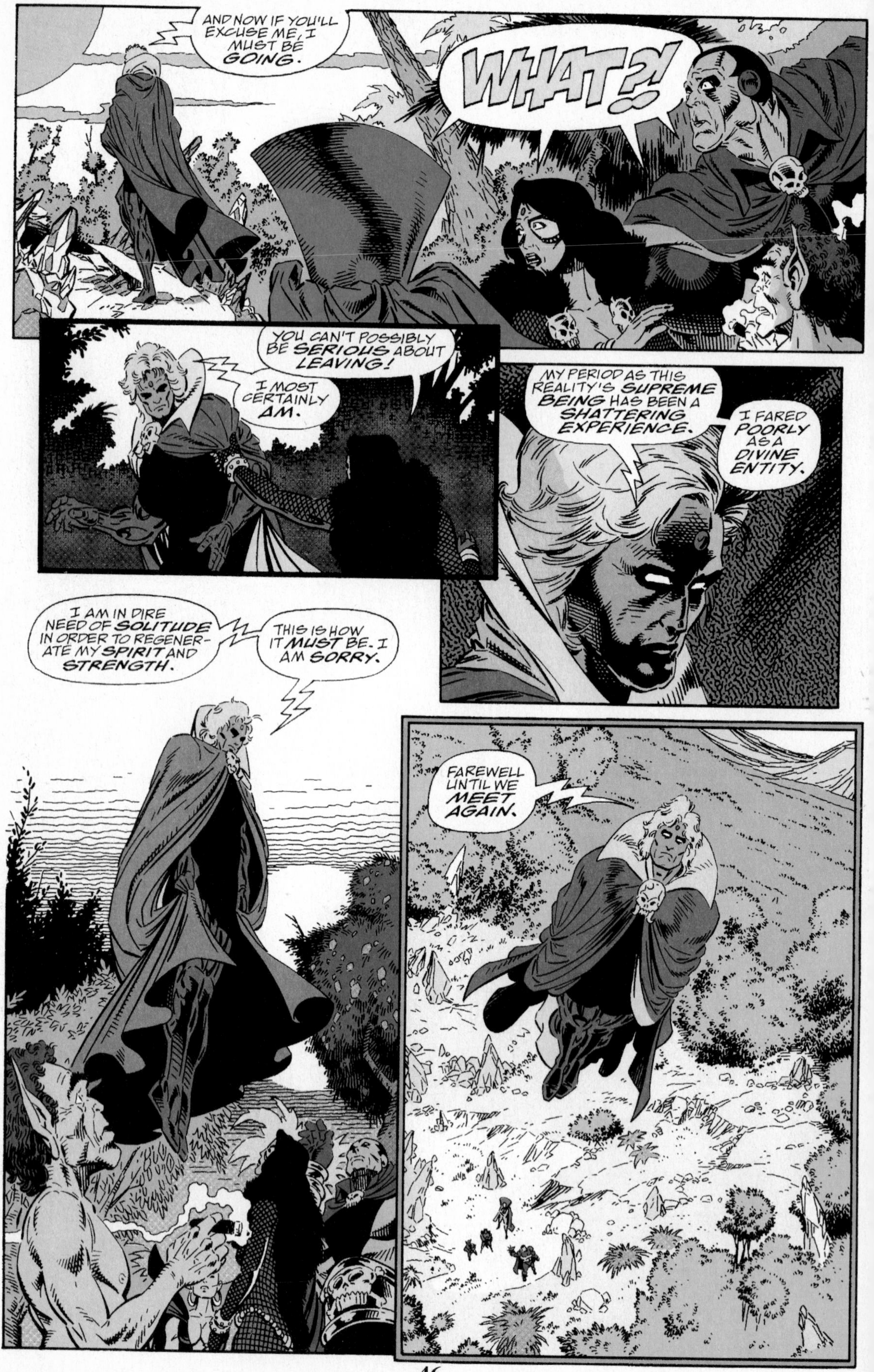
AND NOW IF YOU'LL EXCUSE ME, I MUST BE GOING.
WHAT?!
YOU CAN'T POSSIBLY BE SERIOUS ABOUT LEAVING!
I MOST CERTAINLY AM.
MY PERIOD AS THIS REALITY'S SUPREME BEING HAS BEEN A SHATTERING EXPERIENCE.
I FARED POORLY AS A DIVINE ENTITY.
I AM IN DIRE NEED OF SOLITUDE IN ORDER TO REGENERATE MY SPIRIT AND STRENGTH.
THIS IS HOW IT MUST BE. I AM SORRY.
FAREWELL UNTIL WE MEET AGAIN.

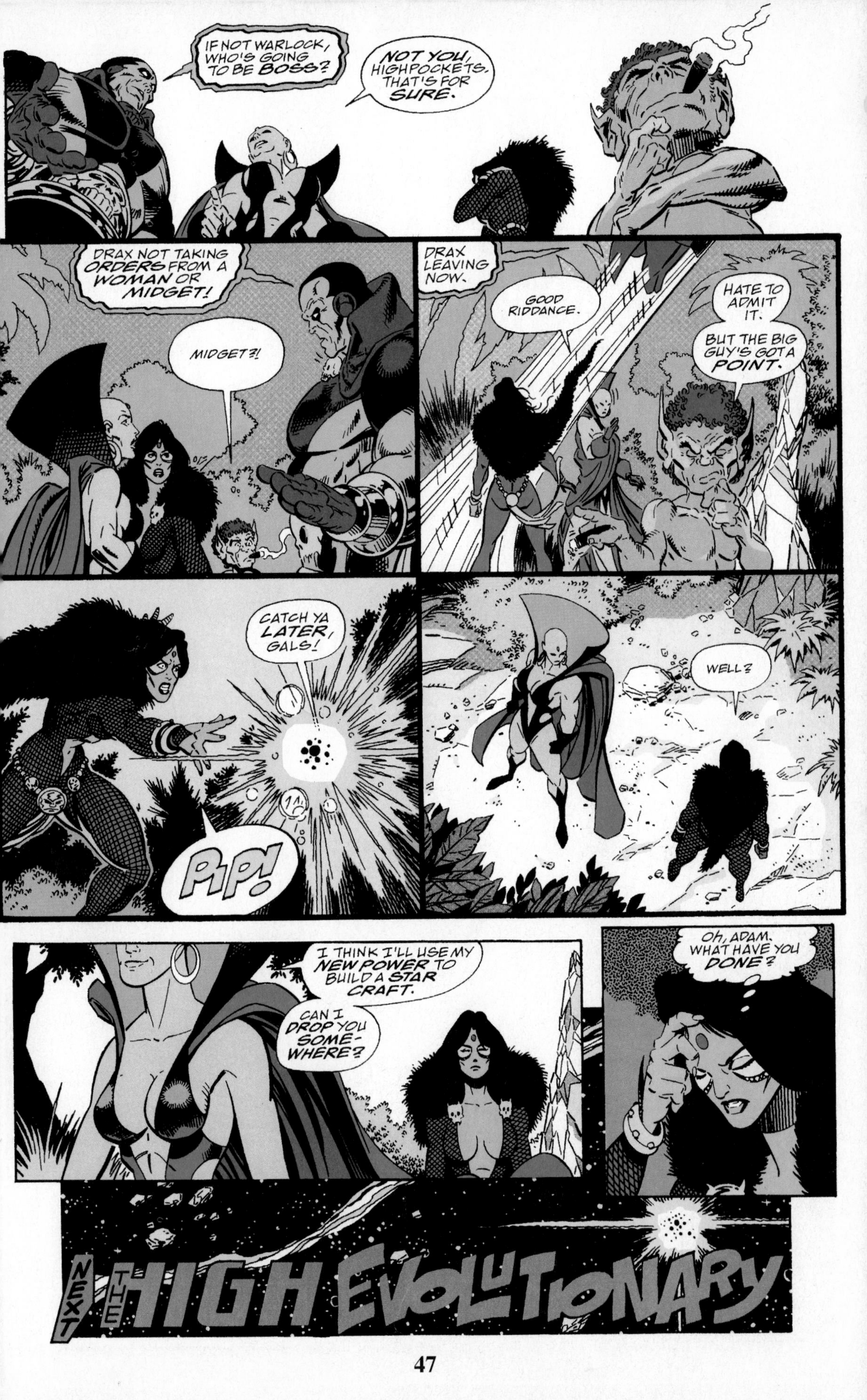
IF NOT WARLOCK, WHO'S GOING TO BE BOSS?
NOT YOU, HIGHPOCKETS. THAT'S FOR SURE.
DRAX NOT TAKING ORDERS FROM A WOMAN OR MIDGET!
MIDGET?!
DRAX LEAVING NOW.
GOOD RIDDANCE.
HATE TO ADMIT IT.
BUT THE BIG GUY'S GOT A POINT.
CATCH YA LATER, GALS!
POP!
WELL?
I THINK I'LL USE MY NEW POWER TO BUILD A STAR CRAFT.
CAN I DROP YOU SOMEWHERE?
Oh, ADAM. WHAT HAVE YOU DONE?
NEXT THE HIGH EVOLUTIONARY

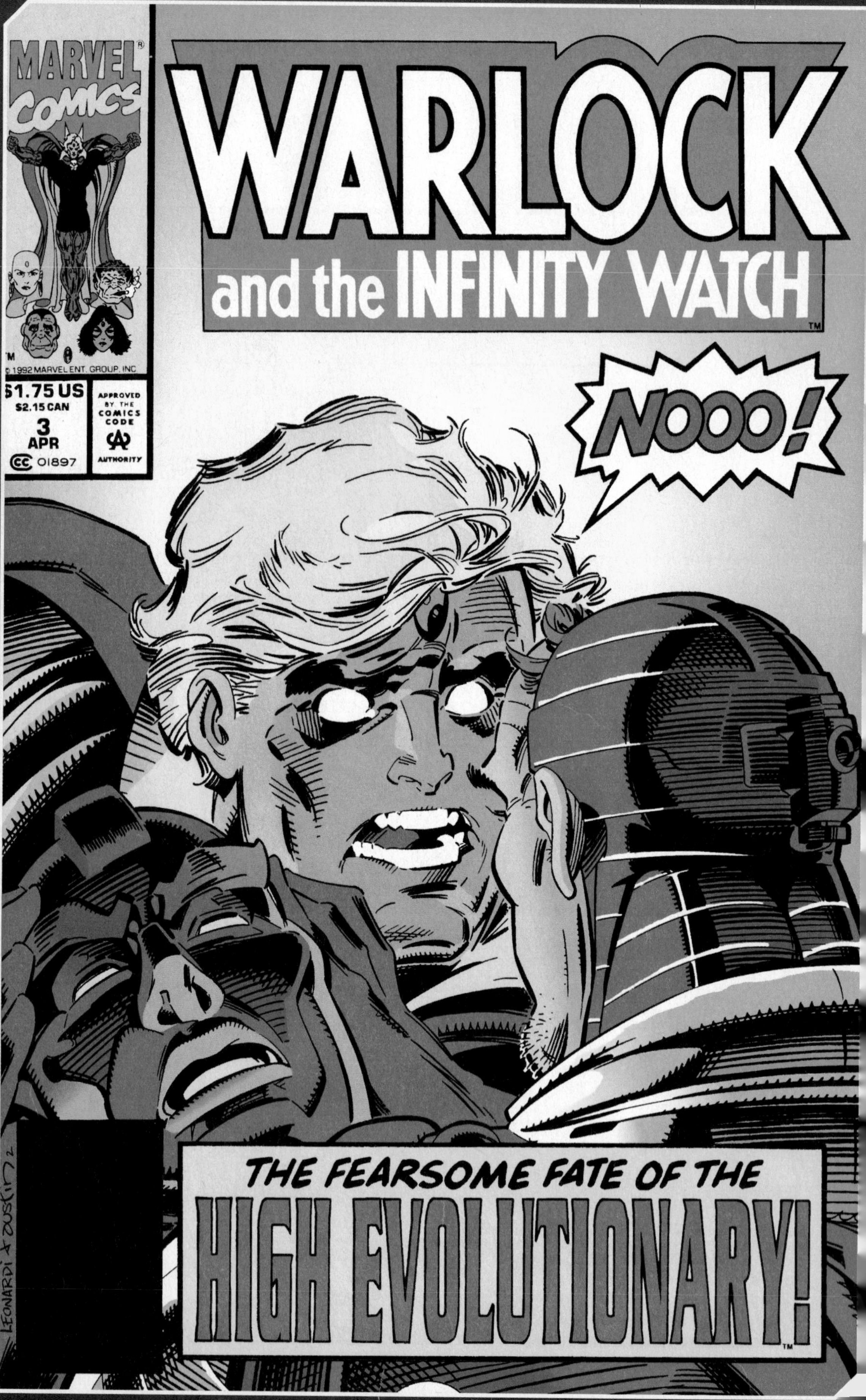
MARVEL COMICS
WARLOCK
and the INFINITY WATCH
© 1992 MARVEL ENT. GROUP, INC.
$1.75 US
$2.15 CAN
3
APR
01897
APPROVED BY THE COMICS CODE AUTHORITY
NOOO!
THE FEARSOME FATE OF THE
HIGH EVOLUTIONARY!
LEONARDI & AUSTIN

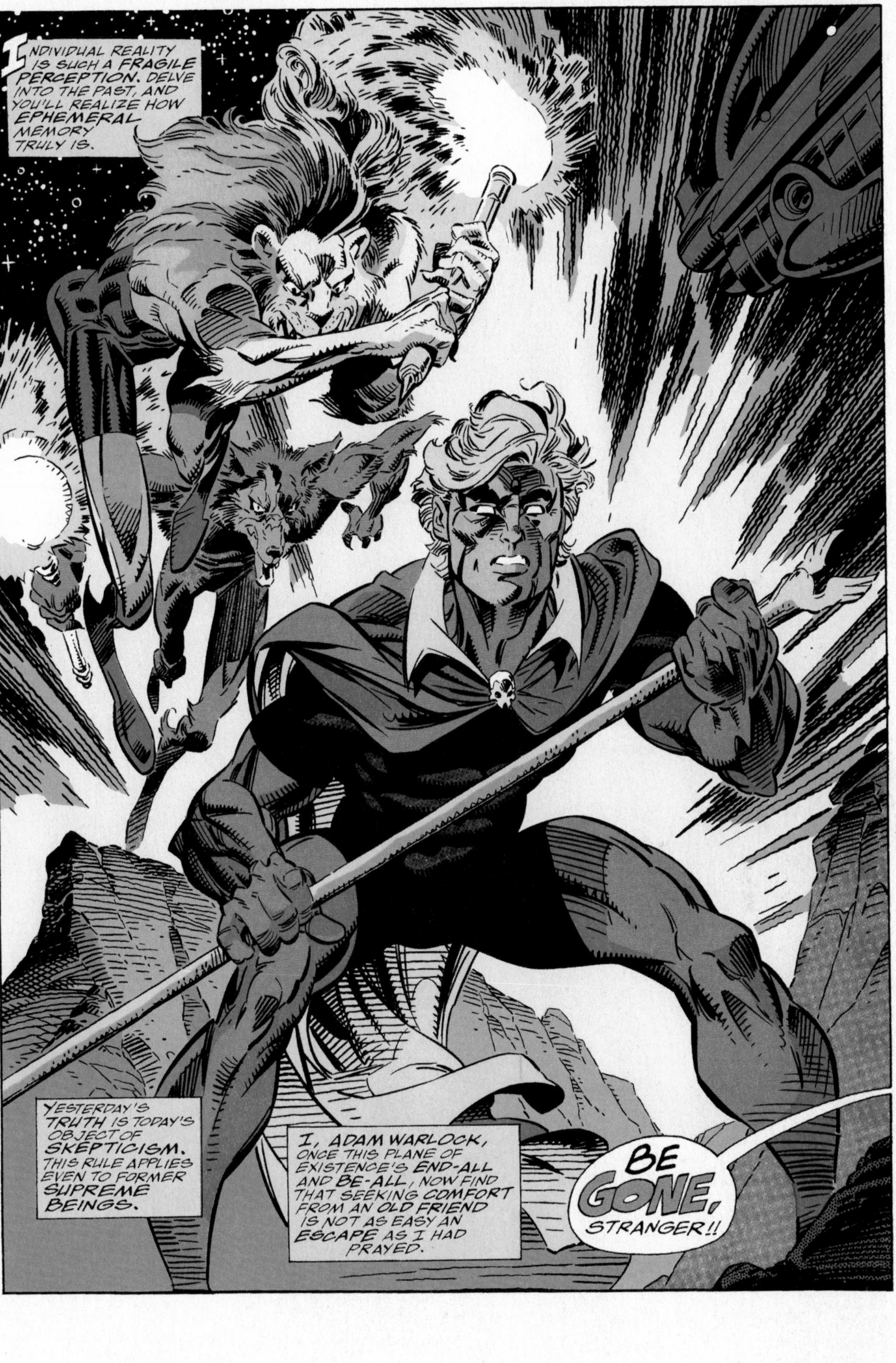
INDIVIDUAL REALITY IS SUCH A FRAGILE PERCEPTION. DELVE INTO THE PAST, AND YOU'LL REALIZE HOW EPHEMERAL MEMORY TRULY IS.
YESTERDAY'S TRUTH IS TODAY'S OBJECT OF SKEPTICISM. THIS RULE APPLIES EVEN TO FORMER SUPREME BEINGS.
I, ADAM WARLOCK, ONCE THIS PLANE OF EXISTENCE'S END-ALL AND BE-ALL, NOW FIND THAT SEEKING COMFORT FROM AN OLD FRIEND IS NOT AS EASY AN ESCAPE AS I HAD PRAYED.
BE GONE, STRANGER!!

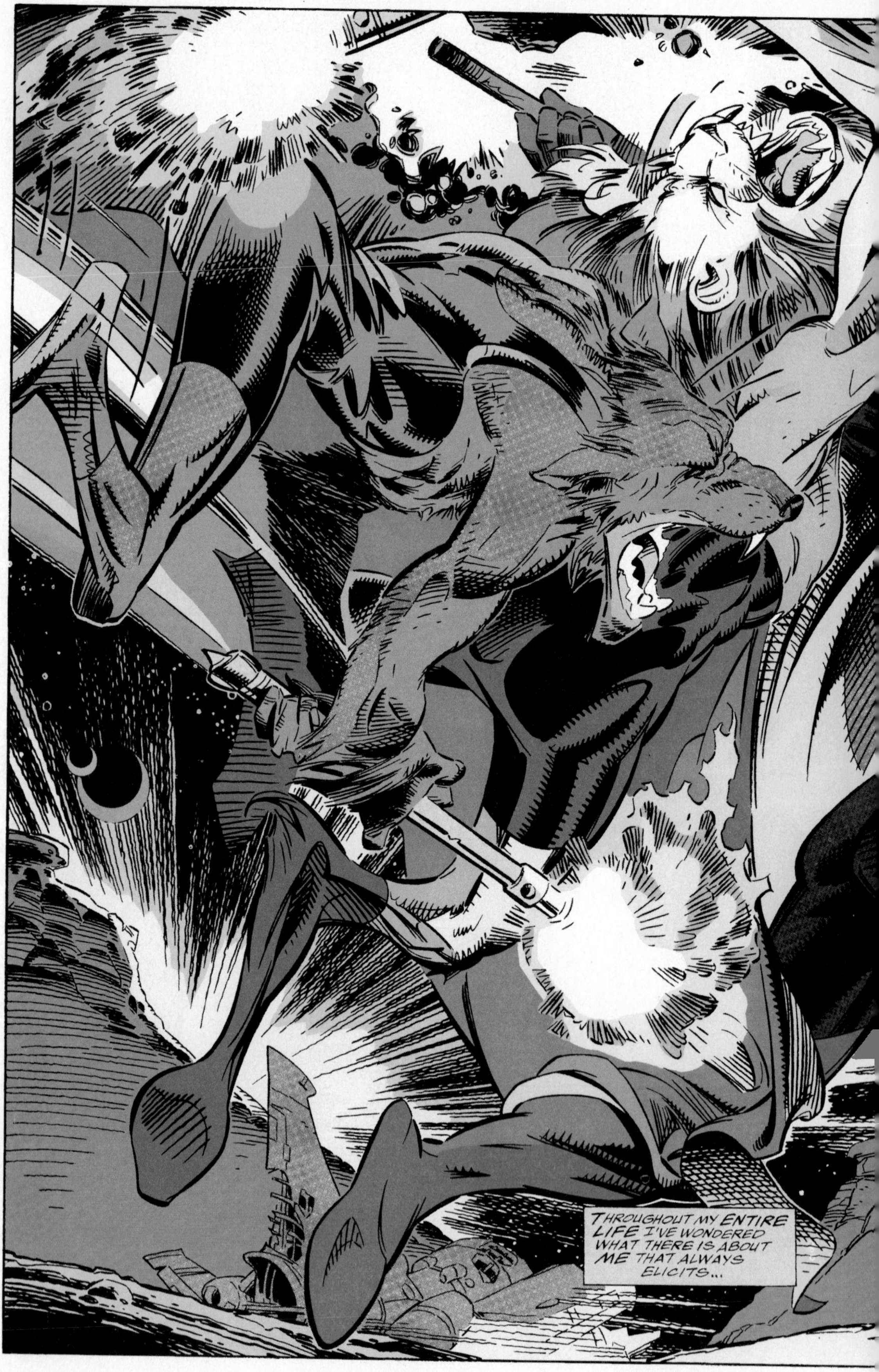
THROUGHOUT MY ENTIRE LIFE I'VE WONDERED WHAT THERE IS ABOUT ME THAT ALWAYS ELICITS...

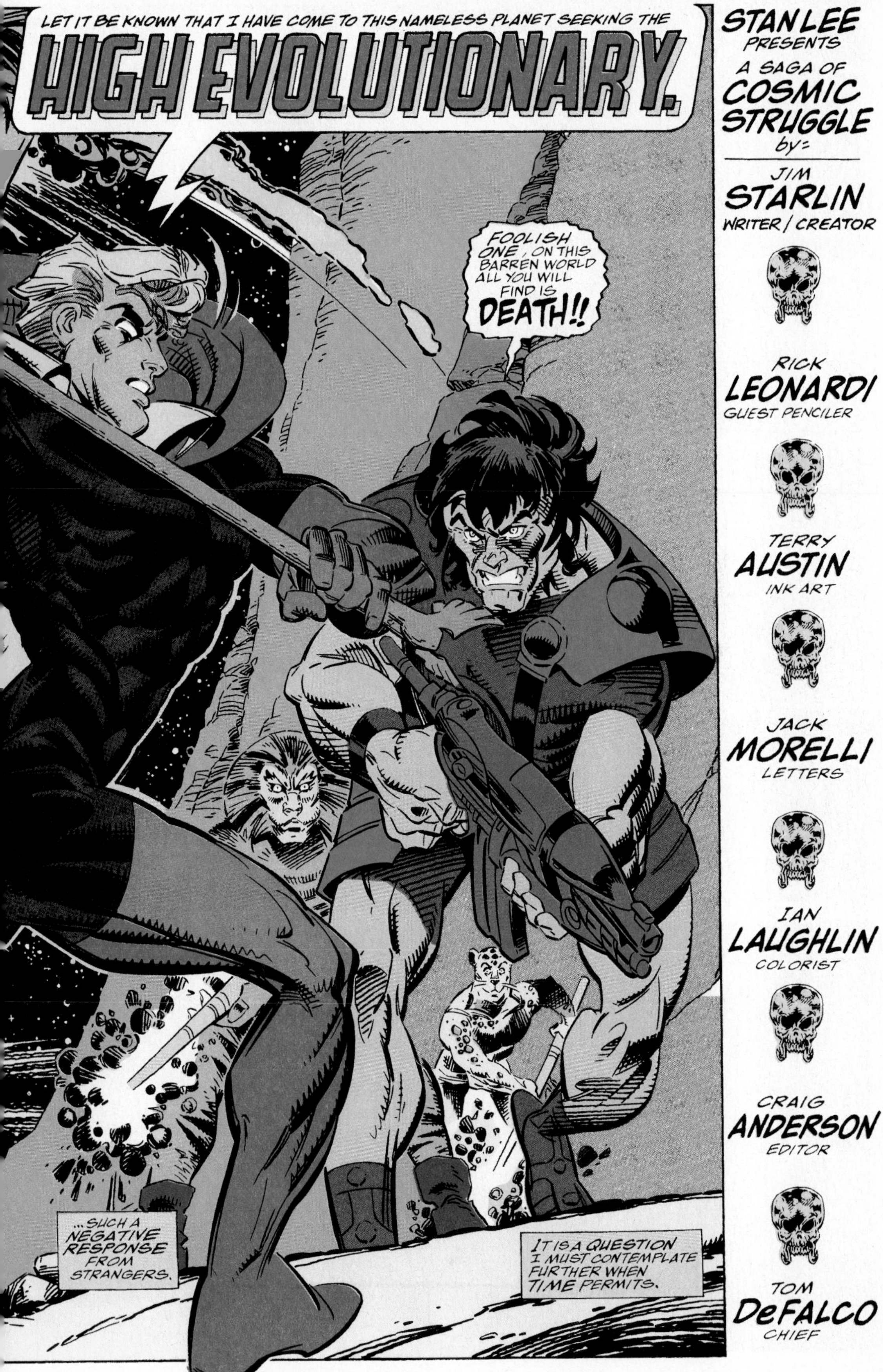
LET IT BE KNOWN THAT I HAVE COME TO THIS NAMELESS PLANET SEEKING THE HIGH EVOLUTIONARY.
FOOLISH ONE, ON THIS BARREN WORLD ALL YOU WILL FIND IS DEATH!!
...SUCH A NEGATIVE RESPONSE FROM STRANGERS.
IT IS A QUESTION I MUST CONTEMPLATE FURTHER WHEN TIME PERMITS.
STAN LEE PRESENTS A SAGA OF COSMIC STRUGGLE by:
JIM STARLIN WRITER / CREATOR
RICK LEONARDI GUEST PENCILER
TERRY AUSTIN INK ART
JACK MORELLI LETTERS
IAN LAUGHLIN COLORIST
CRAIG ANDERSON EDITOR
TOM DeFALCO CHIEF

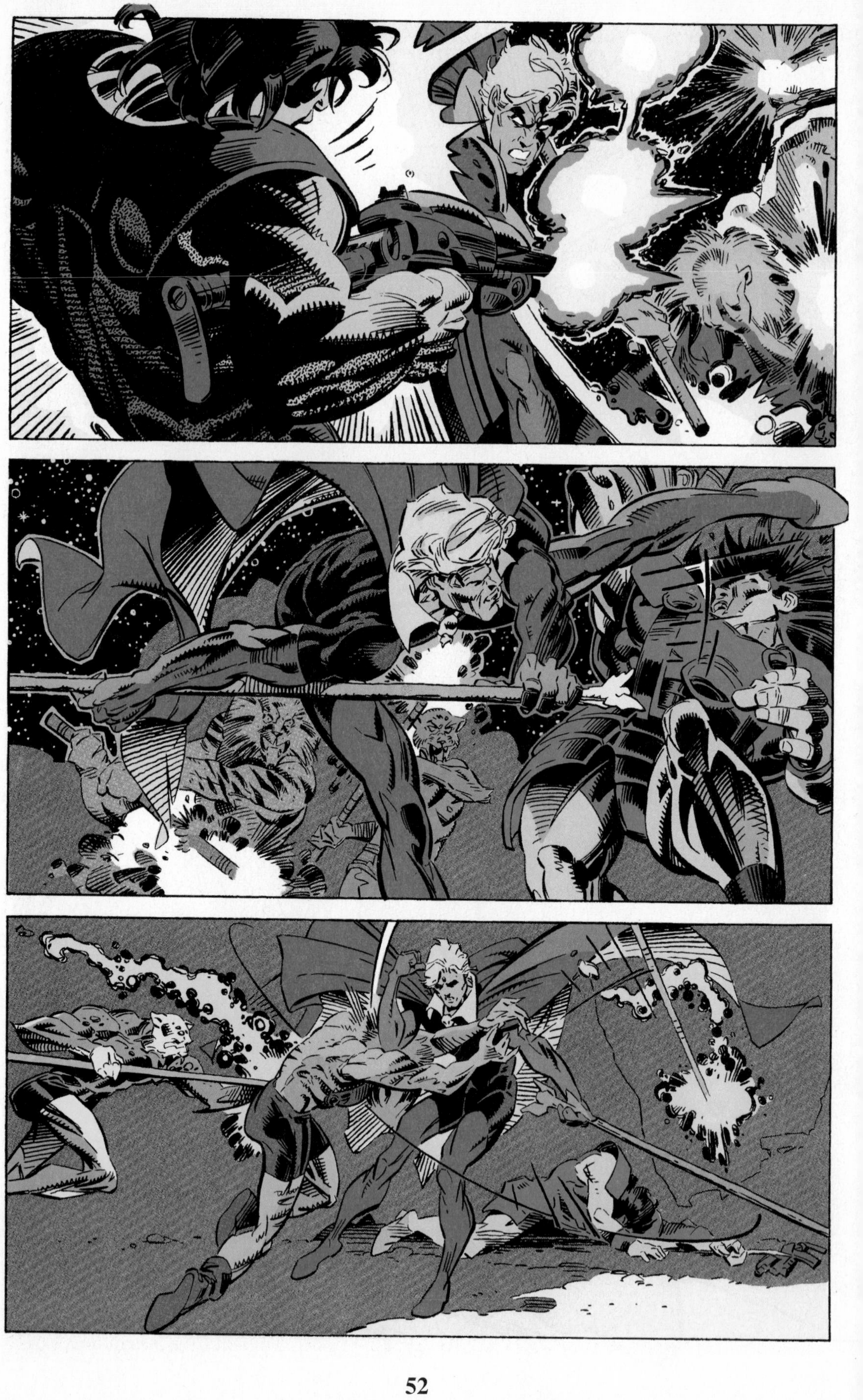

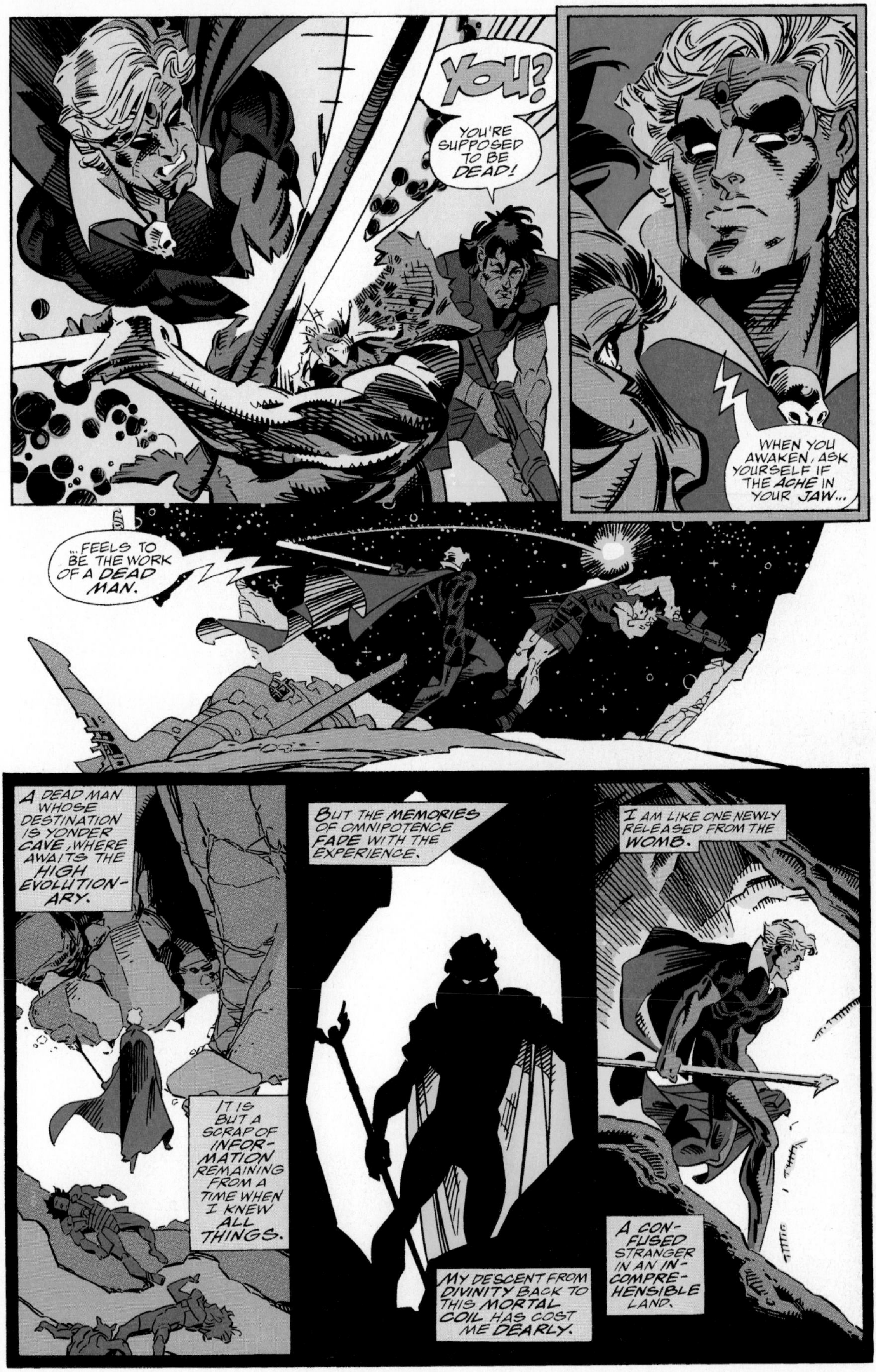
YOU?
YOU'RE SUPPOSED TO BE DEAD!
WHEN YOU AWAKEN, ASK YOURSELF IF THE ACHE IN YOUR JAW...
...FEELS TO BE THE WORK OF A DEAD MAN.
A DEAD MAN WHOSE DESTINATION IS YONDER CAVE, WHERE AWAITS THE HIGH EVOLUTIONARY.
IT IS BUT A SCRAP OF INFORMATION REMAINING FROM A TIME WHEN I KNEW ALL THINGS.
BUT THE MEMORIES OF OMNIPOTENCE FADE WITH THE EXPERIENCE.
MY DESCENT FROM DIVINITY BACK TO THIS MORTAL COIL HAS COST ME DEARLY.
I AM LIKE ONE NEWLY RELEASED FROM THE WOMB.
A CONFUSED STRANGER IN AN INCOMPREHENSIBLE LAND.

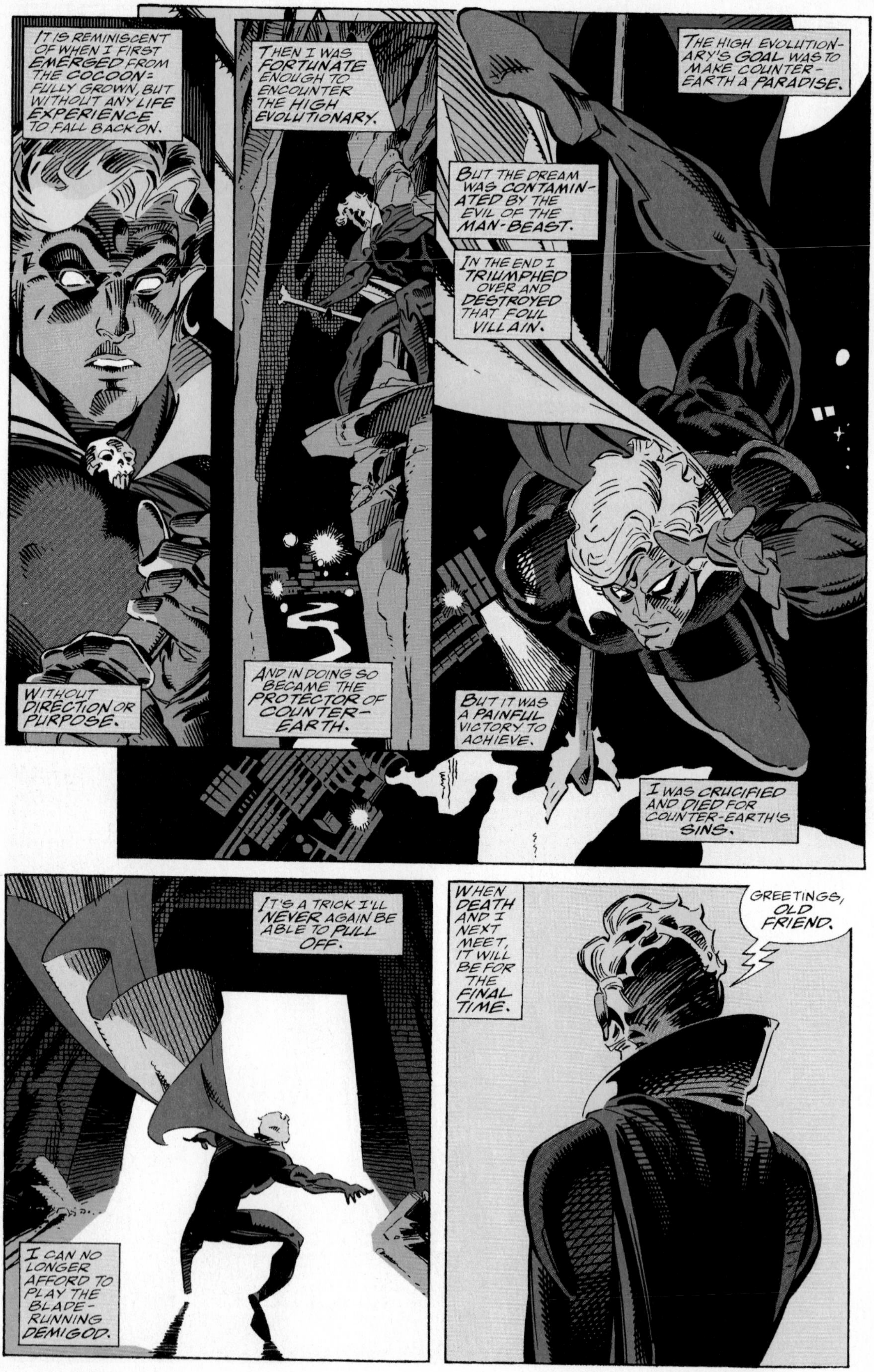

IT IS REMINISCENT OF WHEN I FIRST EMERGED FROM THE COCOON-- FULLY GROWN, BUT WITHOUT ANY LIFE EXPERIENCE TO FALL BACK ON.
WITHOUT DIRECTION OR PURPOSE.
THEN I WAS FORTUNATE ENOUGH TO ENCOUNTER THE HIGH EVOLUTIONARY.
AND IN DOING SO BECAME THE PROTECTOR OF COUNTER-EARTH.
THE HIGH EVOLUTIONARY'S GOAL WAS TO MAKE COUNTER-EARTH A PARADISE.
BUT THE DREAM WAS CONTAMINATED BY THE EVIL OF THE MAN-BEAST.
IN THE END I TRIUMPHED OVER AND DESTROYED THAT FOUL VILLAIN.
BUT IT WAS A PAINFUL VICTORY TO ACHIEVE.
I WAS CRUCIFIED AND DIED FOR COUNTER-EARTH'S SINS.
IT'S A TRICK I'LL NEVER AGAIN BE ABLE TO PULL OFF.
I CAN NO LONGER AFFORD TO PLAY THE BLADE-RUNNING DEMIGOD.
WHEN DEATH AND I NEXT MEET, IT WILL BE FOR THE FINAL TIME.
GREETINGS, OLD FRIEND.

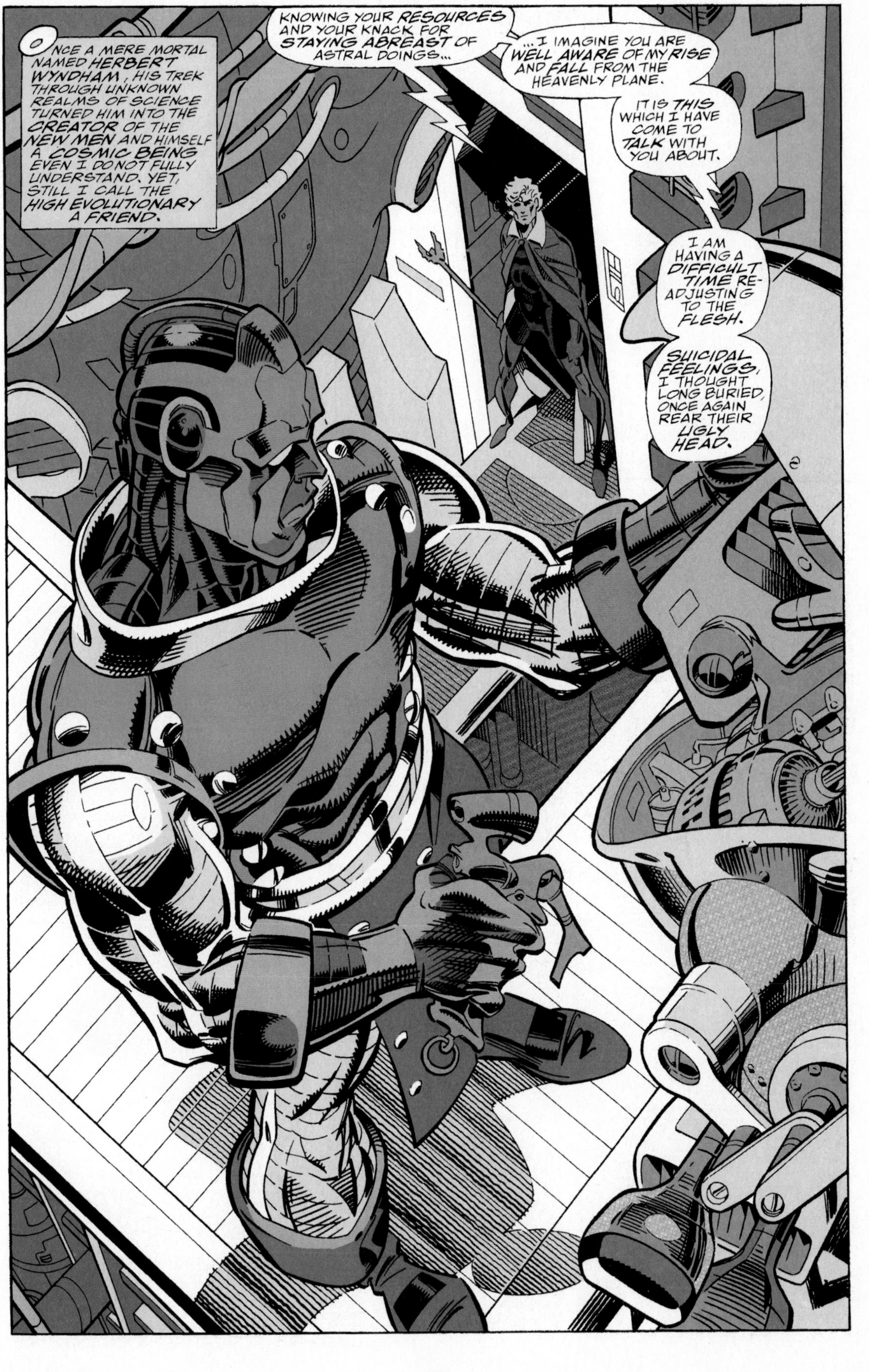

ONCE A MERE MORTAL NAMED HERBERT WYNDHAM, HIS TREK THROUGH UNKNOWN REALMS OF SCIENCE TURNED HIM INTO THE CREATOR OF THE NEW MEN AND HIMSELF A COSMIC BEING EVEN I DO NOT FULLY UNDERSTAND. YET, STILL I CALL THE HIGH EVOLUTIONARY A FRIEND.
KNOWING YOUR RESOURCES AND YOUR KNACK FOR STAYING ABREAST OF ASTRAL DOINGS...
...I IMAGINE YOU ARE WELL AWARE OF MY RISE AND FALL FROM THE HEAVENLY PLANE.
IT IS THIS WHICH I HAVE COME TO TALK WITH YOU ABOUT.
I AM HAVING A DIFFICULT TIME RE-ADJUSTING TO THE FLESH.
SUICIDAL FEELINGS, I THOUGHT LONG BURIED, ONCE AGAIN REAR THEIR UGLY HEAD.

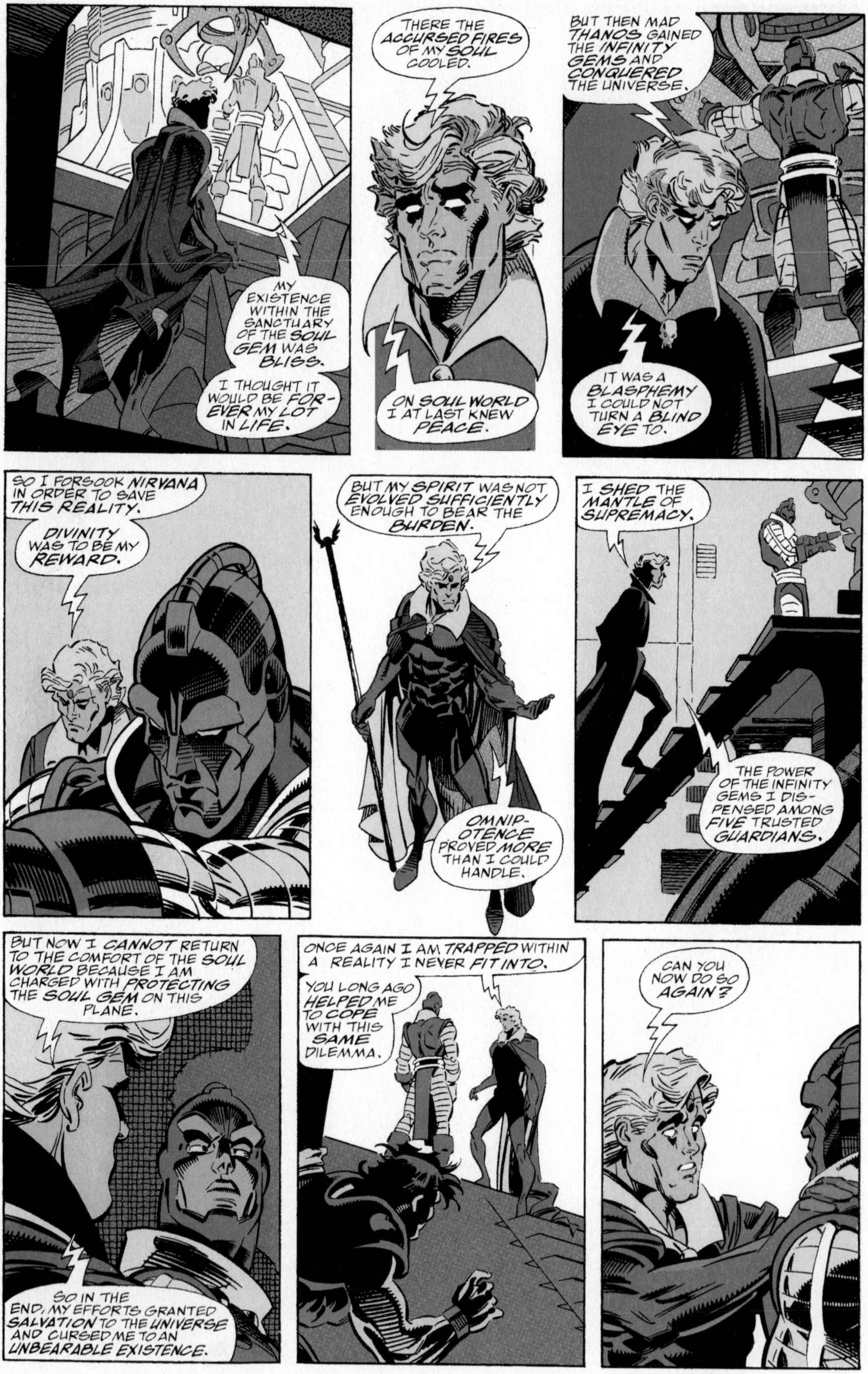

MY EXISTENCE WITHIN THE SANCTUARY OF THE SOUL GEM WAS BLISS.
I THOUGHT IT WOULD BE FOREVER MY LOT IN LIFE.
THERE THE ACCURSED FIRES OF MY SOUL COOLED.
ON SOUL WORLD I AT LAST KNEW PEACE.
BUT THEN MAD THANOS GAINED THE INFINITY GEMS AND CONQUERED THE UNIVERSE.
IT WAS A BLASPHEMY I COULD NOT TURN A BLIND EYE TO.
SO I FORSOOK NIRVANA IN ORDER TO SAVE THIS REALITY.
DIVINITY WAS TO BE MY REWARD.
BUT MY SPIRIT WAS NOT EVOLVED SUFFICIENTLY ENOUGH TO BEAR THE BURDEN.
OMNIPOTENCE PROVED MORE THAN I COULD HANDLE.
I SHED THE MANTLE OF SUPREMACY.
THE POWER OF THE INFINITY GEMS I DISPENSED AMONG FIVE TRUSTED GUARDIANS.
BUT NOW I CANNOT RETURN TO THE COMFORT OF THE SOUL WORLD BECAUSE I AM CHARGED WITH PROTECTING THE SOUL GEM ON THIS PLANE.
SO IN THE END, MY EFFORTS GRANTED SALVATION TO THE UNIVERSE AND CURSED ME TO AN UNBEARABLE EXISTENCE.
ONCE AGAIN I AM TRAPPED WITHIN A REALITY I NEVER FIT INTO.
YOU LONG AGO HELPED ME TO COPE WITH THIS SAME DILEMMA.
CAN YOU NOW DO SO AGAIN?

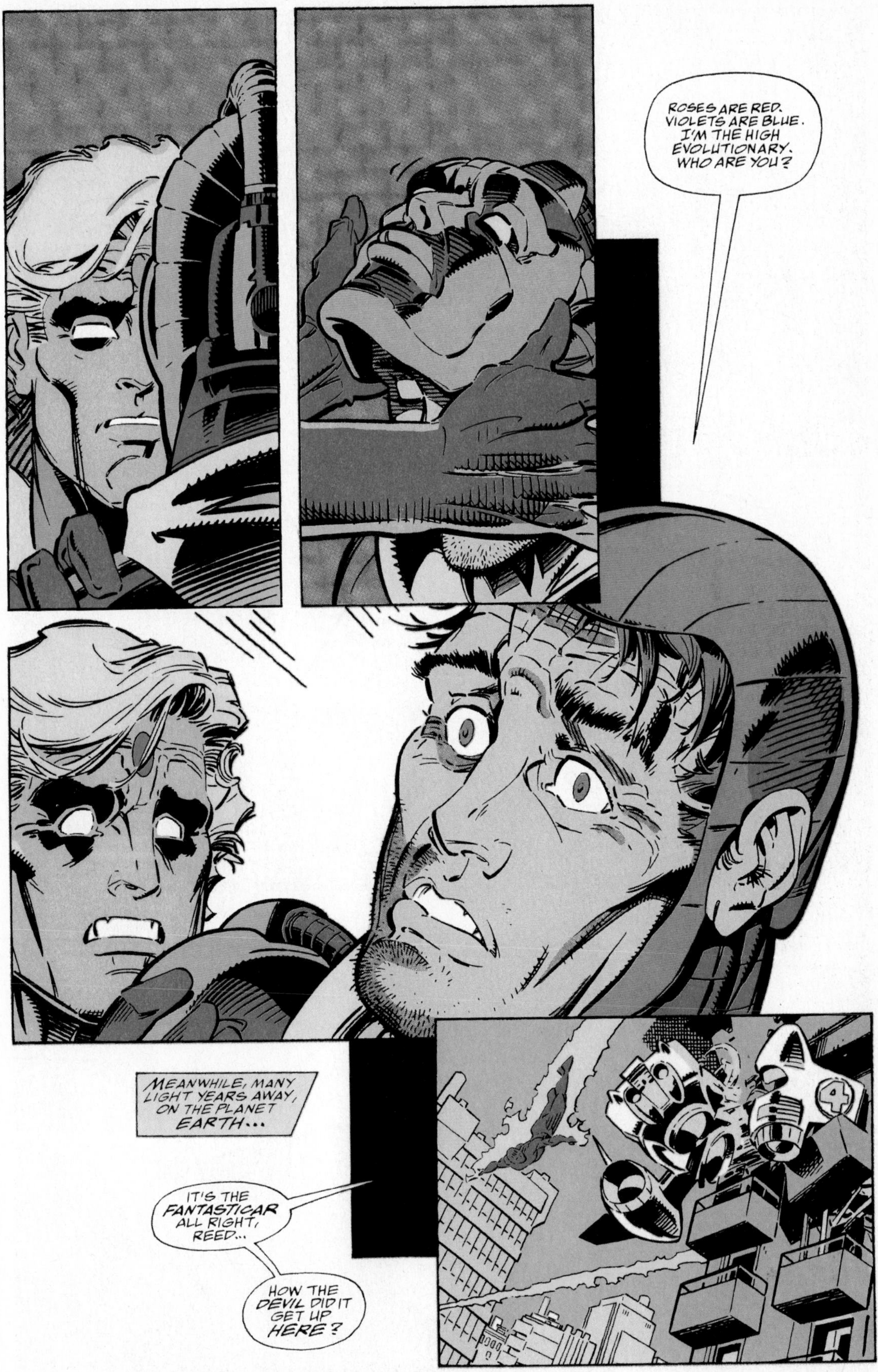
ROSES ARE RED.
VIOLETS ARE BLUE.
I'M THE HIGH EVOLUTIONARY.
WHO ARE YOU?
MEANWHILE, MANY LIGHT YEARS AWAY, ON THE PLANET EARTH...
IT'S THE FANTASTICAR ALL RIGHT, REED...
HOW THE DEVIL DID IT GET UP HERE?

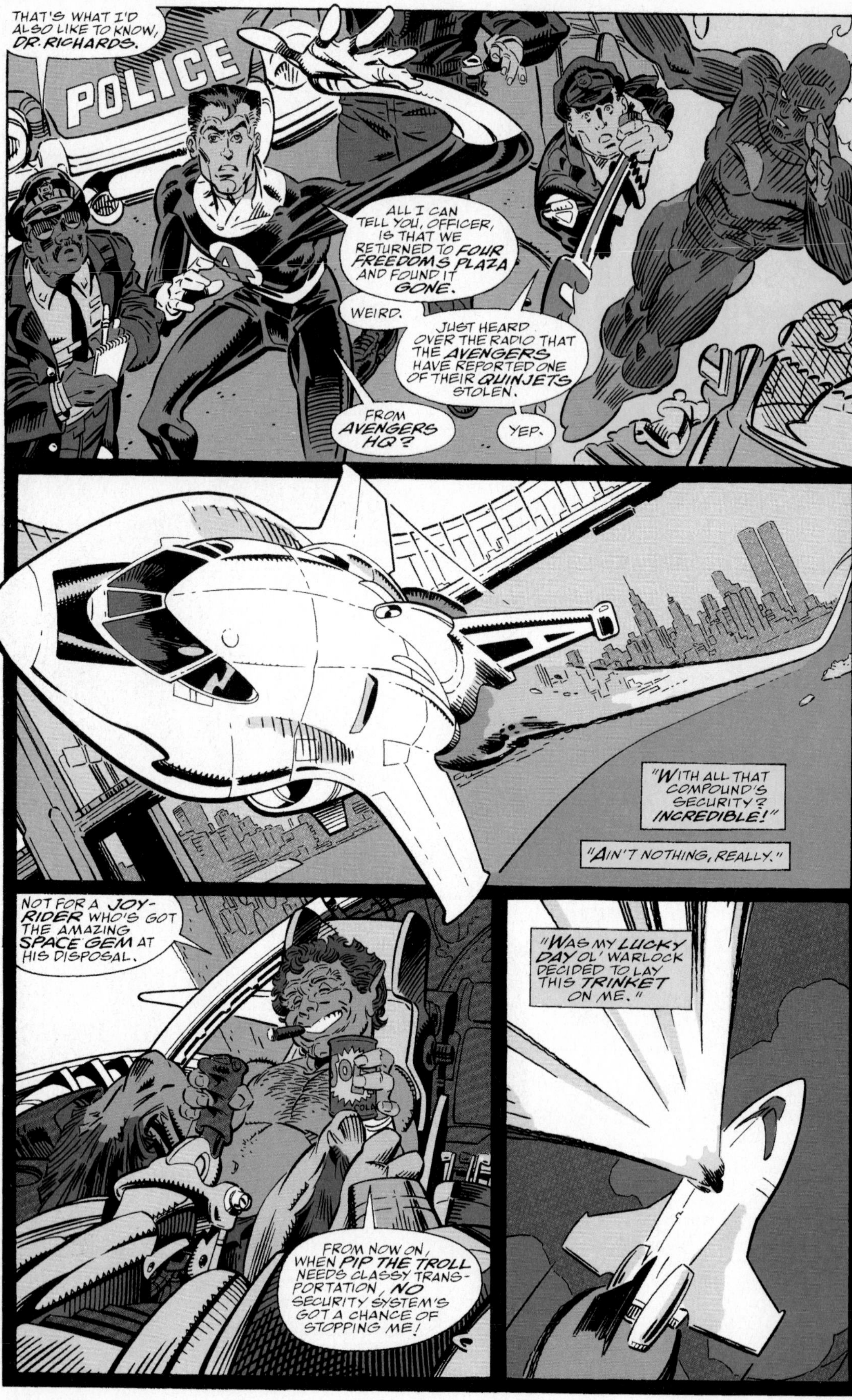
THAT'S WHAT I'D ALSO LIKE TO KNOW, DR. RICHARDS.
POLICE
ALL I CAN TELL YOU, OFFICER, IS THAT WE RETURNED TO FOUR FREEDOMS PLAZA AND FOUND IT GONE.
WEIRD.
JUST HEARD OVER THE RADIO THAT THE AVENGERS HAVE REPORTED ONE OF THEIR QUINJETS STOLEN.
FROM AVENGERS HQ?
YEP.
"WITH ALL THAT COMPOUND'S SECURITY? INCREDIBLE!"
"AIN'T NOTHING, REALLY."
NOT FOR A JOY-RIDER WHO'S GOT THE AMAZING SPACE GEM AT HIS DISPOSAL.
"WAS MY LUCKY DAY OL' WARLOCK DECIDED TO LAY THIS TRINKET ON ME."
FROM NOW ON, WHEN PIP THE TROLL NEEDS CLASSY TRANS-PORTATION, NO SECURITY SYSTEM'S GOT A CHANCE OF STOPPING ME!

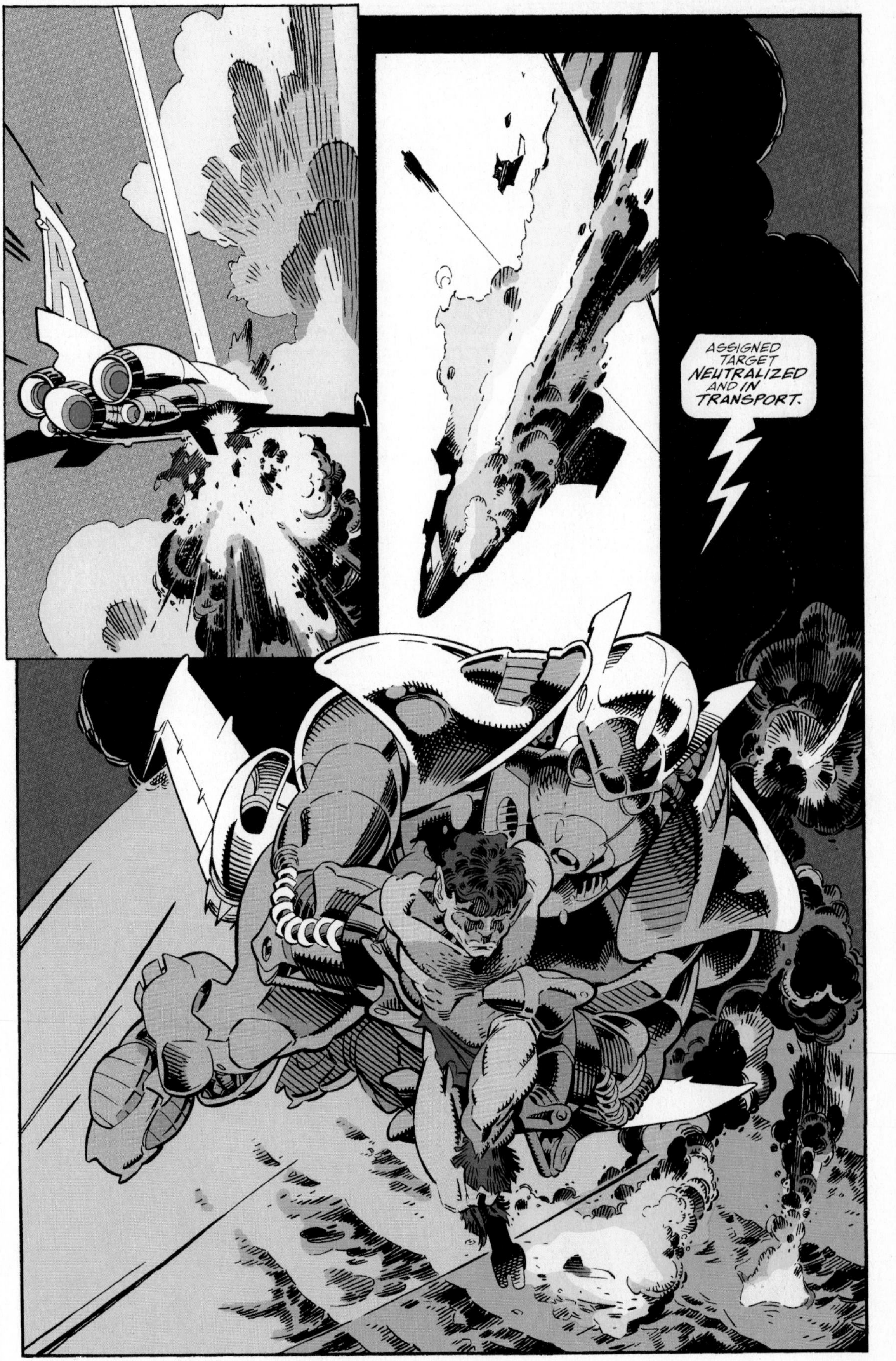
ASSIGNED TARGET NEUTRALIZED AND IN TRANSPORT.

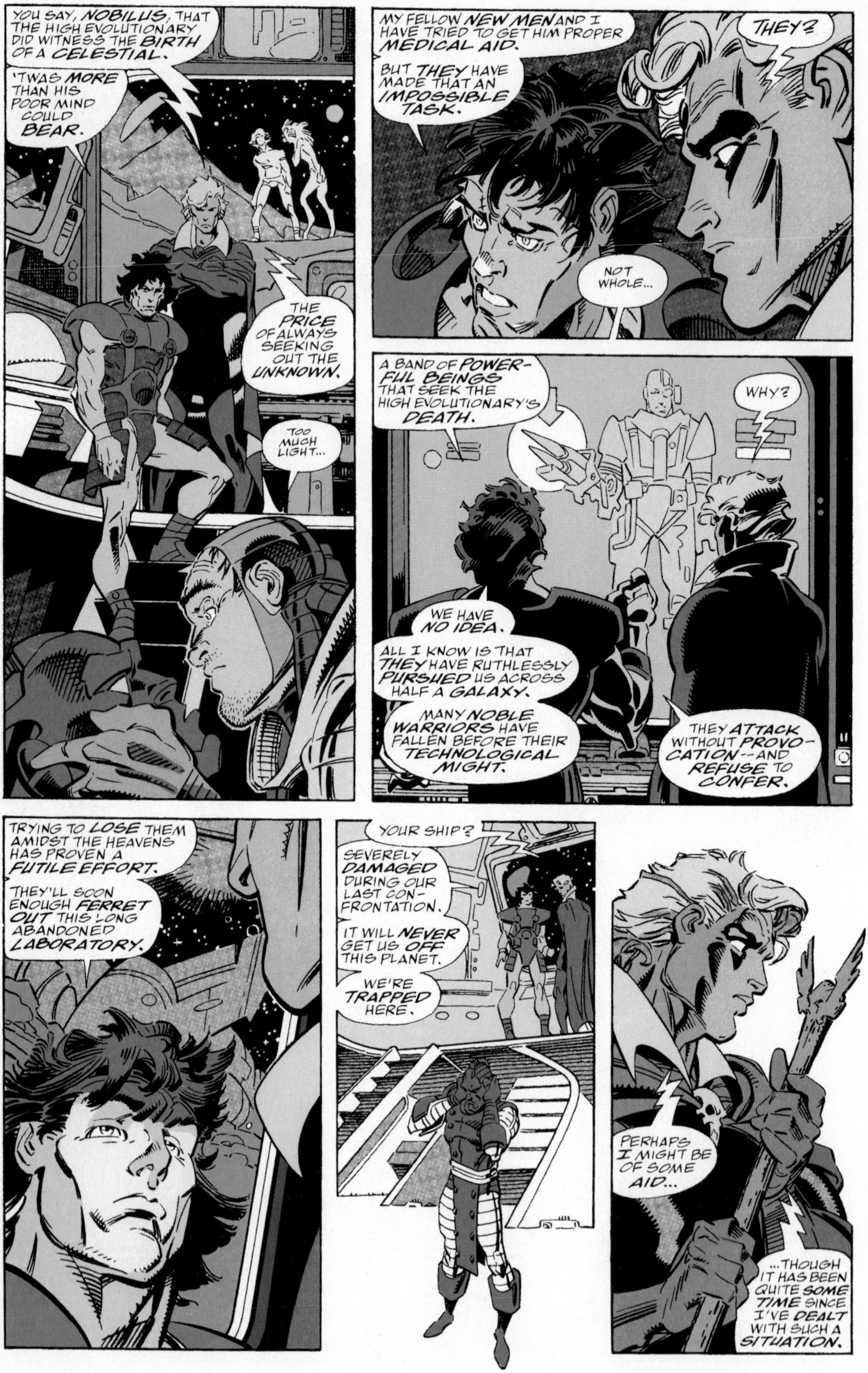
YOU SAY, NOBILUS, THAT THE HIGH EVOLUTIONARY DID WITNESS THE BIRTH OF A CELESTIAL.
'TWAS MORE THAN HIS POOR MIND COULD BEAR.
THE PRICE OF ALWAYS SEEKING OUT THE UNKNOWN.
TOO MUCH LIGHT...
MY FELLOW NEW MEN AND I HAVE TRIED TO GET HIM PROPER MEDICAL AID.
BUT THEY HAVE MADE THAT AN IMPOSSIBLE TASK.
THEY?
NOT WHOLE...
A BAND OF POWERFUL BEINGS THAT SEEK THE HIGH EVOLUTIONARY'S DEATH.
WHY?
WE HAVE NO IDEA.
ALL I KNOW IS THAT THEY HAVE RUTHLESSLY PURSUED US ACROSS HALF A GALAXY.
MANY NOBLE WARRIORS HAVE FALLEN BEFORE THEIR TECHNOLOGICAL MIGHT.
THEY ATTACK WITHOUT PROVOCATION--AND REFUSE TO CONFER.
TRYING TO LOSE THEM AMIDST THE HEAVENS HAS PROVEN A FUTILE EFFORT.
THEY'LL SOON ENOUGH FERRET OUT THIS LONG ABANDONED LABORATORY.
YOUR SHIP?
SEVERELY DAMAGED DURING OUR LAST CONFRONTATION.
IT WILL NEVER GET US OFF THIS PLANET.
WE'RE TRAPPED HERE.
PERHAPS I MIGHT BE OF SOME AID...
...THOUGH IT HAS BEEN QUITE SOME TIME SINCE I'VE DEALT WITH SUCH A SITUATION.

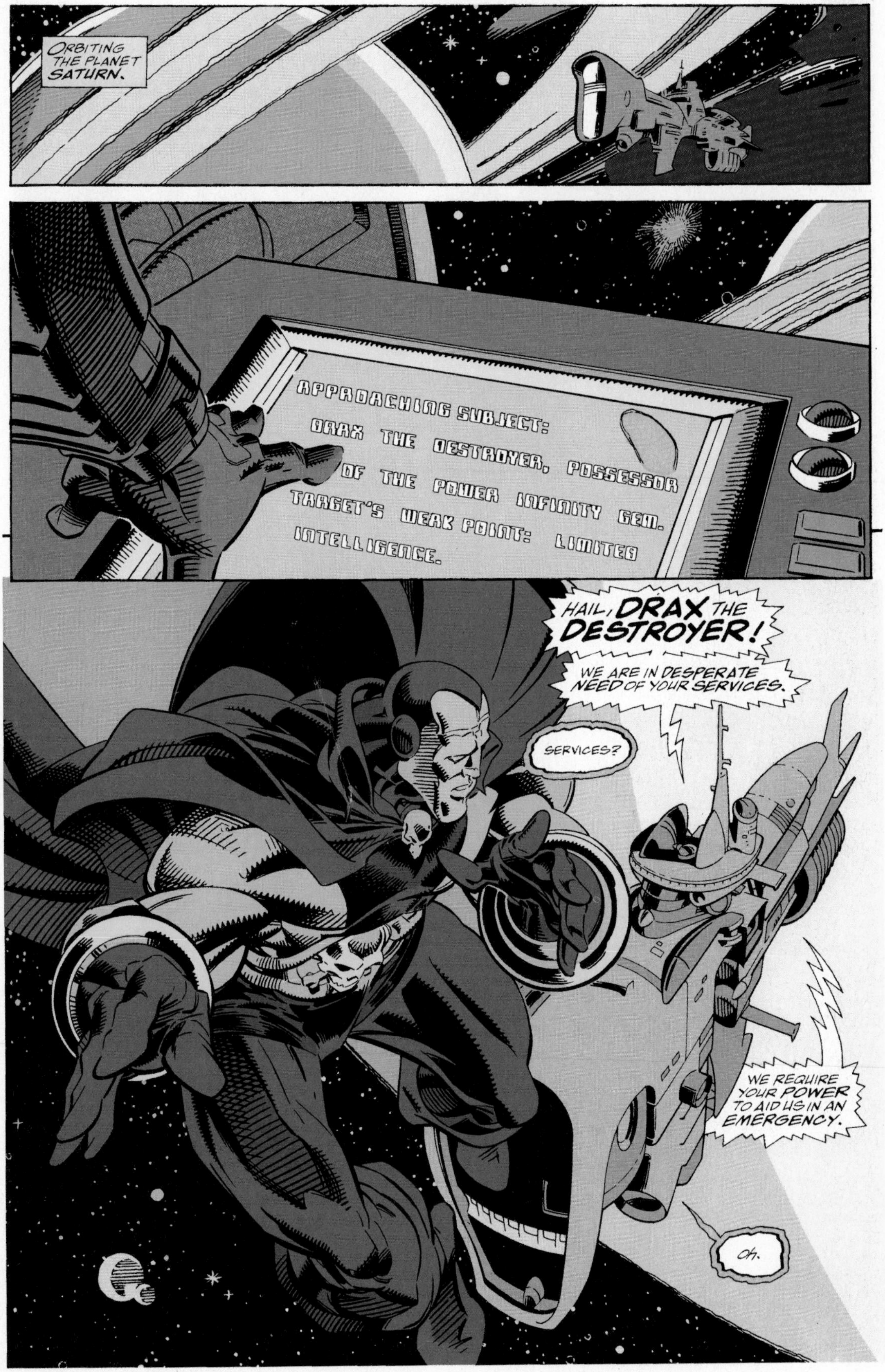
ORBITING THE PLANET SATURN.
APPROACHING SUBJECT:
DRAX THE DESTROYER, POSSESSOR OF THE POWER INFINITY GEM.
TARGET'S WEAK POINT: LIMITED INTELLIGENCE.
HAIL, DRAX THE DESTROYER!
WE ARE IN DESPERATE NEED OF YOUR SERVICES.
SERVICES?
WE REQUIRE YOUR POWER TO AID US IN AN EMERGENCY.
OH.

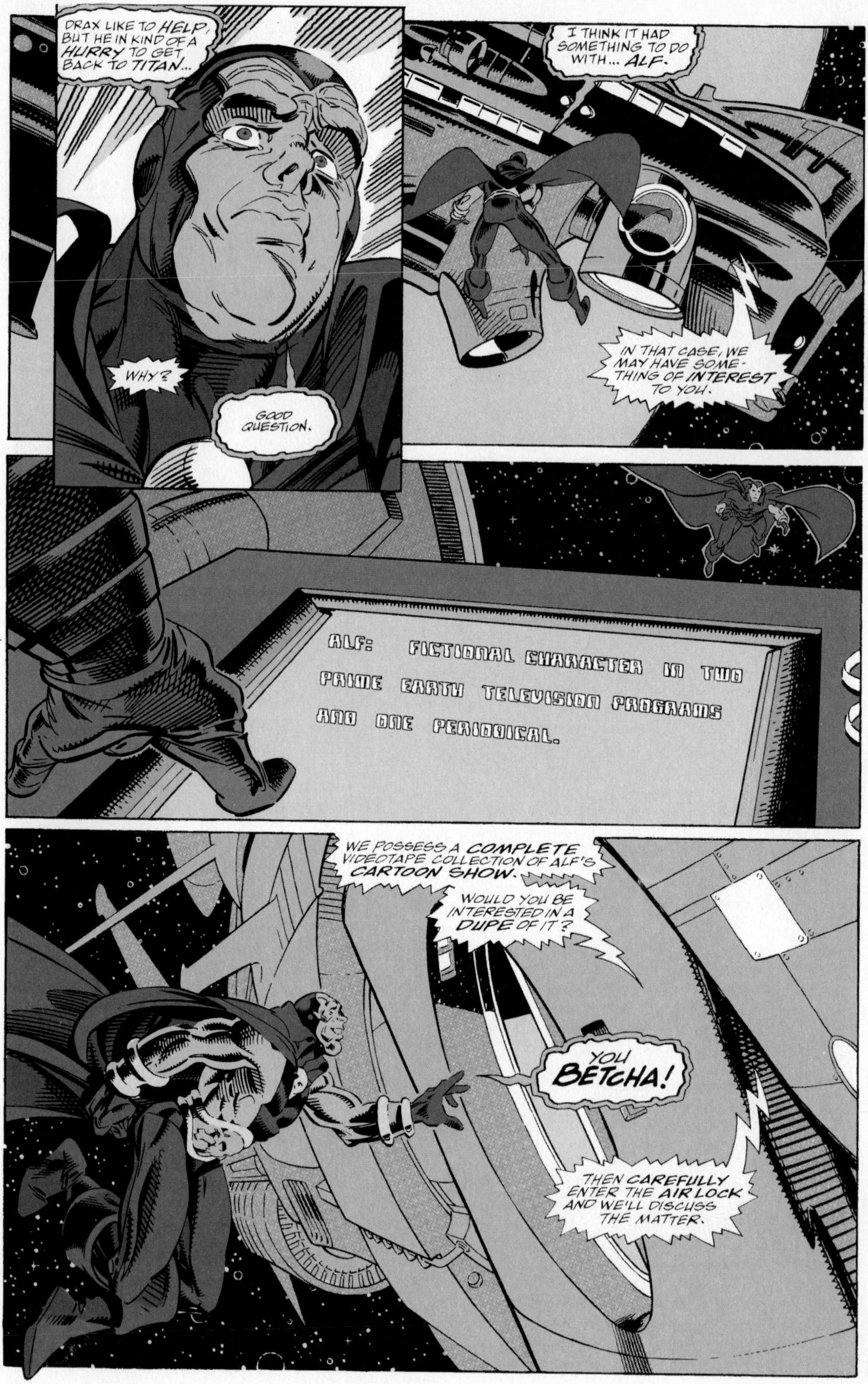
DRAX LIKE TO HELP, BUT HE IN KIND OF A HURRY TO GET BACK TO TITAN...
WHY?
GOOD QUESTION.
I THINK IT HAD SOMETHING TO DO WITH... ALF.
IN THAT CASE, WE MAY HAVE SOMETHING OF INTEREST TO YOU.
ALF: FICTIONAL CHARACTER IN TWO PRIME EARTH TELEVISION PROGRAMS AND ONE PERIODICAL.
WE POSSESS A COMPLETE VIDEOTAPE COLLECTION OF ALF'S CARTOON SHOW.
WOULD YOU BE INTERESTED IN A DUPE OF IT?
YOU BETCHA!
THEN CAREFULLY ENTER THE AIR LOCK AND WE'LL DISCUSS THE MATTER.

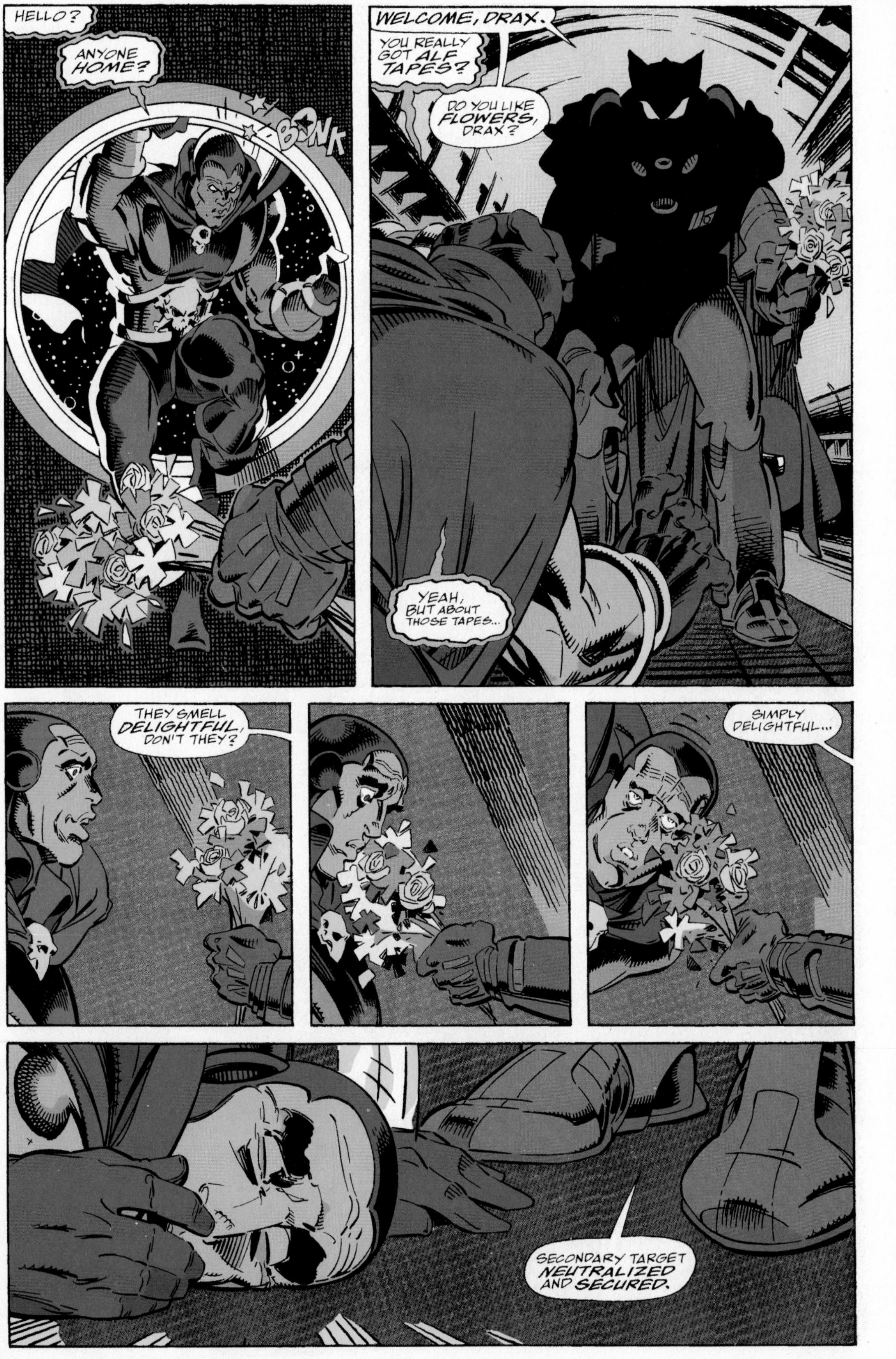
HELLO?
ANYONE HOME?
BONK
WELCOME, DRAX.
YOU REALLY GOT ALF TAPES?
DO YOU LIKE FLOWERS, DRAX?
YEAH, BUT ABOUT THOSE TAPES...
THEY SMELL DELIGHTFUL, DON'T THEY?
SIMPLY DELIGHTFUL...
SECONDARY TARGET NEUTRALIZED AND SECURED.

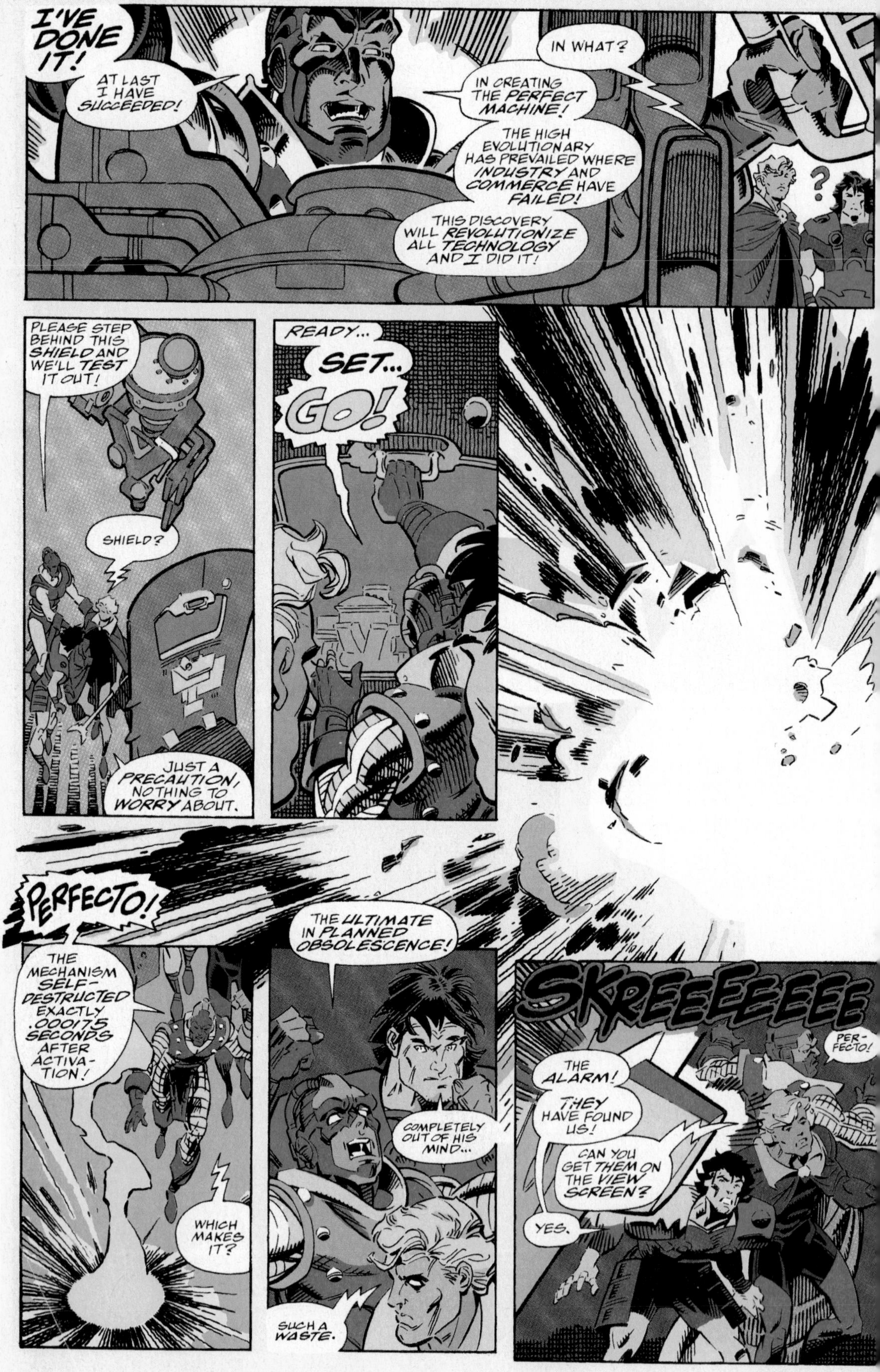
I'VE DONE IT!
AT LAST I HAVE SUCCEEDED!
IN WHAT?
IN CREATING THE PERFECT MACHINE!
THE HIGH EVOLUTIONARY HAS PREVAILED WHERE INDUSTRY AND COMMERCE HAVE FAILED!
THIS DISCOVERY WILL REVOLUTIONIZE ALL TECHNOLOGY AND I DID IT!
?
PLEASE STEP BEHIND THIS SHIELD AND WE'LL TEST IT OUT!
SHIELD?
JUST A PRECAUTION, NOTHING TO WORRY ABOUT.
READY...
SET...
GO!
PERFECTO!
THE MECHANISM SELF-DESTRUCTED EXACTLY .000175 SECONDS AFTER ACTIVATION!
WHICH MAKES IT?
THE ULTIMATE IN PLANNED OBSOLESCENCE!
COMPLETELY OUT OF HIS MIND...
SUCH A WASTE.
SKREEEEEEEE
PERFECTO!
THE ALARM!
THEY HAVE FOUND US!
CAN YOU GET THEM ON THE VIEW SCREEN?
YES.

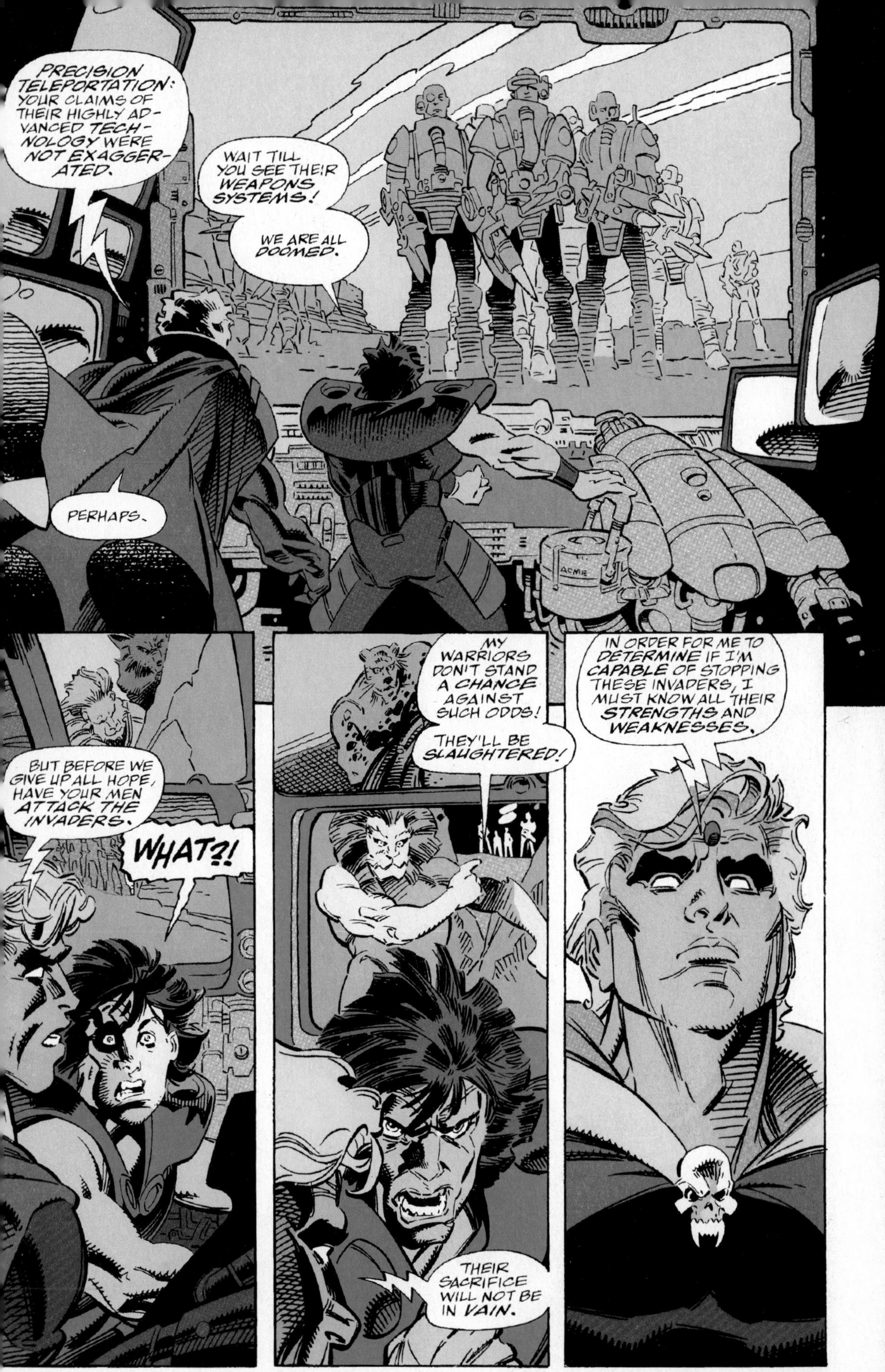
PRECISION TELEPORTATION: YOUR CLAIMS OF THEIR HIGHLY ADVANCED TECHNOLOGY WERE NOT EXAGGERATED.
WAIT TILL YOU SEE THEIR WEAPONS SYSTEMS!
WE ARE ALL DOOMED.
PERHAPS.
ACME
BUT BEFORE WE GIVE UP ALL HOPE, HAVE YOUR MEN ATTACK THE INVADERS.
WHAT?!
MY WARRIORS DON'T STAND A CHANCE AGAINST SUCH ODDS!
THEY'LL BE SLAUGHTERED!
THEIR SACRIFICE WILL NOT BE IN VAIN.
IN ORDER FOR ME TO DETERMINE IF I'M CAPABLE OF STOPPING THESE INVADERS, I MUST KNOW ALL THEIR STRENGTHS AND WEAKNESSES.

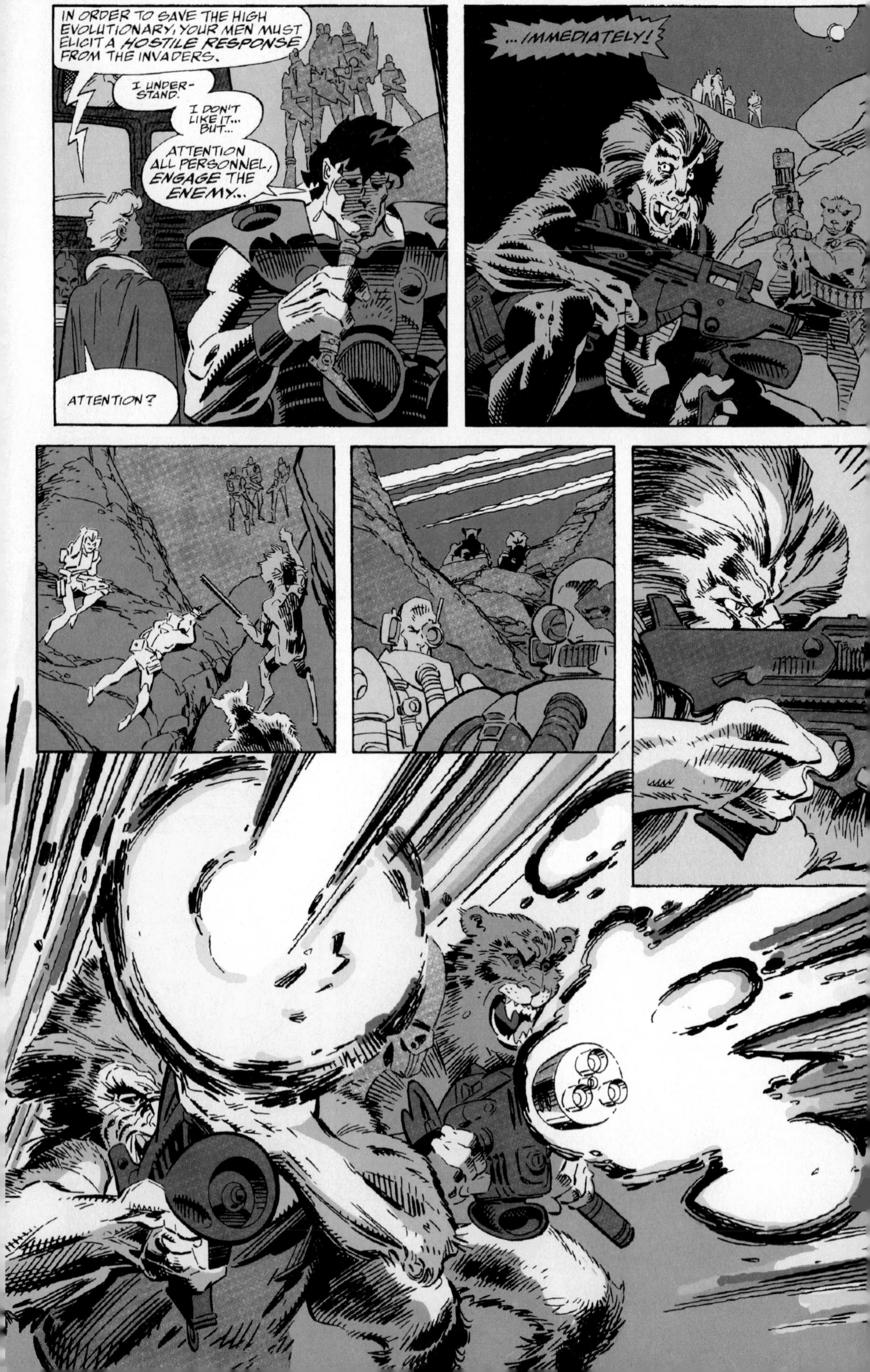
IN ORDER TO SAVE THE HIGH EVOLUTIONARY, YOUR MEN MUST ELICIT A HOSTILE RESPONSE FROM THE INVADERS.
I UNDER-STAND.
I DON'T LIKE IT... BUT...
ATTENTION ALL PERSONNEL, ENGAGE THE ENEMY...
ATTENTION?
...IMMEDIATELY!

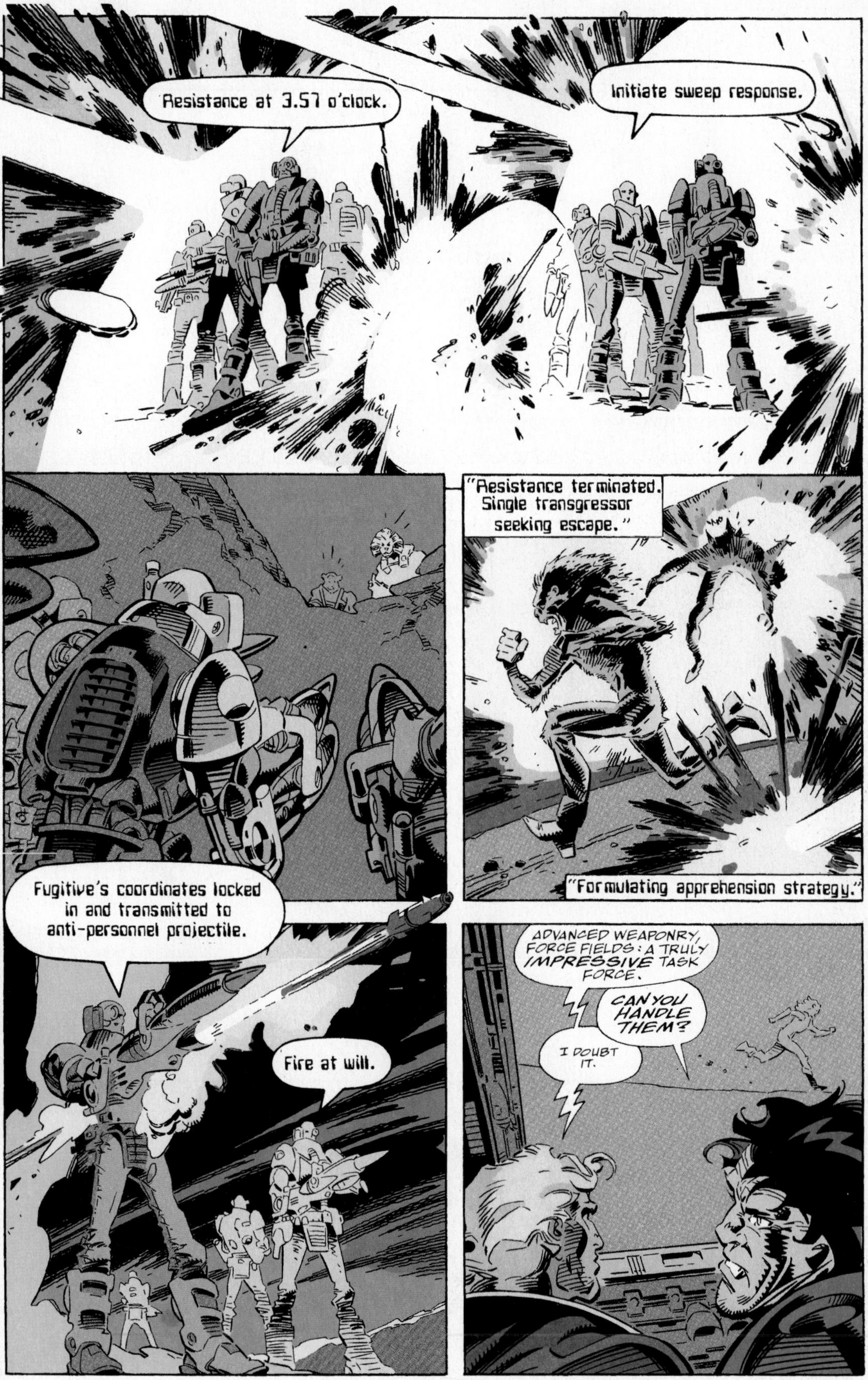

Resistance at 3.57 o'clock.
Initiate sweep response.
"Resistance terminated. Single transgressor seeking escape."
"Formulating apprehension strategy."
Fugitive's coordinates locked in and transmitted to anti-personnel projectile.
Fire at will.
ADVANCED WEAPONRY, FORCE FIELDS: A TRULY IMPRESSIVE TASK FORCE.
CAN YOU HANDLE THEM?
I DOUBT IT.

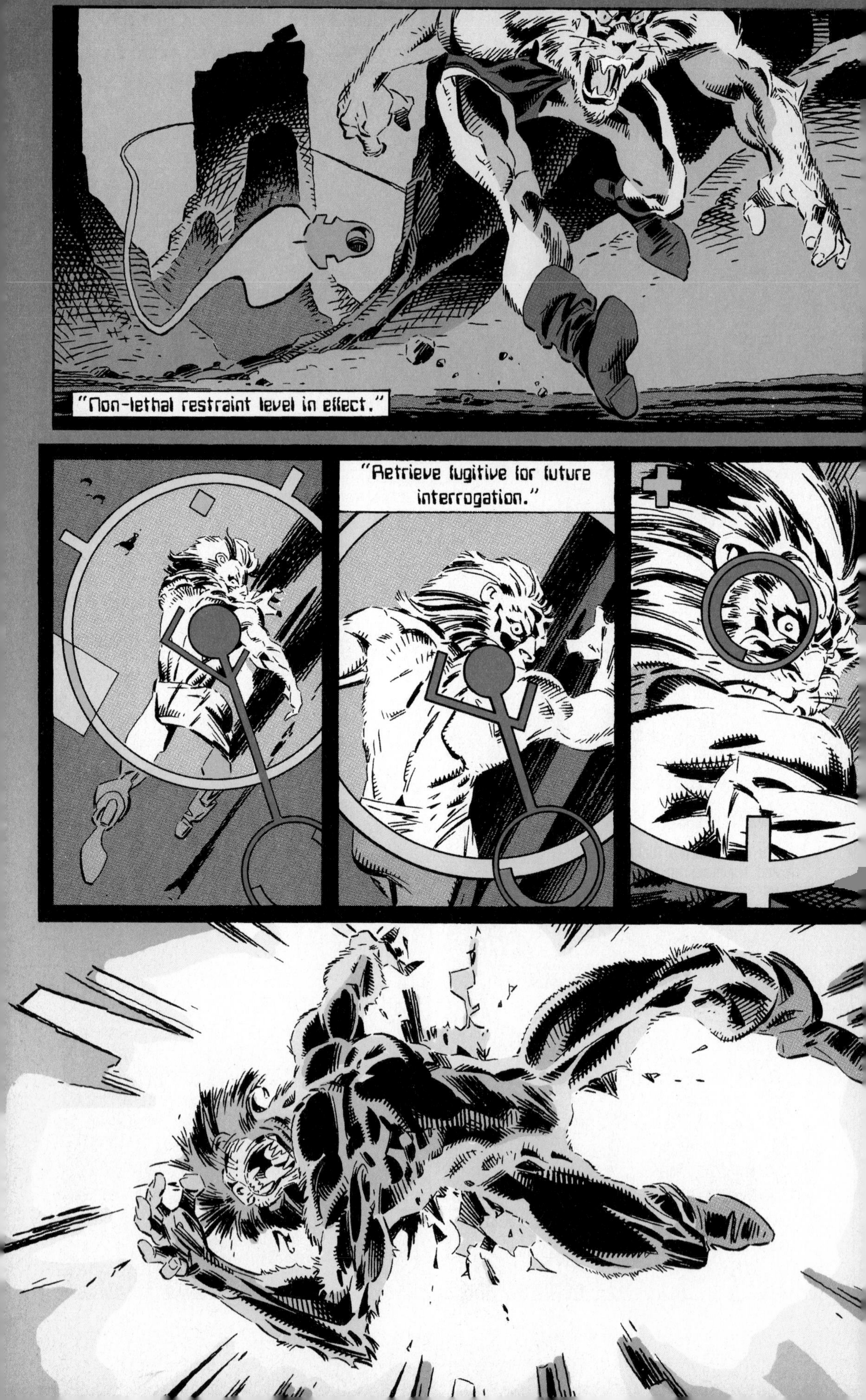
"Non-lethal restraint level in effect."
"Retrieve fugitive for future interrogation."

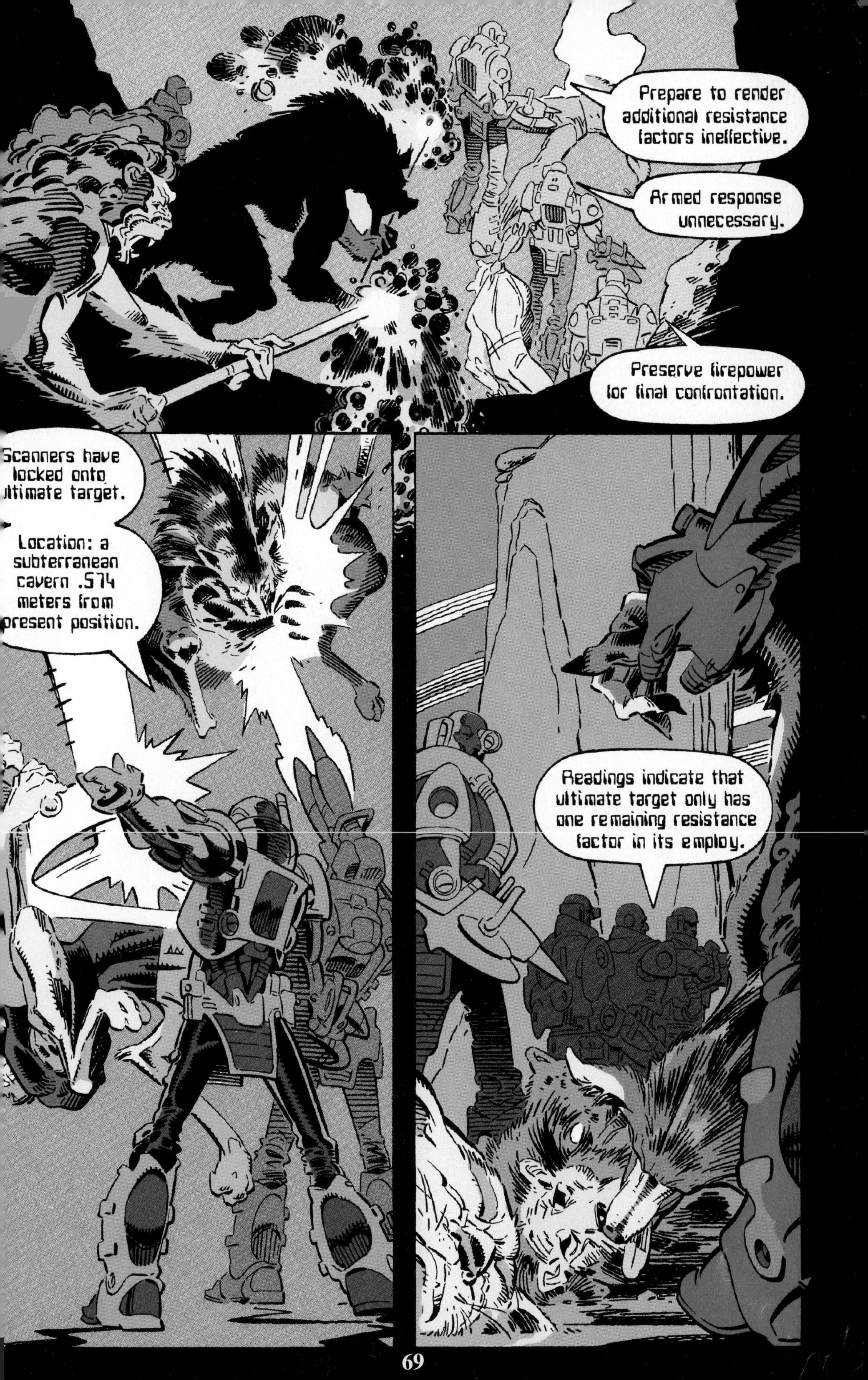
Prepare to render additional resistance factors ineffective.
Armed response unnecessary.
Preserve firepower for final confrontation.
Scanners have locked onto ltimate target.
Location: a subterranean cavern .574 meters from resent position.
Readings indicate that ultimate target only has one remaining resistance factor in its employ.

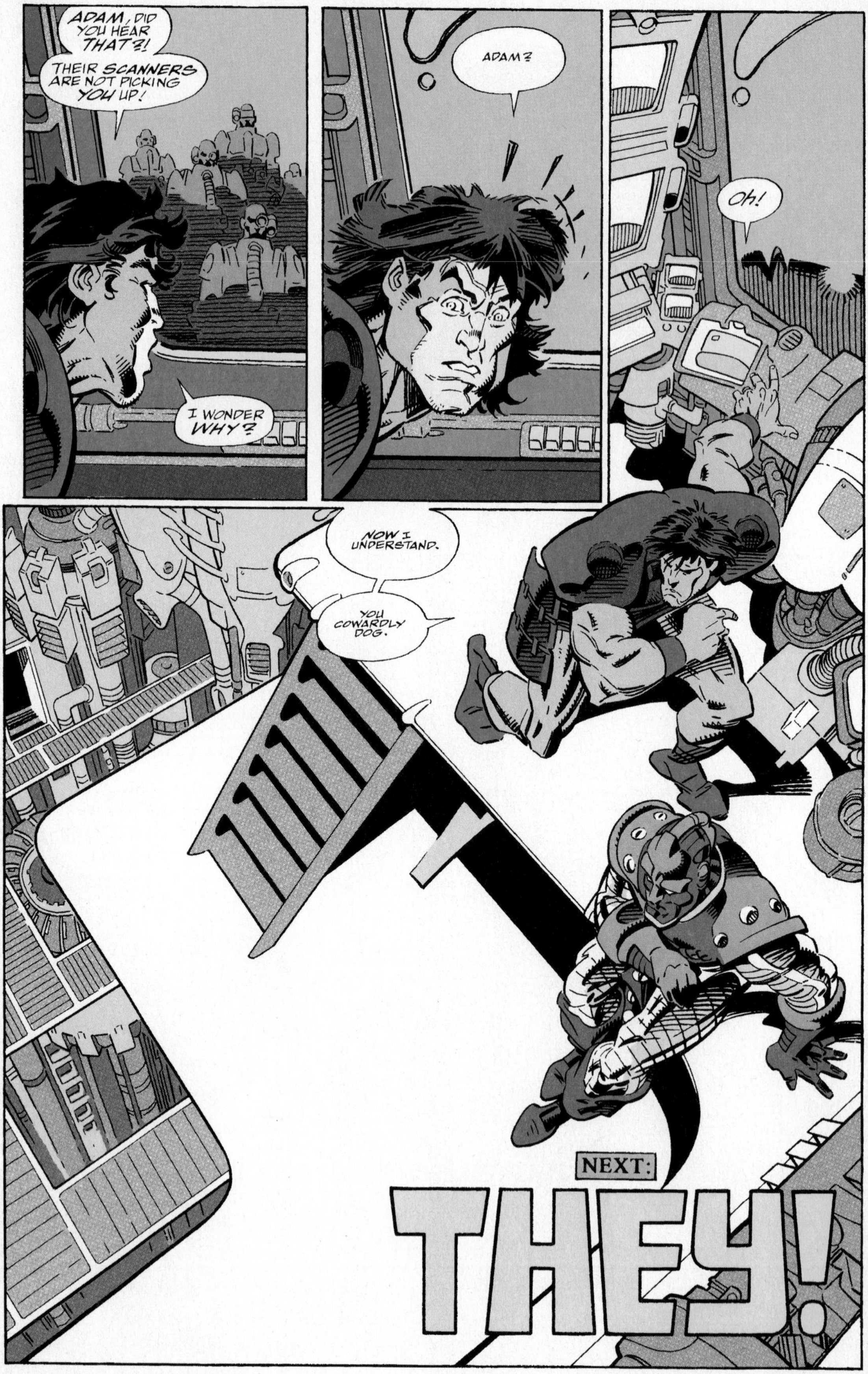
ADAM, DID YOU HEAR THAT?!
THEIR SCANNERS ARE NOT PICKING YOU UP!
I WONDER WHY?
ADAM?
Oh!
NOW I UNDERSTAND.
YOU COWARDLY DOG.
NEXT:
THEY!

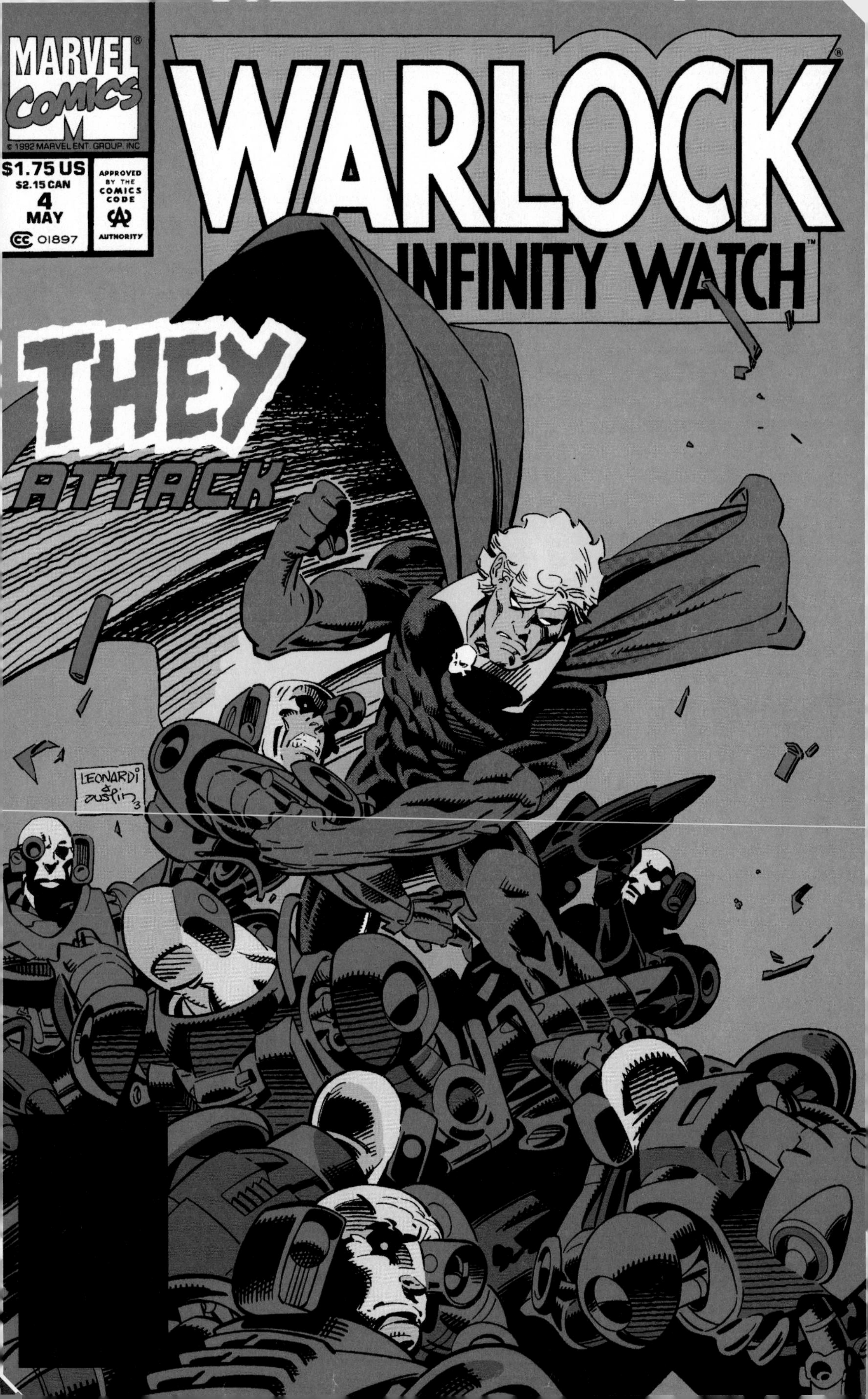

MARVEL COMICS
© 1992 MARVEL ENT. GROUP, INC.
$1.75 US
$2.15 CAN
4
MAY
01897
APPROVED BY THE COMICS CODE AUTHORITY
WARLOCK
INFINITY WATCH
THEY ATTACK
LEONARDI & AUSTIN

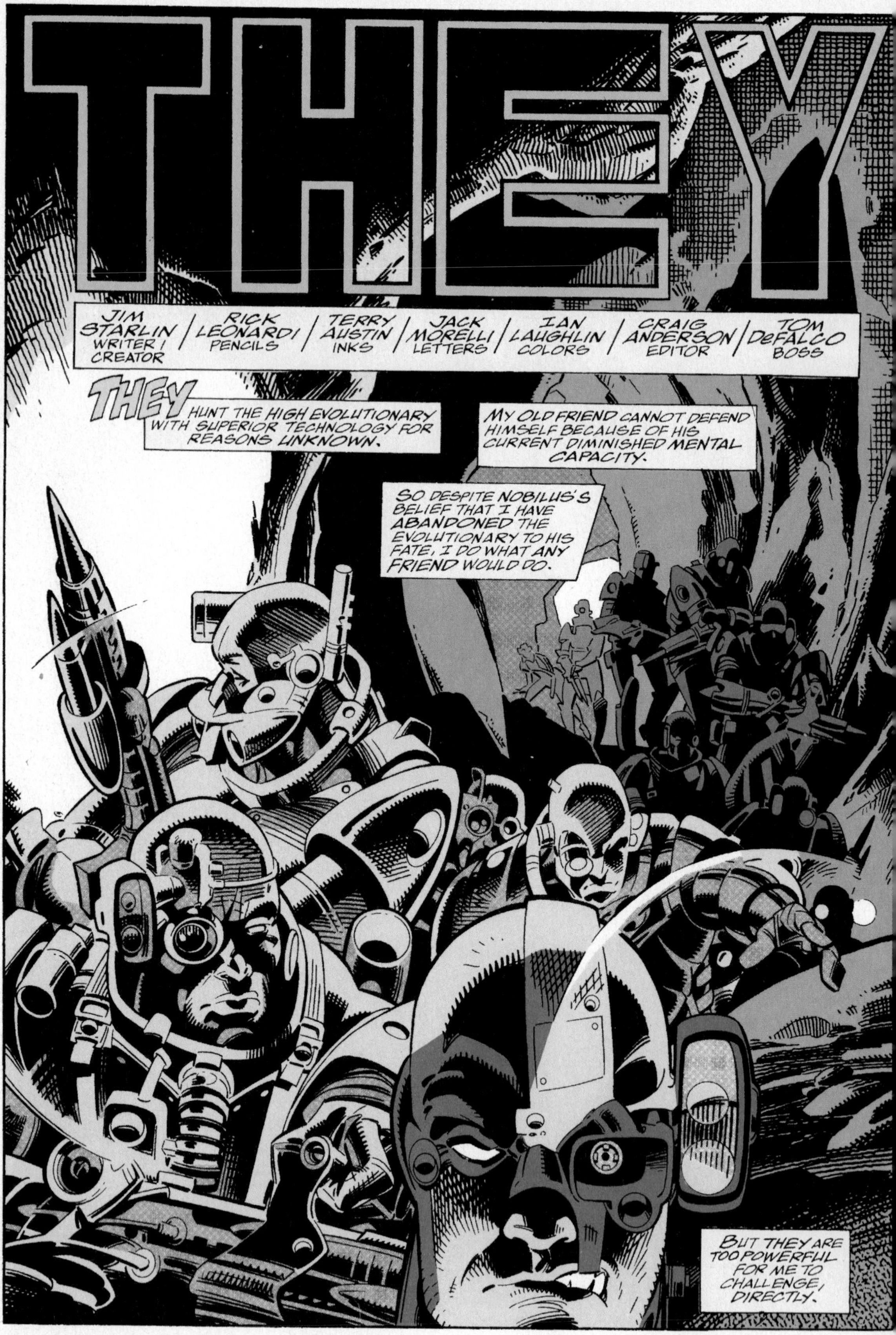
THEY
JIM STARLIN WRITER / CREATOR | RICK LEONARDI PENCILS | TERRY AUSTIN INKS | JACK MORELLI LETTERS | IAN LAUGHLIN COLORS | CRAIG ANDERSON EDITOR | TOM DeFALCO BOSS
THEY HUNT THE HIGH EVOLUTIONARY WITH SUPERIOR TECHNOLOGY FOR REASONS UNKNOWN.
MY OLD FRIEND CANNOT DEFEND HIMSELF BECAUSE OF HIS CURRENT DIMINISHED MENTAL CAPACITY.
SO DESPITE NOBILUS'S BELIEF THAT I HAVE ABANDONED THE EVOLUTIONARY TO HIS FATE, I DO WHAT ANY FRIEND WOULD DO.
BUT THEY ARE TOO POWERFUL FOR ME TO CHALLENGE, DIRECTLY.

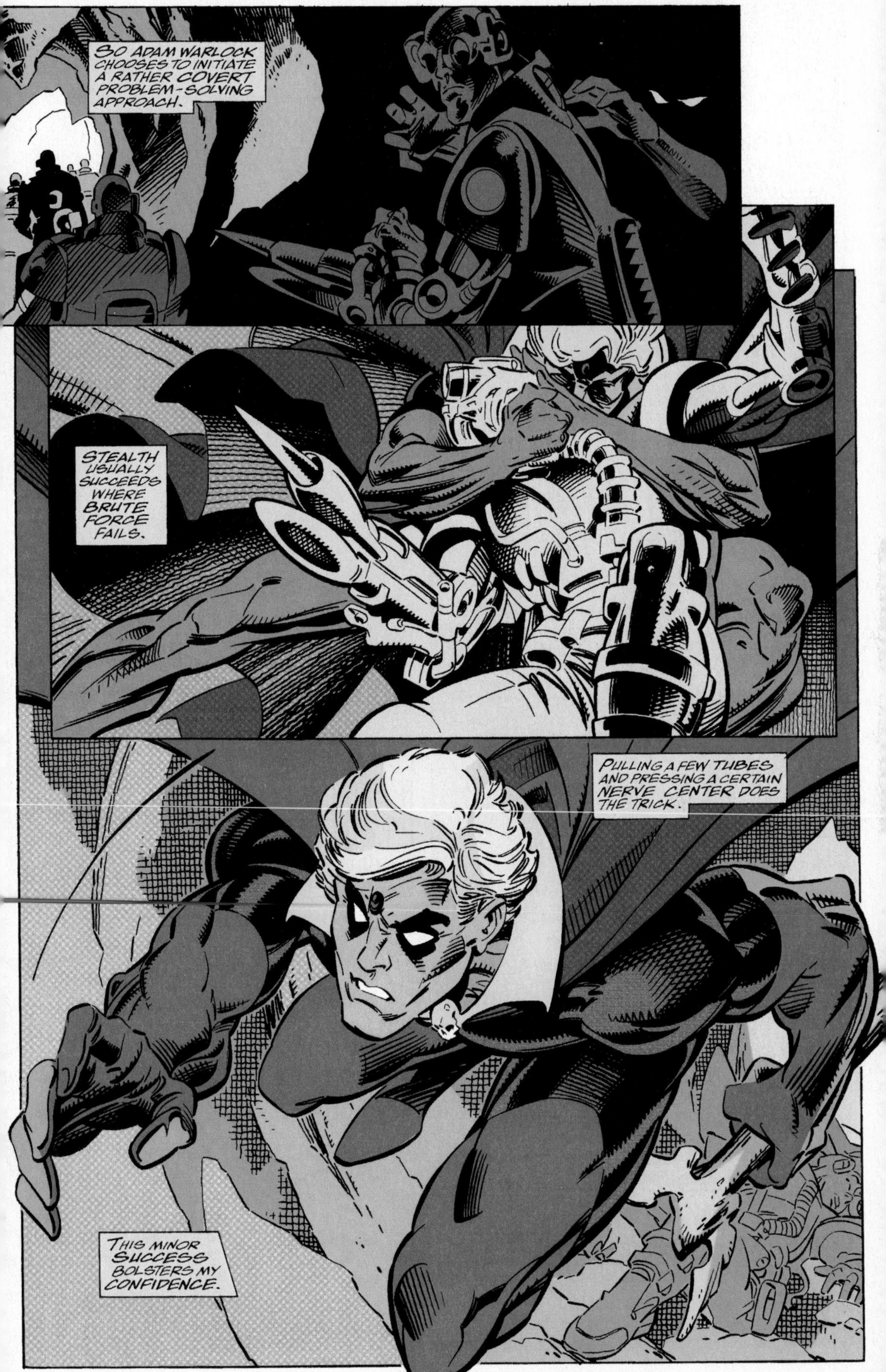
SO ADAM WARLOCK CHOOSES TO INITIATE A RATHER COVERT PROBLEM-SOLVING APPROACH.
STEALTH USUALLY SUCCEEDS WHERE BRUTE FORCE FAILS.
PULLING A FEW TUBES AND PRESSING A CERTAIN NERVE CENTER DOES THE TRICK.
THIS MINOR SUCCESS BOLSTERS MY CONFIDENCE.

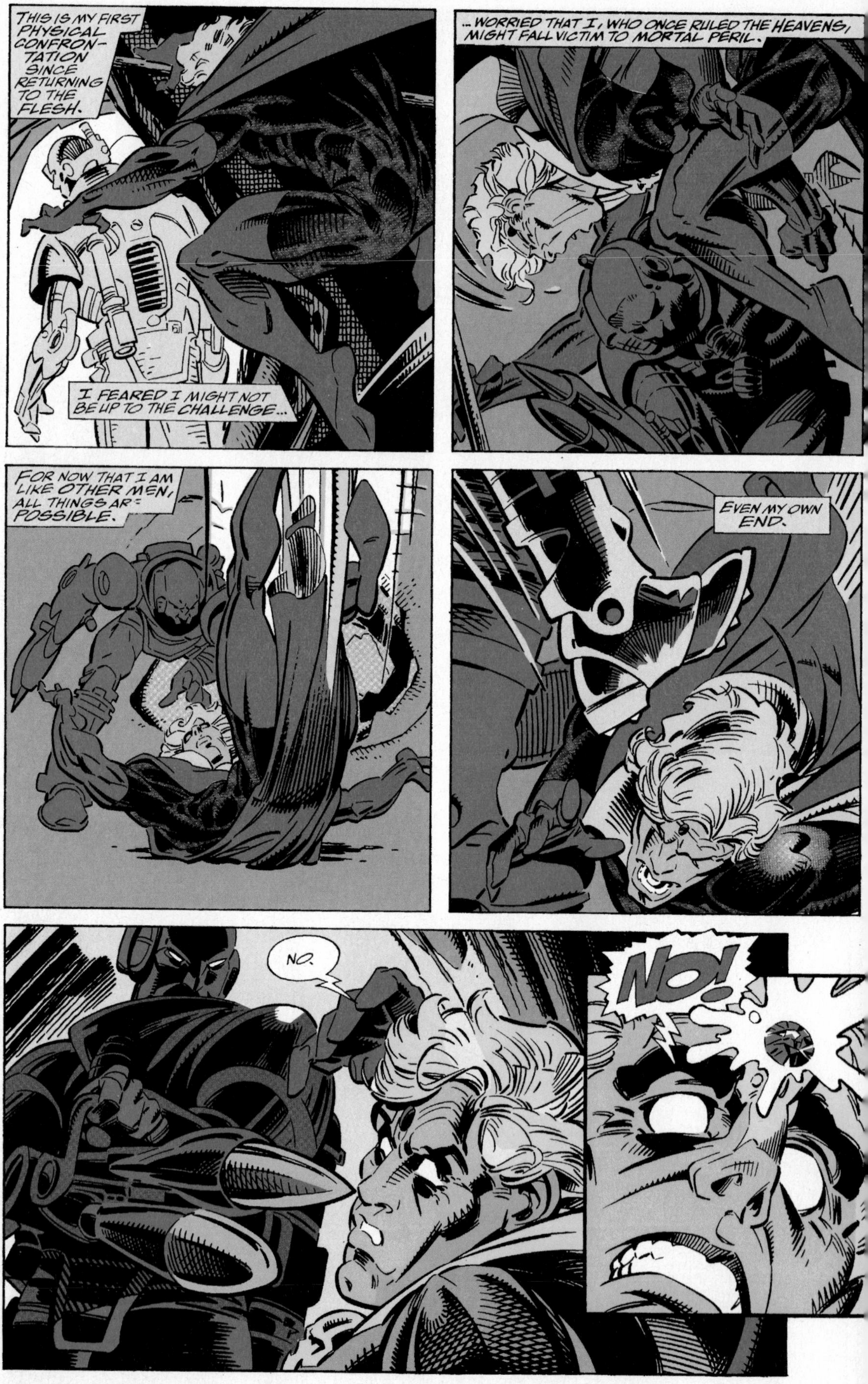
THIS IS MY FIRST PHYSICAL CONFRONTATION SINCE RETURNING TO THE FLESH.
I FEARED I MIGHT NOT BE UP TO THE CHALLENGE...
...WORRIED THAT I, WHO ONCE RULED THE HEAVENS, MIGHT FALL VICTIM TO MORTAL PERIL.
FOR NOW THAT I AM LIKE OTHER MEN, ALL THINGS ARE POSSIBLE.
EVEN MY OWN END.
NO.
NO!

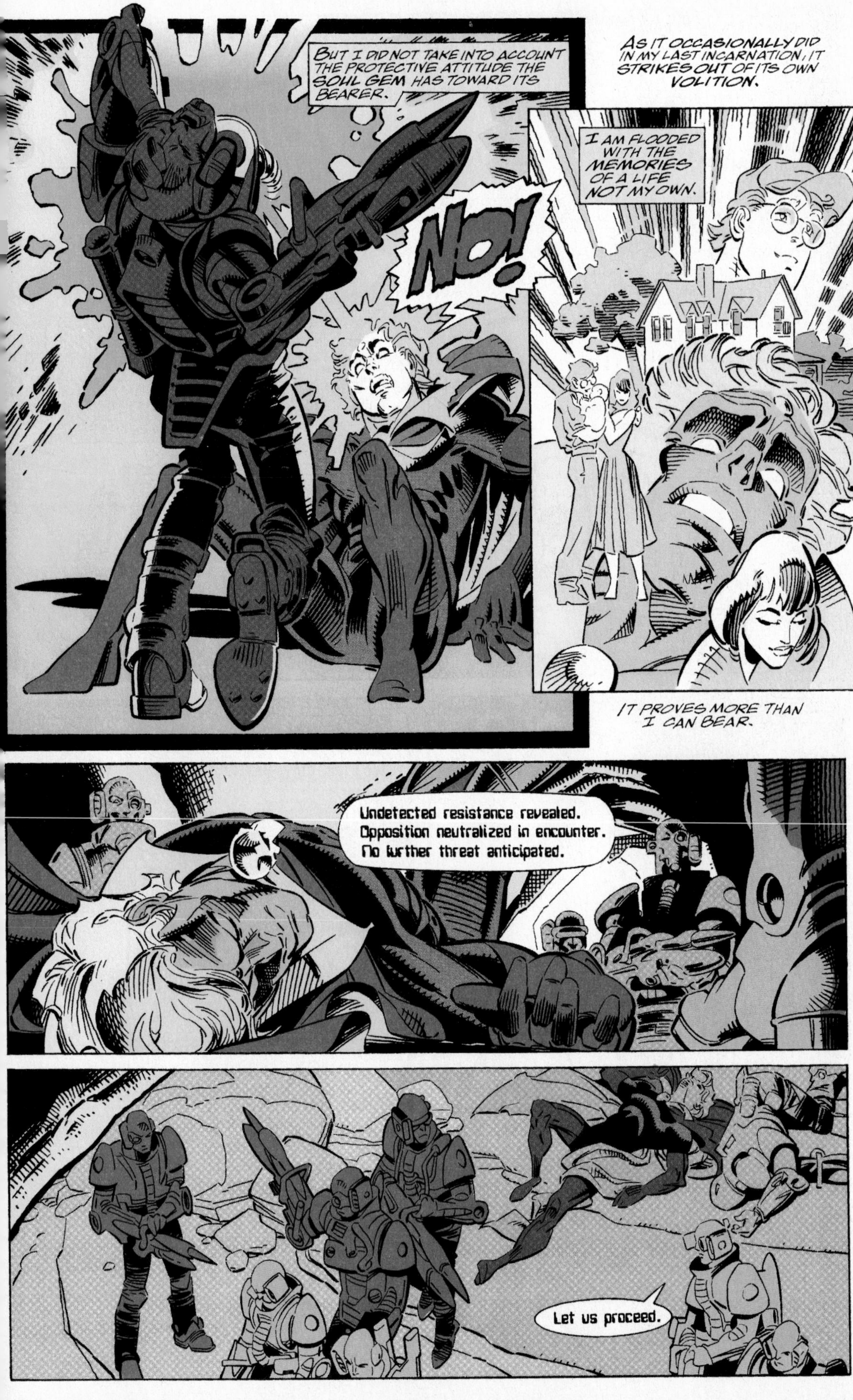

BUT I DID NOT TAKE INTO ACCOUNT THE PROTECTIVE ATTITUDE THE SOUL GEM HAS TOWARD ITS BEARER.
AS IT OCCASIONALLY DID IN MY LAST INCARNATION, IT STRIKES OUT OF ITS OWN VOLITION.
NO!
I AM FLOODED WITH THE MEMORIES OF A LIFE NOT MY OWN.
IT PROVES MORE THAN I CAN BEAR.
Undetected resistance revealed.
Opposition neutralized in encounter.
No further threat anticipated.
Let us proceed.

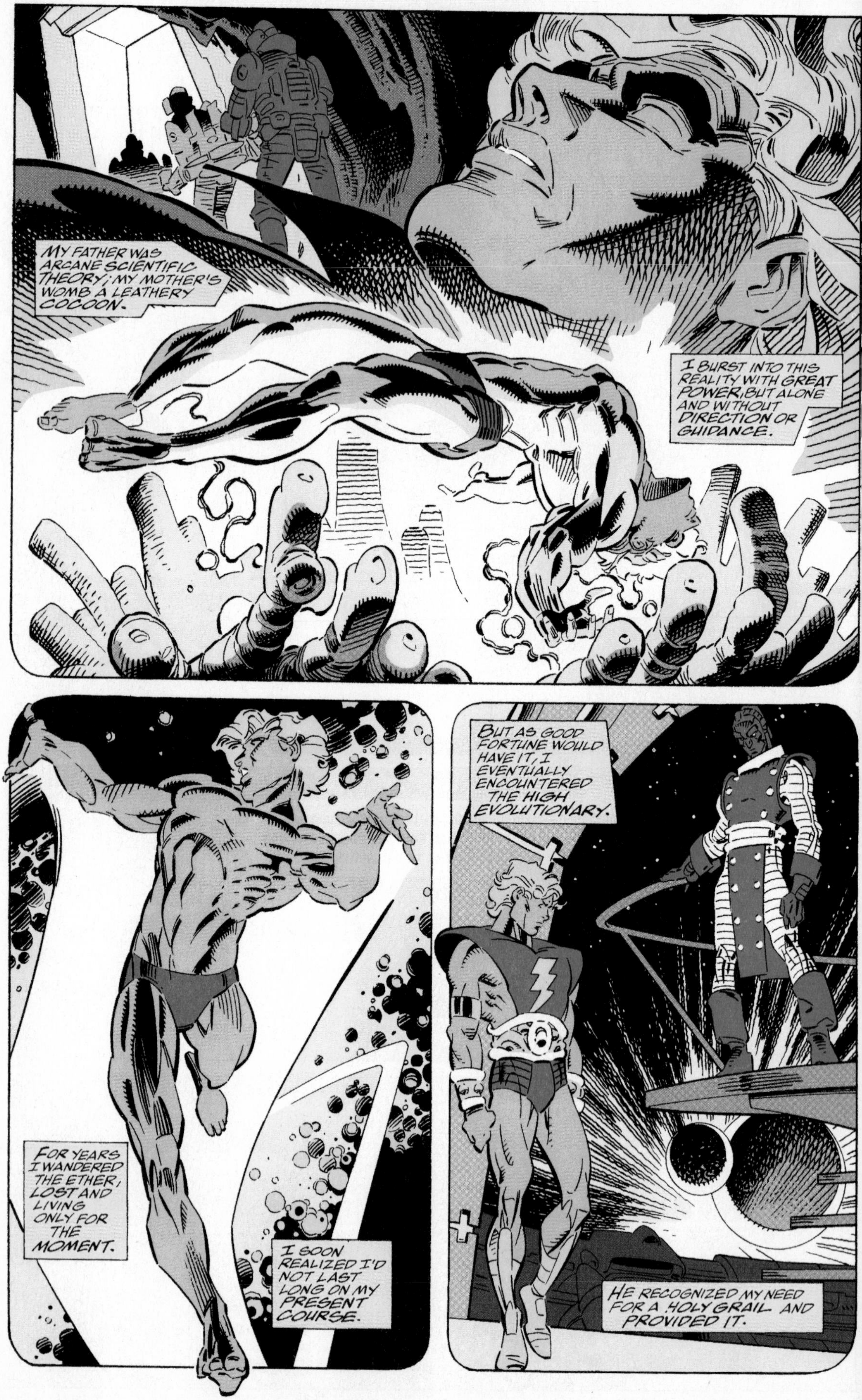
MY FATHER WAS ARCANE SCIENTIFIC THEORY; MY MOTHER'S WOMB A LEATHERY COCOON.
I BURST INTO THIS REALITY WITH GREAT POWER, BUT ALONE AND WITHOUT DIRECTION OR GUIDANCE.
FOR YEARS I WANDERED THE ETHER, LOST AND LIVING ONLY FOR THE MOMENT.
I SOON REALIZED I'D NOT LAST LONG ON MY PRESENT COURSE.
BUT AS GOOD FORTUNE WOULD HAVE IT, I EVENTUALLY ENCOUNTERED THE HIGH EVOLUTIONARY.
HE RECOGNIZED MY NEED FOR A HOLY GRAIL AND PROVIDED IT.

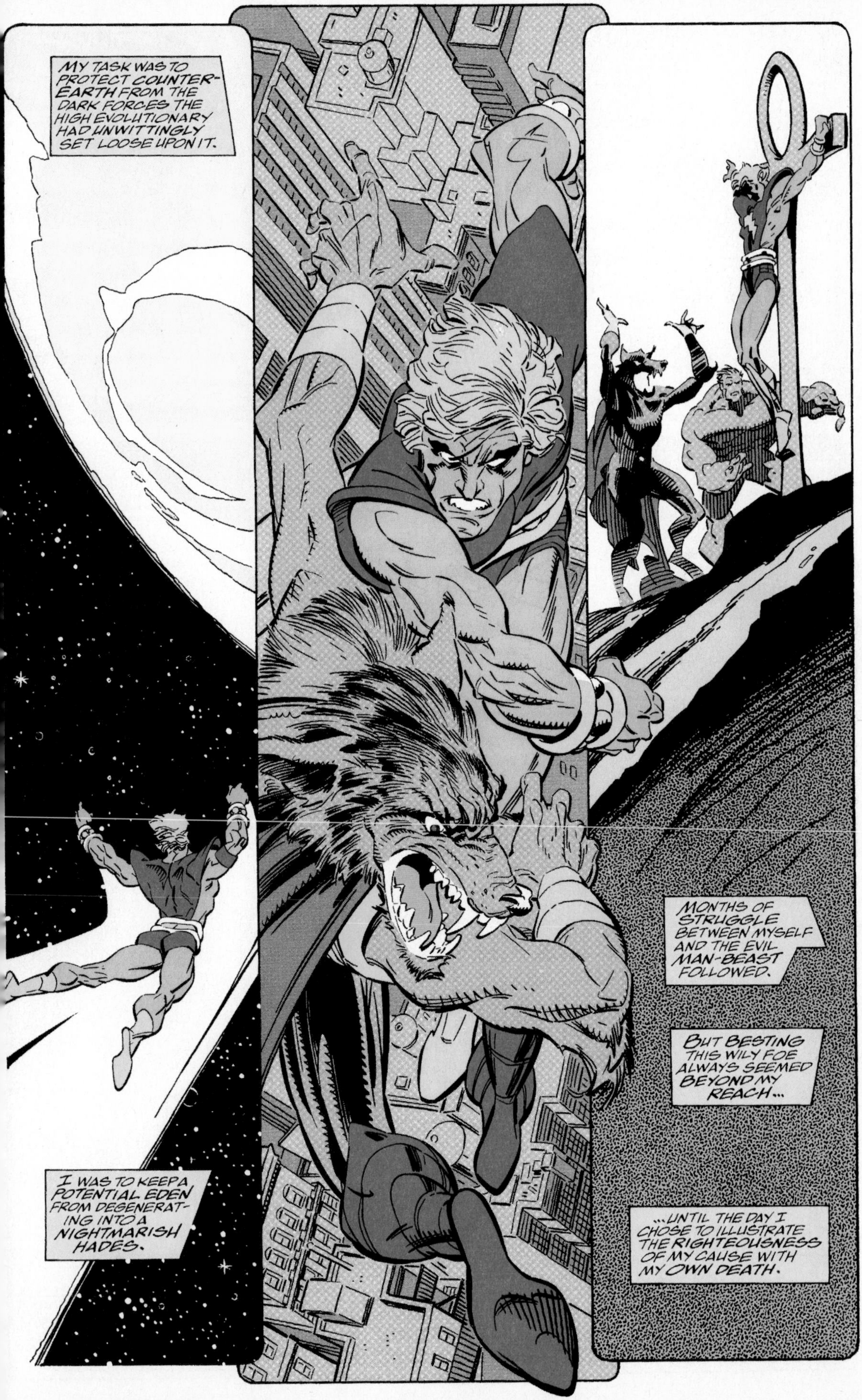
MY TASK WAS TO PROTECT COUNTER-EARTH FROM THE DARK FORCES THE HIGH EVOLUTIONARY HAD UNWITTINGLY SET LOOSE UPON IT.
I WAS TO KEEP A POTENTIAL EDEN FROM DEGENERATING INTO A NIGHTMARISH HADES.
MONTHS OF STRUGGLE BETWEEN MYSELF AND THE EVIL MAN-BEAST FOLLOWED.
BUT BESTING THIS WILY FOE ALWAYS SEEMED BEYOND MY REACH...
...UNTIL THE DAY I CHOSE TO ILLUSTRATE THE RIGHTEOUSNESS OF MY CAUSE WITH MY OWN DEATH.

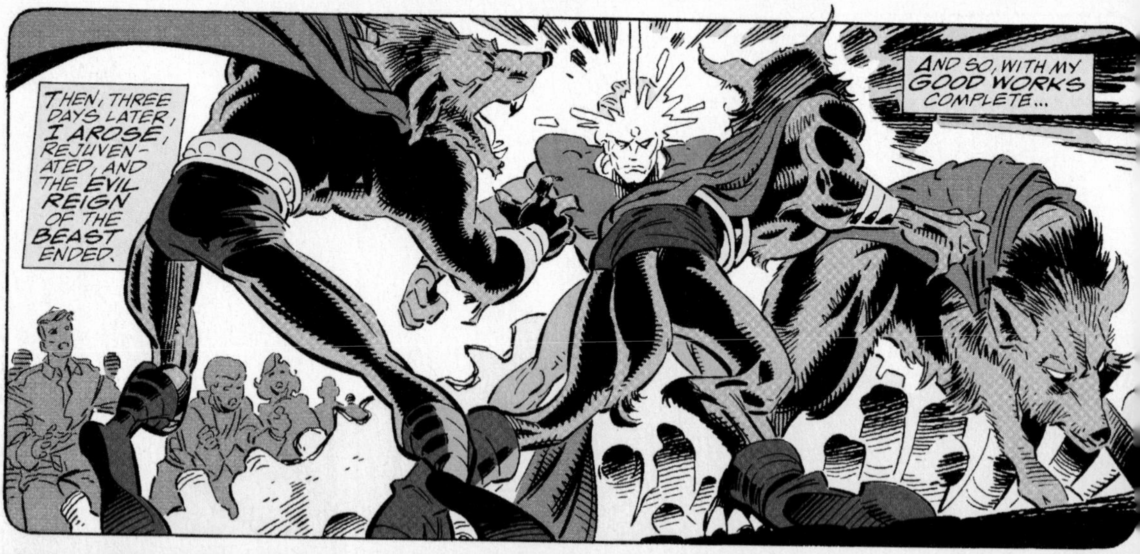
THEN, THREE DAYS LATER, I AROSE, REJUVENATED, AND THE EVIL REIGN OF THE BEAST ENDED.
AND SO, WITH MY GOOD WORKS COMPLETE...

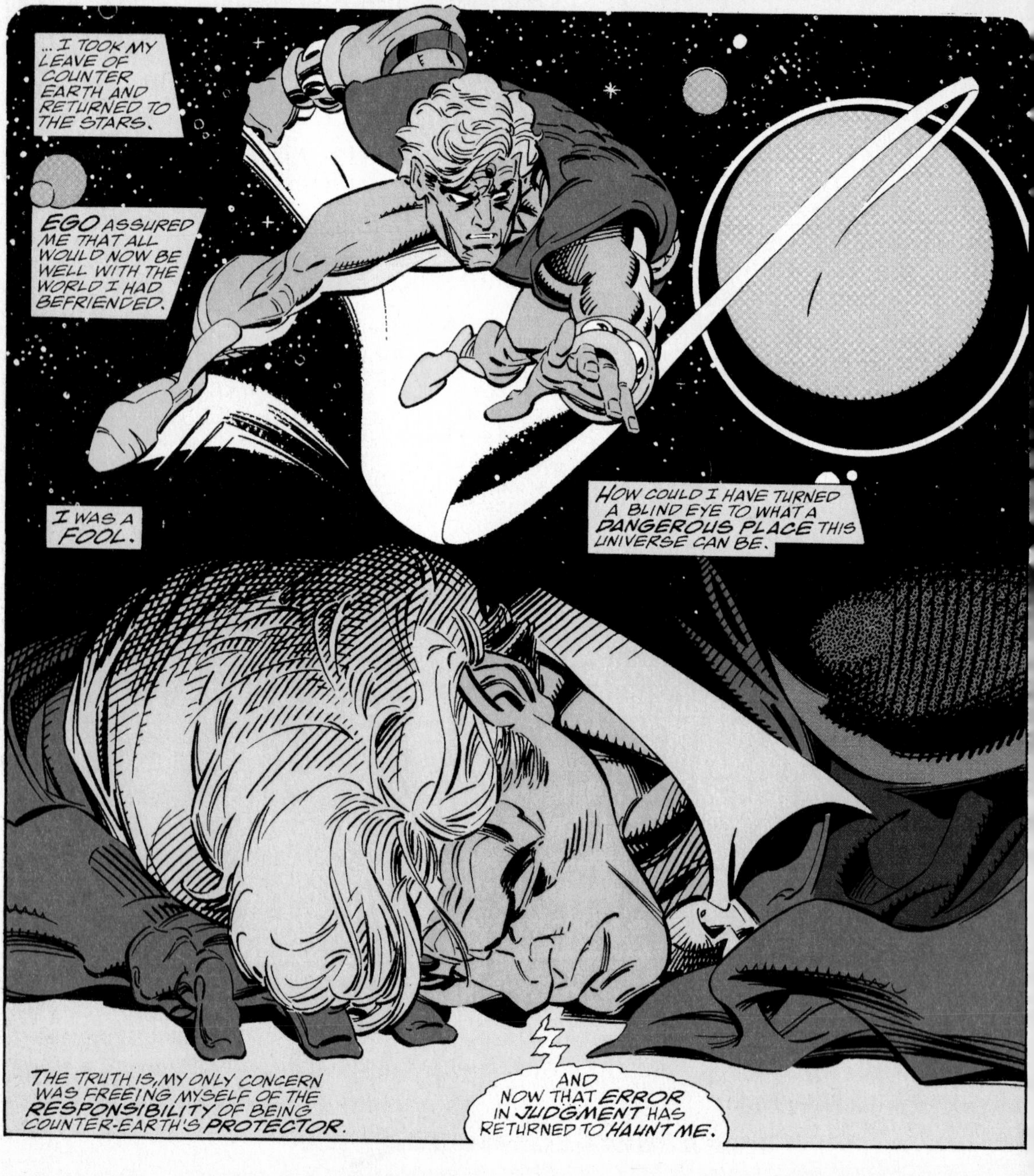
...I TOOK MY LEAVE OF COUNTER EARTH AND RETURNED TO THE STARS.
EGO ASSURED ME THAT ALL WOULD NOW BE WELL WITH THE WORLD I HAD BEFRIENDED.
I WAS A FOOL.
HOW COULD I HAVE TURNED A BLIND EYE TO WHAT A DANGEROUS PLACE THIS UNIVERSE CAN BE.
THE TRUTH IS, MY ONLY CONCERN WAS FREEING MYSELF OF THE RESPONSIBILITY OF BEING COUNTER-EARTH'S PROTECTOR.
AND NOW THAT ERROR IN JUDGMENT HAS RETURNED TO HAUNT ME.

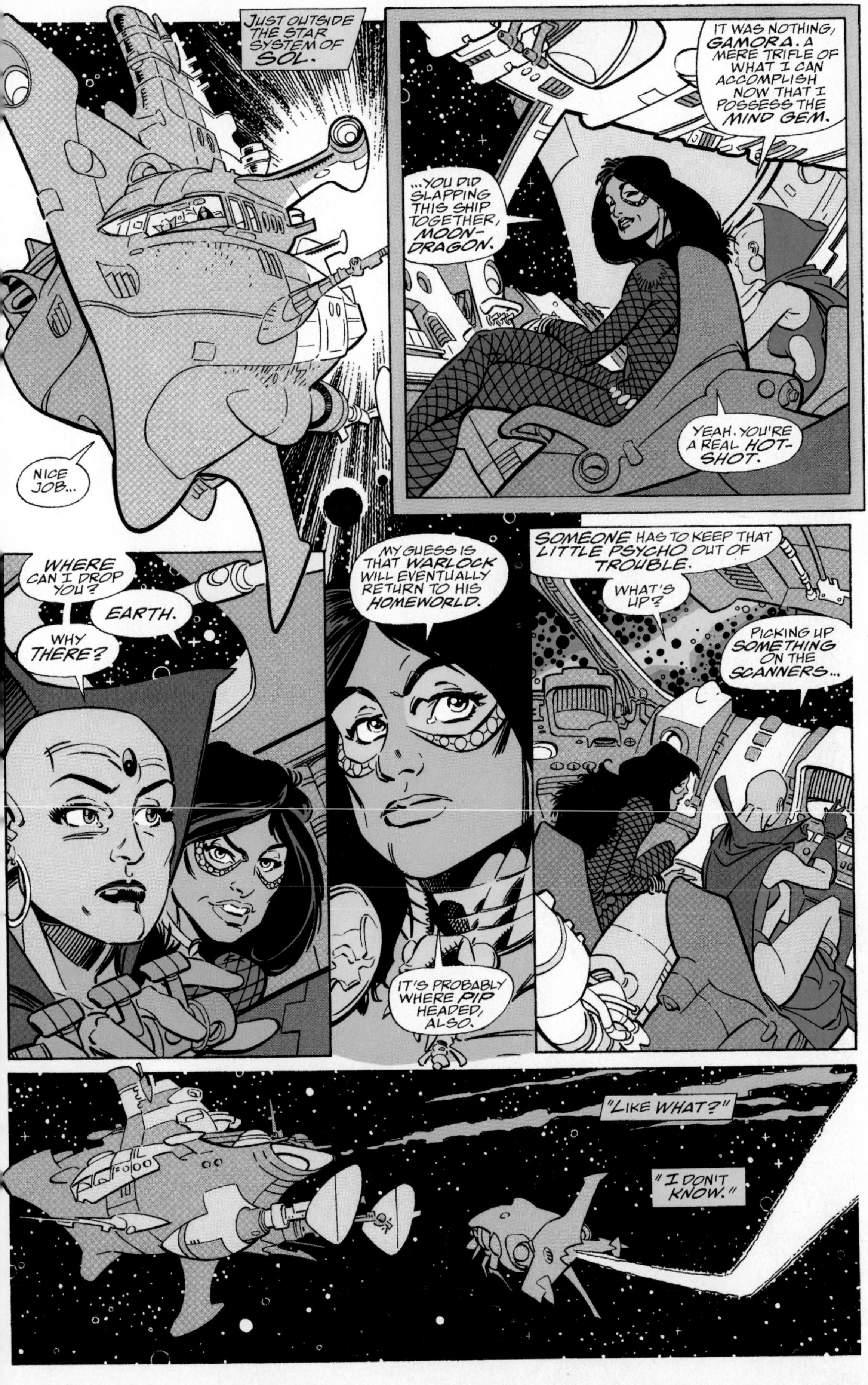

JUST OUTSIDE THE STAR SYSTEM OF SOL.
NICE JOB...
...YOU DID SLAPPING THIS SHIP TOGETHER, MOON-DRAGON.
IT WAS NOTHING, GAMORA. A MERE TRIFLE OF WHAT I CAN ACCOMPLISH NOW THAT I POSSESS THE MIND GEM.
YEAH. YOU'RE A REAL HOT-SHOT.
WHERE CAN I DROP YOU?
EARTH.
WHY THERE?
MY GUESS IS THAT WARLOCK WILL EVENTUALLY RETURN TO HIS HOMEWORLD.
IT'S PROBABLY WHERE PIP HEADED, ALSO.
SOMEONE HAS TO KEEP THAT LITTLE PSYCHO OUT OF TROUBLE.
WHAT'S UP?
PICKING UP SOMETHING ON THE SCANNERS...
"LIKE WHAT?"
"I DON'T KNOW."

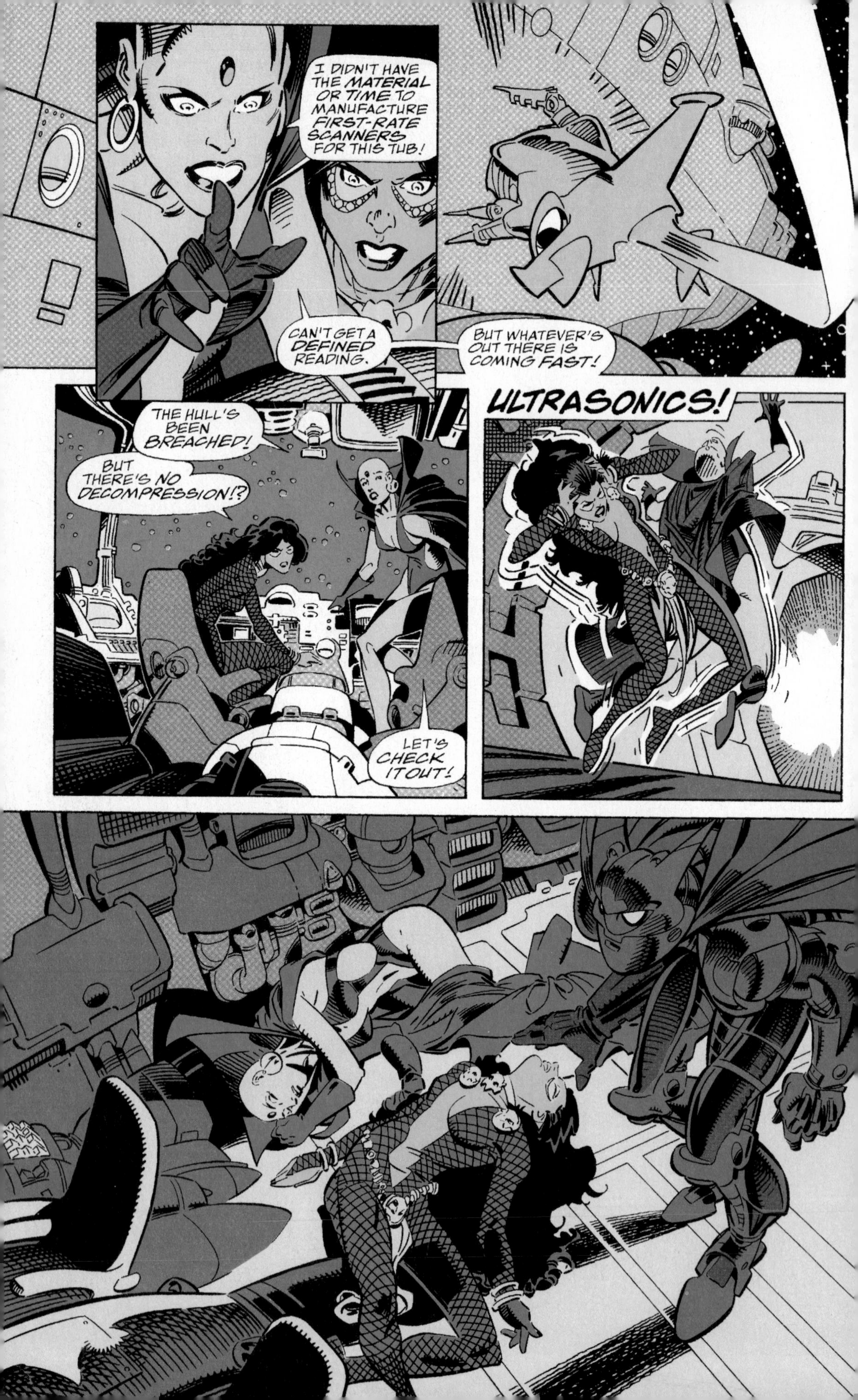
I DIDN'T HAVE THE MATERIAL OR TIME TO MANUFACTURE FIRST-RATE SCANNERS FOR THIS TUB!
CAN'T GET A DEFINED READING.
BUT WHATEVER'S OUT THERE IS COMING FAST!
THE HULL'S BEEN BREACHED!
BUT THERE'S NO DECOMPRESSION!?
LET'S CHECK IT OUT!
ULTRASONICS!

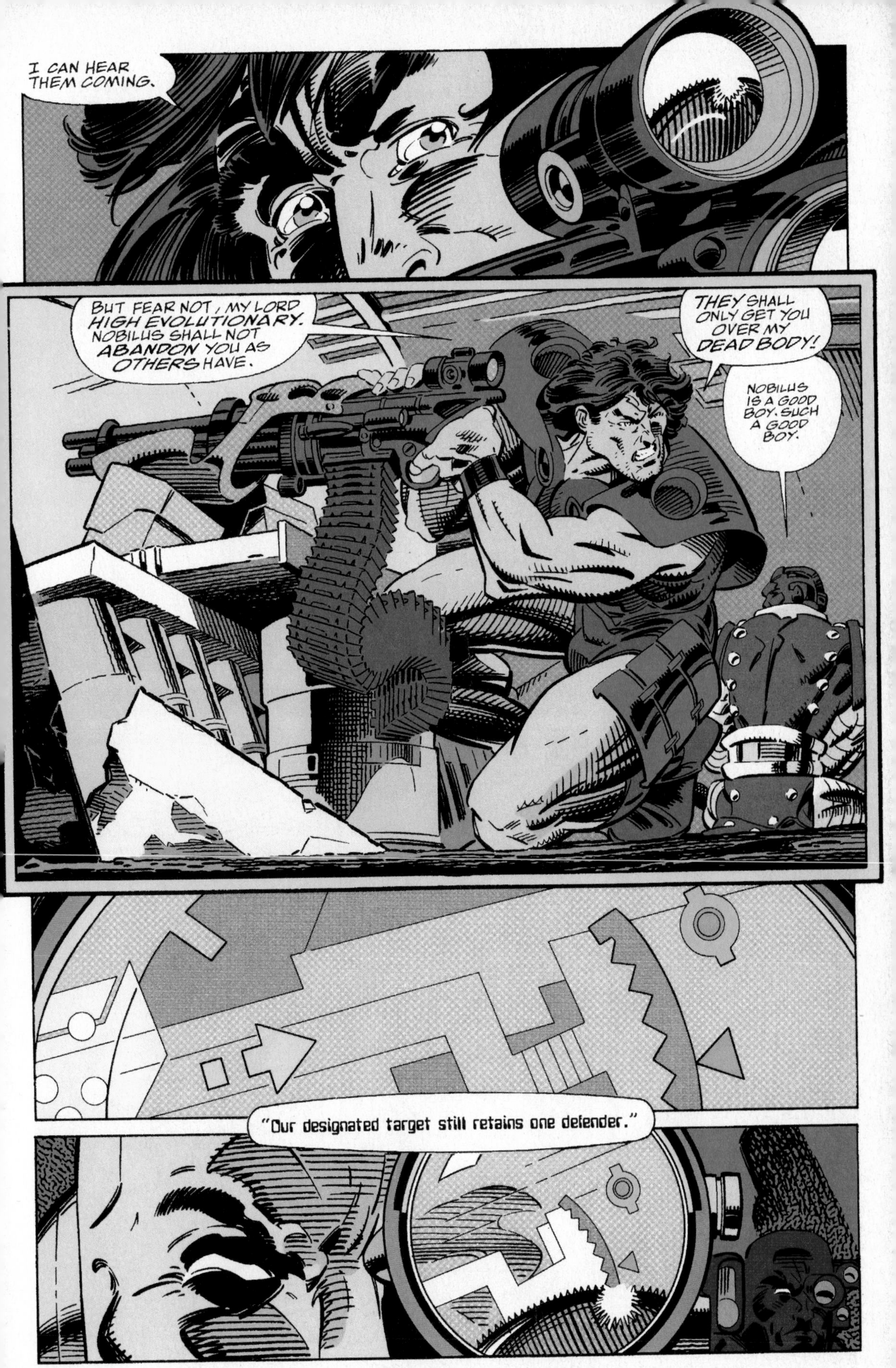
I CAN HEAR THEM COMING.
BUT FEAR NOT, MY LORD HIGH EVOLUTIONARY. NOBILUS SHALL NOT ABANDON YOU AS OTHERS HAVE.
THEY SHALL ONLY GET YOU OVER MY DEAD BODY!
NOBILUS IS A GOOD BOY. SUCH A GOOD BOY.
"Our designated target still retains one defender."

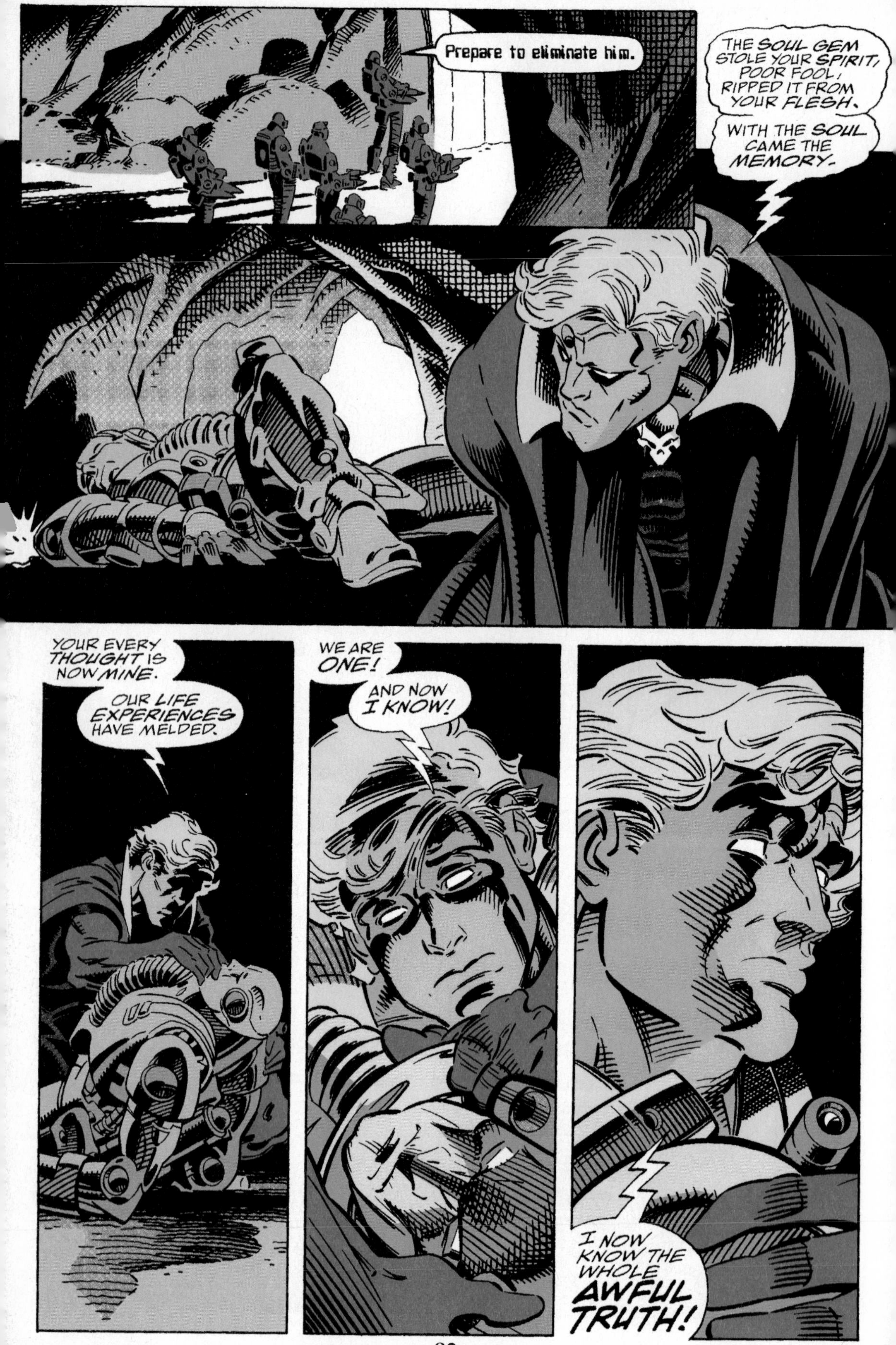
Prepare to eliminate him.
THE SOUL GEM STOLE YOUR SPIRIT, POOR FOOL, RIPPED IT FROM YOUR FLESH.
WITH THE SOUL CAME THE MEMORY.
YOUR EVERY THOUGHT IS NOW MINE.
OUR LIFE EXPERIENCES HAVE MELDED.
WE ARE ONE!
AND NOW I KNOW!
I NOW KNOW THE WHOLE AWFUL TRUTH!

"Institute assault."

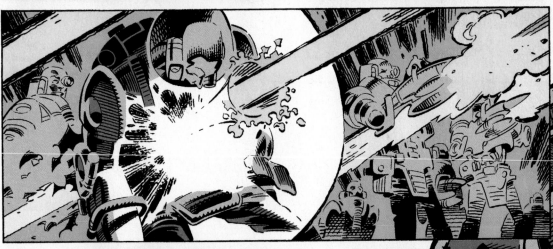

83

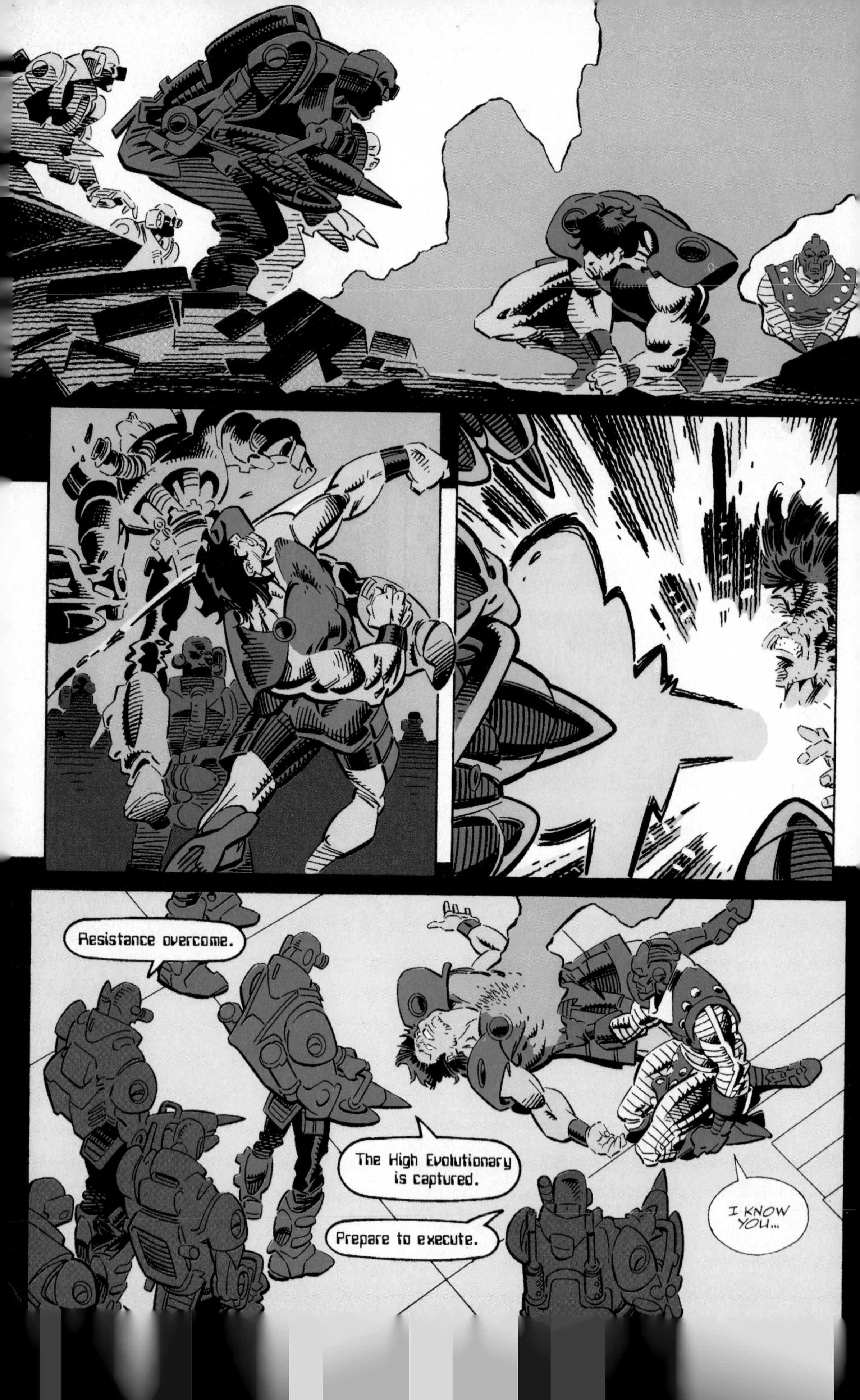
Resistance overcome.
The High Evolutionary is captured.
Prepare to execute.
I KNOW YOU...

COUNTER-EARTH FELL UNDER THE COVETOUS EYE OF ONE SPHINXOR, OF THE PEGASUSIAN MOVING COMPANY.

AND DESPITE THE BEST EFFORTS OF THE HIGH EVOLUTIONARY, THE **THING**, HIS COMPANION ALICIA MASTERS, AND THE MYSTERIOUS STARHAWK, THE PLANET WAS RIPPED FROM ITS ORBIT AND STOLEN.

APPARENTLY SPHINXOR SOLD MY ONE-TIME HOME, AS A CURIOSITY, TO AN INCREDIBLE RACE OF SUPER-BEINGS CALLED THE BEYONDERS.

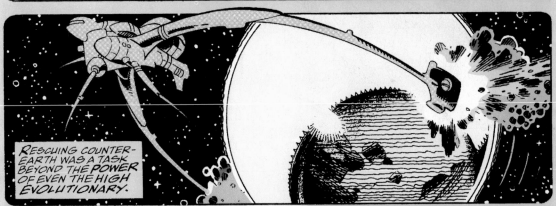

RESCUING COUNTER-EARTH WAS A TASK BEYOND THE POWER OF EVEN THE HIGH EVOLUTIONARY.

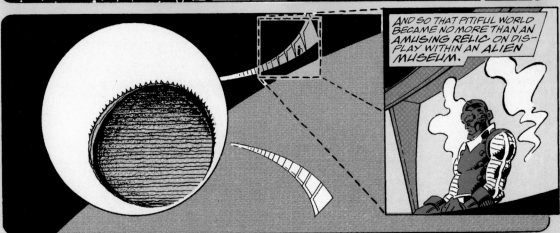

AND SO THAT PITIFUL WORLD BECAME NO MORE THAN AN AMUSING RELIC ON DISPLAY WITHIN AN ALIEN MUSEUM.

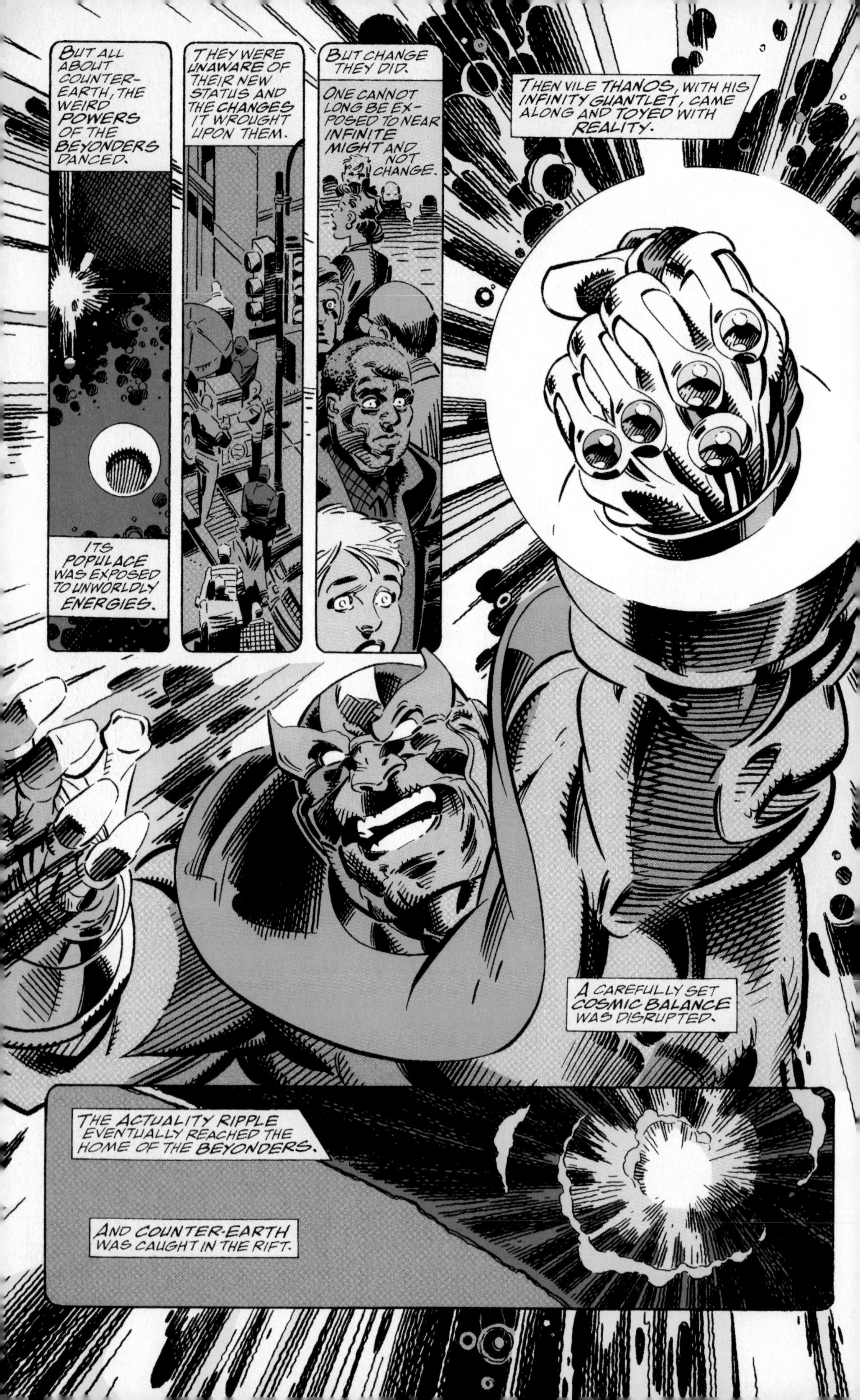
But all about Counter-Earth, the weird powers of the Beyonders danced.
Its populace was exposed to unworldly energies.
They were unaware of their new status and the changes it wrought upon them.
But change they did.
One cannot long be exposed to near infinite might and not change.
Then vile Thanos, with his Infinity Guantlet, came along and toyed with reality.
A carefully set cosmic balance was disrupted.
The Actuality Ripple eventually reached the home of the Beyonders.
And Counter-Earth was caught in the rift.

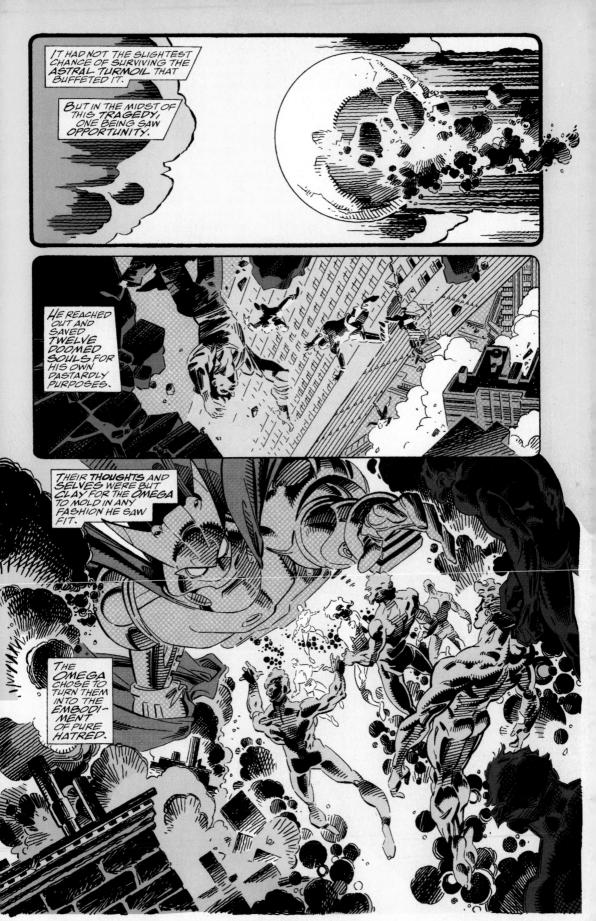

IT HAD NOT THE SLIGHTEST CHANCE OF SURVIVING THE ASTRAL TURMOIL THAT BUFFETED IT.

BUT IN THE MIDST OF THIS TRAGEDY, ONE BEING SAW OPPORTUNITY.

HE REACHED OUT AND SAVED TWELVE DOOMED SOULS FOR HIS OWN DASTARDLY PURPOSES.

THEIR THOUGHTS AND SELVES WERE BUT CLAY FOR THE OMEGA TO MOLD IN ANY FASHION HE SAW FIT.

THE OMEGA CHOSE TO TURN THEM INTO THE EMBODIMENT OF PURE HATRED.

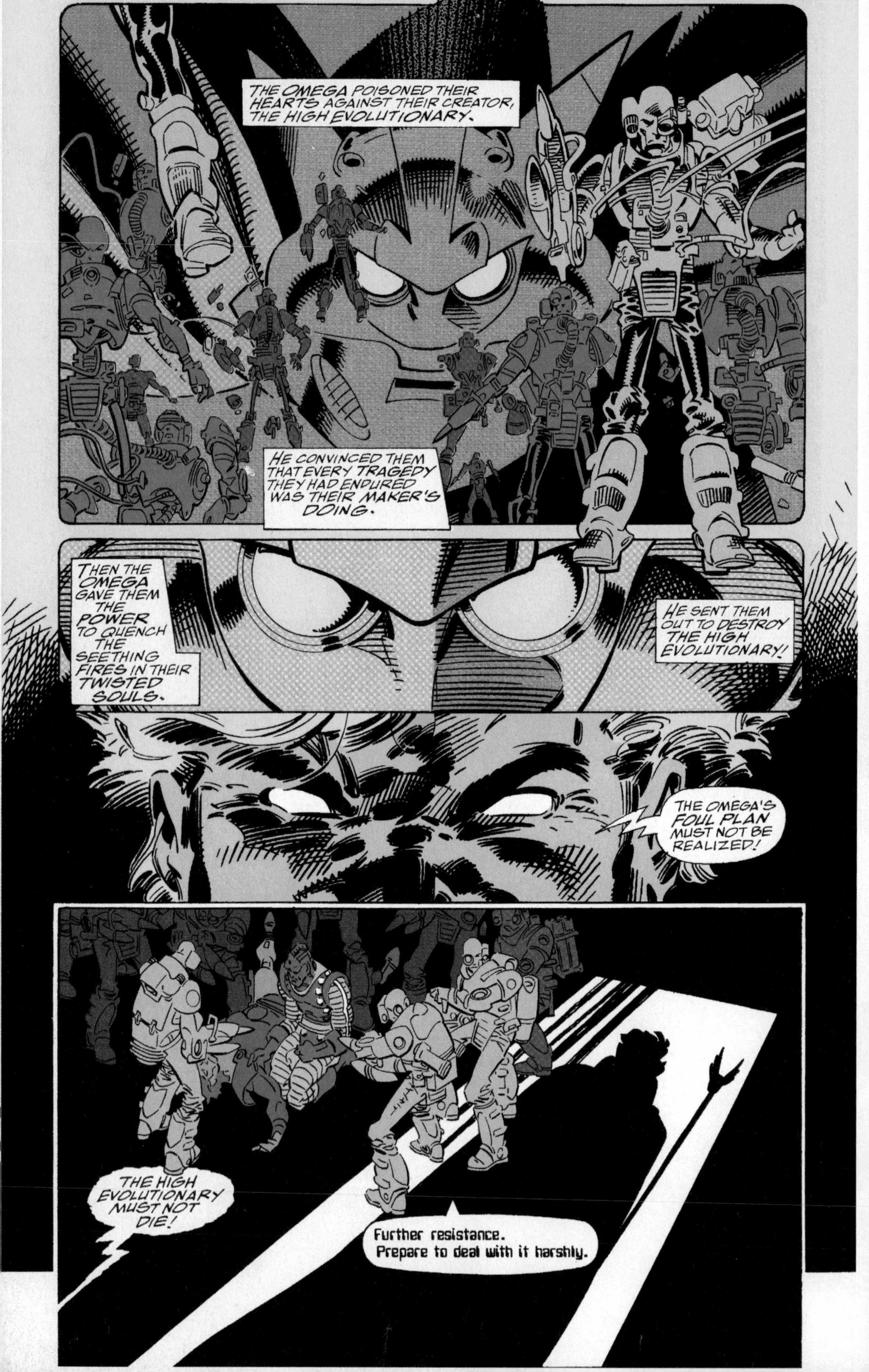
THE OMEGA POISONED THEIR HEARTS AGAINST THEIR CREATOR, THE HIGH EVOLUTIONARY.
HE CONVINCED THEM THAT EVERY TRAGEDY THEY HAD ENDURED WAS THEIR MAKER'S DOING.
THEN THE OMEGA GAVE THEM THE POWER TO QUENCH THE SEETHING FIRES IN THEIR TWISTED SOULS.
HE SENT THEM OUT TO DESTROY THE HIGH EVOLUTIONARY!
THE OMEGA'S FOUL PLAN MUST NOT BE REALIZED!
THE HIGH EVOLUTIONARY MUST NOT DIE!
Further resistance. Prepare to deal with it harshly.

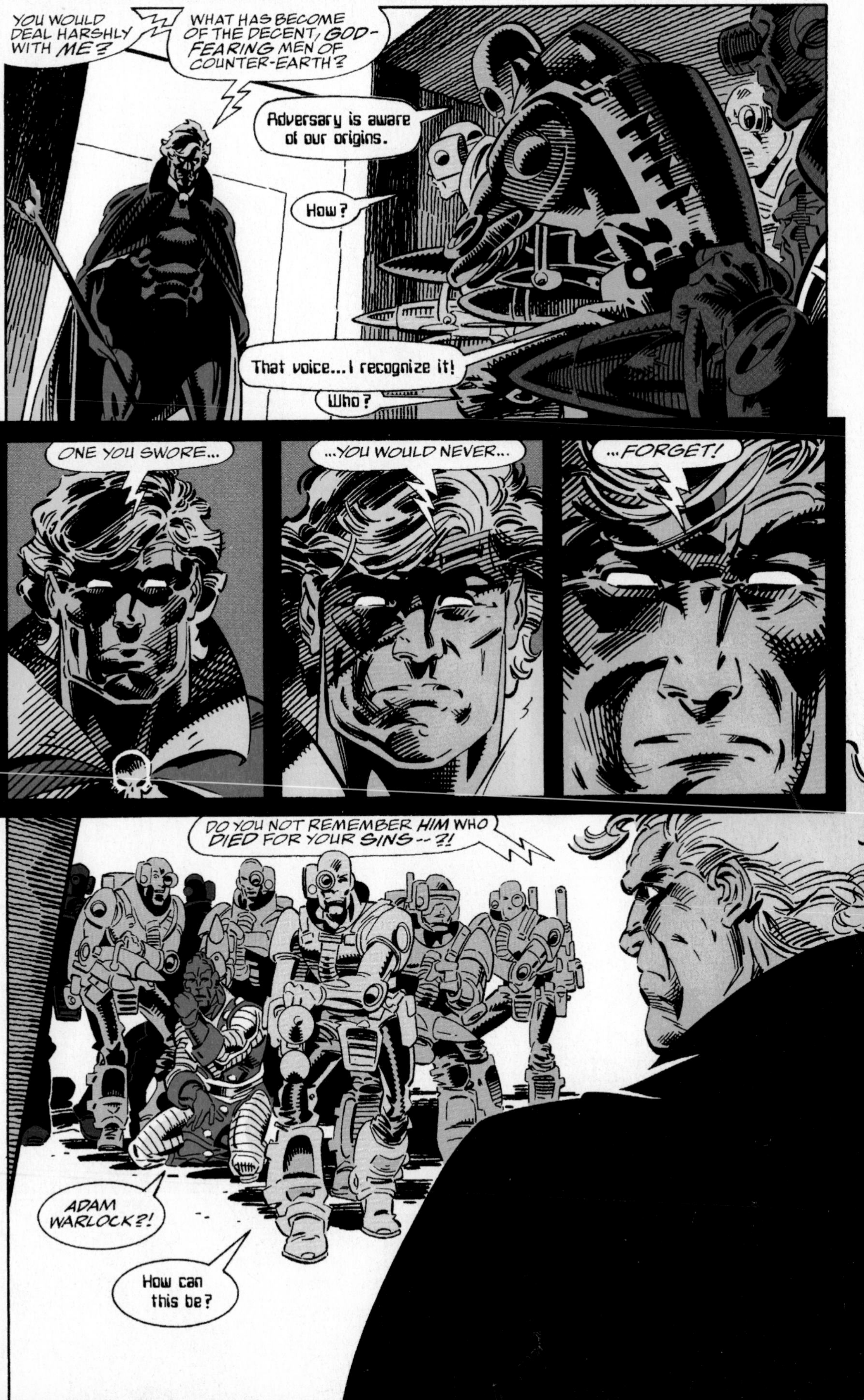
YOU WOULD DEAL HARSHLY WITH ME?
WHAT HAS BECOME OF THE DECENT, GOD-FEARING MEN OF COUNTER-EARTH?
Adversary is aware of our origins.
How?
That voice... I recognize it!
Who?
ONE YOU SWORE...
...YOU WOULD NEVER...
...FORGET!
DO YOU NOT REMEMBER HIM WHO DIED FOR YOUR SINS--?!
ADAM WARLOCK?!
How can this be?

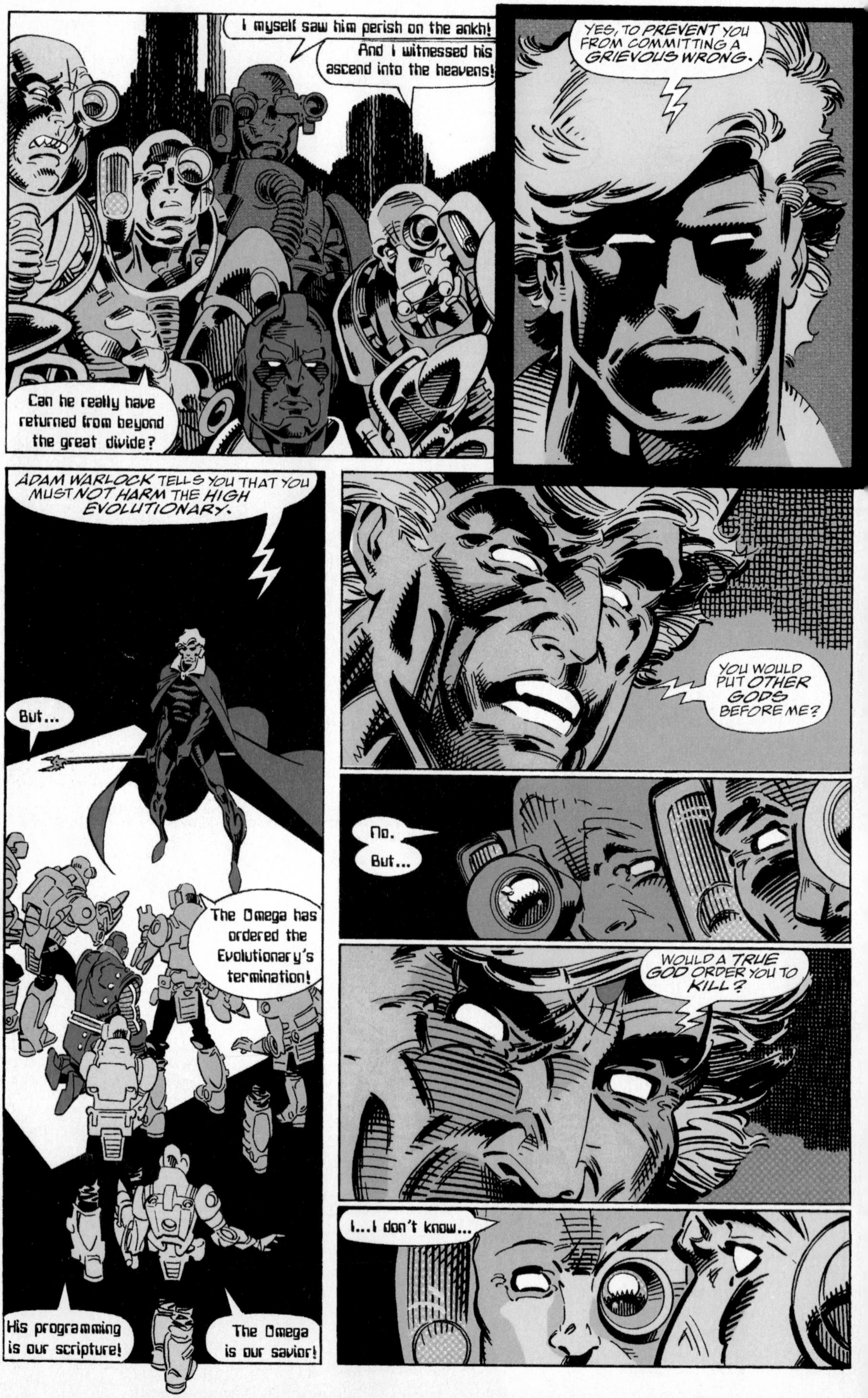
I myself saw him perish on the ankh!
And I witnessed his ascend into the heavens!
Can he really have returned from beyond the great divide?
YES, TO PREVENT YOU FROM COMMITTING A GRIEVOUS WRONG.
ADAM WARLOCK TELLS YOU THAT YOU MUST NOT HARM THE HIGH EVOLUTIONARY.
But...
The Omega has ordered the Evolutionary's termination!
His programming is our scripture!
The Omega is our savior!
YOU WOULD PUT OTHER GODS BEFORE ME?
No.
But...
WOULD A TRUE GOD ORDER YOU TO KILL?
I...I don't know...

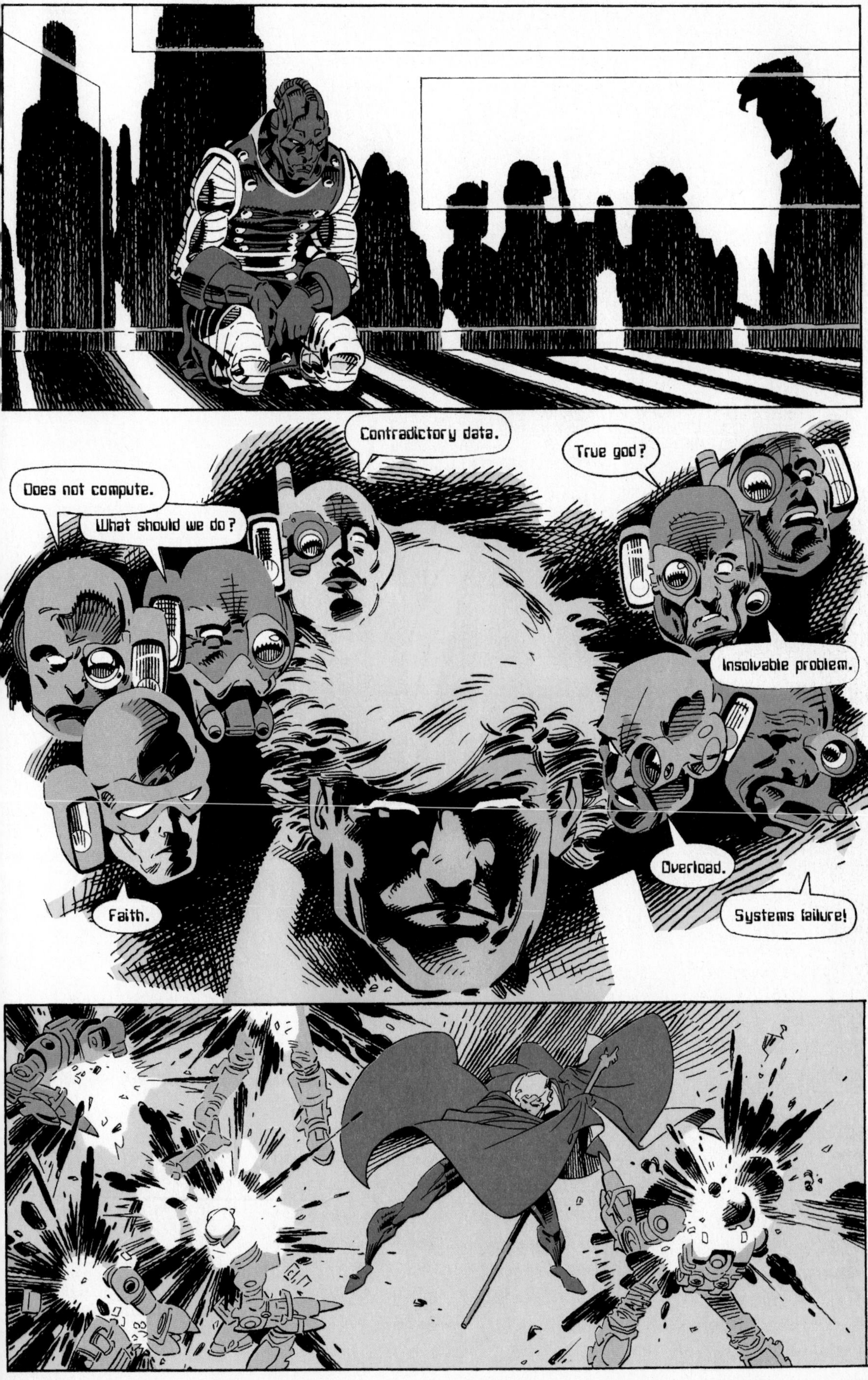
Does not compute.
What should we do?
Contradictory data.
True god?
Insolvable problem.
Faith.
Overload.
Systems failure!

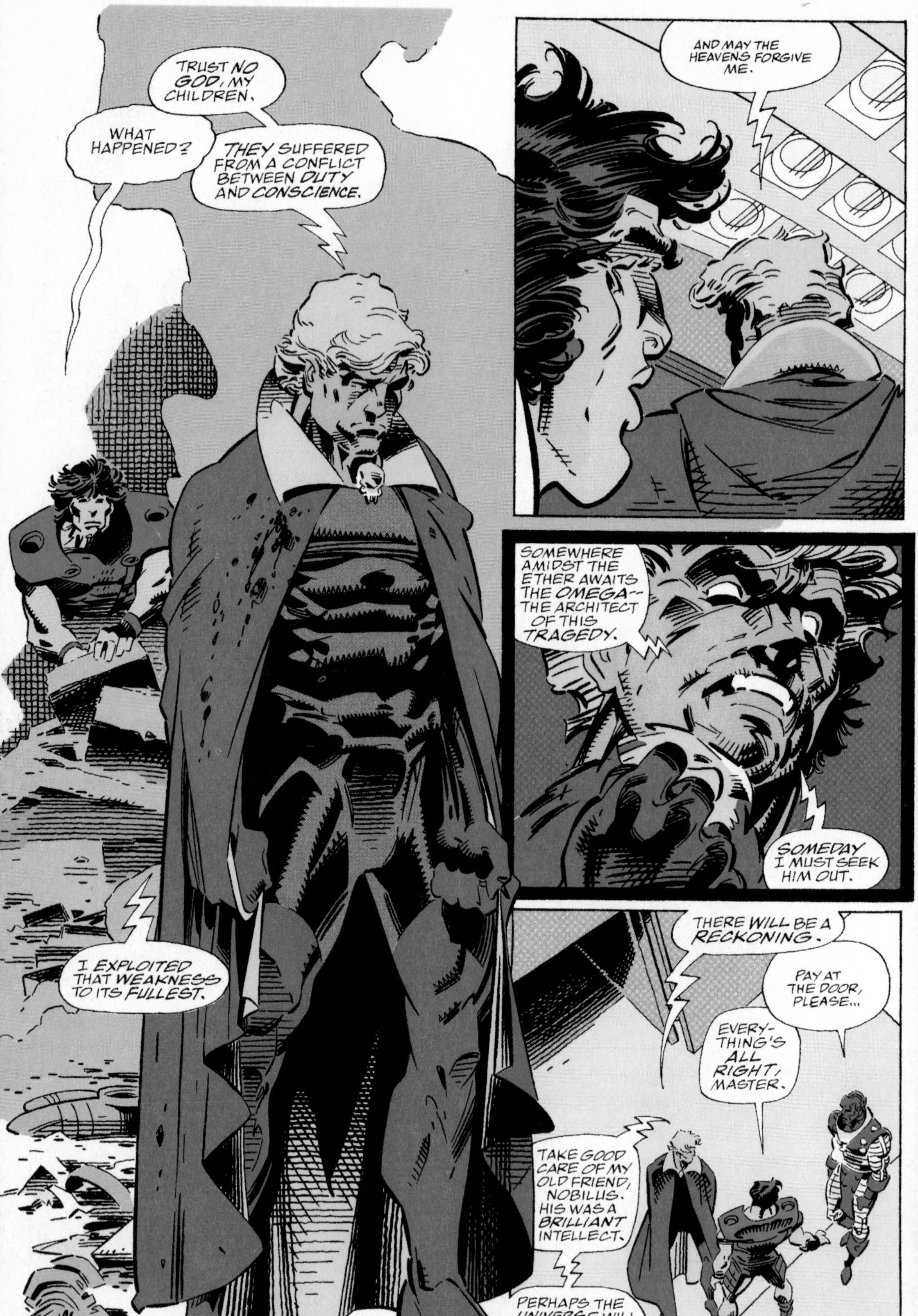

WHAT HAPPENED?
TRUST NO GOD, MY CHILDREN.
THEY SUFFERED FROM A CONFLICT BETWEEN DUTY AND CONSCIENCE.
I EXPLOITED THAT WEAKNESS TO ITS FULLEST.
AND MAY THE HEAVENS FORGIVE ME.
SOMEWHERE AMIDST THE ETHER AWAITS THE OMEGA-- THE ARCHITECT OF THIS TRAGEDY.
SOMEDAY I MUST SEEK HIM OUT.
THERE WILL BE A RECKONING.
PAY AT THE DOOR, PLEASE...
EVERY-THING'S ALL RIGHT, MASTER.
TAKE GOOD CARE OF MY OLD FRIEND, NOBILUS. HIS WAS A BRILLIANT INTELLECT.
PERHAPS THE UNIVERSE WILL AGAIN ONE DAY BENEFIT FROM IT.

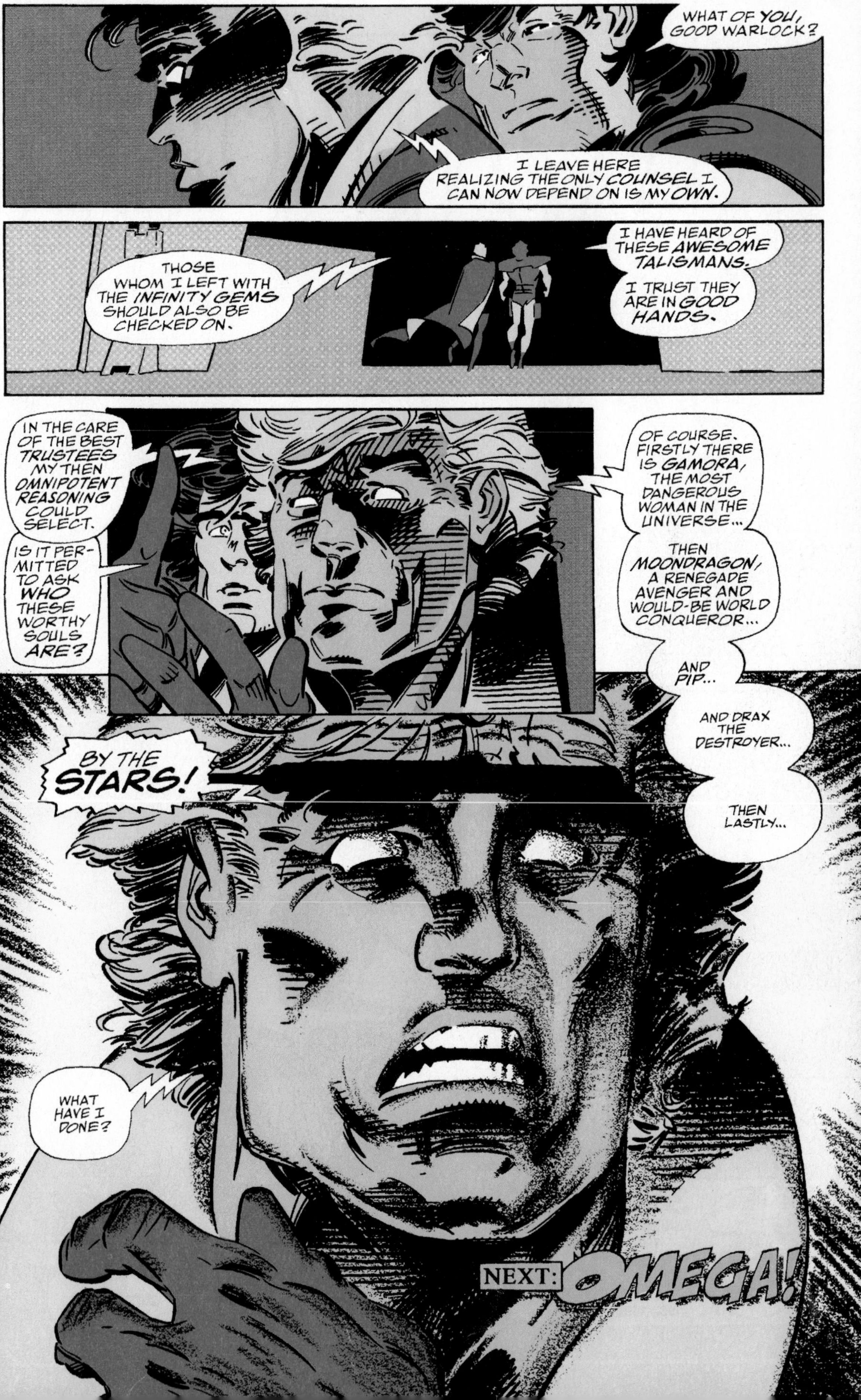

WHAT OF YOU, GOOD WARLOCK?
I LEAVE HERE REALIZING THE ONLY COUNSEL I CAN NOW DEPEND ON IS MY OWN.
THOSE WHOM I LEFT WITH THE INFINITY GEMS SHOULD ALSO BE CHECKED ON.
I HAVE HEARD OF THESE AWESOME TALISMANS.
I TRUST THEY ARE IN GOOD HANDS.
IN THE CARE OF THE BEST TRUSTEES MY THEN OMNIPOTENT REASONING COULD SELECT.
IS IT PERMITTED TO ASK WHO THESE WORTHY SOULS ARE?
OF COURSE. FIRSTLY THERE IS GAMORA, THE MOST DANGEROUS WOMAN IN THE UNIVERSE...
THEN MOONDRAGON, A RENEGADE AVENGER AND WOULD-BE WORLD CONQUEROR...
AND PIP...
AND DRAX THE DESTROYER...
THEN LASTLY...
BY THE STARS!
WHAT HAVE I DONE?
NEXT: OMEGA!

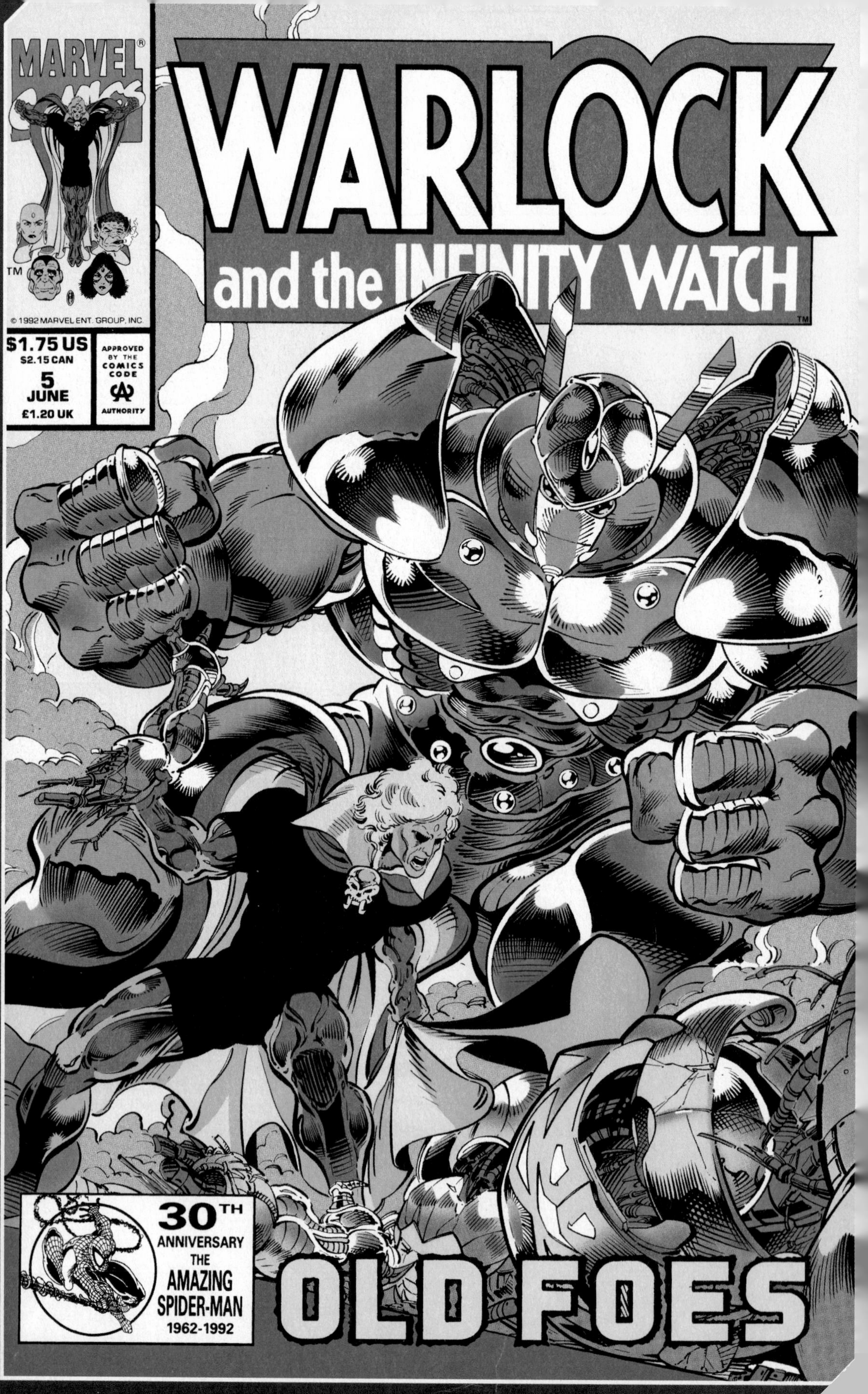
MARVEL COMICS
WARLOCK and the INFINITY WATCH
© 1992 MARVEL ENT. GROUP, INC.
$1.75 US
$2.15 CAN
5
JUNE
£1.20 UK
APPROVED BY THE COMICS CODE AUTHORITY
30TH ANNIVERSARY THE AMAZING SPIDER-MAN 1962-1992
OLD FOES

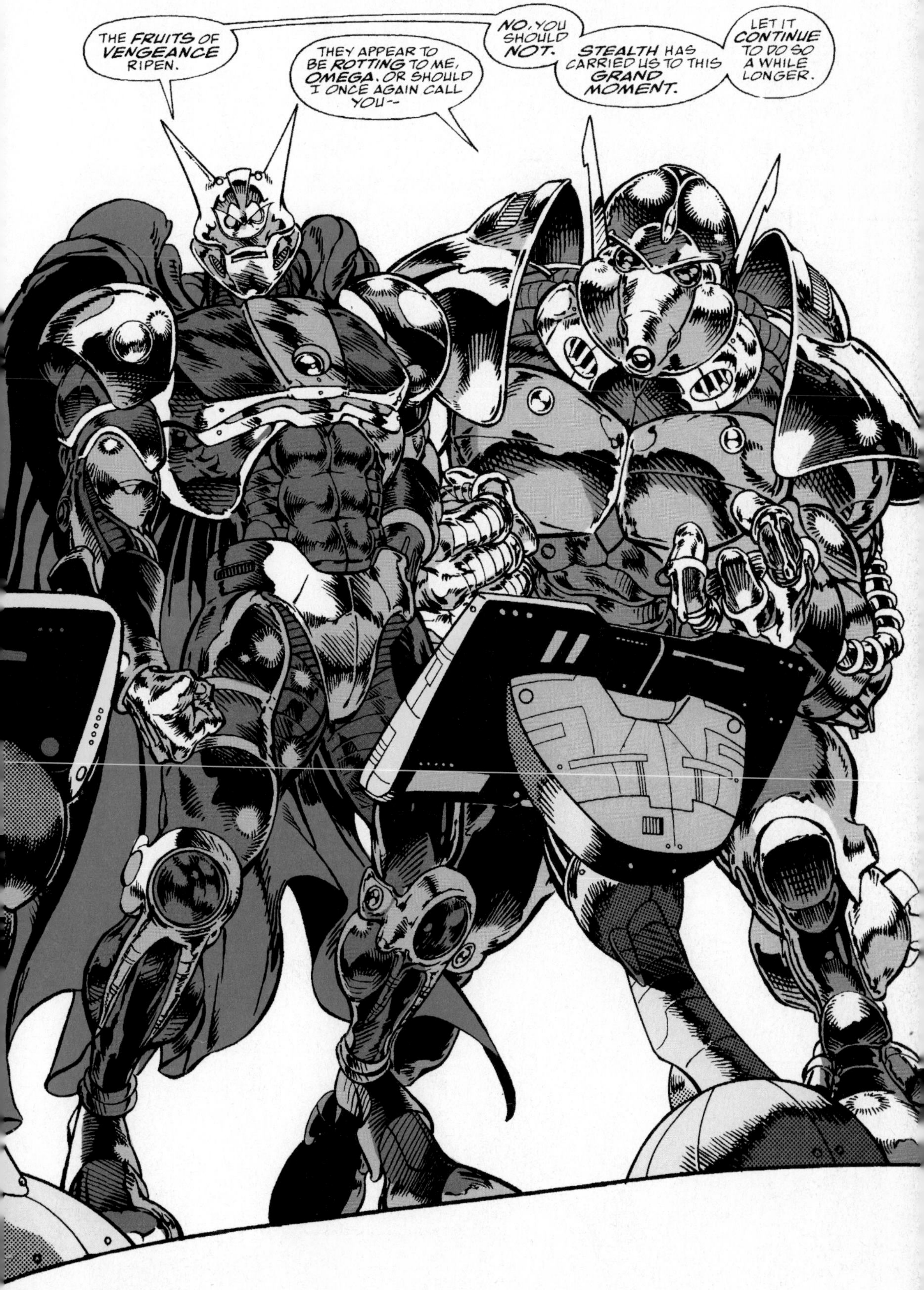
THE FRUITS OF VENGEANCE RIPEN.
THEY APPEAR TO BE ROTTING TO ME, OMEGA. OR SHOULD I ONCE AGAIN CALL YOU--
NO. YOU SHOULD NOT.
STEALTH HAS CARRIED US TO THIS GRAND MOMENT.
LET IT CONTINUE TO DO SO A WHILE LONGER.

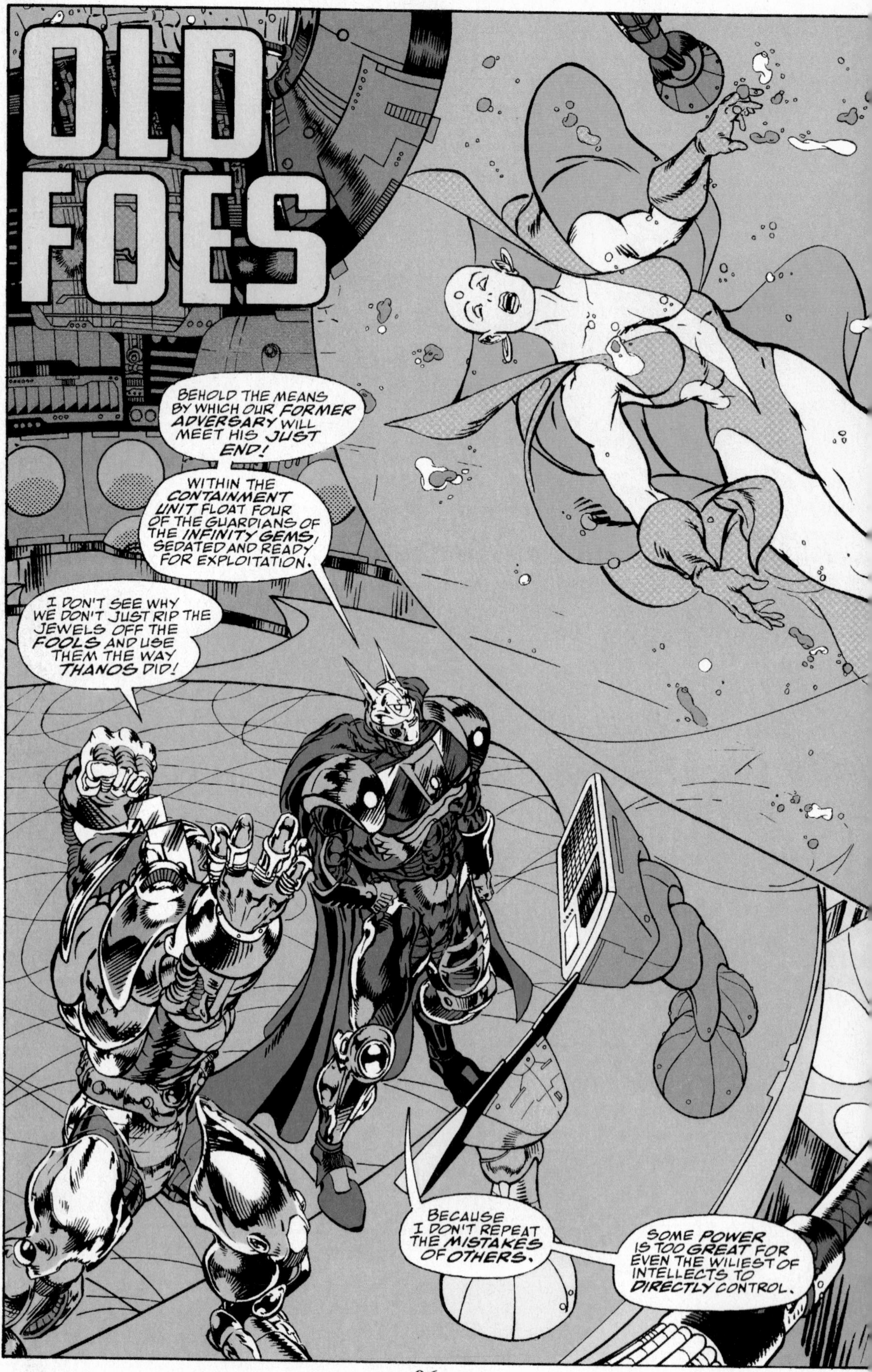
OLD FOES
BEHOLD THE MEANS BY WHICH OUR FORMER ADVERSARY WILL MEET HIS JUST END!
WITHIN THE CONTAINMENT UNIT FLOAT FOUR OF THE GUARDIANS OF THE INFINITY GEMS, SEDATED AND READY FOR EXPLOITATION.
I DON'T SEE WHY WE DON'T JUST RIP THE JEWELS OFF THE FOOLS AND USE THEM THE WAY THANOS DID!
BECAUSE I DON'T REPEAT THE MISTAKES OF OTHERS.
SOME POWER IS TOO GREAT FOR EVEN THE WILIEST OF INTELLECTS TO DIRECTLY CONTROL.

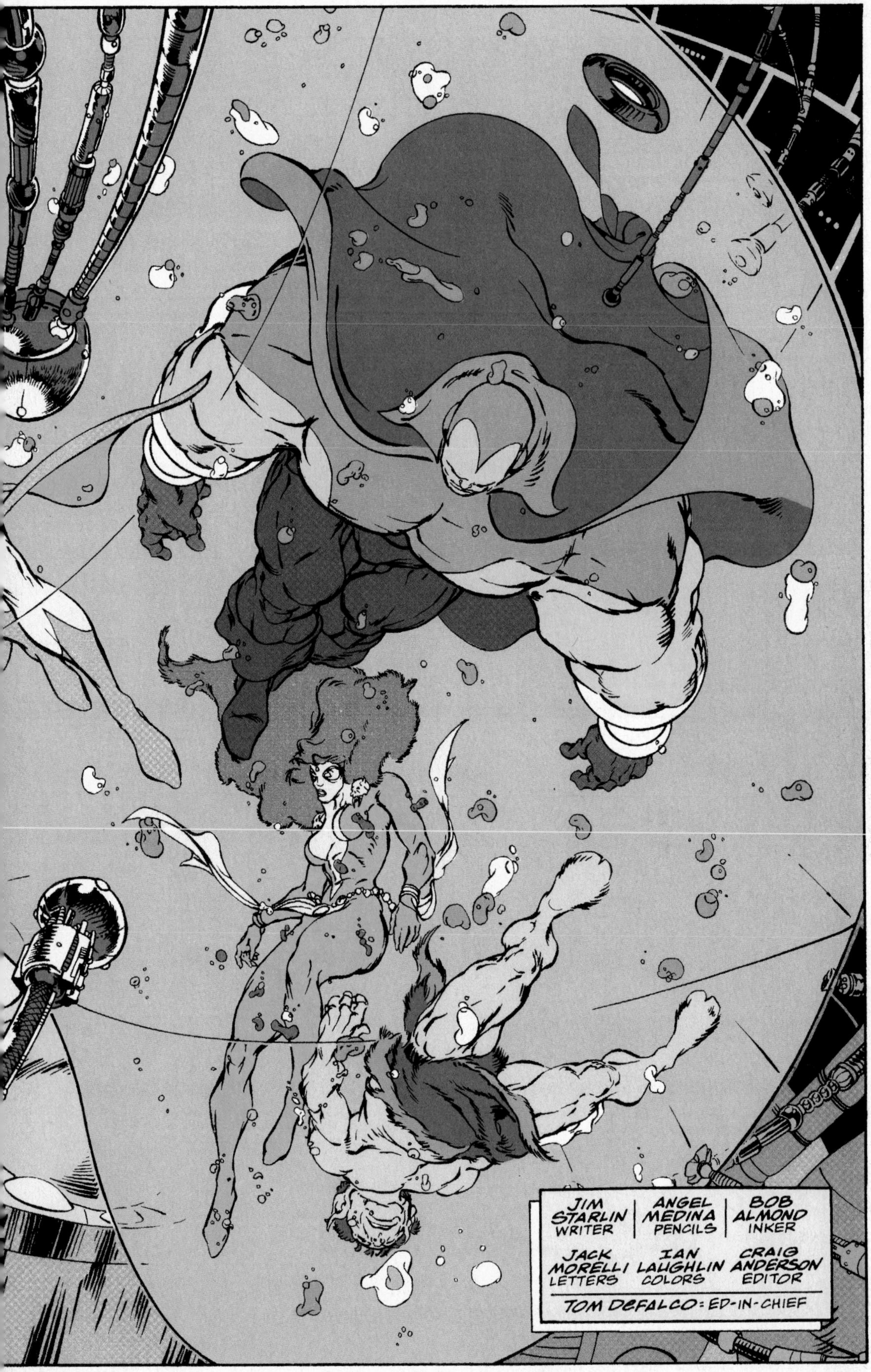
JIM STARLIN WRITER
ANGEL MEDINA PENCILS
BOB ALMOND INKER
JACK MORELLI LETTERS
IAN LAUGHLIN COLORS
CRAIG ANDERSON EDITOR
TOM DEFALCO: ED-IN-CHIEF

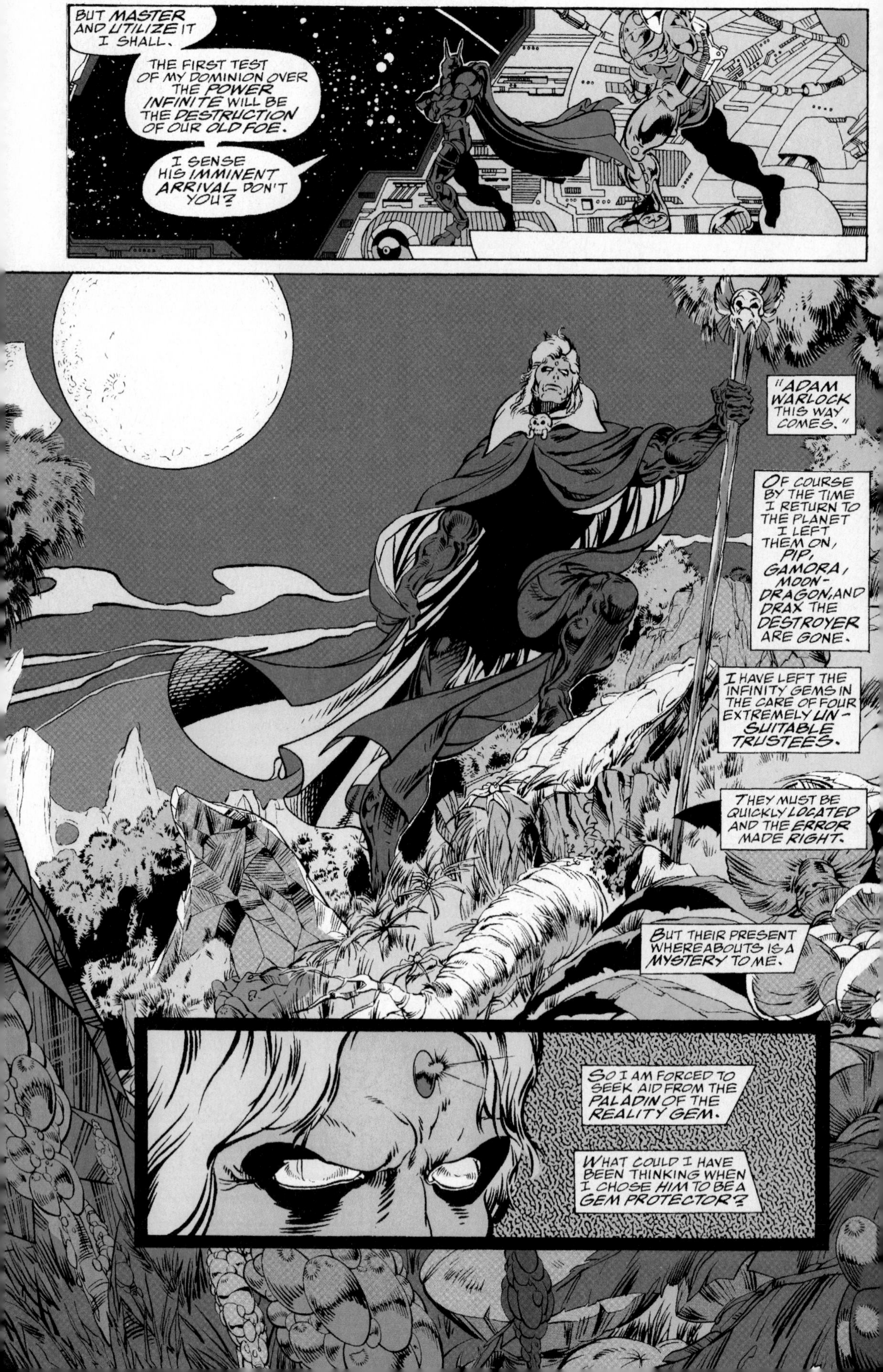

BUT MASTER AND UTILIZE IT I SHALL.
THE FIRST TEST OF MY DOMINION OVER THE POWER INFINITE WILL BE THE DESTRUCTION OF OUR OLD FOE.
I SENSE HIS IMMINENT ARRIVAL, DON'T YOU?
"ADAM WARLOCK THIS WAY COMES."
OF COURSE BY THE TIME I RETURN TO THE PLANET I LEFT THEM ON, PIP, GAMORA, MOON-DRAGON, AND DRAX THE DESTROYER ARE GONE.
I HAVE LEFT THE INFINITY GEMS IN THE CARE OF FOUR EXTREMELY UN-SUITABLE TRUSTEES.
THEY MUST BE QUICKLY LOCATED AND THE ERROR MADE RIGHT.
BUT THEIR PRESENT WHEREABOUTS IS A MYSTERY TO ME.
SO I AM FORCED TO SEEK AID FROM THE PALADIN OF THE REALITY GEM.
WHAT COULD I HAVE BEEN THINKING WHEN I CHOSE HIM TO BE A GEM PROTECTOR?

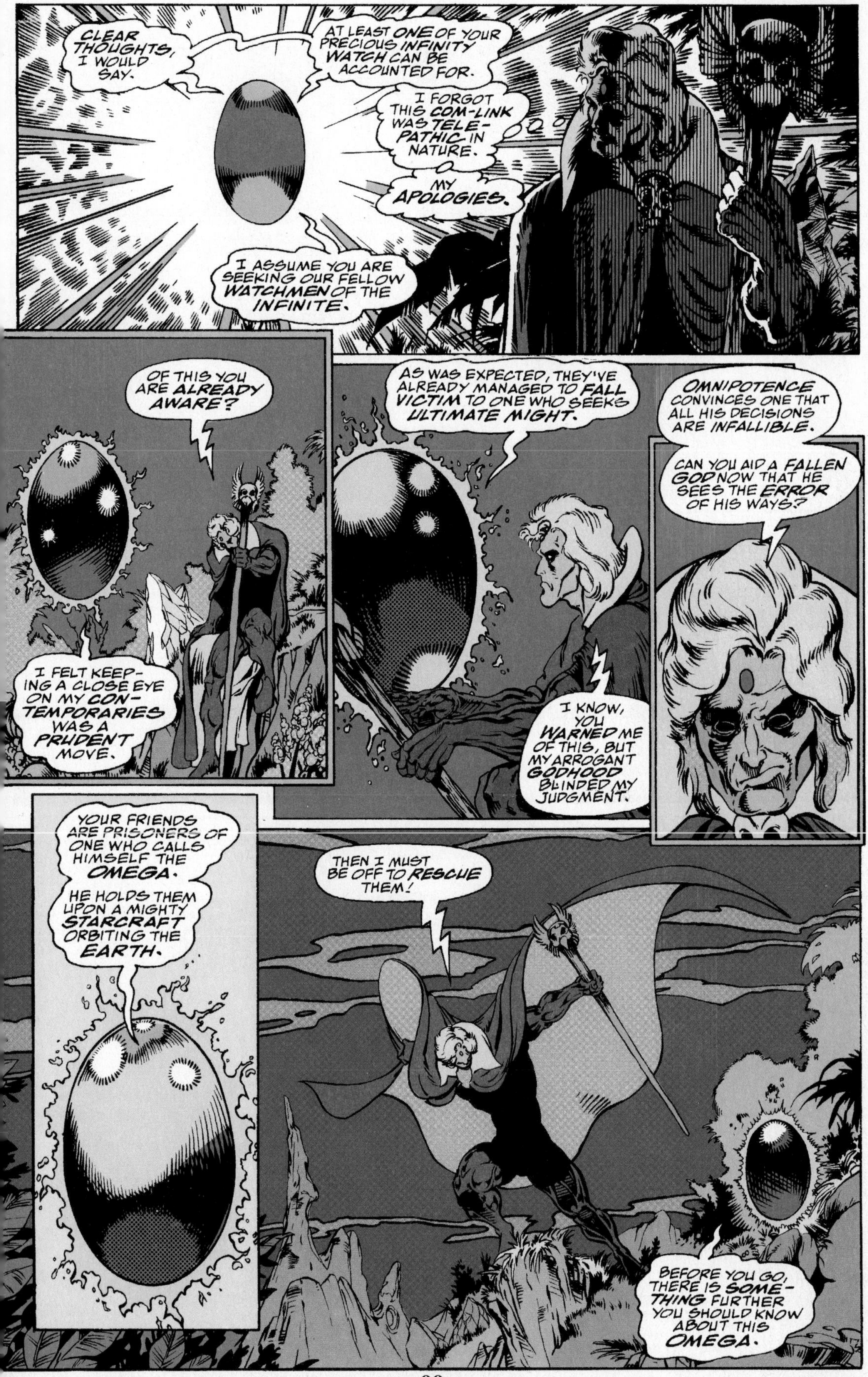
CLEAR THOUGHTS, I WOULD SAY.
AT LEAST ONE OF YOUR PRECIOUS INFINITY WATCH CAN BE ACCOUNTED FOR.
I FORGOT THIS COM-LINK WAS TELE-PATHIC IN NATURE.
MY APOLOGIES.
I ASSUME YOU ARE SEEKING OUR FELLOW WATCHMEN OF THE INFINITE.
OF THIS YOU ARE ALREADY AWARE?
I FELT KEEP-ING A CLOSE EYE ON MY CON-TEMPORARIES WAS A PRUDENT MOVE.
AS WAS EXPECTED, THEY'VE ALREADY MANAGED TO FALL VICTIM TO ONE WHO SEEKS ULTIMATE MIGHT.
I KNOW, YOU WARNED ME OF THIS, BUT MY ARROGANT GODHOOD BLINDED MY JUDGMENT.
OMNIPOTENCE CONVINCES ONE THAT ALL HIS DECISIONS ARE INFALLIBLE.
CAN YOU AID A FALLEN GOD NOW THAT HE SEES THE ERROR OF HIS WAYS?
YOUR FRIENDS ARE PRISONERS OF ONE WHO CALLS HIMSELF THE OMEGA.
HE HOLDS THEM UPON A MIGHTY STARCRAFT ORBITING THE EARTH.
THEN I MUST BE OFF TO RESCUE THEM!
BEFORE YOU GO, THERE IS SOME-THING FURTHER YOU SHOULD KNOW ABOUT THIS OMEGA.

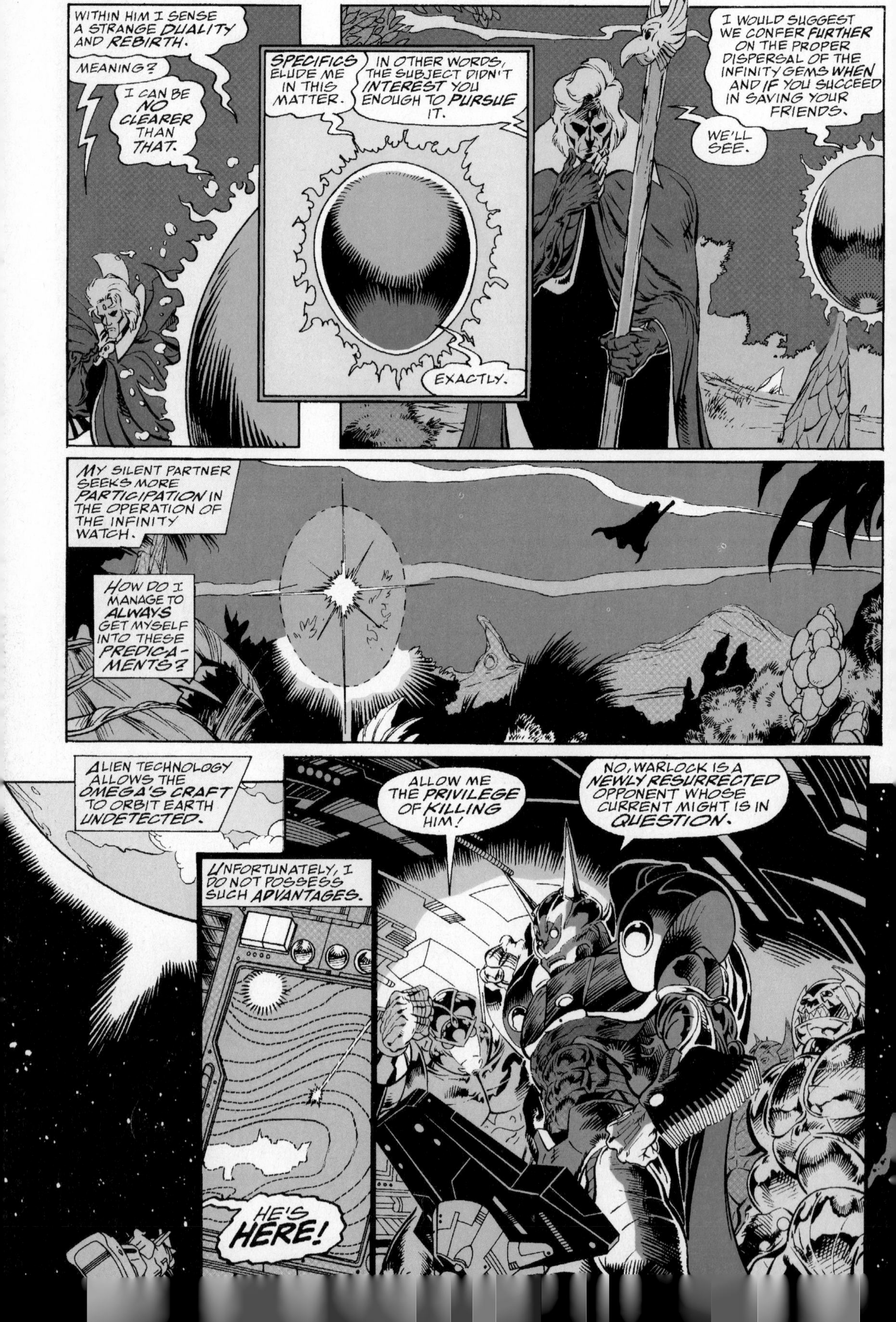
WITHIN HIM I SENSE A STRANGE DUALITY AND REBIRTH.
MEANING?
I CAN BE NO CLEARER THAN THAT.
SPECIFICS ELUDE ME IN THIS MATTER.
IN OTHER WORDS, THE SUBJECT DIDN'T INTEREST YOU ENOUGH TO PURSUE IT.
EXACTLY.
I WOULD SUGGEST WE CONFER FURTHER ON THE PROPER DISPERSAL OF THE INFINITY GEMS WHEN AND IF YOU SUCCEED IN SAVING YOUR FRIENDS.
WE'LL SEE.
MY SILENT PARTNER SEEKS MORE PARTICIPATION IN THE OPERATION OF THE INFINITY WATCH.
HOW DO I MANAGE TO ALWAYS GET MYSELF INTO THESE PREDICA-MENTS?
ALIEN TECHNOLOGY ALLOWS THE OMEGA'S CRAFT TO ORBIT EARTH UNDETECTED.
ALLOW ME THE PRIVILEGE OF KILLING HIM!
NO, WARLOCK IS A NEWLY RESURRECTED OPPONENT WHOSE CURRENT MIGHT IS IN QUESTION.
UNFORTUNATELY, I DO NOT POSSESS SUCH ADVANTAGES.
HE'S HERE!

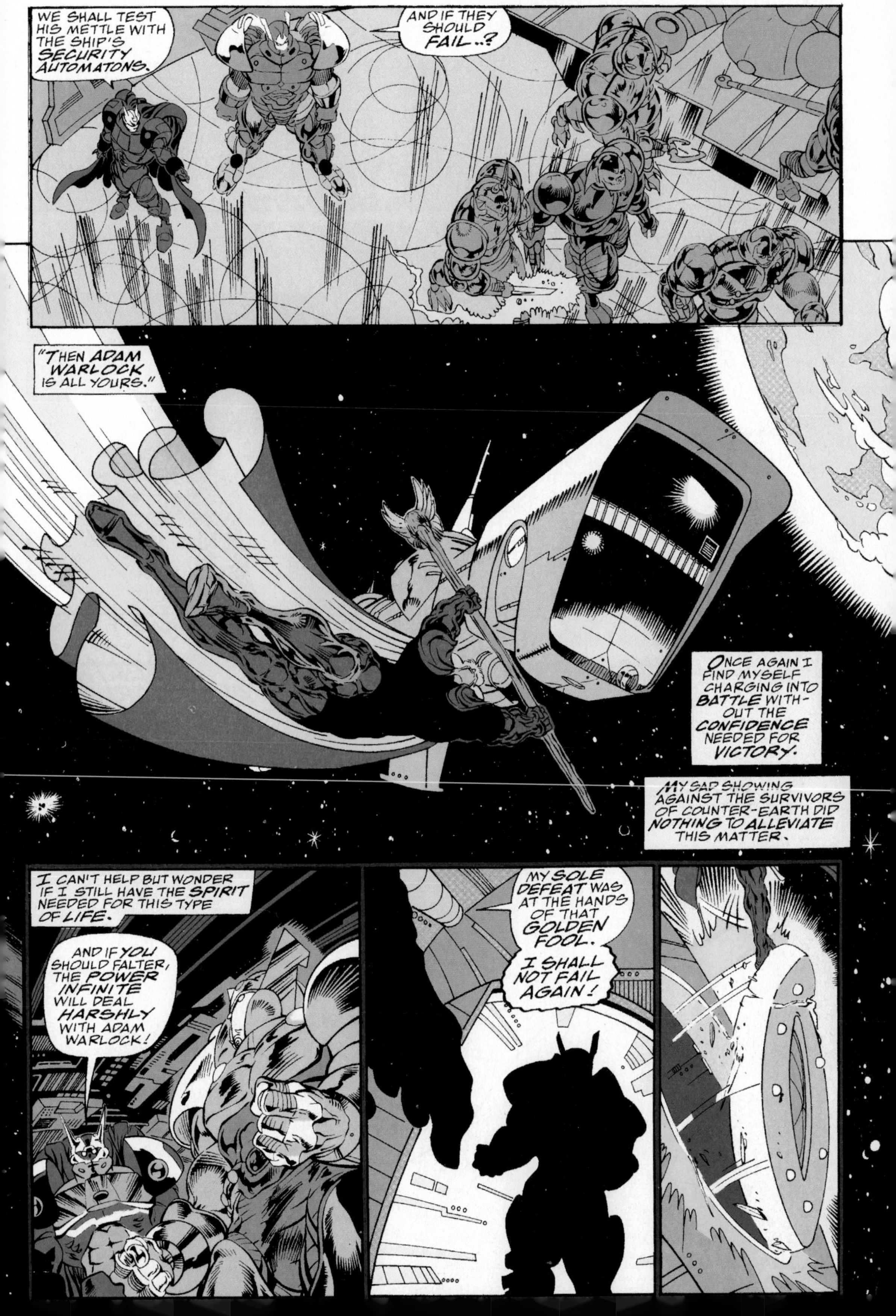
WE SHALL TEST HIS METTLE WITH THE SHIP'S SECURITY AUTOMATONS.
AND IF THEY SHOULD FAIL..?
"THEN ADAM WARLOCK IS ALL YOURS."
ONCE AGAIN I FIND MYSELF CHARGING INTO BATTLE WITH-OUT THE CONFIDENCE NEEDED FOR VICTORY.
MY SAD SHOWING AGAINST THE SURVIVORS OF COUNTER-EARTH DID NOTHING TO ALLEVIATE THIS MATTER.
I CAN'T HELP BUT WONDER IF I STILL HAVE THE SPIRIT NEEDED FOR THIS TYPE OF LIFE.
AND IF YOU SHOULD FALTER, THE POWER INFINITE WILL DEAL HARSHLY WITH ADAM WARLOCK!
MY SOLE DEFEAT WAS AT THE HANDS OF THAT GOLDEN FOOL.
I SHALL NOT FAIL AGAIN!

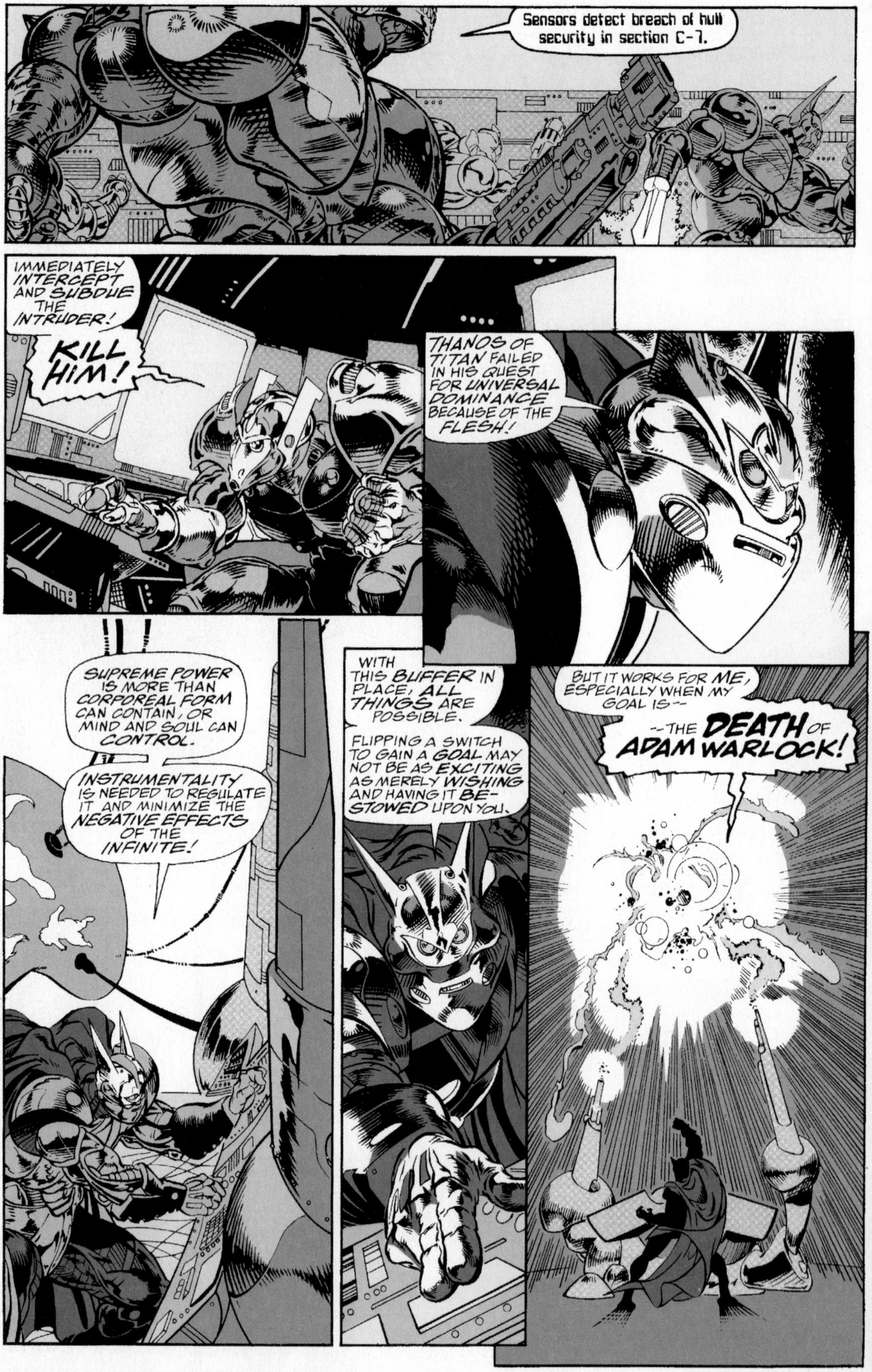

Sensors detect breach of hull security in section C-7.
IMMEDIATELY INTERCEPT AND SUBDUE THE INTRUDER!
KILL HIM!
THANOS OF TITAN FAILED IN HIS QUEST FOR UNIVERSAL DOMINANCE BECAUSE OF THE FLESH!
SUPREME POWER IS MORE THAN CORPOREAL FORM CAN CONTAIN, OR MIND AND SOUL CAN CONTROL.
INSTRUMENTALITY IS NEEDED TO REGULATE IT AND MINIMIZE THE NEGATIVE EFFECTS OF THE INFINITE!
WITH THIS BUFFER IN PLACE, ALL THINGS ARE POSSIBLE.
FLIPPING A SWITCH TO GAIN A GOAL MAY NOT BE AS EXCITING AS MERELY WISHING AND HAVING IT BESTOWED UPON YOU.
BUT IT WORKS FOR ME, ESPECIALLY WHEN MY GOAL IS--
--THE DEATH OF ADAM WARLOCK!

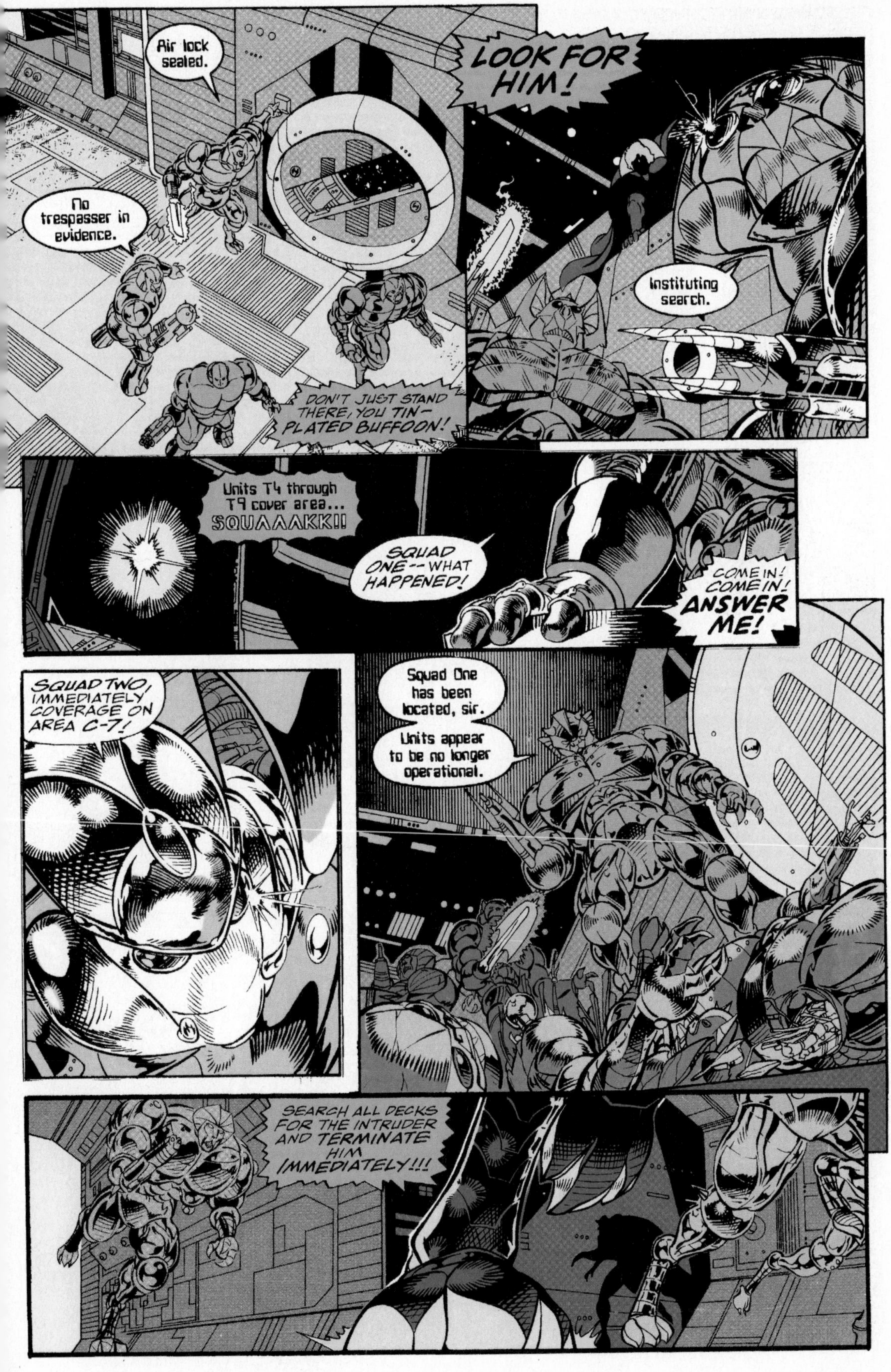
Air lock sealed.
No trespasser in evidence.
LOOK FOR HIM!
Instituting search.
DON'T JUST STAND THERE, YOU TIN-PLATED BUFFOON!
Units T4 through T9 cover area... SQUAAAKK!!
SQUAD ONE -- WHAT HAPPENED!
COME IN! COME IN! ANSWER ME!
SQUAD TWO, IMMEDIATELY COVERAGE ON AREA C-7!
Squad One has been located, sir.
Units appear to be no longer operational.
SEARCH ALL DECKS FOR THE INTRUDER AND TERMINATE HIM IMMEDIATELY!!!

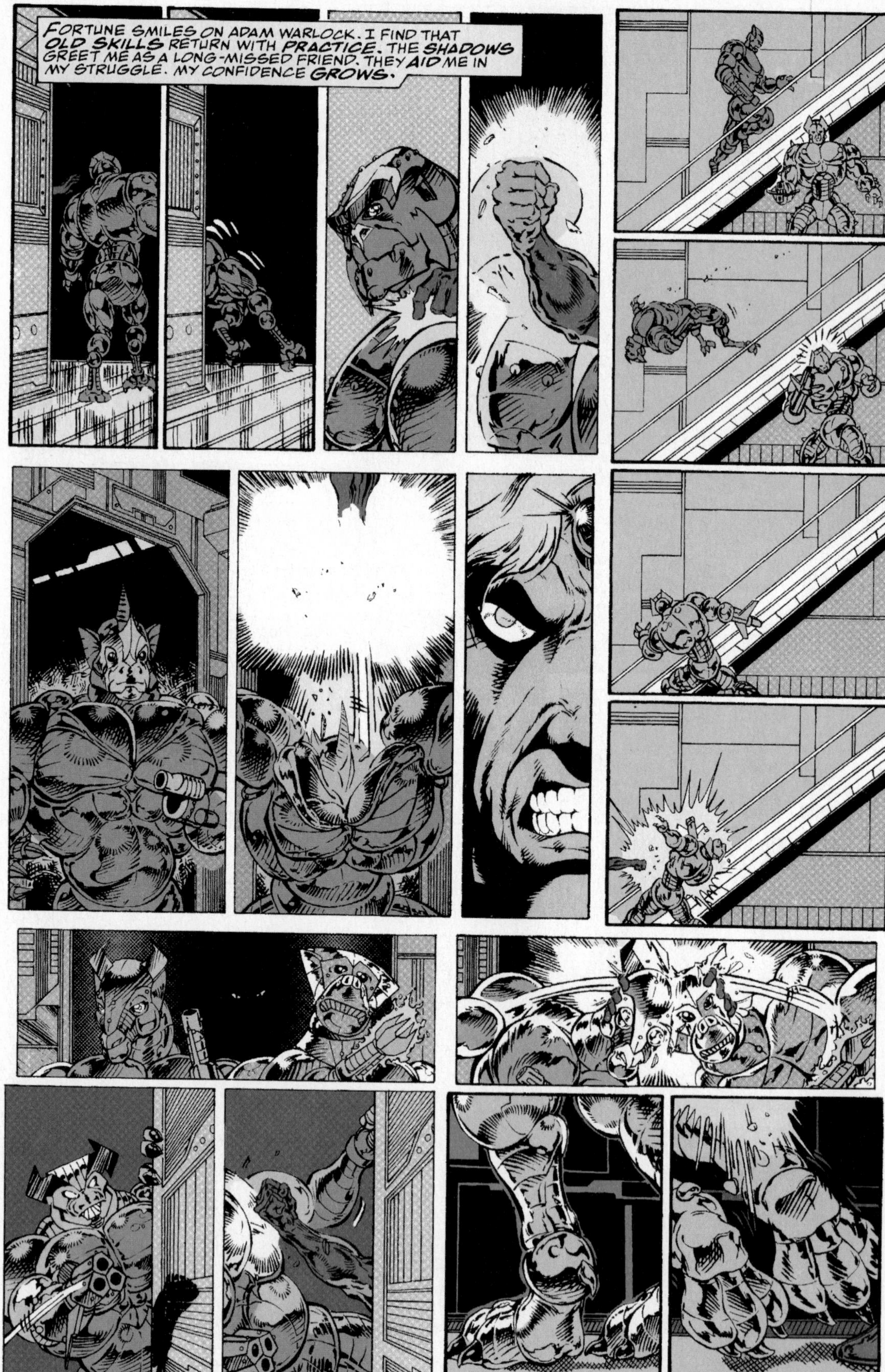
FORTUNE SMILES ON ADAM WARLOCK. I FIND THAT OLD SKILLS RETURN WITH PRACTICE. THE SHADOWS GREET ME AS A LONG-MISSED FRIEND. THEY AID ME IN MY STRUGGLE. MY CONFIDENCE GROWS.

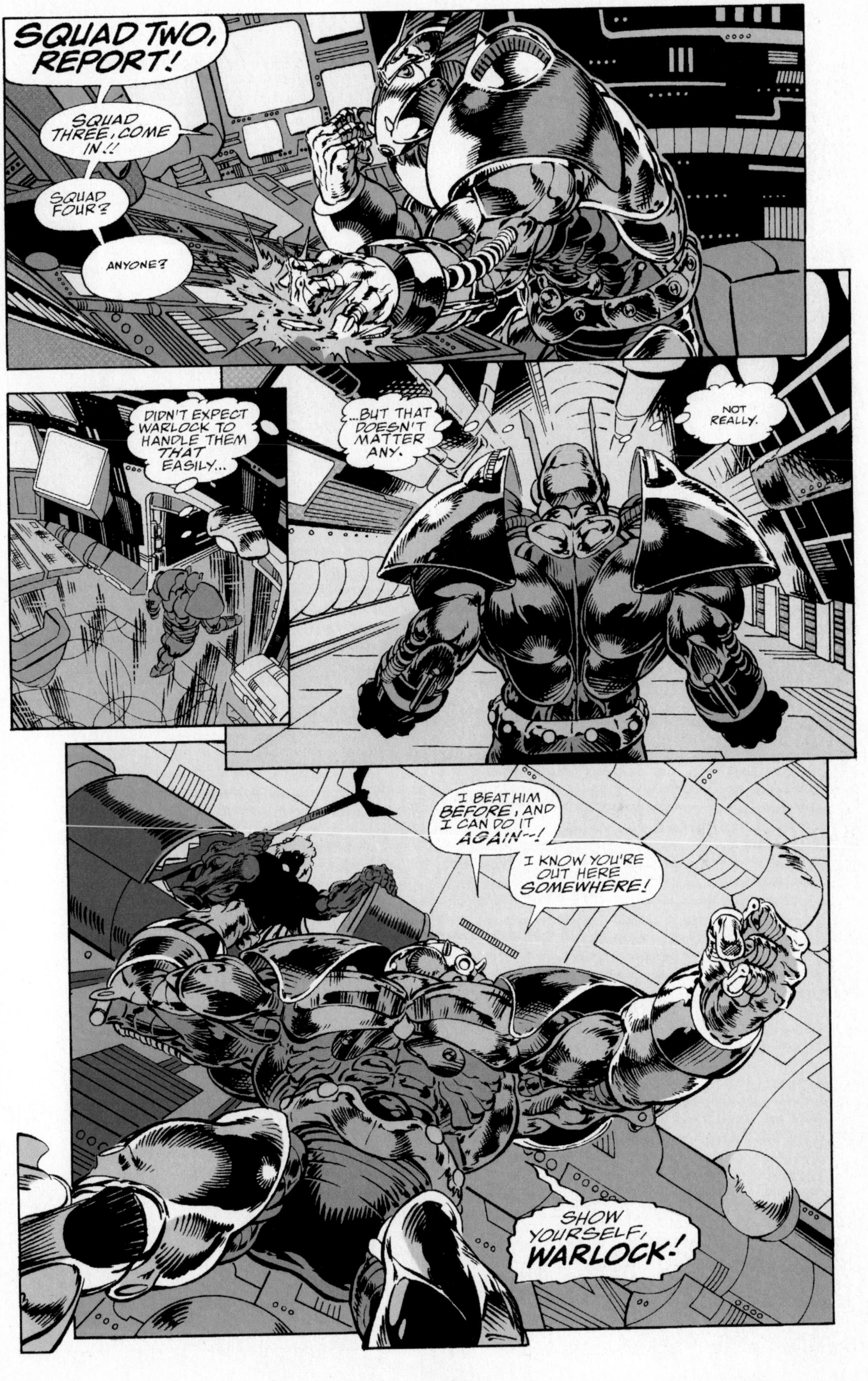
SQUAD TWO, REPORT!
SQUAD THREE, COME IN!!
SQUAD FOUR?
ANYONE?
DIDN'T EXPECT WARLOCK TO HANDLE THEM THAT EASILY...
...BUT THAT DOESN'T MATTER ANY.
NOT REALLY.
I BEAT HIM BEFORE, AND I CAN DO IT AGAIN--!
I KNOW YOU'RE OUT HERE SOMEWHERE!
SHOW YOURSELF, WARLOCK!

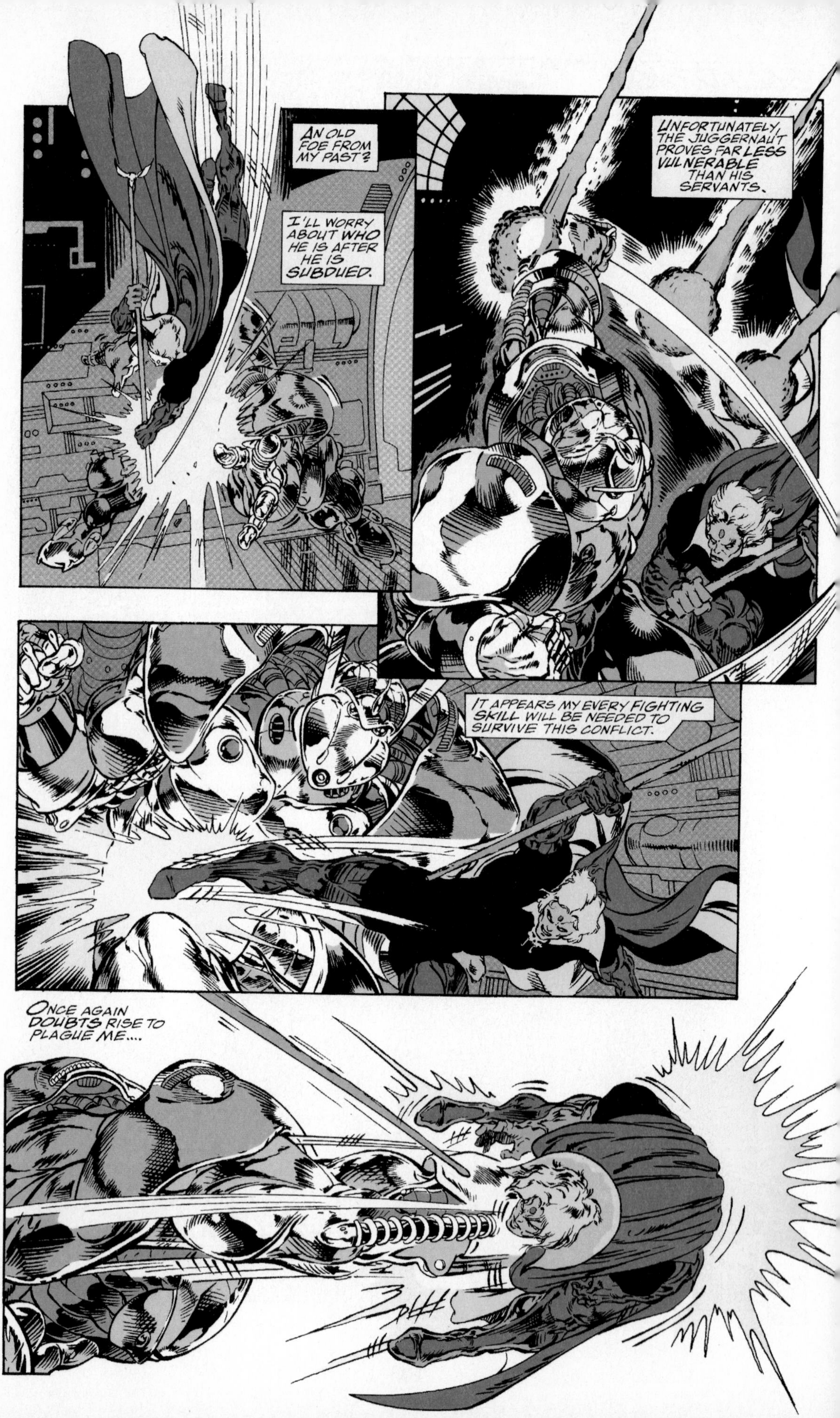
AN OLD FOE FROM MY PAST?
I'LL WORRY ABOUT WHO HE IS AFTER HE IS SUBDUED.
UNFORTUNATELY, THE JUGGERNAUT PROVES FAR LESS VULNERABLE THAN HIS SERVANTS.
IT APPEARS MY EVERY FIGHTING SKILL WILL BE NEEDED TO SURVIVE THIS CONFLICT.
ONCE AGAIN DOUBTS RISE TO PLAGUE ME....

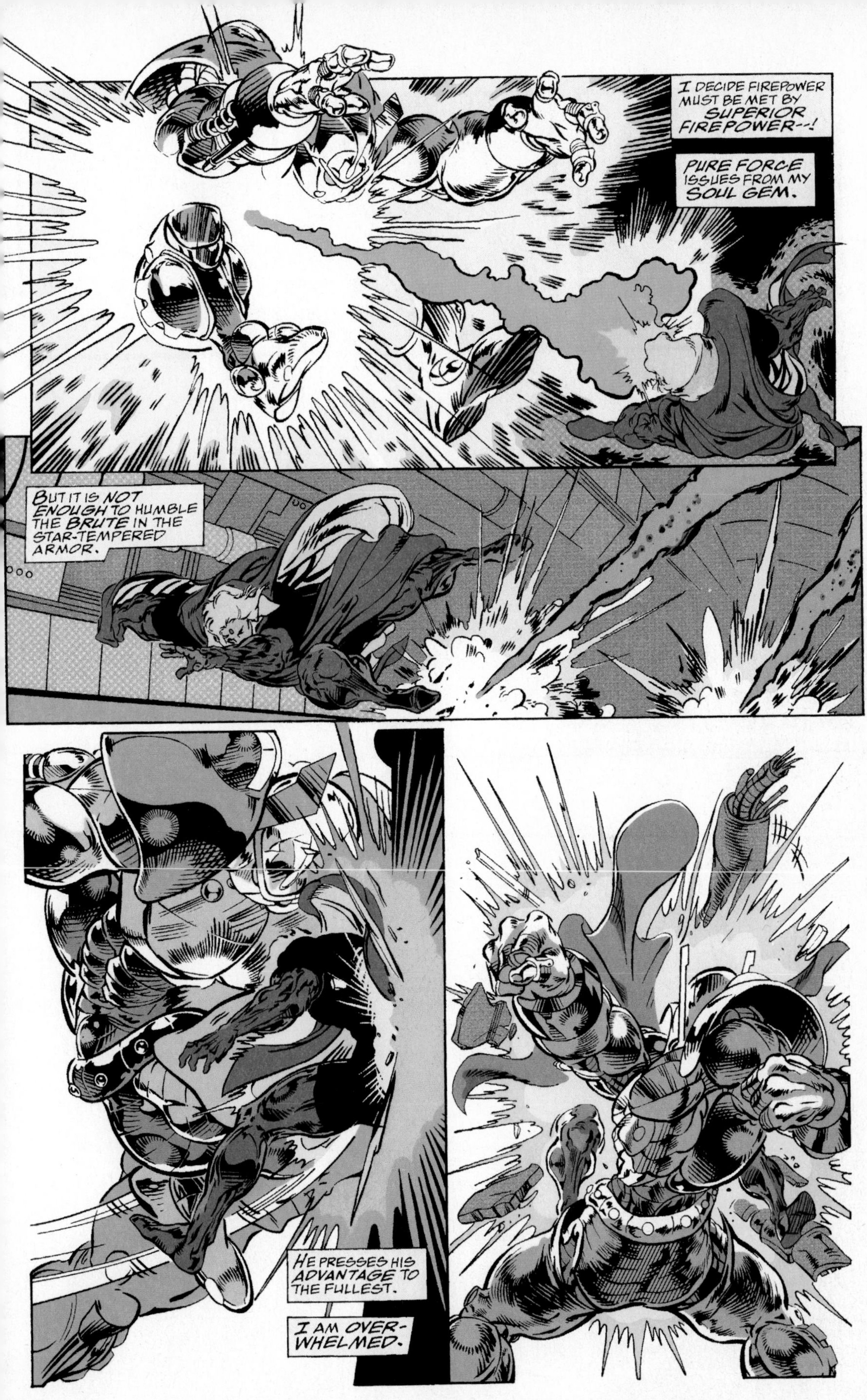
I DECIDE FIREPOWER MUST BE MET BY SUPERIOR FIREPOWER--!
PURE FORCE ISSUES FROM MY SOUL GEM.
BUT IT IS NOT ENOUGH TO HUMBLE THE BRUTE IN THE STAR-TEMPERED ARMOR.
HE PRESSES HIS ADVANTAGE TO THE FULLEST.
I AM OVER-WHELMED.

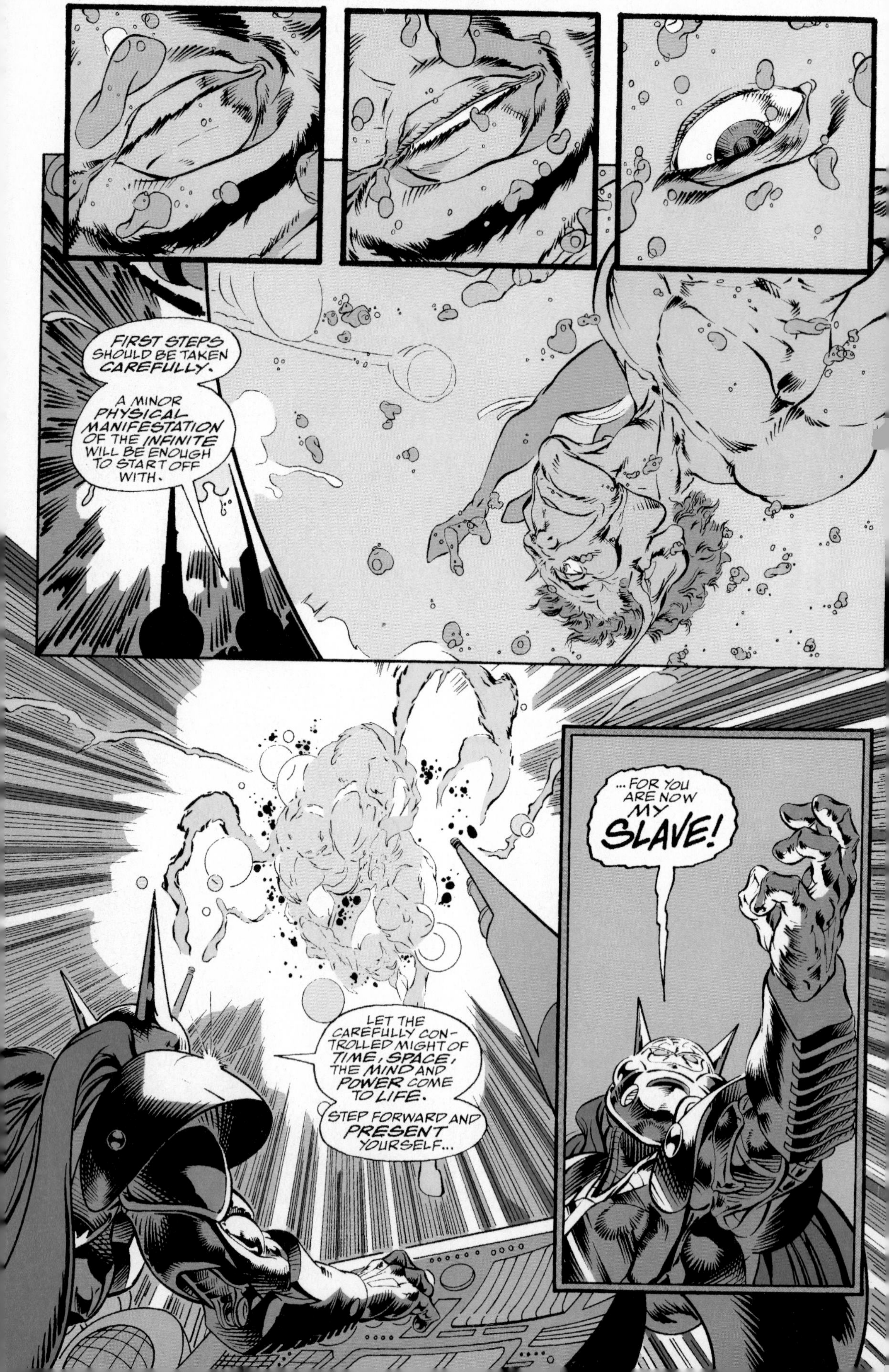
FIRST STEPS SHOULD BE TAKEN CAREFULLY.
A MINOR PHYSICAL MANIFESTATION OF THE INFINITE WILL BE ENOUGH TO START OFF WITH.
LET THE CAREFULLY CONTROLLED MIGHT OF TIME, SPACE, THE MIND AND POWER COME TO LIFE.
STEP FORWARD AND PRESENT YOURSELF...
...FOR YOU ARE NOW MY SLAVE!

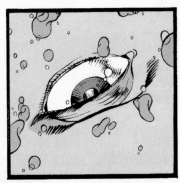

THE DISADVANTAGES OF RETURNING TO THIS PHYSICAL PLANE OF EXISTENCE ARE BECOMING *PAINFULLY* OBVIOUS!

TOO LONG DID I SPEND ON PEACEFUL SOUL WORLD.

HOW DEARLY I WISH TO *RETURN* THERE.

BUT IF I EVER HOPE TO ONCE AGAIN SEE THAT *EMERALD PARADISE,* I MUST ACT *QUICKLY...*

...AND WITH-OUT *MERCY!*

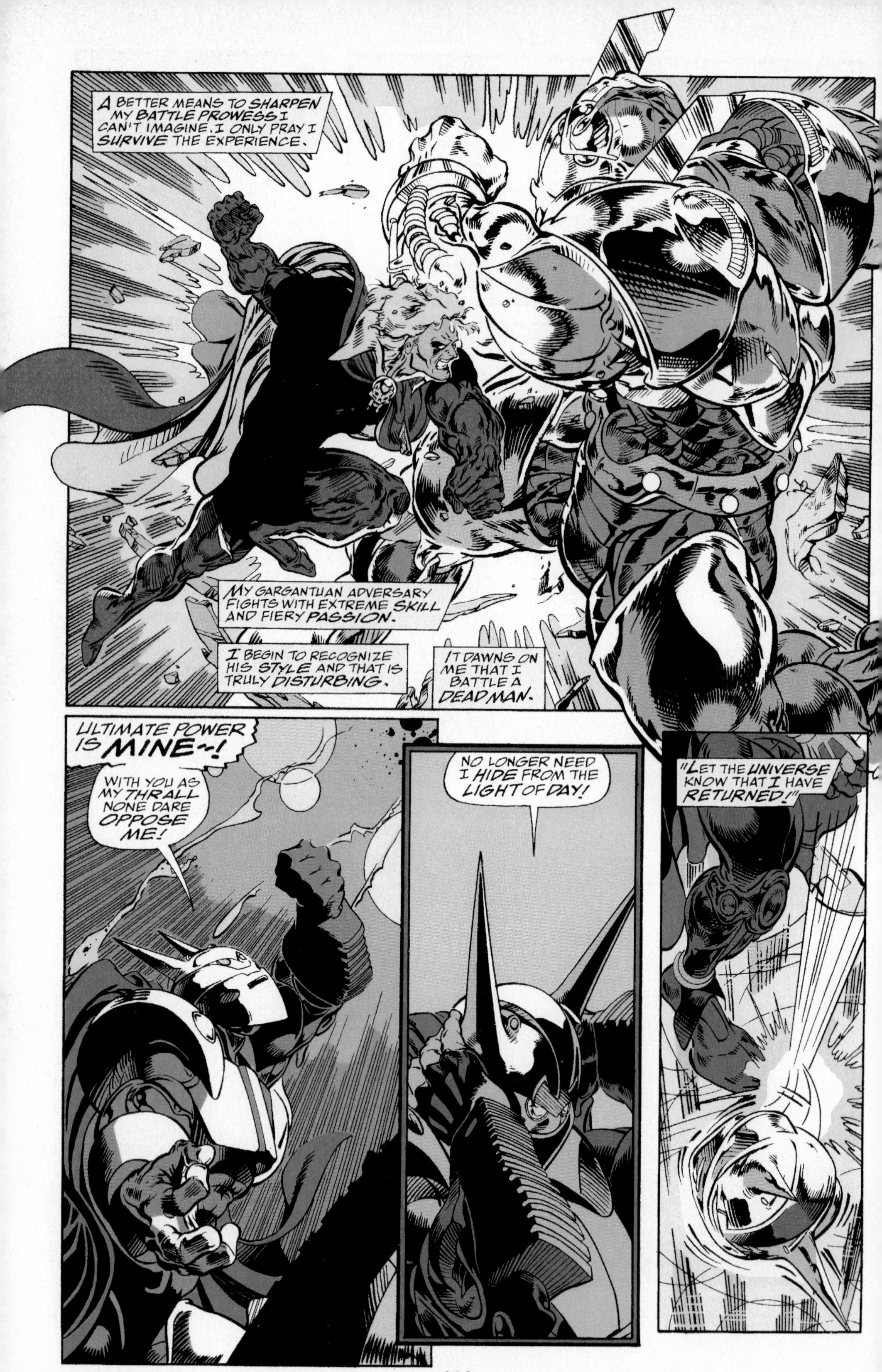
A BETTER MEANS TO SHARPEN MY BATTLE PROWESS I CAN'T IMAGINE. I ONLY PRAY I SURVIVE THE EXPERIENCE.
MY GARGANTUAN ADVERSARY FIGHTS WITH EXTREME SKILL AND FIERY PASSION.
I BEGIN TO RECOGNIZE HIS STYLE AND THAT IS TRULY DISTURBING.
IT DAWNS ON ME THAT I BATTLE A DEAD MAN.
ULTIMATE POWER IS MINE--!
WITH YOU AS MY THRALL NONE DARE OPPOSE ME!
NO LONGER NEED I HIDE FROM THE LIGHT OF DAY!
"LET THE UNIVERSE KNOW THAT I HAVE RETURNED!"

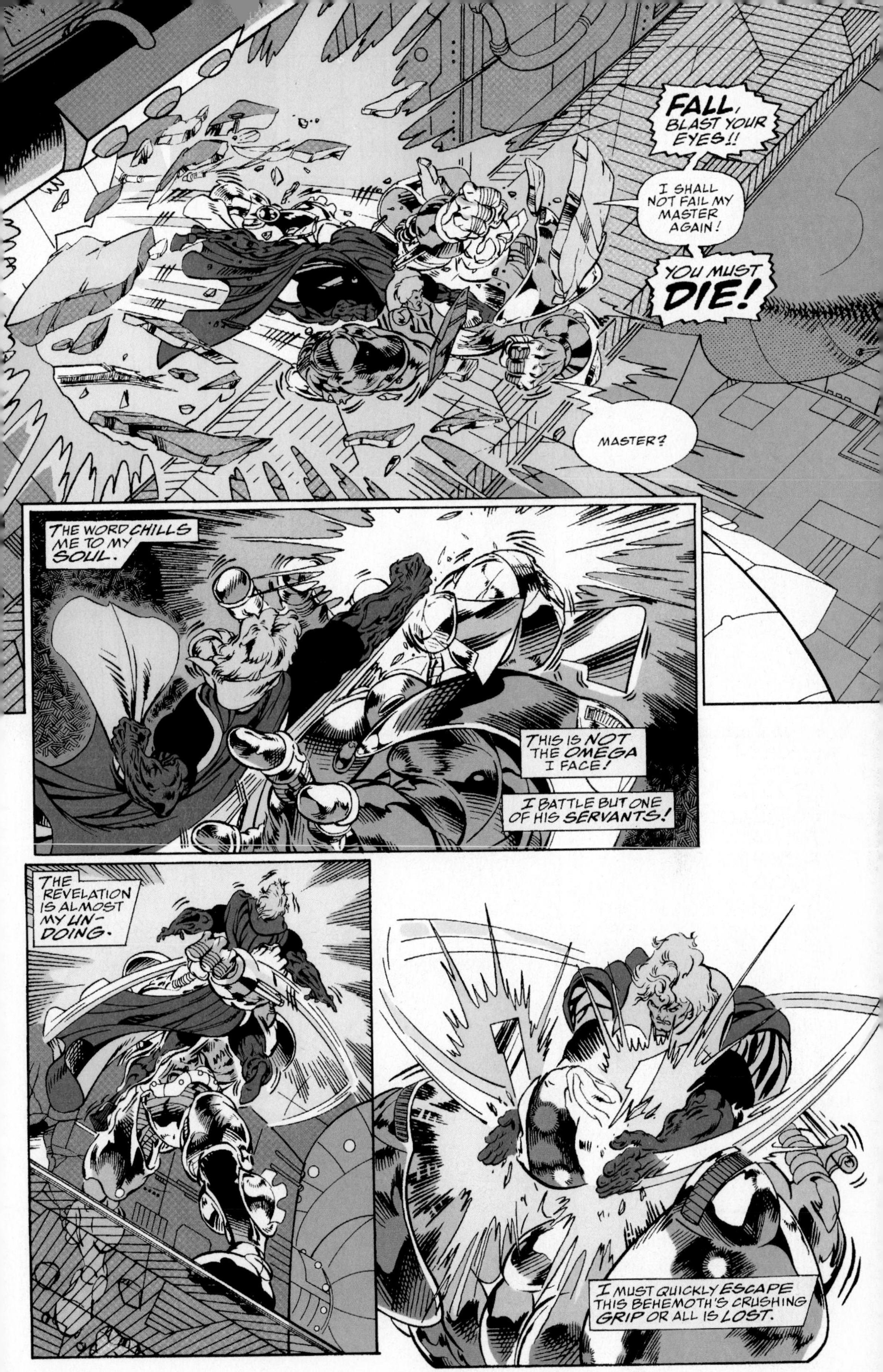
FALL, BLAST YOUR EYES!!
I SHALL NOT FAIL MY MASTER AGAIN!
YOU MUST DIE!
MASTER?
THE WORD CHILLS ME TO MY SOUL.
THIS IS NOT THE OMEGA I FACE!
I BATTLE BUT ONE OF HIS SERVANTS!
THE REVELATION IS ALMOST MY UN-DOING.
I MUST QUICKLY ESCAPE THIS BEHEMOTH'S CRUSHING GRIP OR ALL IS LOST.

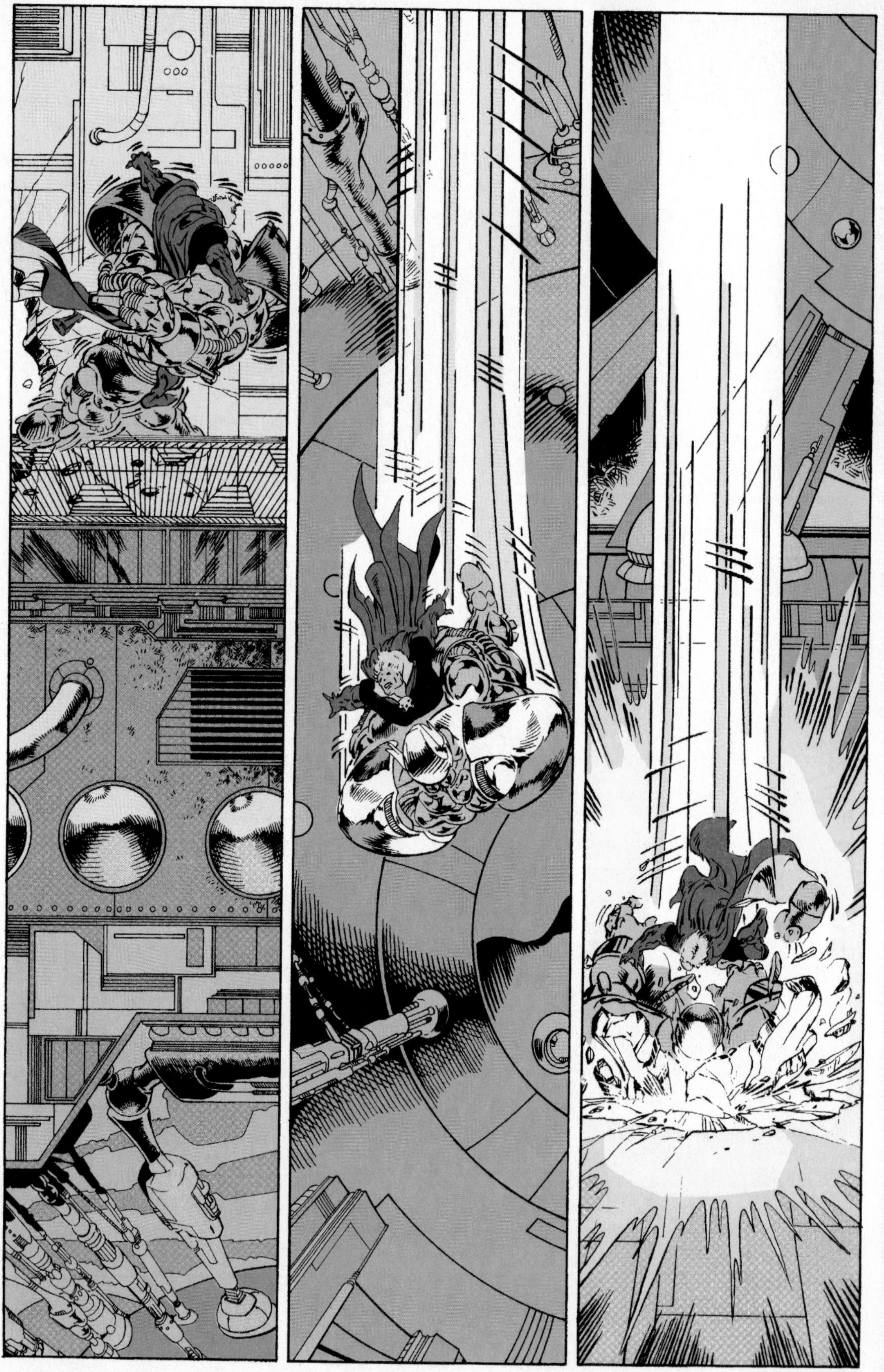

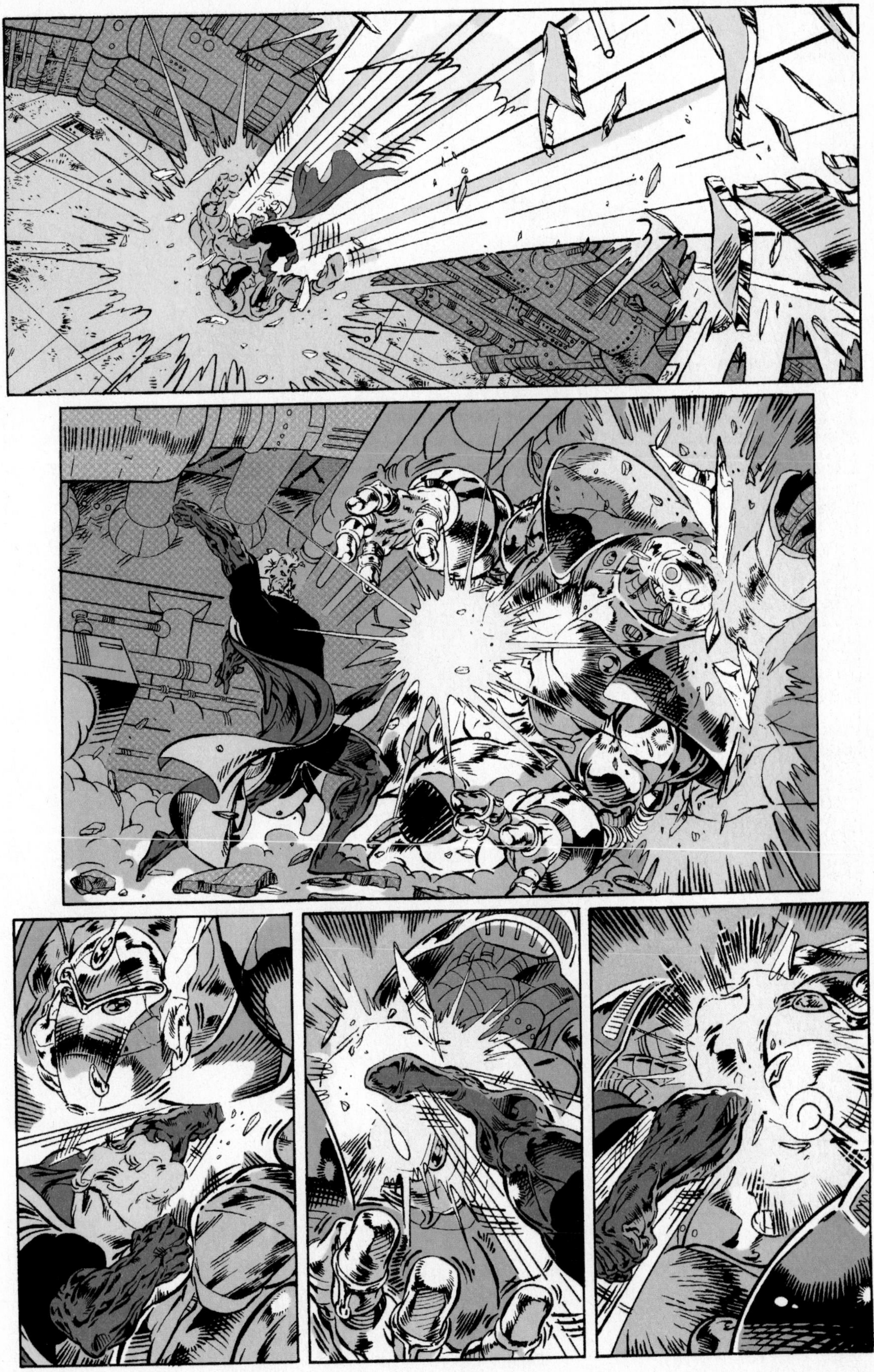

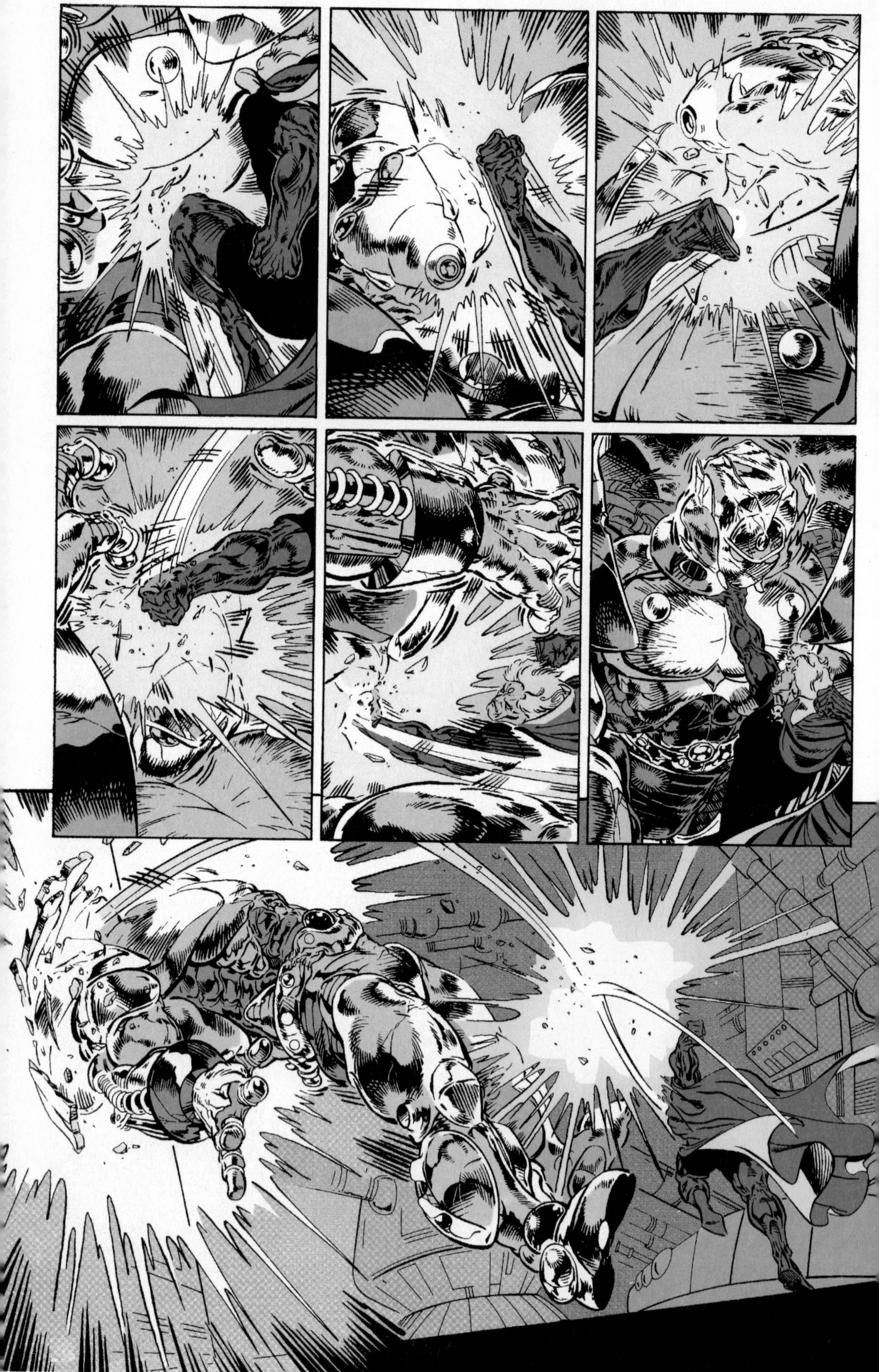

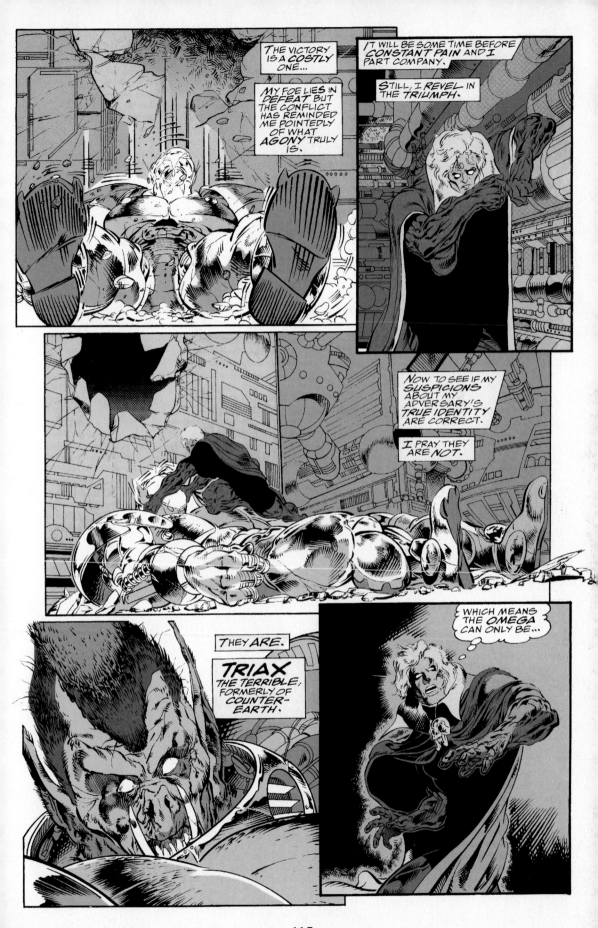

THE VICTORY IS A *COSTLY* ONE...

MY FOE LIES IN *DEFEAT* BUT THE CONFLICT HAS REMINDED ME POINTEDLY OF WHAT *AGONY* TRULY IS.

IT WILL BE SOME TIME BEFORE *CONSTANT PAIN* AND *I* PART COMPANY.

STILL, I *REVEL* IN THE *TRIUMPH.*

NOW TO SEE IF MY *SUSPICIONS* ABOUT MY *ADVERSARY'S TRUE* IDENTITY ARE CORRECT.

I PRAY THEY ARE *NOT.*

WHICH MEANS THE *OMEGA* CAN ONLY BE...

THEY *ARE.*

TRIAX THE TERRIBLE, FORMERLY OF COUNTER-EARTH.

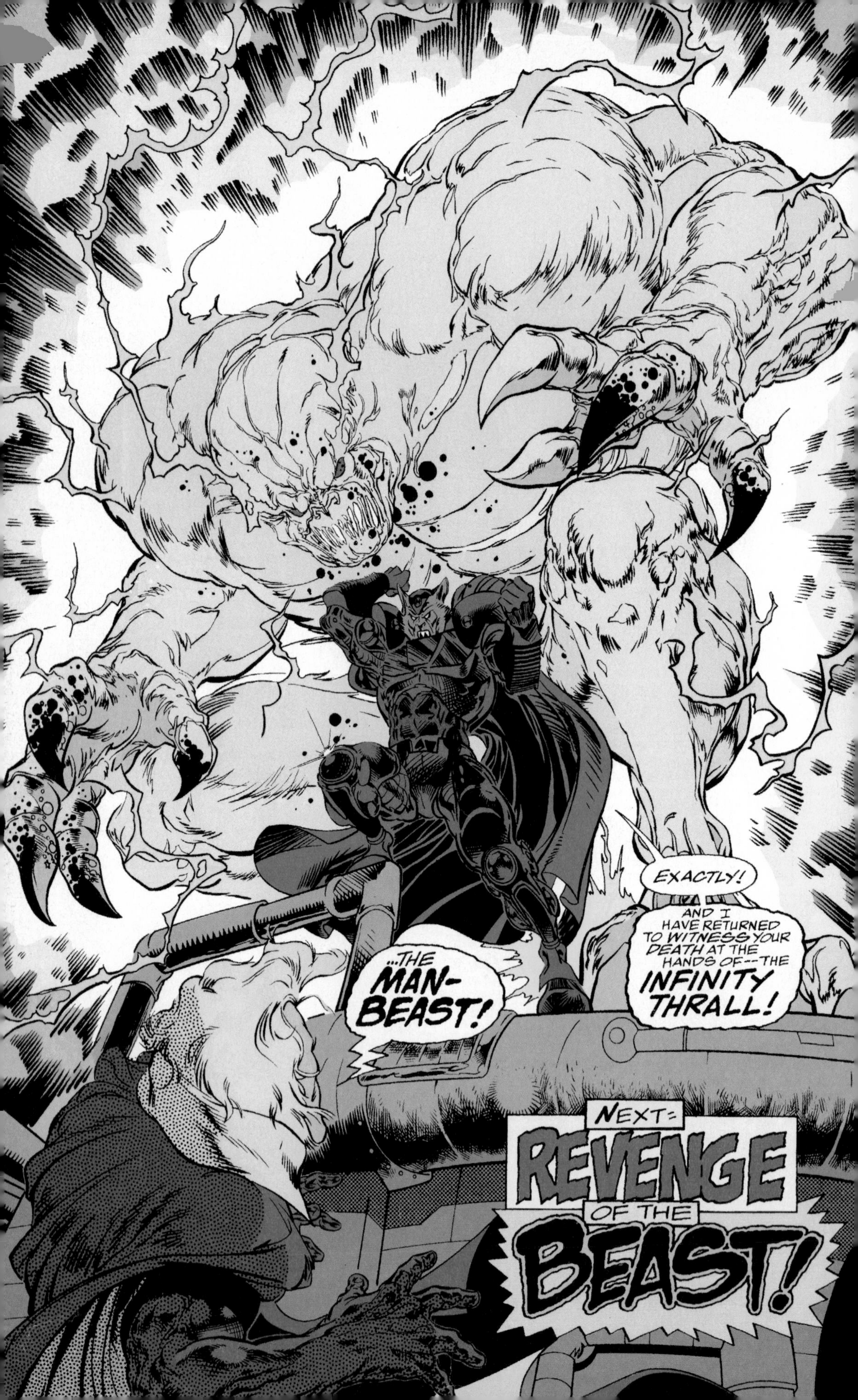
...THE MAN-BEAST!
EXACTLY!
AND I HAVE RETURNED TO WITNESS YOUR DEATH AT THE HANDS OF--THE INFINITY THRALL!
NEXT: REVENGE OF THE BEAST!

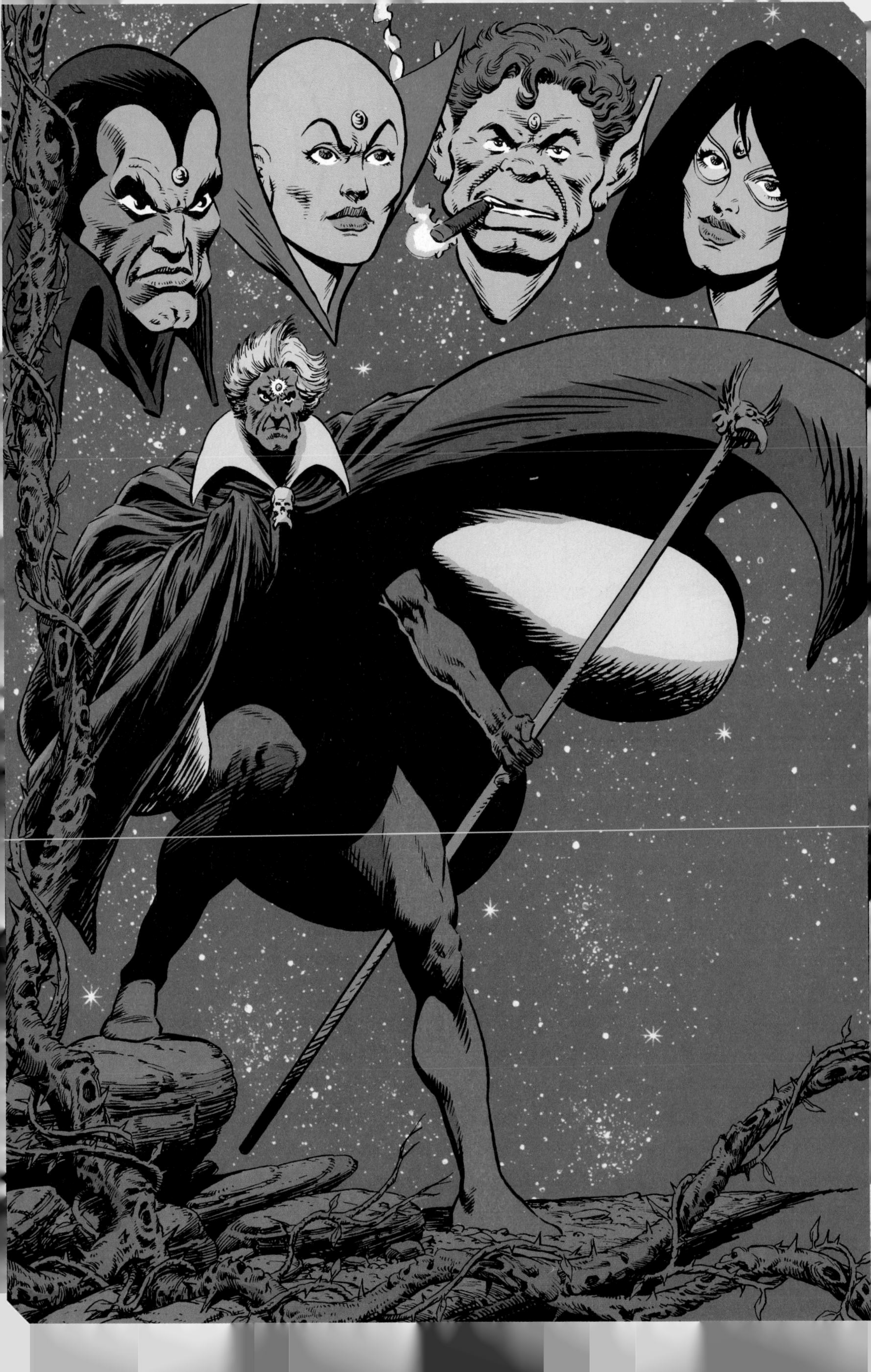

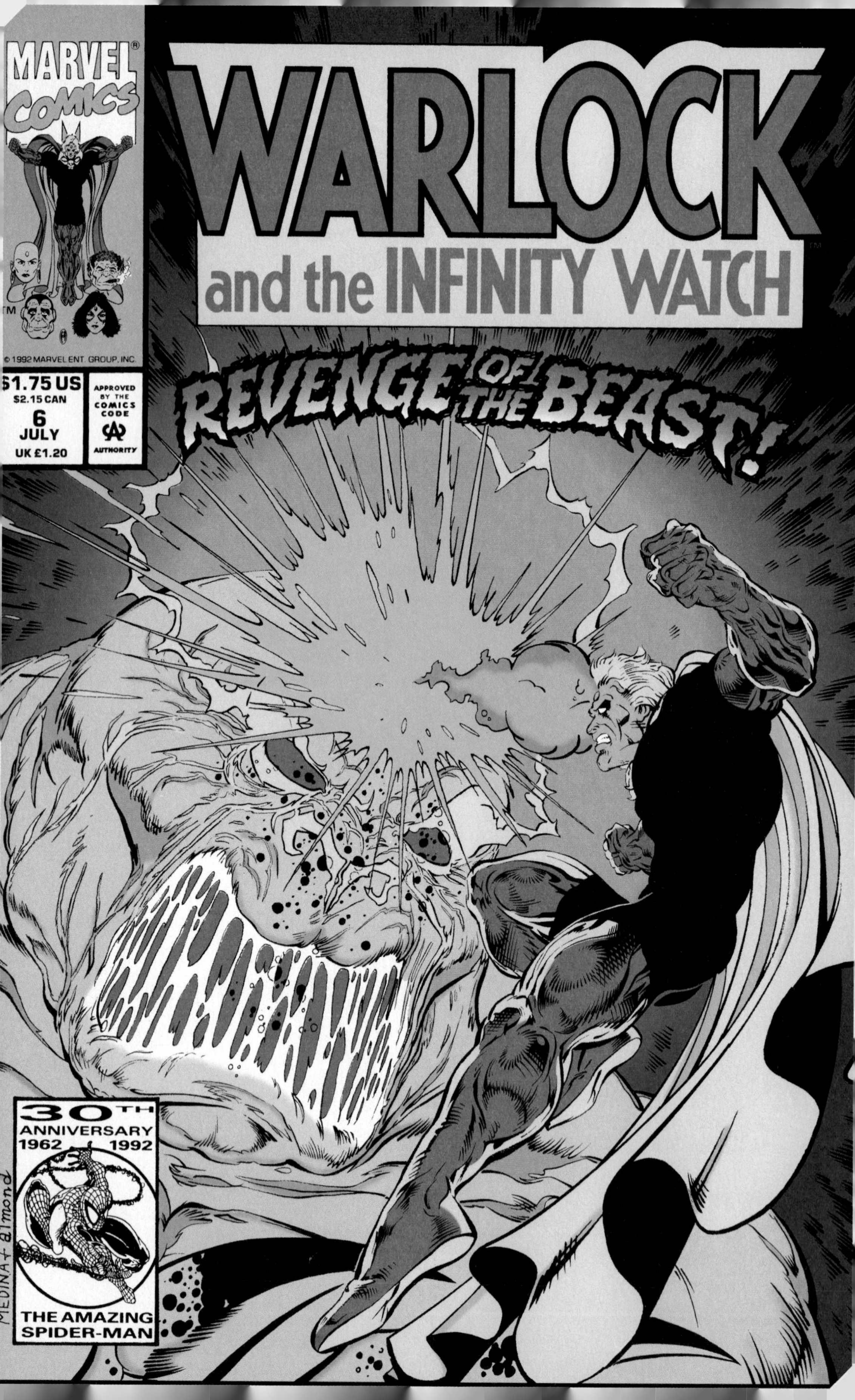
MARVEL COMICS
WARLOCK
and the INFINITY WATCH
© 1992 MARVEL ENT. GROUP, INC.
$1.75 US
$2.15 CAN
6
JULY
UK £1.20
APPROVED BY THE COMICS CODE AUTHORITY
REVENGE OF THE BEAST!
30TH ANNIVERSARY
1962 1992
THE AMAZING SPIDER-MAN
MEDINA + almond

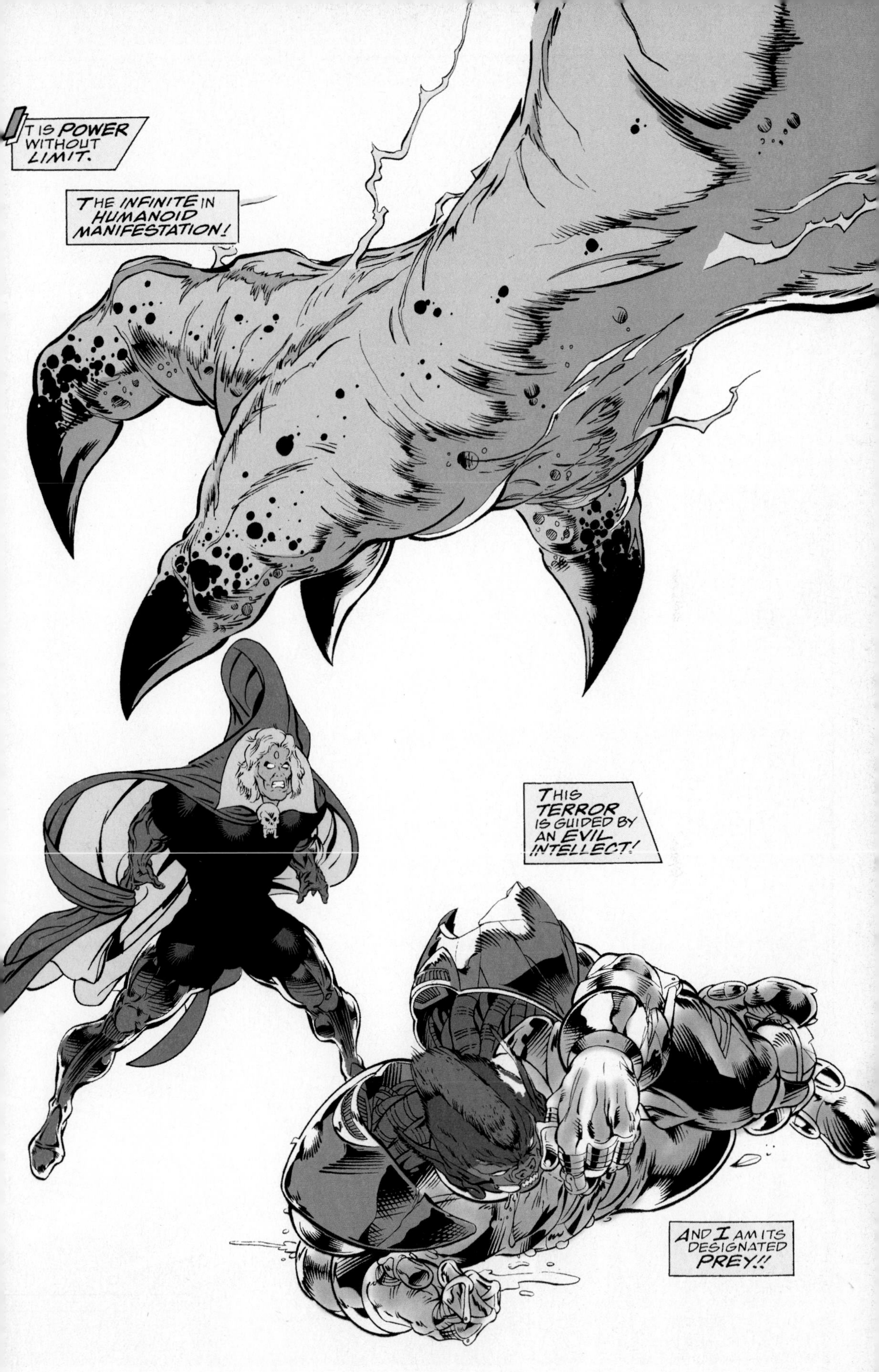
IT IS POWER WITHOUT LIMIT.
THE INFINITE IN HUMANOID MANIFESTATION!
THIS TERROR IS GUIDED BY AN EVIL INTELLECT!
AND I AM ITS DESIGNATED PREY!!

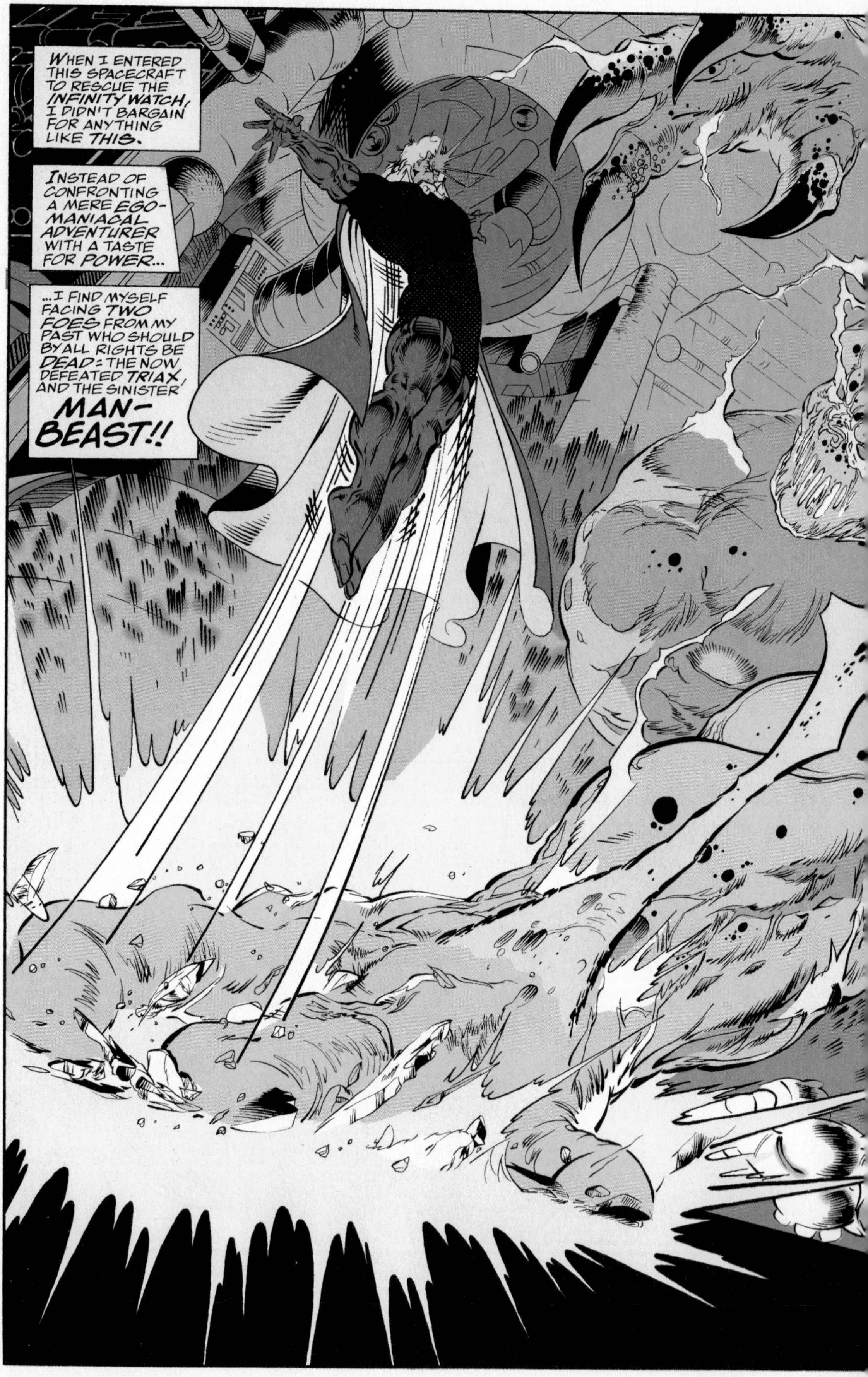
WHEN I ENTERED THIS SPACECRAFT TO RESCUE THE INFINITY WATCH, I DIDN'T BARGAIN FOR ANYTHING LIKE THIS.
INSTEAD OF CONFRONTING A MERE EGO-MANIACAL ADVENTURER WITH A TASTE FOR POWER...
...I FIND MYSELF FACING TWO FOES FROM MY PAST WHO SHOULD BY ALL RIGHTS BE DEAD: THE NOW DEFEATED TRIAX, AND THE SINISTER MAN-BEAST!!

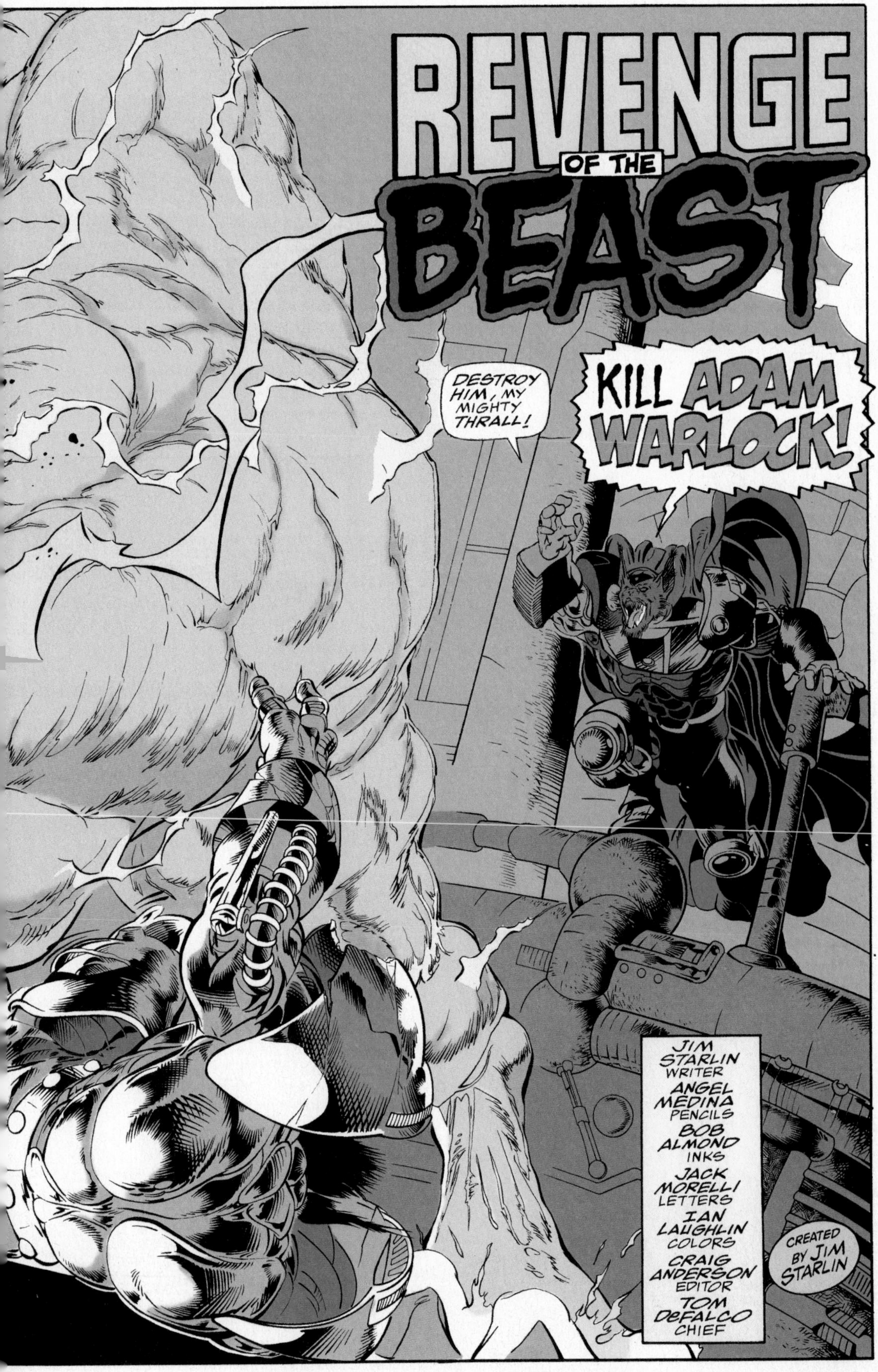
REVENGE
OF THE
BEAST
DESTROY HIM, MY MIGHTY THRALL!
KILL ADAM WARLOCK!
JIM STARLIN WRITER
ANGEL MEDINA PENCILS
BOB ALMOND INKS
JACK MORELLI LETTERS
IAN LAUGHLIN COLORS
CRAIG ANDERSON EDITOR
TOM DeFALCO CHIEF
CREATED BY JIM STARLIN

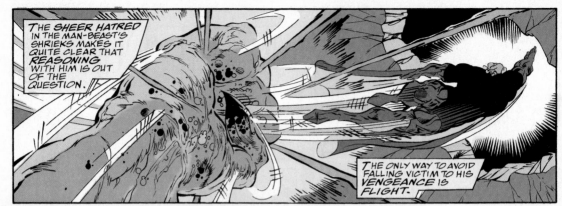

THE SHEER HATRED IN THE MAN-BEAST'S SHRIEKS MAKES IT QUITE CLEAR THAT *REASONING* WITH HIM IS OUT OF THE *QUESTION.*

THE ONLY WAY TO AVOID FALLING VICTIM TO HIS *VENGEANCE* IS *FLIGHT.*

UNFORTUNATELY, ESCAPING A *FIERY ENERGY BEING* WHO CAN GROW AT WILL IS EASIER *SAID* THAN *DONE.*

FORTUNATELY, ADAM WARLOCK IS NOT WITHOUT *RESOURCES* OF HIS *OWN.*

MY WILL FIRES UP THE *SOUL GEM!*

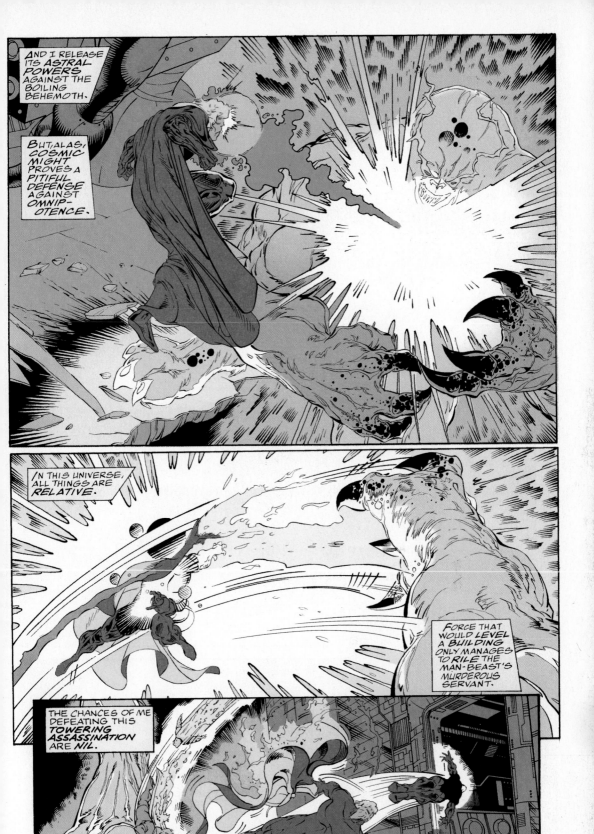

AND I RELEASE ITS *ASTRAL POWERS* AGAINST THE *BOILING BEHEMOTH.*

BUT, ALAS, COSMIC MIGHT PROVES A *PITIFUL* DEFENSE AGAINST *OMNIP-OTENCE.*

IN THIS UNIVERSE, ALL THINGS ARE *RELATIVE.*

FORCE THAT WOULD *LEVEL* A *BUILDING* ONLY MANAGES TO *RILE* THE MAN-BEAST'S *MURDEROUS* SERVANT.

THE CHANCES OF ME DEFEATING THIS *TOWERING ASSASSINATION* ARE *NIL.*

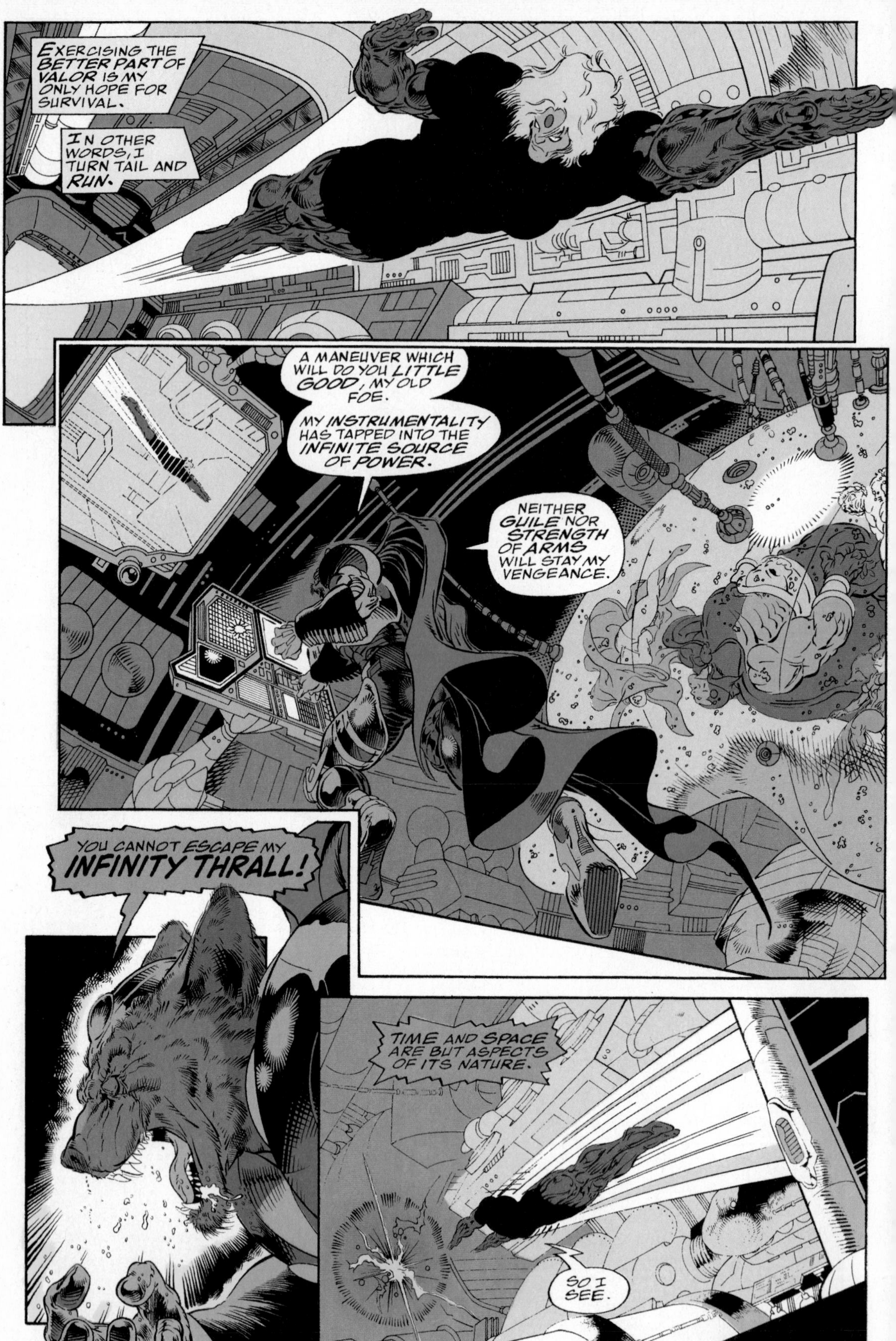
EXERCISING THE BETTER PART OF VALOR IS MY ONLY HOPE FOR SURVIVAL.
IN OTHER WORDS, I TURN TAIL AND RUN.
A MANEUVER WHICH WILL DO YOU LITTLE GOOD, MY OLD FOE.
MY INSTRUMENTALITY HAS TAPPED INTO THE INFINITE SOURCE OF POWER.
NEITHER GUILE NOR STRENGTH OF ARMS WILL STAY MY VENGEANCE.
YOU CANNOT ESCAPE MY INFINITY THRALL!
TIME AND SPACE ARE BUT ASPECTS OF ITS NATURE.
SO I SEE.

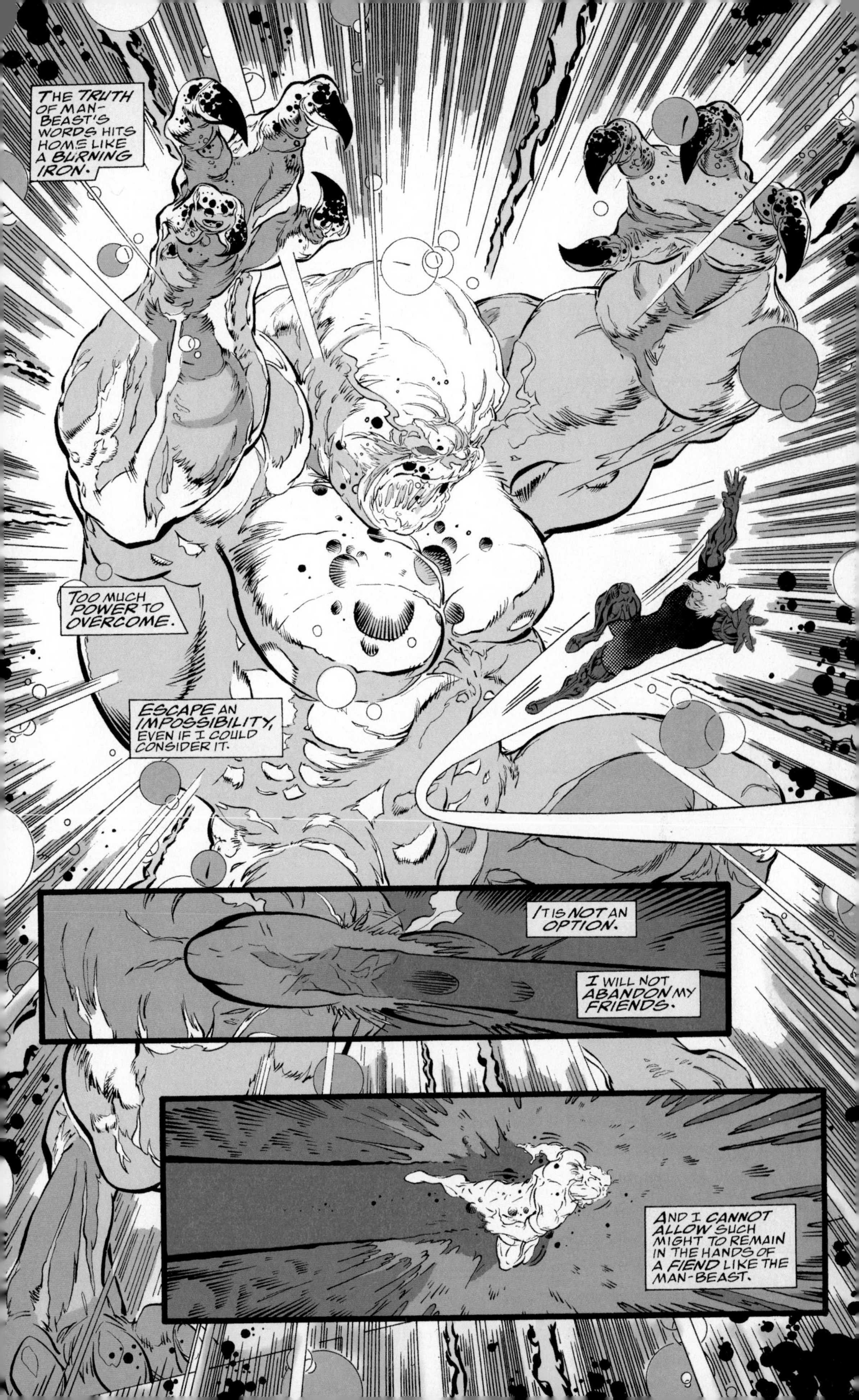

THE TRUTH OF MAN-BEAST'S WORDS HITS HOME LIKE A BURNING IRON.
TOO MUCH POWER TO OVERCOME.
ESCAPE AN IMPOSSIBILITY, EVEN IF I COULD CONSIDER IT.
IT IS NOT AN OPTION.
I WILL NOT ABANDON MY FRIENDS.
AND I CANNOT ALLOW SUCH MIGHT TO REMAIN IN THE HANDS OF A FIEND LIKE THE MAN-BEAST.

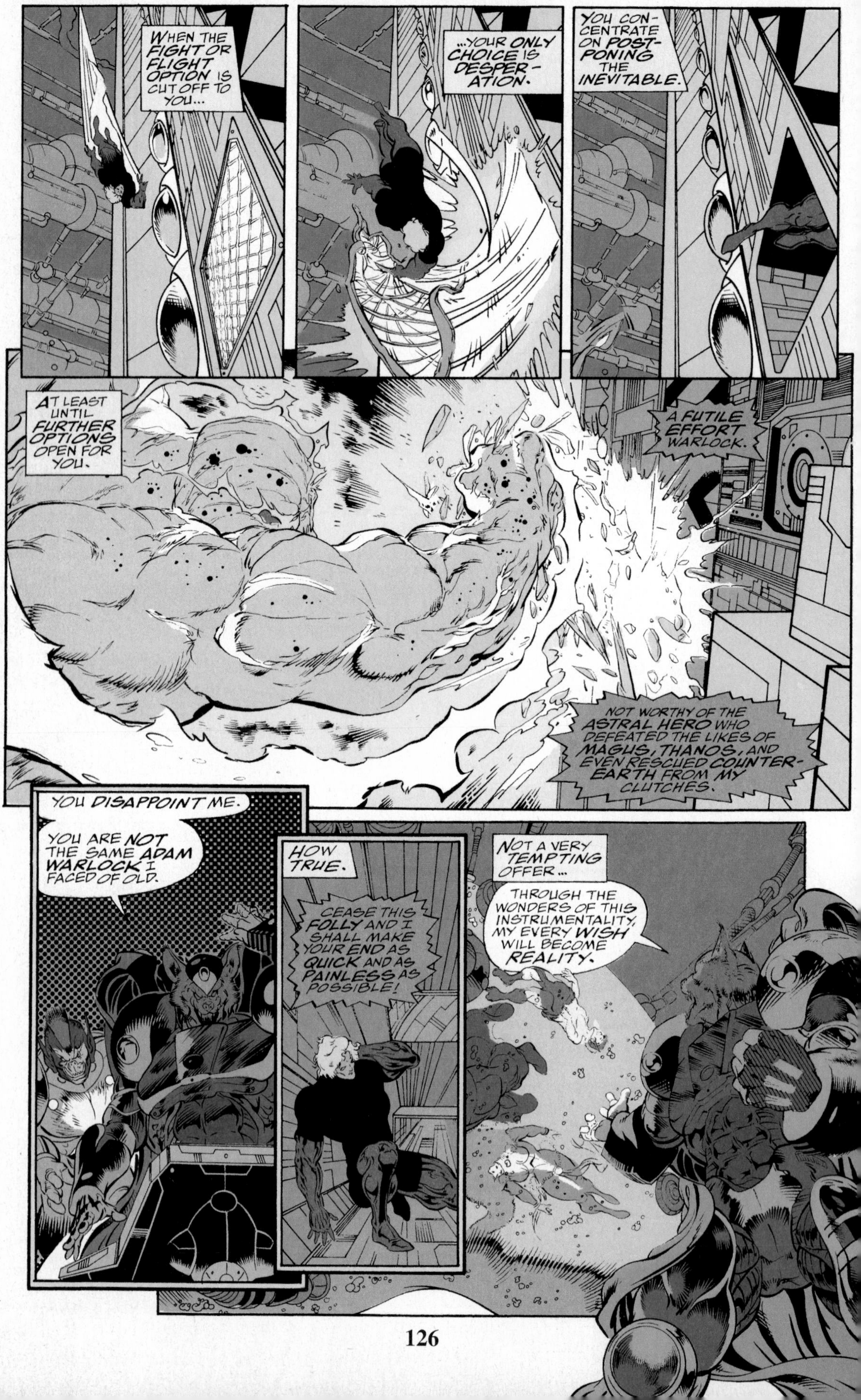

WHEN THE FIGHT OR FLIGHT OPTION IS CUT OFF TO YOU...
...YOUR ONLY CHOICE IS DESPERATION.
YOU CONCENTRATE ON POSTPONING THE INEVITABLE.
AT LEAST UNTIL FURTHER OPTIONS OPEN FOR YOU.
A FUTILE EFFORT WARLOCK.
NOT WORTHY OF THE ASTRAL HERO WHO DEFEATED THE LIKES OF MAGUS, THANOS, AND EVEN RESCUED COUNTER-EARTH FROM MY CLUTCHES.
YOU DISAPPOINT ME.
YOU ARE NOT THE SAME ADAM WARLOCK I FACED OF OLD.
HOW TRUE.
CEASE THIS FOLLY AND I SHALL MAKE YOUR END AS QUICK AND AS PAINLESS AS POSSIBLE!
NOT A VERY TEMPTING OFFER...
THROUGH THE WONDERS OF THIS INSTRUMENTALITY, MY EVERY WISH WILL BECOME REALITY.

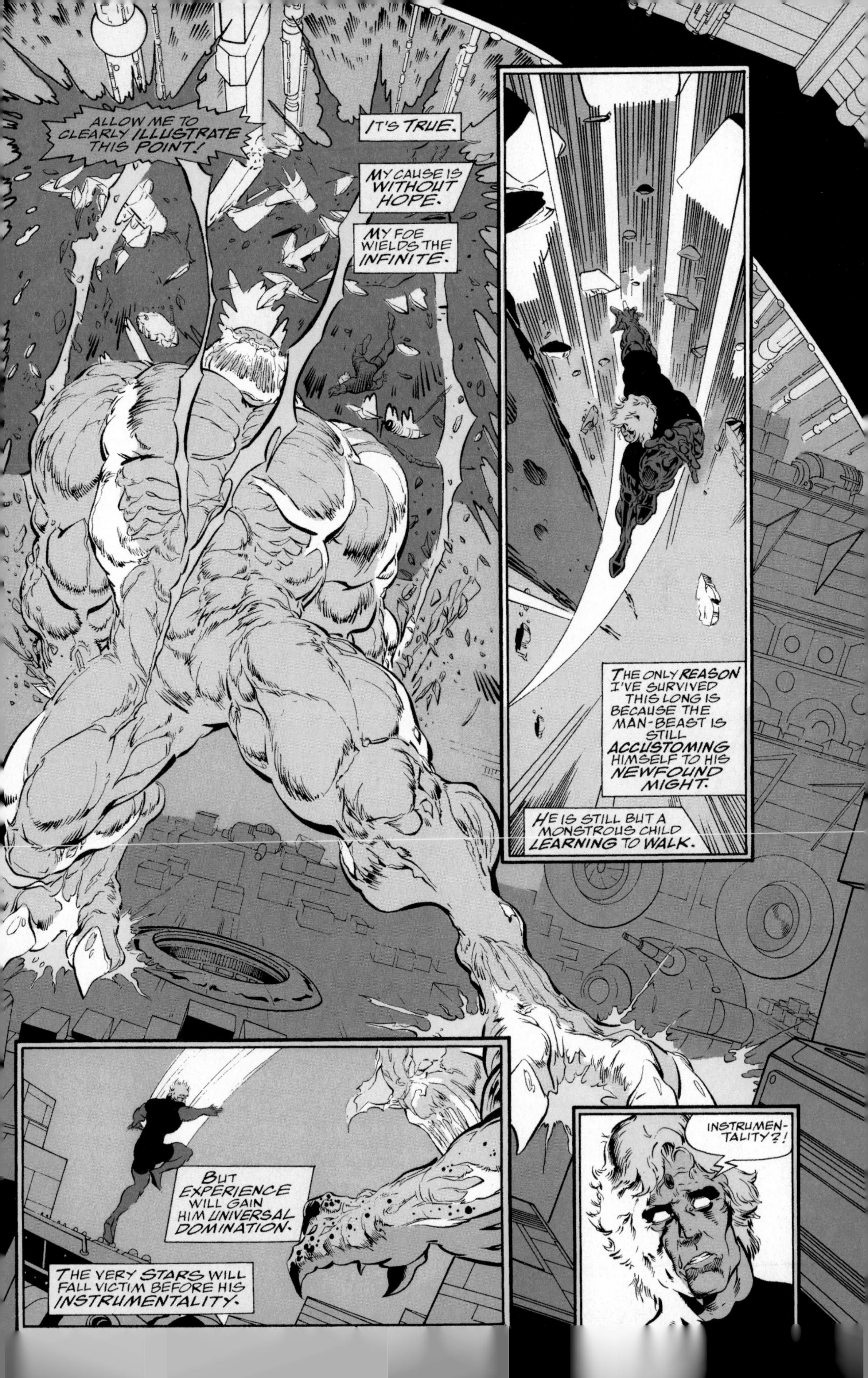

ALLOW ME TO CLEARLY ILLUSTRATE THIS POINT!
IT'S TRUE.
MY CAUSE IS WITHOUT HOPE.
MY FOE WIELDS THE INFINITE.
THE ONLY REASON I'VE SURVIVED THIS LONG IS BECAUSE THE MAN-BEAST IS STILL ACCUSTOMING HIMSELF TO HIS NEWFOUND MIGHT.
HE IS STILL BUT A MONSTROUS CHILD LEARNING TO WALK.
BUT EXPERIENCE WILL GAIN HIM UNIVERSAL DOMINATION.
THE VERY STARS WILL FALL VICTIM BEFORE HIS INSTRUMENTALITY.
INSTRUMENTALITY?!

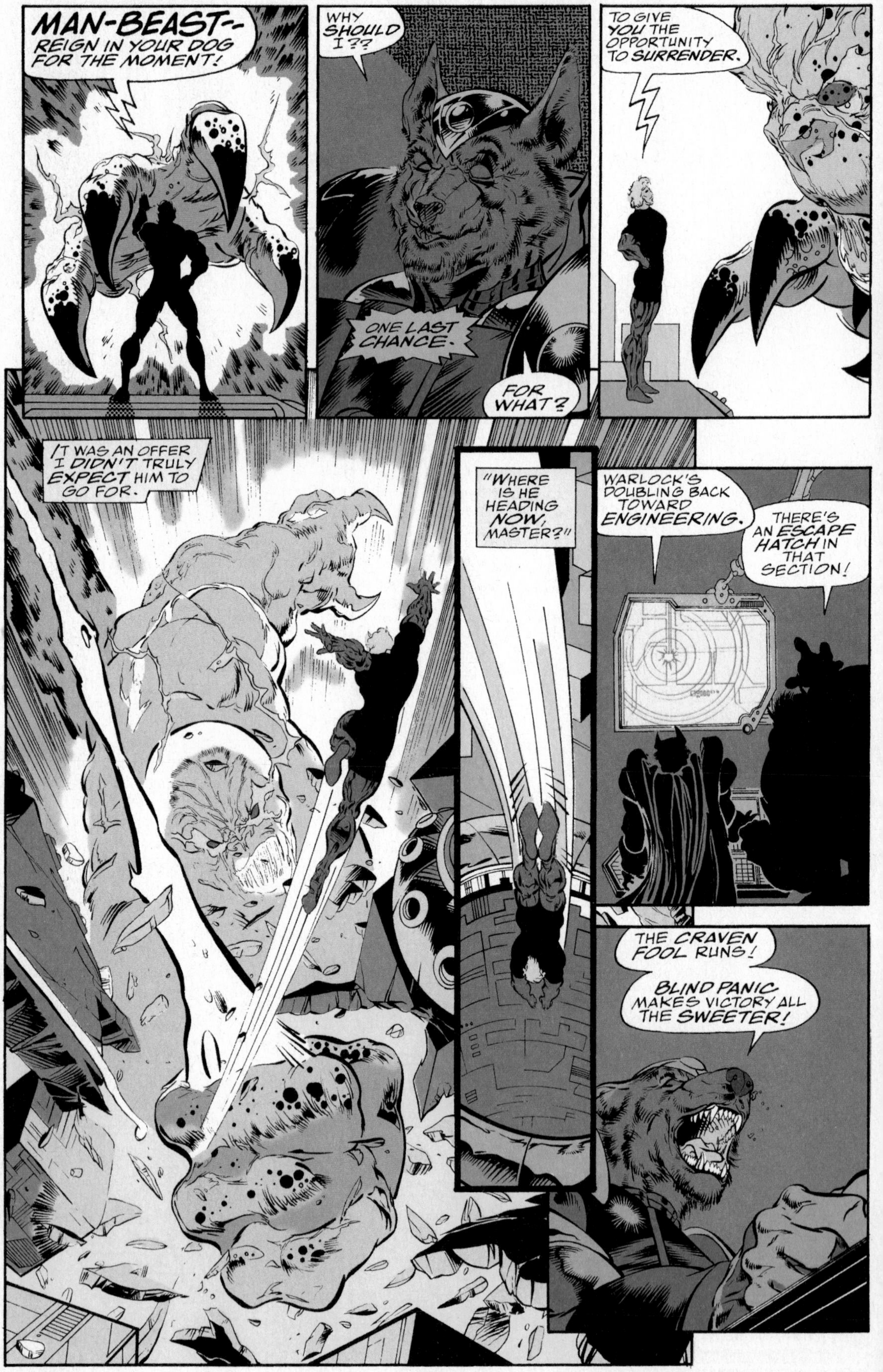
MAN-BEAST-- REIGN IN YOUR DOG FOR THE MOMENT!
WHY SHOULD I??
ONE LAST CHANCE.
FOR WHAT?
TO GIVE YOU THE OPPORTUNITY TO SURRENDER.
IT WAS AN OFFER I DIDN'T TRULY EXPECT HIM TO GO FOR.
"WHERE IS HE HEADING NOW, MASTER?"
WARLOCK'S DOUBLING BACK TOWARD ENGINEERING.
THERE'S AN ESCAPE HATCH IN THAT SECTION!
THE CRAVEN FOOL RUNS!
BLIND PANIC MAKES VICTORY ALL THE SWEETER!

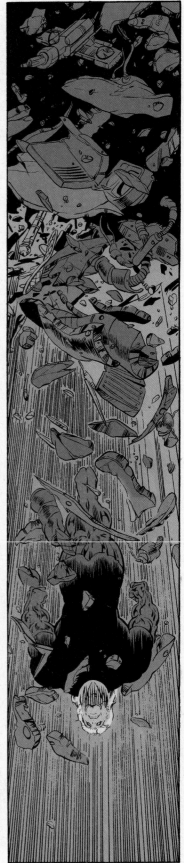

129

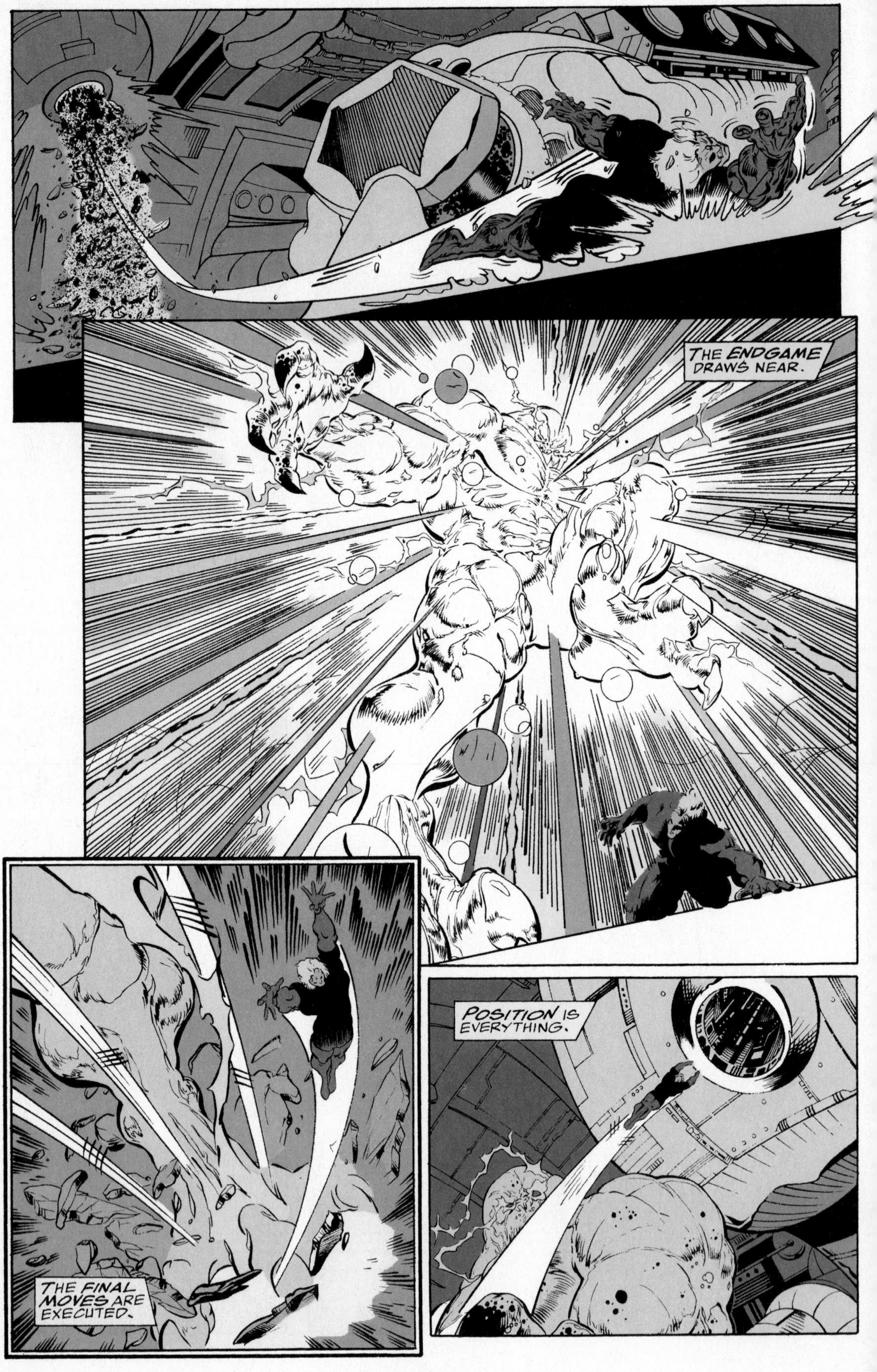
THE ENDGAME DRAWS NEAR.
THE FINAL MOVES ARE EXECUTED.
POSITION IS EVERYTHING.

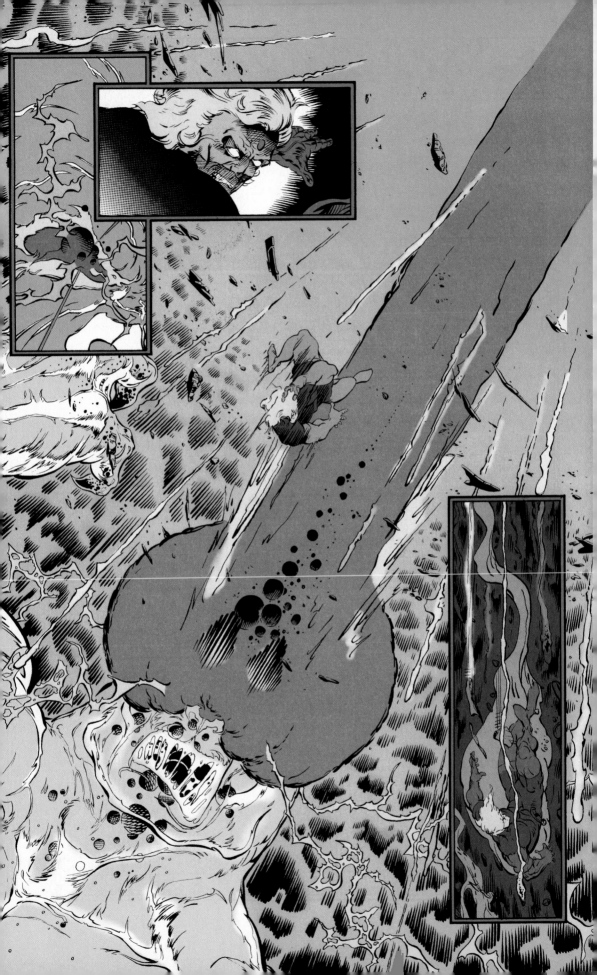

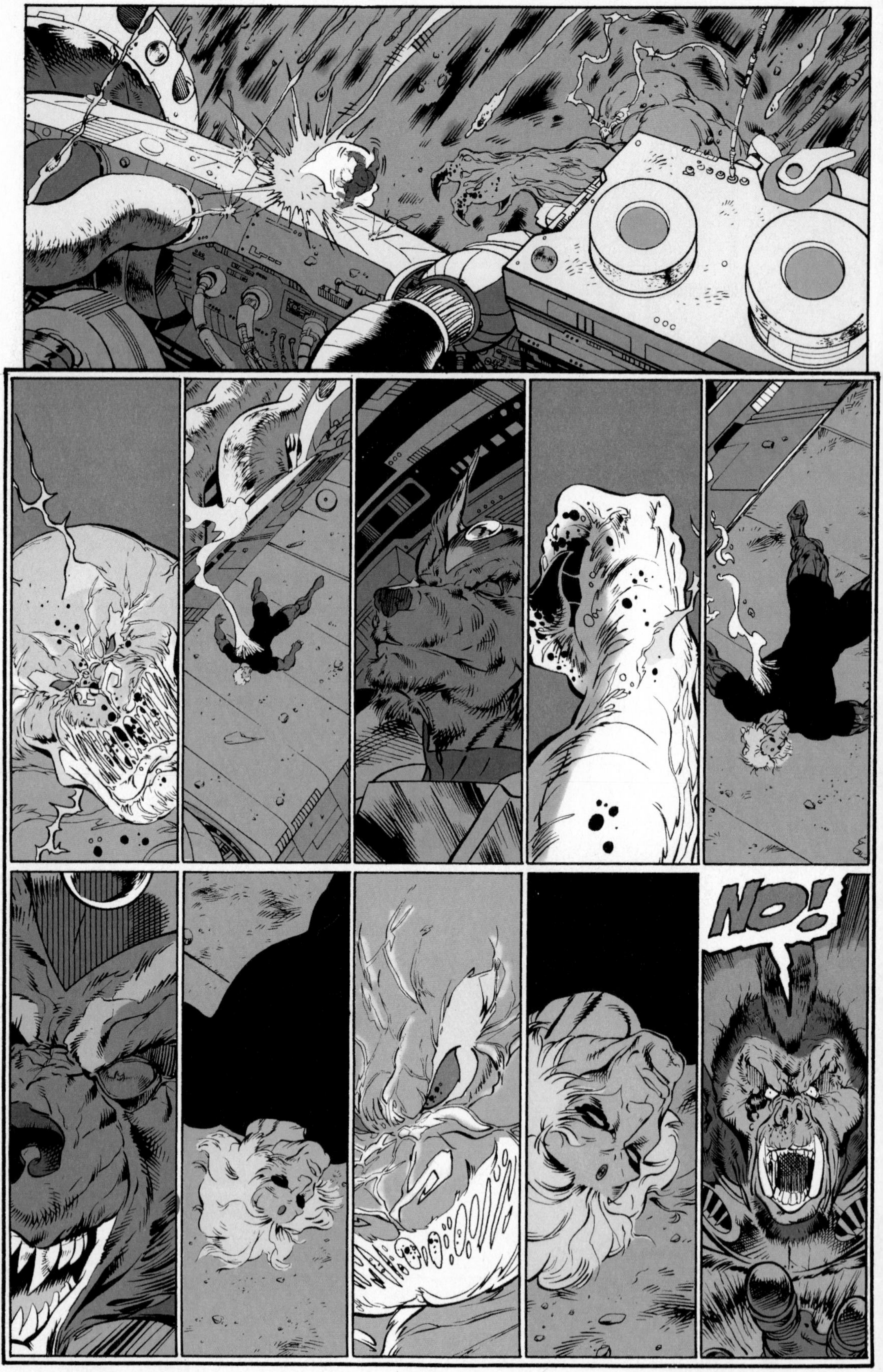
NO!

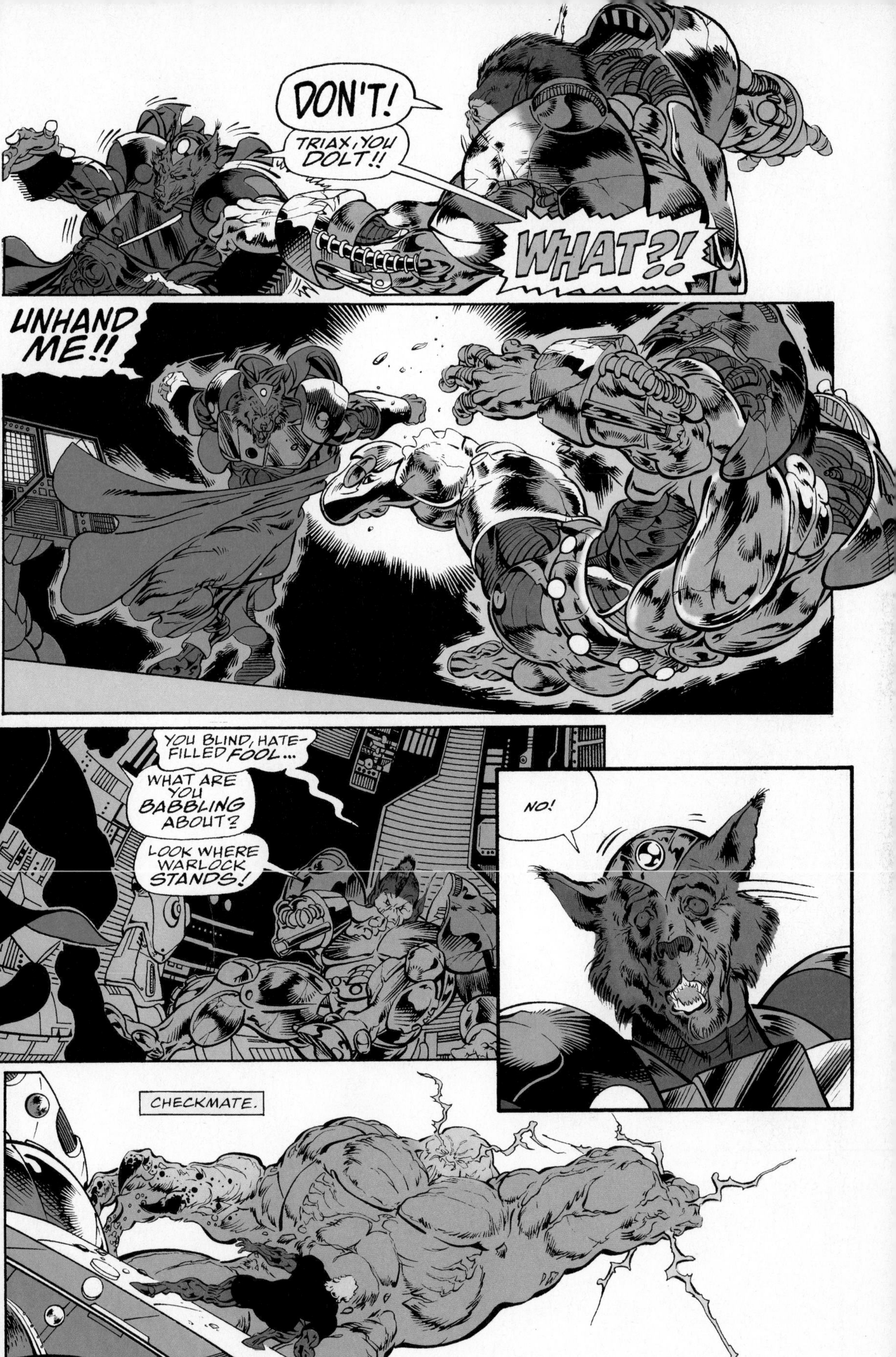
DON'T!
TRIAX, YOU DOLT!!
WHAT?!
UNHAND ME!!
YOU BLIND, HATE-FILLED FOOL...
WHAT ARE YOU BABBLING ABOUT?
LOOK WHERE WARLOCK STANDS!
NO!
CHECKMATE.

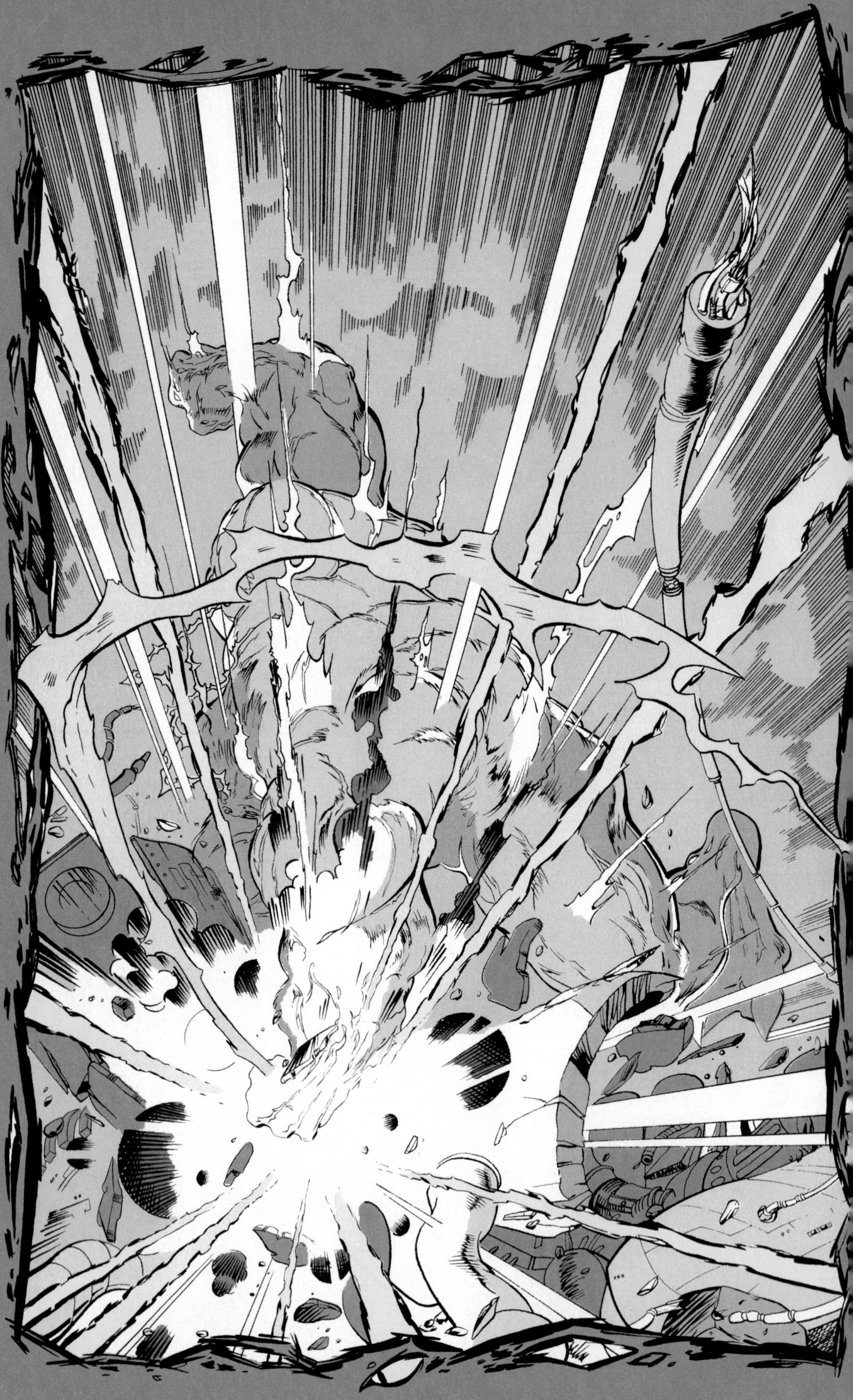

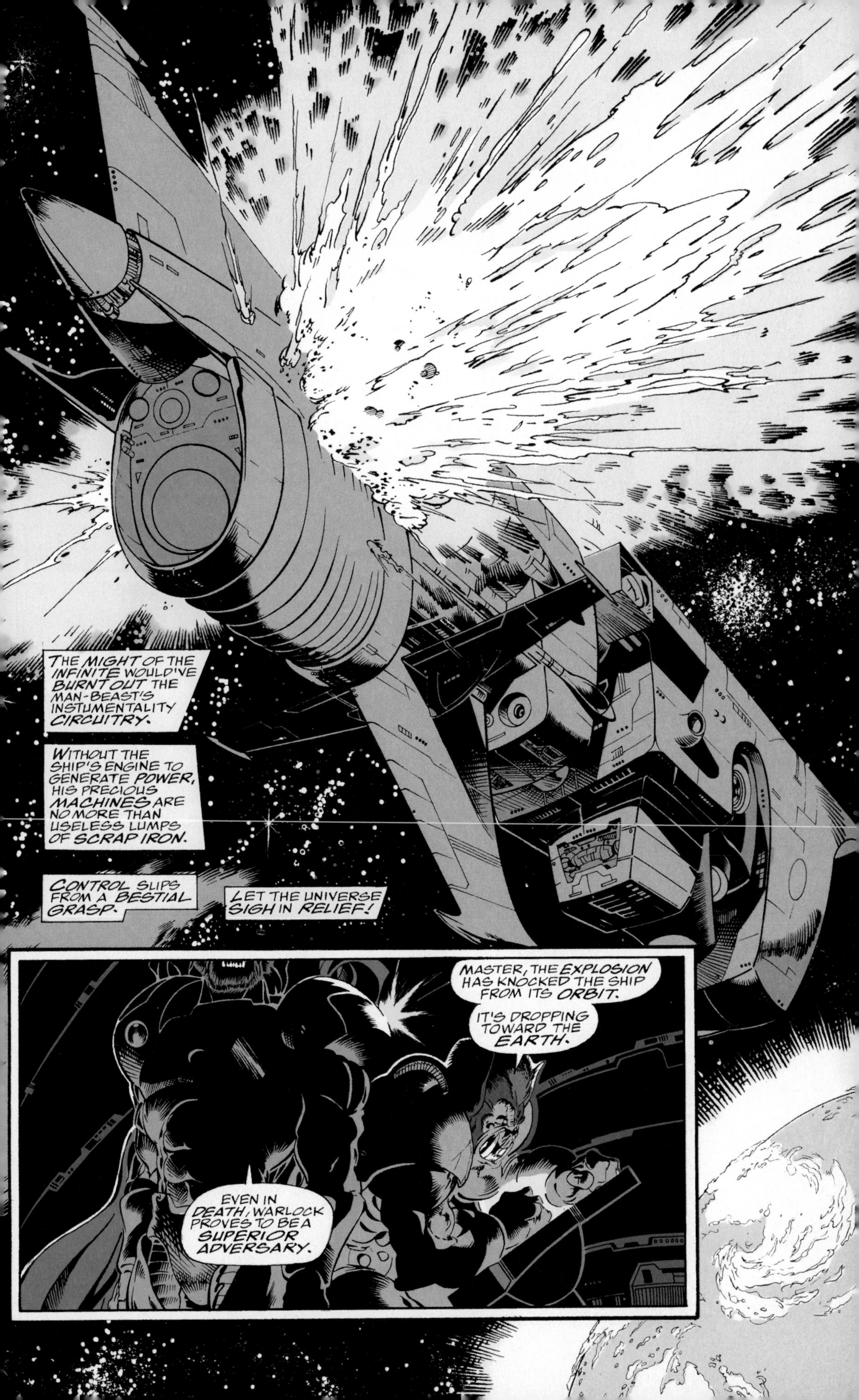
THE MIGHT OF THE INFINITE WOULD'VE BURNT OUT THE MAN-BEAST'S INSTUMENTALITY CIRCUITRY.
WITHOUT THE SHIP'S ENGINE TO GENERATE POWER, HIS PRECIOUS MACHINES ARE NO MORE THAN USELESS LUMPS OF SCRAP IRON.
CONTROL SLIPS FROM A BESTIAL GRASP.
LET THE UNIVERSE SIGH IN RELIEF!
MASTER, THE EXPLOSION HAS KNOCKED THE SHIP FROM ITS ORBIT.
IT'S DROPPING TOWARD THE EARTH.
EVEN IN DEATH, WARLOCK PROVES TO BE A SUPERIOR ADVERSARY.

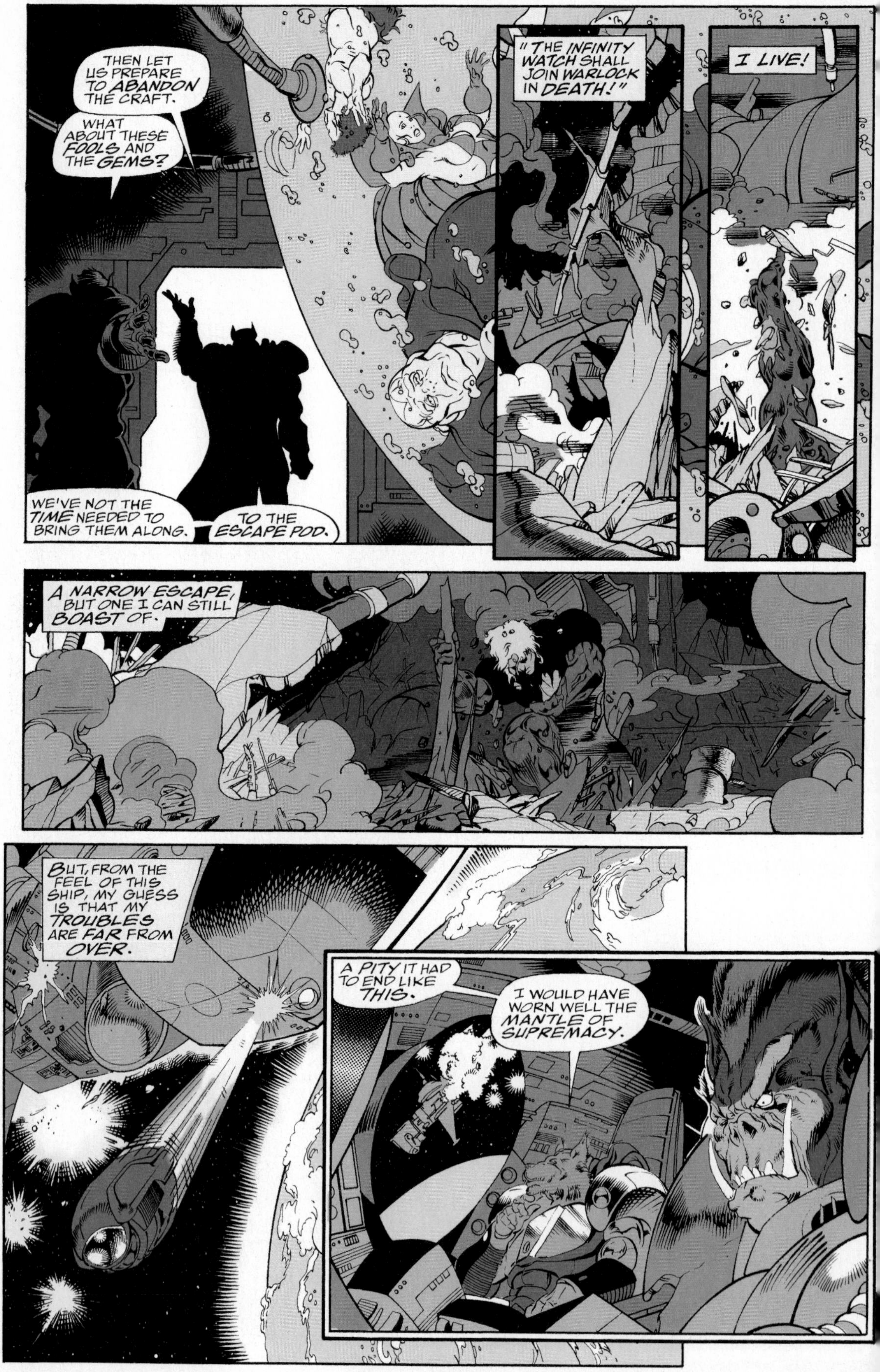
THEN LET US PREPARE TO ABANDON THE CRAFT.
WHAT ABOUT THESE FOOLS AND THE GEMS?
WE'VE NOT THE TIME NEEDED TO BRING THEM ALONG.
TO THE ESCAPE POD.
"THE INFINITY WATCH SHALL JOIN WARLOCK IN DEATH!"
I LIVE!
A NARROW ESCAPE, BUT ONE I CAN STILL BOAST OF.
BUT, FROM THE FEEL OF THIS SHIP, MY GUESS IS THAT MY TROUBLES ARE FAR FROM OVER.
A PITY IT HAD TO END LIKE THIS.
I WOULD HAVE WORN WELL THE MANTLE OF SUPREMACY.

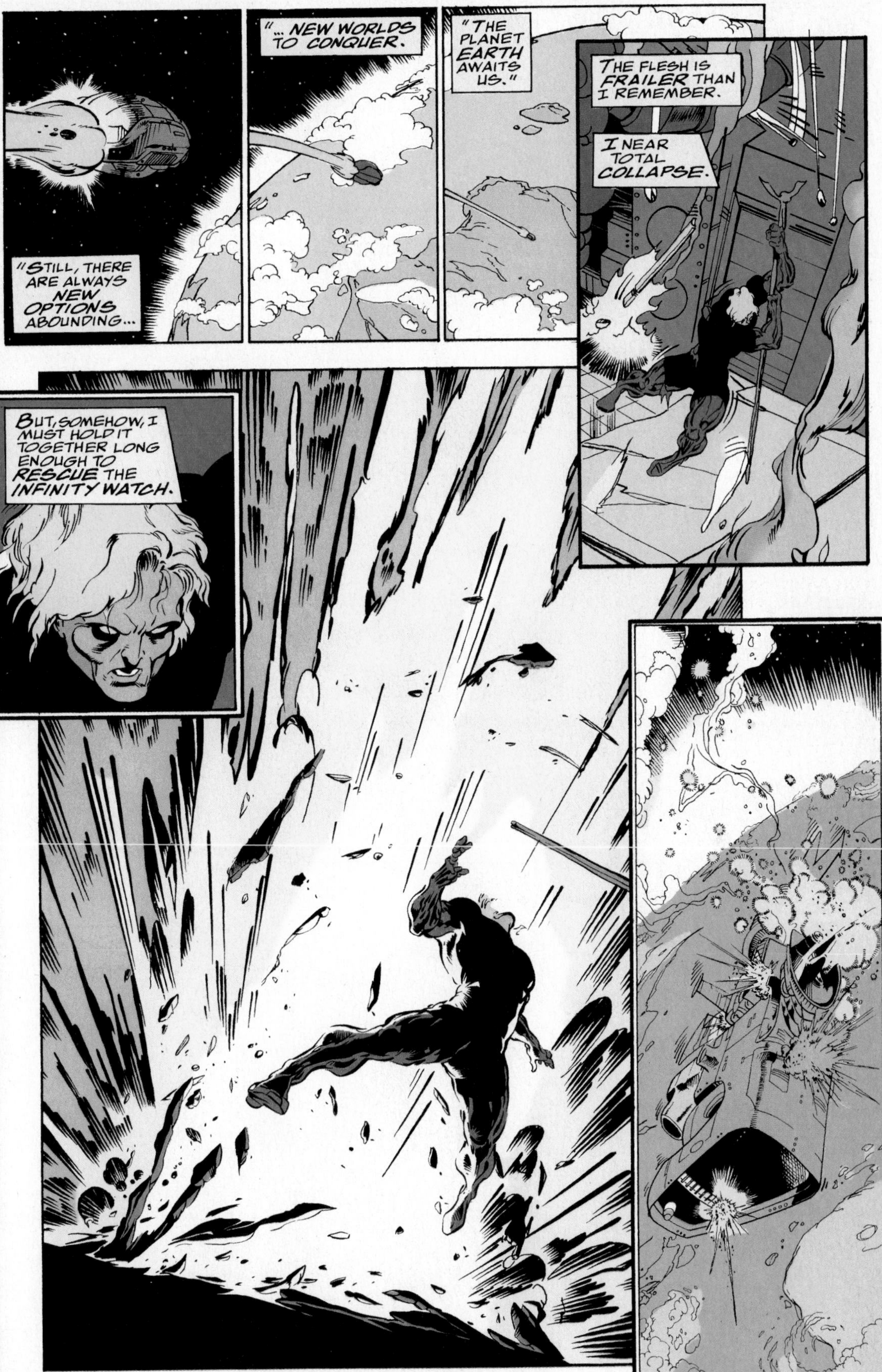
"STILL, THERE ARE ALWAYS NEW OPTIONS ABOUNDING...
"... NEW WORLDS TO CONQUER.
"THE PLANET EARTH AWAITS US."
THE FLESH IS FRAILER THAN I REMEMBER.
I NEAR TOTAL COLLAPSE.
BUT, SOMEHOW, I MUST HOLD IT TOGETHER LONG ENOUGH TO RESCUE THE INFINITY WATCH.

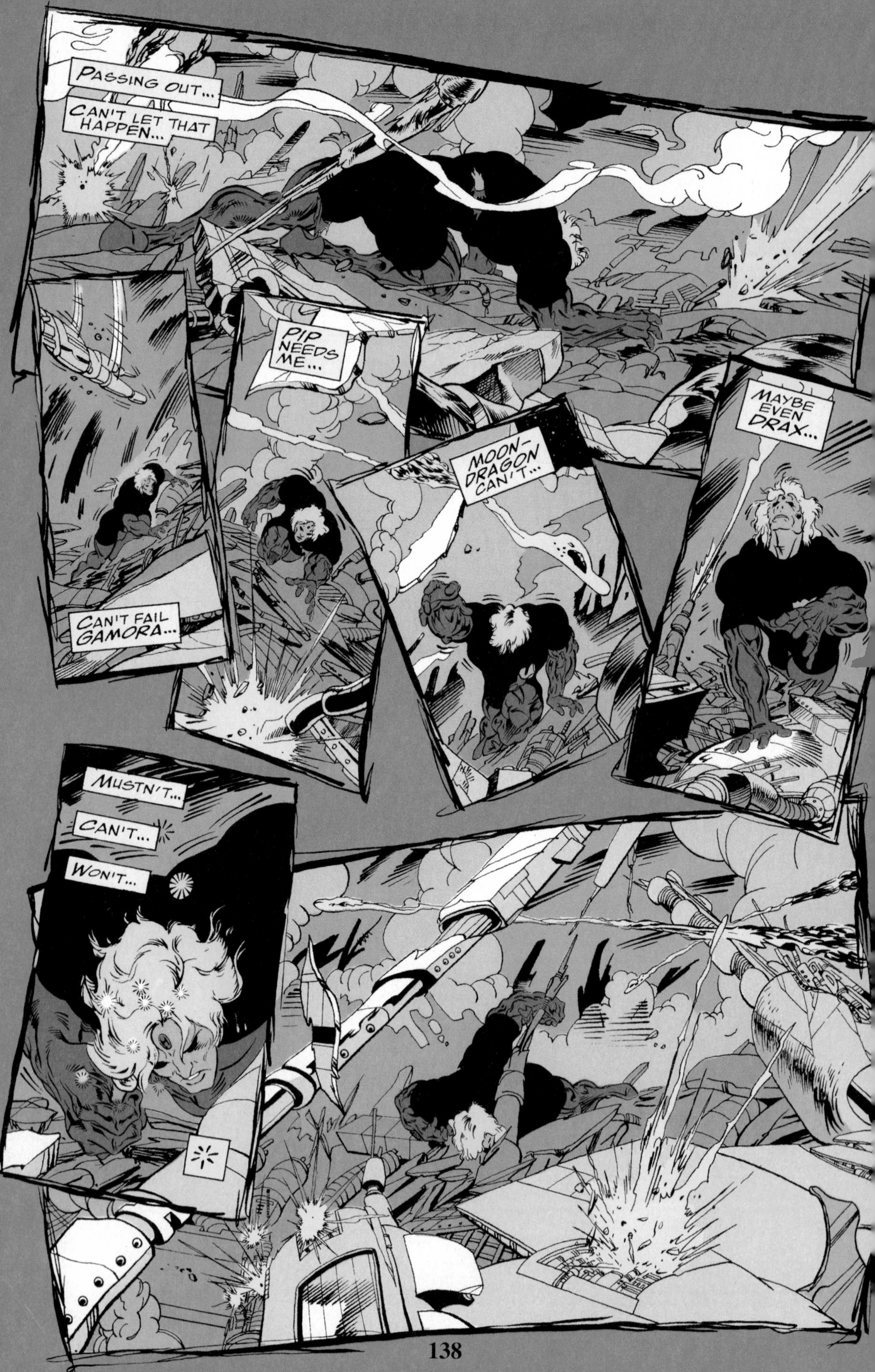

PASSING OUT...
CAN'T LET THAT HAPPEN...
CAN'T FAIL GAMORA...
PIP NEEDS ME...
MOON-DRAGON CAN'T...
MAYBE EVEN DRAX...
MUSTN'T...
CAN'T...
WON'T...

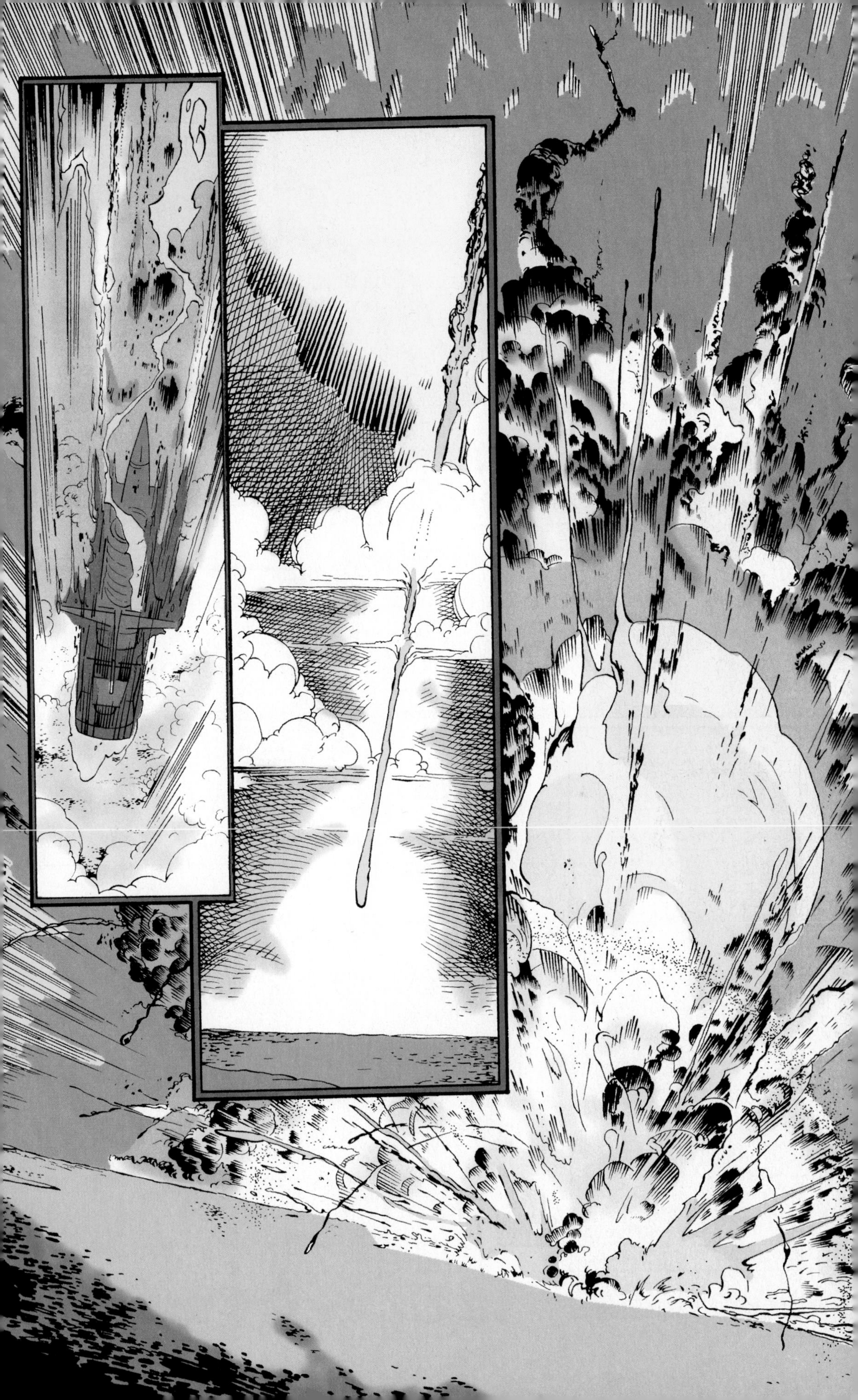

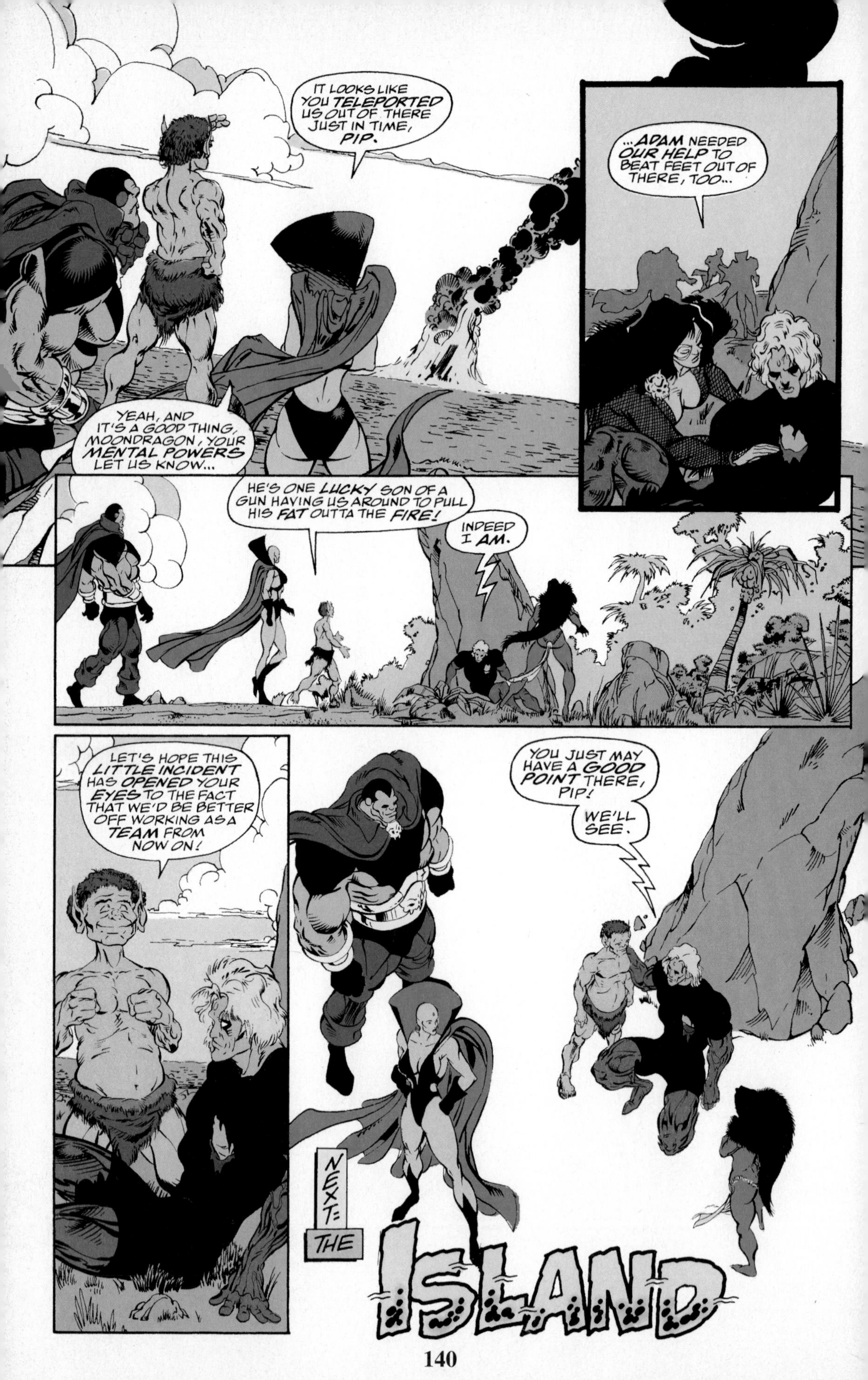
IT LOOKS LIKE YOU TELEPORTED US OUT OF THERE JUST IN TIME, PIP.
YEAH, AND IT'S A GOOD THING, MOONDRAGON, YOUR MENTAL POWERS LET US KNOW...
...ADAM NEEDED OUR HELP TO BEAT FEET OUT OF THERE, TOO...
HE'S ONE LUCKY SON OF A GUN HAVING US AROUND TO PULL HIS FAT OUTTA THE FIRE!
INDEED I AM.
LET'S HOPE THIS LITTLE INCIDENT HAS OPENED YOUR EYES TO THE FACT THAT WE'D BE BETTER OFF WORKING AS A TEAM FROM NOW ON!
YOU JUST MAY HAVE A GOOD POINT THERE, PIP!
WE'LL SEE.
NEXT: THE ISLAND

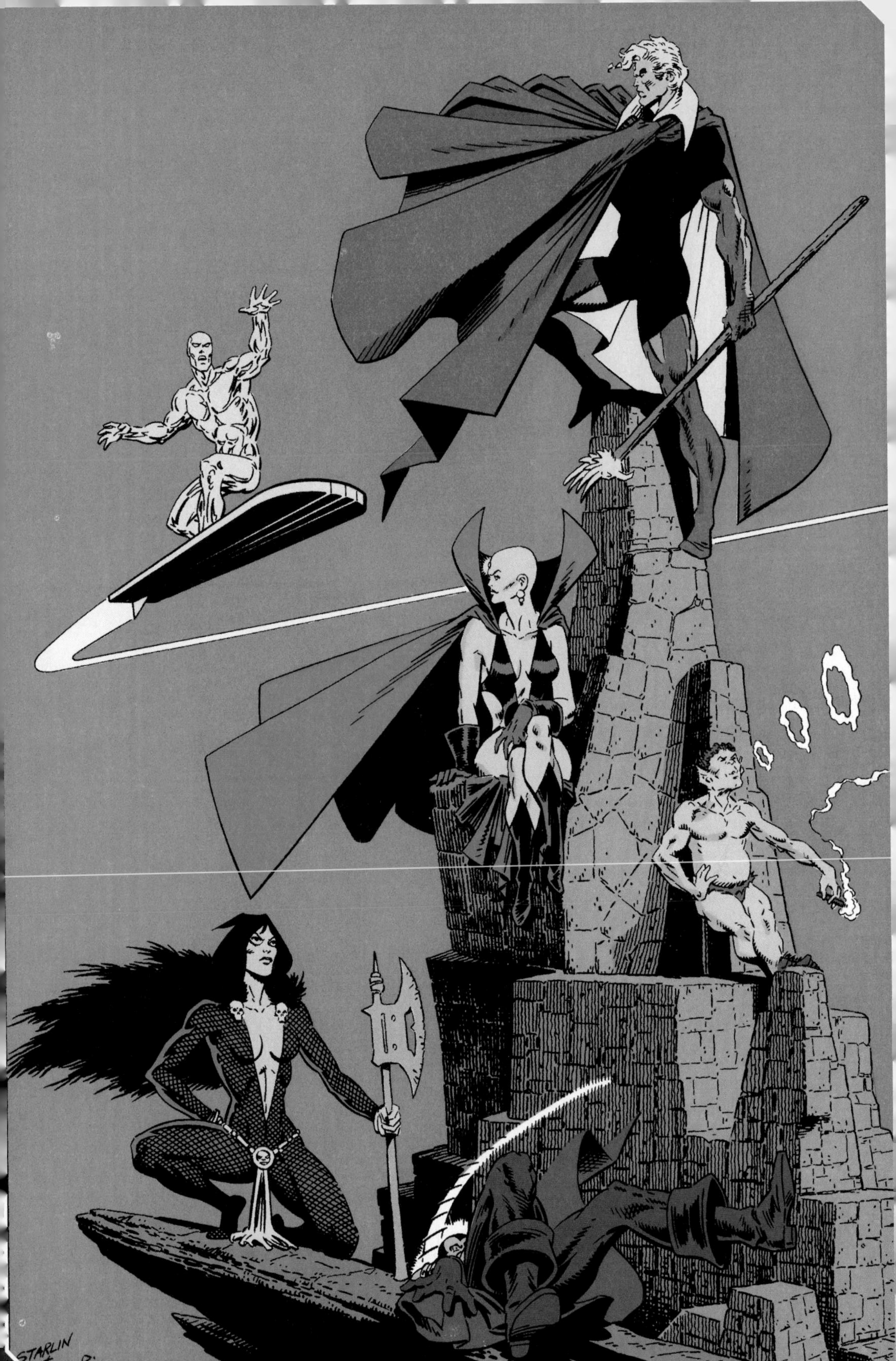
STARLIN
+ austin

SILVER SURFER ANNUAL #5
PINUP BY JIM STARLIN & TERRY AUSTIN

THE *INFINITY WAR* STORYLINE REVEALED THAT WHEN WARLOCK POSSESSED THE INFINITY GAUNTLET, HE SUBCONSCIOUSLY EXPELLED ALL GOOD AND EVIL FROM HIMSELF. WARLOCK'S EVIL COALESCED INTO THE MAGUS — WHO, EMPOWERED BY STOLEN COSMIC CUBES, INCAPACITATED ETERNITY AND ATTACKED EARTH'S HEROES WITH EVIL DOPPELGANGERS, PART OF A MYSTERIOUS PLAN TO GAIN ULTIMATE POWER. *WARLOCK AND THE INFINITY WATCH #7-10* WERE *INFINITY WAR* TIE-INS.

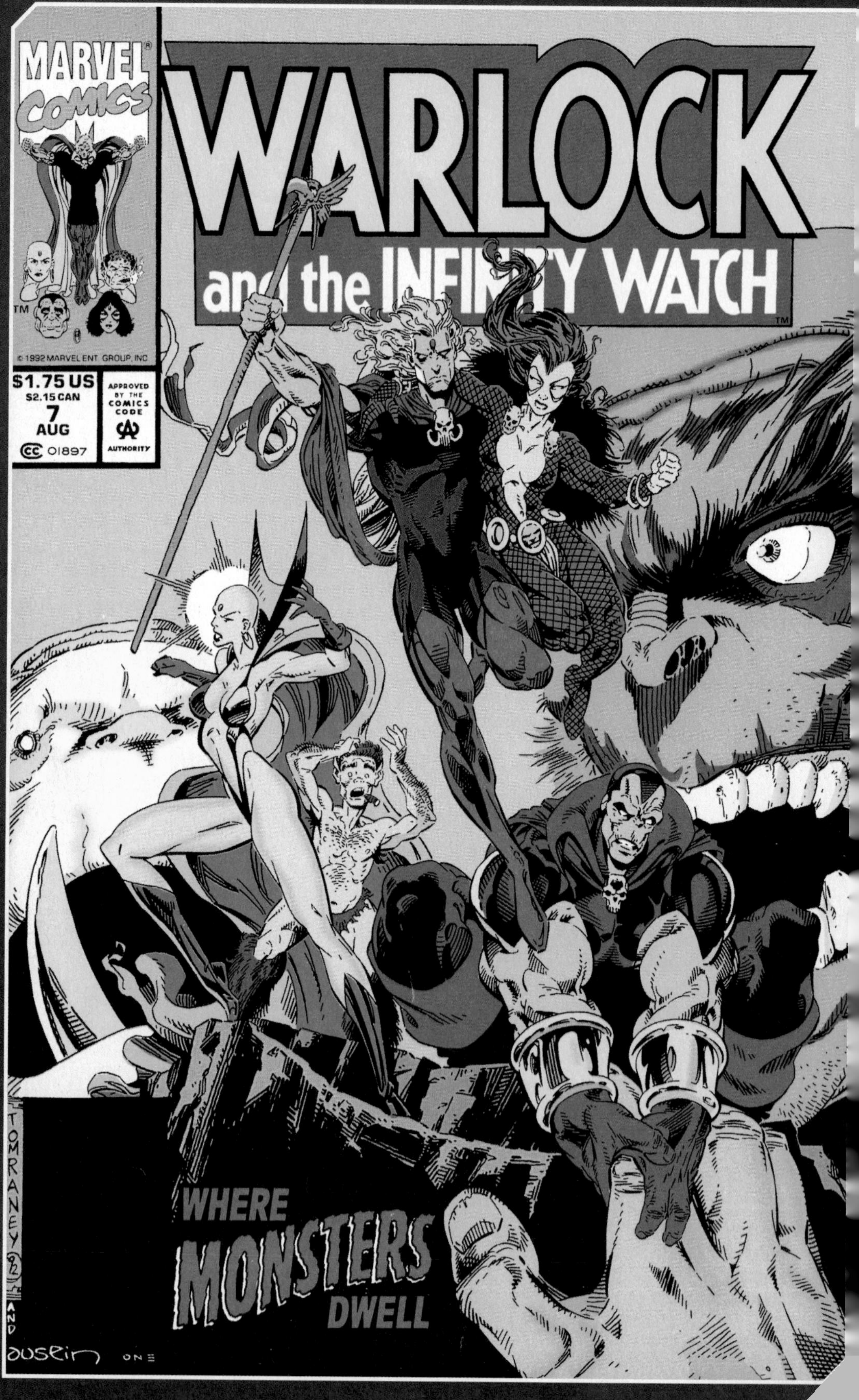
MARVEL COMICS
TM
© 1992 MARVEL ENT. GROUP, INC.
$1.75 US
$2.15 CAN
7
AUG
01897
APPROVED BY THE COMICS CODE AUTHORITY
WARLOCK
WATCH
TM
WHERE
MONSTERS
DWELL
TOM RANEY 92
AND

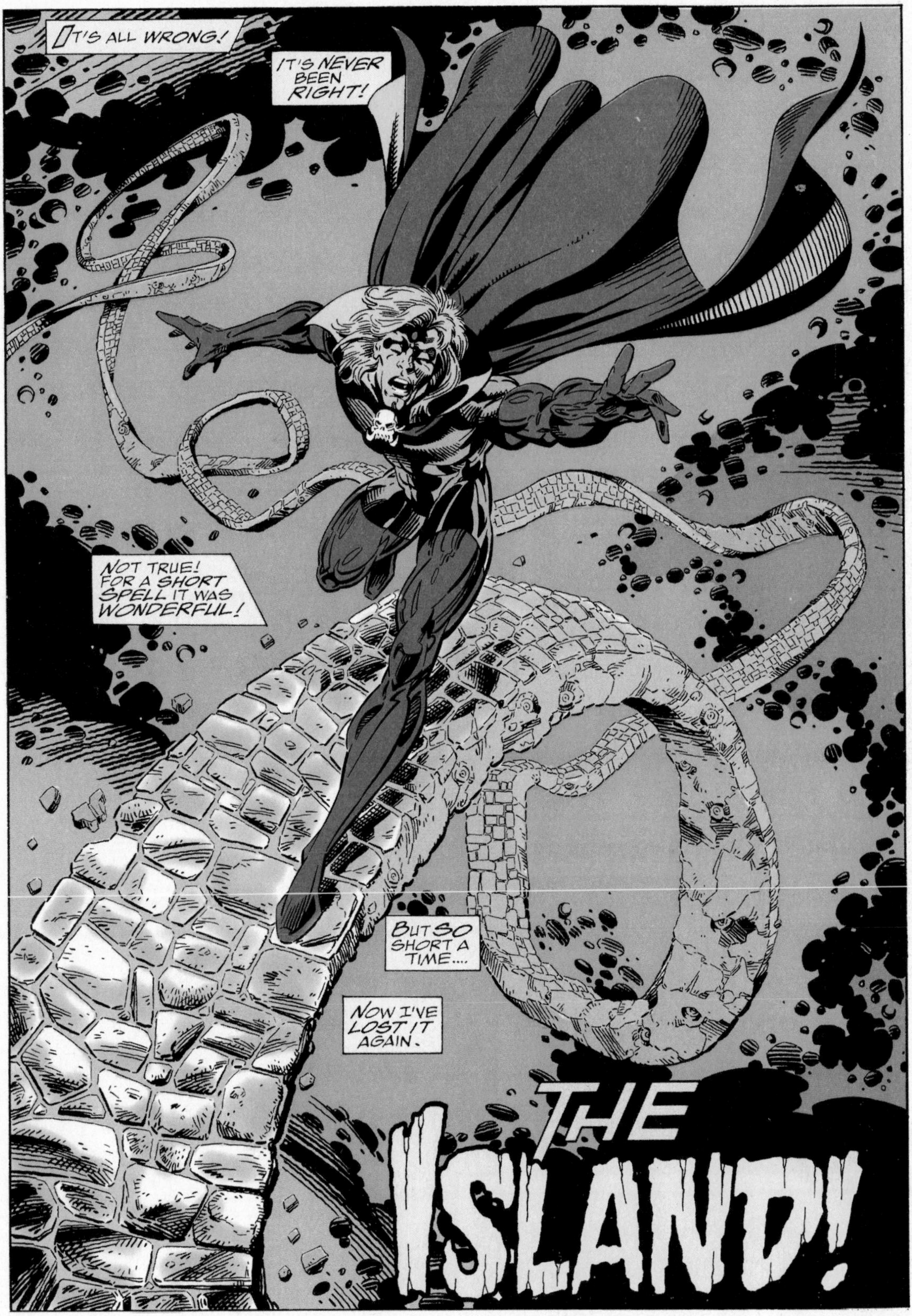
IT'S ALL WRONG!
IT'S NEVER BEEN RIGHT!
NOT TRUE! FOR A SHORT SPELL IT WAS WONDERFUL!
BUT SO SHORT A TIME....
NOW I'VE LOST IT AGAIN.
THE ISLAND!

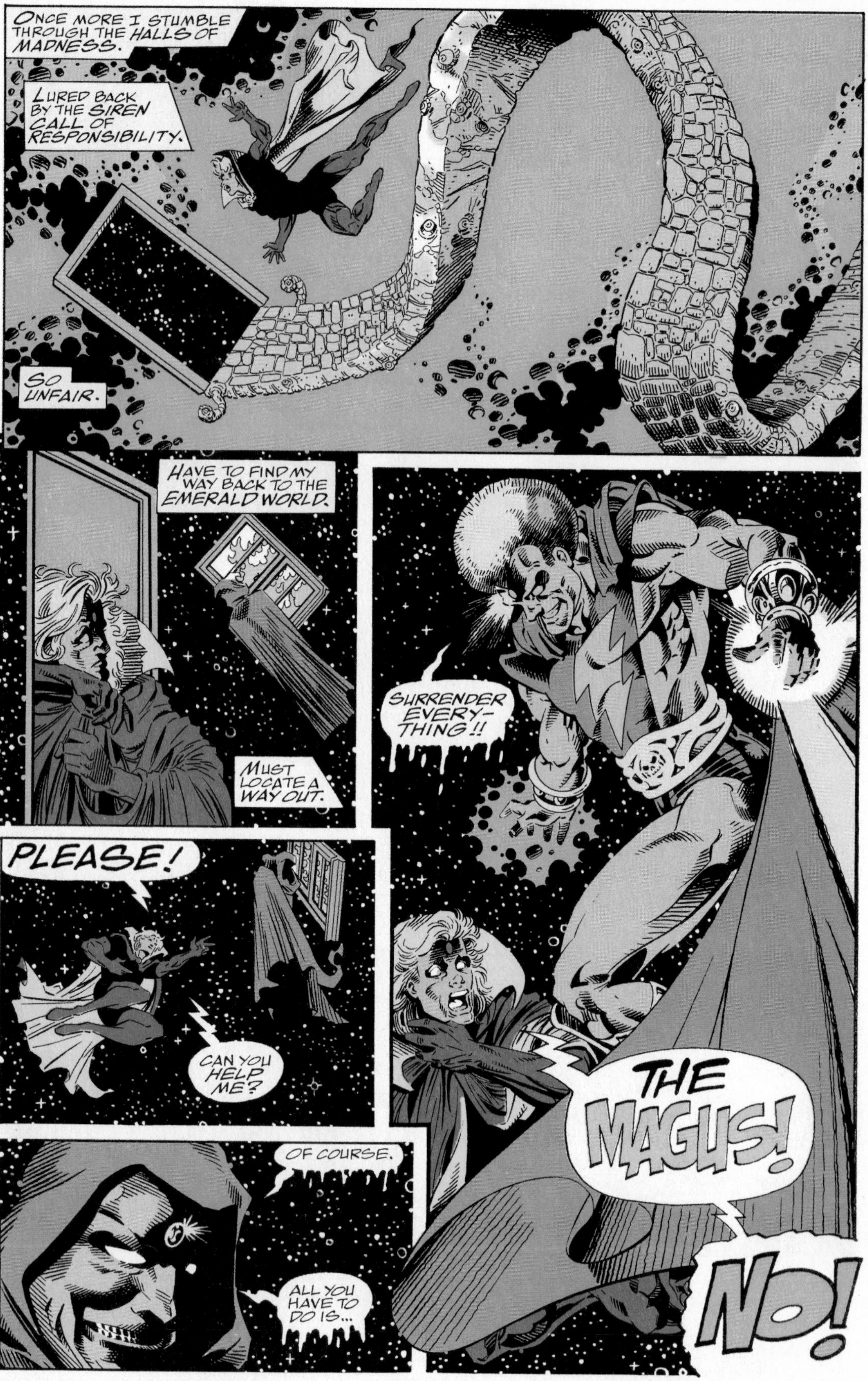

ONCE MORE I STUMBLE THROUGH THE HALLS OF MADNESS.
LURED BACK BY THE SIREN CALL OF RESPONSIBILITY.
SO UNFAIR.
HAVE TO FIND MY WAY BACK TO THE EMERALD WORLD.
MUST LOCATE A WAY OUT.
PLEASE!
CAN YOU HELP ME?
OF COURSE.
ALL YOU HAVE TO DO IS...
SURRENDER EVERY-THING!!
THE MAGUS!
NO!

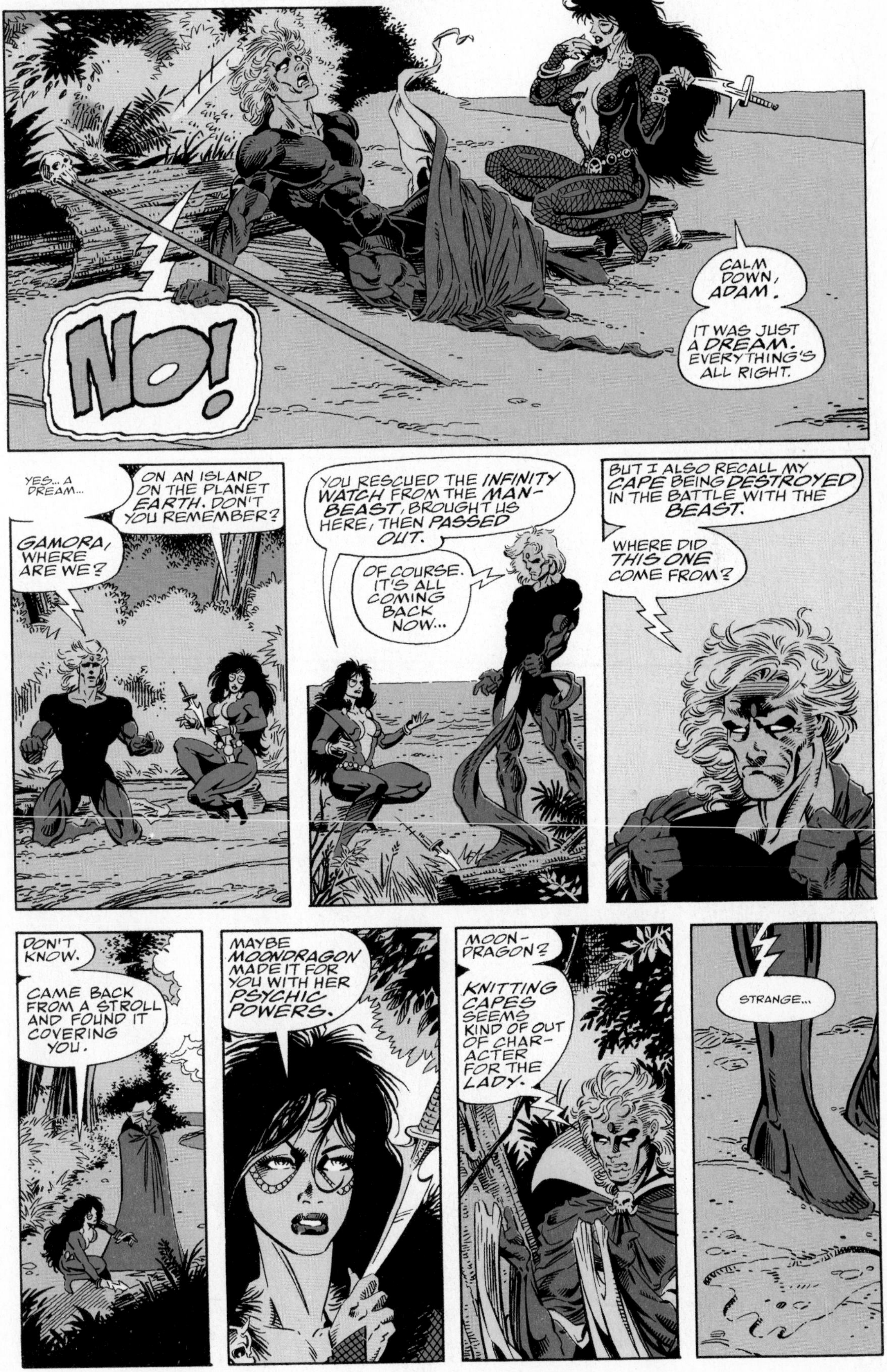
NO!
CALM DOWN, ADAM.
IT WAS JUST A DREAM. EVERYTHING'S ALL RIGHT.
YES... A DREAM...
GAMORA, WHERE ARE WE?
ON AN ISLAND ON THE PLANET EARTH. DON'T YOU REMEMBER?
YOU RESCUED THE INFINITY WATCH FROM THE MAN-BEAST, BROUGHT US HERE, THEN PASSED OUT.
OF COURSE. IT'S ALL COMING BACK NOW...
BUT I ALSO RECALL MY CAPE BEING DESTROYED IN THE BATTLE WITH THE BEAST.
WHERE DID THIS ONE COME FROM?
DON'T KNOW.
CAME BACK FROM A STROLL AND FOUND IT COVERING YOU.
MAYBE MOONDRAGON MADE IT FOR YOU WITH HER PSYCHIC POWERS.
MOON-DRAGON?
KNITTING CAPES SEEMS KIND OF OUT OF CHAR-ACTER FOR THE LADY.
STRANGE...

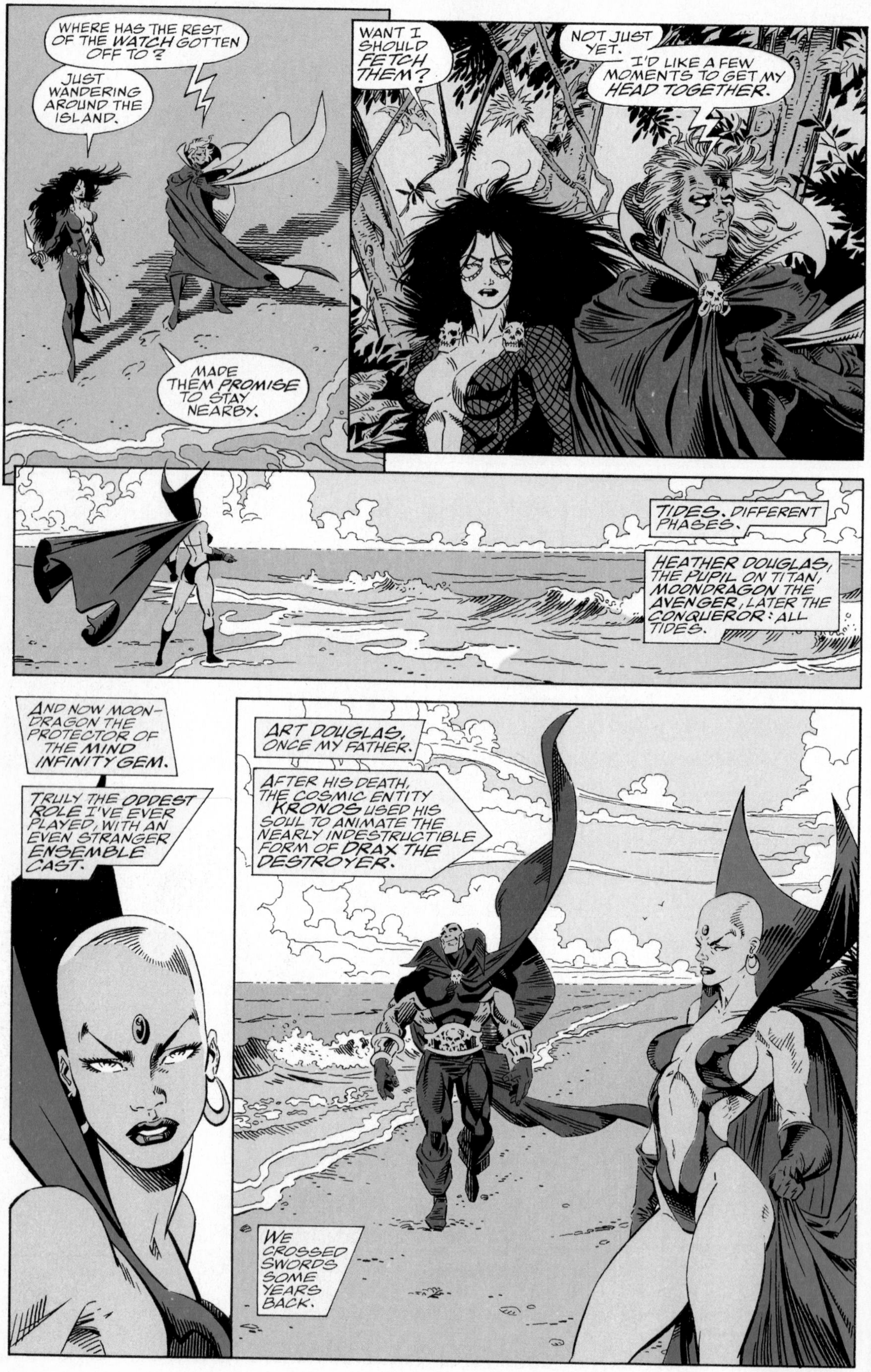
WHERE HAS THE REST OF THE WATCH GOTTEN OFF TO?
JUST WANDERING AROUND THE ISLAND.
MADE THEM PROMISE TO STAY NEARBY.
WANT I SHOULD FETCH THEM?
NOT JUST YET.
I'D LIKE A FEW MOMENTS TO GET MY HEAD TOGETHER.
TIDES. DIFFERENT PHASES.
HEATHER DOUGLAS, THE PUPIL ON TITAN, MOONDRAGON THE AVENGER, LATER THE CONQUEROR: ALL TIDES.
AND NOW MOON-DRAGON THE PROTECTOR OF THE MIND INFINITY GEM.
TRULY THE ODDEST ROLE I'VE EVER PLAYED, WITH AN EVEN STRANGER ENSEMBLE CAST.
ART DOUGLAS, ONCE MY FATHER.
AFTER HIS DEATH, THE COSMIC ENTITY KRONOS USED HIS SOUL TO ANIMATE THE NEARLY INDESTRUCTIBLE FORM OF DRAX THE DESTROYER.
WE CROSSED SWORDS SOME YEARS BACK.

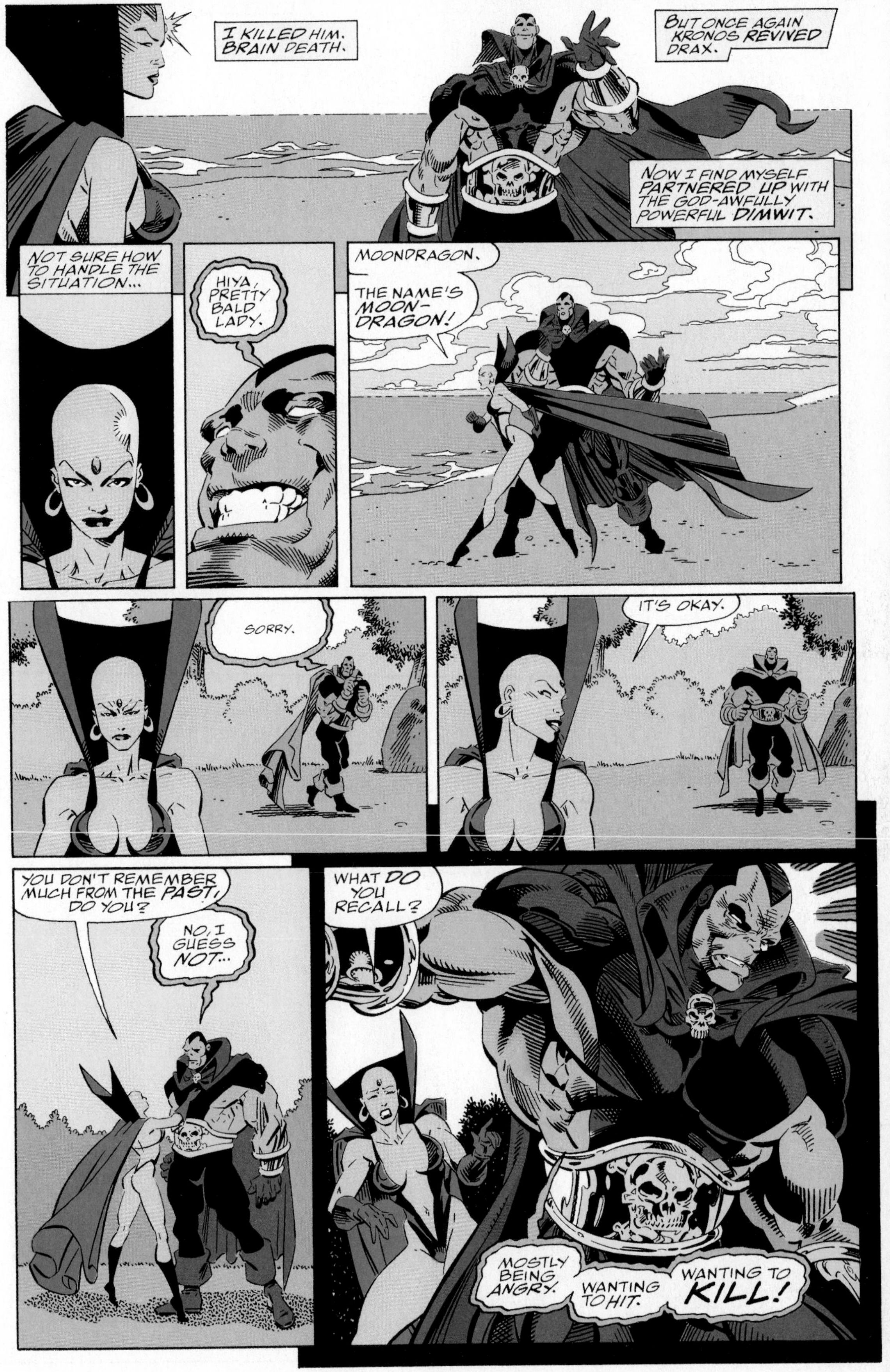
I KILLED HIM. BRAIN DEATH.
BUT ONCE AGAIN KRONOS REVIVED DRAX.
NOW I FIND MYSELF PARTNERED UP WITH THE GOD-AWFULLY POWERFUL DIMWIT.
NOT SURE HOW TO HANDLE THE SITUATION...
HIYA, PRETTY BALD LADY.
MOONDRAGON.
THE NAME'S MOON-DRAGON!
SORRY.
IT'S OKAY.
YOU DON'T REMEMBER MUCH FROM THE PAST, DO YOU?
NO, I GUESS NOT...
WHAT DO YOU RECALL?
MOSTLY BEING ANGRY.
WANTING TO HIT.
WANTING TO KILL!

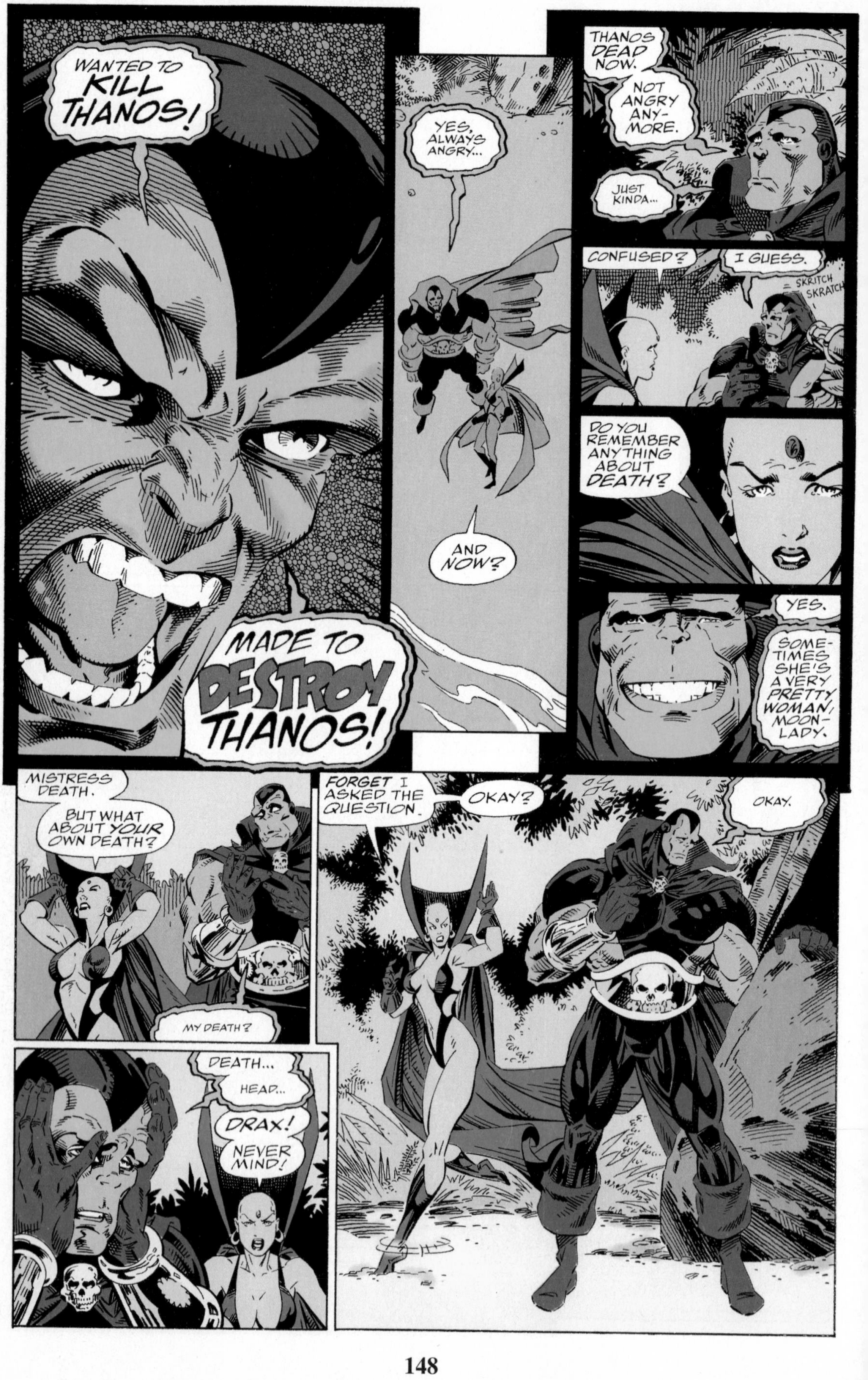
WANTED TO KILL THANOS!
MADE TO DESTROY THANOS!
YES, ALWAYS ANGRY...
AND NOW?
THANOS DEAD NOW.
NOT ANGRY ANY-MORE.
JUST KINDA...
CONFUSED?
I GUESS.
SKRITCH SKRATCH
DO YOU REMEMBER ANYTHING ABOUT DEATH?
YES.
SOME-TIMES SHE'S A VERY PRETTY WOMAN, MOON-LADY.
MISTRESS DEATH.
BUT WHAT ABOUT YOUR OWN DEATH?
MY DEATH?
DEATH...
HEAD...
DRAX!
NEVER MIND!
FORGET I ASKED THE QUESTION.
OKAY?
OKAY.

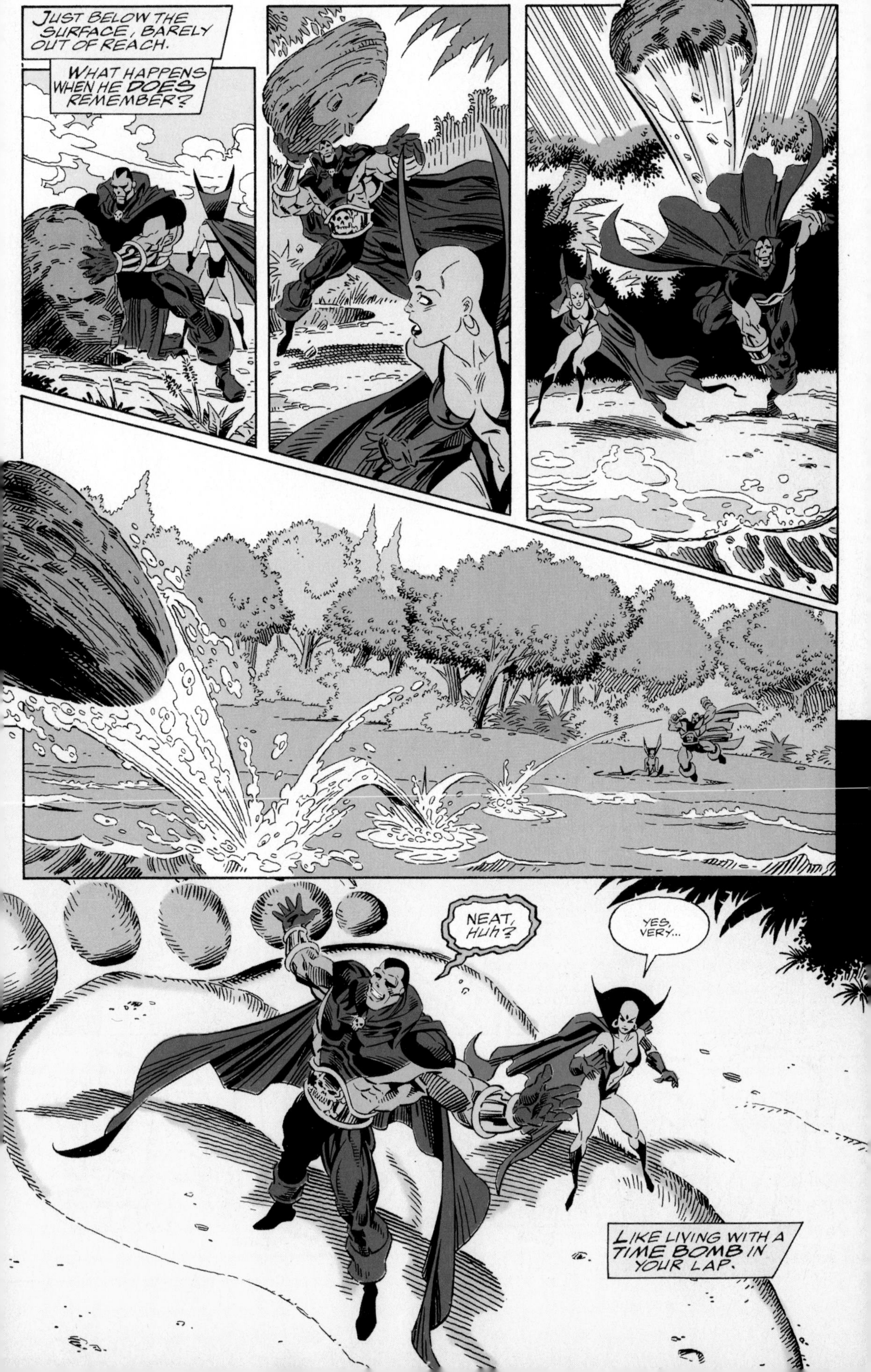
JUST BELOW THE SURFACE, BARELY OUT OF REACH.
WHAT HAPPENS WHEN HE DOES REMEMBER?
NEAT, HUH?
YES, VERY...
LIKE LIVING WITH A TIME BOMB IN YOUR LAP.

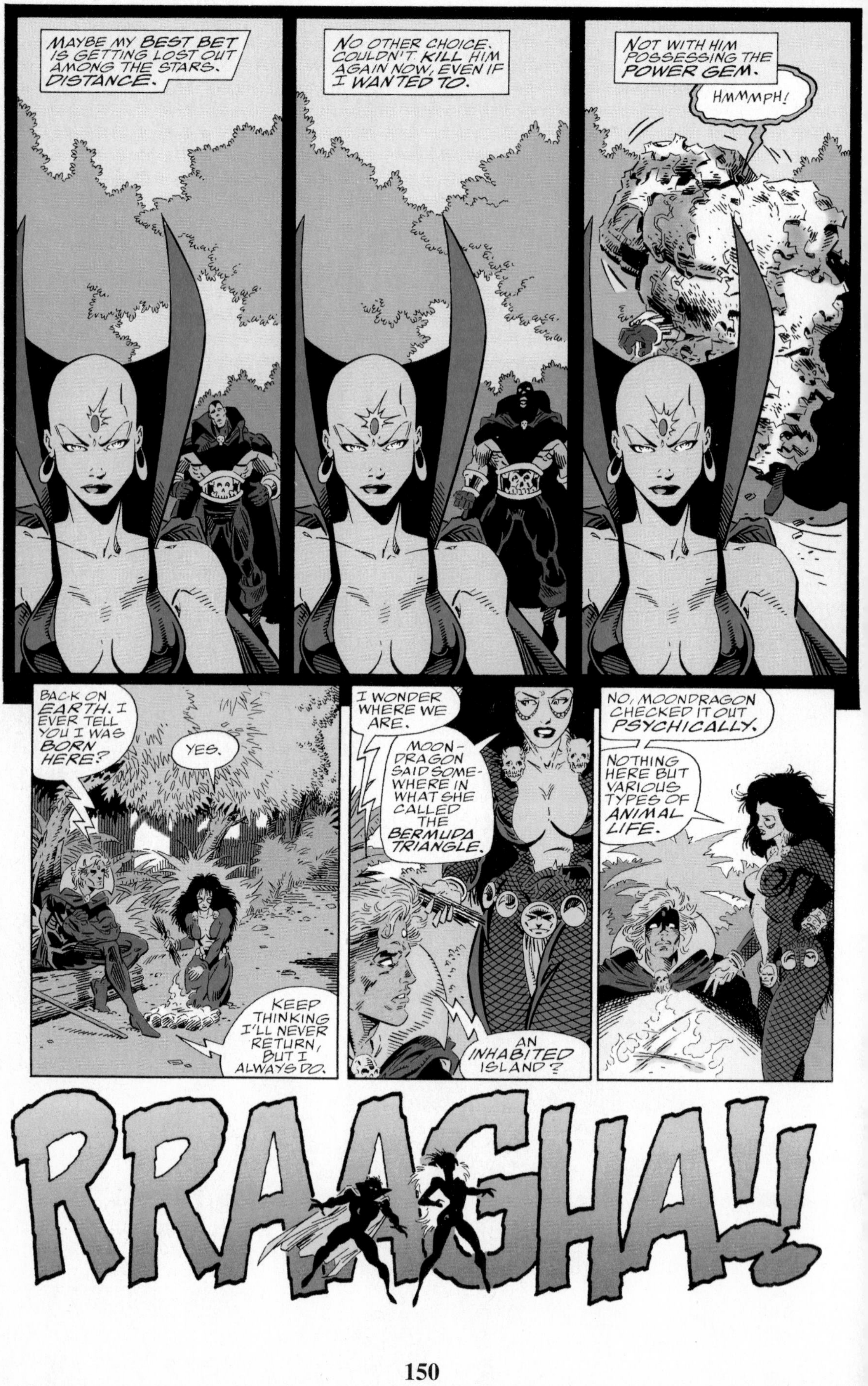
MAYBE MY BEST BET IS GETTING LOST OUT AMONG THE STARS. DISTANCE.
NO OTHER CHOICE. COULDN'T KILL HIM AGAIN NOW, EVEN IF I WANTED TO.
NOT WITH HIM POSSESSING THE POWER GEM.
HMMMPH!
BACK ON EARTH. I EVER TELL YOU I WAS BORN HERE?
YES.
KEEP THINKING I'LL NEVER RETURN, BUT I ALWAYS DO.
I WONDER WHERE WE ARE.
MOON-DRAGON SAID SOME-WHERE IN WHAT SHE CALLED THE BERMUDA TRIANGLE.
AN INHABITED ISLAND?
NO, MOONDRAGON CHECKED IT OUT PSYCHICALLY.
NOTHING HERE BUT VARIOUS TYPES OF ANIMAL LIFE.
RRAAGHA!!

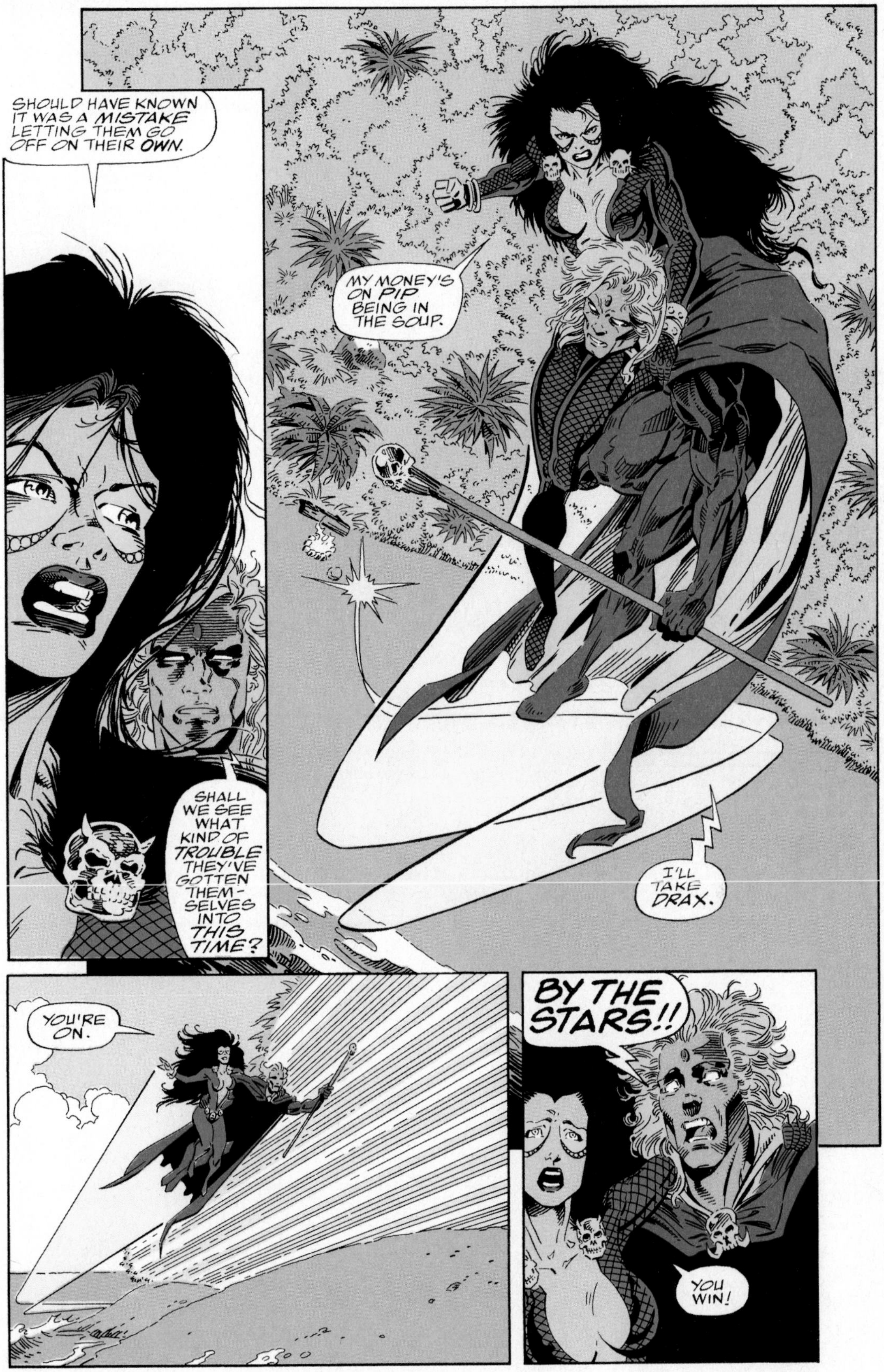
SHOULD HAVE KNOWN IT WAS A MISTAKE LETTING THEM GO OFF ON THEIR OWN.
MY MONEY'S ON PIP BEING IN THE SOUP.
SHALL WE SEE WHAT KIND OF TROUBLE THEY'VE GOTTEN THEM-SELVES INTO THIS TIME?
I'LL TAKE DRAX.
YOU'RE ON.
BY THE STARS!!
YOU WIN!

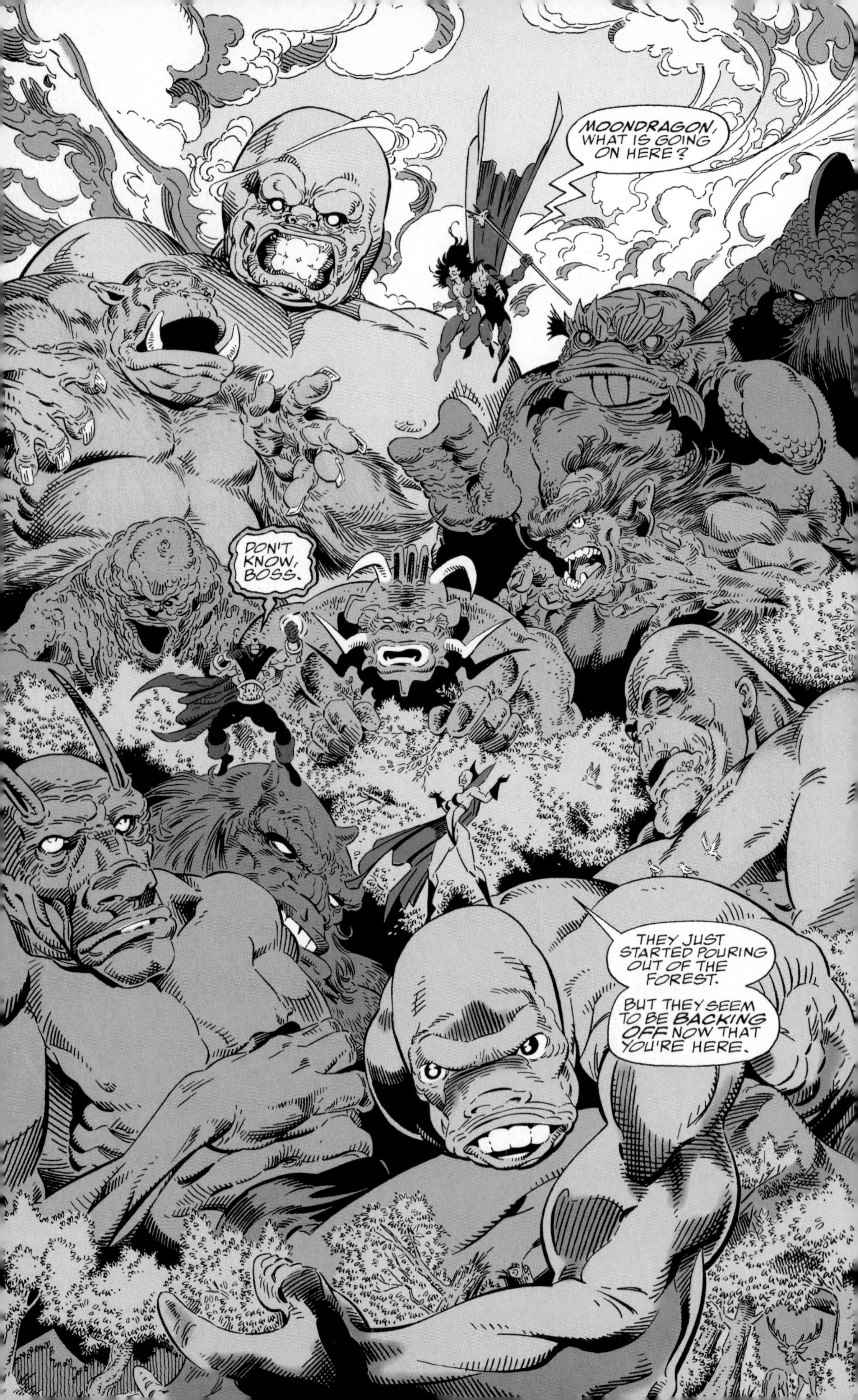
MOONDRAGON, WHAT IS GOING ON HERE?
DON'T KNOW, BOSS.
THEY JUST STARTED POURING OUT OF THE FOREST.
BUT THEY SEEM TO BE BACKING OFF NOW THAT YOU'RE HERE.

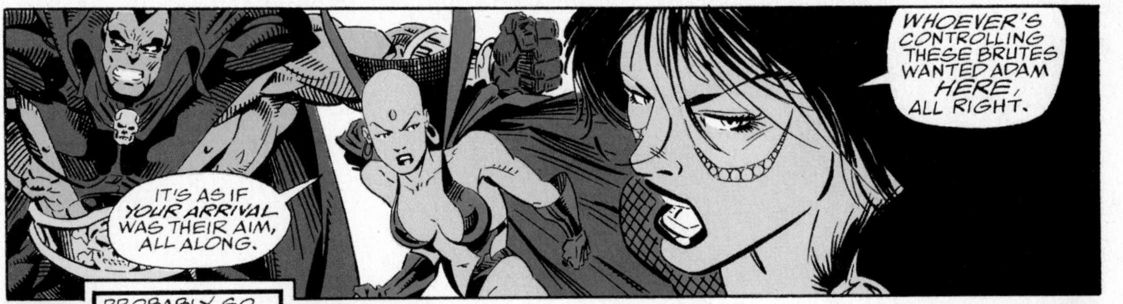
WHOEVER'S CONTROLLING THESE BRUTES WANTED ADAM HERE, ALL RIGHT.
IT'S AS IF YOUR ARRIVAL WAS THEIR AIM, ALL ALONG.

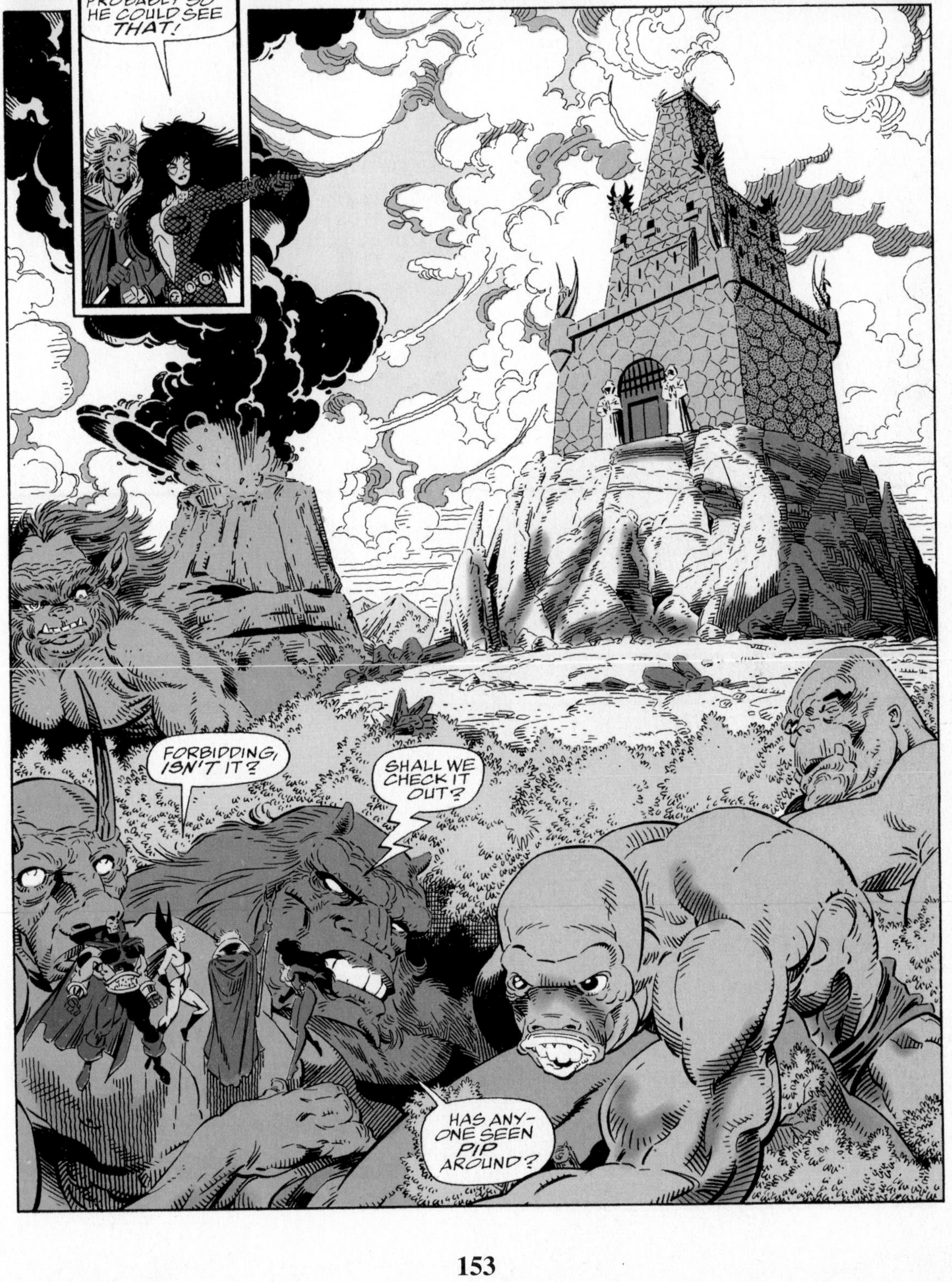
PROBABLY SO HE COULD SEE THAT!
FORBIDDING, ISN'T IT?
SHALL WE CHECK IT OUT?
HAS ANY-ONE SEEN PIP AROUND?

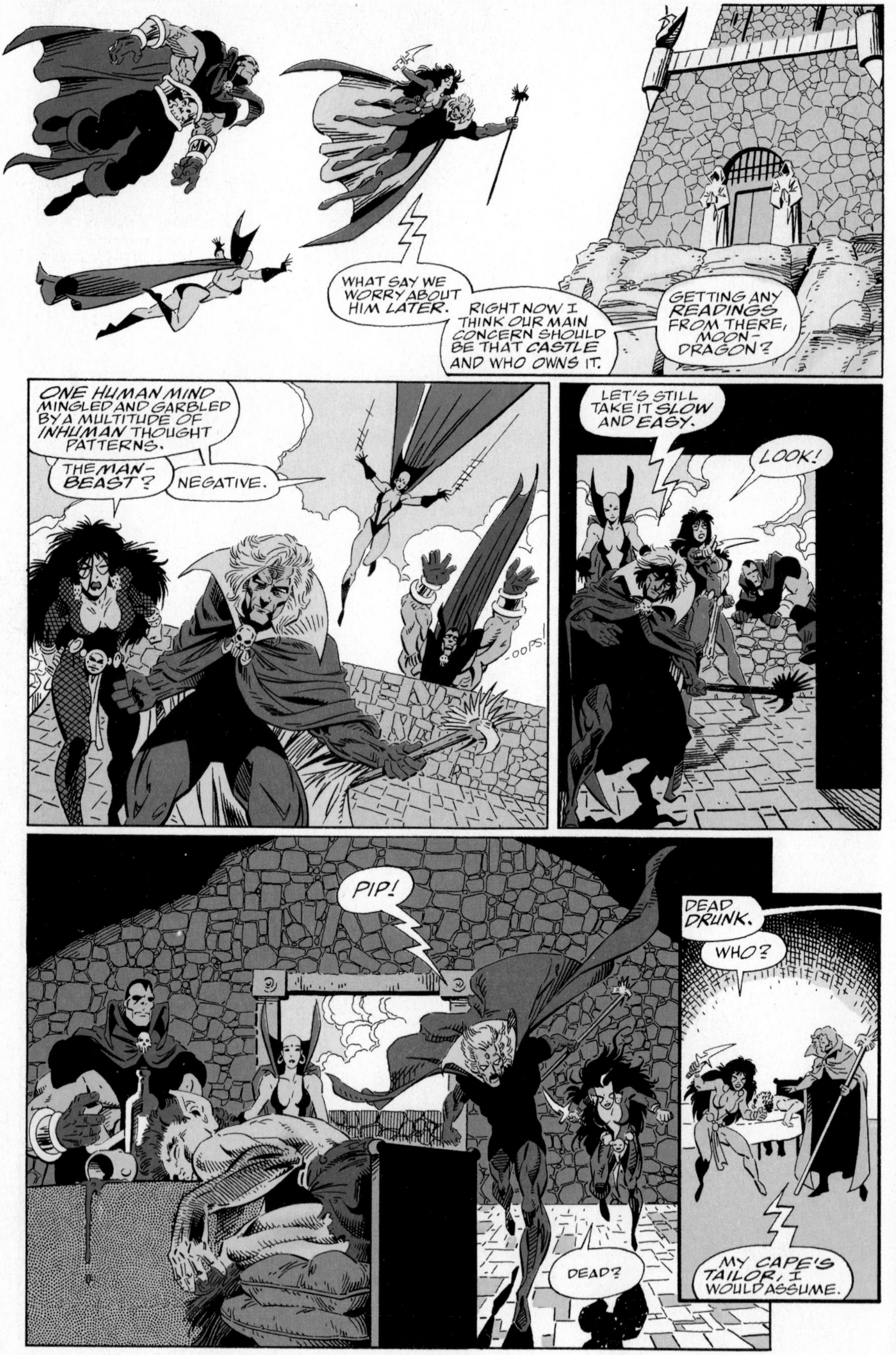
WHAT SAY WE WORRY ABOUT HIM LATER.
RIGHT NOW I THINK OUR MAIN CONCERN SHOULD BE THAT CASTLE AND WHO OWNS IT.
GETTING ANY READINGS FROM THERE, MOON-DRAGON?
ONE HUMAN MIND MINGLED AND GARBLED BY A MULTITUDE OF INHUMAN THOUGHT PATTERNS.
THE MAN-BEAST?
NEGATIVE.
-OOPS!
LET'S STILL TAKE IT SLOW AND EASY.
LOOK!
PIP!
DEAD?
DEAD DRUNK.
WHO?
MY CAPE'S TAILOR, I WOULD ASSUME.

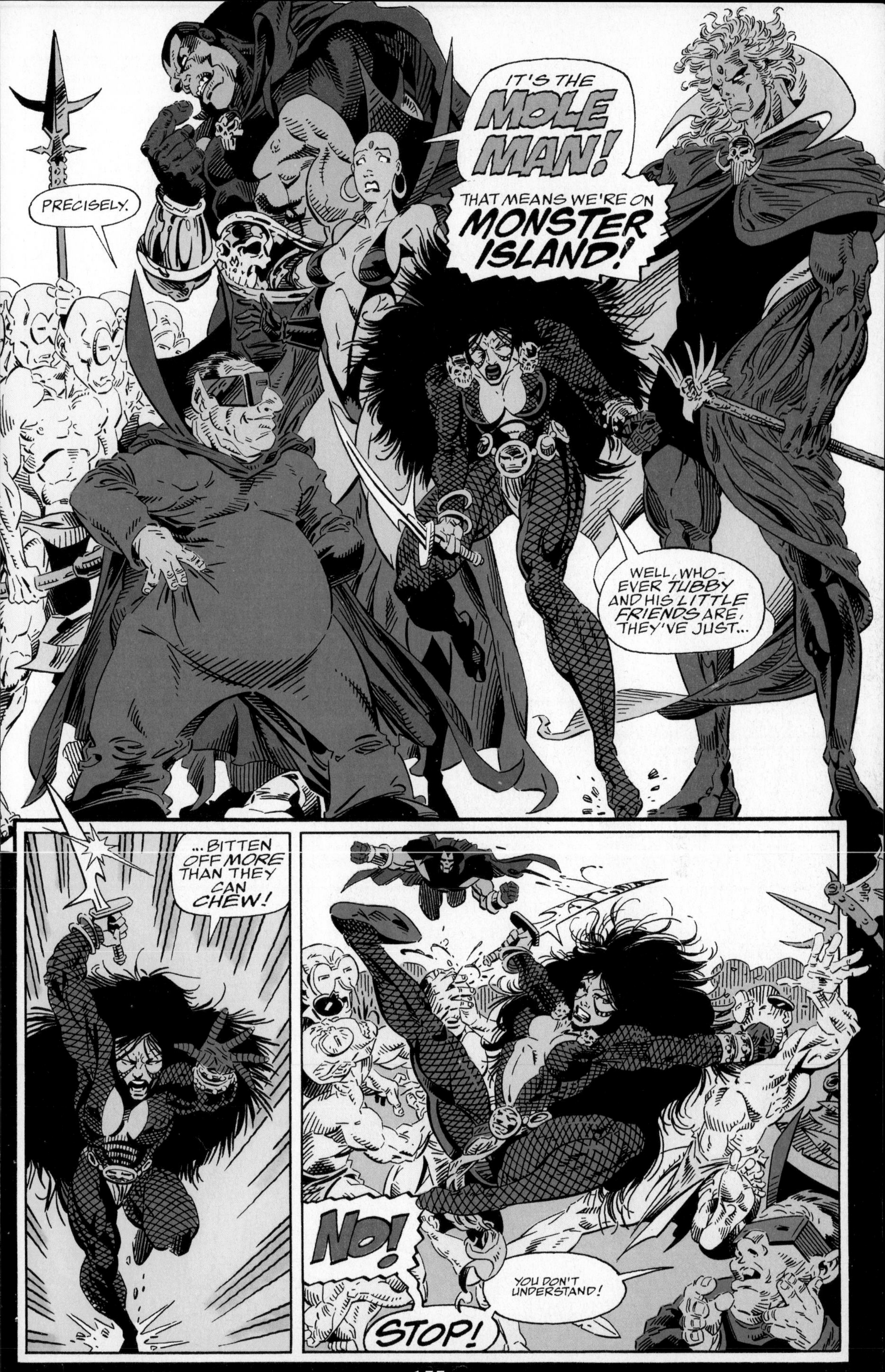

PRECISELY.
IT'S THE MOLE MAN!
THAT MEANS WE'RE ON MONSTER ISLAND!
WELL, WHO-EVER TUBBY AND HIS LITTLE FRIENDS ARE, THEY'VE JUST...
...BITTEN OFF MORE THAN THEY CAN CHEW!
NO!
YOU DON'T UNDERSTAND!
STOP!

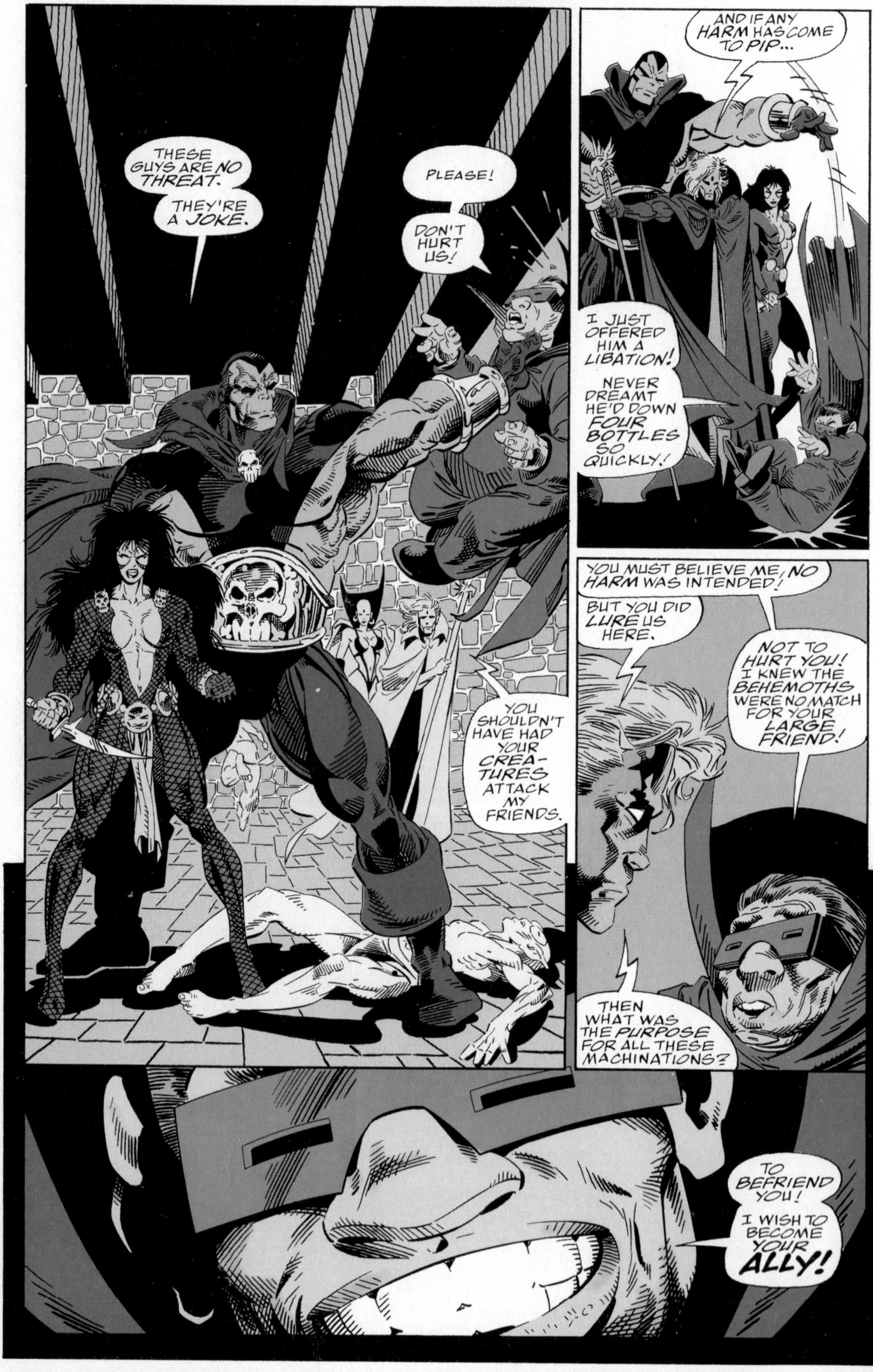
THESE GUYS ARE NO THREAT.
THEY'RE A JOKE.
PLEASE!
DON'T HURT US!
AND IF ANY HARM HAS COME TO PIP...
I JUST OFFERED HIM A LIBATION!
NEVER DREAMT HE'D DOWN FOUR BOTTLES SO QUICKLY!
YOU SHOULDN'T HAVE HAD YOUR CREATURES ATTACK MY FRIENDS.
YOU MUST BELIEVE ME, NO HARM WAS INTENDED!
BUT YOU DID LURE US HERE.
NOT TO HURT YOU! I KNEW THE BEHEMOTHS WERE NO MATCH FOR YOUR LARGE FRIEND!
THEN WHAT WAS THE PURPOSE FOR ALL THESE MACHINATIONS?
TO BEFRIEND YOU!
I WISH TO BECOME YOUR ALLY!

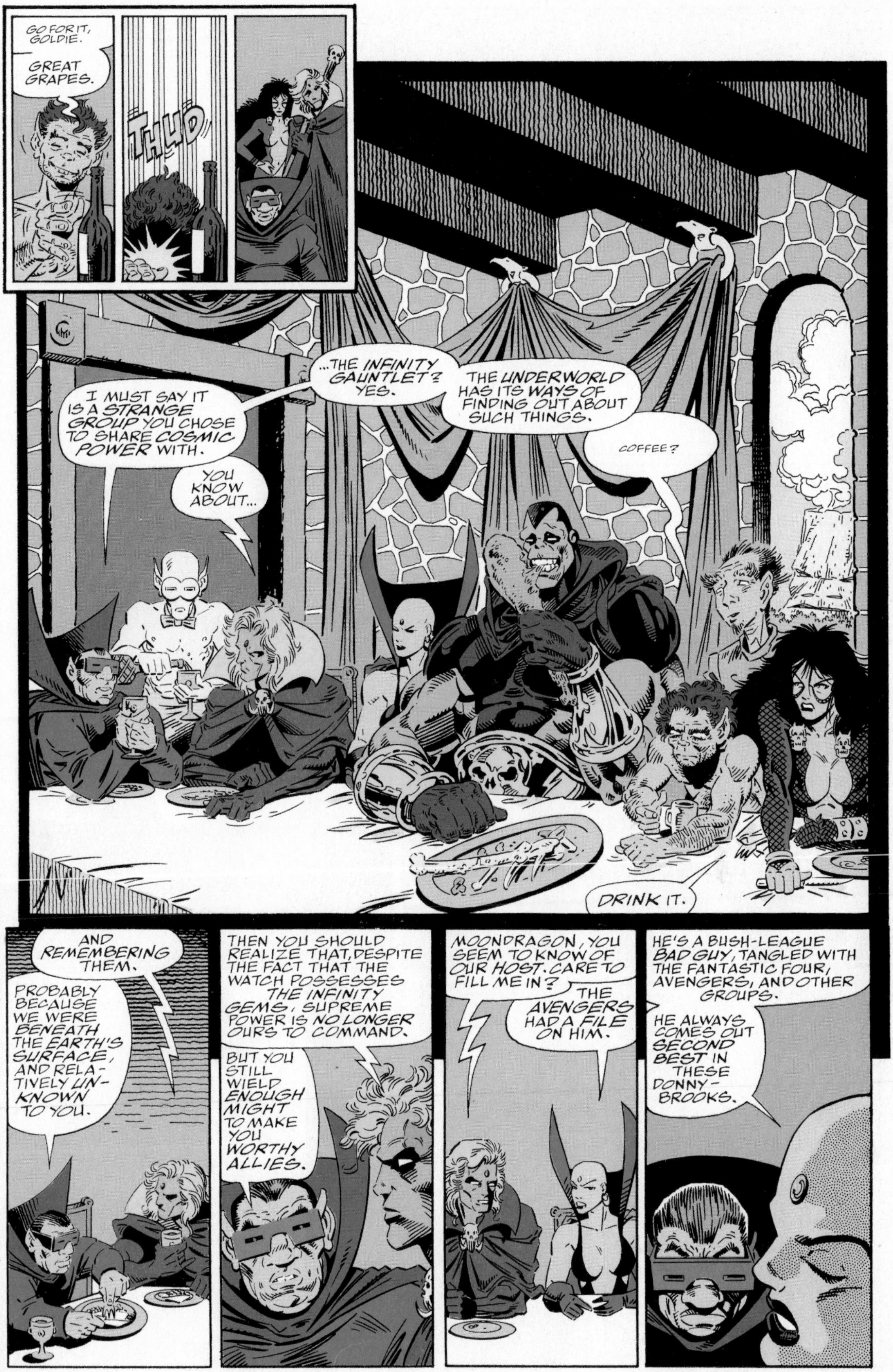
GO FOR IT, GOLDIE.
GREAT GRAPES.
THUD
...THE INFINITY GAUNTLET? YES.
THE UNDERWORLD HAS ITS WAYS OF FINDING OUT ABOUT SUCH THINGS.
I MUST SAY IT IS A STRANGE GROUP YOU CHOSE TO SHARE COSMIC POWER WITH.
YOU KNOW ABOUT...
COFFEE?
DRINK IT.
AND REMEMBERING THEM.
PROBABLY BECAUSE WE WERE BENEATH THE EARTH'S SURFACE, AND RELATIVELY UNKNOWN TO YOU.
THEN YOU SHOULD REALIZE THAT, DESPITE THE FACT THAT THE WATCH POSSESSES THE INFINITY GEMS, SUPREME POWER IS NO LONGER OURS TO COMMAND.
BUT YOU STILL WIELD ENOUGH MIGHT TO MAKE YOU WORTHY ALLIES.
MOONDRAGON, YOU SEEM TO KNOW OF OUR HOST. CARE TO FILL ME IN?
THE AVENGERS HAD A FILE ON HIM.
HE'S A BUSH-LEAGUE BAD GUY, TANGLED WITH THE FANTASTIC FOUR, AVENGERS, AND OTHER GROUPS.
HE ALWAYS COMES OUT SECOND BEST IN THESE DONNYBROOKS.

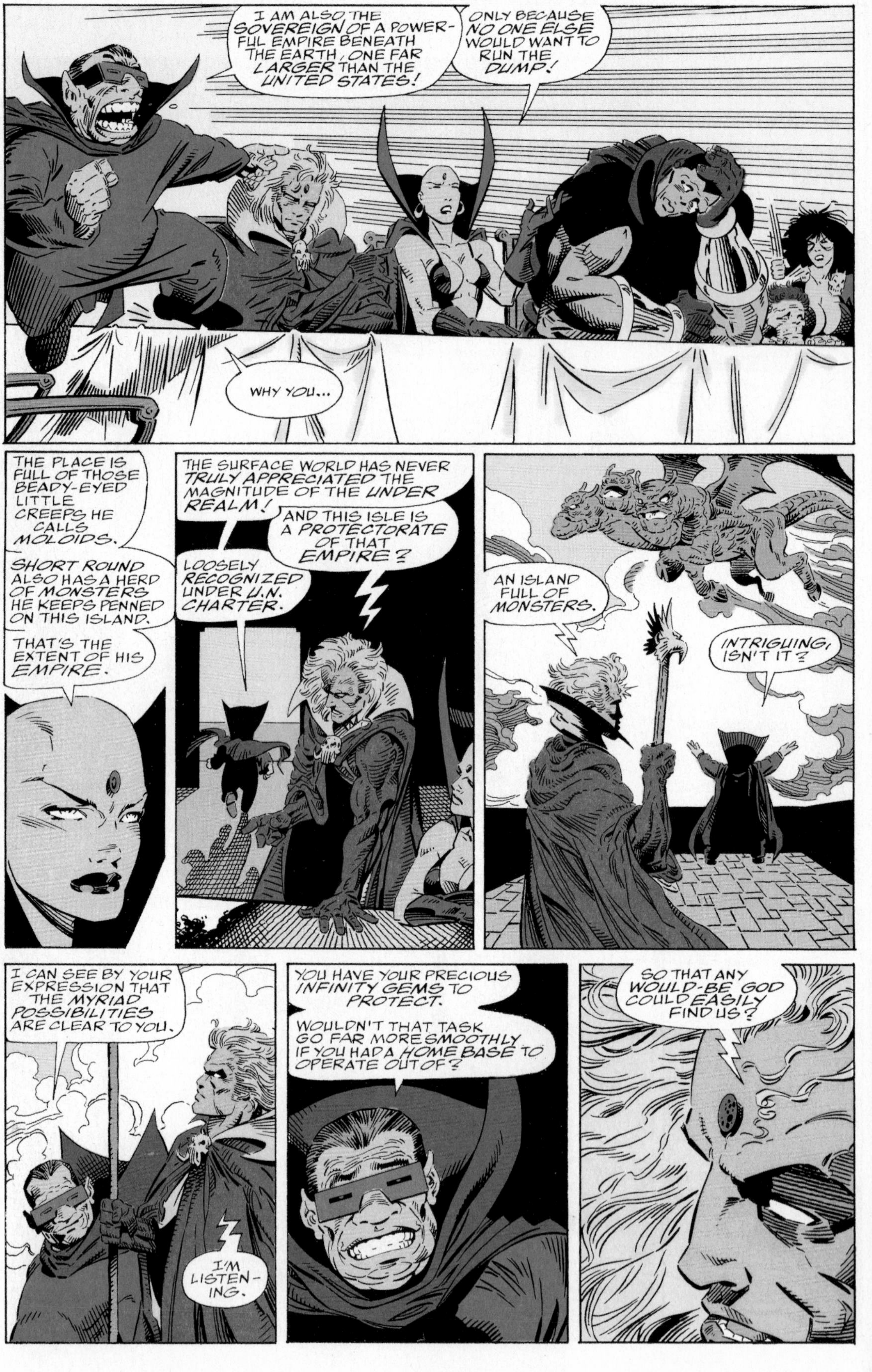
I AM ALSO THE SOVEREIGN OF A POWERFUL EMPIRE BENEATH THE EARTH, ONE FAR LARGER THAN THE UNITED STATES!
ONLY BECAUSE NO ONE ELSE WOULD WANT TO RUN THE DUMP!
WHY YOU...
THE PLACE IS FULL OF THOSE BEADY-EYED LITTLE CREEPS HE CALLS MOLOIDS.
SHORT ROUND ALSO HAS A HERD OF MONSTERS HE KEEPS PENNED ON THIS ISLAND.
THAT'S THE EXTENT OF HIS EMPIRE.
THE SURFACE WORLD HAS NEVER TRULY APPRECIATED THE MAGNITUDE OF THE UNDER REALM!
AND THIS ISLE IS A PROTECTORATE OF THAT EMPIRE?
LOOSELY RECOGNIZED UNDER U.N. CHARTER.
AN ISLAND FULL OF MONSTERS.
INTRIGUING, ISN'T IT?
I CAN SEE BY YOUR EXPRESSION THAT THE MYRIAD POSSIBILITIES ARE CLEAR TO YOU.
I'M LISTENING.
YOU HAVE YOUR PRECIOUS INFINITY GEMS TO PROTECT.
WOULDN'T THAT TASK GO FAR MORE SMOOTHLY IF YOU HAD A HOME BASE TO OPERATE OUT OF?
SO THAT ANY WOULD-BE GOD COULD EASILY FIND US?

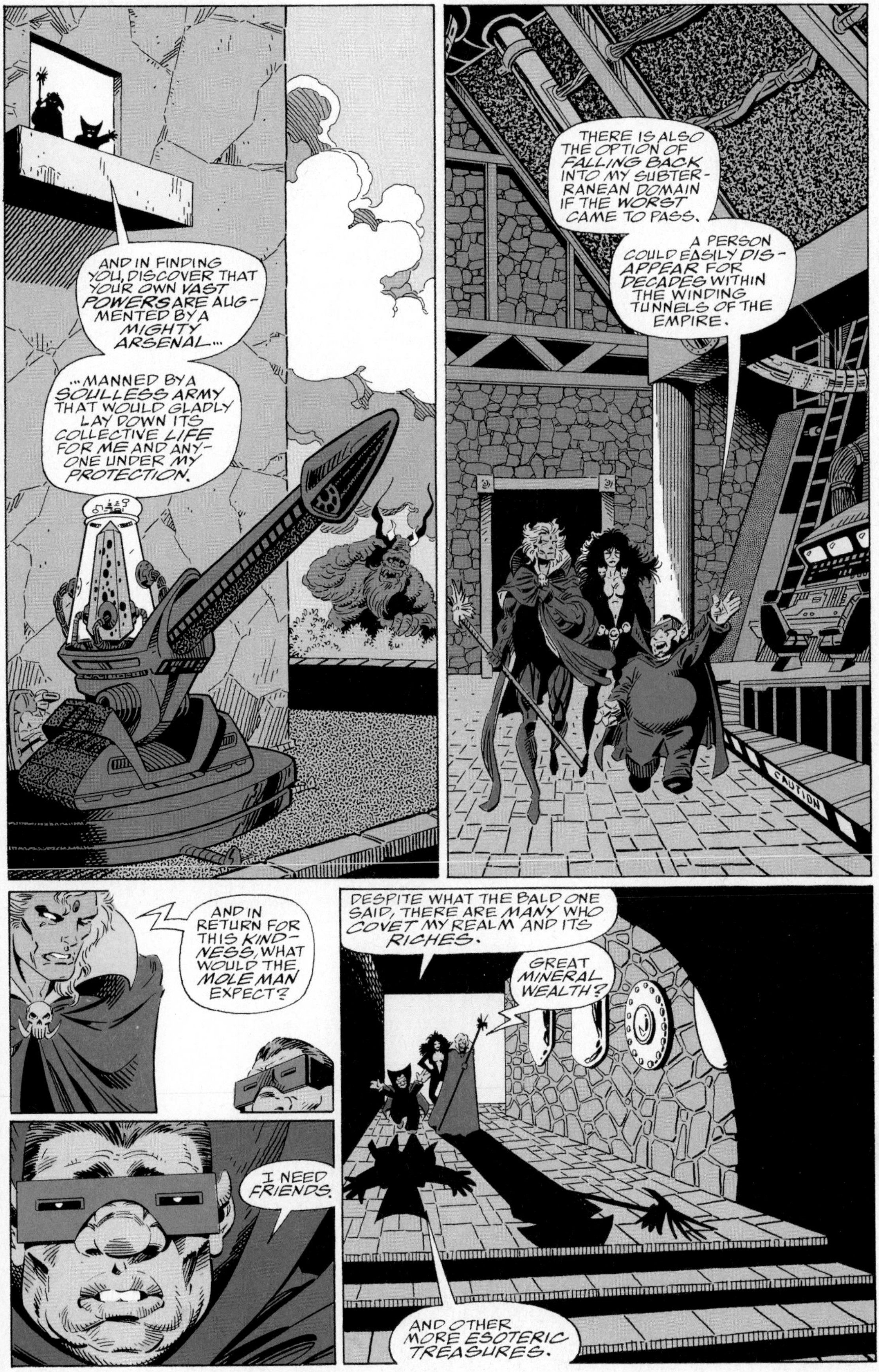
AND IN FINDING YOU, DISCOVER THAT YOUR OWN VAST POWERS ARE AUGMENTED BY A MIGHTY ARSENAL...
...MANNED BY A SOULLESS ARMY THAT WOULD GLADLY LAY DOWN ITS COLLECTIVE LIFE FOR ME AND ANYONE UNDER MY PROTECTION.
THERE IS ALSO THE OPTION OF FALLING BACK INTO MY SUBTERRANEAN DOMAIN IF THE WORST CAME TO PASS.
A PERSON COULD EASILY DISAPPEAR FOR DECADES WITHIN THE WINDING TUNNELS OF THE EMPIRE.
CAUTION
AND IN RETURN FOR THIS KINDNESS, WHAT WOULD THE MOLE MAN EXPECT?
I NEED FRIENDS.
DESPITE WHAT THE BALD ONE SAID, THERE ARE MANY WHO COVET MY REALM AND ITS RICHES.
GREAT MINERAL WEALTH?
AND OTHER MORE ESOTERIC TREASURES.

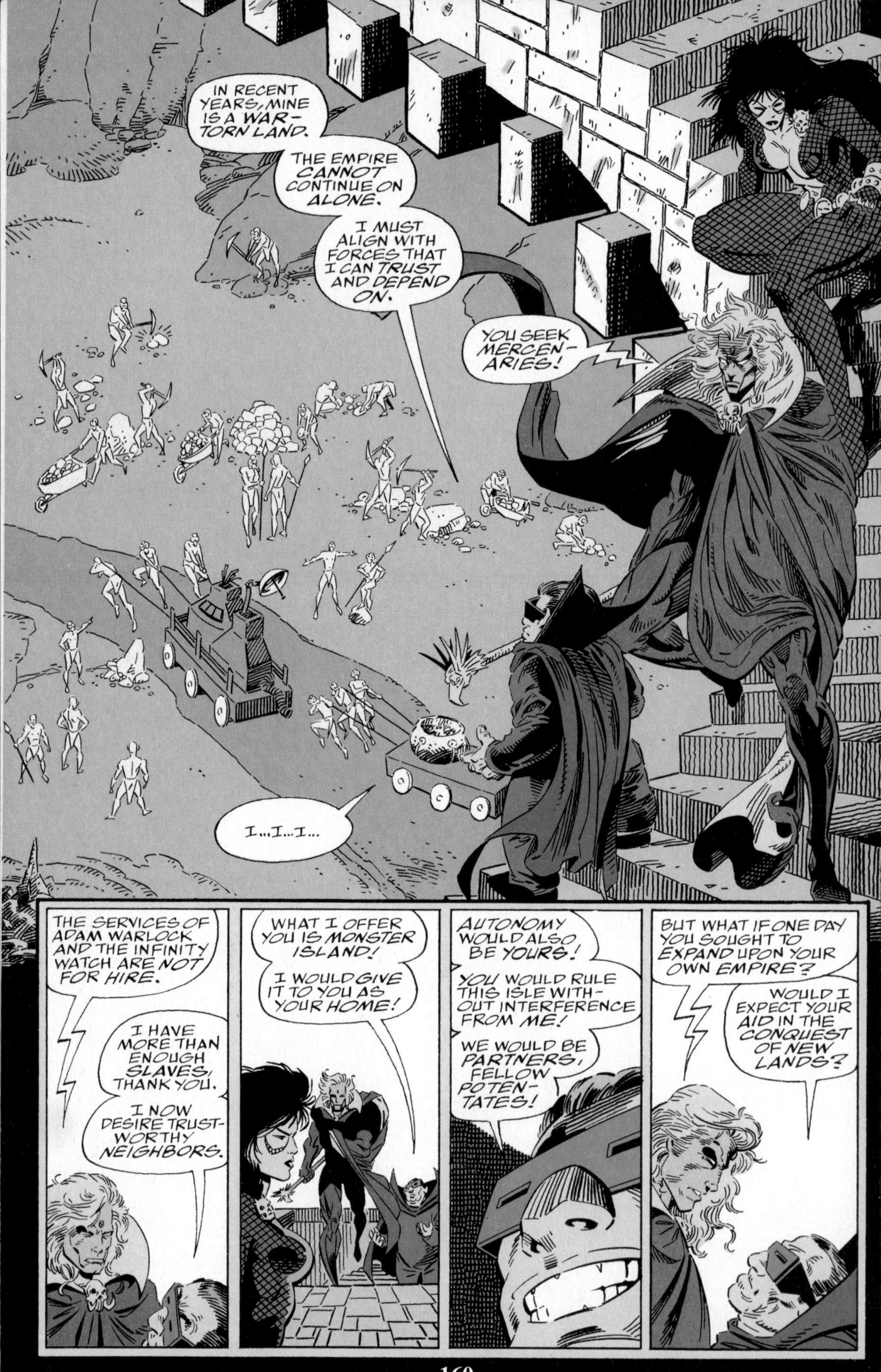
IN RECENT YEARS, MINE IS A WAR-TORN LAND.
THE EMPIRE CANNOT CONTINUE ON ALONE.
I MUST ALIGN WITH FORCES THAT I CAN TRUST AND DEPEND ON.
YOU SEEK MERCEN-ARIES!
I...I...I...
THE SERVICES OF ADAM WARLOCK AND THE INFINITY WATCH ARE NOT FOR HIRE.
I HAVE MORE THAN ENOUGH SLAVES, THANK YOU.
I NOW DESIRE TRUST-WORTHY NEIGHBORS.
WHAT I OFFER YOU IS MONSTER ISLAND!
I WOULD GIVE IT TO YOU AS YOUR HOME!
AUTONOMY WOULD ALSO BE YOURS!
YOU WOULD RULE THIS ISLE WITH-OUT INTERFERENCE FROM ME!
WE WOULD BE PARTNERS, FELLOW POTEN-TATES!
BUT WHAT IF ONE DAY YOU SOUGHT TO EXPAND UPON YOUR OWN EMPIRE?
WOULD I EXPECT YOUR AID IN THE CONQUEST OF NEW LANDS?

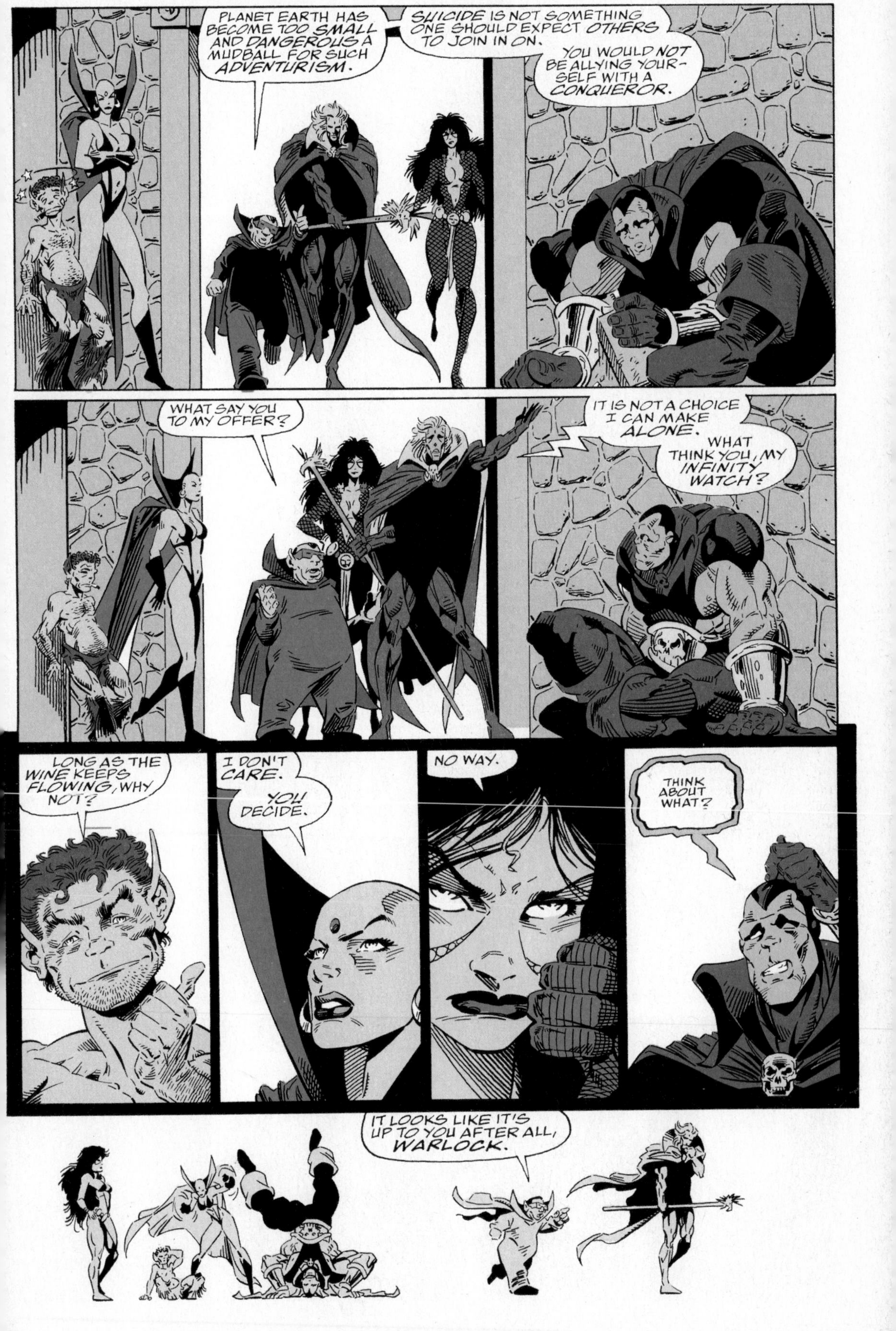
PLANET EARTH HAS BECOME TOO SMALL AND DANGEROUS A MUDBALL FOR SUCH ADVENTURISM.
SUICIDE IS NOT SOMETHING ONE SHOULD EXPECT OTHERS TO JOIN IN ON.
YOU WOULD NOT BE ALLYING YOURSELF WITH A CONQUEROR.
WHAT SAY YOU TO MY OFFER?
IT IS NOT A CHOICE I CAN MAKE ALONE.
WHAT THINK YOU, MY INFINITY WATCH?
LONG AS THE WINE KEEPS FLOWING, WHY NOT?
I DON'T CARE.
YOU DECIDE.
NO WAY.
THINK ABOUT WHAT?
IT LOOKS LIKE IT'S UP TO YOU AFTER ALL, WARLOCK.

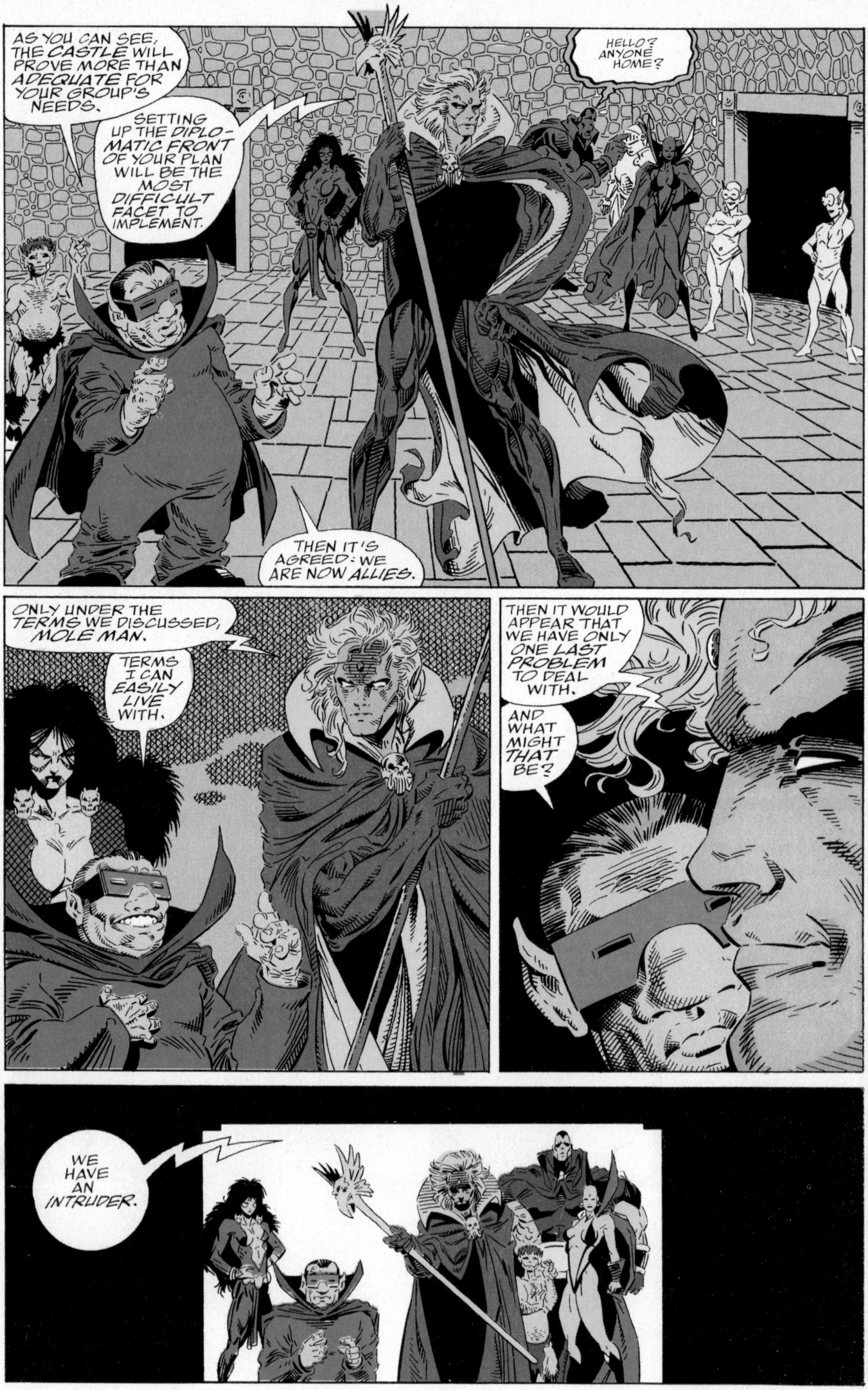
AS YOU CAN SEE, THE CASTLE WILL PROVE MORE THAN ADEQUATE FOR YOUR GROUP'S NEEDS.
SETTING UP THE DIPLOMATIC FRONT OF YOUR PLAN WILL BE THE MOST DIFFICULT FACET TO IMPLEMENT.
HELLO? ANYONE HOME?
THEN IT'S AGREED: WE ARE NOW ALLIES.
ONLY UNDER THE TERMS WE DISCUSSED, MOLE MAN.
TERMS I CAN EASILY LIVE WITH.
THEN IT WOULD APPEAR THAT WE HAVE ONLY ONE LAST PROBLEM TO DEAL WITH.
AND WHAT MIGHT THAT BE?
WE HAVE AN INTRUDER.

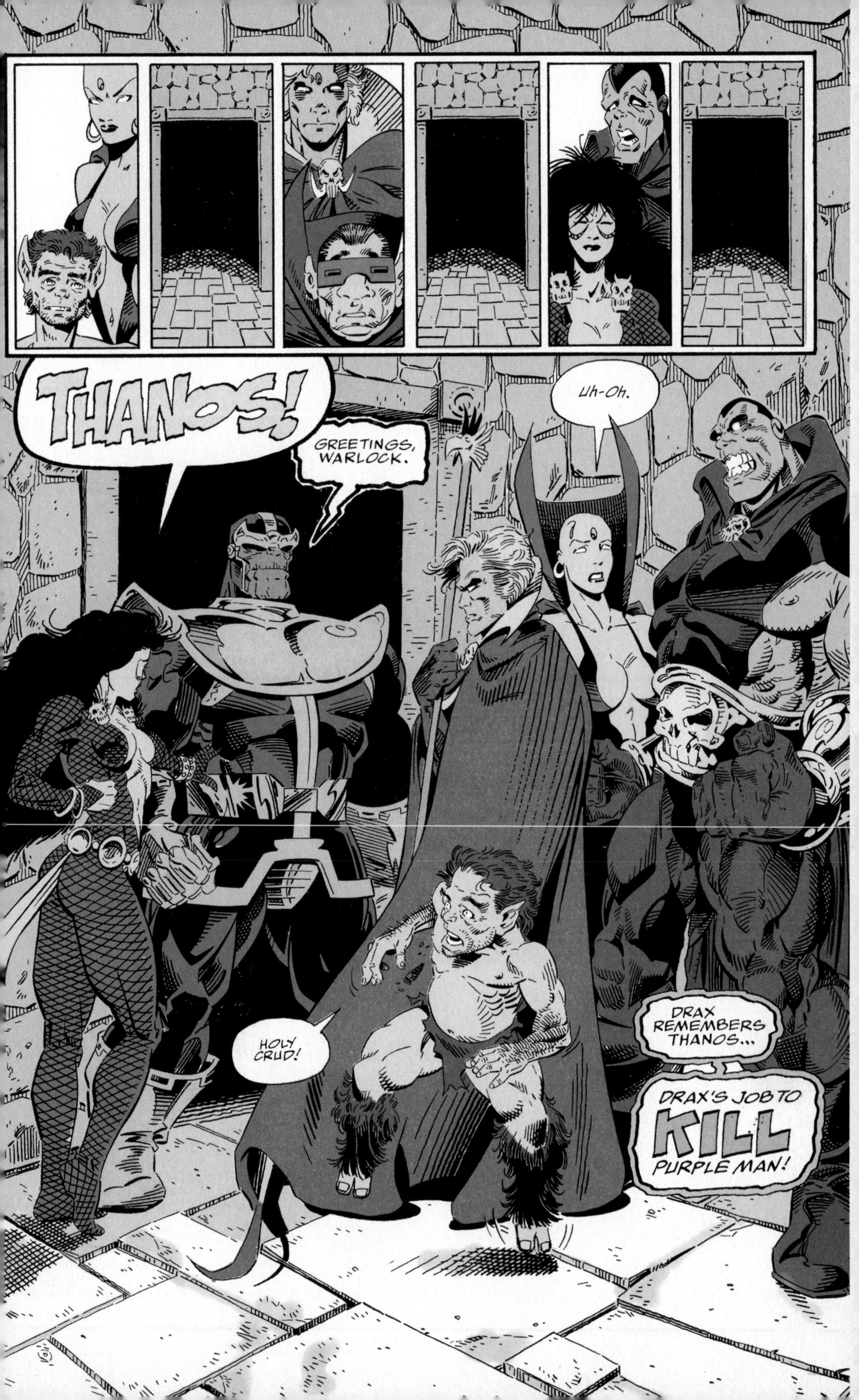
THANOS!
GREETINGS, WARLOCK.
Uh-Oh.
HOLY CRUD!
DRAX REMEMBERS THANOS...
DRAX'S JOB TO KILL PURPLE MAN!

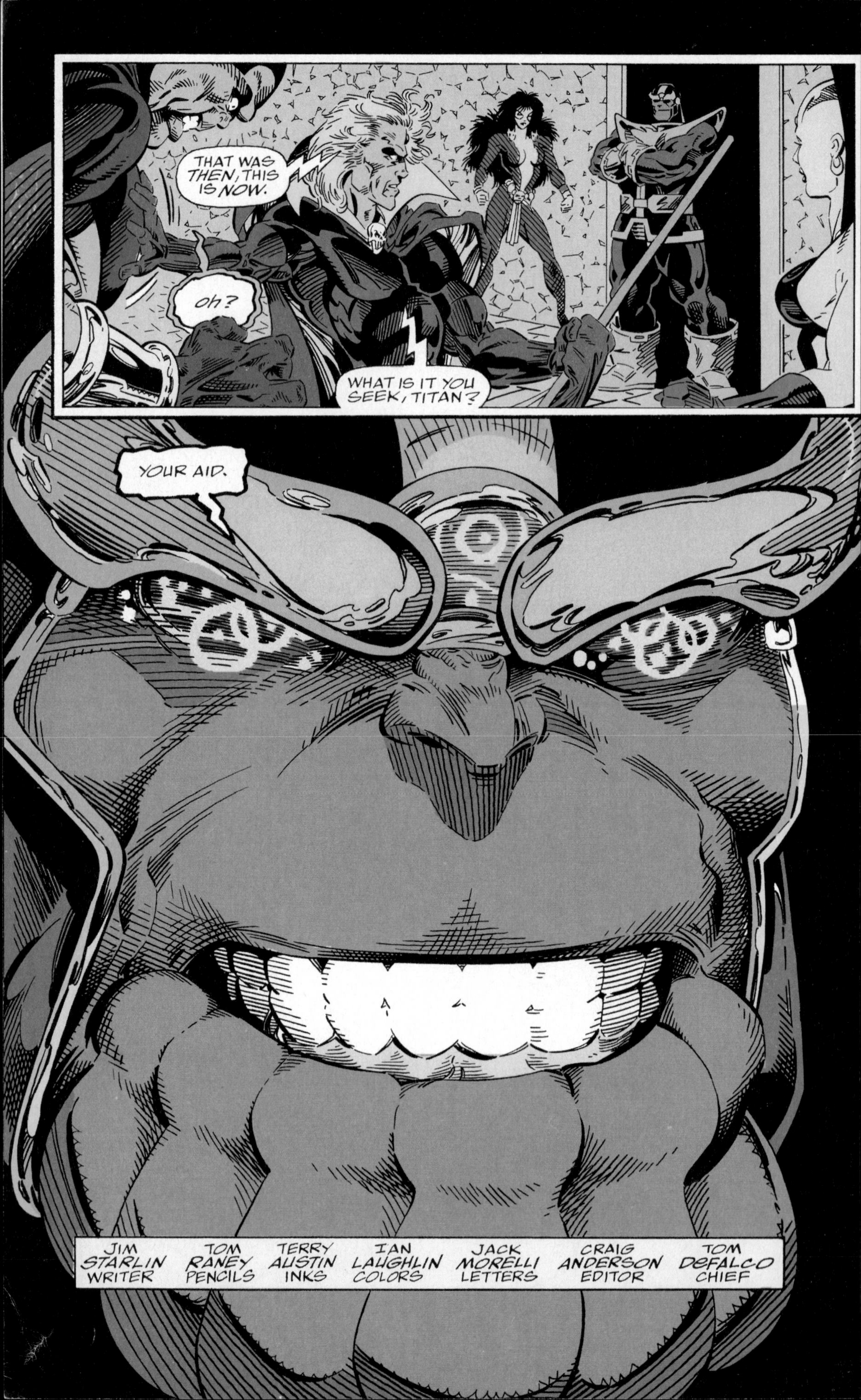
THAT WAS THEN, THIS IS NOW.
oh?
WHAT IS IT YOU SEEK, TITAN?
YOUR AID.
JIM STARLIN WRITER
TOM RANEY PENCILS
TERRY AUSTIN INKS
IAN LAUGHLIN COLORS
JACK MORELLI LETTERS
CRAIG ANDERSON EDITOR
TOM DEFALCO CHIEF

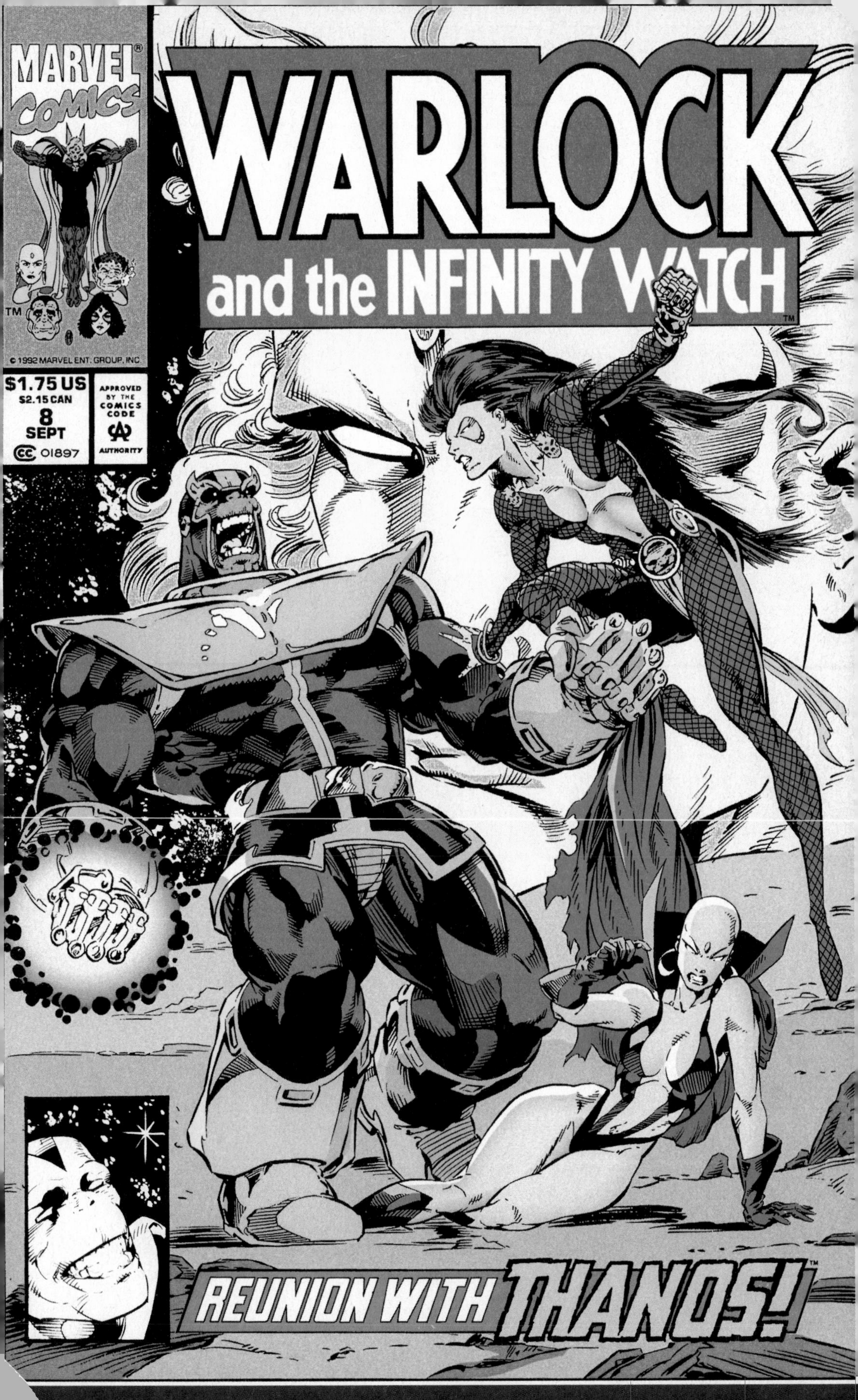
MARVEL® COMICS
WARLOCK and the INFINITY WATCH™
© 1992 MARVEL ENT. GROUP, INC.
$1.75 US
$2.15 CAN
8
SEPT
APPROVED BY THE COMICS CODE AUTHORITY
REUNION WITH THANOS!

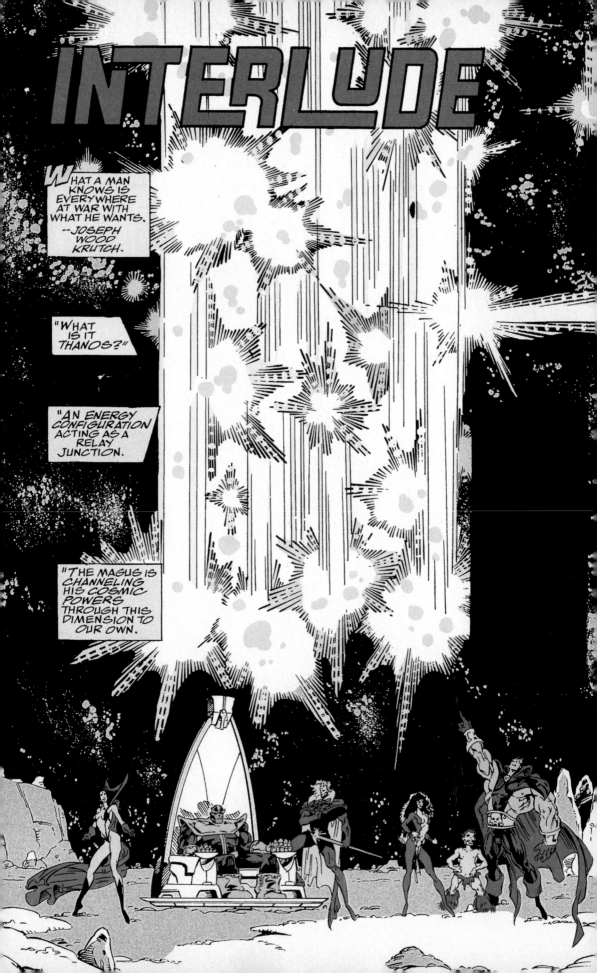

INTERLUDE

WHAT A MAN KNOWS IS EVERYWHERE AT WAR WITH WHAT HE WANTS.
--JOSEPH WOOD KRUTCH.

"WHAT IS IT THANOS?"

"AN ENERGY CONFIGURATION ACTING AS A RELAY JUNCTION.

"THE MAGUS IS CHANNELING HIS COSMIC POWERS THROUGH THIS DIMENSION TO OUR OWN.

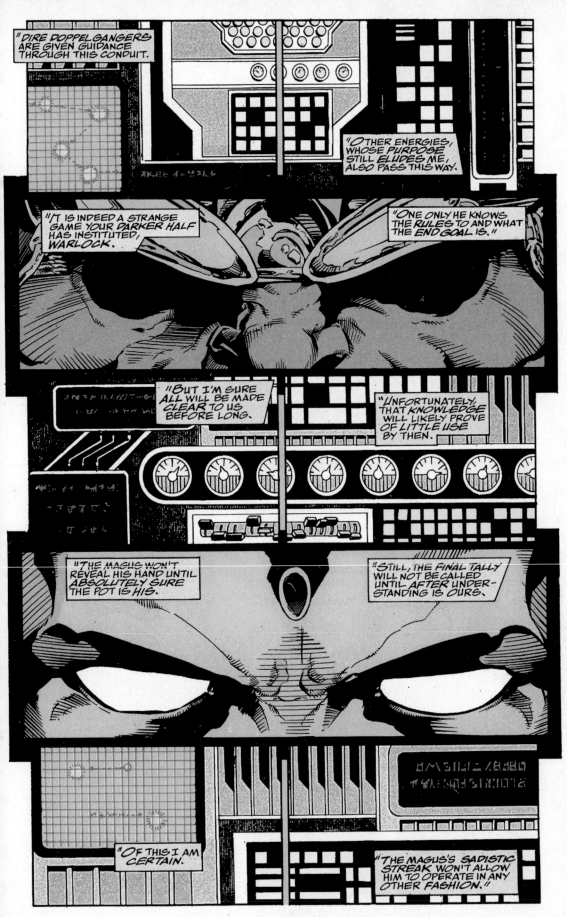

"DIRE DOPPELGANGERS ARE GIVEN GUIDANCE THROUGH THIS CONDUIT."

"OTHER ENERGIES, WHOSE PURPOSE STILL ELUDES ME, ALSO PASS THIS WAY."

"IT IS INDEED A STRANGE GAME YOUR DARKER HALF HAS INSTITUTED, WARLOCK."

"ONE ONLY HE KNOWS THE RULES TO AND WHAT THE END GOAL IS."

"BUT I'M SURE ALL WILL BE MADE CLEAR TO US BEFORE LONG."

"UNFORTUNATELY, THAT KNOWLEDGE WILL LIKELY PROVE OF LITTLE USE BY THEN."

"THE MAGUS WON'T REVEAL HIS HAND UNTIL ABSOLUTELY SURE THE POT IS HIS."

"STILL, THE FINAL TALLY WILL NOT BE CALLED UNTIL AFTER UNDERSTANDING IS OURS."

"OF THIS I AM CERTAIN."

"THE MAGUS'S SADISTIC STREAK WON'T ALLOW HIM TO OPERATE IN ANY OTHER FASHION."

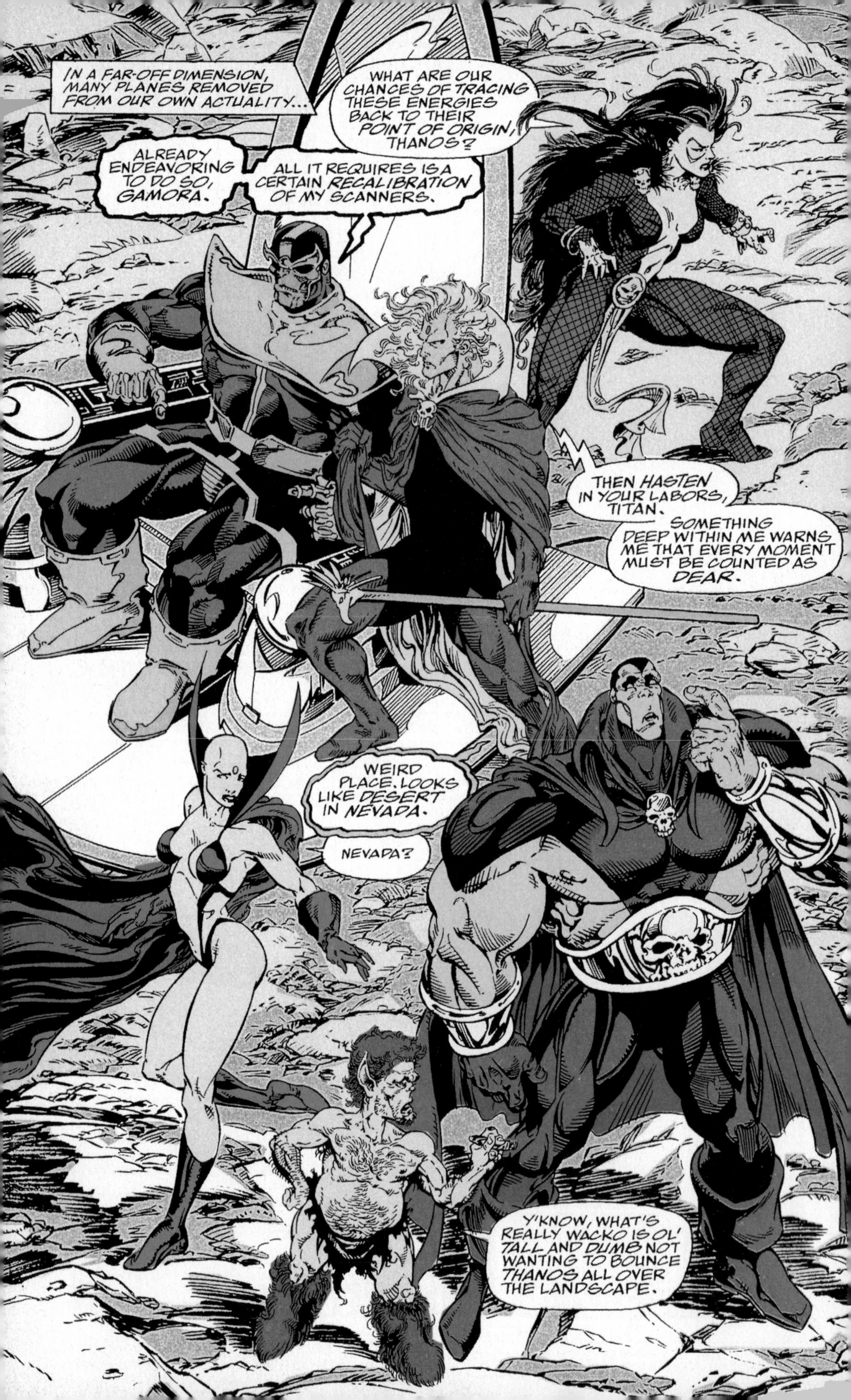
IN A FAR-OFF DIMENSION, MANY PLANES REMOVED FROM OUR OWN ACTUALITY...
WHAT ARE OUR CHANCES OF TRACING THESE ENERGIES BACK TO THEIR POINT OF ORIGIN, THANOS?
ALREADY ENDEAVORING TO DO SO, GAMORA.
ALL IT REQUIRES IS A CERTAIN RECALIBRATION OF MY SCANNERS.
THEN HASTEN IN YOUR LABORS, TITAN.
SOMETHING DEEP WITHIN ME WARNS ME THAT EVERY MOMENT MUST BE COUNTED AS DEAR.
WEIRD PLACE. LOOKS LIKE DESERT IN NEVADA.
NEVADA?
Y'KNOW, WHAT'S REALLY WACKO IS OL' TALL AND DUMB NOT WANTING TO BOUNCE THANOS ALL OVER THE LANDSCAPE.

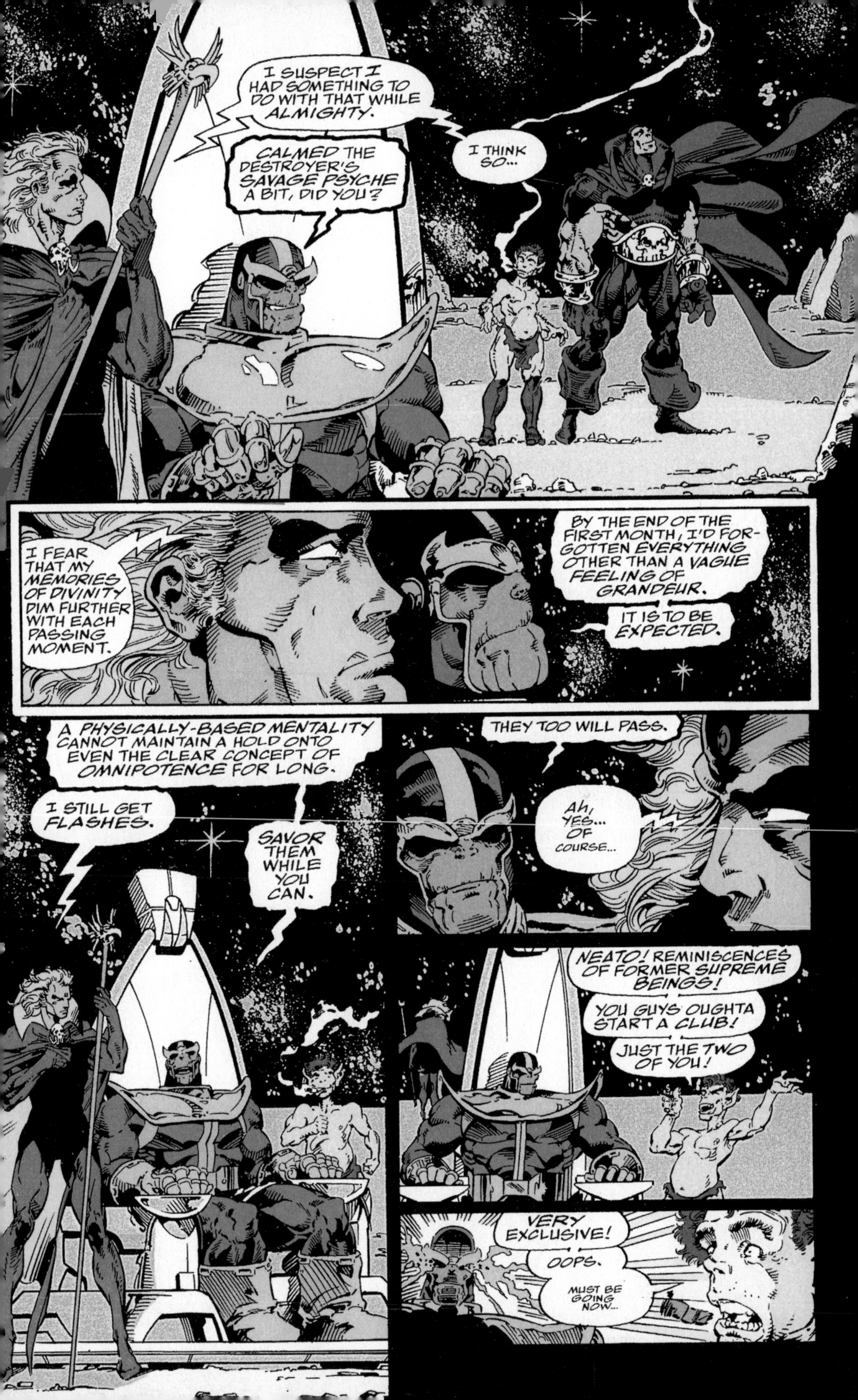
I SUSPECT I HAD SOMETHING TO DO WITH THAT WHILE ALMIGHTY.
CALMED THE DESTROYER'S SAVAGE PSYCHE A BIT, DID YOU?
I THINK SO...
I FEAR THAT MY MEMORIES OF DIVINITY DIM FURTHER WITH EACH PASSING MOMENT.
BY THE END OF THE FIRST MONTH, I'D FORGOTTEN EVERYTHING OTHER THAN A VAGUE FEELING OF GRANDEUR.
IT IS TO BE EXPECTED.
A PHYSICALLY-BASED MENTALITY CANNOT MAINTAIN A HOLD ONTO EVEN THE CLEAR CONCEPT OF OMNIPOTENCE FOR LONG.
I STILL GET FLASHES.
SAVOR THEM WHILE YOU CAN.
THEY TOO WILL PASS.
AH, YES... OF COURSE...
NEATO! REMINISCENCES OF FORMER SUPREME BEINGS!
YOU GUYS OUGHTA START A CLUB!
JUST THE TWO OF YOU!
VERY EXCLUSIVE!
OOPS.
MUST BE GOING NOW...

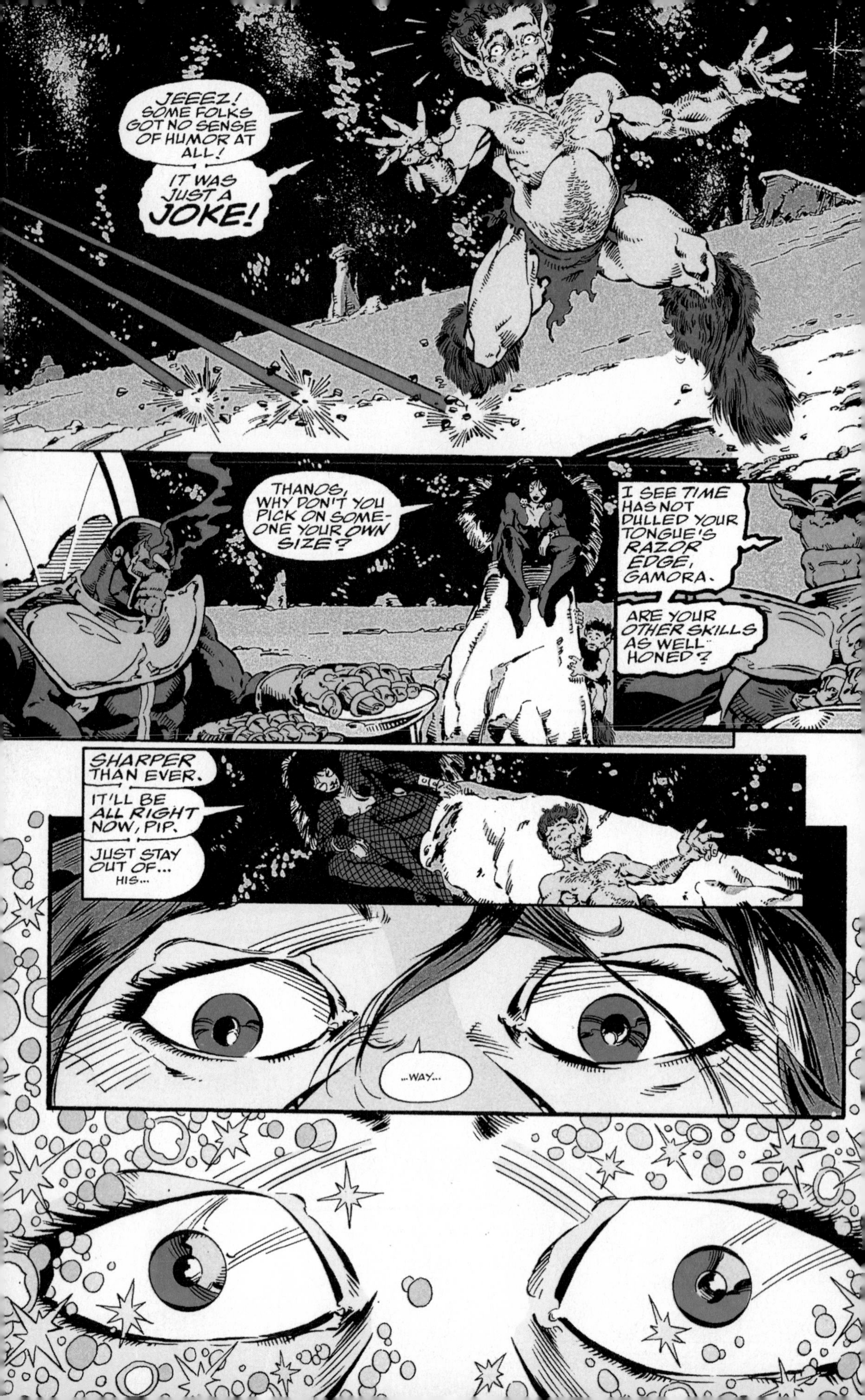
JEEEZ! SOME FOLKS GOT NO SENSE OF HUMOR AT ALL!
IT WAS JUST A JOKE!
THANOS, WHY DON'T YOU PICK ON SOMEONE YOUR OWN SIZE?
I SEE TIME HAS NOT DULLED YOUR TONGUE'S RAZOR EDGE, GAMORA.
ARE YOUR OTHER SKILLS AS WELL HONED?
SHARPER THAN EVER.
IT'LL BE ALL RIGHT NOW, PIP.
JUST STAY OUT OF... HIS...
...WAY...

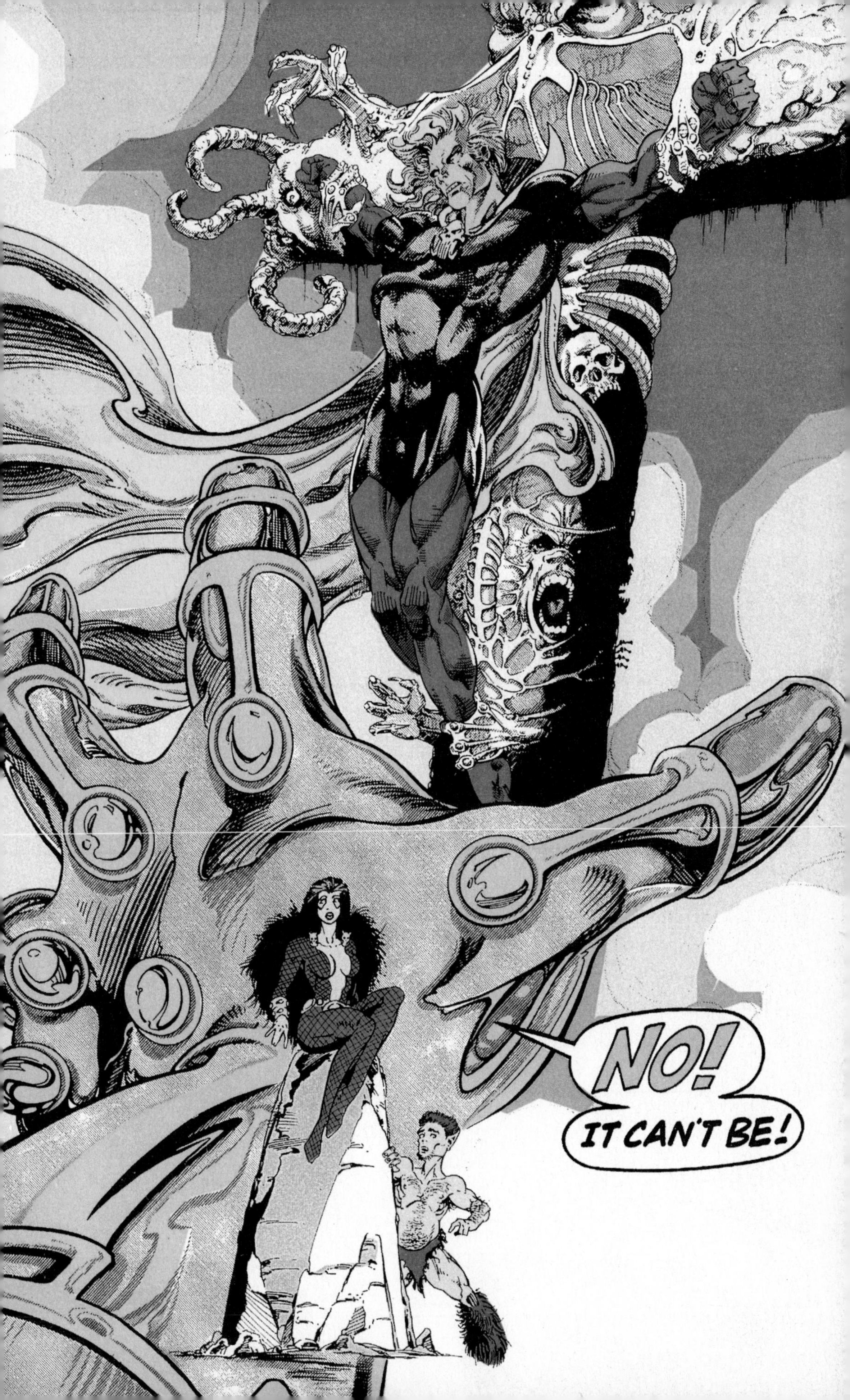
NO!
IT CAN'T BE!

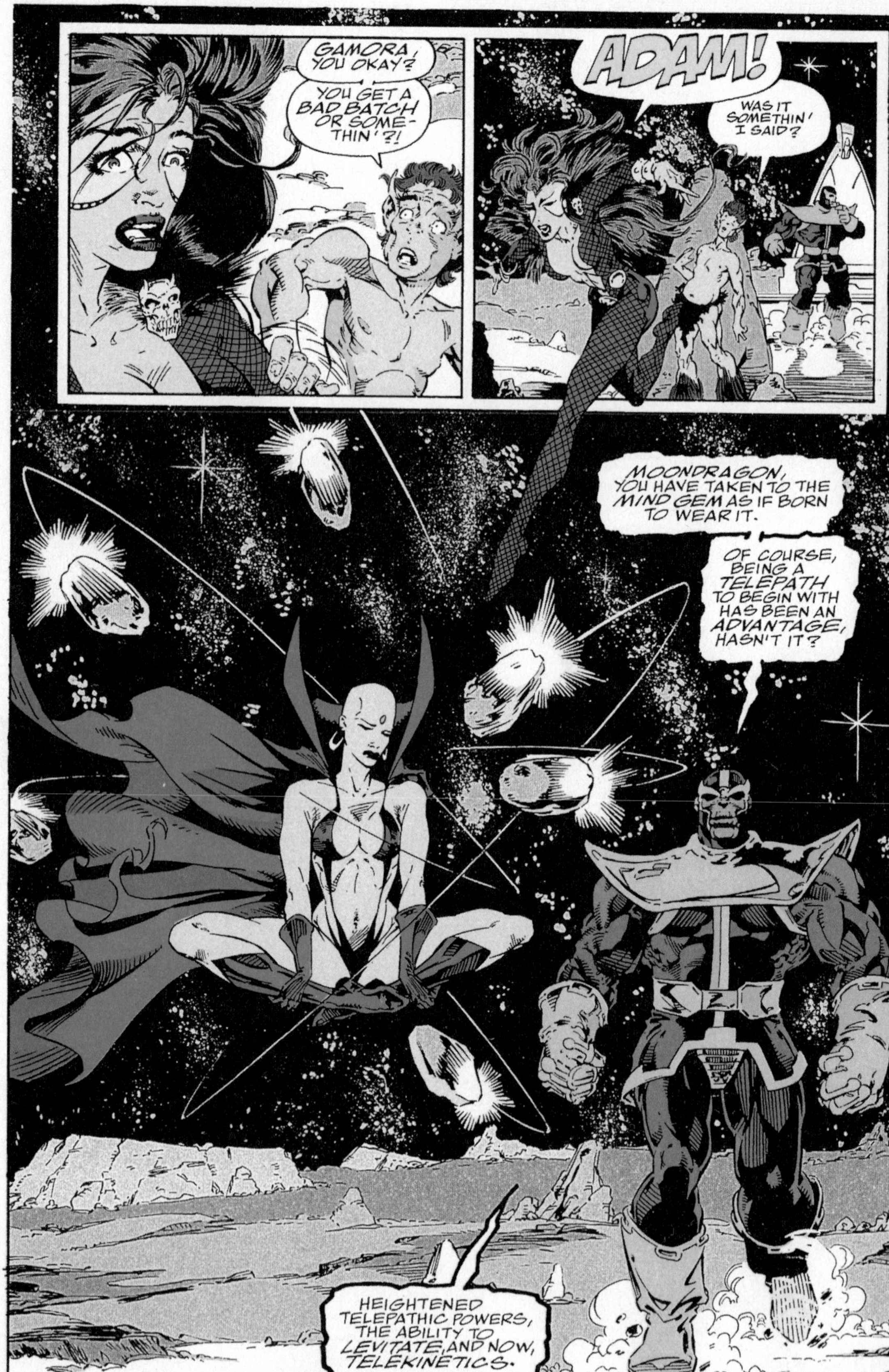
GAMORA, YOU OKAY?
YOU GET A BAD BATCH OR SOMETHIN'?!
ADAM!
WAS IT SOMETHIN' I SAID?
MOONDRAGON, YOU HAVE TAKEN TO THE MIND GEM AS IF BORN TO WEAR IT.
OF COURSE, BEING A TELEPATH TO BEGIN WITH HAS BEEN AN ADVANTAGE, HASN'T IT?
HEIGHTENED TELEPATHIC POWERS, THE ABILITY TO LEVITATE, AND NOW, TELEKINETICS.

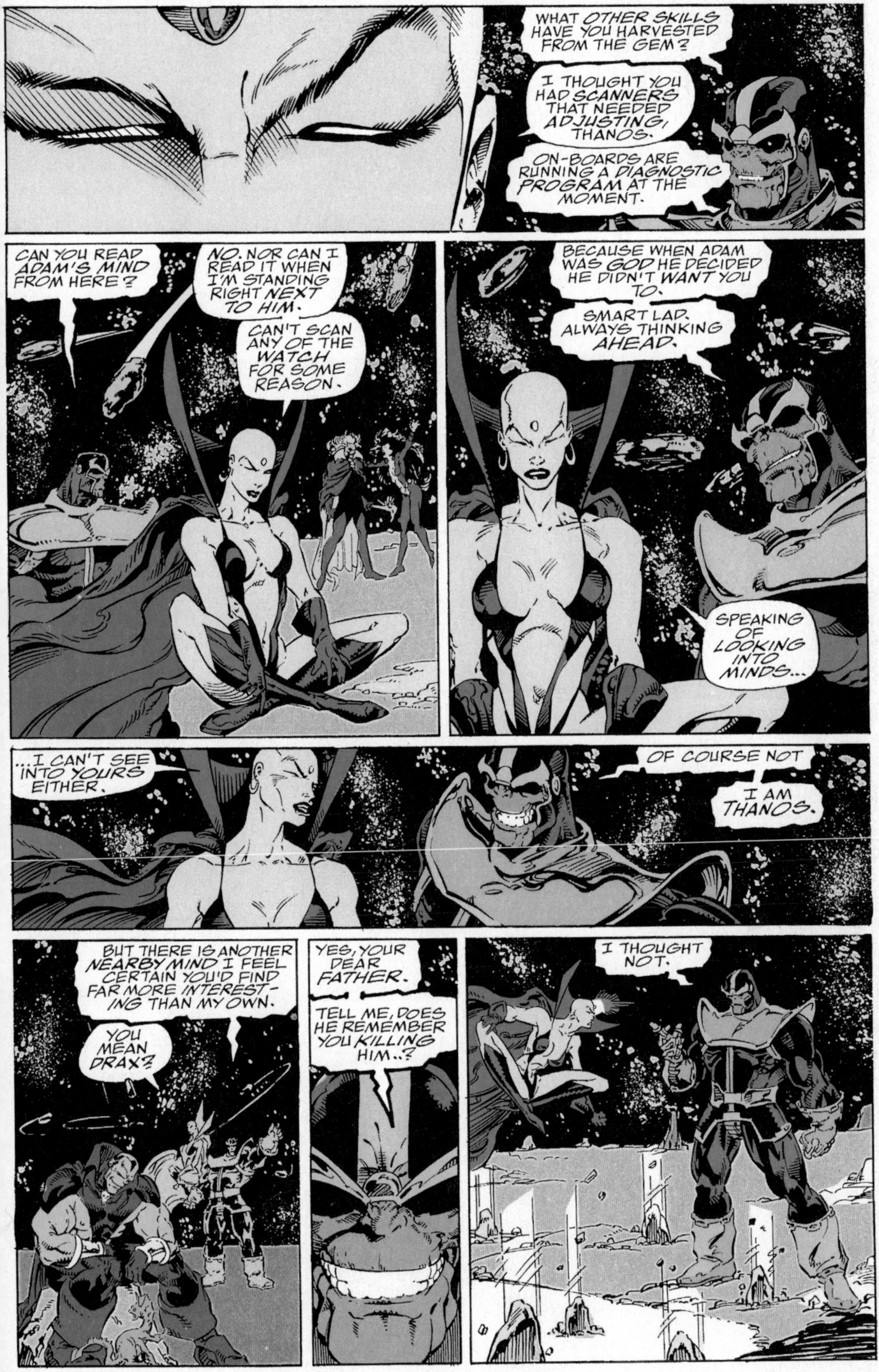
WHAT OTHER SKILLS HAVE YOU HARVESTED FROM THE GEM?
I THOUGHT YOU HAD SCANNERS THAT NEEDED ADJUSTING, THANOS.
ON-BOARDS ARE RUNNING A DIAGNOSTIC PROGRAM AT THE MOMENT.
CAN YOU READ ADAM'S MIND FROM HERE?
NO. NOR CAN I READ IT WHEN I'M STANDING RIGHT NEXT TO HIM.
CAN'T SCAN ANY OF THE WATCH FOR SOME REASON.
BECAUSE WHEN ADAM WAS GOD HE DECIDED HE DIDN'T WANT YOU TO.
SMART LAD. ALWAYS THINKING AHEAD.
SPEAKING OF LOOKING INTO MINDS...
...I CAN'T SEE INTO YOURS EITHER.
OF COURSE NOT
I AM THANOS.
BUT THERE IS ANOTHER NEARBY MIND I FEEL CERTAIN YOU'D FIND FAR MORE INTERESTING THAN MY OWN.
YOU MEAN DRAX?
YES, YOUR DEAR FATHER.
TELL ME, DOES HE REMEMBER YOU KILLING HIM..?
I THOUGHT NOT.

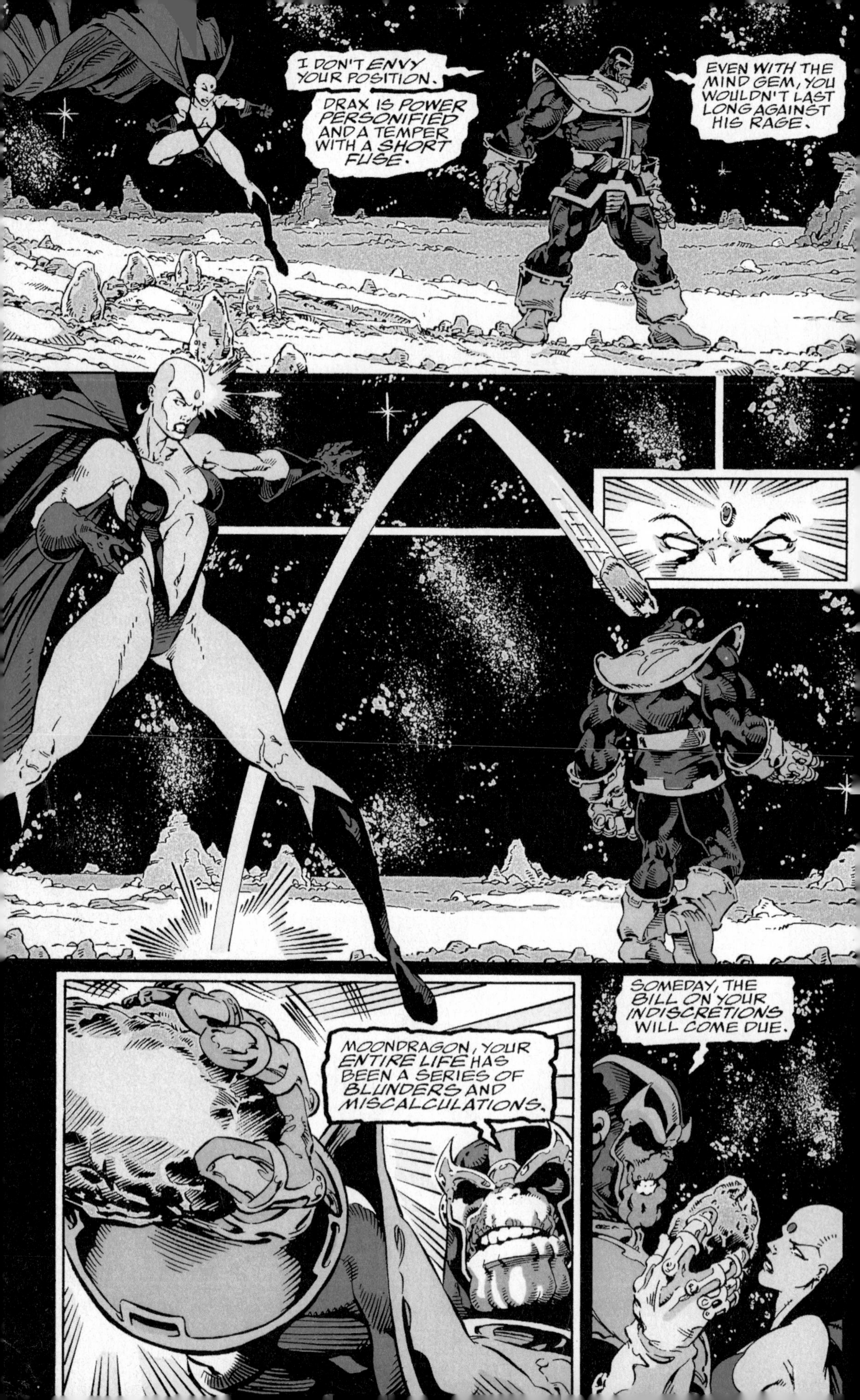
I DON'T ENVY YOUR POSITION.
DRAX IS POWER PERSONIFIED AND A TEMPER WITH A SHORT FUSE.
EVEN WITH THE MIND GEM, YOU WOULDN'T LAST LONG AGAINST HIS RAGE.
MOONDRAGON, YOUR ENTIRE LIFE HAS BEEN A SERIES OF BLUNDERS AND MISCALCULATIONS.
SOMEDAY, THE BILL ON YOUR INDISCRETIONS WILL COME DUE.

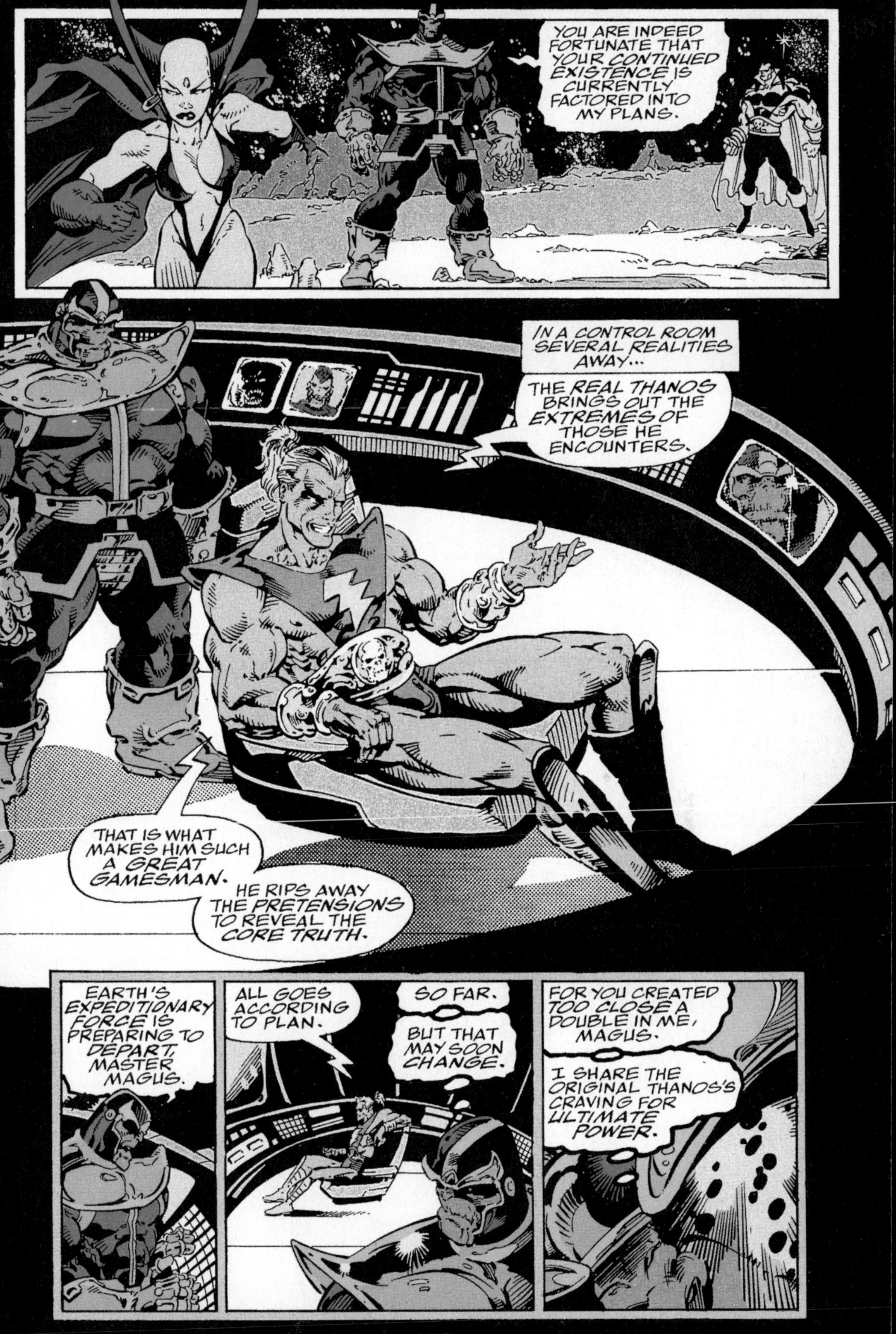
YOU ARE INDEED FORTUNATE THAT YOUR CONTINUED EXISTENCE IS CURRENTLY FACTORED INTO MY PLANS.
IN A CONTROL ROOM SEVERAL REALITIES AWAY...
THE REAL THANOS BRINGS OUT THE EXTREMES OF THOSE HE ENCOUNTERS.
THAT IS WHAT MAKES HIM SUCH A GREAT GAMESMAN.
HE RIPS AWAY THE PRETENSIONS TO REVEAL THE CORE TRUTH.
EARTH'S EXPEDITIONARY FORCE IS PREPARING TO DEPART, MASTER MAGUS.
ALL GOES ACCORDING TO PLAN.
SO FAR.
BUT THAT MAY SOON CHANGE.
FOR YOU CREATED TOO CLOSE A DOUBLE IN ME, MAGUS.
I SHARE THE ORIGINAL THANOS'S CRAVING FOR ULTIMATE POWER.

AND THAT MAY YET PROVE YOU'RE UNDOING.

AN *UNFORESEEN* DEVELOPMENT ON SCREEN #7.

WARLOCK'S *ASTRAL SAMURAI* APPEARS TO BE ACHIEVING A SUBTLE *RELATIONSHIP* WITH HER *TIME GEM!*

HOW *AMUSING.*

I TELL YOU, I CLEARLY SAW A *GAUNTLETED* HAND REACHING OUT TO TOUCH YOU.

INTERESTING. YOU APPEAR TO BE TAPPING INTO THE *INFINITY GEM'S* POWER, GAMORA.

THIS *COMPLICATES* MATTERS.

YOU MEAN I'M ACTUALLY *SEEING* THROUGH *TIME!?*

I BELIEVE SO.

THEN THAT CAN ONLY MEAN THAT THE *INFINITY GAUNTLET* MUST HAVE BEEN WORN BY...

DON'T WORRY ABOUT IT. I'LL HANDLE IT.

YOU'LL HANDLE IT?

YOU WERE HANGING *HELPLESSLY* ON A CROSS, ADAM!

DON'T WALK AWAY FROM ME, MISTER!

ADAM!

176

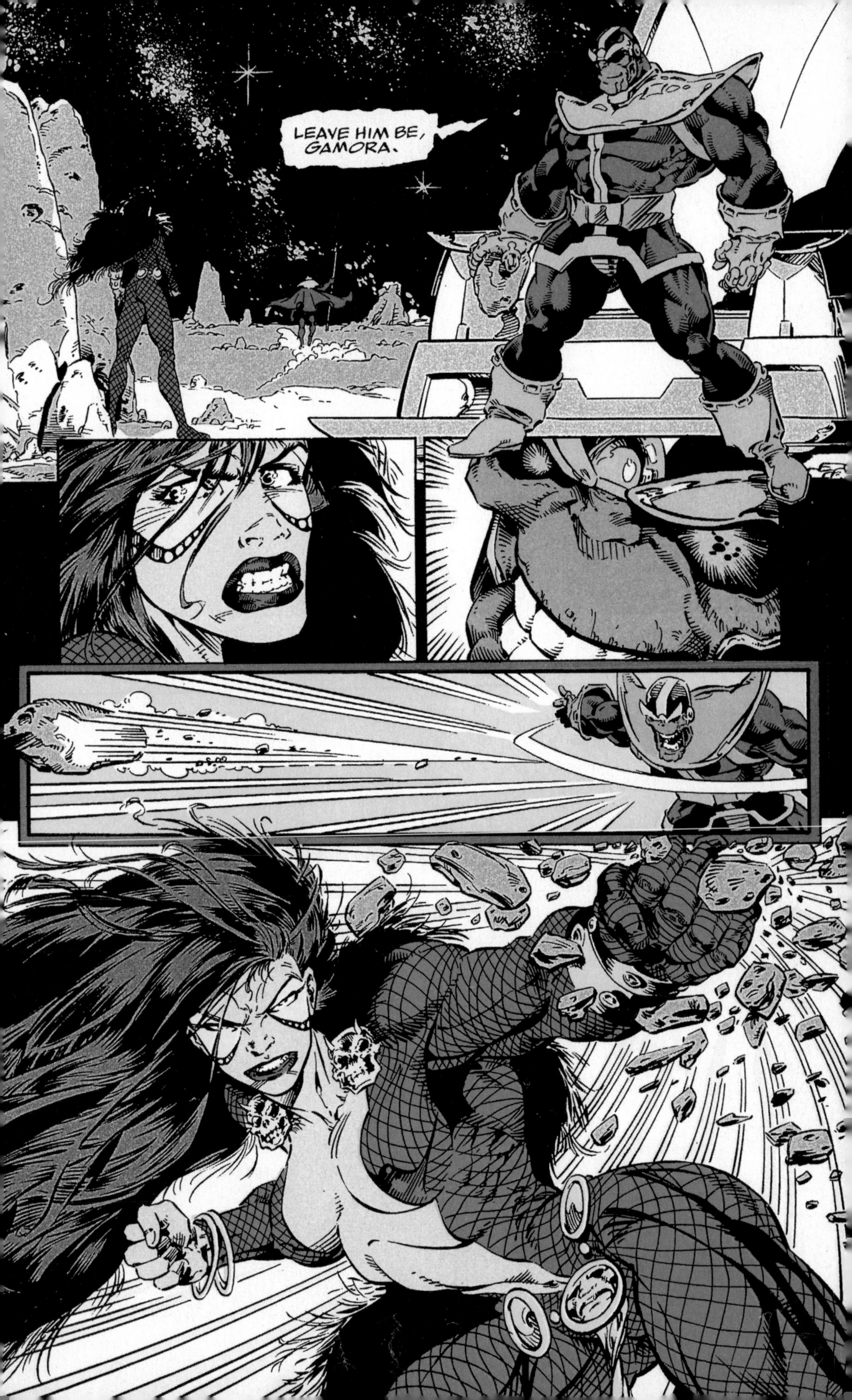
LEAVE HIM BE, GAMORA.

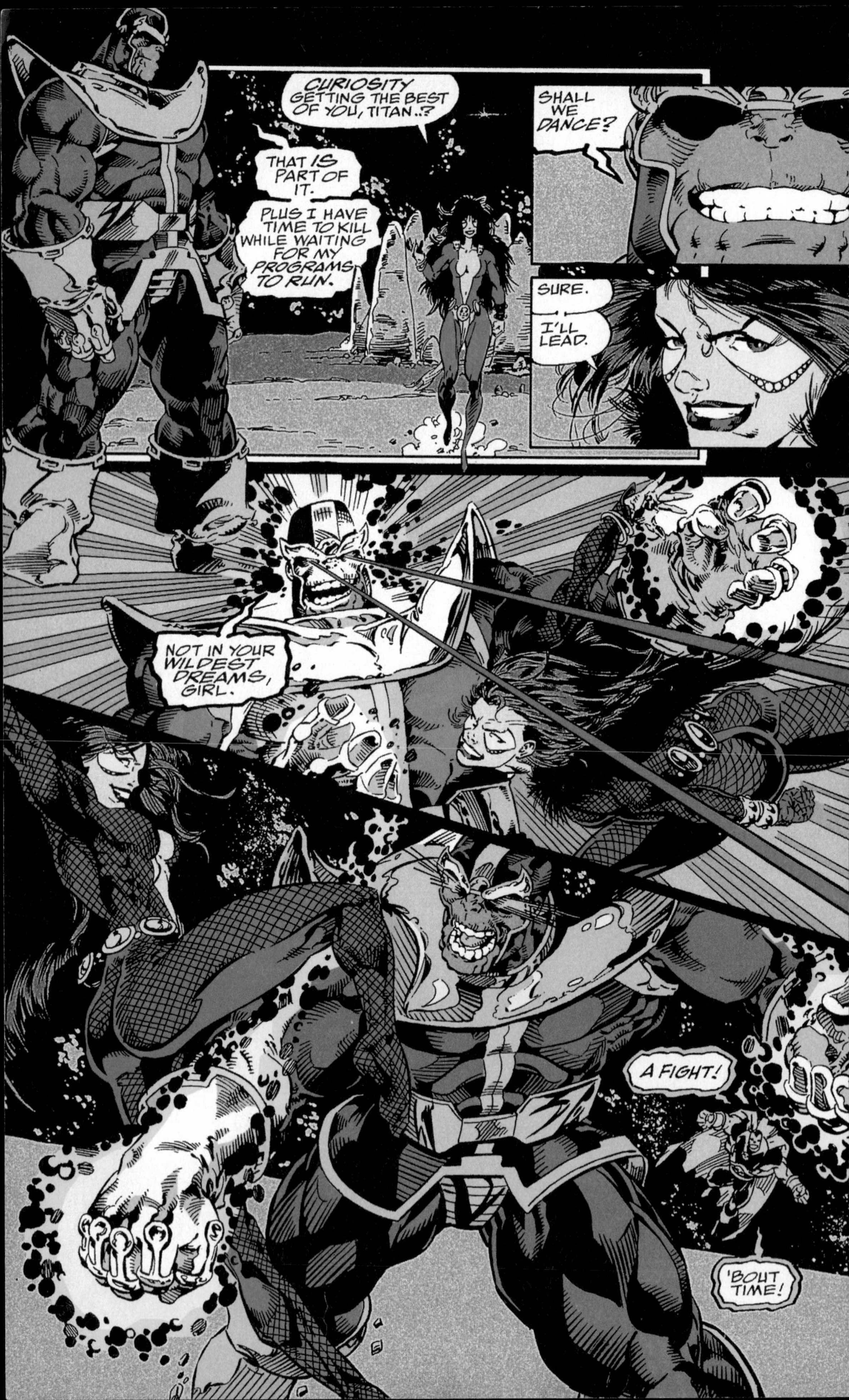
CURIOSITY GETTING THE BEST OF YOU, TITAN..?
THAT IS PART OF IT.
PLUS I HAVE TIME TO KILL WHILE WAITING FOR MY PROGRAMS TO RUN.
SHALL WE DANCE?
SURE.
I'LL LEAD.
NOT IN YOUR WILDEST DREAMS, GIRL.
A FIGHT!
'BOUT TIME!

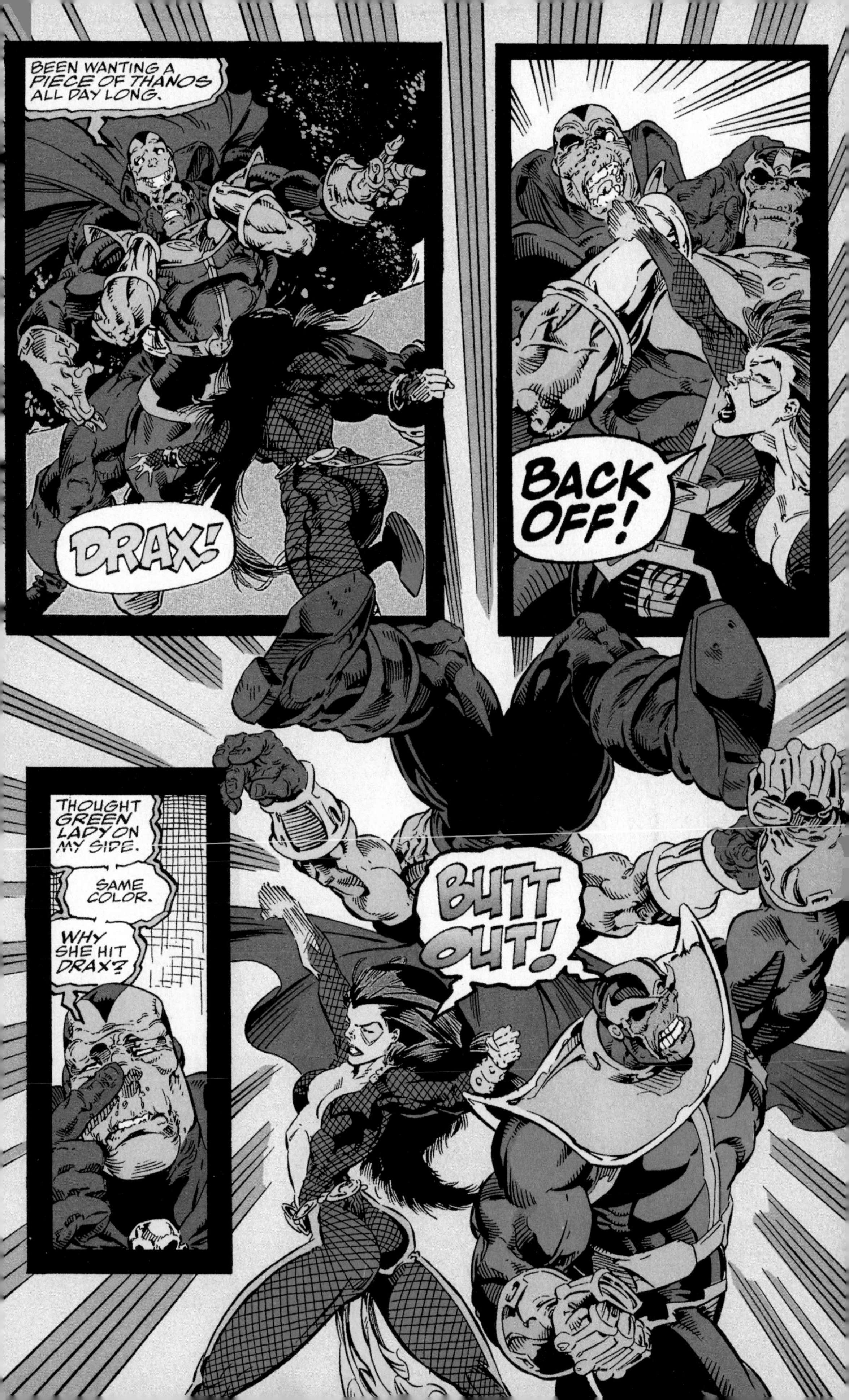
BEEN WANTING A PIECE OF THANOS ALL DAY LONG.
DRAX!
BACK OFF!
THOUGHT GREEN LADY ON MY SIDE.
SAME COLOR.
WHY SHE HIT DRAX?
BUTT OUT!

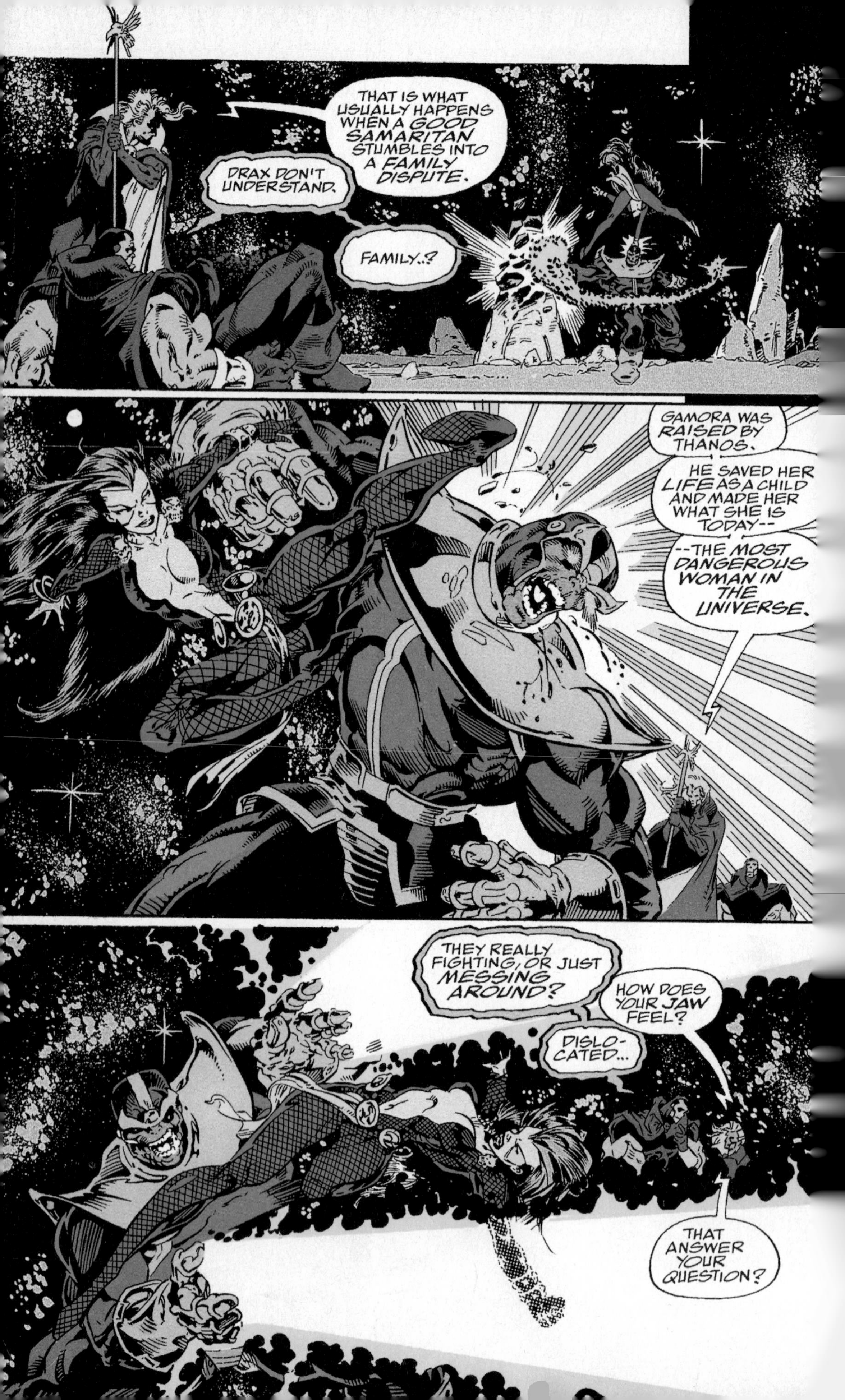

DRAX DON'T UNDERSTAND.
THAT IS WHAT USUALLY HAPPENS WHEN A GOOD SAMARITAN STUMBLES INTO A FAMILY DISPUTE.
FAMILY..?
GAMORA WAS RAISED BY THANOS.
HE SAVED HER LIFE AS A CHILD AND MADE HER WHAT SHE IS TODAY--
--THE MOST DANGEROUS WOMAN IN THE UNIVERSE.
THEY REALLY FIGHTING, OR JUST MESSING AROUND?
HOW DOES YOUR JAW FEEL?
DISLO-CATED...
THAT ANSWER YOUR QUESTION?

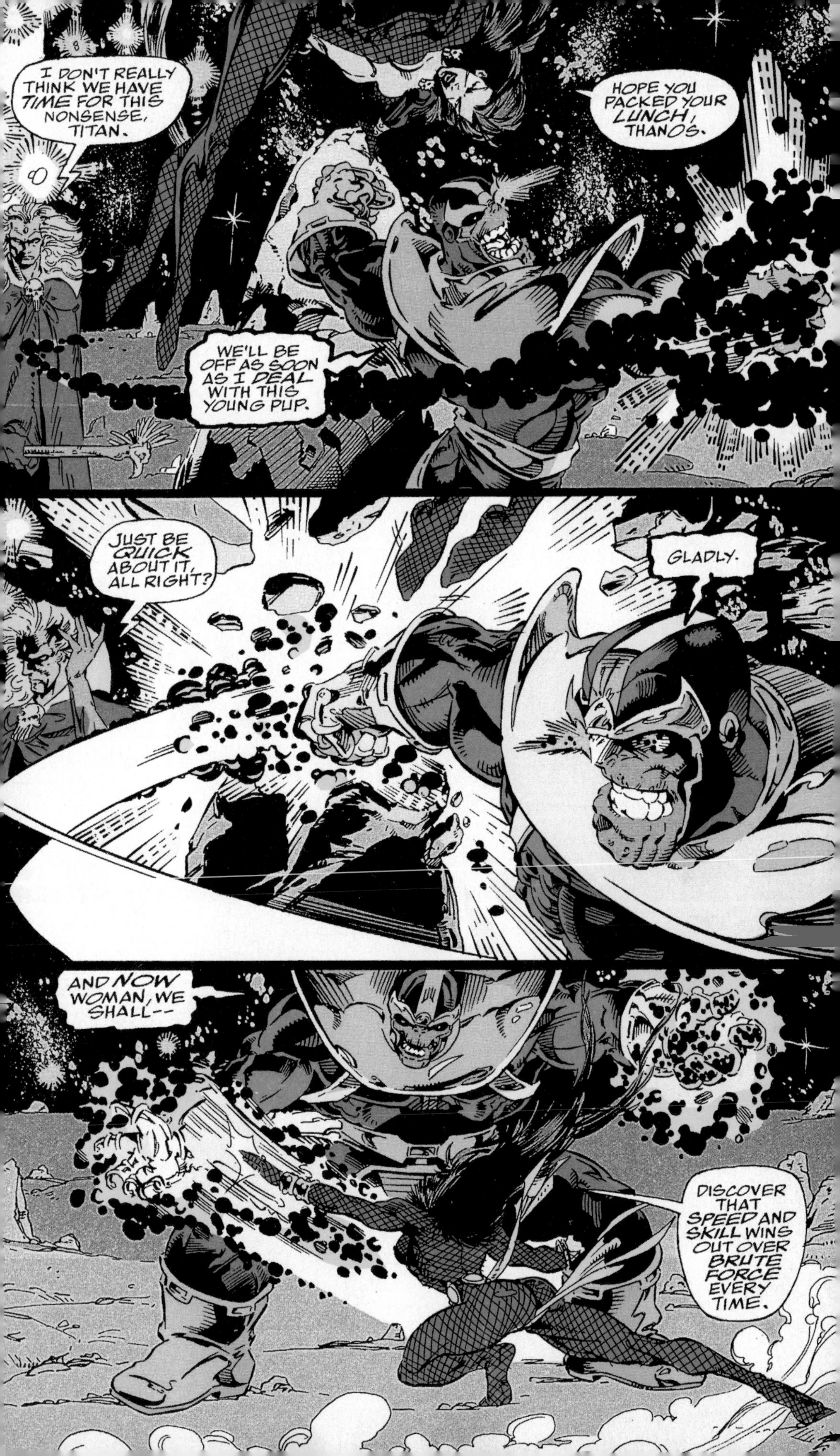
I DON'T REALLY THINK WE HAVE TIME FOR THIS NONSENSE, TITAN.
HOPE YOU PACKED YOUR LUNCH, THANOS.
WE'LL BE OFF AS SOON AS I DEAL WITH THIS YOUNG PUP.
JUST BE QUICK ABOUT IT, ALL RIGHT?
GLADLY.
AND NOW WOMAN, WE SHALL--
DISCOVER THAT SPEED AND SKILL WINS OUT OVER BRUTE FORCE EVERY TIME.

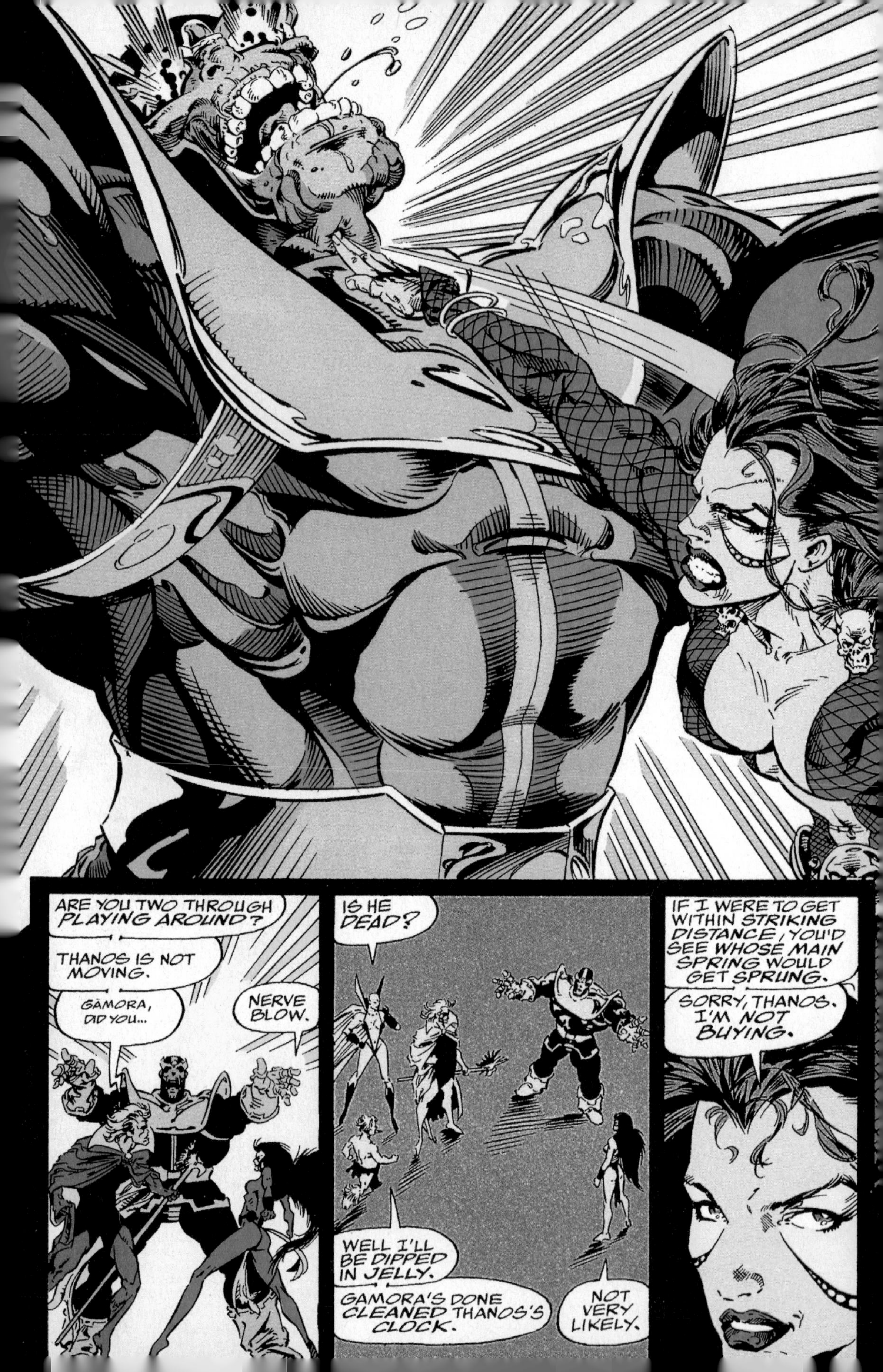
ARE YOU TWO THROUGH PLAYING AROUND?
THANOS IS NOT MOVING.
GAMORA, DID YOU...
NERVE BLOW.
IS HE DEAD?
WELL I'LL BE DIPPED IN JELLY.
GAMORA'S DONE CLEANED THANOS'S CLOCK.
NOT VERY LIKELY.
IF I WERE TO GET WITHIN STRIKING DISTANCE, YOU'D SEE WHOSE MAIN SPRING WOULD GET SPRUNG.
SORRY, THANOS. I'M NOT BUYING.

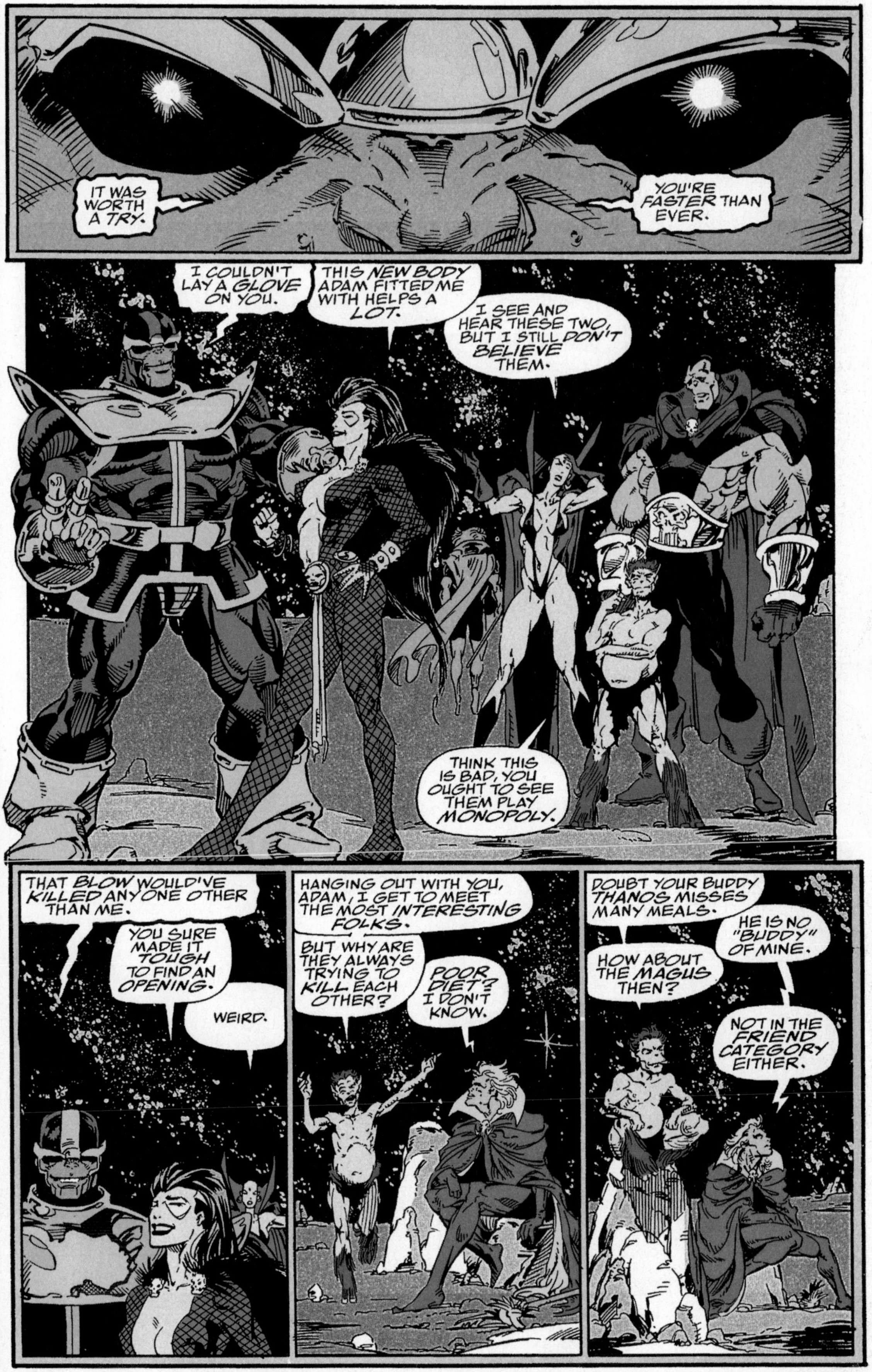
IT WAS WORTH A TRY.
YOU'RE FASTER THAN EVER.
I COULDN'T LAY A GLOVE ON YOU.
THIS NEW BODY ADAM FITTED ME WITH HELPS A LOT.
I SEE AND HEAR THESE TWO, BUT I STILL DON'T BELIEVE THEM.
THINK THIS IS BAD, YOU OUGHT TO SEE THEM PLAY MONOPOLY.
THAT BLOW WOULD'VE KILLED ANYONE OTHER THAN ME.
YOU SURE MADE IT TOUGH TO FIND AN OPENING.
WEIRD.
HANGING OUT WITH YOU, ADAM, I GET TO MEET THE MOST INTERESTING FOLKS.
BUT WHY ARE THEY ALWAYS TRYING TO KILL EACH OTHER?
POOR DIET? I DON'T KNOW.
DOUBT YOUR BUDDY THANOS MISSES MANY MEALS.
HE IS NO "BUDDY" OF MINE.
HOW ABOUT THE MAGUS THEN?
NOT IN THE FRIEND CATEGORY EITHER.

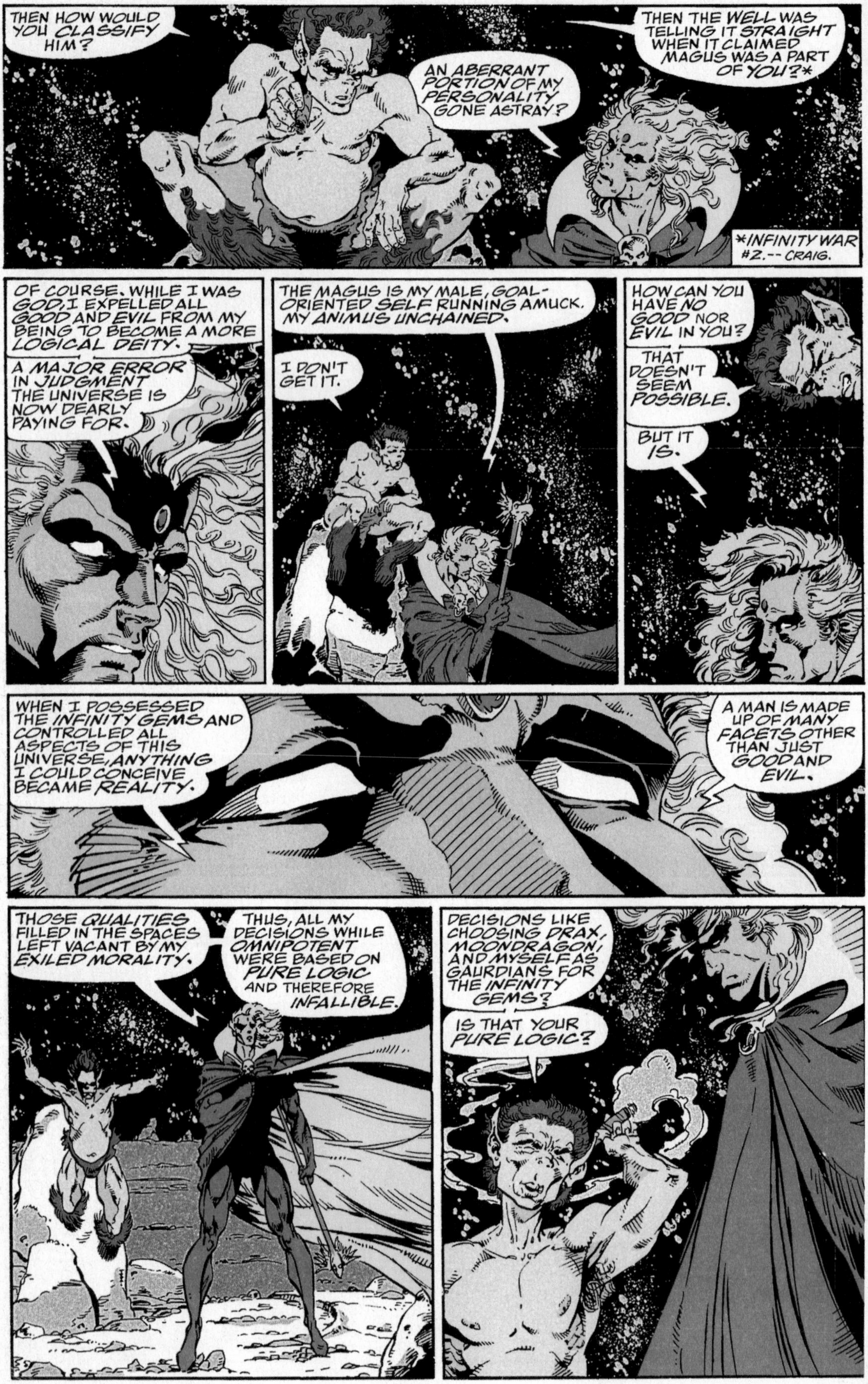
THEN HOW WOULD YOU CLASSIFY HIM?
AN ABERRANT PORTION OF MY PERSONALITY GONE ASTRAY?
THEN THE WELL WAS TELLING IT STRAIGHT WHEN IT CLAIMED MAGUS WAS A PART OF YOU?*
*INFINITY WAR #2.-- CRAIG.
OF COURSE. WHILE I WAS GOD, I EXPELLED ALL GOOD AND EVIL FROM MY BEING TO BECOME A MORE LOGICAL DEITY.
A MAJOR ERROR IN JUDGMENT THE UNIVERSE IS NOW DEARLY PAYING FOR.
THE MAGUS IS MY MALE, GOAL-ORIENTED SELF RUNNING AMUCK. MY ANIMUS UNCHAINED.
I DON'T GET IT.
HOW CAN YOU HAVE NO GOOD NOR EVIL IN YOU?
THAT DOESN'T SEEM POSSIBLE.
BUT IT IS.
WHEN I POSSESSED THE INFINITY GEMS AND CONTROLLED ALL ASPECTS OF THIS UNIVERSE, ANYTHING I COULD CONCEIVE BECAME REALITY.
A MAN IS MADE UP OF MANY FACETS OTHER THAN JUST GOOD AND EVIL.
THOSE QUALITIES FILLED IN THE SPACES LEFT VACANT BY MY EXILED MORALITY.
THUS, ALL MY DECISIONS WHILE OMNIPOTENT WERE BASED ON PURE LOGIC AND THEREFORE INFALLIBLE.
DECISIONS LIKE CHOOSING DRAX, MOONDRAGON, AND MYSELF AS GAURDIANS FOR THE INFINITY GEMS?
IS THAT YOUR PURE LOGIC?

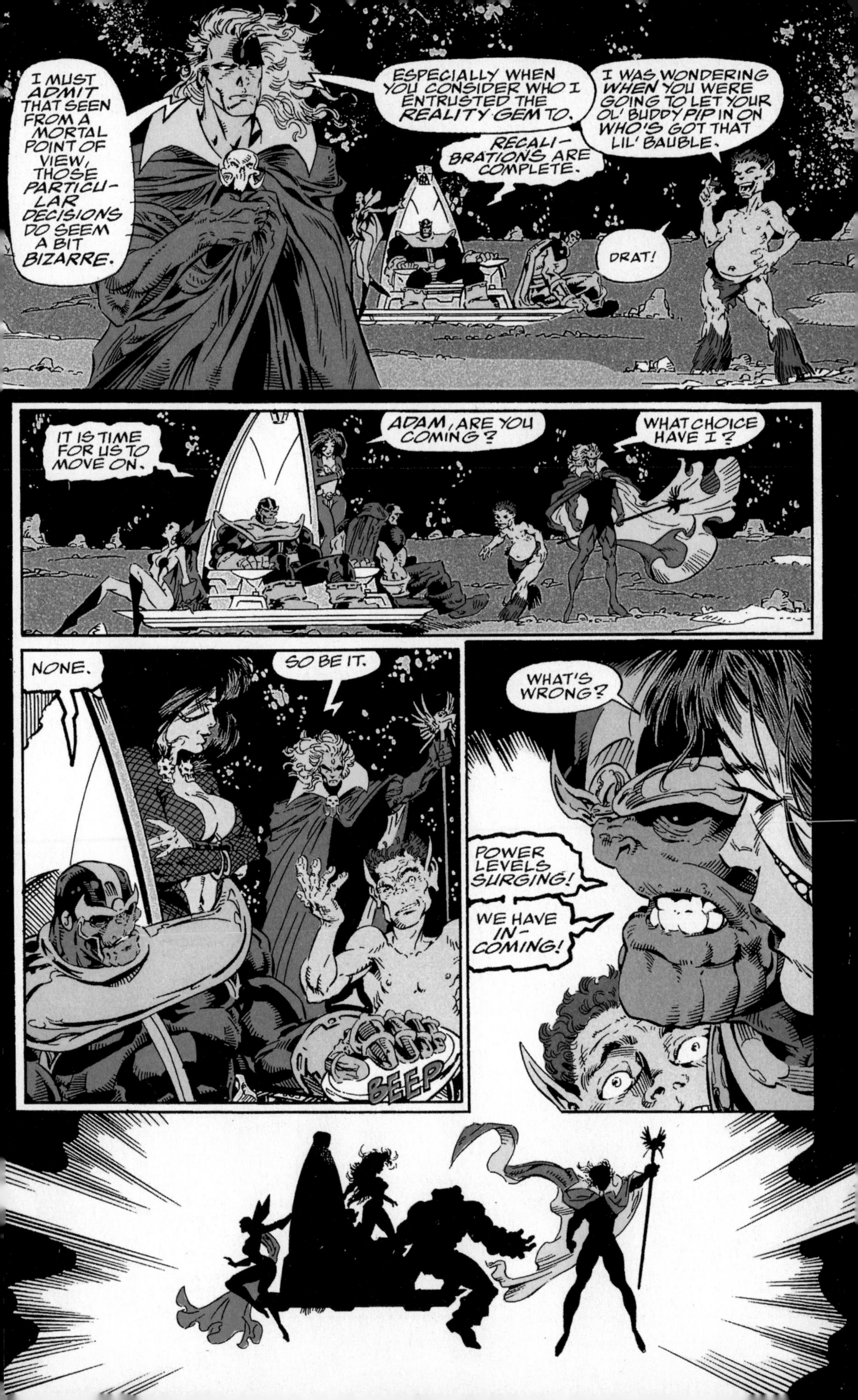
I MUST ADMIT THAT SEEN FROM A MORTAL POINT OF VIEW, THOSE PARTICULAR DECISIONS DO SEEM A BIT BIZARRE.
ESPECIALLY WHEN YOU CONSIDER WHO I ENTRUSTED THE REALITY GEM TO.
I WAS WONDERING WHEN YOU WERE GOING TO LET YOUR OL' BUDDY PIP IN ON WHO'S GOT THAT LIL' BAUBLE.
RECALIBRATIONS ARE COMPLETE.
DRAT!
IT IS TIME FOR US TO MOVE ON.
ADAM, ARE YOU COMING?
WHAT CHOICE HAVE I?
NONE.
SO BE IT.
BEEP
WHAT'S WRONG?
POWER LEVELS SURGING!
WE HAVE INCOMING!

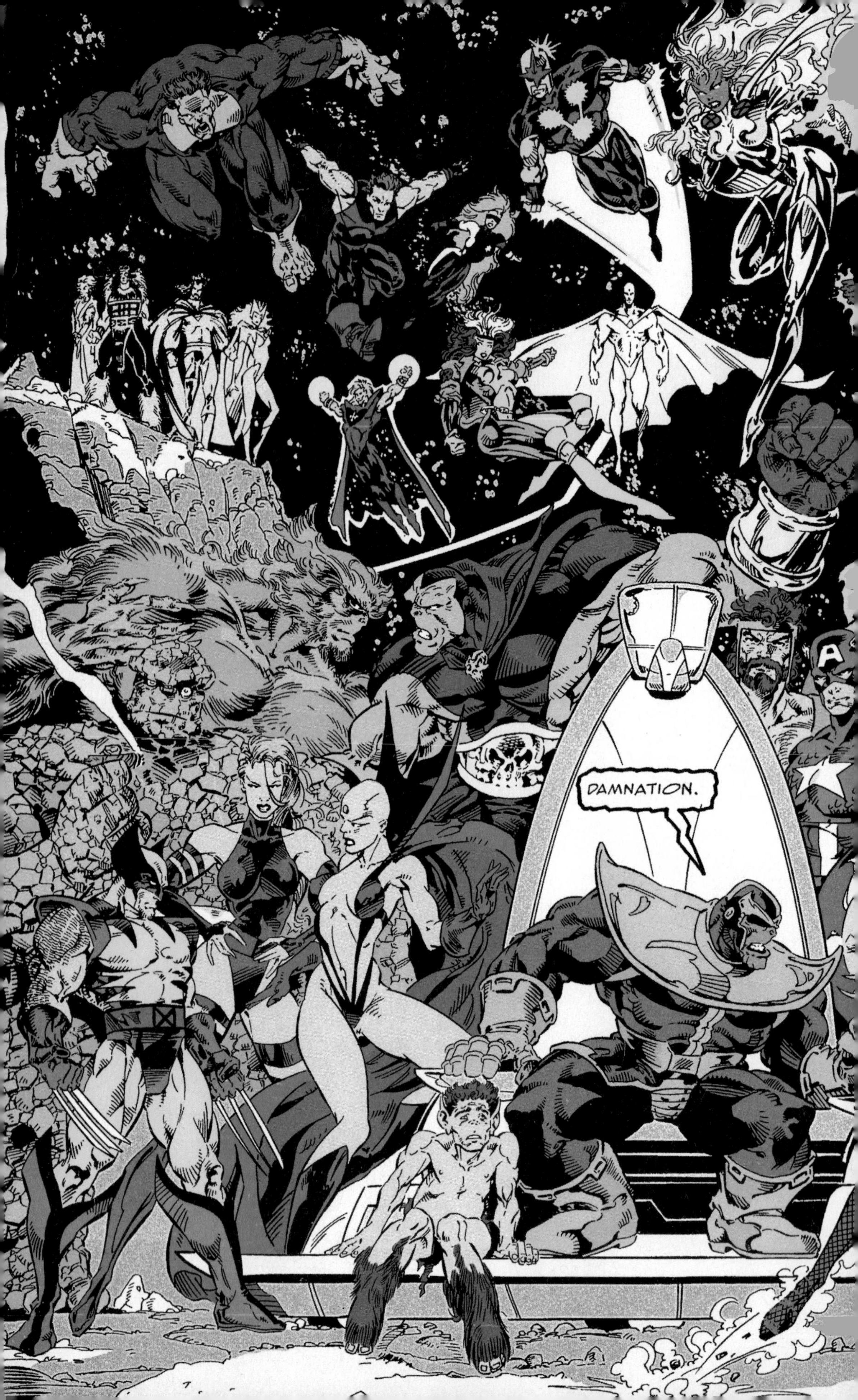
DAMNATION.

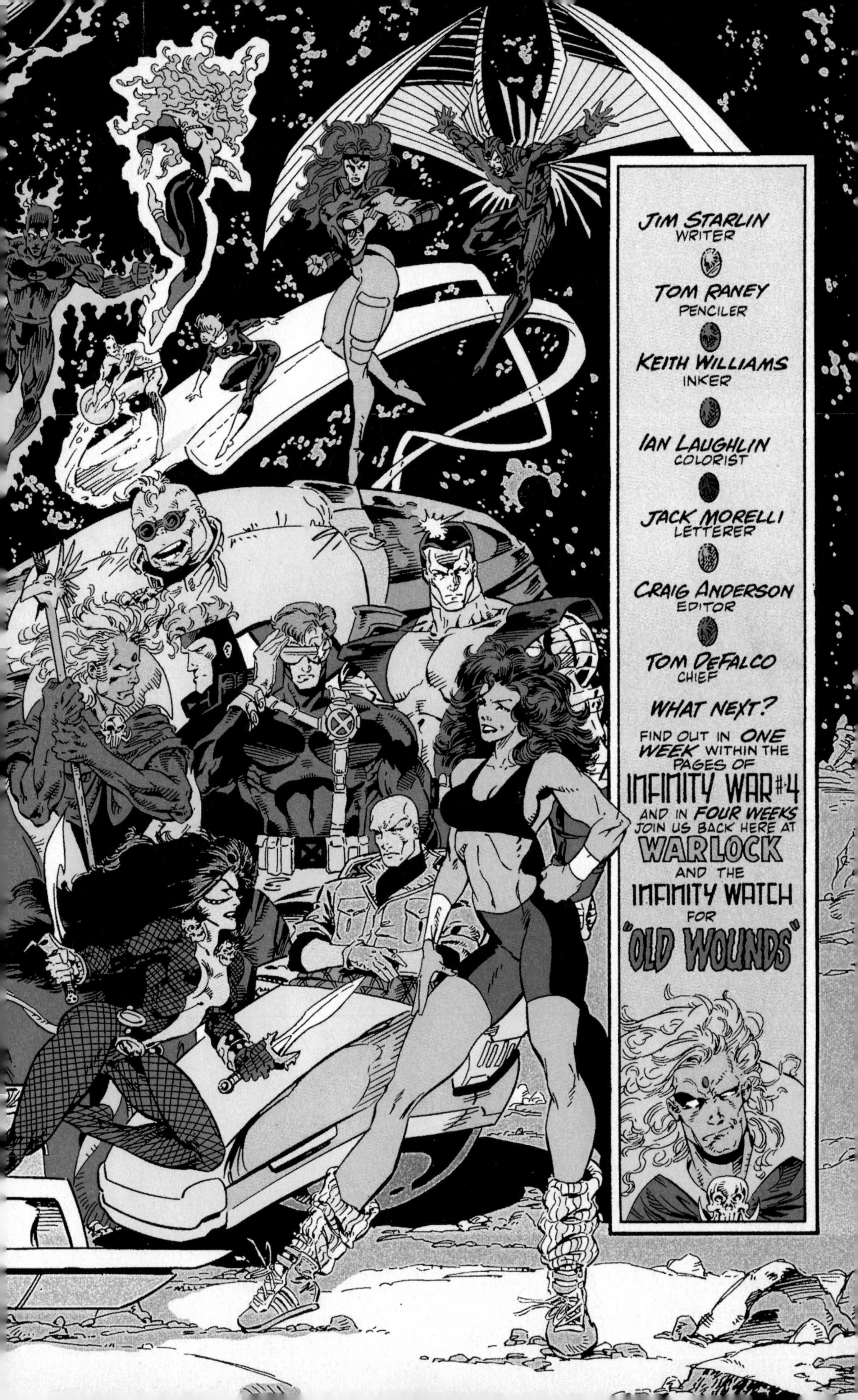

JIM STARLIN
WRITER
TOM RANEY
PENCILER
KEITH WILLIAMS
INKER
IAN LAUGHLIN
COLORIST
JACK MORELLI
LETTERER
CRAIG ANDERSON
EDITOR
TOM DEFALCO
CHIEF
WHAT NEXT?
FIND OUT IN ONE WEEK WITHIN THE PAGES OF
INFINITY WAR #4
AND IN FOUR WEEKS JOIN US BACK HERE AT
WARLOCK
AND THE
INFINITY WATCH
FOR
"OLD WOUNDS"

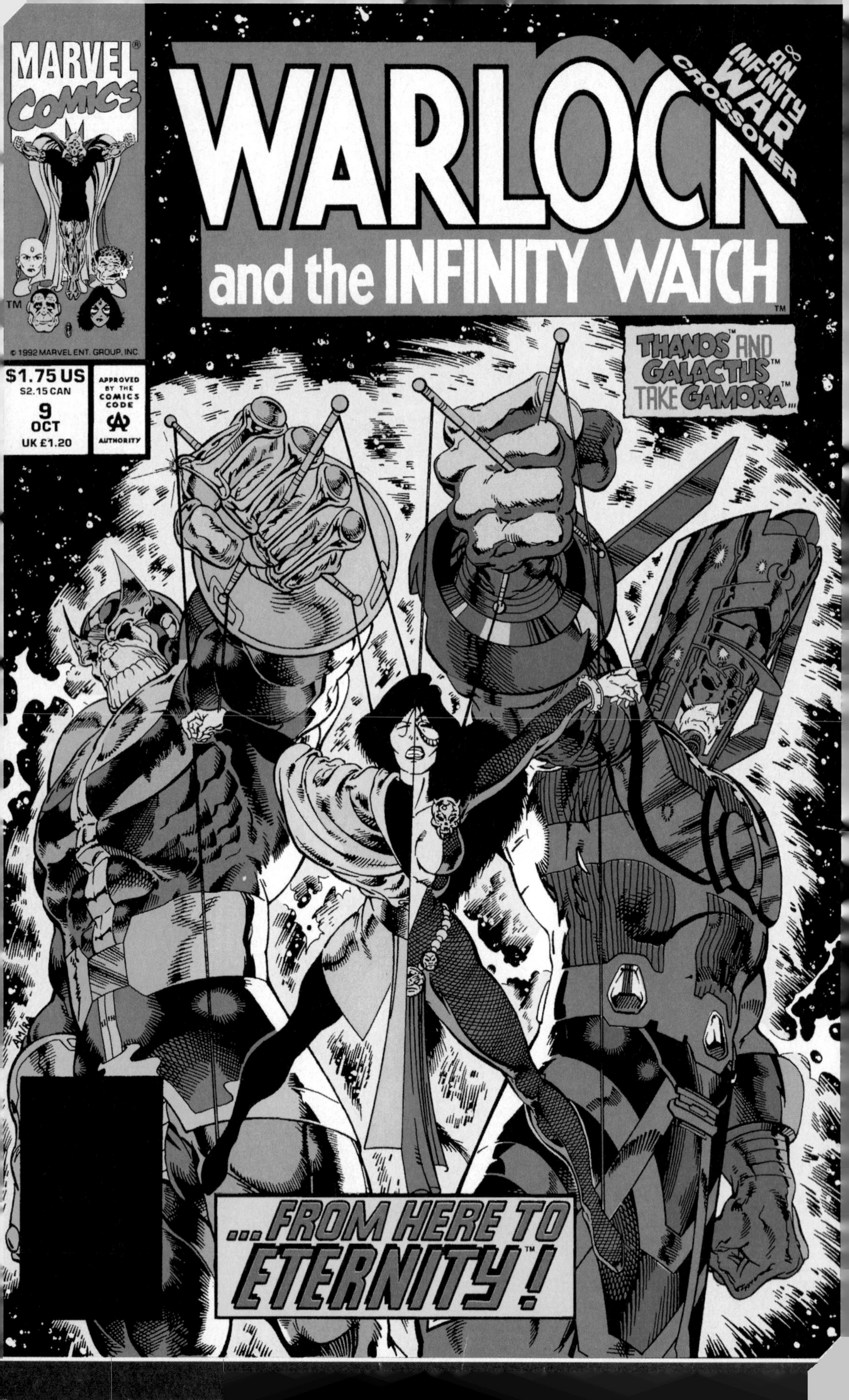
MARVEL® COMICS
WARLOCK and the INFINITY WATCH™
AN INFINITY WAR CROSSOVER
THANOS™ AND GALACTUS™ TAKE GAMORA™...
TM
© 1992 MARVEL ENT. GROUP, INC.
$1.75 US
$2.15 CAN
9
OCT
UK £1.20
APPROVED BY THE COMICS CODE AUTHORITY
...FROM HERE TO ETERNITY™!

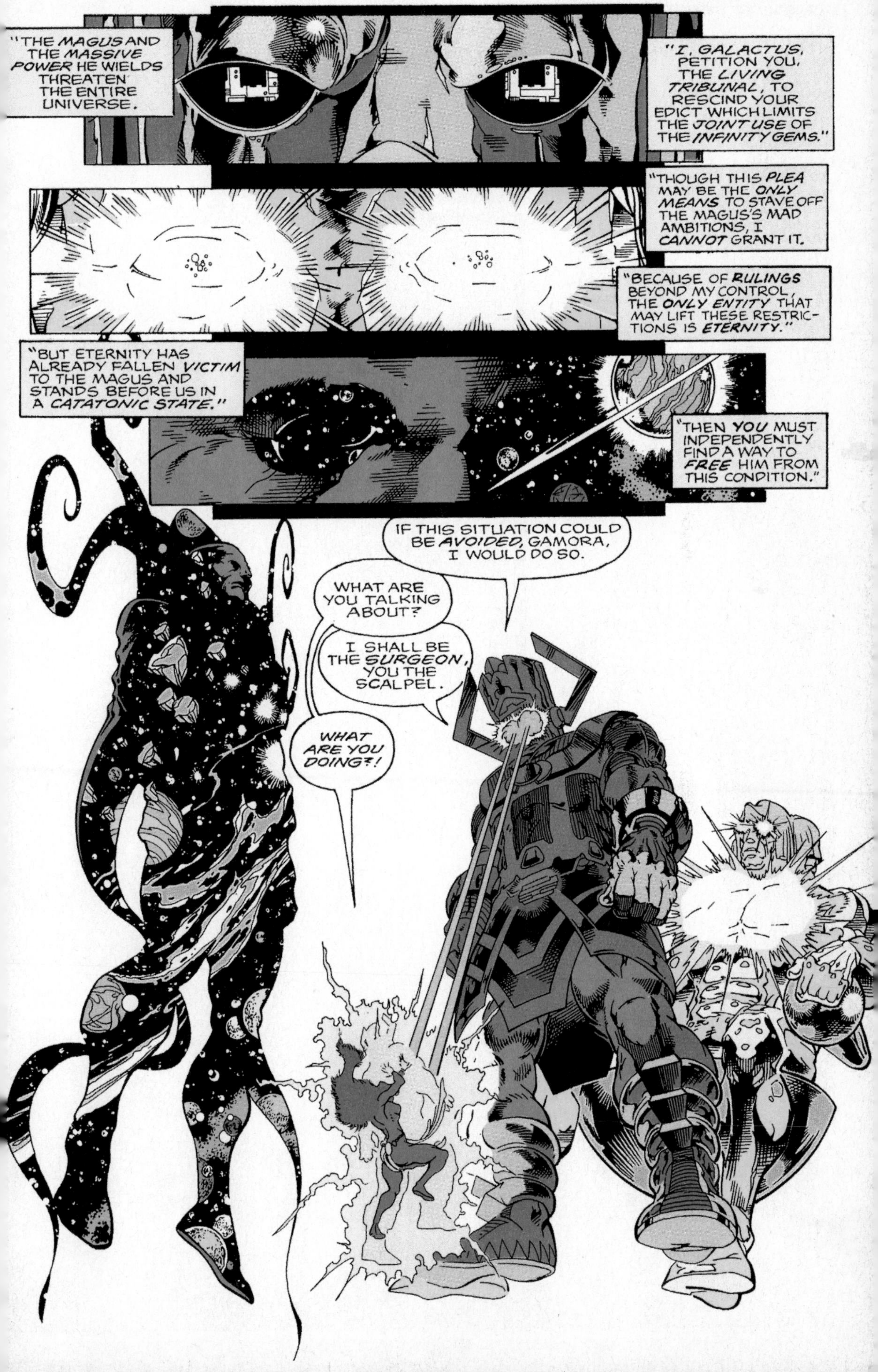
"THE MAGUS AND THE MASSIVE POWER HE WIELDS THREATEN THE ENTIRE UNIVERSE.
"I, GALACTUS, PETITION YOU, THE LIVING TRIBUNAL, TO RESCIND YOUR EDICT WHICH LIMITS THE JOINT USE OF THE INFINITY GEMS."
"THOUGH THIS PLEA MAY BE THE ONLY MEANS TO STAVE OFF THE MAGUS'S MAD AMBITIONS, I CANNOT GRANT IT.
"BECAUSE OF RULINGS BEYOND MY CONTROL, THE ONLY ENTITY THAT MAY LIFT THESE RESTRICTIONS IS ETERNITY."
"BUT ETERNITY HAS ALREADY FALLEN VICTIM TO THE MAGUS AND STANDS BEFORE US IN A CATATONIC STATE."
"THEN YOU MUST INDEPENDENTLY FIND A WAY TO FREE HIM FROM THIS CONDITION."
IF THIS SITUATION COULD BE AVOIDED, GAMORA, I WOULD DO SO.
WHAT ARE YOU TALKING ABOUT?
I SHALL BE THE SURGEON, YOU THE SCALPEL.
WHAT ARE YOU DOING?!

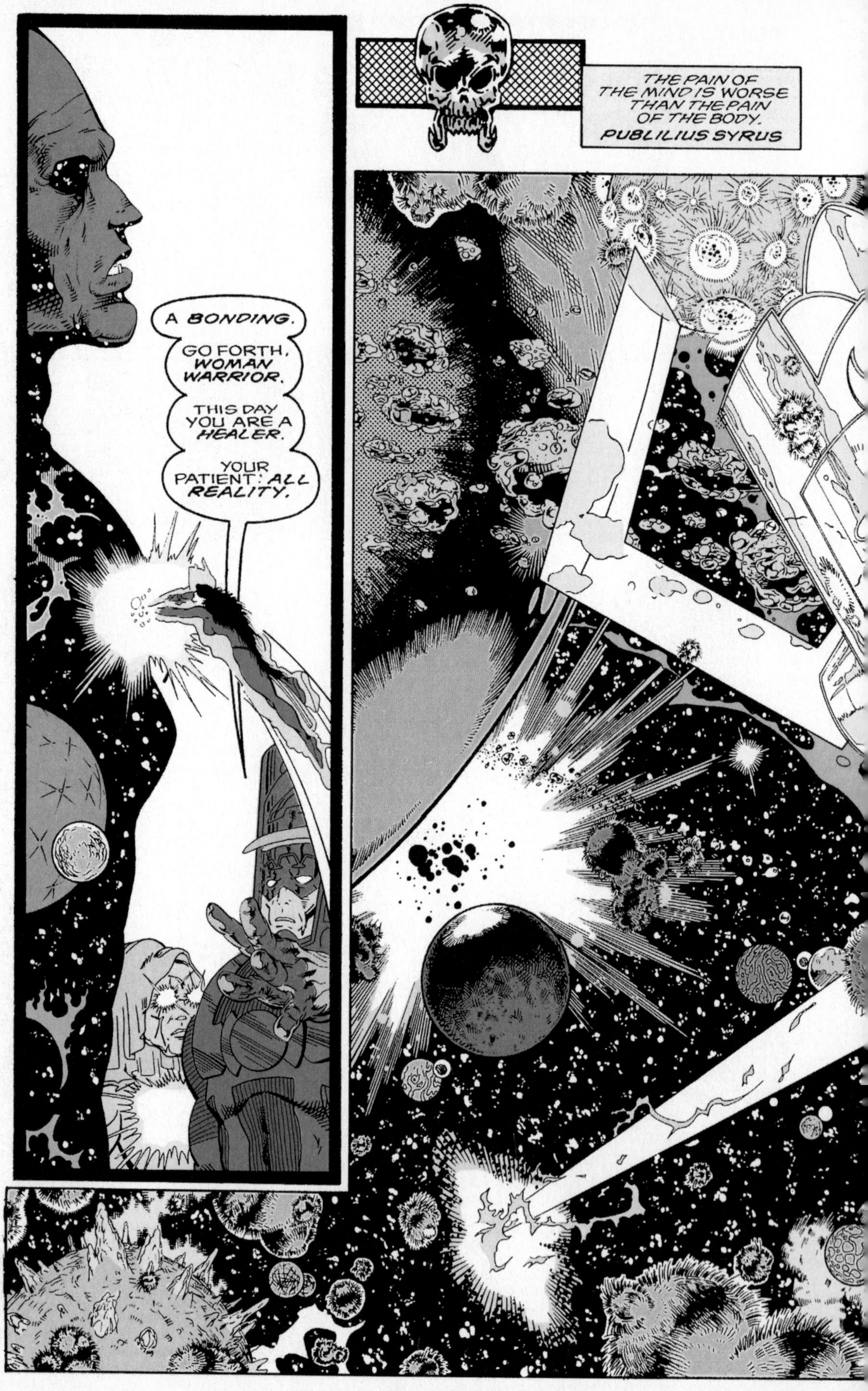
THE PAIN OF THE MIND IS WORSE THAN THE PAIN OF THE BODY. PUBLILIUS SYRUS
A BONDING.
GO FORTH, WOMAN WARRIOR.
THIS DAY YOU ARE A HEALER.
YOUR PATIENT: ALL REALITY.

OLD WOUNDS

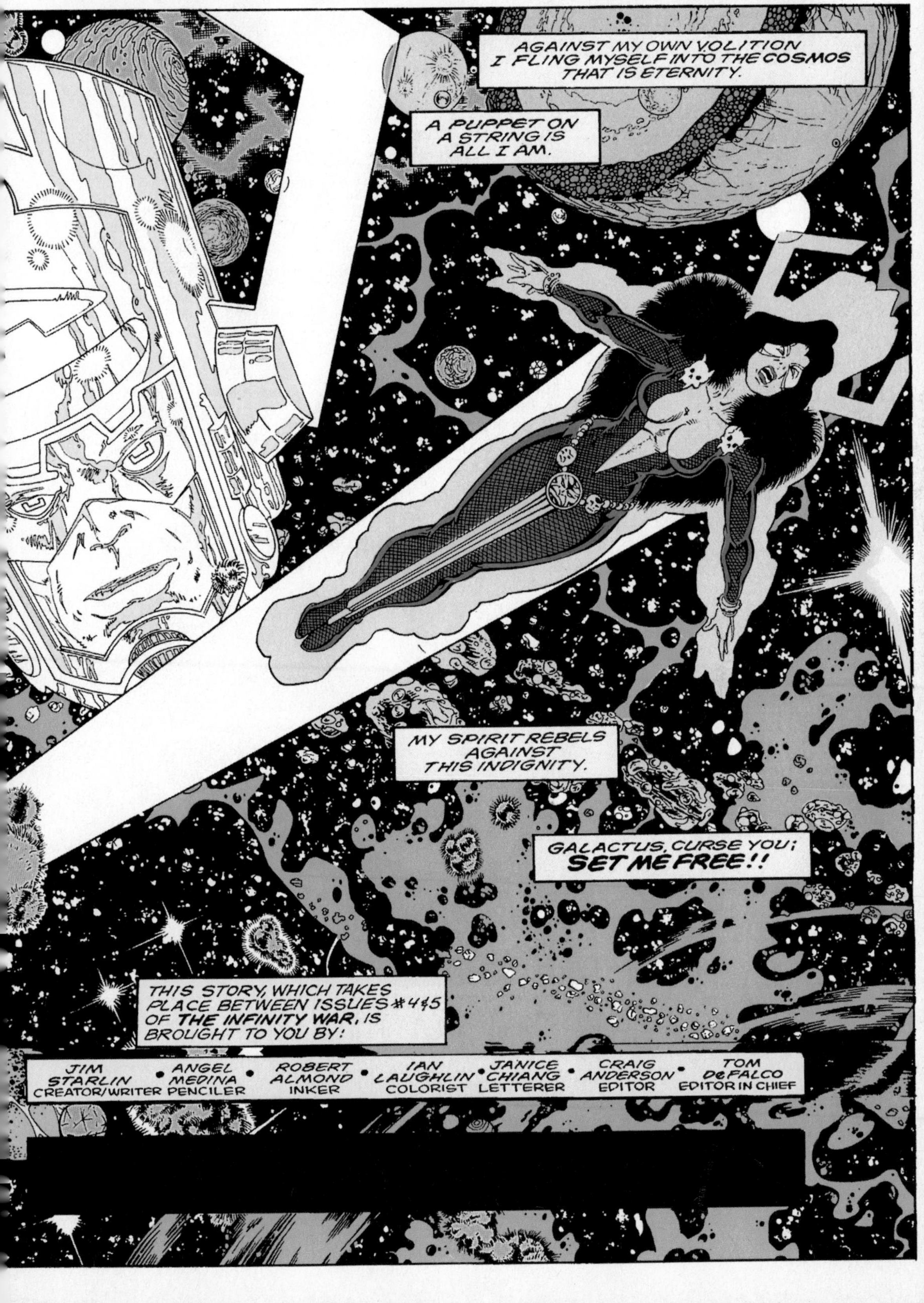
AGAINST MY OWN VOLITION I FLING MYSELF INTO THE COSMOS THAT IS ETERNITY.
A PUPPET ON A STRING IS ALL I AM.
MY SPIRIT REBELS AGAINST THIS INDIGNITY.
GALACTUS, CURSE YOU; SET ME FREE!!
THIS STORY, WHICH TAKES PLACE BETWEEN ISSUES #4&5 OF THE INFINITY WAR, IS BROUGHT TO YOU BY:
JIM STARLIN CREATOR/WRITER • ANGEL MEDINA PENCILER • ROBERT ALMOND INKER • IAN LAUGHLIN COLORIST • JANICE CHIANG LETTERER • CRAIG ANDERSON EDITOR • TOM DeFALCO EDITOR IN CHIEF
[redacted]

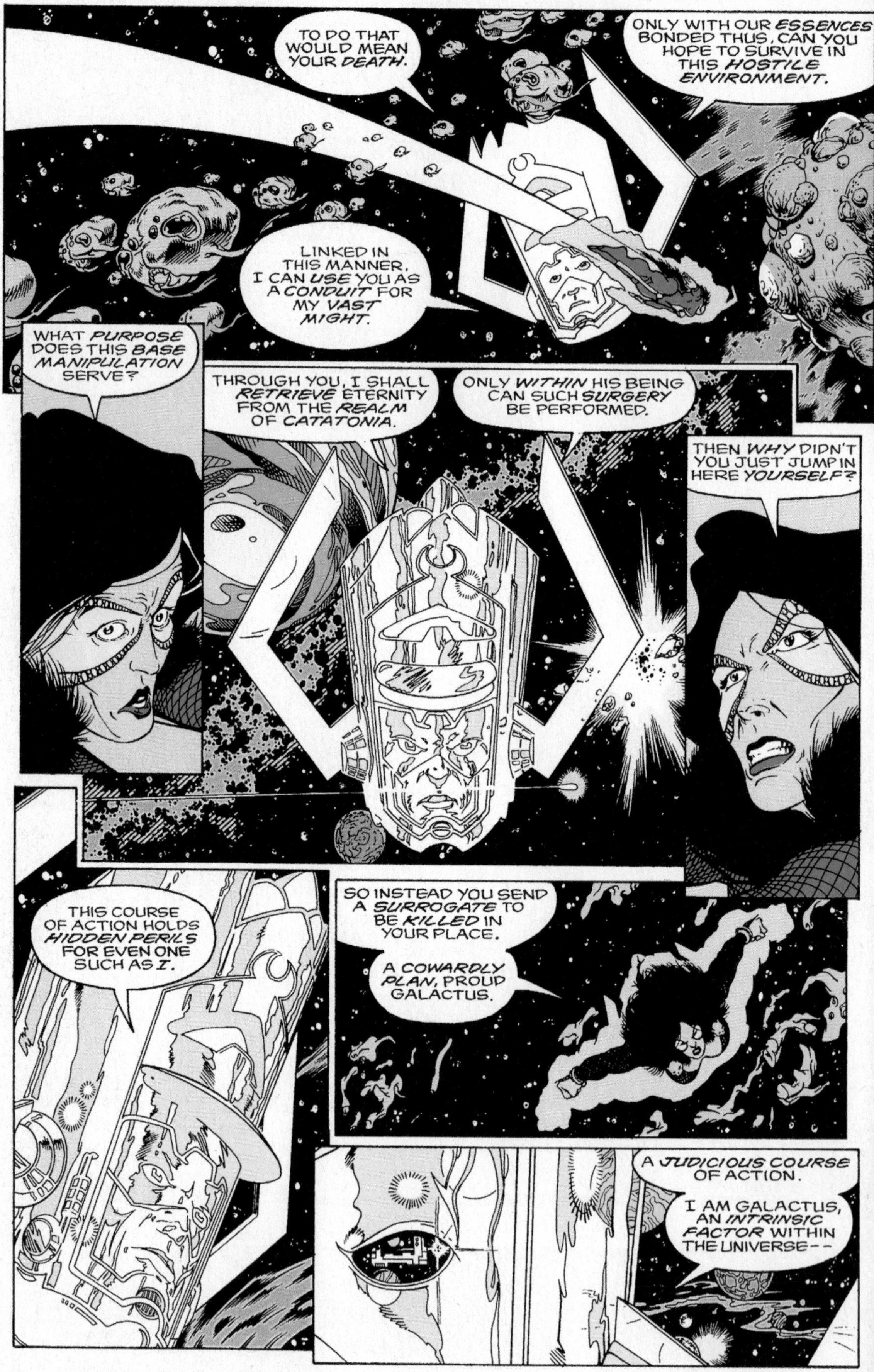
TO DO THAT WOULD MEAN YOUR DEATH.
ONLY WITH OUR ESSENCES BONDED THUS, CAN YOU HOPE TO SURVIVE IN THIS HOSTILE ENVIRONMENT.
LINKED IN THIS MANNER, I CAN USE YOU AS A CONDUIT FOR MY VAST MIGHT.
WHAT PURPOSE DOES THIS BASE MANIPULATION SERVE?
THROUGH YOU, I SHALL RETRIEVE ETERNITY FROM THE REALM OF CATATONIA.
ONLY WITHIN HIS BEING CAN SUCH SURGERY BE PERFORMED.
THEN WHY DIDN'T YOU JUST JUMP IN HERE YOURSELF?
THIS COURSE OF ACTION HOLDS HIDDEN PERILS FOR EVEN ONE SUCH AS I.
SO INSTEAD YOU SEND A SURROGATE TO BE KILLED IN YOUR PLACE.
A COWARDLY PLAN, PROUD GALACTUS.
A JUDICIOUS COURSE OF ACTION.
I AM GALACTUS, AN INTRINSIC FACTOR WITHIN THE UNIVERSE--

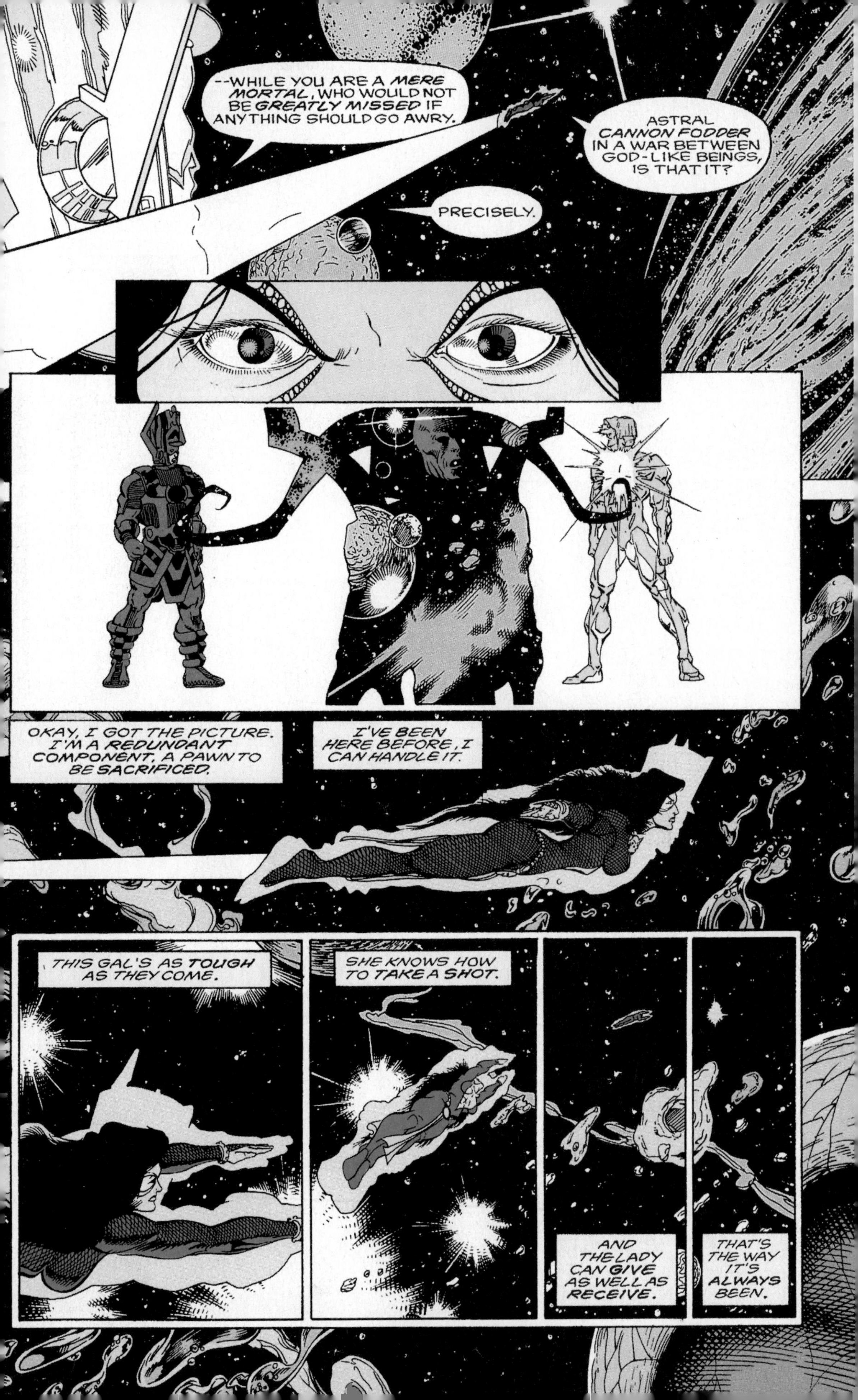

--WHILE YOU ARE A MERE MORTAL, WHO WOULD NOT BE GREATLY MISSED IF ANYTHING SHOULD GO AWRY.
ASTRAL CANNON FODDER IN A WAR BETWEEN GOD-LIKE BEINGS, IS THAT IT?
PRECISELY.
OKAY, I GOT THE PICTURE. I'M A REDUNDANT COMPONENT, A PAWN TO BE SACRIFICED.
I'VE BEEN HERE BEFORE, I CAN HANDLE IT.
THIS GAL'S AS TOUGH AS THEY COME.
SHE KNOWS HOW TO TAKE A SHOT.
AND THE LADY CAN GIVE AS WELL AS RECEIVE.
THAT'S THE WAY IT'S ALWAYS BEEN.

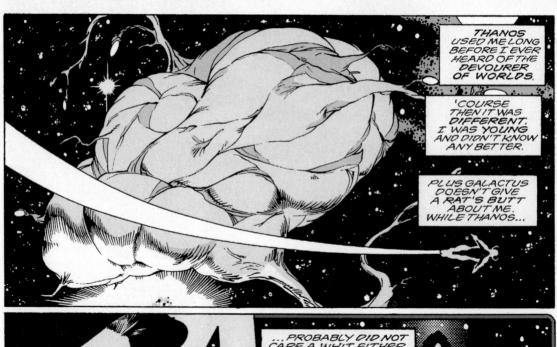

THANOS USED ME LONG BEFORE I EVER HEARD OF THE DEVOURER OF WORLDS.

'COURSE THEN IT WAS DIFFERENT. I WAS YOUNG AND DIDN'T KNOW ANY BETTER.

PLUS GALACTUS DOESN'T GIVE A RAT'S BUTT ABOUT ME. WHILE THANOS...

...PROBABLY DID NOT CARE A WHIT EITHER, DESPITE THE FACT HE SAVED MY LIFE AND RAISED ME.

HE HAD HIS REASONS, I'M SURE, ALL OF THEM SELFISH.

PRETTY OBVIOUS FROM THE START HE WAS PREPARING ME TO BE HIS OWN PERSONAL ASTRAL SAMURAI.

BY THE TIME I WAS 15 I COULD TAKE OUT A COMBAT DROID WITHOUT WORKING UP A SWEAT.

STILL THERE WERE TIMES WHEN I FELT THERE WAS MORE TO IT THAN JUST THAT.

I KNOW, PROBABLY ONLY FOOLING MYSELF.

STILL REMEMBER THE TIME WE CAME INTO THAT SPACEPORT AT TARTOONLA #7

NO WAY I'LL EVER FORGET THAT DAY.

194

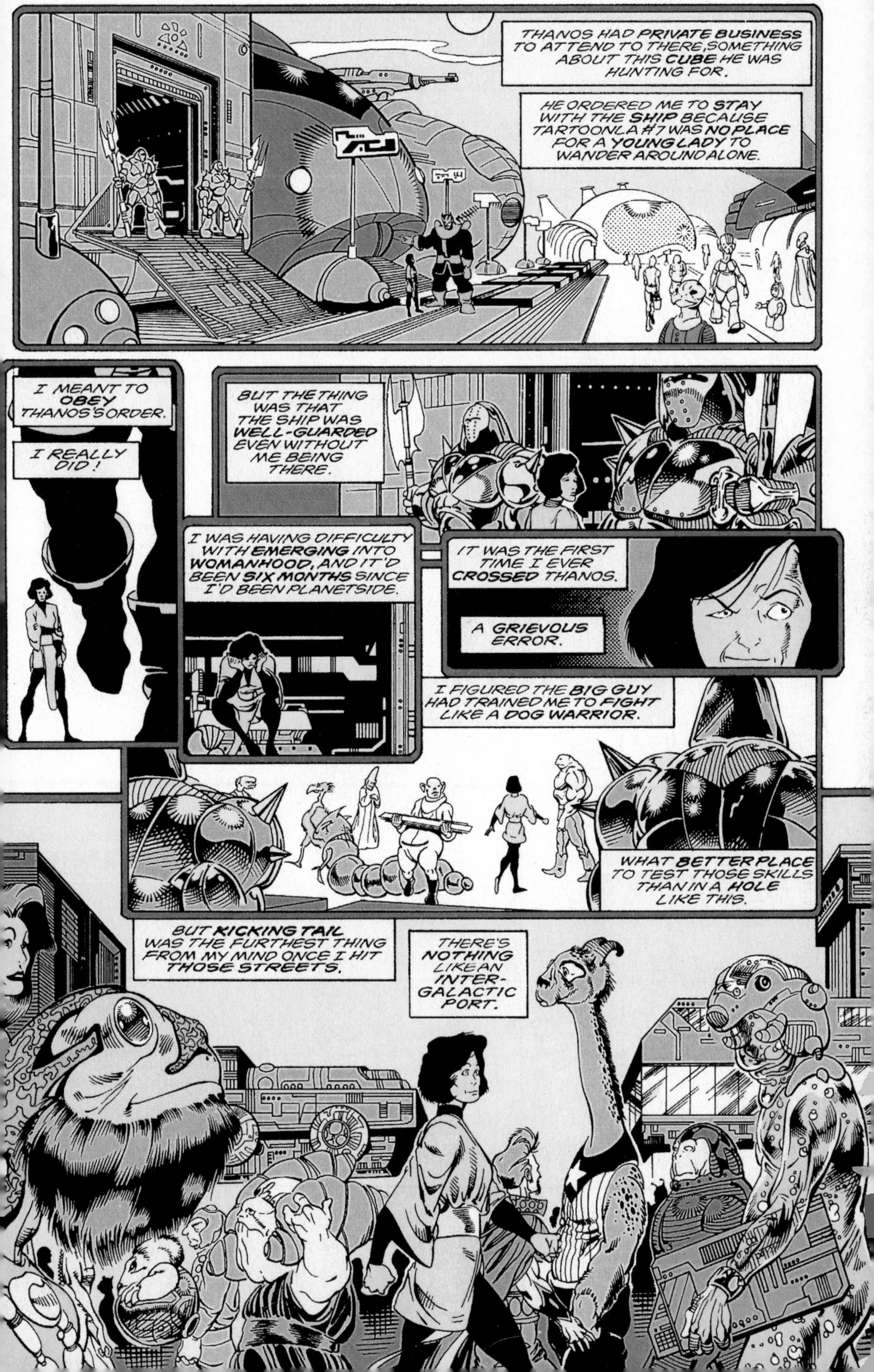
THANOS HAD PRIVATE BUSINESS TO ATTEND TO THERE, SOMETHING ABOUT THIS CUBE HE WAS HUNTING FOR.
HE ORDERED ME TO STAY WITH THE SHIP BECAUSE TARTOONLA #7 WAS NO PLACE FOR A YOUNG LADY TO WANDER AROUND ALONE.
I MEANT TO OBEY THANOS'S ORDER.
I REALLY DID!
BUT THE THING WAS THAT THE SHIP WAS WELL-GUARDED EVEN WITHOUT ME BEING THERE.
I WAS HAVING DIFFICULTY WITH EMERGING INTO WOMANHOOD, AND IT'D BEEN SIX MONTHS SINCE I'D BEEN PLANETSIDE.
IT WAS THE FIRST TIME I EVER CROSSED THANOS.
A GRIEVOUS ERROR.
I FIGURED THE BIG GUY HAD TRAINED ME TO FIGHT LIKE A DOG WARRIOR.
WHAT BETTER PLACE TO TEST THOSE SKILLS THAN IN A HOLE LIKE THIS.
BUT KICKING TAIL WAS THE FURTHEST THING FROM MY MIND ONCE I HIT THOSE STREETS.
THERE'S NOTHING LIKE AN INTER-GALACTIC PORT.

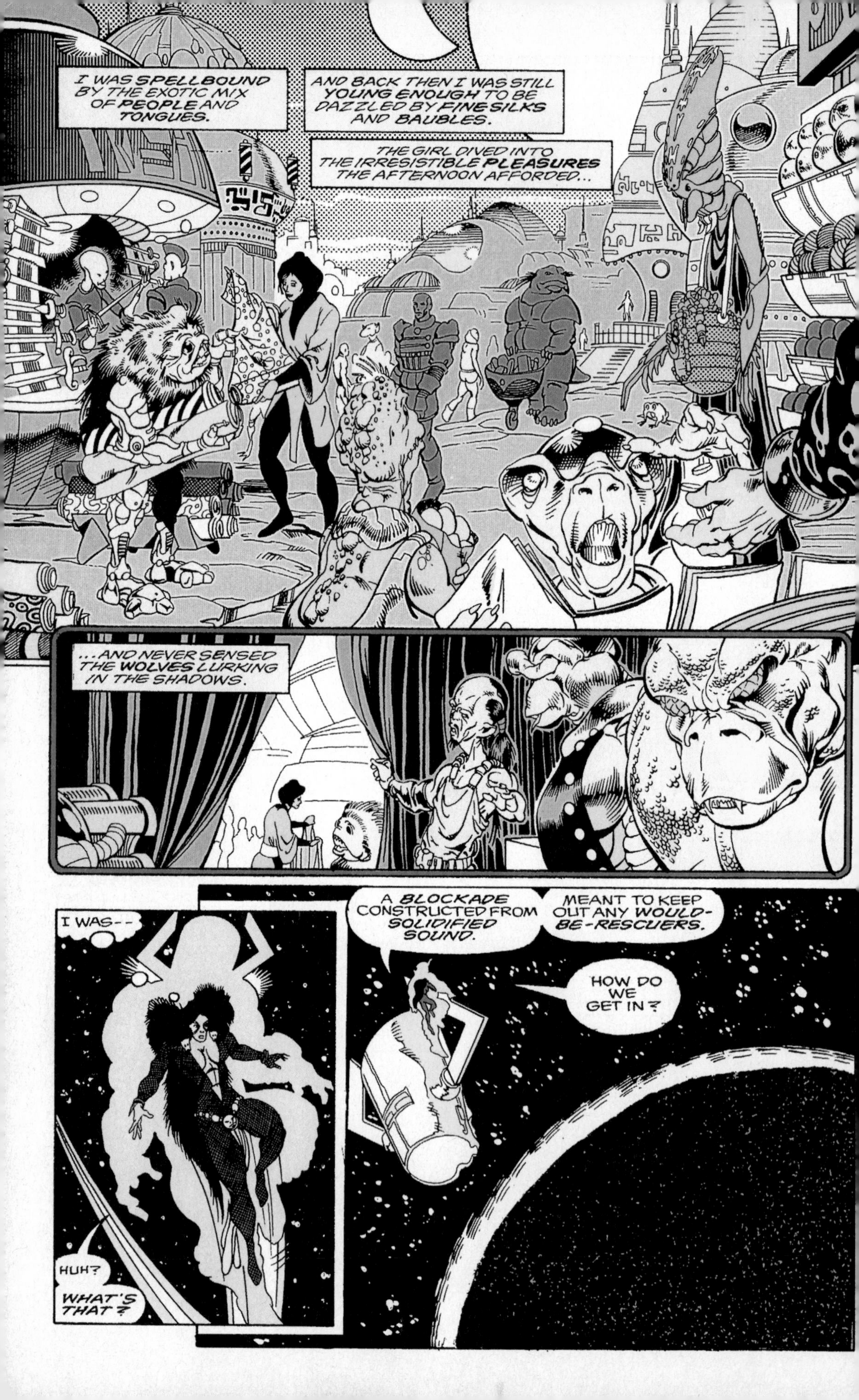
I WAS SPELLBOUND BY THE EXOTIC MIX OF PEOPLE AND TONGUES.
AND BACK THEN I WAS STILL YOUNG ENOUGH TO BE DAZZLED BY FINE SILKS AND BAUBLES.
THE GIRL DIVED INTO THE IRRESISTIBLE PLEASURES THE AFTERNOON AFFORDED...
...AND NEVER SENSED THE WOLVES LURKING IN THE SHADOWS.
I WAS--
A BLOCKADE CONSTRUCTED FROM SOLIDIFIED SOUND.
MEANT TO KEEP OUT ANY WOULD-BE-RESCUERS.
HOW DO WE GET IN?
HUH?
WHAT'S THAT?

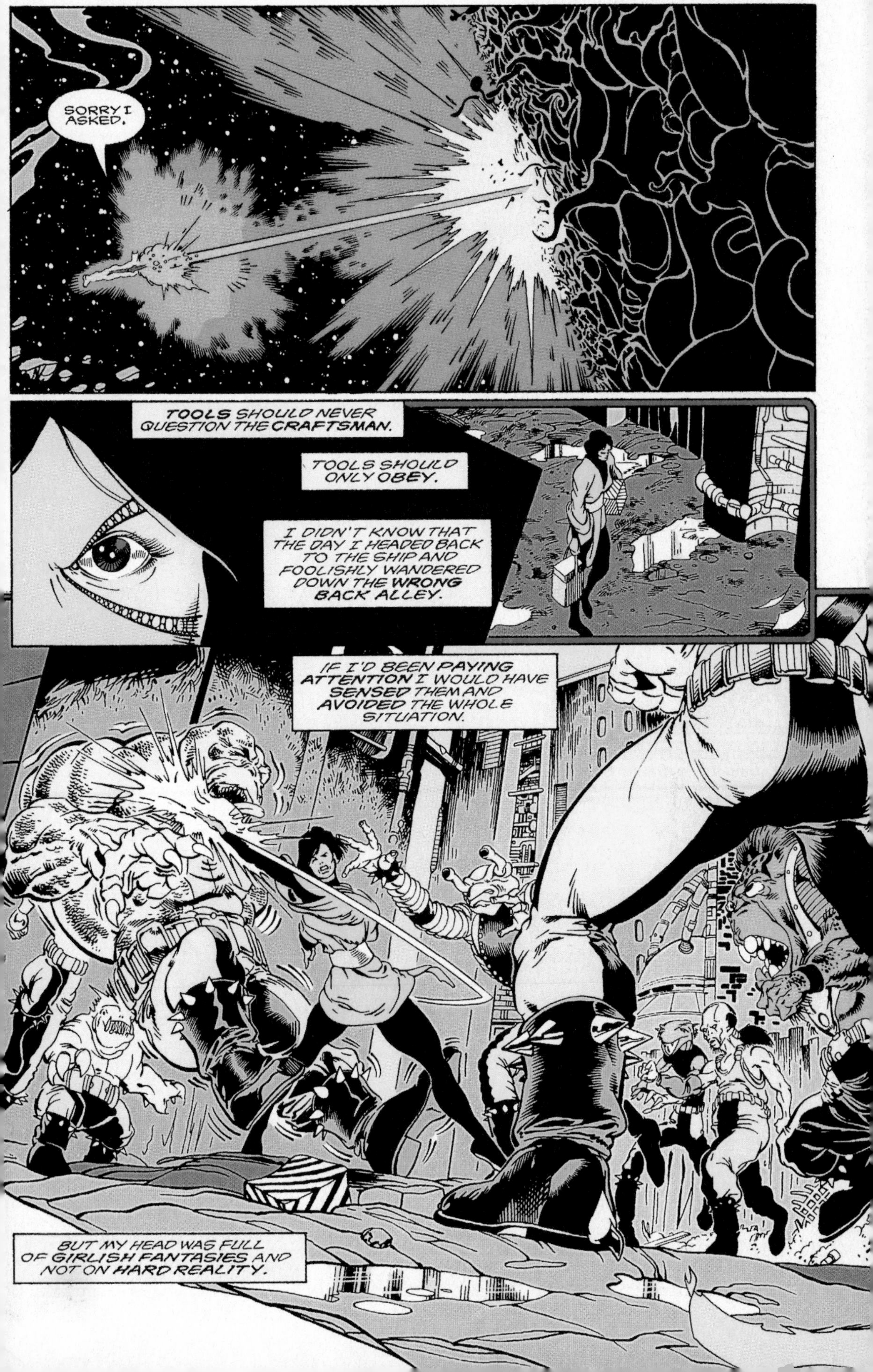
SORRY I ASKED.
TOOLS SHOULD NEVER QUESTION THE CRAFTSMAN.
TOOLS SHOULD ONLY OBEY.
I DIDN'T KNOW THAT THE DAY I HEADED BACK TO THE SHIP AND FOOLISHLY WANDERED DOWN THE WRONG BACK ALLEY.
IF I'D BEEN PAYING ATTENTION I WOULD HAVE SENSED THEM AND AVOIDED THE WHOLE SITUATION.
BUT MY HEAD WAS FULL OF GIRLISH FANTASIES AND NOT ON HARD REALITY.

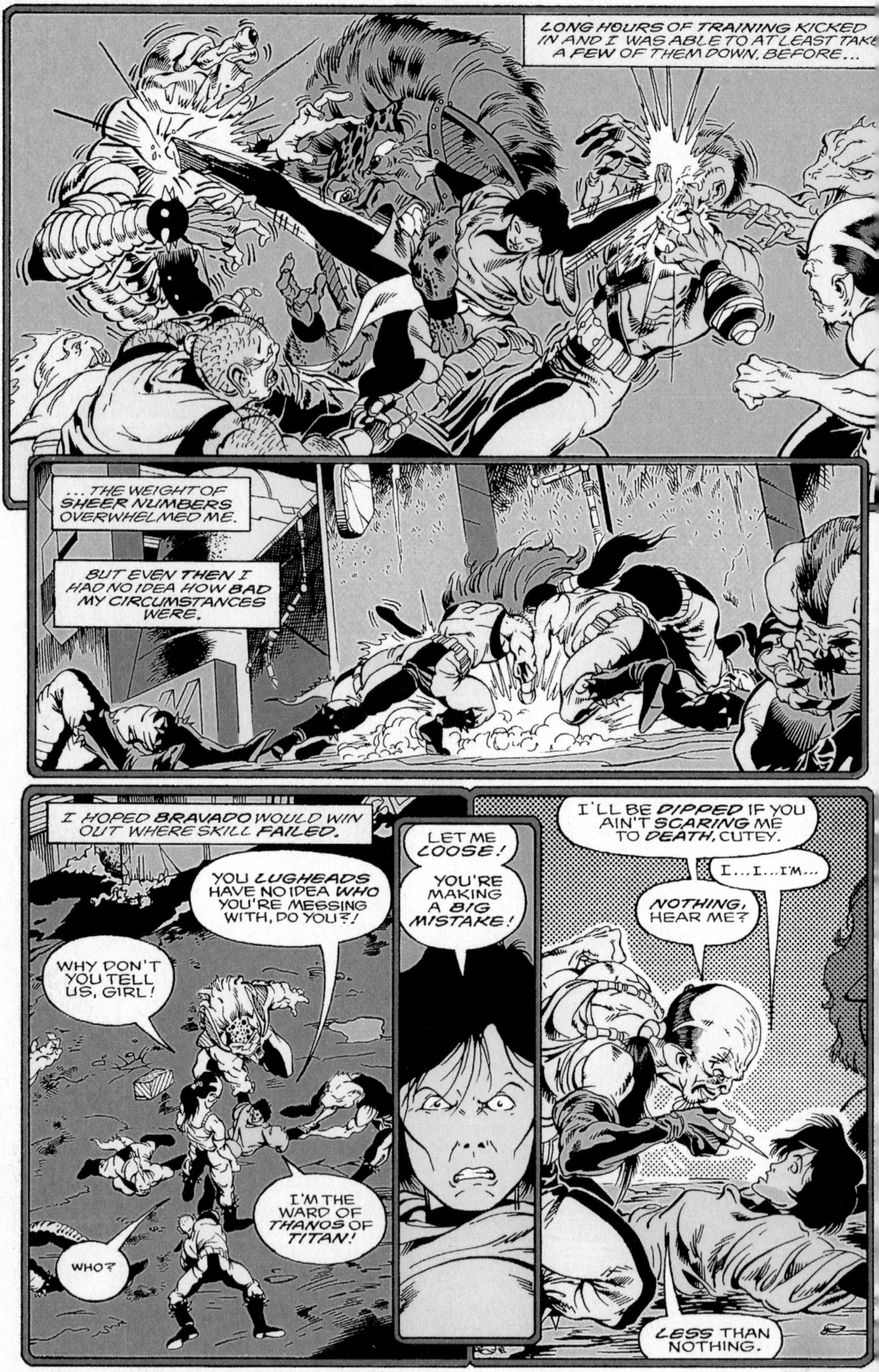

LONG HOURS OF TRAINING KICKED IN AND I WAS ABLE TO AT LEAST TAKE A FEW OF THEM DOWN, BEFORE...
...THE WEIGHT OF SHEER NUMBERS OVERWHELMED ME.
BUT EVEN THEN I HAD NO IDEA HOW BAD MY CIRCUMSTANCES WERE.
I HOPED BRAVADO WOULD WIN OUT WHERE SKILL FAILED.
YOU LUGHEADS HAVE NO IDEA WHO YOU'RE MESSING WITH, DO YOU?!
WHY DON'T YOU TELL US, GIRL!
I'M THE WARD OF THANOS OF TITAN!
WHO?
LET ME LOOSE!
YOU'RE MAKING A BIG MISTAKE!
I'LL BE DIPPED IF YOU AIN'T SCARING ME TO DEATH, CUTEY.
I...I...I'M...
NOTHING, HEAR ME?
LESS THAN NOTHING.

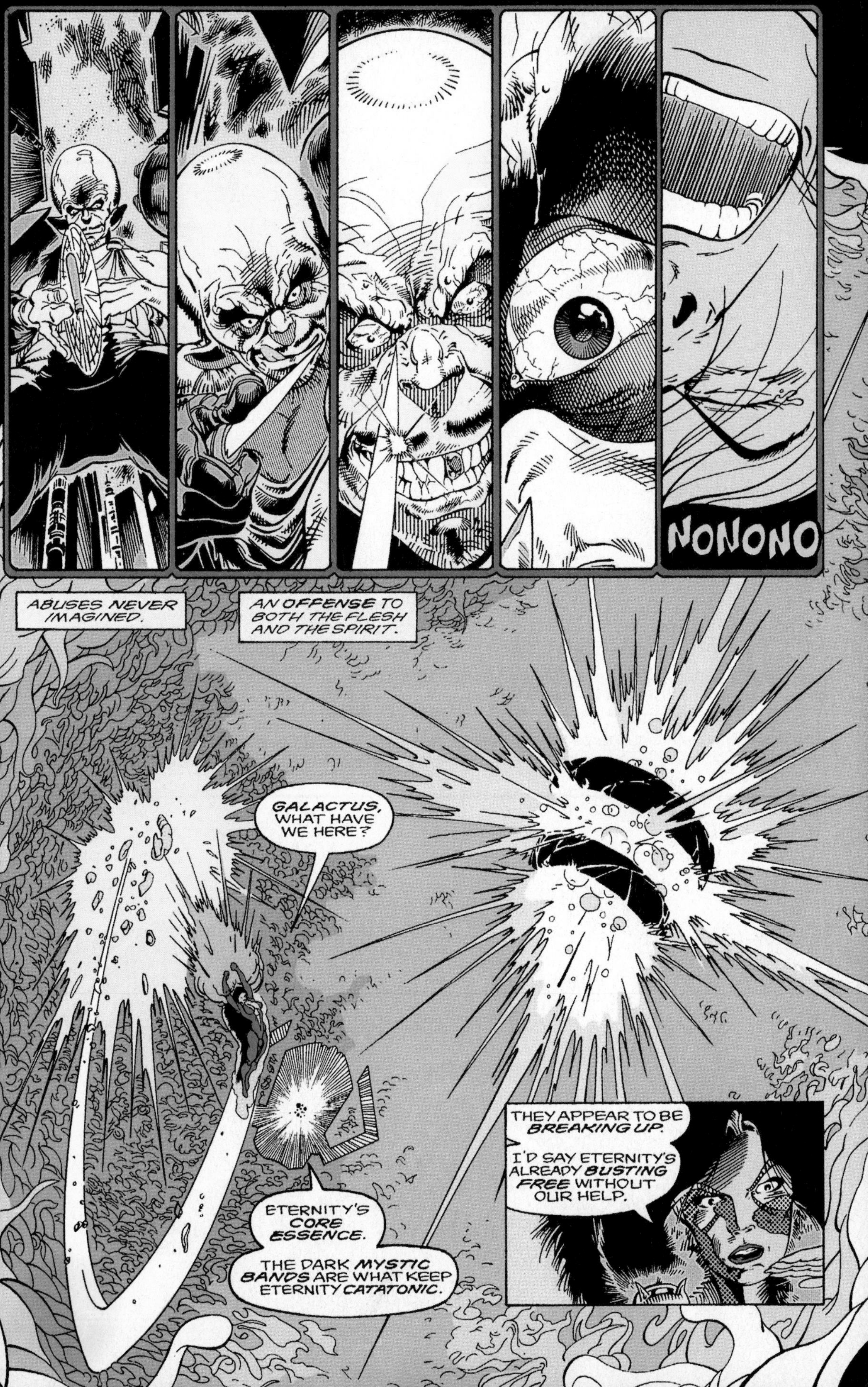
NONONO
ABUSES NEVER IMAGINED.
AN OFFENSE TO BOTH THE FLESH AND THE SPIRIT.
GALACTUS, WHAT HAVE WE HERE?
ETERNITY'S CORE ESSENCE.
THE DARK MYSTIC BANDS ARE WHAT KEEP ETERNITY CATATONIC.
THEY APPEAR TO BE BREAKING UP.
I'D SAY ETERNITY'S ALREADY BUSTING FREE WITHOUT OUR HELP.

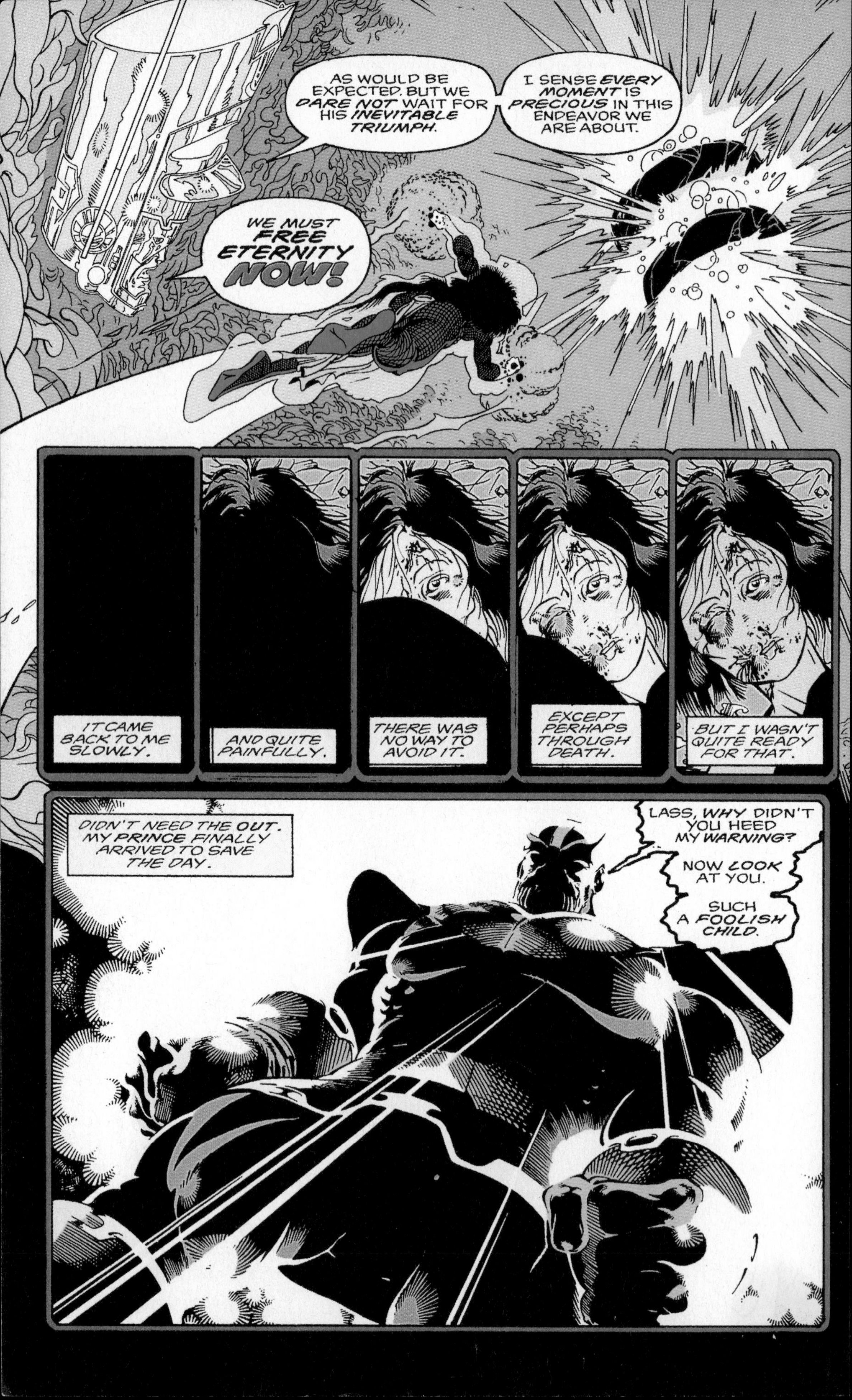
AS WOULD BE EXPECTED. BUT WE DARE NOT WAIT FOR HIS INEVITABLE TRIUMPH.
I SENSE EVERY MOMENT IS PRECIOUS IN THIS ENDEAVOR WE ARE ABOUT.
WE MUST FREE ETERNITY NOW!
IT CAME BACK TO ME SLOWLY.
AND QUITE PAINFULLY.
THERE WAS NO WAY TO AVOID IT.
EXCEPT PERHAPS THROUGH DEATH.
BUT I WASN'T QUITE READY FOR THAT.
DIDN'T NEED THE OUT. MY PRINCE FINALLY ARRIVED TO SAVE THE DAY.
LASS, WHY DIDN'T YOU HEED MY WARNING?
NOW LOOK AT YOU.
SUCH A FOOLISH CHILD.

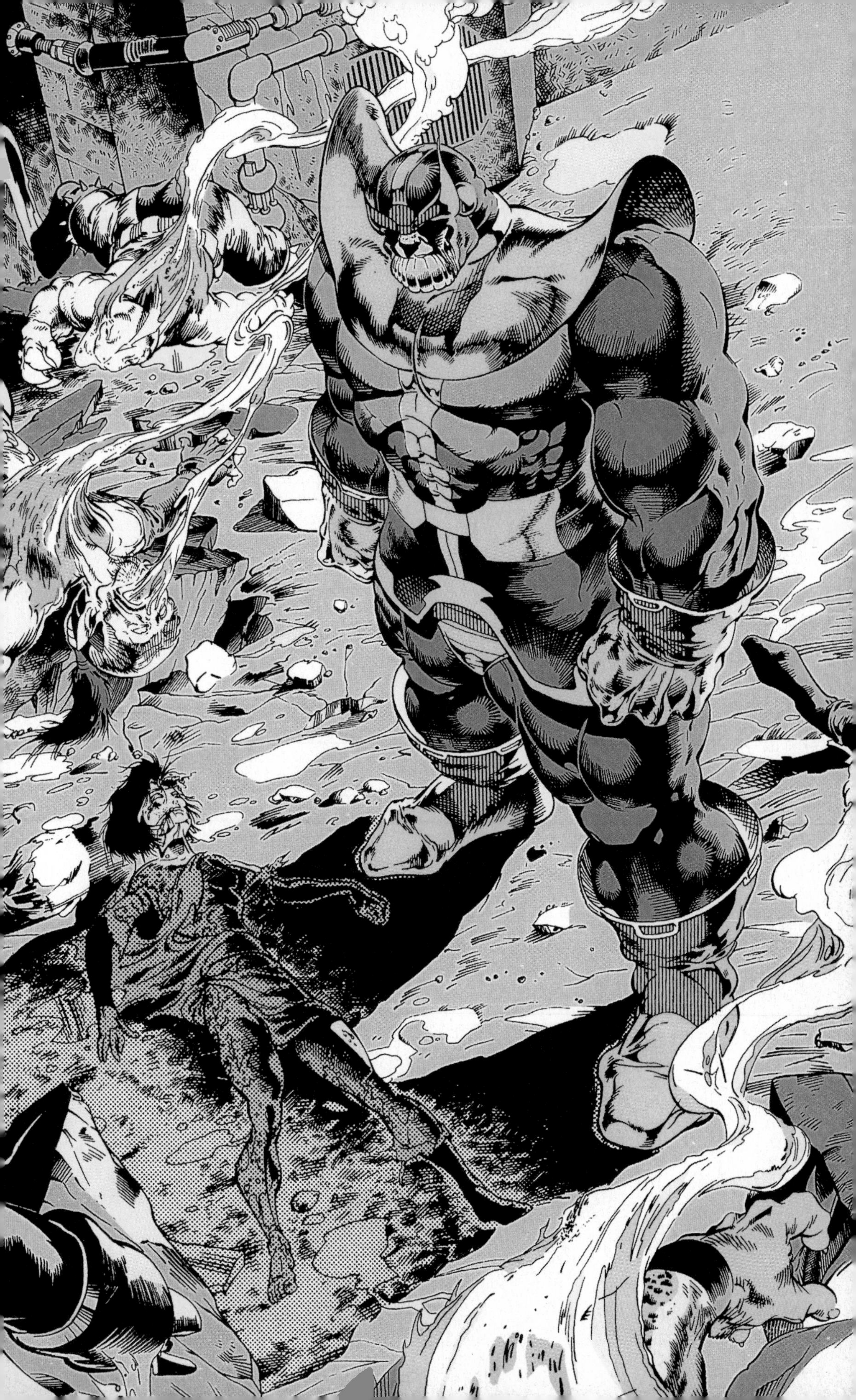

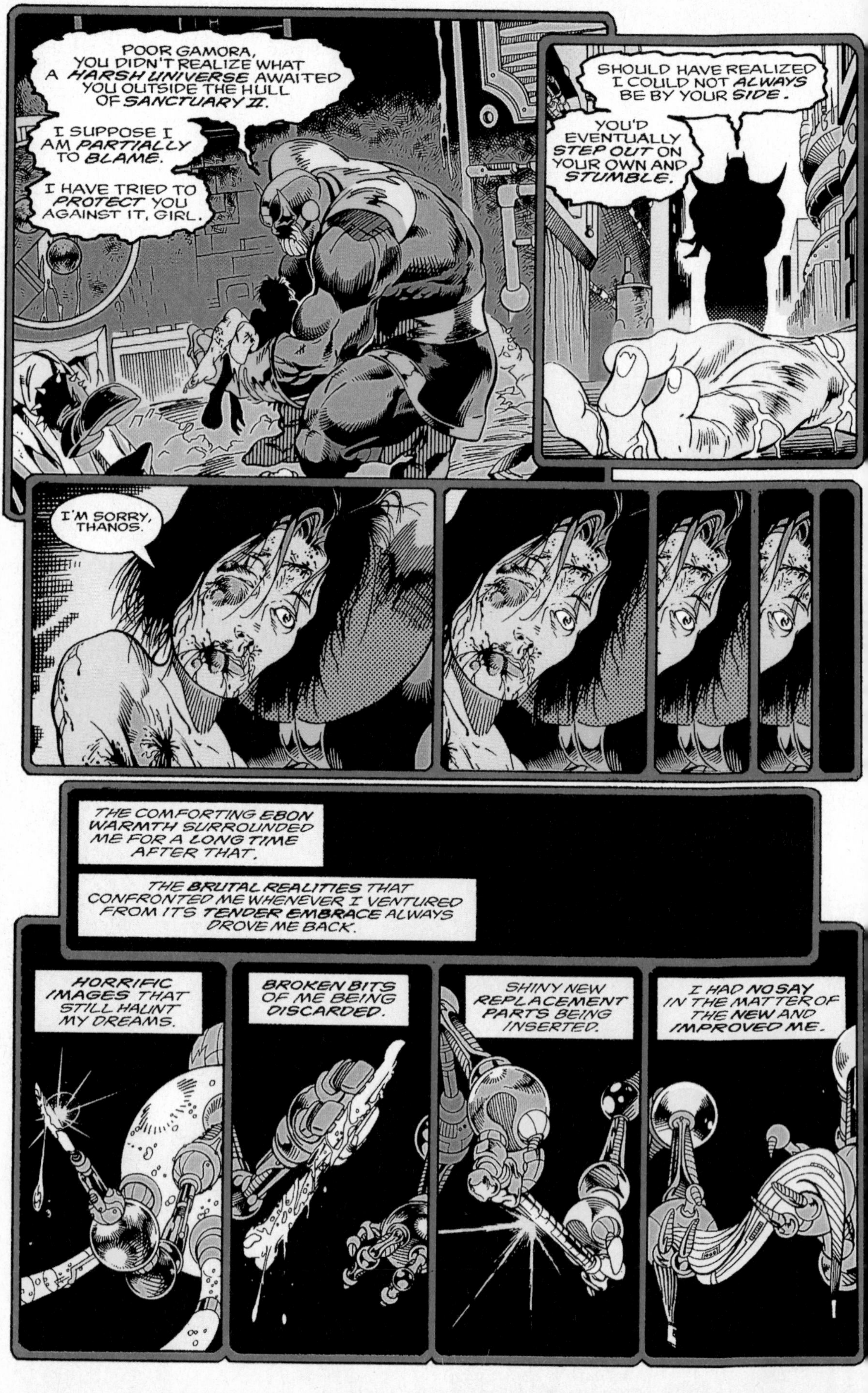
POOR GAMORA, YOU DIDN'T REALIZE WHAT A HARSH UNIVERSE AWAITED YOU OUTSIDE THE HULL OF SANCTUARY II.
I SUPPOSE I AM PARTIALLY TO BLAME.
I HAVE TRIED TO PROTECT YOU AGAINST IT, GIRL.
SHOULD HAVE REALIZED I COULD NOT ALWAYS BE BY YOUR SIDE.
YOU'D EVENTUALLY STEP OUT ON YOUR OWN AND STUMBLE.
I'M SORRY, THANOS.
THE COMFORTING EBON WARMTH SURROUNDED ME FOR A LONG TIME AFTER THAT.
THE BRUTAL REALITIES THAT CONFRONTED ME WHENEVER I VENTURED FROM ITS TENDER EMBRACE ALWAYS DROVE ME BACK.
HORRIFIC IMAGES THAT STILL HAUNT MY DREAMS.
BROKEN BITS OF ME BEING DISCARDED.
SHINY NEW REPLACEMENT PARTS BEING INSERTED.
I HAD NO SAY IN THE MATTER OF THE NEW AND IMPROVED ME.

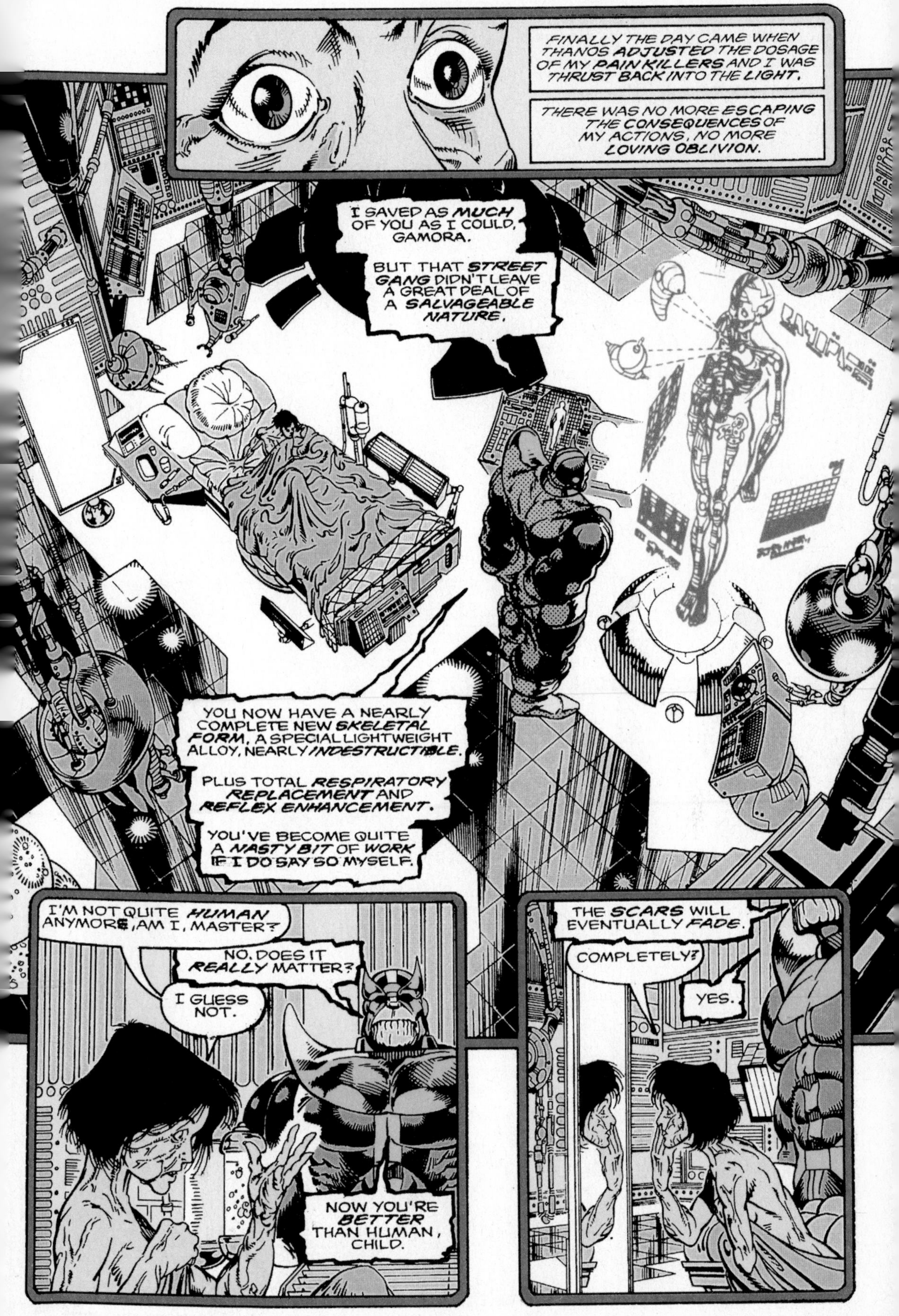

FINALLY THE DAY CAME WHEN THANOS ADJUSTED THE DOSAGE OF MY PAIN KILLERS AND I WAS THRUST BACK INTO THE LIGHT.
THERE WAS NO MORE ESCAPING THE CONSEQUENCES OF MY ACTIONS, NO MORE LOVING OBLIVION.
I SAVED AS MUCH OF YOU AS I COULD, GAMORA.
BUT THAT STREET GANG DIDN'T LEAVE A GREAT DEAL OF A SALVAGEABLE NATURE.
YOU NOW HAVE A NEARLY COMPLETE NEW SKELETAL FORM, A SPECIAL LIGHTWEIGHT ALLOY, NEARLY INDESTRUCTIBLE.
PLUS TOTAL RESPIRATORY REPLACEMENT AND REFLEX ENHANCEMENT.
YOU'VE BECOME QUITE A NASTY BIT OF WORK IF I DO SAY SO MYSELF.
I'M NOT QUITE HUMAN ANYMORE, AM I, MASTER?
NO. DOES IT REALLY MATTER?
I GUESS NOT.
NOW YOU'RE BETTER THAN HUMAN, CHILD.
THE SCARS WILL EVENTUALLY FADE.
COMPLETELY?
YES.

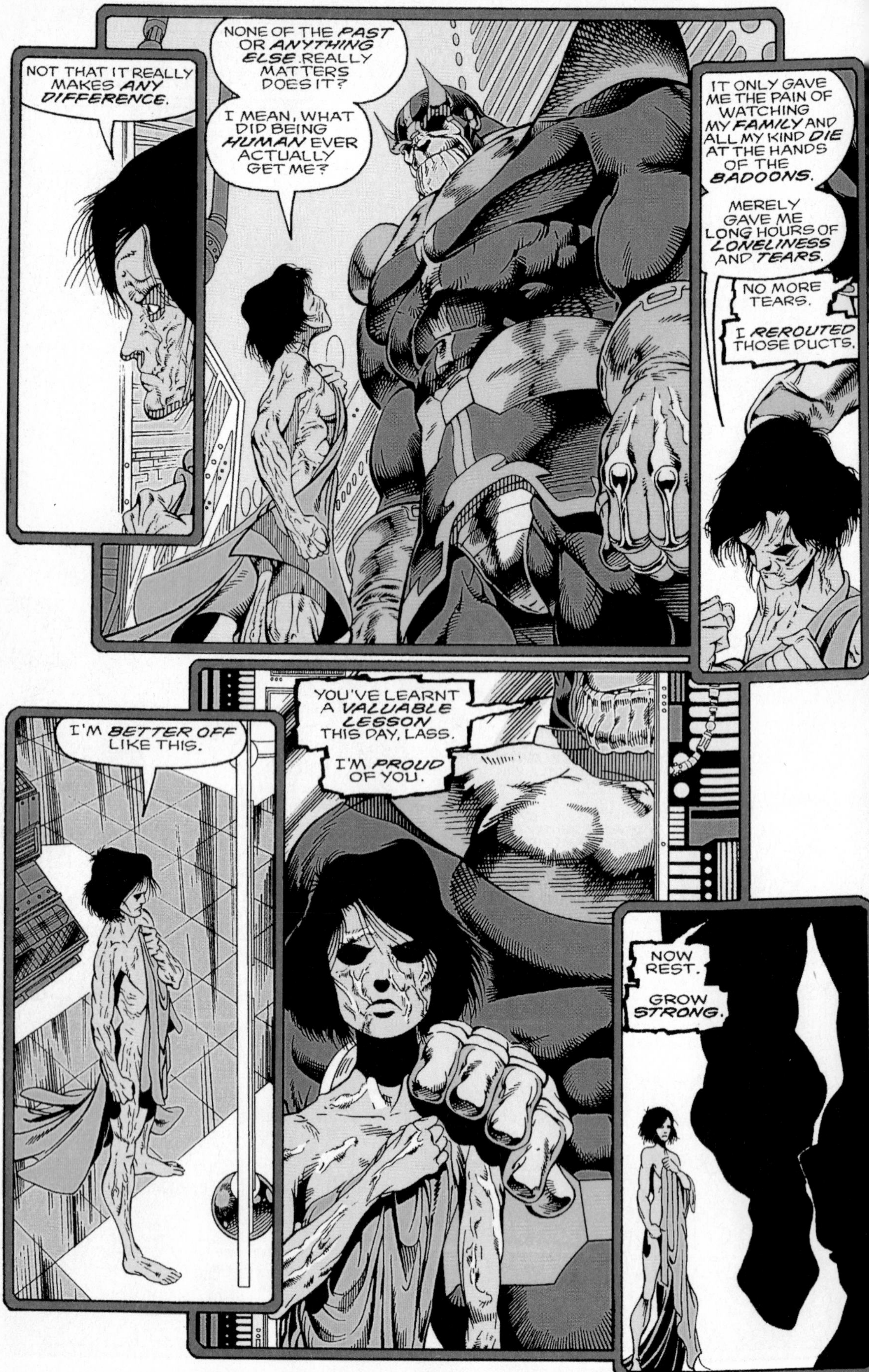

NOT THAT IT REALLY MAKES ANY DIFFERENCE.
NONE OF THE PAST OR ANYTHING ELSE REALLY MATTERS DOES IT?
I MEAN, WHAT DID BEING HUMAN EVER ACTUALLY GET ME?
IT ONLY GAVE ME THE PAIN OF WATCHING MY FAMILY AND ALL MY KIND DIE AT THE HANDS OF THE BADOONS.
MERELY GAVE ME LONG HOURS OF LONELINESS AND TEARS.
NO MORE TEARS.
I REROUTED THOSE DUCTS.
I'M BETTER OFF LIKE THIS.
YOU'VE LEARNT A VALUABLE LESSON THIS DAY, LASS.
I'M PROUD OF YOU.
NOW REST.
GROW STRONG.

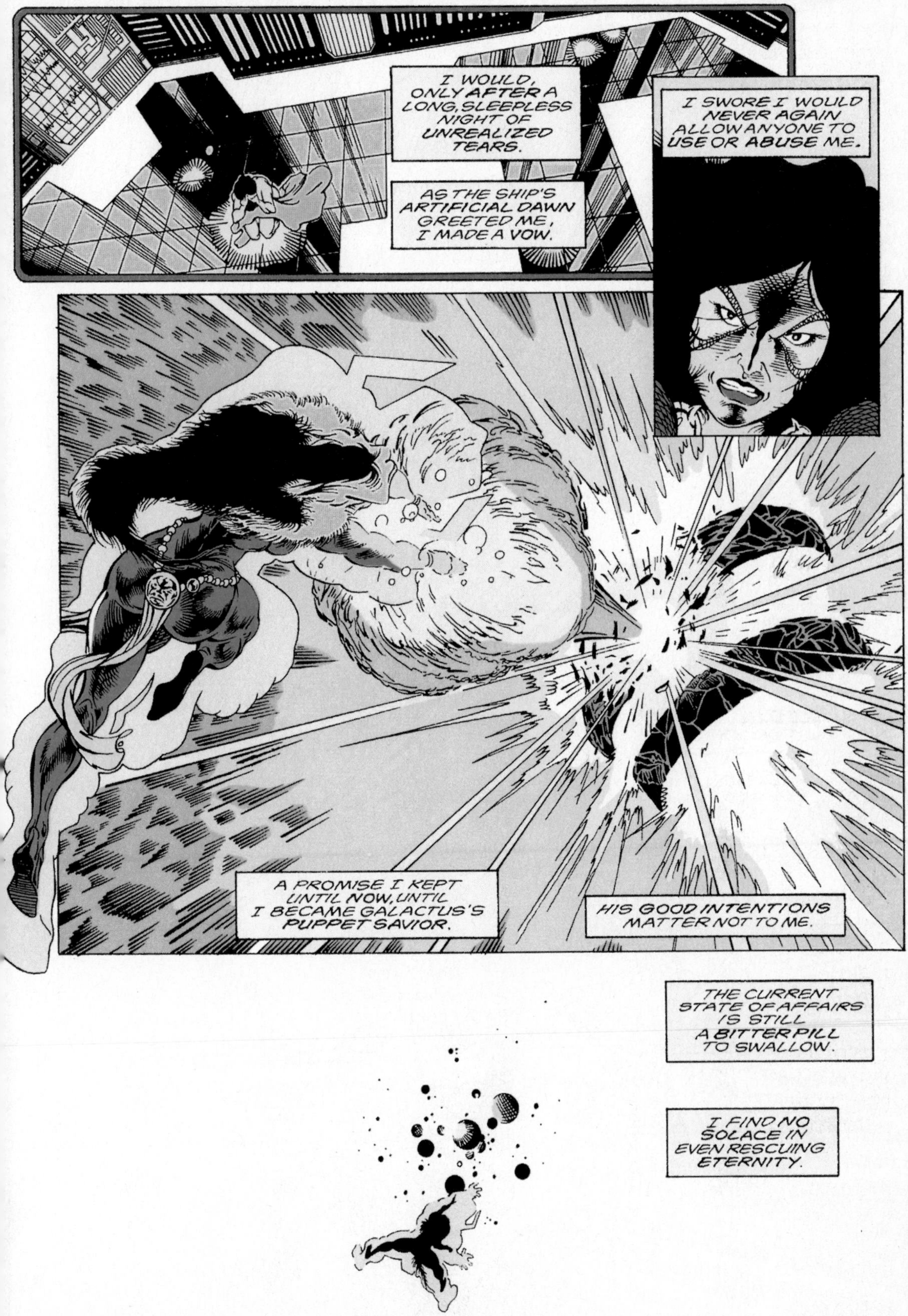
I WOULD, ONLY AFTER A LONG, SLEEPLESS NIGHT OF UNREALIZED TEARS.
AS THE SHIP'S ARTIFICIAL DAWN GREETED ME, I MADE A VOW.
I SWORE I WOULD NEVER AGAIN ALLOW ANYONE TO USE OR ABUSE ME.
A PROMISE I KEPT UNTIL NOW, UNTIL I BECAME GALACTUS'S PUPPET SAVIOR.
HIS GOOD INTENTIONS MATTER NOT TO ME.
THE CURRENT STATE OF AFFAIRS IS STILL A BITTER PILL TO SWALLOW.
I FIND NO SOLACE IN EVEN RESCUING ETERNITY.

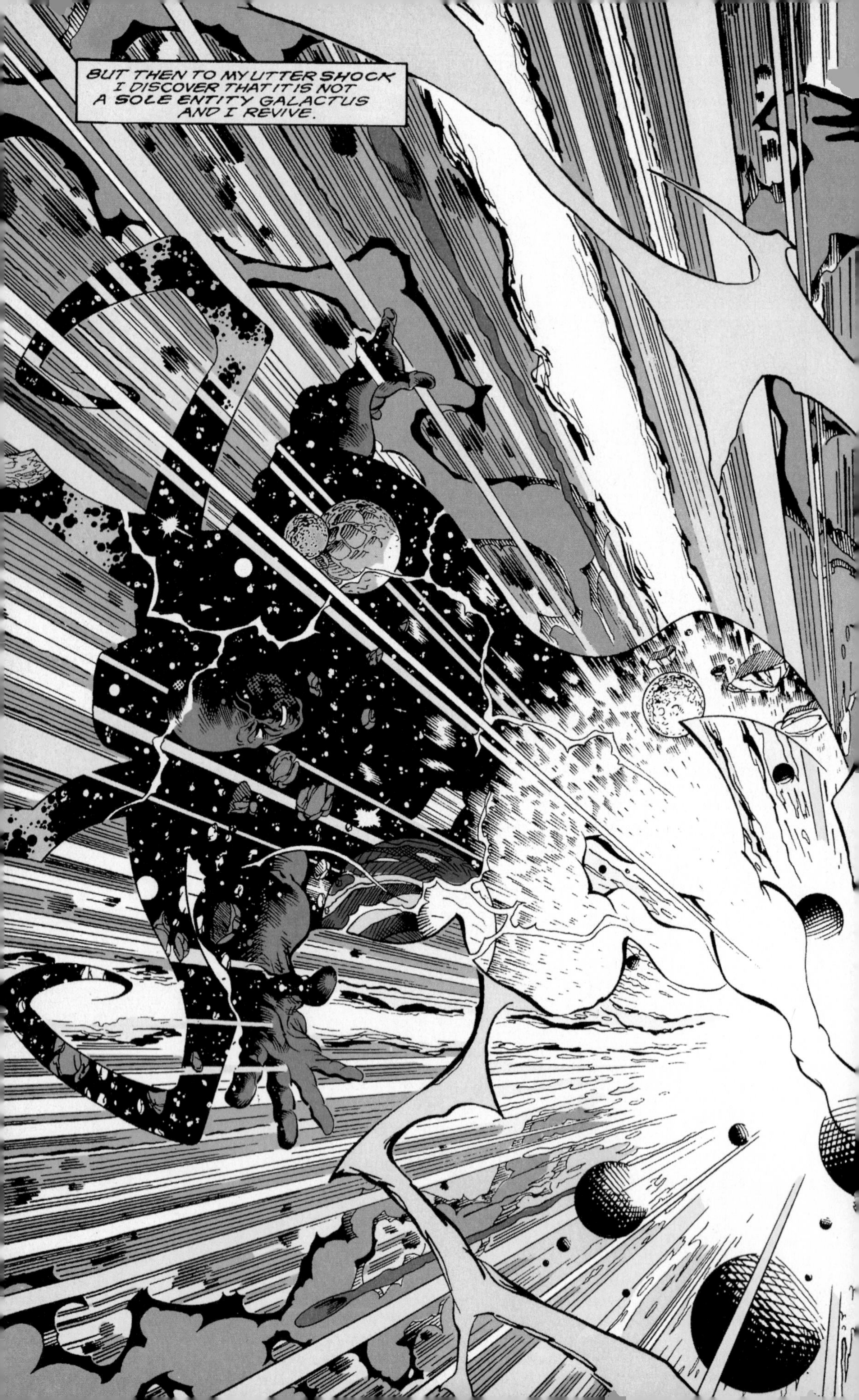
BUT THEN TO MY UTTER SHOCK I DISCOVER THAT IT IS NOT A SOLE ENTITY GALACTUS AND I REVIVE.

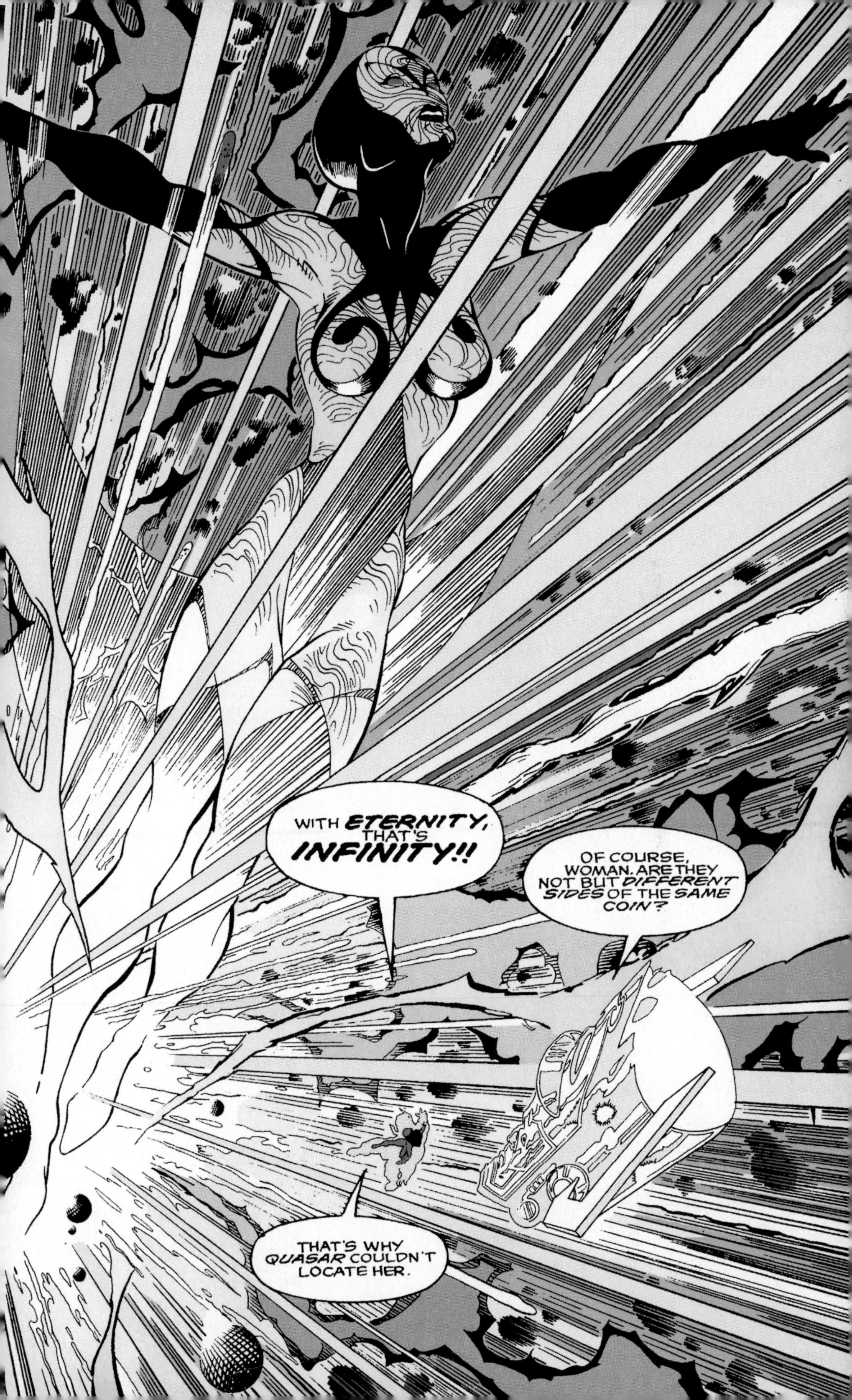
WITH ETERNITY, THAT'S INFINITY!!
OF COURSE, WOMAN. ARE THEY NOT BUT DIFFERENT SIDES OF THE SAME COIN?
THAT'S WHY QUASAR COULDN'T LOCATE HER.

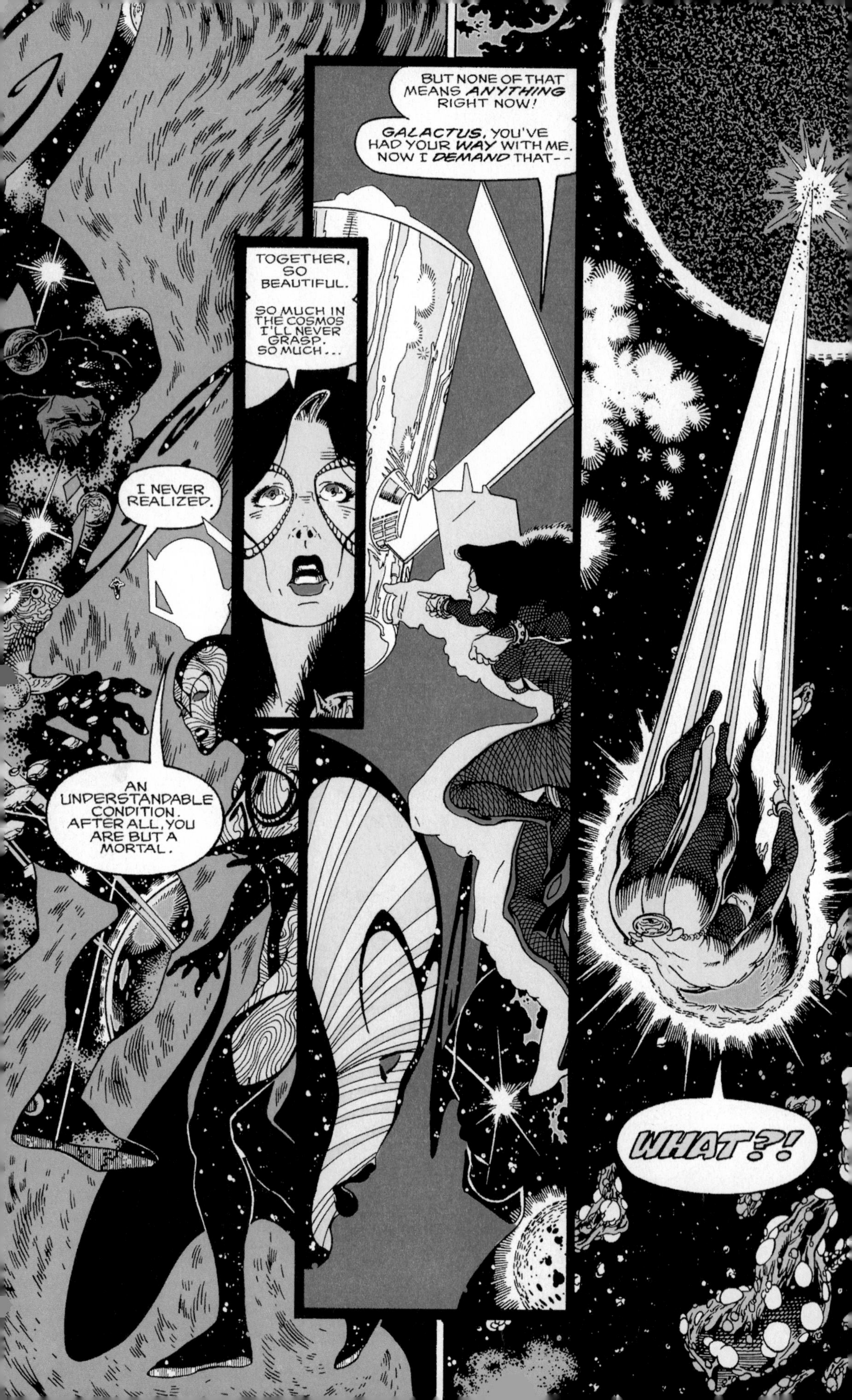
BUT NONE OF THAT MEANS ANYTHING RIGHT NOW!
GALACTUS, YOU'VE HAD YOUR WAY WITH ME. NOW I DEMAND THAT--
TOGETHER, SO BEAUTIFUL.
SO MUCH IN THE COSMOS I'LL NEVER GRASP. SO MUCH...
I NEVER REALIZED.
AN UNDERSTANDABLE CONDITION. AFTER ALL, YOU ARE BUT A MORTAL.
WHAT?!

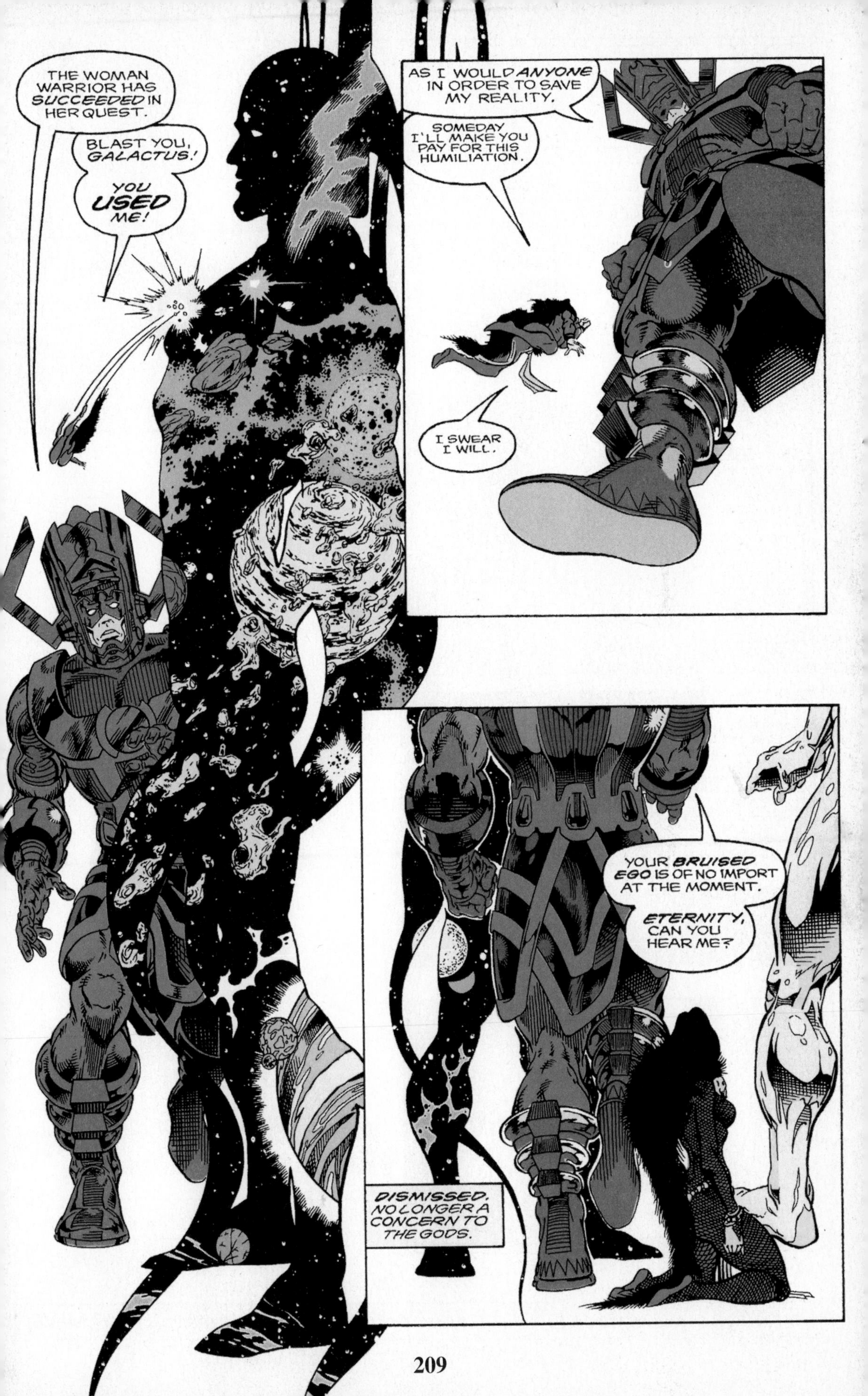

THE WOMAN WARRIOR HAS SUCCEEDED IN HER QUEST.
BLAST YOU, GALACTUS!
YOU USED ME!
AS I WOULD ANYONE IN ORDER TO SAVE MY REALITY.
SOMEDAY I'LL MAKE YOU PAY FOR THIS HUMILIATION.
I SWEAR I WILL.
YOUR BRUISED EGO IS OF NO IMPORT AT THE MOMENT.
ETERNITY, CAN YOU HEAR ME?
DISMISSED. NO LONGER A CONCERN TO THE GODS.

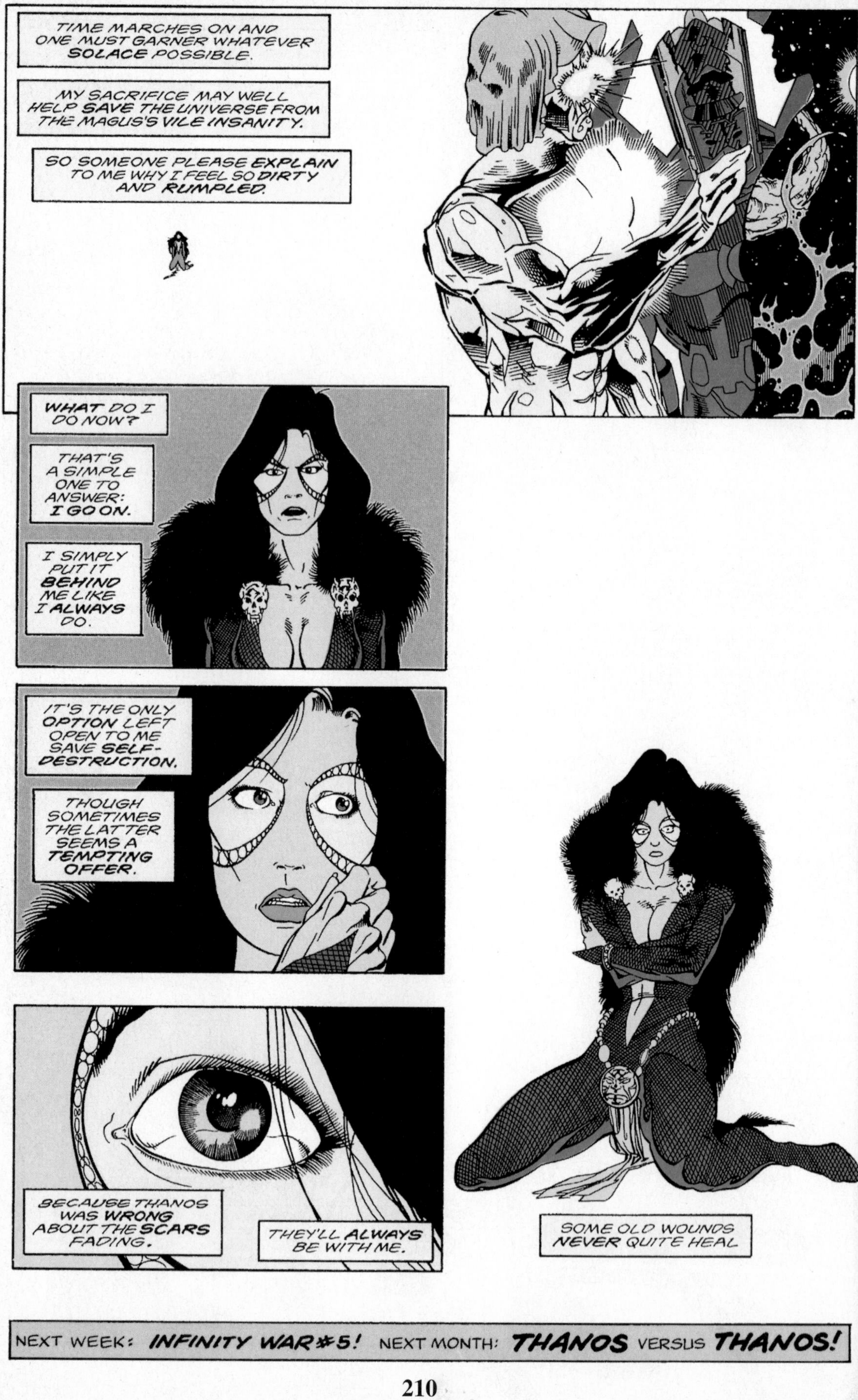
TIME MARCHES ON AND ONE MUST GARNER WHATEVER SOLACE POSSIBLE.
MY SACRIFICE MAY WELL HELP SAVE THE UNIVERSE FROM THE MAGUS'S VILE INSANITY.
SO SOMEONE PLEASE EXPLAIN TO ME WHY I FEEL SO DIRTY AND RUMPLED.
WHAT DO I DO NOW?
THAT'S A SIMPLE ONE TO ANSWER: I GO ON.
I SIMPLY PUT IT BEHIND ME LIKE I ALWAYS DO.
IT'S THE ONLY OPTION LEFT OPEN TO ME SAVE SELF-DESTRUCTION.
THOUGH SOMETIMES THE LATTER SEEMS A TEMPTING OFFER.
BECAUSE THANOS WAS WRONG ABOUT THE SCARS FADING.
THEY'LL ALWAYS BE WITH ME.
SOME OLD WOUNDS NEVER QUITE HEAL
NEXT WEEK: INFINITY WAR #5! NEXT MONTH: THANOS VERSUS THANOS!

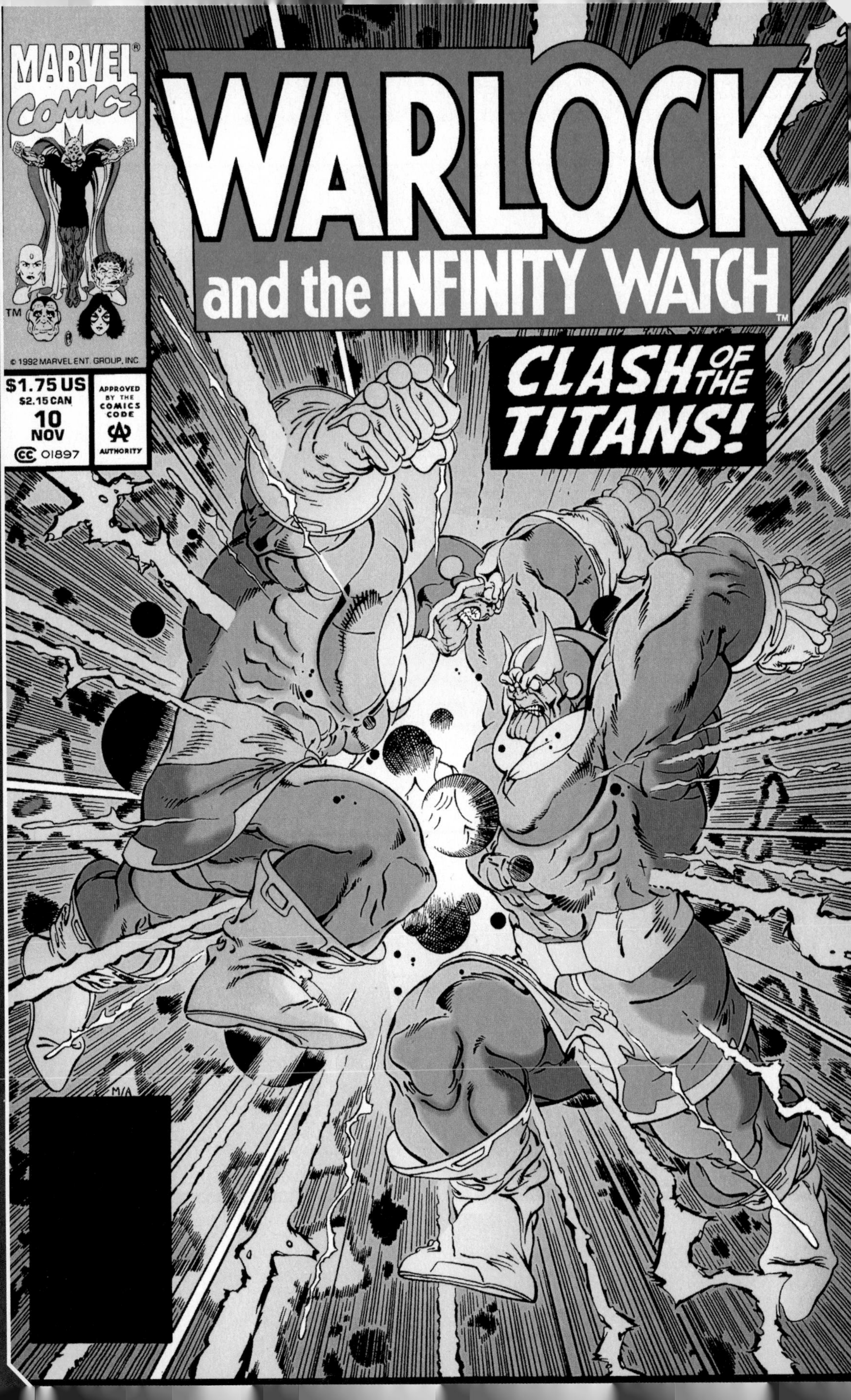

MARVEL® COMICS
WARLOCK
and the INFINITY WATCH™
™
© 1992 MARVEL ENT. GROUP, INC.
$1.75 US
$2.15 CAN
10
NOV
APPROVED BY THE COMICS CODE AUTHORITY
01897
CLASH OF THE TITANS!
M/A

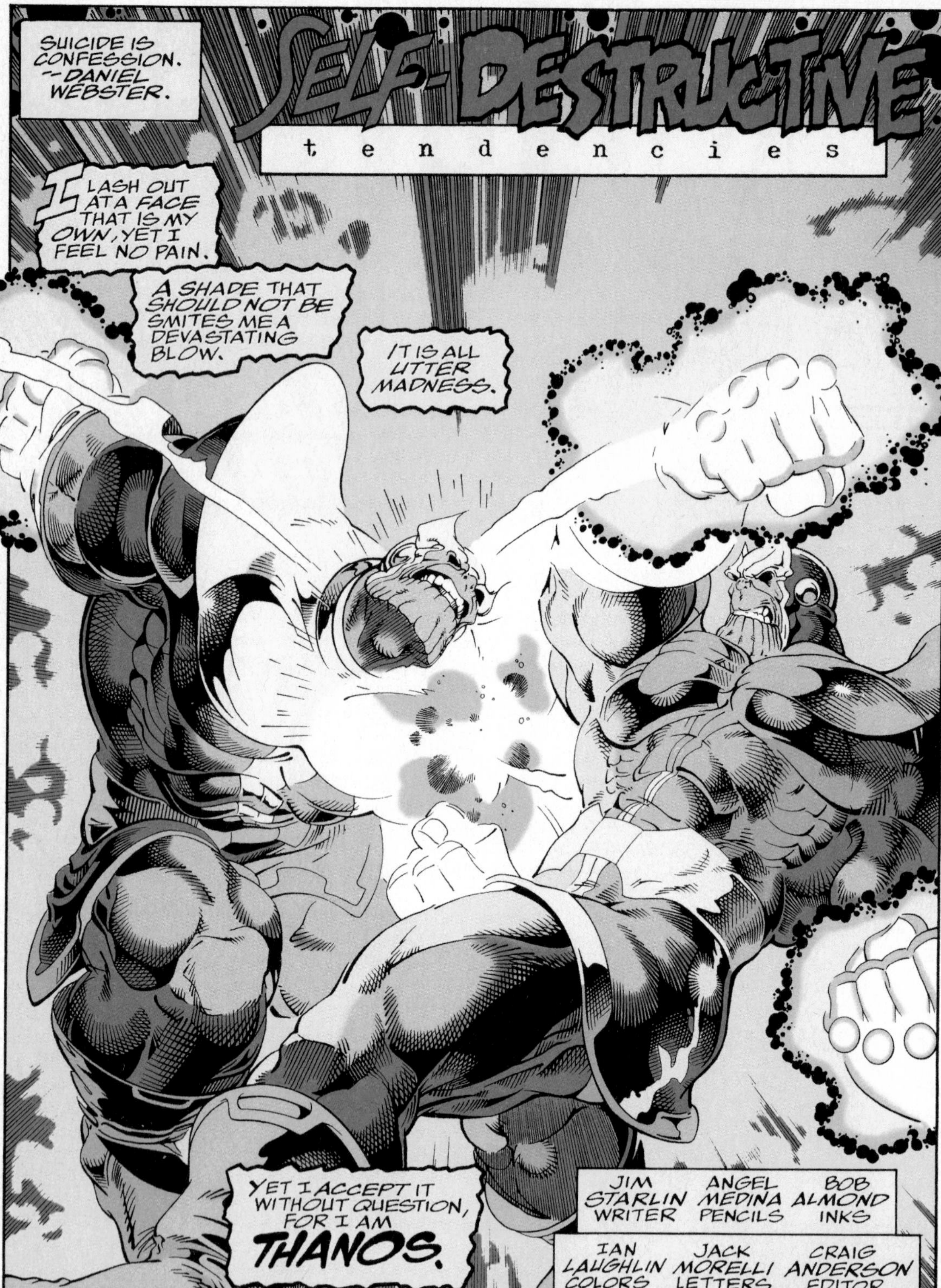
SUICIDE IS CONFESSION. --DANIEL WEBSTER.
SELF-DESTRUCTIVE
tendencies
I LASH OUT AT A FACE THAT IS MY OWN, YET I FEEL NO PAIN.
A SHADE THAT SHOULD NOT BE SMITES ME A DEVASTATING BLOW.
IT IS ALL UTTER MADNESS.
YET I ACCEPT IT WITHOUT QUESTION, FOR I AM THANOS.
JIM STARLIN WRITER
ANGEL MEDINA PENCILS
BOB ALMOND INKS
IAN LAUGHLIN COLORS
JACK MORELLI LETTERS
CRAIG ANDERSON EDITOR
TOM DEFALCO--BOSS
CREATED BY JIM STARLIN

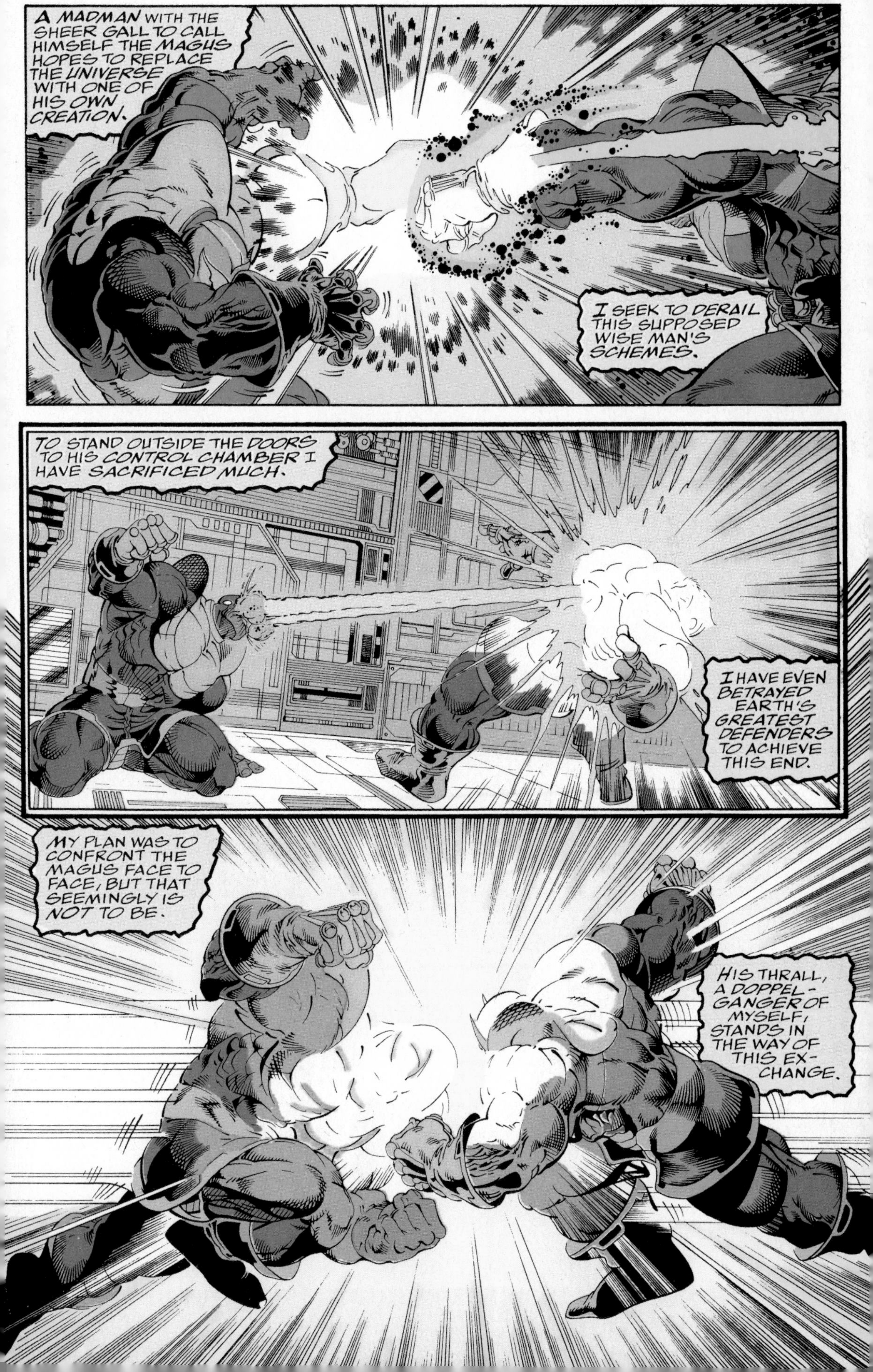
A MADMAN WITH THE SHEER GALL TO CALL HIMSELF THE MAGUS HOPES TO REPLACE THE UNIVERSE WITH ONE OF HIS OWN CREATION.
I SEEK TO DERAIL THIS SUPPOSED WISE MAN'S SCHEMES.
TO STAND OUTSIDE THE DOORS TO HIS CONTROL CHAMBER I HAVE SACRIFICED MUCH.
I HAVE EVEN BETRAYED EARTH'S GREATEST DEFENDERS TO ACHIEVE THIS END.
MY PLAN WAS TO CONFRONT THE MAGUS FACE TO FACE, BUT THAT SEEMINGLY IS NOT TO BE.
HIS THRALL, A DOPPEL-GANGER OF MYSELF, STANDS IN THE WAY OF THIS EX-CHANGE.

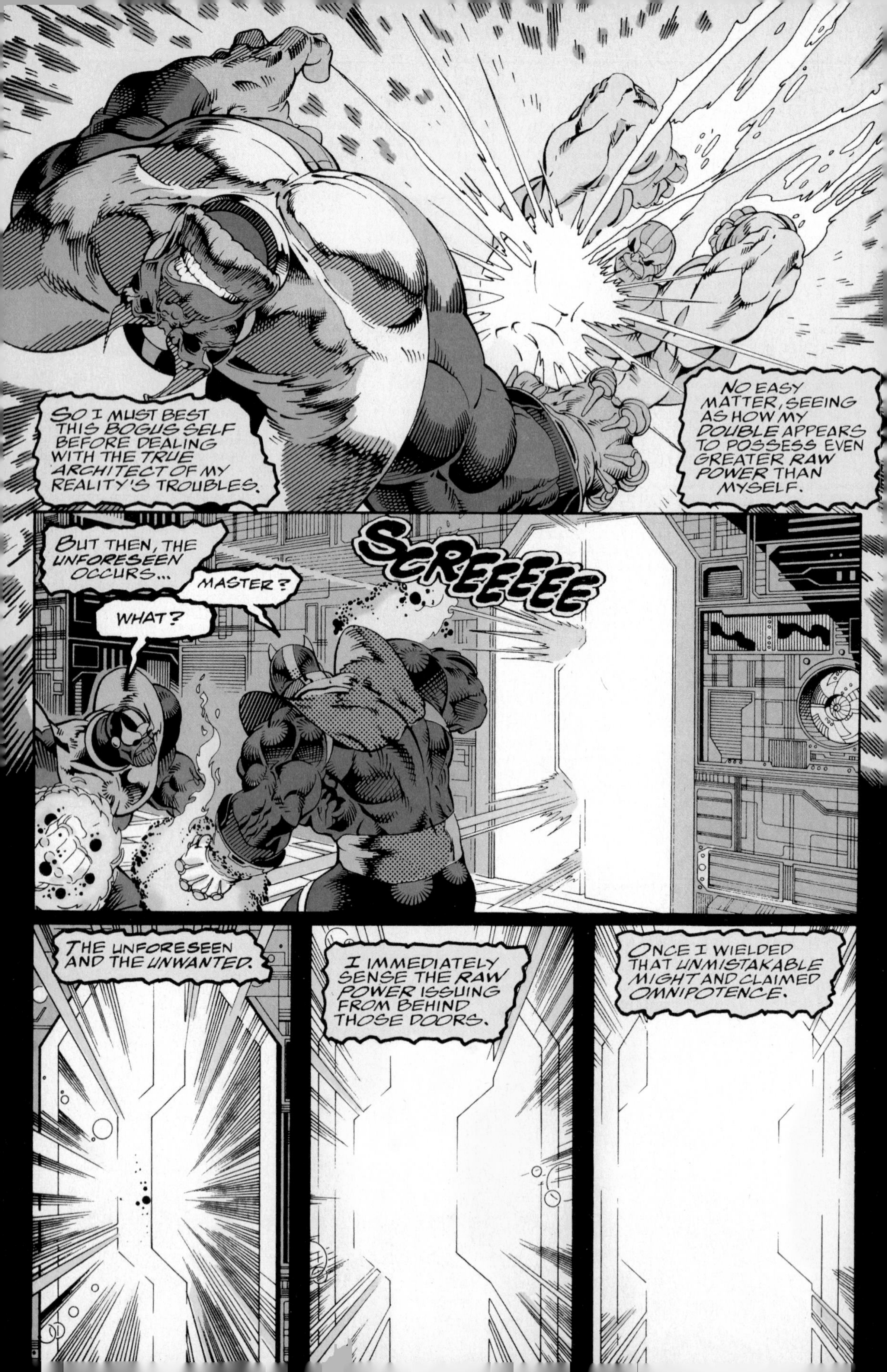
SO I MUST BEST THIS BOGUS SELF BEFORE DEALING WITH THE TRUE ARCHITECT OF MY REALITY'S TROUBLES.
NO EASY MATTER, SEEING AS HOW MY DOUBLE APPEARS TO POSSESS EVEN GREATER RAW POWER THAN MYSELF.
BUT THEN, THE UNFORESEEN OCCURS...
SCREEEEEE
MASTER?
WHAT?
THE UNFORESEEN AND THE UNWANTED.
I IMMEDIATELY SENSE THE RAW POWER ISSUING FROM BEHIND THOSE DOORS.
ONCE I WIELDED THAT UNMISTAKABLE MIGHT AND CLAIMED OMNIPOTENCE.

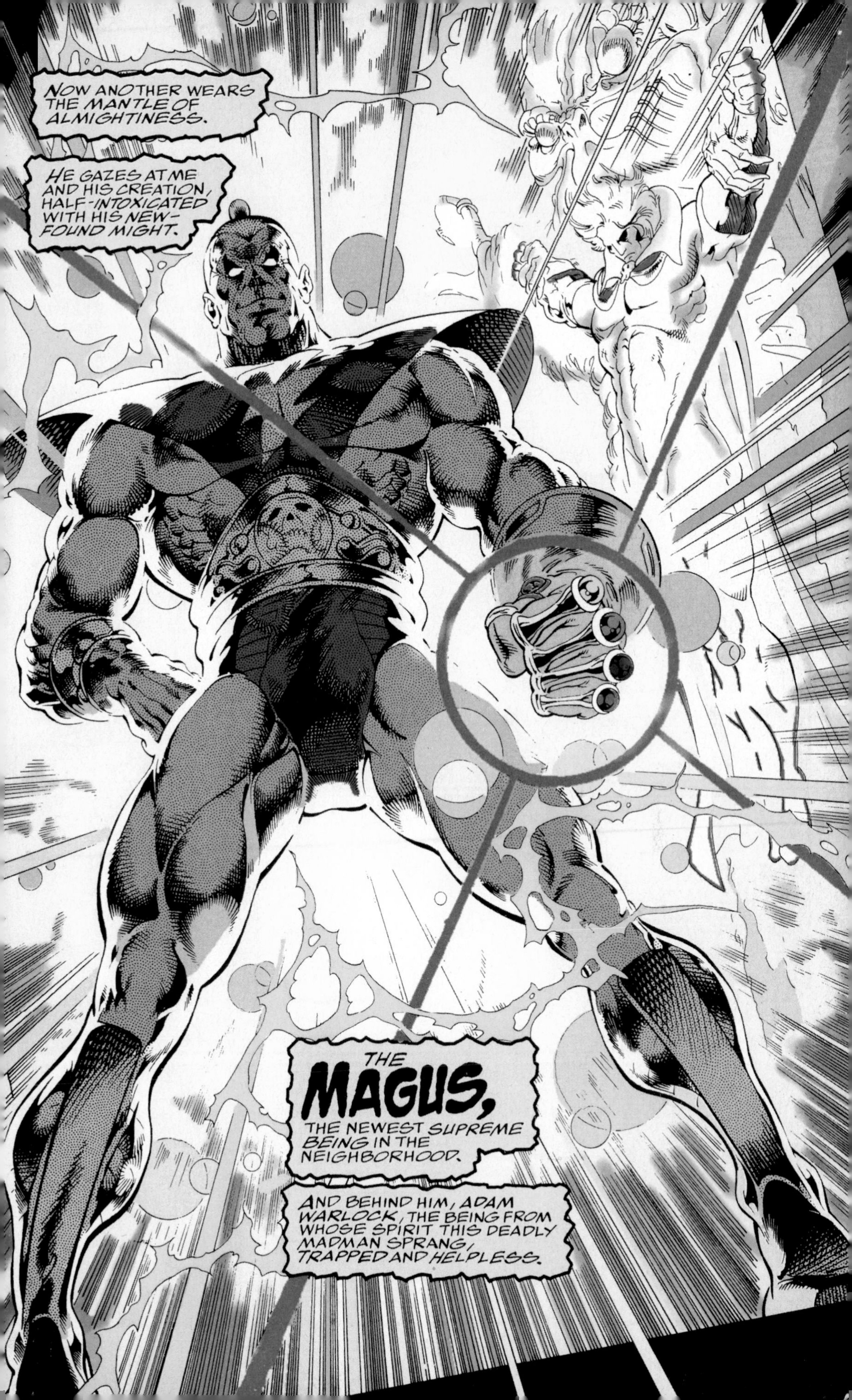
NOW ANOTHER WEARS THE MANTLE OF ALMIGHTINESS.
HE GAZES AT ME AND HIS CREATION, HALF-INTOXICATED WITH HIS NEW-FOUND MIGHT.
THE MAGUS, THE NEWEST SUPREME BEING IN THE NEIGHBORHOOD.
AND BEHIND HIM, ADAM WARLOCK, THE BEING FROM WHOSE SPIRIT THIS DEADLY MADMAN SPRANG, TRAPPED AND HELPLESS.

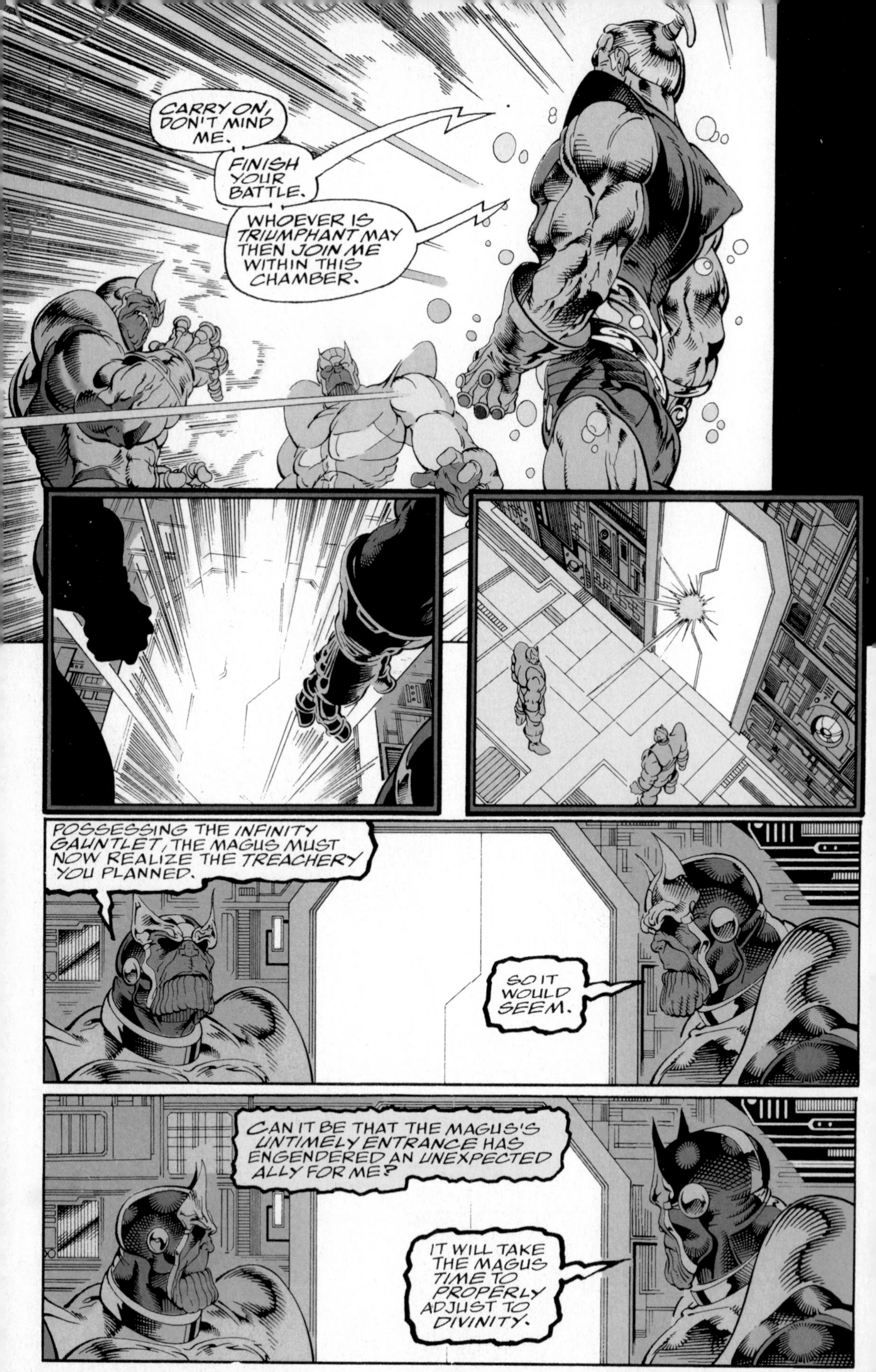

CARRY ON, DON'T MIND ME.
FINISH YOUR BATTLE.
WHOEVER IS TRIUMPHANT MAY THEN JOIN ME WITHIN THIS CHAMBER.
POSSESSING THE INFINITY GAUNTLET, THE MAGUS MUST NOW REALIZE THE TREACHERY YOU PLANNED.
SO IT WOULD SEEM.
CAN IT BE THAT THE MAGUS'S UNTIMELY ENTRANCE HAS ENGENDERED AN UNEXPECTED ALLY FOR ME?
IT WILL TAKE THE MAGUS TIME TO PROPERLY ADJUST TO DIVINITY.

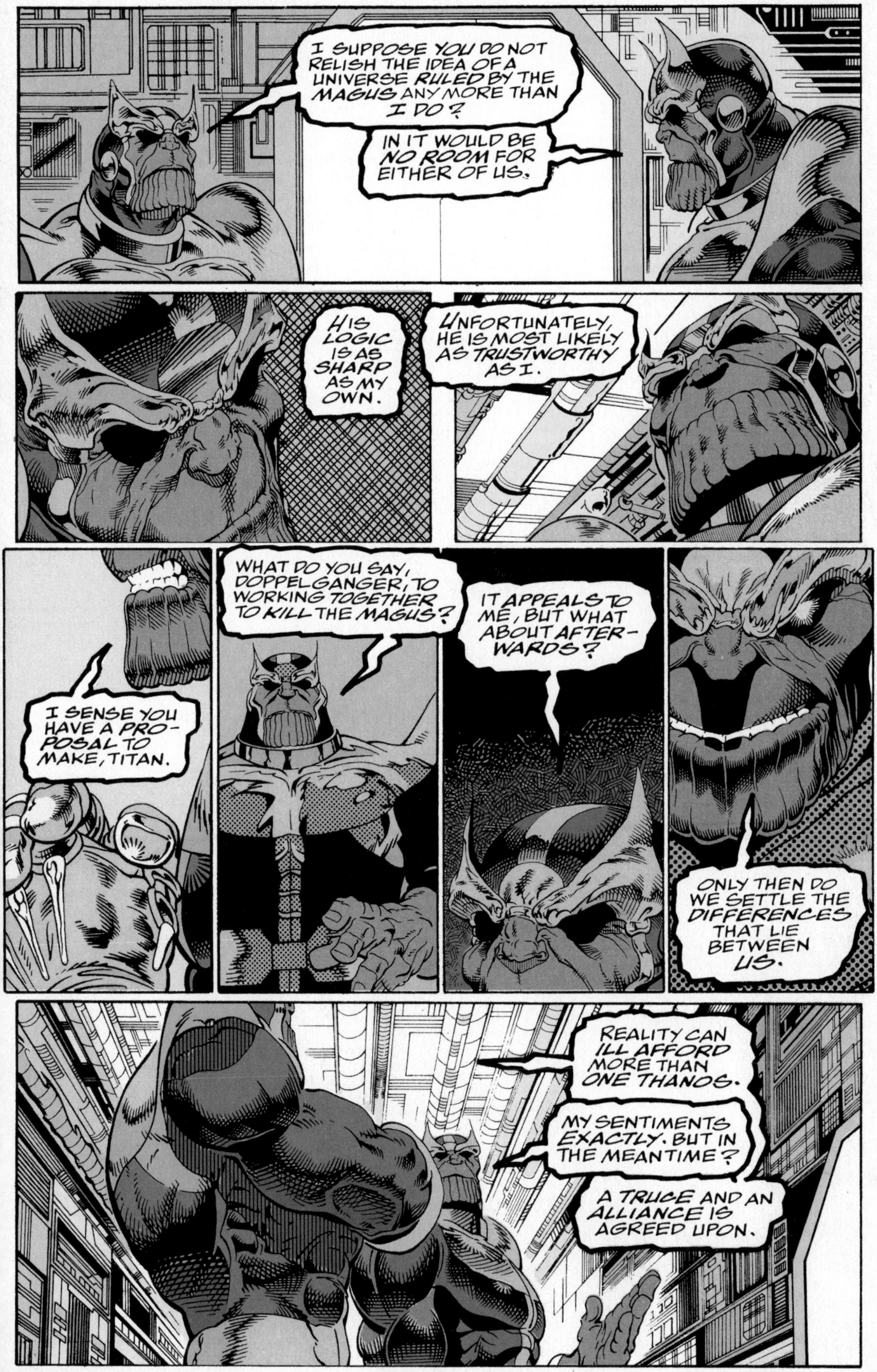
I SUPPOSE YOU DO NOT RELISH THE IDEA OF A UNIVERSE RULED BY THE MAGUS ANY MORE THAN I DO?
IN IT WOULD BE NO ROOM FOR EITHER OF US.
HIS LOGIC IS AS SHARP AS MY OWN.
UNFORTUNATELY, HE IS MOST LIKELY AS TRUSTWORTHY AS I.
I SENSE YOU HAVE A PROPOSAL TO MAKE, TITAN.
WHAT DO YOU SAY, DOPPELGANGER, TO WORKING TOGETHER TO KILL THE MAGUS?
IT APPEALS TO ME, BUT WHAT ABOUT AFTERWARDS?
ONLY THEN DO WE SETTLE THE DIFFERENCES THAT LIE BETWEEN US.
REALITY CAN ILL AFFORD MORE THAN ONE THANOS.
MY SENTIMENTS EXACTLY. BUT IN THE MEANTIME?
A TRUCE AND AN ALLIANCE IS AGREED UPON.

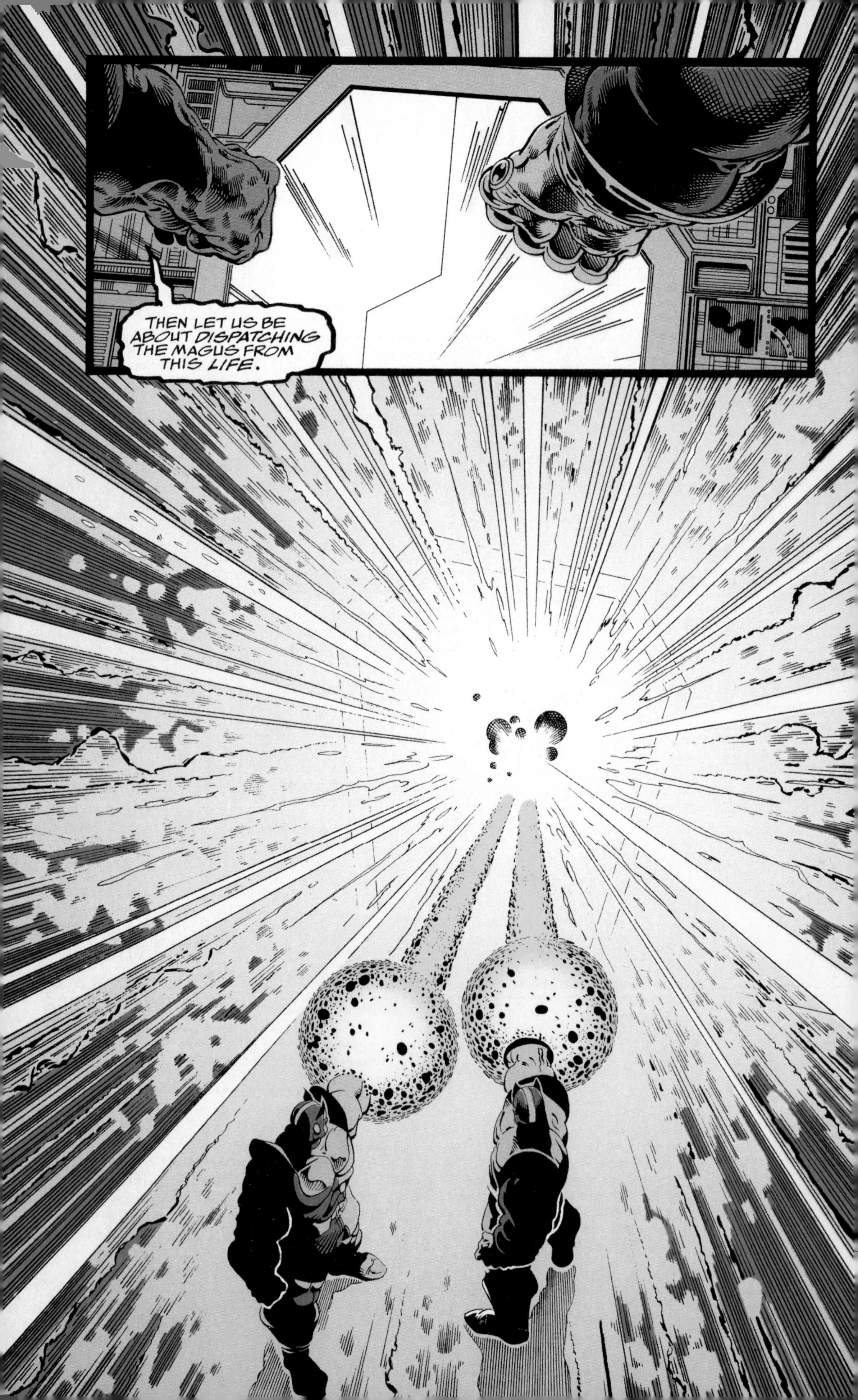
THEN LET US BE ABOUT DISPATCHING THE MAGUS FROM THIS LIFE.

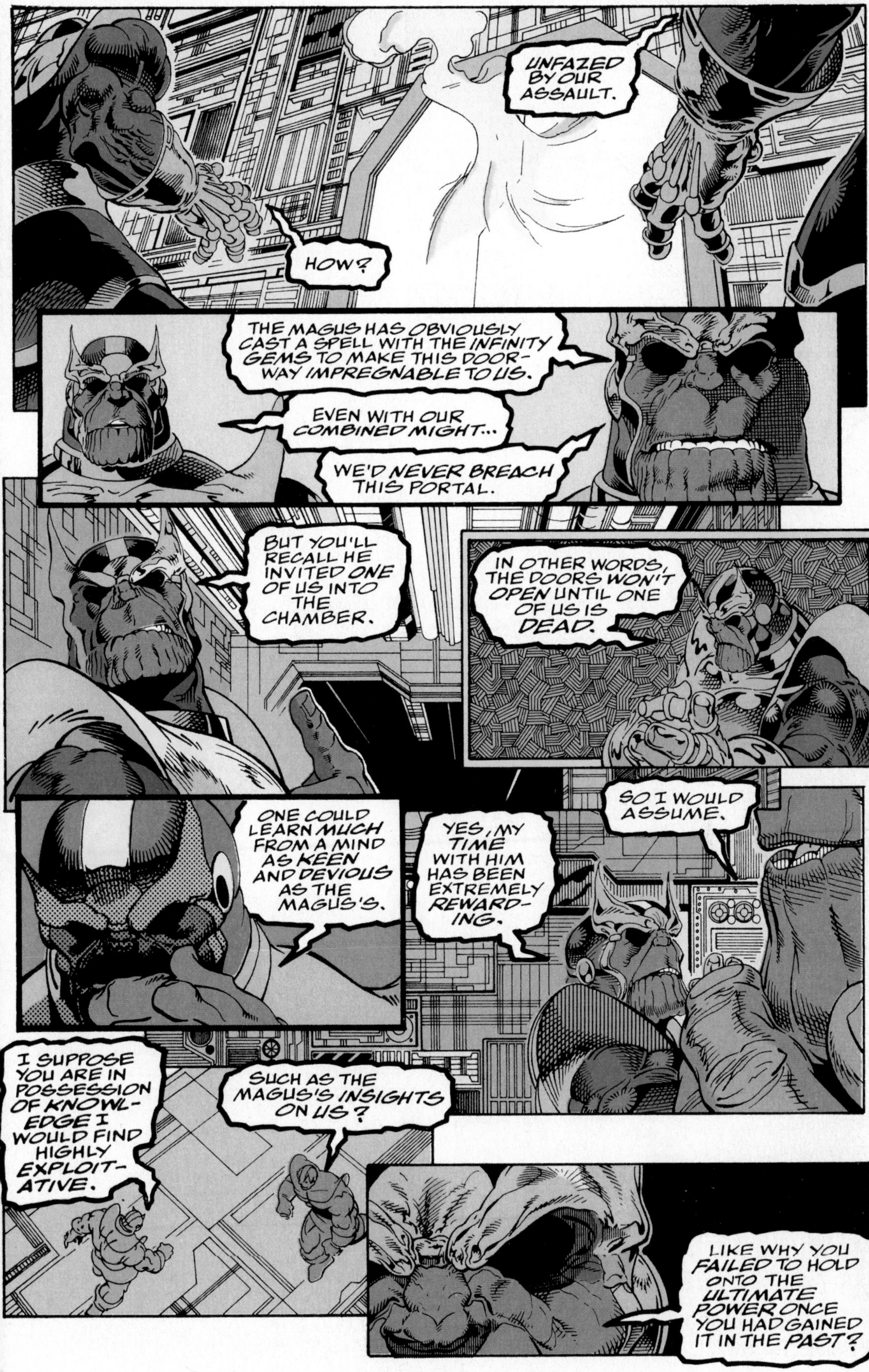
UNFAZED BY OUR ASSAULT.
HOW?
THE MAGUS HAS OBVIOUSLY CAST A SPELL WITH THE INFINITY GEMS TO MAKE THIS DOORWAY IMPREGNABLE TO US.
EVEN WITH OUR COMBINED MIGHT...
WE'D NEVER BREACH THIS PORTAL.
BUT YOU'LL RECALL HE INVITED ONE OF US INTO THE CHAMBER.
IN OTHER WORDS, THE DOORS WON'T OPEN UNTIL ONE OF US IS DEAD.
ONE COULD LEARN MUCH FROM A MIND AS KEEN AND DEVIOUS AS THE MAGUS'S.
YES, MY TIME WITH HIM HAS BEEN EXTREMELY REWARDING.
SO I WOULD ASSUME.
I SUPPOSE YOU ARE IN POSSESSION OF KNOWLEDGE I WOULD FIND HIGHLY EXPLOITATIVE.
SUCH AS THE MAGUS'S INSIGHTS ON US?
LIKE WHY YOU FAILED TO HOLD ONTO THE ULTIMATE POWER ONCE YOU HAD GAINED IT IN THE PAST?

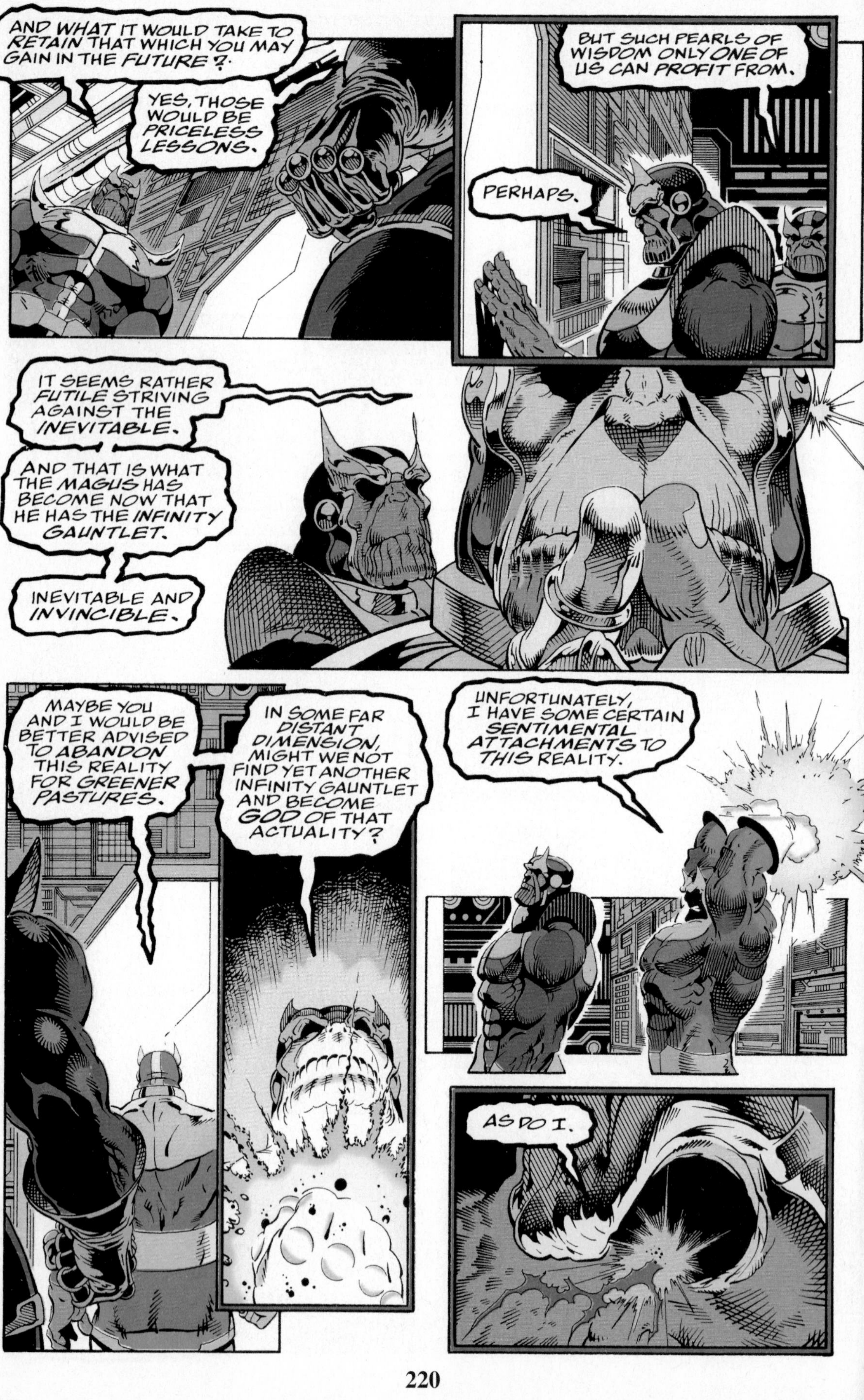
AND WHAT IT WOULD TAKE TO RETAIN THAT WHICH YOU MAY GAIN IN THE FUTURE?
YES, THOSE WOULD BE PRICELESS LESSONS.
BUT SUCH PEARLS OF WISDOM ONLY ONE OF US CAN PROFIT FROM.
PERHAPS.
IT SEEMS RATHER FUTILE STRIVING AGAINST THE INEVITABLE.
AND THAT IS WHAT THE MAGUS HAS BECOME NOW THAT HE HAS THE INFINITY GAUNTLET.
INEVITABLE AND INVINCIBLE.
MAYBE YOU AND I WOULD BE BETTER ADVISED TO ABANDON THIS REALITY FOR GREENER PASTURES.
IN SOME FAR DISTANT DIMENSION, MIGHT WE NOT FIND YET ANOTHER INFINITY GAUNTLET AND BECOME GOD OF THAT ACTUALITY?
UNFORTUNATELY, I HAVE SOME CERTAIN SENTIMENTAL ATTACHMENTS TO THIS REALITY.
AS DO I.

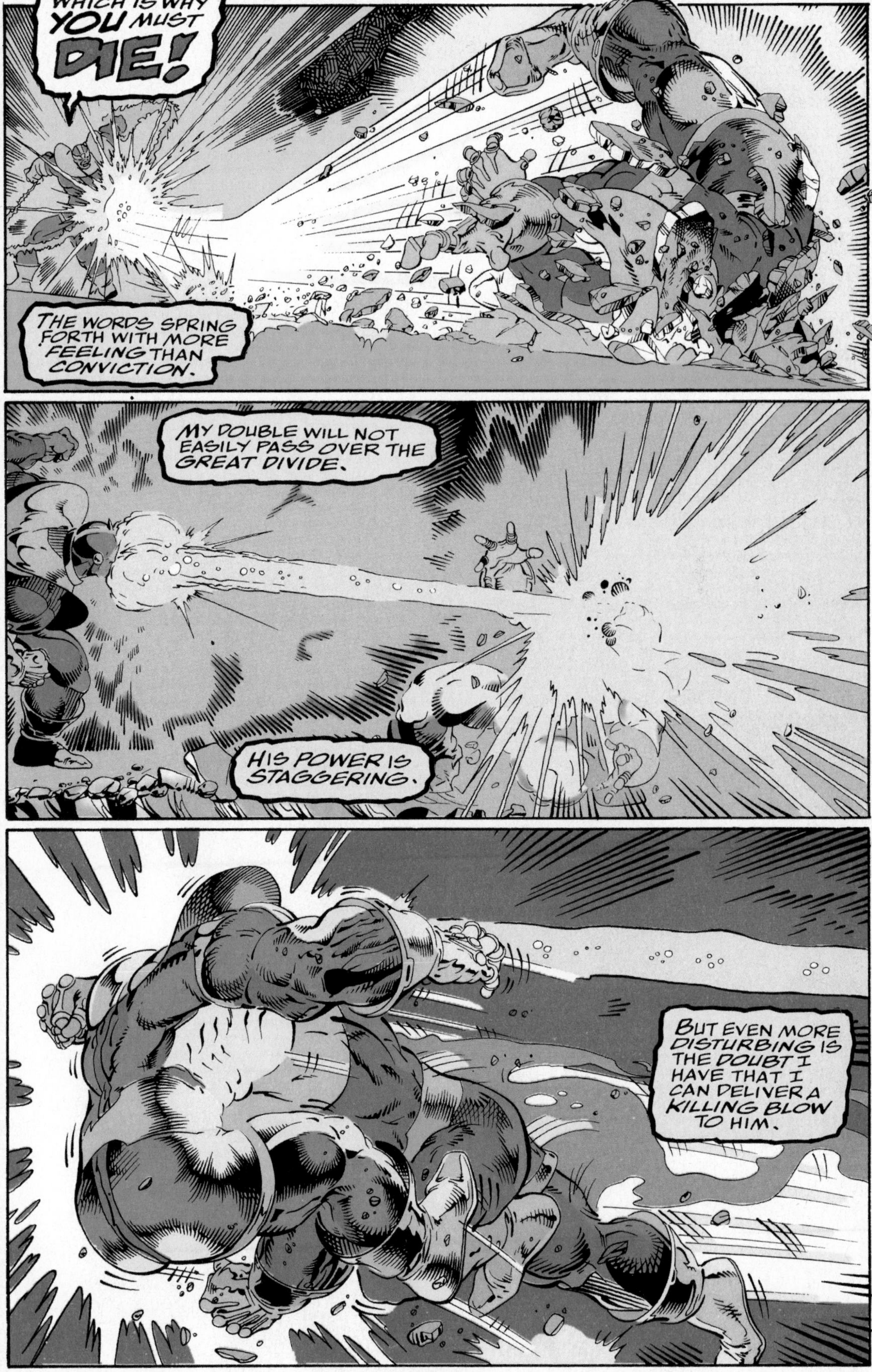
WHICH IS WHY YOU MUST DIE!
THE WORDS SPRING FORTH WITH MORE FEELING THAN CONVICTION.
MY DOUBLE WILL NOT EASILY PASS OVER THE GREAT DIVIDE.
HIS POWER IS STAGGERING.
BUT EVEN MORE DISTURBING IS THE DOUBT I HAVE THAT I CAN DELIVER A KILLING BLOW TO HIM.

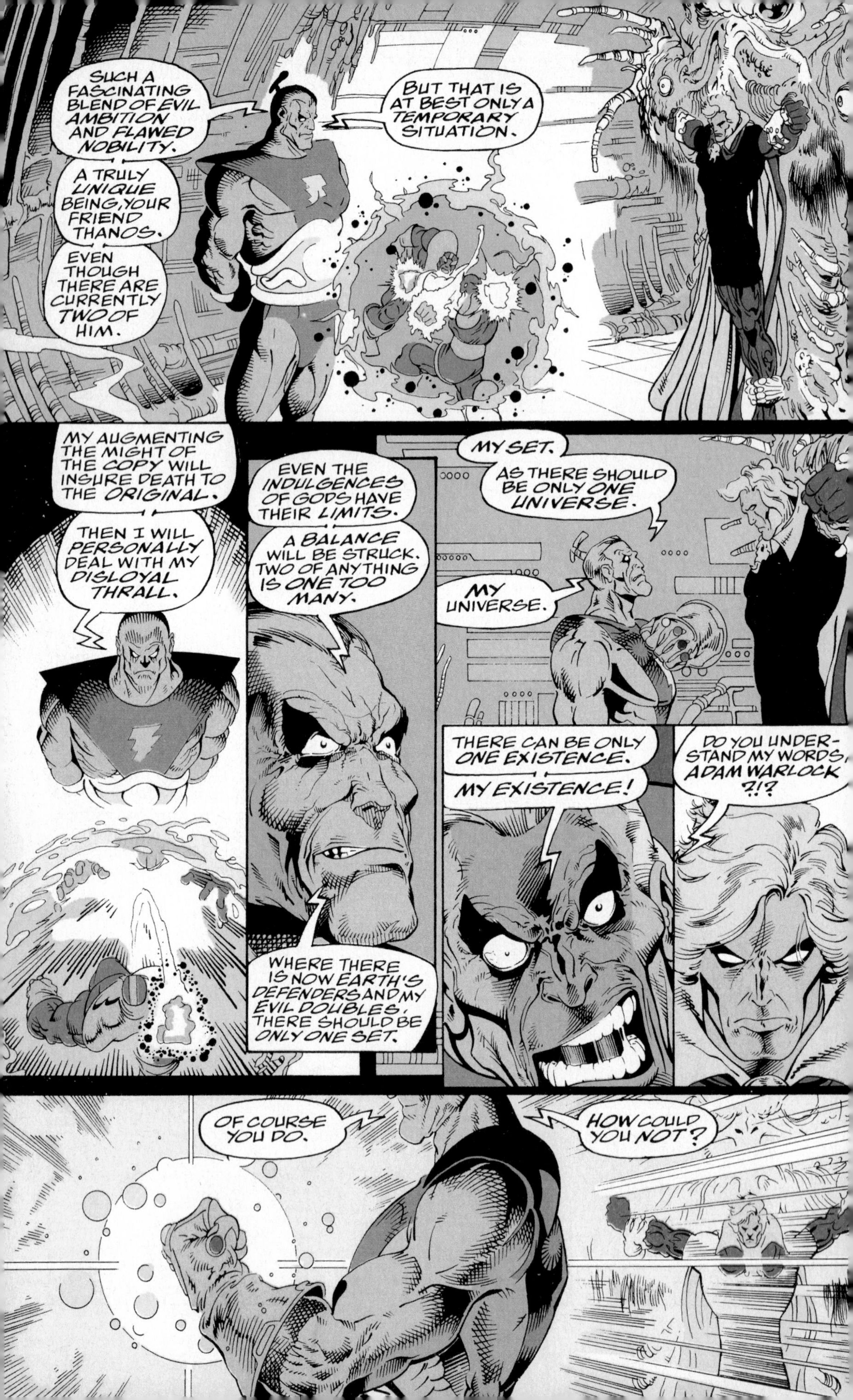
SUCH A FASCINATING BLEND OF EVIL AMBITION AND FLAWED NOBILITY.
A TRULY UNIQUE BEING, YOUR FRIEND THANOS.
EVEN THOUGH THERE ARE CURRENTLY TWO OF HIM.
BUT THAT IS AT BEST ONLY A TEMPORARY SITUATION.
MY AUGMENTING THE MIGHT OF THE COPY WILL INSURE DEATH TO THE ORIGINAL.
THEN I WILL PERSONALLY DEAL WITH MY DISLOYAL THRALL.
EVEN THE INDULGENCES OF GODS HAVE THEIR LIMITS.
A BALANCE WILL BE STRUCK. TWO OF ANYTHING IS ONE TOO MANY.
WHERE THERE IS NOW EARTH'S DEFENDERS AND MY EVIL DOUBLES, THERE SHOULD BE ONLY ONE SET.
MY SET.
AS THERE SHOULD BE ONLY ONE UNIVERSE.
MY UNIVERSE.
THERE CAN BE ONLY ONE EXISTENCE.
MY EXISTENCE!
DO YOU UNDER-STAND MY WORDS, ADAM WARLOCK ?!?
OF COURSE YOU DO.
HOW COULD YOU NOT?

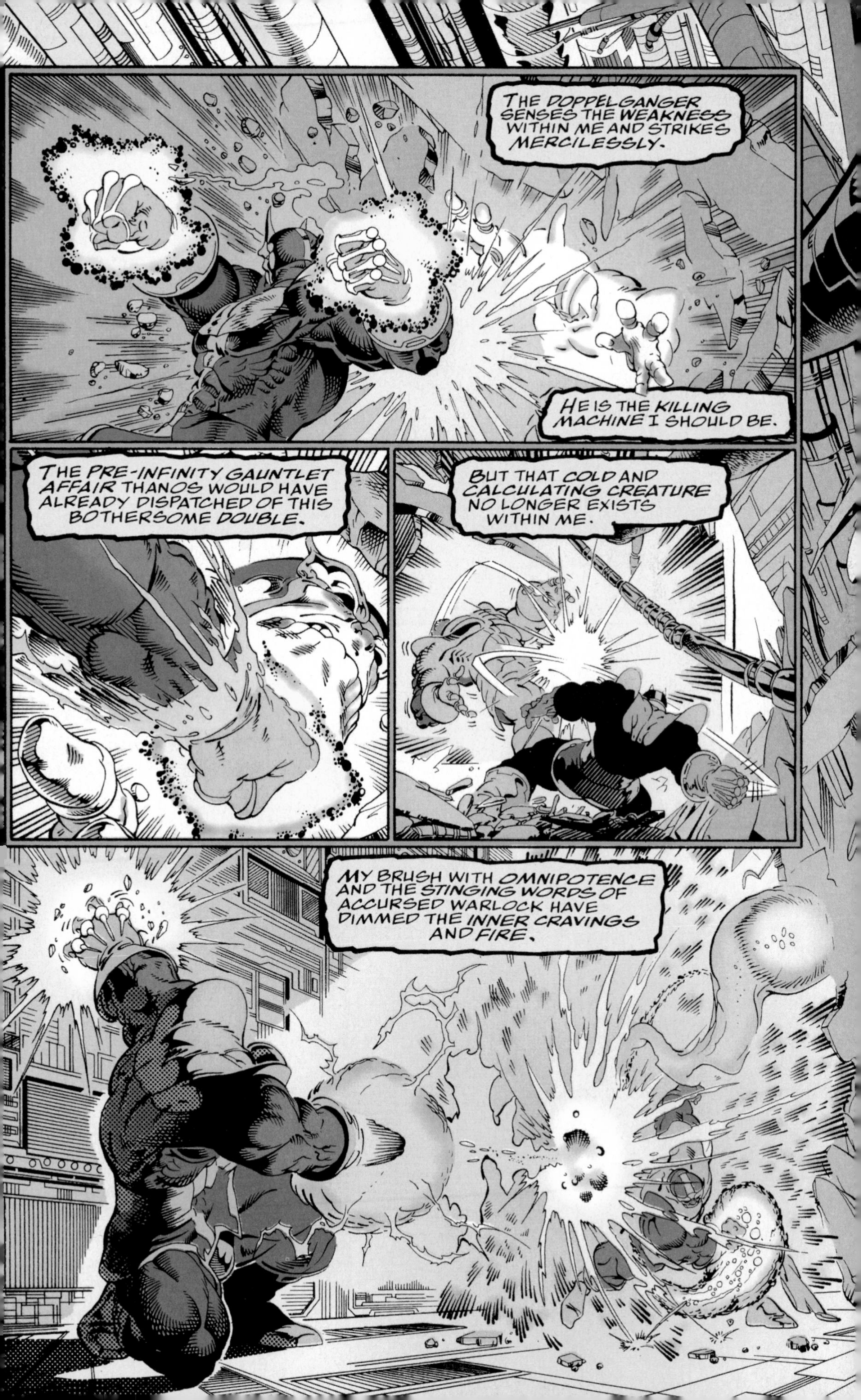
THE DOPPELGANGER SENSES THE WEAKNESS WITHIN ME AND STRIKES MERCILESSLY.
HE IS THE KILLING MACHINE I SHOULD BE.
THE PRE-INFINITY GAUNTLET AFFAIR THANOS WOULD HAVE ALREADY DISPATCHED OF THIS BOTHERSOME DOUBLE.
BUT THAT COLD AND CALCULATING CREATURE NO LONGER EXISTS WITHIN ME.
MY BRUSH WITH OMNIPOTENCE AND THE STINGING WORDS OF ACCURSED WARLOCK HAVE DIMMED THE INNER CRAVINGS AND FIRE.

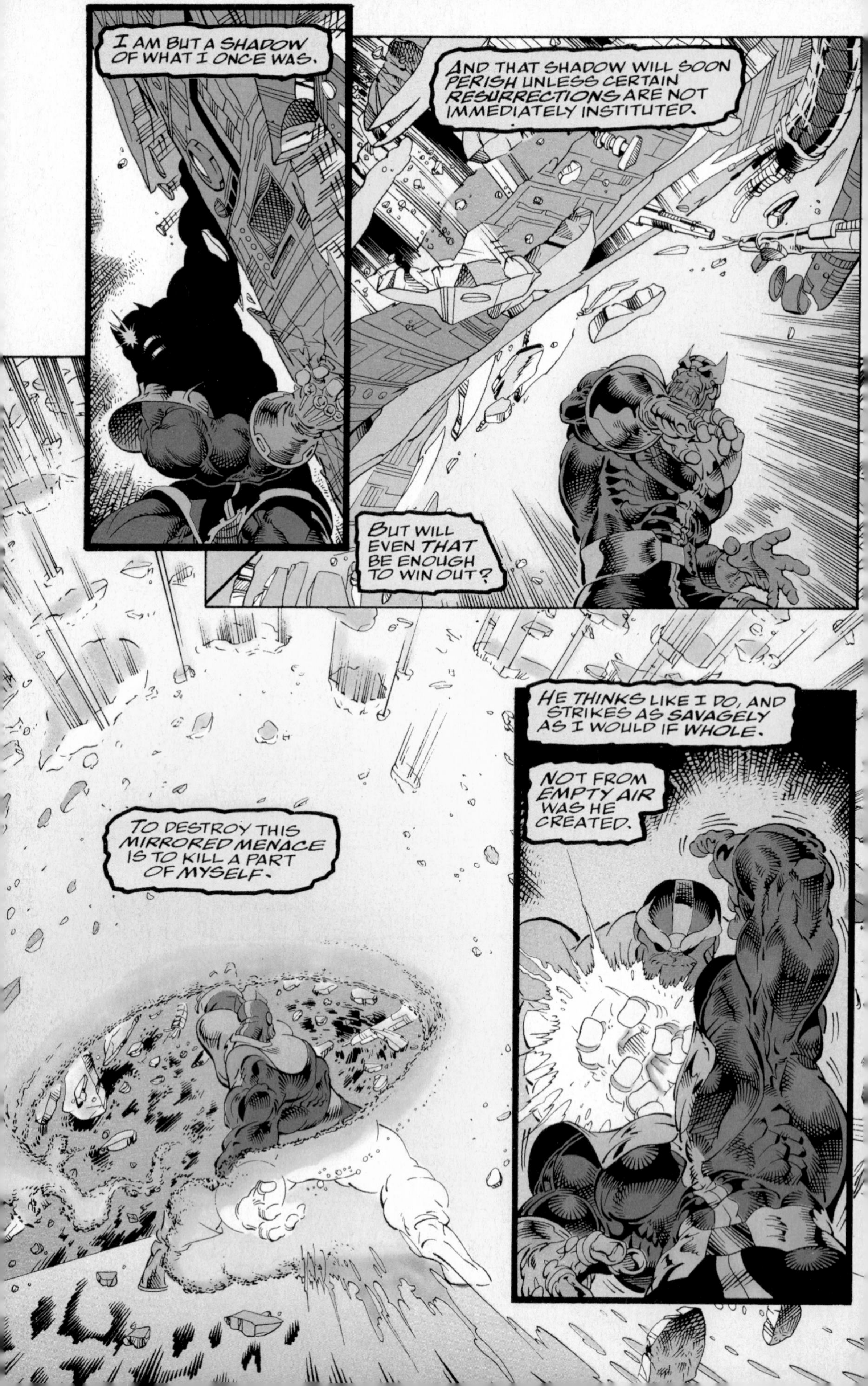
I AM BUT A SHADOW OF WHAT I ONCE WAS.
AND THAT SHADOW WILL SOON PERISH UNLESS CERTAIN RESURRECTIONS ARE NOT IMMEDIATELY INSTITUTED.
BUT WILL EVEN THAT BE ENOUGH TO WIN OUT?
HE THINKS LIKE I DO, AND STRIKES AS SAVAGELY AS I WOULD IF WHOLE.
NOT FROM EMPTY AIR WAS HE CREATED.
TO DESTROY THIS MIRRORED MENACE IS TO KILL A PART OF MYSELF.

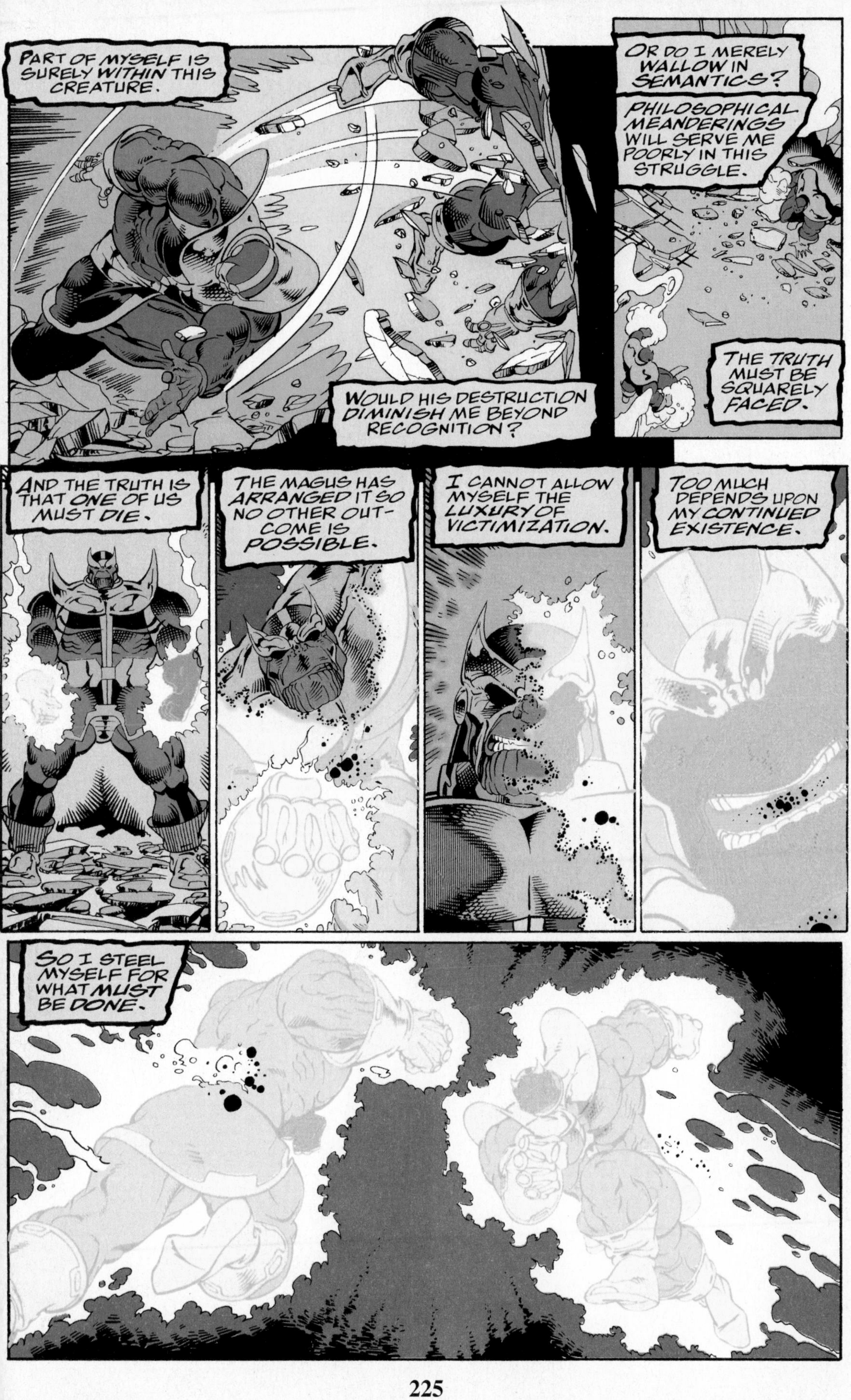
PART OF MYSELF IS SURELY WITHIN THIS CREATURE.
WOULD HIS DESTRUCTION DIMINISH ME BEYOND RECOGNITION?
OR DO I MERELY WALLOW IN SEMANTICS?
PHILOSOPHICAL MEANDERINGS WILL SERVE ME POORLY IN THIS STRUGGLE.
THE TRUTH MUST BE SQUARELY FACED.
AND THE TRUTH IS THAT ONE OF US MUST DIE.
THE MAGUS HAS ARRANGED IT SO NO OTHER OUT-COME IS POSSIBLE.
I CANNOT ALLOW MYSELF THE LUXURY OF VICTIMIZATION.
TOO MUCH DEPENDS UPON MY CONTINUED EXISTENCE.
SO I STEEL MYSELF FOR WHAT MUST BE DONE.

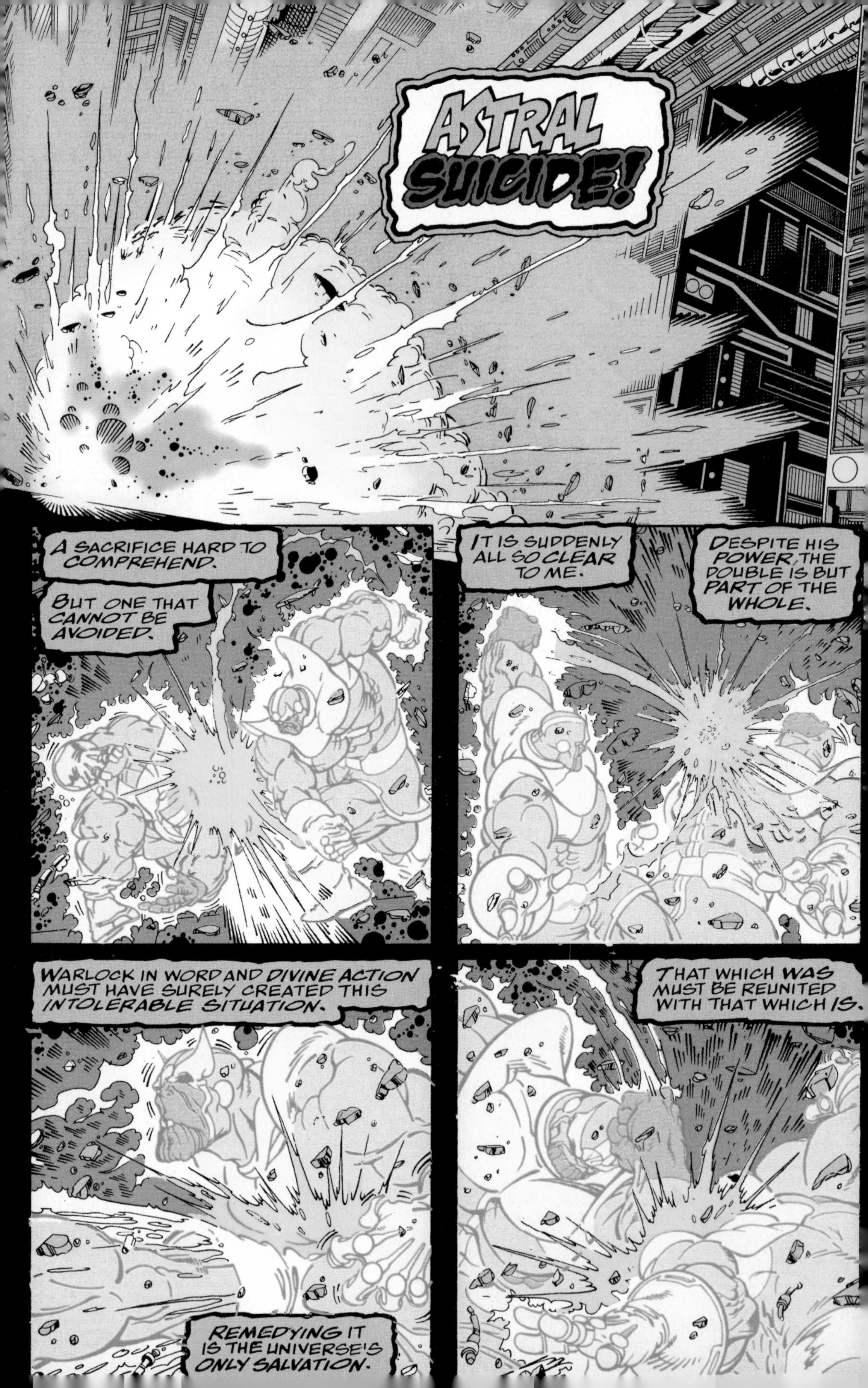
ASTRAL SUICIDE!
A SACRIFICE HARD TO COMPREHEND.
BUT ONE THAT CANNOT BE AVOIDED.
IT IS SUDDENLY ALL SO CLEAR TO ME.
DESPITE HIS POWER, THE DOUBLE IS BUT PART OF THE WHOLE.
WARLOCK IN WORD AND DIVINE ACTION MUST HAVE SURELY CREATED THIS INTOLERABLE SITUATION.
REMEDYING IT IS THE UNIVERSE'S ONLY SALVATION.
THAT WHICH WAS MUST BE REUNITED WITH THAT WHICH IS.

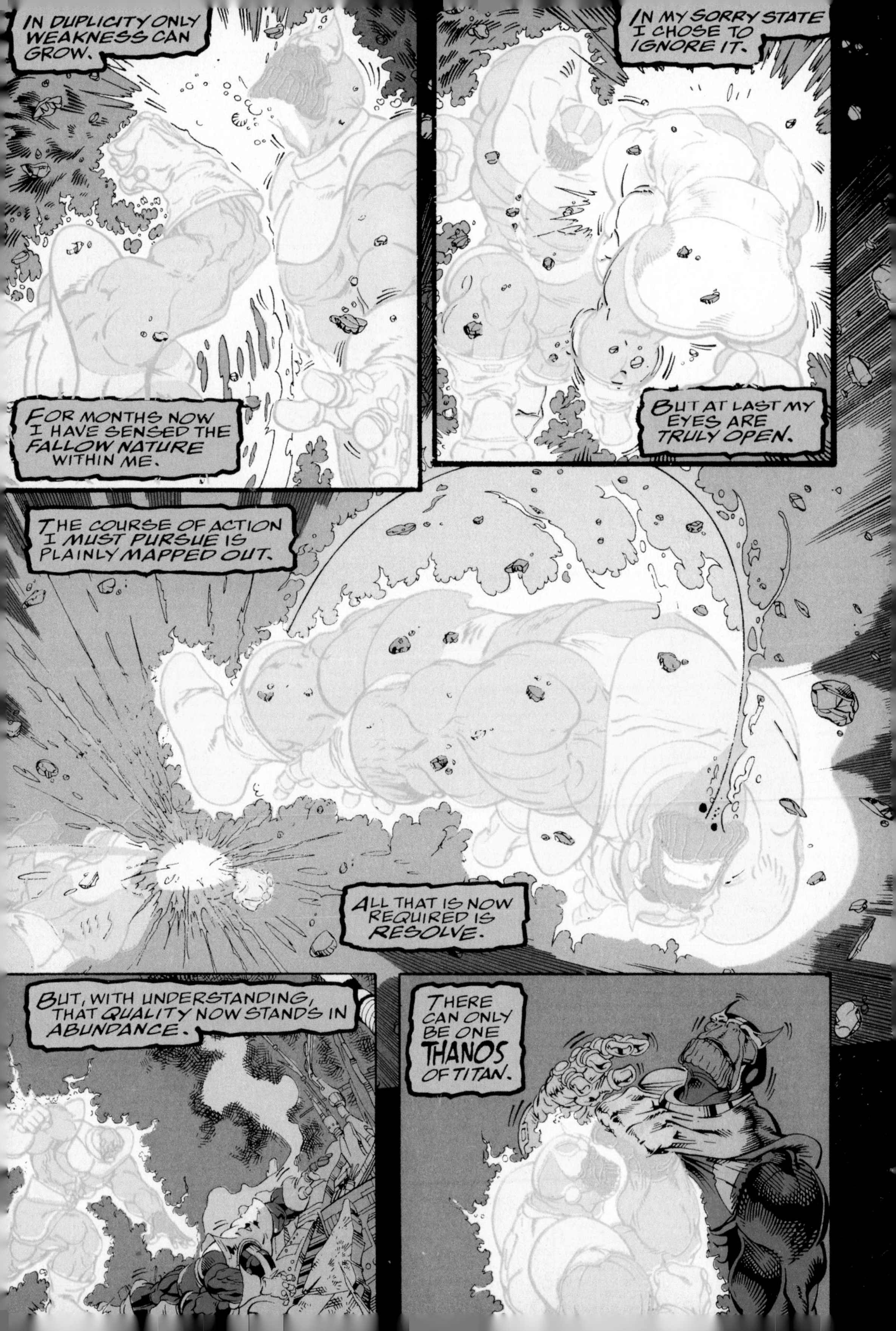
IN DUPLICITY ONLY WEAKNESS CAN GROW.
FOR MONTHS NOW I HAVE SENSED THE FALLOW NATURE WITHIN ME.
IN MY SORRY STATE I CHOSE TO IGNORE IT.
BUT AT LAST MY EYES ARE TRULY OPEN.
THE COURSE OF ACTION I MUST PURSUE IS PLAINLY MAPPED OUT.
ALL THAT IS NOW REQUIRED IS RESOLVE.
BUT, WITH UNDERSTANDING, THAT QUALITY NOW STANDS IN ABUNDANCE.
THERE CAN ONLY BE ONE THANOS OF TITAN.

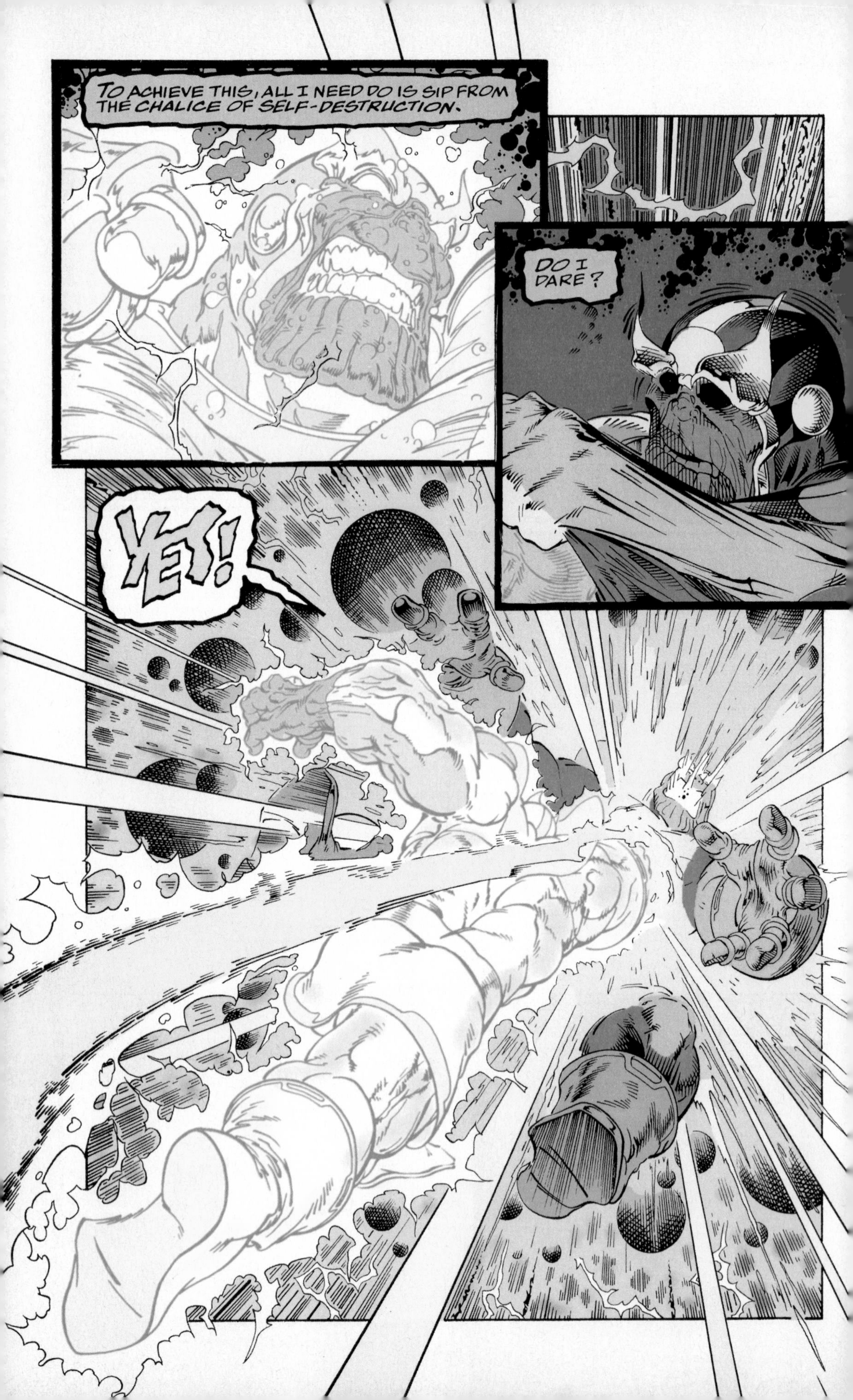

TO ACHIEVE THIS, ALL I NEED DO IS SIP FROM THE CHALICE OF SELF-DESTRUCTION.
DO I DARE?
YET!

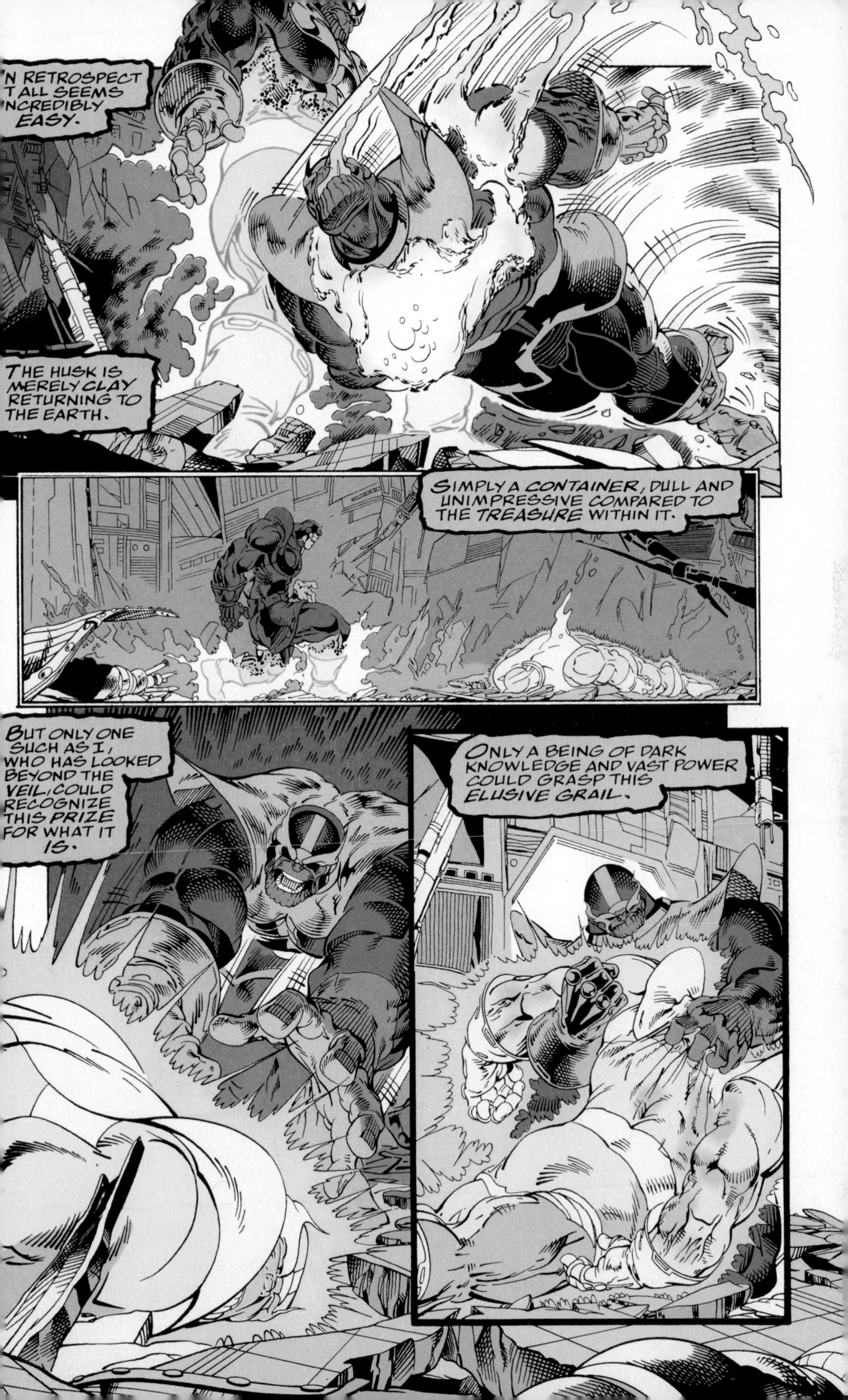
N RETROSPECT T ALL SEEMS NCREDIBLY EASY.
THE HUSK IS MERELY CLAY RETURNING TO THE EARTH.
SIMPLY A CONTAINER, DULL AND UNIMPRESSIVE COMPARED TO THE TREASURE WITHIN IT.
BUT ONLY ONE SUCH AS I, WHO HAS LOOKED BEYOND THE VEIL, COULD RECOGNIZE THIS PRIZE FOR WHAT IT IS.
ONLY A BEING OF DARK KNOWLEDGE AND VAST POWER COULD GRASP THIS ELUSIVE GRAIL.

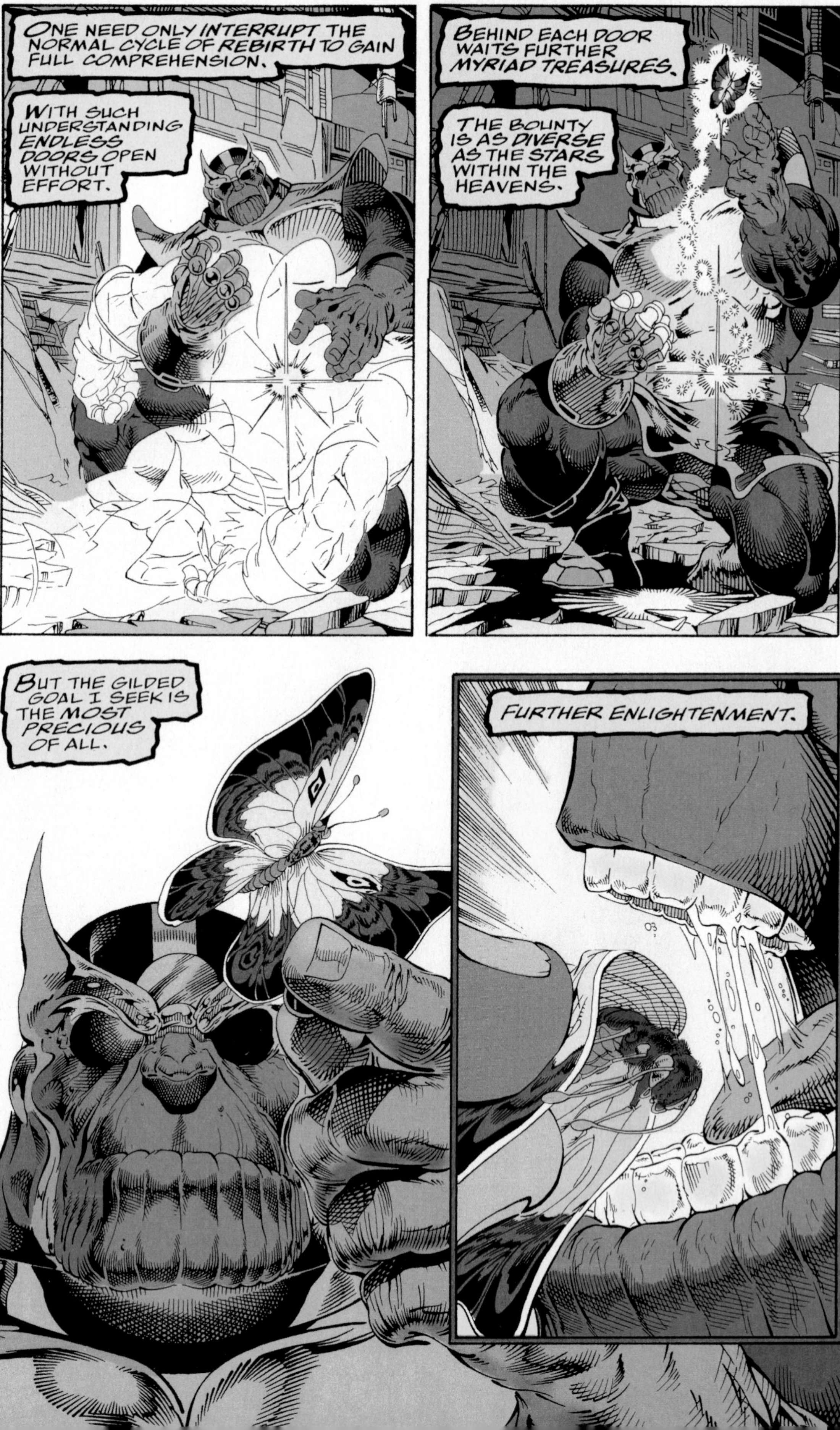
ONE NEED ONLY INTERRUPT THE NORMAL CYCLE OF REBIRTH TO GAIN FULL COMPREHENSION.
WITH SUCH UNDERSTANDING ENDLESS DOORS OPEN WITHOUT EFFORT.
BEHIND EACH DOOR WAITS FURTHER MYRIAD TREASURES.
THE BOUNTY IS AS DIVERSE AS THE STARS WITHIN THE HEAVENS.
BUT THE GILDED GOAL I SEEK IS THE MOST PRECIOUS OF ALL.
FURTHER ENLIGHTENMENT.

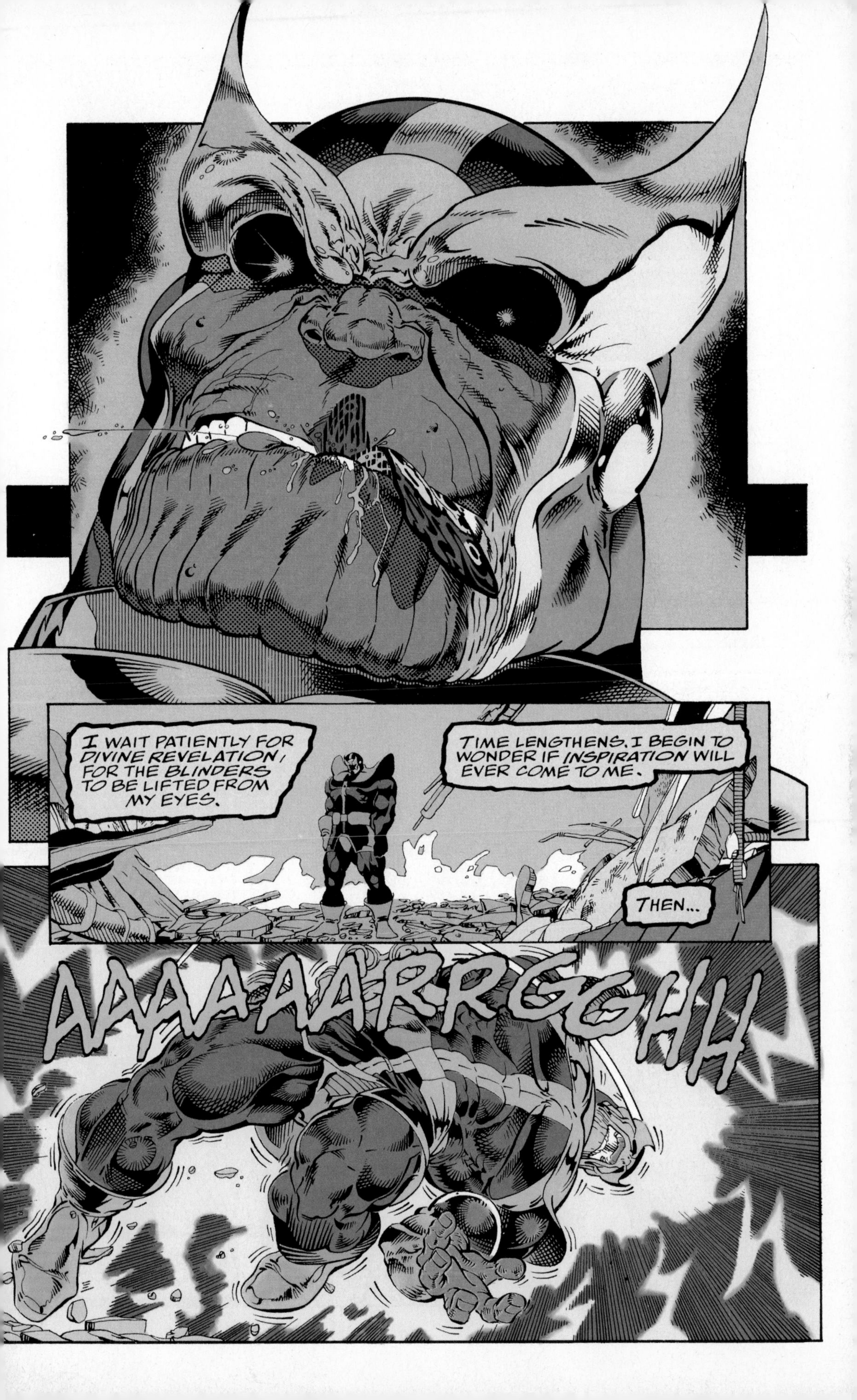
I WAIT PATIENTLY FOR DIVINE REVELATION, FOR THE BLINDERS TO BE LIFTED FROM MY EYES.
TIME LENGTHENS. I BEGIN TO WONDER IF INSPIRATION WILL EVER COME TO ME.
THEN...
AAAAAARRGGHH

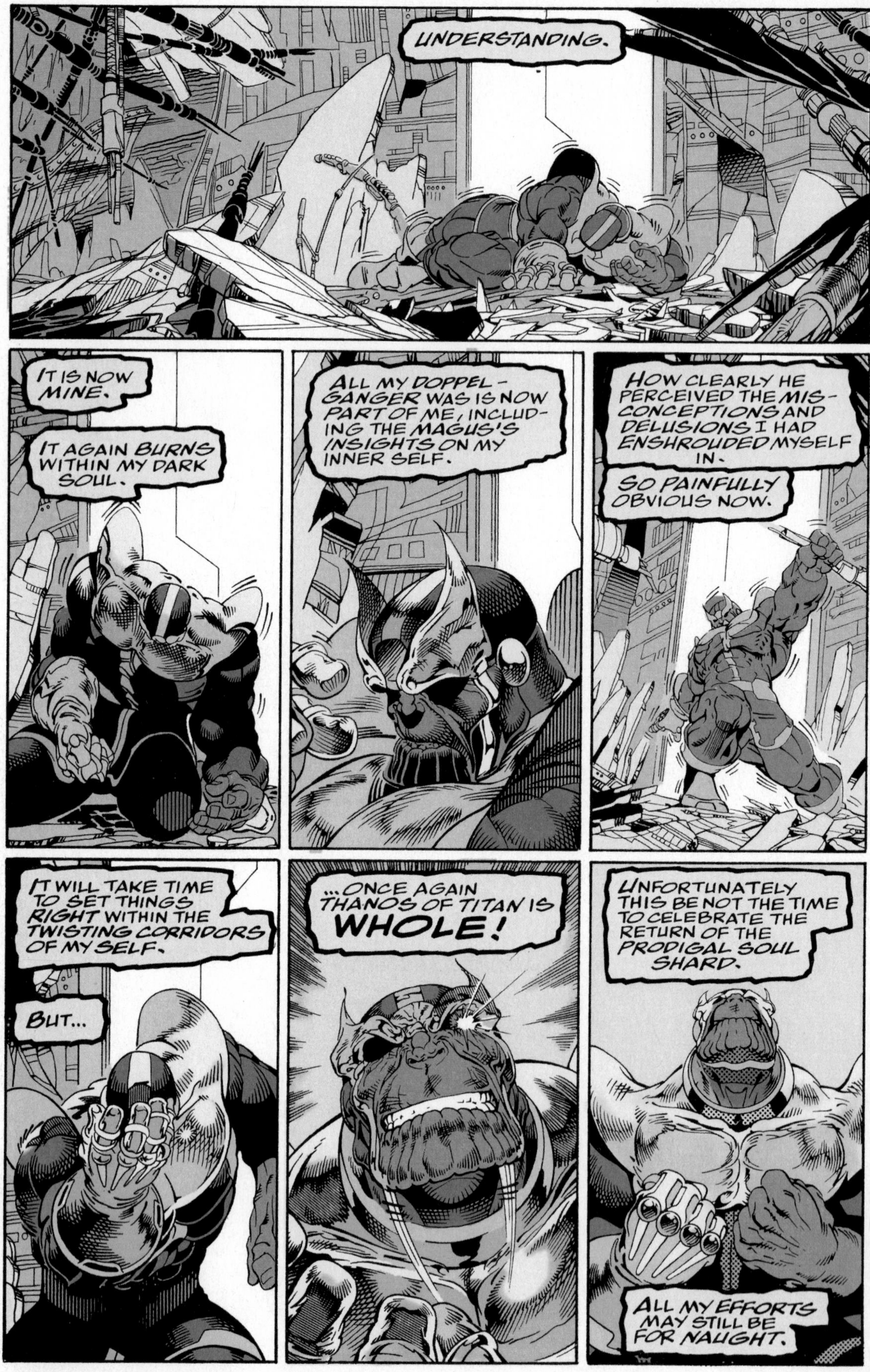
UNDERSTANDING.
IT IS NOW MINE.
IT AGAIN BURNS WITHIN MY DARK SOUL.
ALL MY DOPPELGANGER WAS IS NOW PART OF ME, INCLUDING THE MAGUS'S INSIGHTS ON MY INNER SELF.
HOW CLEARLY HE PERCEIVED THE MISCONCEPTIONS AND DELUSIONS I HAD ENSHROUDED MYSELF IN.
SO PAINFULLY OBVIOUS NOW.
IT WILL TAKE TIME TO SET THINGS RIGHT WITHIN THE TWISTING CORRIDORS OF MY SELF.
BUT...
...ONCE AGAIN THANOS OF TITAN IS WHOLE!
UNFORTUNATELY THIS BE NOT THE TIME TO CELEBRATE THE RETURN OF THE PRODIGAL SOUL SHARD.
ALL MY EFFORTS MAY STILL BE FOR NAUGHT.

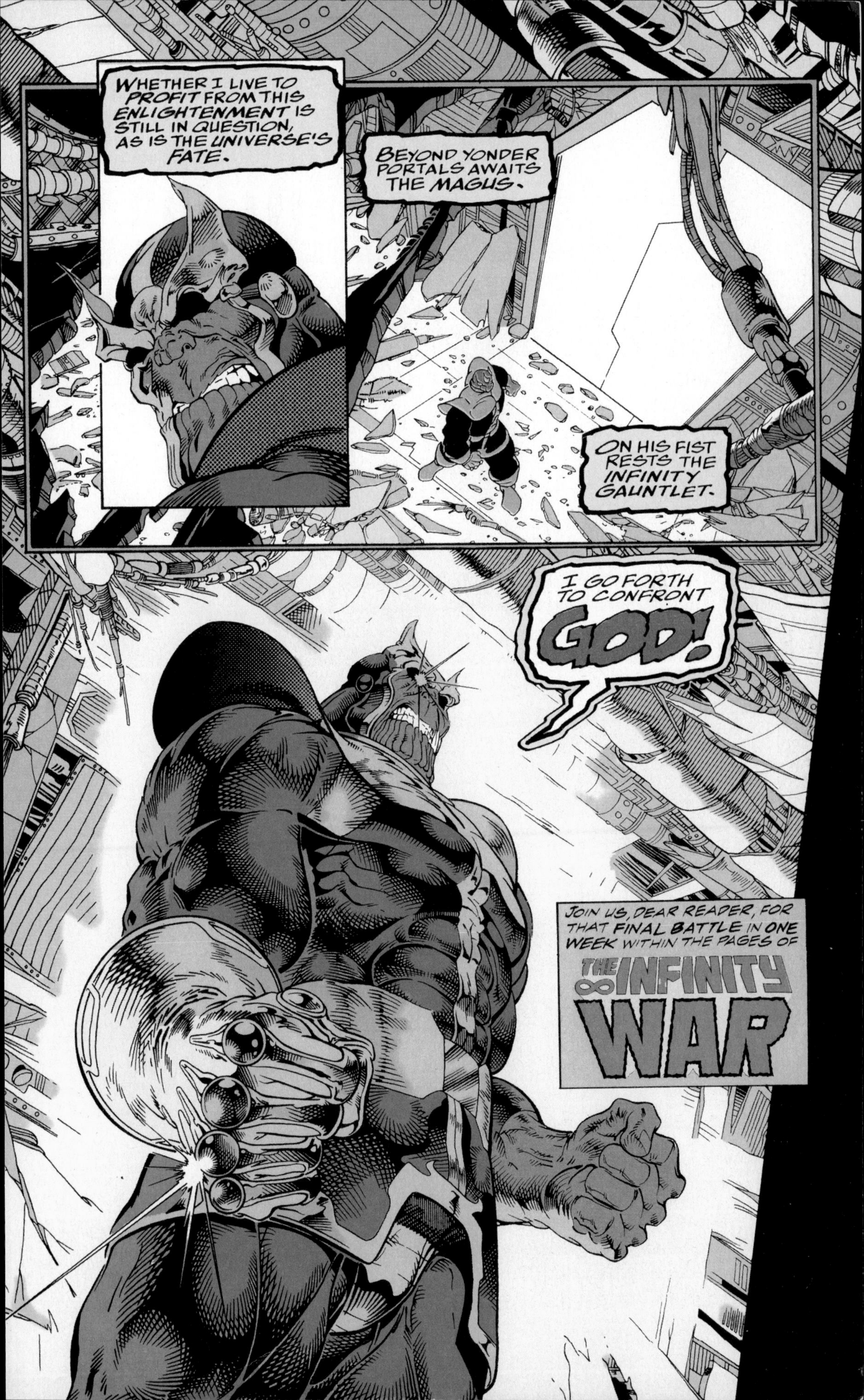
WHETHER I LIVE TO PROFIT FROM THIS ENLIGHTENMENT IS STILL IN QUESTION, AS IS THE UNIVERSE'S FATE.
BEYOND YONDER PORTALS AWAITS THE MAGUS.
ON HIS FIST RESTS THE INFINITY GAUNTLET.
I GO FORTH TO CONFRONT GOD!
JOIN US, DEAR READER, FOR THAT FINAL BATTLE IN ONE WEEK WITHIN THE PAGES OF
THE INFINITY WAR

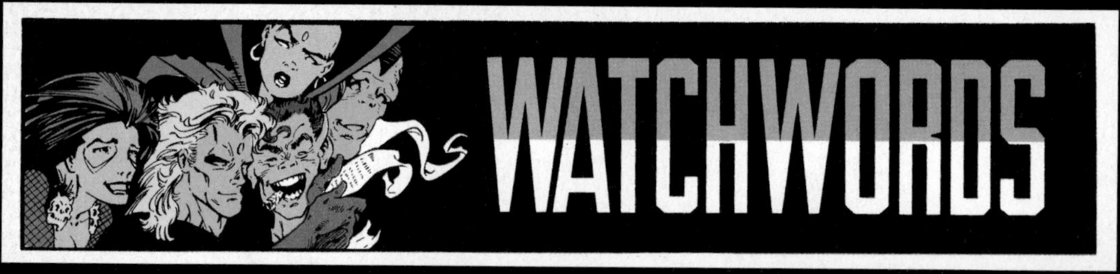
WATCHWORDS

WARLOCK AND THE INFINITY WATCH
LETTERS-PAGE LOGO BY TOM RANEY

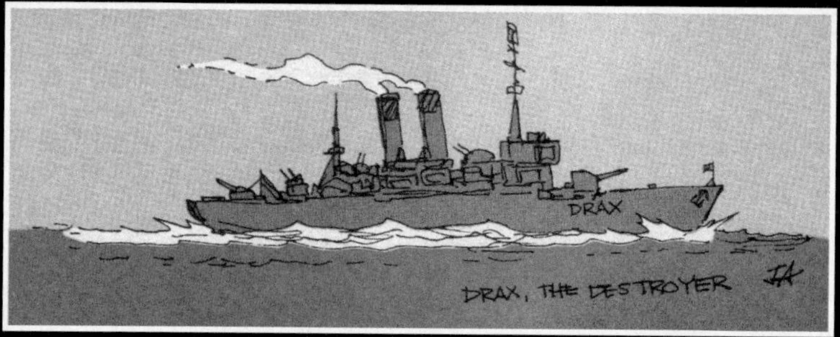
DRAX
DRAX, THE DESTROYER

"DRAX THE DESTROYER" PARODY ILLUSTRATION
BY JACK ABEL, FROM WARLOCK AND THE INFINITY WATCH #21 LETTERS PAGE

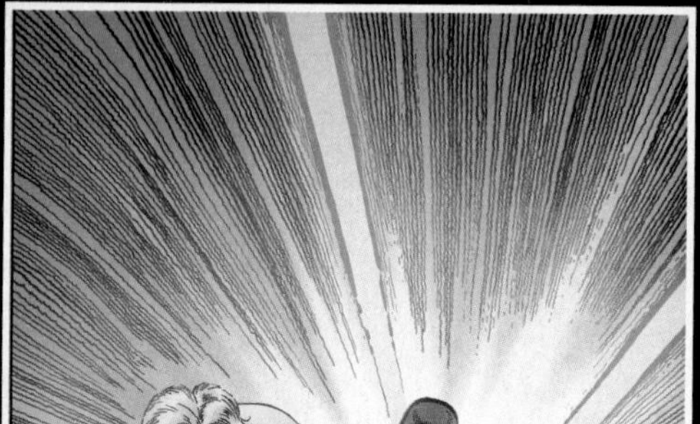

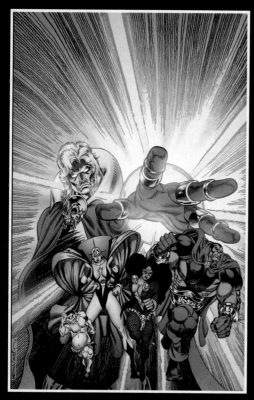

INFINITY GAUNTLET AFTERMATH
***TPB* COVER ART**
BY ANGEL MEDINA, TERRY AUSTIN
& THOMAS MASON

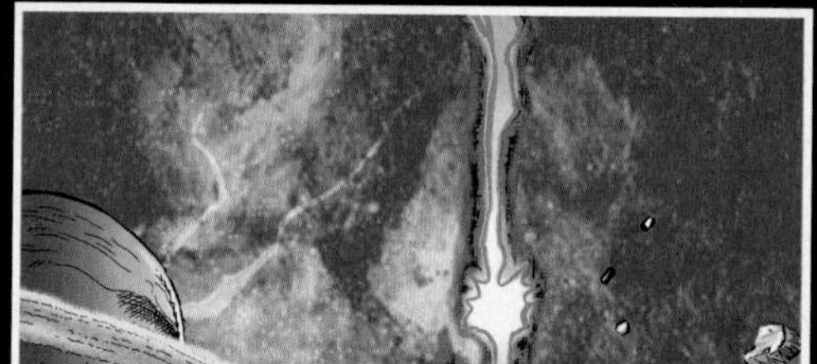

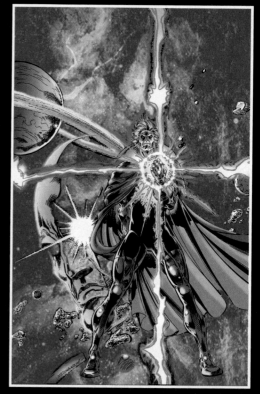

INFINITY GAUNTLET AFTERMATH
***TPB* BACK-COVER ART**
BY ANGEL MEDINA, TERRY AUSTIN
& TOM SMITH

THOUGH THE MAGUS HAD STOLEN THE RESTORED INFINITY GAUNTLET, HE SOON DISCOVERED THAT THE REALITY GEM WAS A FACSIMILE, CREATED TO TRICK HIM INTO THINKING HE HAD BECOME SUPREME. WARLOCK AND THANOS DEFEATED THE MAGUS AND THE VILLAIN'S SPIRIT WAS ABSORBED INTO THE SOUL GEM, BUT THE BATTLE LEFT WARLOCK IN A COMA.

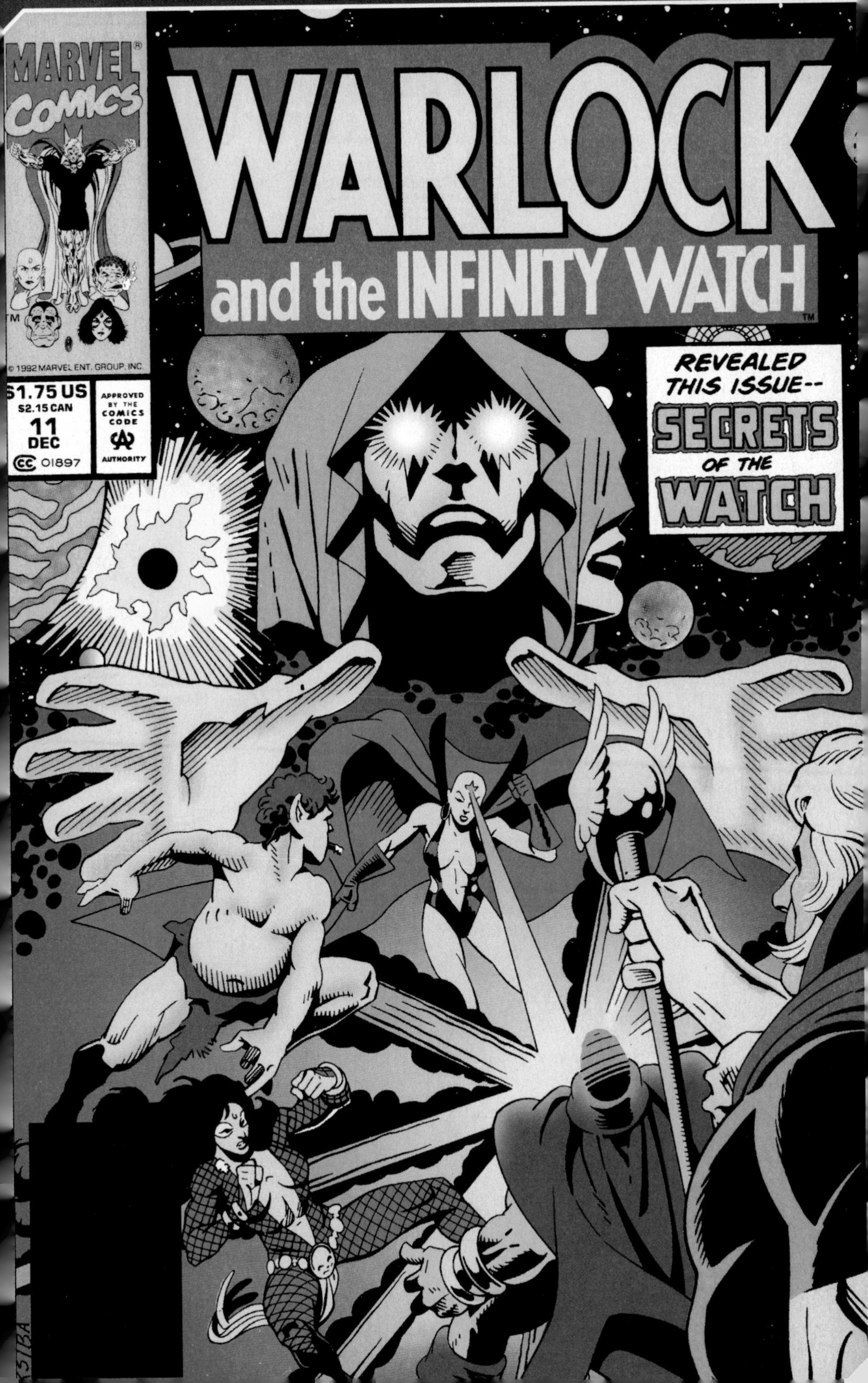
MARVEL COMICS
WARLOCK and the INFINITY WATCH
© 1992 MARVEL ENT. GROUP, INC.
$1.75 US
$2.15 CAN
11
DEC
01897
APPROVED BY THE COMICS CODE AUTHORITY
REVEALED THIS ISSUE--
SECRETS OF THE WATCH

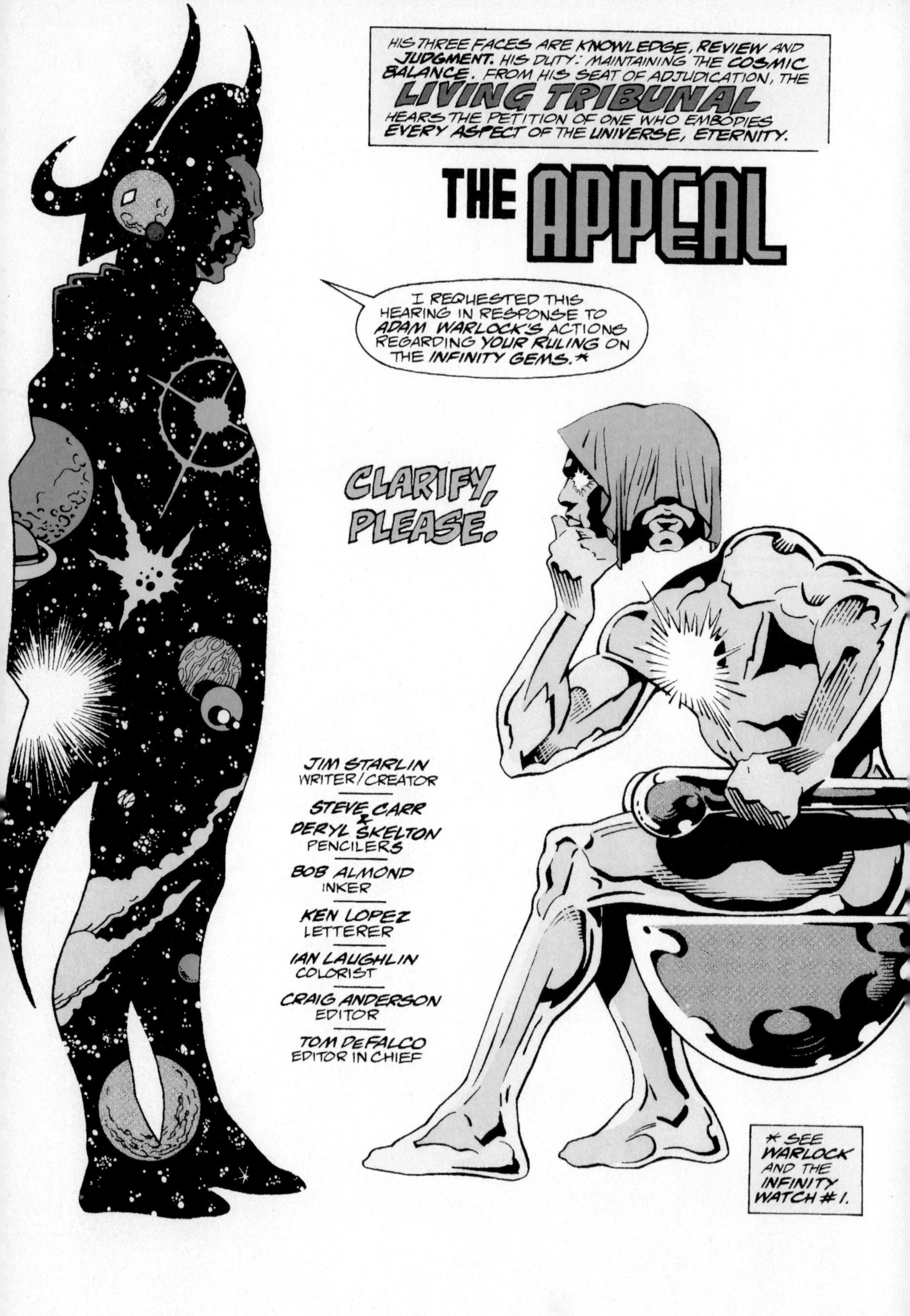
HIS THREE FACES ARE KNOWLEDGE, REVIEW AND JUDGMENT. HIS DUTY: MAINTAINING THE COSMIC BALANCE. FROM HIS SEAT OF ADJUDICATION, THE LIVING TRIBUNAL HEARS THE PETITION OF ONE WHO EMBODIES EVERY ASPECT OF THE UNIVERSE, ETERNITY.
THE APPEAL
I REQUESTED THIS HEARING IN RESPONSE TO ADAM WARLOCK'S ACTIONS REGARDING YOUR RULING ON THE INFINITY GEMS.*
CLARIFY, PLEASE.
JIM STARLIN WRITER/CREATOR
STEVE CARR & DERYL SKELTON PENCILERS
BOB ALMOND INKER
KEN LOPEZ LETTERER
IAN LAUGHLIN COLORIST
CRAIG ANDERSON EDITOR
TOM DEFALCO EDITOR IN CHIEF
* SEE WARLOCK AND THE INFINITY WATCH #1.

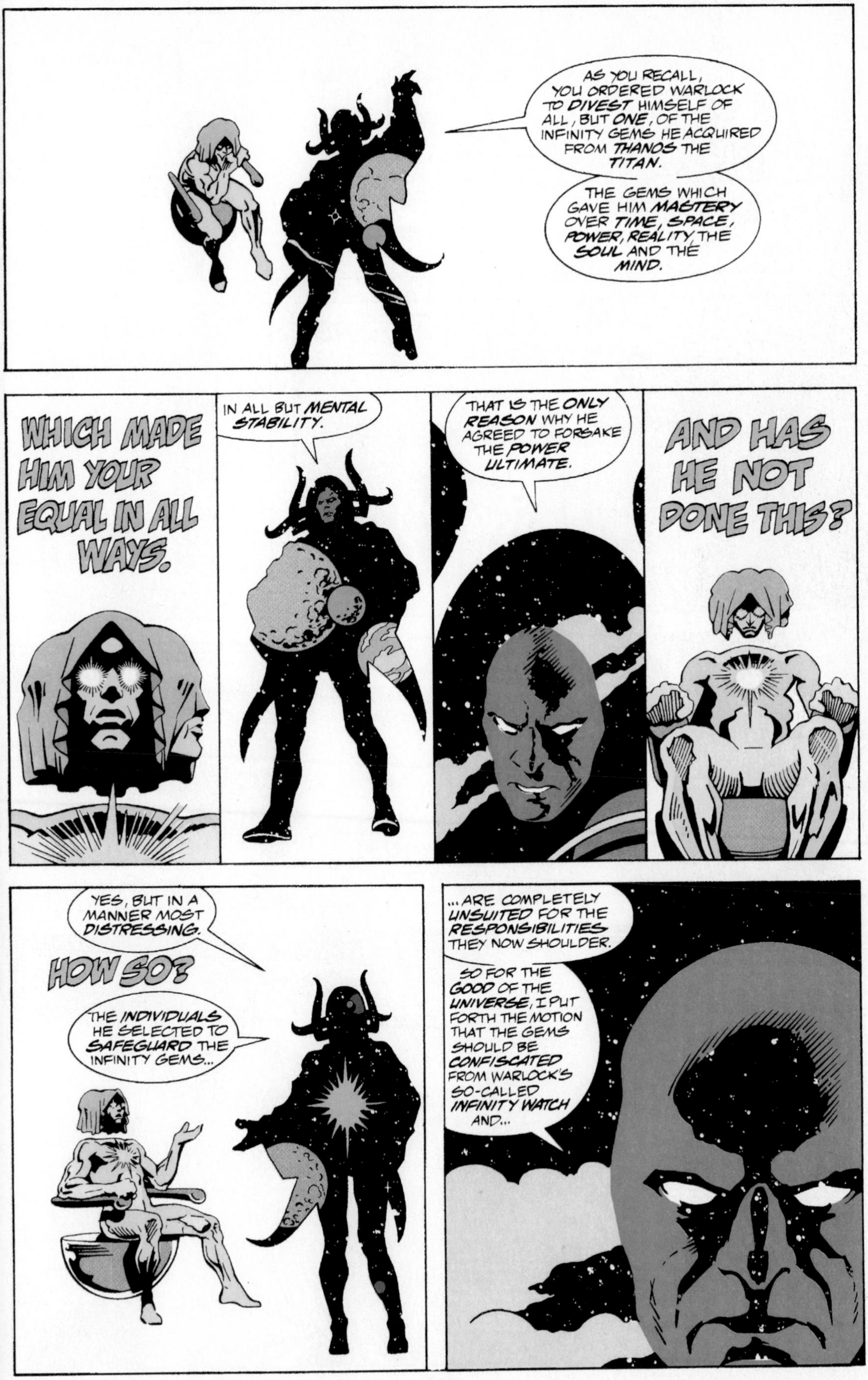
AS YOU RECALL, YOU ORDERED WARLOCK TO DIVEST HIMSELF OF ALL, BUT ONE, OF THE INFINITY GEMS HE ACQUIRED FROM THANOS THE TITAN.
THE GEMS WHICH GAVE HIM MASTERY OVER TIME, SPACE, POWER, REALITY, THE SOUL AND THE MIND.
WHICH MADE HIM YOUR EQUAL IN ALL WAYS.
IN ALL BUT MENTAL STABILITY.
THAT IS THE ONLY REASON WHY HE AGREED TO FORSAKE THE POWER ULTIMATE.
AND HAS HE NOT DONE THIS?
YES, BUT IN A MANNER MOST DISTRESSING.
HOW SO?
THE INDIVIDUALS HE SELECTED TO SAFEGUARD THE INFINITY GEMS...
...ARE COMPLETELY UNSUITED FOR THE RESPONSIBILITIES THEY NOW SHOULDER.
SO FOR THE GOOD OF THE UNIVERSE, I PUT FORTH THE MOTION THAT THE GEMS SHOULD BE CONFISCATED FROM WARLOCK'S SO-CALLED INFINITY WATCH AND...

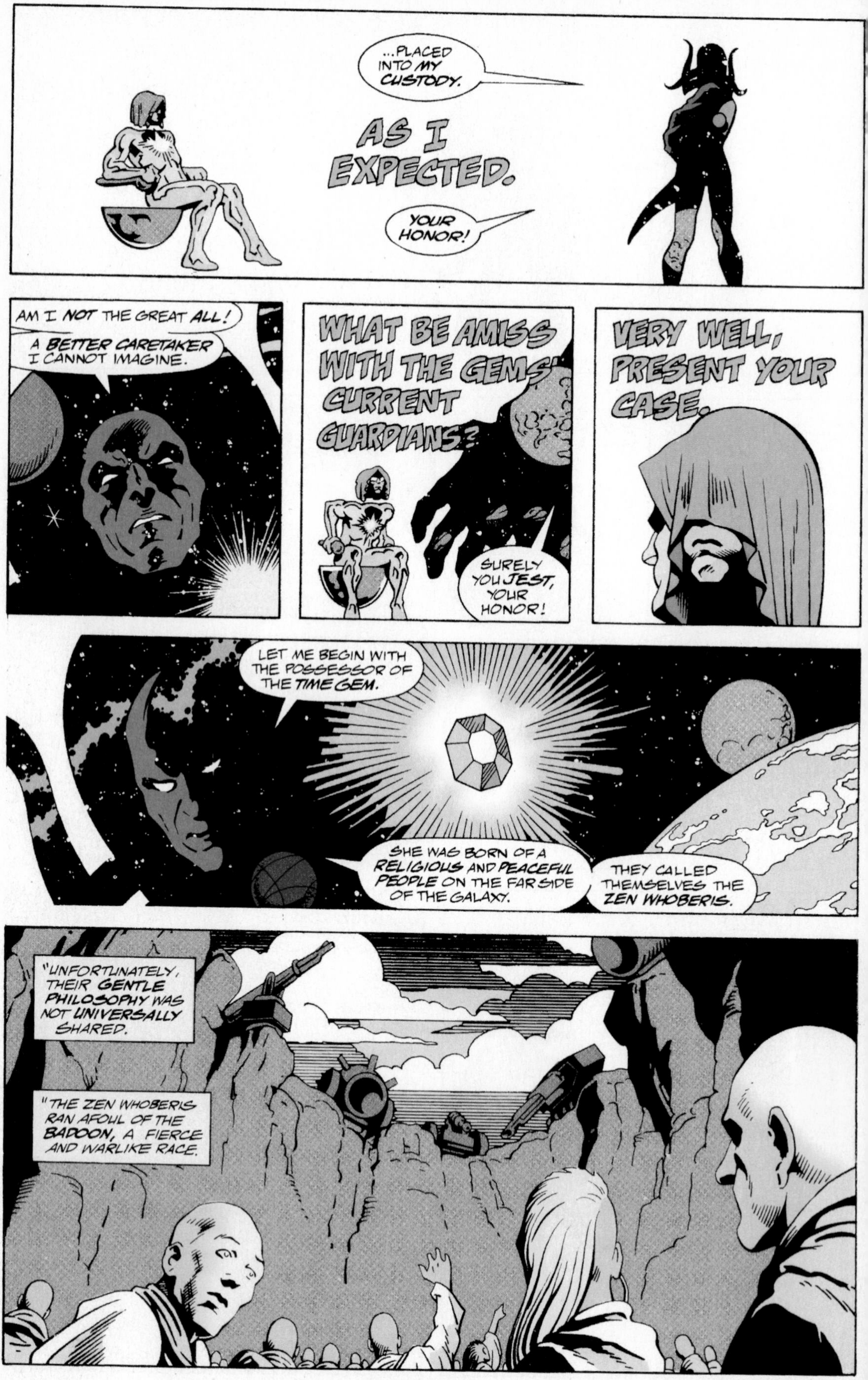
...PLACED INTO MY CUSTODY.
AS I EXPECTED.
YOUR HONOR!
AM I NOT THE GREAT ALL!
A BETTER CARETAKER I CANNOT IMAGINE.
WHAT BE AMISS WITH THE GEMS' CURRENT GUARDIANS?
SURELY YOU JEST, YOUR HONOR!
VERY WELL, PRESENT YOUR CASE.
LET ME BEGIN WITH THE POSSESSOR OF THE TIME GEM.
SHE WAS BORN OF A RELIGIOUS AND PEACEFUL PEOPLE ON THE FAR SIDE OF THE GALAXY.
THEY CALLED THEMSELVES THE ZEN WHOBERIS.
"UNFORTUNATELY, THEIR GENTLE PHILOSOPHY WAS NOT UNIVERSALLY SHARED.
"THE ZEN WHOBERIS RAN AFOUL OF THE BADOON, A FIERCE AND WARLIKE RACE.

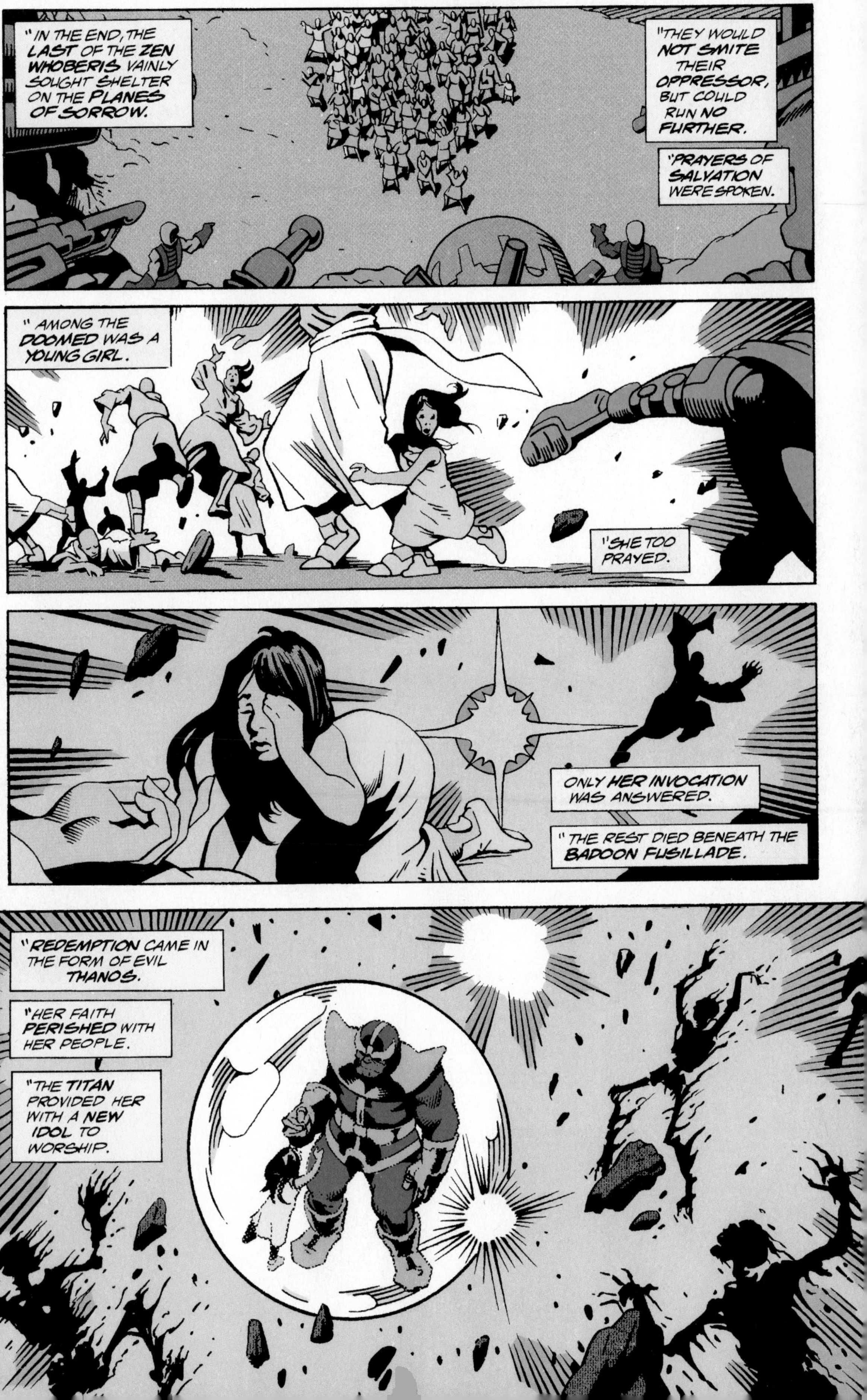
"IN THE END, THE LAST OF THE ZEN WHOBERIS VAINLY SOUGHT SHELTER ON THE PLANES OF SORROW.
"THEY WOULD NOT SMITE THEIR OPPRESSOR, BUT COULD RUN NO FURTHER.
"PRAYERS OF SALVATION WERE SPOKEN.
"AMONG THE DOOMED WAS A YOUNG GIRL.
"SHE TOO PRAYED.
ONLY HER INVOCATION WAS ANSWERED.
"THE REST DIED BENEATH THE BADOON FUSILLADE.
"REDEMPTION CAME IN THE FORM OF EVIL THANOS.
"HER FAITH PERISHED WITH HER PEOPLE.
"THE TITAN PROVIDED HER WITH A NEW IDOL TO WORSHIP.

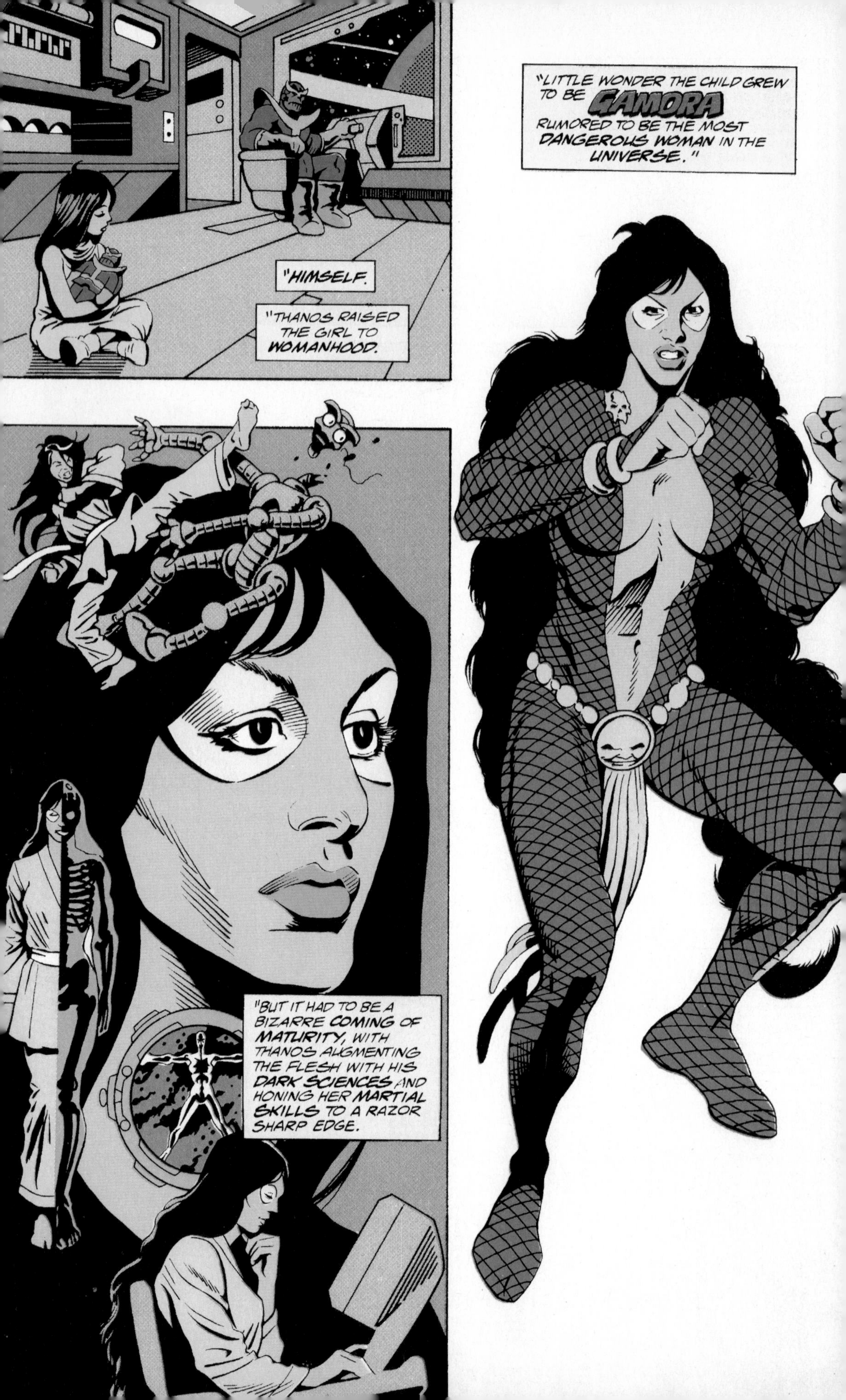
"HIMSELF.
"THANOS RAISED THE GIRL TO WOMANHOOD.
"BUT IT HAD TO BE A BIZARRE COMING OF MATURITY, WITH THANOS AUGMENTING THE FLESH WITH HIS DARK SCIENCES AND HONING HER MARTIAL SKILLS TO A RAZOR SHARP EDGE.
"LITTLE WONDER THE CHILD GREW TO BE GAMORA RUMORED TO BE THE MOST DANGEROUS WOMAN IN THE UNIVERSE."

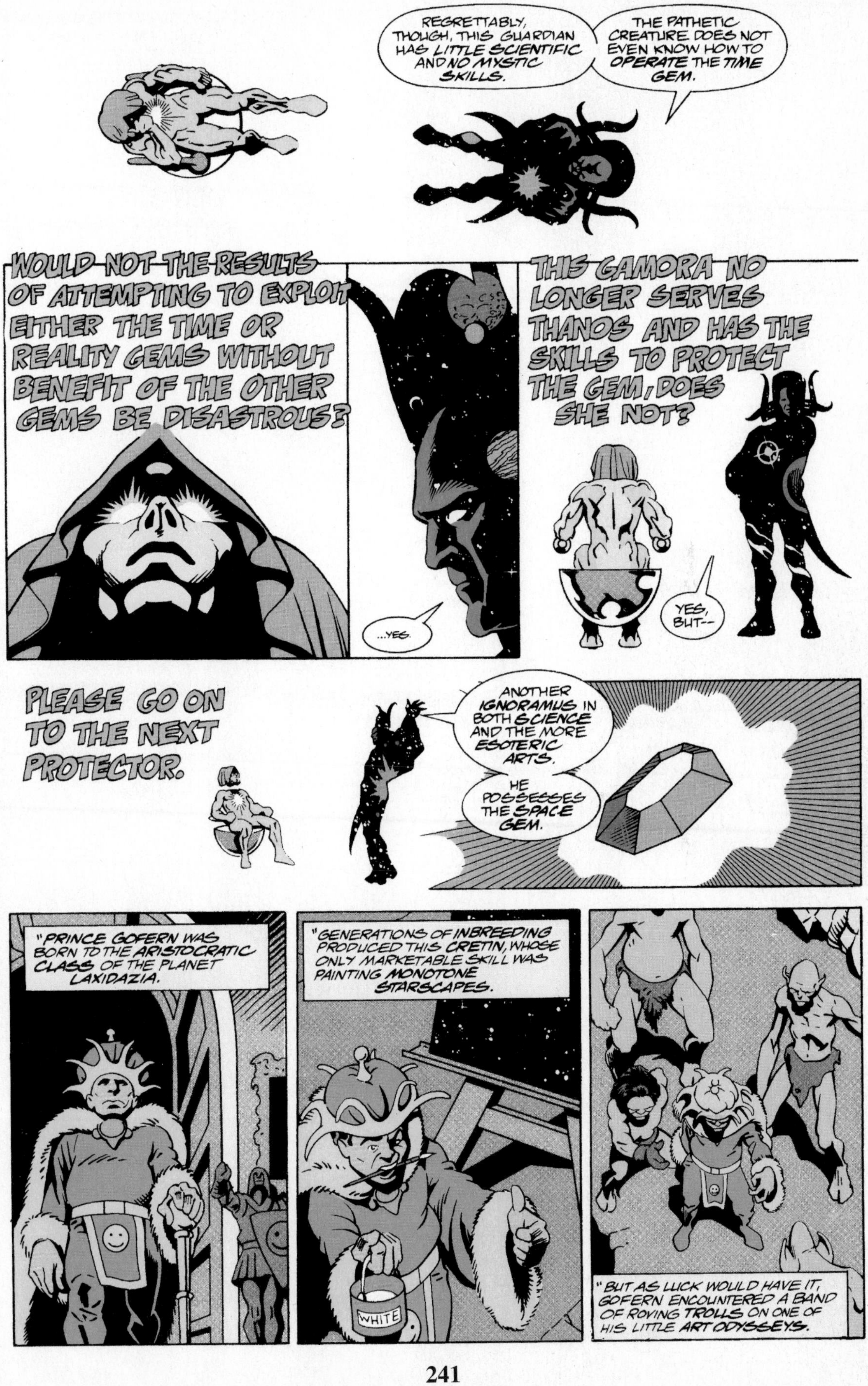

REGRETTABLY, THOUGH, THIS GUARDIAN HAS LITTLE SCIENTIFIC AND NO MYSTIC SKILLS.
THE PATHETIC CREATURE DOES NOT EVEN KNOW HOW TO OPERATE THE TIME GEM.
WOULD NOT THE RESULTS OF ATTEMPTING TO EXPLOIT EITHER THE TIME OR REALITY GEMS WITHOUT BENEFIT OF THE OTHER GEMS BE DISASTROUS?
...YES.
THIS GAMORA NO LONGER SERVES THANOS AND HAS THE SKILLS TO PROTECT THE GEM, DOES SHE NOT?
YES, BUT--
PLEASE GO ON TO THE NEXT PROTECTOR.
ANOTHER IGNORAMUS IN BOTH SCIENCE AND THE MORE ESOTERIC ARTS.
HE POSSESSES THE SPACE GEM.
"PRINCE GOFERN WAS BORN TO THE ARISTOCRATIC CLASS OF THE PLANET LAXIDAZIA.
"GENERATIONS OF INBREEDING PRODUCED THIS CRETIN, WHOSE ONLY MARKETABLE SKILL WAS PAINTING MONOTONE STARSCAPES.
WHITE
"BUT AS LUCK WOULD HAVE IT, GOFERN ENCOUNTERED A BAND OF ROVING TROLLS ON ONE OF HIS LITTLE ART ODYSSEYS.

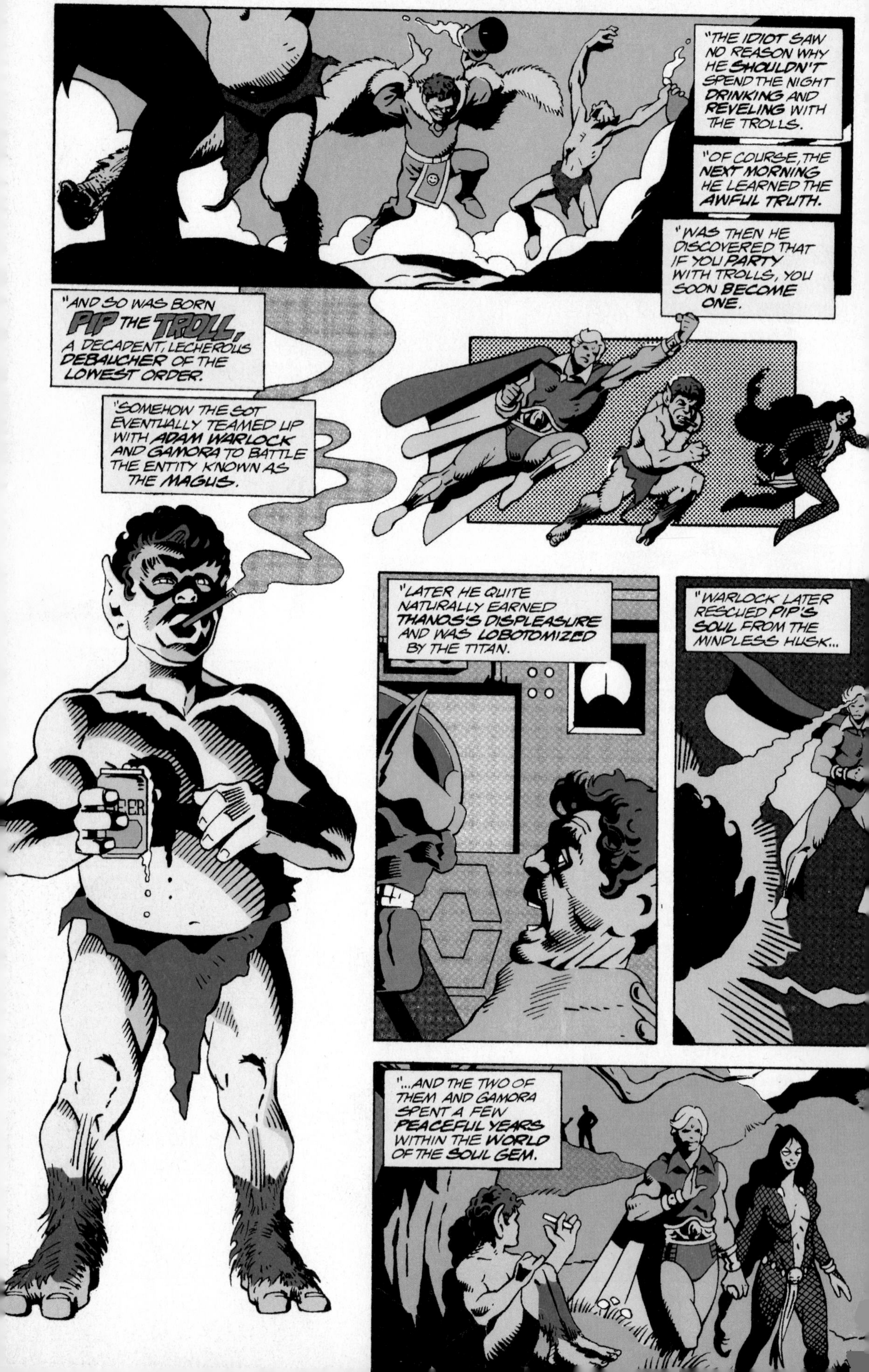
"THE IDIOT SAW NO REASON WHY HE SHOULDN'T SPEND THE NIGHT DRINKING AND REVELING WITH THE TROLLS.
"OF COURSE, THE NEXT MORNING HE LEARNED THE AWFUL TRUTH.
"WAS THEN HE DISCOVERED THAT IF YOU PARTY WITH TROLLS, YOU SOON BECOME ONE.
"AND SO WAS BORN PIP THE TROLL, A DECADENT, LECHEROUS DEBAUCHER OF THE LOWEST ORDER.
"SOMEHOW THE SOT EVENTUALLY TEAMED UP WITH ADAM WARLOCK AND GAMORA TO BATTLE THE ENTITY KNOWN AS THE MAGUS.
BEER
"LATER HE QUITE NATURALLY EARNED THANOS'S DISPLEASURE AND WAS LOBOTOMIZED BY THE TITAN.
"WARLOCK LATER RESCUED PIP'S SOUL FROM THE MINDLESS HUSK...
"...AND THE TWO OF THEM AND GAMORA SPENT A FEW PEACEFUL YEARS WITHIN THE WORLD OF THE SOUL GEM.

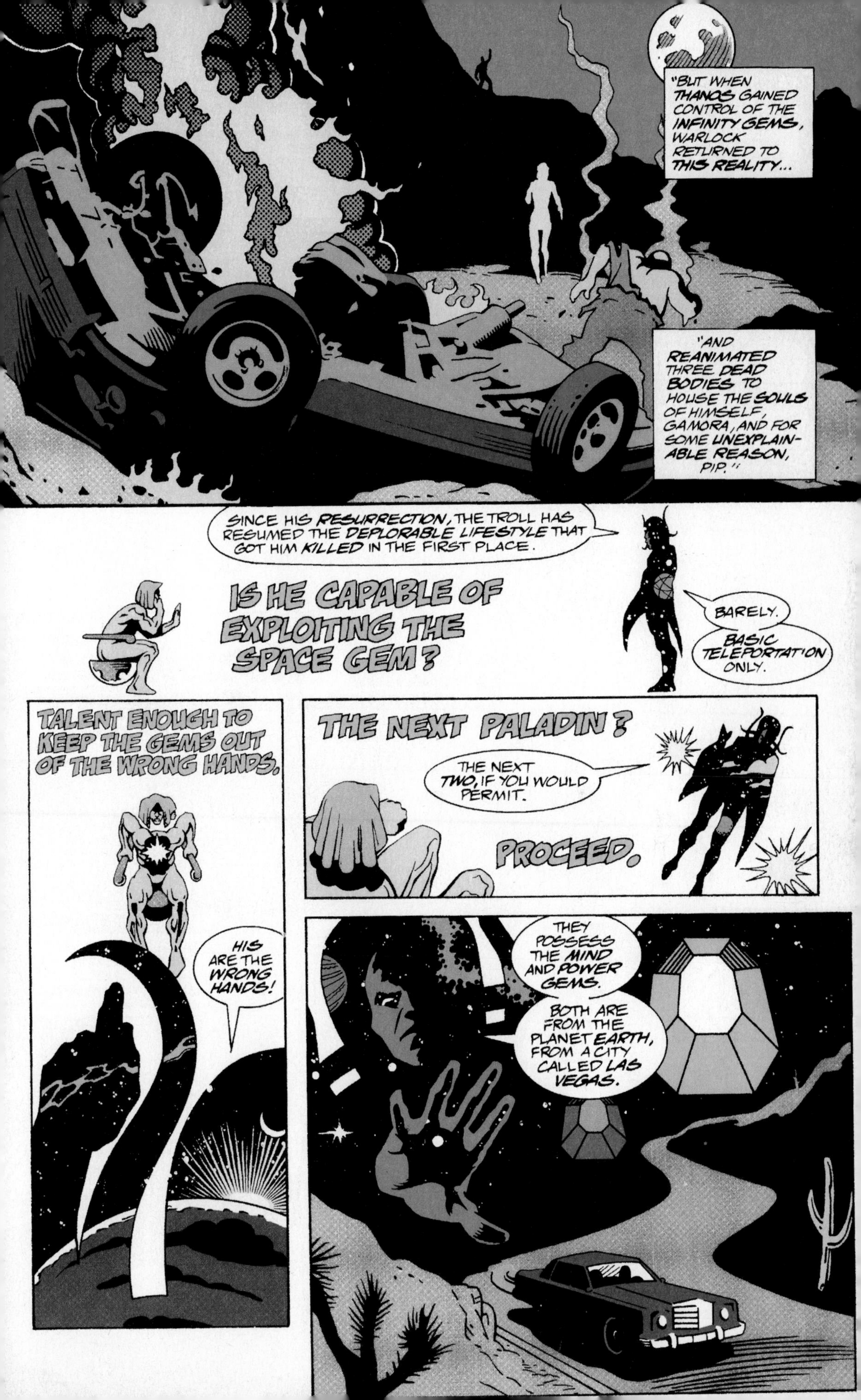
"BUT WHEN THANOS GAINED CONTROL OF THE INFINITY GEMS, WARLOCK RETURNED TO THIS REALITY...
"AND REANIMATED THREE DEAD BODIES TO HOUSE THE SOULS OF HIMSELF, GAMORA, AND FOR SOME UNEXPLAINABLE REASON, PIP."
SINCE HIS RESURRECTION, THE TROLL HAS RESUMED THE DEPLORABLE LIFESTYLE THAT GOT HIM KILLED IN THE FIRST PLACE.
IS HE CAPABLE OF EXPLOITING THE SPACE GEM?
BARELY.
BASIC TELEPORTATION ONLY.
TALENT ENOUGH TO KEEP THE GEMS OUT OF THE WRONG HANDS.
HIS ARE THE WRONG HANDS!
THE NEXT PALADIN?
THE NEXT TWO, IF YOU WOULD PERMIT.
PROCEED.
THEY POSSESS THE MIND AND POWER GEMS.
BOTH ARE FROM THE PLANET EARTH, FROM A CITY CALLED LAS VEGAS.

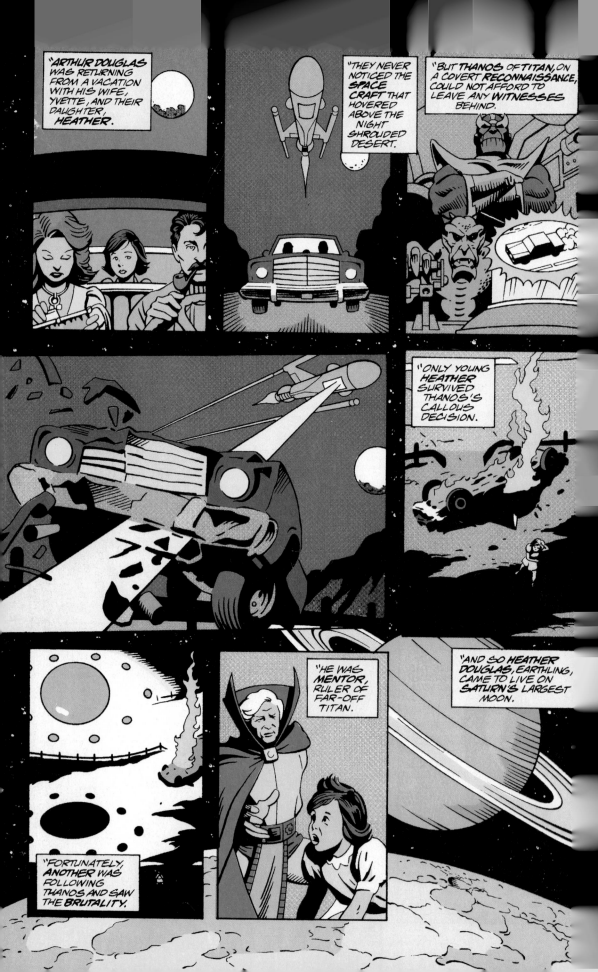

"ARTHUR DOUGLAS WAS RETURNING FROM A VACATION WITH HIS WIFE, YVETTE, AND THEIR DAUGHTER, HEATHER.

"THEY NEVER NOTICED THE SPACE CRAFT THAT HOVERED ABOVE THE NIGHT SHROUDED DESERT.

"BUT THANOS OF TITAN, ON A COVERT RECONNAISSANCE, COULD NOT AFFORD TO LEAVE ANY WITNESSES BEHIND.

"ONLY YOUNG HEATHER SURVIVED THANOS'S CALLOUS DECISION.

"FORTUNATELY, ANOTHER WAS FOLLOWING THANOS AND SAW THE BRUTALITY.

"HE WAS MENTOR, RULER OF FAR-OFF TITAN.

"AND SO HEATHER DOUGLAS, EARTHLING, CAME TO LIVE ON SATURN'S LARGEST MOON.

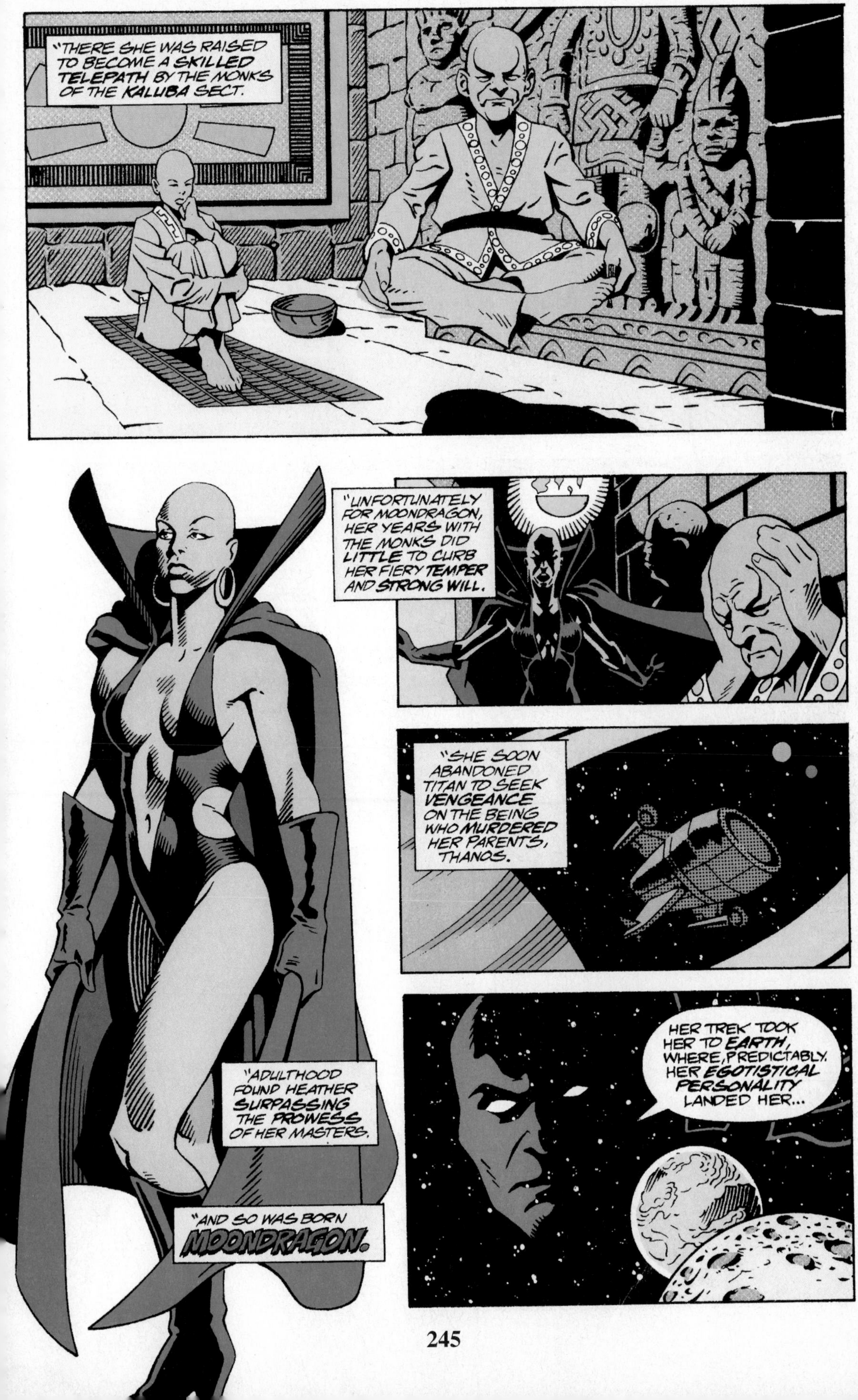
"THERE SHE WAS RAISED TO BECOME A SKILLED TELEPATH BY THE MONKS OF THE KALUBA SECT.
"ADULTHOOD FOUND HEATHER SURPASSING THE PROWESS OF HER MASTERS.
"AND SO WAS BORN MOONDRAGON.
"UNFORTUNATELY FOR MOONDRAGON, HER YEARS WITH THE MONKS DID LITTLE TO CURB HER FIERY TEMPER AND STRONG WILL.
"SHE SOON ABANDONED TITAN TO SEEK VENGEANCE ON THE BEING WHO MURDERED HER PARENTS, THANOS.
HER TREK TOOK HER TO EARTH, WHERE, PREDICTABLY, HER EGOTISTICAL PERSONALITY LANDED HER...

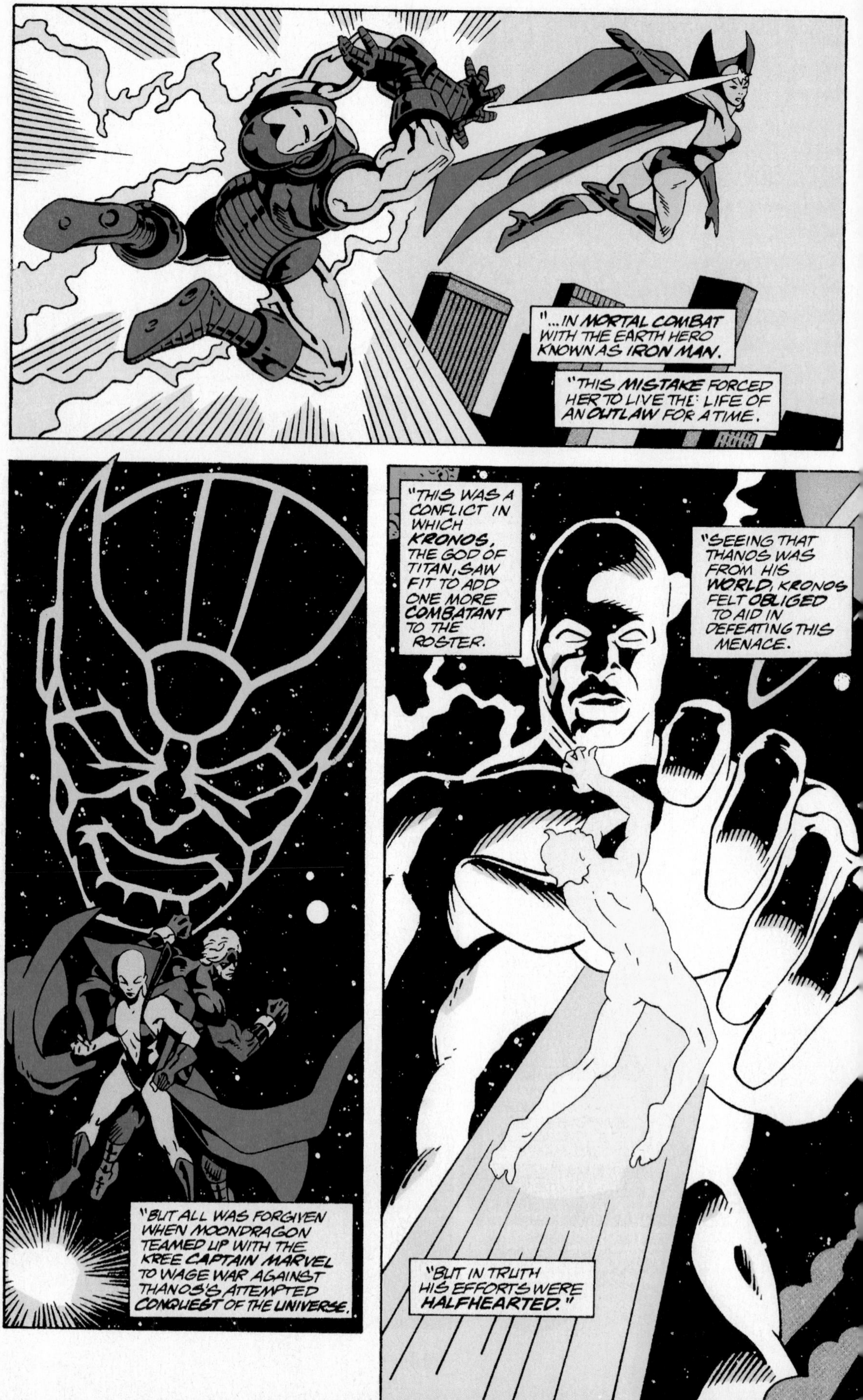
"...IN MORTAL COMBAT WITH THE EARTH HERO KNOWN AS IRON MAN.
"THIS MISTAKE FORCED HER TO LIVE THE LIFE OF AN OUTLAW FOR A TIME.
"THIS WAS A CONFLICT IN WHICH KRONOS, THE GOD OF TITAN, SAW FIT TO ADD ONE MORE COMBATANT TO THE ROSTER.
"SEEING THAT THANOS WAS FROM HIS WORLD, KRONOS FELT OBLIGED TO AID IN DEFEATING THIS MENACE.
"BUT ALL WAS FORGIVEN WHEN MOONDRAGON TEAMED UP WITH THE KREE CAPTAIN MARVEL TO WAGE WAR AGAINST THANOS'S ATTEMPTED CONQUEST OF THE UNIVERSE.
"BUT IN TRUTH HIS EFFORTS WERE HALFHEARTED."

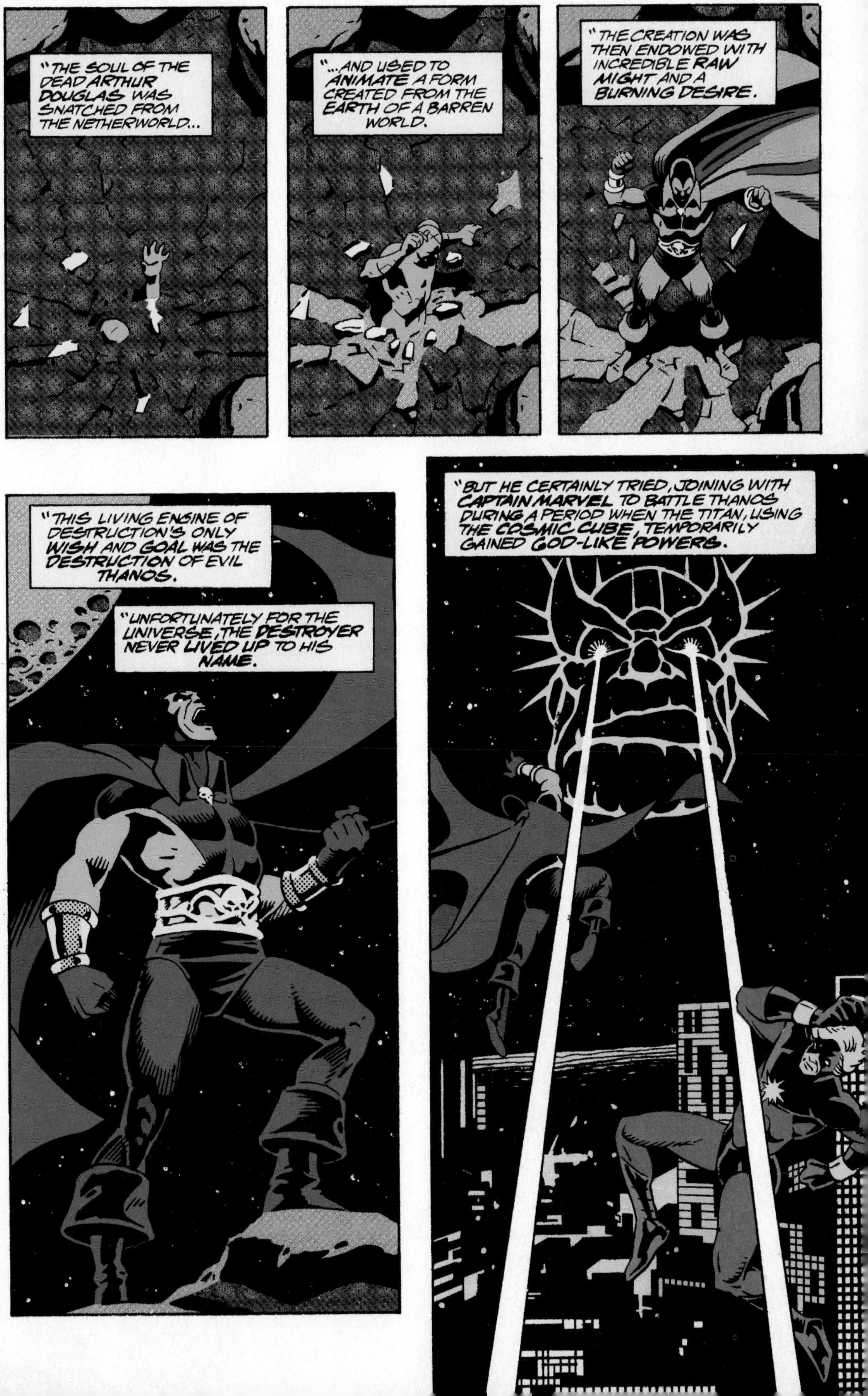
"THE SOUL OF THE DEAD ARTHUR DOUGLAS WAS SNATCHED FROM THE NETHERWORLD...
"...AND USED TO ANIMATE A FORM CREATED FROM THE EARTH OF A BARREN WORLD.
"THE CREATION WAS THEN ENDOWED WITH INCREDIBLE RAW MIGHT AND A BURNING DESIRE.
"THIS LIVING ENGINE OF DESTRUCTION'S ONLY WISH AND GOAL WAS THE DESTRUCTION OF EVIL THANOS.
"UNFORTUNATELY FOR THE UNIVERSE, THE DESTROYER NEVER LIVED UP TO HIS NAME.
"BUT HE CERTAINLY TRIED, JOINING WITH CAPTAIN MARVEL TO BATTLE THANOS DURING A PERIOD WHEN THE TITAN, USING THE COSMIC CUBE, TEMPORARILY GAINED GOD-LIKE POWERS.

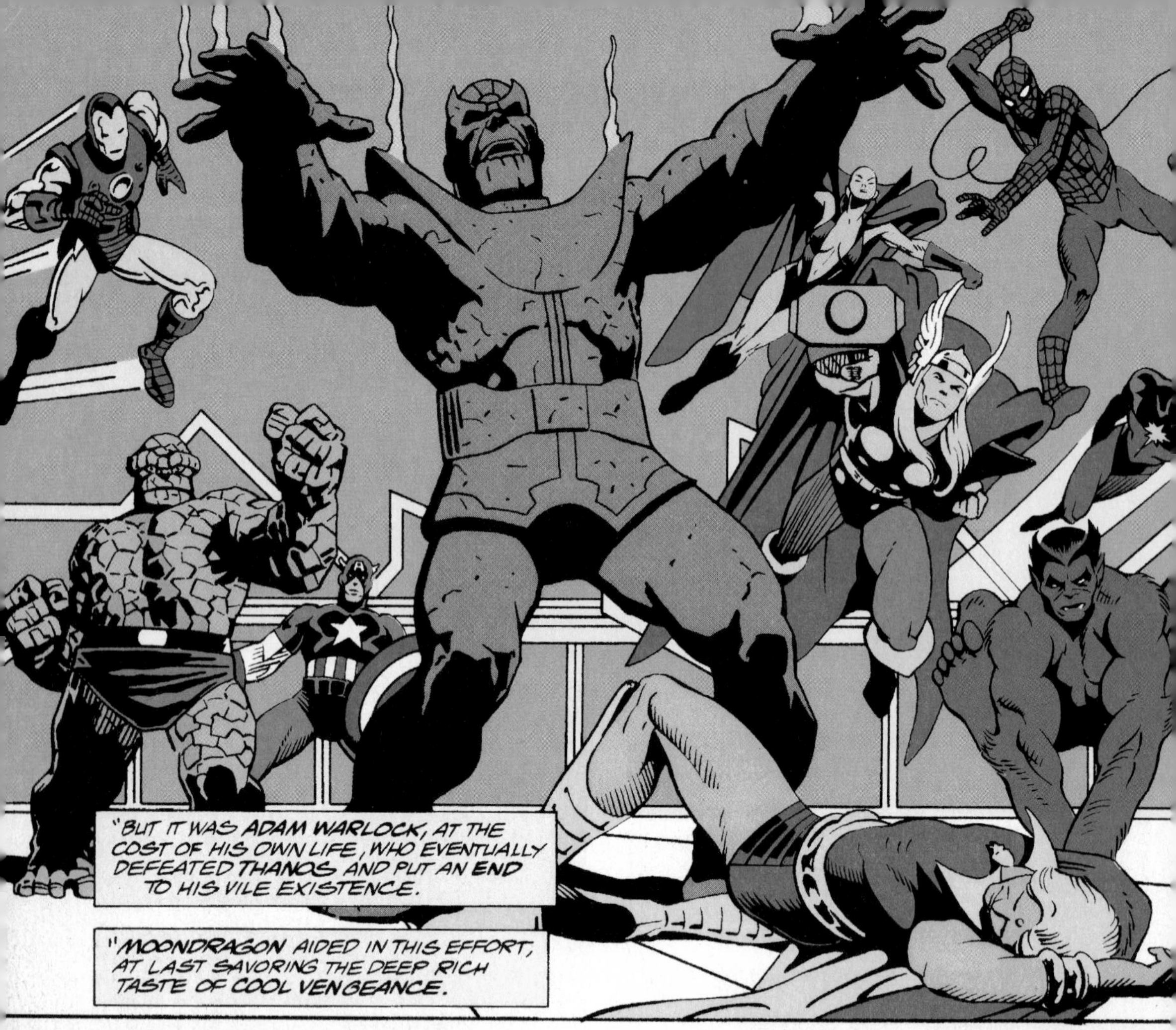
"BUT IT WAS ADAM WARLOCK, AT THE COST OF HIS OWN LIFE, WHO EVENTUALLY DEFEATED THANOS AND PUT AN END TO HIS VILE EXISTENCE.
"MOONDRAGON AIDED IN THIS EFFORT, AT LAST SAVORING THE DEEP RICH TASTE OF COOL VENGEANCE.

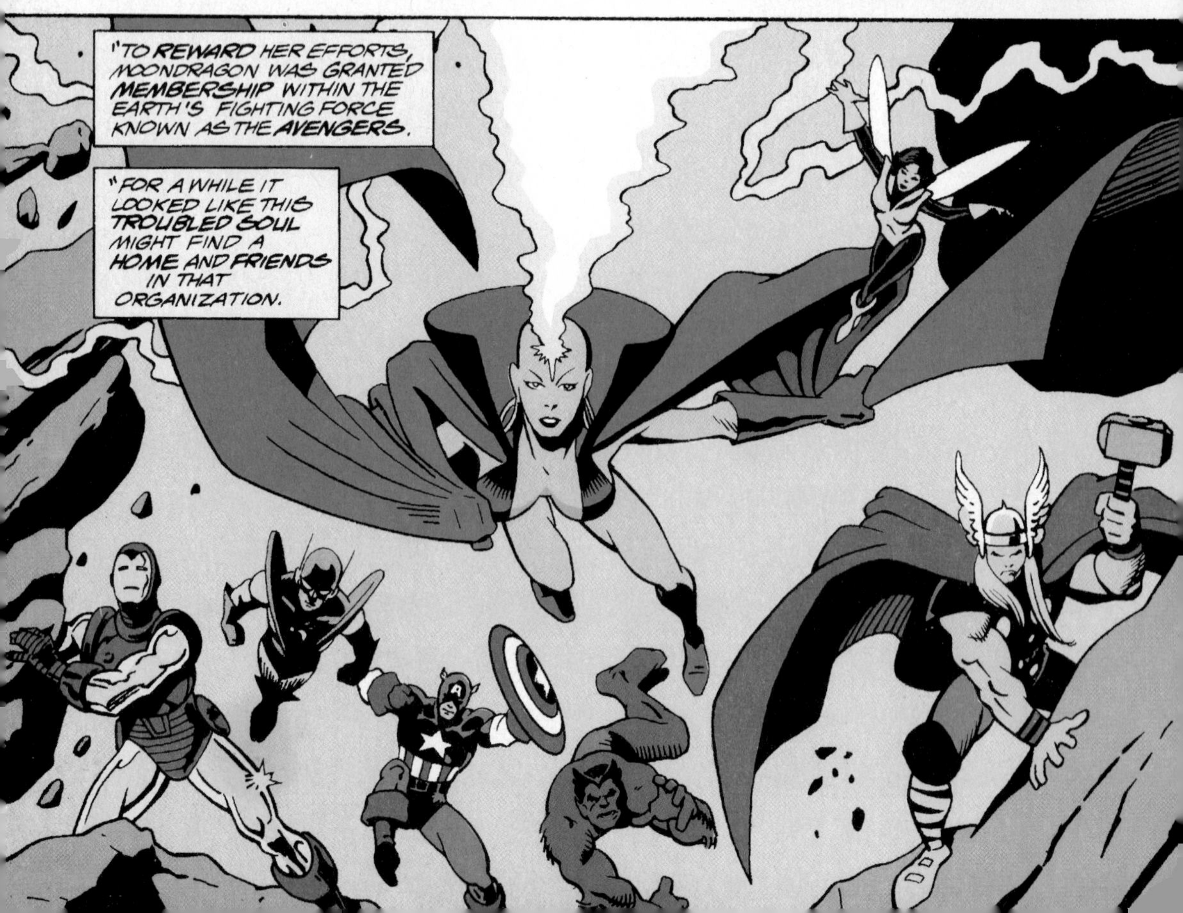
"TO REWARD HER EFFORTS, MOONDRAGON WAS GRANTED MEMBERSHIP WITHIN THE EARTH'S FIGHTING FORCE KNOWN AS THE AVENGERS.
"FOR A WHILE IT LOOKED LIKE THIS TROUBLED SOUL MIGHT FIND A HOME AND FRIENDS IN THAT ORGANIZATION.

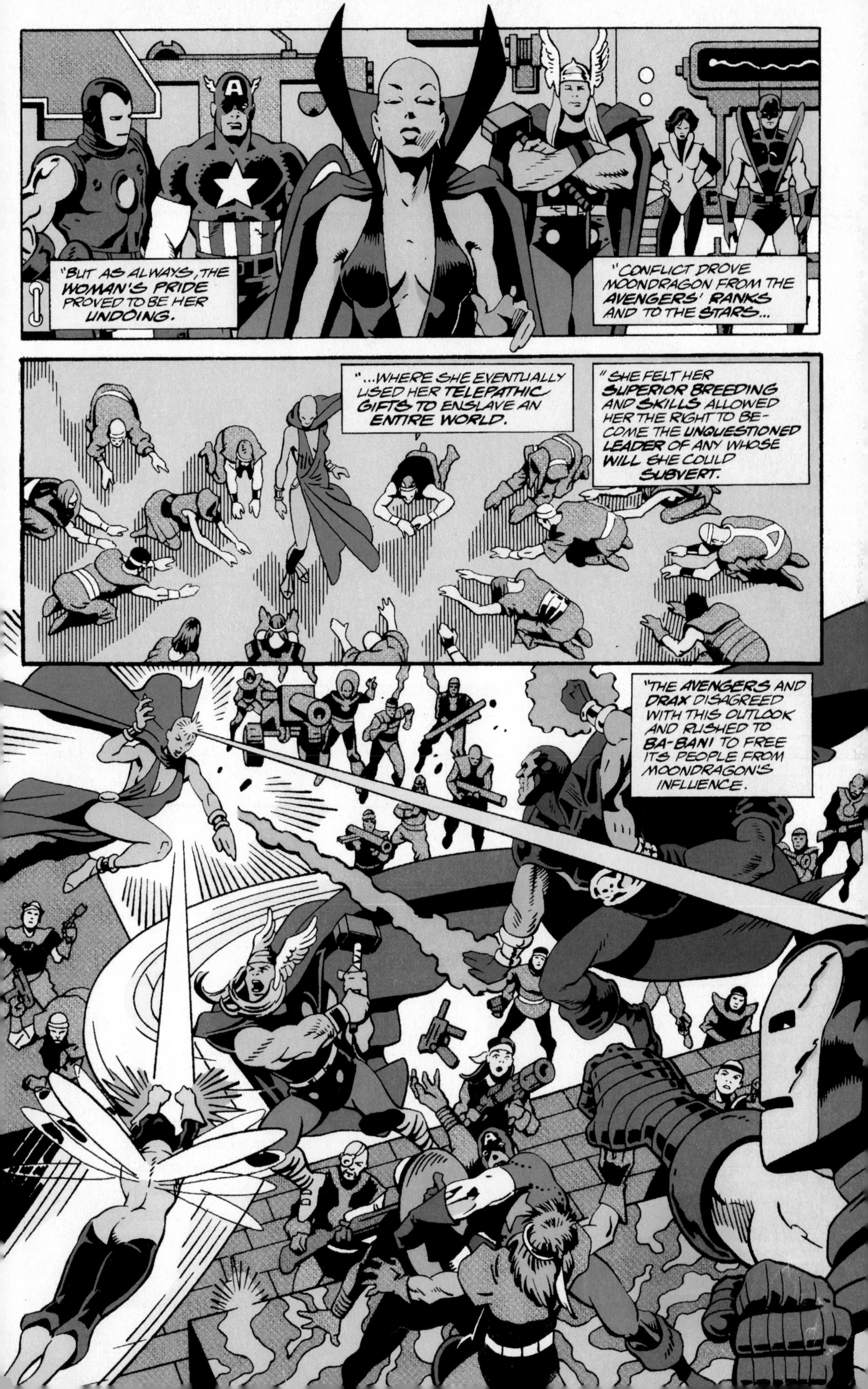
"BUT AS ALWAYS, THE WOMAN'S PRIDE PROVED TO BE HER UNDOING.
"CONFLICT DROVE MOONDRAGON FROM THE AVENGERS' RANKS AND TO THE STARS...
"...WHERE SHE EVENTUALLY USED HER TELEPATHIC GIFTS TO ENSLAVE AN ENTIRE WORLD.
"SHE FELT HER SUPERIOR BREEDING AND SKILLS ALLOWED HER THE RIGHT TO BE-COME THE UNQUESTIONED LEADER OF ANY WHOSE WILL SHE COULD SUBVERT.
"THE AVENGERS AND DRAX DISAGREED WITH THIS OUTLOOK AND RUSHED TO BA-BANI TO FREE ITS PEOPLE FROM MOONDRAGON'S INFLUENCE.

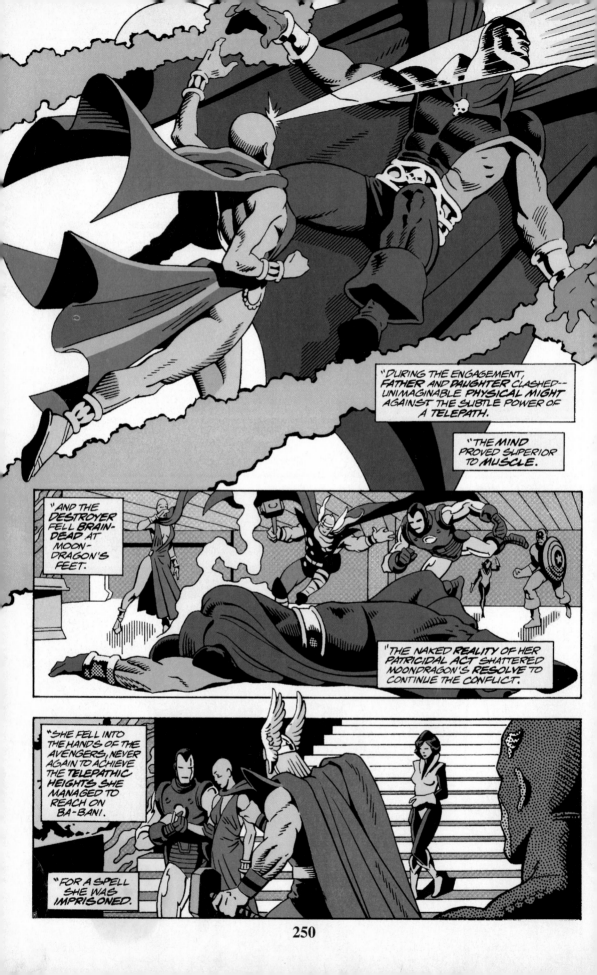

"DURING THE ENGAGEMENT, FATHER AND DAUGHTER CLASHED-- UNIMAGINABLE PHYSICAL MIGHT AGAINST THE SUBTLE POWER OF A TELEPATH.

"THE MIND PROVED SUPERIOR TO MUSCLE.

"AND THE DESTROYER FELL BRAIN- DEAD AT MOON- DRAGON'S FEET.

"THE NAKED REALITY OF HER PATRICIDAL ACT SHATTERED MOONDRAGON'S RESOLVE TO CONTINUE THE CONFLICT.

"SHE FELL INTO THE HANDS OF THE AVENGERS, NEVER AGAIN TO ACHIEVE THE TELEPATHIC HEIGHTS SHE MANAGED TO REACH ON BA-BANI.

"FOR A SPELL SHE WAS IMPRISONED.

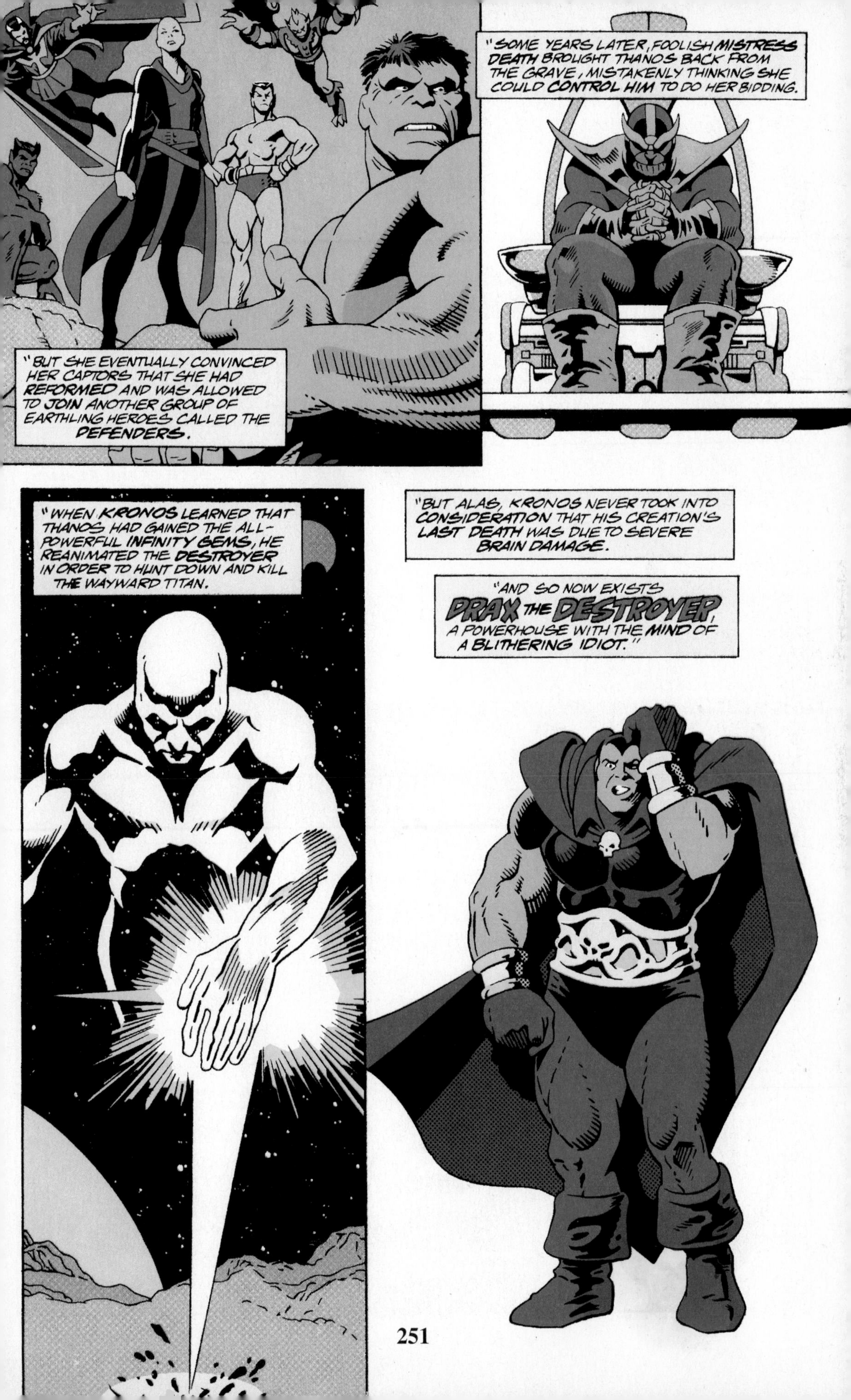
"BUT SHE EVENTUALLY CONVINCED HER CAPTORS THAT SHE HAD REFORMED AND WAS ALLOWED TO JOIN ANOTHER GROUP OF EARTHLING HEROES CALLED THE DEFENDERS.
"SOME YEARS LATER, FOOLISH MISTRESS DEATH BROUGHT THANOS BACK FROM THE GRAVE, MISTAKENLY THINKING SHE COULD CONTROL HIM TO DO HER BIDDING.
"WHEN KRONOS LEARNED THAT THANOS HAD GAINED THE ALL-POWERFUL INFINITY GEMS, HE REANIMATED THE DESTROYER IN ORDER TO HUNT DOWN AND KILL THE WAYWARD TITAN.
"BUT ALAS, KRONOS NEVER TOOK INTO CONSIDERATION THAT HIS CREATION'S LAST DEATH WAS DUE TO SEVERE BRAIN DAMAGE.
"AND SO NOW EXISTS DRAX THE DESTROYER, A POWERHOUSE WITH THE MIND OF A BLITHERING IDIOT."

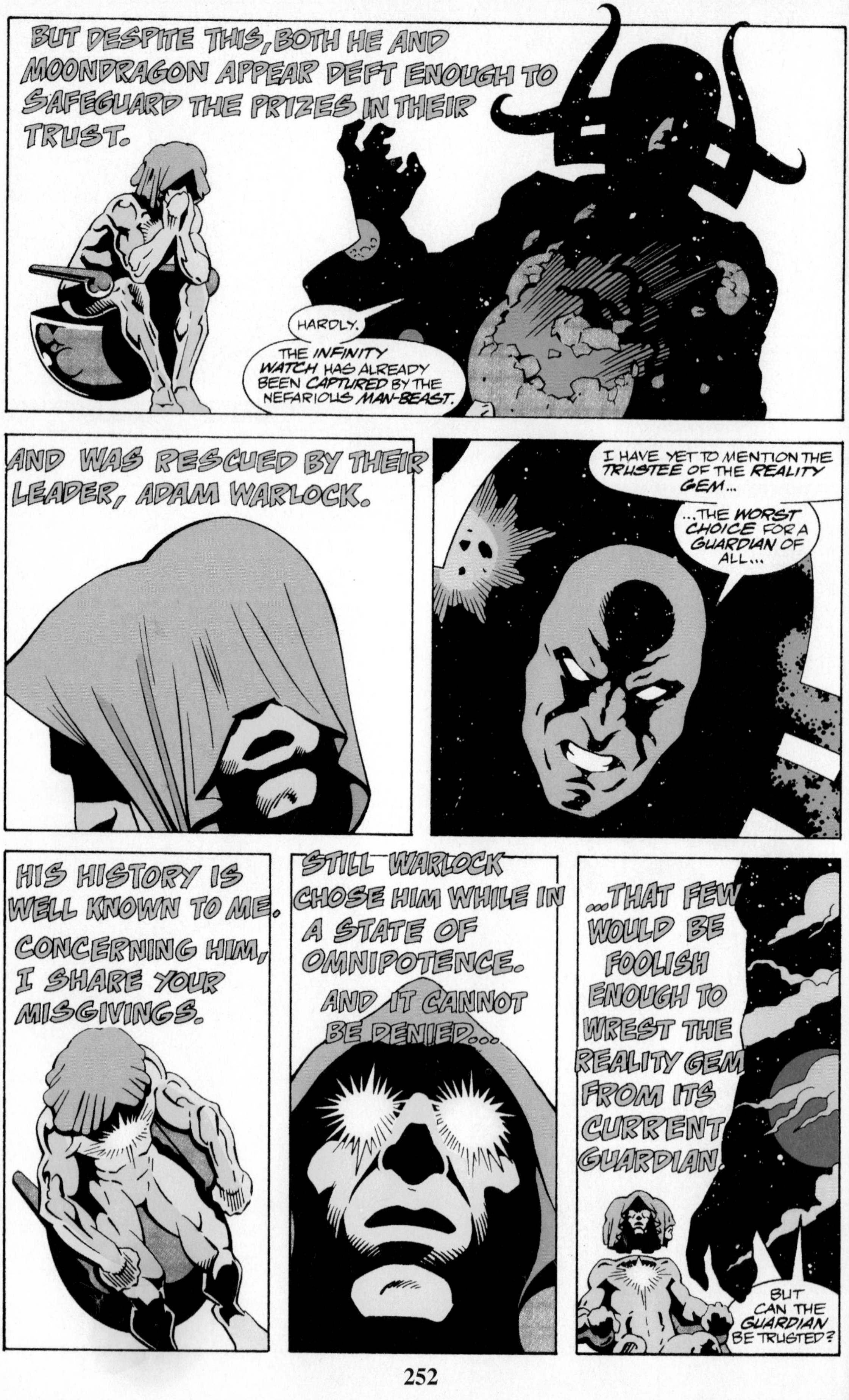
BUT DESPITE THIS, BOTH HE AND MOONDRAGON APPEAR DEFT ENOUGH TO SAFEGUARD THE PRIZES IN THEIR TRUST.
HARDLY.
THE INFINITY WATCH HAS ALREADY BEEN CAPTURED BY THE NEFARIOUS MAN-BEAST.
AND WAS RESCUED BY THEIR LEADER, ADAM WARLOCK.
I HAVE YET TO MENTION THE TRUSTEE OF THE REALITY GEM...
...THE WORST CHOICE FOR A GUARDIAN OF ALL...
HIS HISTORY IS WELL KNOWN TO ME.
CONCERNING HIM, I SHARE YOUR MISGIVINGS.
STILL WARLOCK CHOSE HIM WHILE IN A STATE OF OMNIPOTENCE.
AND IT CANNOT BE DENIED...
...THAT FEW WOULD BE FOOLISH ENOUGH TO WREST THE REALITY GEM FROM ITS CURRENT GUARDIAN.
BUT CAN THE GUARDIAN BE TRUSTED?

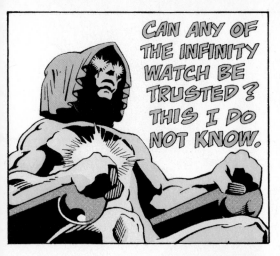

CAN ANY OF THE INFINITY WATCH BE TRUSTED? THIS I DO NOT KNOW.

THEN YOUR RULING IS?

ETERNITY, BEFORE THE INFINITY GEMS RESURFACED YOU WERE THE UNCHALLENGED LORD OF ALL THERE IS.

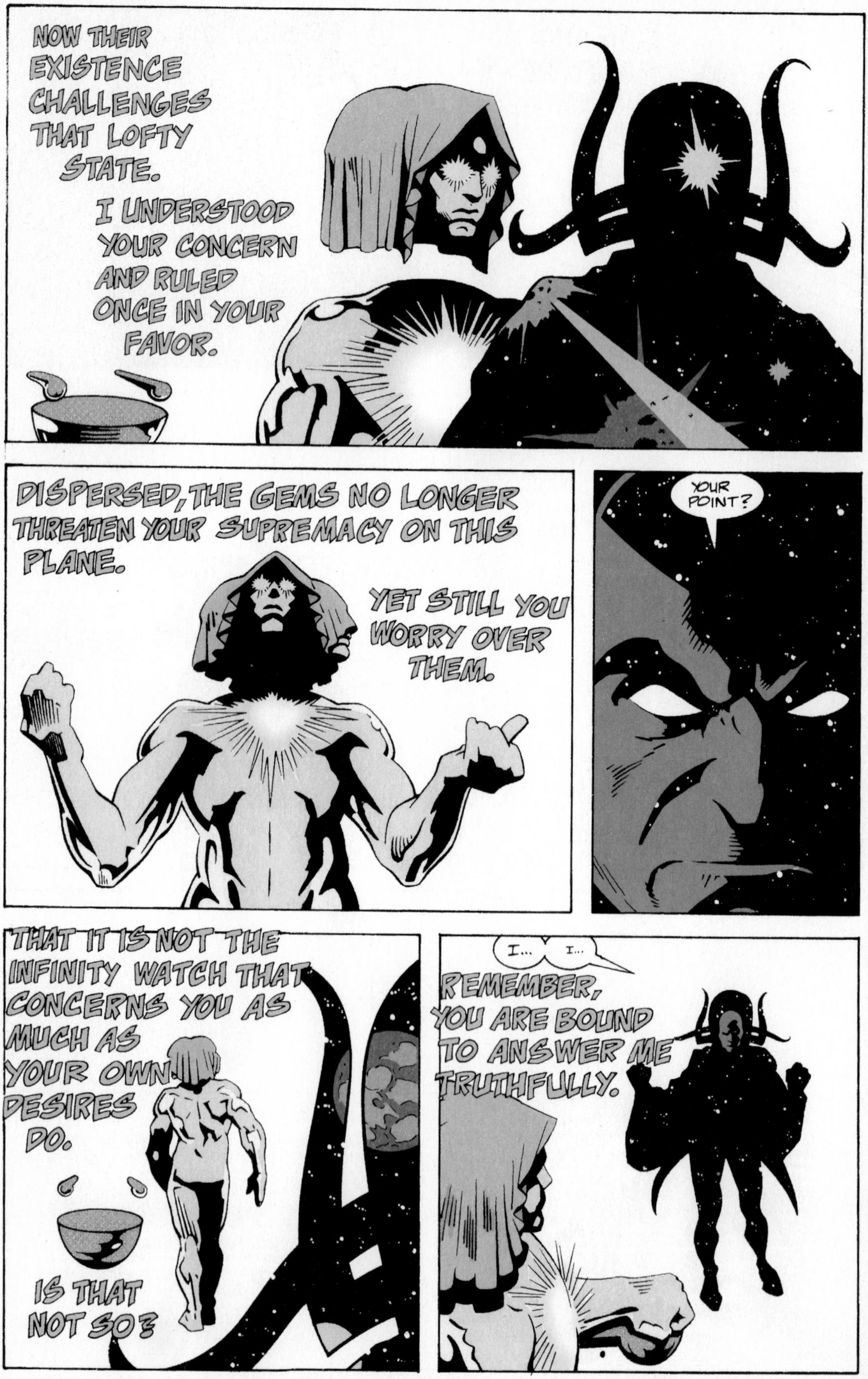
NOW THEIR EXISTENCE CHALLENGES THAT LOFTY STATE.
I UNDERSTOOD YOUR CONCERN AND RULED ONCE IN YOUR FAVOR.
DISPERSED, THE GEMS NO LONGER THREATEN YOUR SUPREMACY ON THIS PLANE.
YET STILL YOU WORRY OVER THEM.
YOUR POINT?
THAT IT IS NOT THE INFINITY WATCH THAT CONCERNS YOU AS MUCH AS YOUR OWN DESIRES DO.
IS THAT NOT SO?
I...
I...
REMEMBER, YOU ARE BOUND TO ANSWER ME TRUTHFULLY.

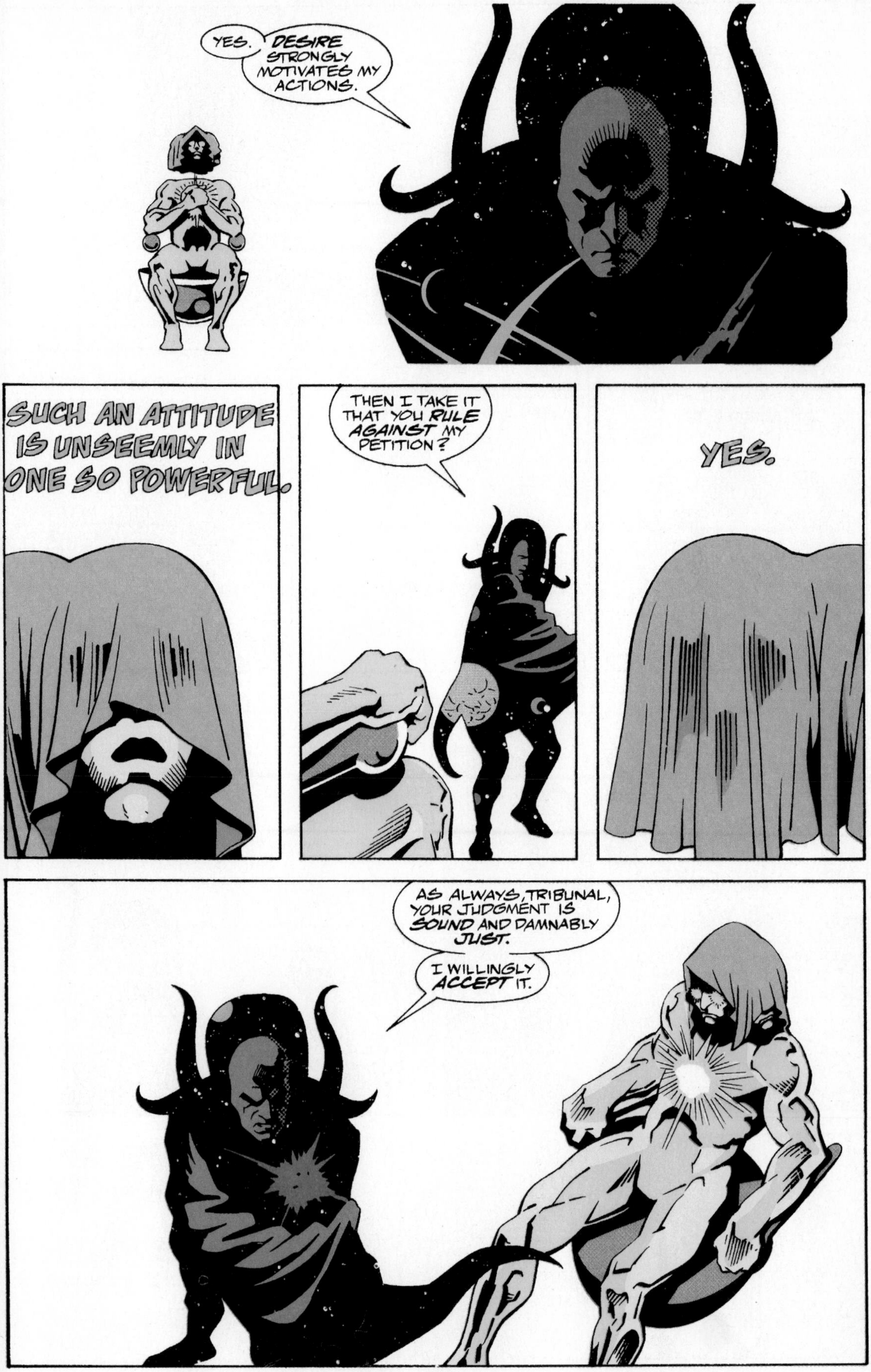
YES. DESIRE STRONGLY MOTIVATES MY ACTIONS.
SUCH AN ATTITUDE IS UNSEEMLY IN ONE SO POWERFUL.
THEN I TAKE IT THAT YOU RULE AGAINST MY PETITION?
YES.
AS ALWAYS, TRIBUNAL, YOUR JUDGMENT IS SOUND AND DAMNABLY JUST.
I WILLINGLY ACCEPT IT.

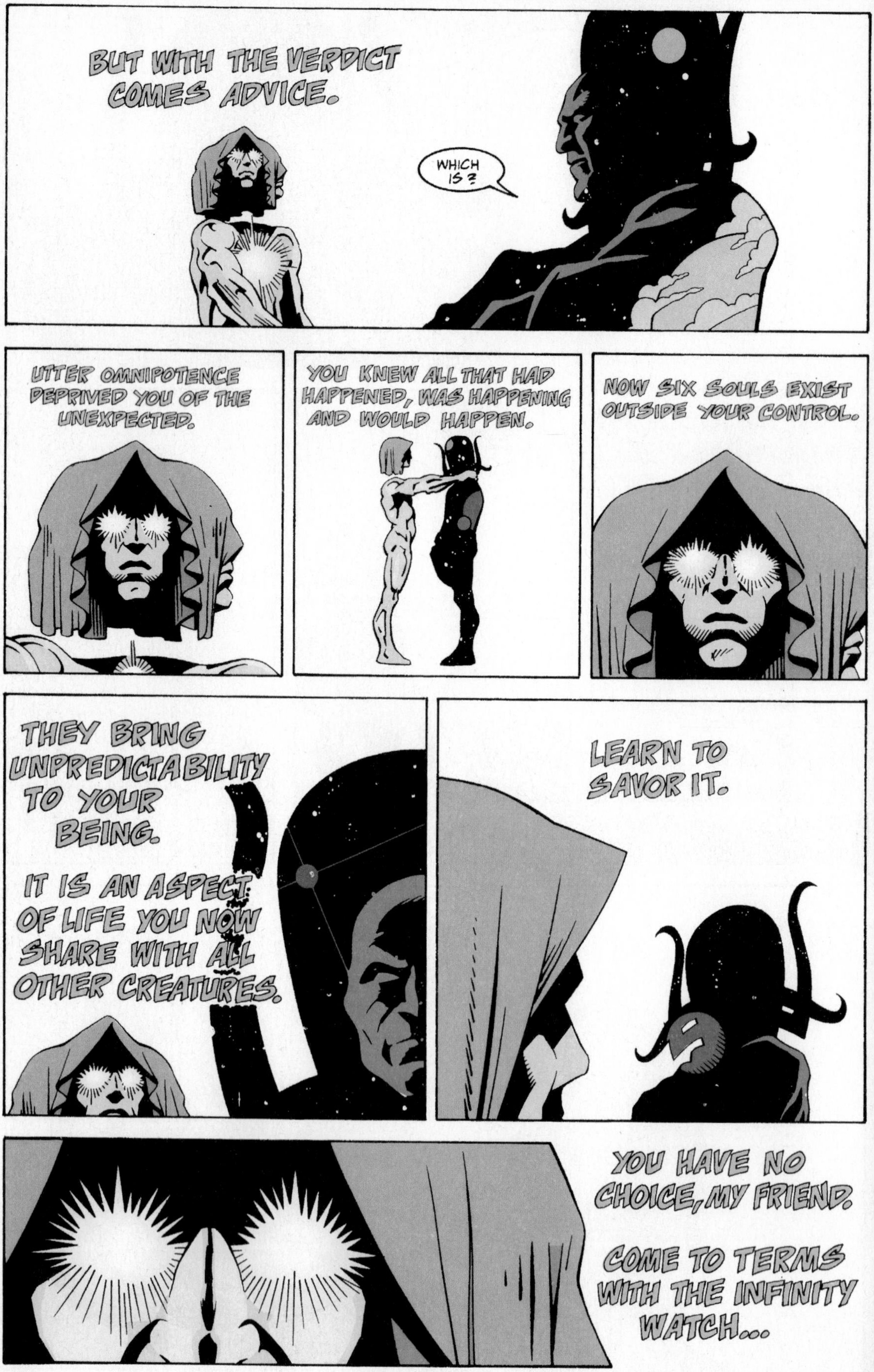
BUT WITH THE VERDICT COMES ADVICE.
WHICH IS?
UTTER OMNIPOTENCE DEPRIVED YOU OF THE UNEXPECTED.
YOU KNEW ALL THAT HAD HAPPENED, WAS HAPPENING AND WOULD HAPPEN.
NOW SIX SOULS EXIST OUTSIDE YOUR CONTROL.
THEY BRING UNPREDICTABILITY TO YOUR BEING.
IT IS AN ASPECT OF LIFE YOU NOW SHARE WITH ALL OTHER CREATURES.
LEARN TO SAVOR IT.
YOU HAVE NO CHOICE, MY FRIEND.
COME TO TERMS WITH THE INFINITY WATCH...

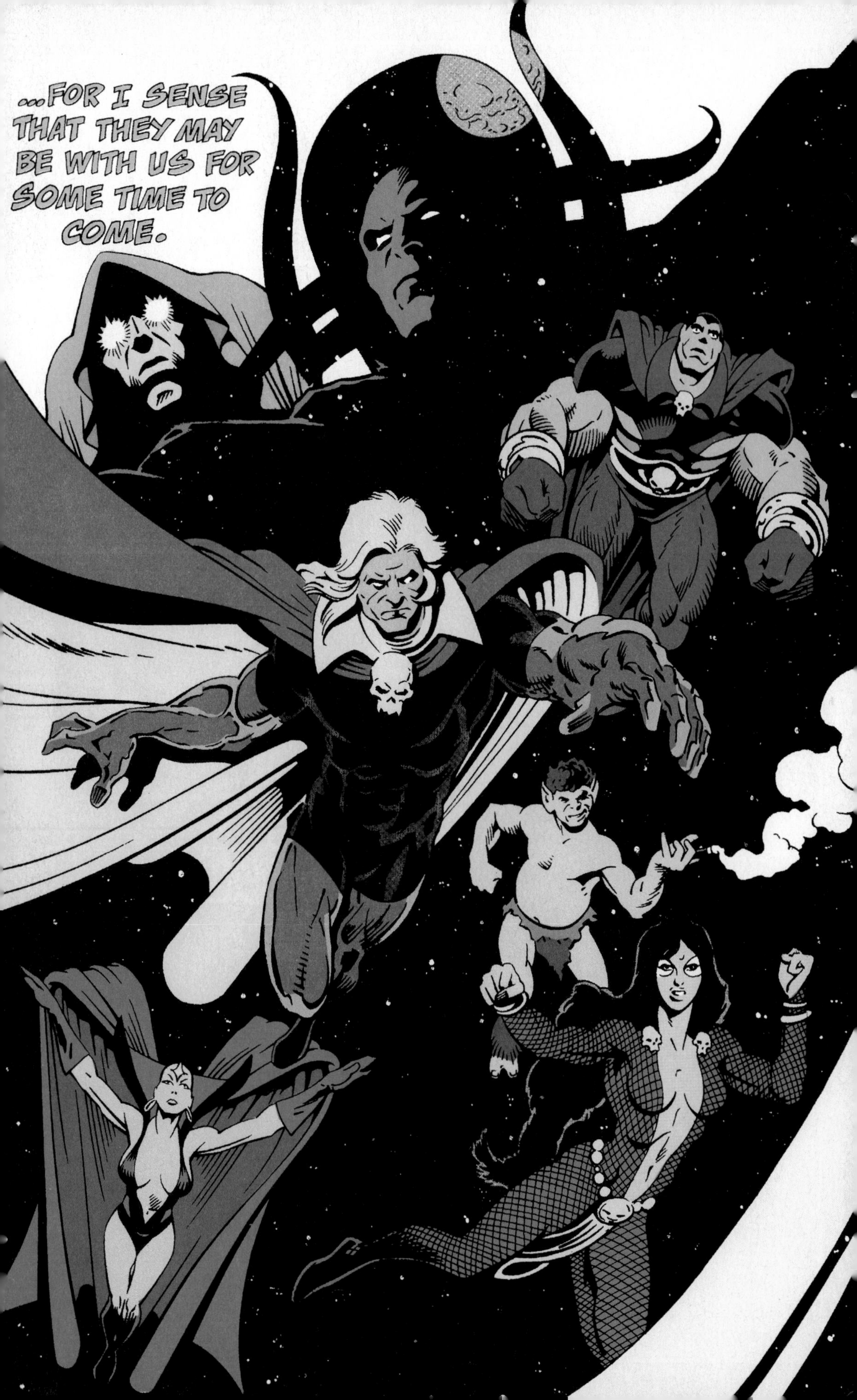
...FOR I SENSE THAT THEY MAY BE WITH US FOR SOME TIME TO COME.

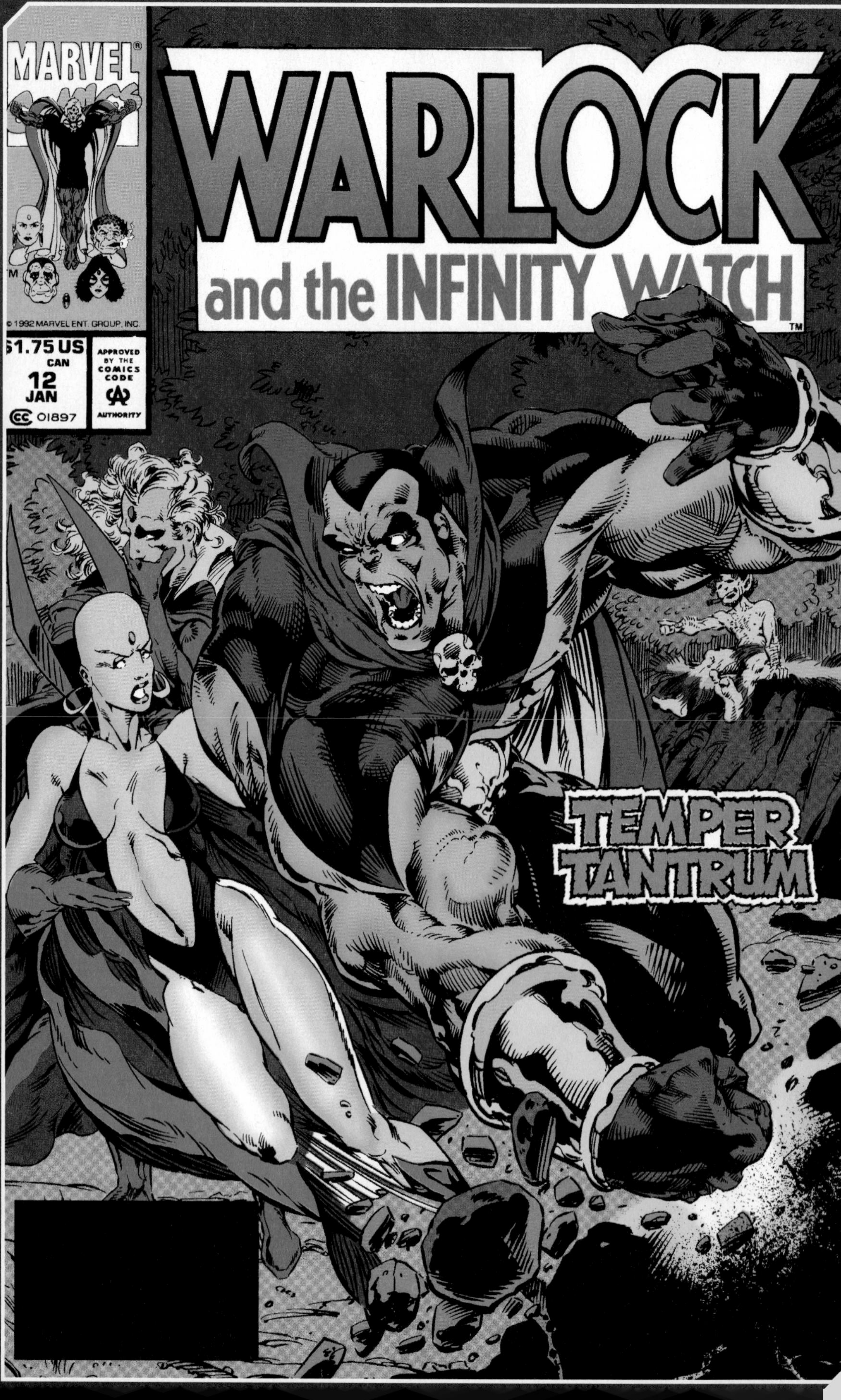
MARVEL
WARLOCK
and the INFINITY WATCH
© 1992 MARVEL ENT. GROUP, INC.
$1.75 US
CAN
12
JAN
01897
APPROVED BY THE COMICS CODE AUTHORITY
TEMPER TANTRUM

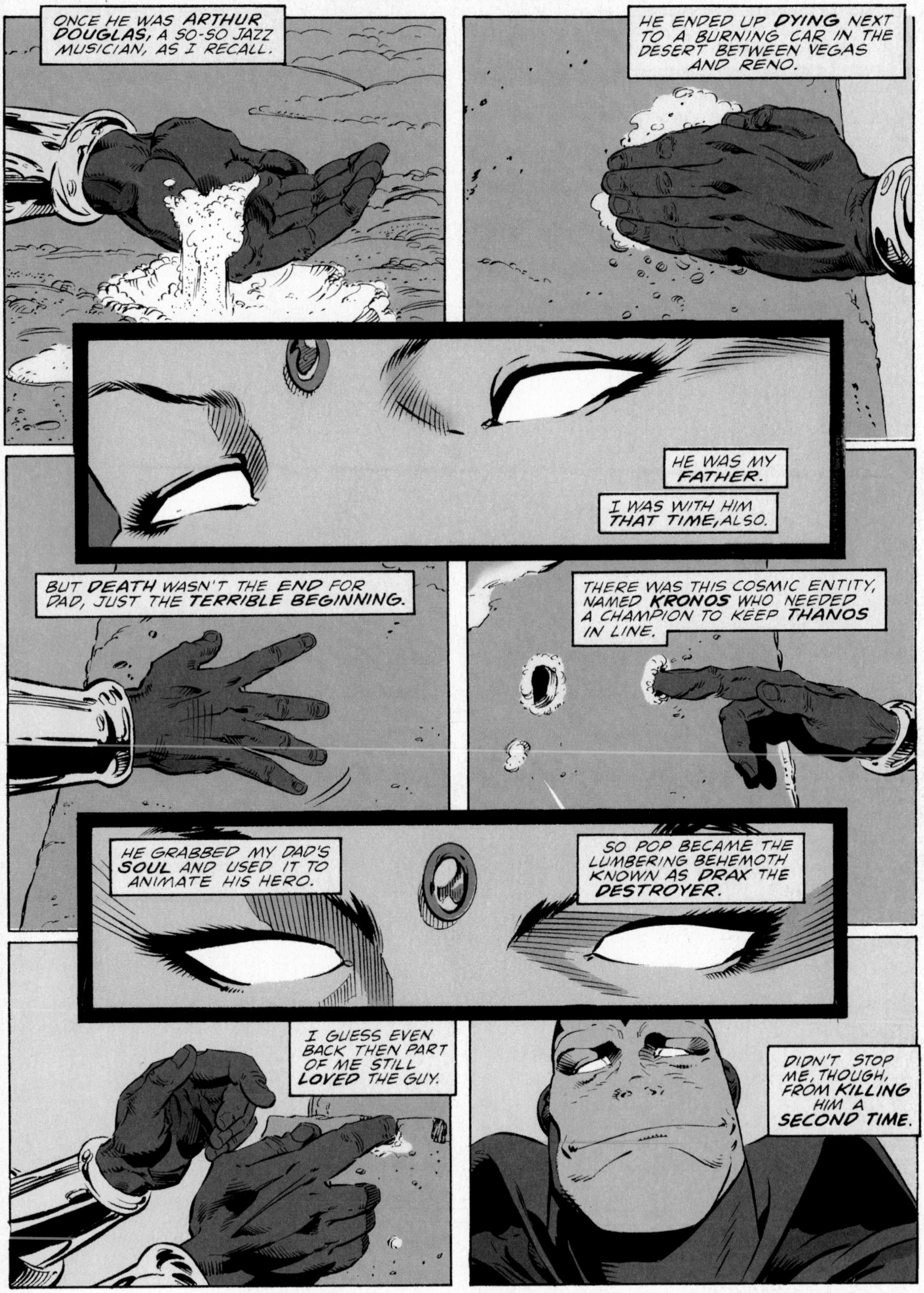
ONCE HE WAS ARTHUR DOUGLAS, A SO-SO JAZZ MUSICIAN, AS I RECALL.
HE ENDED UP DYING NEXT TO A BURNING CAR IN THE DESERT BETWEEN VEGAS AND RENO.
HE WAS MY FATHER.
I WAS WITH HIM THAT TIME, ALSO.
BUT DEATH WASN'T THE END FOR DAD, JUST THE TERRIBLE BEGINNING.
THERE WAS THIS COSMIC ENTITY, NAMED KRONOS WHO NEEDED A CHAMPION TO KEEP THANOS IN LINE.
HE GRABBED MY DAD'S SOUL AND USED IT TO ANIMATE HIS HERO.
SO POP BECAME THE LUMBERING BEHEMOTH KNOWN AS DRAX THE DESTROYER.
I GUESS EVEN BACK THEN PART OF ME STILL LOVED THE GUY.
DIDN'T STOP ME, THOUGH, FROM KILLING HIM A SECOND TIME.

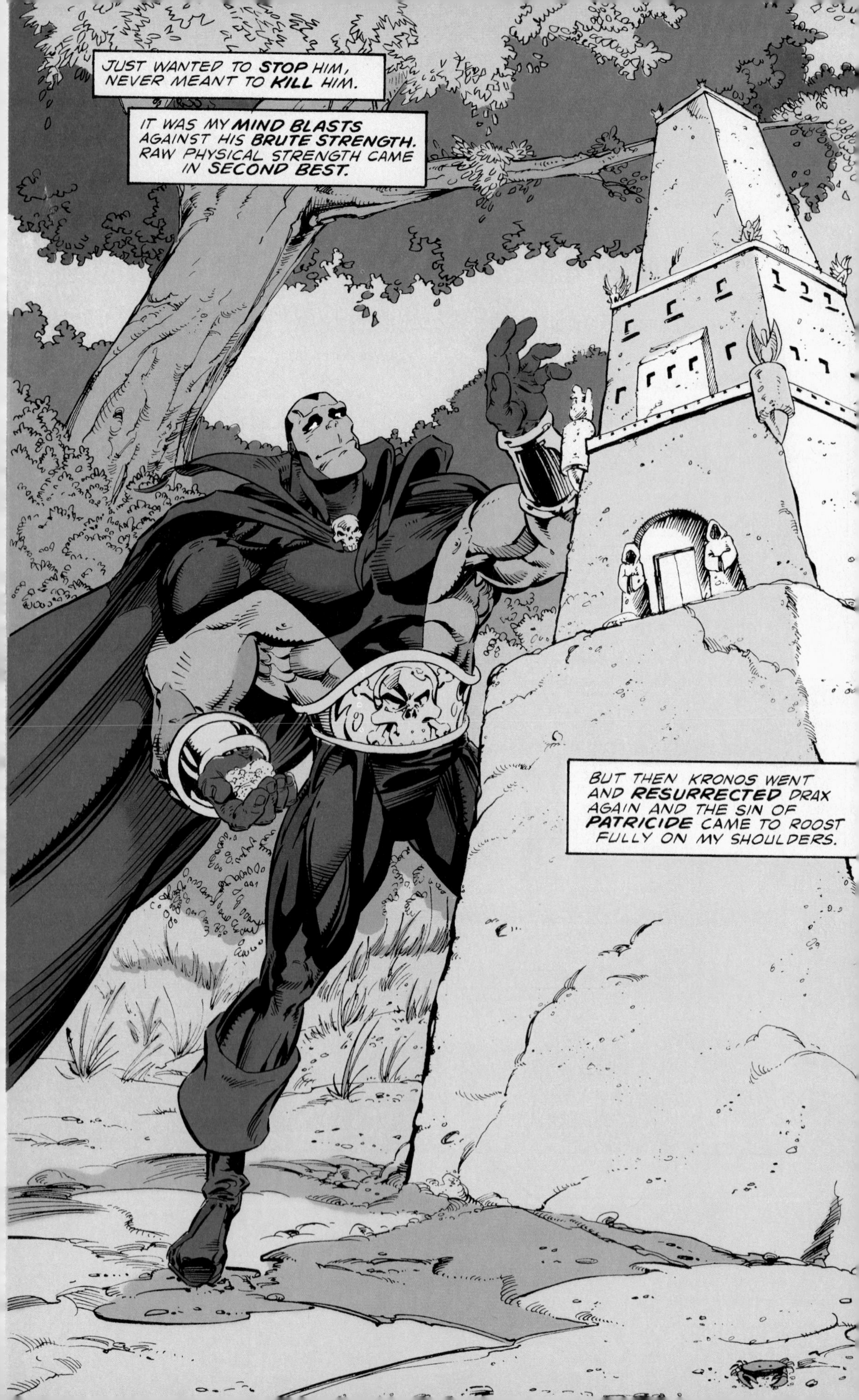
JUST WANTED TO STOP HIM, NEVER MEANT TO KILL HIM.
IT WAS MY MIND BLASTS AGAINST HIS BRUTE STRENGTH. RAW PHYSICAL STRENGTH CAME IN SECOND BEST.
BUT THEN KRONOS WENT AND RESURRECTED DRAX AGAIN AND THE SIN OF PATRICIDE CAME TO ROOST FULLY ON MY SHOULDERS.

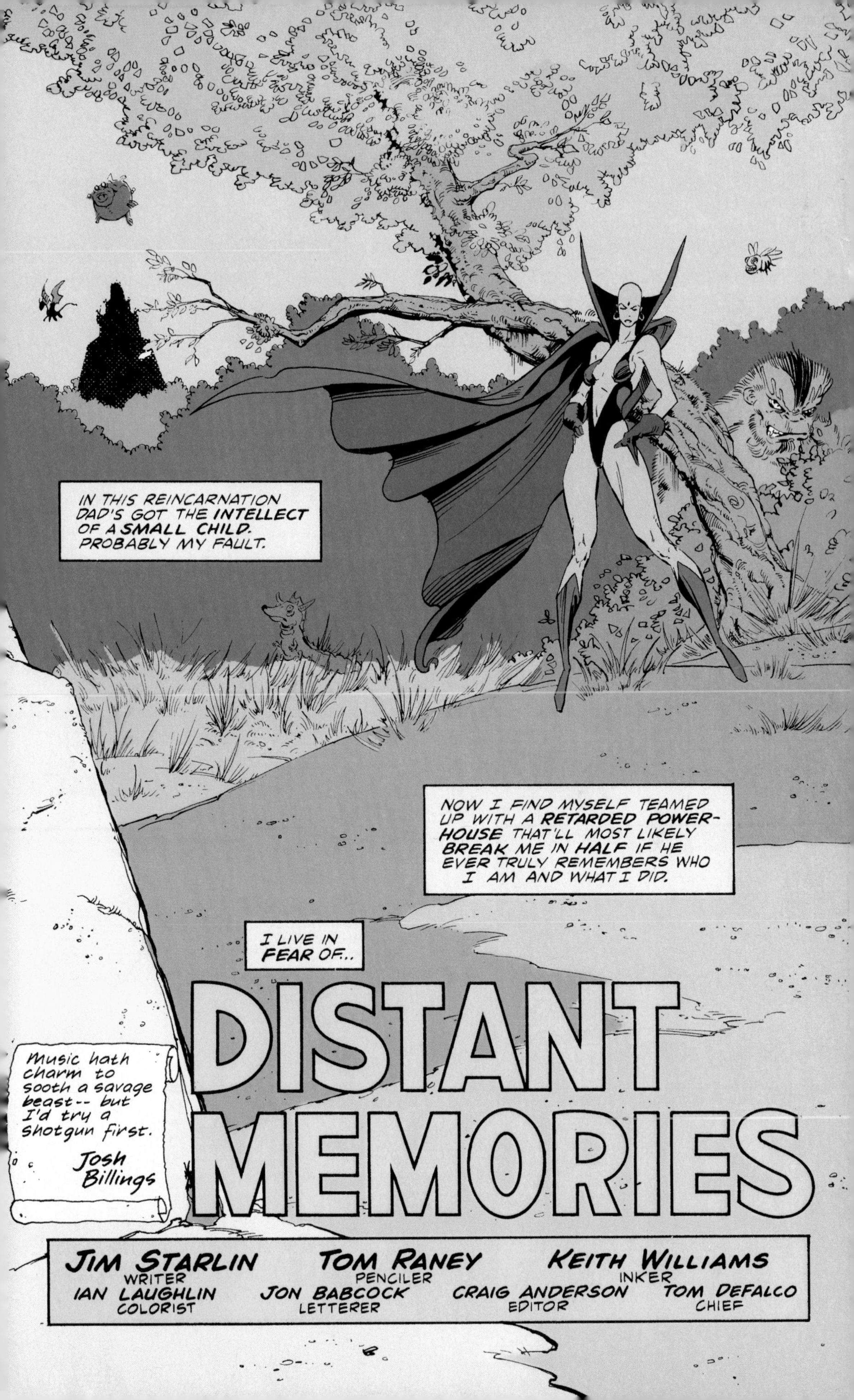
IN THIS REINCARNATION DAD'S GOT THE INTELLECT OF A SMALL CHILD. PROBABLY MY FAULT.
NOW I FIND MYSELF TEAMED UP WITH A RETARDED POWER-HOUSE THAT'LL MOST LIKELY BREAK ME IN HALF IF HE EVER TRULY REMEMBERS WHO I AM AND WHAT I DID.
I LIVE IN FEAR OF...
DISTANT MEMORIES
Music hath charm to sooth a savage beast-- but I'd try a shotgun first. Josh Billings
JIM STARLIN WRITER
TOM RANEY PENCILER
KEITH WILLIAMS INKER
IAN LAUGHLIN COLORIST
JON BABCOCK LETTERER
CRAIG ANDERSON EDITOR
TOM DEFALCO CHIEF

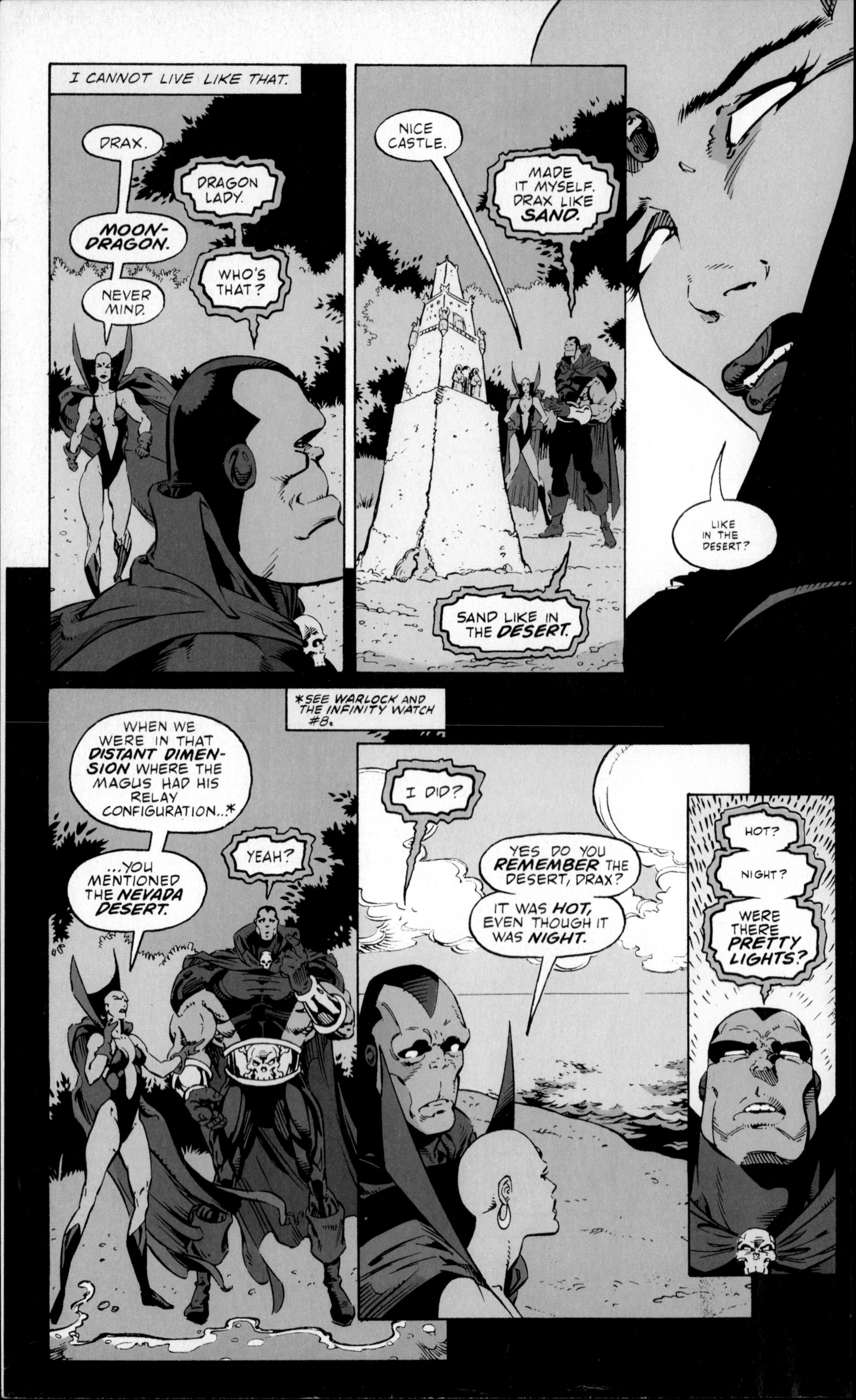
I CANNOT LIVE LIKE THAT.
DRAX.
DRAGON LADY.
MOON-DRAGON.
WHO'S THAT?
NEVER MIND.
NICE CASTLE.
MADE IT MYSELF. DRAX LIKE SAND.
LIKE IN THE DESERT?
SAND LIKE IN THE DESERT.
*SEE WARLOCK AND THE INFINITY WATCH #8.
WHEN WE WERE IN THAT DISTANT DIMENSION WHERE THE MAGUS HAD HIS RELAY CONFIGURATION...*
...YOU MENTIONED THE NEVADA DESERT.
YEAH?
I DID?
YES DO YOU REMEMBER THE DESERT, DRAX?
IT WAS HOT, EVEN THOUGH IT WAS NIGHT.
HOT?
NIGHT?
WERE THERE PRETTY LIGHTS?

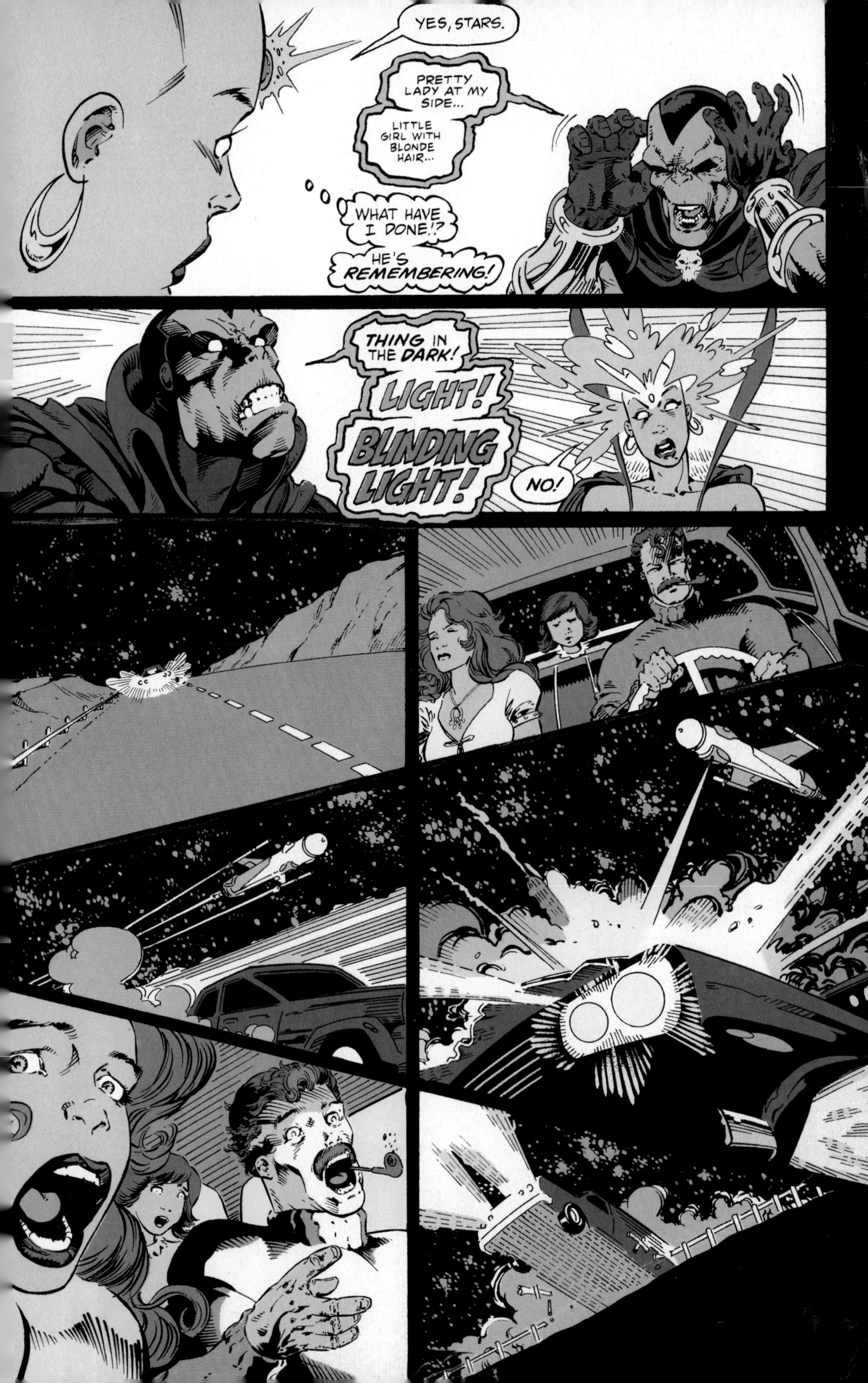
YES, STARS.
PRETTY LADY AT MY SIDE...
LITTLE GIRL WITH BLONDE HAIR...
WHAT HAVE I DONE!?
HE'S REMEMBERING!
THING IN THE DARK!
LIGHT! BLINDING LIGHT!
NO!

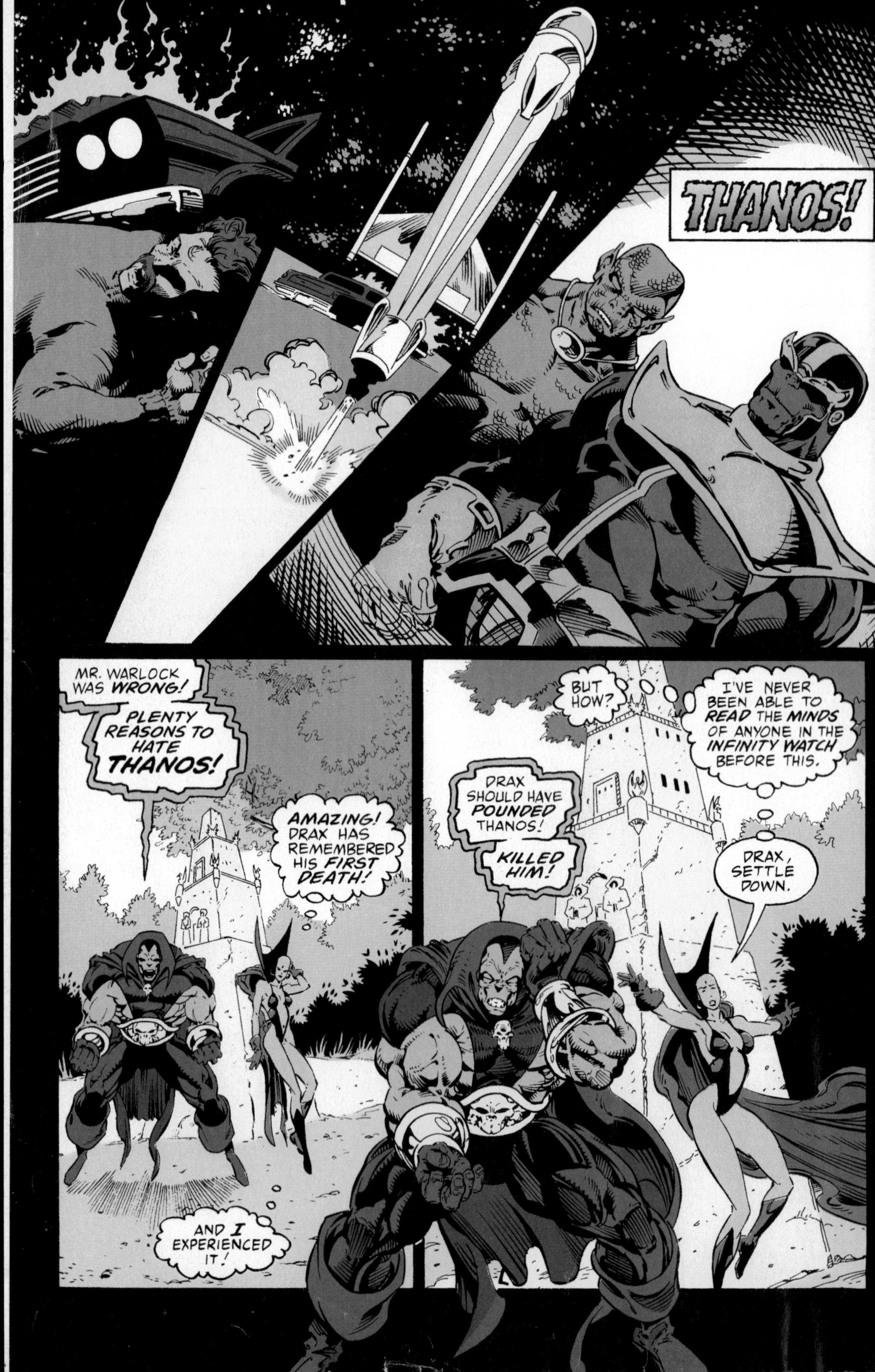

THANOS!
MR. WARLOCK WAS WRONG!
PLENTY REASONS TO HATE THANOS!
AMAZING! DRAX HAS REMEMBERED HIS FIRST DEATH!
AND I EXPERIENCED IT!
BUT HOW?
I'VE NEVER BEEN ABLE TO READ THE MINDS OF ANYONE IN THE INFINITY WATCH BEFORE THIS.
DRAX SHOULD HAVE POUNDED THANOS!
KILLED HIM!
DRAX, SETTLE DOWN.

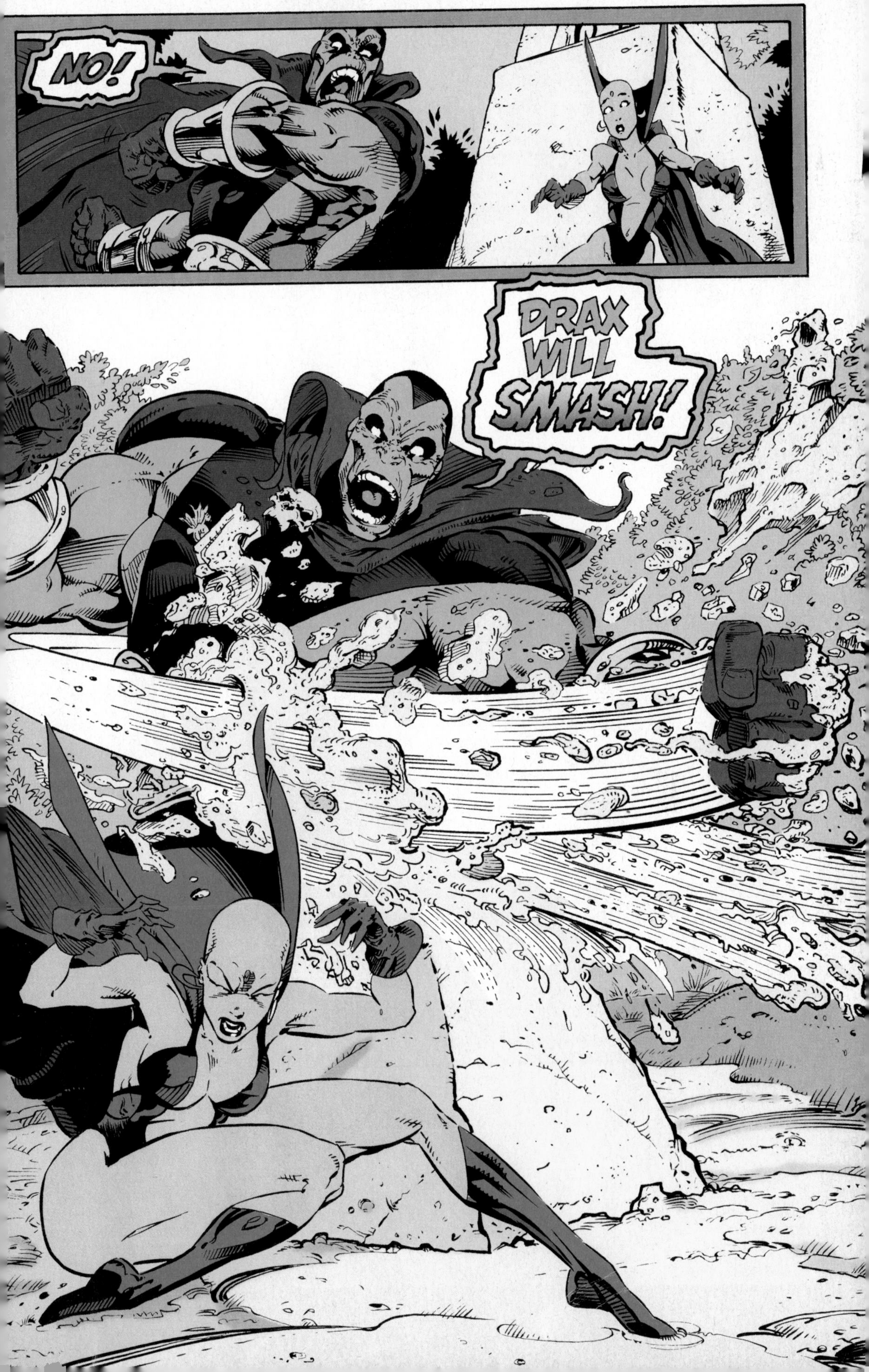
NO!
DRAX WILL SMASH!

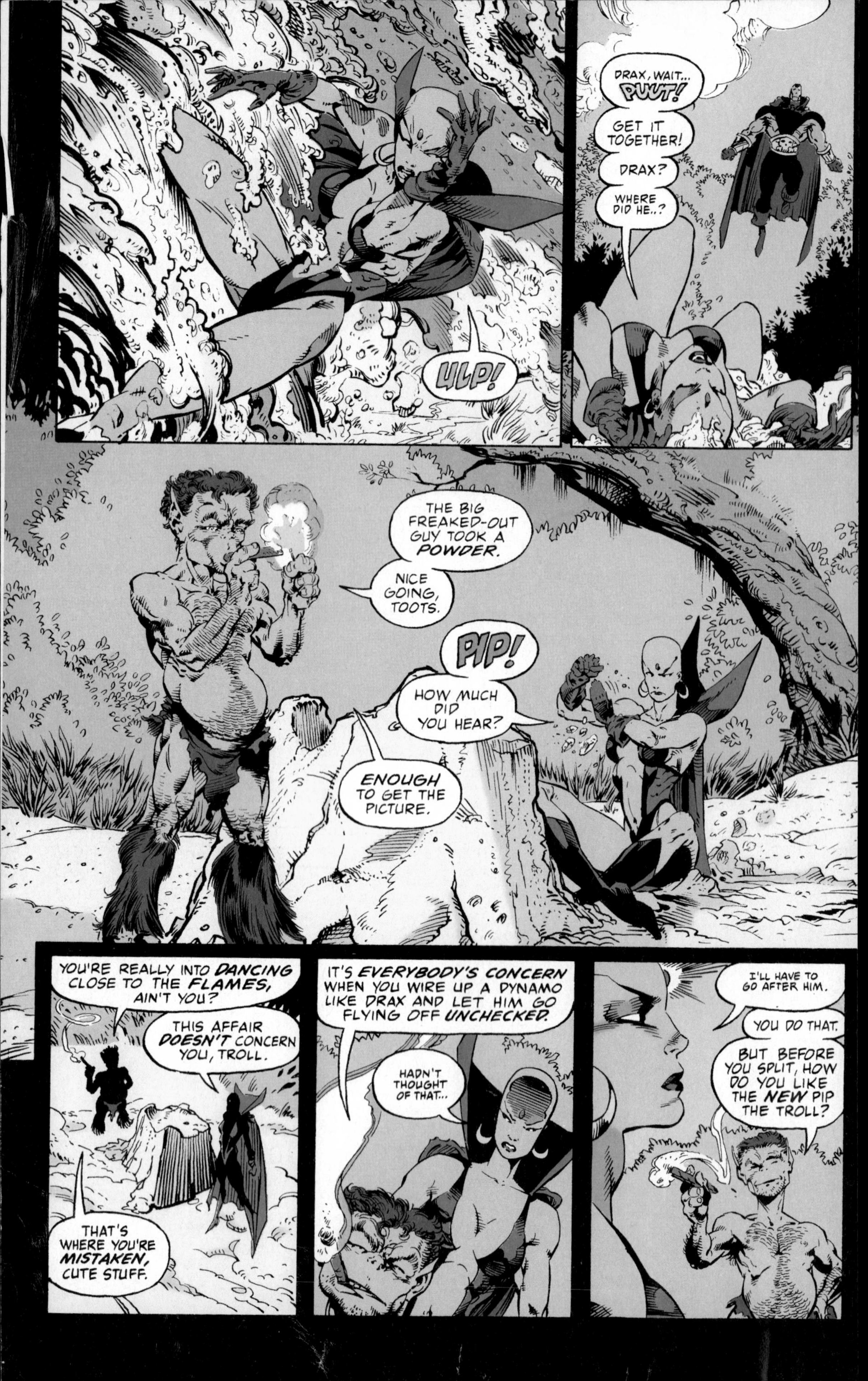

ULP!
DRAX, WAIT...
PUUT!
GET IT TOGETHER!
DRAX?
WHERE DID HE..?
THE BIG FREAKED-OUT GUY TOOK A POWDER.
NICE GOING, TOOTS.
PIP!
HOW MUCH DID YOU HEAR?
ENOUGH TO GET THE PICTURE.
YOU'RE REALLY INTO DANCING CLOSE TO THE FLAMES, AIN'T YOU?
THIS AFFAIR DOESN'T CONCERN YOU, TROLL.
THAT'S WHERE YOU'RE MISTAKEN, CUTE STUFF.
IT'S EVERYBODY'S CONCERN WHEN YOU WIRE UP A DYNAMO LIKE DRAX AND LET HIM GO FLYING OFF UNCHECKED.
HADN'T THOUGHT OF THAT...
I'LL HAVE TO GO AFTER HIM.
YOU DO THAT.
BUT BEFORE YOU SPLIT, HOW DO YOU LIKE THE NEW PIP THE TROLL?

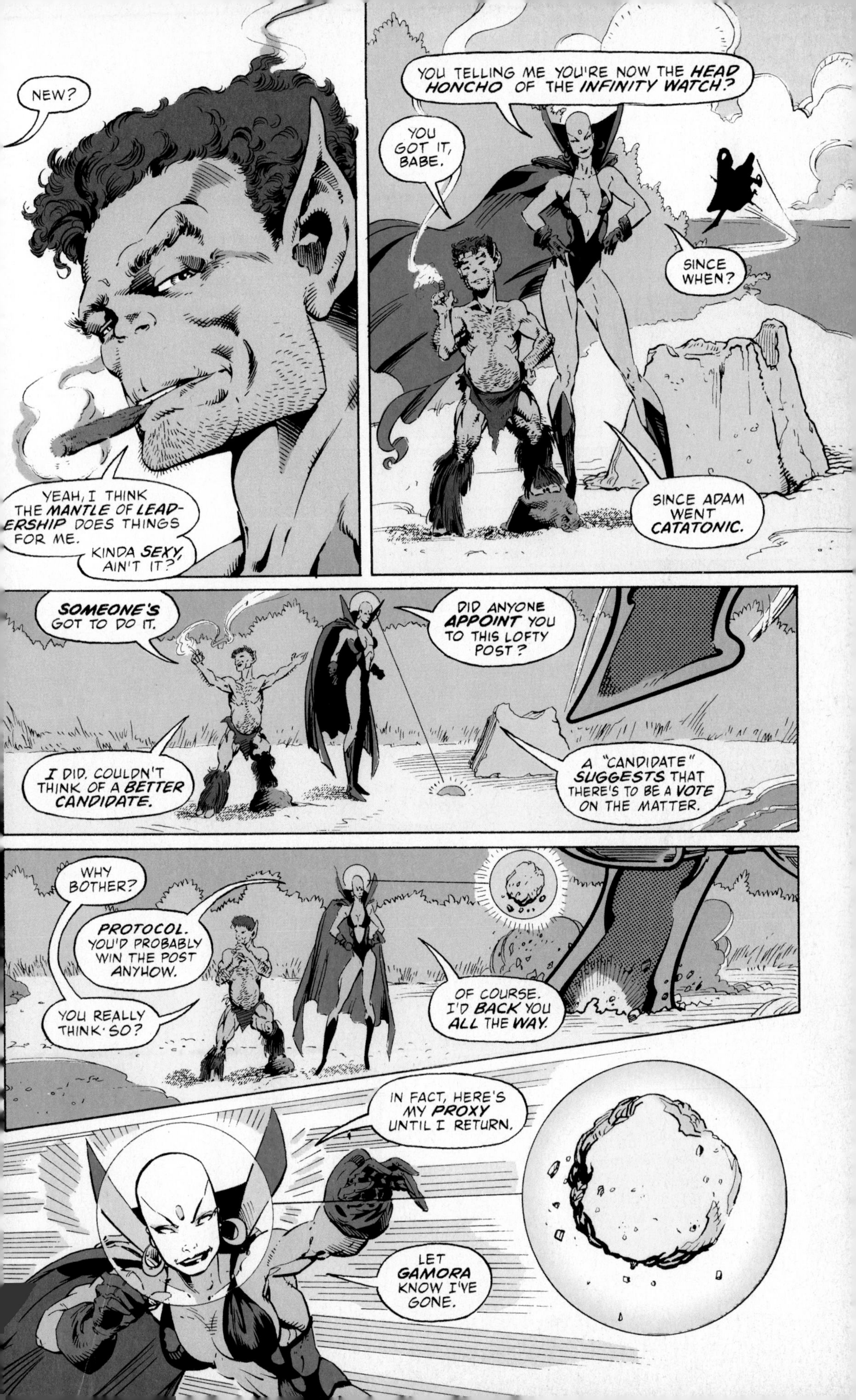
NEW?
YEAH, I THINK THE MANTLE OF LEADERSHIP DOES THINGS FOR ME.
KINDA SEXY, AIN'T IT?
YOU TELLING ME YOU'RE NOW THE HEAD HONCHO OF THE INFINITY WATCH?
YOU GOT IT, BABE.
SINCE WHEN?
SINCE ADAM WENT CATATONIC.
SOMEONE'S GOT TO DO IT.
DID ANYONE APPOINT YOU TO THIS LOFTY POST?
I DID. COULDN'T THINK OF A BETTER CANDIDATE.
A "CANDIDATE" SUGGESTS THAT THERE'S TO BE A VOTE ON THE MATTER.
WHY BOTHER?
PROTOCOL. YOU'D PROBABLY WIN THE POST ANYHOW.
YOU REALLY THINK SO?
OF COURSE. I'D BACK YOU ALL THE WAY.
IN FACT, HERE'S MY PROXY UNTIL I RETURN.
LET GAMORA KNOW I'VE GONE.

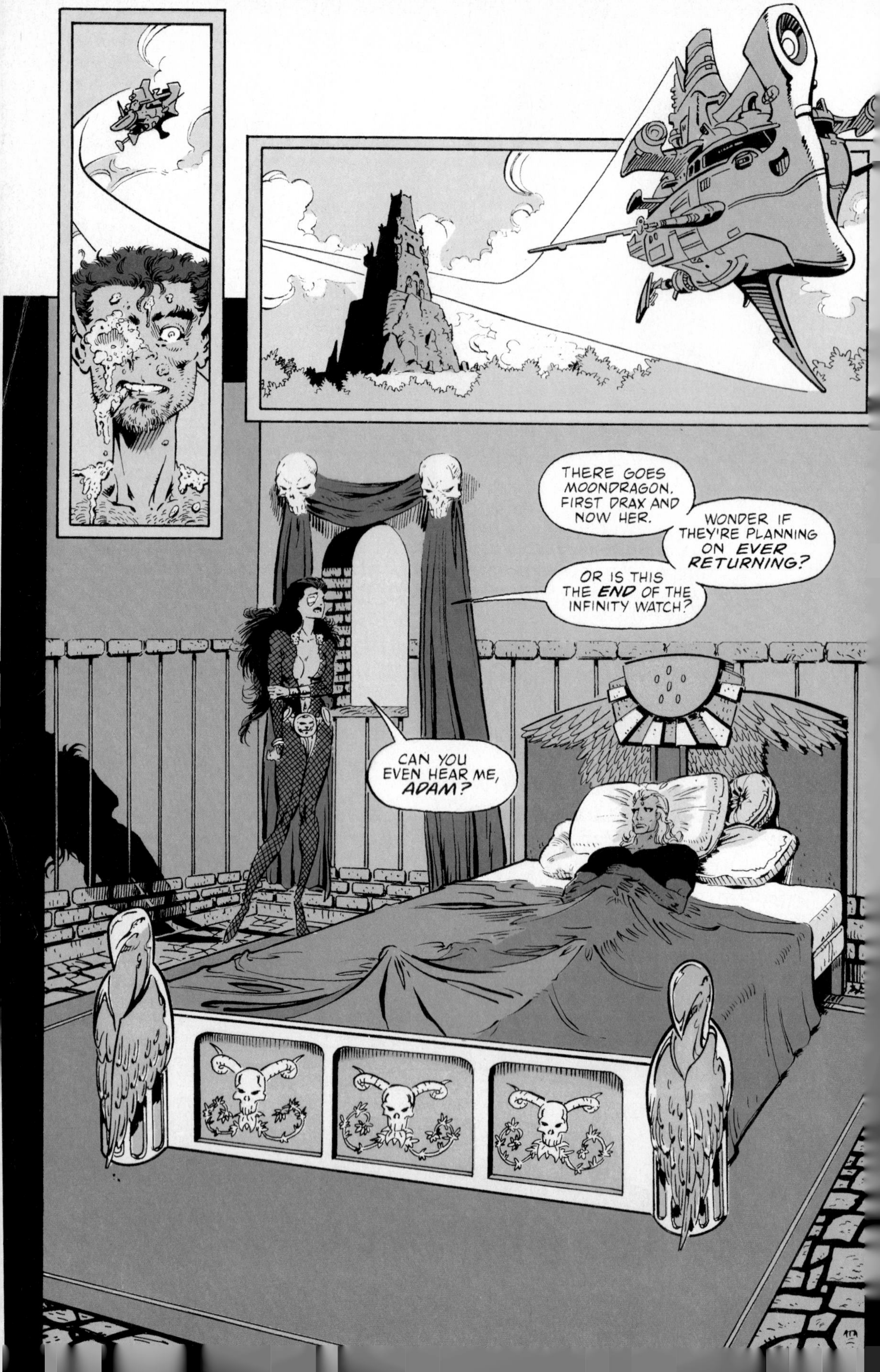
THERE GOES MOONDRAGON. FIRST DRAX AND NOW HER.
WONDER IF THEY'RE PLANNING ON EVER RETURNING?
OR IS THIS THE END OF THE INFINITY WATCH?
CAN YOU EVEN HEAR ME, ADAM?

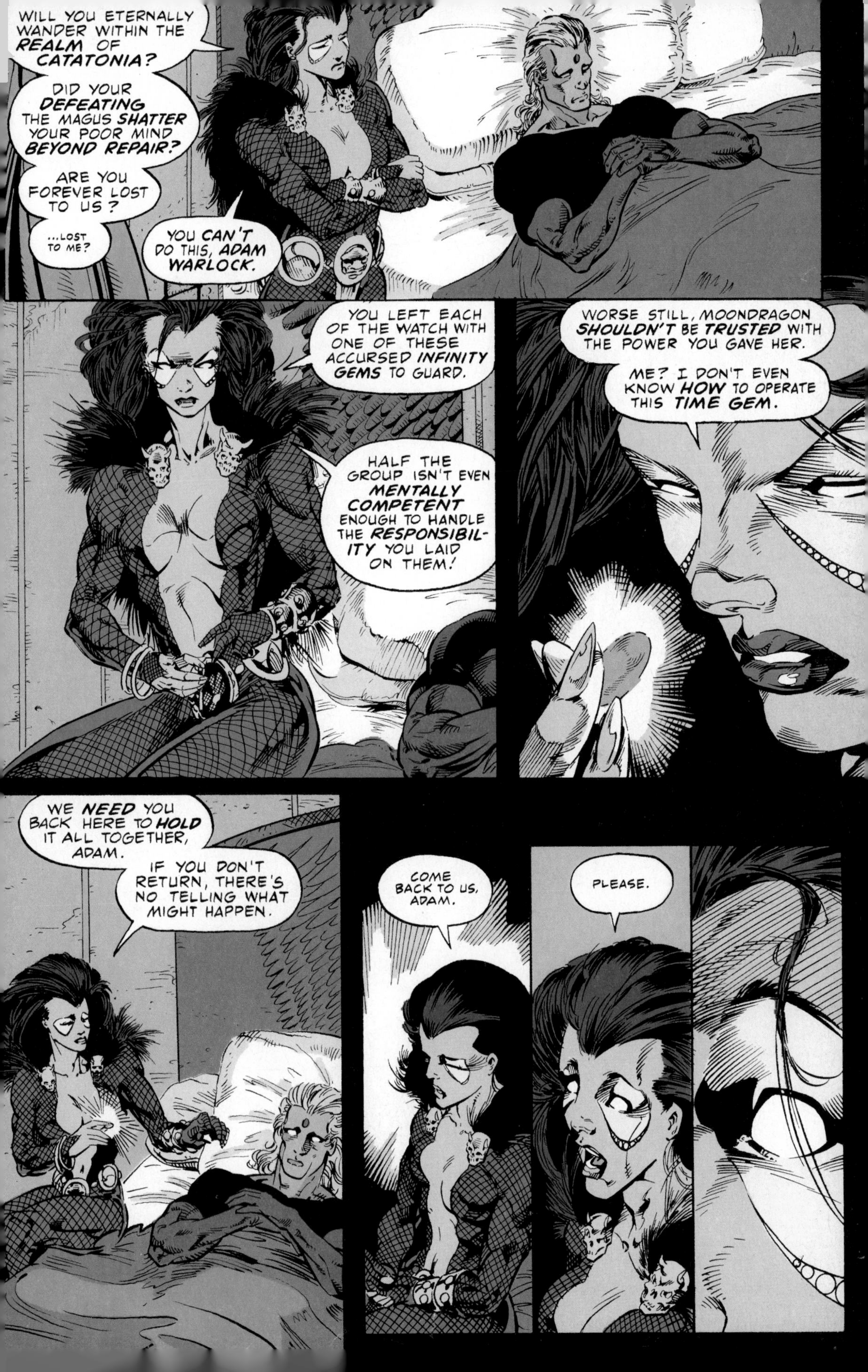

WILL YOU ETERNALLY WANDER WITHIN THE REALM OF CATATONIA?
DID YOUR DEFEATING THE MAGUS SHATTER YOUR POOR MIND BEYOND REPAIR?
ARE YOU FOREVER LOST TO US?
...LOST TO ME?
YOU CAN'T DO THIS, ADAM WARLOCK.
YOU LEFT EACH OF THE WATCH WITH ONE OF THESE ACCURSED INFINITY GEMS TO GUARD.
HALF THE GROUP ISN'T EVEN MENTALLY COMPETENT ENOUGH TO HANDLE THE RESPONSIBIL-ITY YOU LAID ON THEM!
WORSE STILL, MOONDRAGON SHOULDN'T BE TRUSTED WITH THE POWER YOU GAVE HER.
ME? I DON'T EVEN KNOW HOW TO OPERATE THIS TIME GEM.
WE NEED YOU BACK HERE TO HOLD IT ALL TOGETHER, ADAM.
IF YOU DON'T RETURN, THERE'S NO TELLING WHAT MIGHT HAPPEN.
COME BACK TO US, ADAM.
PLEASE.

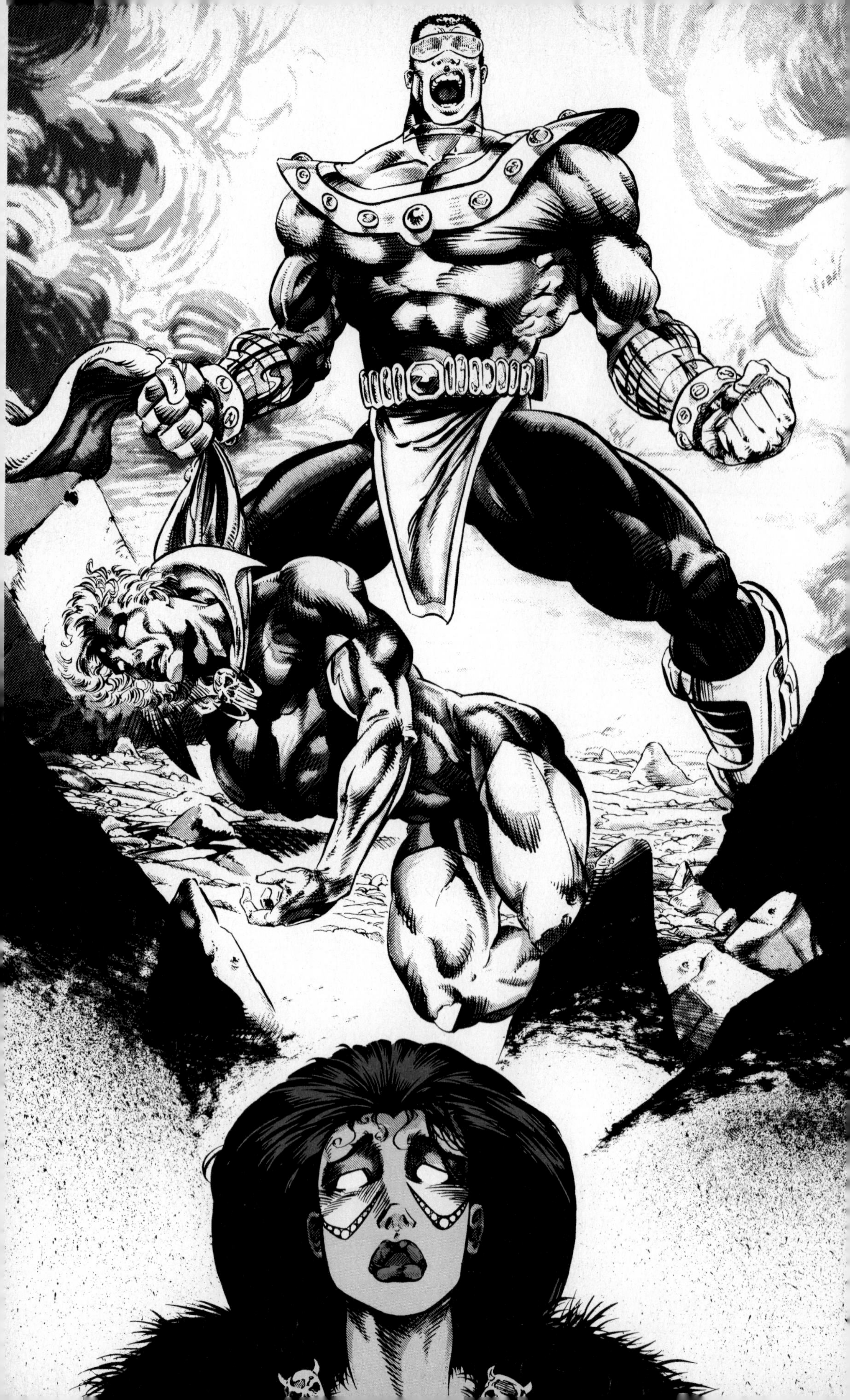

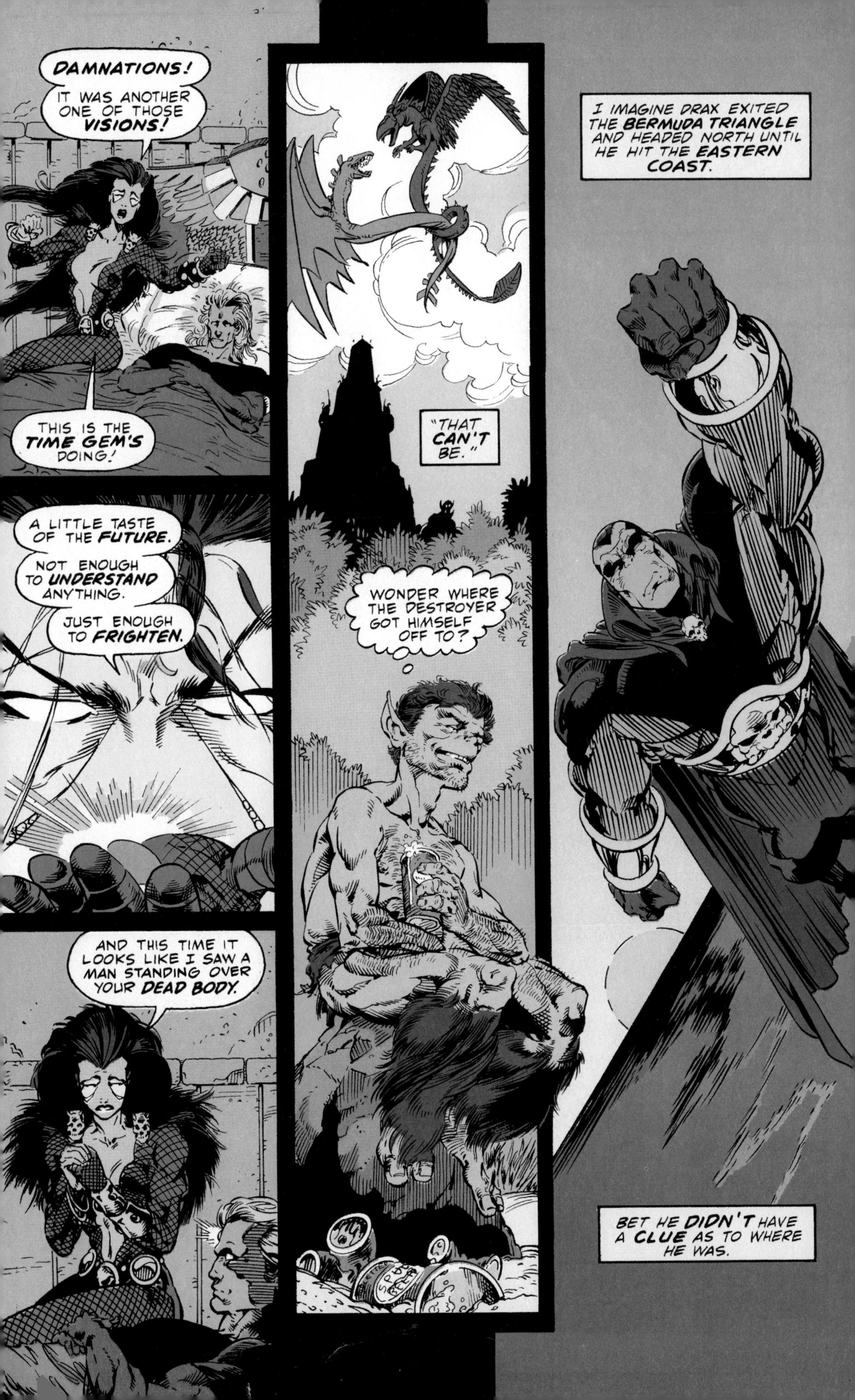
DAMNATIONS!
IT WAS ANOTHER ONE OF THOSE VISIONS!
THIS IS THE TIME GEM'S DOING!
A LITTLE TASTE OF THE FUTURE.
NOT ENOUGH TO UNDERSTAND ANYTHING.
JUST ENOUGH TO FRIGHTEN.
AND THIS TIME IT LOOKS LIKE I SAW A MAN STANDING OVER YOUR DEAD BODY.
"THAT CAN'T BE."
WONDER WHERE THE DESTROYER GOT HIMSELF OFF TO?
I IMAGINE DRAX EXITED THE BERMUDA TRIANGLE AND HEADED NORTH UNTIL HE HIT THE EASTERN COAST.
BET HE DIDN'T HAVE A CLUE AS TO WHERE HE WAS.

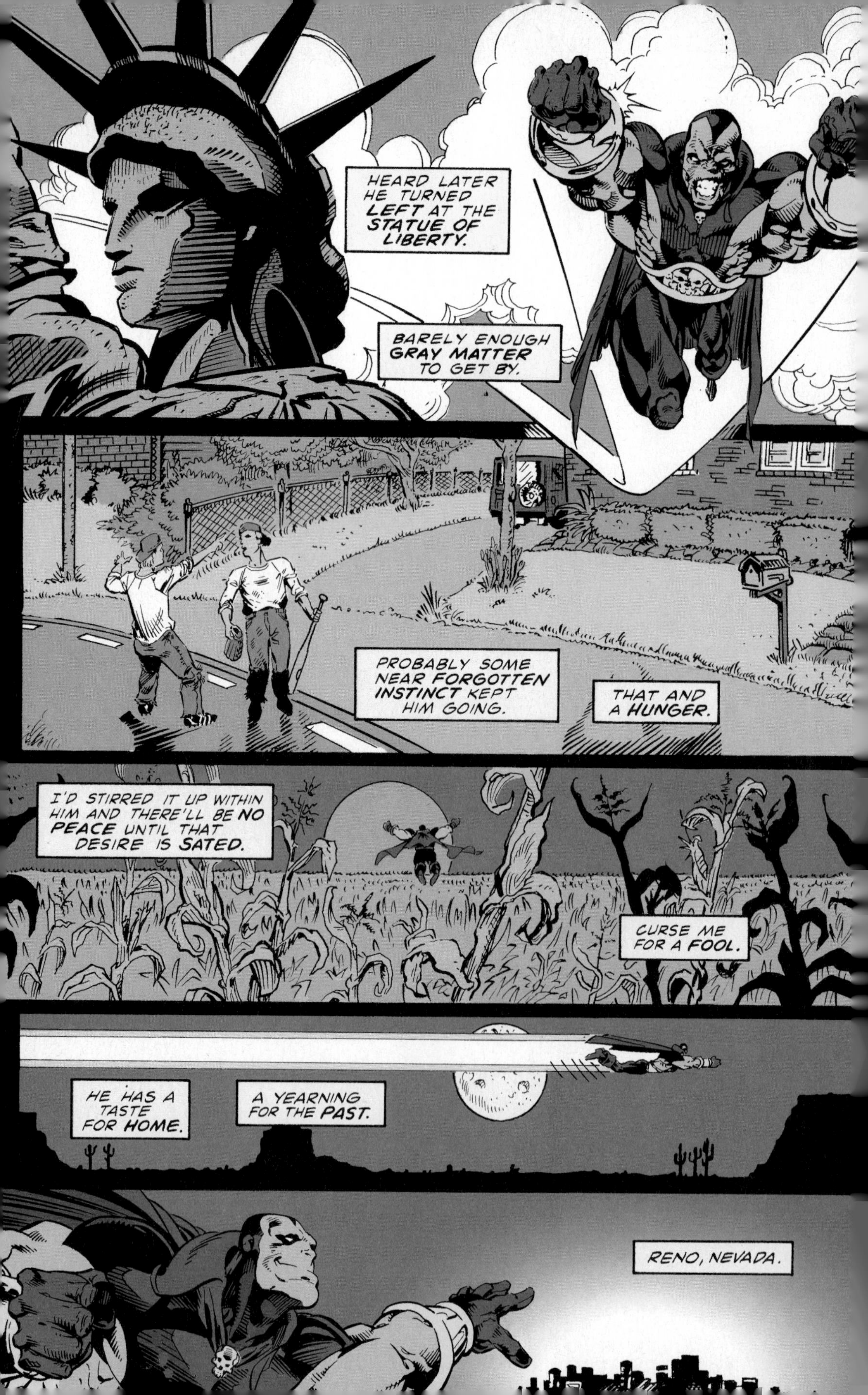
HEARD LATER HE TURNED LEFT AT THE STATUE OF LIBERTY.
BARELY ENOUGH GRAY MATTER TO GET BY.
PROBABLY SOME NEAR FORGOTTEN INSTINCT KEPT HIM GOING.
THAT AND A HUNGER.
I'D STIRRED IT UP WITHIN HIM AND THERE'LL BE NO PEACE UNTIL THAT DESIRE IS SATED.
CURSE ME FOR A FOOL.
HE HAS A TASTE FOR HOME.
A YEARNING FOR THE PAST.
RENO, NEVADA.

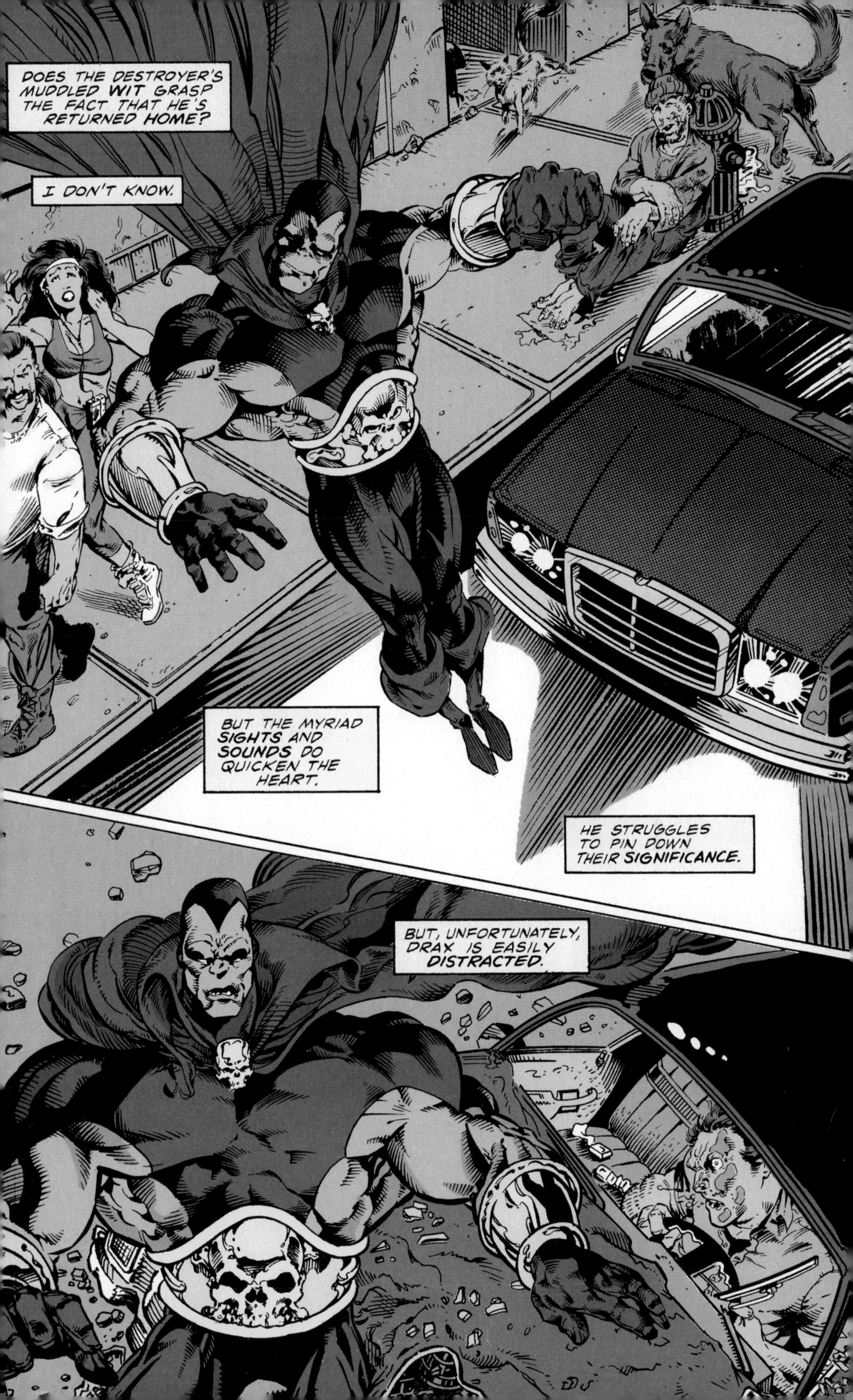
DOES THE DESTROYER'S MUDDLED WIT GRASP THE FACT THAT HE'S RETURNED HOME?
I DON'T KNOW.
BUT THE MYRIAD SIGHTS AND SOUNDS DO QUICKEN THE HEART.
HE STRUGGLES TO PIN DOWN THEIR SIGNIFICANCE.
BUT, UNFORTUNATELY, DRAX IS EASILY DISTRACTED.

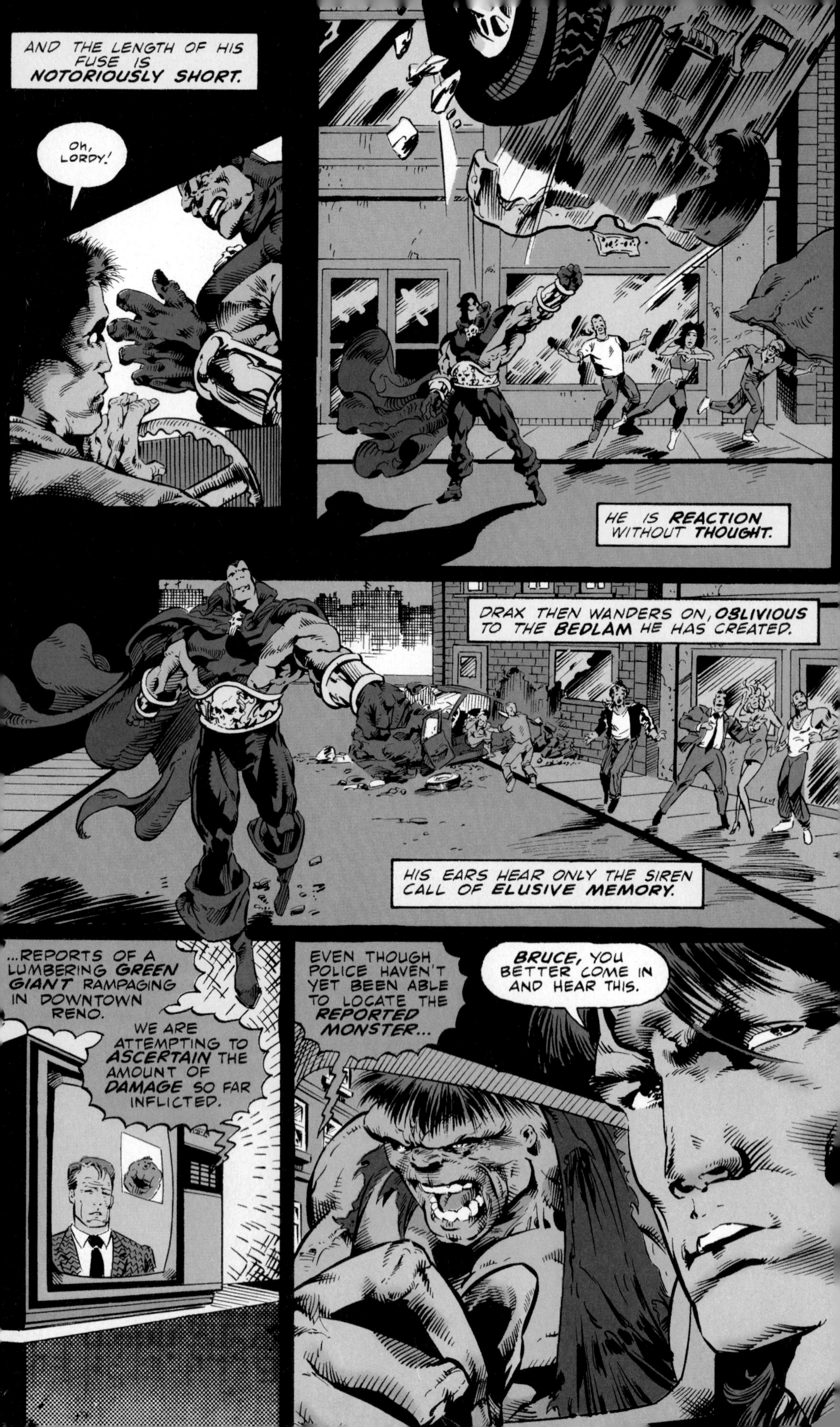
AND THE LENGTH OF HIS FUSE IS NOTORIOUSLY SHORT.
OH, LORDY!
HE IS REACTION WITHOUT THOUGHT.
DRAX THEN WANDERS ON, OBLIVIOUS TO THE BEDLAM HE HAS CREATED.
HIS EARS HEAR ONLY THE SIREN CALL OF ELUSIVE MEMORY.
...REPORTS OF A LUMBERING GREEN GIANT RAMPAGING IN DOWNTOWN RENO.
WE ARE ATTEMPTING TO ASCERTAIN THE AMOUNT OF DAMAGE SO FAR INFLICTED.
EVEN THOUGH POLICE HAVEN'T YET BEEN ABLE TO LOCATE THE REPORTED MONSTER...
BRUCE, YOU BETTER COME IN AND HEAR THIS.

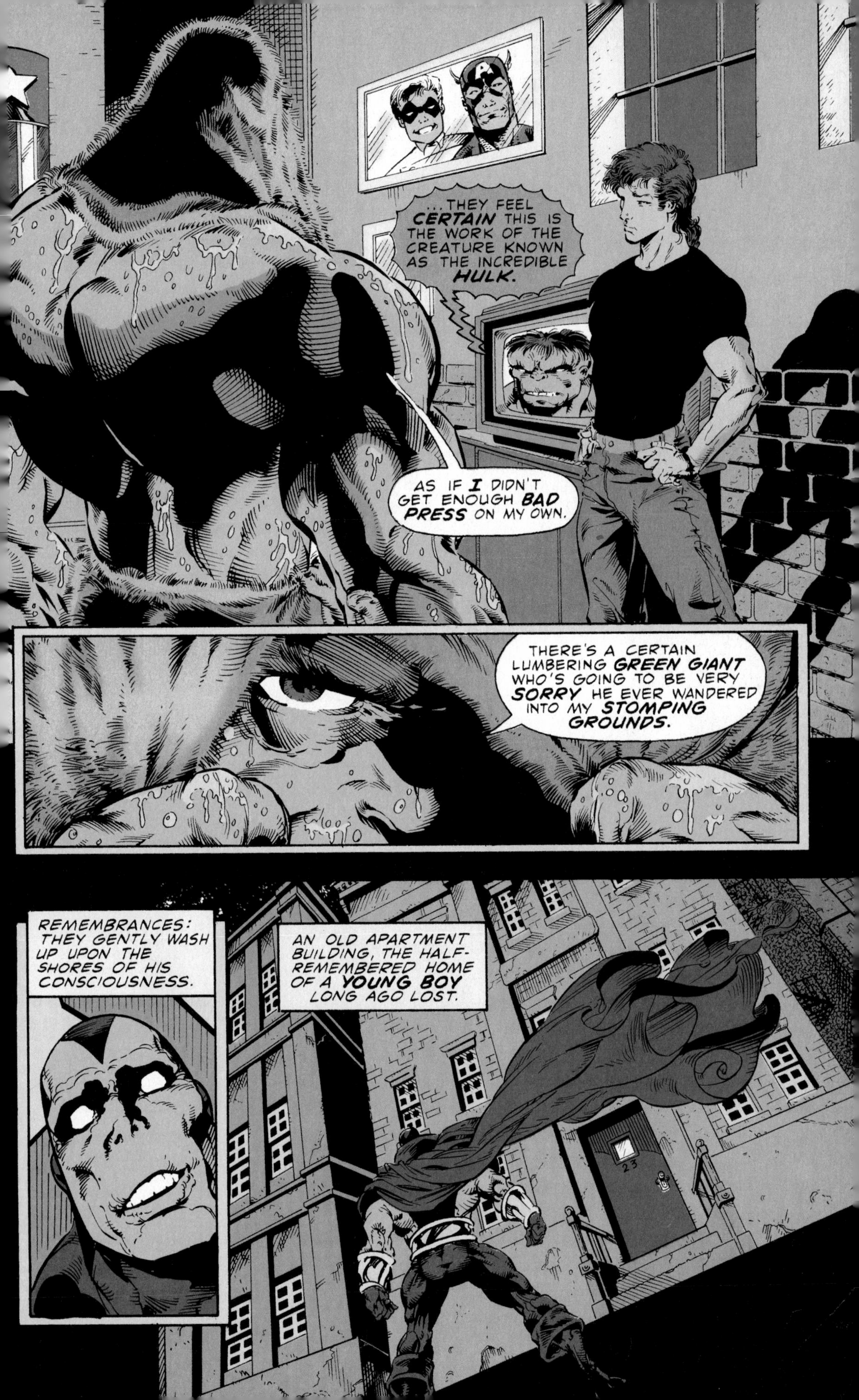
...THEY FEEL CERTAIN THIS IS THE WORK OF THE CREATURE KNOWN AS THE INCREDIBLE HULK.
AS IF I DIDN'T GET ENOUGH BAD PRESS ON MY OWN.
THERE'S A CERTAIN LUMBERING GREEN GIANT WHO'S GOING TO BE VERY SORRY HE EVER WANDERED INTO MY STOMPING GROUNDS.
REMEMBRANCES: THEY GENTLY WASH UP UPON THE SHORES OF HIS CONSCIOUSNESS.
AN OLD APARTMENT BUILDING, THE HALF-REMEMBERED HOME OF A YOUNG BOY LONG AGO LOST.
23

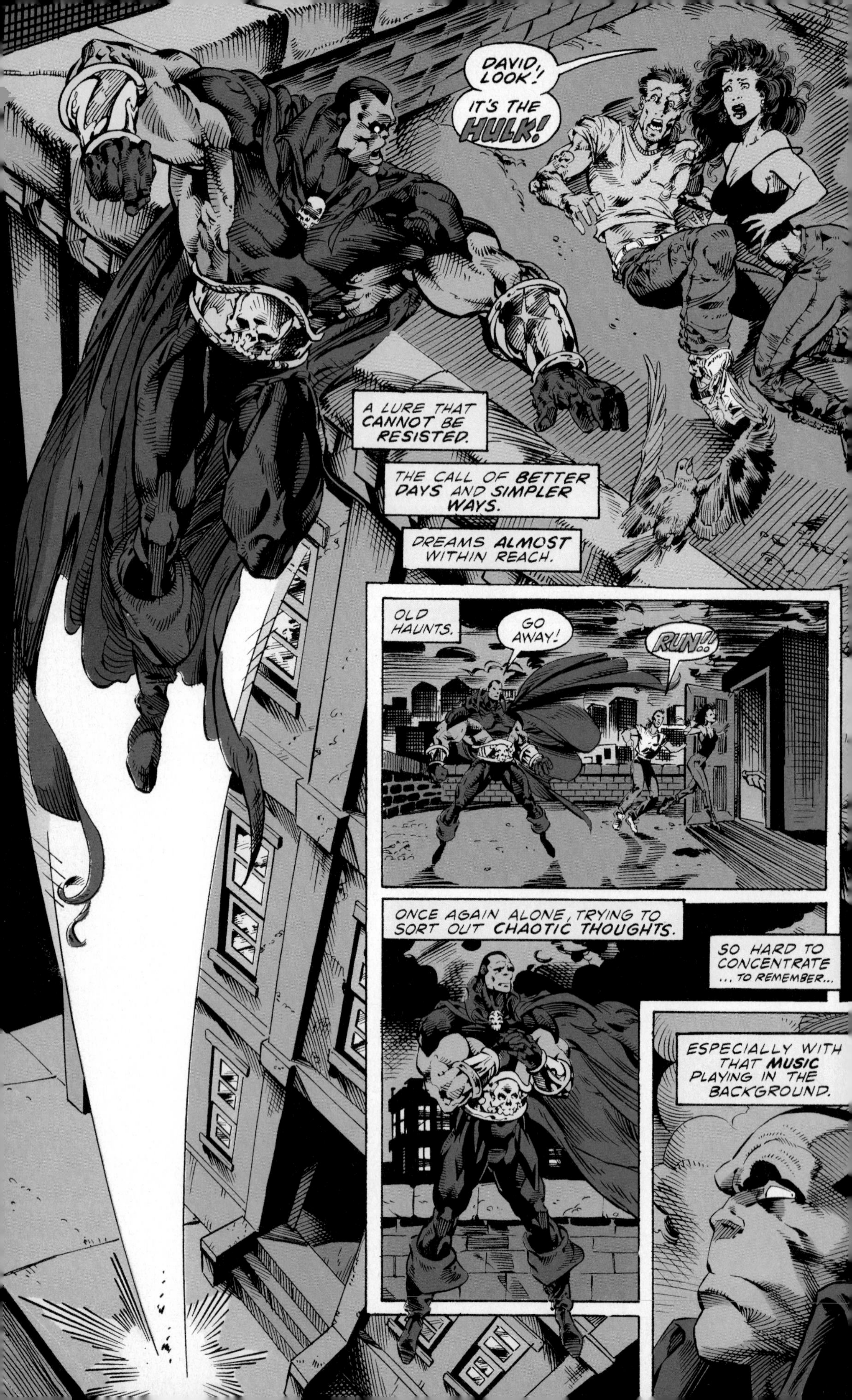
DAVID, LOOK!
IT'S THE HULK!
A LURE THAT CANNOT BE RESISTED.
THE CALL OF BETTER DAYS AND SIMPLER WAYS.
DREAMS ALMOST WITHIN REACH.
OLD HAUNTS.
GO AWAY!
RUN!!
ONCE AGAIN ALONE, TRYING TO SORT OUT CHAOTIC THOUGHTS.
SO HARD TO CONCENTRATE ...TO REMEMBER...
ESPECIALLY WITH THAT MUSIC PLAYING IN THE BACKGROUND.

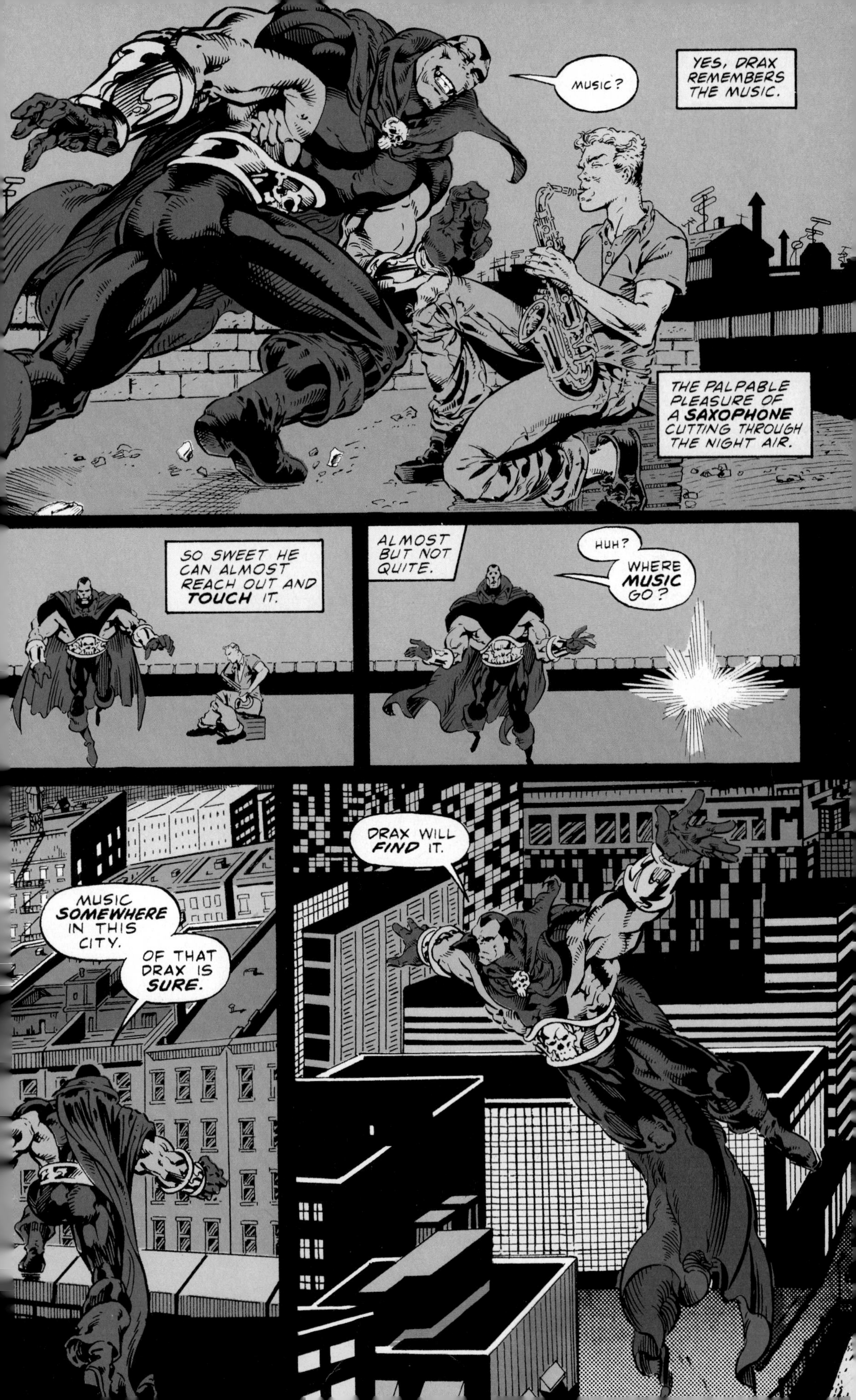

YES, DRAX REMEMBERS THE MUSIC.
MUSIC?
THE PALPABLE PLEASURE OF A **SAXOPHONE** CUTTING THROUGH THE NIGHT AIR.
SO SWEET HE CAN ALMOST REACH OUT AND **TOUCH** IT.
ALMOST BUT NOT QUITE.
HUH?
WHERE **MUSIC** GO?
MUSIC **SOMEWHERE** IN THIS CITY.
OF THAT DRAX IS **SURE.**
DRAX WILL **FIND** IT.

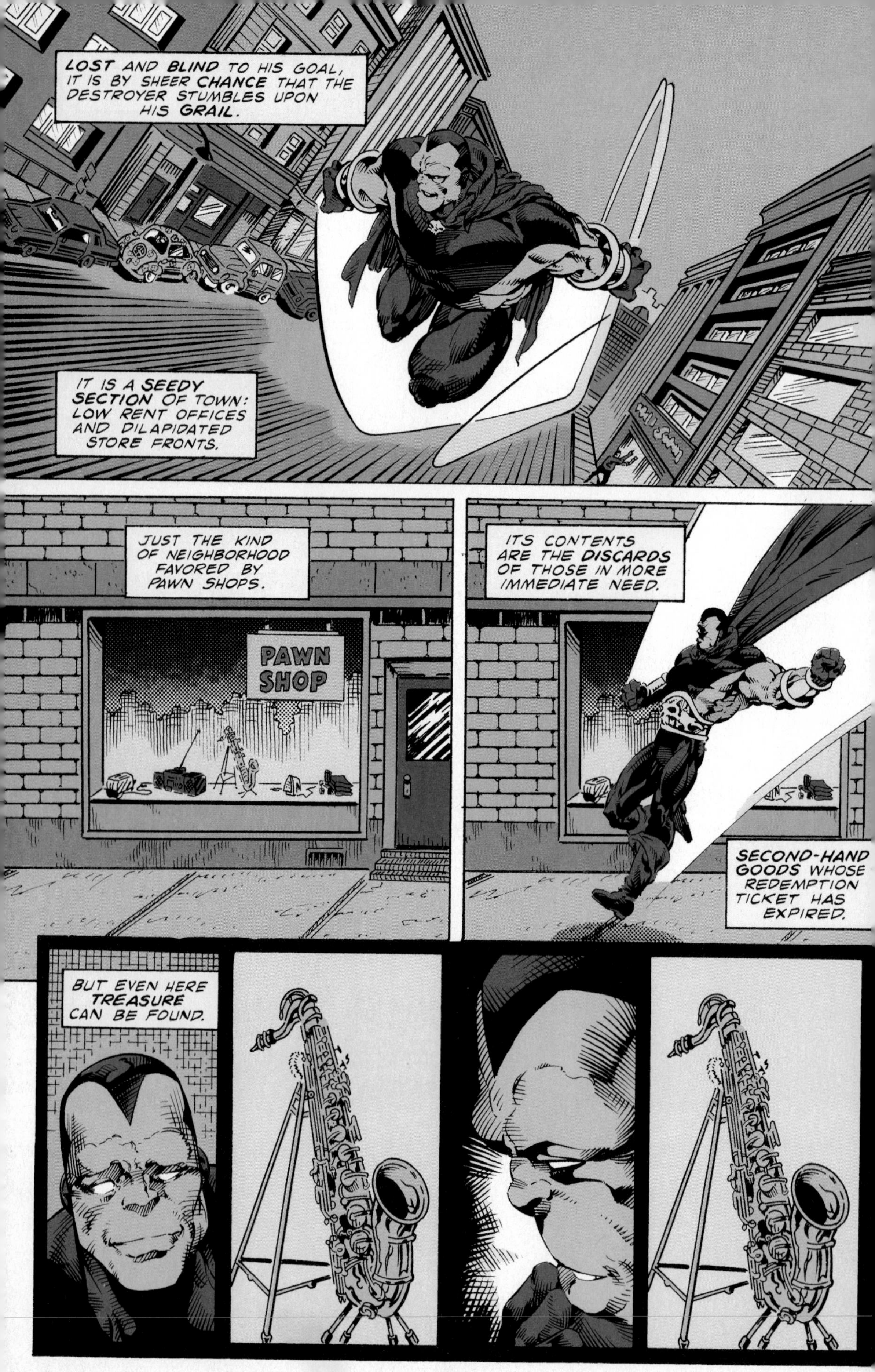
LOST AND BLIND TO HIS GOAL, IT IS BY SHEER CHANCE THAT THE DESTROYER STUMBLES UPON HIS GRAIL.
IT IS A SEEDY SECTION OF TOWN: LOW RENT OFFICES AND DILAPIDATED STORE FRONTS.
JUST THE KIND OF NEIGHBORHOOD FAVORED BY PAWN SHOPS.
PAWN SHOP
ITS CONTENTS ARE THE DISCARDS OF THOSE IN MORE IMMEDIATE NEED.
SECOND-HAND GOODS WHOSE REDEMPTION TICKET HAS EXPIRED.
BUT EVEN HERE TREASURE CAN BE FOUND.

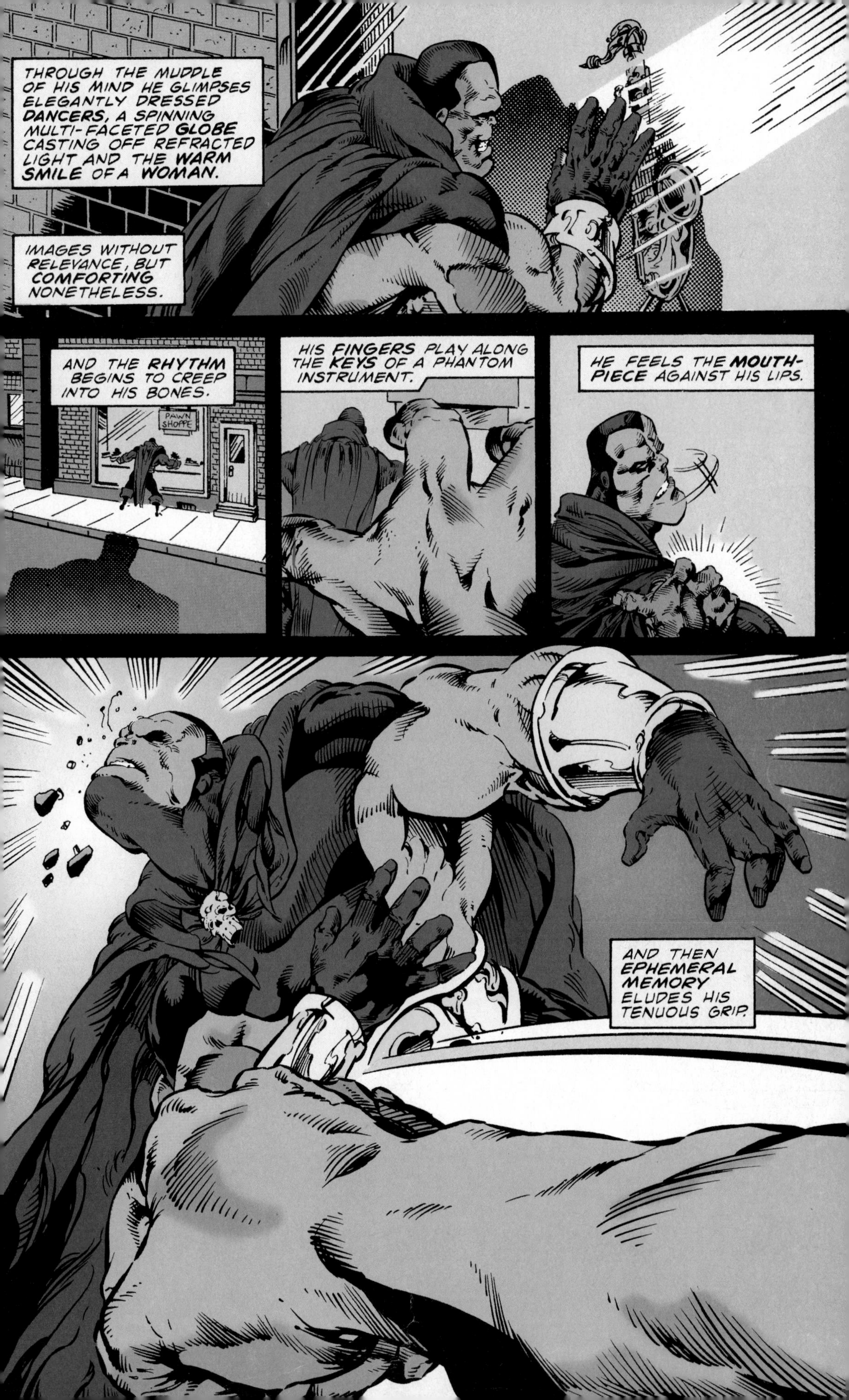

THROUGH THE MUDDLE OF HIS MIND HE GLIMPSES ELEGANTLY DRESSED DANCERS, A SPINNING MULTI-FACETED GLOBE CASTING OFF REFRACTED LIGHT AND THE WARM SMILE OF A WOMAN.
IMAGES WITHOUT RELEVANCE, BUT COMFORTING NONETHELESS.
AND THE RHYTHM BEGINS TO CREEP INTO HIS BONES.
PAWN SHOPPE
HIS FINGERS PLAY ALONG THE KEYS OF A PHANTOM INSTRUMENT.
HE FEELS THE MOUTH-PIECE AGAINST HIS LIPS.
AND THEN EPHEMERAL MEMORY ELUDES HIS TENUOUS GRIP.

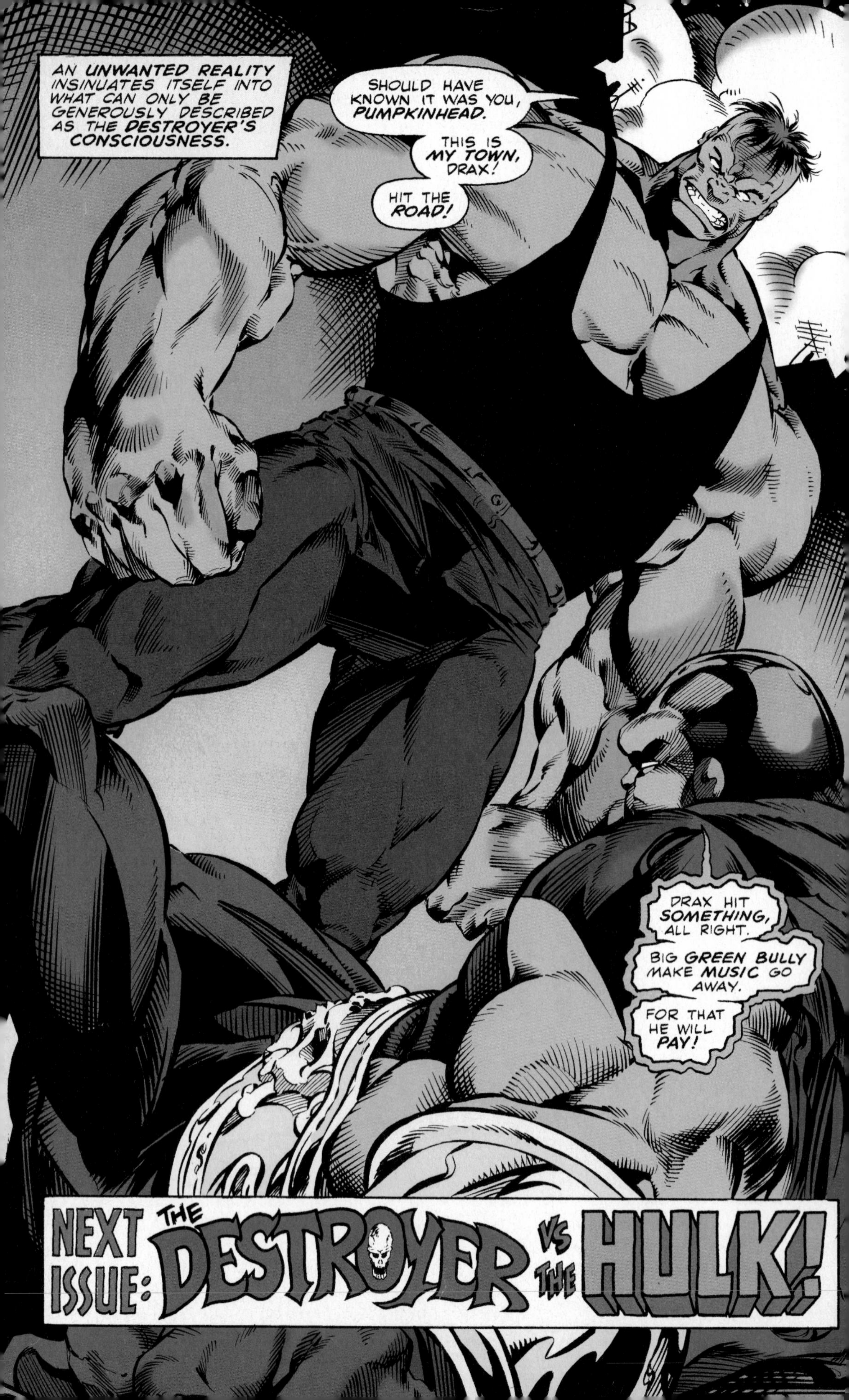

AN UNWANTED REALITY INSINUATES ITSELF INTO WHAT CAN ONLY BE GENEROUSLY DESCRIBED AS THE DESTROYER'S CONSCIOUSNESS.
SHOULD HAVE KNOWN IT WAS YOU, PUMPKINHEAD.
THIS IS MY TOWN, DRAX!
HIT THE ROAD!
DRAX HIT SOMETHING, ALL RIGHT.
BIG GREEN BULLY MAKE MUSIC GO AWAY.
FOR THAT HE WILL PAY!
NEXT ISSUE: THE DESTROYER VS THE HULK!

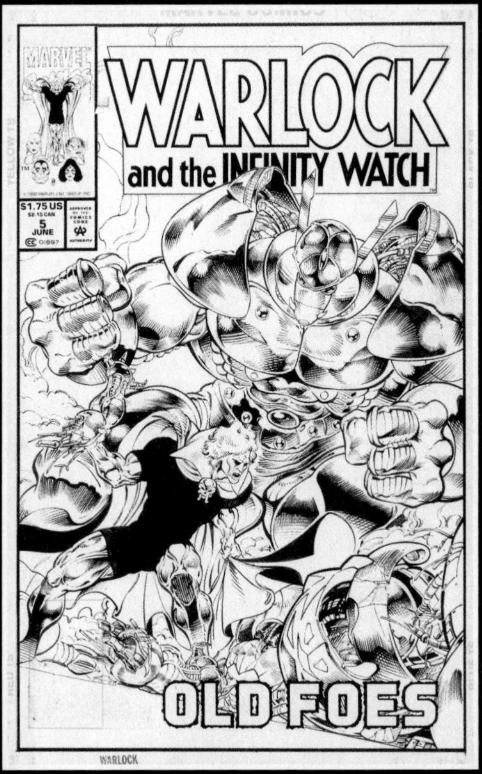
MARVEL COMICS
WARLOCK
and the INFINITY WATCH
$1.75 US
5
JUNE
OLD FOES

WARLOCK AND THE INFINITY WATCH #5

COVER ART BY ANGEL MEDINA

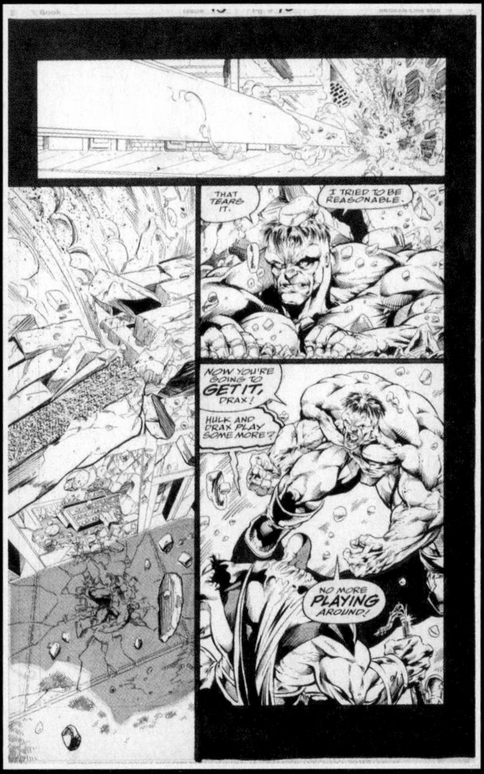
THAT TEARS IT.
I TRIED TO BE REASONABLE.
NOW YOU'RE GOING TO GET IT, DRAX!
HULK AND DRAX PLAY SOME MORE?
NO MORE PLAYING AROUND!

WARLOCK AND THE INFINITY WATCH #13

PAGE 15 ART BY TOM RANEY & KEITH WILLIAMS

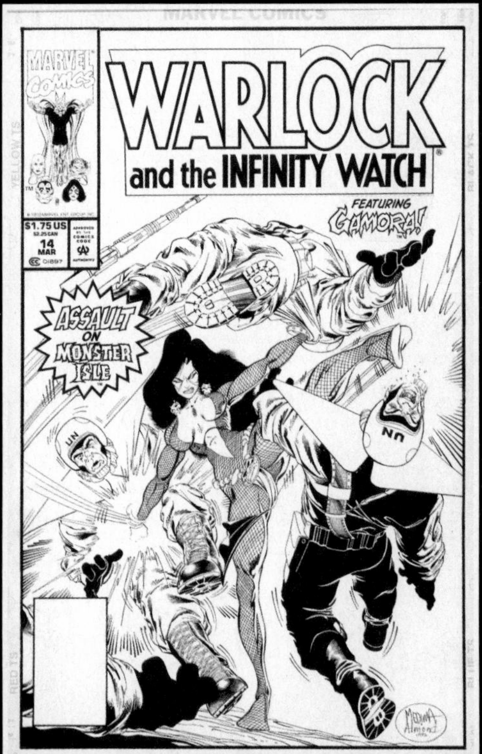
MARVEL COMICS
WARLOCK
and the INFINITY WATCH
$1.75 US
14
MAR
FEATURING GAMORA!
ASSAULT ON MONSTER ISLE

WARLOCK AND THE INFINITY WATCH #14

COVER ART BY ANGEL MEDINA & BOB ALMOND

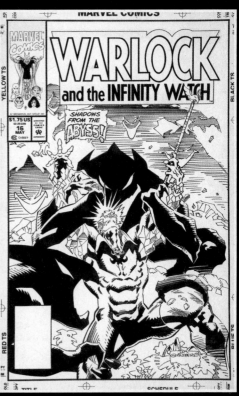

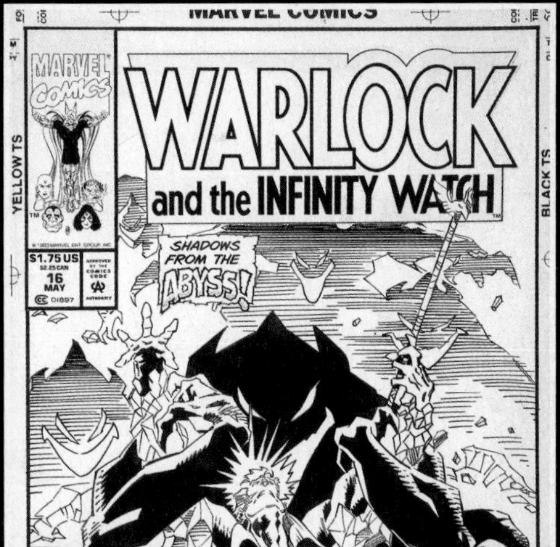
MARVEL COMICS
WARLOCK
and the INFINITY WATCH
$1.75 US
16
MAY
SHADOWS FROM THE ABYSS!

WARLOCK AND THE INFINITY WATCH #16

COVER ART BY TOM GRINDBERG

COURTESY OF *HERITAGEAUCTIONS.COM*

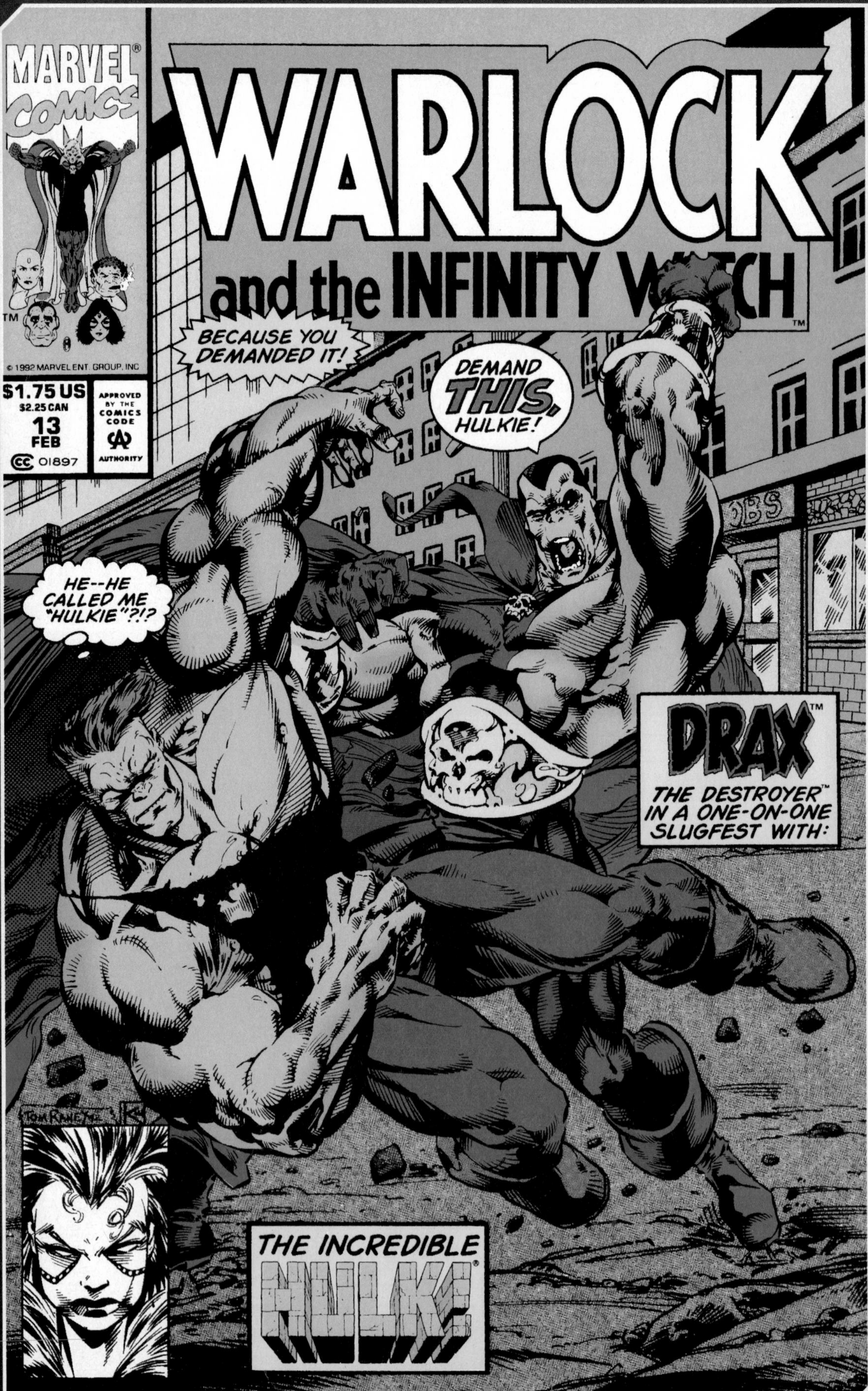
MARVEL COMICS
WARLOCK
and the INFINITY WATCH
© 1992 MARVEL ENT. GROUP, INC
$1.75 US
$2.25 CAN
13
FEB
APPROVED BY THE COMICS CODE AUTHORITY
BECAUSE YOU DEMANDED IT!
DEMAND THIS, HULKIE!
HE--HE CALLED ME "HULKIE"?!?
DRAX
THE DESTROYER IN A ONE-ON-ONE SLUGFEST WITH:
THE INCREDIBLE
HULK!

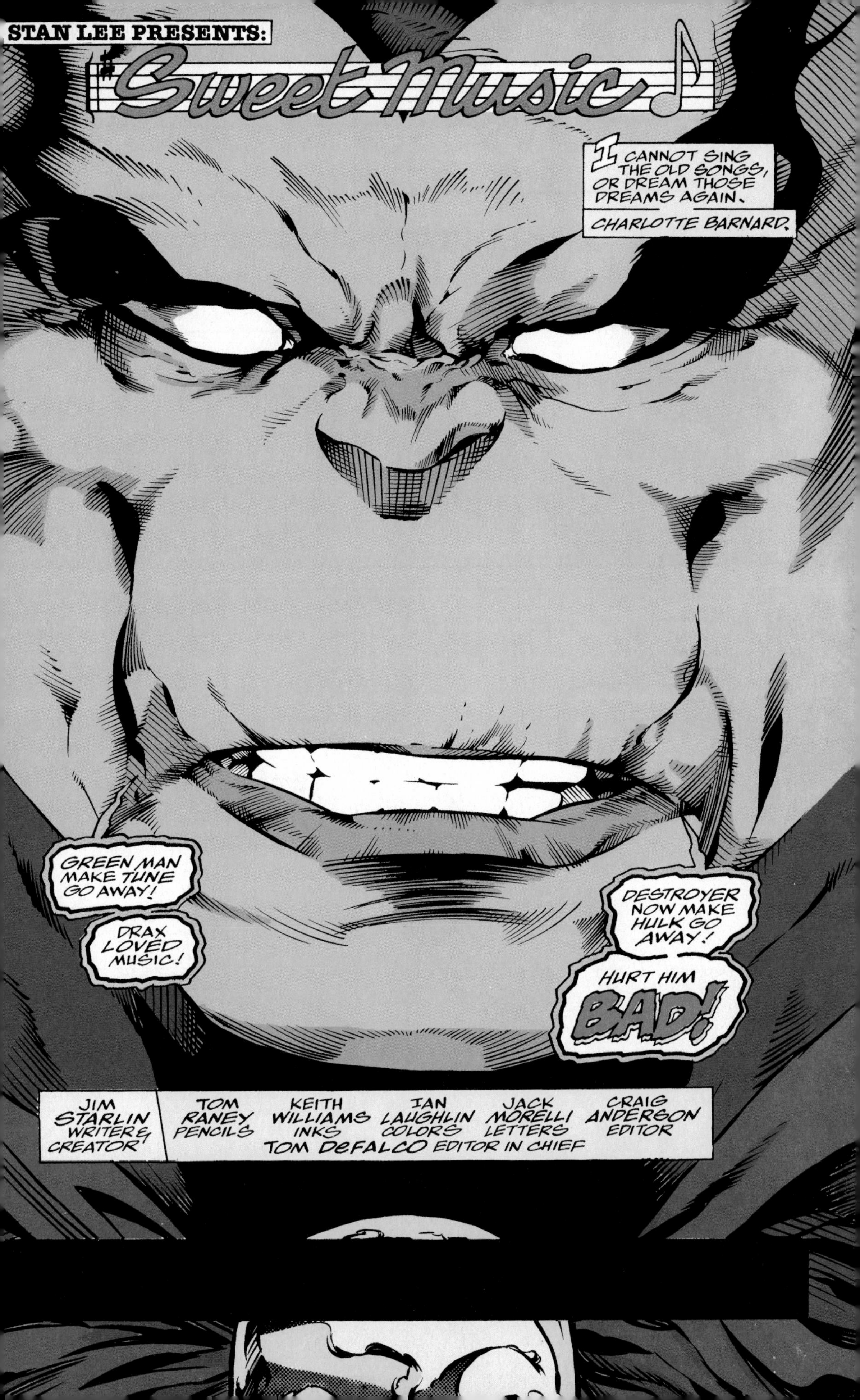
STAN LEE PRESENTS:
Sweet Music
I CANNOT SING THE OLD SONGS, OR DREAM THOSE DREAMS AGAIN.
CHARLOTTE BARNARD.
GREEN MAN MAKE TUNE GO AWAY!
DRAX LOVED MUSIC!
DESTROYER NOW MAKE HULK GO AWAY!
HURT HIM BAD!
JIM STARLIN WRITER & CREATOR
TOM RANEY PENCILS
KEITH WILLIAMS INKS
IAN LAUGHLIN COLORS
JACK MORELLI LETTERS
CRAIG ANDERSON EDITOR
TOM DeFALCO EDITOR IN CHIEF

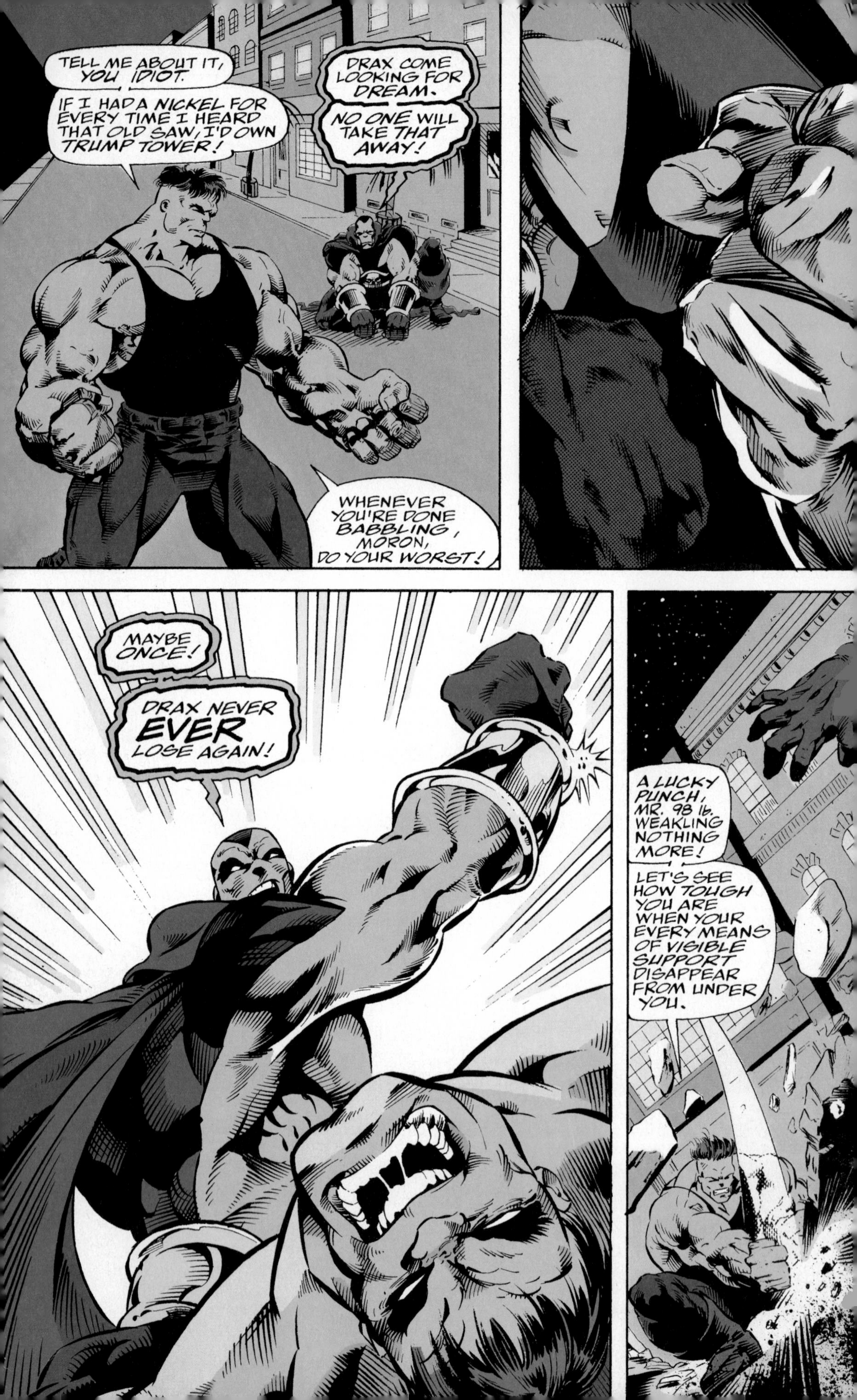
TELL ME ABOUT IT, YOU IDIOT.
IF I HAD A NICKEL FOR EVERY TIME I HEARD THAT OLD SAW, I'D OWN TRUMP TOWER!
DRAX COME LOOKING FOR DREAM.
NO ONE WILL TAKE THAT AWAY!
WHENEVER YOU'RE DONE BABBLING, MORON, DO YOUR WORST!
MAYBE ONCE!
DRAX NEVER EVER LOSE AGAIN!
A LUCKY PUNCH, MR. 98 lb. WEAKLING NOTHING MORE!
LET'S SEE HOW TOUGH YOU ARE WHEN YOUR EVERY MEANS OF VISIBLE SUPPORT DISAPPEAR FROM UNDER YOU.

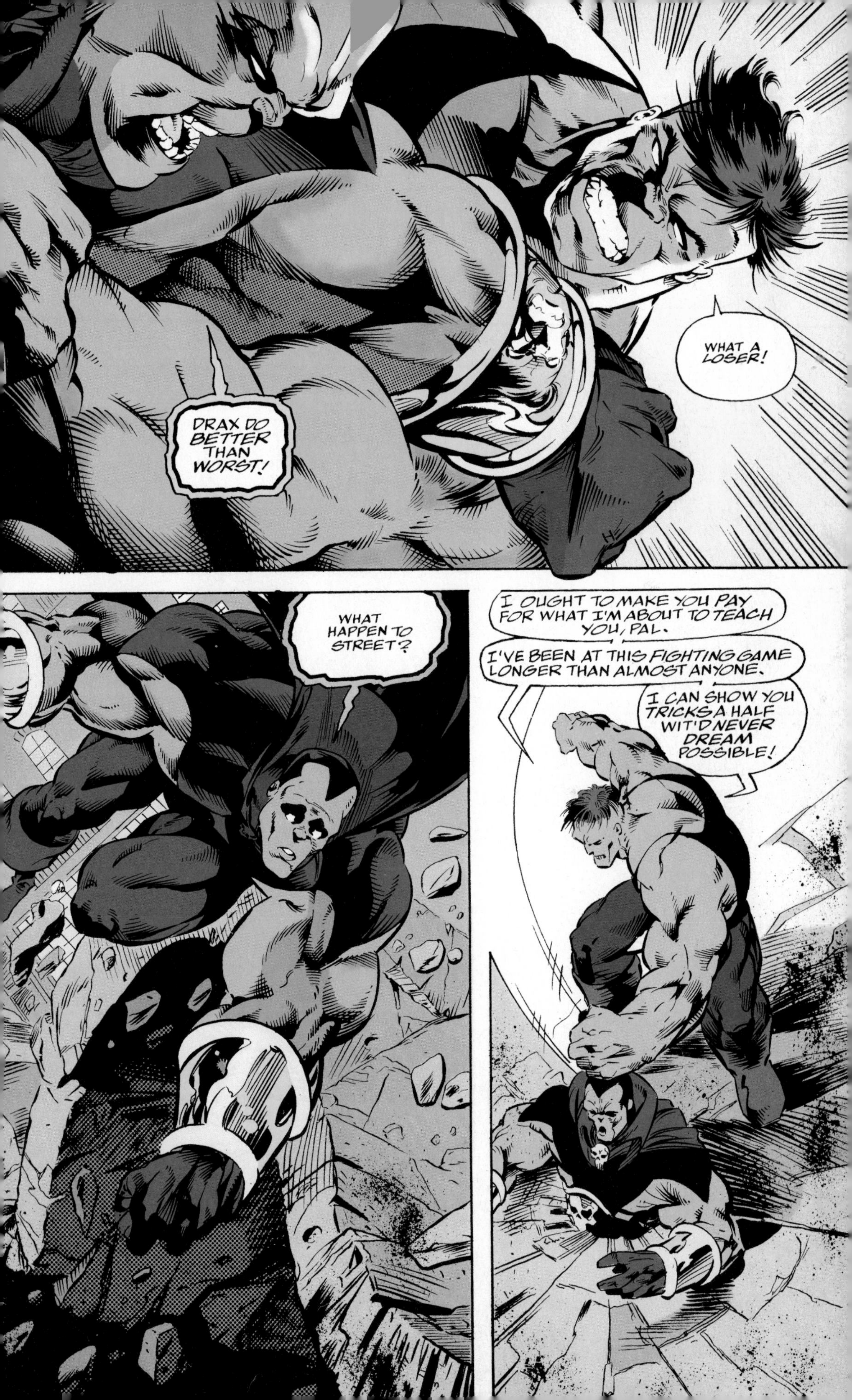
WHAT A LOSER!
DRAX DO BETTER THAN WORST!
WHAT HAPPEN TO STREET?
I OUGHT TO MAKE YOU PAY FOR WHAT I'M ABOUT TO TEACH YOU, PAL.
I'VE BEEN AT THIS FIGHTING GAME LONGER THAN ALMOST ANYONE.
I CAN SHOW YOU TRICKS A HALF WIT'D NEVER DREAM POSSIBLE!

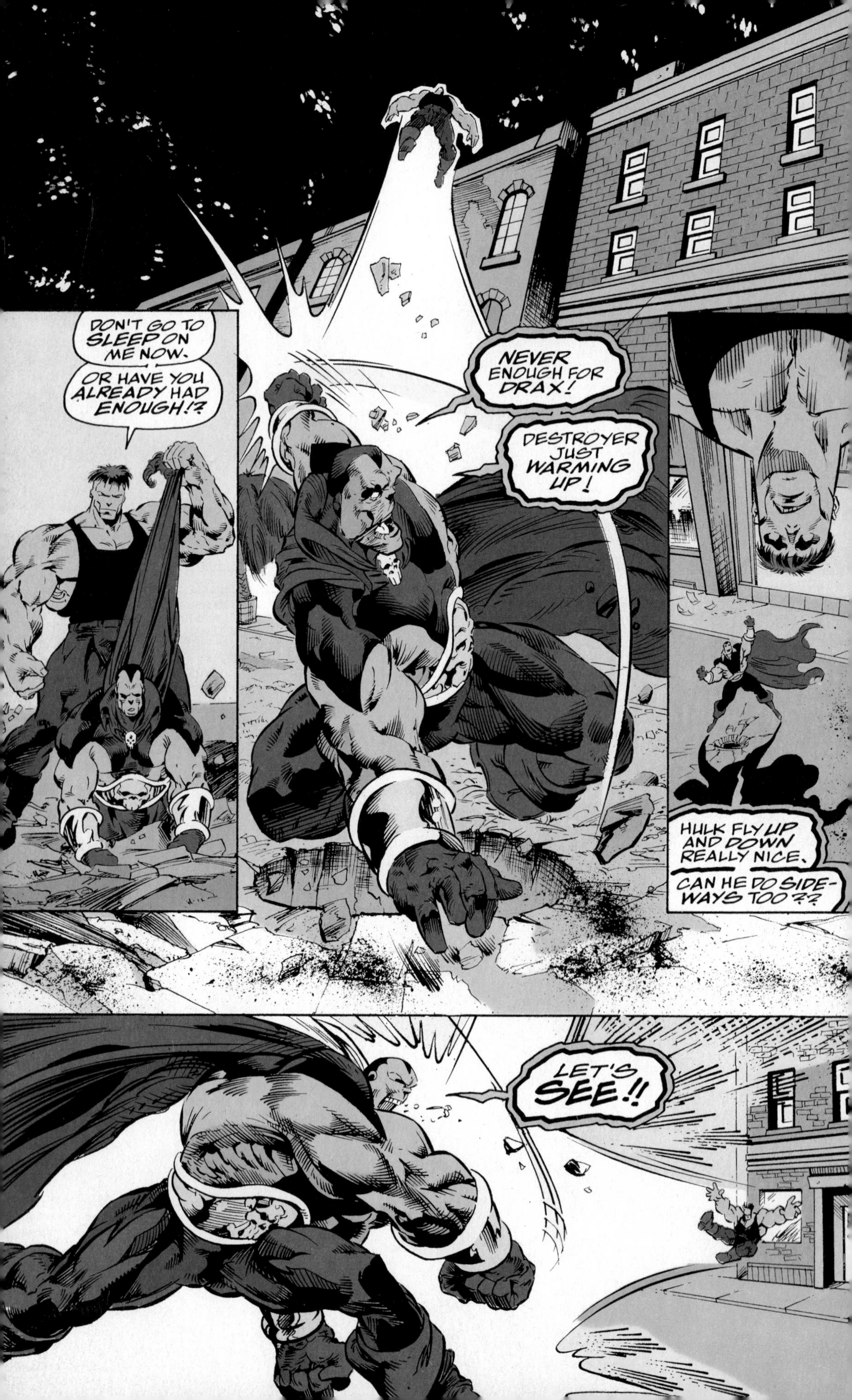
DON'T GO TO SLEEP ON ME NOW.
OR HAVE YOU ALREADY HAD ENOUGH!?
NEVER ENOUGH FOR DRAX!
DESTROYER JUST WARMING UP!
HULK FLY UP AND DOWN REALLY NICE.
CAN HE DO SIDE-WAYS TOO??
LET'S SEE!!

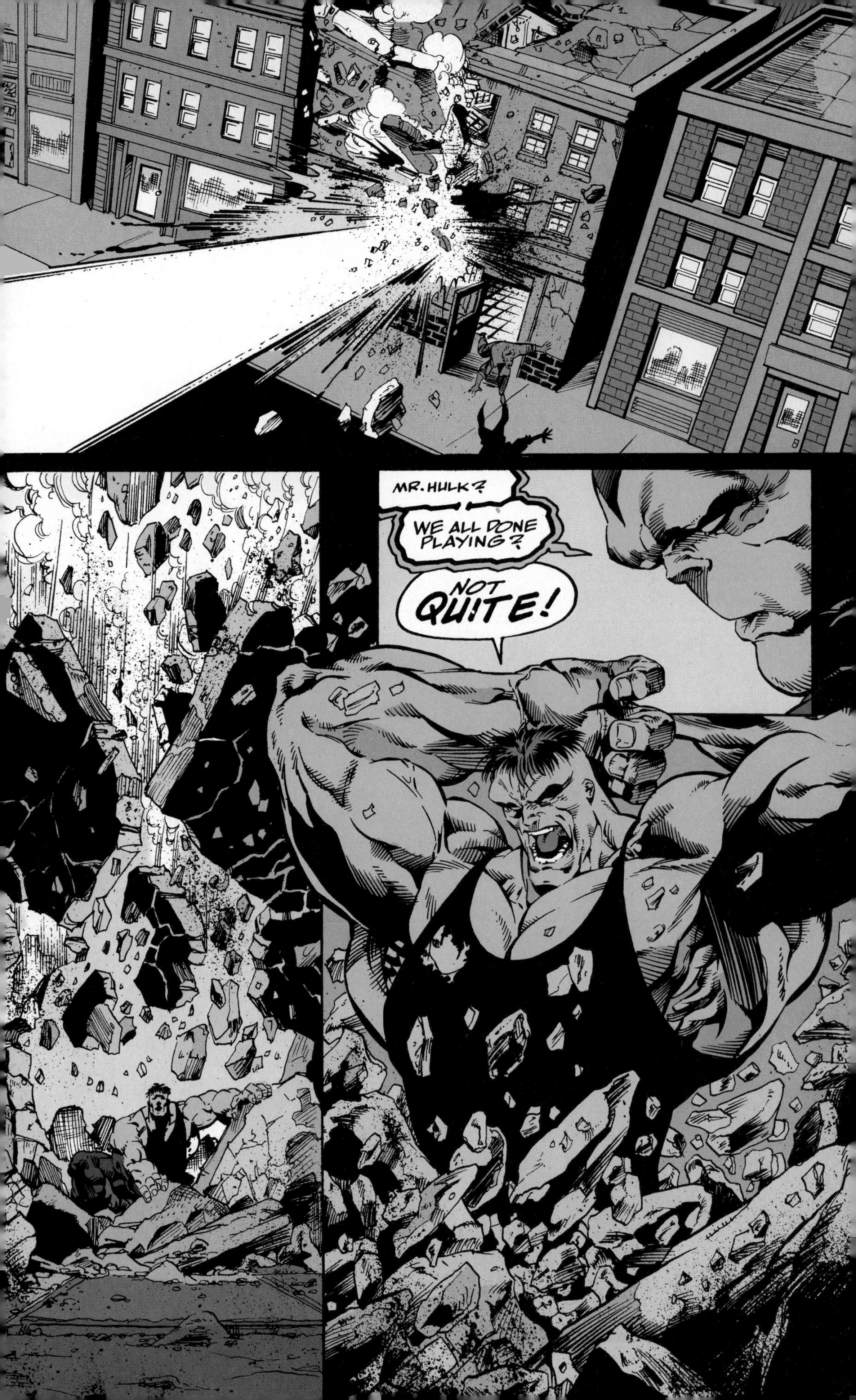
MR. HULK?
WE ALL DONE PLAYING?
NOT QUITE!

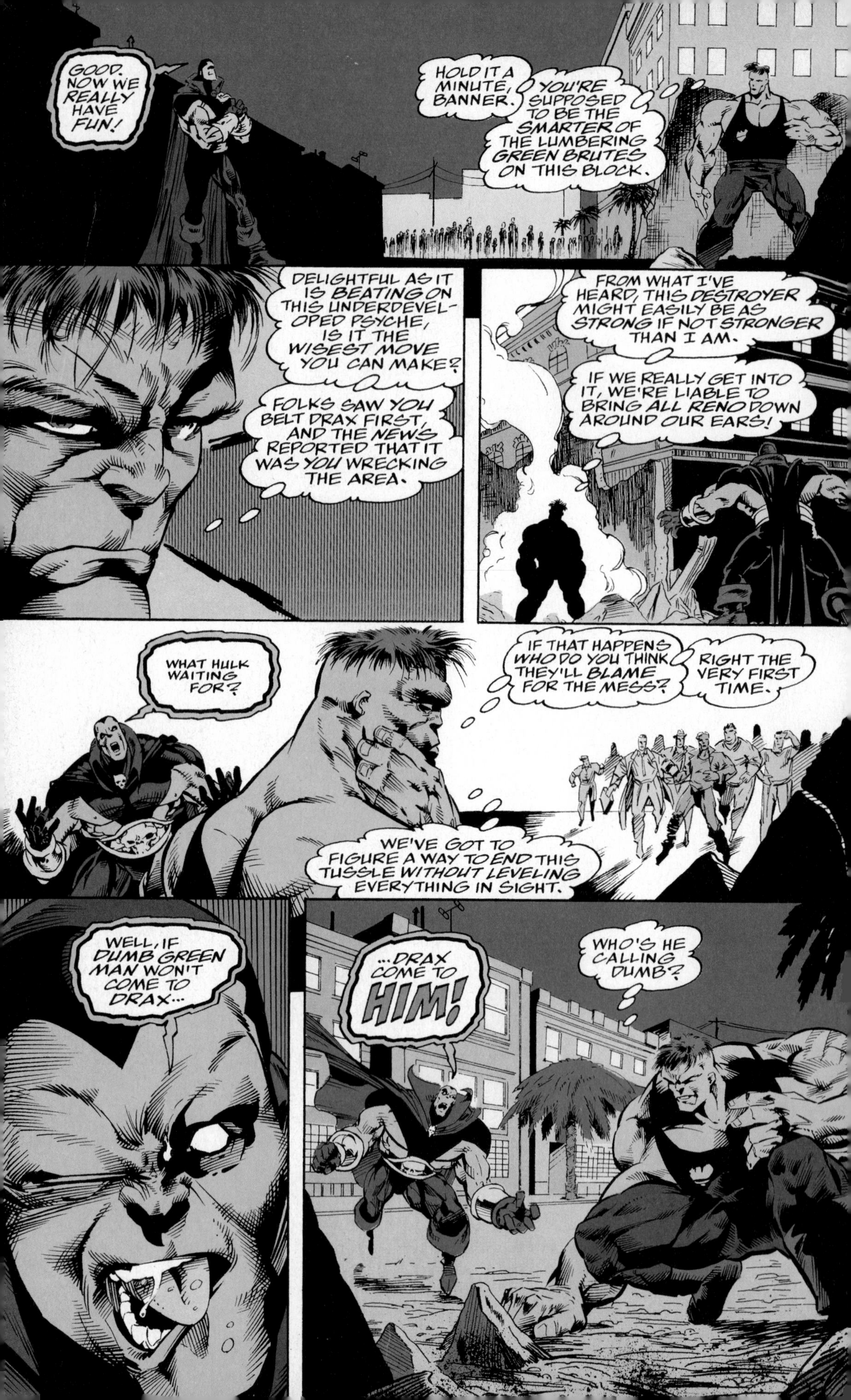
GOOD. NOW WE REALLY HAVE FUN!
HOLD IT A MINUTE, BANNER.
YOU'RE SUPPOSED TO BE THE SMARTER OF THE LUMBERING GREEN BRUTES ON THIS BLOCK.
DELIGHTFUL AS IT IS BEATING ON THIS UNDERDEVEL-OPED PSYCHE, IS IT THE WISEST MOVE YOU CAN MAKE?
FOLKS SAW YOU BELT DRAX FIRST, AND THE NEWS REPORTED THAT IT WAS YOU WRECKING THE AREA.
FROM WHAT I'VE HEARD, THIS DESTROYER MIGHT EASILY BE AS STRONG IF NOT STRONGER THAN I AM.
IF WE REALLY GET INTO IT, WE'RE LIABLE TO BRING ALL RENO DOWN AROUND OUR EARS!
WHAT HULK WAITING FOR?
IF THAT HAPPENS WHO DO YOU THINK THEY'LL BLAME FOR THE MESS?
RIGHT THE VERY FIRST TIME.
WE'VE GOT TO FIGURE A WAY TO END THIS TUSSLE WITHOUT LEVELING EVERYTHING IN SIGHT.
WELL, IF DUMB GREEN MAN WON'T COME TO DRAX...
...DRAX COME TO HIM!
WHO'S HE CALLING DUMB?

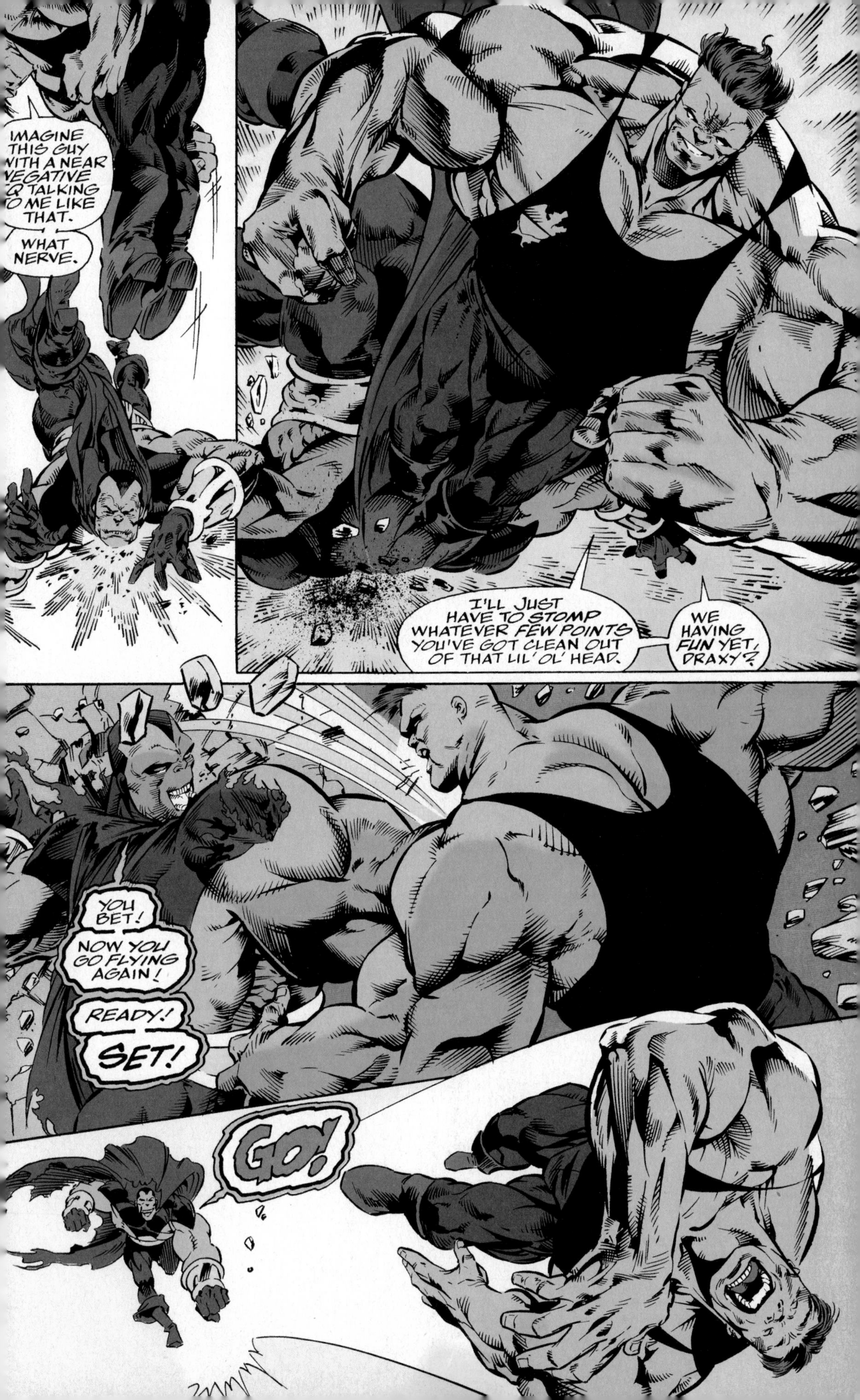
IMAGINE THIS GUY WITH A NEAR NEGATIVE IQ TALKING TO ME LIKE THAT.
WHAT NERVE.
I'LL JUST HAVE TO STOMP WHATEVER FEW POINTS YOU'VE GOT CLEAN OUT OF THAT LIL' OL' HEAD.
WE HAVING FUN YET, DRAXY?
YOU BET!
NOW YOU GO FLYING AGAIN!
READY!
SET!
GO!

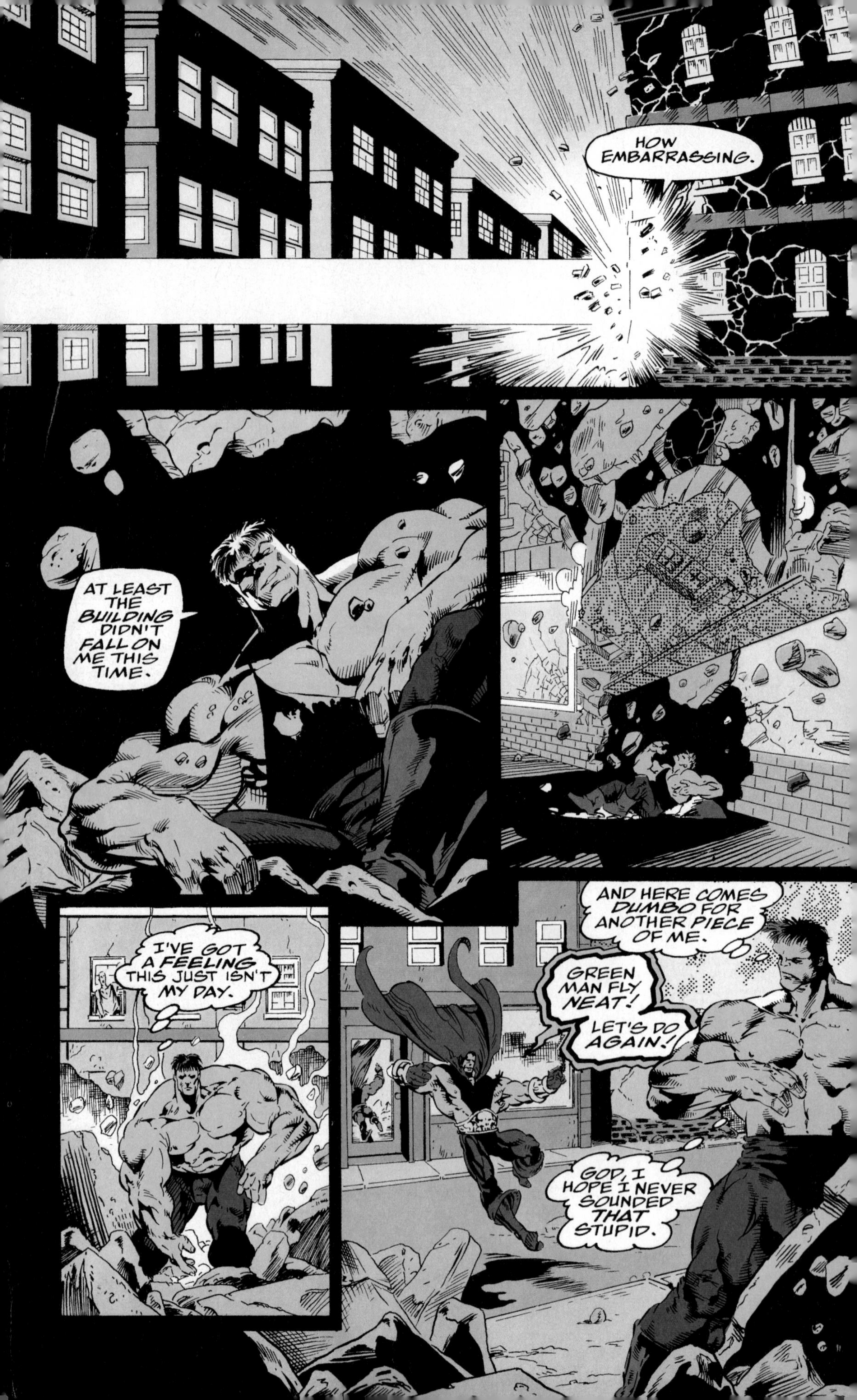
HOW EMBARRASSING.
AT LEAST THE BUILDING DIDN'T FALL ON ME THIS TIME.
I'VE GOT A FEELING THIS JUST ISN'T MY DAY.
AND HERE COMES DUMBO FOR ANOTHER PIECE OF ME.
GREEN MAN FLY NEAT!
LET'S DO AGAIN!
GOD, I HOPE I NEVER SOUNDED THAT STUPID.

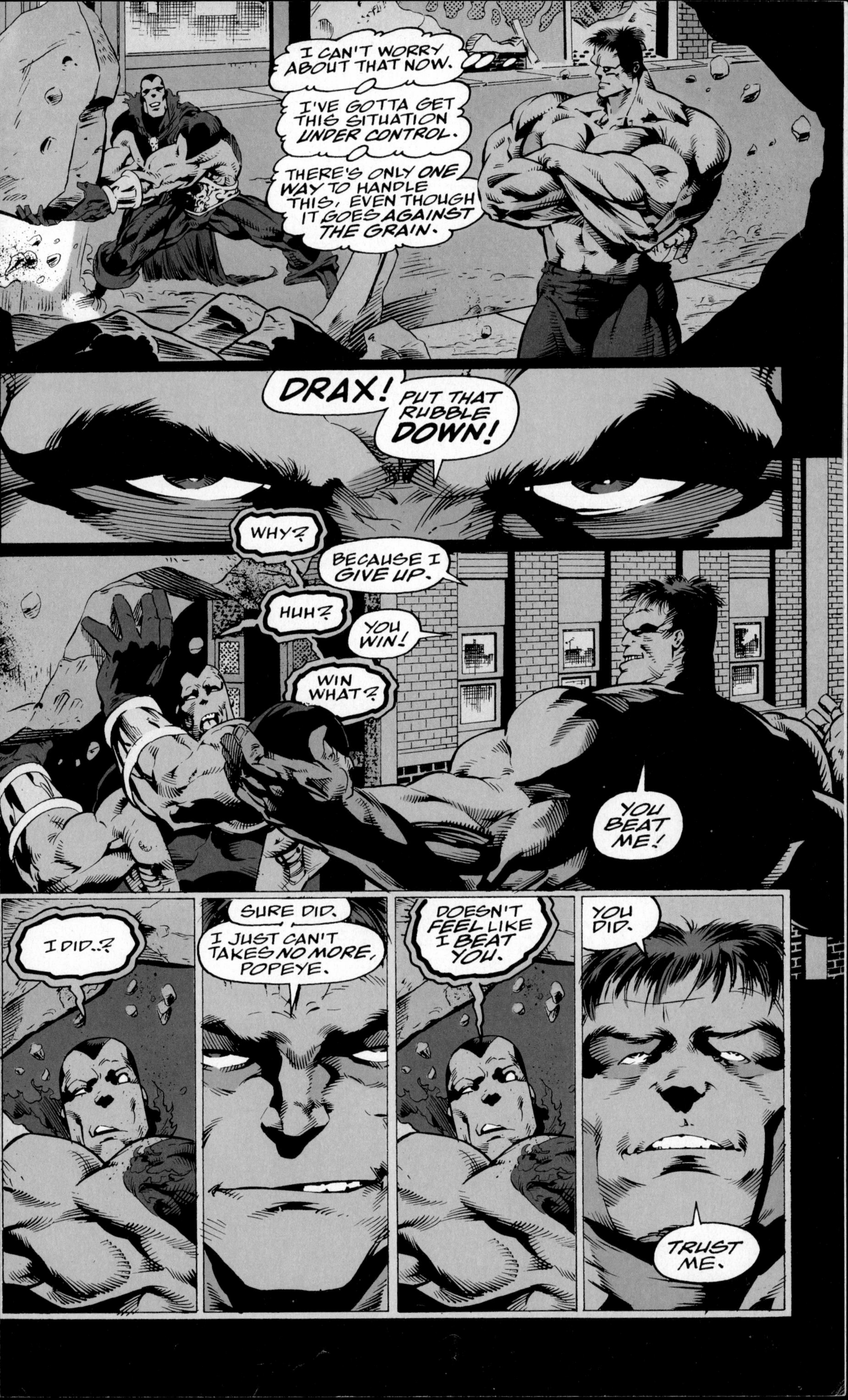

I CAN'T WORRY ABOUT THAT NOW.
I'VE GOTTA GET THIS SITUATION UNDER CONTROL.
THERE'S ONLY ONE WAY TO HANDLE THIS, EVEN THOUGH IT GOES AGAINST THE GRAIN.
DRAX!
PUT THAT RUBBLE DOWN!
WHY?
BECAUSE I GIVE UP.
HUH?
YOU WIN!
WIN WHAT?
YOU BEAT ME!
I DID..?
SURE DID.
I JUST CAN'T TAKES NO MORE, POPEYE.
DOESN'T FEEL LIKE I BEAT YOU.
YOU DID.
TRUST ME.

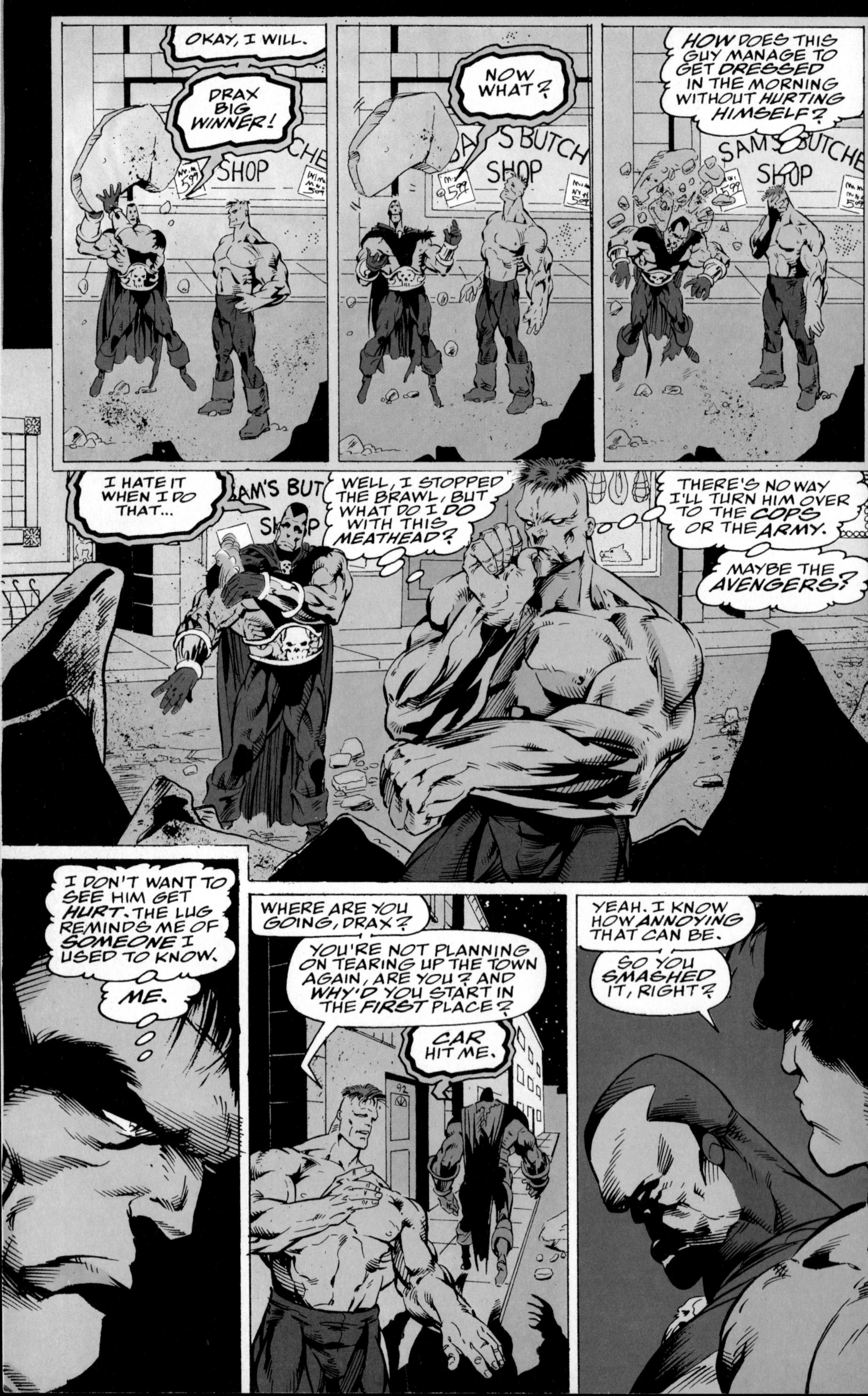
OKAY, I WILL.
DRAX BIG WINNER!
SAM'S BUTCHER SHOP
NOW WHAT?
HOW DOES THIS GUY MANAGE TO GET DRESSED IN THE MORNING WITHOUT HURTING HIMSELF?
I HATE IT WHEN I DO THAT...
WELL, I STOPPED THE BRAWL, BUT WHAT DO I DO WITH THIS MEATHEAD?
THERE'S NO WAY I'LL TURN HIM OVER TO THE COPS OR THE ARMY.
MAYBE THE AVENGERS?
I DON'T WANT TO SEE HIM GET HURT. THE LUG REMINDS ME OF SOMEONE I USED TO KNOW.
ME.
WHERE ARE YOU GOING, DRAX?
YOU'RE NOT PLANNING ON TEARING UP THE TOWN AGAIN, ARE YOU? AND WHY'D YOU START IN THE FIRST PLACE?
CAR HIT ME.
YEAH. I KNOW HOW ANNOYING THAT CAN BE.
SO YOU SMASHED IT, RIGHT?

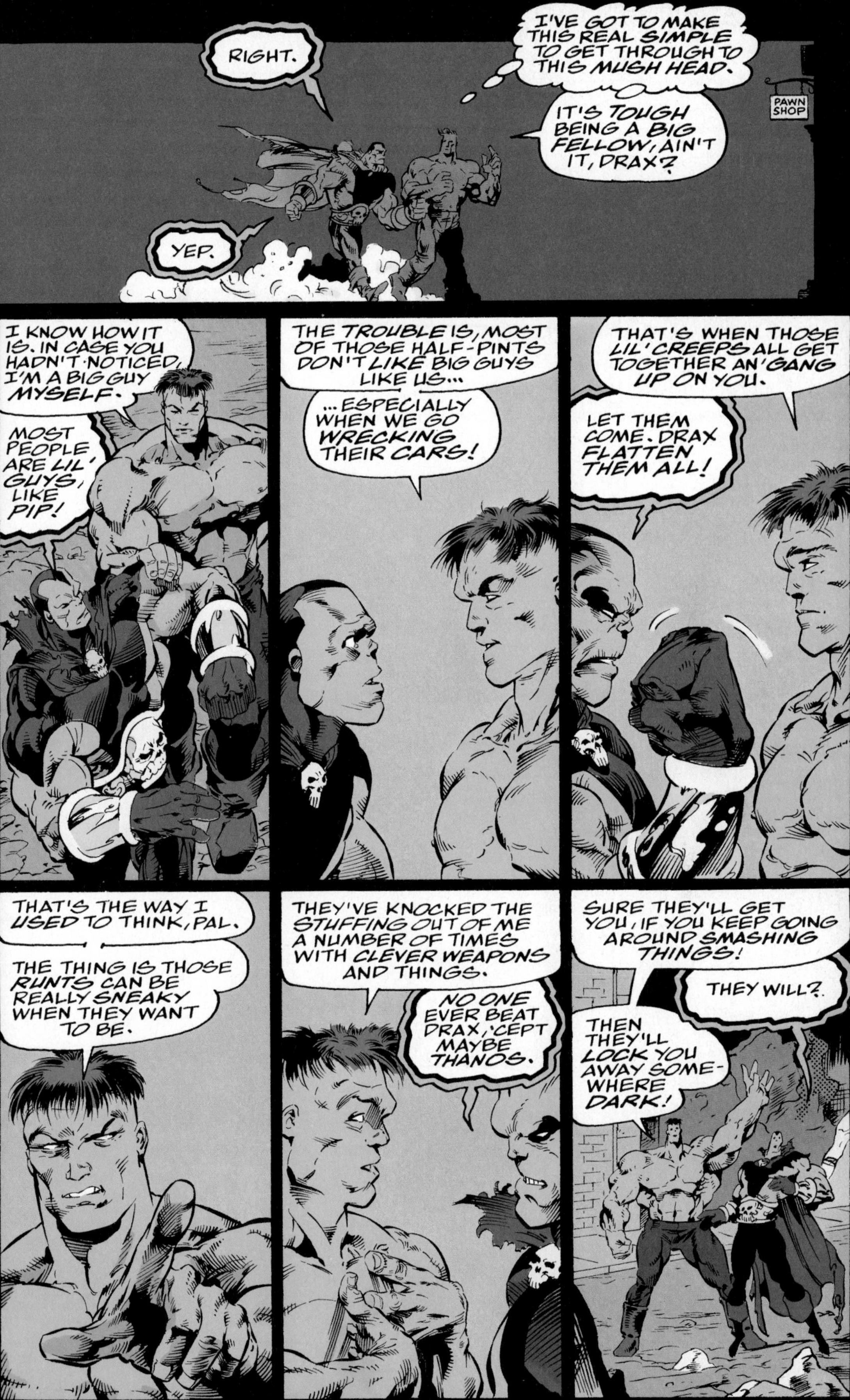
RIGHT.
I'VE GOT TO MAKE THIS REAL SIMPLE TO GET THROUGH TO THIS MUSH HEAD.
IT'S TOUGH BEING A BIG FELLOW, AIN'T IT, DRAX?
PAWN SHOP
YEP.
I KNOW HOW IT IS. IN CASE YOU HADN'T NOTICED, I'M A BIG GUY MYSELF.
MOST PEOPLE ARE LIL' GUYS, LIKE PIP!
THE TROUBLE IS, MOST OF THOSE HALF-PINTS DON'T LIKE BIG GUYS LIKE US...
...ESPECIALLY WHEN WE GO WRECKING THEIR CARS!
THAT'S WHEN THOSE LIL' CREEPS ALL GET TOGETHER AN' GANG UP ON YOU.
LET THEM COME. DRAX FLATTEN THEM ALL!
THAT'S THE WAY I USED TO THINK, PAL.
THE THING IS THOSE RUNTS CAN BE REALLY SNEAKY WHEN THEY WANT TO BE.
THEY'VE KNOCKED THE STUFFING OUT OF ME A NUMBER OF TIMES WITH CLEVER WEAPONS AND THINGS.
NO ONE EVER BEAT DRAX, 'CEPT MAYBE THANOS.
SURE THEY'LL GET YOU, IF YOU KEEP GOING AROUND SMASHING THINGS!
THEY WILL?
THEN THEY'LL LOCK YOU AWAY SOME-WHERE DARK!

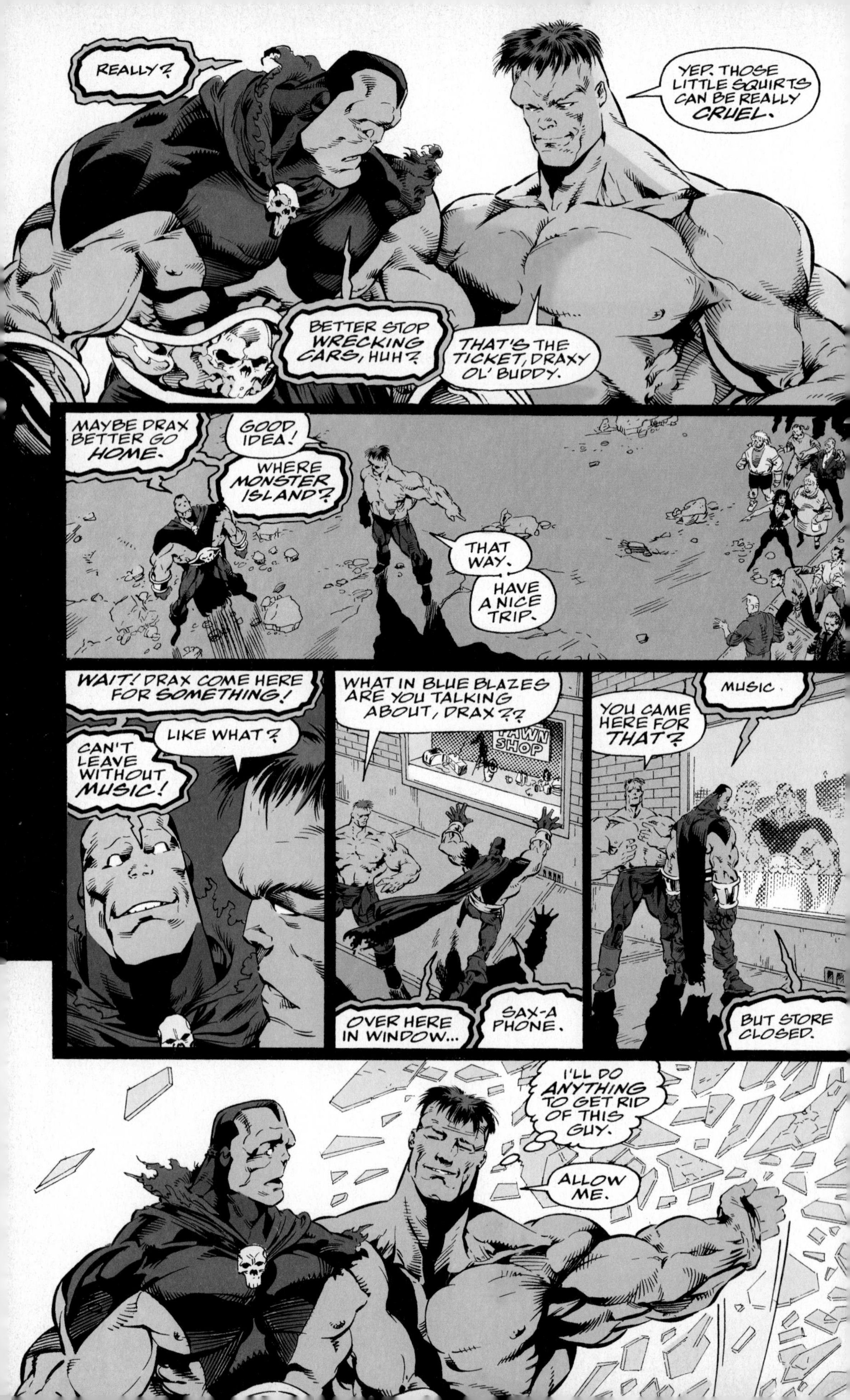

REALLY?
YEP. THOSE LITTLE SQUIRTS CAN BE REALLY CRUEL.
BETTER STOP WRECKING CARS, HUH?
THAT'S THE TICKET, DRAXY OL' BUDDY.
MAYBE DRAX BETTER GO HOME.
GOOD IDEA!
WHERE MONSTER ISLAND?
THAT WAY.
HAVE A NICE TRIP.
WAIT! DRAX COME HERE FOR SOMETHING!
LIKE WHAT?
CAN'T LEAVE WITHOUT MUSIC!
WHAT IN BLUE BLAZES ARE YOU TALKING ABOUT, DRAX??
PAWN SHOP
OVER HERE IN WINDOW...
SAX-A PHONE.
MUSIC.
YOU CAME HERE FOR THAT?
BUT STORE CLOSED.
I'LL DO ANYTHING TO GET RID OF THIS GUY.
ALLOW ME.

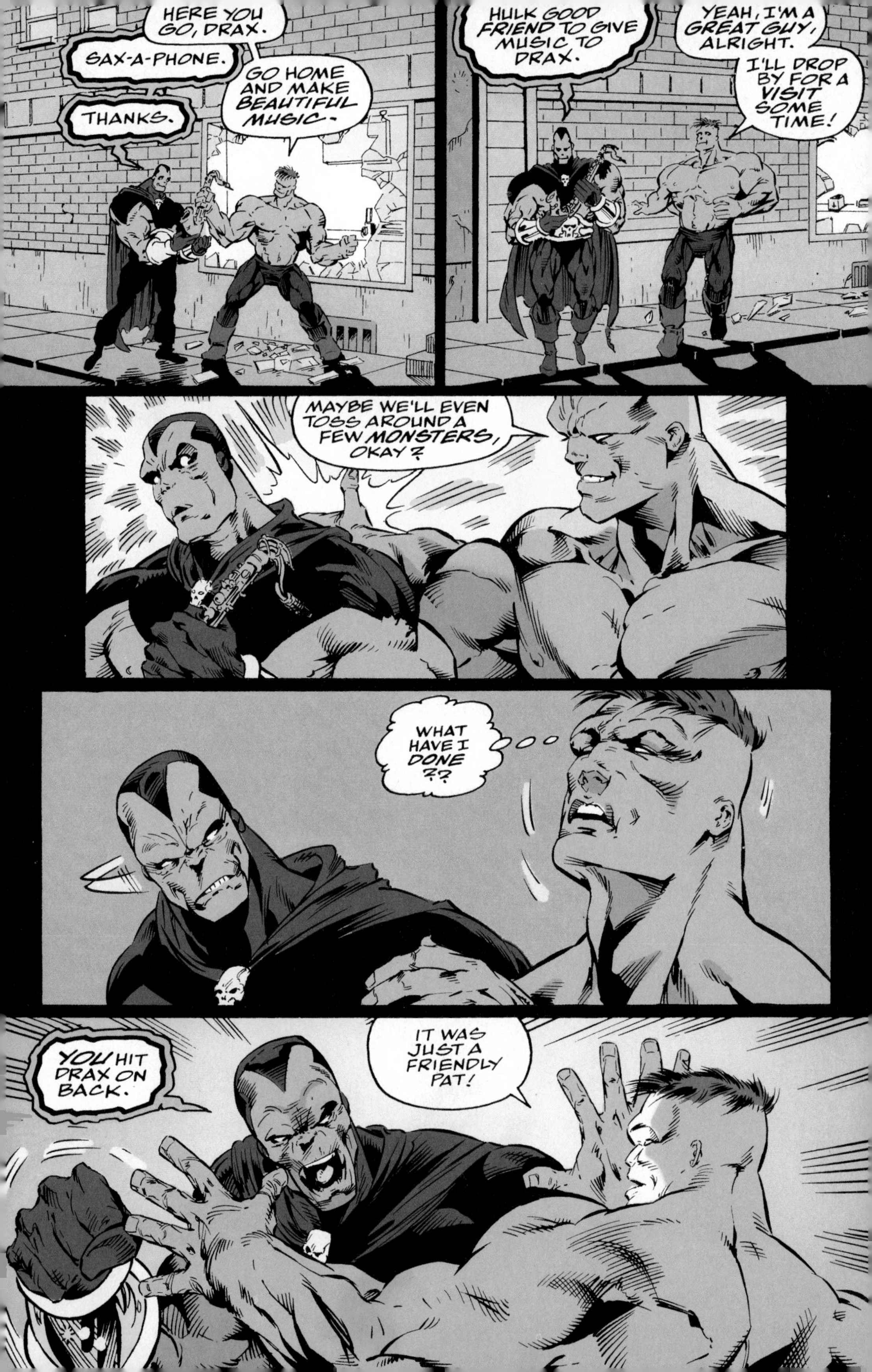
HERE YOU GO, DRAX.
SAX-A-PHONE.
THANKS.
GO HOME AND MAKE BEAUTIFUL MUSIC-
HULK GOOD FRIEND TO GIVE MUSIC TO DRAX.
YEAH, I'M A GREAT GUY, ALRIGHT.
I'LL DROP BY FOR A VISIT SOME TIME!
MAYBE WE'LL EVEN TOSS AROUND A FEW MONSTERS, OKAY?
WHAT HAVE I DONE ??
YOU HIT DRAX ON BACK.
IT WAS JUST A FRIENDLY PAT!

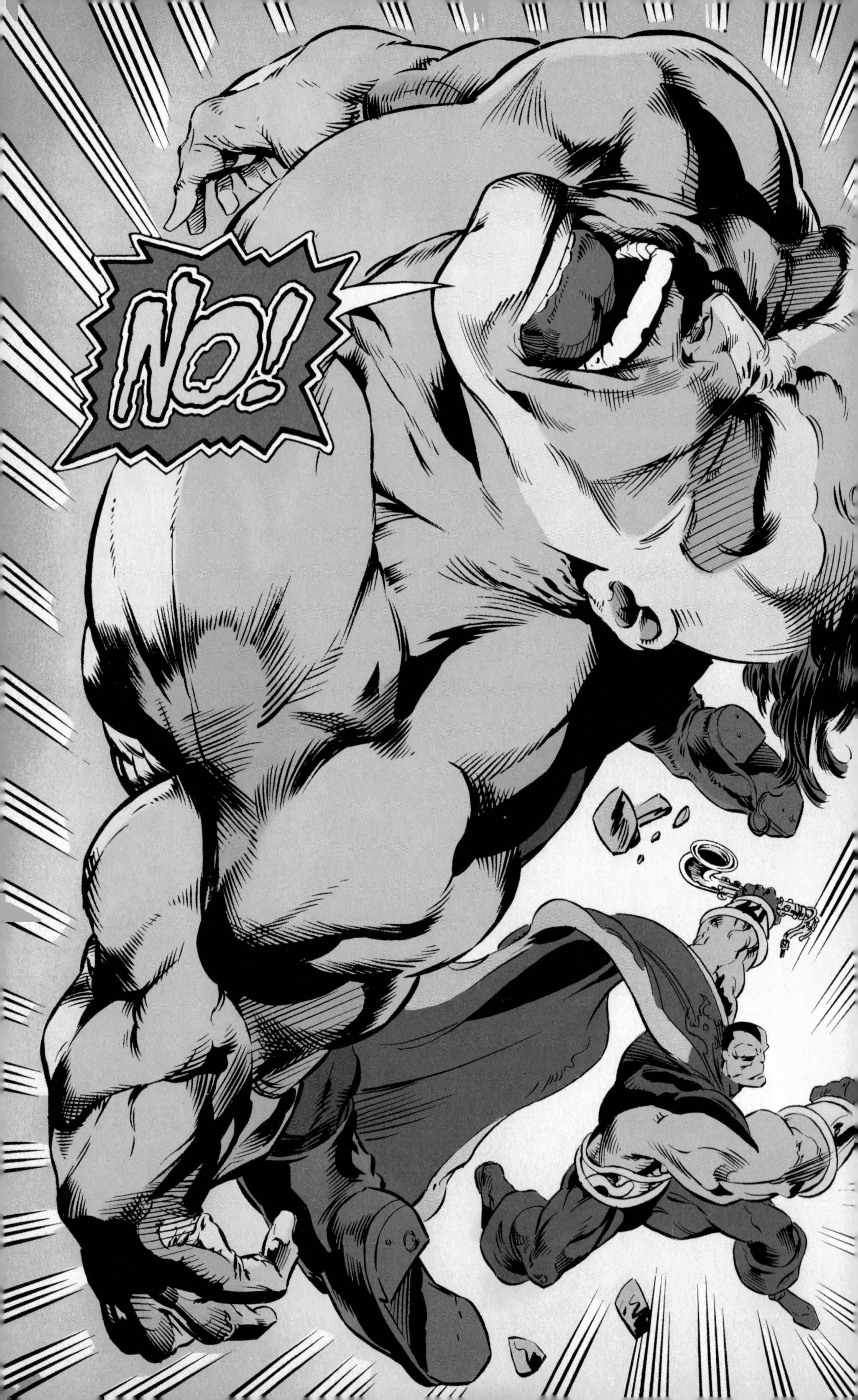
NO!

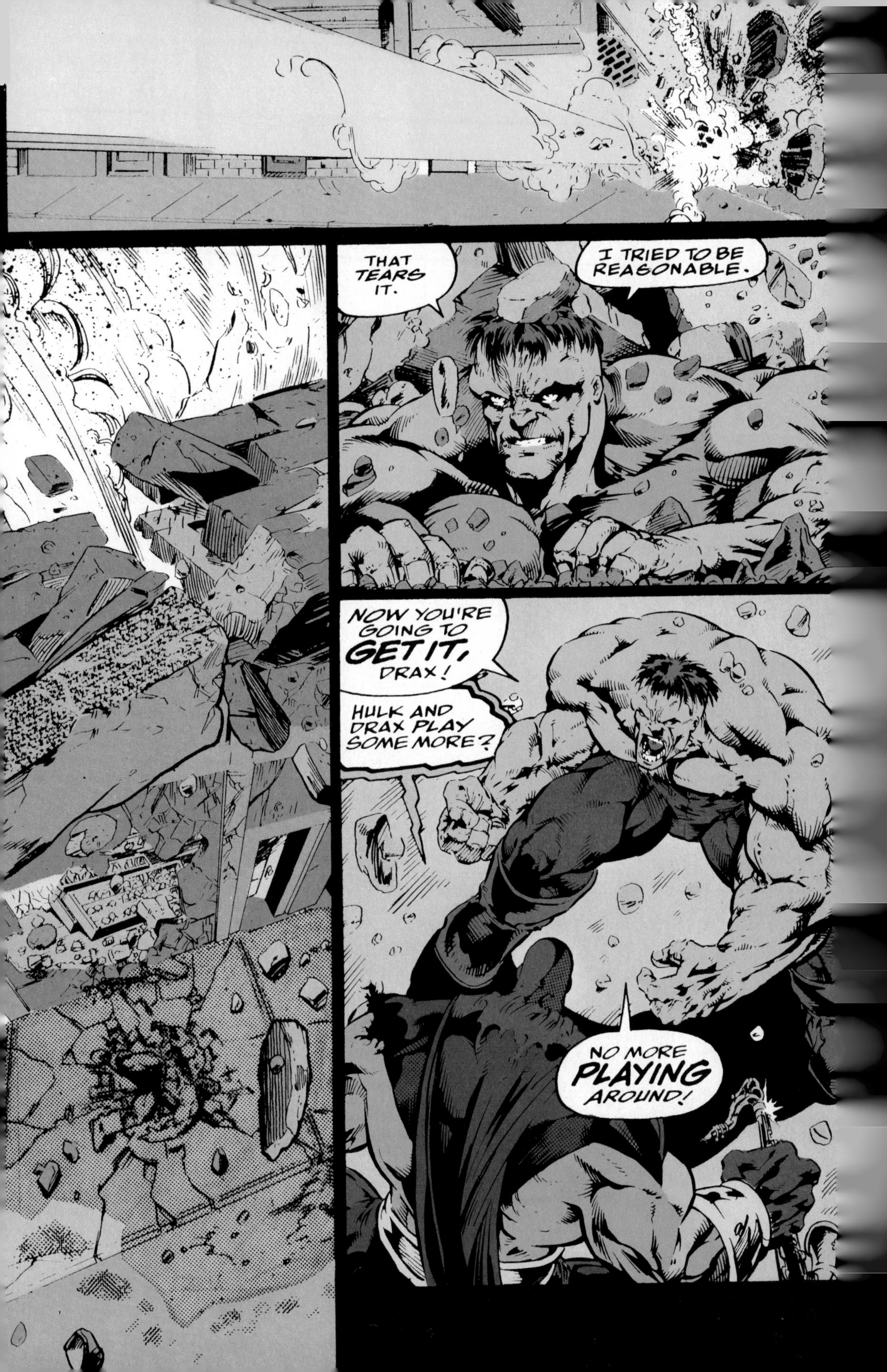
THAT TEARS IT.
I TRIED TO BE REASONABLE.
NOW YOU'RE GOING TO GET IT, DRAX!
HULK AND DRAX PLAY SOME MORE?
NO MORE PLAYING AROUND!

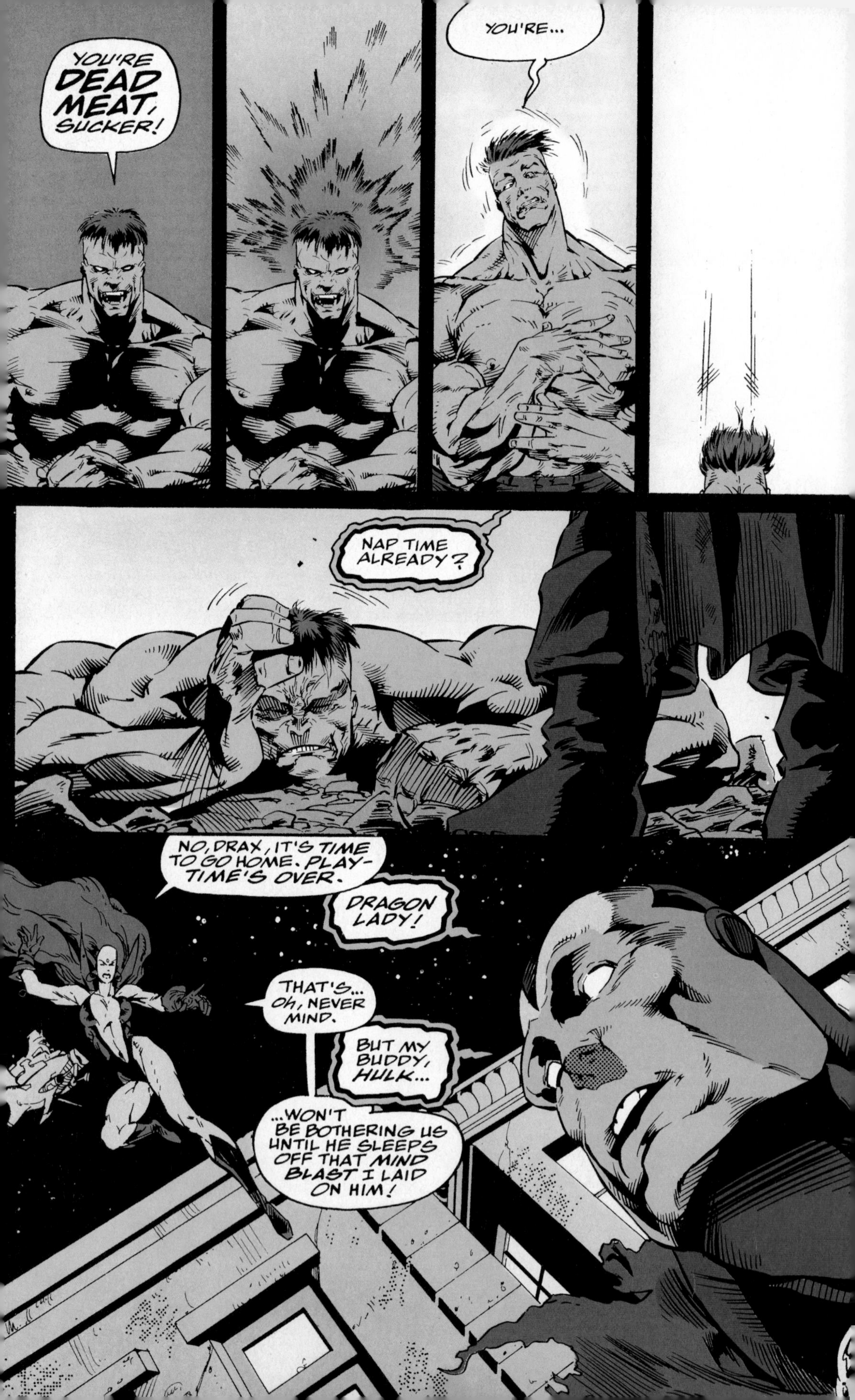

YOU'RE DEAD MEAT, SUCKER!
YOU'RE...
NAP TIME ALREADY?
NO, DRAX, IT'S TIME TO GO HOME. PLAY-TIME'S OVER.
DRAGON LADY!
THAT'S... OH, NEVER MIND.
BUT MY BUDDY, HULK...
...WON'T BE BOTHERING US UNTIL HE SLEEPS OFF THAT MIND BLAST I LAID ON HIM!

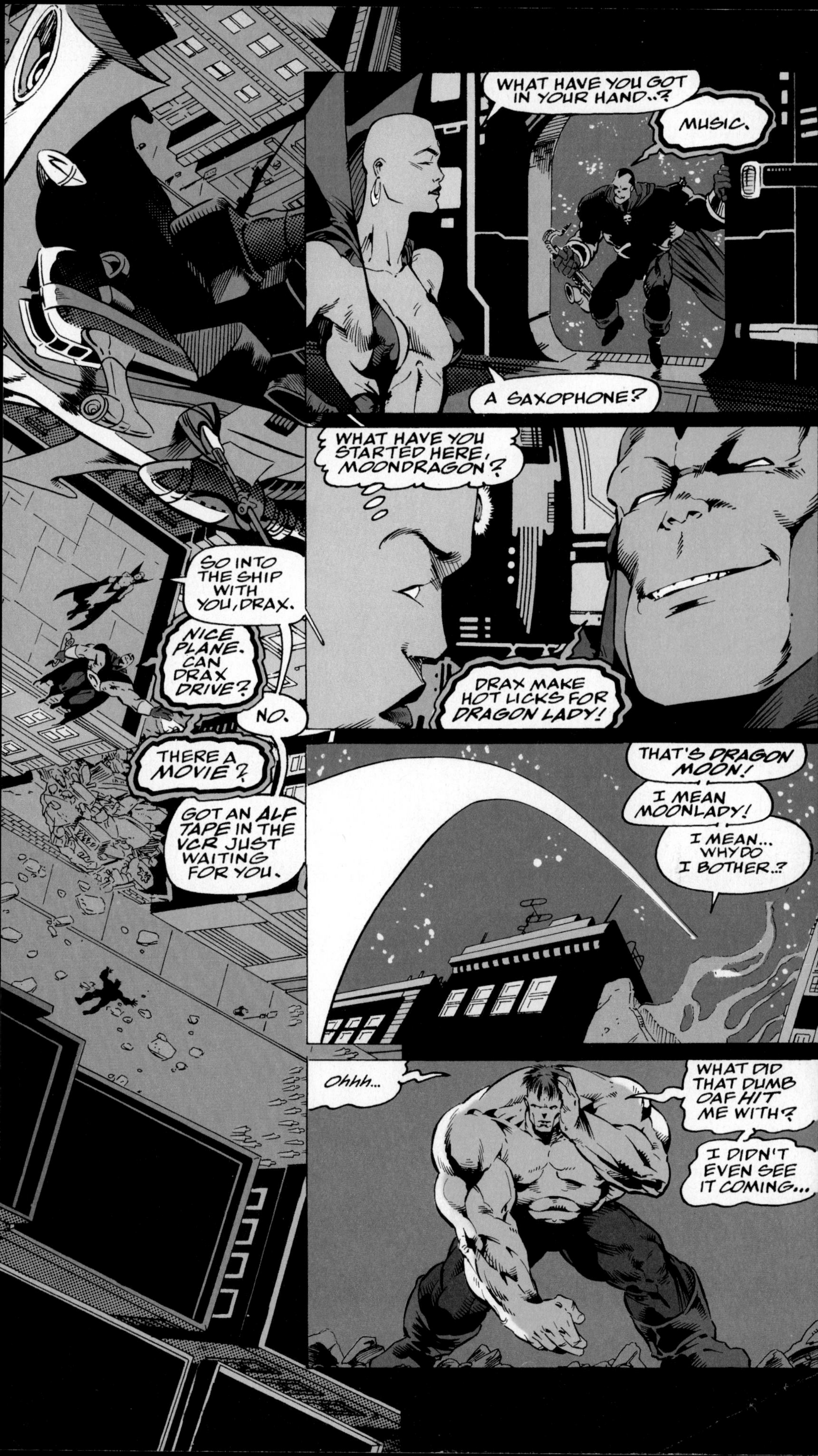
WHAT HAVE YOU GOT IN YOUR HAND..?
MUSIC.
A SAXOPHONE?
WHAT HAVE YOU STARTED HERE, MOONDRAGON?
DRAX MAKE HOT LICKS FOR DRAGON LADY!
SO INTO THE SHIP WITH YOU, DRAX.
NICE PLANE. CAN DRAX DRIVE?
NO.
THERE A MOVIE?
GOT AN ALF TAPE IN THE VCR JUST WAITING FOR YOU.
THAT'S DRAGON MOON!
I MEAN MOONLADY!
I MEAN... WHY DO I BOTHER..?
Ohhh...
WHAT DID THAT DUMB OAF HIT ME WITH?
I DIDN'T EVEN SEE IT COMING...

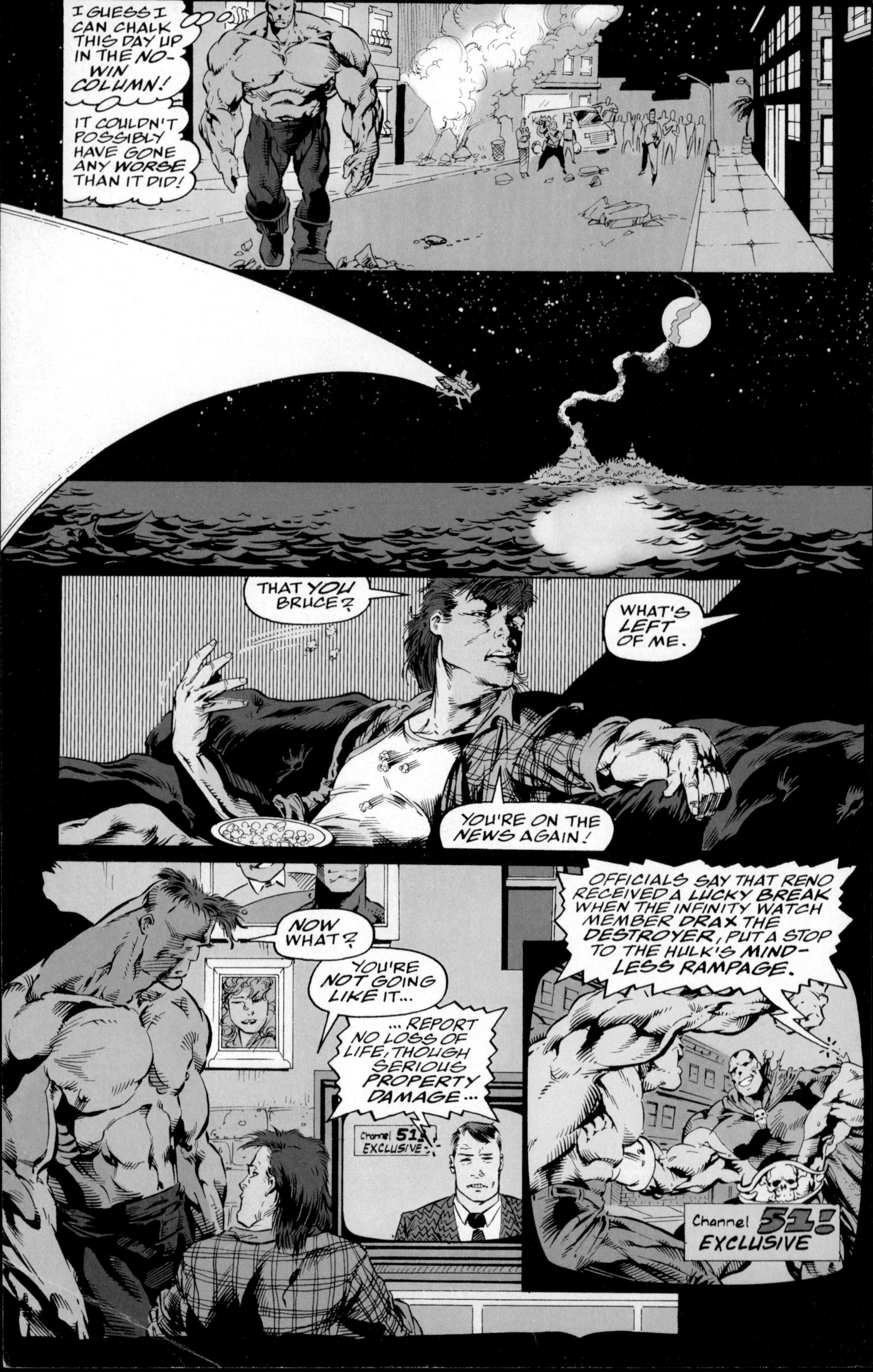
I GUESS I CAN CHALK THIS DAY UP IN THE NO-WIN COLUMN!
IT COULDN'T POSSIBLY HAVE GONE ANY WORSE THAN IT DID!
THAT YOU BRUCE?
WHAT'S LEFT OF ME.
YOU'RE ON THE NEWS AGAIN!
NOW WHAT?
YOU'RE NOT GOING LIKE IT...
... REPORT NO LOSS OF LIFE, THOUGH SERIOUS PROPERTY DAMAGE...
Channel 51! EXCLUSIVE
OFFICIALS SAY THAT RENO RECEIVED A LUCKY BREAK WHEN THE INFINITY WATCH MEMBER DRAX THE DESTROYER, PUT A STOP TO THE HULK'S MINDLESS RAMPAGE.
Channel 51! EXCLUSIVE

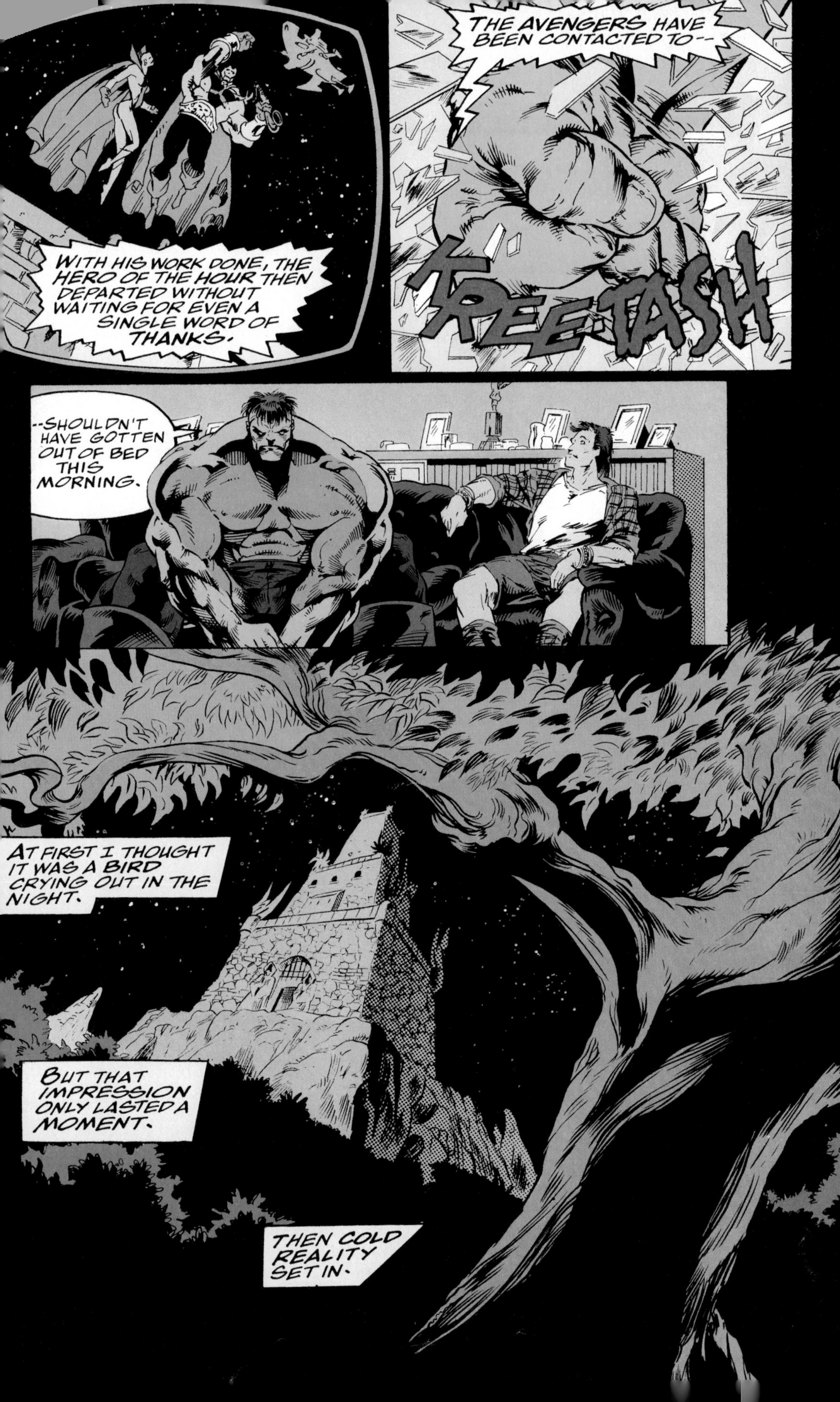
WITH HIS WORK DONE, THE HERO OF THE HOUR THEN DEPARTED WITHOUT WAITING FOR EVEN A SINGLE WORD OF THANKS.
THE AVENGERS HAVE BEEN CONTACTED TO--
KREE-TASH
--SHOULDN'T HAVE GOTTEN OUT OF BED THIS MORNING.
AT FIRST I THOUGHT IT WAS A BIRD CRYING OUT IN THE NIGHT.
BUT THAT IMPRESSION ONLY LASTED A MOMENT.
THEN COLD REALITY SET IN.

OVER THE PAST FEW WEEKS, EVER SINCE THE INFINITY WATCH WAS FORMED, MY THOUGHTS HAVE OFTEN DRIFTED TO MY FATHER ARTHUR DOUGLAS, A.K.A. DRAX THE DESTROYER.

I WONDER HOW MUCH, IF ANY, OF DAD NOW SURVIVES WITHIN THAT TOWERING BEHEMOTH.

IF ASKED, I'M SURE MY ANSWER WOULD HAVE BEEN: NONE.

TO THINK OTHERWISE WAS TOO TERRIBLE TO EVEN CONTEMPLATE.

THE THOUGHT OF THAT ONCE REFINED AND GENTLE MAN TRAPPED WITHIN DRAX'S RUDE FRAME IS THE STUFF OF NIGHTMARES.

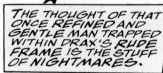

NO FATE COULD BE SO CRUEL.

HOW WOULD IT FEEL TO HAVE ONE'S KEEN INTELLECT REDUCED TO THAT OF A CHILD?

WOULD THERE BE HORRIFIC MOMENTS OF CLARITY TO TORMENT HE WHO WAS?

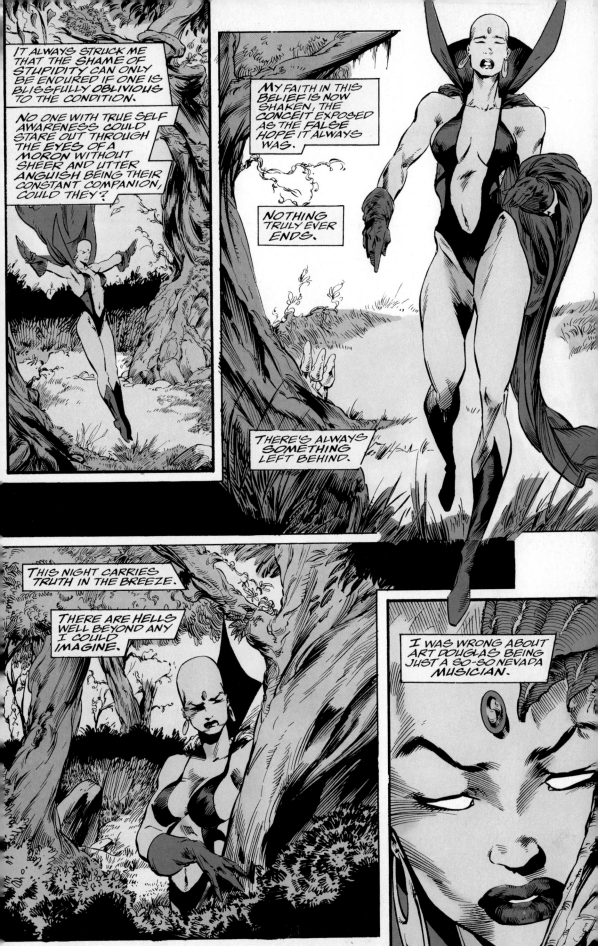

IT ALWAYS STRUCK ME THAT THE SHAME OF STUPIDITY CAN ONLY BE ENDURED IF ONE IS BLISSFULLY OBLIVIOUS TO THE CONDITION.

NO ONE WITH TRUE SELF AWARENESS COULD STARE OUT THROUGH THE EYES OF A MORON WITHOUT SHEER AND UTTER ANGUISH BEING THEIR CONSTANT COMPANION, COULD THEY?

MY FAITH IN THIS BELIEF IS NOW SHAKEN, THE CONCEIT EXPOSED AS THE FALSE HOPE IT ALWAYS WAS.

NOTHING TRULY EVER ENDS.

THERE'S ALWAYS SOMETHING LEFT BEHIND.

THIS NIGHT CARRIES TRUTH IN THE BREEZE.

THERE ARE HELLS WELL BEYOND ANY I COULD IMAGINE.

I WAS WRONG ABOUT ART DOUGLAS BEING JUST A SO-SO NEVADA MUSICIAN.

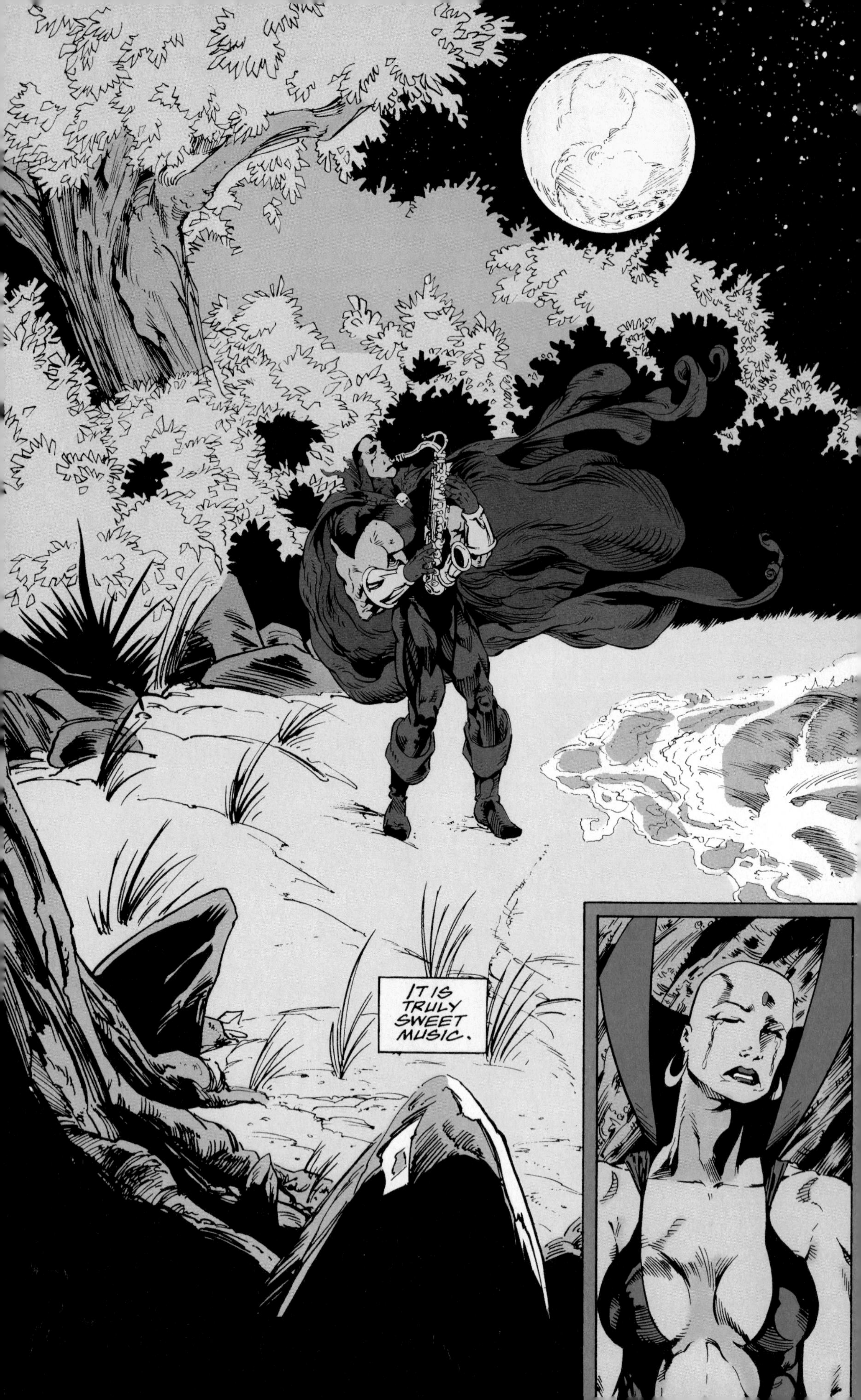
IT IS TRULY SWEET MUSIC.

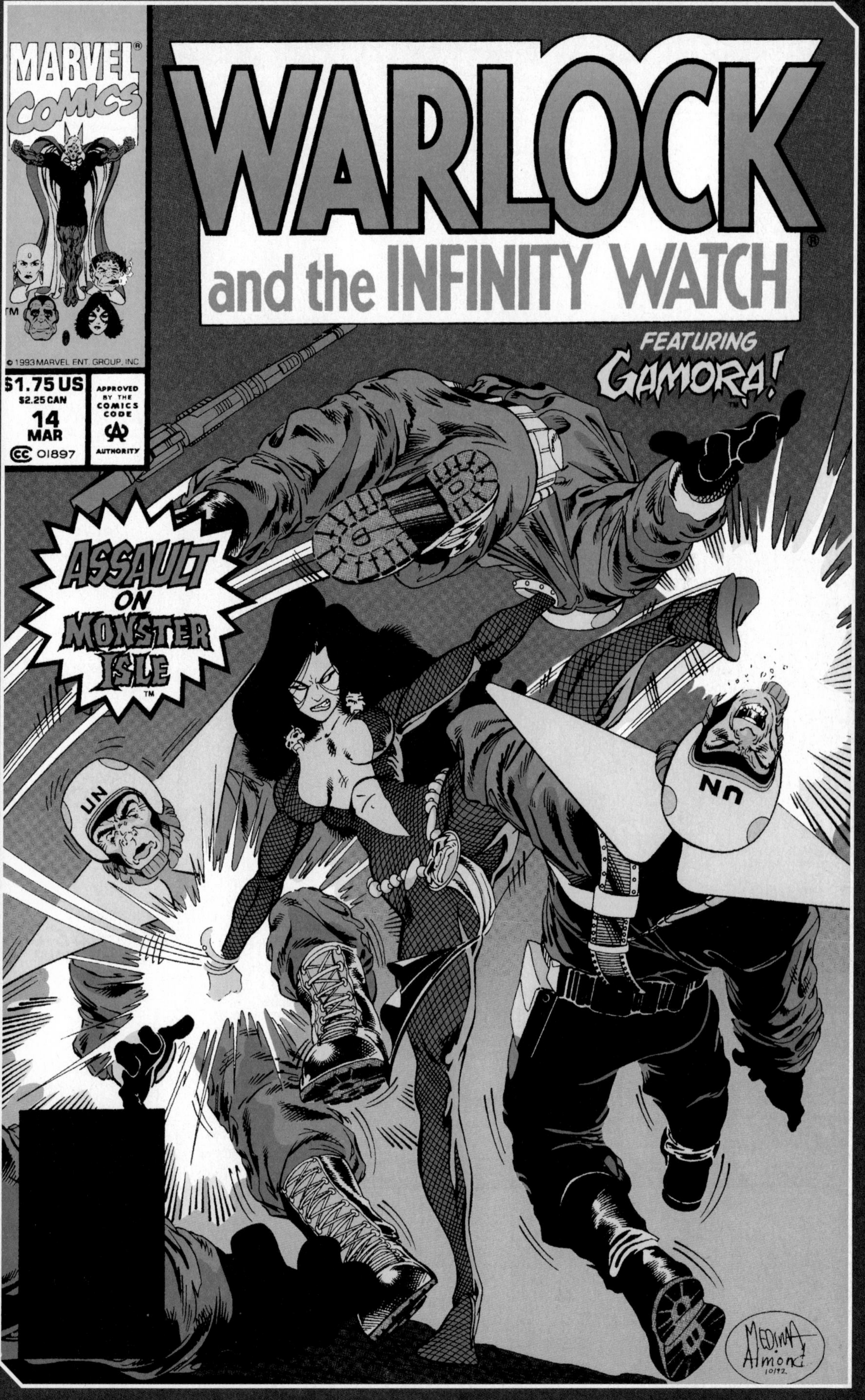
MARVEL COMICS
WARLOCK and the INFINITY WATCH
© 1993 MARVEL ENT. GROUP, INC.
$1.75 US
$2.25 CAN
14
MAR
01897
APPROVED BY THE COMICS CODE AUTHORITY
FEATURING GAMORA!
ASSAULT ON MONSTER ISLE
UN
UN

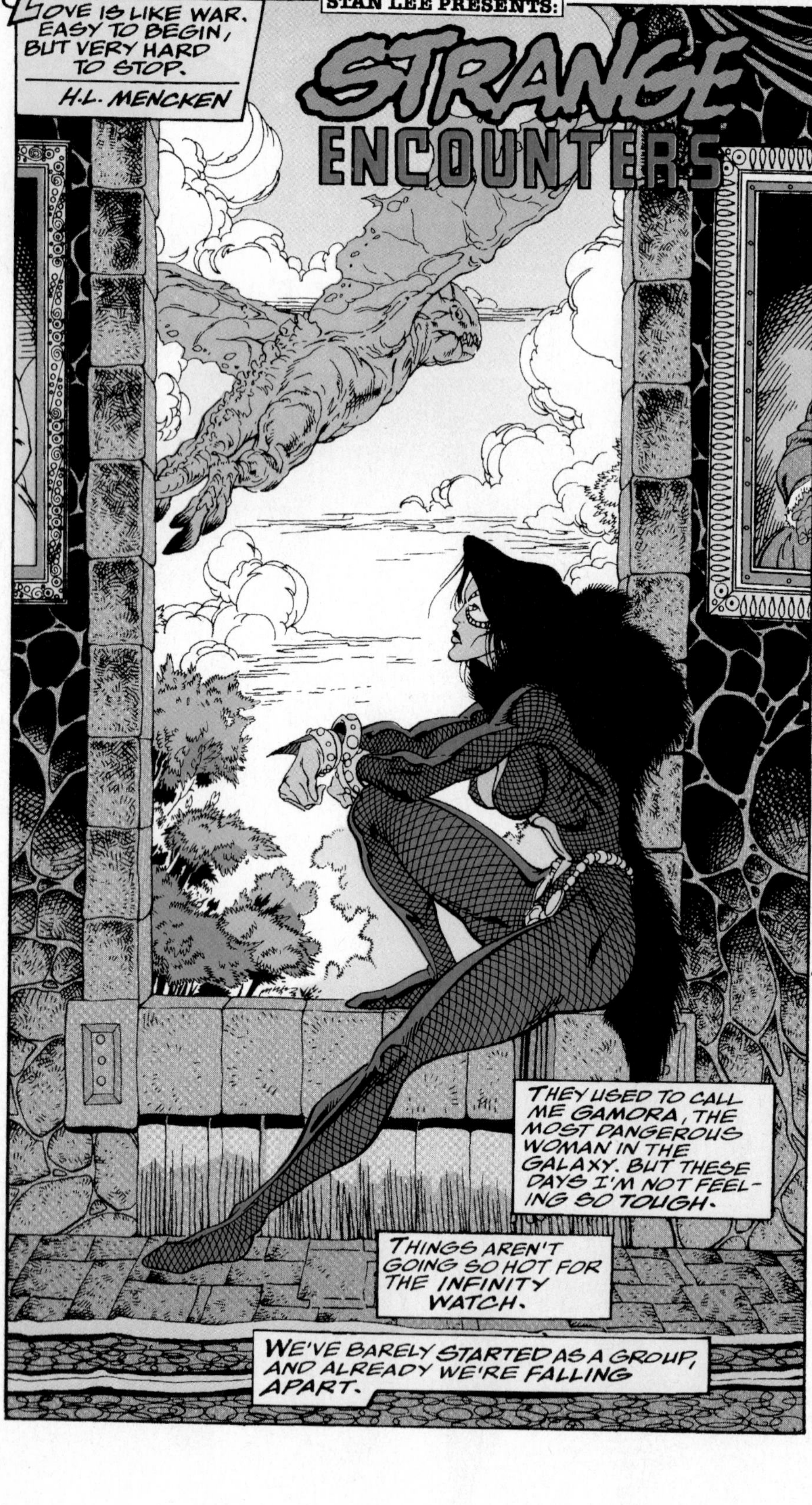
LOVE IS LIKE WAR. EASY TO BEGIN, BUT VERY HARD TO STOP.
H.L. MENCKEN
STAN LEE PRESENTS:
STRANGE ENCOUNTERS
THEY USED TO CALL ME GAMORA, THE MOST DANGEROUS WOMAN IN THE GALAXY. BUT THESE DAYS I'M NOT FEELING SO TOUGH.
THINGS AREN'T GOING SO HOT FOR THE INFINITY WATCH.
WE'VE BARELY STARTED AS A GROUP, AND ALREADY WE'RE FALLING APART.

JIM STARLIN WRITER

ANGEL MEDINA PENCILS

BOB ALMOND INKER

JACK MORELLI LETTERS

IAN LAUGHLIN COLORS

CRAIG ANDERSON EDITOR

TOM DeFALCO CHIEFTAIN

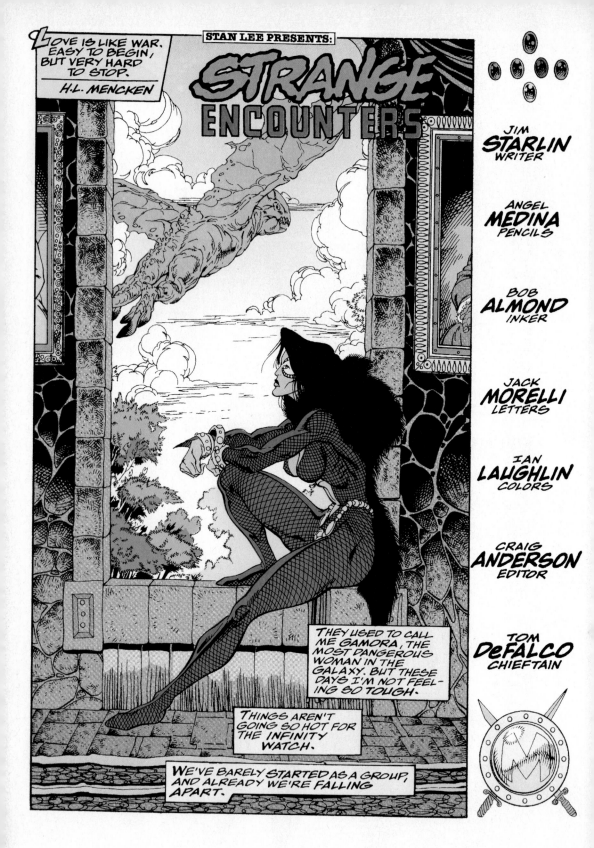

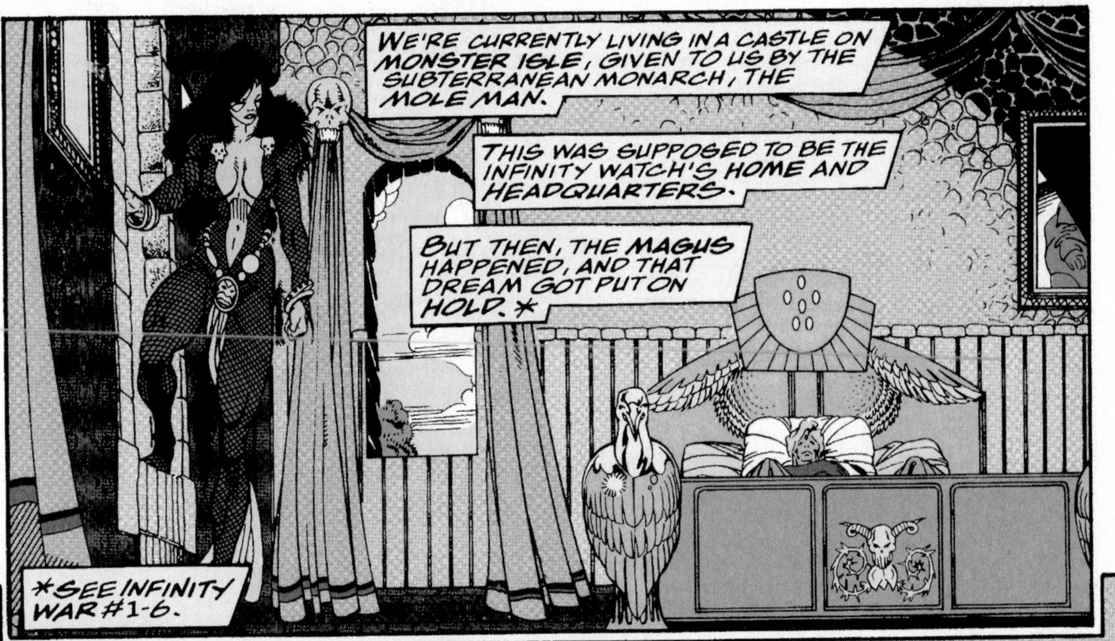

WE'RE CURRENTLY LIVING IN A CASTLE ON MONSTER ISLE, GIVEN TO US BY THE SUBTERRANEAN MONARCH, THE MOLE MAN.
THIS WAS SUPPOSED TO BE THE INFINITY WATCH'S HOME AND HEADQUARTERS.
BUT THEN, THE MAGUS HAPPENED, AND THAT DREAM GOT PUT ON HOLD.*
*SEE INFINITY WAR #1-6.

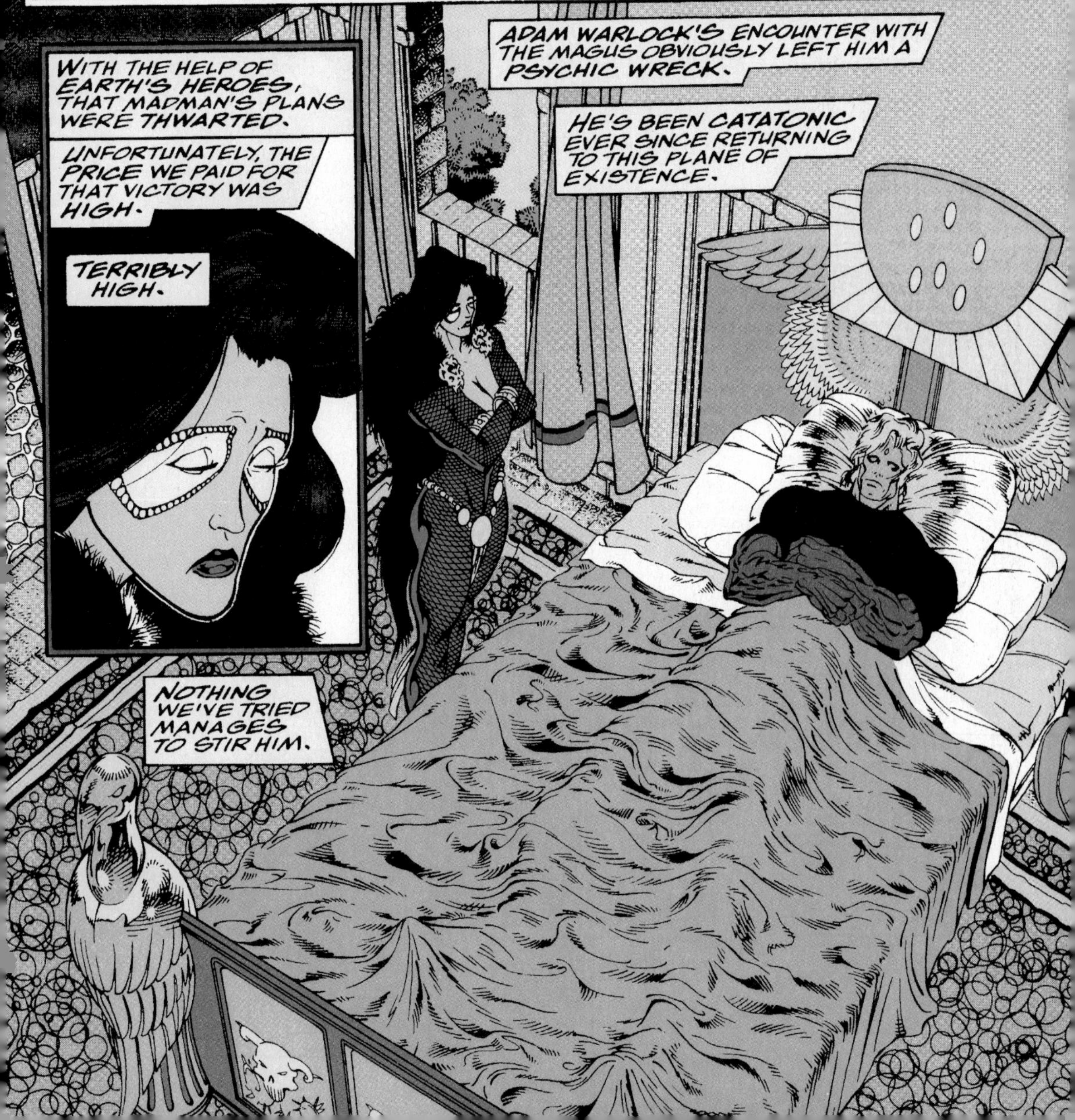

WITH THE HELP OF EARTH'S HEROES, THAT MADMAN'S PLANS WERE THWARTED.
UNFORTUNATELY, THE PRICE WE PAID FOR THAT VICTORY WAS HIGH.
TERRIBLY HIGH.
ADAM WARLOCK'S ENCOUNTER WITH THE MAGUS OBVIOUSLY LEFT HIM A PSYCHIC WRECK.
HE'S BEEN CATATONIC EVER SINCE RETURNING TO THIS PLANE OF EXISTENCE.
NOTHING WE'VE TRIED MANAGES TO STIR HIM.

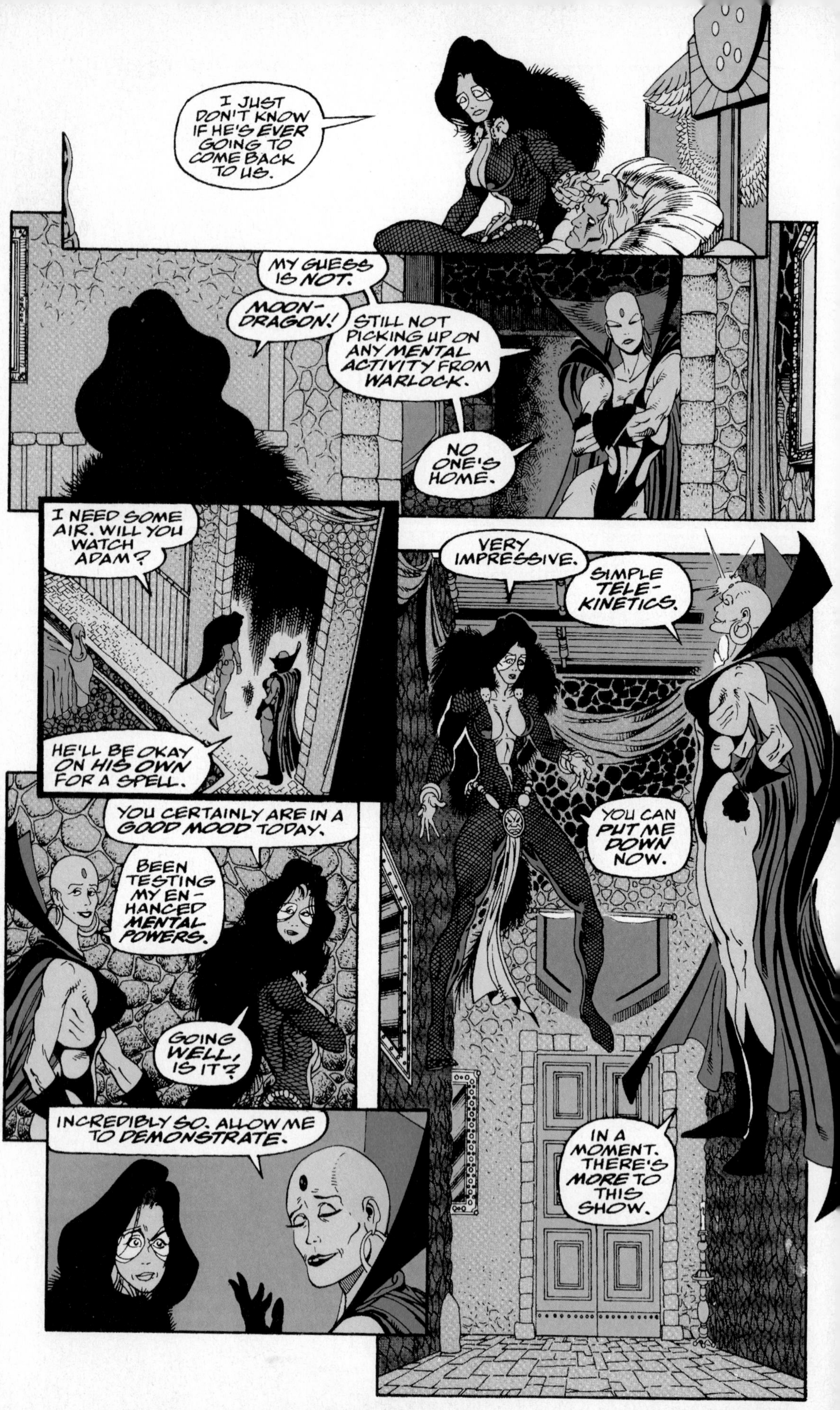
I JUST DON'T KNOW IF HE'S EVER GOING TO COME BACK TO US.
MY GUESS IS NOT.
MOON-DRAGON!
STILL NOT PICKING UP ON ANY MENTAL ACTIVITY FROM WARLOCK.
NO ONE'S HOME.
I NEED SOME AIR. WILL YOU WATCH ADAM?
HE'LL BE OKAY ON HIS OWN FOR A SPELL.
YOU CERTAINLY ARE IN A GOOD MOOD TODAY.
BEEN TESTING MY EN-HANCED MENTAL POWERS.
GOING WELL, IS IT?
INCREDIBLY SO. ALLOW ME TO DEMONSTRATE.
VERY IMPRESSIVE.
SIMPLE TELE-KINETICS.
YOU CAN PUT ME DOWN NOW.
IN A MOMENT. THERE'S MORE TO THIS SHOW.

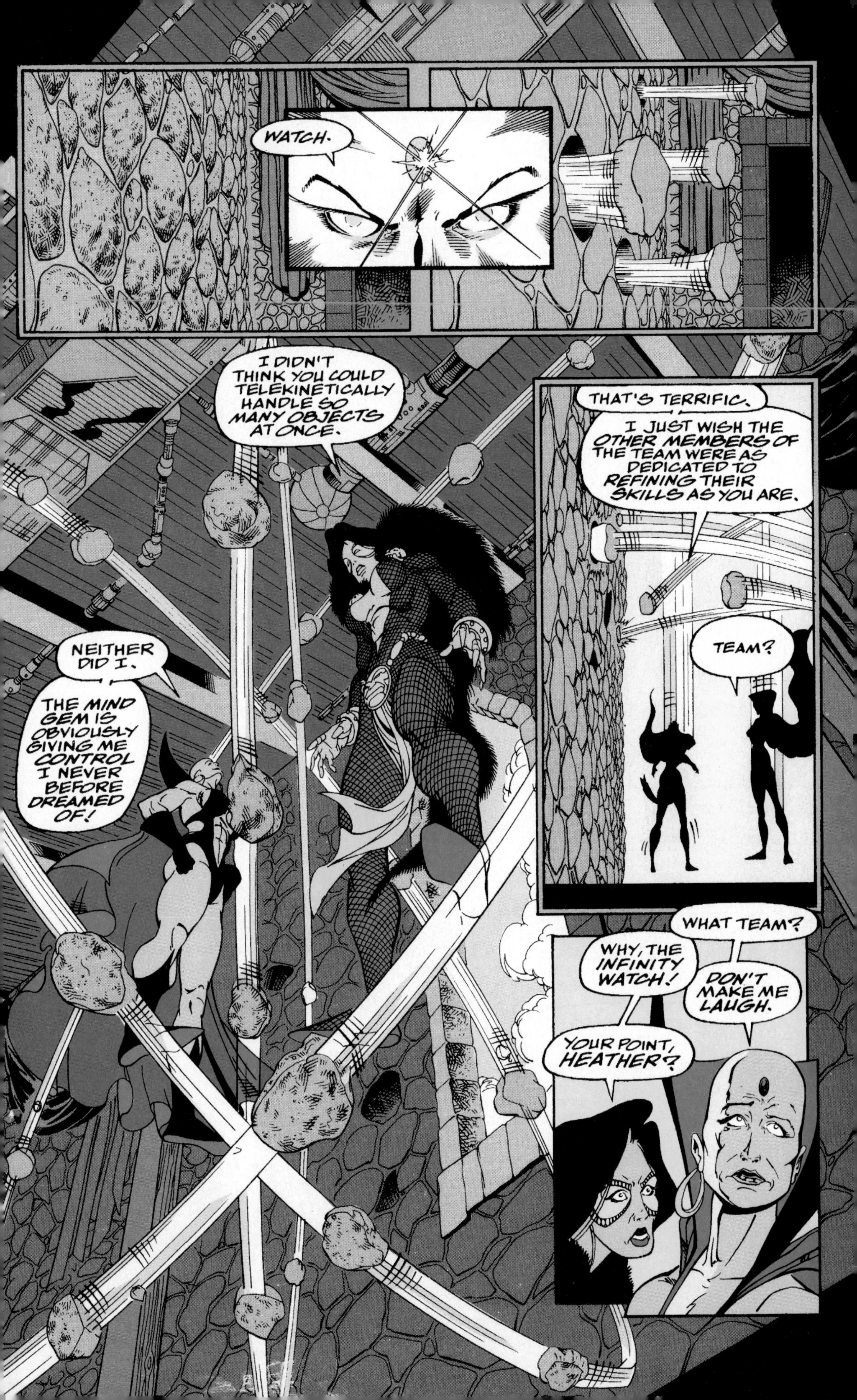
WATCH.
I DIDN'T THINK YOU COULD TELEKINETICALLY HANDLE SO MANY OBJECTS AT ONCE.
NEITHER DID I.
THE MIND GEM IS OBVIOUSLY GIVING ME CONTROL I NEVER BEFORE DREAMED OF!
THAT'S TERRIFIC.
I JUST WISH THE OTHER MEMBERS OF THE TEAM WERE AS DEDICATED TO REFINING THEIR SKILLS AS YOU ARE.
TEAM?
WHAT TEAM?
WHY, THE INFINITY WATCH!
DON'T MAKE ME LAUGH.
YOUR POINT, HEATHER?

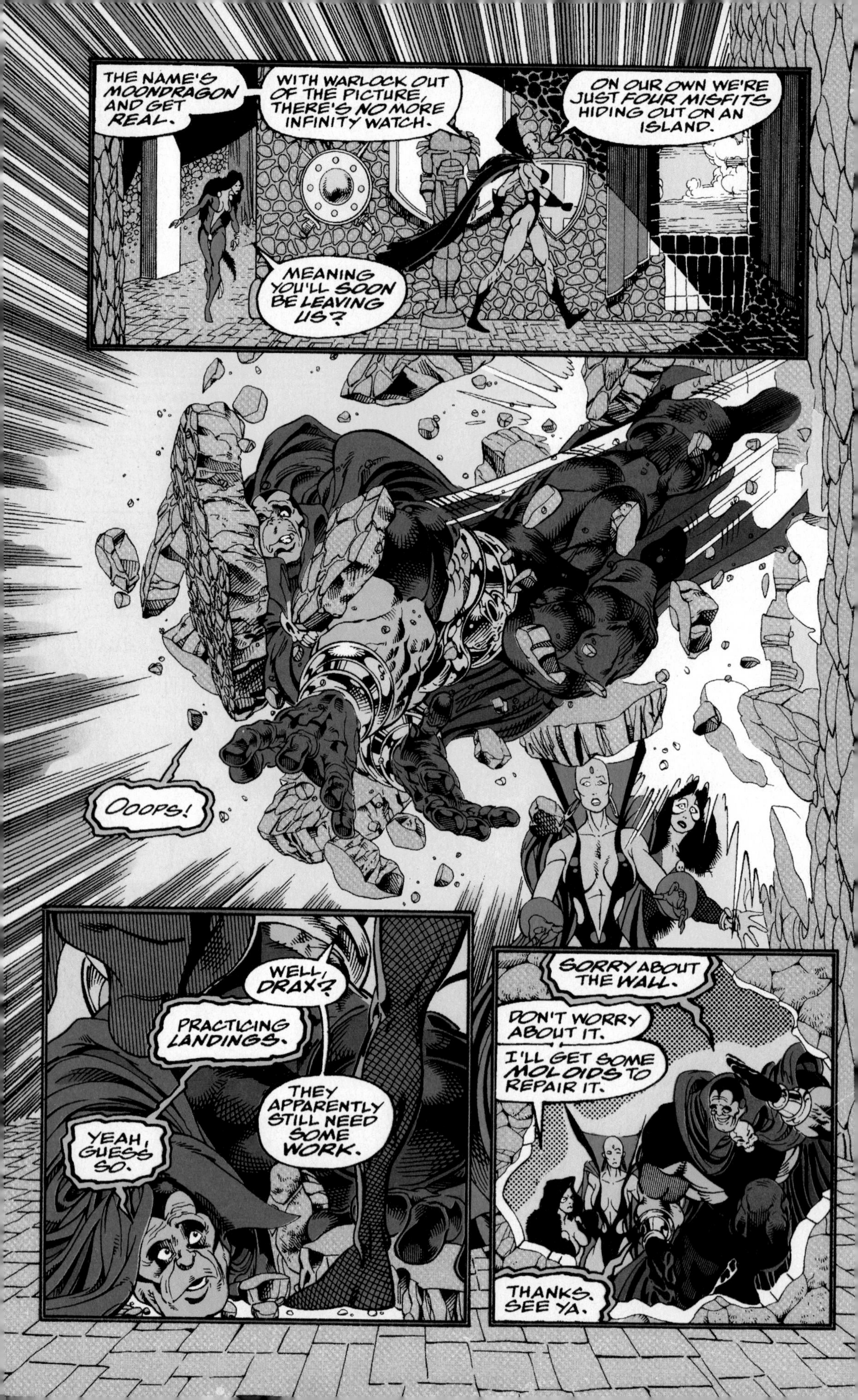
THE NAME'S MOONDRAGON AND GET REAL.
WITH WARLOCK OUT OF THE PICTURE, THERE'S NO MORE INFINITY WATCH.
ON OUR OWN WE'RE JUST FOUR MISFITS HIDING OUT ON AN ISLAND.
MEANING YOU'LL SOON BE LEAVING US?
OOOPS!
WELL, DRAX?
PRACTICING LANDINGS.
THEY APPARENTLY STILL NEED SOME WORK.
YEAH, GUESS SO.
SORRY ABOUT THE WALL.
DON'T WORRY ABOUT IT.
I'LL GET SOME MOLOIDS TO REPAIR IT.
THANKS. SEE YA.

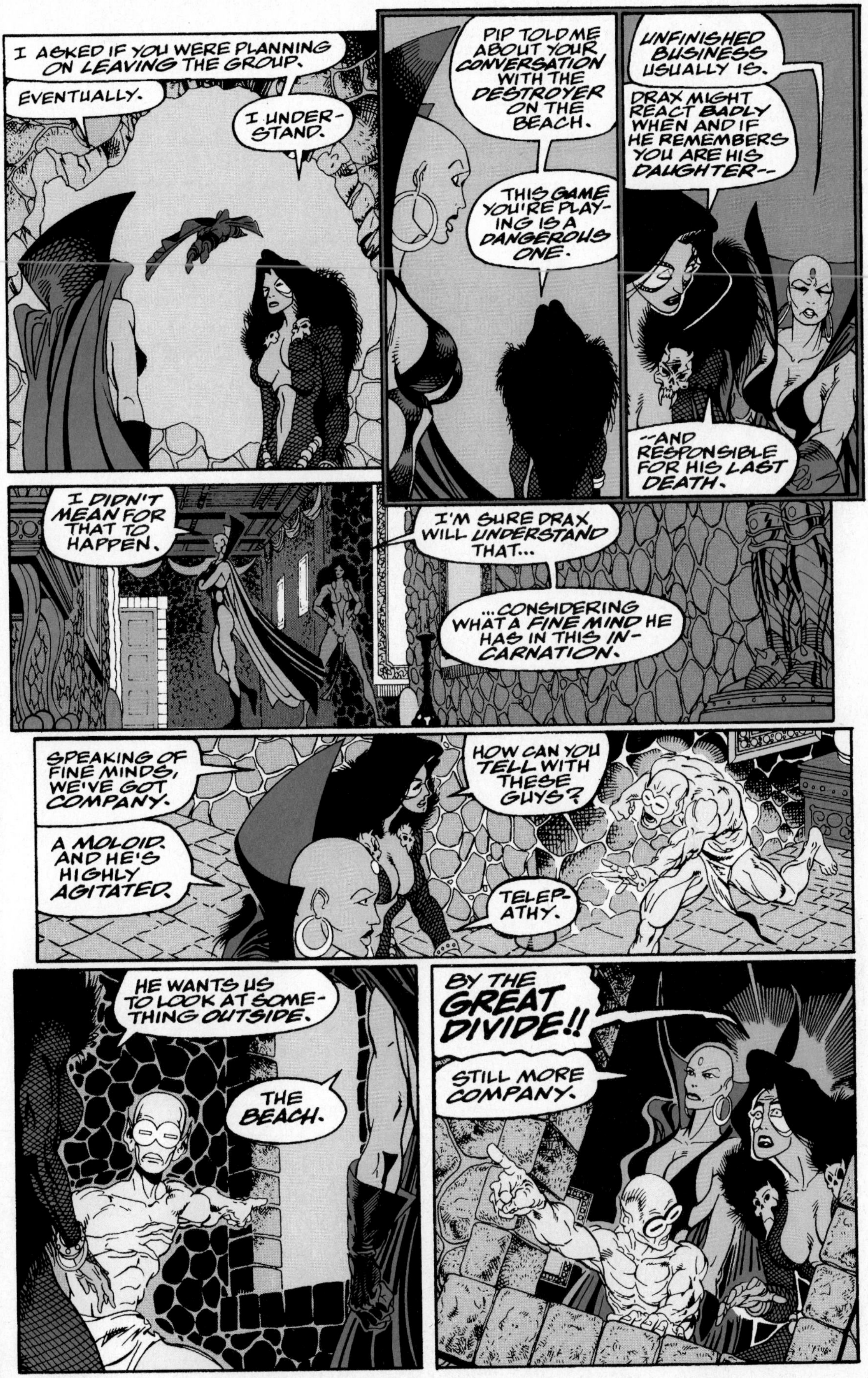
I ASKED IF YOU WERE PLANNING ON LEAVING THE GROUP.
EVENTUALLY.
I UNDERSTAND.
PIP TOLD ME ABOUT YOUR CONVERSATION WITH THE DESTROYER ON THE BEACH.
THIS GAME YOU'RE PLAYING IS A DANGEROUS ONE.
UNFINISHED BUSINESS USUALLY IS.
DRAX MIGHT REACT BADLY WHEN AND IF HE REMEMBERS YOU ARE HIS DAUGHTER--
--AND RESPONSIBLE FOR HIS LAST DEATH.
I DIDN'T MEAN FOR THAT TO HAPPEN.
I'M SURE DRAX WILL UNDERSTAND THAT...
...CONSIDERING WHAT A FINE MIND HE HAS IN THIS INCARNATION.
SPEAKING OF FINE MINDS, WE'VE GOT COMPANY.
A MOLOID. AND HE'S HIGHLY AGITATED.
HOW CAN YOU TELL WITH THESE GUYS?
TELEPATHY.
HE WANTS US TO LOOK AT SOMETHING OUTSIDE.
THE BEACH.
BY THE GREAT DIVIDE!!
STILL MORE COMPANY.

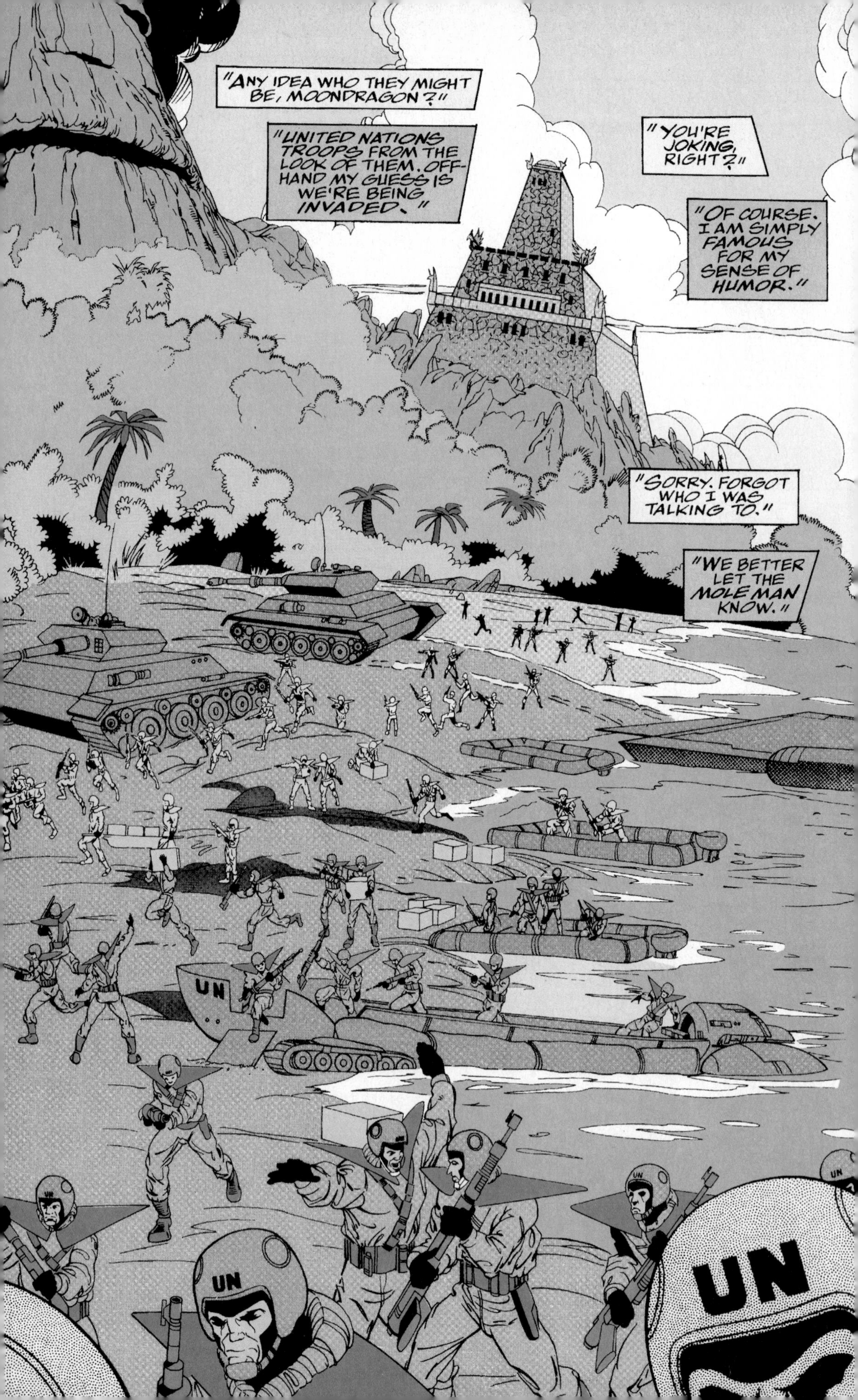
"ANY IDEA WHO THEY MIGHT BE, MOONDRAGON?"
"UNITED NATIONS TROOPS FROM THE LOOK OF THEM. OFF-HAND MY GUESS IS WE'RE BEING INVADED."
"YOU'RE JOKING, RIGHT?"
"OF COURSE. I AM SIMPLY FAMOUS FOR MY SENSE OF HUMOR."
"SORRY. FORGOT WHO I WAS TALKING TO."
"WE BETTER LET THE MOLE MAN KNOW."
UN

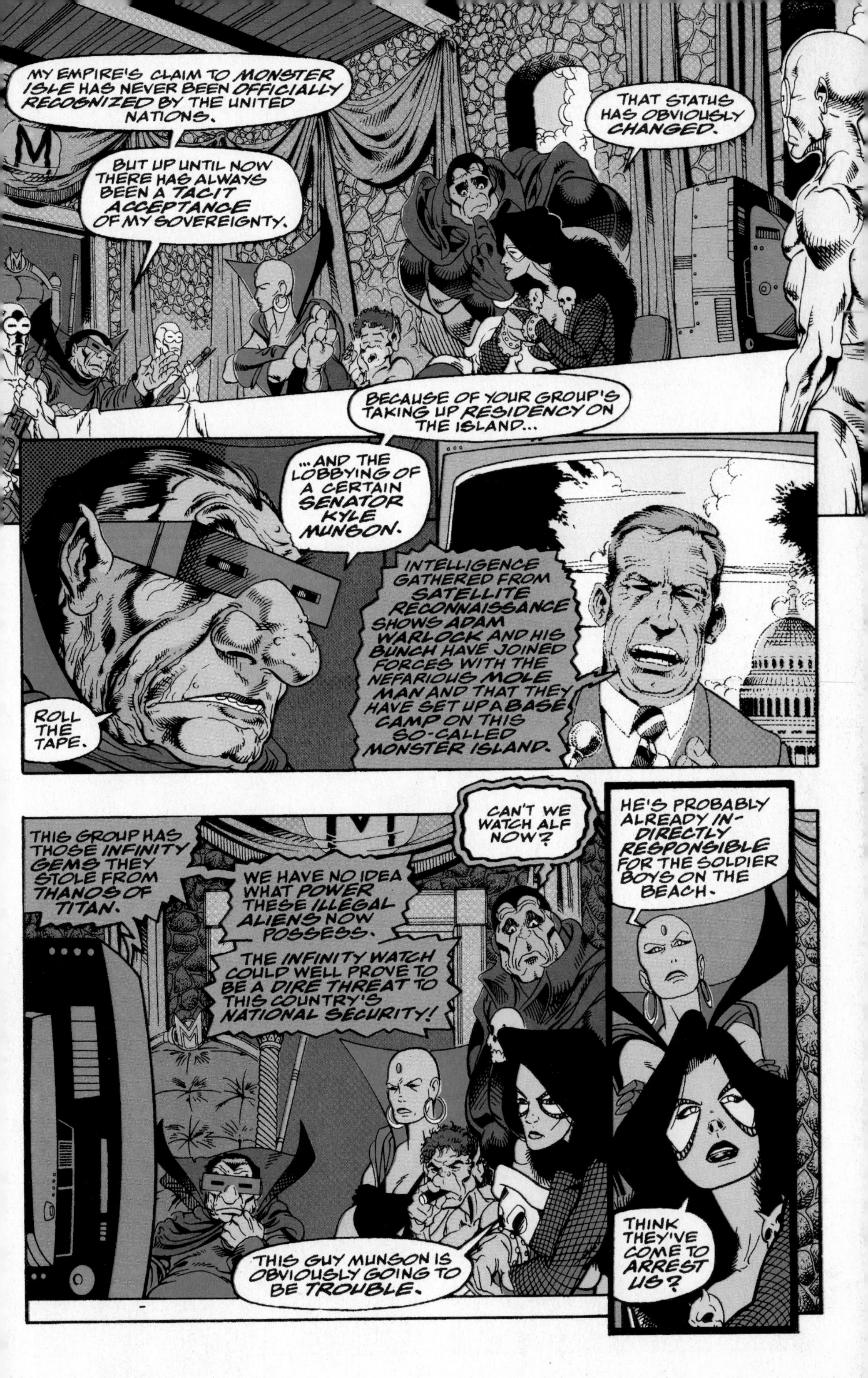
MY EMPIRE'S CLAIM TO MONSTER ISLE HAS NEVER BEEN OFFICIALLY RECOGNIZED BY THE UNITED NATIONS.
BUT UP UNTIL NOW THERE HAS ALWAYS BEEN A TACIT ACCEPTANCE OF MY SOVEREIGNTY.
THAT STATUS HAS OBVIOUSLY CHANGED.
BECAUSE OF YOUR GROUP'S TAKING UP RESIDENCY ON THE ISLAND...
...AND THE LOBBYING OF A CERTAIN SENATOR KYLE MUNSON.
ROLL THE TAPE.
INTELLIGENCE GATHERED FROM SATELLITE RECONNAISSANCE SHOWS ADAM WARLOCK AND HIS BUNCH HAVE JOINED FORCES WITH THE NEFARIOUS MOLE MAN AND THAT THEY HAVE SET UP A BASE CAMP ON THIS SO-CALLED MONSTER ISLAND.
THIS GROUP HAS THOSE INFINITY GEMS THEY STOLE FROM THANOS OF TITAN.
WE HAVE NO IDEA WHAT POWER THESE ILLEGAL ALIENS NOW POSSESS.
THE INFINITY WATCH COULD WELL PROVE TO BE A DIRE THREAT TO THIS COUNTRY'S NATIONAL SECURITY!
CAN'T WE WATCH ALF NOW?
HE'S PROBABLY ALREADY INDIRECTLY RESPONSIBLE FOR THE SOLDIER BOYS ON THE BEACH.
THIS GUY MUNSON IS OBVIOUSLY GOING TO BE TROUBLE.
THINK THEY'VE COME TO ARREST US?

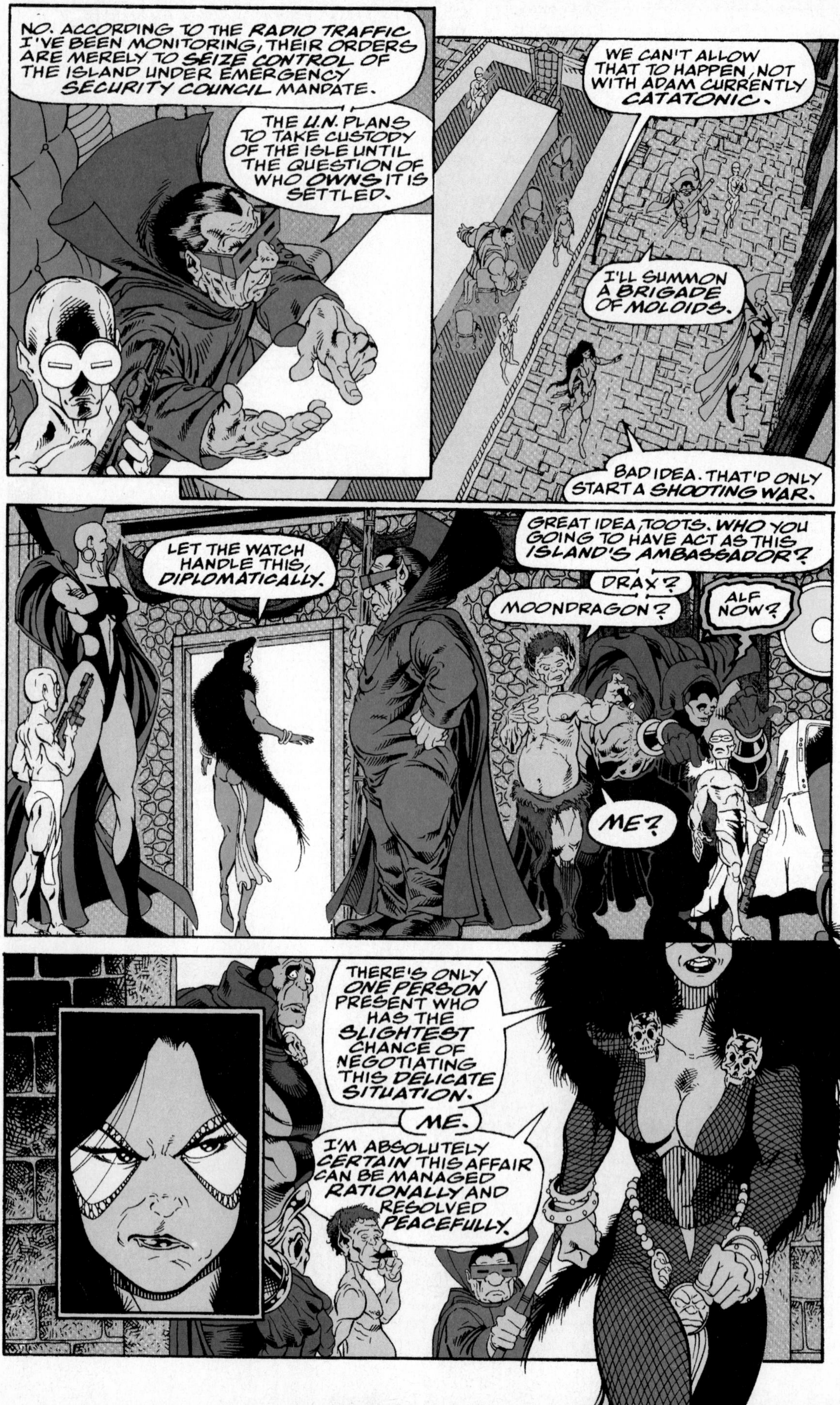
NO. ACCORDING TO THE RADIO TRAFFIC I'VE BEEN MONITORING, THEIR ORDERS ARE MERELY TO SEIZE CONTROL OF THE ISLAND UNDER EMERGENCY SECURITY COUNCIL MANDATE.
THE U.N. PLANS TO TAKE CUSTODY OF THE ISLE UNTIL THE QUESTION OF WHO OWNS IT IS SETTLED.
WE CAN'T ALLOW THAT TO HAPPEN, NOT WITH ADAM CURRENTLY CATATONIC.
I'LL SUMMON A BRIGADE OF MOLOIDS.
BAD IDEA. THAT'D ONLY START A SHOOTING WAR.
LET THE WATCH HANDLE THIS, DIPLOMATICALLY.
GREAT IDEA, TOOTS. WHO YOU GOING TO HAVE ACT AS THIS ISLAND'S AMBASSADOR?
DRAX?
MOONDRAGON?
ALF NOW?
ME?
THERE'S ONLY ONE PERSON PRESENT WHO HAS THE SLIGHTEST CHANCE OF NEGOTIATING THIS DELICATE SITUATION.
ME.
I'M ABSOLUTELY CERTAIN THIS AFFAIR CAN BE MANAGED RATIONALLY AND RESOLVED PEACEFULLY.

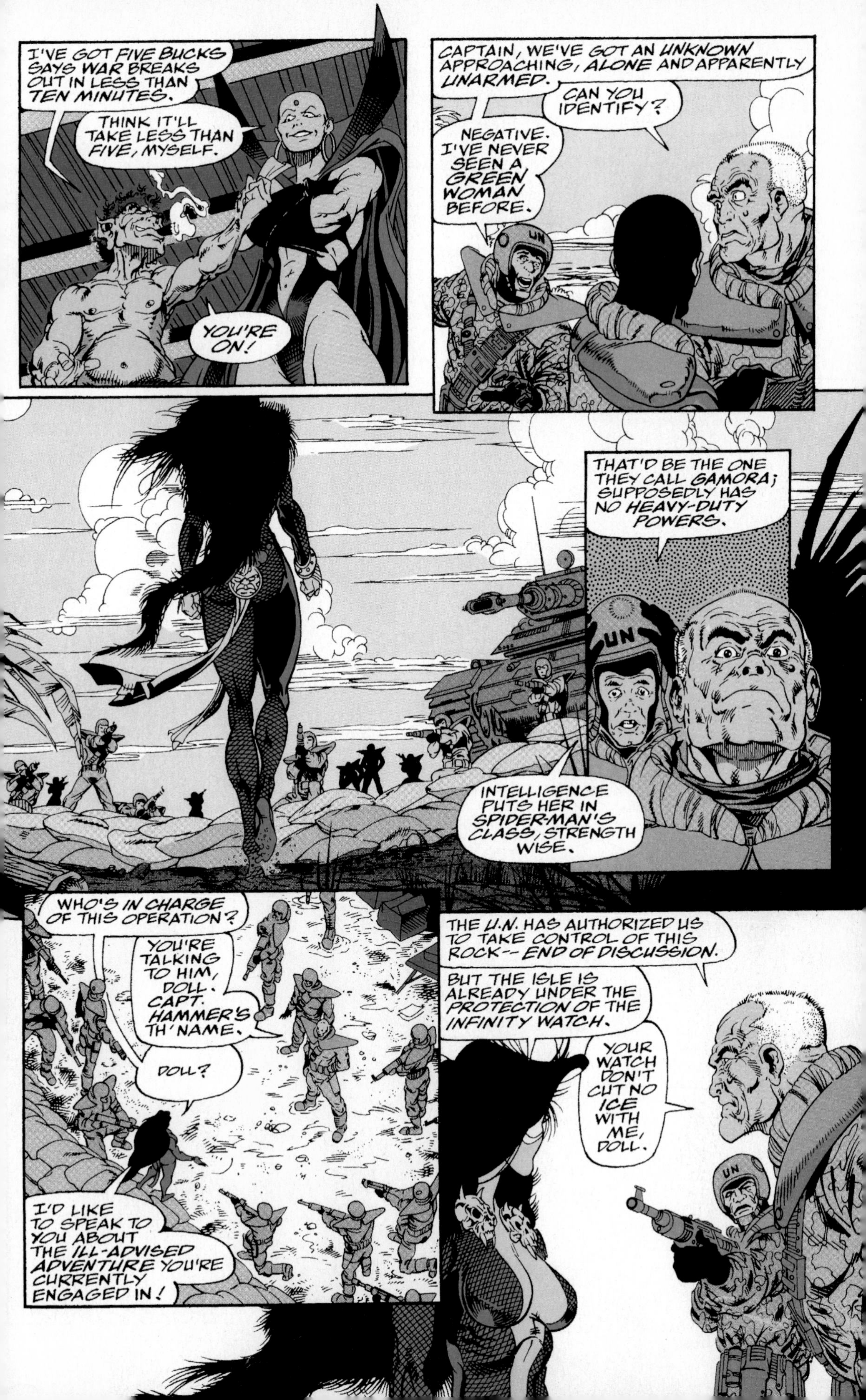
I'VE GOT FIVE BUCKS SAYS WAR BREAKS OUT IN LESS THAN TEN MINUTES.
THINK IT'LL TAKE LESS THAN FIVE, MYSELF.
YOU'RE ON!
CAPTAIN, WE'VE GOT AN UNKNOWN APPROACHING, ALONE AND APPARENTLY UNARMED.
CAN YOU IDENTIFY?
NEGATIVE. I'VE NEVER SEEN A GREEN WOMAN BEFORE.
THAT'D BE THE ONE THEY CALL GAMORA; SUPPOSEDLY HAS NO HEAVY-DUTY POWERS.
INTELLIGENCE PUTS HER IN SPIDER-MAN'S CLASS, STRENGTH WISE.
WHO'S IN CHARGE OF THIS OPERATION?
YOU'RE TALKING TO HIM, DOLL. CAPT. HAMMER'S TH' NAME.
DOLL?
I'D LIKE TO SPEAK TO YOU ABOUT THE ILL-ADVISED ADVENTURE YOU'RE CURRENTLY ENGAGED IN!
THE U.N. HAS AUTHORIZED US TO TAKE CONTROL OF THIS ROCK-- END OF DISCUSSION.
BUT THE ISLE IS ALREADY UNDER THE PROTECTION OF THE INFINITY WATCH.
YOUR WATCH DON'T CUT NO ICE WITH ME, DOLL.
UN

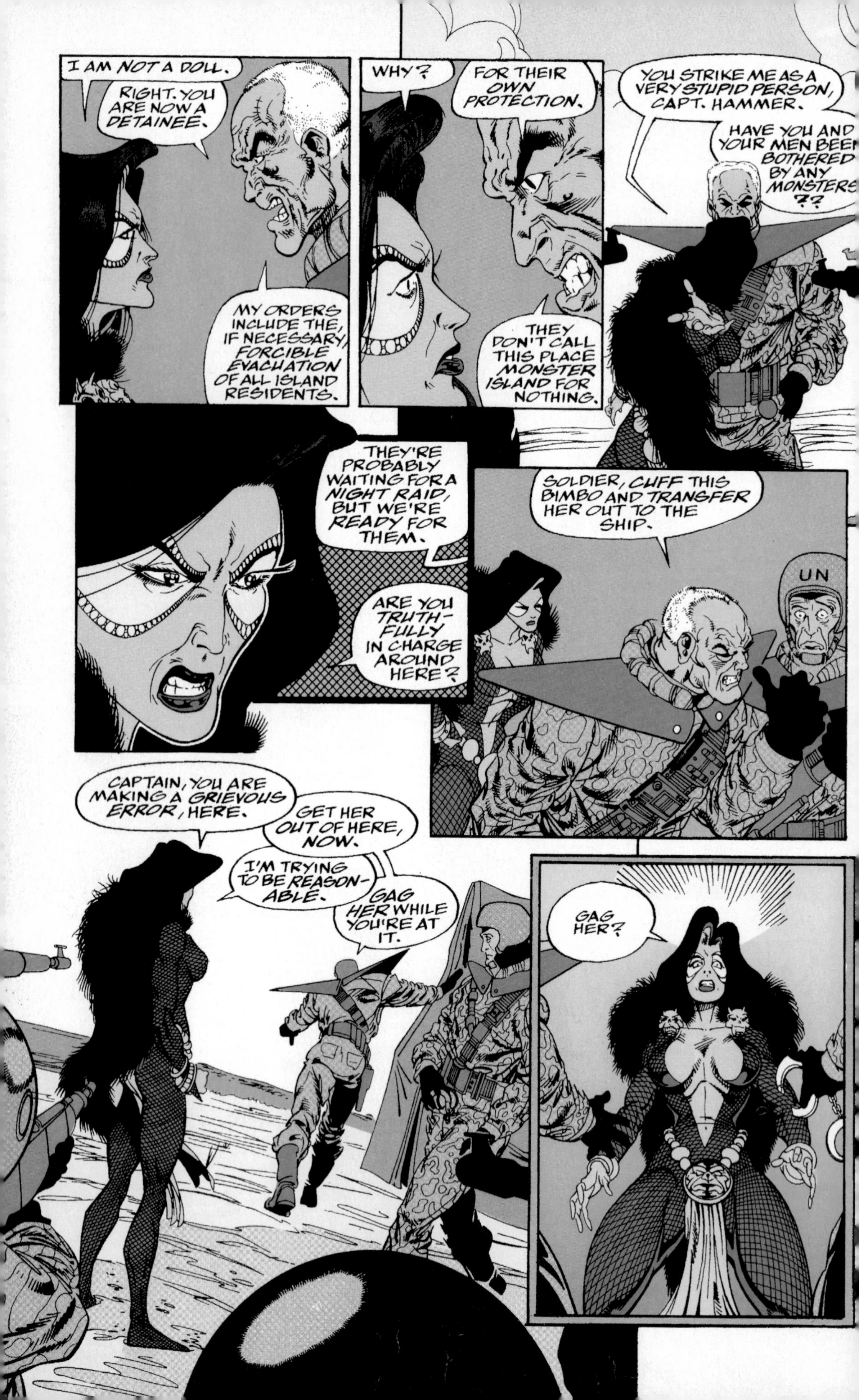
I AM NOT A DOLL.
RIGHT. YOU ARE NOW A DETAINEE.
MY ORDERS INCLUDE THE, IF NECESSARY, FORCIBLE EVACUATION OF ALL ISLAND RESIDENTS.
WHY?
FOR THEIR OWN PROTECTION.
THEY DON'T CALL THIS PLACE MONSTER ISLAND FOR NOTHING.
YOU STRIKE ME AS A VERY STUPID PERSON, CAPT. HAMMER.
HAVE YOU AND YOUR MEN BEEN BOTHERED BY ANY MONSTERS??
THEY'RE PROBABLY WAITING FOR A NIGHT RAID, BUT WE'RE READY FOR THEM.
ARE YOU TRUTHFULLY IN CHARGE AROUND HERE?
SOLDIER, CUFF THIS BIMBO AND TRANSFER HER OUT TO THE SHIP.
UN
CAPTAIN, YOU ARE MAKING A GRIEVOUS ERROR, HERE.
GET HER OUT OF HERE, NOW.
I'M TRYING TO BE REASONABLE.
GAG HER WHILE YOU'RE AT IT.
GAG HER?

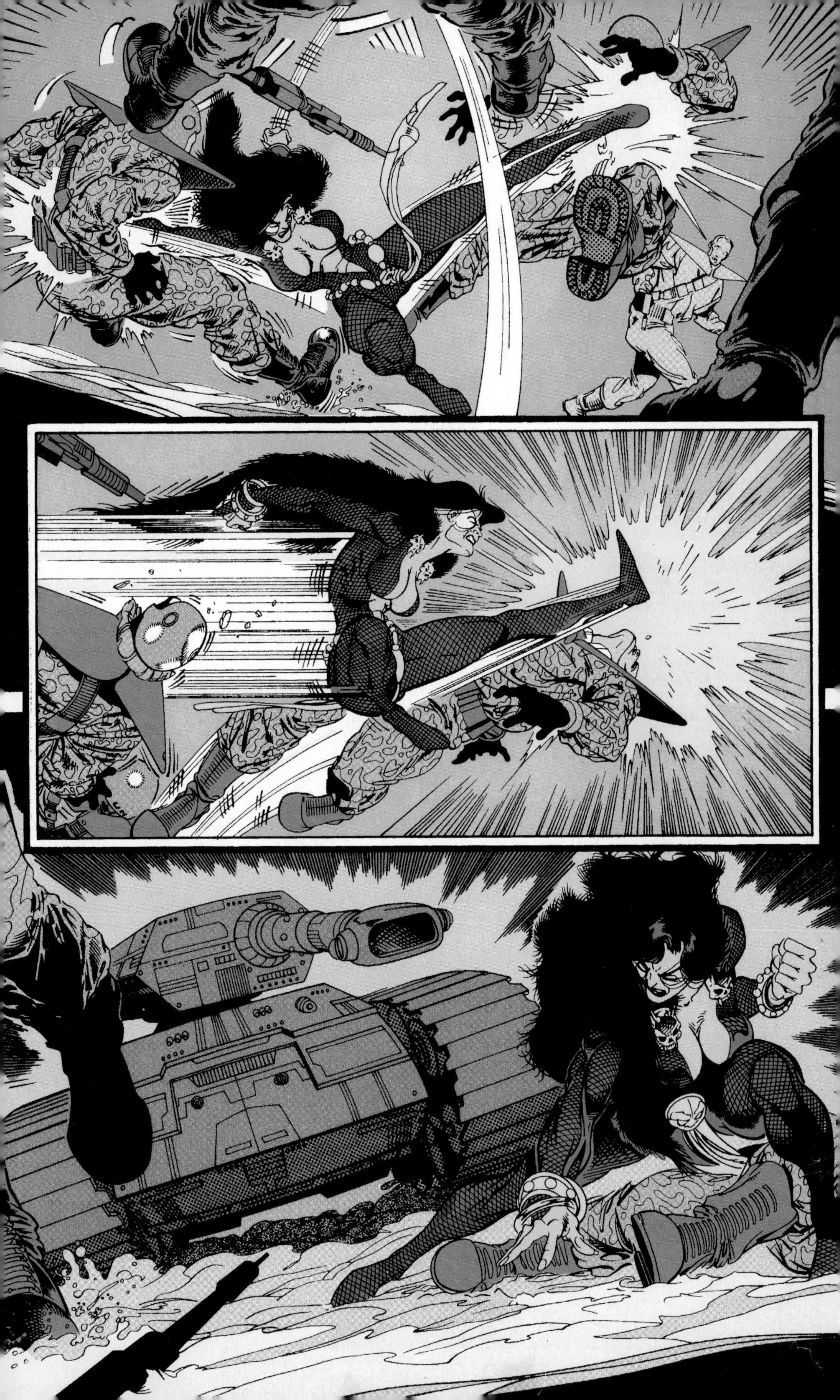

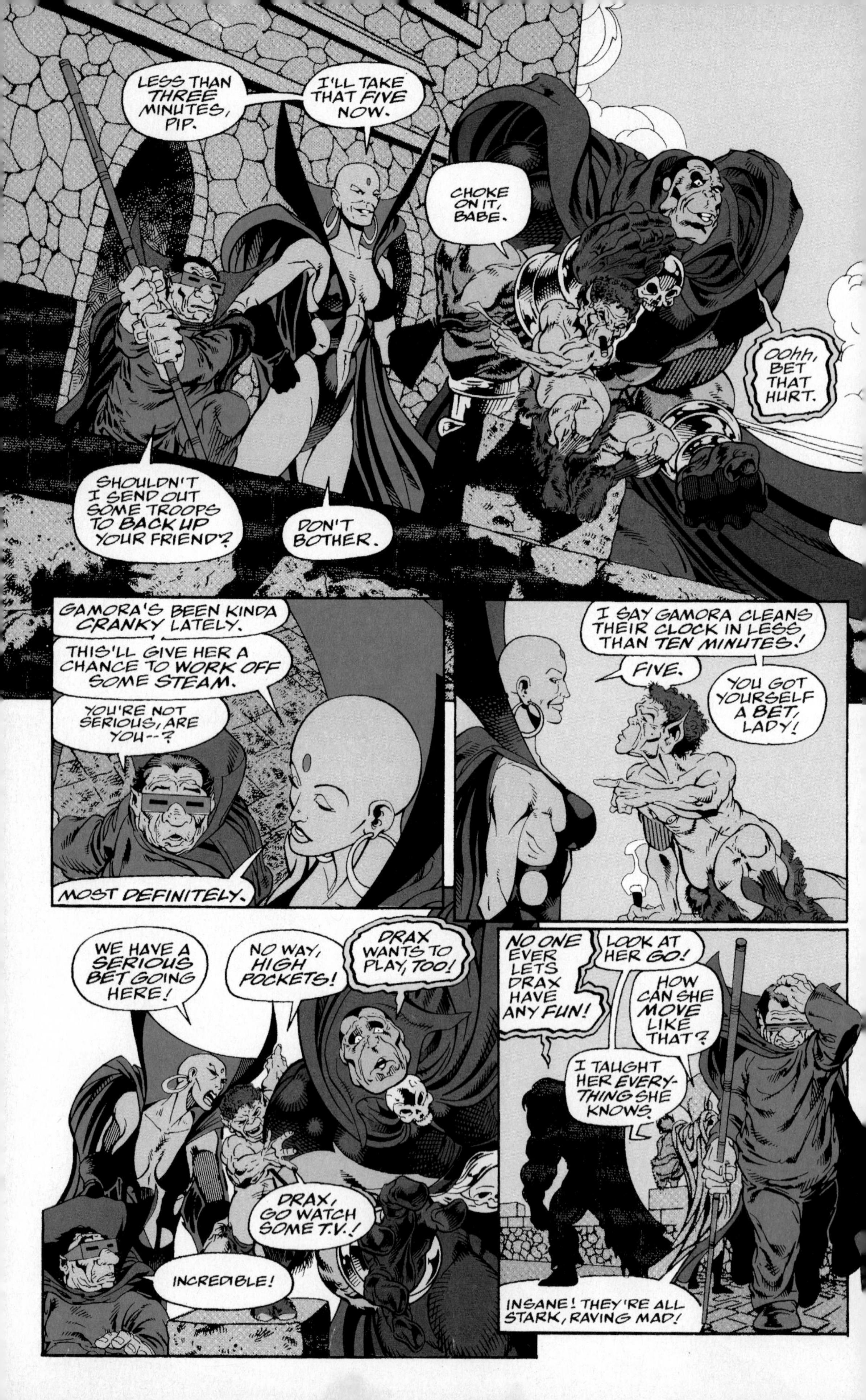
LESS THAN THREE MINUTES, PIP.
I'LL TAKE THAT FIVE NOW.
CHOKE ON IT, BABE.
Oohh, BET THAT HURT.
SHOULDN'T I SEND OUT SOME TROOPS TO BACK UP YOUR FRIEND?
DON'T BOTHER.
GAMORA'S BEEN KINDA CRANKY LATELY.
THIS'LL GIVE HER A CHANCE TO WORK OFF SOME STEAM.
YOU'RE NOT SERIOUS, ARE YOU--?
MOST DEFINITELY.
I SAY GAMORA CLEANS THEIR CLOCK IN LESS THAN TEN MINUTES!
FIVE.
YOU GOT YOURSELF A BET, LADY!
WE HAVE A SERIOUS BET GOING HERE!
NO WAY, HIGH POCKETS!
DRAX WANTS TO PLAY, TOO!
DRAX, GO WATCH SOME T.V.!
INCREDIBLE!
NO ONE EVER LETS DRAX HAVE ANY FUN!
LOOK AT HER GO!
HOW CAN SHE MOVE LIKE THAT?
I TAUGHT HER EVERY-THING SHE KNOWS.
INSANE! THEY'RE ALL STARK, RAVING MAD!

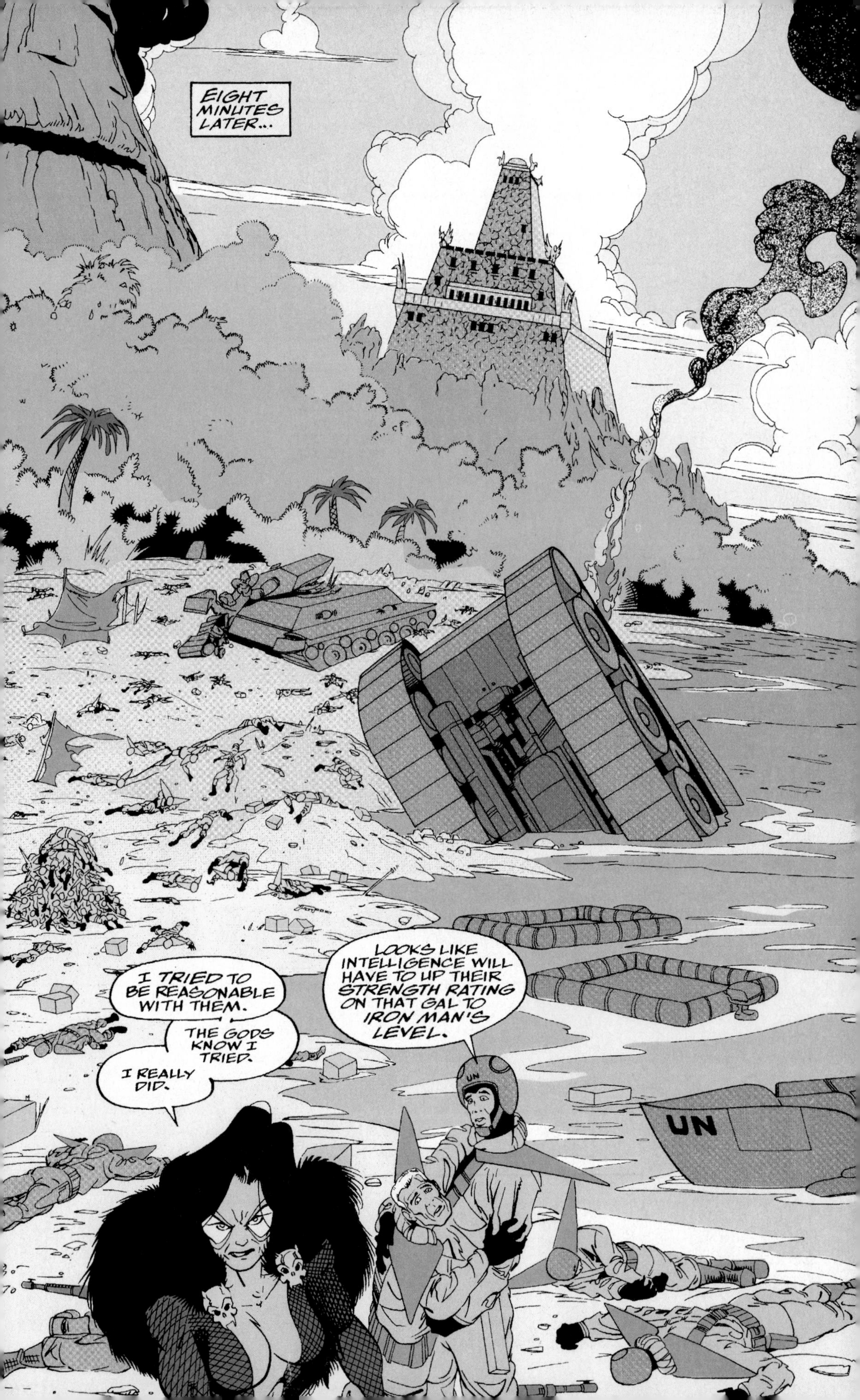
EIGHT MINUTES LATER...
I TRIED TO BE REASONABLE WITH THEM.
THE GODS KNOW I TRIED.
I REALLY DID.
LOOKS LIKE INTELLIGENCE WILL HAVE TO UP THEIR STRENGTH RATING ON THAT GAL TO IRON MAN'S LEVEL.
UN
UN

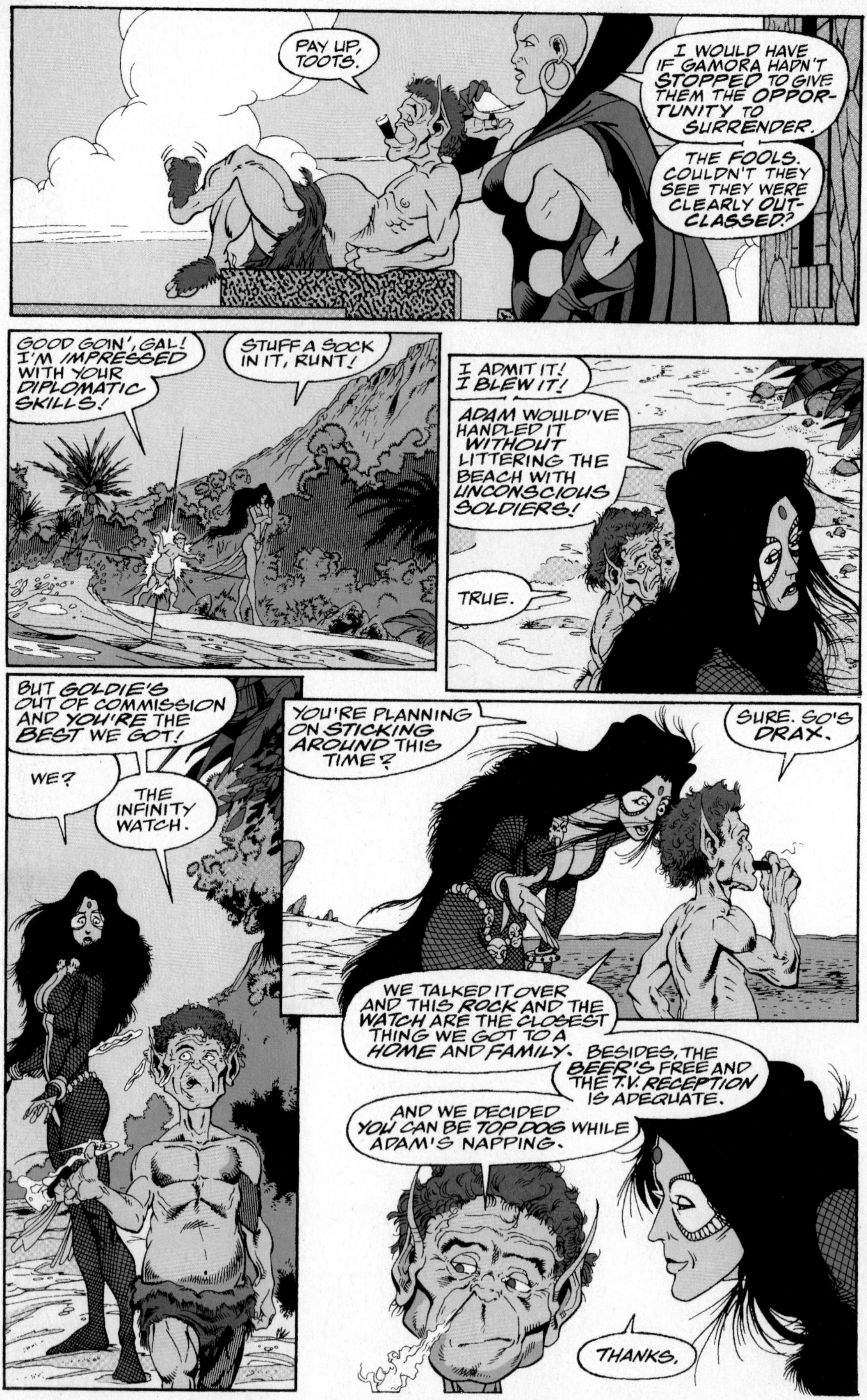
PAY UP, TOOTS.
I WOULD HAVE IF GAMORA HADN'T STOPPED TO GIVE THEM THE OPPORTUNITY TO SURRENDER.
THE FOOLS. COULDN'T THEY SEE THEY WERE CLEARLY OUTCLASSED?
GOOD GOIN', GAL! I'M IMPRESSED WITH YOUR DIPLOMATIC SKILLS!
STUFF A SOCK IN IT, RUNT!
I ADMIT IT! I BLEW IT!
ADAM WOULD'VE HANDLED IT WITHOUT LITTERING THE BEACH WITH UNCONSCIOUS SOLDIERS!
TRUE.
BUT GOLDIE'S OUT OF COMMISSION AND YOU'RE THE BEST WE GOT!
WE?
THE INFINITY WATCH.
YOU'RE PLANNING ON STICKING AROUND THIS TIME?
SURE. SO'S DRAX.
WE TALKED IT OVER AND THIS ROCK AND THE WATCH ARE THE CLOSEST THING WE GOT TO A HOME AND FAMILY.
BESIDES, THE BEER'S FREE AND THE T.V. RECEPTION IS ADEQUATE.
AND WE DECIDED YOU CAN BE TOP DOG WHILE ADAM'S NAPPING.
THANKS.

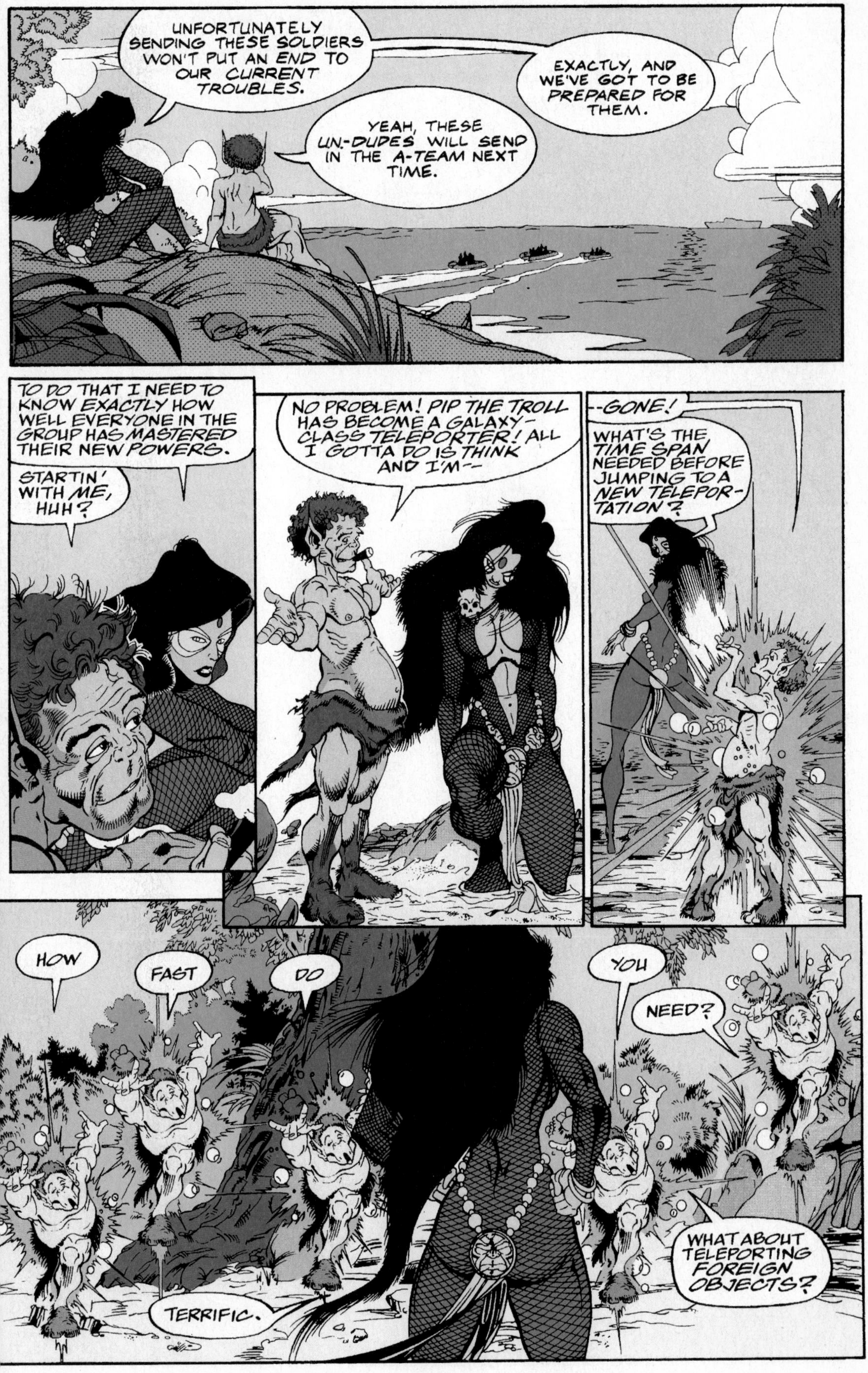
UNFORTUNATELY SENDING THESE SOLDIERS WON'T PUT AN END TO OUR CURRENT TROUBLES.
YEAH, THESE UN-DUDES WILL SEND IN THE A-TEAM NEXT TIME.
EXACTLY, AND WE'VE GOT TO BE PREPARED FOR THEM.
TO DO THAT I NEED TO KNOW EXACTLY HOW WELL EVERYONE IN THE GROUP HAS MASTERED THEIR NEW POWERS.
STARTIN' WITH ME, HUH?
NO PROBLEM! PIP THE TROLL HAS BECOME A GALAXY-CLASS TELEPORTER! ALL I GOTTA DO IS THINK AND I'M--
--GONE!
WHAT'S THE TIME SPAN NEEDED BEFORE JUMPING TO A NEW TELEPORTATION?
HOW
FAST
DO
YOU
NEED?
TERRIFIC.
WHAT ABOUT TELEPORTING FOREIGN OBJECTS?

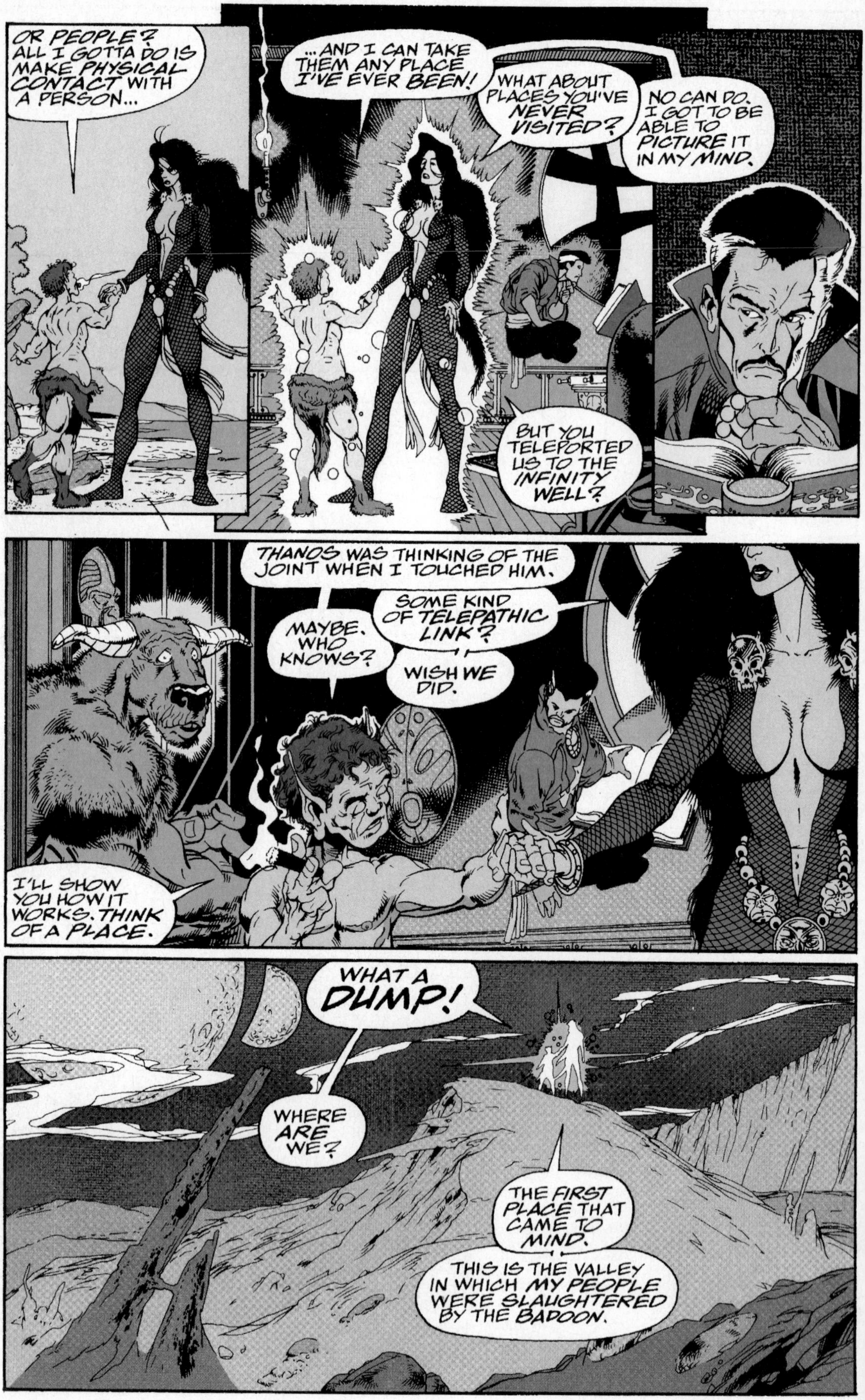
OR PEOPLE? ALL I GOTTA DO IS MAKE PHYSICAL CONTACT WITH A PERSON...
...AND I CAN TAKE THEM ANY PLACE I'VE EVER BEEN!
WHAT ABOUT PLACES YOU'VE NEVER VISITED?
NO CAN DO. I GOT TO BE ABLE TO PICTURE IT IN MY MIND.
BUT YOU TELEPORTED US TO THE INFINITY WELL?
THANOS WAS THINKING OF THE JOINT WHEN I TOUCHED HIM.
SOME KIND OF TELEPATHIC LINK?
MAYBE. WHO KNOWS?
WISH WE DID.
I'LL SHOW YOU HOW IT WORKS. THINK OF A PLACE.
WHAT A DUMP!
WHERE ARE WE?
THE FIRST PLACE THAT CAME TO MIND.
THIS IS THE VALLEY IN WHICH MY PEOPLE WERE SLAUGHTERED BY THE BADOON.

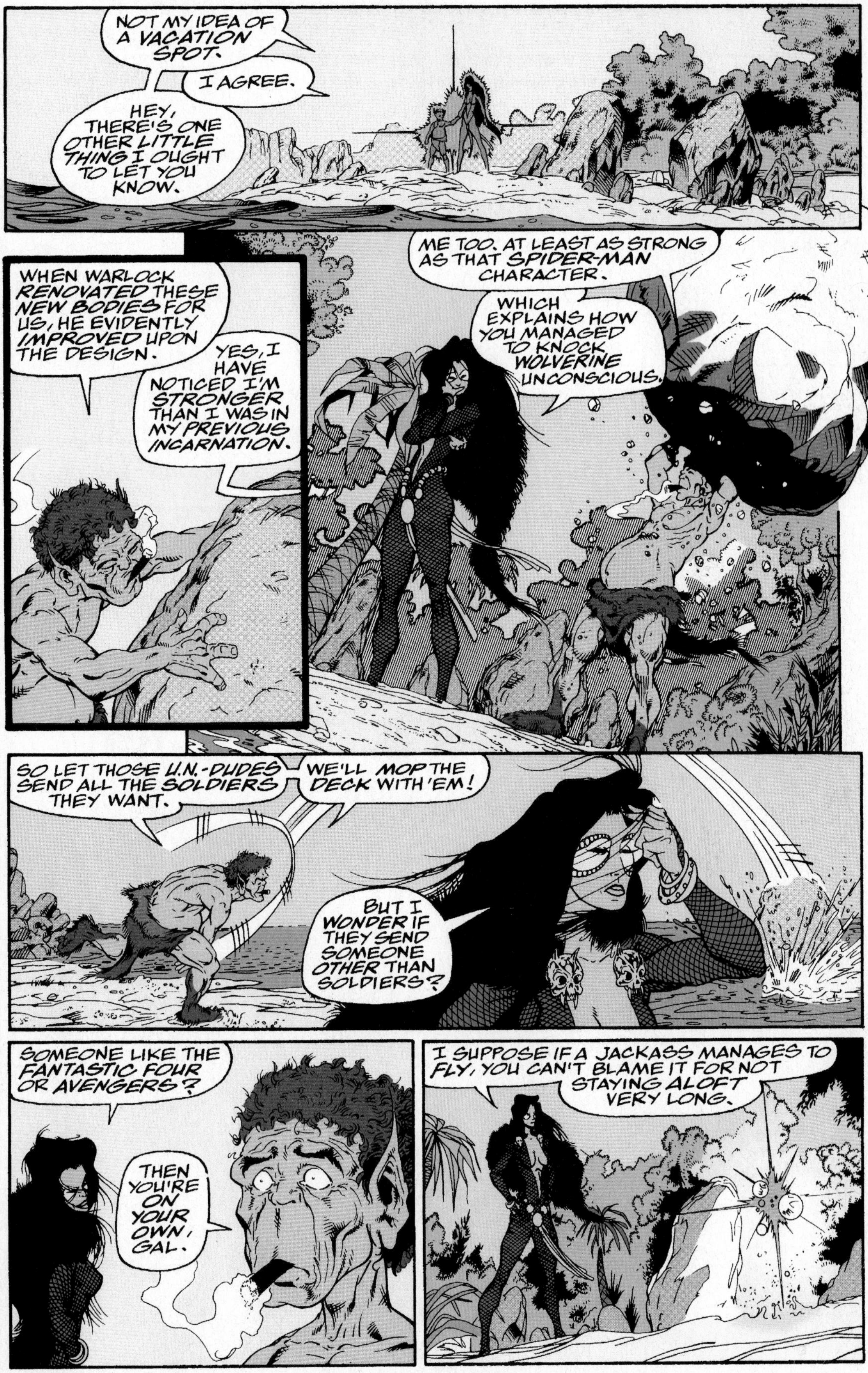
NOT MY IDEA OF A VACATION SPOT.
I AGREE.
HEY, THERE'S ONE OTHER LITTLE THING I OUGHT TO LET YOU KNOW.
WHEN WARLOCK RENOVATED THESE NEW BODIES FOR US, HE EVIDENTLY IMPROVED UPON THE DESIGN.
YES, I HAVE NOTICED I'M STRONGER THAN I WAS IN MY PREVIOUS INCARNATION.
ME TOO. AT LEAST AS STRONG AS THAT SPIDER-MAN CHARACTER.
WHICH EXPLAINS HOW YOU MANAGED TO KNOCK WOLVERINE UNCONSCIOUS.
SO LET THOSE U.N.-DUDES SEND ALL THE SOLDIERS THEY WANT.
WE'LL MOP THE DECK WITH 'EM!
BUT I WONDER IF THEY SEND SOMEONE OTHER THAN SOLDIERS?
SOMEONE LIKE THE FANTASTIC FOUR OR AVENGERS?
THEN YOU'RE ON YOUR OWN, GAL.
I SUPPOSE IF A JACKASS MANAGES TO FLY, YOU CAN'T BLAME IT FOR NOT STAYING ALOFT VERY LONG.

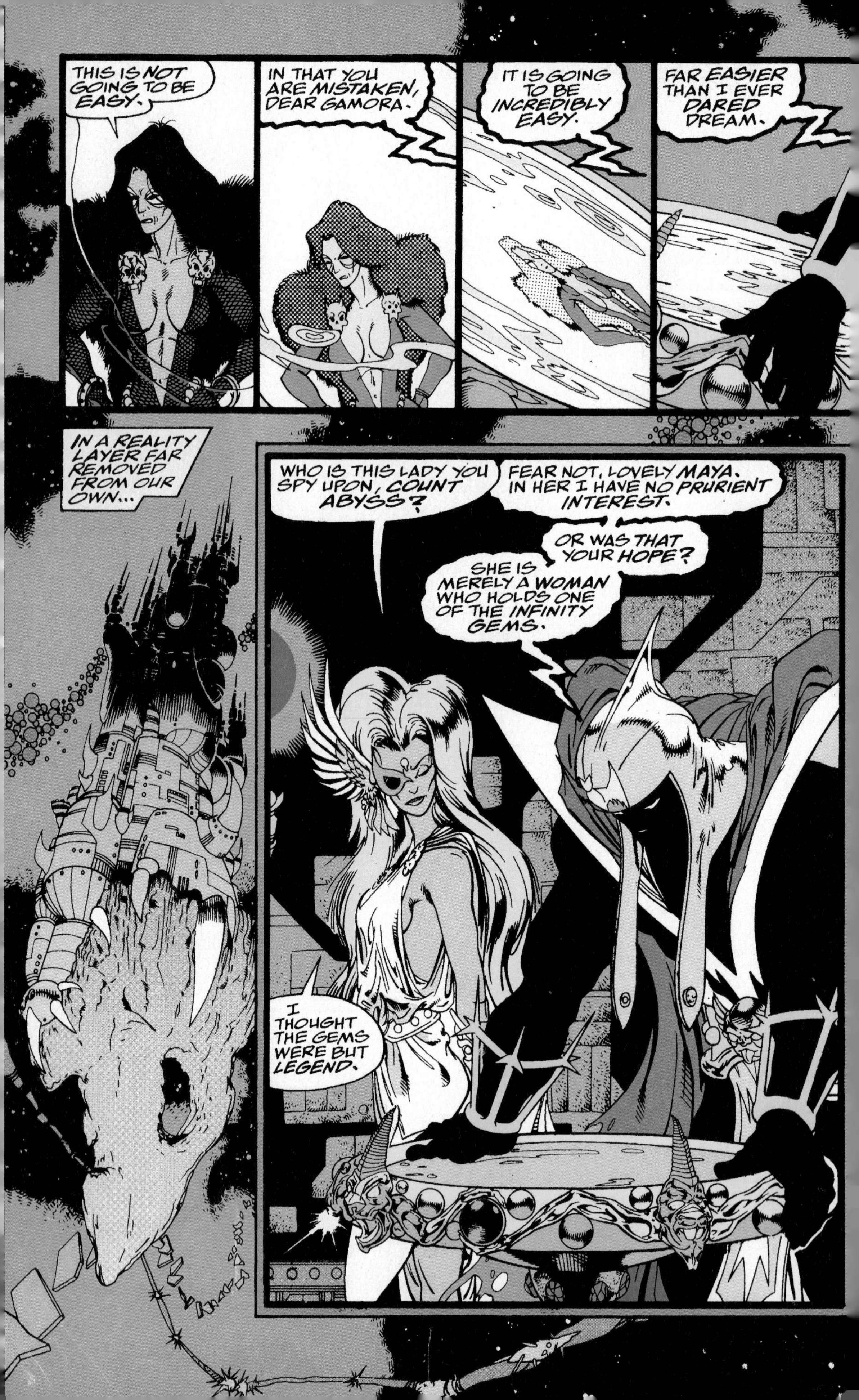
THIS IS NOT GOING TO BE EASY.
IN THAT YOU ARE MISTAKEN, DEAR GAMORA.
IT IS GOING TO BE INCREDIBLY EASY.
FAR EASIER THAN I EVER DARED DREAM.
IN A REALITY LAYER FAR REMOVED FROM OUR OWN...
WHO IS THIS LADY YOU SPY UPON, COUNT ABYSS?
FEAR NOT, LOVELY MAYA. IN HER I HAVE NO PRURIENT INTEREST.
OR WAS THAT YOUR HOPE?
SHE IS MERELY A WOMAN WHO HOLDS ONE OF THE INFINITY GEMS.
I THOUGHT THE GEMS WERE BUT LEGEND.

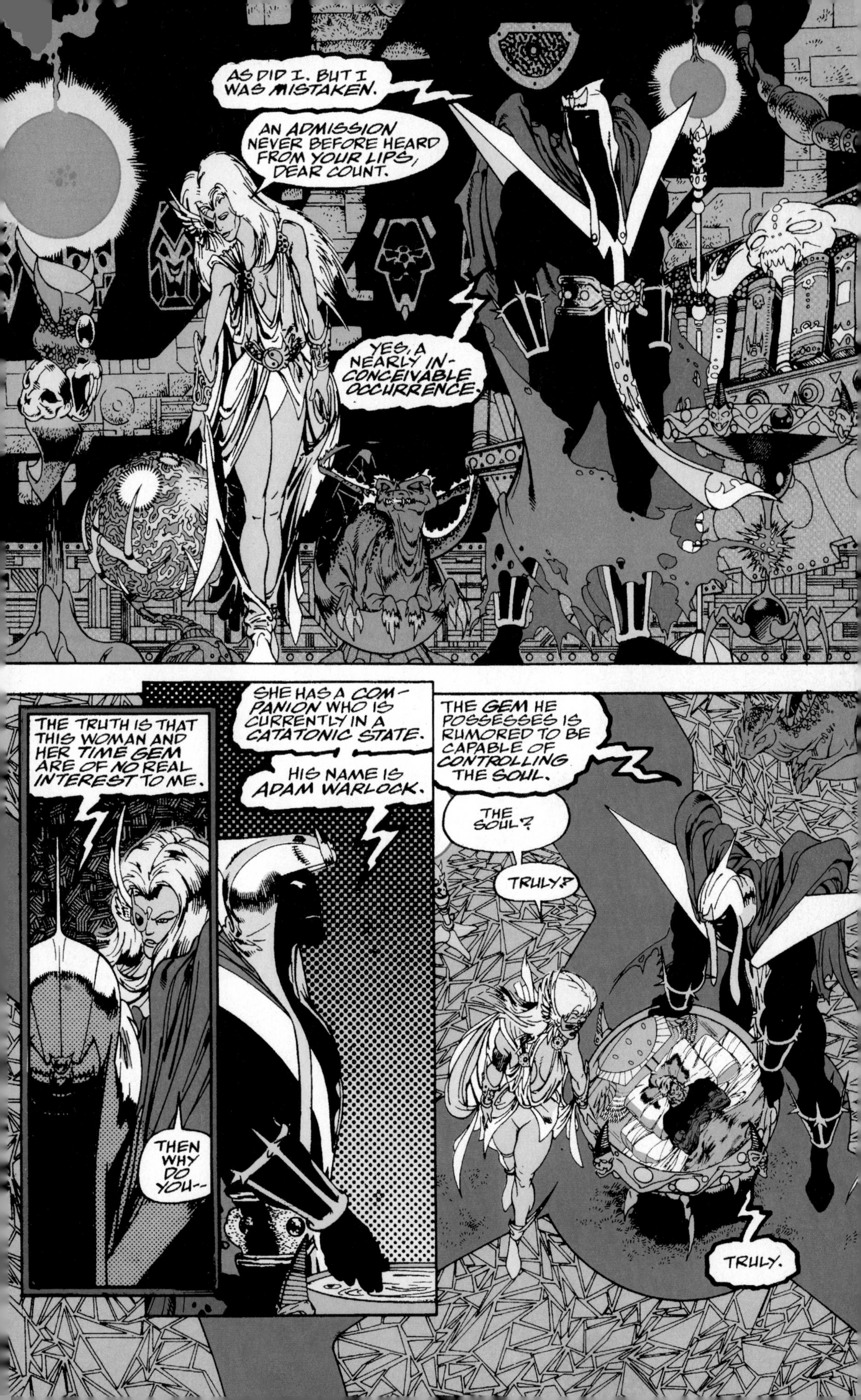
AS DID I. BUT I WAS MISTAKEN.
AN ADMISSION NEVER BEFORE HEARD FROM YOUR LIPS, DEAR COUNT.
YES, A NEARLY INCONCEIVABLE OCCURRENCE.
THE TRUTH IS THAT THIS WOMAN AND HER TIME GEM ARE OF NO REAL INTEREST TO ME.
THEN WHY DO YOU--
SHE HAS A COMPANION WHO IS CURRENTLY IN A CATATONIC STATE.
HIS NAME IS ADAM WARLOCK.
THE GEM HE POSSESSES IS RUMORED TO BE CAPABLE OF CONTROLLING THE SOUL.
THE SOUL?
TRULY?
TRULY.

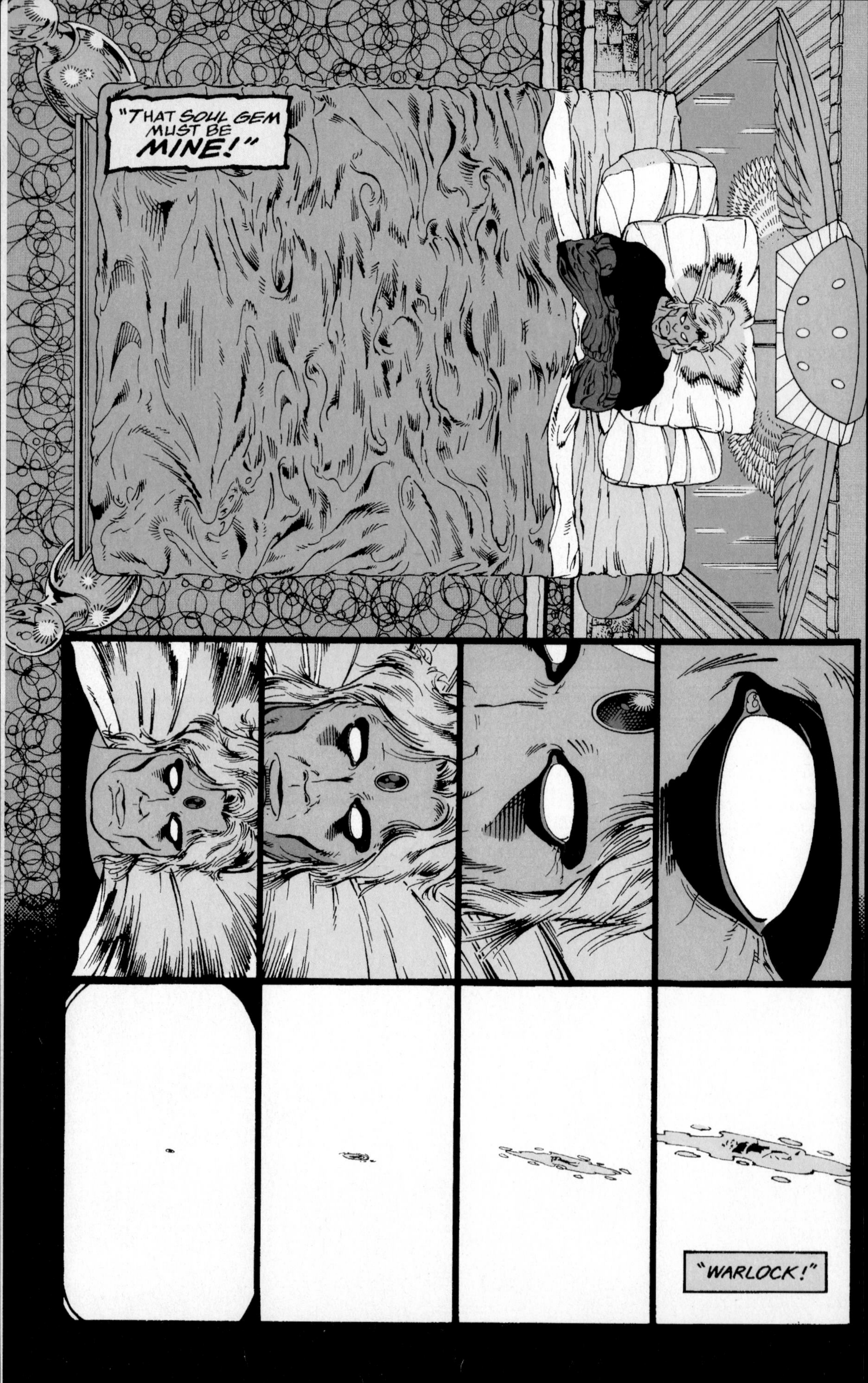
"THAT SOUL GEM MUST BE MINE!"
"WARLOCK!"

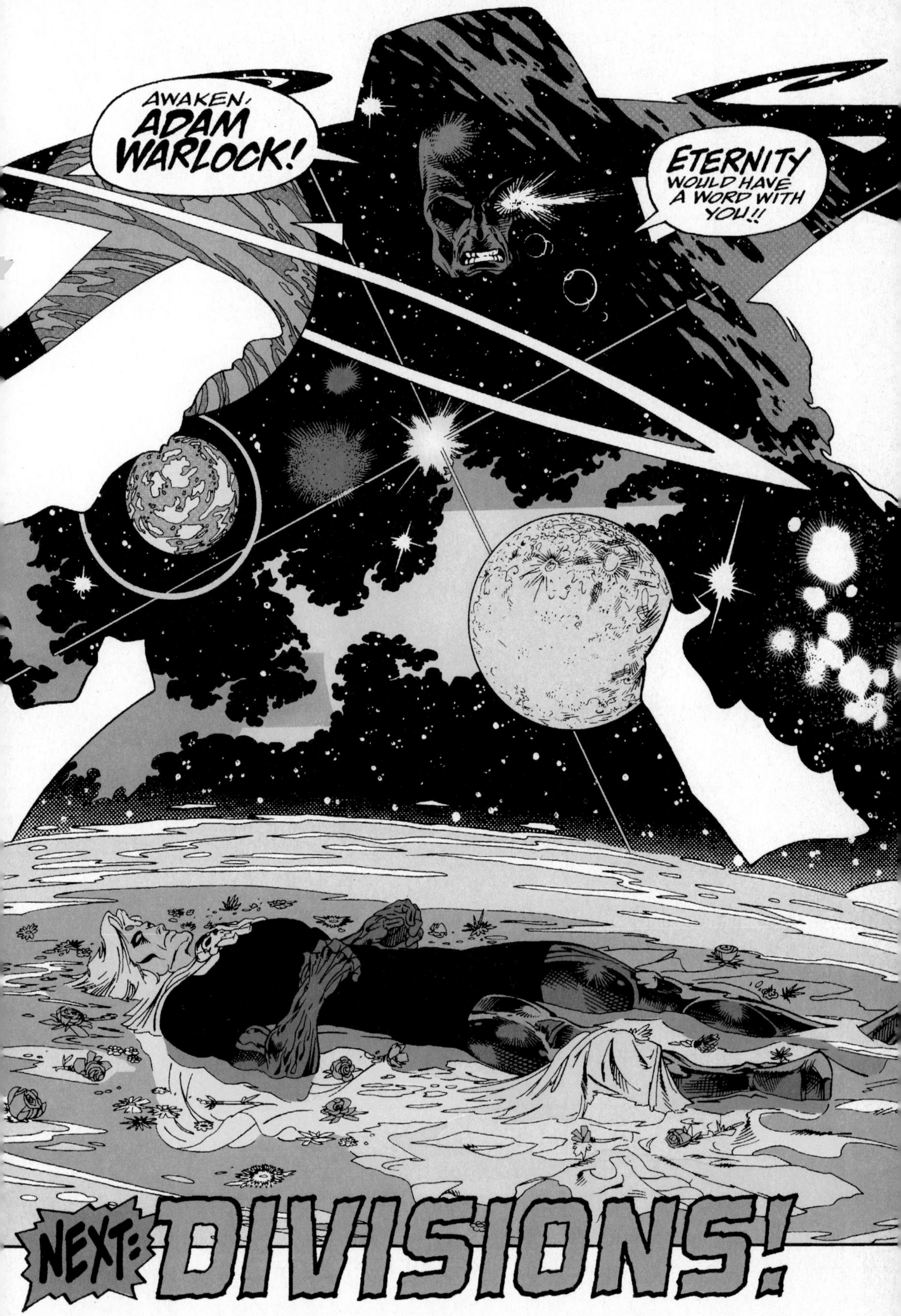
AWAKEN, ADAM WARLOCK!
ETERNITY WOULD HAVE A WORD WITH YOU!!
NEXT: DIVISIONS!

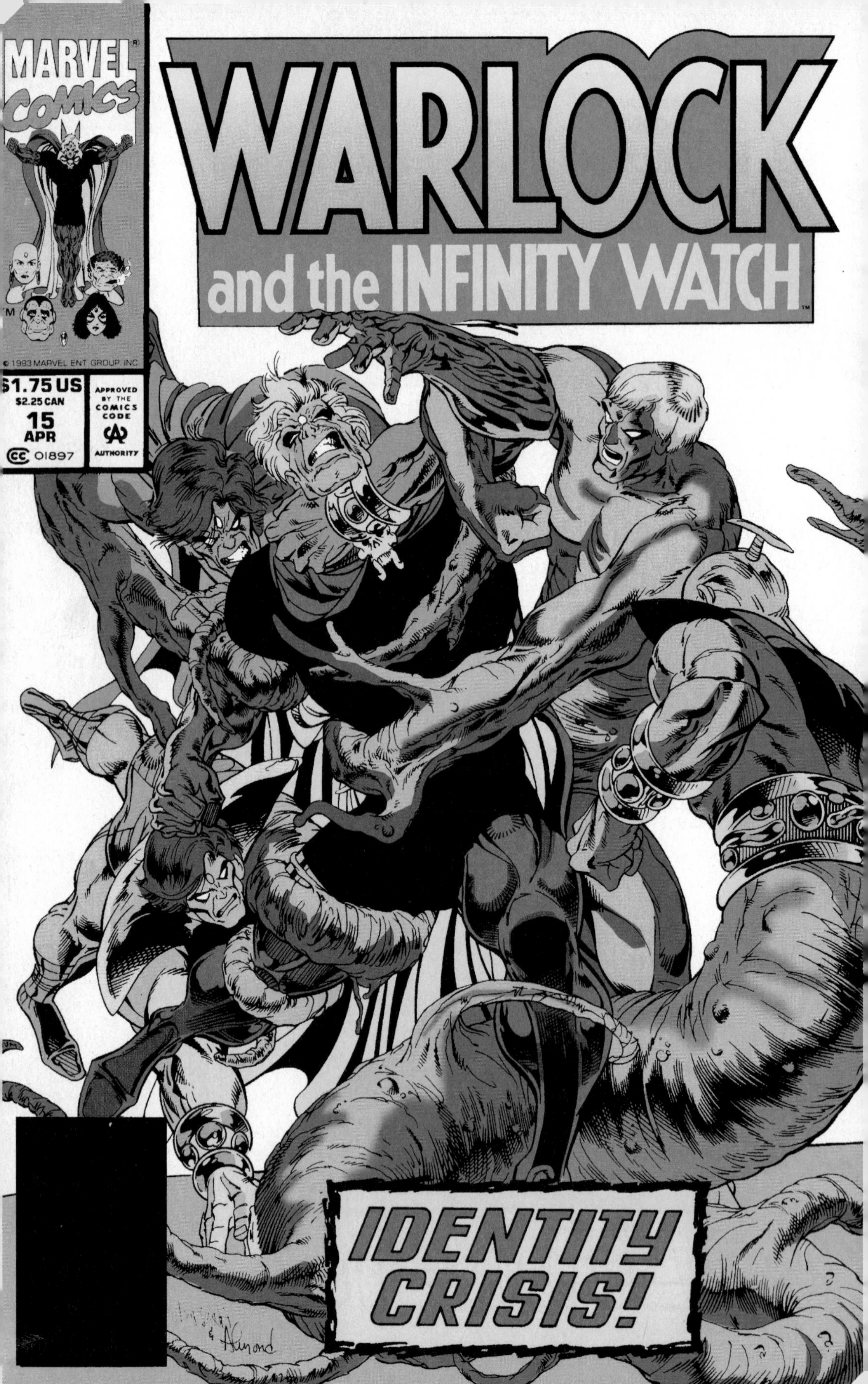
MARVEL COMICS
WARLOCK
and the INFINITY WATCH
© 1993 MARVEL ENT. GROUP, INC.
$1.75 US
$2.25 CAN
15
APR
01897
APPROVED BY THE COMICS CODE AUTHORITY
IDENTITY CRISIS!

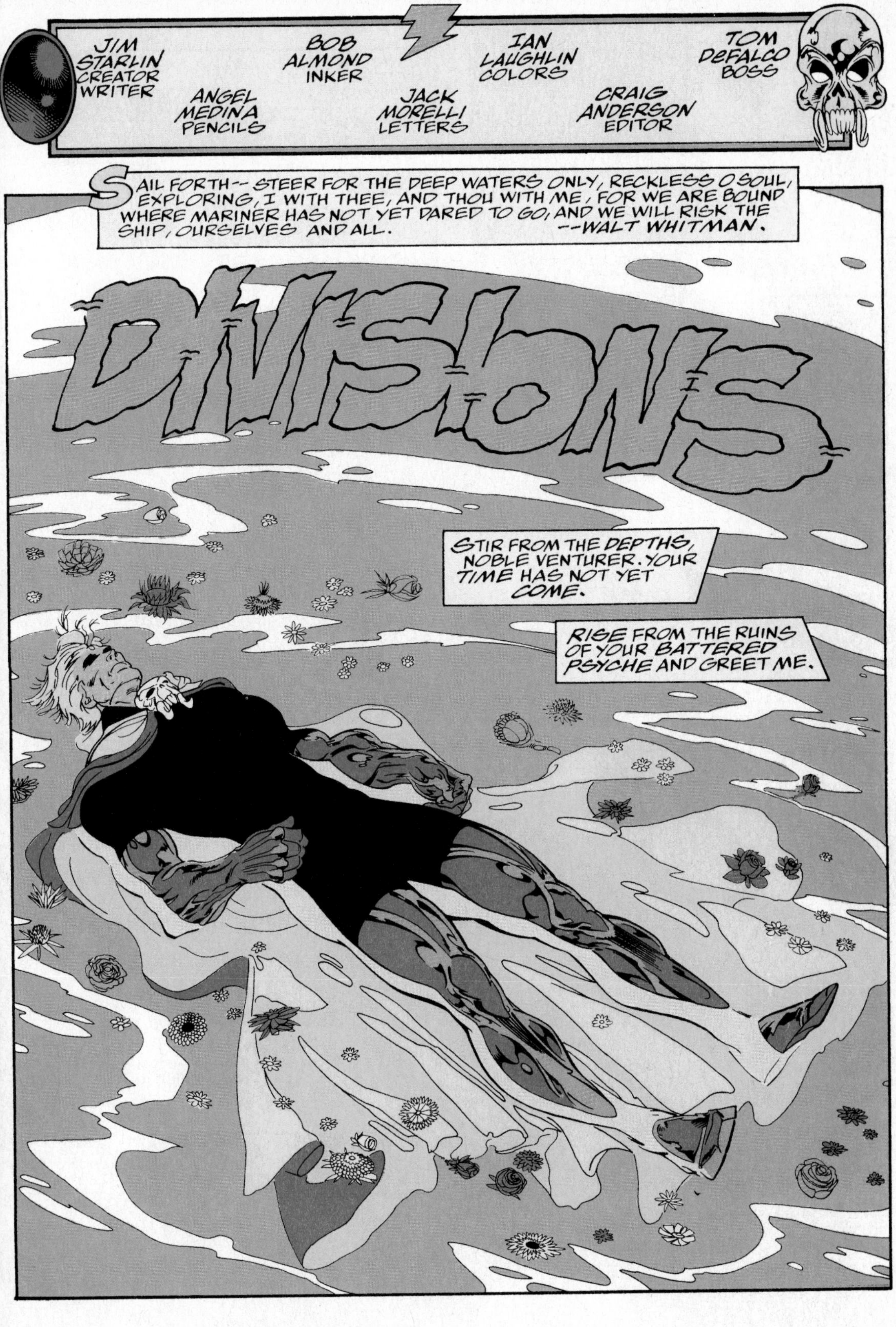
JIM STARLIN CREATOR WRITER
ANGEL MEDINA PENCILS
BOB ALMOND INKER
JACK MORELLI LETTERS
IAN LAUGHLIN COLORS
CRAIG ANDERSON EDITOR
TOM DeFALCO BOSS
SAIL FORTH-- STEER FOR THE DEEP WATERS ONLY, RECKLESS O SOUL, EXPLORING, I WITH THEE, AND THOU WITH ME, FOR WE ARE BOUND WHERE MARINER HAS NOT YET DARED TO GO, AND WE WILL RISK THE SHIP, OURSELVES AND ALL. --WALT WHITMAN.
DIVISIONS
STIR FROM THE DEPTHS, NOBLE VENTURER. YOUR TIME HAS NOT YET COME.
RISE FROM THE RUINS OF YOUR BATTERED PSYCHE AND GREET ME.

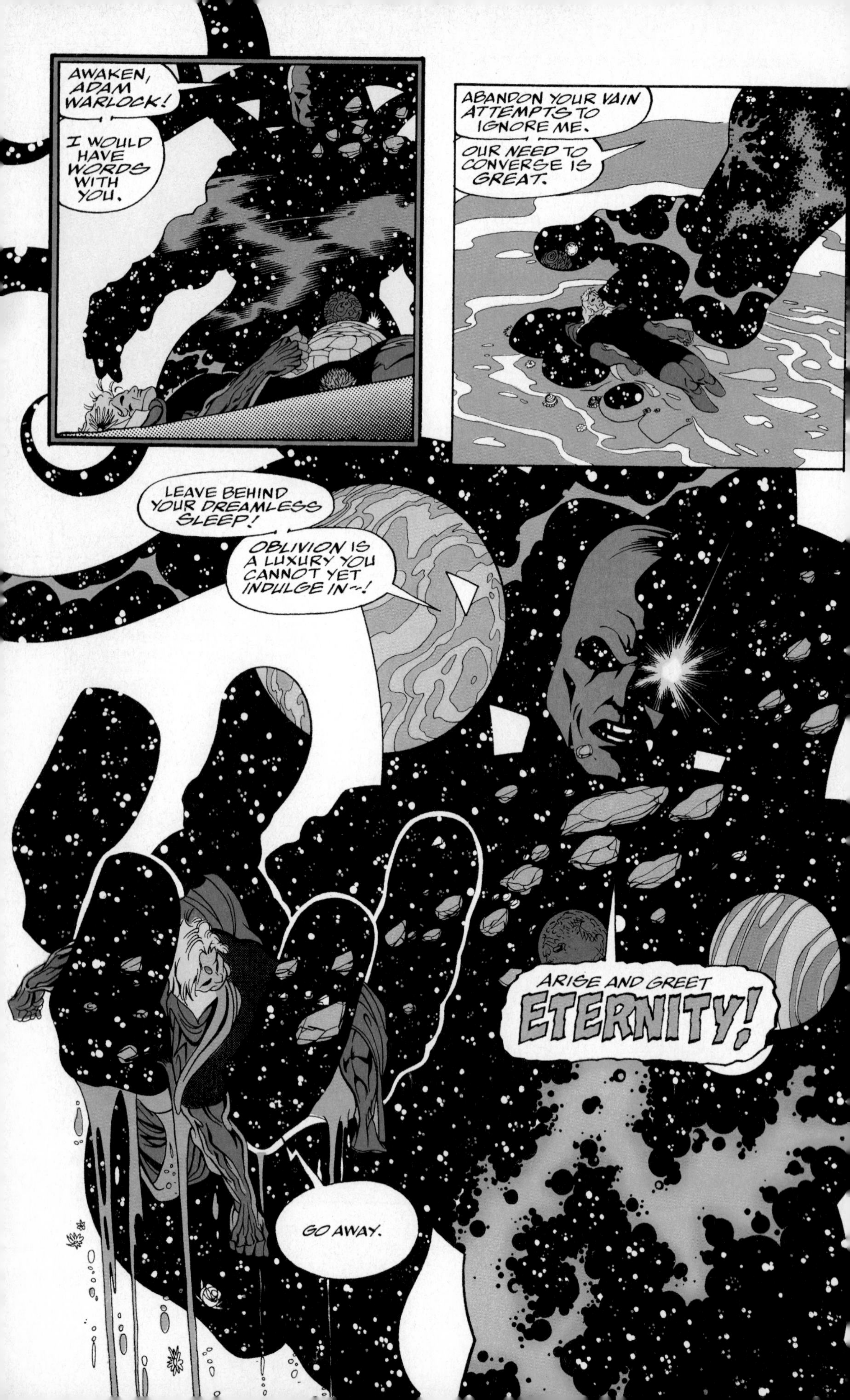
AWAKEN, ADAM WARLOCK!
I WOULD HAVE WORDS WITH YOU.
ABANDON YOUR VAIN ATTEMPTS TO IGNORE ME.
OUR NEED TO CONVERSE IS GREAT.
LEAVE BEHIND YOUR DREAMLESS SLEEP!
OBLIVION IS A LUXURY YOU CANNOT YET INDULGE IN--!
ARISE AND GREET ETERNITY!
GO AWAY.

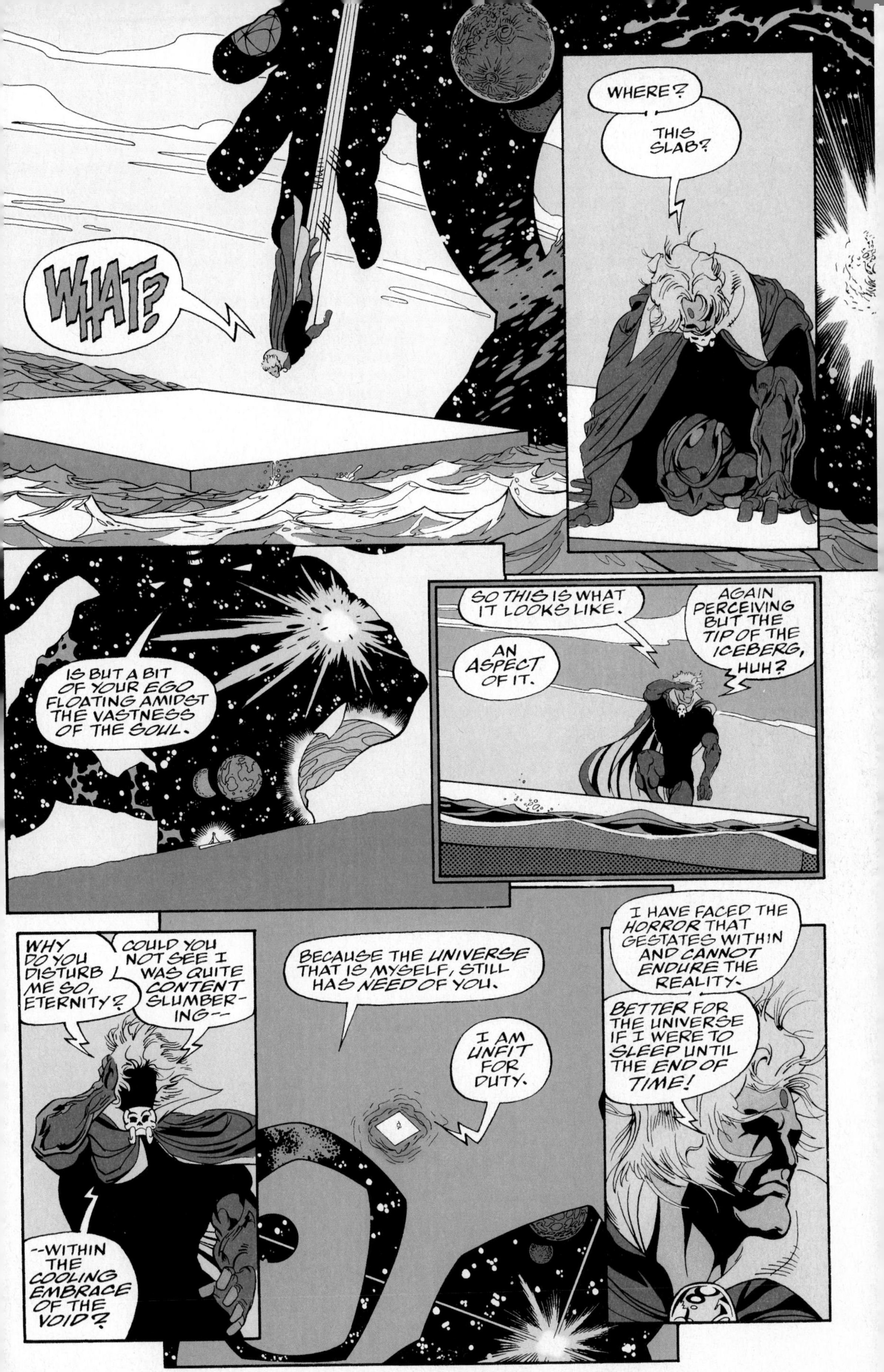

WHAT?
WHERE?
THIS SLAB?
IS BUT A BIT OF YOUR EGO FLOATING AMIDST THE VASTNESS OF THE SOUL.
SO THIS IS WHAT IT LOOKS LIKE.
AN ASPECT OF IT.
AGAIN PERCEIVING BUT THE TIP OF THE ICEBERG, HUH?
WHY DO YOU DISTURB ME SO, ETERNITY?
COULD YOU NOT SEE I WAS QUITE CONTENT SLUMBERING--
--WITHIN THE COOLING EMBRACE OF THE VOID?
BECAUSE THE UNIVERSE THAT IS MYSELF, STILL HAS NEED OF YOU.
I AM UNFIT FOR DUTY.
I HAVE FACED THE HORROR THAT GESTATES WITHIN AND CANNOT ENDURE THE REALITY.
BETTER FOR THE UNIVERSE IF I WERE TO SLEEP UNTIL THE END OF TIME!

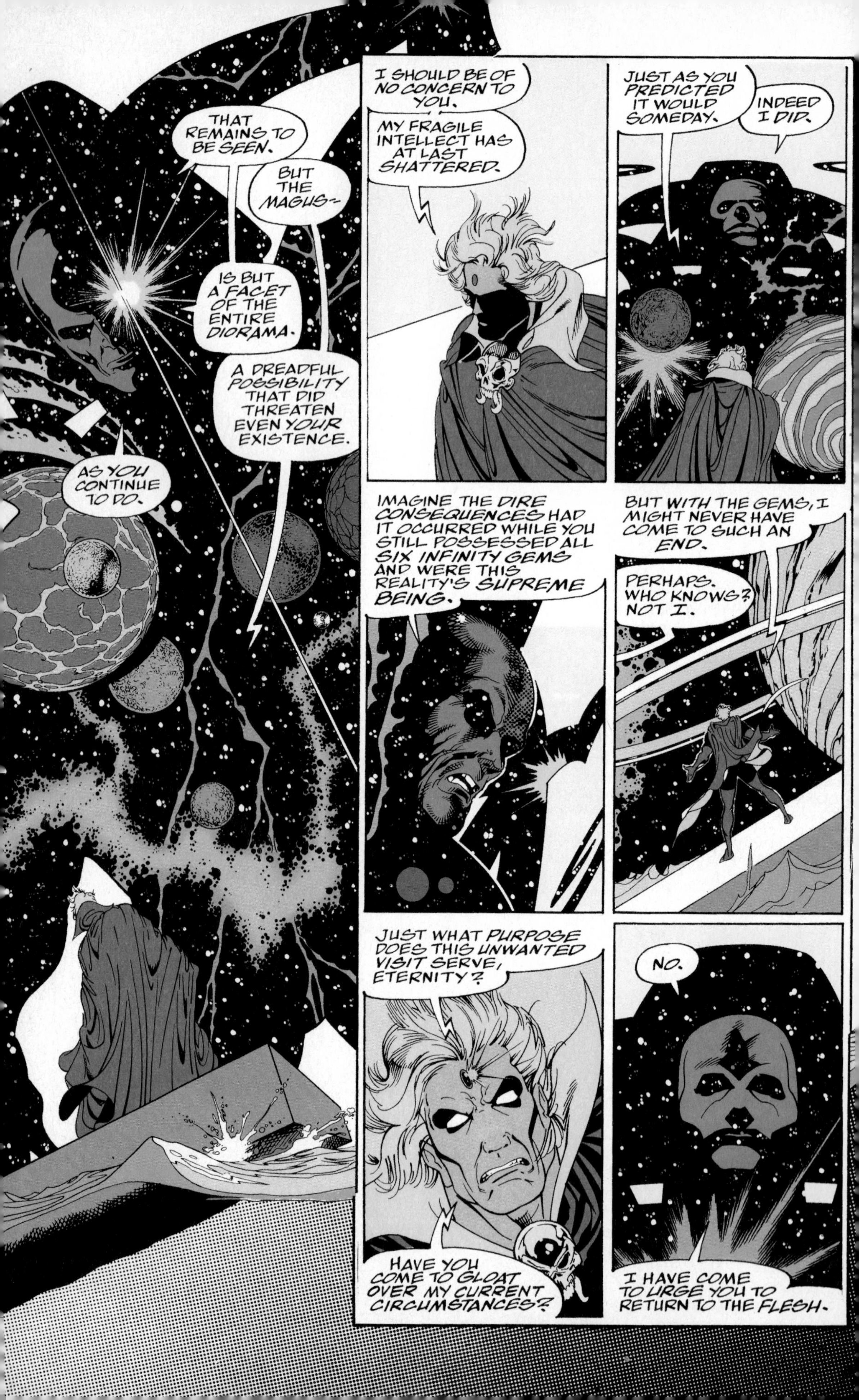
THAT REMAINS TO BE SEEN.
BUT THE MAGUS--
IS BUT A FACET OF THE ENTIRE DIORAMA.
A DREADFUL POSSIBILITY THAT DID THREATEN EVEN YOUR EXISTENCE.
AS YOU CONTINUE TO DO.
I SHOULD BE OF NO CONCERN TO YOU.
MY FRAGILE INTELLECT HAS AT LAST SHATTERED.
JUST AS YOU PREDICTED IT WOULD SOMEDAY.
INDEED I DID.
IMAGINE THE DIRE CONSEQUENCES HAD IT OCCURRED WHILE YOU STILL POSSESSED ALL SIX INFINITY GEMS AND WERE THIS REALITY'S SUPREME BEING.
BUT WITH THE GEMS, I MIGHT NEVER HAVE COME TO SUCH AN END.
PERHAPS. WHO KNOWS? NOT I.
JUST WHAT PURPOSE DOES THIS UNWANTED VISIT SERVE, ETERNITY?
HAVE YOU COME TO GLOAT OVER MY CURRENT CIRCUMSTANCES?
NO.
I HAVE COME TO URGE YOU TO RETURN TO THE FLESH.

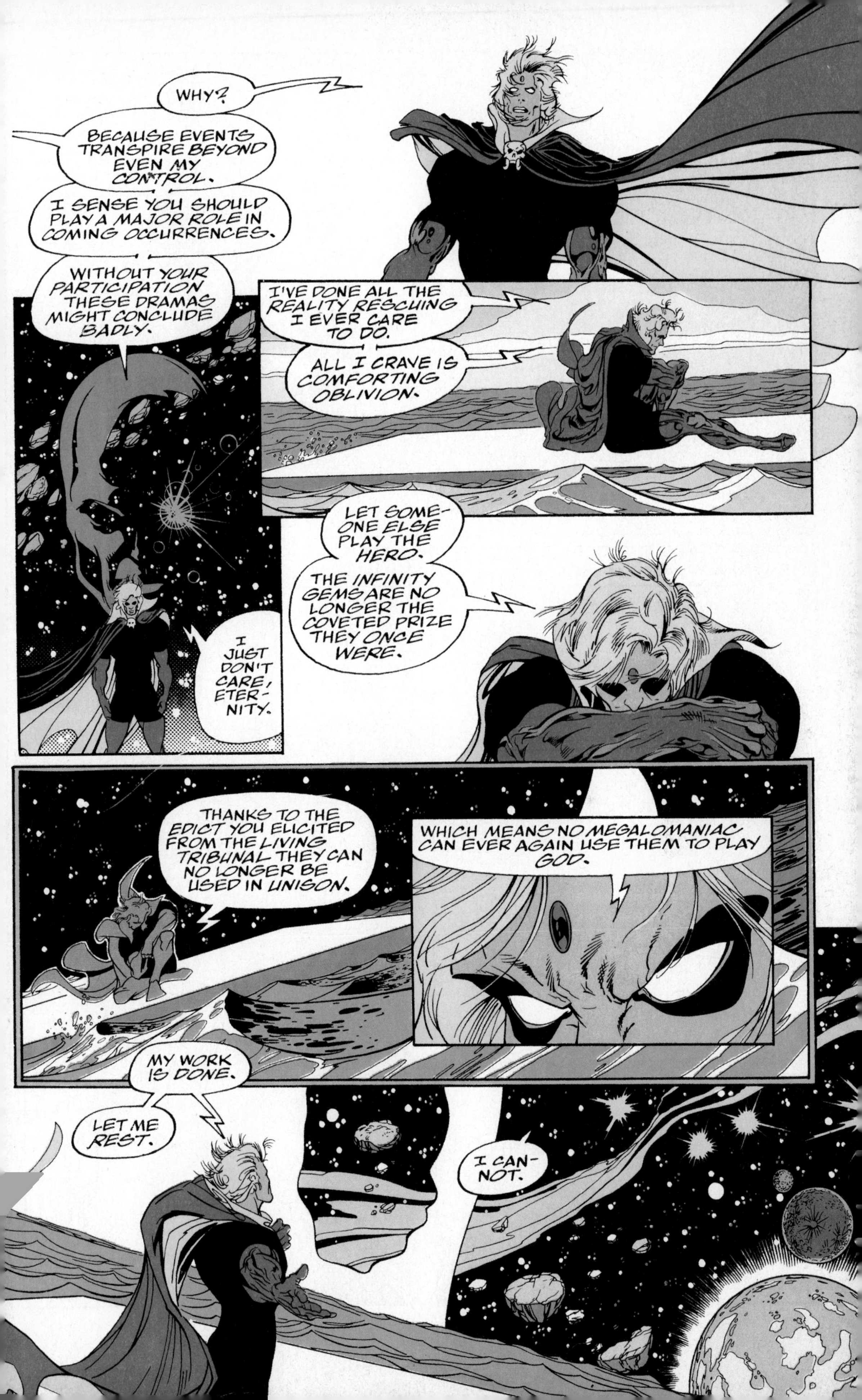
WHY?
BECAUSE EVENTS TRANSPIRE BEYOND EVEN MY CONTROL.
I SENSE YOU SHOULD PLAY A MAJOR ROLE IN COMING OCCURRENCES.
WITHOUT YOUR PARTICIPATION THESE DRAMAS MIGHT CONCLUDE BADLY.
I'VE DONE ALL THE REALITY RESCUING I EVER CARE TO DO.
ALL I CRAVE IS COMFORTING OBLIVION.
I JUST DON'T CARE, ETERNITY.
LET SOMEONE ELSE PLAY THE HERO.
THE INFINITY GEMS ARE NO LONGER THE COVETED PRIZE THEY ONCE WERE.
THANKS TO THE EDICT YOU ELICITED FROM THE LIVING TRIBUNAL THEY CAN NO LONGER BE USED IN UNISON.
WHICH MEANS NO MEGALOMANIAC CAN EVER AGAIN USE THEM TO PLAY GOD.
MY WORK IS DONE.
LET ME REST.
I CANNOT.

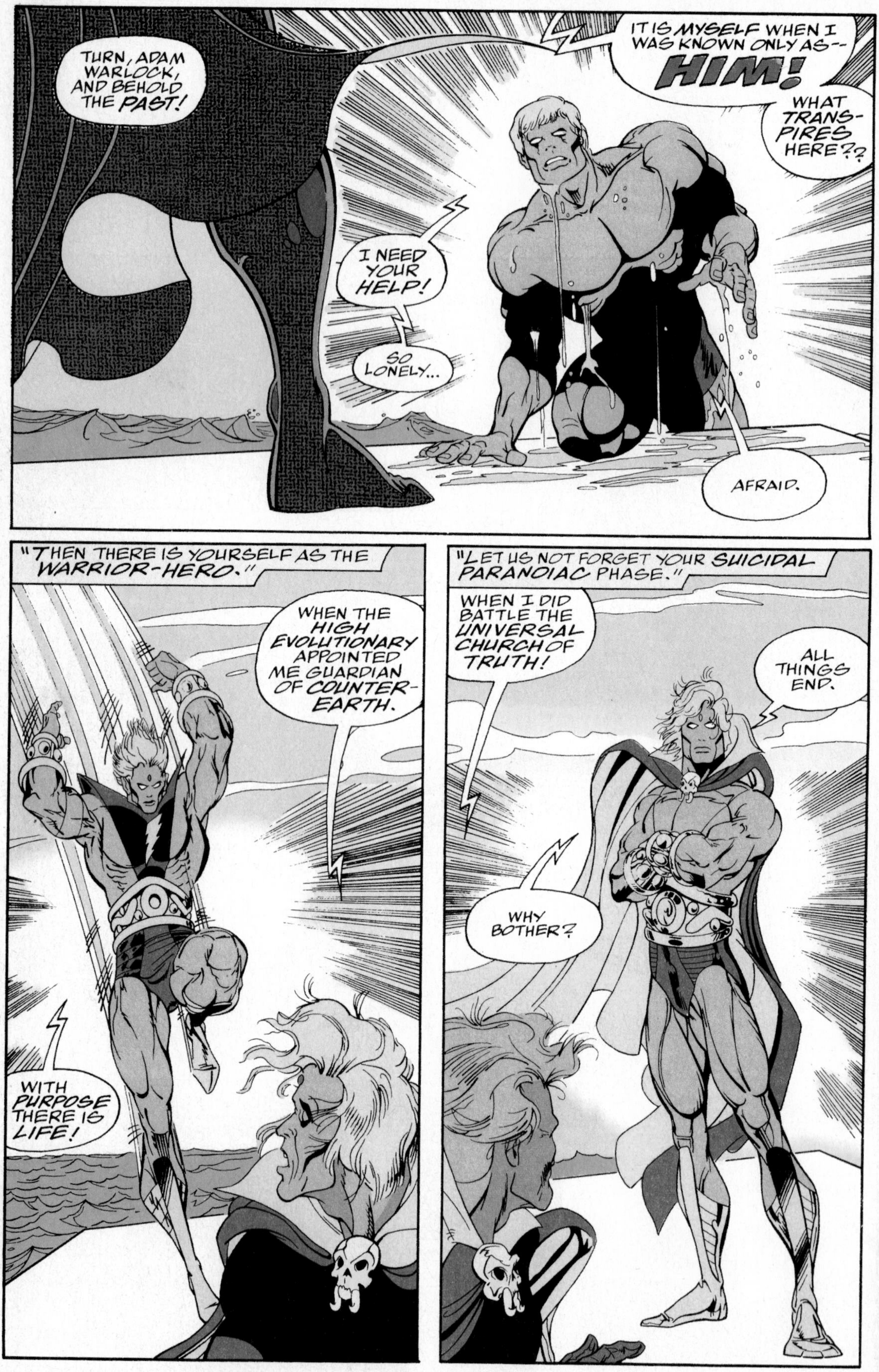
TURN, ADAM WARLOCK, AND BEHOLD THE PAST!
IT IS MYSELF WHEN I WAS KNOWN ONLY AS-- HIM!
WHAT TRANSPIRES HERE??
I NEED YOUR HELP!
SO LONELY...
AFRAID.
"THEN THERE IS YOURSELF AS THE WARRIOR-HERO."
WHEN THE HIGH EVOLUTIONARY APPOINTED ME GUARDIAN OF COUNTER-EARTH.
WITH PURPOSE THERE IS LIFE!
"LET US NOT FORGET YOUR SUICIDAL PARANOIAC PHASE."
WHEN I DID BATTLE THE UNIVERSAL CHURCH OF TRUTH!
ALL THINGS END.
WHY BOTHER?

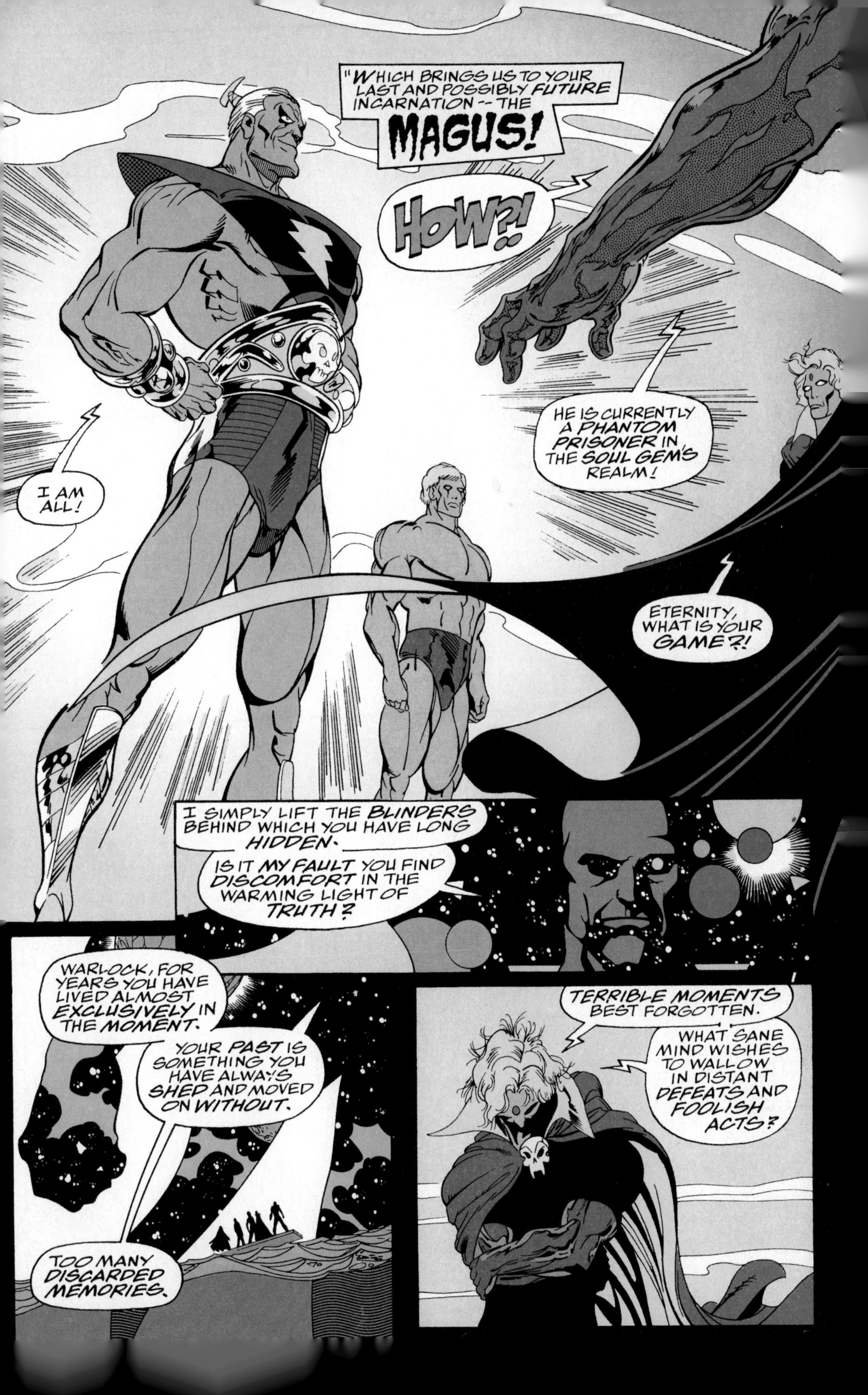
"WHICH BRINGS US TO YOUR LAST AND POSSIBLY FUTURE INCARNATION -- THE MAGUS!
HOW?!
I AM ALL!
HE IS CURRENTLY A PHANTOM PRISONER IN THE SOUL GEM'S REALM!
ETERNITY, WHAT IS YOUR GAME?!
I SIMPLY LIFT THE BLINDERS BEHIND WHICH YOU HAVE LONG HIDDEN.
IS IT MY FAULT YOU FIND DISCOMFORT IN THE WARMING LIGHT OF TRUTH?
WARLOCK, FOR YEARS YOU HAVE LIVED ALMOST EXCLUSIVELY IN THE MOMENT.
YOUR PAST IS SOMETHING YOU HAVE ALWAYS SHED AND MOVED ON WITHOUT.
TOO MANY DISCARDED MEMORIES.
TERRIBLE MOMENTS BEST FORGOTTEN.
WHAT SANE MIND WISHES TO WALLOW IN DISTANT DEFEATS AND FOOLISH ACTS?

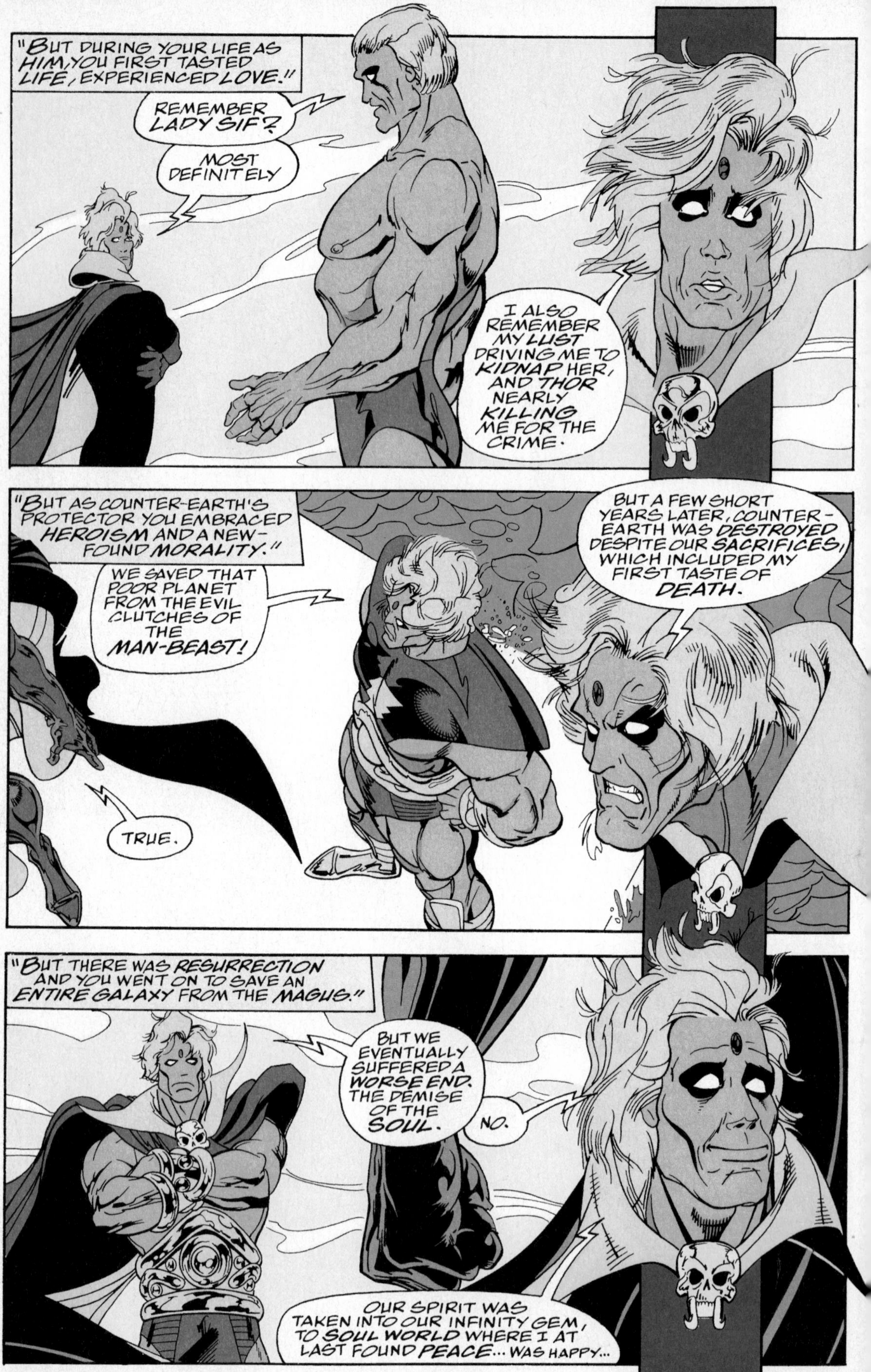
"BUT DURING YOUR LIFE AS HIM, YOU FIRST TASTED LIFE, EXPERIENCED LOVE."
REMEMBER LADY SIF?
MOST DEFINITELY.
I ALSO REMEMBER MY LUST DRIVING ME TO KIDNAP HER, AND THOR NEARLY KILLING ME FOR THE CRIME.
"BUT AS COUNTER-EARTH'S PROTECTOR YOU EMBRACED HEROISM AND A NEW-FOUND MORALITY."
WE SAVED THAT POOR PLANET FROM THE EVIL CLUTCHES OF THE MAN-BEAST!
BUT A FEW SHORT YEARS LATER, COUNTER-EARTH WAS DESTROYED DESPITE OUR SACRIFICES, WHICH INCLUDED MY FIRST TASTE OF DEATH.
TRUE.
"BUT THERE WAS RESURRECTION AND YOU WENT ON TO SAVE AN ENTIRE GALAXY FROM THE MAGUS."
BUT WE EVENTUALLY SUFFERED A WORSE END. THE DEMISE OF THE SOUL.
NO.
OUR SPIRIT WAS TAKEN INTO OUR INFINITY GEM, TO SOUL WORLD WHERE I AT LAST FOUND PEACE... WAS HAPPY...

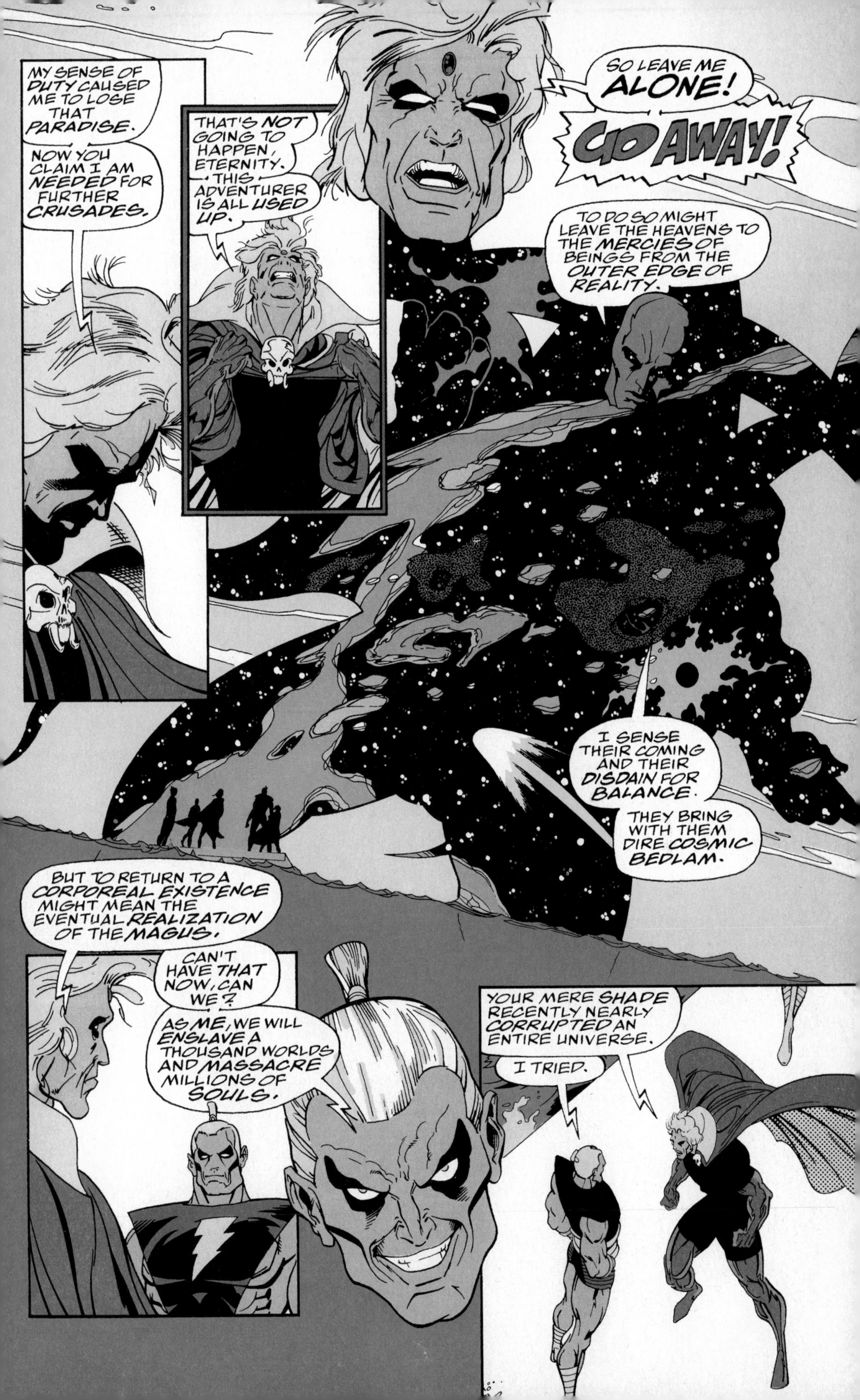
MY SENSE OF DUTY CAUSED ME TO LOSE THAT PARADISE.
NOW YOU CLAIM I AM NEEDED FOR FURTHER CRUSADES.
THAT'S NOT GOING TO HAPPEN, ETERNITY. THIS ADVENTURER IS ALL USED UP.
SO LEAVE ME ALONE!
GO AWAY!
TO DO SO MIGHT LEAVE THE HEAVENS TO THE MERCIES OF BEINGS FROM THE OUTER EDGE OF REALITY.
I SENSE THEIR COMING AND THEIR DISDAIN FOR BALANCE.
THEY BRING WITH THEM DIRE COSMIC BEDLAM.
BUT TO RETURN TO A CORPOREAL EXISTENCE MIGHT MEAN THE EVENTUAL REALIZATION OF THE MAGUS.
CAN'T HAVE THAT NOW, CAN WE?
AS ME, WE WILL ENSLAVE A THOUSAND WORLDS AND MASSACRE MILLIONS OF SOULS.
YOUR MERE SHADE RECENTLY NEARLY CORRUPTED AN ENTIRE UNIVERSE.
I TRIED.

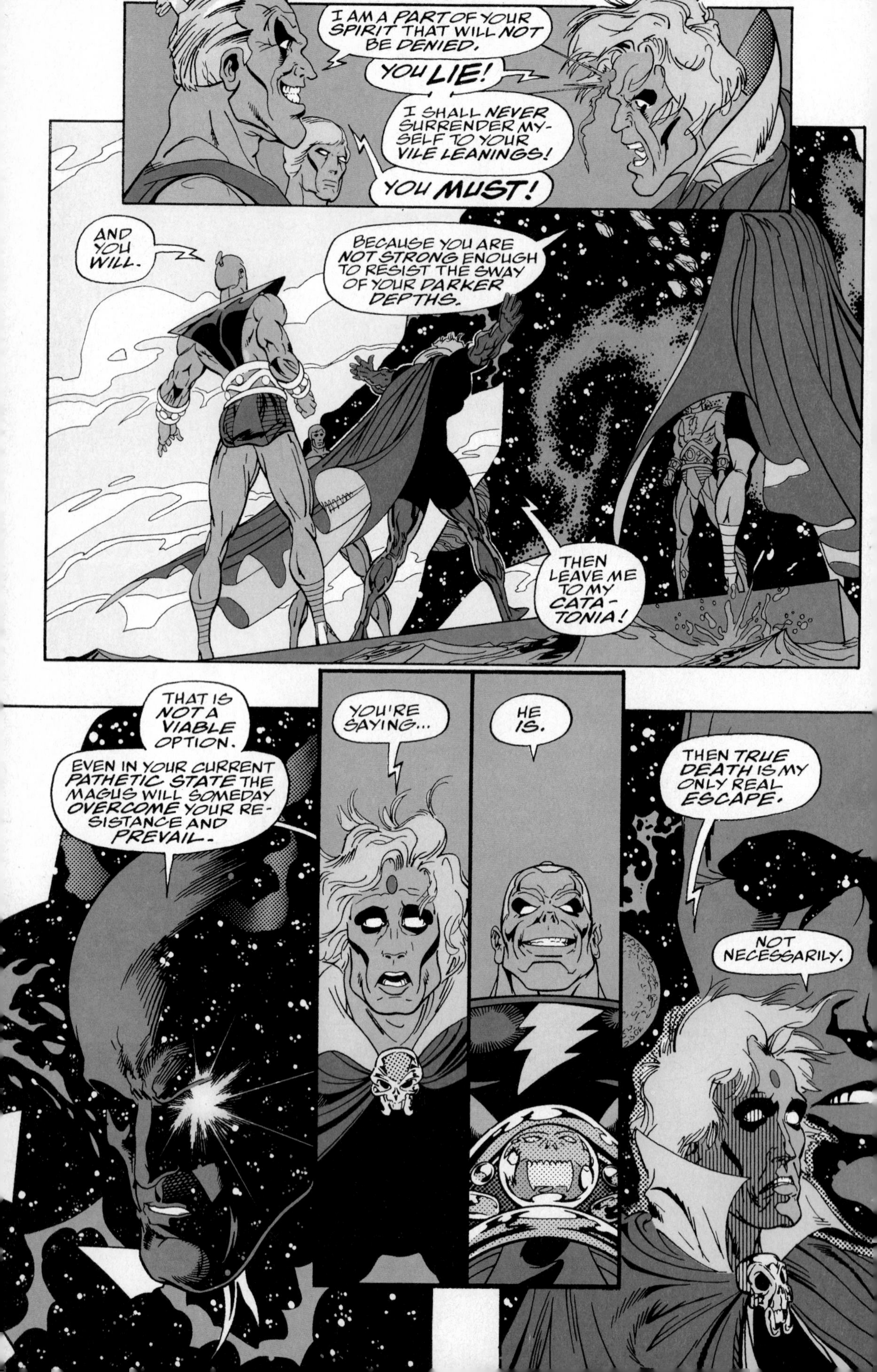

I AM A PART OF YOUR SPIRIT THAT WILL NOT BE DENIED.
YOU LIE!
I SHALL NEVER SURRENDER MY-SELF TO YOUR VILE LEANINGS!
YOU MUST!
AND YOU WILL.
BECAUSE YOU ARE NOT STRONG ENOUGH TO RESIST THE SWAY OF YOUR DARKER DEPTHS.
THEN LEAVE ME TO MY CATA-TONIA!
THAT IS NOT A VIABLE OPTION.
EVEN IN YOUR CURRENT PATHETIC STATE THE MAGUS WILL SOMEDAY OVERCOME YOUR RE-SISTANCE AND PREVAIL.
YOU'RE SAYING...
HE IS.
THEN TRUE DEATH IS MY ONLY REAL ESCAPE.
NOT NECESSARILY.

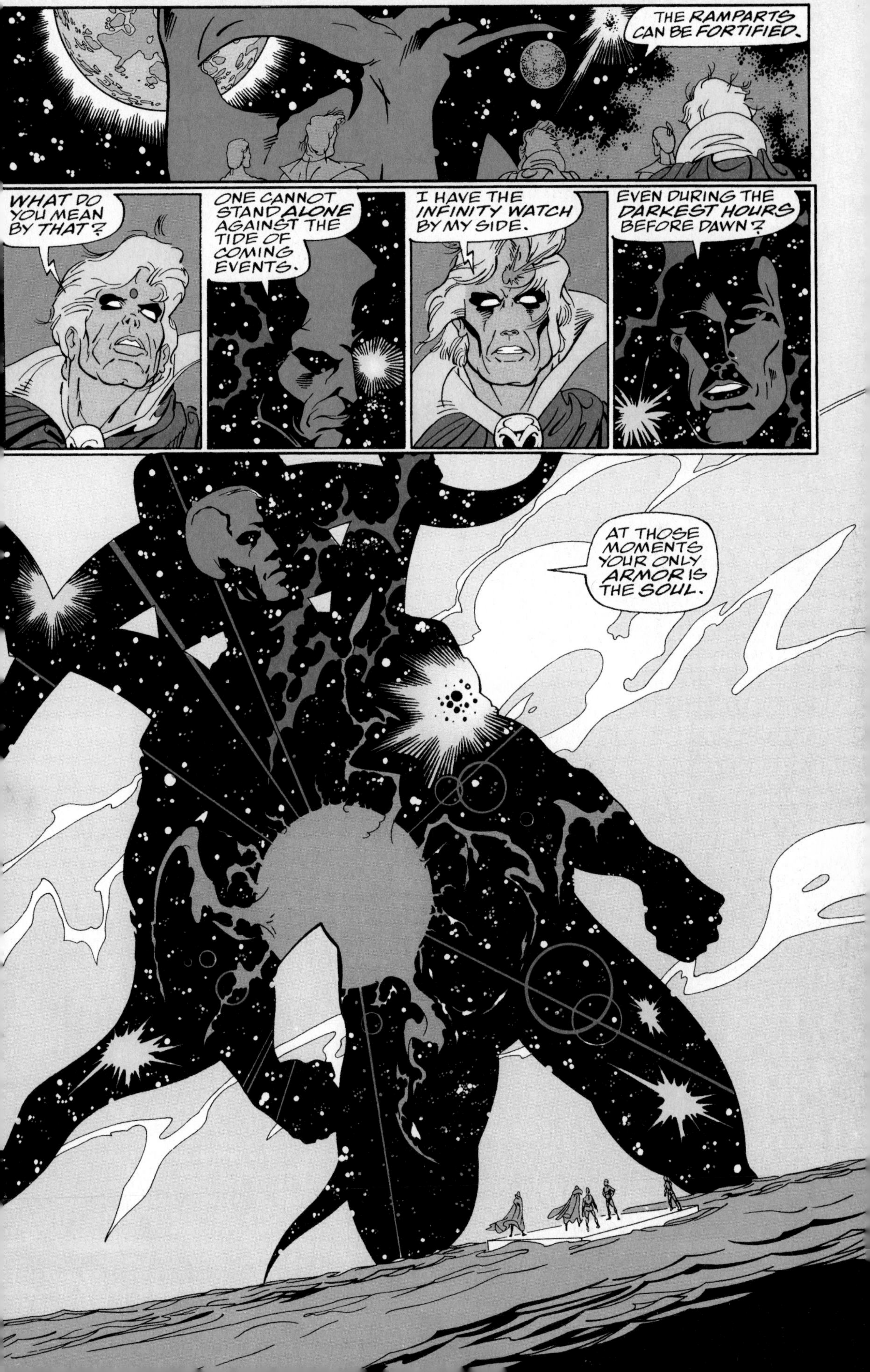
THE RAMPARTS CAN BE FORTIFIED.
WHAT DO YOU MEAN BY THAT?
ONE CANNOT STAND ALONE AGAINST THE TIDE OF COMING EVENTS.
I HAVE THE INFINITY WATCH BY MY SIDE.
EVEN DURING THE DARKEST HOURS BEFORE DAWN?
AT THOSE MOMENTS YOUR ONLY ARMOR IS THE SOUL.

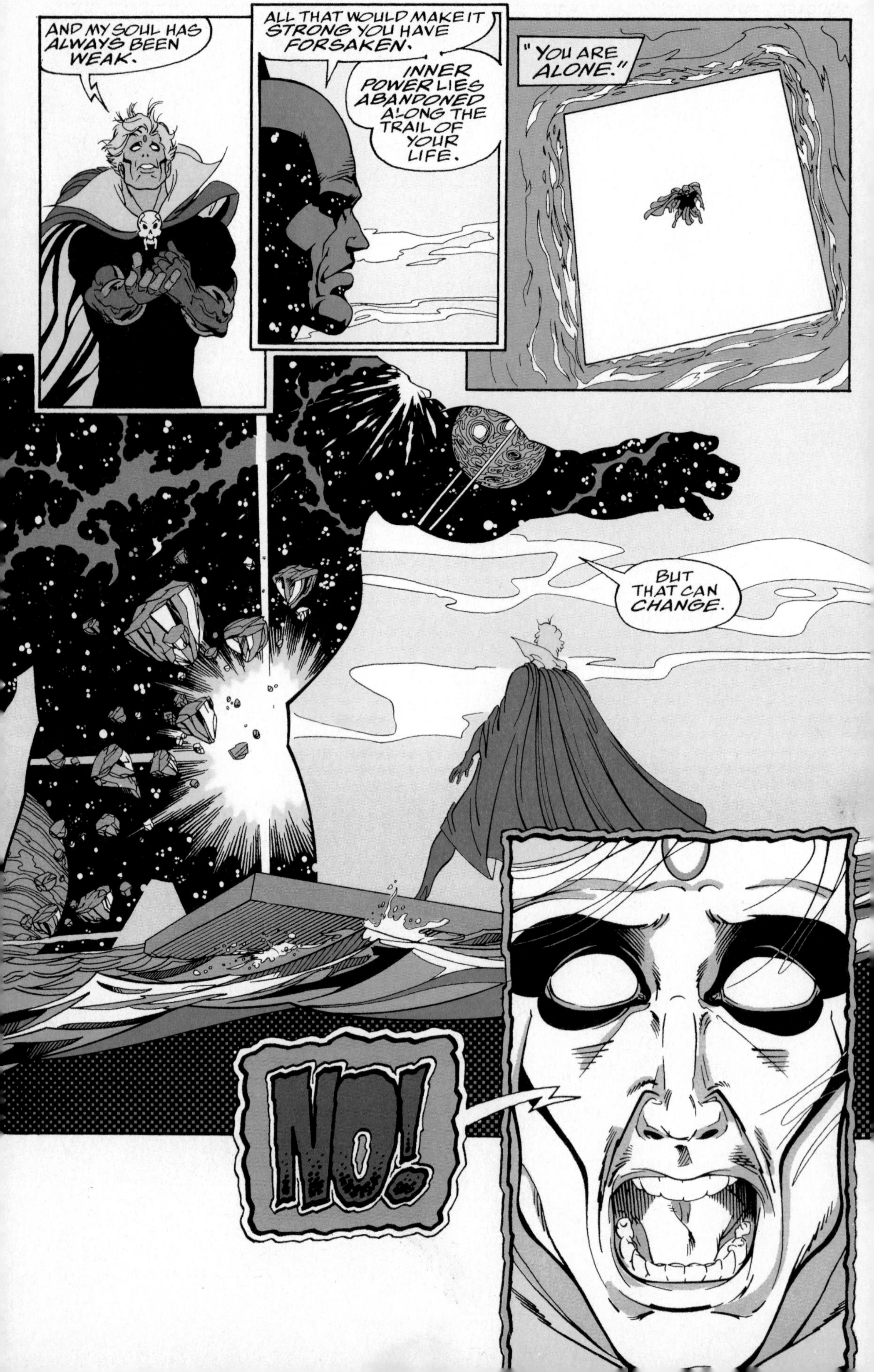
AND MY SOUL HAS ALWAYS BEEN WEAK.
ALL THAT WOULD MAKE IT STRONG YOU HAVE FORSAKEN.
INNER POWER LIES ABANDONED ALONG THE TRAIL OF YOUR LIFE.
"YOU ARE ALONE."
BUT THAT CAN CHANGE.
NO!

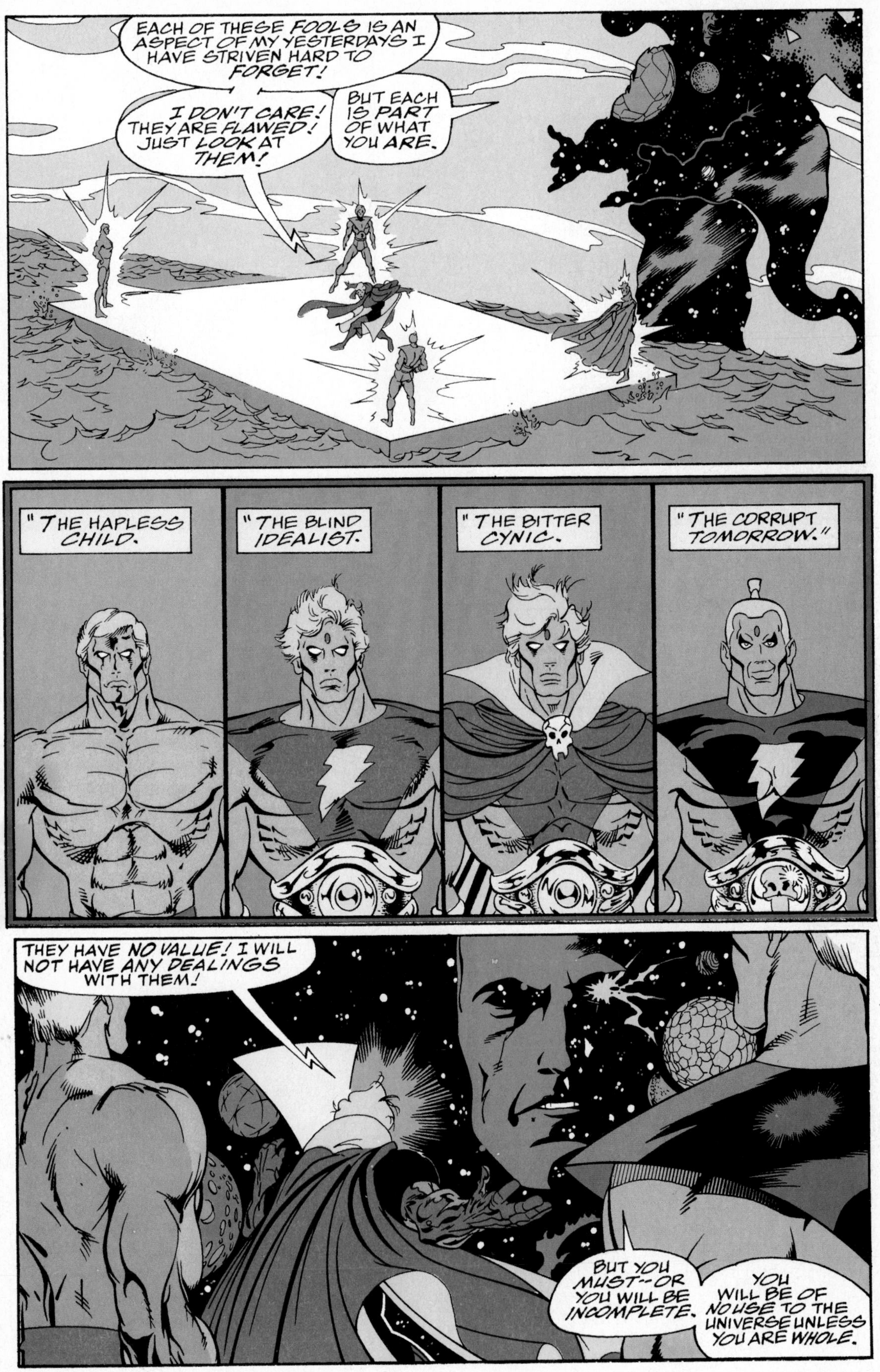
EACH OF THESE FOOLS IS AN ASPECT OF MY YESTERDAYS I HAVE STRIVEN HARD TO FORGET!
I DON'T CARE! THEY ARE FLAWED! JUST LOOK AT THEM!
BUT EACH IS PART OF WHAT YOU ARE.
"THE HAPLESS CHILD.
"THE BLIND IDEALIST.
"THE BITTER CYNIC.
"THE CORRUPT TOMORROW."
THEY HAVE NO VALUE! I WILL NOT HAVE ANY DEALINGS WITH THEM!
BUT YOU MUST--OR YOU WILL BE INCOMPLETE.
YOU WILL BE OF NO USE TO THE UNIVERSE UNLESS YOU ARE WHOLE.

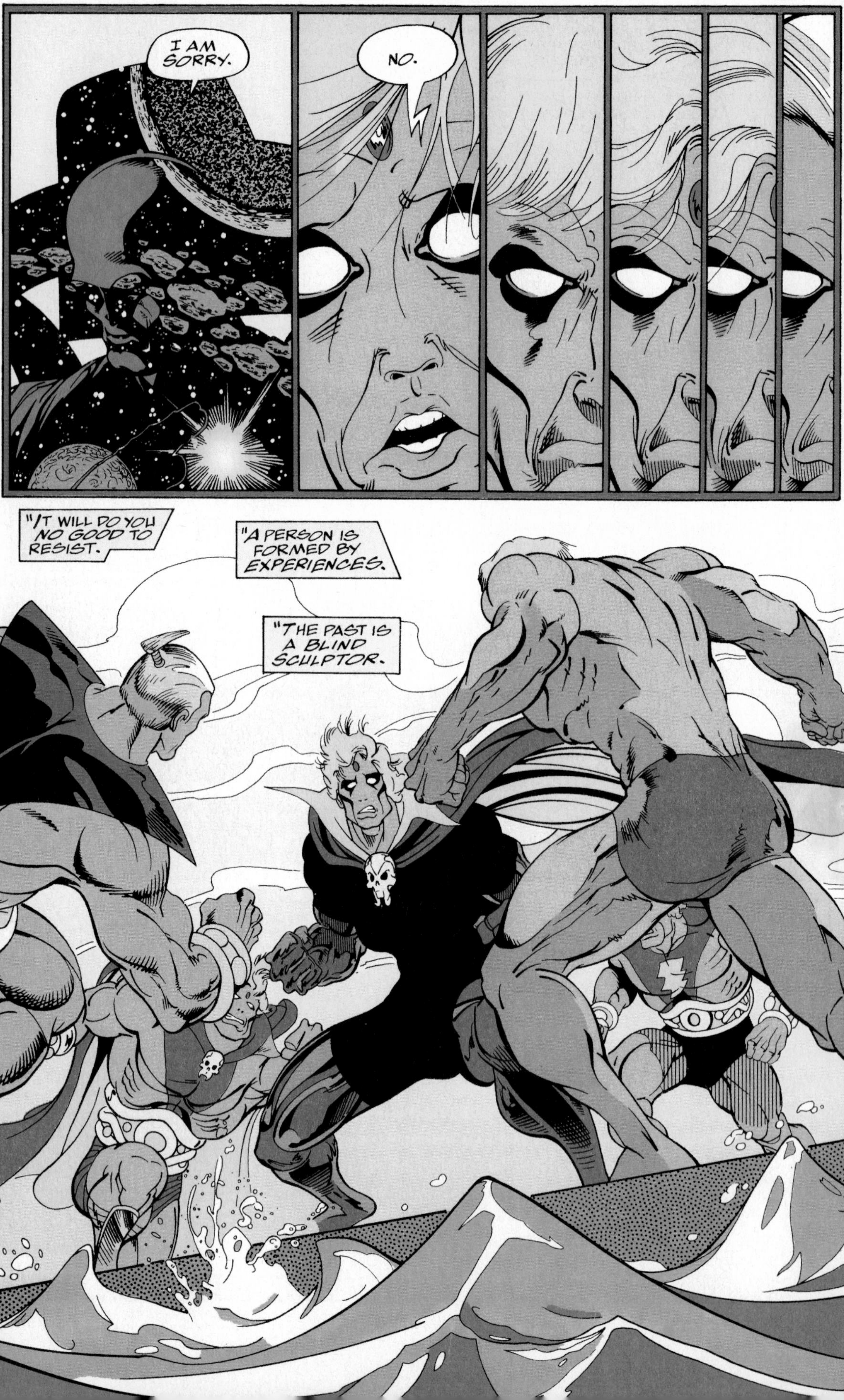
I AM SORRY.
NO.
"IT WILL DO YOU NO GOOD TO RESIST.
"A PERSON IS FORMED BY EXPERIENCES.
"THE PAST IS A BLIND SCULPTOR.

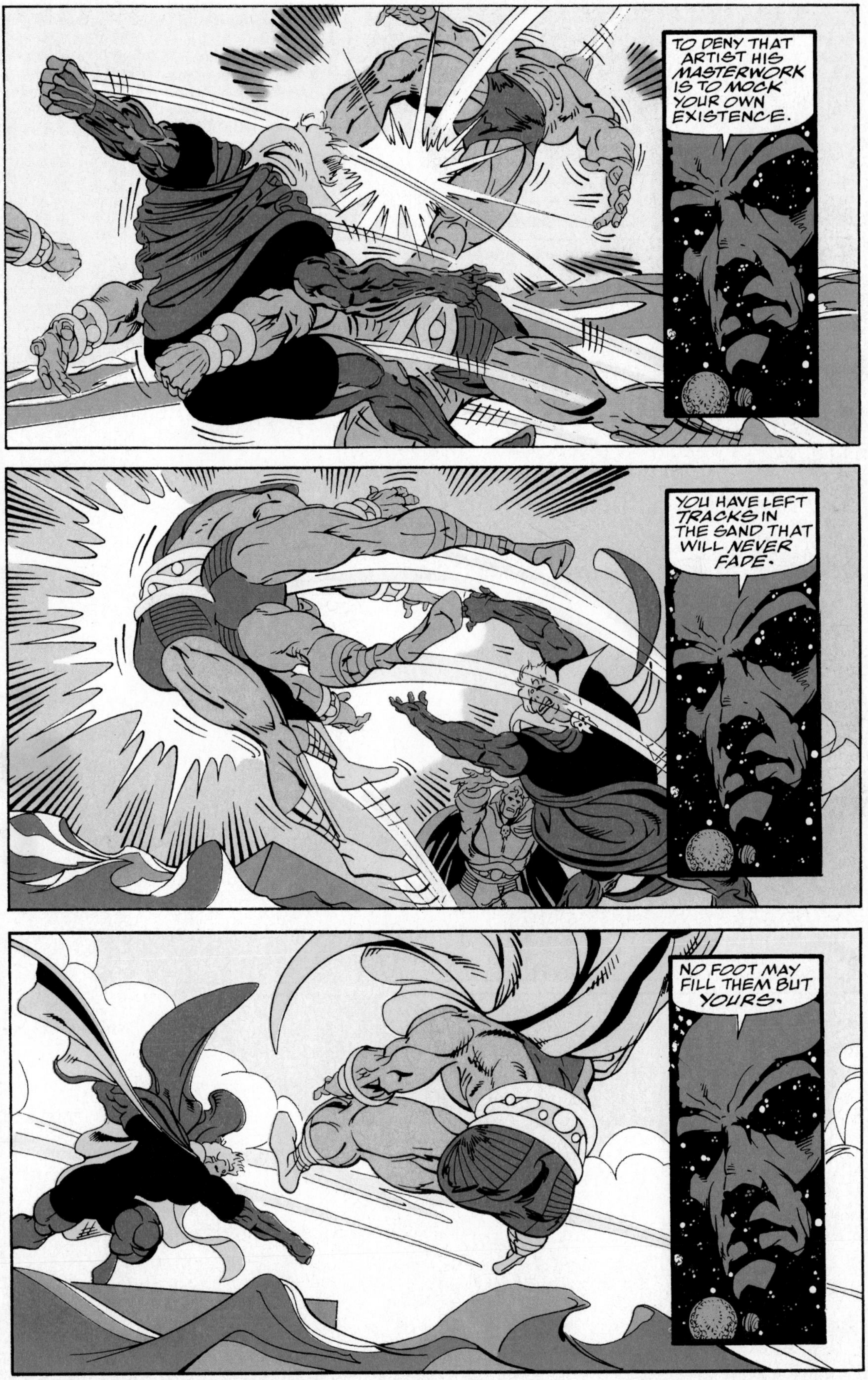
TO DENY THAT ARTIST HIS MASTERWORK IS TO MOCK YOUR OWN EXISTENCE.
YOU HAVE LEFT TRACKS IN THE SAND THAT WILL NEVER FADE.
NO FOOT MAY FILL THEM BUT YOURS.

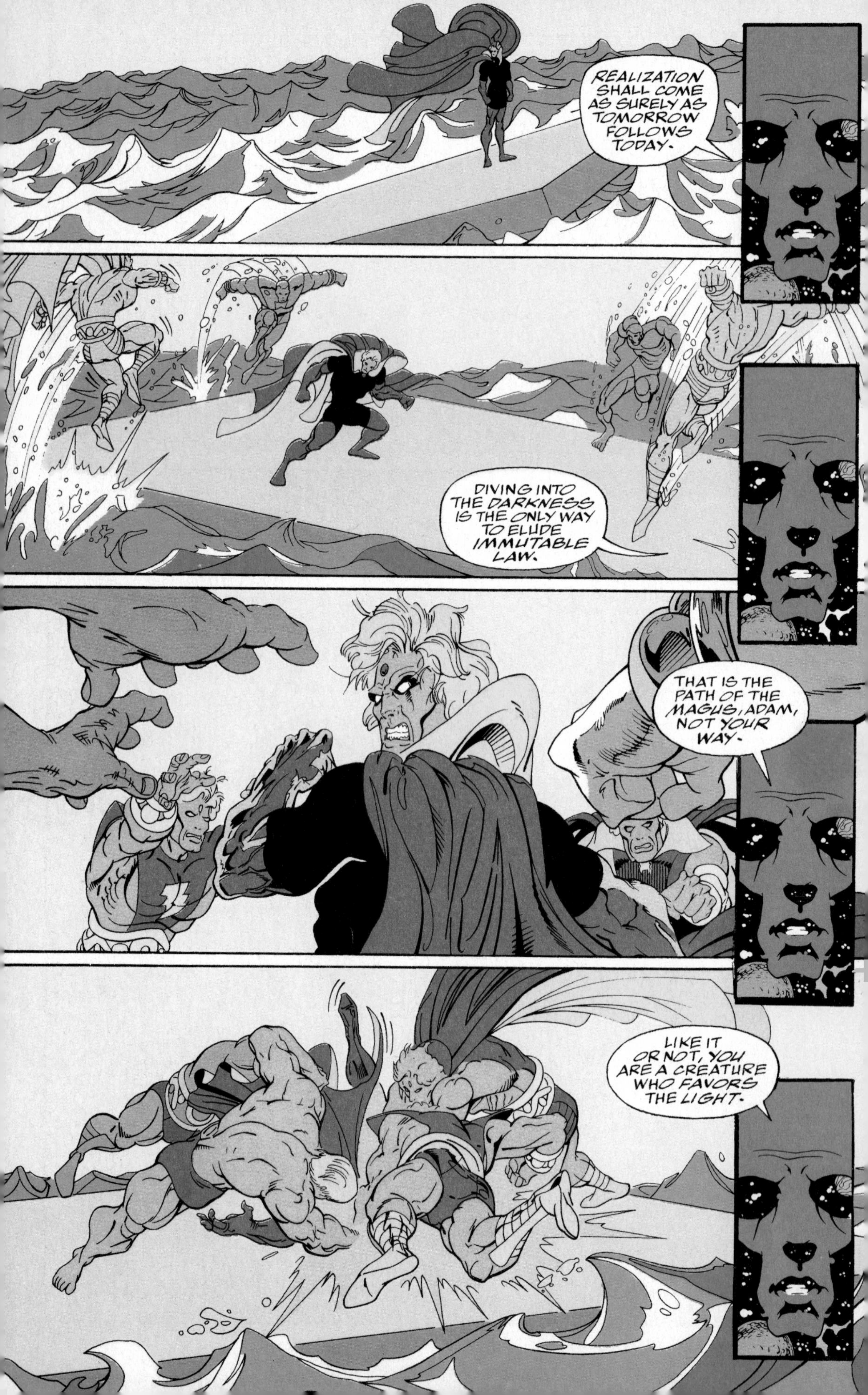
REALIZATION SHALL COME AS SURELY AS TOMORROW FOLLOWS TODAY.
DIVING INTO THE DARKNESS IS THE ONLY WAY TO ELUDE IMMUTABLE LAW.
THAT IS THE PATH OF THE MAGUS, ADAM, NOT YOUR WAY.
LIKE IT OR NOT, YOU ARE A CREATURE WHO FAVORS THE LIGHT.

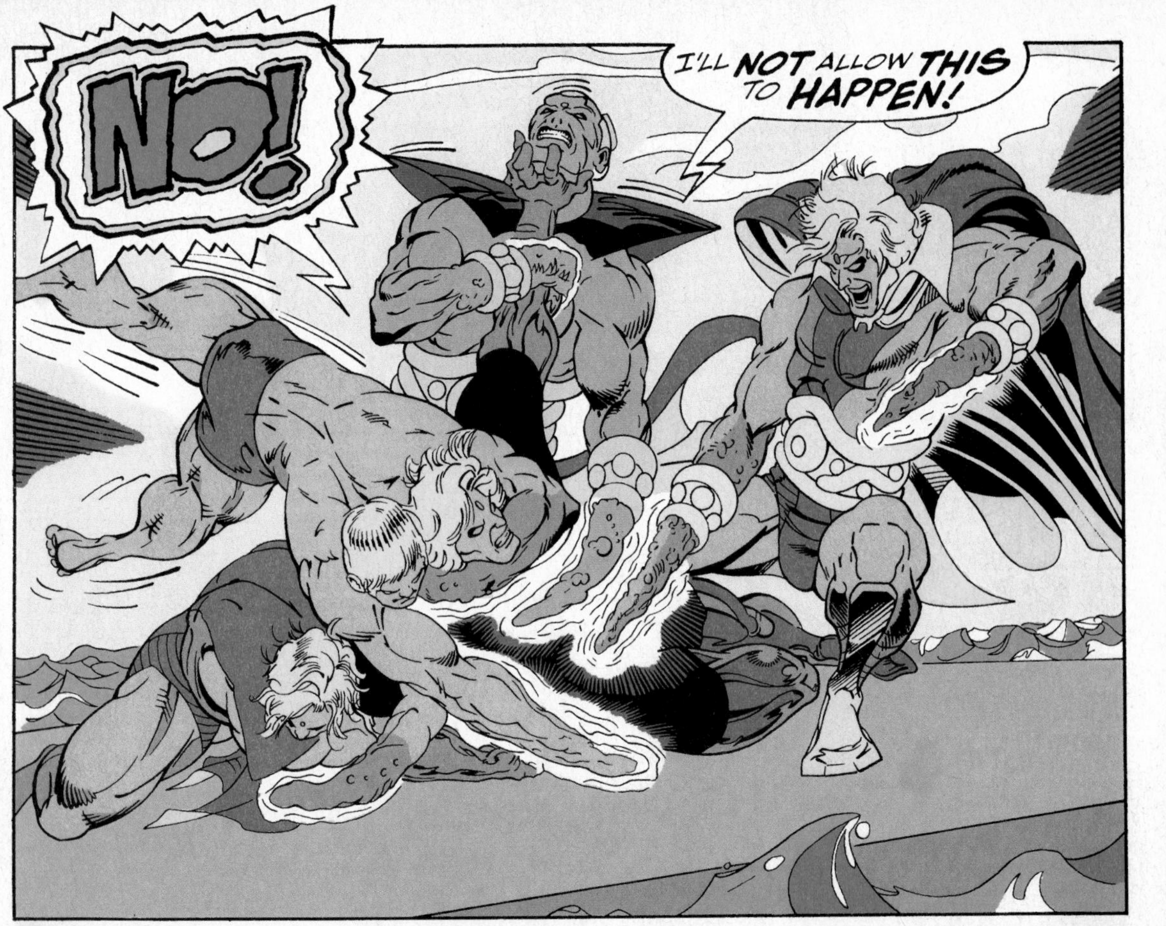
NO!
I'LL NOT ALLOW THIS TO HAPPEN!

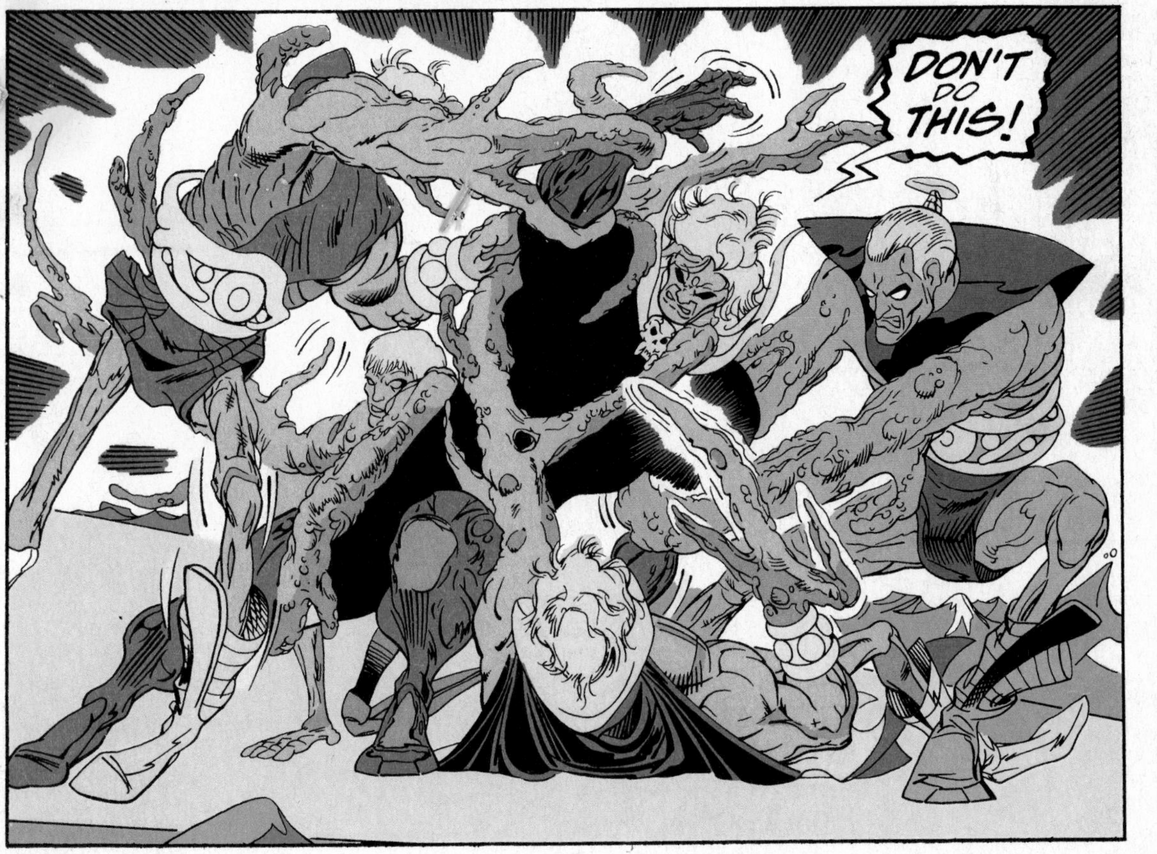
DON'T DO THIS!

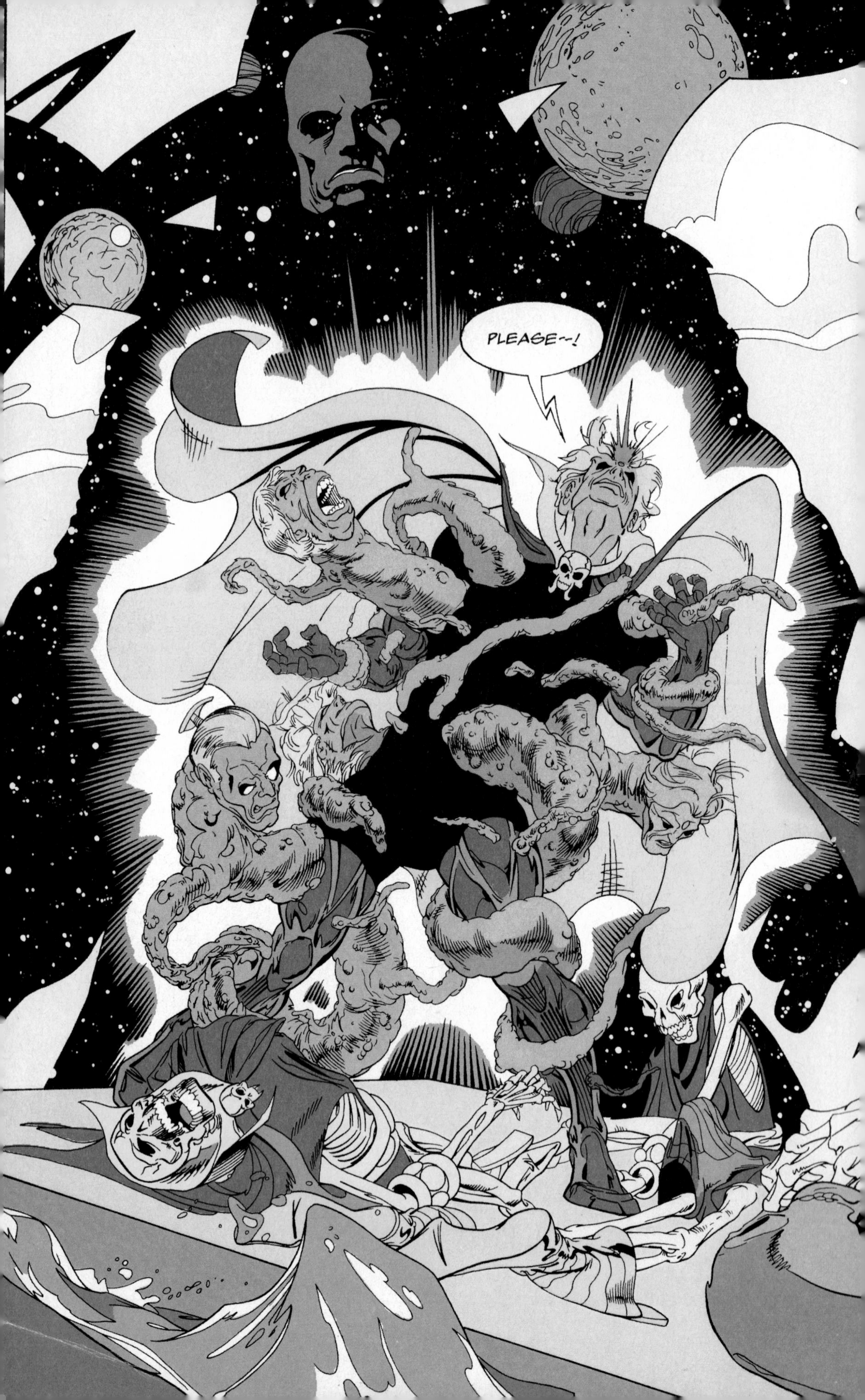
PLEASE--!

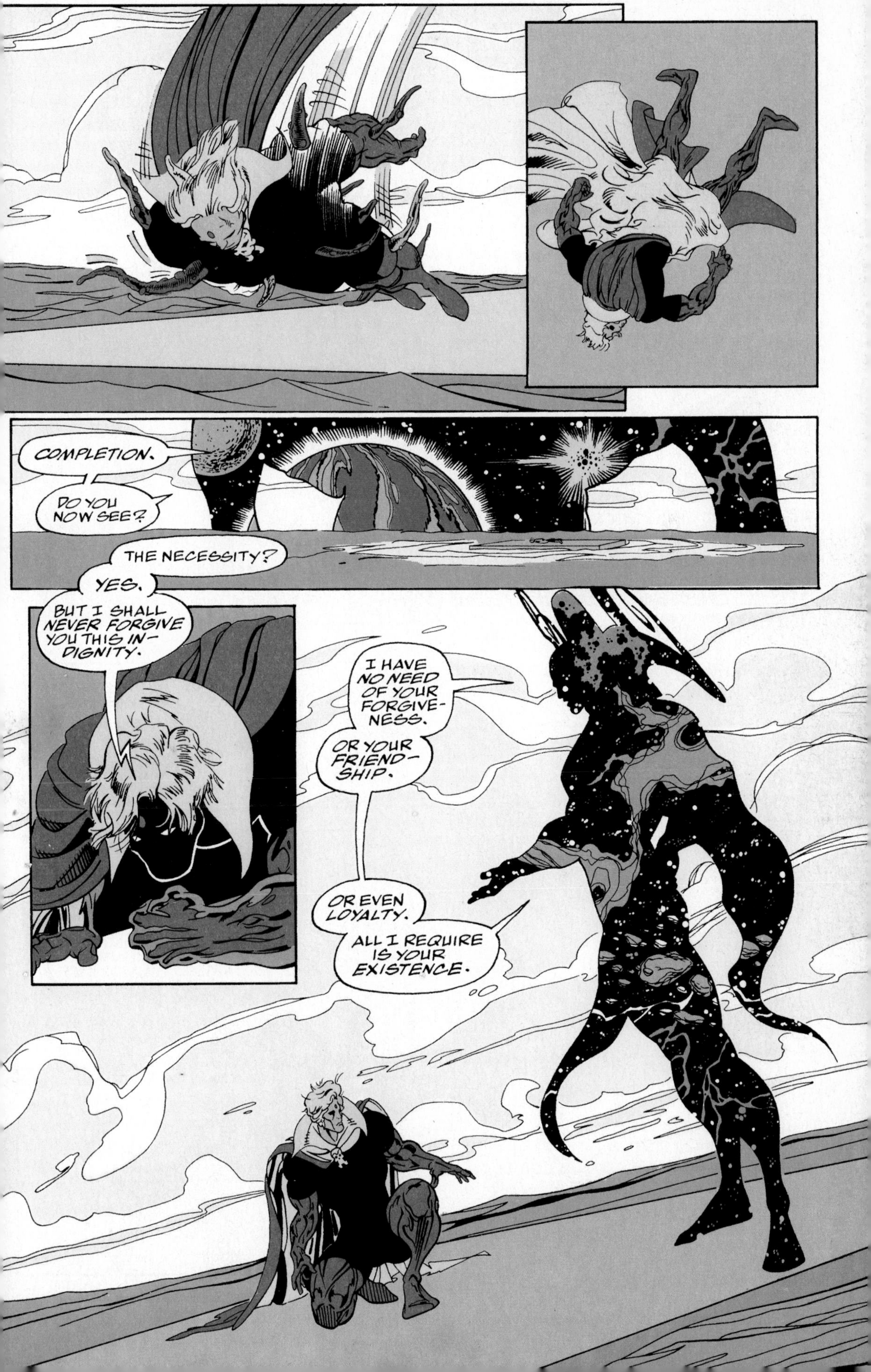
COMPLETION.
DO YOU NOW SEE?
THE NECESSITY?
YES.
BUT I SHALL NEVER FORGIVE YOU THIS IN-DIGNITY.
I HAVE NO NEED OF YOUR FORGIVE-NESS.
OR YOUR FRIEND-SHIP.
OR EVEN LOYALTY.
ALL I REQUIRE IS YOUR EXISTENCE.

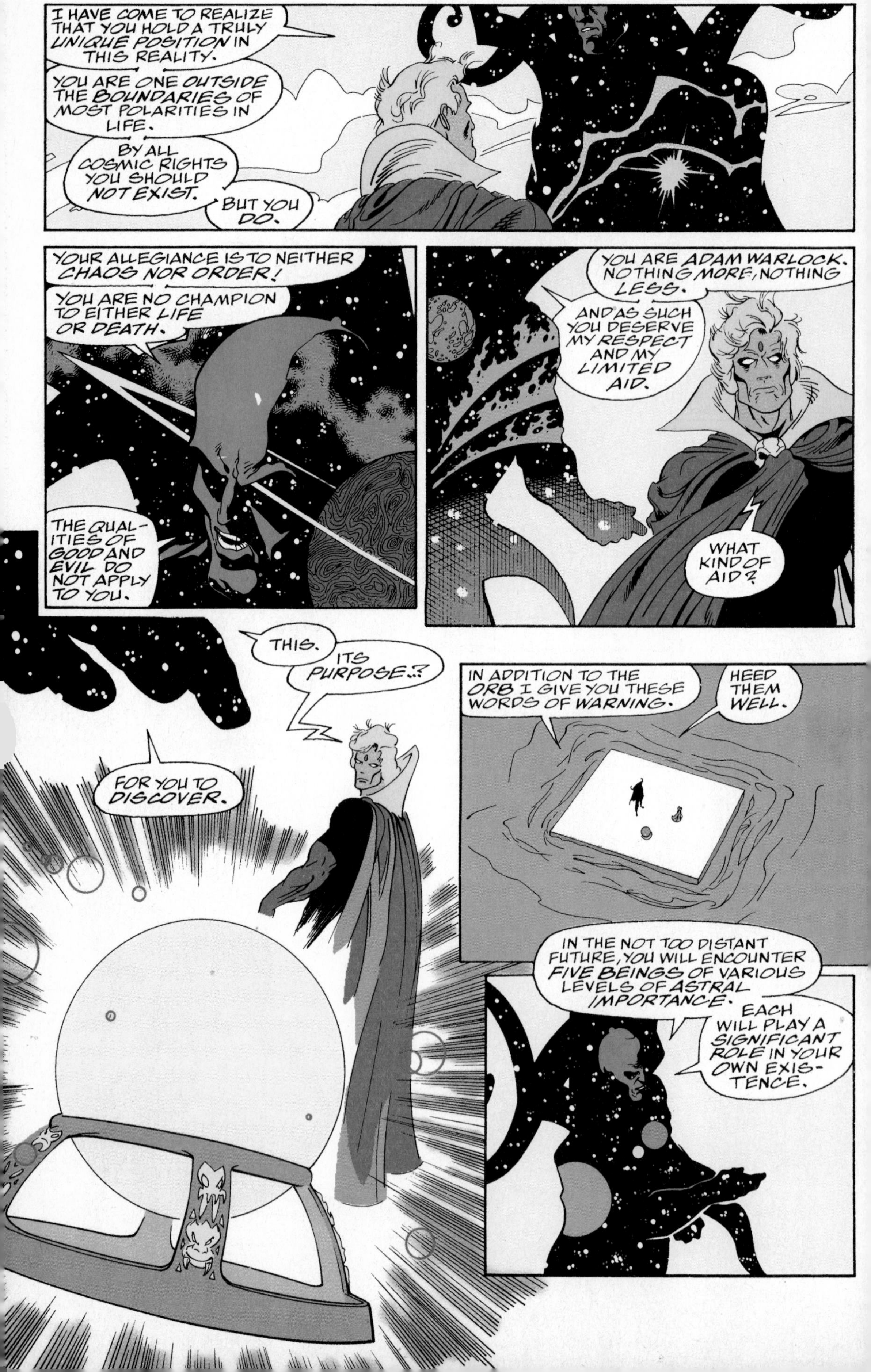
I HAVE COME TO REALIZE THAT YOU HOLD A TRULY UNIQUE POSITION IN THIS REALITY.
YOU ARE ONE OUTSIDE THE BOUNDARIES OF MOST POLARITIES IN LIFE.
BY ALL COSMIC RIGHTS YOU SHOULD NOT EXIST.
BUT YOU DO.
YOUR ALLEGIANCE IS TO NEITHER CHAOS NOR ORDER!
YOU ARE NO CHAMPION TO EITHER LIFE OR DEATH.
THE QUALITIES OF GOOD AND EVIL DO NOT APPLY TO YOU.
YOU ARE ADAM WARLOCK. NOTHING MORE, NOTHING LESS.
AND AS SUCH YOU DESERVE MY RESPECT AND MY LIMITED AID.
WHAT KIND OF AID?
THIS.
ITS PURPOSE..?
FOR YOU TO DISCOVER.
IN ADDITION TO THE ORB I GIVE YOU THESE WORDS OF WARNING.
HEED THEM WELL.
IN THE NOT TOO DISTANT FUTURE, YOU WILL ENCOUNTER FIVE BEINGS OF VARIOUS LEVELS OF ASTRAL IMPORTANCE.
EACH WILL PLAY A SIGNIFICANT ROLE IN YOUR OWN EXISTENCE.

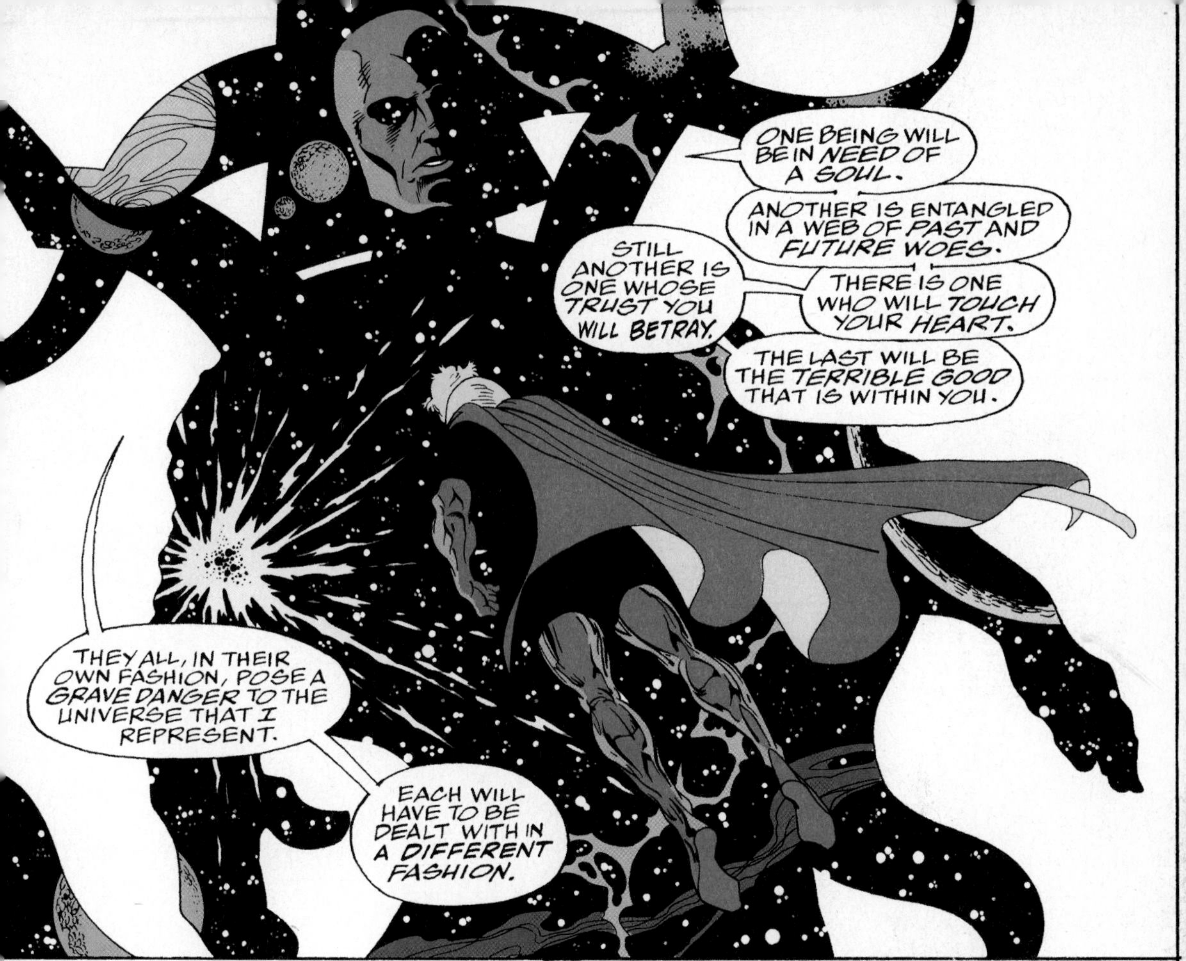

ONE BEING WILL BE IN NEED OF A SOUL.
ANOTHER IS ENTANGLED IN A WEB OF PAST AND FUTURE WOES.
STILL ANOTHER IS ONE WHOSE TRUST YOU WILL BETRAY.
THERE IS ONE WHO WILL TOUCH YOUR HEART.
THE LAST WILL BE THE TERRIBLE GOOD THAT IS WITHIN YOU.
THEY ALL, IN THEIR OWN FASHION, POSE A GRAVE DANGER TO THE UNIVERSE THAT I REPRESENT.
EACH WILL HAVE TO BE DEALT WITH IN A DIFFERENT FASHION.

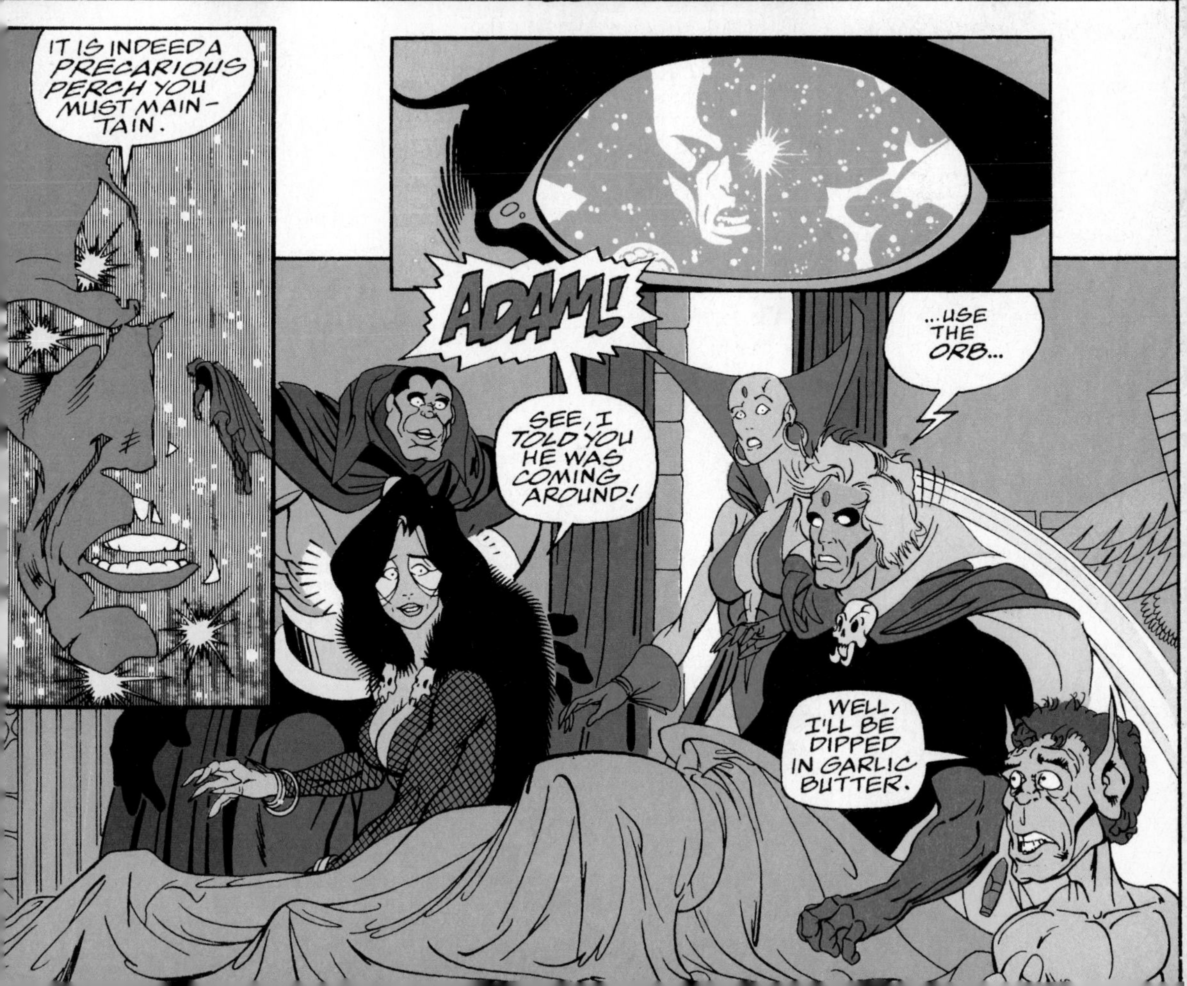

IT IS INDEED A PRECARIOUS PERCH YOU MUST MAIN-TAIN.
ADAM!
...USE THE ORB...
SEE, I TOLD YOU HE WAS COMING AROUND!
WELL, I'LL BE DIPPED IN GARLIC BUTTER.

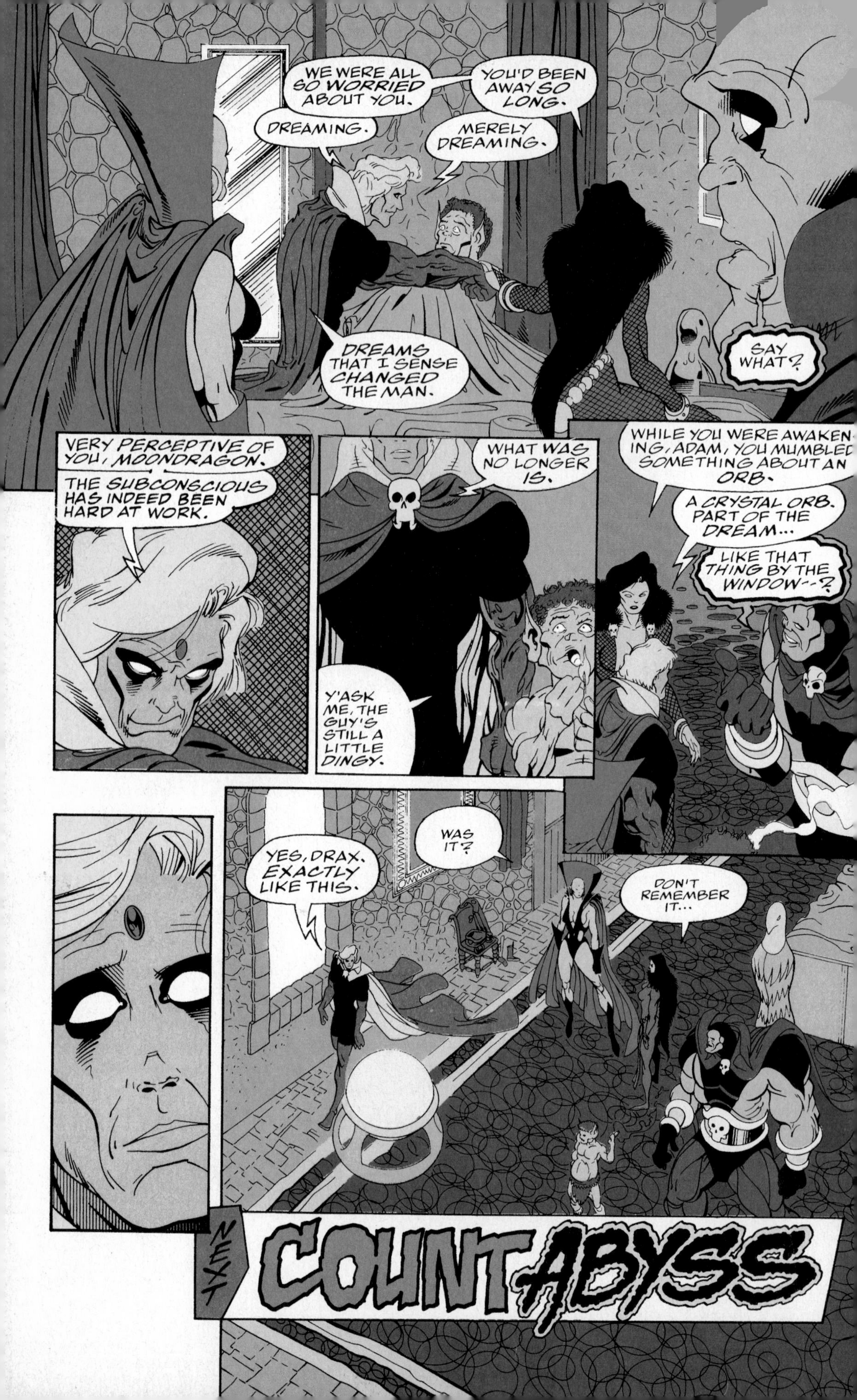
WE WERE ALL SO WORRIED ABOUT YOU.
YOU'D BEEN AWAY SO LONG.
DREAMING.
MERELY DREAMING.
DREAMS THAT I SENSE CHANGED THE MAN.
SAY WHAT?
VERY PERCEPTIVE OF YOU, MOONDRAGON.
THE SUBCONSCIOUS HAS INDEED BEEN HARD AT WORK.
WHAT WAS NO LONGER IS.
Y'ASK ME, THE GUY'S STILL A LITTLE DINGY.
WHILE YOU WERE AWAKENING, ADAM, YOU MUMBLED SOMETHING ABOUT AN ORB.
A CRYSTAL ORB. PART OF THE DREAM...
LIKE THAT THING BY THE WINDOW--?
WAS IT?
YES, DRAX. EXACTLY LIKE THIS.
DON'T REMEMBER IT...
NEXT
COUNT ABYSS

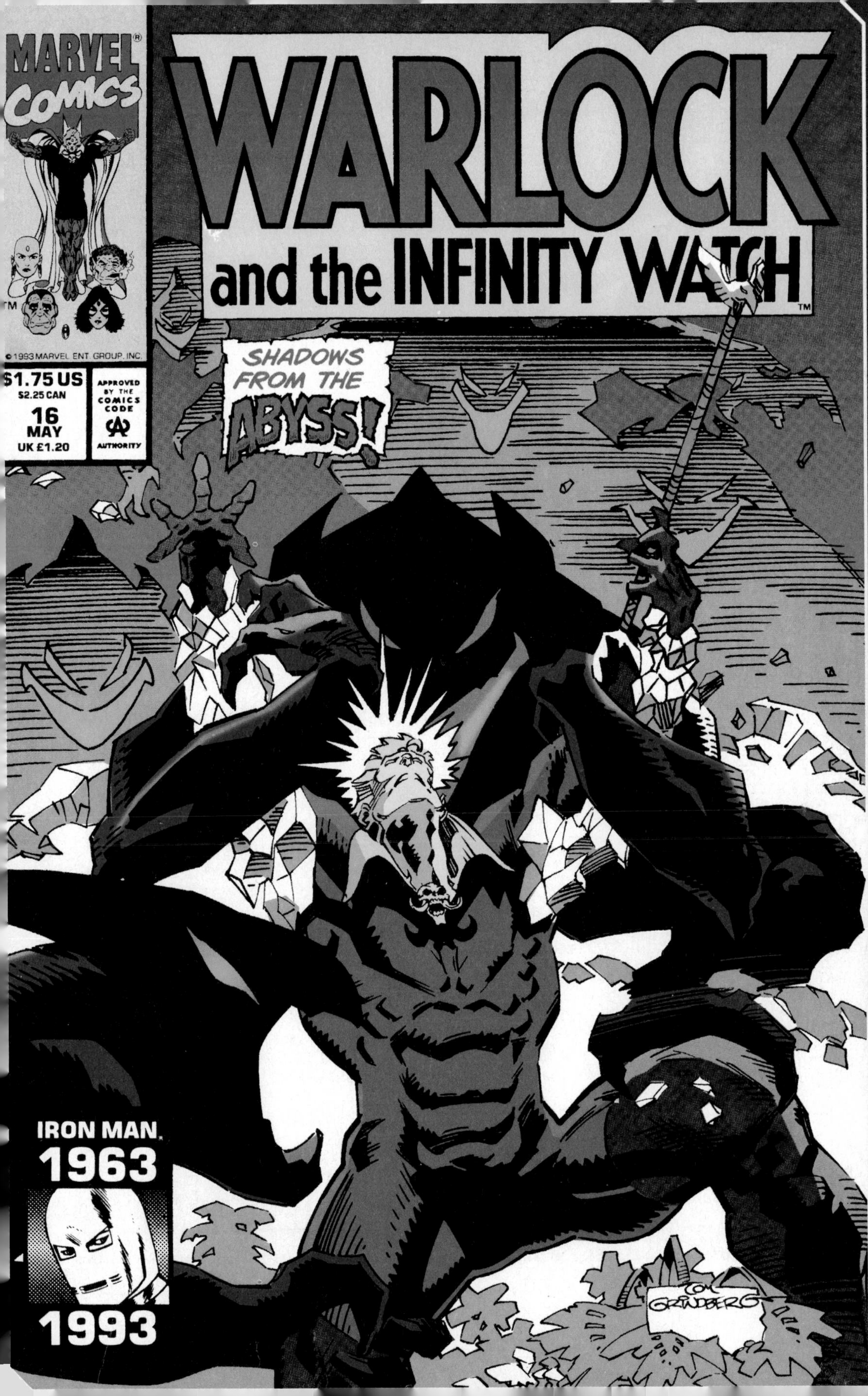
MARVEL COMICS
WARLOCK and the INFINITY WATCH
©1993 MARVEL ENT. GROUP, INC.
$1.75 US
$2.25 CAN
16
MAY
UK £1.20
APPROVED BY THE COMICS CODE AUTHORITY
SHADOWS FROM THE ABYSS!
IRON MAN
1963
1993

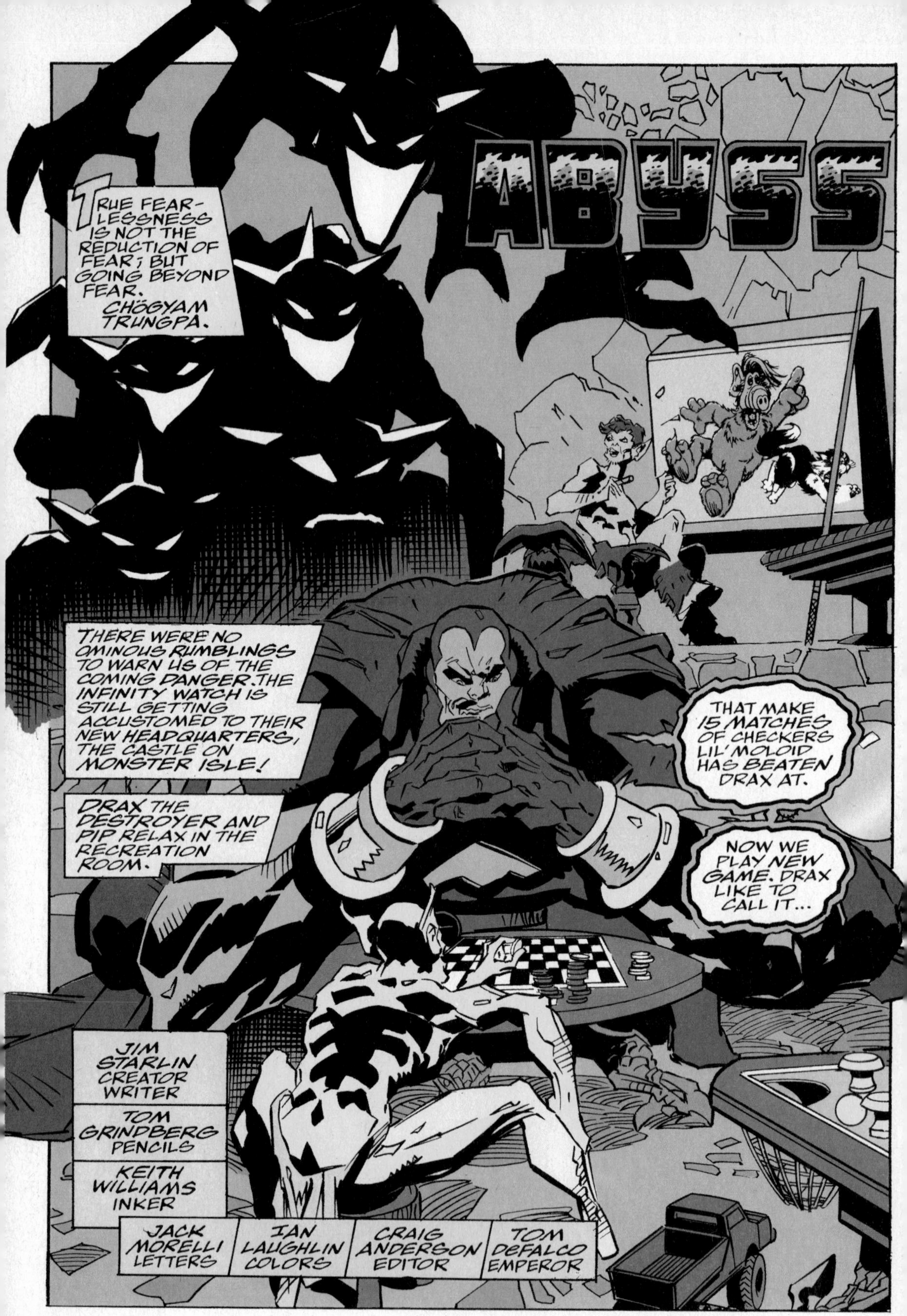
ABYSS
TRUE FEARLESSNESS IS NOT THE REDUCTION OF FEAR; BUT GOING BEYOND FEAR. CHÖGYAM TRUNGPA.
THERE WERE NO OMINOUS RUMBLINGS TO WARN US OF THE COMING DANGER. THE INFINITY WATCH IS STILL GETTING ACCUSTOMED TO THEIR NEW HEADQUARTERS, THE CASTLE ON MONSTER ISLE!
DRAX THE DESTROYER AND PIP RELAX IN THE RECREATION ROOM.
THAT MAKE 15 MATCHES OF CHECKERS LIL' MOLOID HAS BEATEN DRAX AT.
NOW WE PLAY NEW GAME. DRAX LIKE TO CALL IT...
JIM STARLIN CREATOR WRITER
TOM GRINDBERG PENCILS
KEITH WILLIAMS INKER
JACK MORELLI LETTERS
IAN LAUGHLIN COLORS
CRAIG ANDERSON EDITOR
TOM DEFALCO EMPEROR

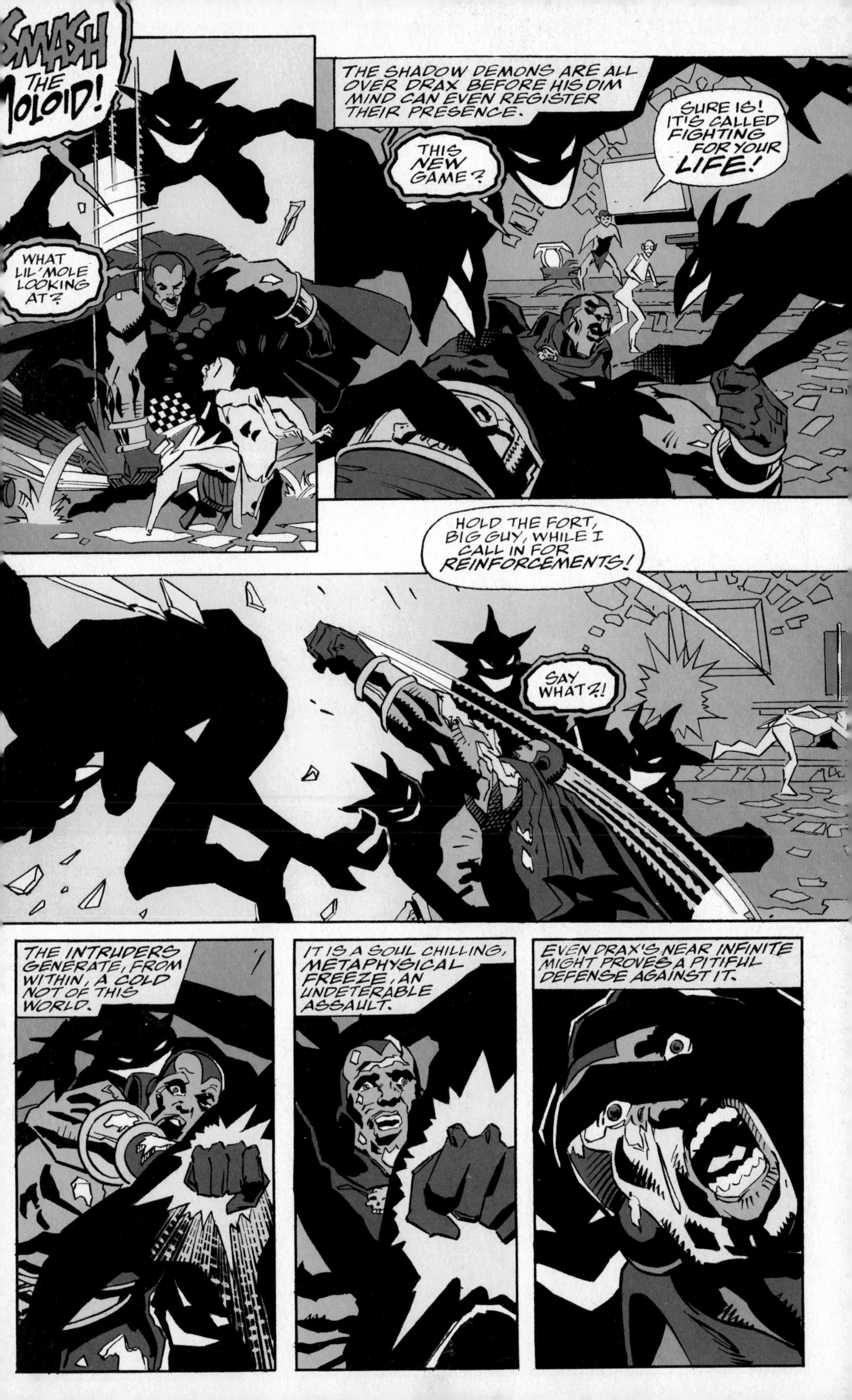
SMASH THE MOLOID!
WHAT LIL' MOLE LOOKING AT?
THE SHADOW DEMONS ARE ALL OVER DRAX BEFORE HIS DIM MIND CAN EVEN REGISTER THEIR PRESENCE.
THIS NEW GAME?
SURE IS! IT'S CALLED FIGHTING FOR YOUR LIFE!
HOLD THE FORT, BIG GUY, WHILE I CALL IN FOR REINFORCEMENTS!
SAY WHAT?!
THE INTRUDERS GENERATE, FROM WITHIN, A COLD NOT OF THIS WORLD.
IT IS A SOUL CHILLING, METAPHYSICAL FREEZE, AN UNDETERABLE ASSAULT.
EVEN DRAX'S NEAR INFINITE MIGHT PROVES A PITIFUL DEFENSE AGAINST IT.

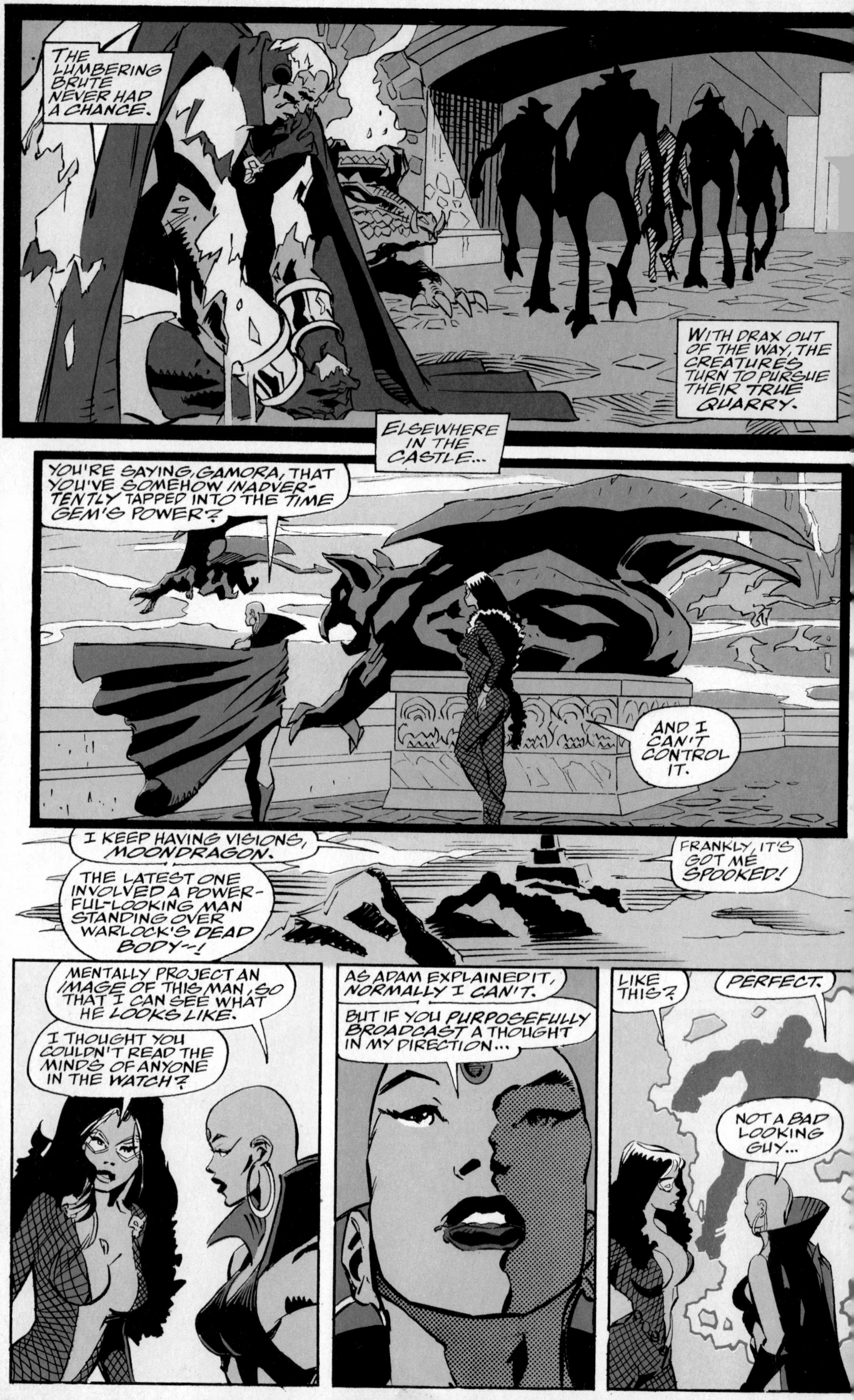

THE LUMBERING BRUTE NEVER HAD A CHANCE.
WITH DRAX OUT OF THE WAY, THE CREATURES TURN TO PURSUE THEIR TRUE QUARRY.
ELSEWHERE IN THE CASTLE...
YOU'RE SAYING, GAMORA, THAT YOU'VE SOMEHOW INADVERTENTLY TAPPED INTO THE TIME GEM'S POWER?
AND I CAN'T CONTROL IT.
I KEEP HAVING VISIONS, MOONDRAGON.
THE LATEST ONE INVOLVED A POWERFUL-LOOKING MAN STANDING OVER WARLOCK'S DEAD BODY--!
FRANKLY, IT'S GOT ME SPOOKED!
MENTALLY PROJECT AN IMAGE OF THIS MAN, SO THAT I CAN SEE WHAT HE LOOKS LIKE.
I THOUGHT YOU COULDN'T READ THE MINDS OF ANYONE IN THE WATCH?
AS ADAM EXPLAINED IT, NORMALLY I CAN'T.
BUT IF YOU PURPOSEFULLY BROADCAST A THOUGHT IN MY DIRECTION...
LIKE THIS?
PERFECT.
NOT A BAD LOOKING GUY...

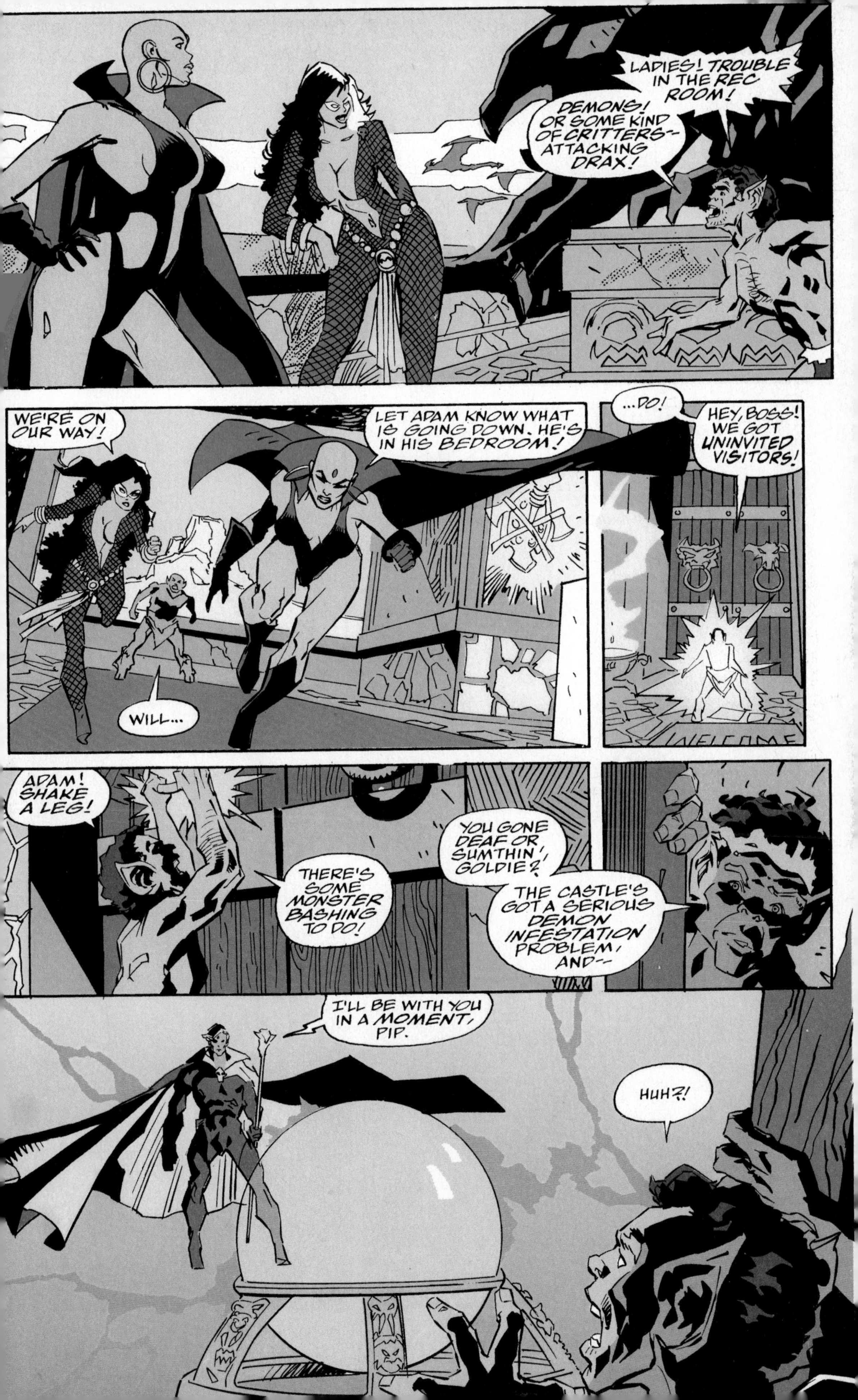
LADIES! TROUBLE IN THE REC ROOM!
DEMONS! OR SOME KIND OF CRITTERS-- ATTACKING DRAX!
WE'RE ON OUR WAY!
LET ADAM KNOW WHAT IS GOING DOWN. HE'S IN HIS BEDROOM!
WILL...
...DO!
HEY, BOSS! WE GOT UNINVITED VISITORS!
WELCOME
ADAM! SHAKE A LEG!
THERE'S SOME MONSTER BASHING TO DO!
YOU GONE DEAF OR SUMTHIN', GOLDIE?
THE CASTLE'S GOT A SERIOUS DEMON INFESTATION PROBLEM, AND--
I'LL BE WITH YOU IN A MOMENT, PIP.
HUH?!

NOW WHAT WAS THAT YOU WERE SAYING ABOUT DEMONS?

"UNBEKNOWNST TO ME, THE BATTLE HAS ALREADY BEEN JOINED.

"AT FIRST THE GODS SEEM TO BE ON GAMORA'S SIDE.

THEN THE TABLES TURN AND DISASTER STRIKES...

WHAT THE?

BUT DELIVERANCE COMES IN THE FORM OF AN UNEXPECTED TELEKINETIC EXTRACTION.

WHO?

WHAT?

HOW?

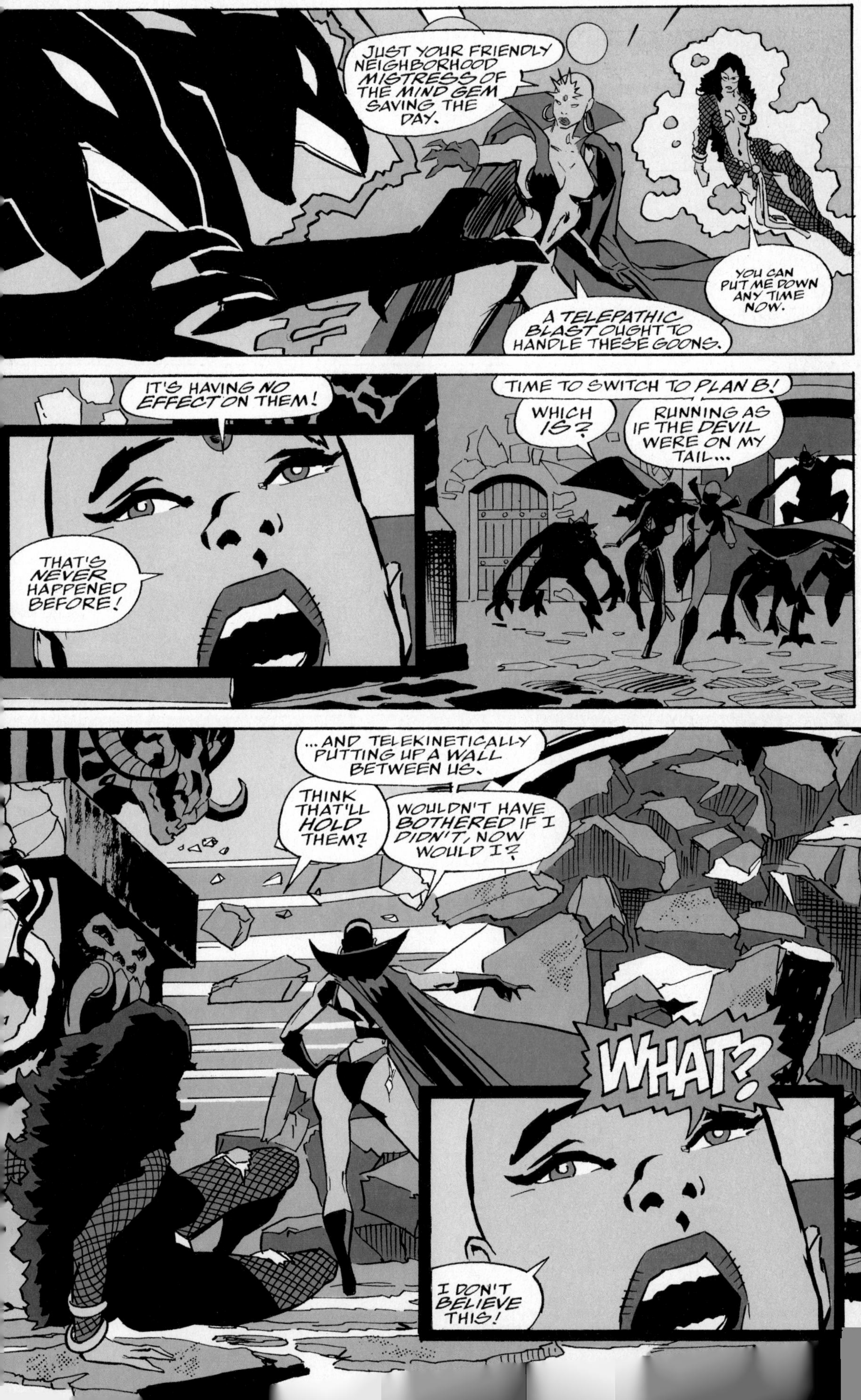
JUST YOUR FRIENDLY NEIGHBORHOOD MISTRESS OF THE MIND GEM SAVING THE DAY.
A TELEPATHIC BLAST OUGHT TO HANDLE THESE GOONS.
YOU CAN PUT ME DOWN ANY TIME NOW.
IT'S HAVING NO EFFECT ON THEM!
THAT'S NEVER HAPPENED BEFORE!
TIME TO SWITCH TO PLAN B!
WHICH IS?
RUNNING AS IF THE DEVIL WERE ON MY TAIL...
...AND TELEKINETICALLY PUTTING UP A WALL BETWEEN US.
THINK THAT'LL HOLD THEM?
WOULDN'T HAVE BOTHERED IF I DIDN'T, NOW WOULD I?
WHAT?
I DON'T BELIEVE THIS!

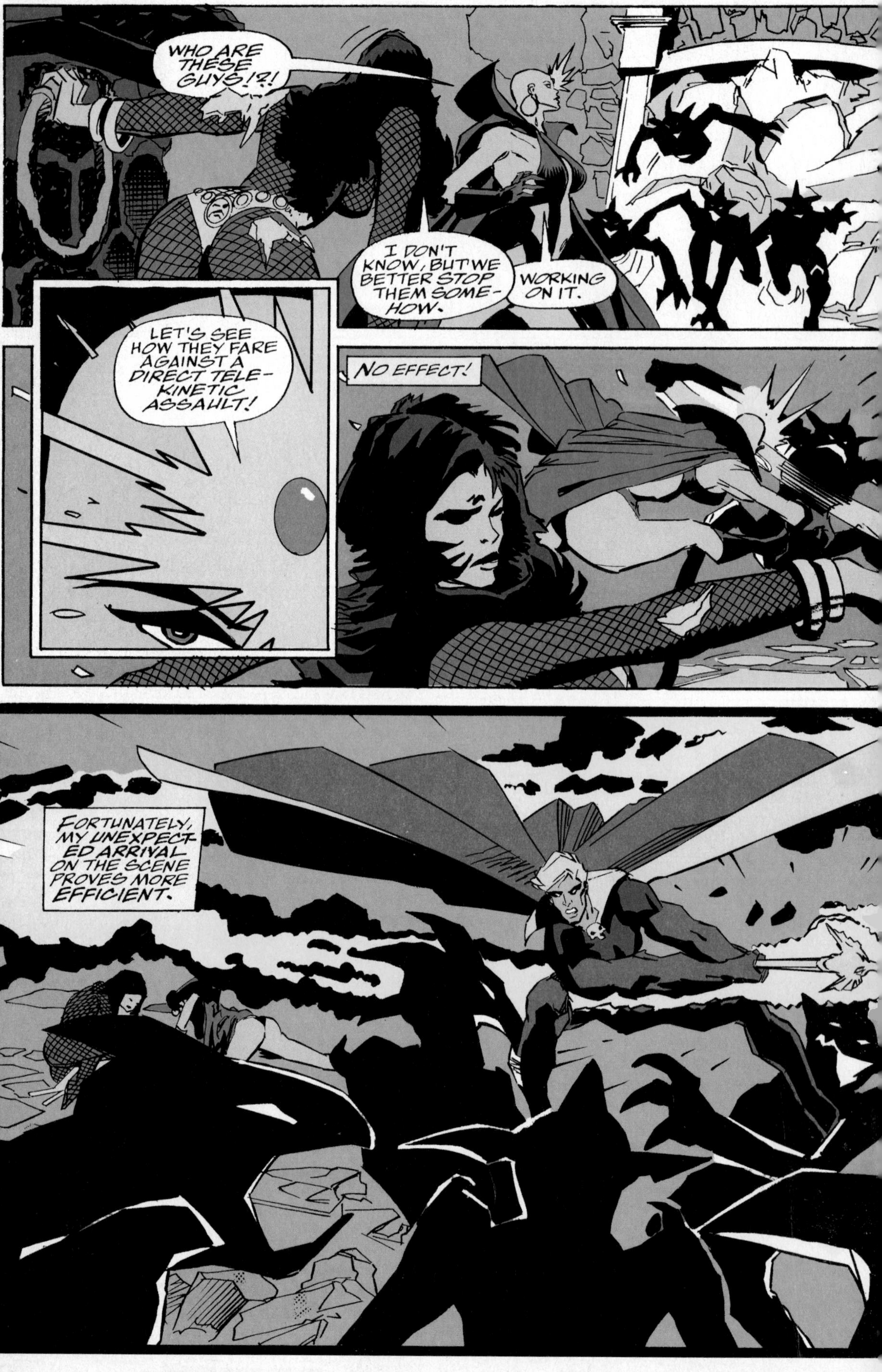
WHO ARE THESE GUYS!?!
I DON'T KNOW, BUT WE BETTER STOP THEM SOME-HOW.
WORKING ON IT.
LET'S SEE HOW THEY FARE AGAINST A DIRECT TELE-KINETIC ASSAULT!
NO EFFECT!
FORTUNATELY, MY UNEXPECT-ED ARRIVAL ON THE SCENE PROVES MORE EFFICIENT.

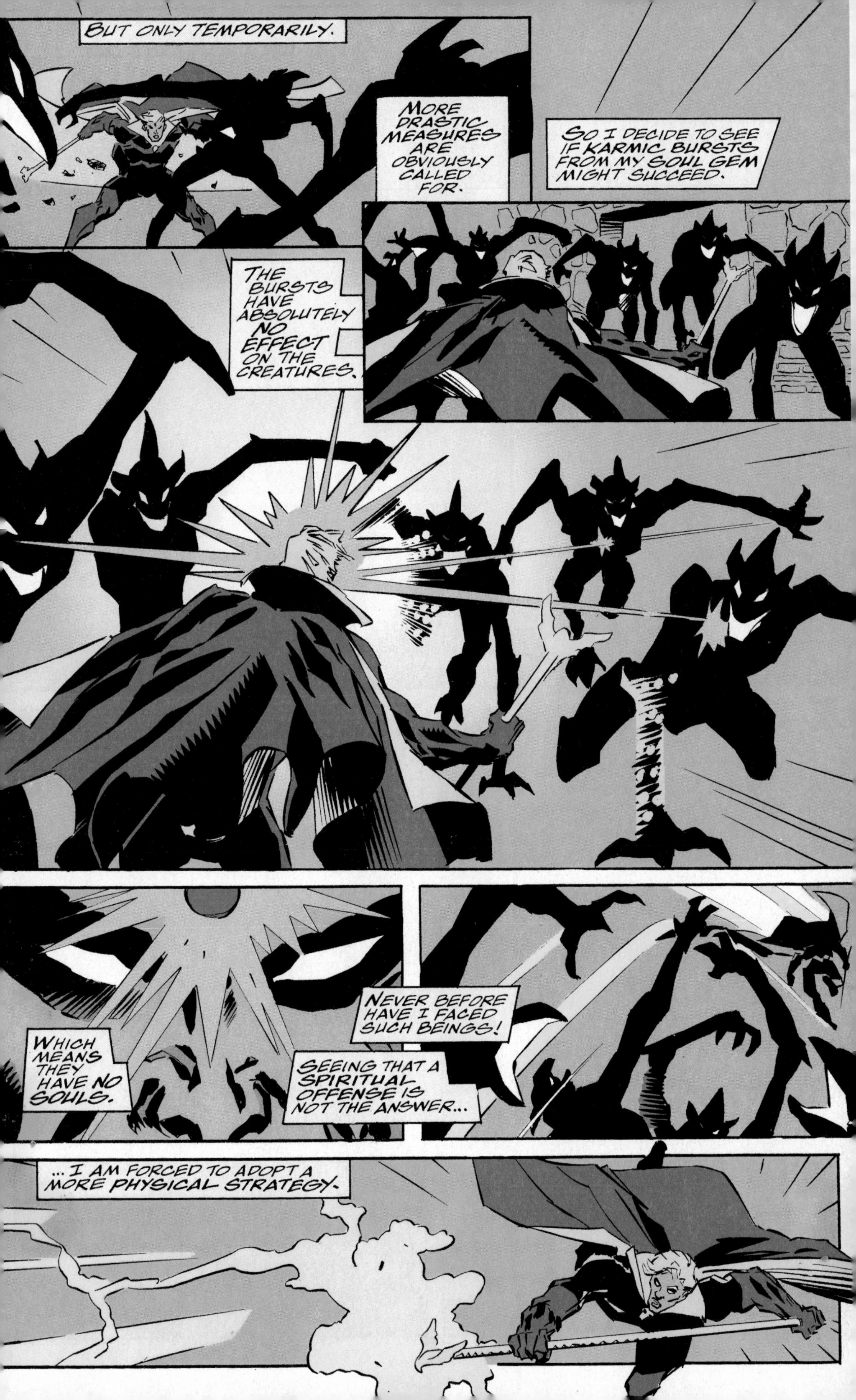
BUT ONLY TEMPORARILY.
MORE DRASTIC MEASURES ARE OBVIOUSLY CALLED FOR.
SO I DECIDE TO SEE IF KARMIC BURSTS FROM MY SOUL GEM MIGHT SUCCEED.
THE BURSTS HAVE ABSOLUTELY NO EFFECT ON THE CREATURES.
WHICH MEANS THEY HAVE NO SOULS.
NEVER BEFORE HAVE I FACED SUCH BEINGS!
SEEING THAT A SPIRITUAL OFFENSE IS NOT THE ANSWER...
... I AM FORCED TO ADOPT A MORE PHYSICAL STRATEGY.

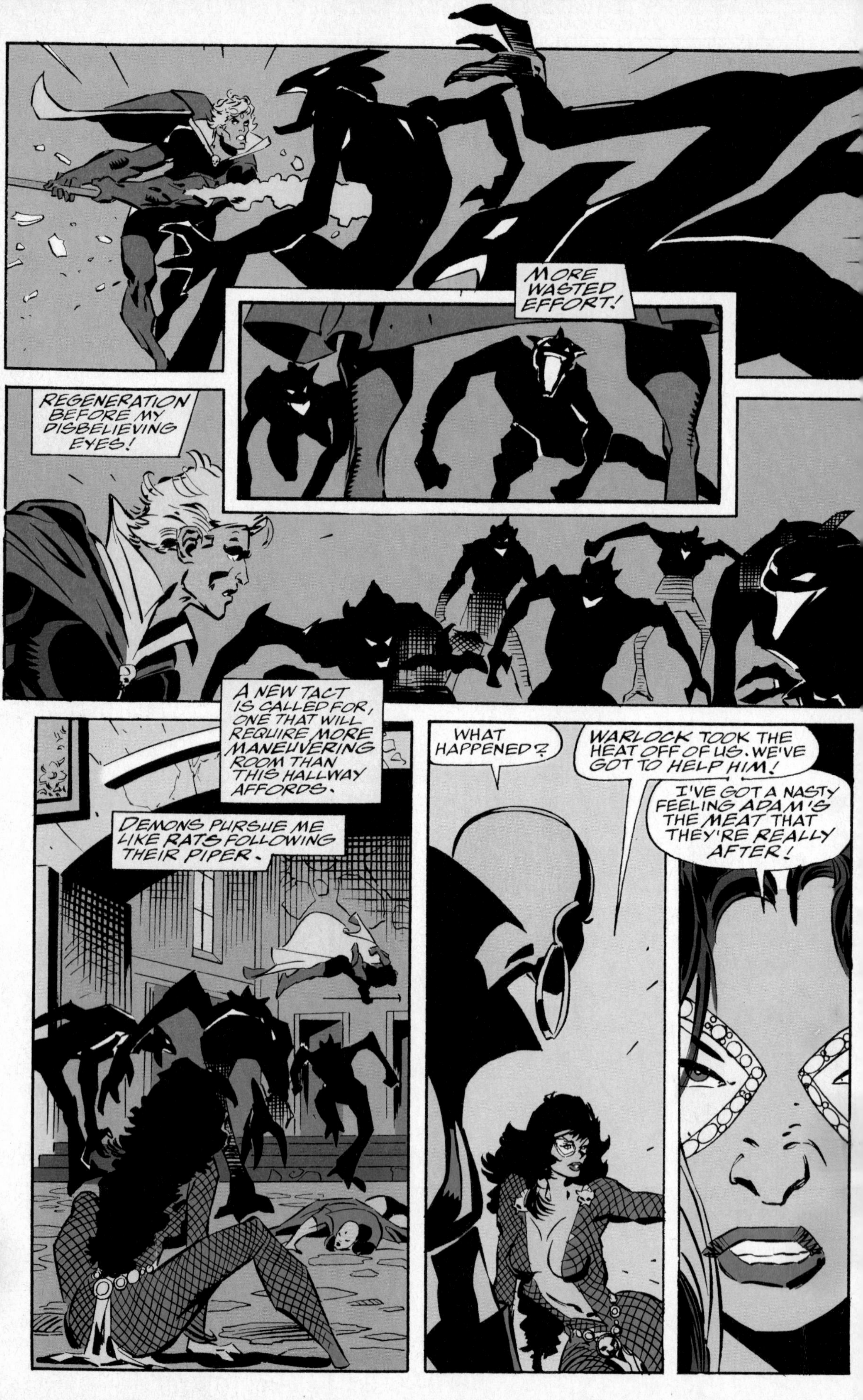
MORE WASTED EFFORT!
REGENERATION BEFORE MY DISBELIEVING EYES!
A NEW TACT IS CALLED FOR, ONE THAT WILL REQUIRE MORE MANEUVERING ROOM THAN THIS HALLWAY AFFORDS.
DEMONS PURSUE ME LIKE RATS FOLLOWING THEIR PIPER.
WHAT HAPPENED?
WARLOCK TOOK THE HEAT OFF OF US. WE'VE GOT TO HELP HIM!
I'VE GOT A NASTY FEELING ADAM'S THE MEAT THAT THEY'RE REALLY AFTER!

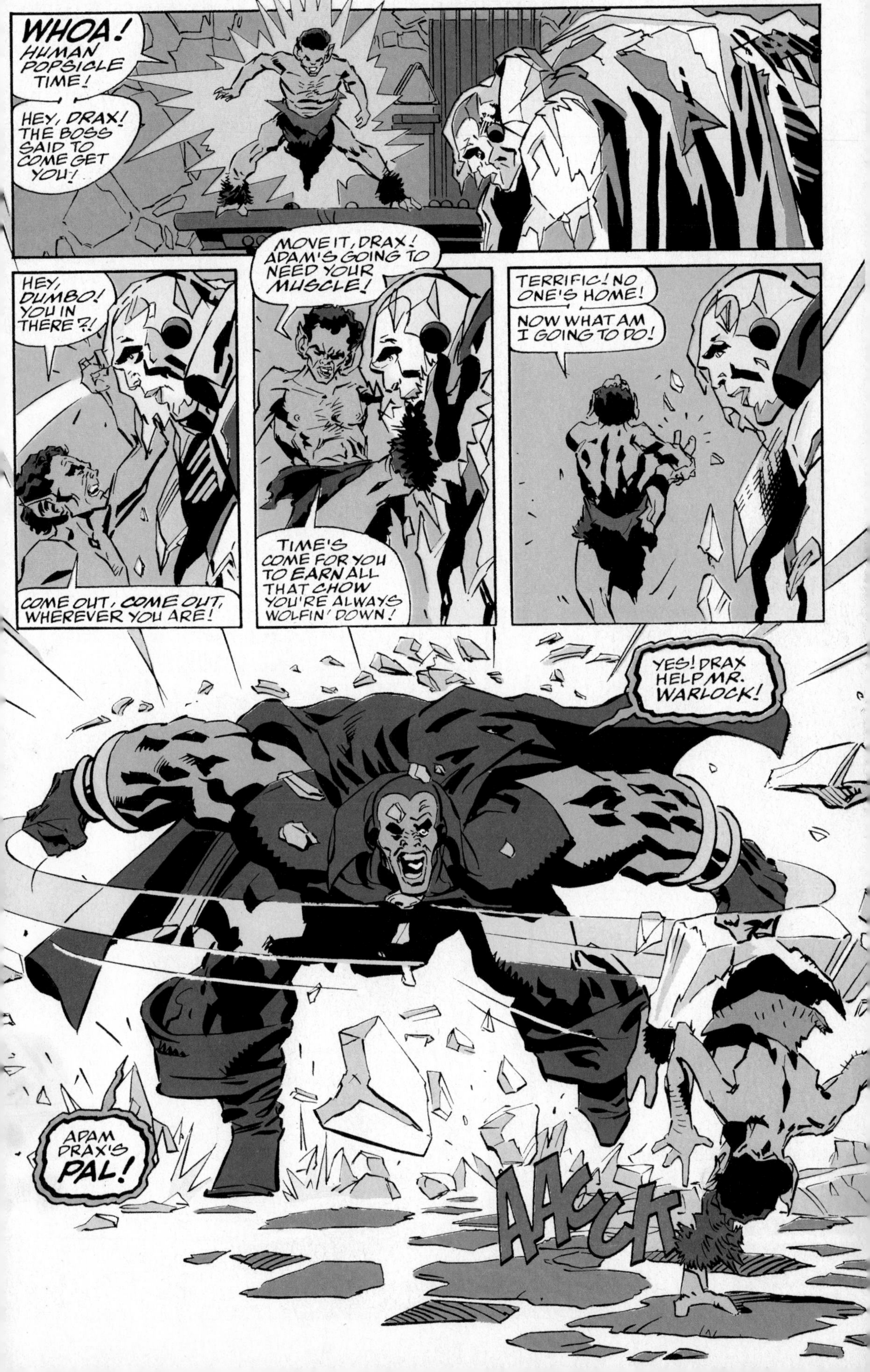

WHOA! HUMAN POPSICLE TIME!
HEY, DRAX! THE BOSS SAID TO COME GET YOU!
HEY, DUMBO! YOU IN THERE?!
COME OUT, COME OUT, WHEREVER YOU ARE!
MOVE IT, DRAX! ADAM'S GOING TO NEED YOUR MUSCLE!
TIME'S COME FOR YOU TO EARN ALL THAT CHOW YOU'RE ALWAYS WOLFIN' DOWN!
TERRIFIC! NO ONE'S HOME!
NOW WHAT AM I GOING TO DO!
YES! DRAX HELP MR. WARLOCK!
ADAM DRAX'S PAL!
AACCK

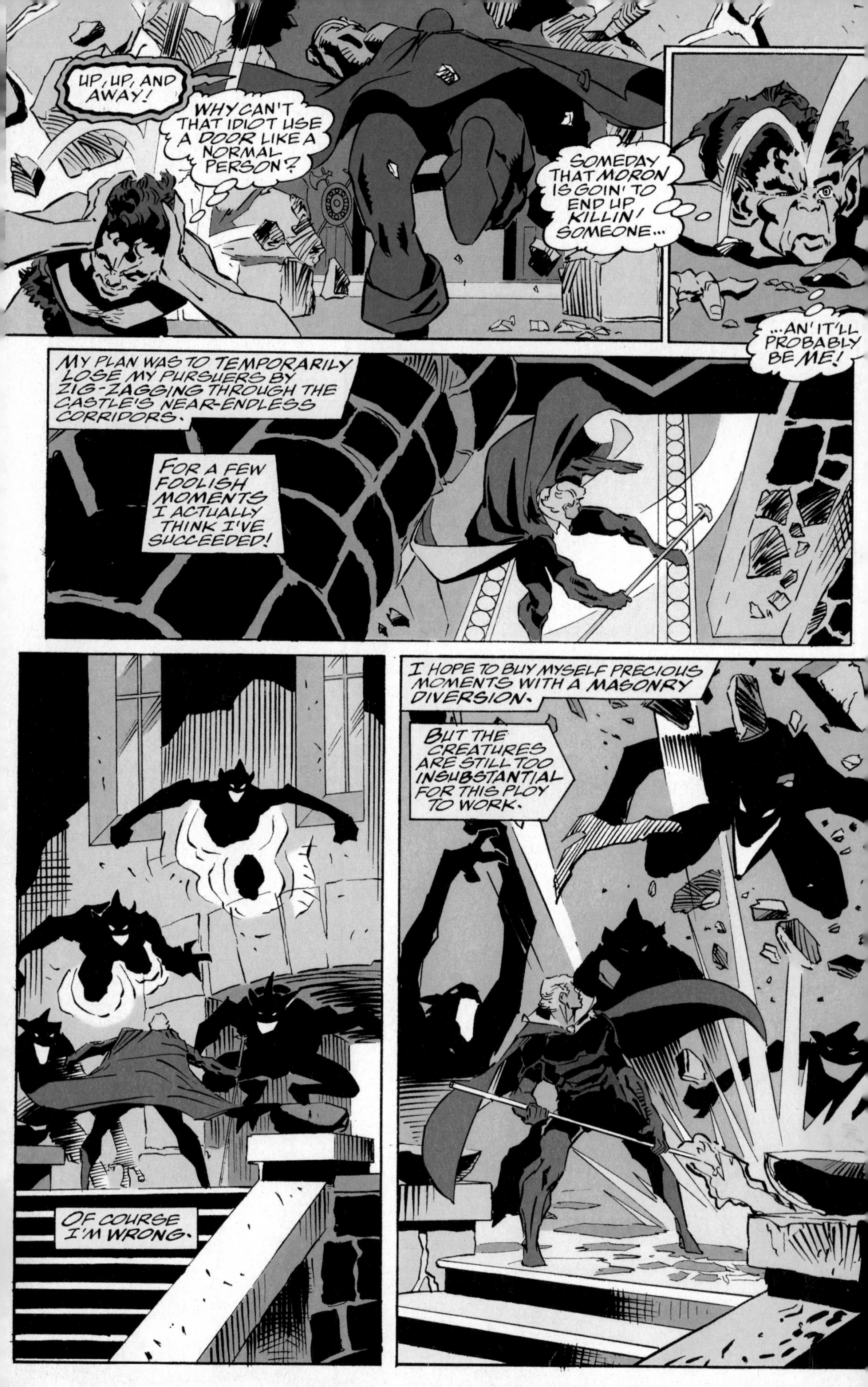
UP, UP, AND AWAY!
WHY CAN'T THAT IDIOT USE A DOOR LIKE A NORMAL PERSON?
SOMEDAY THAT MORON IS GOIN' TO END UP KILLIN' SOMEONE...
...AN' IT'LL PROBABLY BE ME!
MY PLAN WAS TO TEMPORARILY LOSE MY PURSUERS BY ZIG-ZAGGING THROUGH THE CASTLE'S NEAR-ENDLESS CORRIDORS.
FOR A FEW FOOLISH MOMENTS I ACTUALLY THINK I'VE SUCCEEDED!
OF COURSE I'M WRONG.
I HOPE TO BUY MYSELF PRECIOUS MOMENTS WITH A MASONRY DIVERSION.
BUT THE CREATURES ARE STILL TOO INSUBSTANTIAL FOR THIS PLOY TO WORK.

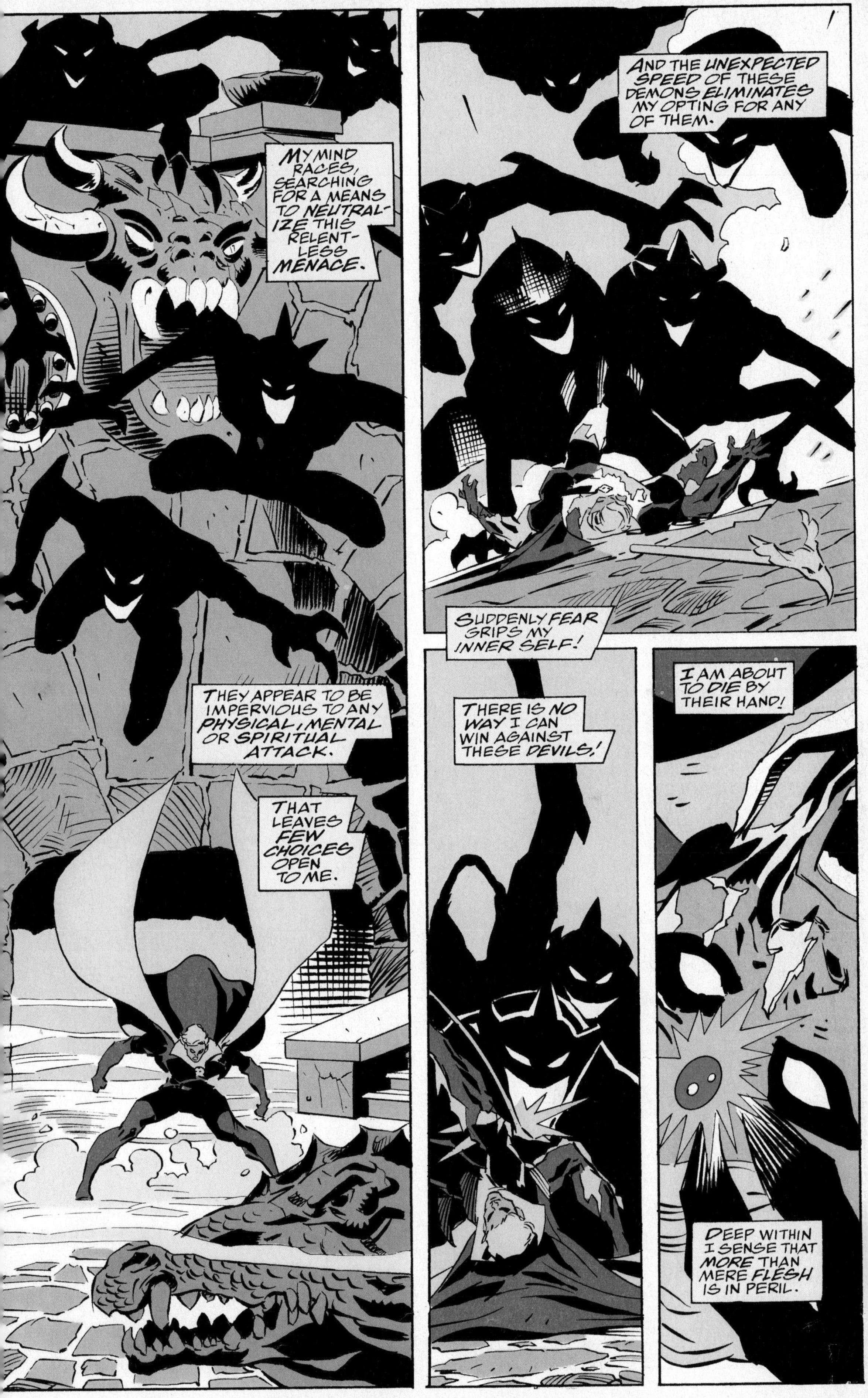
MY MIND RACES, SEARCHING FOR A MEANS TO NEUTRALIZE THIS RELENTLESS MENACE.
THEY APPEAR TO BE IMPERVIOUS TO ANY PHYSICAL, MENTAL OR SPIRITUAL ATTACK.
THAT LEAVES FEW CHOICES OPEN TO ME.
AND THE UNEXPECTED SPEED OF THESE DEMONS ELIMINATES MY OPTING FOR ANY OF THEM.
SUDDENLY FEAR GRIPS MY INNER SELF!
THERE IS NO WAY I CAN WIN AGAINST THESE DEVILS!
I AM ABOUT TO DIE BY THEIR HAND!
DEEP WITHIN I SENSE THAT MORE THAN MERE FLESH IS IN PERIL.

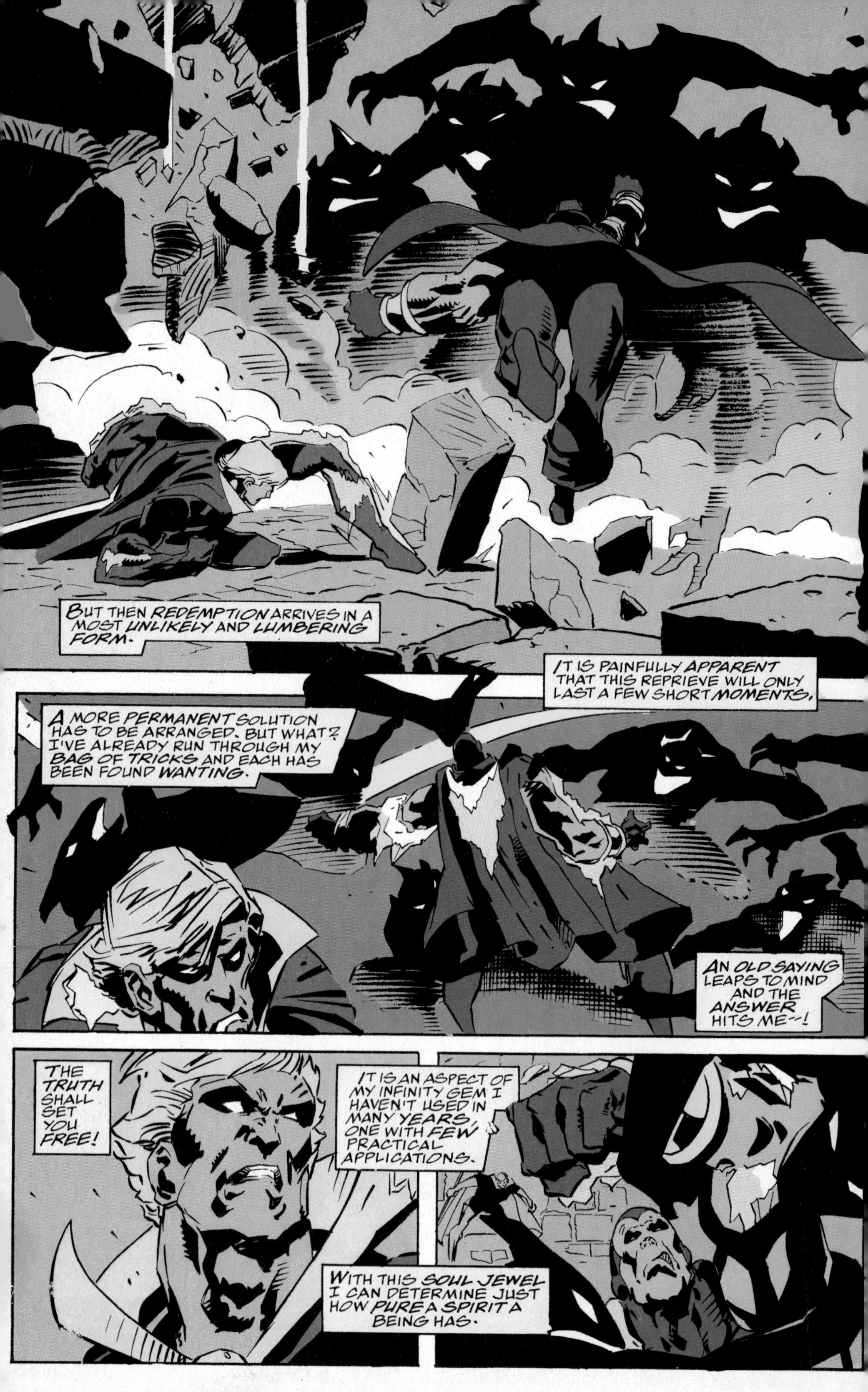

BUT THEN REDEMPTION ARRIVES IN A MOST UNLIKELY AND LUMBERING FORM.
IT IS PAINFULLY APPARENT THAT THIS REPRIEVE WILL ONLY LAST A FEW SHORT MOMENTS.
A MORE PERMANENT SOLUTION HAS TO BE ARRANGED. BUT WHAT? I'VE ALREADY RUN THROUGH MY BAG OF TRICKS AND EACH HAS BEEN FOUND WANTING.
AN OLD SAYING LEAPS TO MIND AND THE ANSWER HITS ME--!
THE TRUTH SHALL SET YOU FREE!
IT IS AN ASPECT OF MY INFINITY GEM I HAVEN'T USED IN MANY YEARS, ONE WITH FEW PRACTICAL APPLICATIONS.
WITH THIS SOUL JEWEL I CAN DETERMINE JUST HOW PURE A SPIRIT A BEING HAS.

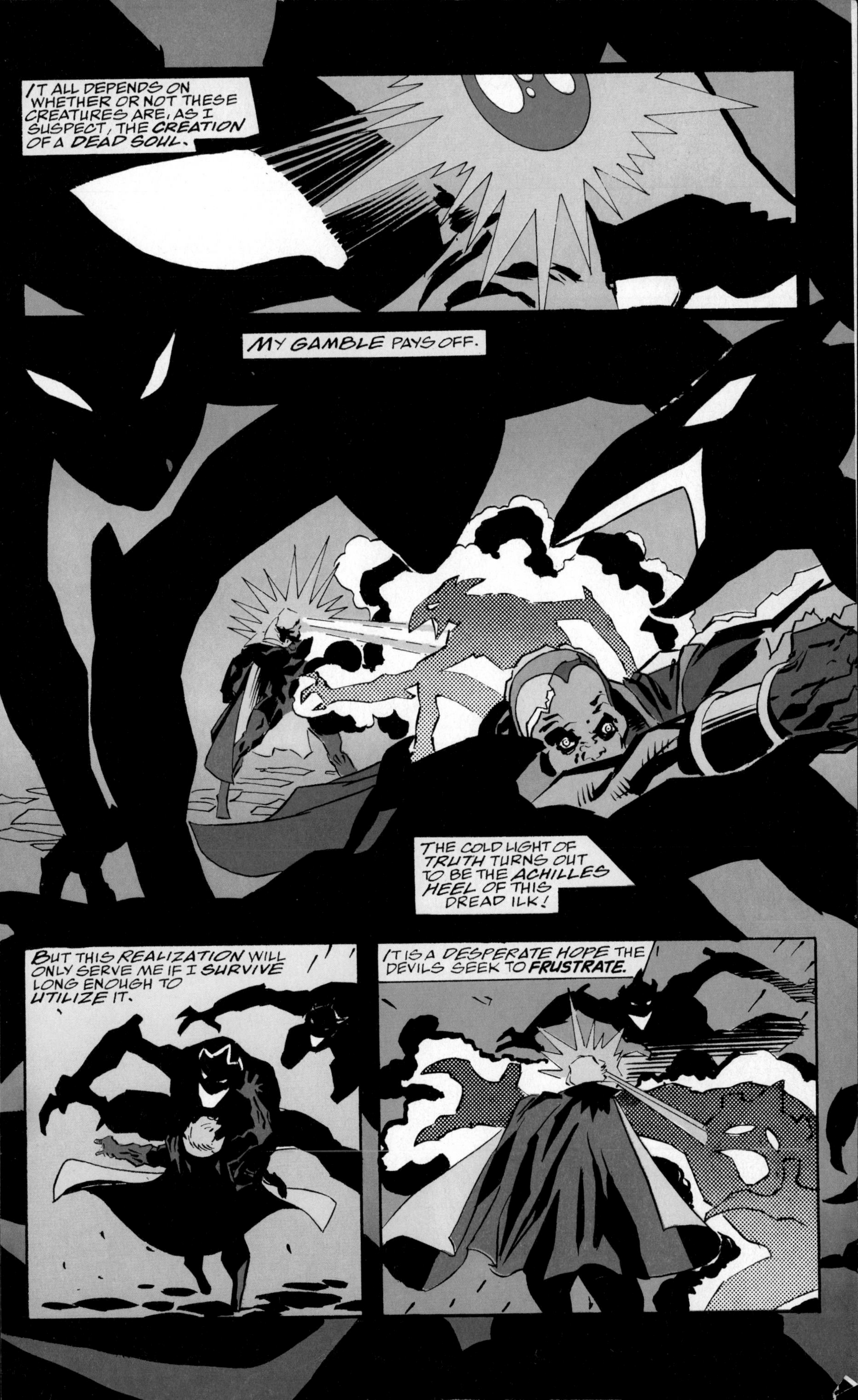
IT ALL DEPENDS ON WHETHER OR NOT THESE CREATURES ARE, AS I SUSPECT, THE CREATION OF A DEAD SOUL.
MY GAMBLE PAYS OFF.
THE COLD LIGHT OF TRUTH TURNS OUT TO BE THE ACHILLES HEEL OF THIS DREAD ILK!
BUT THIS REALIZATION WILL ONLY SERVE ME IF I SURVIVE LONG ENOUGH TO UTILIZE IT.
IT IS A DESPERATE HOPE THE DEVILS SEEK TO FRUSTRATE.

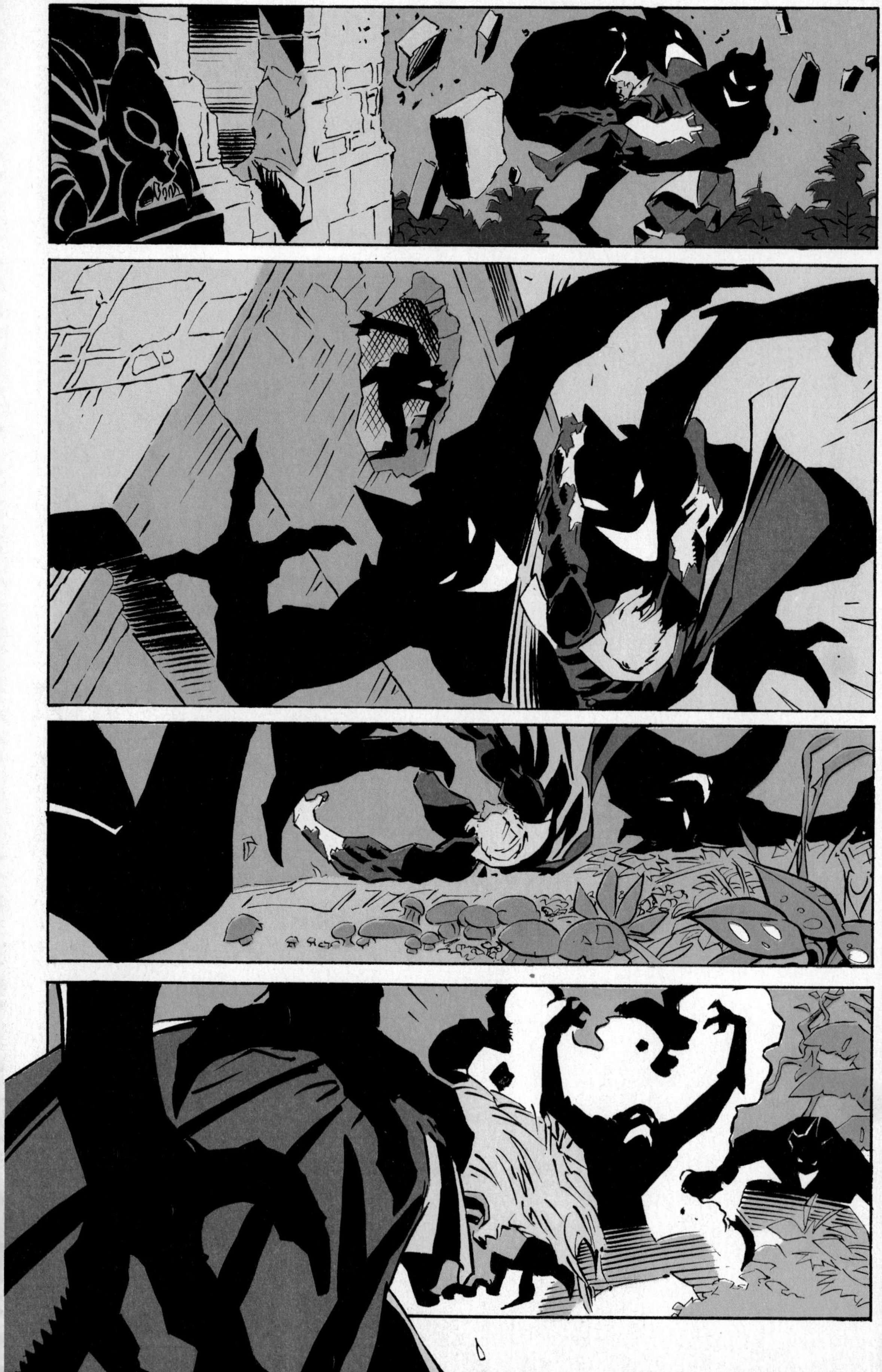

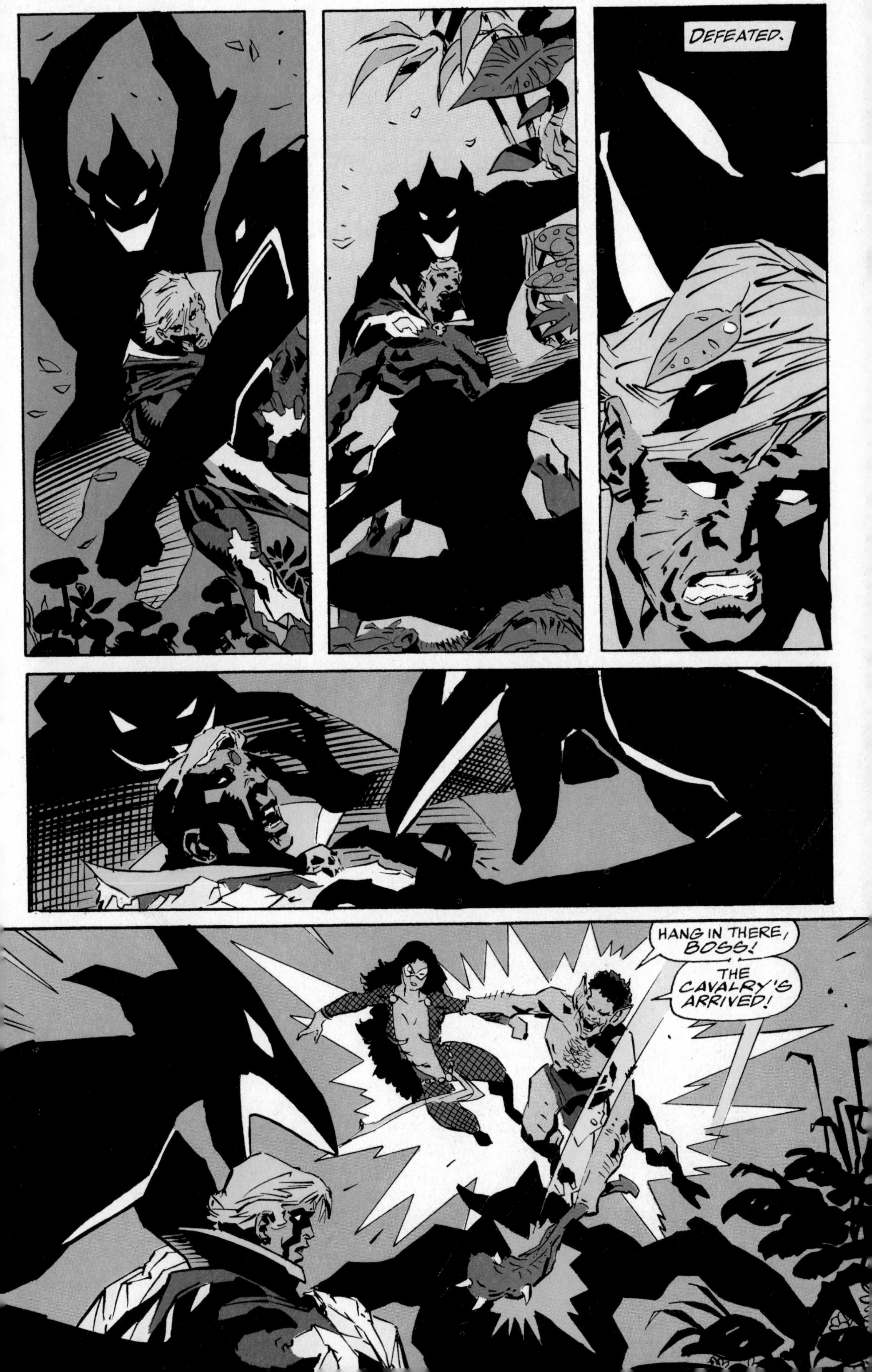
DEFEATED.
HANG IN THERE, BOSS!
THE CAVALRY'S ARRIVED!

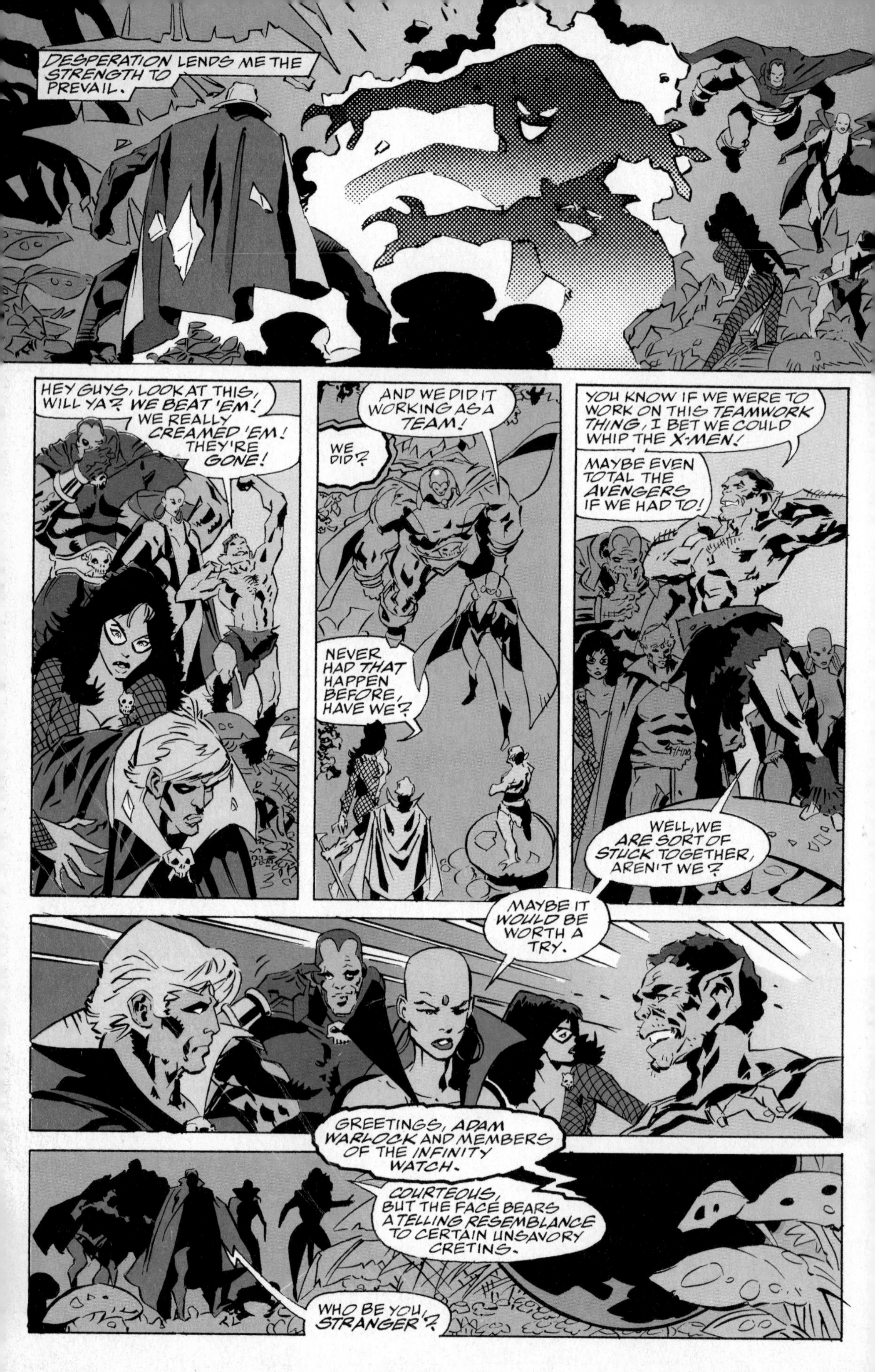
DESPERATION LENDS ME THE STRENGTH TO PREVAIL.
HEY GUYS, LOOK AT THIS, WILL YA? WE BEAT 'EM! WE REALLY CREAMED 'EM! THEY'RE GONE!
AND WE DID IT WORKING AS A TEAM!
WE DID?
NEVER HAD THAT HAPPEN BEFORE, HAVE WE?
YOU KNOW IF WE WERE TO WORK ON THIS TEAMWORK THING, I BET WE COULD WHIP THE X-MEN!
MAYBE EVEN TOTAL THE AVENGERS IF WE HAD TO!
WELL, WE ARE SORT OF STUCK TOGETHER, AREN'T WE?
MAYBE IT WOULD BE WORTH A TRY.
GREETINGS, ADAM WARLOCK AND MEMBERS OF THE INFINITY WATCH.
COURTEOUS, BUT THE FACE BEARS A TELLING RESEMBLANCE TO CERTAIN UNSAVORY CRETINS.
WHO BE YOU, STRANGER?

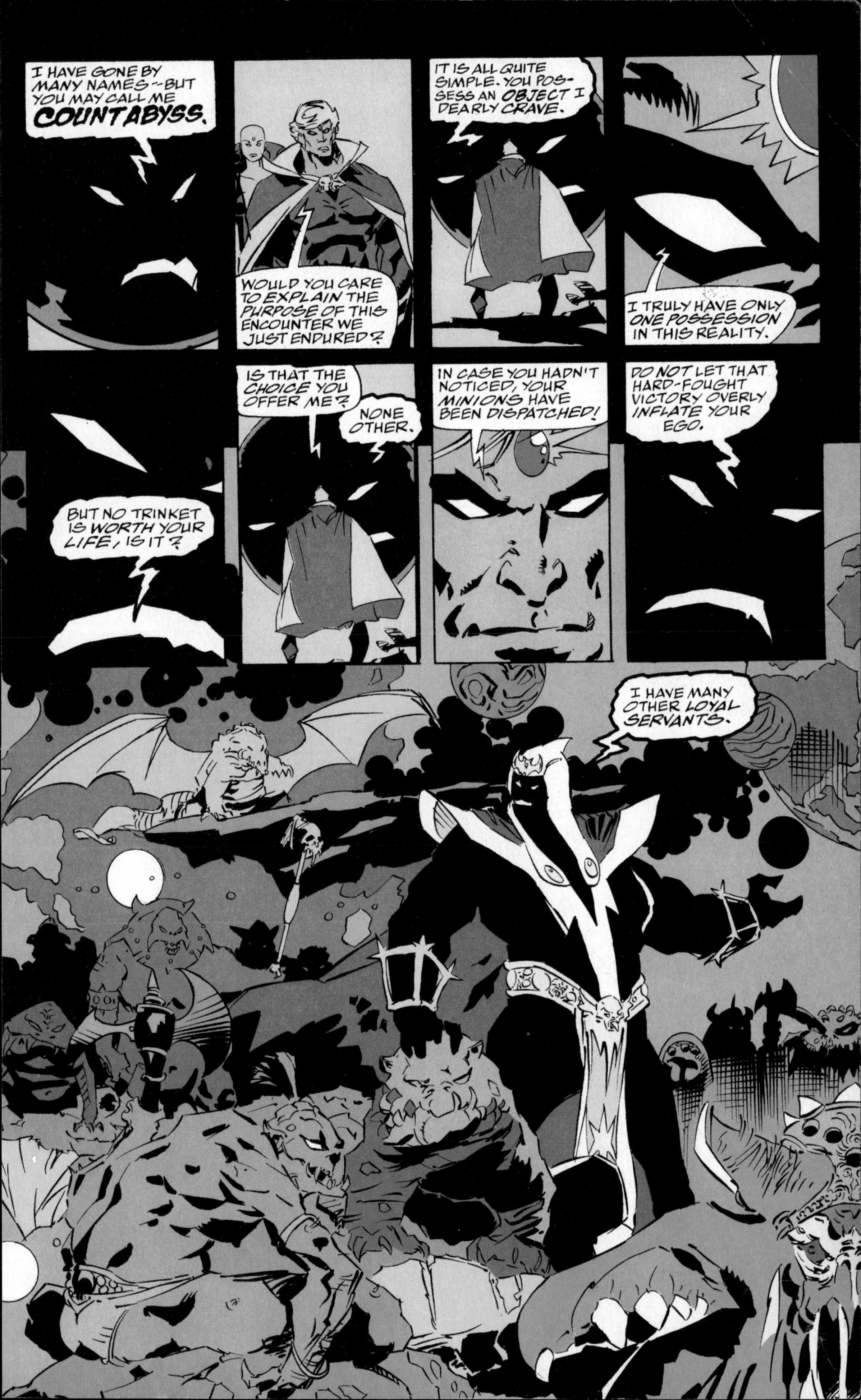
I HAVE GONE BY MANY NAMES--BUT YOU MAY CALL ME COUNT ABYSS.
WOULD YOU CARE TO EXPLAIN THE PURPOSE OF THIS ENCOUNTER WE JUST ENDURED?
IT IS ALL QUITE SIMPLE. YOU POSSESS AN OBJECT I DEARLY CRAVE.
I TRULY HAVE ONLY ONE POSSESSION IN THIS REALITY.
BUT NO TRINKET IS WORTH YOUR LIFE, IS IT?
IS THAT THE CHOICE YOU OFFER ME?
NONE OTHER.
IN CASE YOU HADN'T NOTICED, YOUR MINIONS HAVE BEEN DISPATCHED!
DO NOT LET THAT HARD-FOUGHT VICTORY OVERLY INFLATE YOUR EGO.
I HAVE MANY OTHER LOYAL SERVANTS.

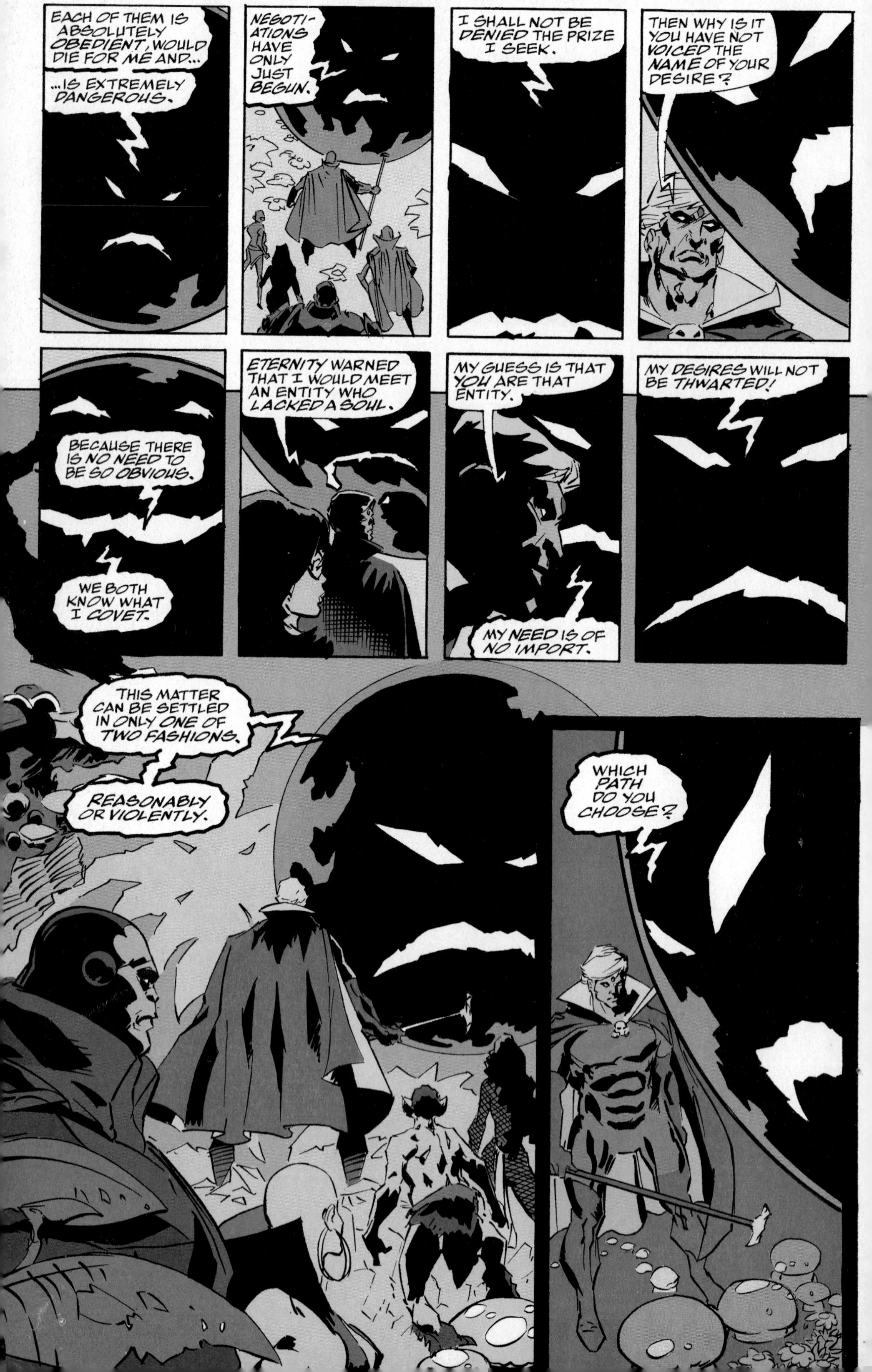
EACH OF THEM IS ABSOLUTELY OBEDIENT, WOULD DIE FOR ME AND...
...IS EXTREMELY DANGEROUS.
NEGOTIATIONS HAVE ONLY JUST BEGUN.
I SHALL NOT BE DENIED THE PRIZE I SEEK.
THEN WHY IS IT YOU HAVE NOT VOICED THE NAME OF YOUR DESIRE?
BECAUSE THERE IS NO NEED TO BE SO OBVIOUS.
WE BOTH KNOW WHAT I COVET.
ETERNITY WARNED THAT I WOULD MEET AN ENTITY WHO LACKED A SOUL.
MY GUESS IS THAT YOU ARE THAT ENTITY.
MY NEED IS OF NO IMPORT.
MY DESIRES WILL NOT BE THWARTED!
THIS MATTER CAN BE SETTLED IN ONLY ONE OF TWO FASHIONS.
REASONABLY OR VIOLENTLY.
WHICH PATH DO YOU CHOOSE?

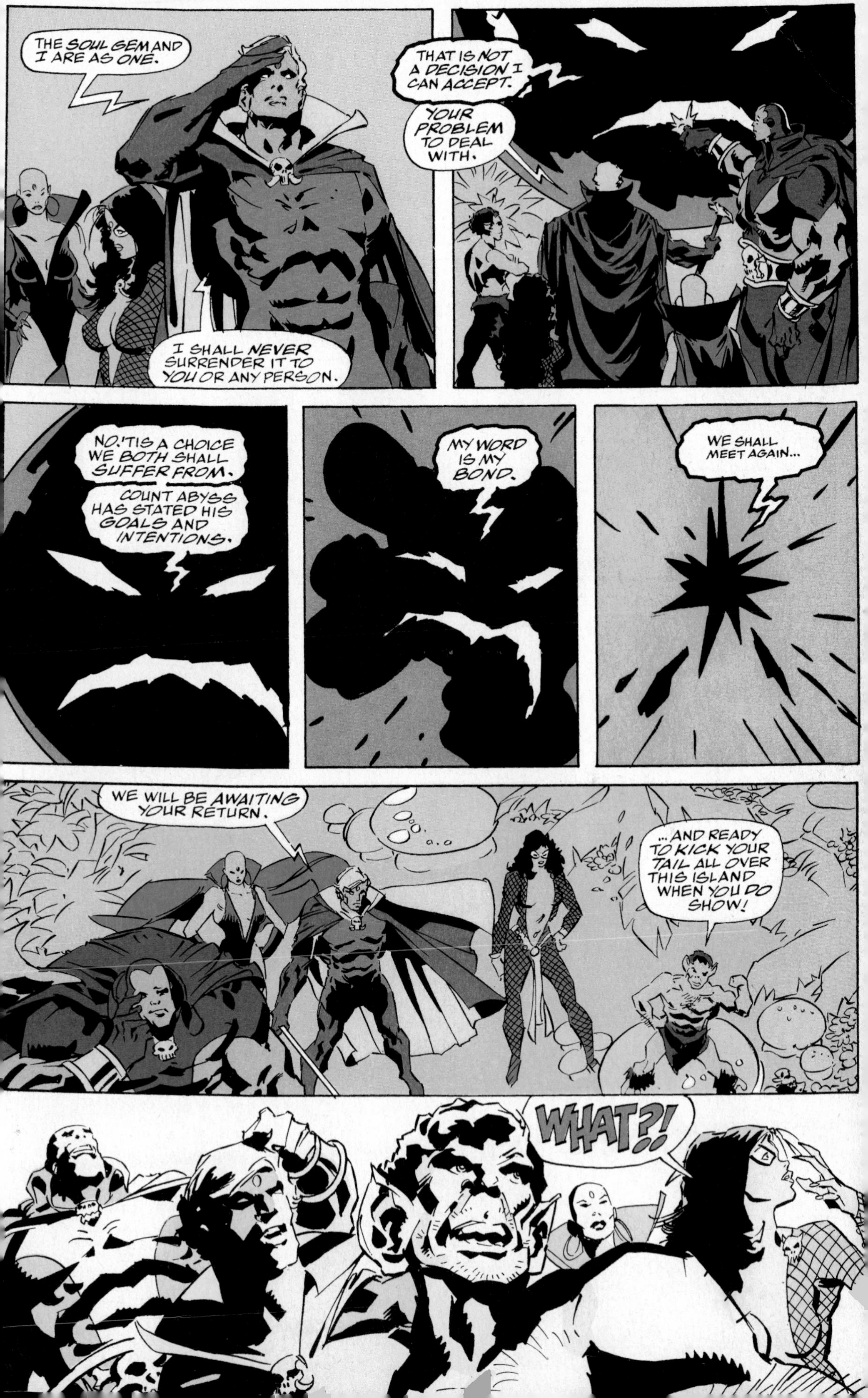
THE SOUL GEM AND I ARE AS ONE.
I SHALL NEVER SURRENDER IT TO YOU OR ANY PERSON.
THAT IS NOT A DECISION I CAN ACCEPT.
YOUR PROBLEM TO DEAL WITH.
NO.'TIS A CHOICE WE BOTH SHALL SUFFER FROM.
COUNT ABYSS HAS STATED HIS GOALS AND INTENTIONS.
MY WORD IS MY BOND.
WE SHALL MEET AGAIN...
WE WILL BE AWAITING YOUR RETURN.
...AND READY TO KICK YOUR TAIL ALL OVER THIS ISLAND WHEN YOU DO SHOW!
WHAT?!

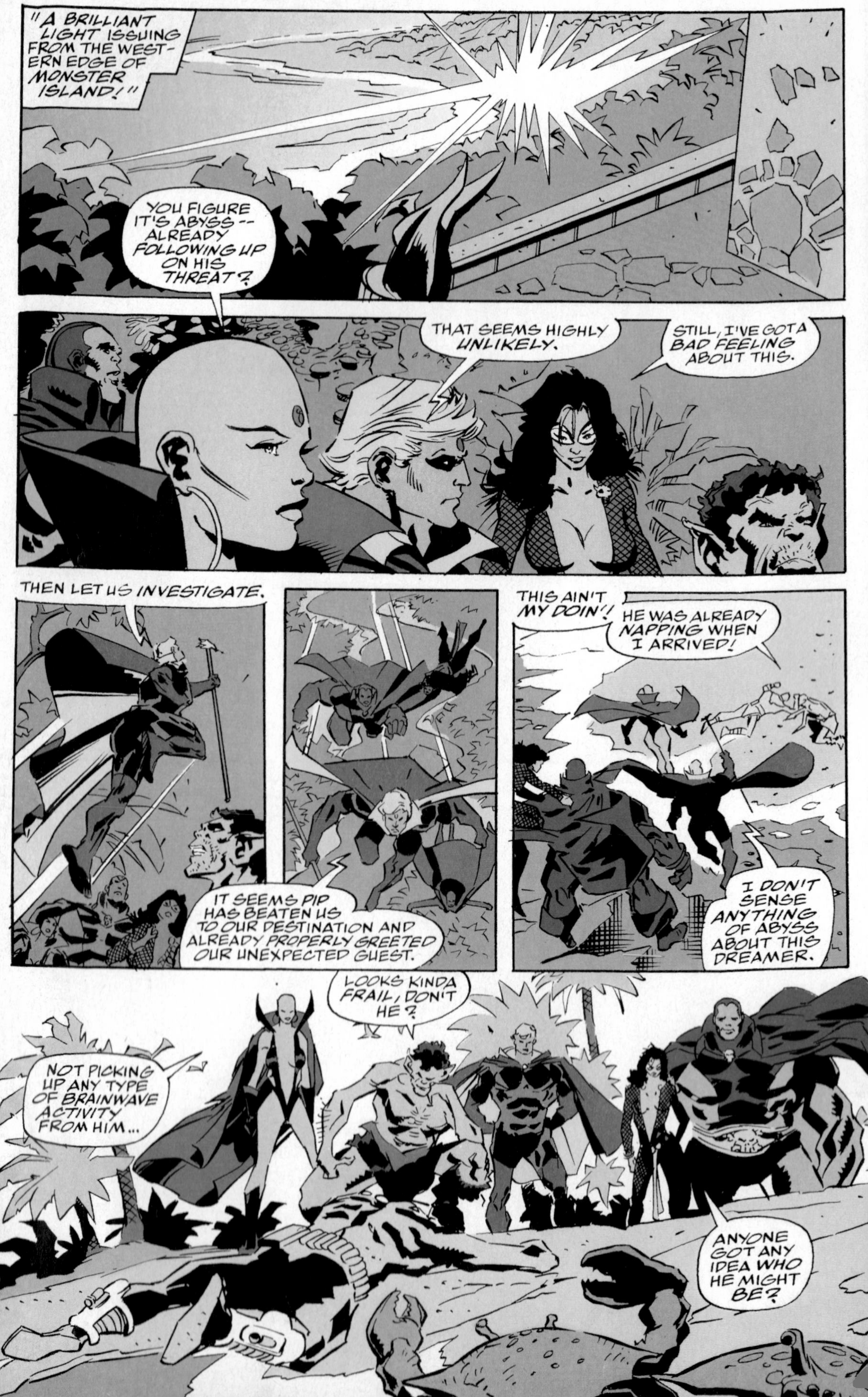
"A BRILLIANT LIGHT ISSUING FROM THE WESTERN EDGE OF MONSTER ISLAND!"
YOU FIGURE IT'S ABYSS -- ALREADY FOLLOWING UP ON HIS THREAT?
THAT SEEMS HIGHLY UNLIKELY.
STILL, I'VE GOT A BAD FEELING ABOUT THIS.
THEN LET US INVESTIGATE.
IT SEEMS PIP HAS BEATEN US TO OUR DESTINATION AND ALREADY PROPERLY GREETED OUR UNEXPECTED GUEST.
THIS AIN'T MY DOIN'!
HE WAS ALREADY NAPPING WHEN I ARRIVED!
I DON'T SENSE ANYTHING OF ABYSS ABOUT THIS DREAMER.
LOOKS KINDA FRAIL, DON'T HE?
NOT PICKING UP ANY TYPE OF BRAINWAVE ACTIVITY FROM HIM...
ANYONE GOT ANY IDEA WHO HE MIGHT BE?

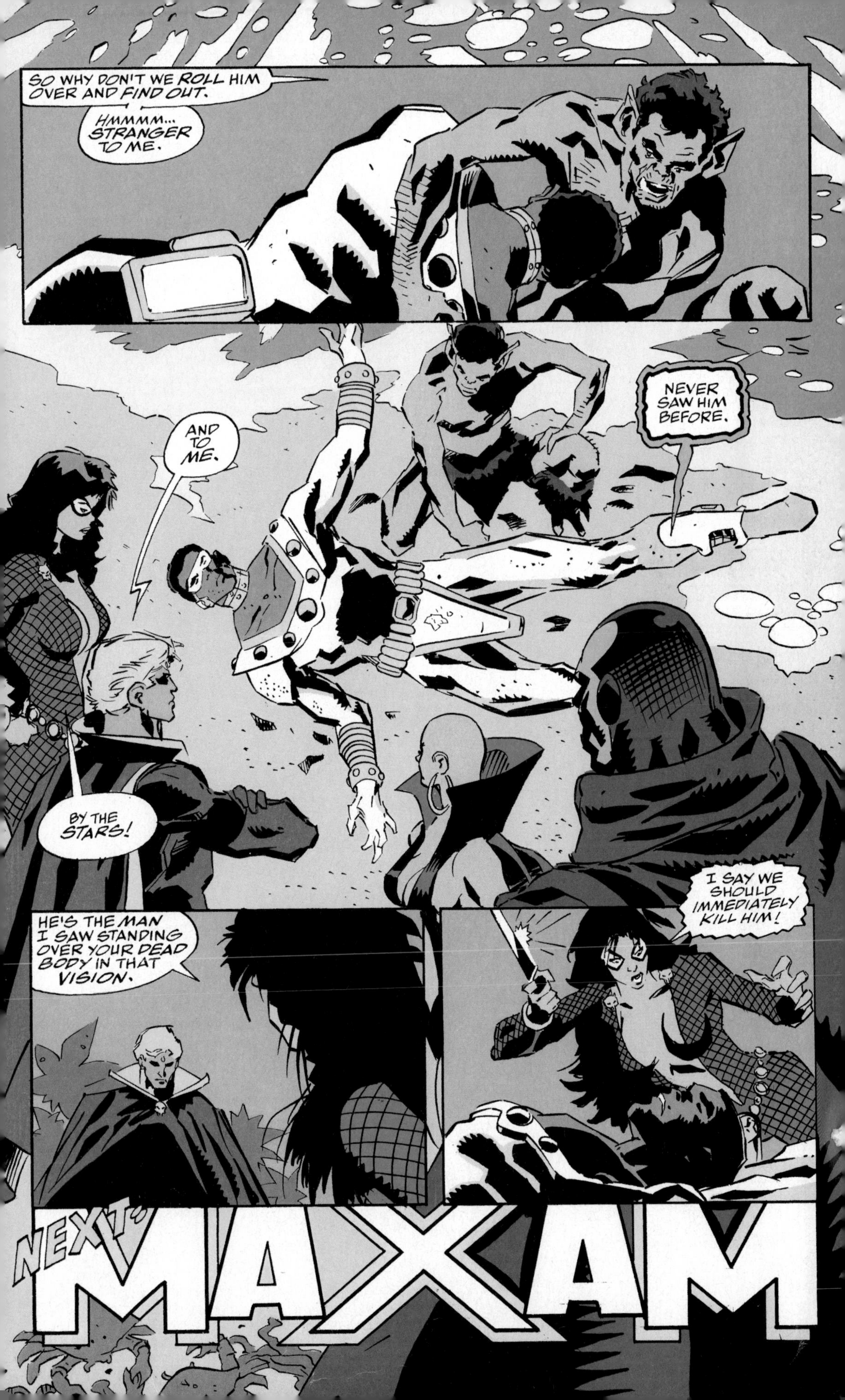
SO WHY DON'T WE ROLL HIM OVER AND FIND OUT.
HMMMM... STRANGER TO ME.
AND TO ME.
NEVER SAW HIM BEFORE.
BY THE STARS!
HE'S THE MAN I SAW STANDING OVER YOUR DEAD BODY IN THAT VISION.
I SAY WE SHOULD IMMEDIATELY KILL HIM!
NEXT:
MAXAM

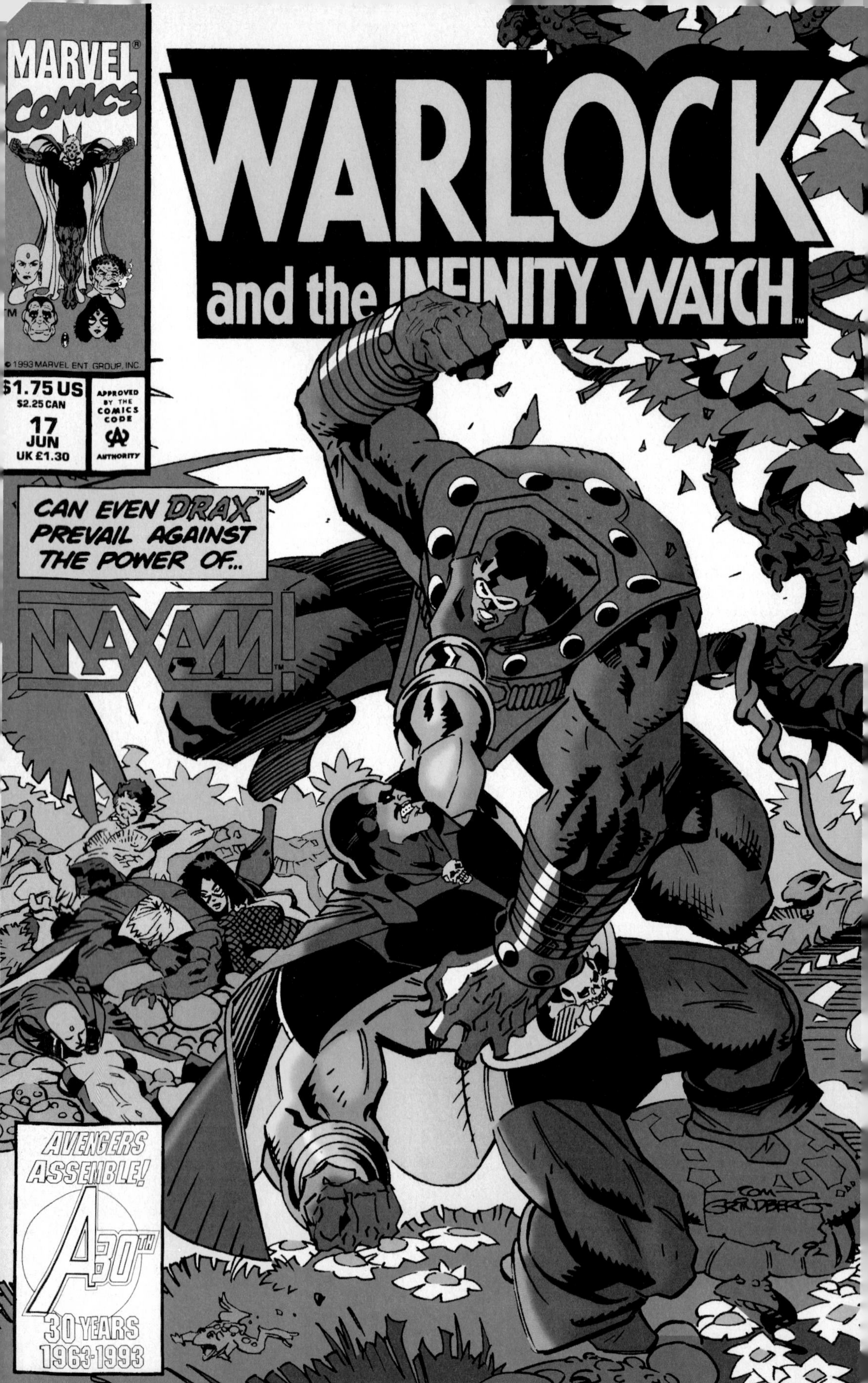
MARVEL® COMICS
WARLOCK
and the INFINITY WATCH™
© 1993 MARVEL ENT. GROUP, INC.
$1.75 US
$2.25 CAN
17
JUN
UK £1.30
APPROVED BY THE COMICS CODE AUTHORITY
CAN EVEN DRAX™ PREVAIL AGAINST THE POWER OF...
MAXAM!™
AVENGERS ASSEMBLE!
30TH
30 YEARS
1963-1993

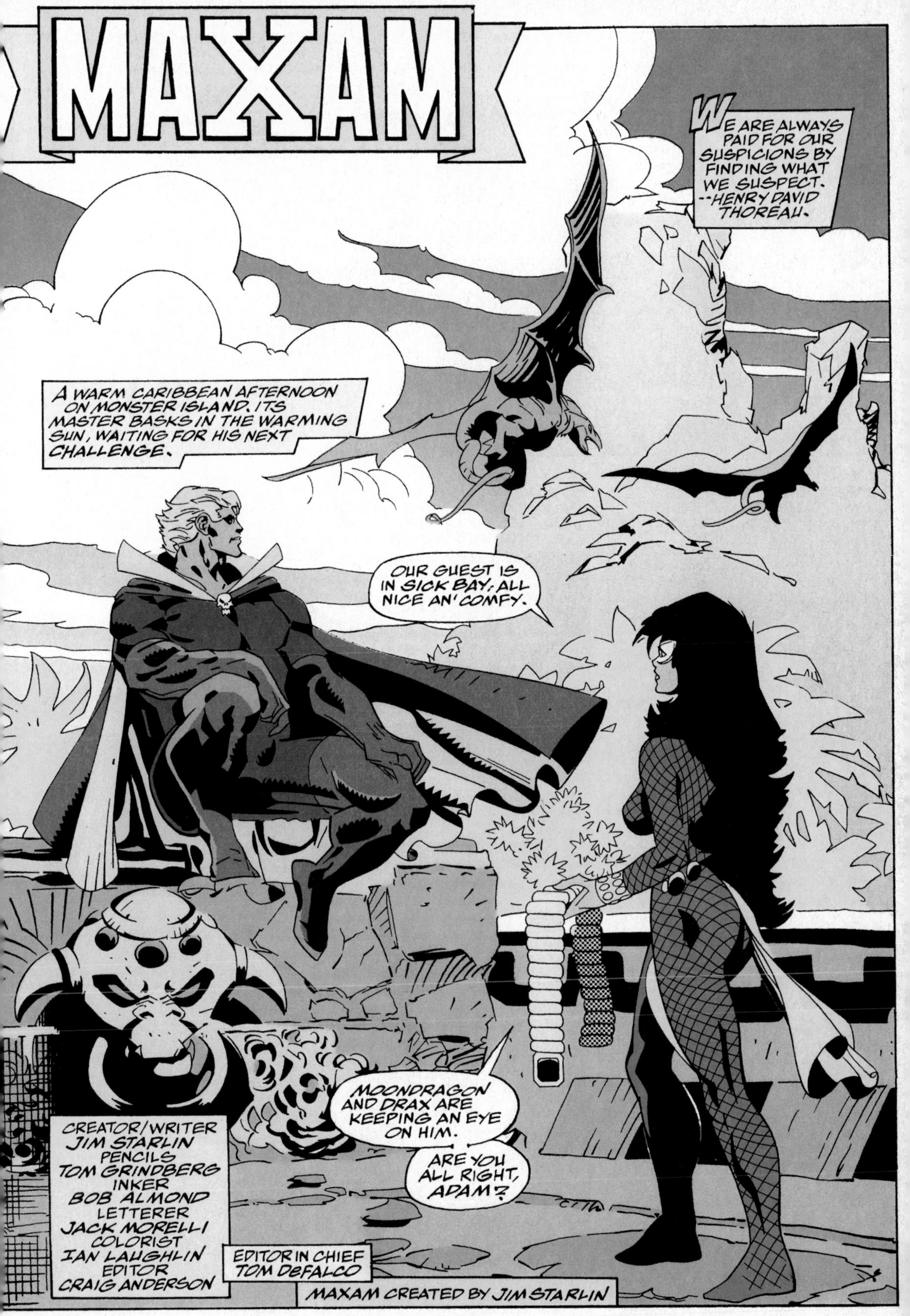
MAXAM
WE ARE ALWAYS PAID FOR OUR SUSPICIONS BY FINDING WHAT WE SUSPECT. --HENRY DAVID THOREAU.
A WARM CARIBBEAN AFTERNOON ON MONSTER ISLAND. ITS MASTER BASKS IN THE WARMING SUN, WAITING FOR HIS NEXT CHALLENGE.
OUR GUEST IS IN SICK BAY, ALL NICE AN' COMFY.
MOONDRAGON AND DRAX ARE KEEPING AN EYE ON HIM.
ARE YOU ALL RIGHT, ADAM?
CREATOR/WRITER JIM STARLIN PENCILS TOM GRINDBERG INKER BOB ALMOND LETTERER JACK MORELLI COLORIST IAN LAUGHLIN EDITOR CRAIG ANDERSON
EDITOR IN CHIEF TOM DEFALCO
MAXAM CREATED BY JIM STARLIN

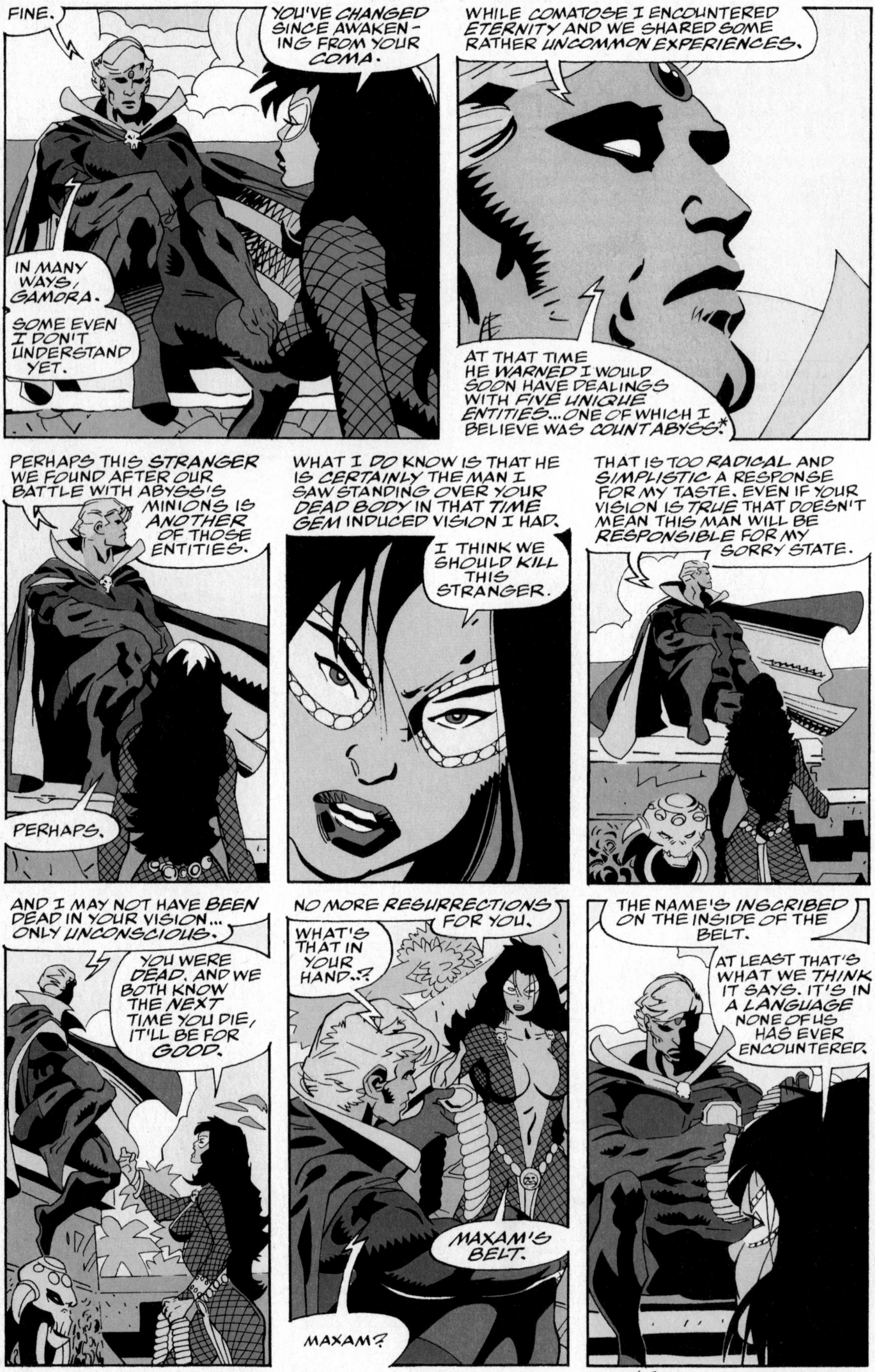
FINE.
YOU'VE CHANGED SINCE AWAKENING FROM YOUR COMA.
IN MANY WAYS, GAMORA.
SOME EVEN I DON'T UNDERSTAND YET.
WHILE COMATOSE I ENCOUNTERED ETERNITY AND WE SHARED SOME RATHER UNCOMMON EXPERIENCES.
AT THAT TIME HE WARNED I WOULD SOON HAVE DEALINGS WITH FIVE UNIQUE ENTITIES...ONE OF WHICH I BELIEVE WAS COUNT ABYSS.*
PERHAPS THIS STRANGER WE FOUND AFTER OUR BATTLE WITH ABYSS'S MINIONS IS ANOTHER OF THOSE ENTITIES.
PERHAPS.
WHAT I DO KNOW IS THAT HE IS CERTAINLY THE MAN I SAW STANDING OVER YOUR DEAD BODY IN THAT TIME GEM INDUCED VISION I HAD.
I THINK WE SHOULD KILL THIS STRANGER.
THAT IS TOO RADICAL AND SIMPLISTIC A RESPONSE FOR MY TASTE. EVEN IF YOUR VISION IS TRUE THAT DOESN'T MEAN THIS MAN WILL BE RESPONSIBLE FOR MY SORRY STATE.
AND I MAY NOT HAVE BEEN DEAD IN YOUR VISION... ONLY UNCONSCIOUS.
YOU WERE DEAD. AND WE BOTH KNOW THE NEXT TIME YOU DIE, IT'LL BE FOR GOOD.
NO MORE RESURRECTIONS FOR YOU.
WHAT'S THAT IN YOUR HAND..?
MAXAM'S BELT.
MAXAM?
THE NAME'S INSCRIBED ON THE INSIDE OF THE BELT.
AT LEAST THAT'S WHAT WE THINK IT SAYS. IT'S IN A LANGUAGE NONE OF US HAS EVER ENCOUNTERED.
*SEE LAST ISSUE.--C.

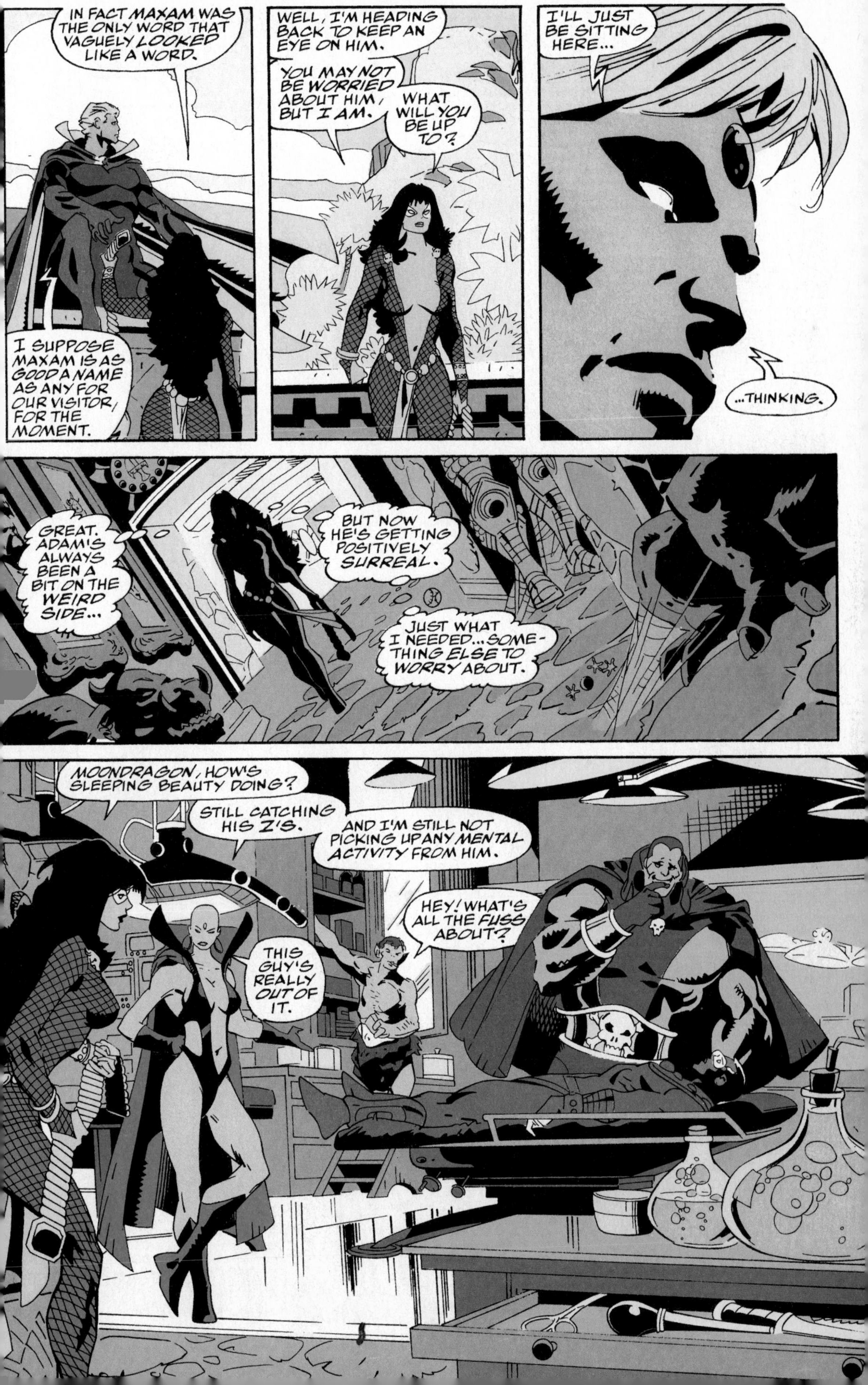

IN FACT MAXAM WAS THE ONLY WORD THAT VAGUELY LOOKED LIKE A WORD.
I SUPPOSE MAXAM IS AS GOOD A NAME AS ANY FOR OUR VISITOR, FOR THE MOMENT.
WELL, I'M HEADING BACK TO KEEP AN EYE ON HIM.
YOU MAY NOT BE WORRIED ABOUT HIM, BUT I AM.
WHAT WILL YOU BE UP TO?
I'LL JUST BE SITTING HERE...
...THINKING.
GREAT. ADAM'S ALWAYS BEEN A BIT ON THE WEIRD SIDE...
BUT NOW HE'S GETTING POSITIVELY SURREAL.
JUST WHAT I NEEDED... SOMETHING ELSE TO WORRY ABOUT.
MOONDRAGON, HOW'S SLEEPING BEAUTY DOING?
STILL CATCHING HIS Z'S.
AND I'M STILL NOT PICKING UP ANY MENTAL ACTIVITY FROM HIM.
HEY! WHAT'S ALL THE FUSS ABOUT?
THIS GUY'S REALLY OUT OF IT.

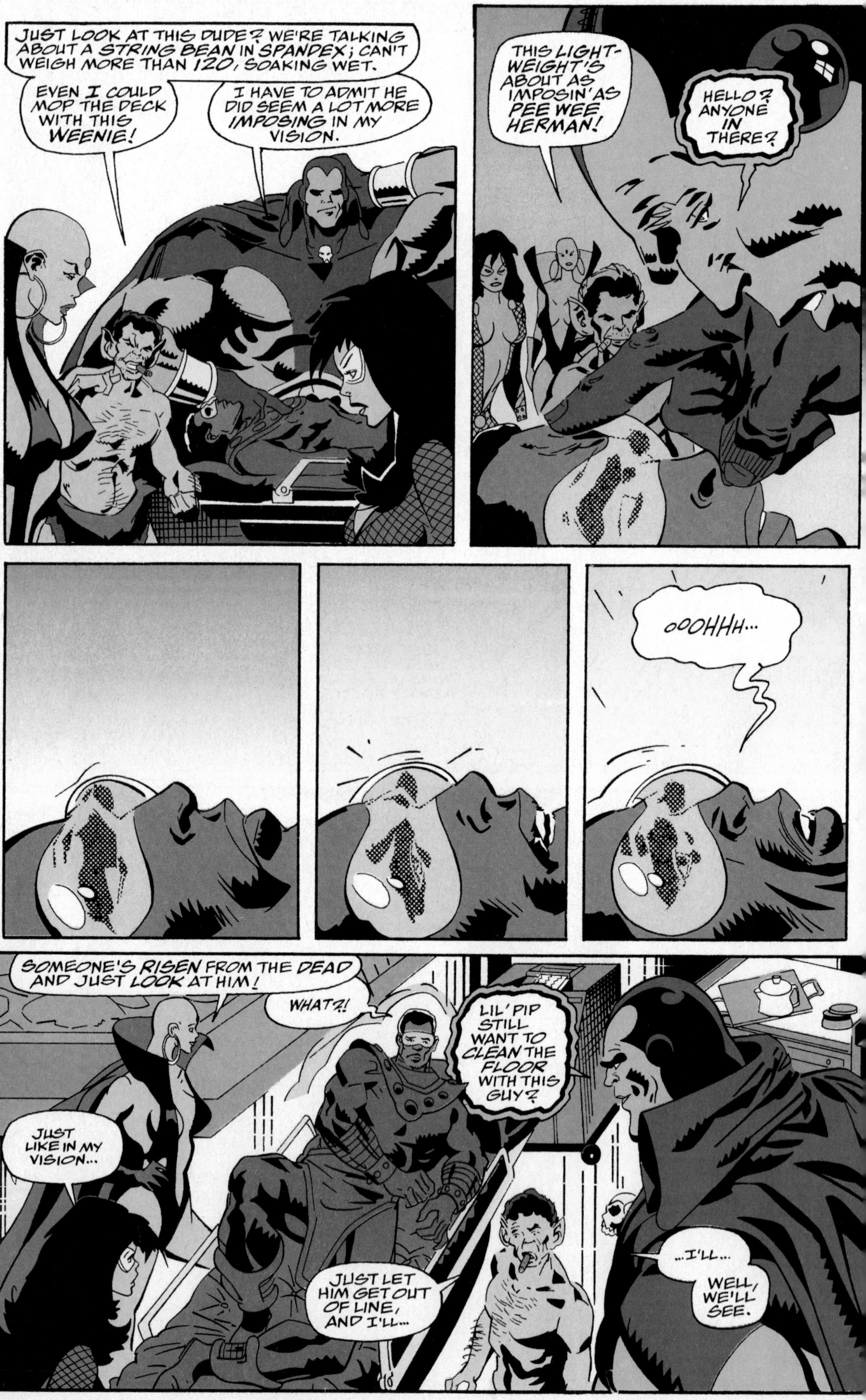
JUST LOOK AT THIS DUDE?! WE'RE TALKING ABOUT A STRING BEAN IN SPANDEX; CAN'T WEIGH MORE THAN 120, SOAKING WET.
EVEN I COULD MOP THE DECK WITH THIS WEENIE!
I HAVE TO ADMIT HE DID SEEM A LOT MORE IMPOSING IN MY VISION.
THIS LIGHT-WEIGHT'S ABOUT AS IMPOSIN' AS PEE WEE HERMAN!
HELLO?! ANYONE IN THERE?
OOOHHH...
SOMEONE'S RISEN FROM THE DEAD AND JUST LOOK AT HIM!
WHAT?!
LIL' PIP STILL WANT TO CLEAN THE FLOOR WITH THIS GUY?
JUST LIKE IN MY VISION...
JUST LET HIM GET OUT OF LINE, AND I'LL...
...I'LL...
WELL, WE'LL SEE.

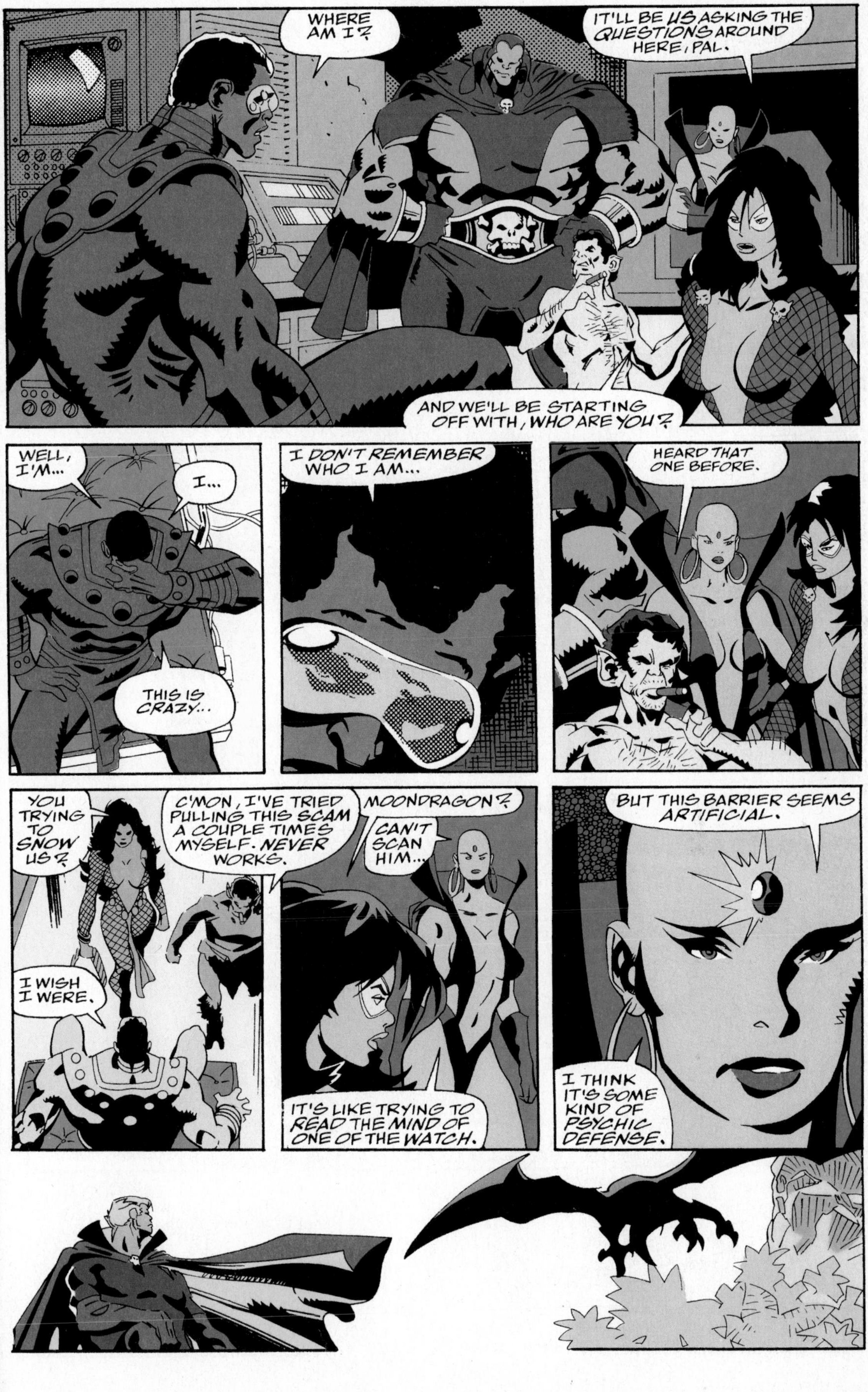
WHERE AM I?
IT'LL BE US ASKING THE QUESTIONS AROUND HERE, PAL.
AND WE'LL BE STARTING OFF WITH, WHO ARE YOU?
WELL, I'M...
I...
THIS IS CRAZY...
I DON'T REMEMBER WHO I AM...
HEARD THAT ONE BEFORE.
YOU TRYING TO SNOW US?
C'MON, I'VE TRIED PULLING THIS SCAM A COUPLE TIMES MYSELF. NEVER WORKS.
I WISH I WERE.
MOONDRAGON?
CAN'T SCAN HIM...
IT'S LIKE TRYING TO READ THE MIND OF ONE OF THE WATCH.
BUT THIS BARRIER SEEMS ARTIFICIAL.
I THINK IT'S SOME KIND OF PSYCHIC DEFENSE.

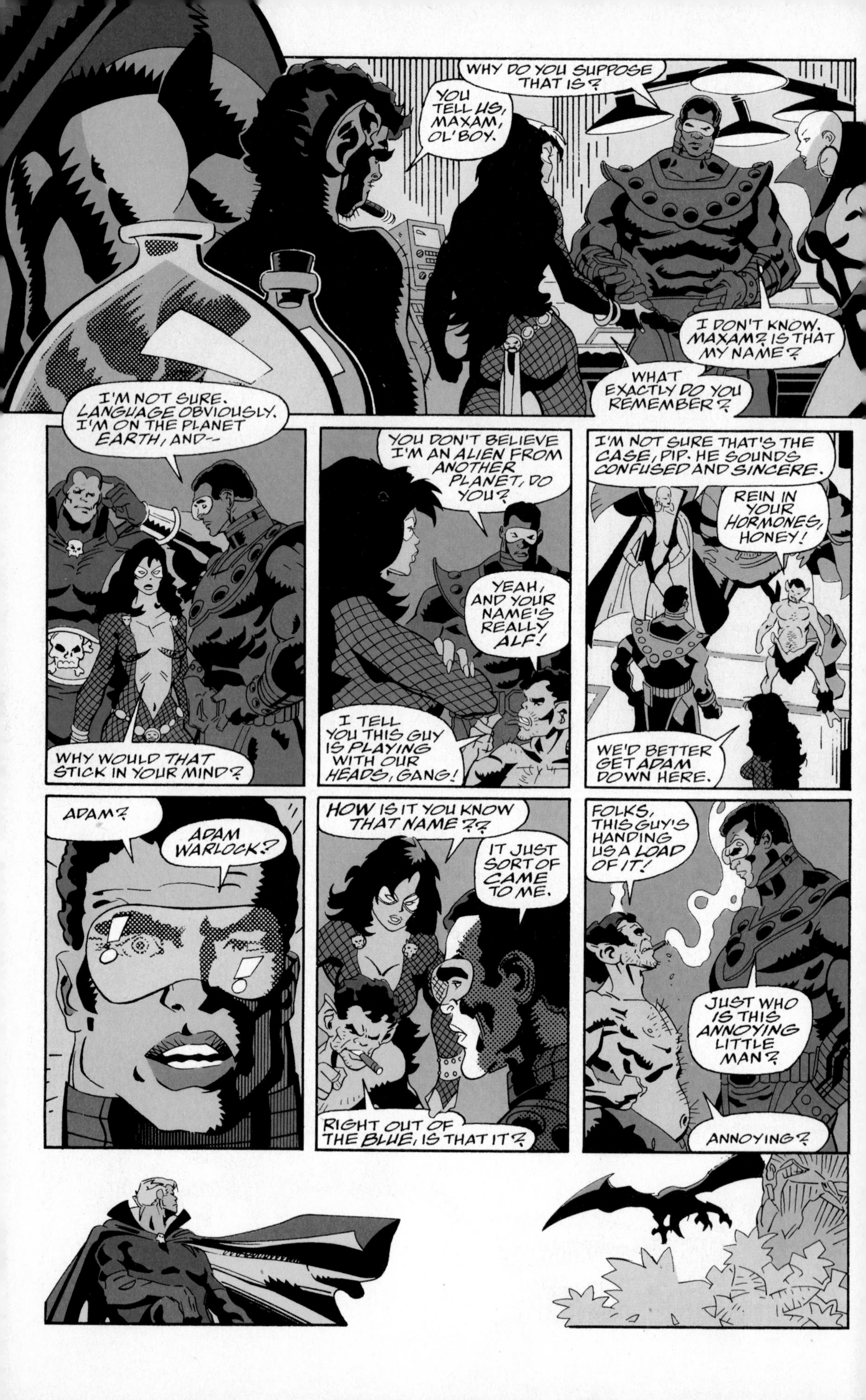
WHY DO YOU SUPPOSE THAT IS?
YOU TELL US, MAXAM, OL' BOY.
I DON'T KNOW. MAXAM? IS THAT MY NAME?
WHAT EXACTLY DO YOU REMEMBER?
I'M NOT SURE. LANGUAGE OBVIOUSLY. I'M ON THE PLANET EARTH, AND--
WHY WOULD THAT STICK IN YOUR MIND?
YOU DON'T BELIEVE I'M AN ALIEN FROM ANOTHER PLANET, DO YOU?
YEAH, AND YOUR NAME'S REALLY ALF!
I TELL YOU THIS GUY IS PLAYING WITH OUR HEADS, GANG!
I'M NOT SURE THAT'S THE CASE, PIP. HE SOUNDS CONFUSED AND SINCERE.
REIN IN YOUR HORMONES, HONEY!
WE'D BETTER GET ADAM DOWN HERE.
ADAM?
ADAM WARLOCK?
HOW IS IT YOU KNOW THAT NAME??
IT JUST SORT OF CAME TO ME.
RIGHT OUT OF THE BLUE, IS THAT IT?
FOLKS, THIS GUY'S HANDING US A LOAD OF IT!
JUST WHO IS THIS ANNOYING LITTLE MAN?
ANNOYING?

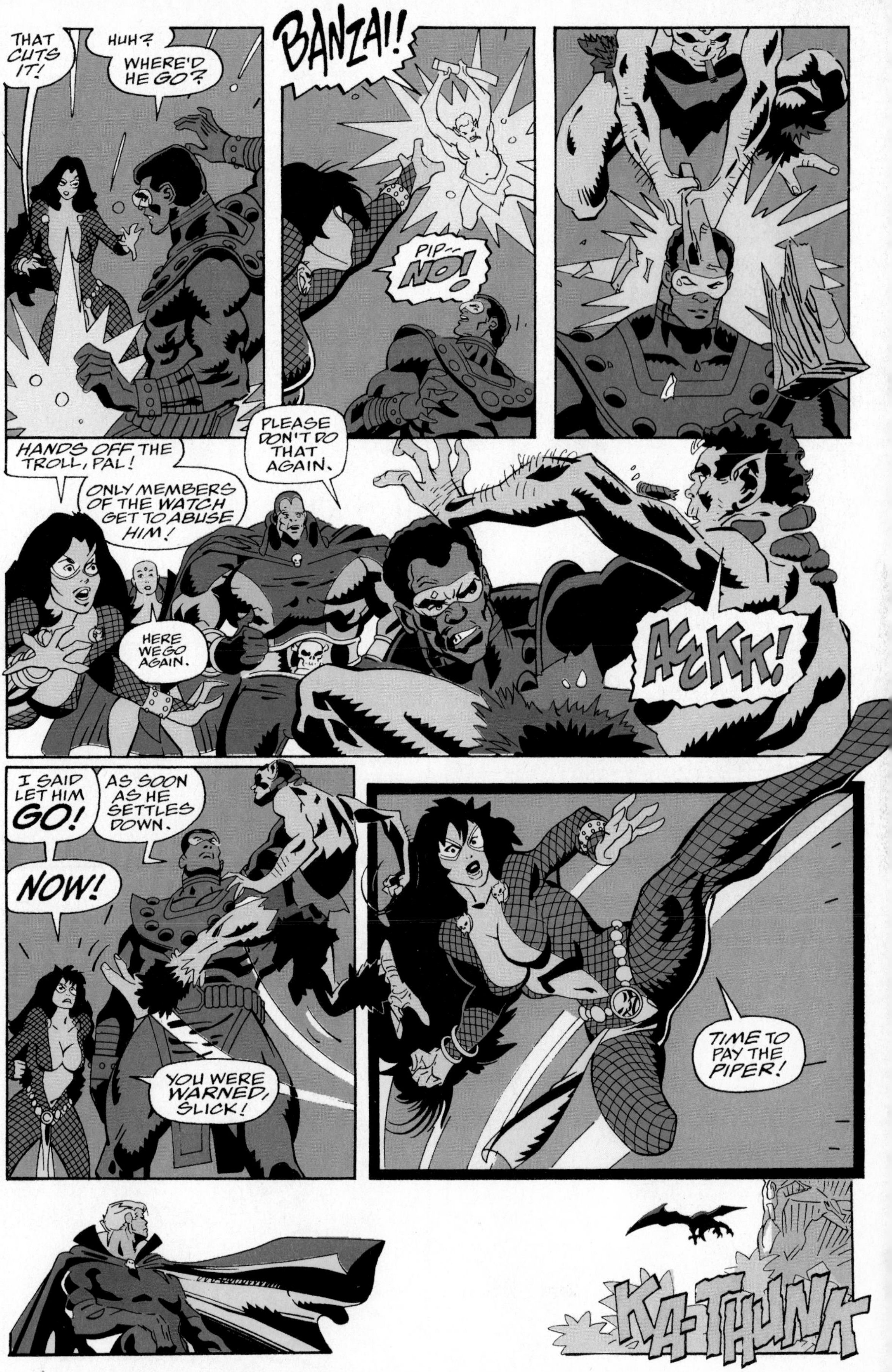
THAT CUTS IT!
HUH? WHERE'D HE GO?
BANZAI!!
PIP-- NO!
HANDS OFF THE TROLL, PAL!
ONLY MEMBERS OF THE WATCH GET TO ABUSE HIM!
PLEASE DON'T DO THAT AGAIN.
HERE WE GO AGAIN.
AECKK!
I SAID LET HIM GO!
AS SOON AS HE SETTLES DOWN.
NOW!
YOU WERE WARNED, SLICK!
TIME TO PAY THE PIPER!
KA-THUNK

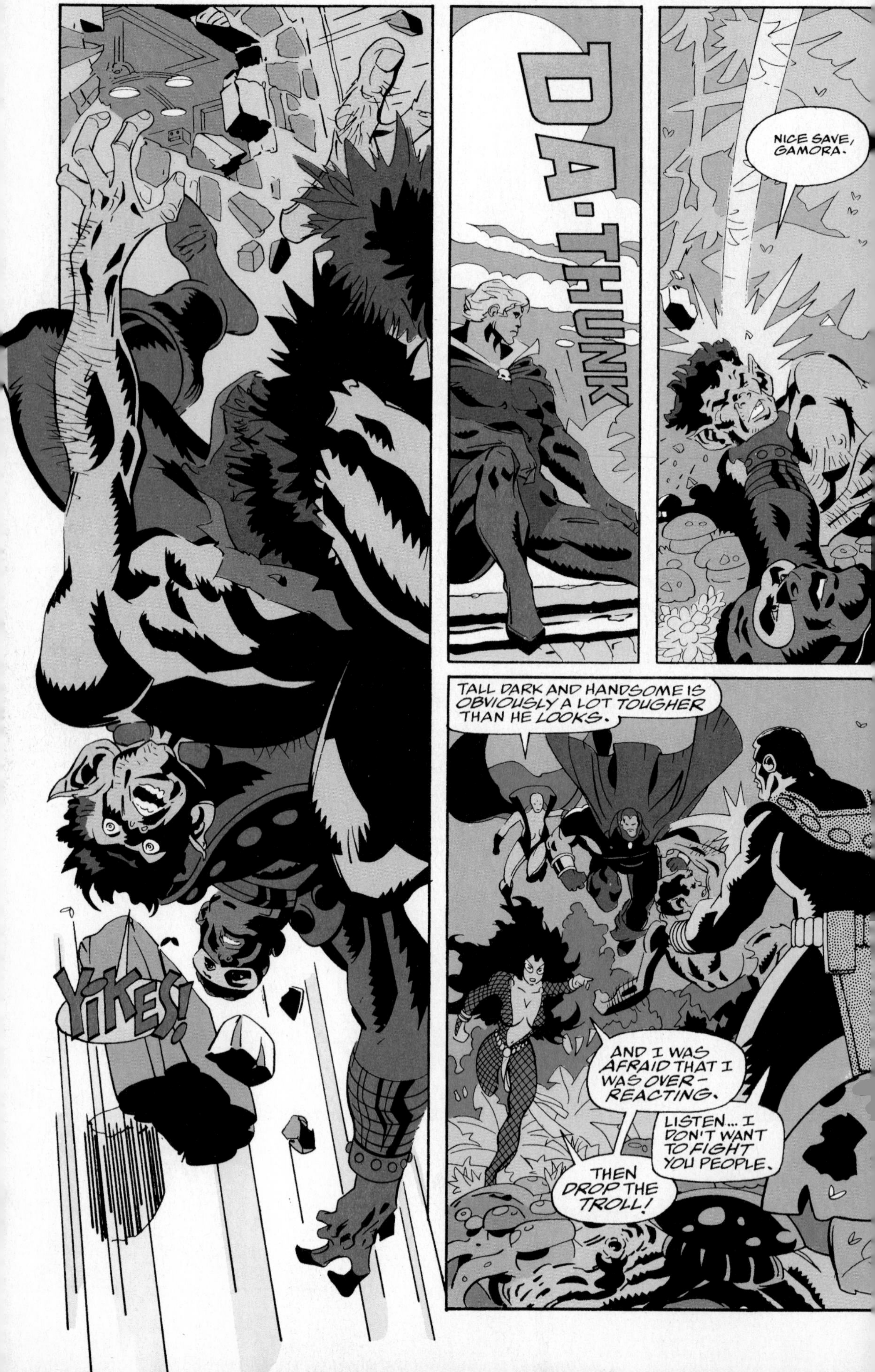
YIKES!
DA-THUNK
NICE SAVE, GAMORA.
TALL DARK AND HANDSOME IS OBVIOUSLY A LOT TOUGHER THAN HE LOOKS.
AND I WAS AFRAID THAT I WAS OVER-REACTING.
LISTEN... I DON'T WANT TO FIGHT YOU PEOPLE.
THEN DROP THE TROLL!

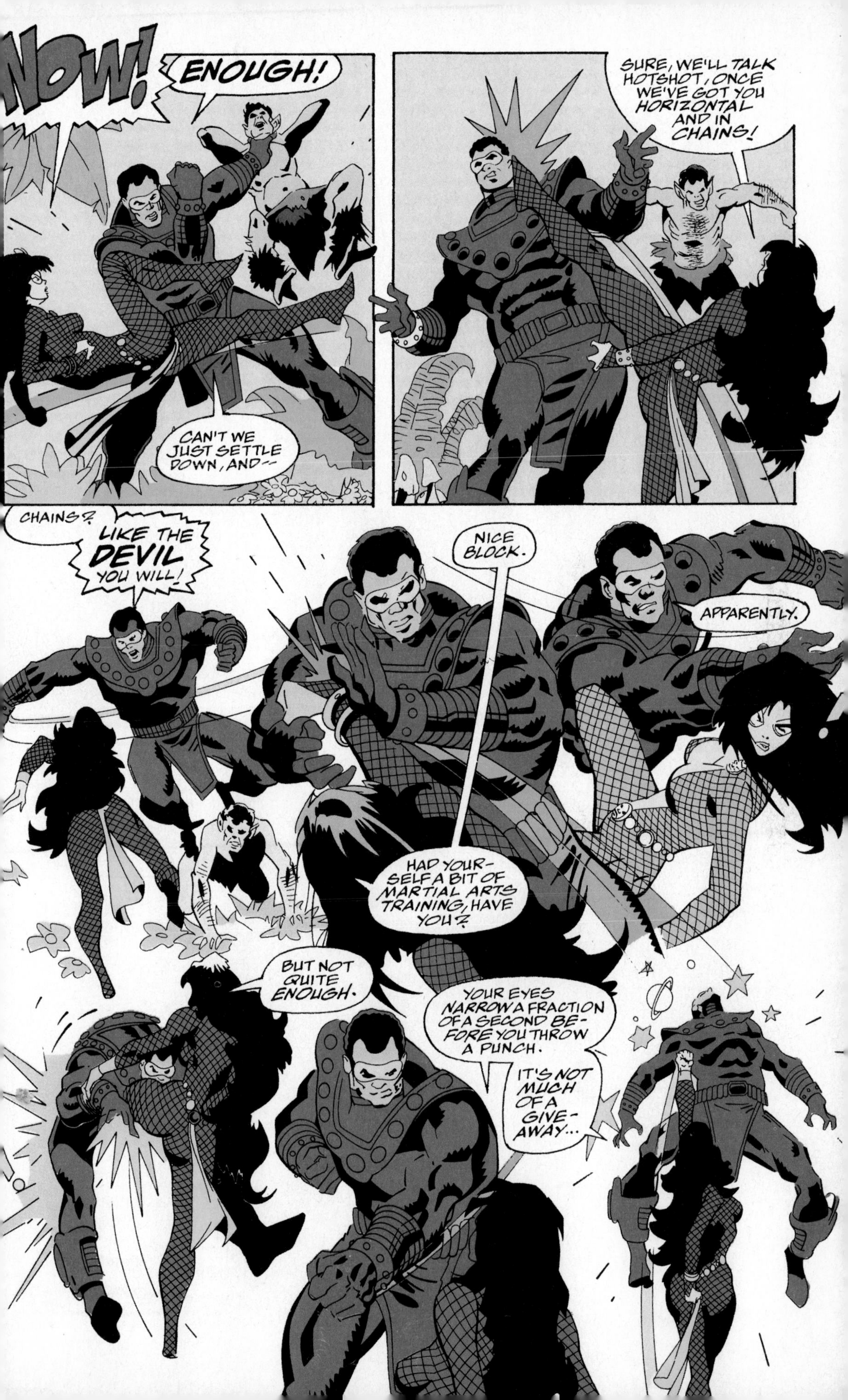
NOW!
ENOUGH!
CAN'T WE JUST SETTLE DOWN, AND--
SURE, WE'LL TALK HOTSHOT, ONCE WE'VE GOT YOU HORIZONTAL AND IN CHAINS!
CHAINS?
LIKE THE DEVIL YOU WILL!
NICE BLOCK.
APPARENTLY.
HAD YOURSELF A BIT OF MARTIAL ARTS TRAINING, HAVE YOU?
BUT NOT QUITE ENOUGH.
YOUR EYES NARROW A FRACTION OF A SECOND BEFORE YOU THROW A PUNCH.
IT'S NOT MUCH OF A GIVE-AWAY...

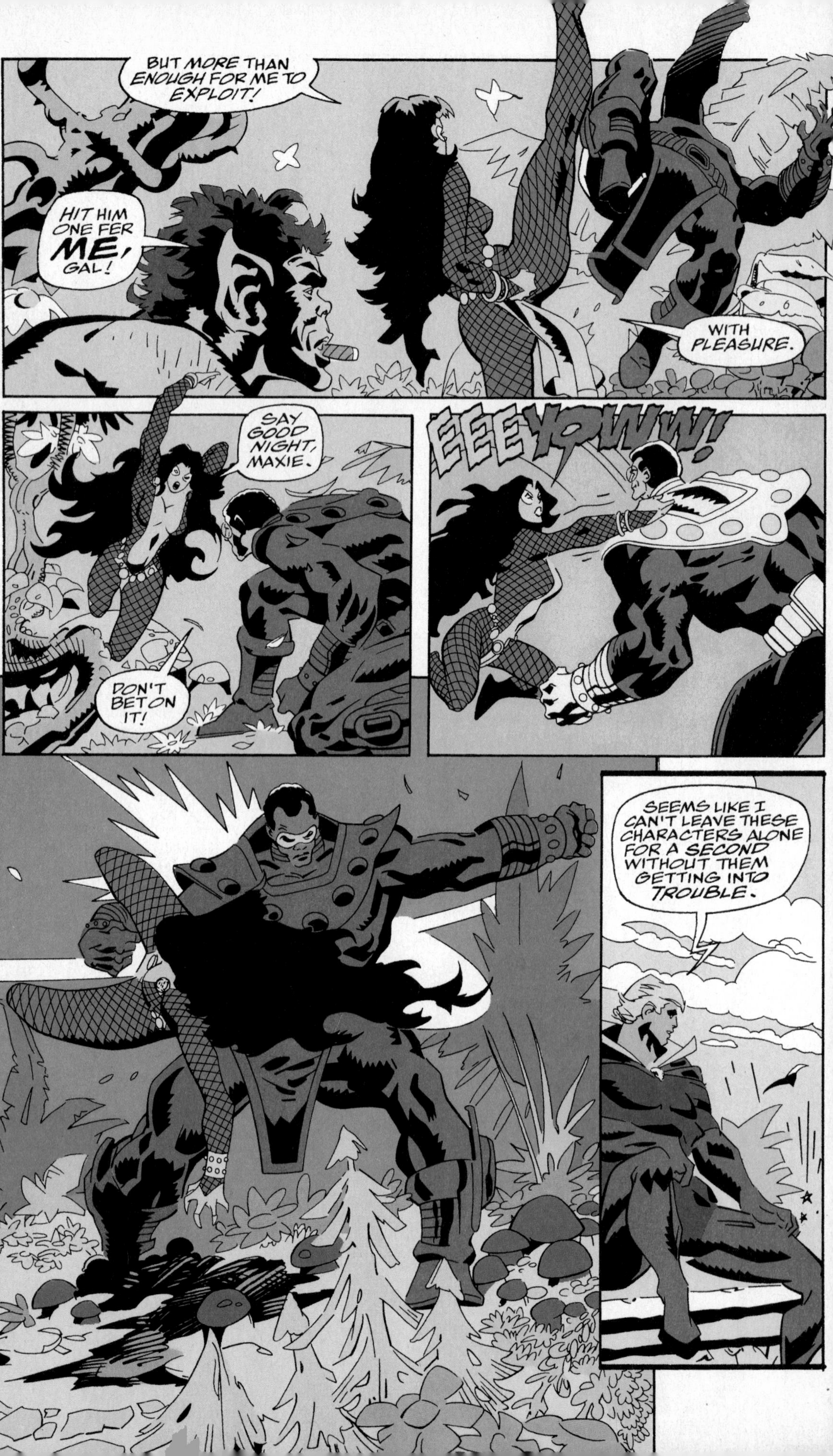
BUT MORE THAN ENOUGH FOR ME TO EXPLOIT!
HIT HIM ONE FER ME, GAL!
WITH PLEASURE.
SAY GOOD NIGHT, MAXIE.
DON'T BET ON IT!
EEEYOWW!
SEEMS LIKE I CAN'T LEAVE THESE CHARACTERS ALONE FOR A SECOND WITHOUT THEM GETTING INTO TROUBLE.

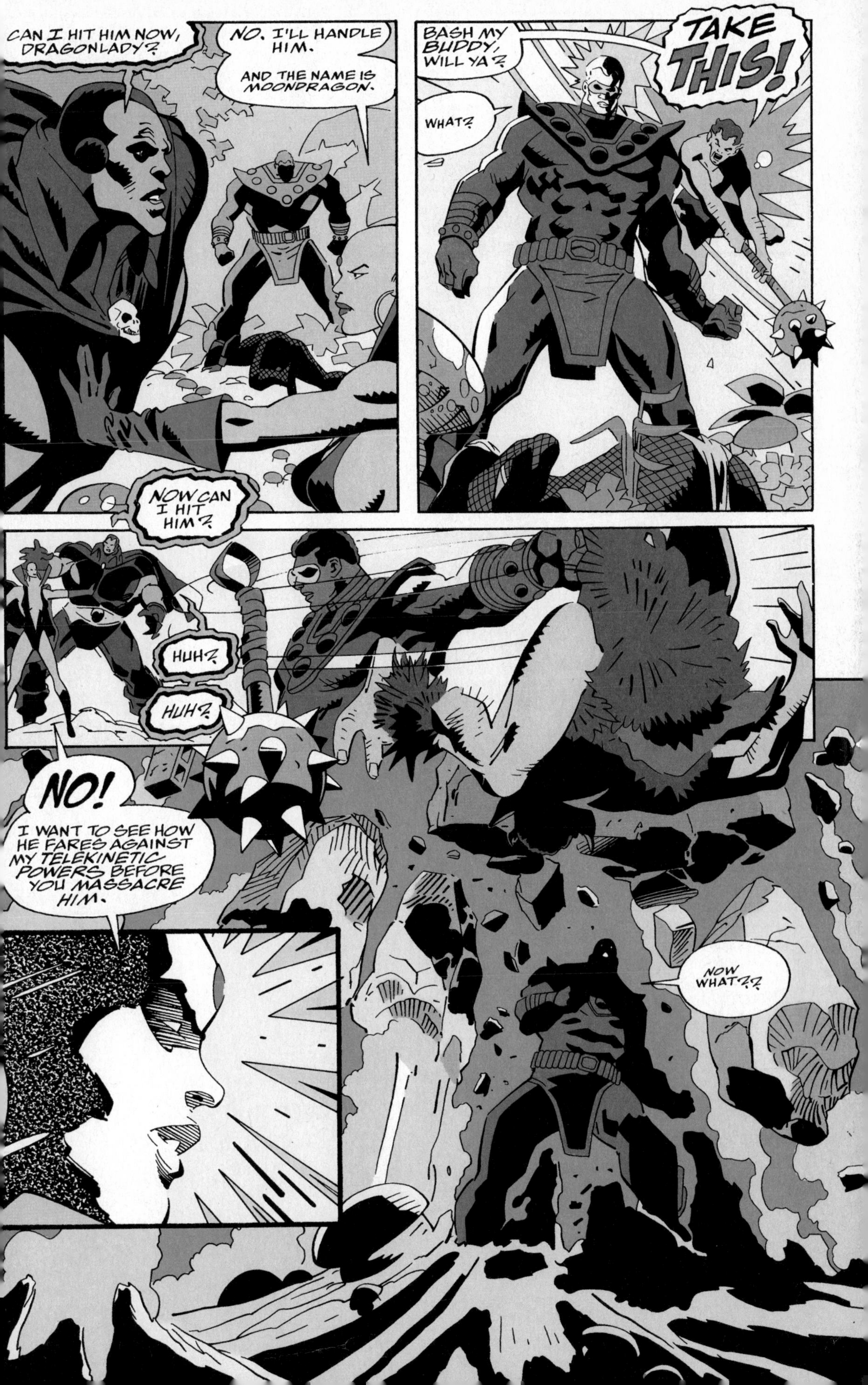
CAN I HIT HIM NOW, DRAGONLADY?
NO. I'LL HANDLE HIM.
AND THE NAME IS MOONDRAGON.
BASH MY BUDDY, WILL YA?
TAKE THIS!
WHAT?
NOW CAN I HIT HIM?
HUH?
HUH?
NO!
I WANT TO SEE HOW HE FARES AGAINST MY TELEKINETIC POWERS BEFORE YOU MASSACRE HIM.
NOW WHAT??

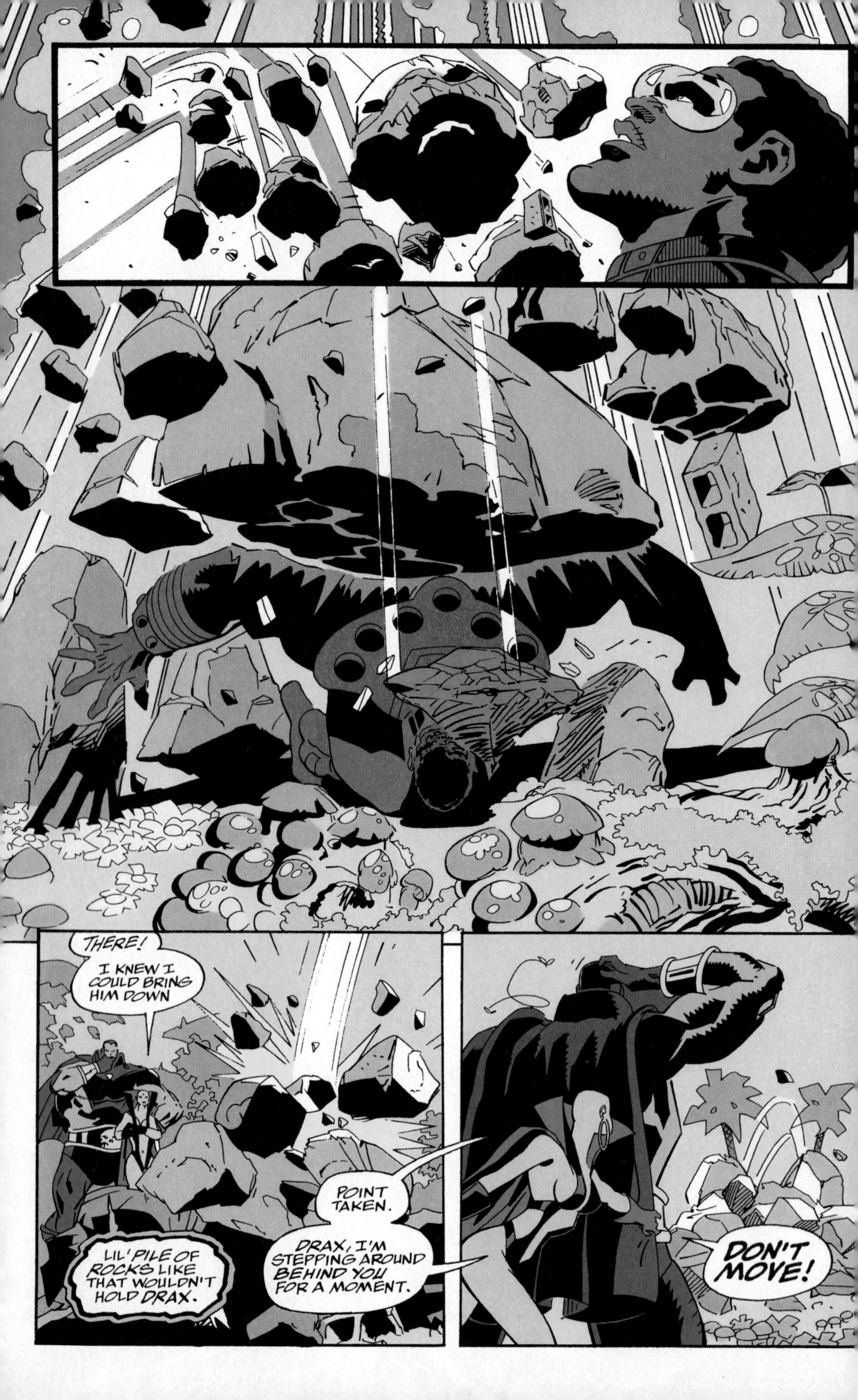
THERE!
I KNEW I COULD BRING HIM DOWN
LIL' PILE OF ROCKS LIKE THAT WOULDN'T HOLD DRAX.
POINT TAKEN.
DRAX, I'M STEPPING AROUND BEHIND YOU FOR A MOMENT.
DON'T MOVE!

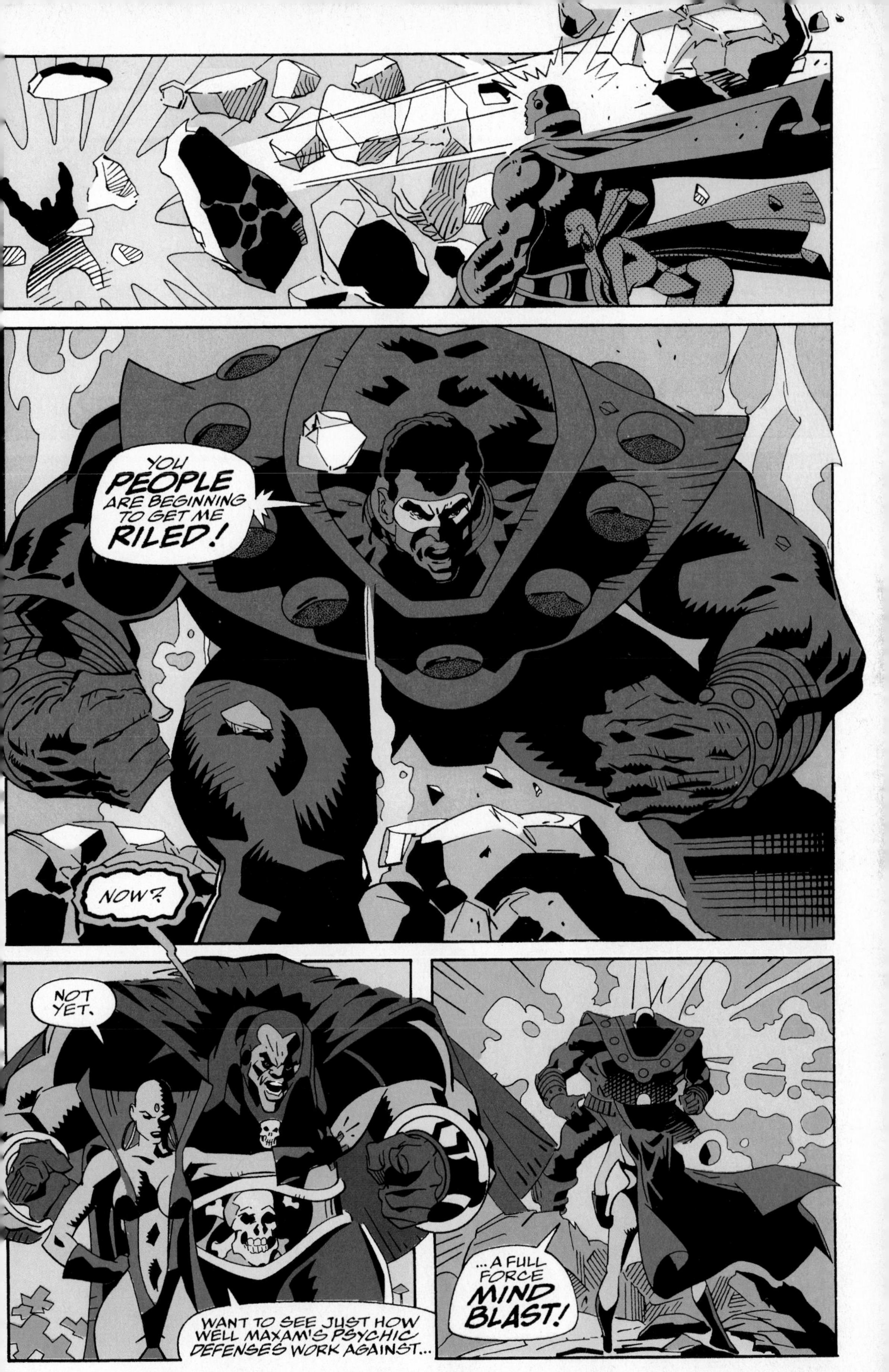

YOU PEOPLE ARE BEGINNING TO GET ME RILED!
NOW?
NOT YET.
WANT TO SEE JUST HOW WELL MAXAM'S PSYCHIC DEFENSES WORK AGAINST...
...A FULL FORCE MIND BLAST!

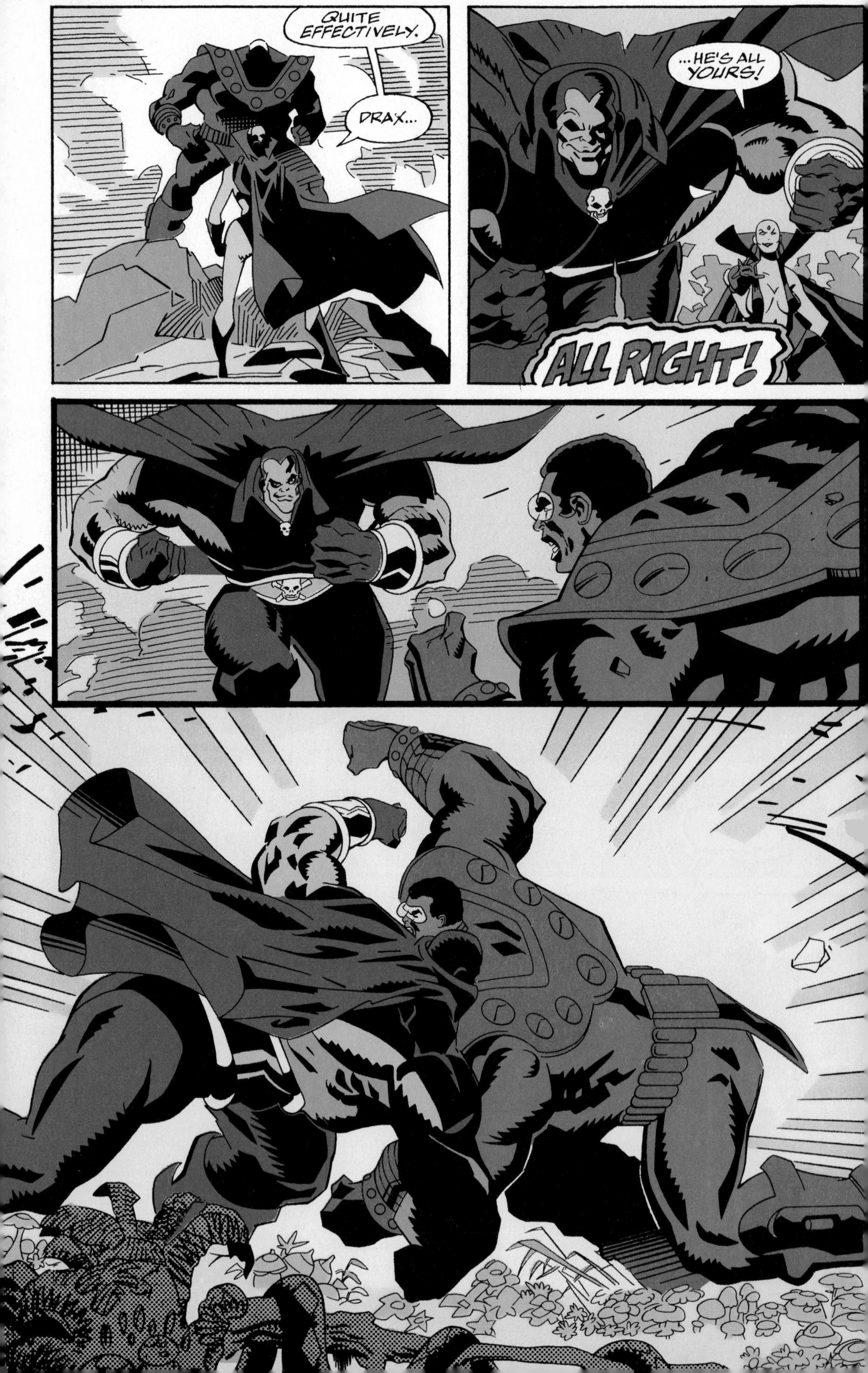
QUITE EFFECTIVELY.
DRAX...
...HE'S ALL YOURS!
ALL RIGHT!

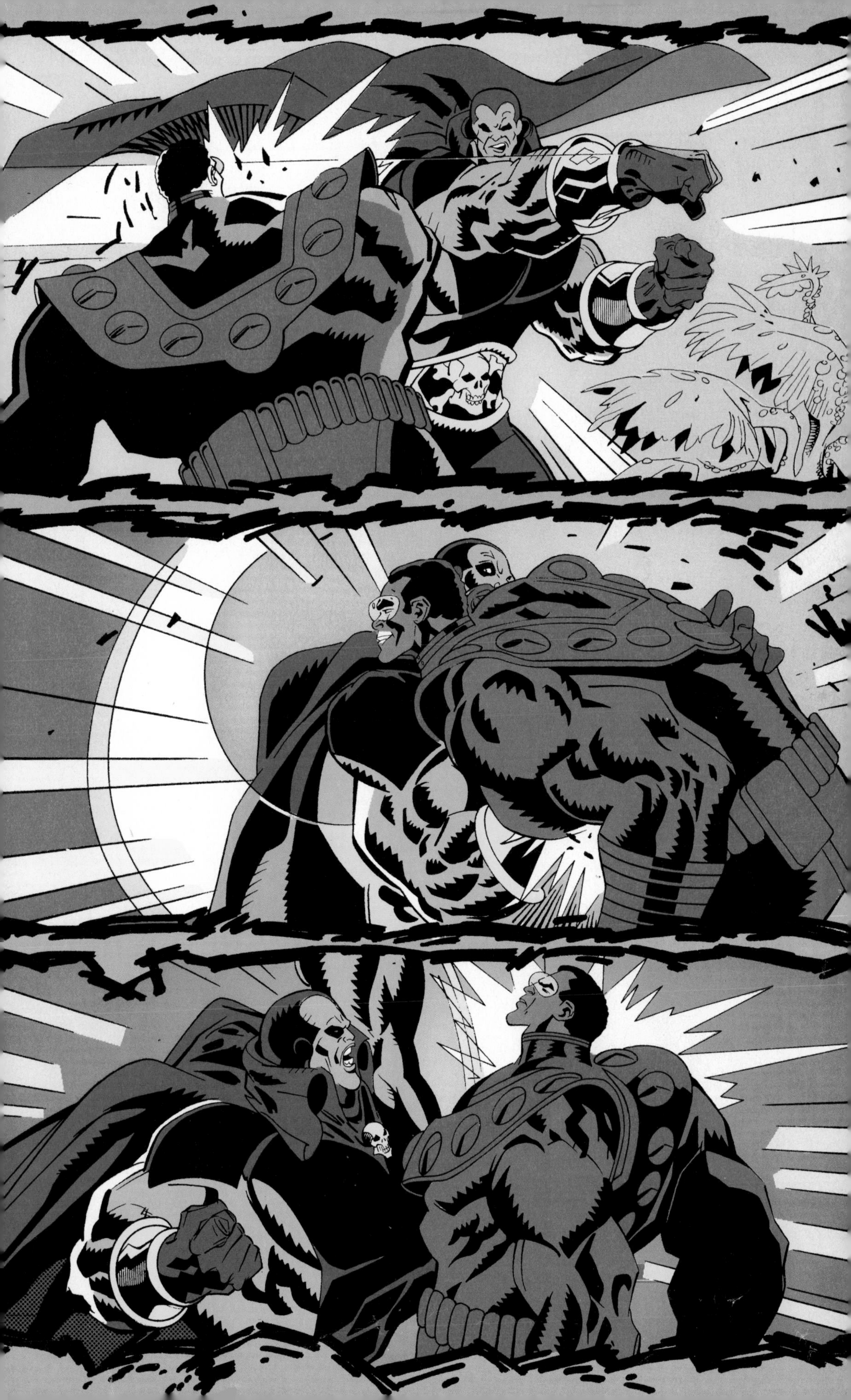

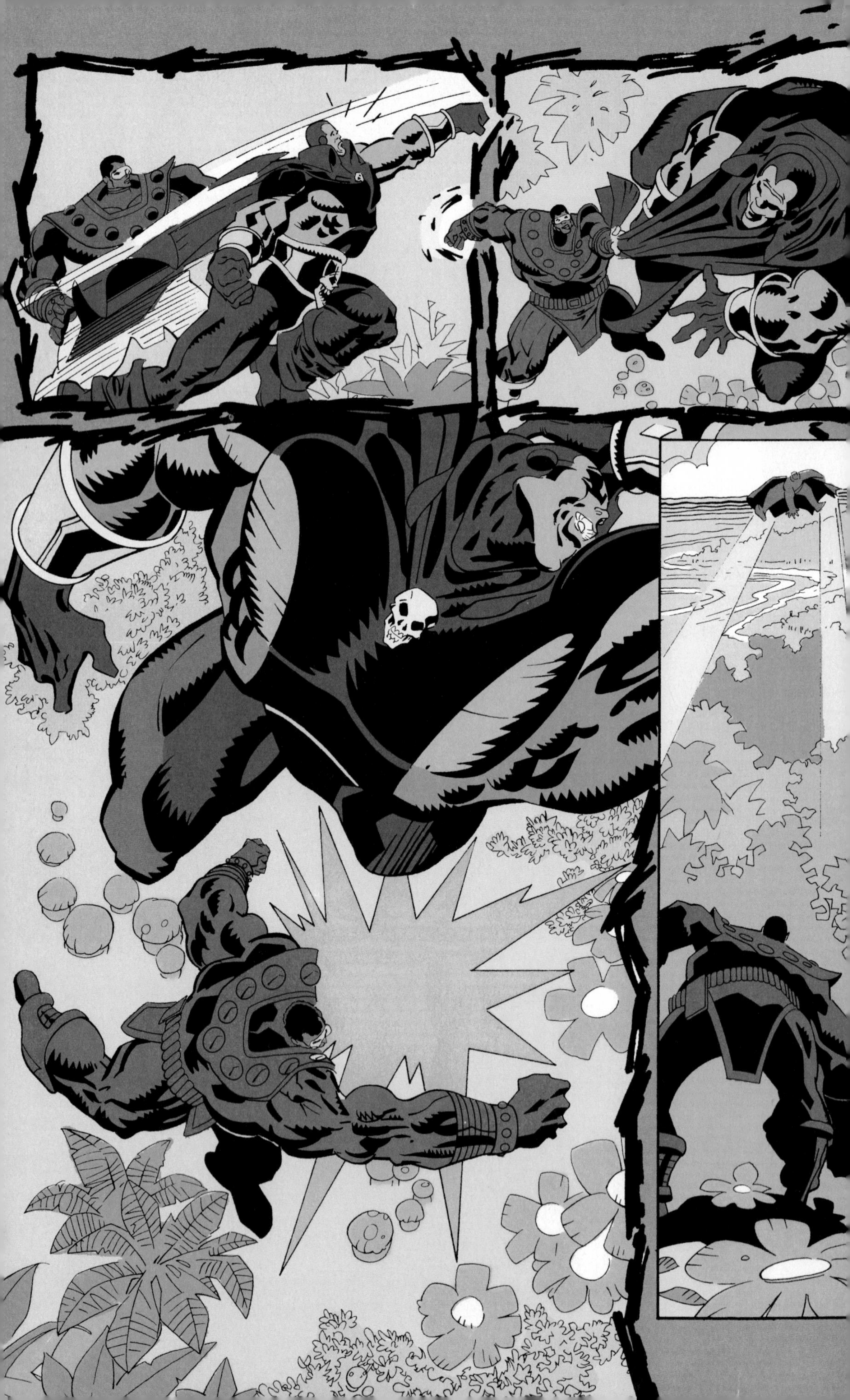

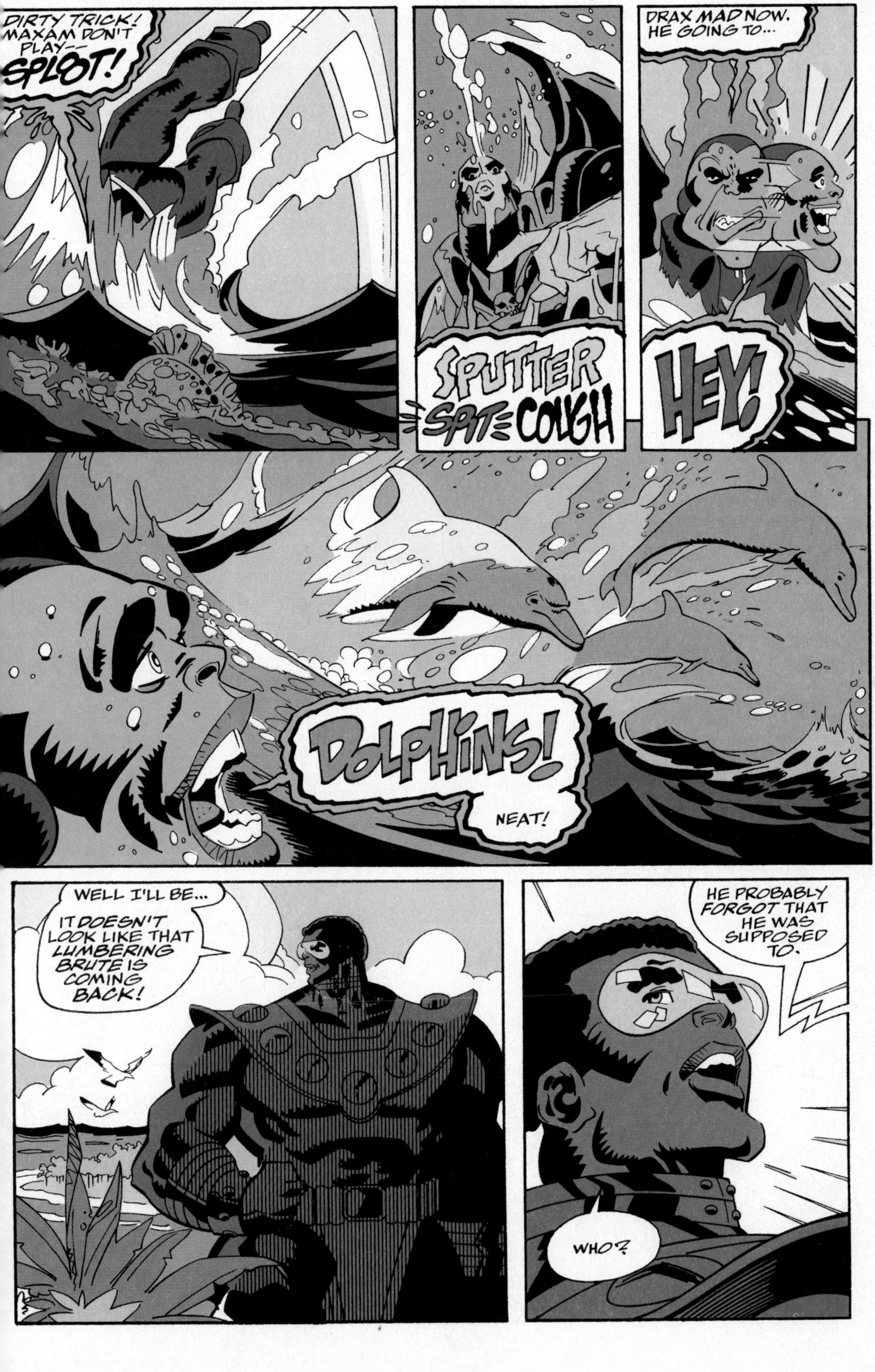
DIRTY TRICK! MAXAM DON'T PLAY--
SPLOT!
SPUTTER
SPIT COUGH
DRAX MAD NOW. HE GOING TO...
HEY!
DOLPHINS!
NEAT!
WELL I'LL BE...
IT DOESN'T LOOK LIKE THAT LUMBERING BRUTE IS COMING BACK!
HE PROBABLY FORGOT THAT HE WAS SUPPOSED TO.
WHO?

GETTING DISTRACTED IS A BIG PROBLEM WITH DRAX.

ADAM WARLOCK!

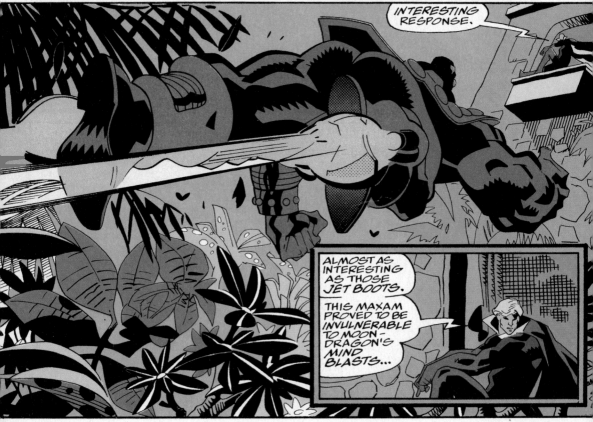

INTERESTING RESPONSE.

ALMOST AS INTERESTING AS THOSE JET BOOTS.

THIS MAXAM PROVED TO BE INVULNERABLE TO MOON-DRAGON'S MIND BLASTS...

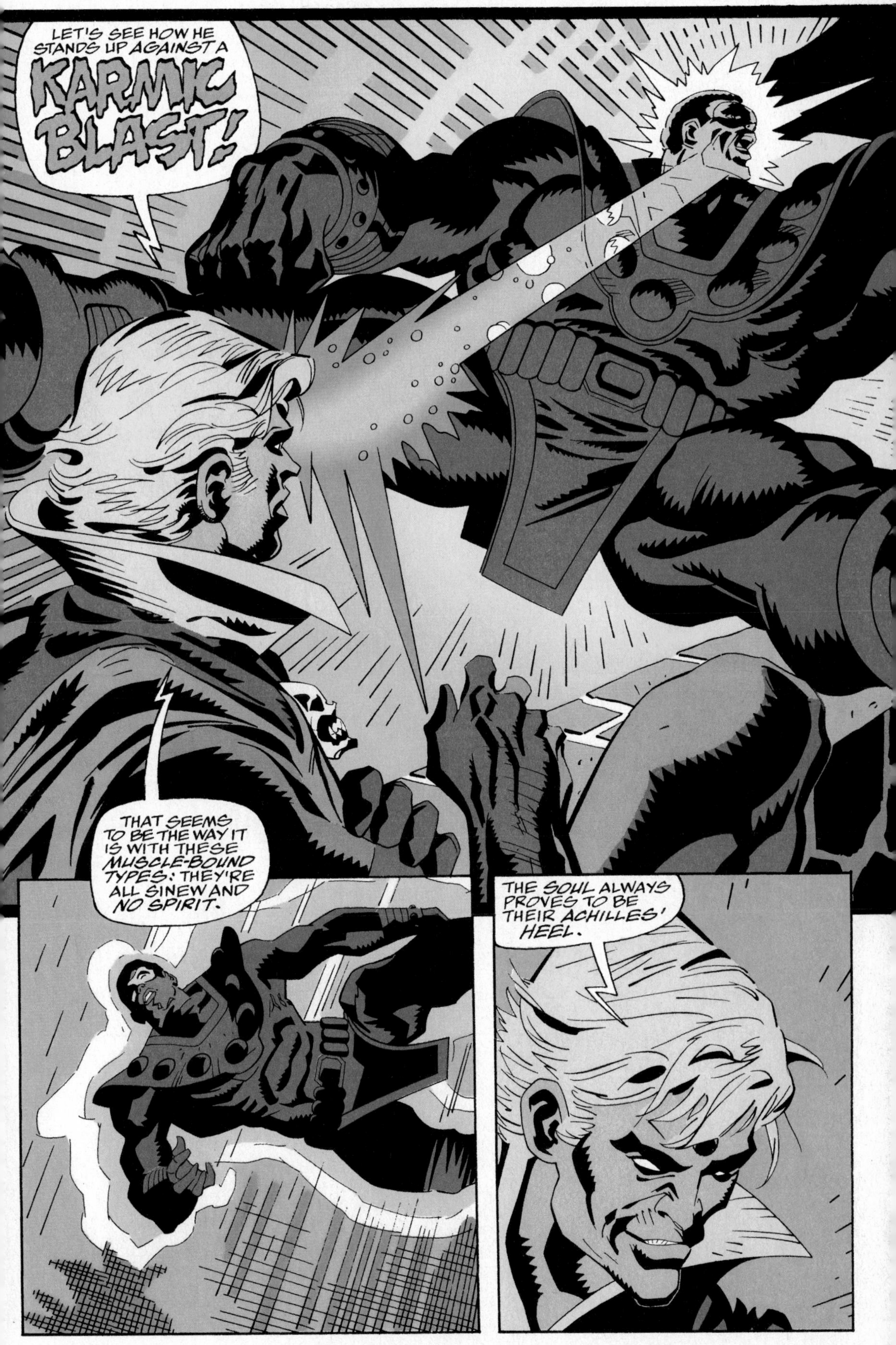
LET'S SEE HOW HE STANDS UP AGAINST A KARMIC BLAST!
THAT SEEMS TO BE THE WAY IT IS WITH THESE MUSCLE-BOUND TYPES: THEY'RE ALL SINEW AND NO SPIRIT.
THE SOUL ALWAYS PROVES TO BE THEIR ACHILLES' HEEL.

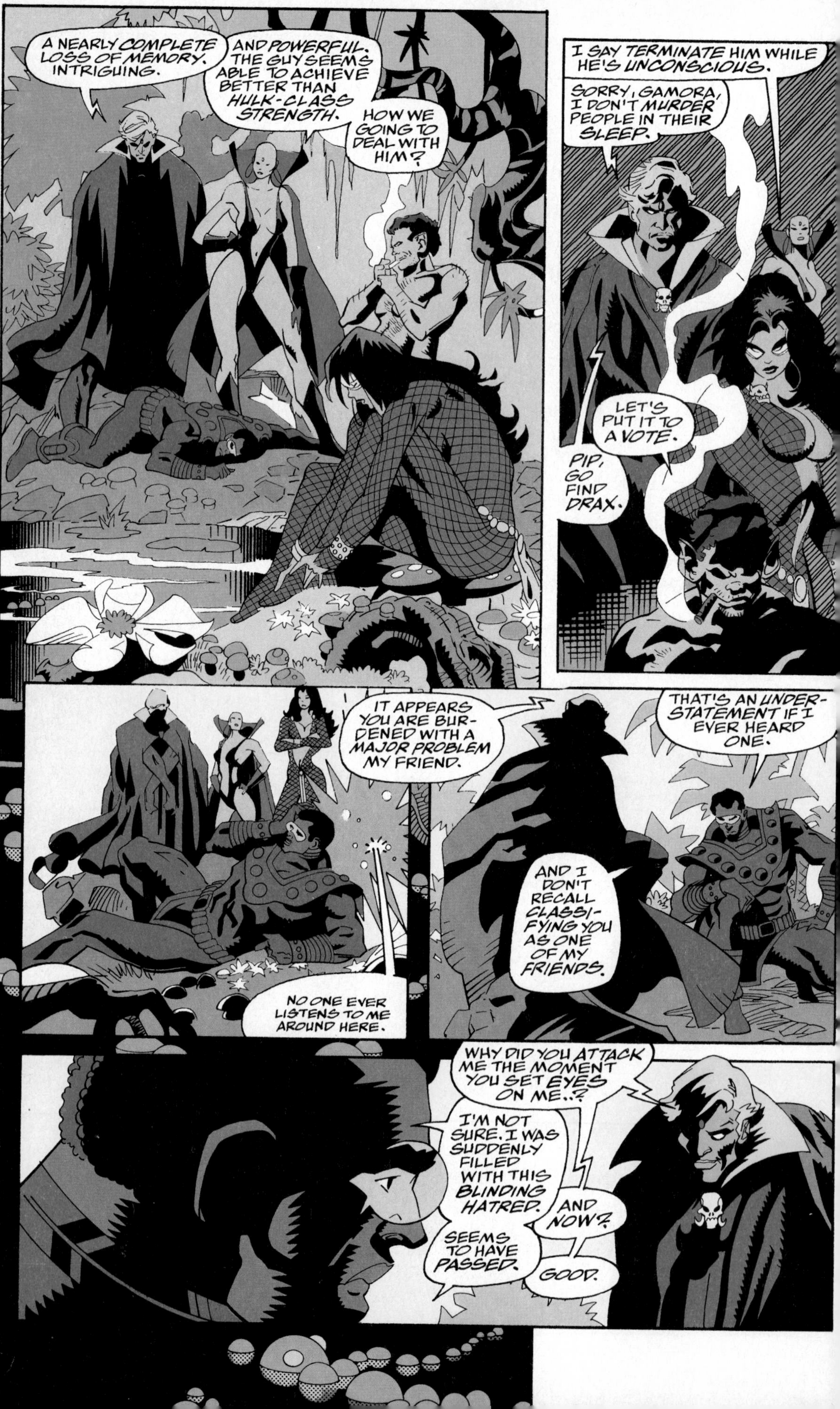
A NEARLY COMPLETE LOSS OF MEMORY. INTRIGUING.
AND POWERFUL. THE GUY SEEMS ABLE TO ACHIEVE BETTER THAN HULK-CLASS STRENGTH.
HOW WE GOING TO DEAL WITH HIM?
I SAY TERMINATE HIM WHILE HE'S UNCONSCIOUS.
SORRY, GAMORA, I DON'T MURDER PEOPLE IN THEIR SLEEP.
LET'S PUT IT TO A VOTE.
PIP, GO FIND DRAX.
IT APPEARS YOU ARE BURDENED WITH A MAJOR PROBLEM MY FRIEND.
NO ONE EVER LISTENS TO ME AROUND HERE.
THAT'S AN UNDERSTATEMENT IF I EVER HEARD ONE.
AND I DON'T RECALL CLASSIFYING YOU AS ONE OF MY FRIENDS.
WHY DID YOU ATTACK ME THE MOMENT YOU SET EYES ON ME..?
I'M NOT SURE. I WAS SUDDENLY FILLED WITH THIS BLINDING HATRED.
AND NOW?
SEEMS TO HAVE PASSED.
GOOD.

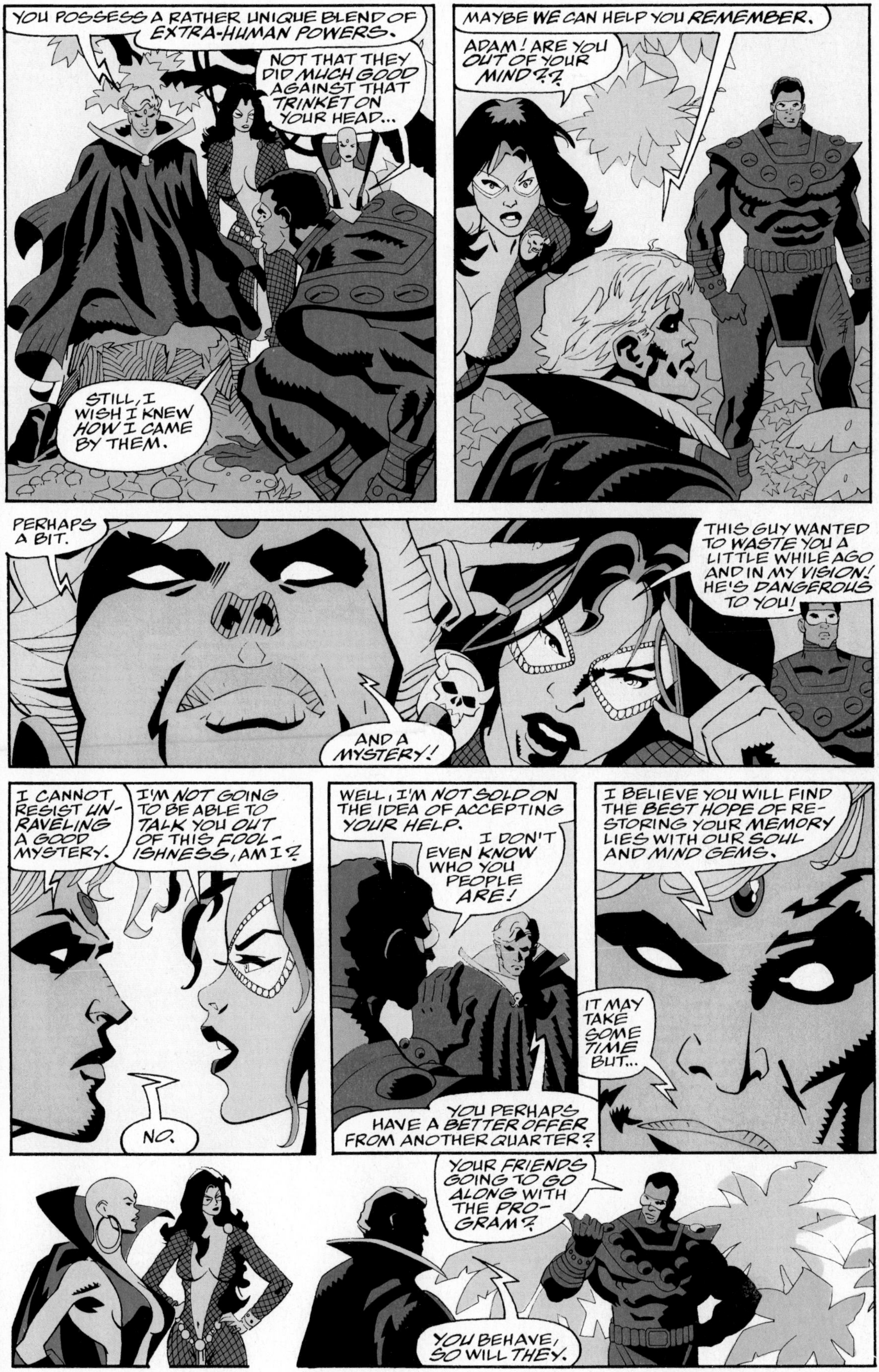
YOU POSSESS A RATHER UNIQUE BLEND OF EXTRA-HUMAN POWERS.
NOT THAT THEY DID MUCH GOOD AGAINST THAT TRINKET ON YOUR HEAD...
STILL, I WISH I KNEW HOW I CAME BY THEM.
MAYBE WE CAN HELP YOU REMEMBER.
ADAM! ARE YOU OUT OF YOUR MIND?!?
PERHAPS A BIT.
AND A MYSTERY!
THIS GUY WANTED TO WASTE YOU A LITTLE WHILE AGO AND IN MY VISION! HE'S DANGEROUS TO YOU!
I CANNOT RESIST UNRAVELING A GOOD MYSTERY.
I'M NOT GOING TO BE ABLE TO TALK YOU OUT OF THIS FOOLISHNESS, AM I?
NO.
WELL, I'M NOT SOLD ON THE IDEA OF ACCEPTING YOUR HELP.
I DON'T EVEN KNOW WHO YOU PEOPLE ARE!
YOU PERHAPS HAVE A BETTER OFFER FROM ANOTHER QUARTER?
I BELIEVE YOU WILL FIND THE BEST HOPE OF RESTORING YOUR MEMORY LIES WITH OUR SOUL AND MIND GEMS.
IT MAY TAKE SOME TIME BUT...
YOUR FRIENDS GOING TO GO ALONG WITH THE PROGRAM?
YOU BEHAVE, SO WILL THEY.

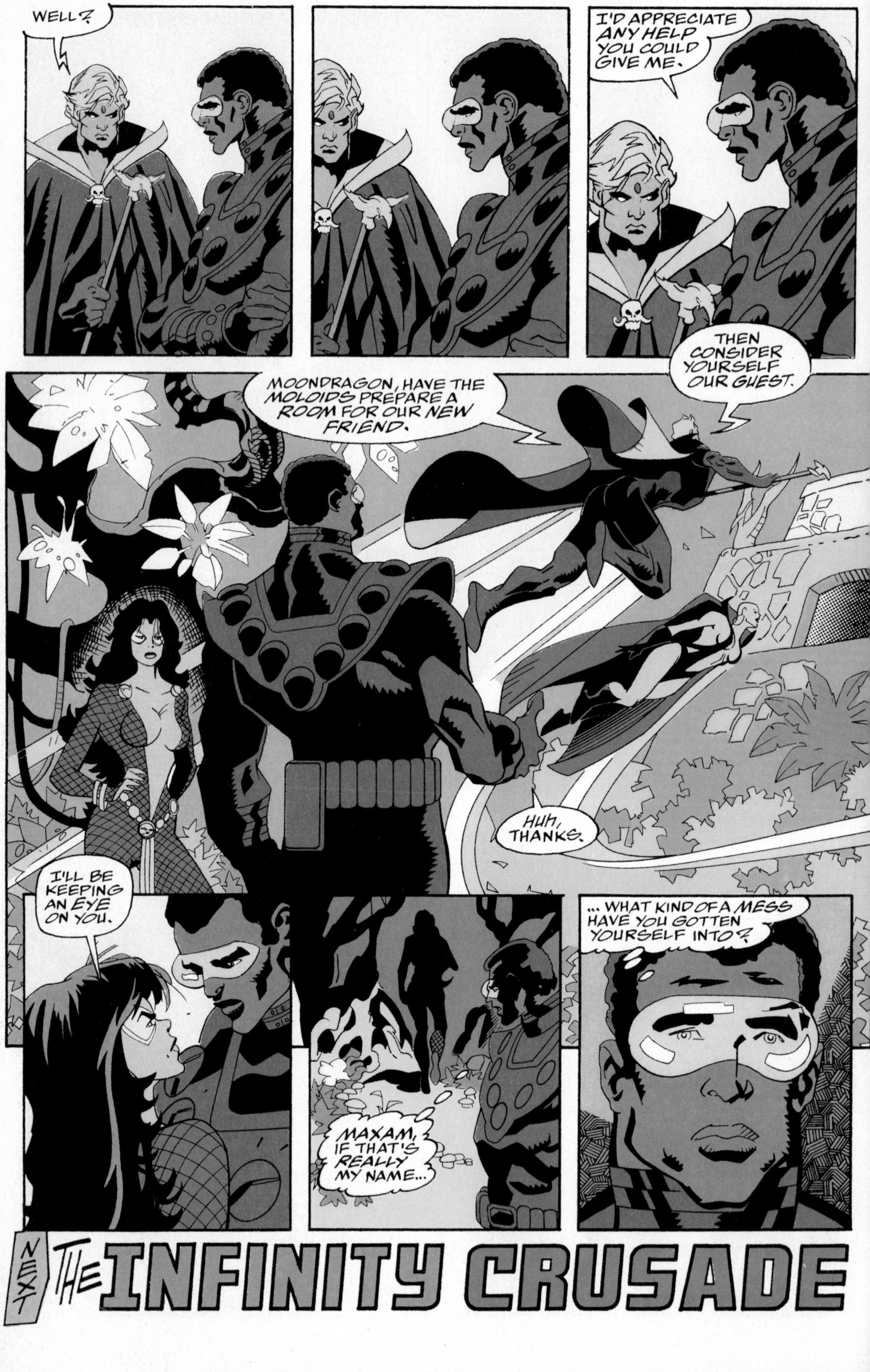

WELL?
I'D APPRECIATE ANY HELP YOU COULD GIVE ME.
THEN CONSIDER YOURSELF OUR GUEST.
MOONDRAGON, HAVE THE MOLOIDS PREPARE A ROOM FOR OUR NEW FRIEND.
HUH, THANKS.
I'LL BE KEEPING AN EYE ON YOU.
MAXAM, IF THAT'S REALLY MY NAME...
... WHAT KIND OF A MESS HAVE YOU GOTTEN YOURSELF INTO?
NEXT THE INFINITY CRUSADE

N THE *INFINITY CRUSADE* STORYLINE, WARLOCK'S GOOD SIDE, THE GODDESS, MERGED THE MAGUS' STOLEN COSMIC CUBES INTO AN ALL-POWERFUL COSMIC EGG. WITH IT SHE CREATED THE PLANET PARADISE MEGA AND TELEPATHICALLY BRAINWASHED SPIRITUALLY INCLINED HEROES TO JOIN HER ARMY, PART OF A AR-REACHING PLAN TO WIPE OUT ALL SIN IN THE UNIVERSE. *WARLOCK AND THE INFINITY WATCH* #18-22 WERE NFINITY CRUSADE TIE-INS.

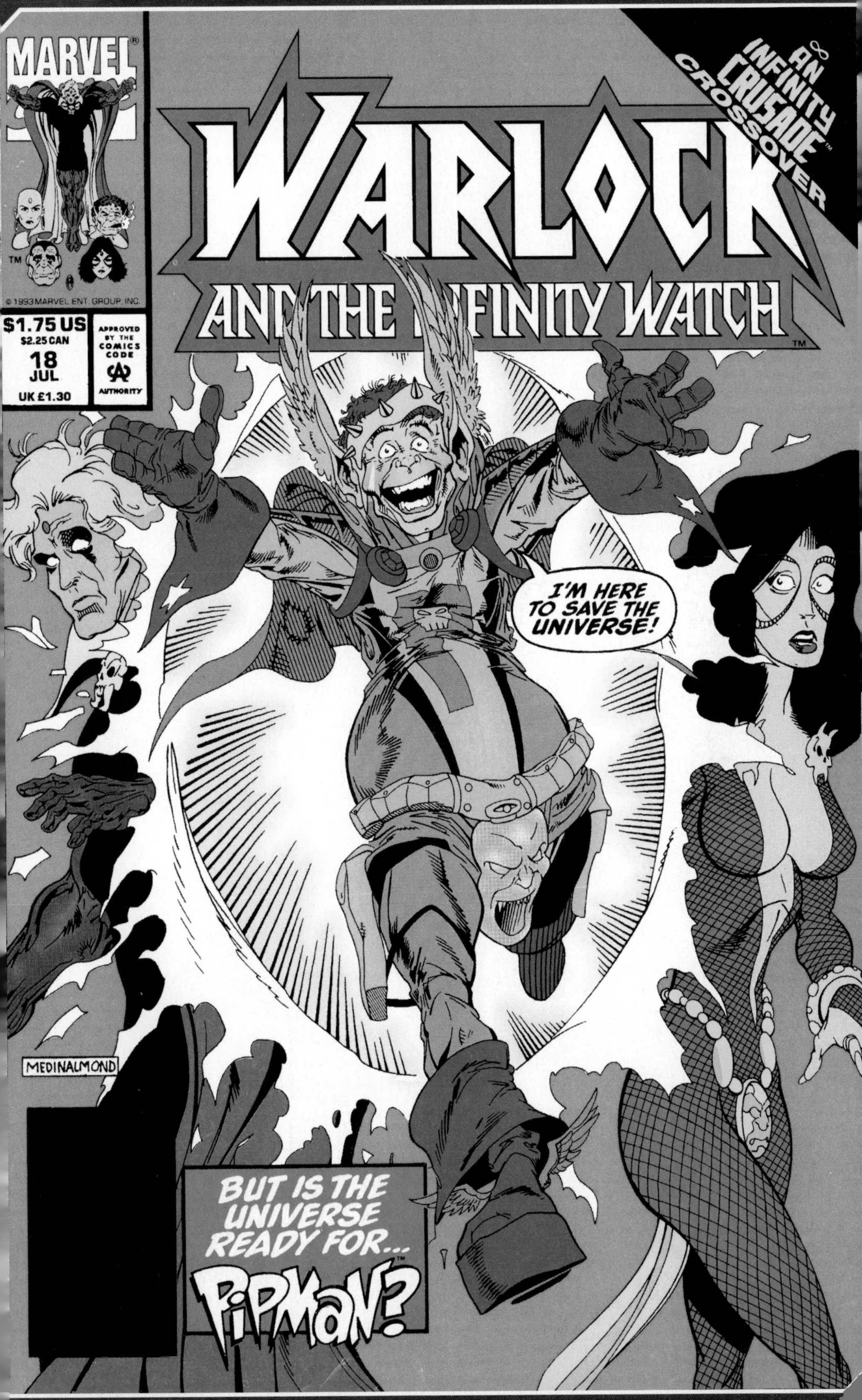

MARVEL
WARLOCK
AND THE INFINITY WATCH
AN INFINITY CRUSADE CROSSOVER
© 1993 MARVEL ENT. GROUP, INC.
$1.75 US
$2.25 CAN
18
JUL
UK £1.30
APPROVED BY THE COMICS CODE AUTHORITY
I'M HERE TO SAVE THE UNIVERSE!
MEDINA/ALMOND
BUT IS THE UNIVERSE READY FOR...
PIPMAN?

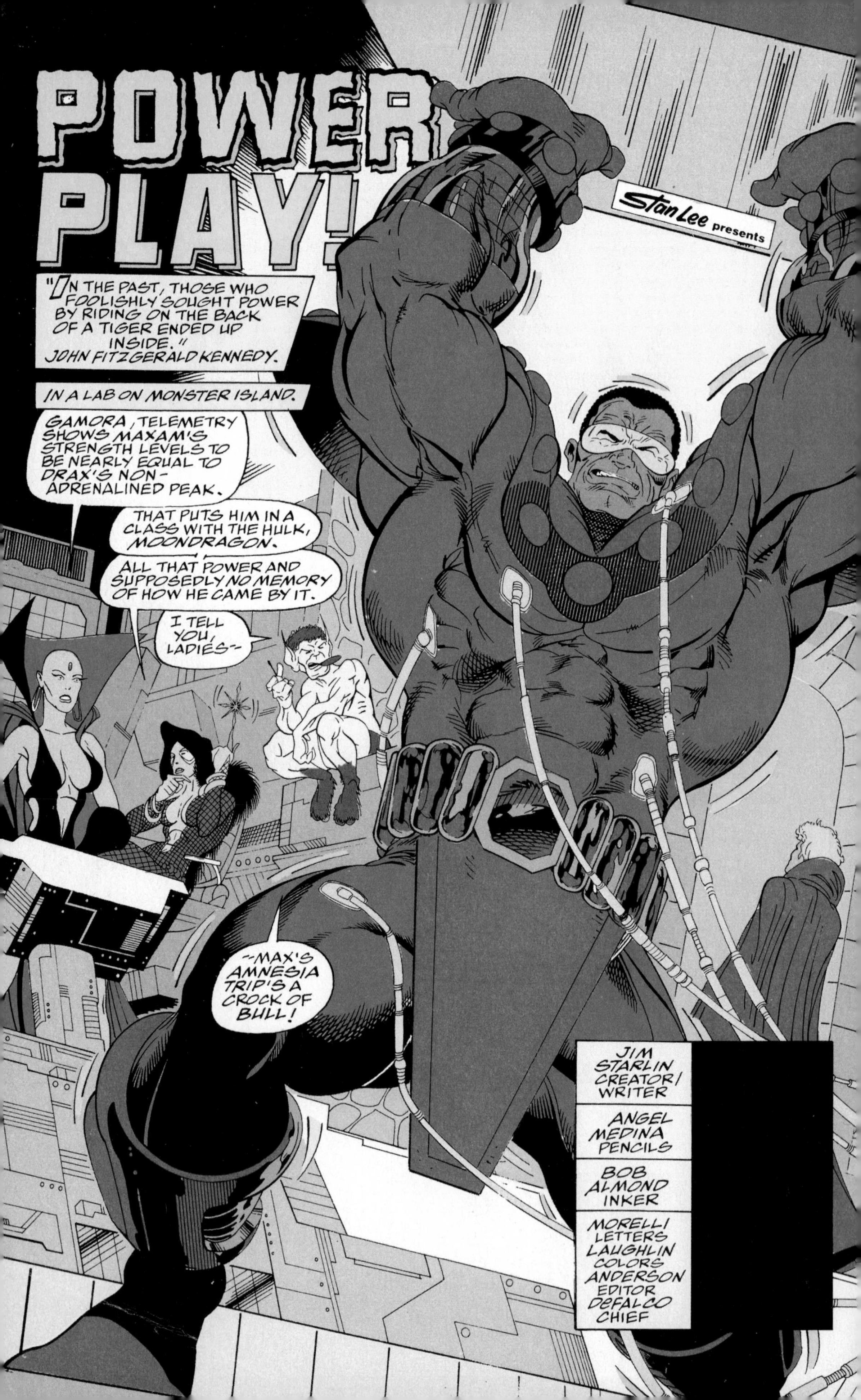
POWER PLAY!
Stan Lee presents
"IN THE PAST, THOSE WHO FOOLISHLY SOUGHT POWER BY RIDING ON THE BACK OF A TIGER ENDED UP INSIDE." JOHN FITZGERALD KENNEDY.
IN A LAB ON MONSTER ISLAND.
GAMORA, TELEMETRY SHOWS MAXAM'S STRENGTH LEVELS TO BE NEARLY EQUAL TO DRAX'S NON-ADRENALINED PEAK.
THAT PUTS HIM IN A CLASS WITH THE HULK, MOONDRAGON.
ALL THAT POWER AND SUPPOSEDLY NO MEMORY OF HOW HE CAME BY IT.
I TELL YOU, LADIES--
--MAX'S AMNESIA TRIP'S A CROCK OF BULL!
JIM STARLIN CREATOR/WRITER
ANGEL MEDINA PENCILS
BOB ALMOND INKER
MORELLI LETTERS
LAUGHLIN COLORS
ANDERSON EDITOR
DEFALCO CHIEF

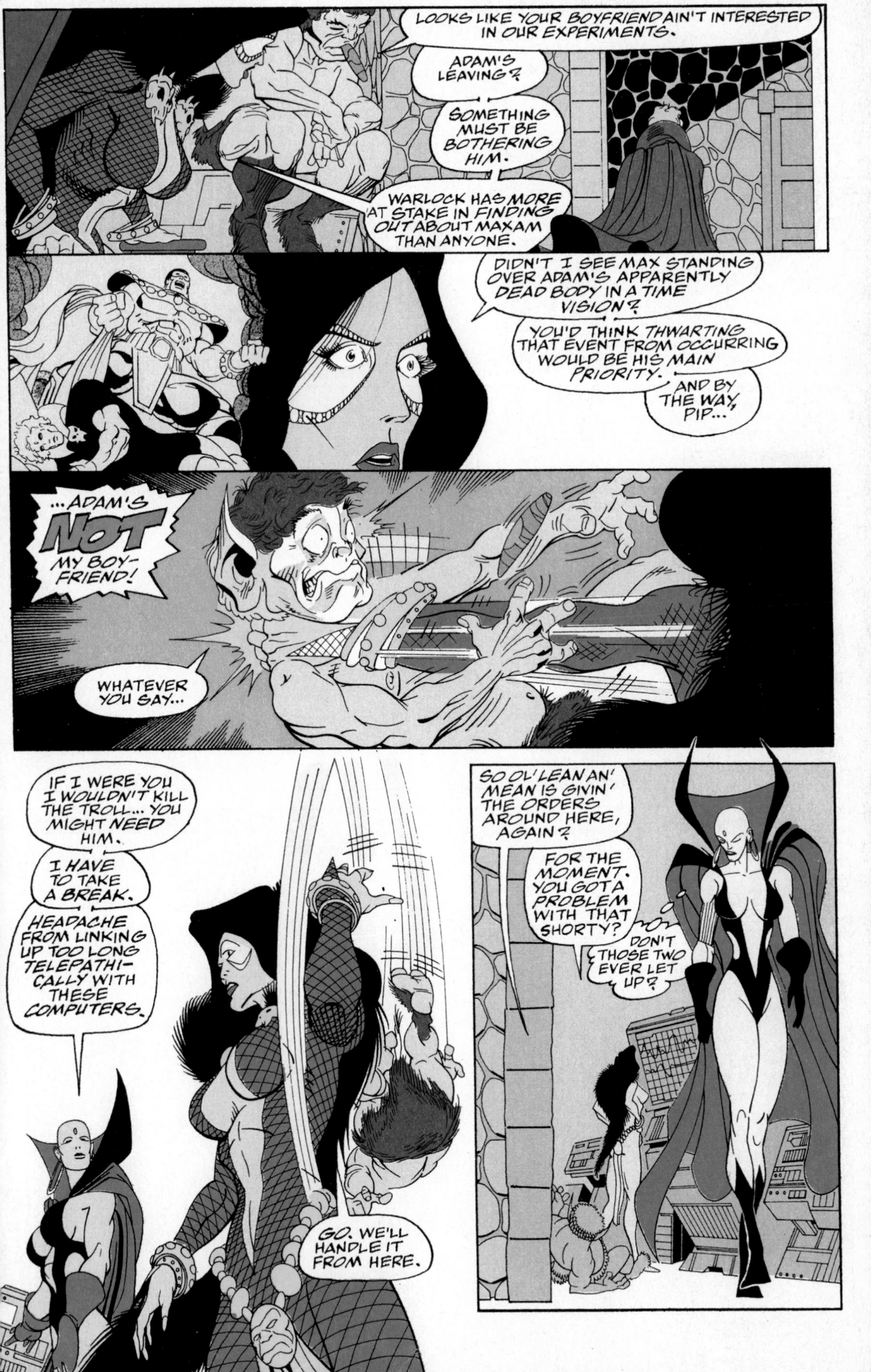
LOOKS LIKE YOUR BOYFRIEND AIN'T INTERESTED IN OUR EXPERIMENTS.
ADAM'S LEAVING?
SOMETHING MUST BE BOTHERING HIM.
WARLOCK HAS MORE AT STAKE IN FINDING OUT ABOUT MAXAM THAN ANYONE.
DIDN'T I SEE MAX STANDING OVER ADAM'S APPARENTLY DEAD BODY IN A TIME VISION?
YOU'D THINK THWARTING THAT EVENT FROM OCCURRING WOULD BE HIS MAIN PRIORITY.
AND BY THE WAY, PIP...
...ADAM'S NOT MY BOY-FRIEND!
WHATEVER YOU SAY...
IF I WERE YOU I WOULDN'T KILL THE TROLL... YOU MIGHT NEED HIM.
I HAVE TO TAKE A BREAK.
HEADACHE FROM LINKING UP TOO LONG TELEPATHICALLY WITH THESE COMPUTERS.
GO. WE'LL HANDLE IT FROM HERE.
SO OL' LEAN AN' MEAN IS GIVIN' THE ORDERS AROUND HERE, AGAIN?
FOR THE MOMENT. YOU GOT A PROBLEM WITH THAT SHORTY?
DON'T THOSE TWO EVER LET UP?

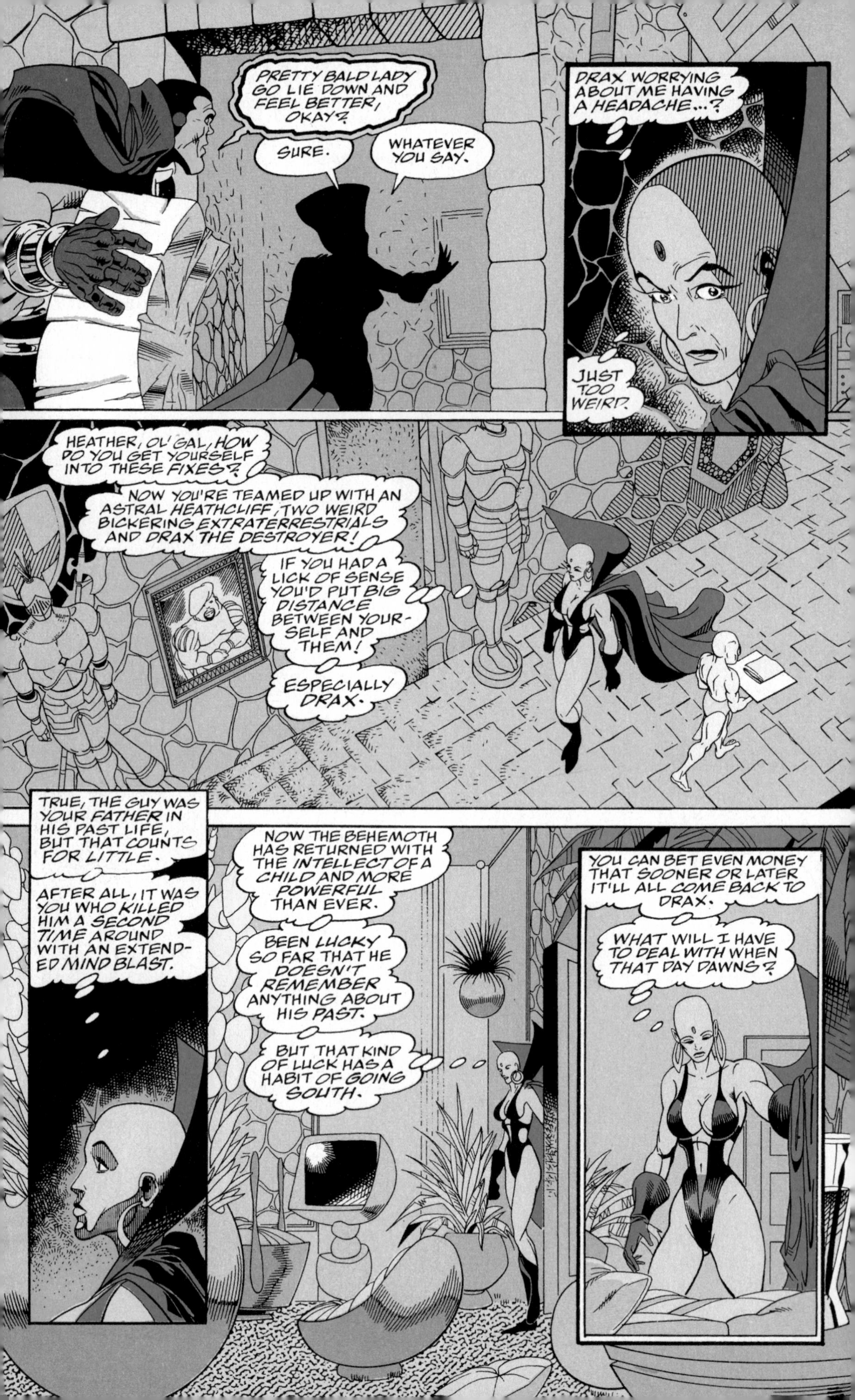

PRETTY BALD LADY GO LIE DOWN AND FEEL BETTER, OKAY?
SURE.
WHATEVER YOU SAY.
DRAX WORRYING ABOUT ME HAVING A HEADACHE...?
JUST TOO WEIRD.
HEATHER, OL' GAL, HOW DO YOU GET YOURSELF INTO THESE FIXES?
NOW YOU'RE TEAMED UP WITH AN ASTRAL HEATHCLIFF, TWO WEIRD BICKERING EXTRATERRESTRIALS AND DRAX THE DESTROYER!
IF YOU HAD A LICK OF SENSE YOU'D PUT BIG DISTANCE BETWEEN YOURSELF AND THEM!
ESPECIALLY DRAX.
TRUE, THE GUY WAS YOUR FATHER IN HIS PAST LIFE, BUT THAT COUNTS FOR LITTLE.
AFTER ALL, IT WAS YOU WHO KILLED HIM A SECOND TIME AROUND WITH AN EXTENDED MIND BLAST.
NOW THE BEHEMOTH HAS RETURNED WITH THE INTELLECT OF A CHILD AND MORE POWERFUL THAN EVER.
BEEN LUCKY SO FAR THAT HE DOESN'T REMEMBER ANYTHING ABOUT HIS PAST.
BUT THAT KIND OF LUCK HAS A HABIT OF GOING SOUTH.
YOU CAN BET EVEN MONEY THAT SOONER OR LATER IT'LL ALL COME BACK TO DRAX.
WHAT WILL I HAVE TO DEAL WITH WHEN THAT DAY DAWNS?

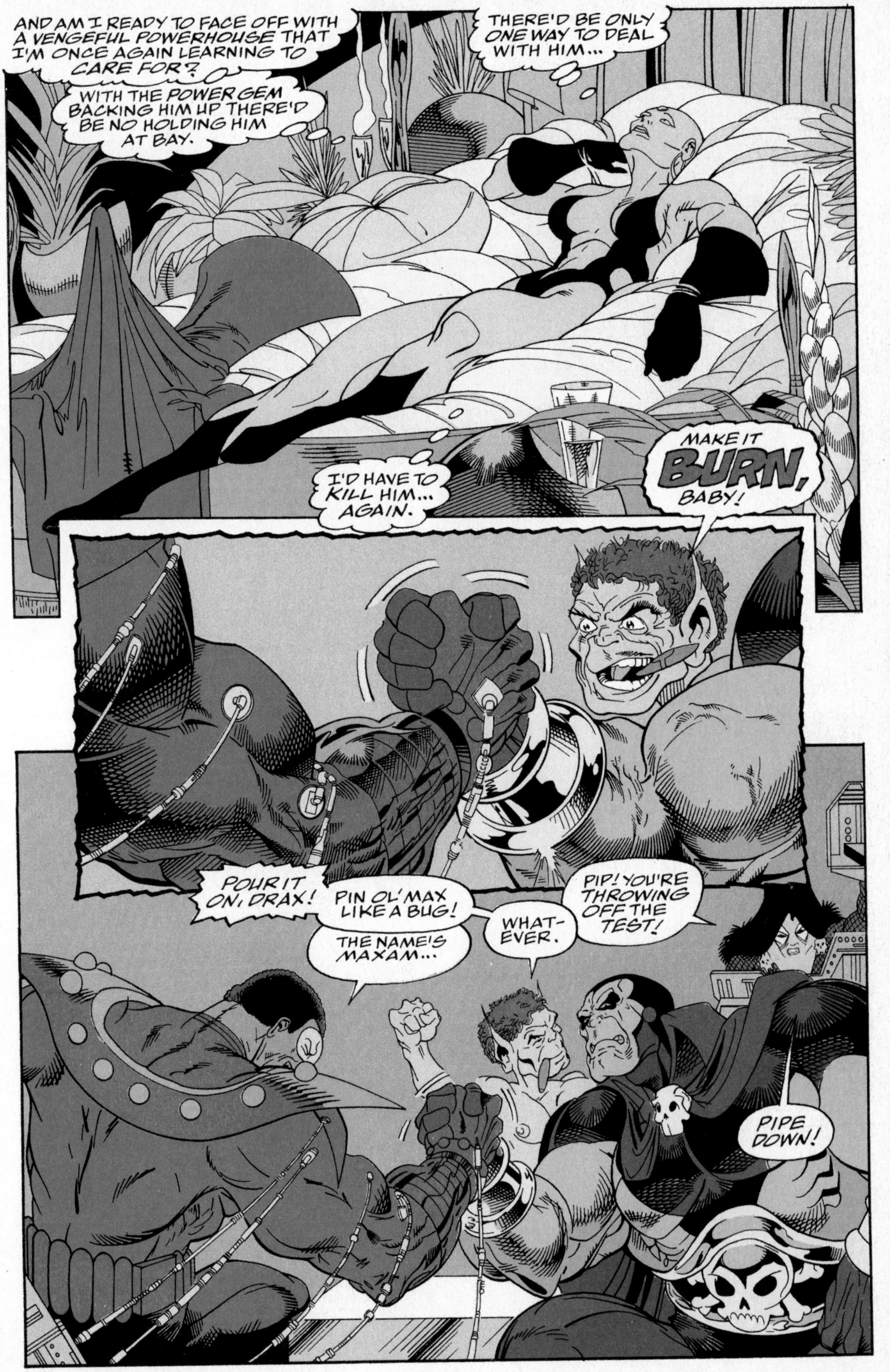
AND AM I READY TO FACE OFF WITH A VENGEFUL POWERHOUSE THAT I'M ONCE AGAIN LEARNING TO CARE FOR?
WITH THE POWER GEM BACKING HIM UP THERE'D BE NO HOLDING HIM AT BAY.
THERE'D BE ONLY ONE WAY TO DEAL WITH HIM...
I'D HAVE TO KILL HIM... AGAIN.
MAKE IT BURN, BABY!
POUR IT ON, DRAX!
PIN OL' MAX LIKE A BUG!
THE NAME'S MAXAM...
WHAT-EVER.
PIP! YOU'RE THROWING OFF THE TEST!
PIPE DOWN!

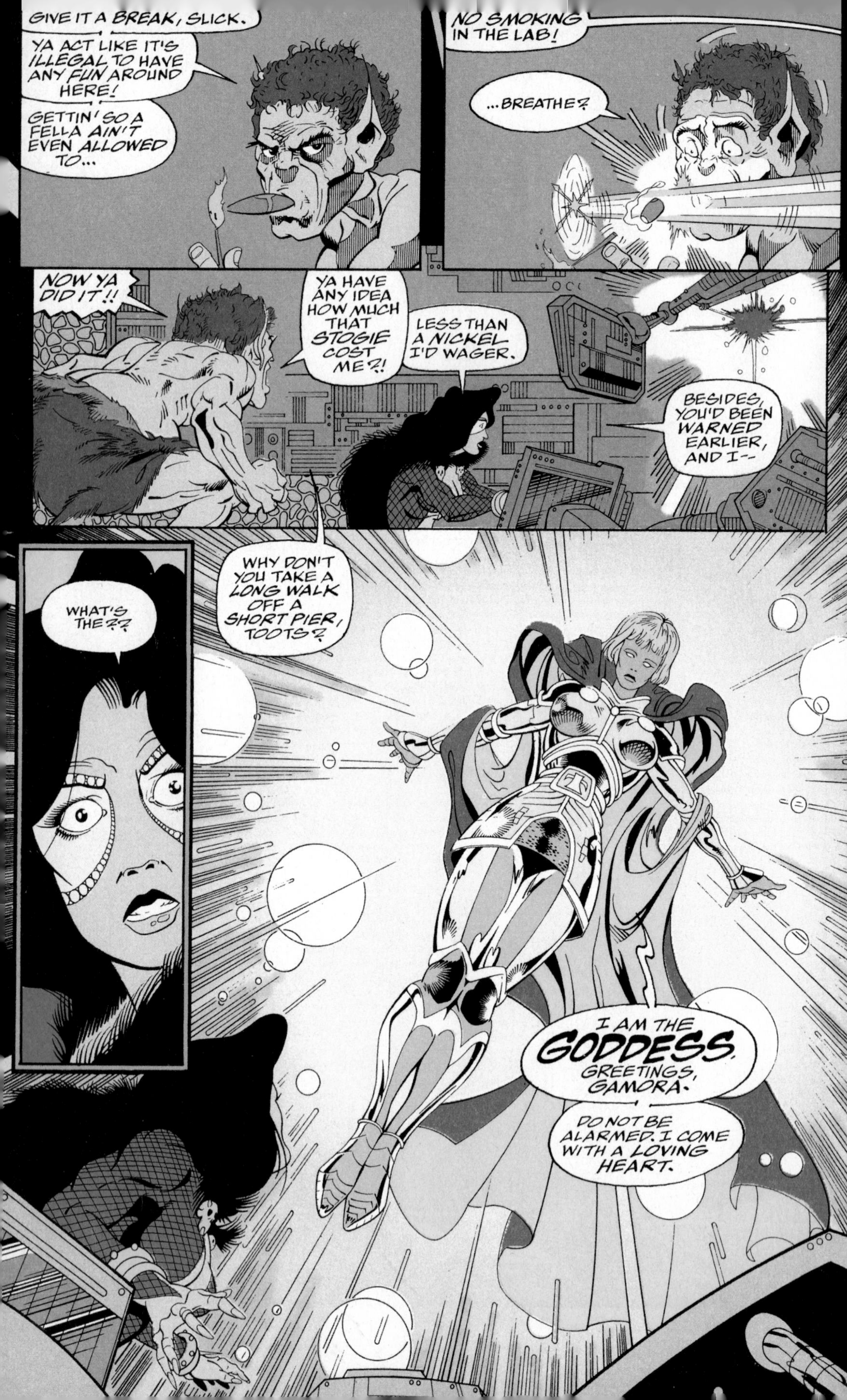
GIVE IT A BREAK, SLICK.
YA ACT LIKE IT'S ILLEGAL TO HAVE ANY FUN AROUND HERE!
GETTIN' SO A FELLA AIN'T EVEN ALLOWED TO...
NO SMOKING IN THE LAB!
...BREATHE?
NOW YA DID IT!!
YA HAVE ANY IDEA HOW MUCH THAT STOGIE COST ME?!
LESS THAN A NICKEL I'D WAGER.
BESIDES, YOU'D BEEN WARNED EARLIER, AND I--
WHY DON'T YOU TAKE A LONG WALK OFF A SHORT PIER, TOOTS?
WHAT'S THE??
I AM THE GODDESS. GREETINGS, GAMORA.
DO NOT BE ALARMED. I COME WITH A LOVING HEART.

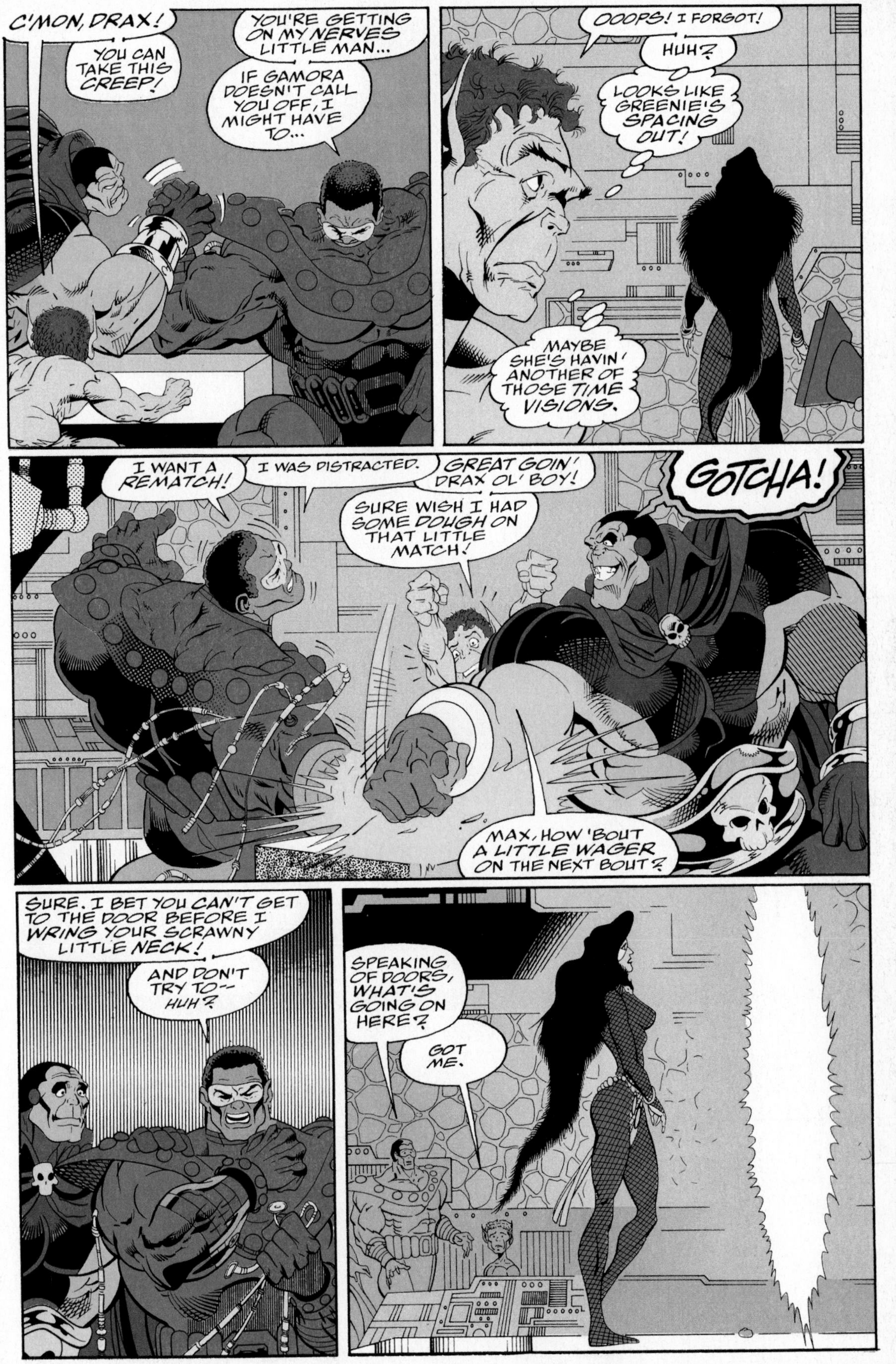

C'MON, DRAX!
YOU CAN TAKE THIS CREEP!
YOU'RE GETTING ON MY NERVES LITTLE MAN...
IF GAMORA DOESN'T CALL YOU OFF, I MIGHT HAVE TO...
OOOPS! I FORGOT!
HUH?
LOOKS LIKE GREENIE'S SPACING OUT!
MAYBE SHE'S HAVIN' ANOTHER OF THOSE TIME VISIONS.
I WANT A REMATCH!
I WAS DISTRACTED.
GREAT GOIN' DRAX OL' BOY!
SURE WISH I HAD SOME DOUGH ON THAT LITTLE MATCH!
GOTCHA!
MAX, HOW 'BOUT A LITTLE WAGER ON THE NEXT BOUT?
SURE. I BET YOU CAN'T GET TO THE DOOR BEFORE I WRING YOUR SCRAWNY LITTLE NECK!
AND DON'T TRY TO-- HUH?
SPEAKING OF DOORS, WHAT'S GOING ON HERE?
GOT ME.

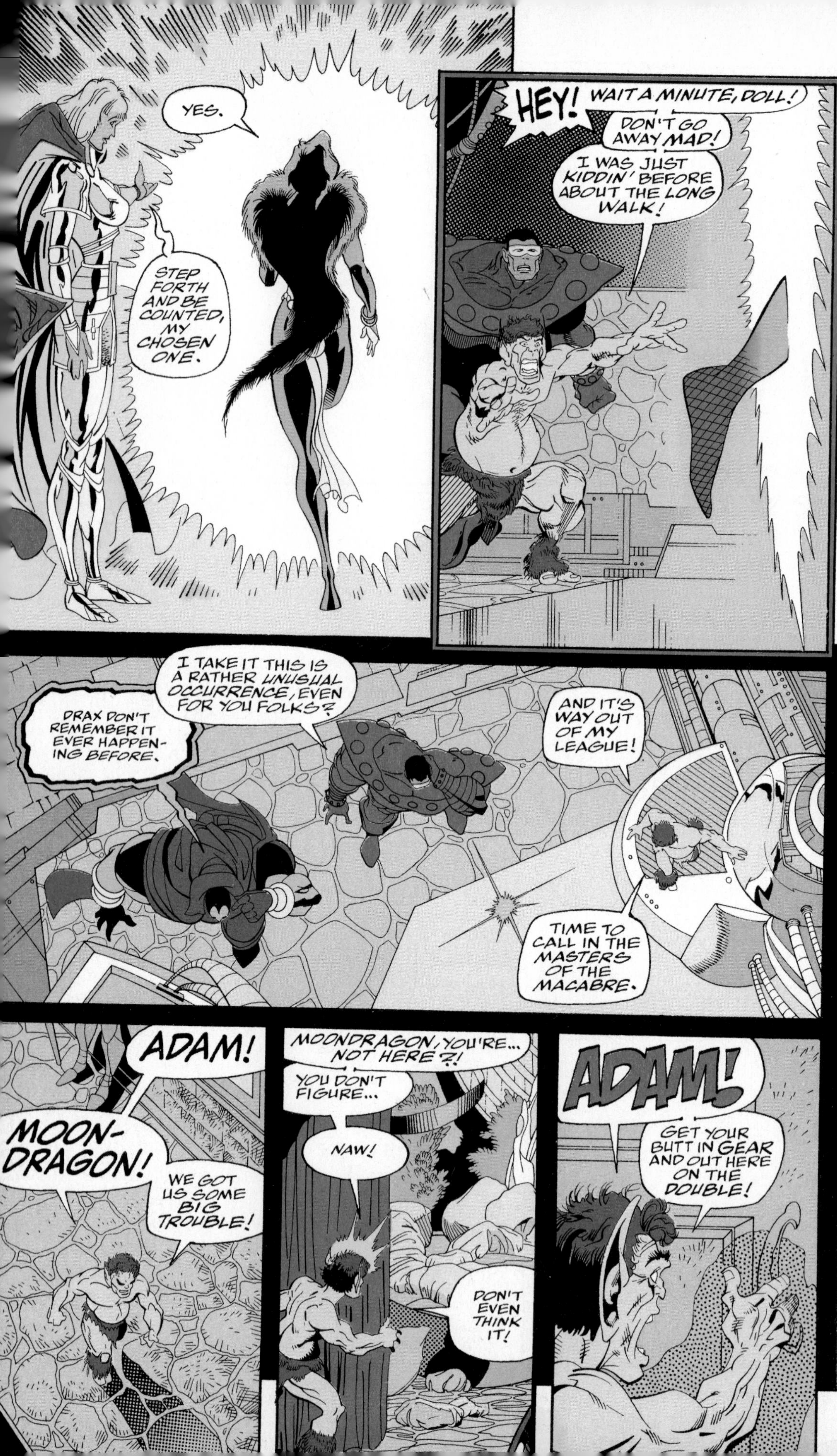
YES.
STEP FORTH AND BE COUNTED, MY CHOSEN ONE.
HEY!
WAIT A MINUTE, DOLL!
DON'T GO AWAY MAD!
I WAS JUST KIDDIN' BEFORE ABOUT THE LONG WALK!
I TAKE IT THIS IS A RATHER UNUSUAL OCCURRENCE, EVEN FOR YOU FOLKS?
DRAX DON'T REMEMBER IT EVER HAPPENING BEFORE.
AND IT'S WAY OUT OF MY LEAGUE!
TIME TO CALL IN THE MASTERS OF THE MACABRE.
ADAM!
MOON-DRAGON!
WE GOT US SOME BIG TROUBLE!
MOONDRAGON, YOU'RE... NOT HERE?!
YOU DON'T FIGURE...
NAW!
DON'T EVEN THINK IT!
ADAM!
GET YOUR BUTT IN GEAR AND OUT HERE ON THE DOUBLE!

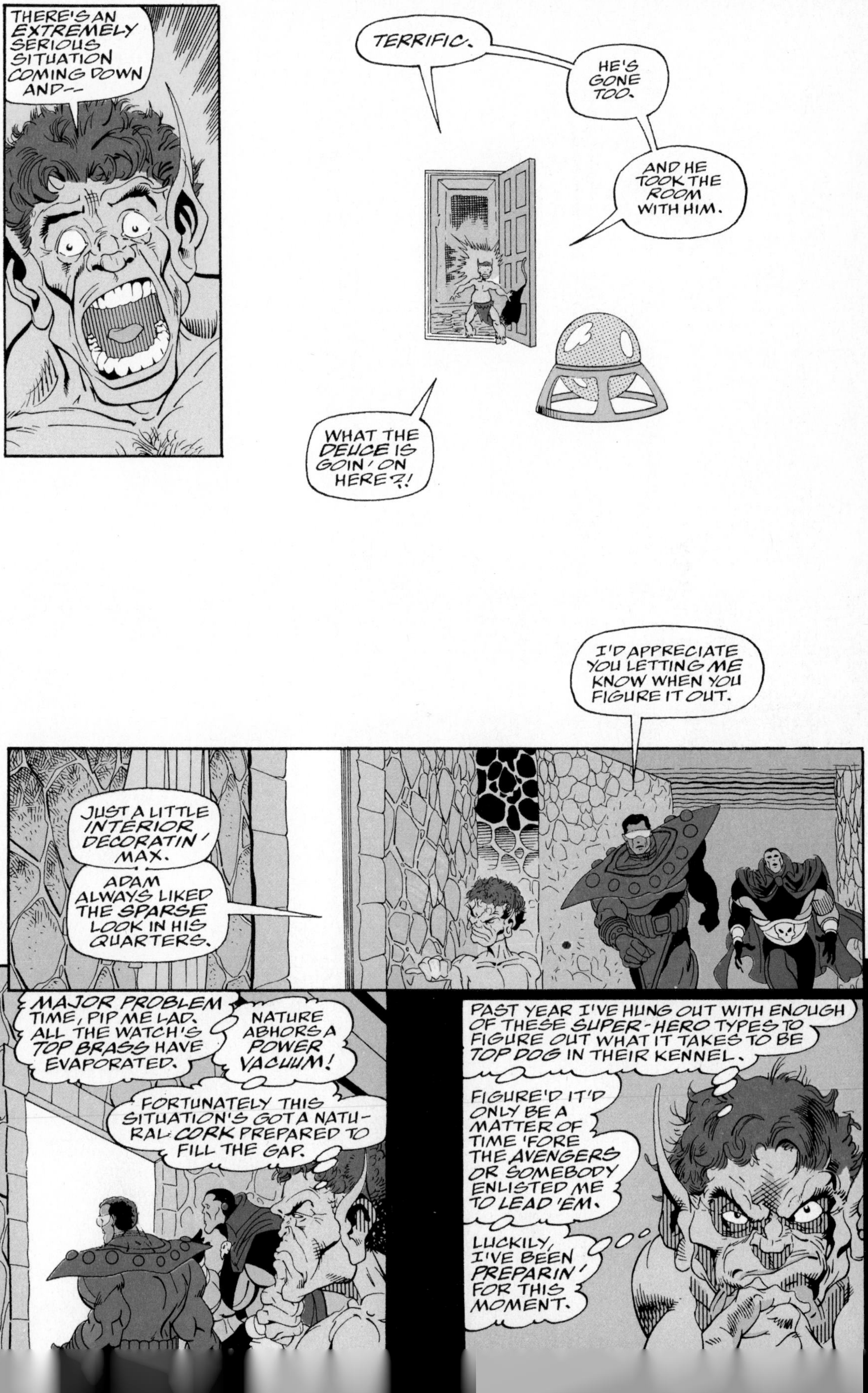
THERE'S AN EXTREMELY SERIOUS SITUATION COMING DOWN AND--
TERRIFIC.
HE'S GONE TOO.
AND HE TOOK THE ROOM WITH HIM.
WHAT THE DEUCE IS GOIN' ON HERE?!
I'D APPRECIATE YOU LETTING ME KNOW WHEN YOU FIGURE IT OUT.
JUST A LITTLE INTERIOR DECORATIN', MAX.
ADAM ALWAYS LIKED THE SPARSE LOOK IN HIS QUARTERS.
MAJOR PROBLEM TIME, PIP ME LAD. ALL THE WATCH'S TOP BRASS HAVE EVAPORATED.
NATURE ABHORS A POWER VACUUM!
FORTUNATELY THIS SITUATION'S GOT A NATURAL CORK PREPARED TO FILL THE GAP.
PAST YEAR I'VE HUNG OUT WITH ENOUGH OF THESE SUPER-HERO TYPES TO FIGURE OUT WHAT IT TAKES TO BE TOP DOG IN THEIR KENNEL.
FIGURE'D IT'D ONLY BE A MATTER OF TIME 'FORE THE AVENGERS OR SOMEBODY ENLISTED ME TO LEAD 'EM.
LUCKILY, I'VE BEEN PREPARIN' FOR THIS MOMENT.

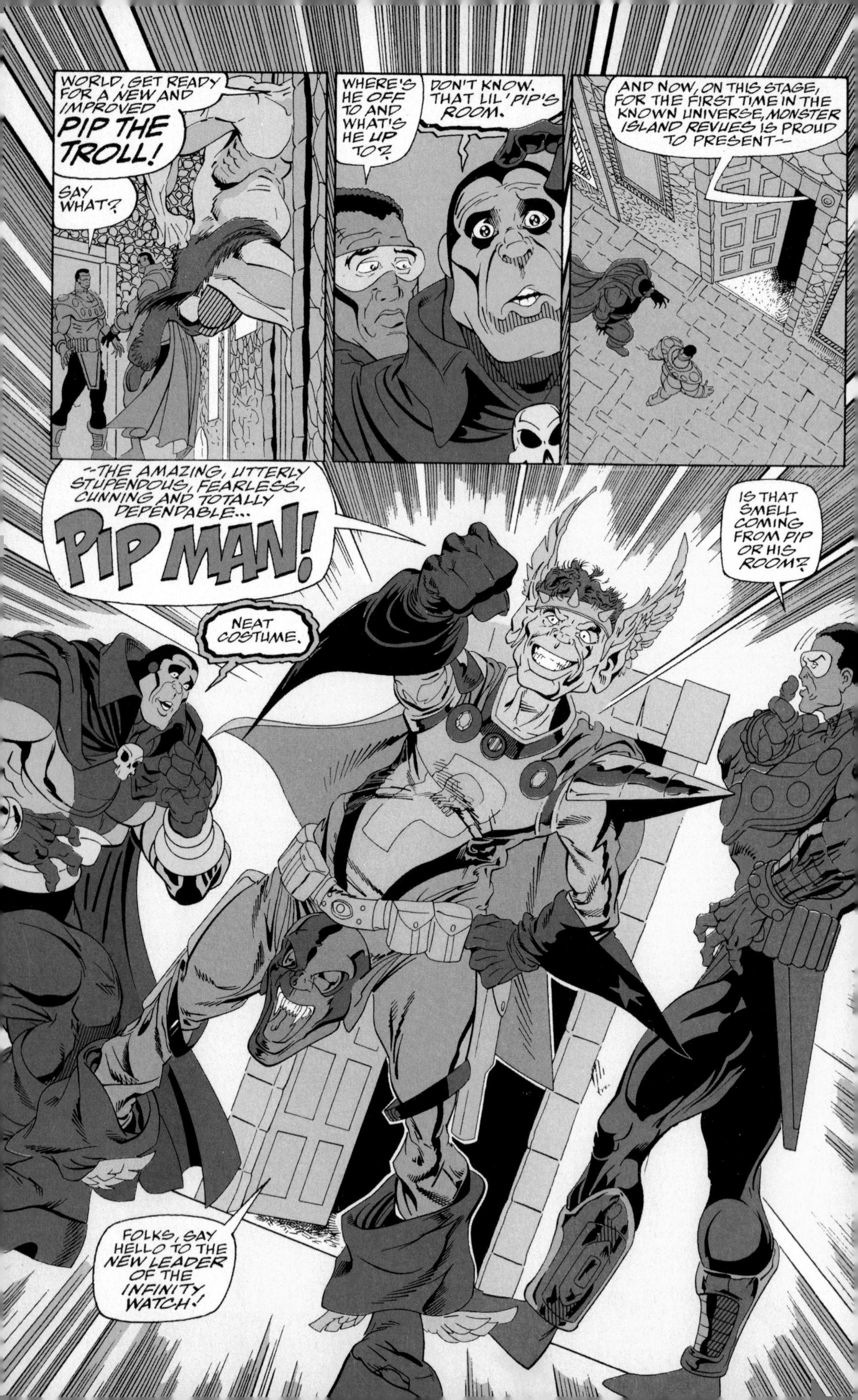
WORLD, GET READY FOR A NEW AND IMPROVED PIP THE TROLL!
SAY WHAT?
WHERE'S HE OFF TO AND WHAT'S HE UP TO?
DON'T KNOW. THAT LIL' PIP'S ROOM.
AND NOW, ON THIS STAGE, FOR THE FIRST TIME IN THE KNOWN UNIVERSE, MONSTER ISLAND REVUES IS PROUD TO PRESENT--
--THE AMAZING, UTTERLY STUPENDOUS, FEARLESS, CUNNING AND TOTALLY DEPENDABLE... PIP MAN!
IS THAT SMELL COMING FROM PIP OR HIS ROOM?
NEAT COSTUME.
FOLKS, SAY HELLO TO THE NEW LEADER OF THE INFINITY WATCH!

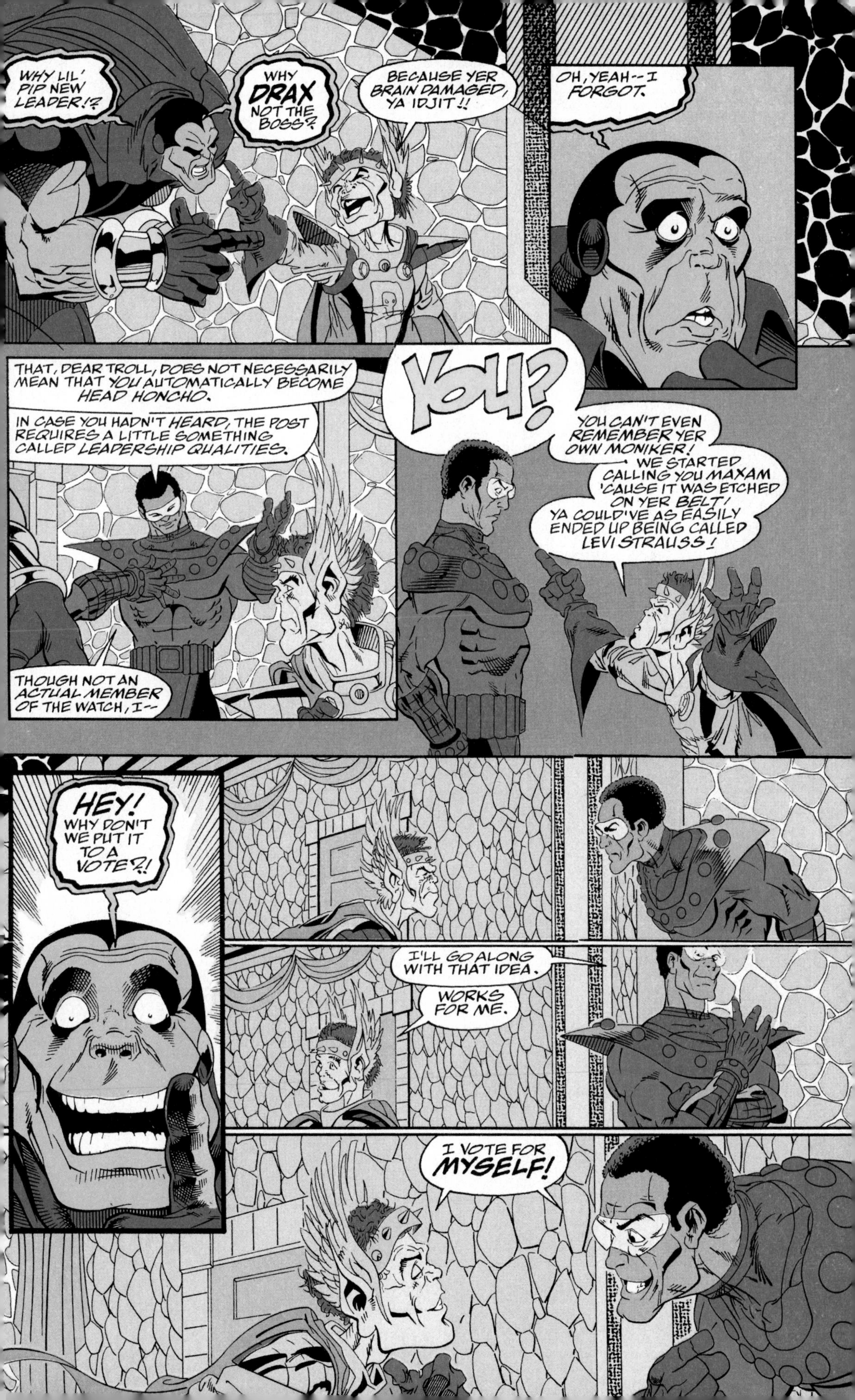
WHY LIL' PIP NEW LEADER!?
WHY DRAX NOT THE BOSS?
BECAUSE YER BRAIN DAMAGED, YA IDJIT!!
OH, YEAH-- I FORGOT.
THAT, DEAR TROLL, DOES NOT NECESSARILY MEAN THAT YOU AUTOMATICALLY BECOME HEAD HONCHO.
IN CASE YOU HADN'T HEARD, THE POST REQUIRES A LITTLE SOMETHING CALLED LEADERSHIP QUALITIES.
THOUGH NOT AN ACTUAL MEMBER OF THE WATCH, I--
YOU?
YOU CAN'T EVEN REMEMBER YER OWN MONIKER!
WE STARTED CALLING YOU MAXAM 'CAUSE IT WAS ETCHED ON YER BELT!
YA COULD'VE AS EASILY ENDED UP BEING CALLED LEVI STRAUSS!
HEY! WHY DON'T WE PUT IT TO A VOTE?!
I'LL GO ALONG WITH THAT IDEA.
WORKS FOR ME.
I VOTE FOR MYSELF!

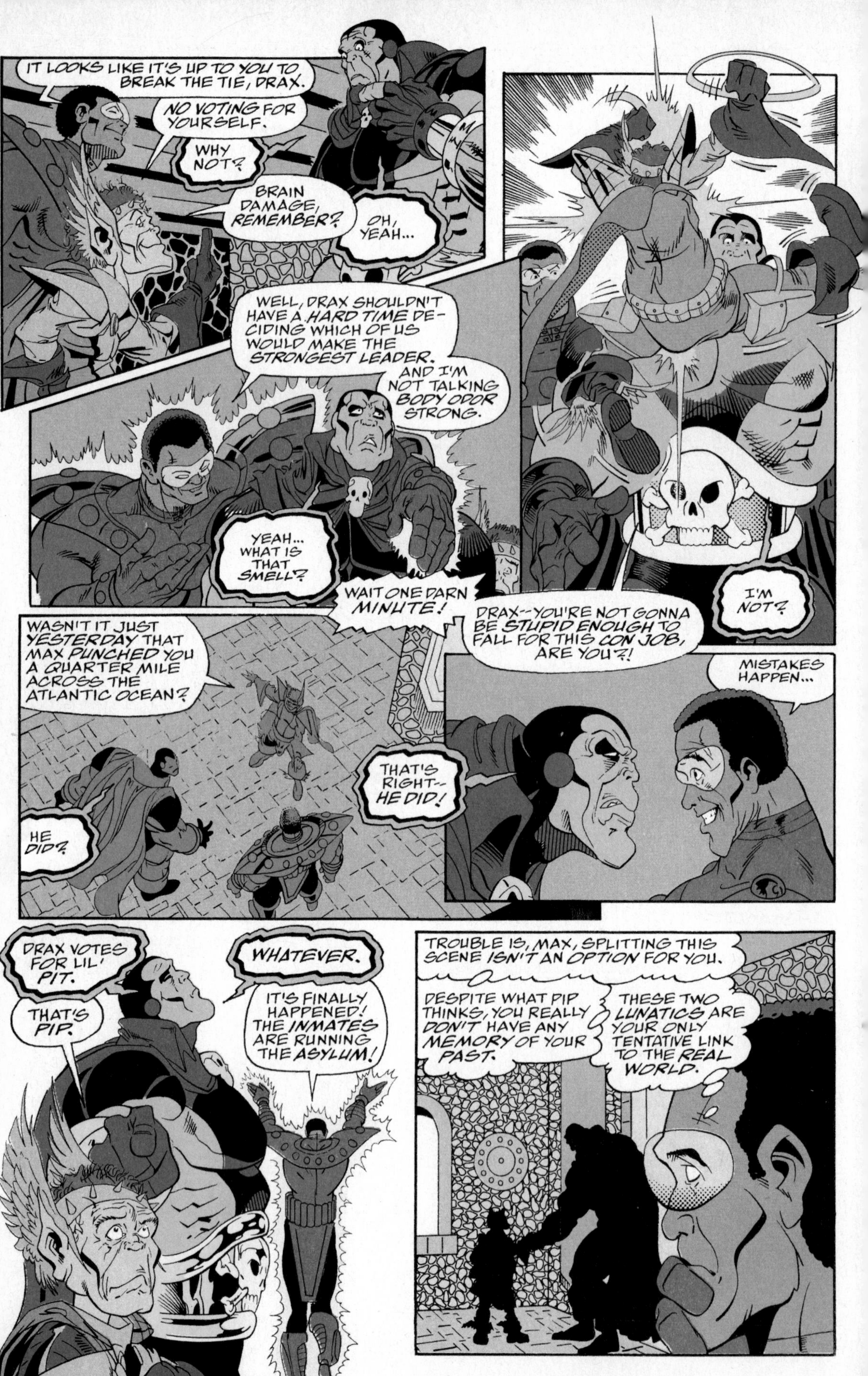
IT LOOKS LIKE IT'S UP TO YOU TO BREAK THE TIE, DRAX.
NO VOTING FOR YOURSELF.
WHY NOT?
BRAIN DAMAGE, REMEMBER?
OH, YEAH...
WELL, DRAX SHOULDN'T HAVE A HARD TIME DECIDING WHICH OF US WOULD MAKE THE STRONGEST LEADER.
AND I'M NOT TALKING BODY ODOR STRONG.
YEAH... WHAT IS THAT SMELL?
WAIT ONE DARN MINUTE!
DRAX--YOU'RE NOT GONNA BE STUPID ENOUGH TO FALL FOR THIS CON JOB, ARE YOU?!
I'M NOT?
WASN'T IT JUST YESTERDAY THAT MAX PUNCHED YOU A QUARTER MILE ACROSS THE ATLANTIC OCEAN?
HE DID?
THAT'S RIGHT-- HE DID!
MISTAKES HAPPEN...
DRAX VOTES FOR LIL' PIT.
THAT'S PIP.
WHATEVER.
IT'S FINALLY HAPPENED! THE INMATES ARE RUNNING THE ASYLUM!
TROUBLE IS, MAX, SPLITTING THIS SCENE ISN'T AN OPTION FOR YOU.
DESPITE WHAT PIP THINKS, YOU REALLY DON'T HAVE ANY MEMORY OF YOUR PAST.
THESE TWO LUNATICS ARE YOUR ONLY TENTATIVE LINK TO THE REAL WORLD.

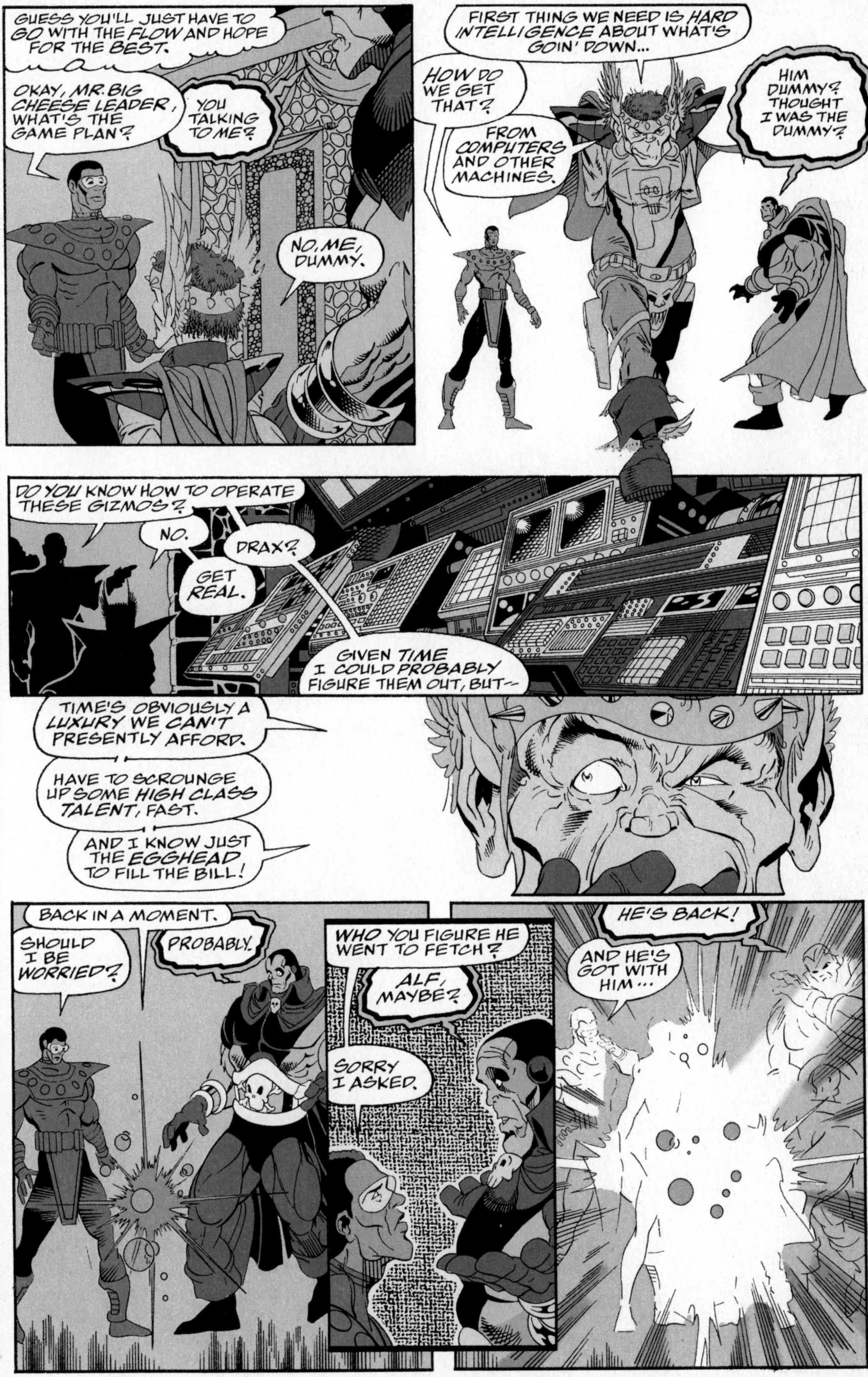
GUESS YOU'LL JUST HAVE TO GO WITH THE FLOW AND HOPE FOR THE BEST.
OKAY, MR. BIG CHEESE LEADER, WHAT'S THE GAME PLAN?
YOU TALKING TO ME?
NO, ME, DUMMY.
FIRST THING WE NEED IS HARD INTELLIGENCE ABOUT WHAT'S GOIN' DOWN...
HOW DO WE GET THAT?
FROM COMPUTERS AND OTHER MACHINES.
HIM DUMMY? THOUGHT I WAS THE DUMMY?
DO YOU KNOW HOW TO OPERATE THESE GIZMOS?
NO.
DRAX?
GET REAL.
GIVEN TIME I COULD PROBABLY FIGURE THEM OUT, BUT--
TIME'S OBVIOUSLY A LUXURY WE CAN'T PRESENTLY AFFORD.
HAVE TO SCROUNGE UP SOME HIGH CLASS TALENT, FAST.
AND I KNOW JUST THE EGGHEAD TO FILL THE BILL!
BACK IN A MOMENT.
SHOULD I BE WORRIED?
PROBABLY.
WHO YOU FIGURE HE WENT TO FETCH?
ALF, MAYBE?
SORRY I ASKED.
HE'S BACK!
AND HE'S GOT WITH HIM...

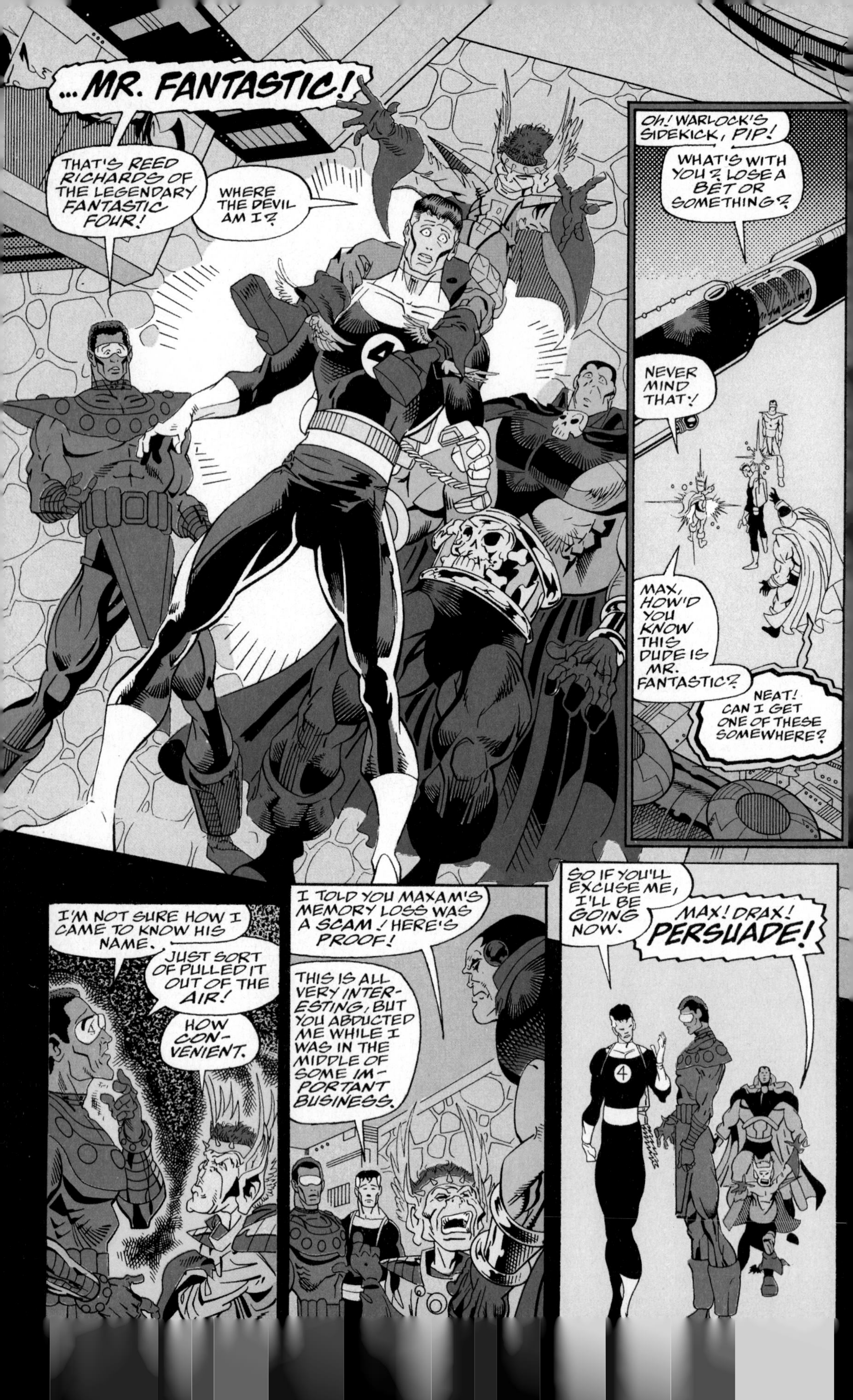

...MR. FANTASTIC!
THAT'S REED RICHARDS OF THE LEGENDARY FANTASTIC FOUR!
WHERE THE DEVIL AM I?
OH! WARLOCK'S SIDEKICK, PIP!
WHAT'S WITH YOU? LOSE A BET OR SOMETHING?
NEVER MIND THAT!
MAX, HOW'D YOU KNOW THIS DUDE IS MR. FANTASTIC?
NEAT! CAN I GET ONE OF THESE SOMEWHERE?
I'M NOT SURE HOW I CAME TO KNOW HIS NAME.
JUST SORT OF PULLED IT OUT OF THE AIR!
HOW CON-VENIENT.
I TOLD YOU MAXAM'S MEMORY LOSS WAS A SCAM! HERE'S PROOF!
THIS IS ALL VERY INTER-ESTING, BUT YOU ABDUCTED ME WHILE I WAS IN THE MIDDLE OF SOME IM-PORTANT BUSINESS.
SO IF YOU'LL EXCUSE ME, I'LL BE GOING NOW.
MAX! DRAX! PERSUADE!

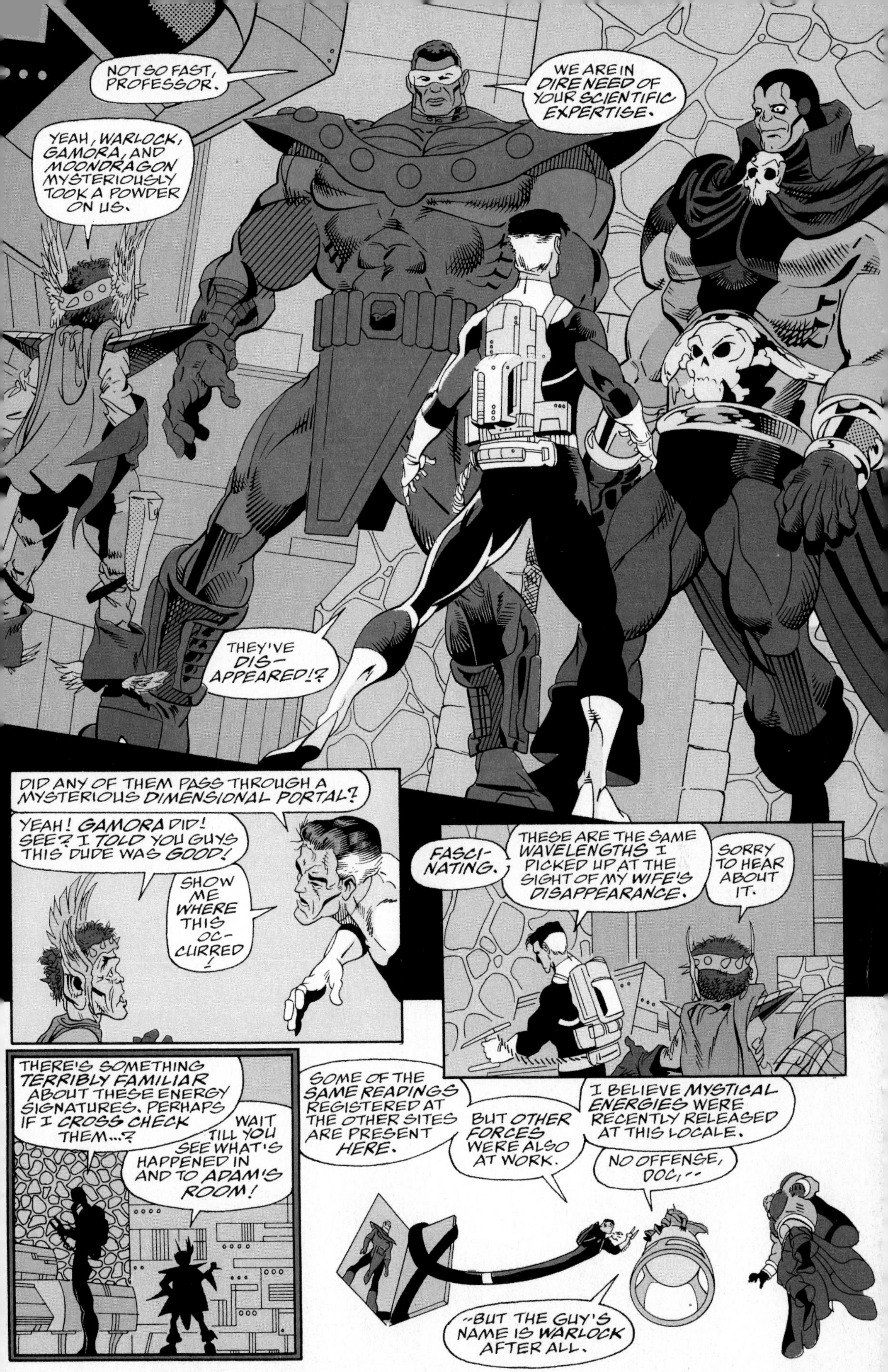

NOT SO FAST, PROFESSOR.
WE ARE IN DIRE NEED OF YOUR SCIENTIFIC EXPERTISE.
YEAH, WARLOCK, GAMORA, AND MOONDRAGON MYSTERIOUSLY TOOK A POWDER ON US.
THEY'VE DIS-APPEARED!?
DID ANY OF THEM PASS THROUGH A MYSTERIOUS DIMENSIONAL PORTAL?
YEAH! GAMORA DID! SEE? I TOLD YOU GUYS THIS DUDE WAS GOOD!
SHOW ME WHERE THIS OC-CURRED!
FASCI-NATING.
THESE ARE THE SAME WAVELENGTHS I PICKED UP AT THE SIGHT OF MY WIFE'S DISAPPEARANCE.
SORRY TO HEAR ABOUT IT.
THERE'S SOMETHING TERRIBLY FAMILIAR ABOUT THESE ENERGY SIGNATURES. PERHAPS IF I CROSS CHECK THEM...?
WAIT TILL YOU SEE WHAT'S HAPPENED IN AND TO ADAM'S ROOM!
SOME OF THE SAME READINGS REGISTERED AT THE OTHER SITES ARE PRESENT HERE.
BUT OTHER FORCES WERE ALSO AT WORK.
I BELIEVE MYSTICAL ENERGIES WERE RECENTLY RELEASED AT THIS LOCALE.
NO OFFENSE, DOC,--
--BUT THE GUY'S NAME IS WARLOCK AFTER ALL.

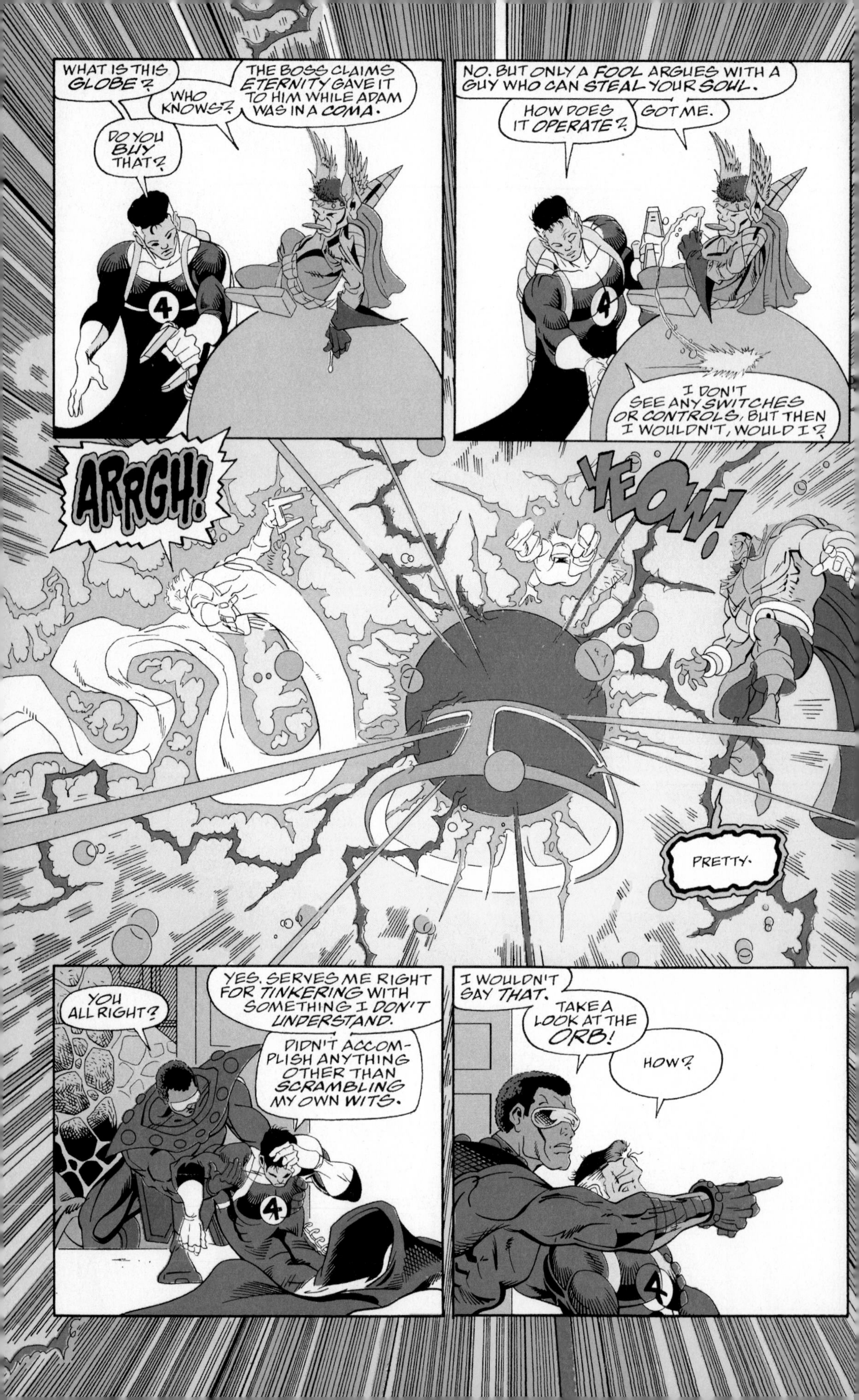
WHAT IS THIS GLOBE?
THE BOSS CLAIMS ETERNITY GAVE IT TO HIM WHILE ADAM WAS IN A COMA.
WHO KNOWS?
DO YOU BUY THAT?
NO. BUT ONLY A FOOL ARGUES WITH A GUY WHO CAN STEAL YOUR SOUL.
HOW DOES IT OPERATE?
GOT ME.
I DON'T SEE ANY SWITCHES OR CONTROLS, BUT THEN I WOULDN'T, WOULD I?
ARRGH!
YEOW!
PRETTY.
YOU ALL RIGHT?
YES. SERVES ME RIGHT FOR TINKERING WITH SOMETHING I DON'T UNDERSTAND.
DIDN'T ACCOMPLISH ANYTHING OTHER THAN SCRAMBLING MY OWN WITS.
I WOULDN'T SAY THAT.
TAKE A LOOK AT THE ORB!
HOW?

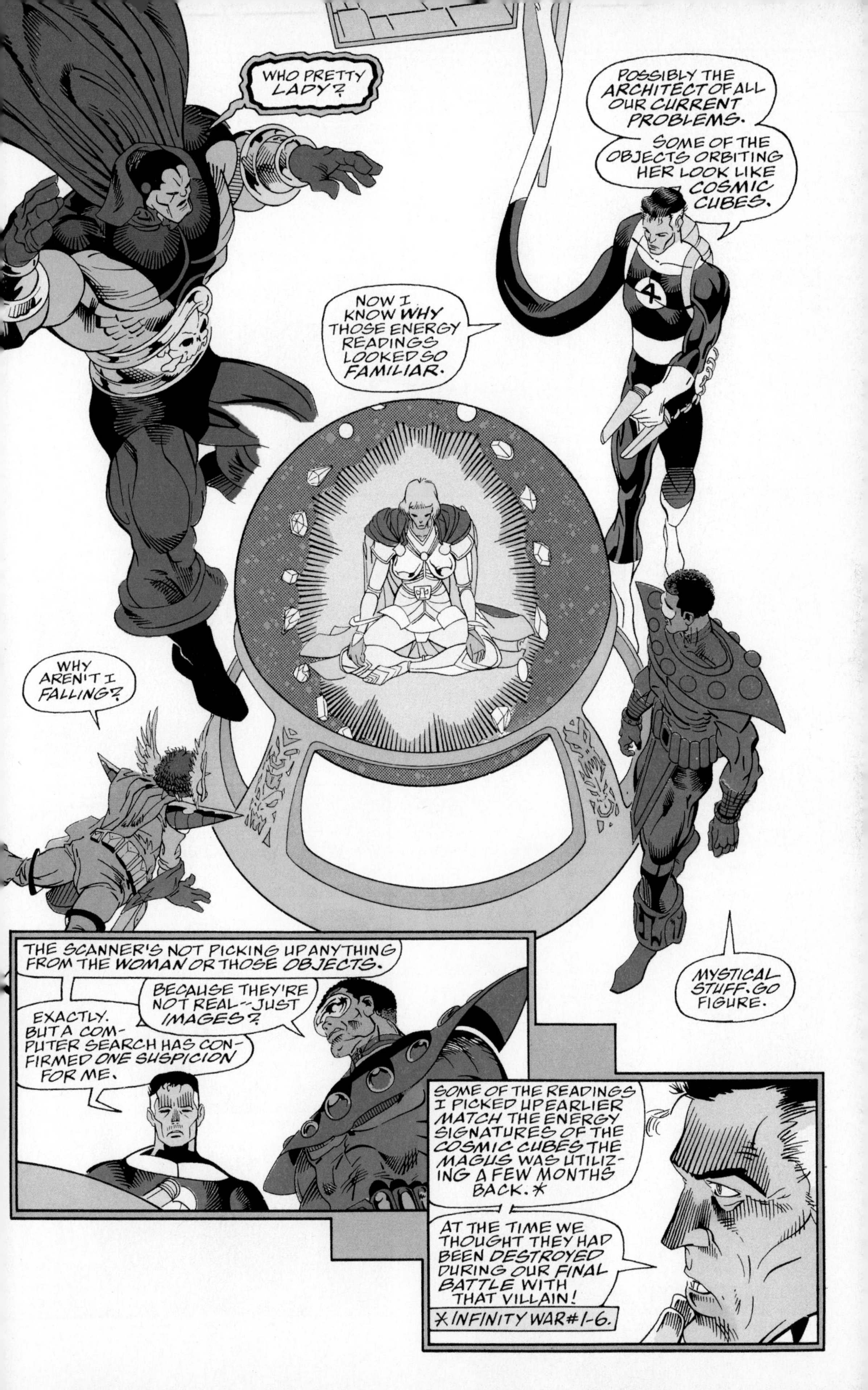
WHO PRETTY LADY?
POSSIBLY THE ARCHITECT OF ALL OUR CURRENT PROBLEMS.
SOME OF THE OBJECTS ORBITING HER LOOK LIKE COSMIC CUBES.
NOW I KNOW WHY THOSE ENERGY READINGS LOOKED SO FAMILIAR.
WHY AREN'T I FALLING?
MYSTICAL STUFF. GO FIGURE.
THE SCANNER'S NOT PICKING UP ANYTHING FROM THE WOMAN OR THOSE OBJECTS.
BECAUSE THEY'RE NOT REAL--JUST IMAGES?
EXACTLY. BUT A COMPUTER SEARCH HAS CONFIRMED ONE SUSPICION FOR ME.
SOME OF THE READINGS I PICKED UP EARLIER MATCH THE ENERGY SIGNATURES OF THE COSMIC CUBES THE MAGUS WAS UTILIZING A FEW MONTHS BACK.*
AT THE TIME WE THOUGHT THEY HAD BEEN DESTROYED DURING OUR FINAL BATTLE WITH THAT VILLAIN!
*INFINITY WAR #1-6.

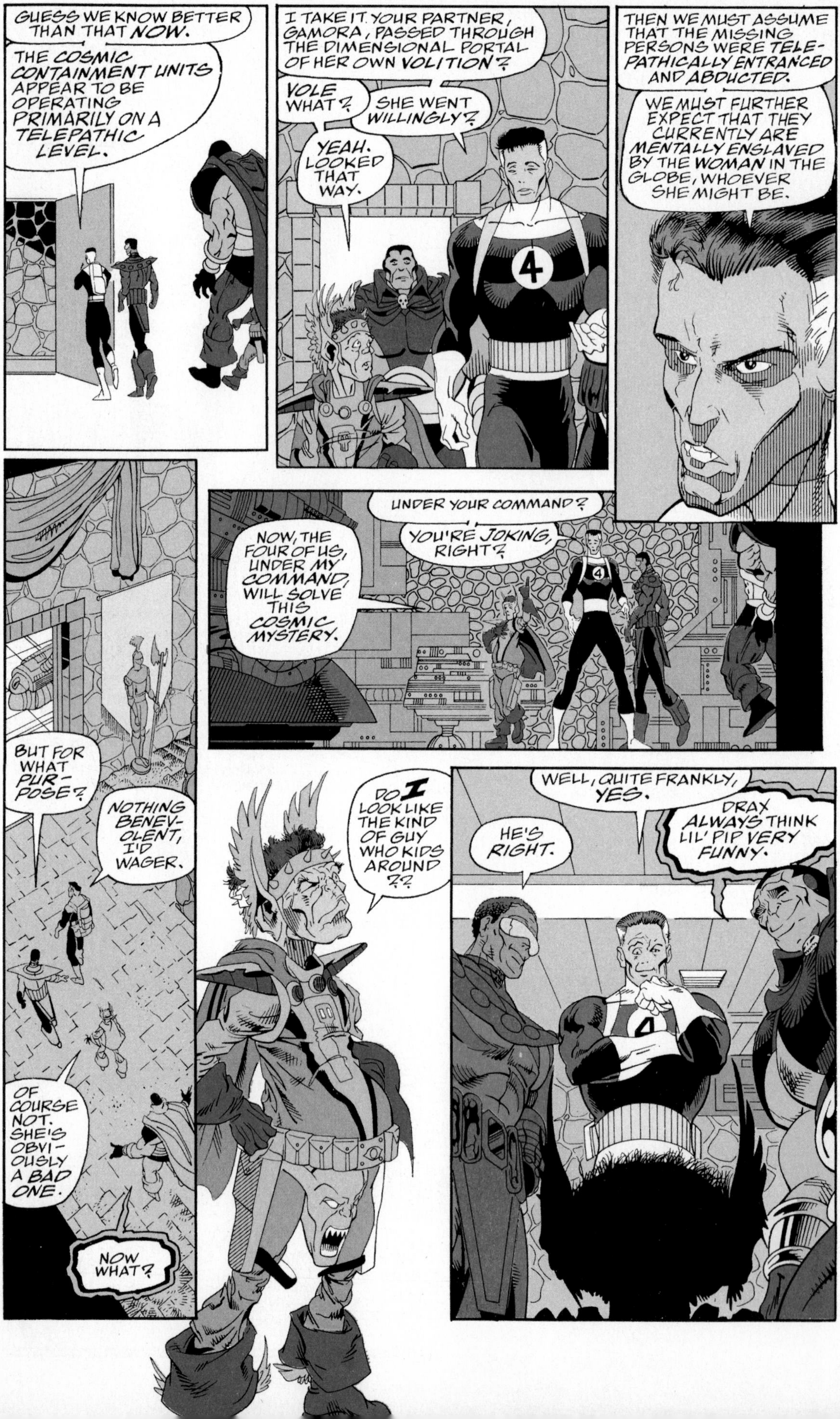
GUESS WE KNOW BETTER THAN THAT NOW.
THE COSMIC CONTAINMENT UNITS APPEAR TO BE OPERATING PRIMARILY ON A TELEPATHIC LEVEL.
I TAKE IT YOUR PARTNER, GAMORA, PASSED THROUGH THE DIMENSIONAL PORTAL OF HER OWN VOLITION?
VOLE WHAT?
SHE WENT WILLINGLY?
YEAH. LOOKED THAT WAY.
THEN WE MUST ASSUME THAT THE MISSING PERSONS WERE TELEPATHICALLY ENTRANCED AND ABDUCTED.
WE MUST FURTHER EXPECT THAT THEY CURRENTLY ARE MENTALLY ENSLAVED BY THE WOMAN IN THE GLOBE, WHOEVER SHE MIGHT BE.
NOW, THE FOUR OF US, UNDER MY COMMAND, WILL SOLVE THIS COSMIC MYSTERY.
UNDER YOUR COMMAND?
YOU'RE JOKING, RIGHT?
BUT FOR WHAT PURPOSE?
NOTHING BENEVOLENT, I'D WAGER.
OF COURSE NOT. SHE'S OBVIOUSLY A BAD ONE.
NOW WHAT?
DO I LOOK LIKE THE KIND OF GUY WHO KIDS AROUND??
WELL, QUITE FRANKLY, YES.
HE'S RIGHT.
DRAX ALWAYS THINK LIL' PIP VERY FUNNY.

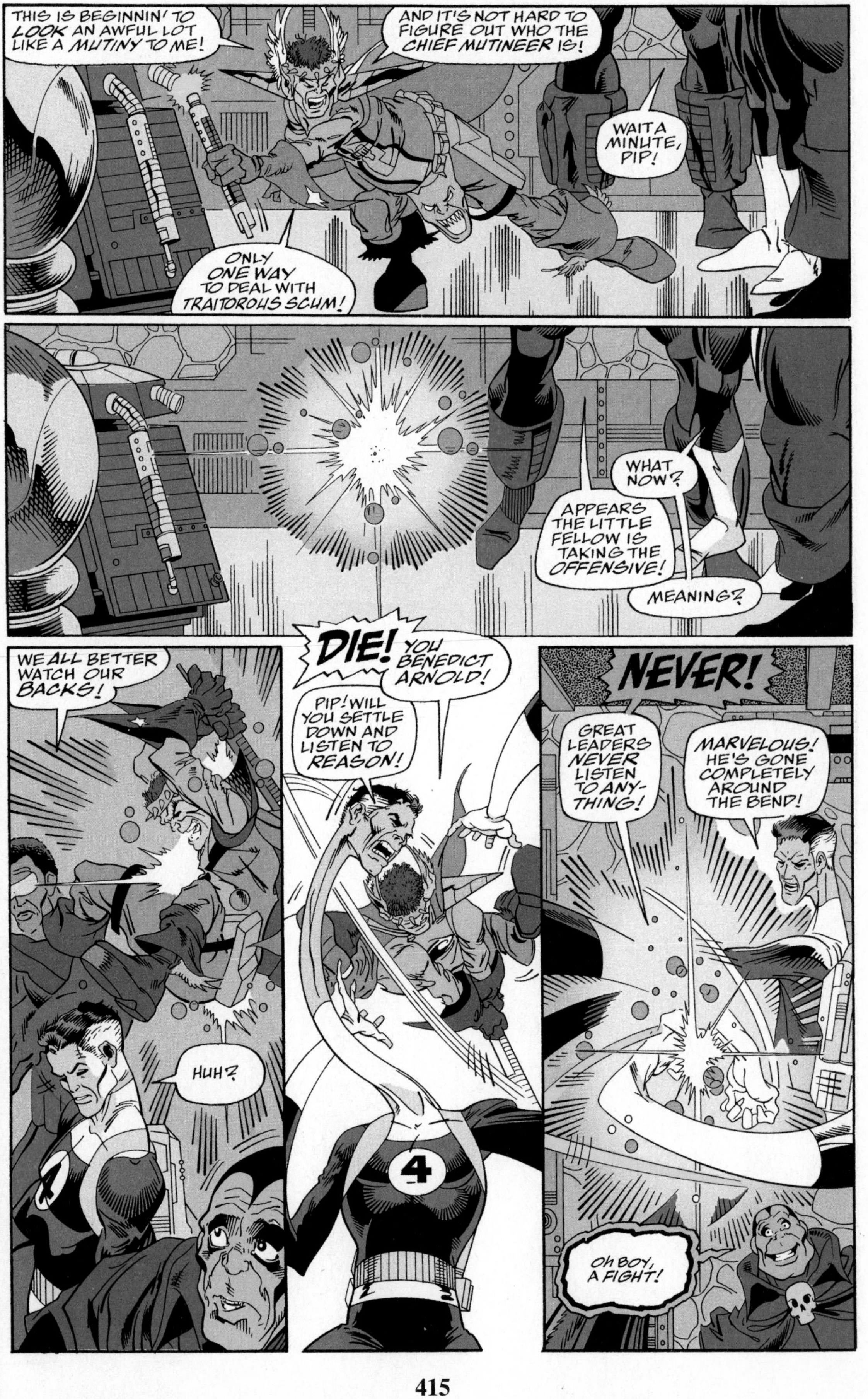
THIS IS BEGINNIN' TO LOOK AN AWFUL LOT LIKE A MUTINY TO ME!
AND IT'S NOT HARD TO FIGURE OUT WHO THE CHIEF MUTINEER IS!
WAIT A MINUTE, PIP!
ONLY ONE WAY TO DEAL WITH TRAITOROUS SCUM!
WHAT NOW?
APPEARS THE LITTLE FELLOW IS TAKING THE OFFENSIVE!
MEANING?
WE ALL BETTER WATCH OUR BACKS!
HUH?
DIE! YOU BENEDICT ARNOLD!
PIP! WILL YOU SETTLE DOWN AND LISTEN TO REASON!
NEVER!
GREAT LEADERS NEVER LISTEN TO ANY-THING!
MARVELOUS! HE'S GONE COMPLETELY AROUND THE BEND!
Oh BOY, A FIGHT!

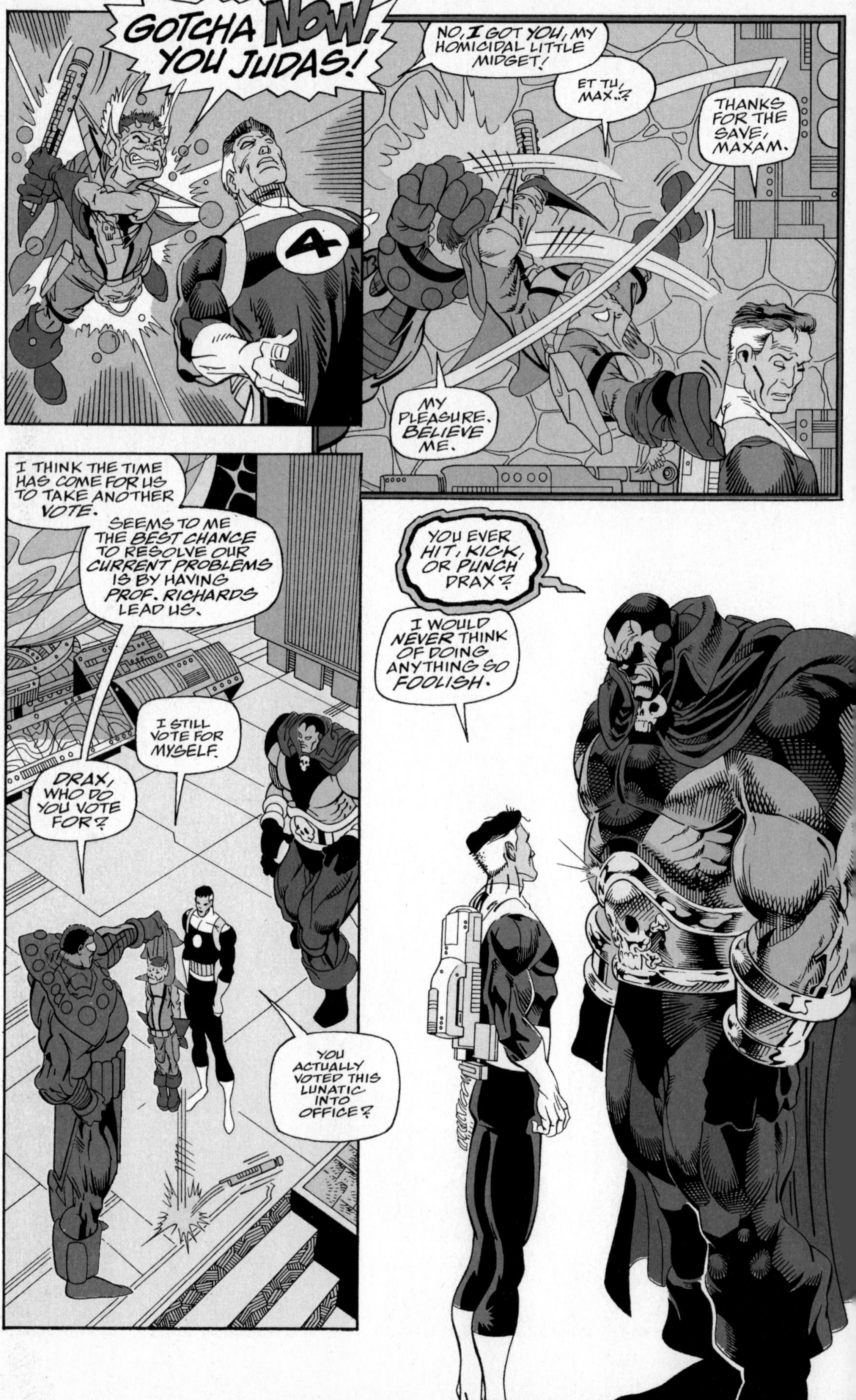
GOTCHA NOW, YOU JUDAS!
NO, I GOT YOU, MY HOMICIDAL LITTLE MIDGET!
ET TU, MAX..?
THANKS FOR THE SAVE, MAXAM.
MY PLEASURE. BELIEVE ME.
I THINK THE TIME HAS COME FOR US TO TAKE ANOTHER VOTE.
SEEMS TO ME THE BEST CHANCE TO RESOLVE OUR CURRENT PROBLEMS IS BY HAVING PROF. RICHARDS LEAD US.
I STILL VOTE FOR MYSELF.
DRAX, WHO DO YOU VOTE FOR?
YOU ACTUALLY VOTED THIS LUNATIC INTO OFFICE?
YOU EVER HIT, KICK, OR PUNCH DRAX?
I WOULD NEVER THINK OF DOING ANYTHING SO FOOLISH.

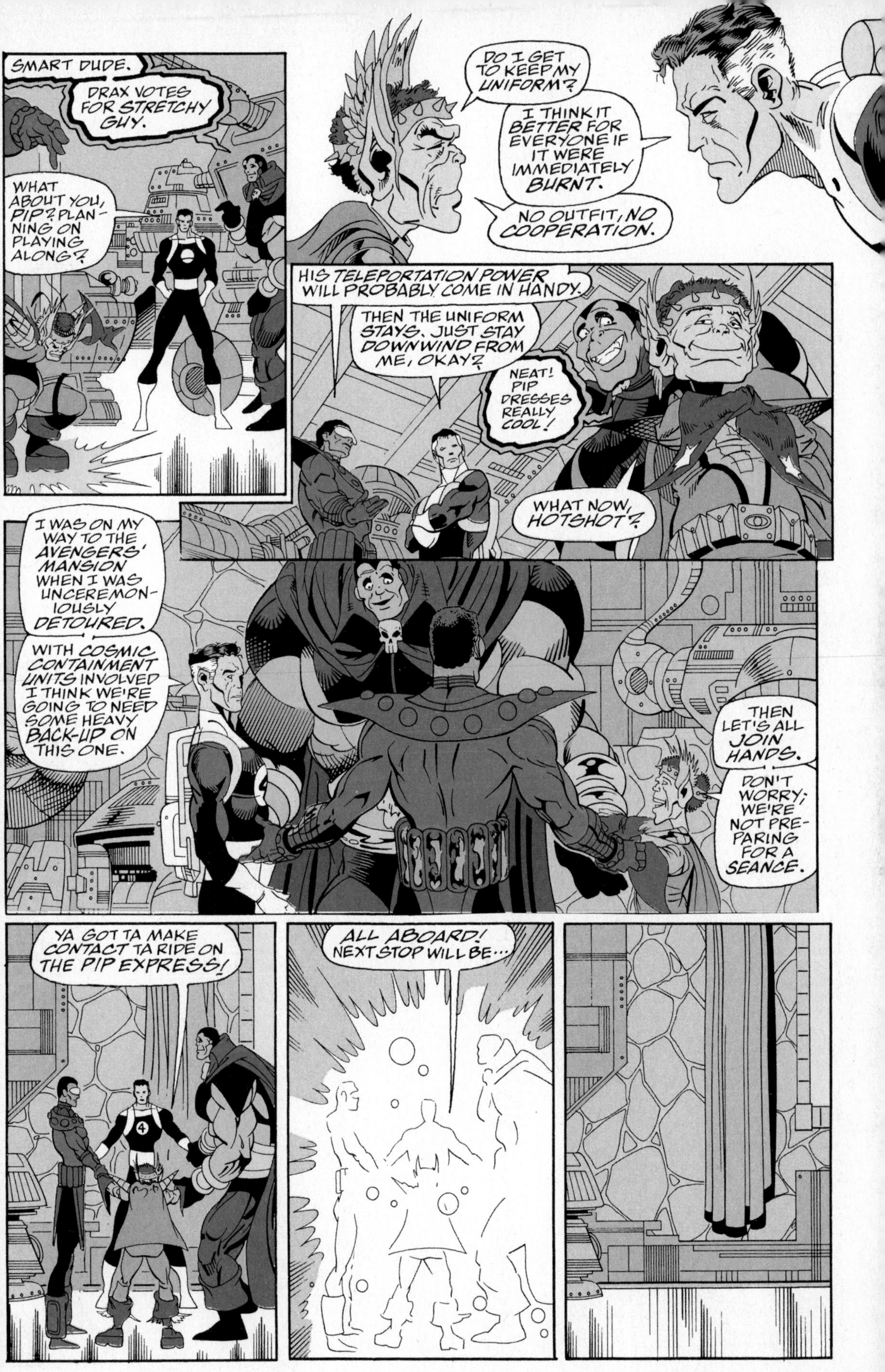
SMART DUDE.
DRAX VOTES FOR STRETCHY GUY.
WHAT ABOUT YOU, PIP? PLANNING ON PLAYING ALONG?
DO I GET TO KEEP MY UNIFORM?
I THINK IT BETTER FOR EVERYONE IF IT WERE IMMEDIATELY BURNT.
NO OUTFIT, NO COOPERATION.
HIS TELEPORTATION POWER WILL PROBABLY COME IN HANDY.
THEN THE UNIFORM STAYS. JUST STAY DOWNWIND FROM ME, OKAY?
NEAT! PIP DRESSES REALLY COOL!
WHAT NOW, HOTSHOT?
I WAS ON MY WAY TO THE AVENGERS' MANSION WHEN I WAS UNCEREMONIOUSLY DETOURED.
WITH COSMIC CONTAINMENT UNITS INVOLVED I THINK WE'RE GOING TO NEED SOME HEAVY BACK-UP ON THIS ONE.
THEN LET'S ALL JOIN HANDS.
DON'T WORRY; WE'RE NOT PREPARING FOR A SEANCE.
YA GOTTA MAKE CONTACT TA RIDE ON THE PIP EXPRESS!
ALL ABOARD! NEXT STOP WILL BE...

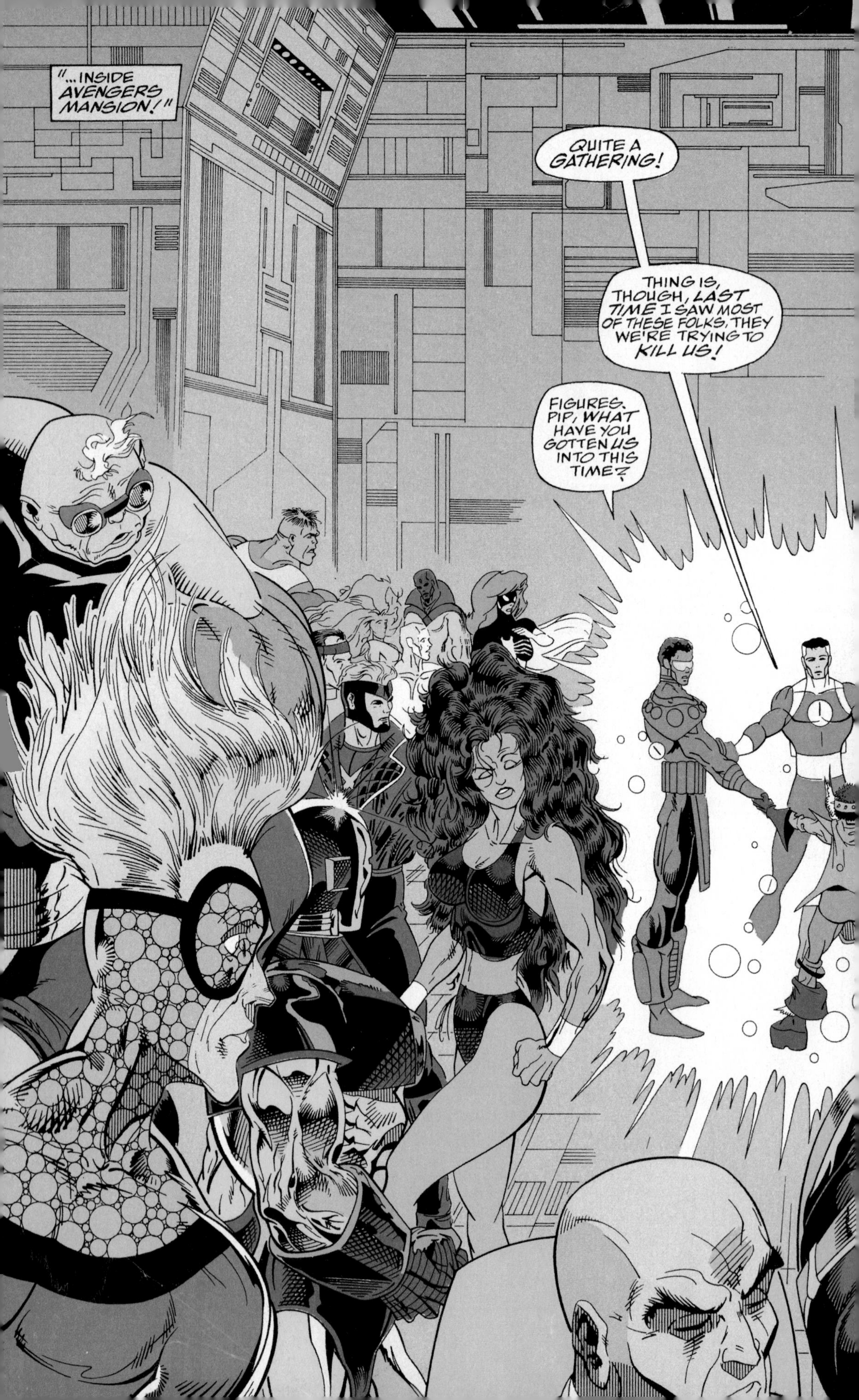
"...INSIDE AVENGERS MANSION!"
QUITE A GATHERING!
THING IS, THOUGH, LAST TIME I SAW MOST OF THESE FOLKS, THEY WE'RE TRYING TO KILL US!
FIGURES. PIP, WHAT HAVE YOU GOTTEN US INTO THIS TIME?

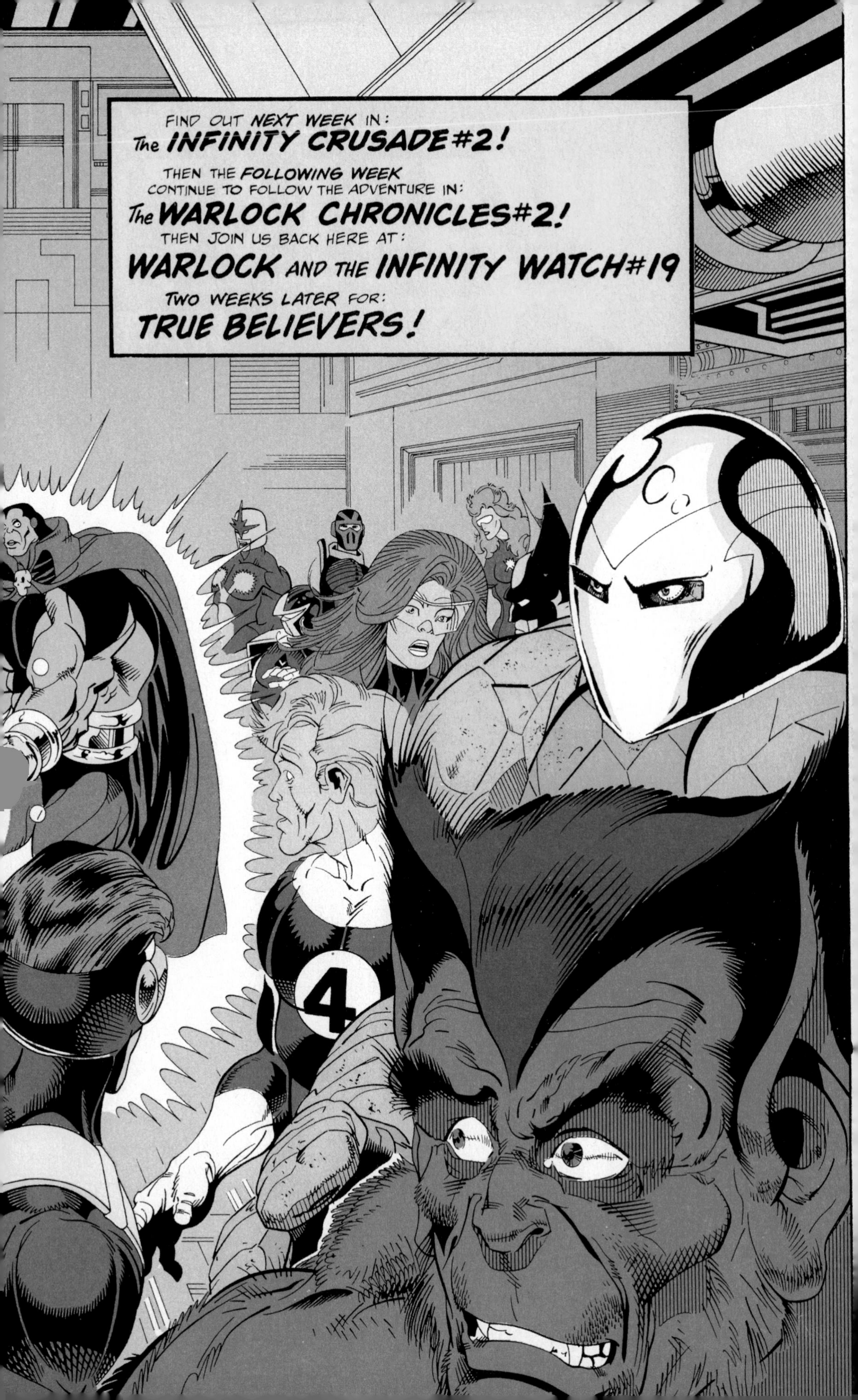
FIND OUT NEXT WEEK IN:
The INFINITY CRUSADE #2!
THEN THE FOLLOWING WEEK
CONTINUE TO FOLLOW THE ADVENTURE IN:
The WARLOCK CHRONICLES #2!
THEN JOIN US BACK HERE AT:
WARLOCK AND THE INFINITY WATCH #19
TWO WEEKS LATER FOR:
TRUE BELIEVERS!

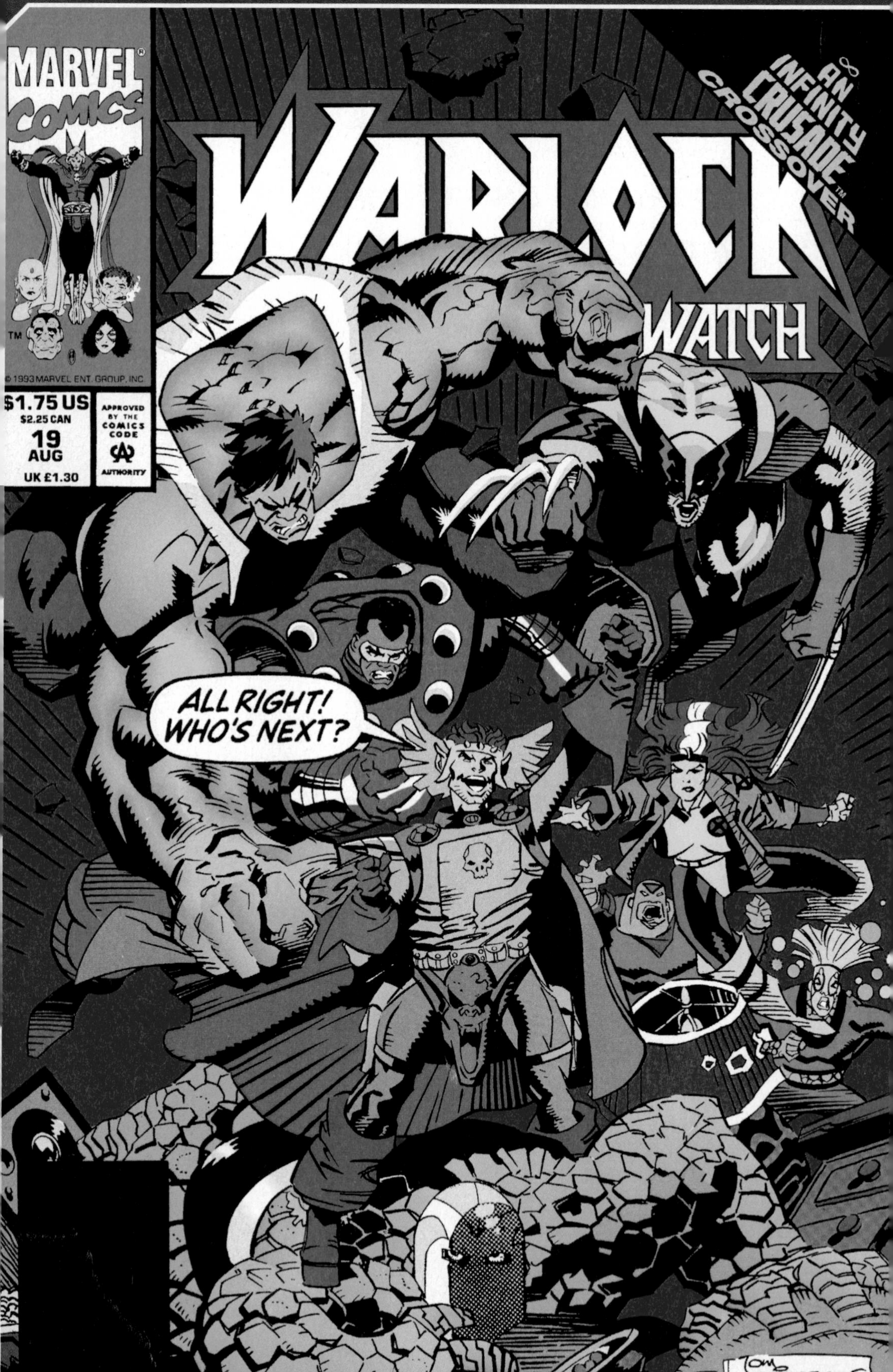
MARVEL COMICS
WARLOCK
WATCH
AN INFINITY CRUSADE CROSSOVER
© 1993 MARVEL ENT. GROUP, INC.
$1.75 US
$2.25 CAN
19
AUG
UK £1.30
APPROVED BY THE COMICS CODE AUTHORITY
ALL RIGHT! WHO'S NEXT?
TOM GRINDBERG '93

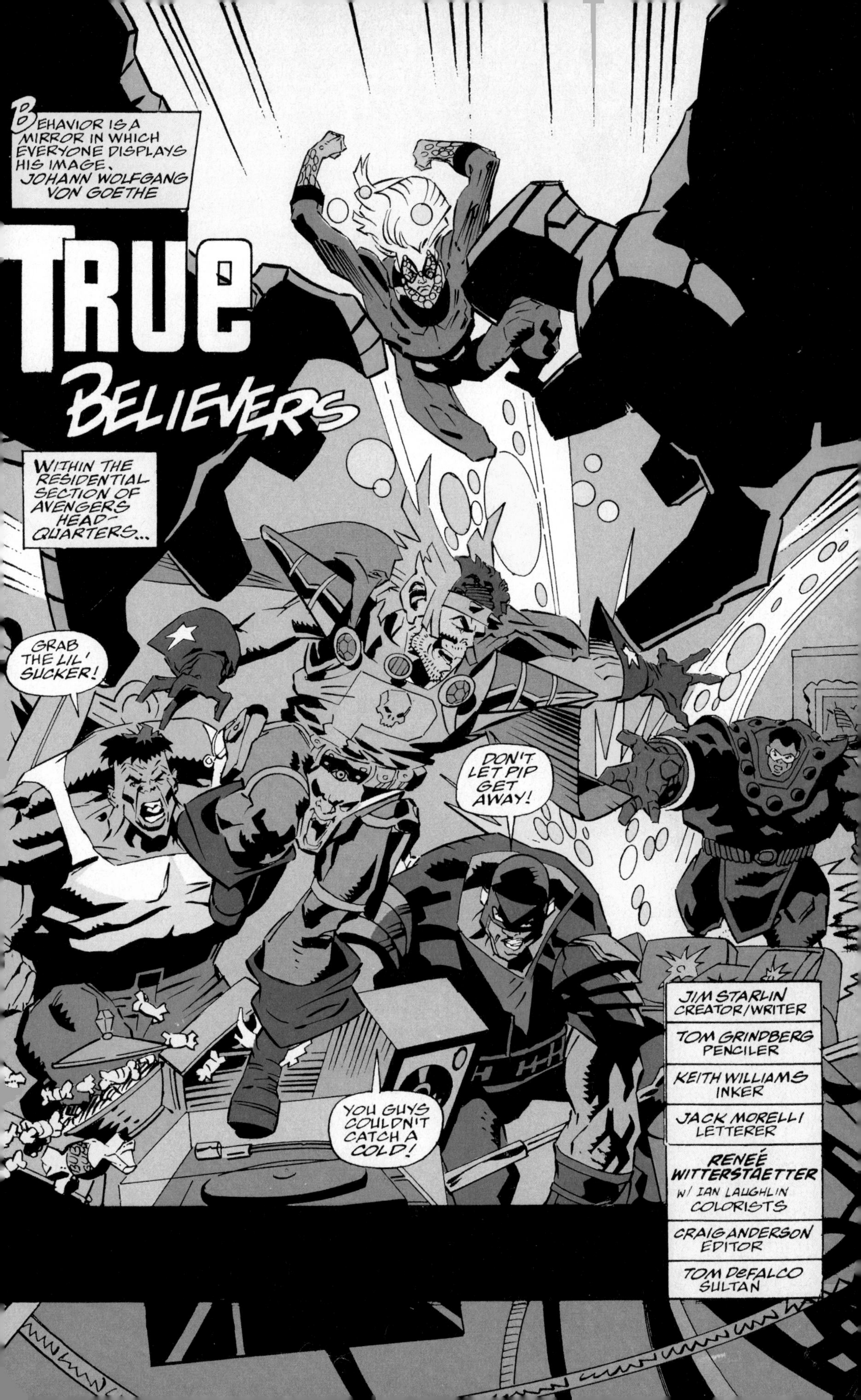
BEHAVIOR IS A MIRROR IN WHICH EVERYONE DISPLAYS HIS IMAGE. JOHANN WOLFGANG VON GOETHE
TRUE BELIEVERS
WITHIN THE RESIDENTIAL SECTION OF AVENGERS HEAD-QUARTERS...
GRAB THE LIL' SUCKER!
DON'T LET PIP GET AWAY!
YOU GUYS COULDN'T CATCH A COLD!
JIM STARLIN CREATOR/WRITER
TOM GRINDBERG PENCILER
KEITH WILLIAMS INKER
JACK MORELLI LETTERER
RENEÉ WITTERSTAETTER W/ IAN LAUGHLIN COLORISTS
CRAIG ANDERSON EDITOR
TOM DeFALCO SULTAN

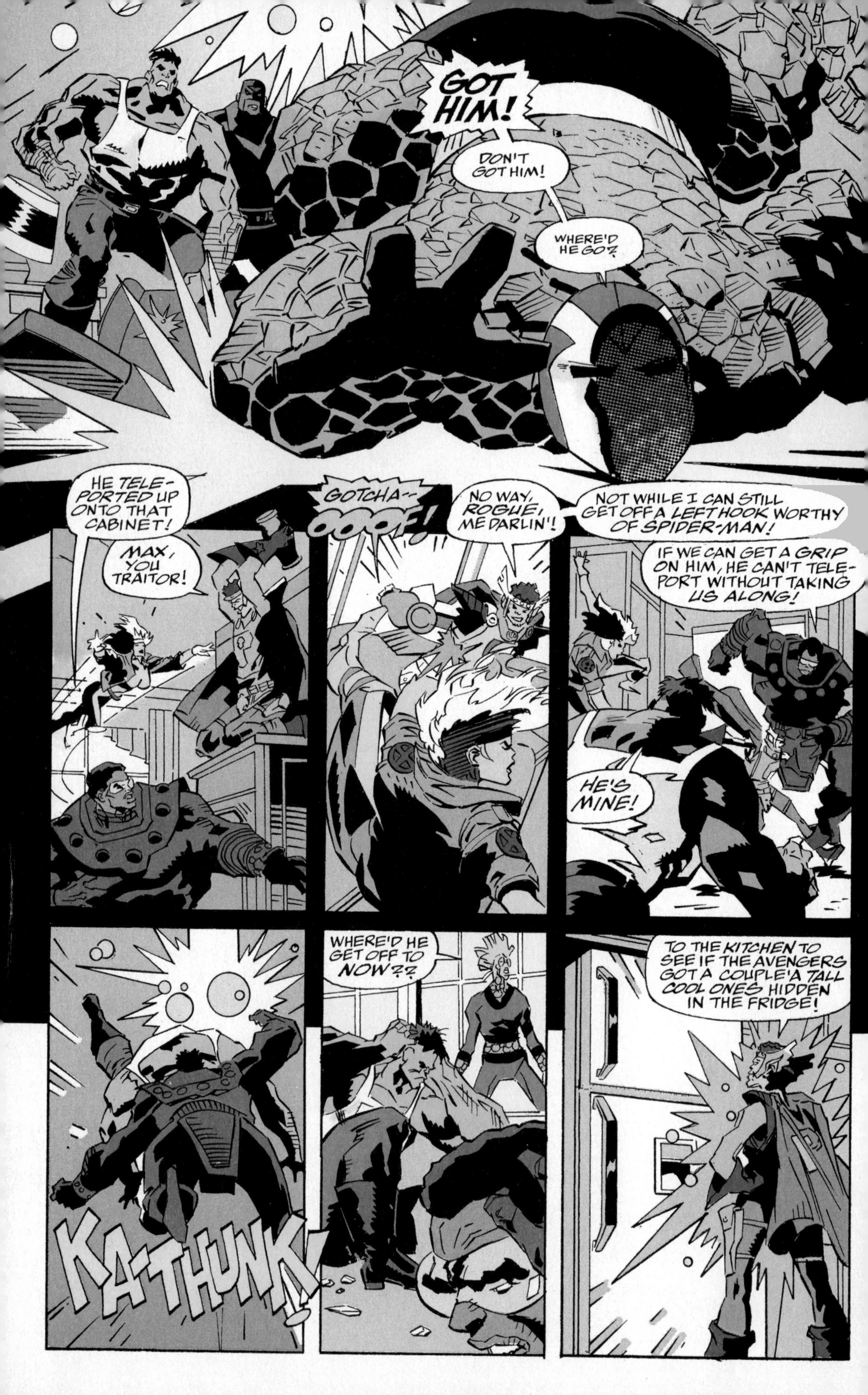

GOT HIM!
DON'T GOT HIM!
WHERE'D HE GO?
HE TELEPORTED UP ONTO THAT CABINET!
MAX, YOU TRAITOR!
GOTCHA--
OOOF!
NO WAY, ROGUE, ME DARLIN'!
NOT WHILE I CAN STILL GET OFF A LEFT HOOK WORTHY OF SPIDER-MAN!
IF WE CAN GET A GRIP ON HIM, HE CAN'T TELEPORT WITHOUT TAKING US ALONG!
HE'S MINE!
KA-THUNK!
WHERE'D HE GET OFF TO NOW??
TO THE KITCHEN TO SEE IF THE AVENGERS GOT A COUPLE'A TALL COOL ONES HIDDEN IN THE FRIDGE!

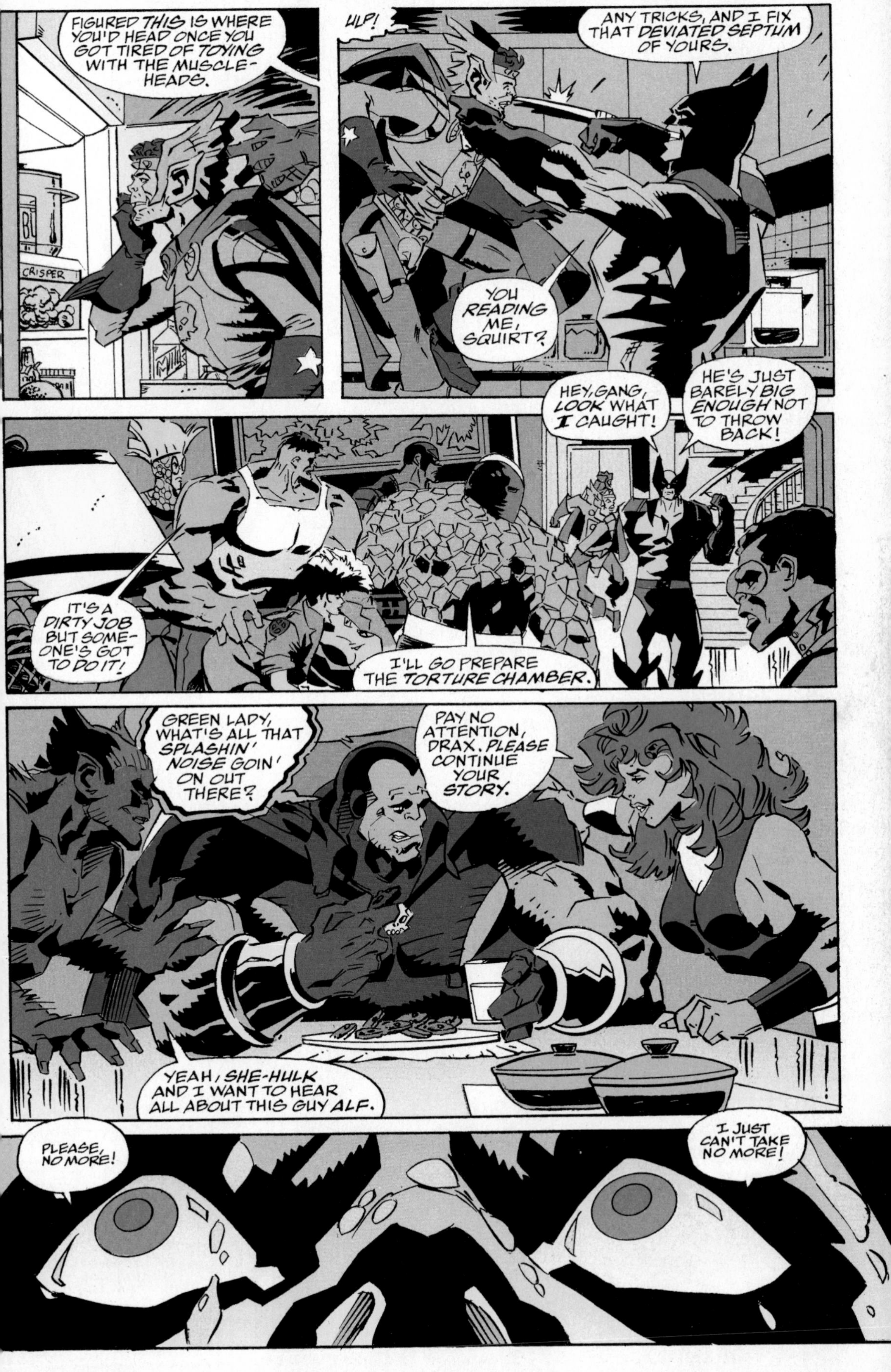

FIGURED THIS IS WHERE YOU'D HEAD ONCE YOU GOT TIRED OF TOYING WITH THE MUSCLE-HEADS.
ULP!
ANY TRICKS, AND I FIX THAT DEVIATED SEPTUM OF YOURS.
YOU READING ME, SQUIRT?
CRISPER
HEY, GANG, LOOK WHAT I CAUGHT!
HE'S JUST BARELY BIG ENOUGH NOT TO THROW BACK!
IT'S A DIRTY JOB BUT SOME-ONE'S GOT TO DO IT!
I'LL GO PREPARE THE TORTURE CHAMBER.
GREEN LADY, WHAT'S ALL THAT SPLASHIN' NOISE GOIN' ON OUT THERE?
PAY NO ATTENTION, DRAX. PLEASE CONTINUE YOUR STORY.
YEAH, SHE-HULK AND I WANT TO HEAR ALL ABOUT THIS GUY ALF.
PLEASE, NO MORE!
I JUST CAN'T TAKE NO MORE!

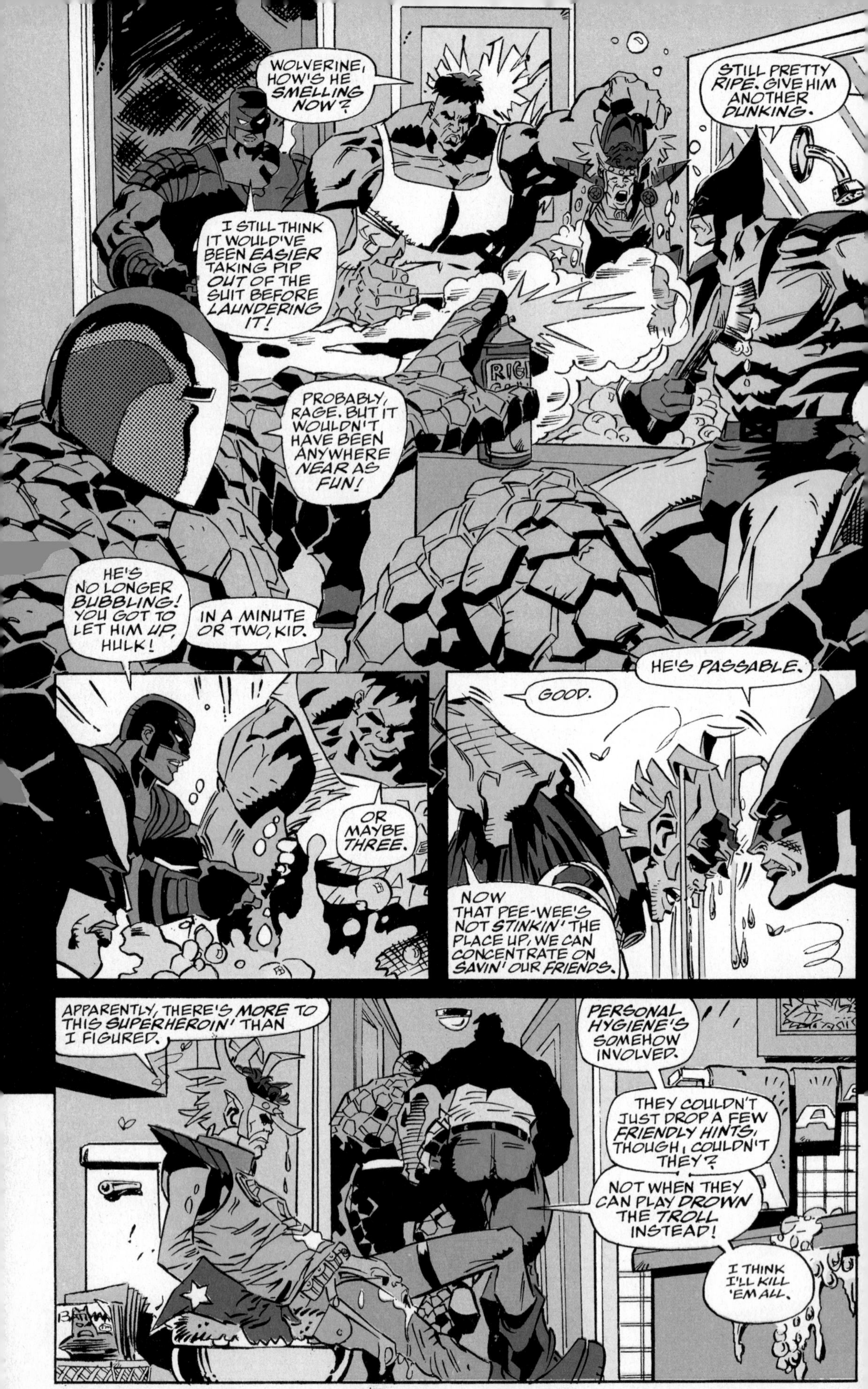
WOLVERINE, HOW'S HE SMELLING NOW?
STILL PRETTY RIPE. GIVE HIM ANOTHER DUNKING.
I STILL THINK IT WOULD'VE BEEN EASIER TAKING PIP OUT OF THE SUIT BEFORE LAUNDERING IT!
PROBABLY, RAGE. BUT IT WOULDN'T HAVE BEEN ANYWHERE NEAR AS FUN!
HE'S NO LONGER BUBBLING! YOU GOT TO LET HIM UP, HULK!
IN A MINUTE OR TWO, KID.
OR MAYBE THREE.
GOOD.
HE'S PASSABLE.
NOW THAT PEE-WEE'S NOT STINKIN' THE PLACE UP, WE CAN CONCENTRATE ON SAVIN' OUR FRIENDS.
APPARENTLY, THERE'S MORE TO THIS SUPERHEROIN' THAN I FIGURED.
PERSONAL HYGIENE'S SOMEHOW INVOLVED.
THEY COULDN'T JUST DROP A FEW FRIENDLY HINTS, THOUGH, COULDN'T THEY?
NOT WHEN THEY CAN PLAY DROWN THE TROLL INSTEAD!
I THINK I'LL KILL 'EM ALL.

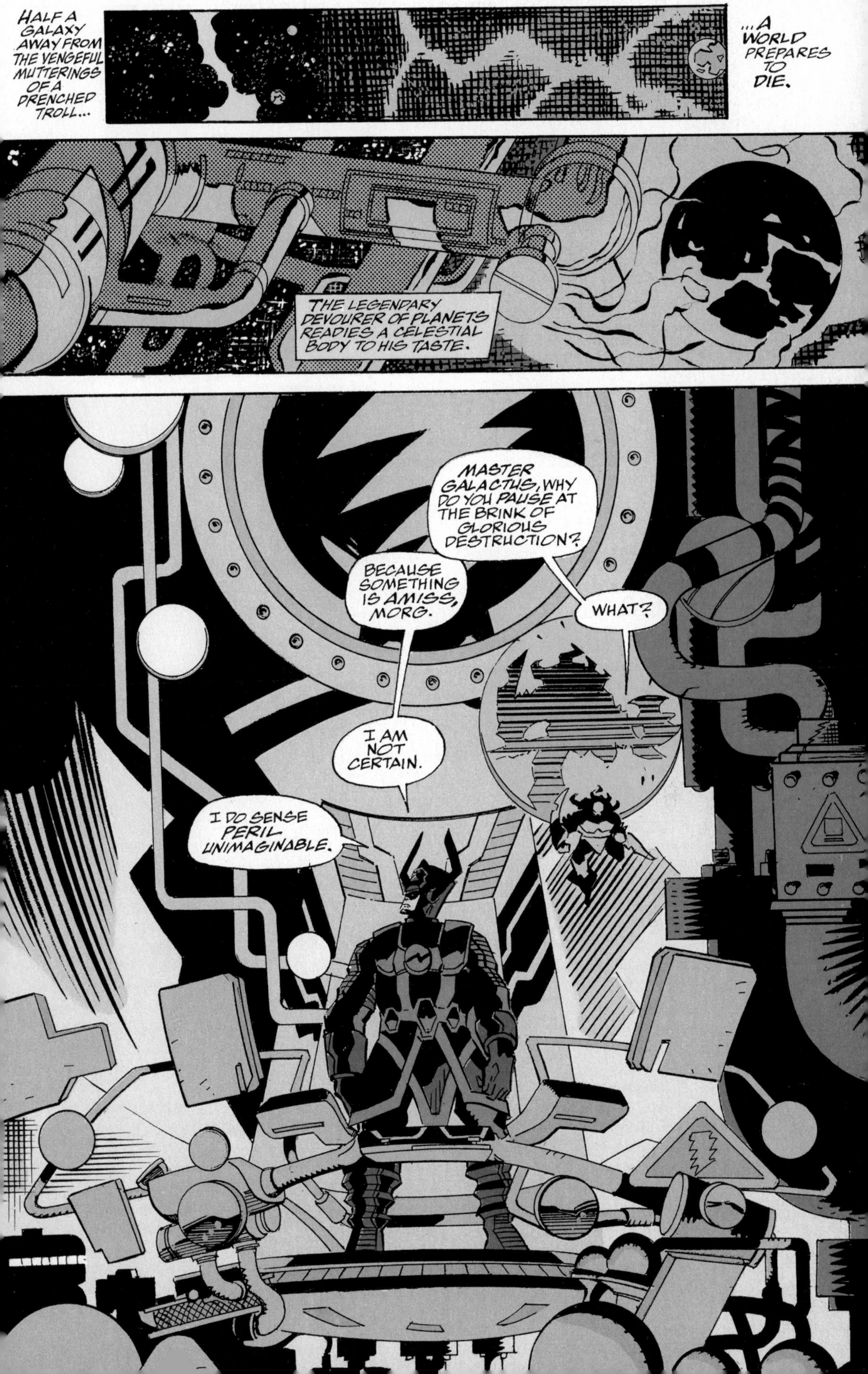
HALF A GALAXY AWAY FROM THE VENGEFUL MUTTERINGS OF A DRENCHED TROLL...
...A WORLD PREPARES TO DIE.
THE LEGENDARY DEVOURER OF PLANETS READIES A CELESTIAL BODY TO HIS TASTE.
MASTER GALACTUS, WHY DO YOU PAUSE AT THE BRINK OF GLORIOUS DESTRUCTION?
BECAUSE SOMETHING IS AMISS, MORG.
WHAT?
I AM NOT CERTAIN.
I DO SENSE PERIL UNIMAGINABLE.

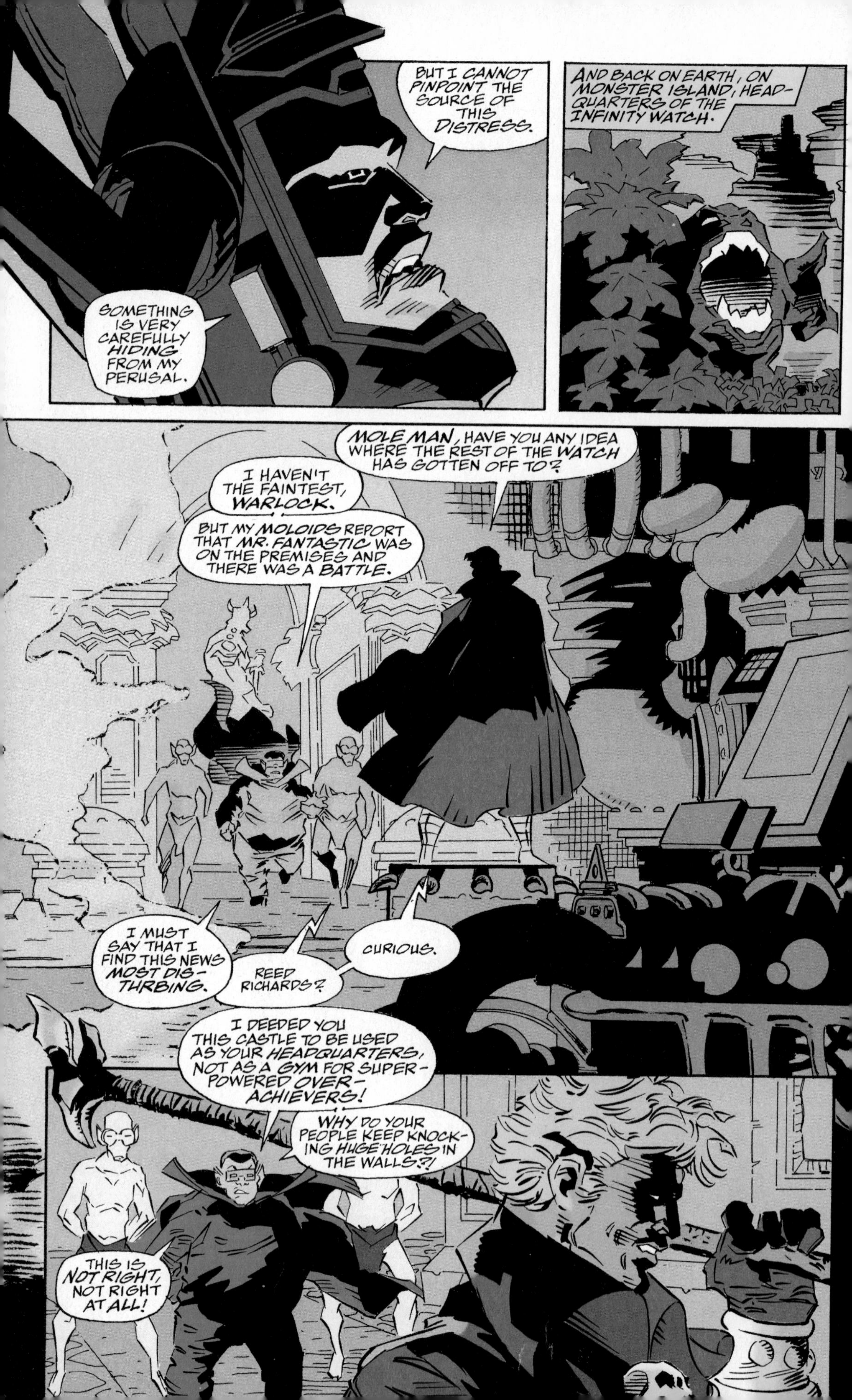
BUT I CANNOT PINPOINT THE SOURCE OF THIS DISTRESS.
SOMETHING IS VERY CAREFULLY HIDING FROM MY PERUSAL.
AND BACK ON EARTH, ON MONSTER ISLAND, HEAD-QUARTERS OF THE INFINITY WATCH.
MOLE MAN, HAVE YOU ANY IDEA WHERE THE REST OF THE WATCH HAS GOTTEN OFF TO?
I HAVEN'T THE FAINTEST, WARLOCK.
BUT MY MOLOIDS REPORT THAT MR. FANTASTIC WAS ON THE PREMISES AND THERE WAS A BATTLE.
I MUST SAY THAT I FIND THIS NEWS MOST DIS-TURBING.
REED RICHARDS?
CURIOUS.
I DEEDED YOU THIS CASTLE TO BE USED AS YOUR HEADQUARTERS, NOT AS A GYM FOR SUPER-POWERED OVER-ACHIEVERS!
WHY DO YOUR PEOPLE KEEP KNOCK-ING HUGE HOLES IN THE WALLS?!
THIS IS NOT RIGHT, NOT RIGHT AT ALL!

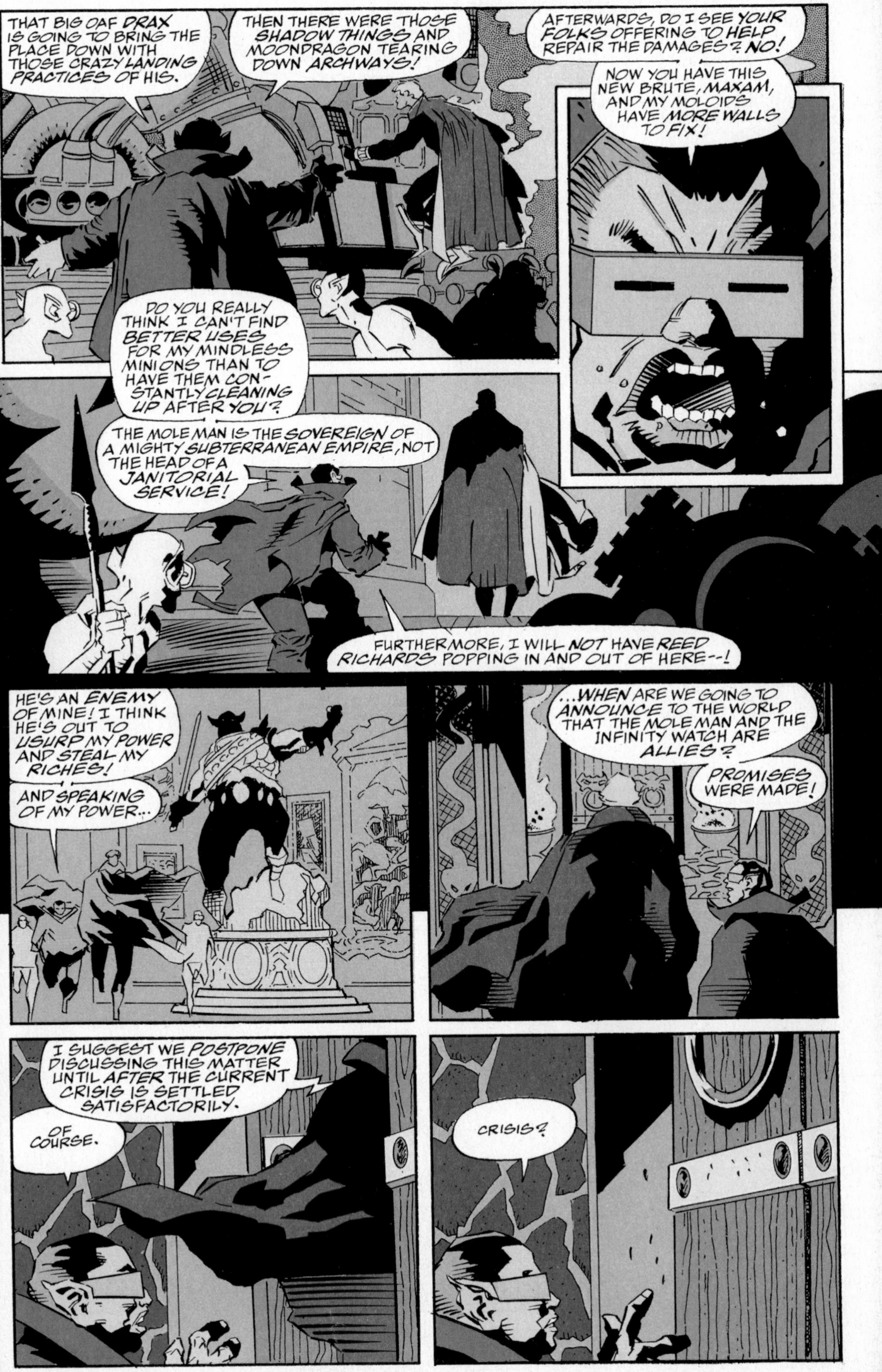
THAT BIG OAF DRAX IS GOING TO BRING THE PLACE DOWN WITH THOSE CRAZY LANDING PRACTICES OF HIS.
THEN THERE WERE THOSE SHADOW THINGS AND MOONDRAGON TEARING DOWN ARCHWAYS!
AFTERWARDS, DO I SEE YOUR FOLKS OFFERING TO HELP REPAIR THE DAMAGES? NO!
NOW YOU HAVE THIS NEW BRUTE, MAXAM, AND MY MOLOIDS HAVE MORE WALLS TO FIX!
DO YOU REALLY THINK I CAN'T FIND BETTER USES FOR MY MINDLESS MINIONS THAN TO HAVE THEM CON-STANTLY CLEANING UP AFTER YOU?
THE MOLE MAN IS THE SOVEREIGN OF A MIGHTY SUBTERRANEAN EMPIRE, NOT THE HEAD OF A JANITORIAL SERVICE!
FURTHERMORE, I WILL NOT HAVE REED RICHARDS POPPING IN AND OUT OF HERE--!
HE'S AN ENEMY OF MINE! I THINK HE'S OUT TO USURP MY POWER AND STEAL MY RICHES!
AND SPEAKING OF MY POWER...
...WHEN ARE WE GOING TO ANNOUNCE TO THE WORLD THAT THE MOLE MAN AND THE INFINITY WATCH ARE ALLIES?
PROMISES WERE MADE!
I SUGGEST WE POSTPONE DISCUSSING THIS MATTER UNTIL AFTER THE CURRENT CRISIS IS SETTLED SATISFACTORILY.
OF COURSE.
CRISIS?

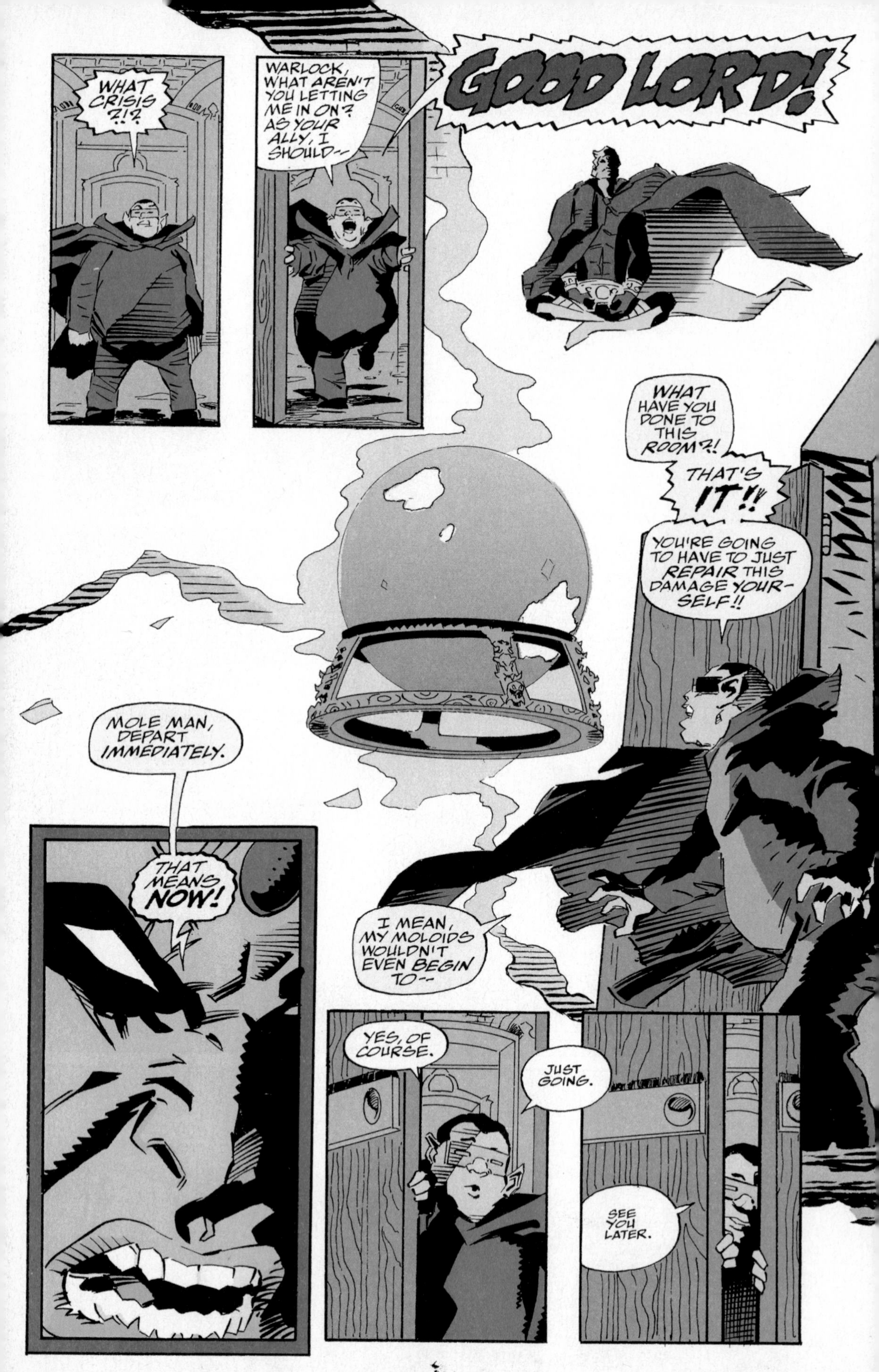
WHAT CRISIS ?!?
WARLOCK, WHAT AREN'T YOU LETTING ME IN ON? AS YOUR ALLY, I SHOULD--
GOOD LORD!
WHAT HAVE YOU DONE TO THIS ROOM?!
THAT'S IT!!
YOU'RE GOING TO HAVE TO JUST REPAIR THIS DAMAGE YOURSELF!!
I MEAN, MY MOLOIDS WOULDN'T EVEN BEGIN TO--
MOLE MAN, DEPART IMMEDIATELY.
THAT MEANS NOW!
YES, OF COURSE.
JUST GOING.
SEE YOU LATER.

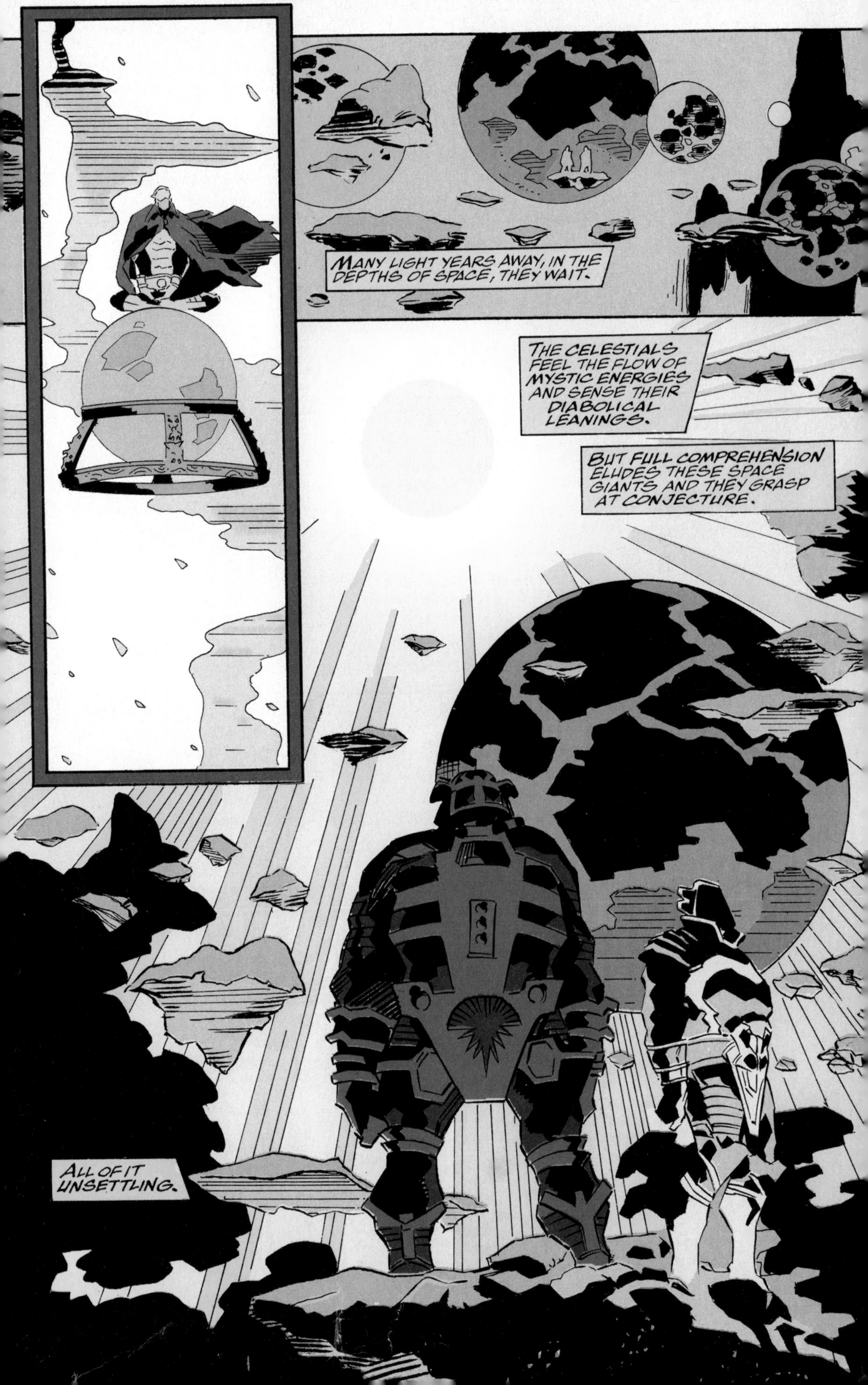
MANY LIGHT YEARS AWAY, IN THE DEPTHS OF SPACE, THEY WAIT.
THE CELESTIALS FEEL THE FLOW OF MYSTIC ENERGIES AND SENSE THEIR DIABOLICAL LEANINGS.
BUT FULL COMPREHENSION ELUDES THESE SPACE GIANTS AND THEY GRASP AT CONJECTURE.
ALL OF IT UNSETTLING.

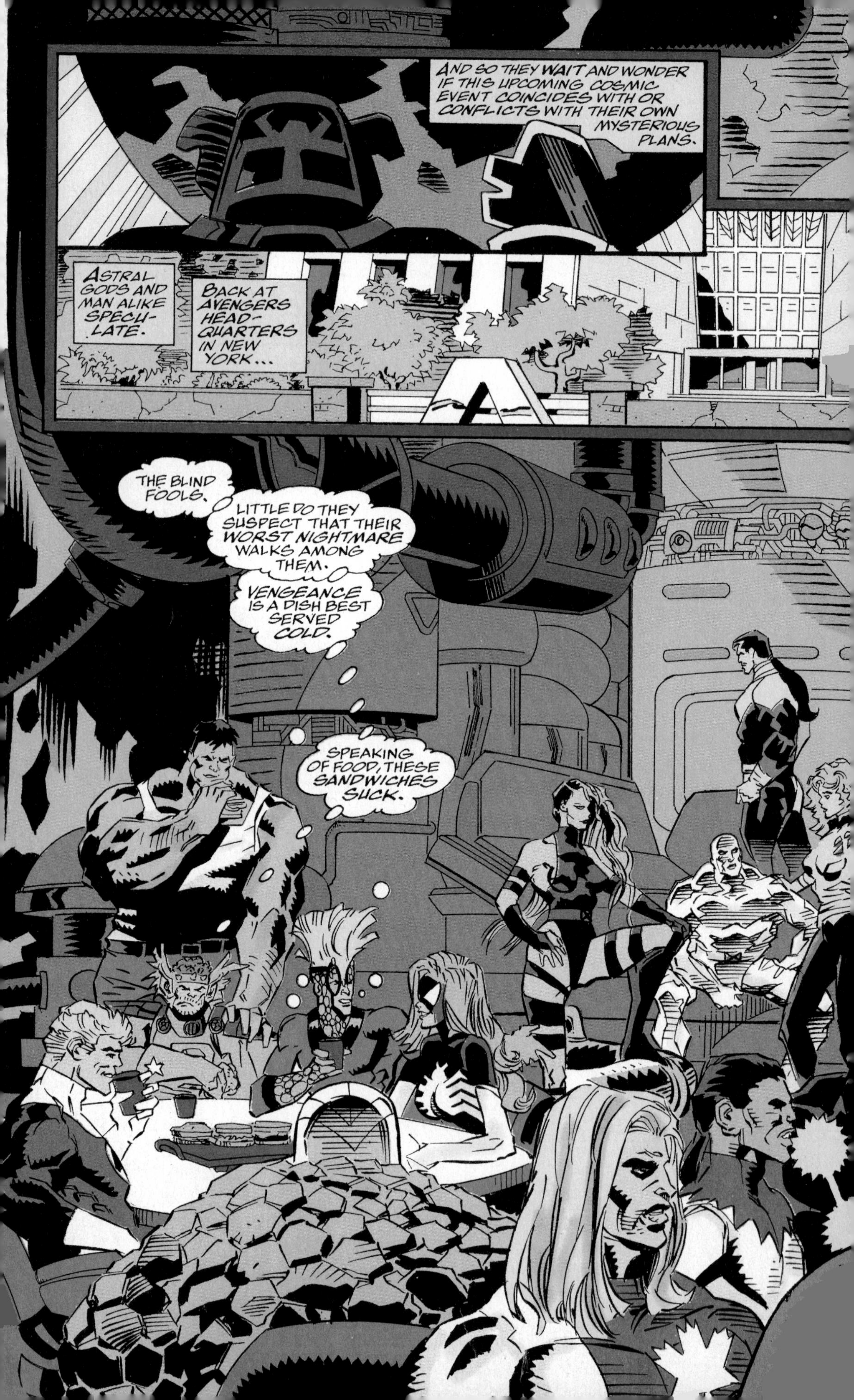
AND SO THEY WAIT AND WONDER IF THIS UPCOMING COSMIC EVENT COINCIDES WITH OR CONFLICTS WITH THEIR OWN MYSTERIOUS PLANS.
ASTRAL GODS AND MAN ALIKE SPECULATE.
BACK AT AVENGERS HEADQUARTERS IN NEW YORK...
THE BLIND FOOLS.
LITTLE DO THEY SUSPECT THAT THEIR WORST NIGHTMARE WALKS AMONG THEM.
VENGEANCE IS A DISH BEST SERVED COLD.
SPEAKING OF FOOD, THESE SANDWICHES SUCK.

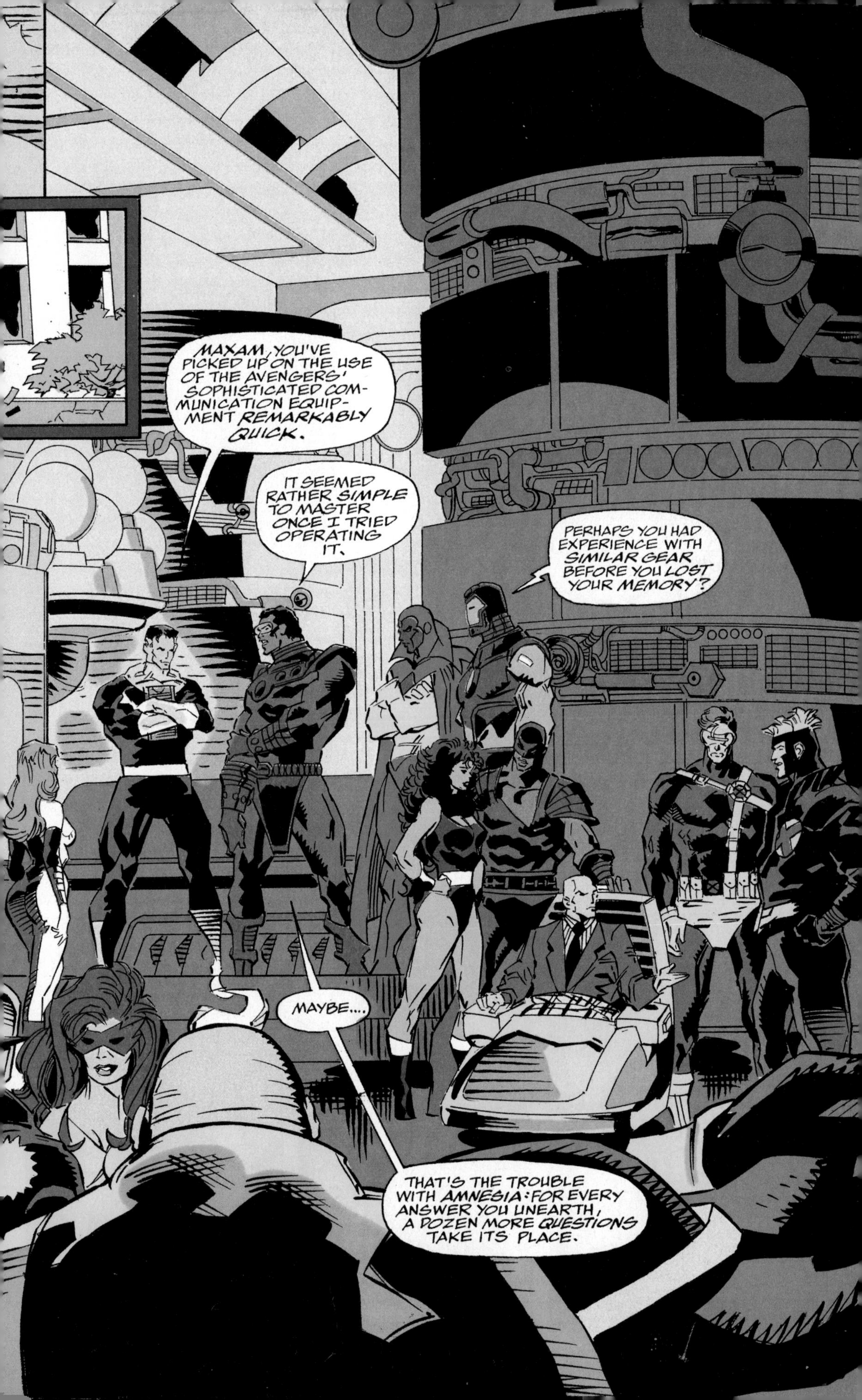
MAXAM, YOU'VE PICKED UP ON THE USE OF THE AVENGERS' SOPHISTICATED COMMUNICATION EQUIPMENT REMARKABLY QUICK.
IT SEEMED RATHER SIMPLE TO MASTER ONCE I TRIED OPERATING IT.
PERHAPS YOU HAD EXPERIENCE WITH SIMILAR GEAR BEFORE YOU LOST YOUR MEMORY?
MAYBE....
THAT'S THE TROUBLE WITH AMNESIA: FOR EVERY ANSWER YOU UNEARTH, A DOZEN MORE QUESTIONS TAKE ITS PLACE.

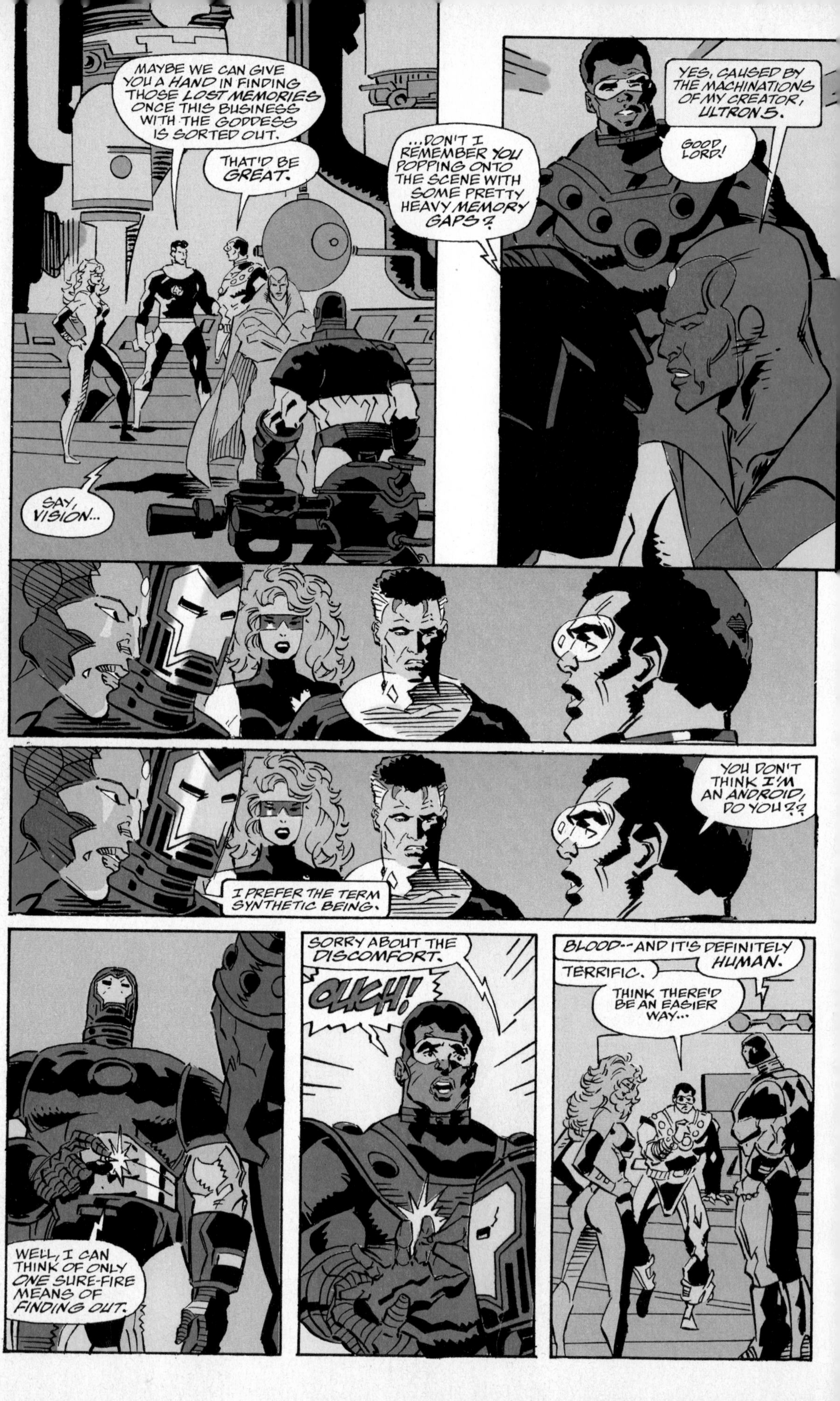
MAYBE WE CAN GIVE YOU A HAND IN FINDING THOSE LOST MEMORIES ONCE THIS BUSINESS WITH THE GODDESS IS SORTED OUT.
THAT'D BE GREAT.
SAY, VISION...
...DON'T I REMEMBER YOU POPPING ONTO THE SCENE WITH SOME PRETTY HEAVY MEMORY GAPS?
YES, CAUSED BY THE MACHINATIONS OF MY CREATOR, ULTRON 5.
GOOD LORD!
YOU DON'T THINK I'M AN ANDROID, DO YOU??
I PREFER THE TERM SYNTHETIC BEING.
WELL, I CAN THINK OF ONLY ONE SURE-FIRE MEANS OF FINDING OUT.
SORRY ABOUT THE DISCOMFORT.
OUCH!
BLOOD--AND IT'S DEFINITELY HUMAN.
TERRIFIC.
THINK THERE'D BE AN EASIER WAY...

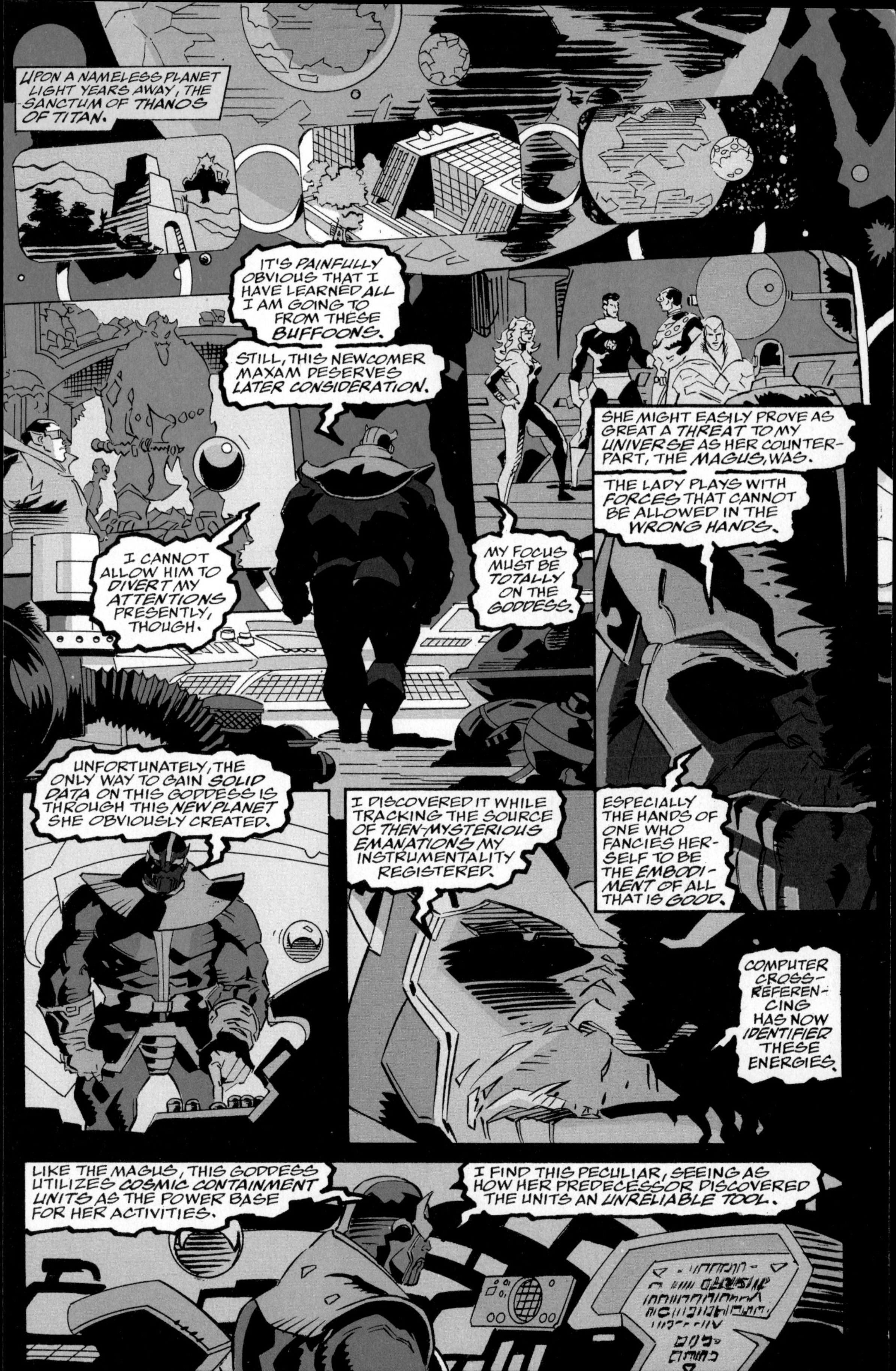

UPON A NAMELESS PLANET LIGHT YEARS AWAY, THE SANCTUM OF THANOS OF TITAN.
IT'S PAINFULLY OBVIOUS THAT I HAVE LEARNED ALL I AM GOING TO FROM THESE BUFFOONS.
STILL, THIS NEWCOMER MAXAM DESERVES LATER CONSIDERATION.
I CANNOT ALLOW HIM TO DIVERT MY ATTENTIONS PRESENTLY, THOUGH.
MY FOCUS MUST BE TOTALLY ON THE GODDESS.
SHE MIGHT EASILY PROVE AS GREAT A THREAT TO MY UNIVERSE AS HER COUNTER-PART, THE MAGUS, WAS.
THE LADY PLAYS WITH FORCES THAT CANNOT BE ALLOWED IN THE WRONG HANDS.
ESPECIALLY THE HANDS OF ONE WHO FANCIES HER-SELF TO BE THE EMBODI-MENT OF ALL THAT IS GOOD.
UNFORTUNATELY, THE ONLY WAY TO GAIN SOLID DATA ON THIS GODDESS IS THROUGH THIS NEW PLANET SHE OBVIOUSLY CREATED.
I DISCOVERED IT WHILE TRACKING THE SOURCE OF THEN-MYSTERIOUS EMANATIONS MY INSTRUMENTALITY REGISTERED.
COMPUTER CROSS-REFEREN-CING HAS NOW IDENTIFIER THESE ENERGIES.
LIKE THE MAGUS, THIS GODDESS UTILIZES COSMIC CONTAINMENT UNITS AS THE POWER BASE FOR HER ACTIVITIES.
I FIND THIS PECULIAR, SEEING AS HOW HER PREDECESSOR DISCOVERED THE UNITS AN UNRELIABLE TOOL.

THE GODDESS MUST BE *AWARE* OF THE LIMITS OF THE *UNITS'* USEFUL- NESS.

MANY HAVE PREVIOUSLY TRIED TO GAIN *UNIVERSAL DOMINATION* WITH THEM AND *FAILED.*

YET ONE MUST ASSUME THAT WARLOCK'S *FEMININE SELF* SHARES HIS SKILL AS A *SCHEMER.*

THE GODDESS WOULD *NEVER* PURSUE A TACTIC THAT WAS SO *PREDESTINED* TO *FAILURE.*

THUS, THE ONLY *LOGICAL* CONCLUSION I CAN REACH ON THIS MATTER IS THAT I AM *MISSING THE POINT* OF IT.

OBVIOUSLY I CANNOT PROPERLY *FATHOM* THE GODDESS'S *INTENTIONS* WITH THE *MEAGER INTELLIGENCE* --

--CURRENTLY AT MY DISPOSAL.

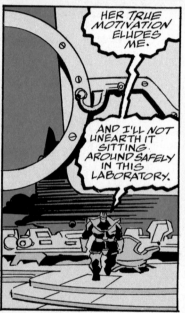

HER *TRUE MOTIVATION* ELUDES ME.

AND I'LL *NOT* UNEARTH IT SITTING AROUND SAFELY IN THIS LABORATORY.

NONE OF MY SPY PROBES HAVE BEEN ABLE TO PENE- TRATE HER *PLANETARY DEFENSES.*

SOMETHING IS HAPPENING ON THAT *MUDBALL* THE GODDESS DOES *NOT* WANT THE REST OF THE GALAXY TO *WITNESS.*

HOW CAN I POSSIBLY RESIST SUCH A *CHALLENGE* ..?

I *CAN'T.*

INTELLECTUAL CURIOSITY WILL YET BE THE DOWNFALL OF ME.

HAVE ALL *PREPARATIONS* FOR MY *DEPARTURE* BEEN COMPLETED..?

Yes, sir.

CONTINUE TO MONITOR *COM-FREQUENCY BC-7.*

I HAVE MY *SUSPICIONS* THAT *HEAVY-DUTY ARMA- MENT* MAY BE NEEDED IN THIS ENGAGEMENT.

HAVE STORAGE UNIT *#D-666* POWERED UP AND READY FOR DELIVERY.

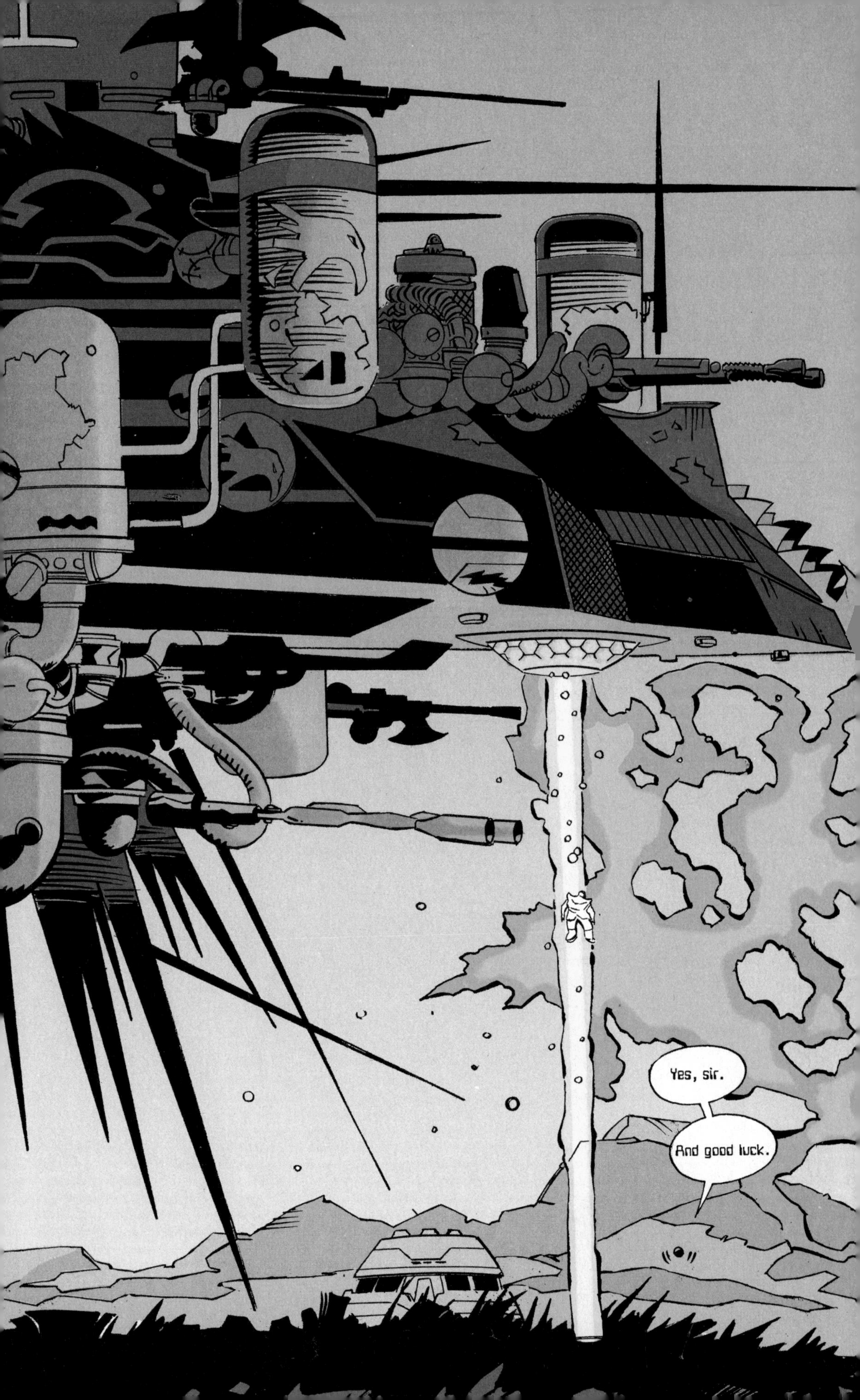
Yes, sir.
And good luck.

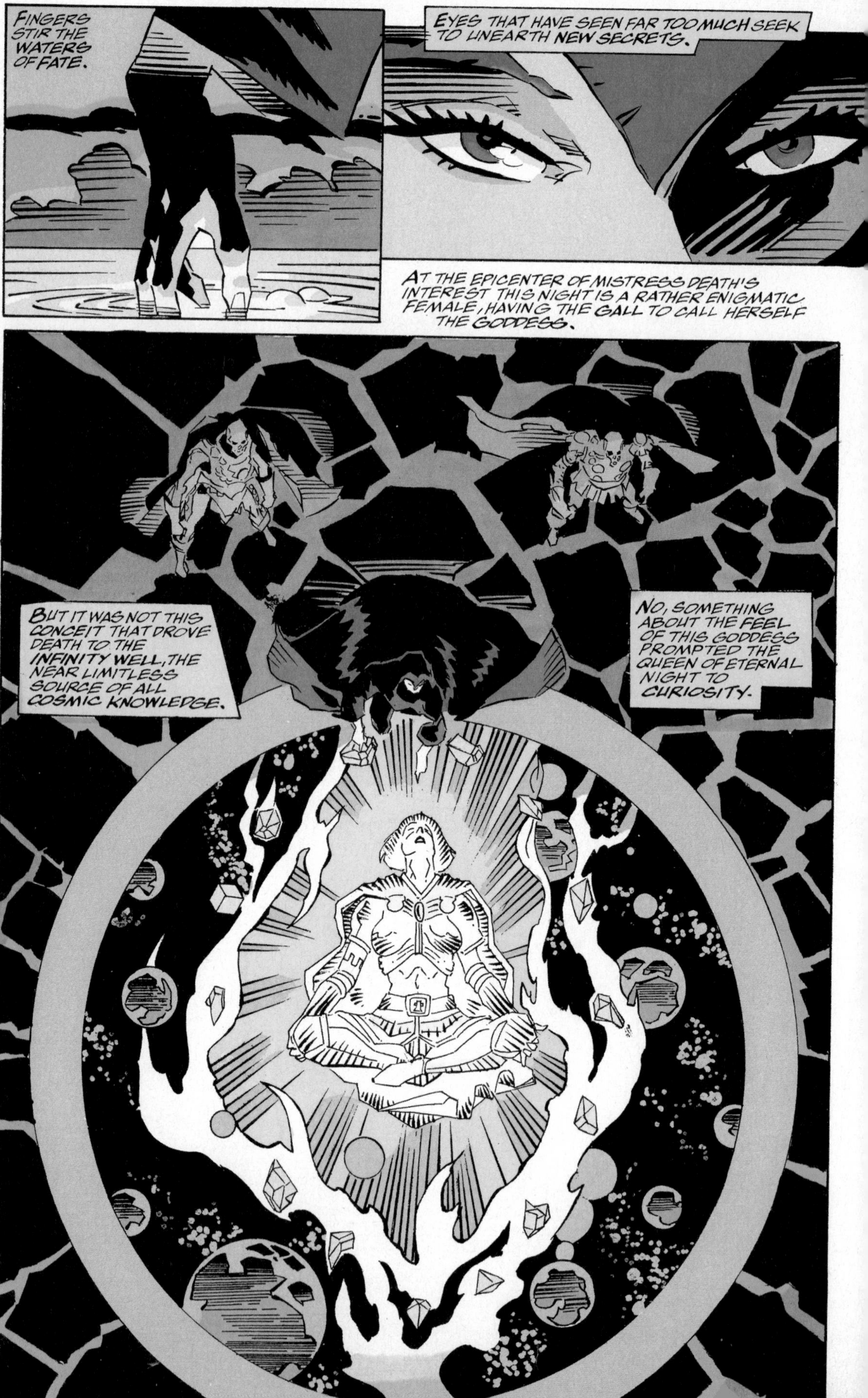
FINGERS STIR THE WATERS OF FATE.
EYES THAT HAVE SEEN FAR TOO MUCH SEEK TO UNEARTH NEW SECRETS.
AT THE EPICENTER OF MISTRESS DEATH'S INTEREST THIS NIGHT IS A RATHER ENIGMATIC FEMALE, HAVING THE GALL TO CALL HERSELF THE GODDESS.
BUT IT WAS NOT THIS CONCEIT THAT DROVE DEATH TO THE INFINITY WELL, THE NEAR LIMITLESS SOURCE OF ALL COSMIC KNOWLEDGE.
NO, SOMETHING ABOUT THE FEEL OF THIS GODDESS PROMPTED THE QUEEN OF ETERNAL NIGHT TO CURIOSITY.

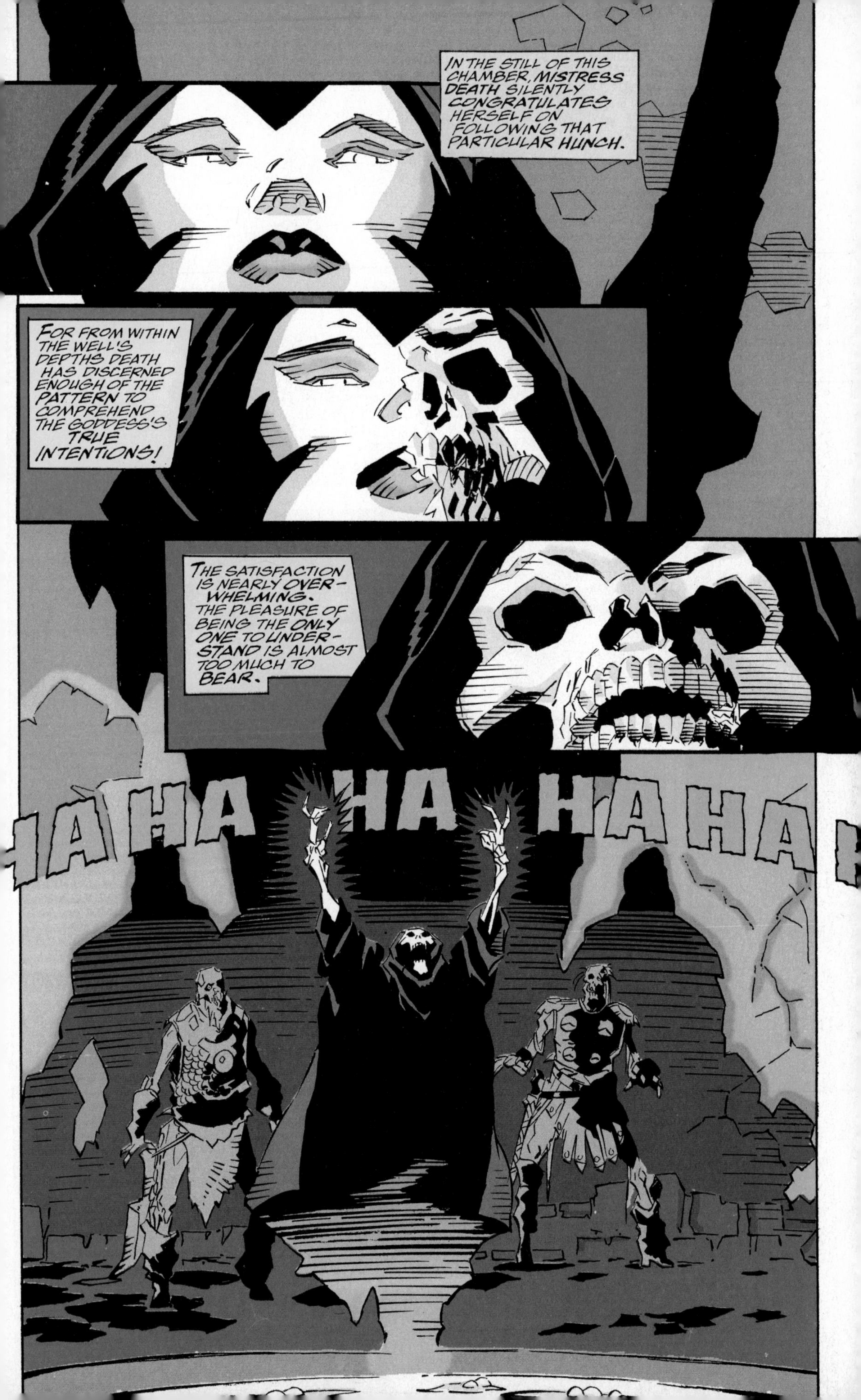
IN THE STILL OF THIS CHAMBER, MISTRESS DEATH SILENTLY CONGRATULATES HERSELF ON FOLLOWING THAT PARTICULAR HUNCH.
FOR FROM WITHIN THE WELL'S DEPTHS DEATH HAS DISCERNED ENOUGH OF THE PATTERN TO COMPREHEND THE GODDESS'S TRUE INTENTIONS!
THE SATISFACTION IS NEARLY OVER-WHELMING. THE PLEASURE OF BEING THE ONLY ONE TO UNDER-STAND IS ALMOST TOO MUCH TO BEAR.
HAHA HA HAHA!

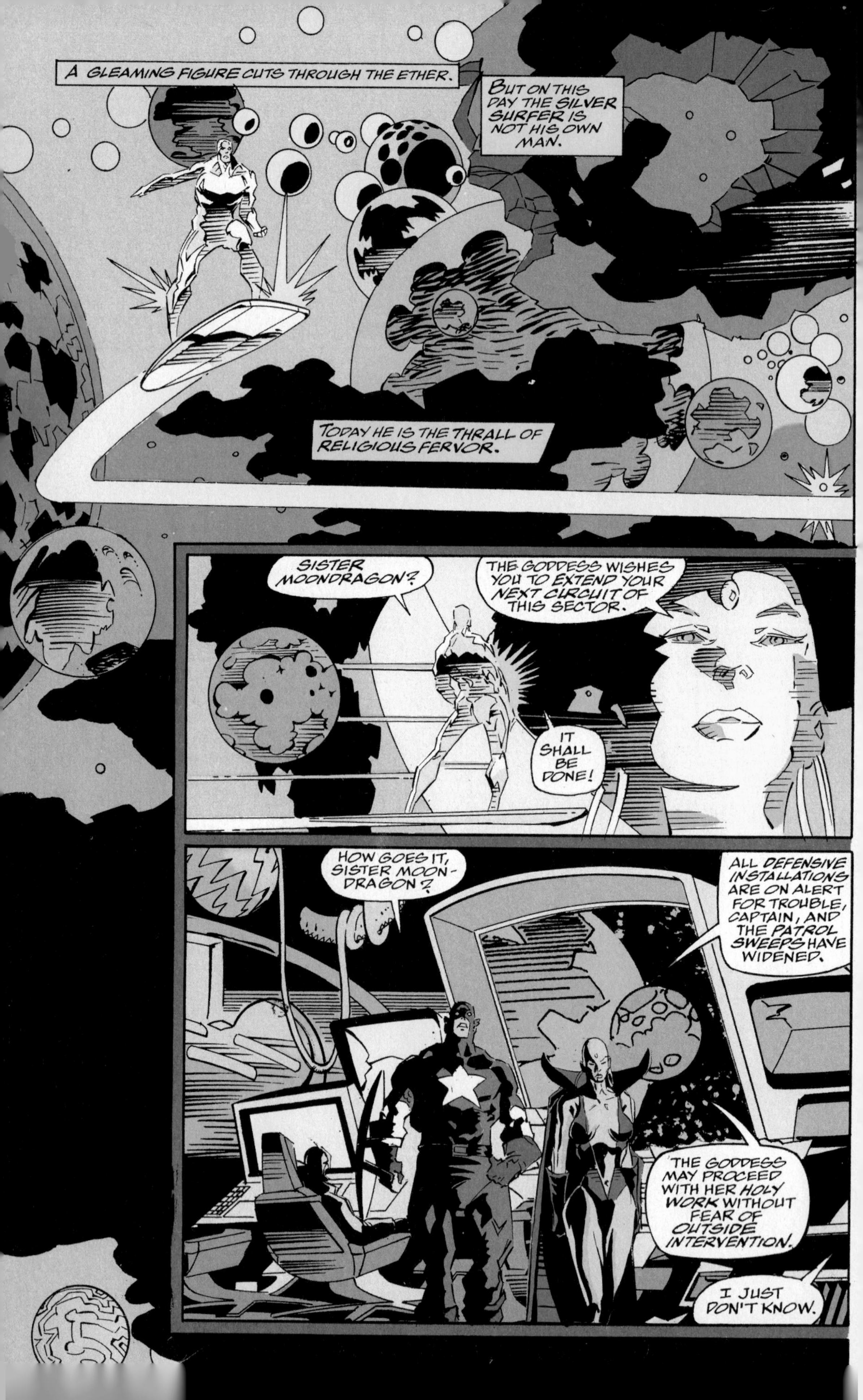
A GLEAMING FIGURE CUTS THROUGH THE ETHER.
BUT ON THIS DAY THE SILVER SURFER IS NOT HIS OWN MAN.
TODAY HE IS THE THRALL OF RELIGIOUS FERVOR.
SISTER MOONDRAGON?
THE GODDESS WISHES YOU TO EXTEND YOUR NEXT CIRCUIT OF THIS SECTOR.
IT SHALL BE DONE!
HOW GOES IT, SISTER MOON-DRAGON?
ALL DEFENSIVE INSTALLATIONS ARE ON ALERT FOR TROUBLE, CAPTAIN, AND THE PATROL SWEEPS HAVE WIDENED.
THE GODDESS MAY PROCEED WITH HER HOLY WORK WITHOUT FEAR OF OUTSIDE INTERVENTION.
I JUST DON'T KNOW.

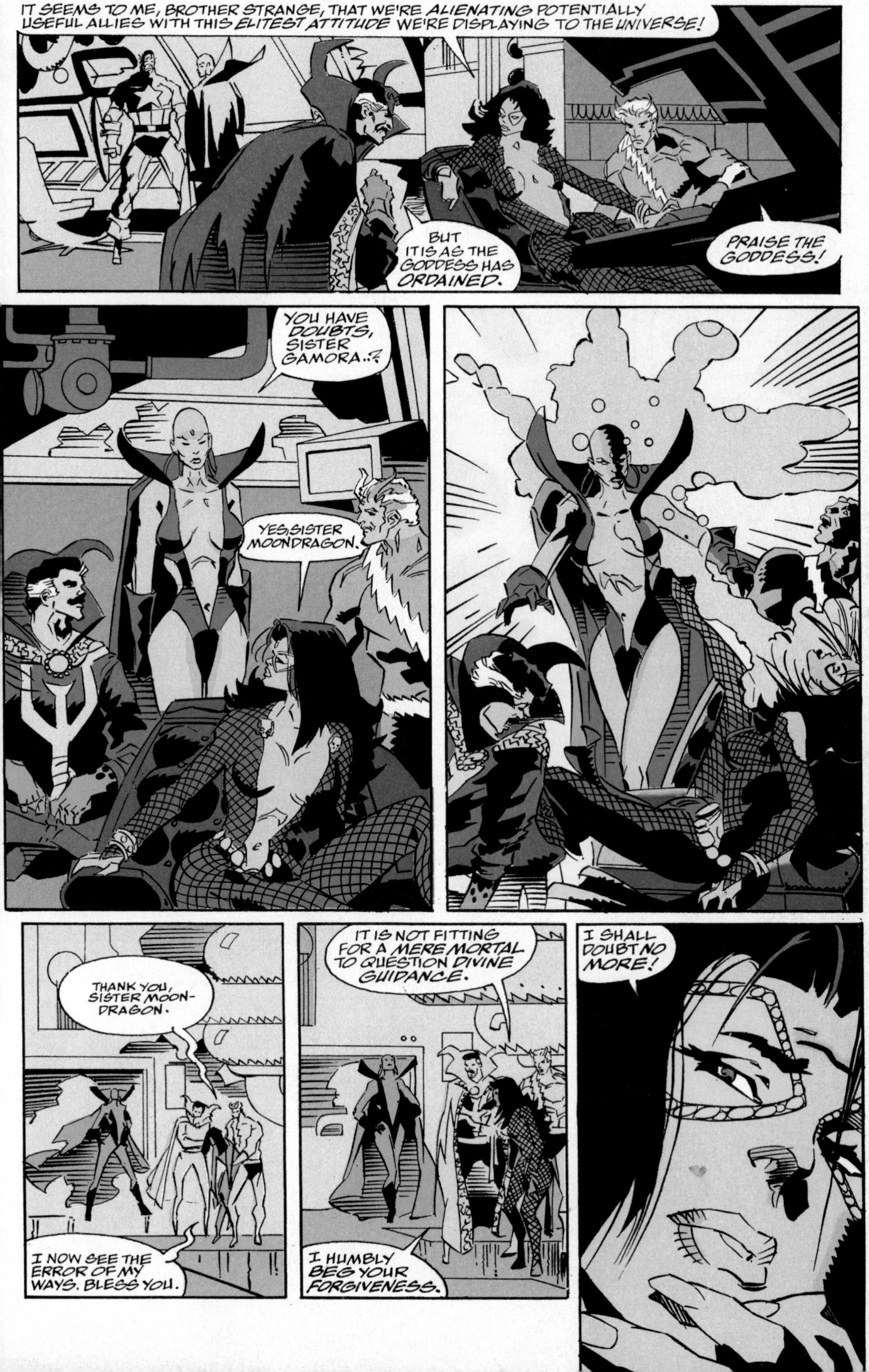

IT SEEMS TO ME, BROTHER STRANGE, THAT WE'RE ALIENATING POTENTIALLY USEFUL ALLIES WITH THIS ELITEST ATTITUDE WE'RE DISPLAYING TO THE UNIVERSE!
BUT IT IS AS THE GODDESS HAS ORDAINED.
PRAISE THE GODDESS!
YOU HAVE DOUBTS, SISTER GAMORA..?
YES, SISTER MOONDRAGON.
THANK YOU, SISTER MOON-DRAGON.
I NOW SEE THE ERROR OF MY WAYS. BLESS YOU.
IT IS NOT FITTING FOR A MERE MORTAL TO QUESTION DIVINE GUIDANCE.
I HUMBLY BEG YOUR FORGIVENESS.
I SHALL DOUBT NO MORE!

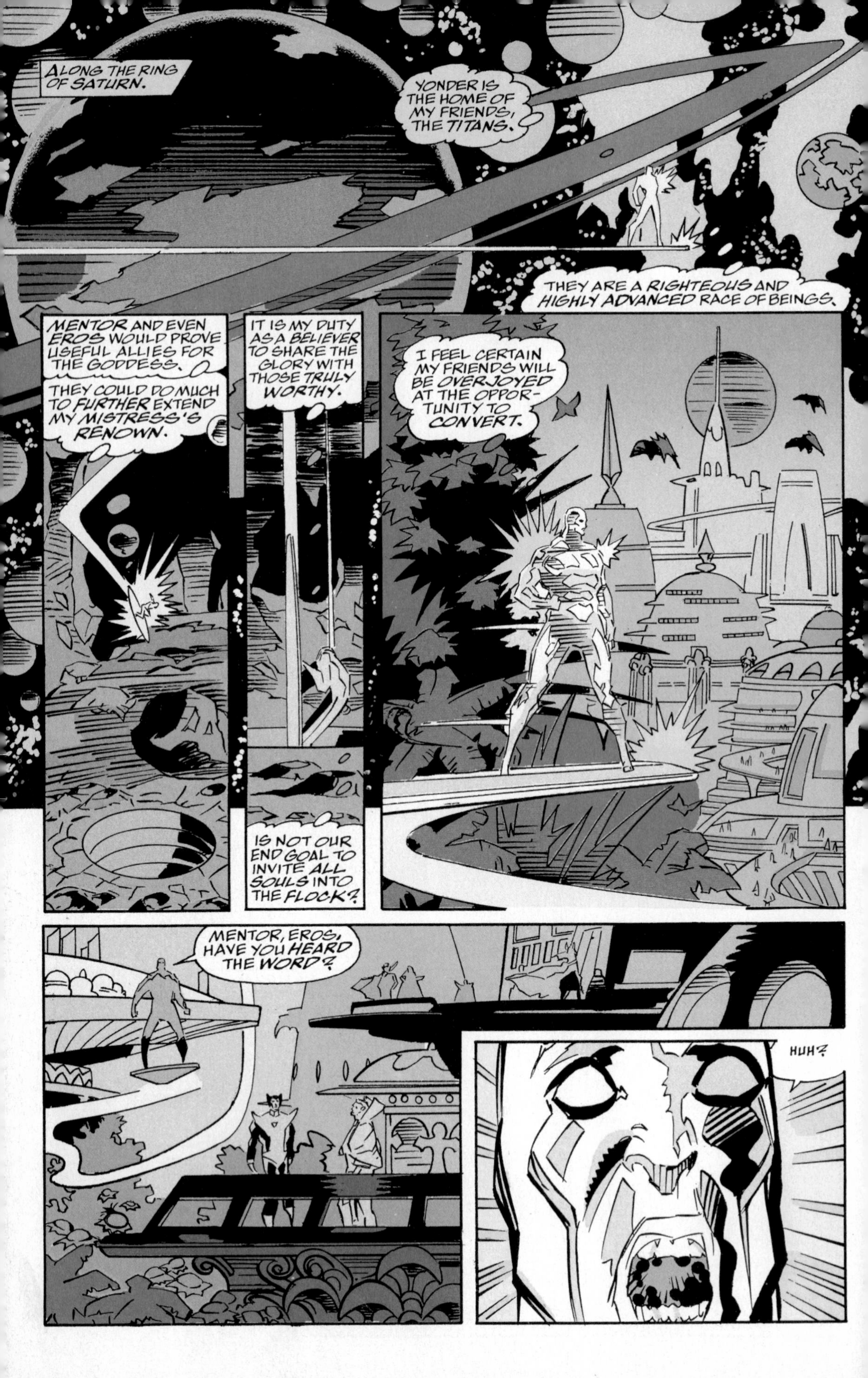

ALONG THE RING OF SATURN.
YONDER IS THE HOME OF MY FRIENDS, THE TITANS.
THEY ARE A RIGHTEOUS AND HIGHLY ADVANCED RACE OF BEINGS.
MENTOR AND EVEN EROS WOULD PROVE USEFUL ALLIES FOR THE GODDESS.
THEY COULD DO MUCH TO FURTHER EXTEND MY MISTRESS'S RENOWN.
IT IS MY DUTY AS A BELIEVER TO SHARE THE GLORY WITH THOSE TRULY WORTHY.
IS NOT OUR END GOAL TO INVITE ALL SOULS INTO THE FLOCK?
I FEEL CERTAIN MY FRIENDS WILL BE OVERJOYED AT THE OPPORTUNITY TO CONVERT.
MENTOR, EROS, HAVE YOU HEARD THE WORD?
HUH?

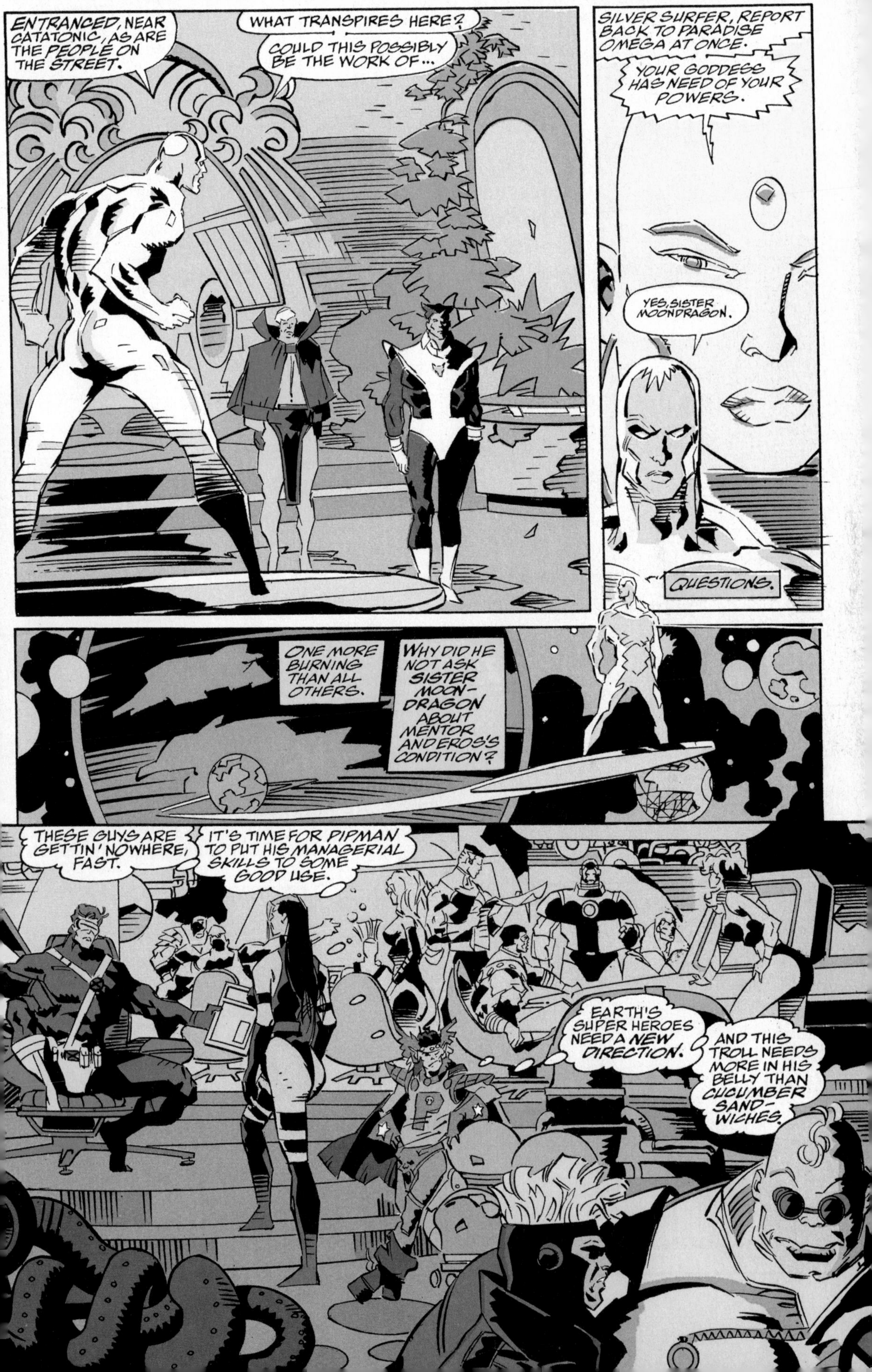
ENTRANCED, NEAR CATATONIC, AS ARE THE PEOPLE ON THE STREET.
WHAT TRANSPIRES HERE?
COULD THIS POSSIBLY BE THE WORK OF...
SILVER SURFER, REPORT BACK TO PARADISE OMEGA AT ONCE.
YOUR GODDESS HAS NEED OF YOUR POWERS.
YES, SISTER MOONDRAGON.
QUESTIONS.
ONE MORE BURNING THAN ALL OTHERS.
WHY DID HE NOT ASK SISTER MOON-DRAGON ABOUT MENTOR AND EROS'S CONDITION?
THESE GUYS ARE GETTIN' NOWHERE, FAST.
IT'S TIME FOR PIPMAN TO PUT HIS MANAGERIAL SKILLS TO SOME GOOD USE.
EARTH'S SUPER HEROES NEED A NEW DIRECTION.
AND THIS TROLL NEEDS MORE IN HIS BELLY THAN CUCUMBER SAND-WICHES.

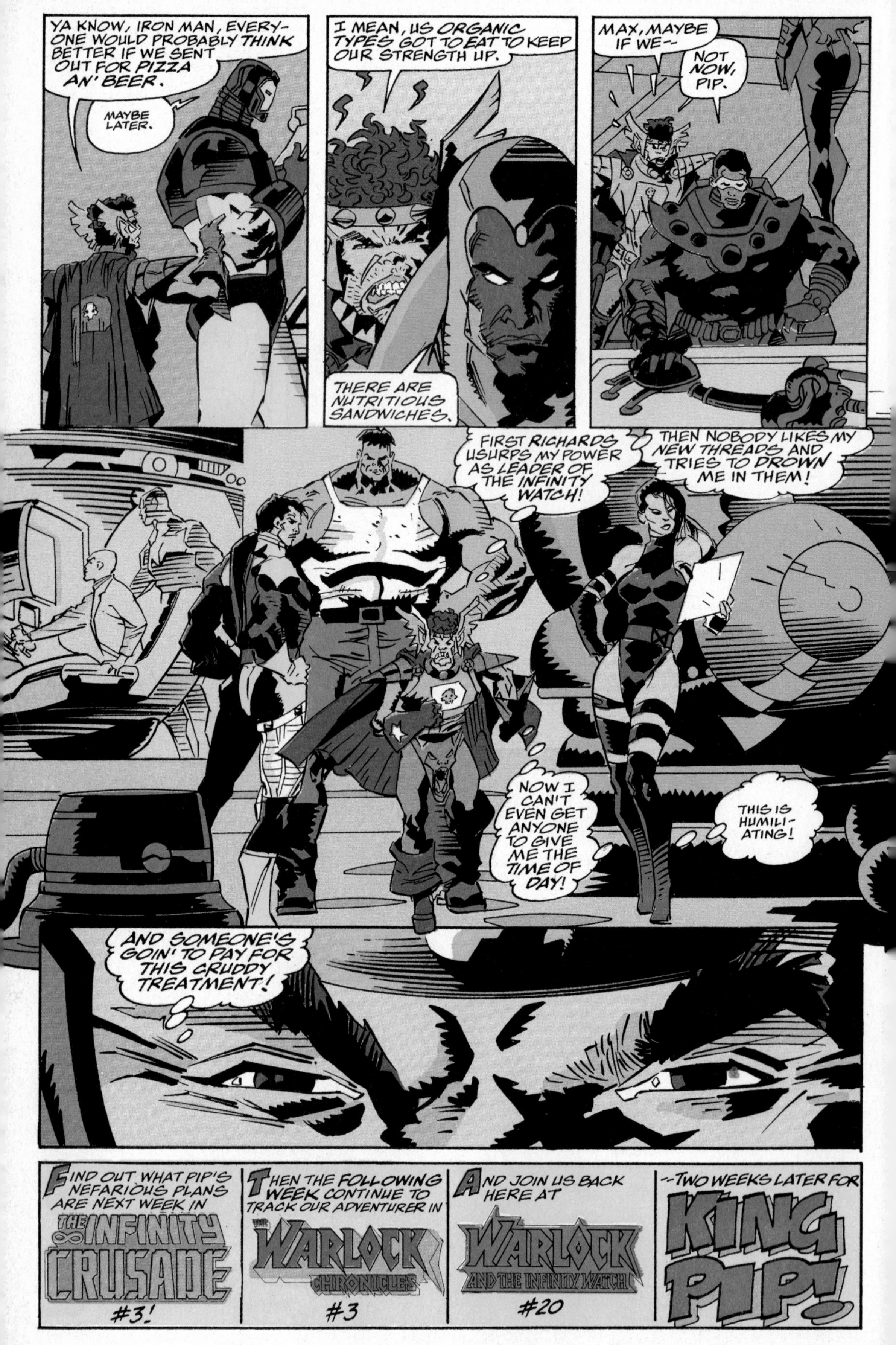
YA KNOW, IRON MAN, EVERYONE WOULD PROBABLY THINK BETTER IF WE SENT OUT FOR PIZZA AN' BEER.
MAYBE LATER.
I MEAN, US ORGANIC TYPES GOT TO EAT TO KEEP OUR STRENGTH UP.
THERE ARE NUTRITIOUS SANDWICHES.
MAX, MAYBE IF WE--
NOT NOW, PIP.
FIRST RICHARDS USURPS MY POWER AS LEADER OF THE INFINITY WATCH!
THEN NOBODY LIKES MY NEW THREADS AND TRIES TO DROWN ME IN THEM!
NOW I CAN'T EVEN GET ANYONE TO GIVE ME THE TIME OF DAY!
THIS IS HUMILIATING!
AND SOMEONE'S GOIN' TO PAY FOR THIS CRUDDY TREATMENT!
FIND OUT WHAT PIP'S NEFARIOUS PLANS ARE NEXT WEEK IN
THE INFINITY CRUSADE
#3!
THEN THE FOLLOWING WEEK CONTINUE TO TRACK OUR ADVENTURER IN
WARLOCK CHRONICLES
#3
AND JOIN US BACK HERE AT
WARLOCK AND THE INFINITY WATCH
#20
--TWO WEEKS LATER FOR
KING PIP!

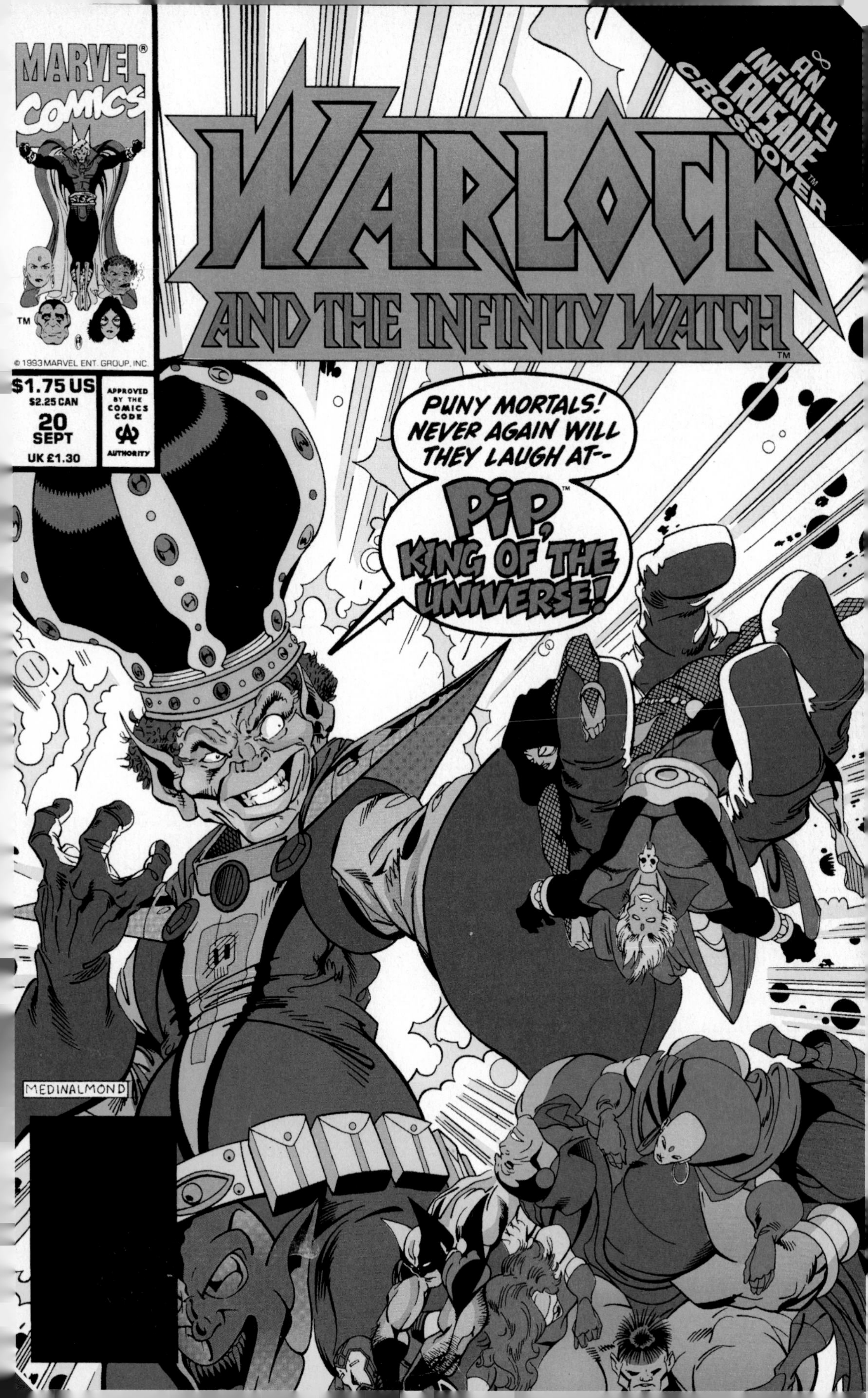
MARVEL COMICS
AN INFINITY CRUSADE CROSSOVER
WARLOCK
AND THE INFINITY WATCH
© 1993 MARVEL ENT. GROUP, INC.
$1.75 US
$2.25 CAN
20
SEPT
UK £1.30
APPROVED BY THE COMICS CODE AUTHORITY
PUNY MORTALS! NEVER AGAIN WILL THEY LAUGH AT--
PIP, KING OF THE UNIVERSE!
MEDINALMOND

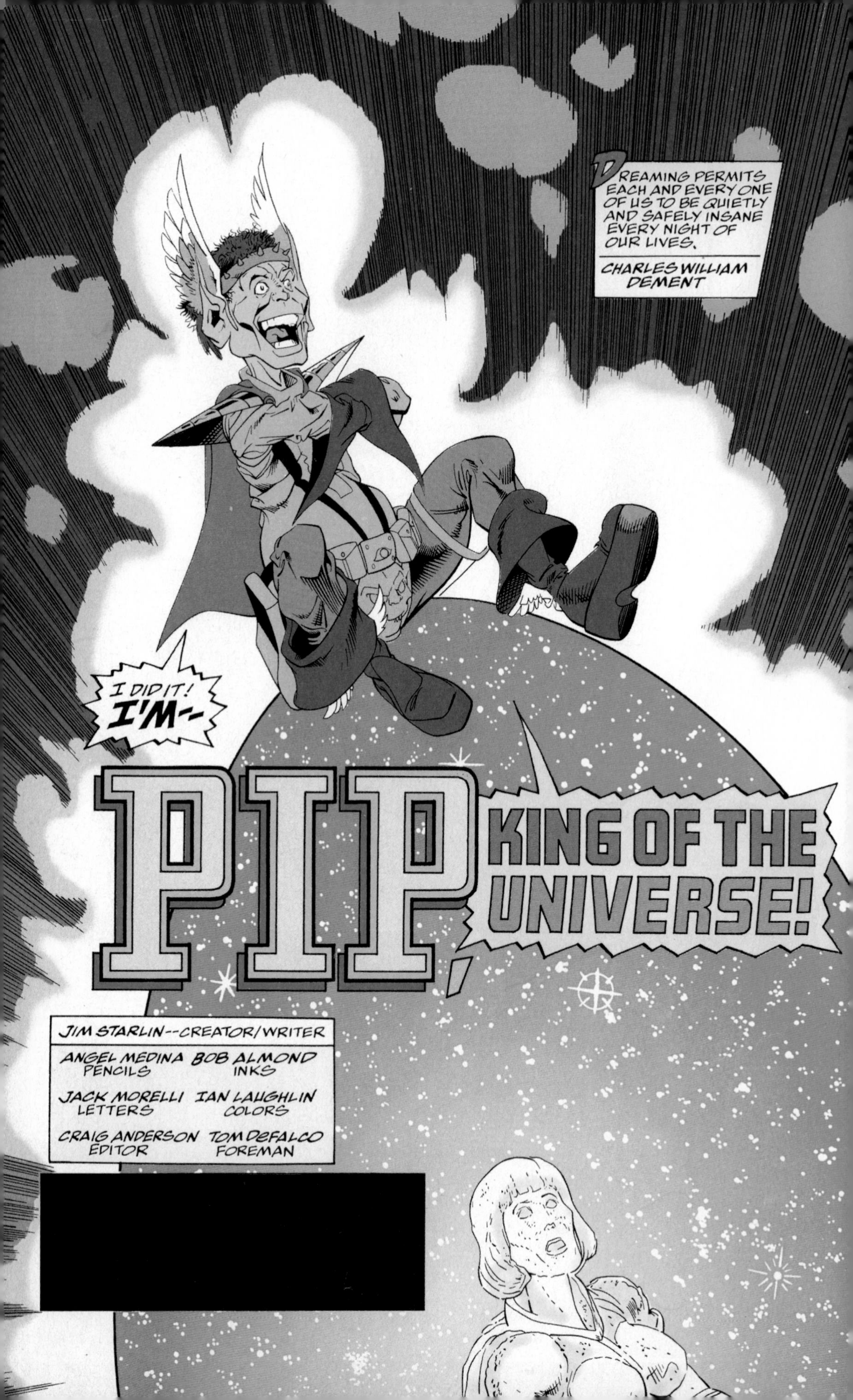
DREAMING PERMITS EACH AND EVERY ONE OF US TO BE QUIETLY AND SAFELY INSANE EVERY NIGHT OF OUR LIVES.
CHARLES WILLIAM DEMENT
I DID IT! I'M--
PIP, KING OF THE UNIVERSE!
JIM STARLIN--CREATOR/WRITER
ANGEL MEDINA PENCILS
BOB ALMOND INKS
JACK MORELLI LETTERS
IAN LAUGHLIN COLORS
CRAIG ANDERSON EDITOR
TOM DeFALCO FOREMAN
[redacted]

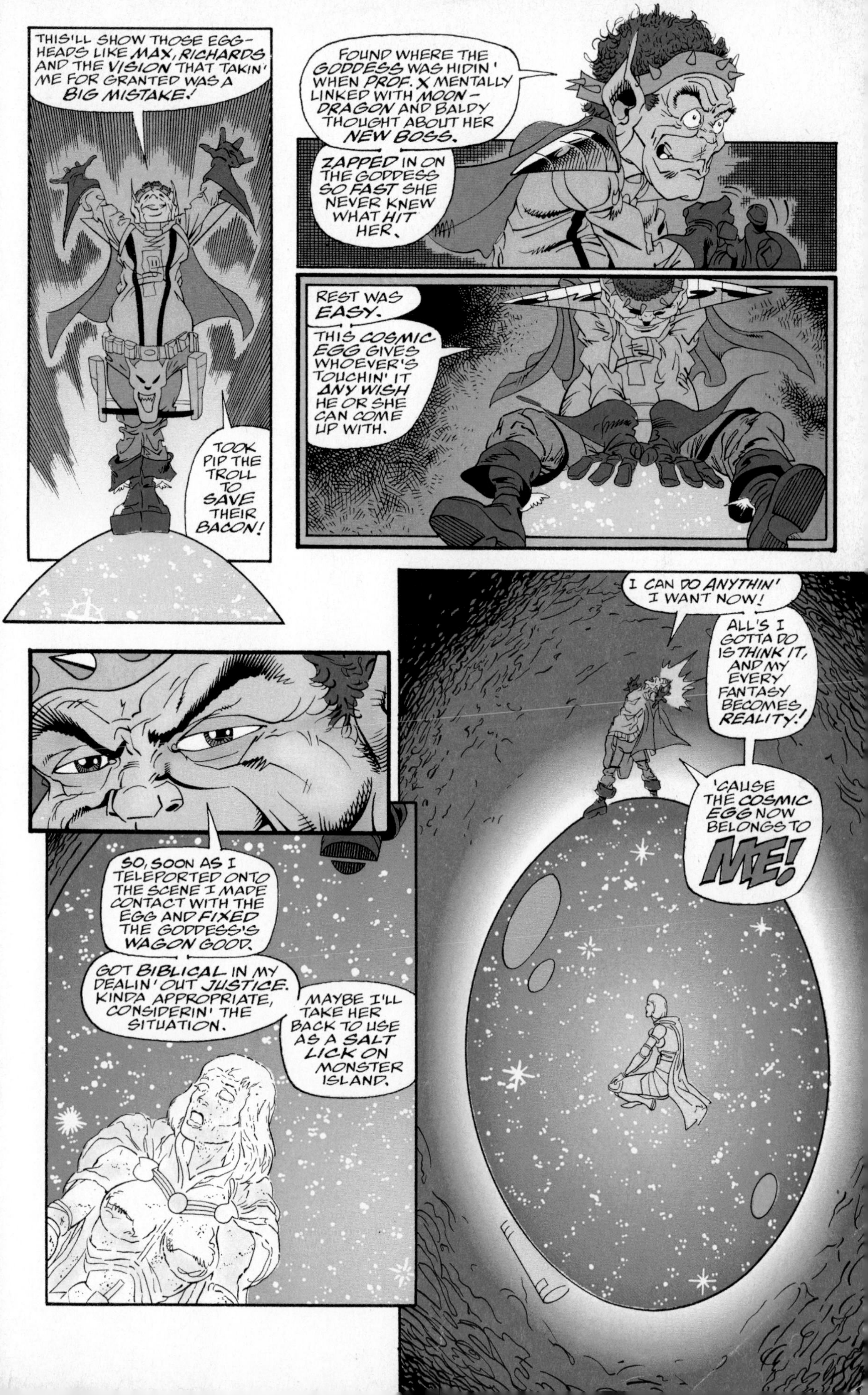
THIS'LL SHOW THOSE EGG-HEADS LIKE MAX, RICHARDS AND THE VISION THAT TAKIN' ME FOR GRANTED WAS A BIG MISTAKE!
TOOK PIP THE TROLL TO SAVE THEIR BACON!
FOUND WHERE THE GODDESS WAS HIDIN' WHEN PROF. X MENTALLY LINKED WITH MOON-DRAGON AND BALDY THOUGHT ABOUT HER NEW BOSS.
ZAPPED IN ON THE GODDESS SO FAST SHE NEVER KNEW WHAT HIT HER.
REST WAS EASY.
THIS COSMIC EGG GIVES WHOEVER'S TOUCHIN' IT ANY WISH HE OR SHE CAN COME UP WITH.
SO, SOON AS I TELEPORTED ONTO THE SCENE I MADE CONTACT WITH THE EGG AND FIXED THE GODDESS'S WAGON GOOD.
GOT BIBLICAL IN MY DEALIN' OUT JUSTICE. KINDA APPROPRIATE, CONSIDERIN' THE SITUATION.
MAYBE I'LL TAKE HER BACK TO USE AS A SALT LICK ON MONSTER ISLAND.
I CAN DO ANYTHIN' I WANT NOW!
ALL'S I GOTTA DO IS THINK IT, AND MY EVERY FANTASY BECOMES REALITY!
'CAUSE THE COSMIC EGG NOW BELONGS TO ME!

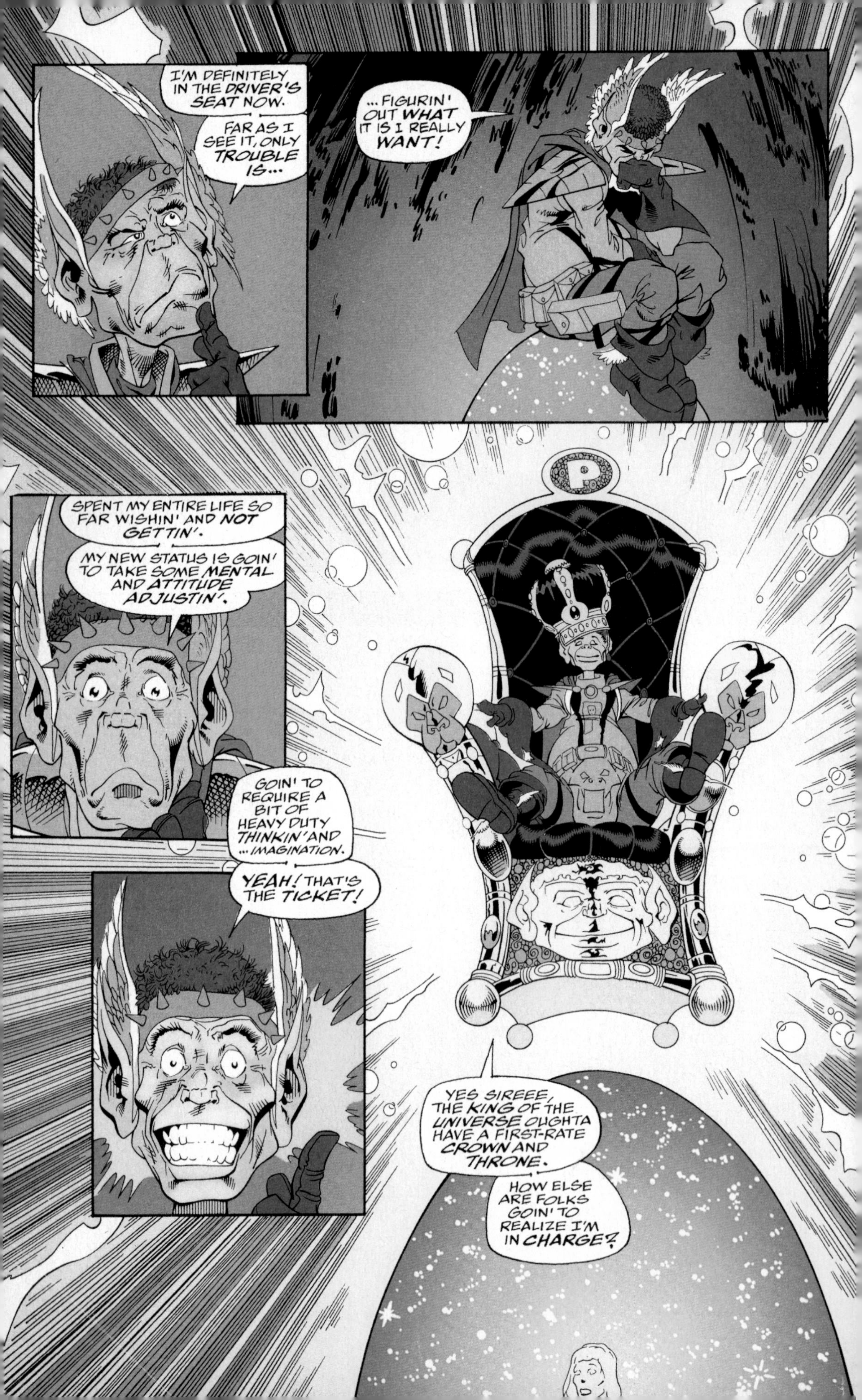
I'M DEFINITELY IN THE DRIVER'S SEAT NOW.
FAR AS I SEE IT, ONLY TROUBLE IS...
...FIGURIN' OUT WHAT IT IS I REALLY WANT!
SPENT MY ENTIRE LIFE SO FAR WISHIN' AND NOT GETTIN'.
MY NEW STATUS IS GOIN' TO TAKE SOME MENTAL AND ATTITUDE ADJUSTIN'.
GOIN' TO REQUIRE A BIT OF HEAVY DUTY THINKIN' AND ...IMAGINATION.
YEAH! THAT'S THE TICKET!
YES SIREEE, THE KING OF THE UNIVERSE OUGHTA HAVE A FIRST-RATE CROWN AND THRONE.
HOW ELSE ARE FOLKS GOIN' TO REALIZE I'M IN CHARGE?

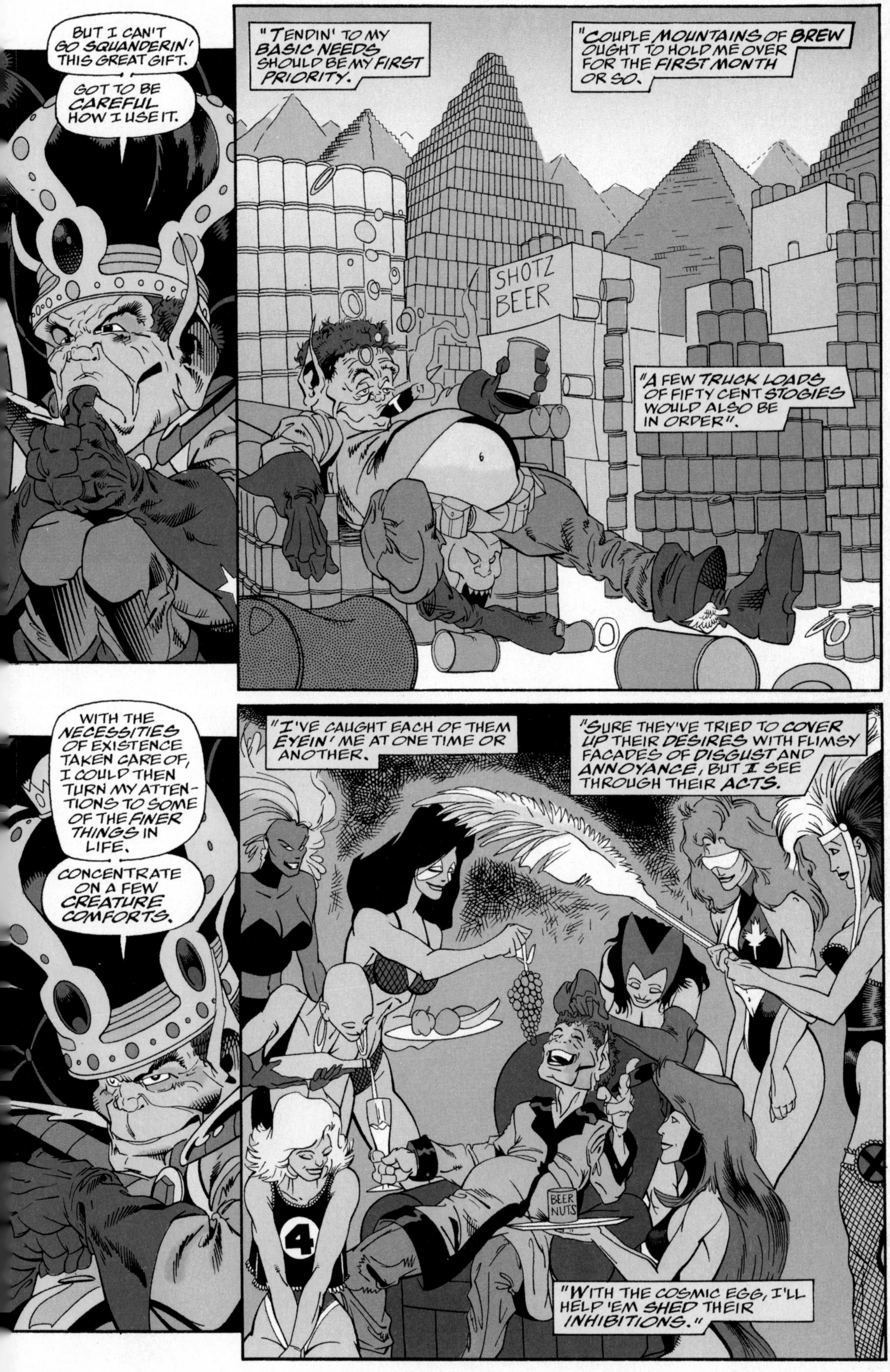
BUT I CAN'T GO SQUANDERIN' THIS GREAT GIFT.
GOT TO BE CAREFUL HOW I USE IT.
"TENDIN' TO MY BASIC NEEDS SHOULD BE MY FIRST PRIORITY.
"COUPLE MOUNTAINS OF BREW OUGHT TO HOLD ME OVER FOR THE FIRST MONTH OR SO.
SHOTZ BEER
"A FEW TRUCK LOADS OF FIFTY CENT STOGIES WOULD ALSO BE IN ORDER".
WITH THE NECESSITIES OF EXISTENCE TAKEN CARE OF, I COULD THEN TURN MY ATTENTIONS TO SOME OF THE FINER THINGS IN LIFE.
CONCENTRATE ON A FEW CREATURE COMFORTS.
"I'VE CAUGHT EACH OF THEM EYEIN' ME AT ONE TIME OR ANOTHER.
"SURE THEY'VE TRIED TO COVER UP THEIR DESIRES WITH FLIMSY FACADES OF DISGUST AND ANNOYANCE, BUT I SEE THROUGH THEIR ACTS.
BEER NUTS
"WITH THE COSMIC EGG, I'LL HELP 'EM SHED THEIR INHIBITIONS."

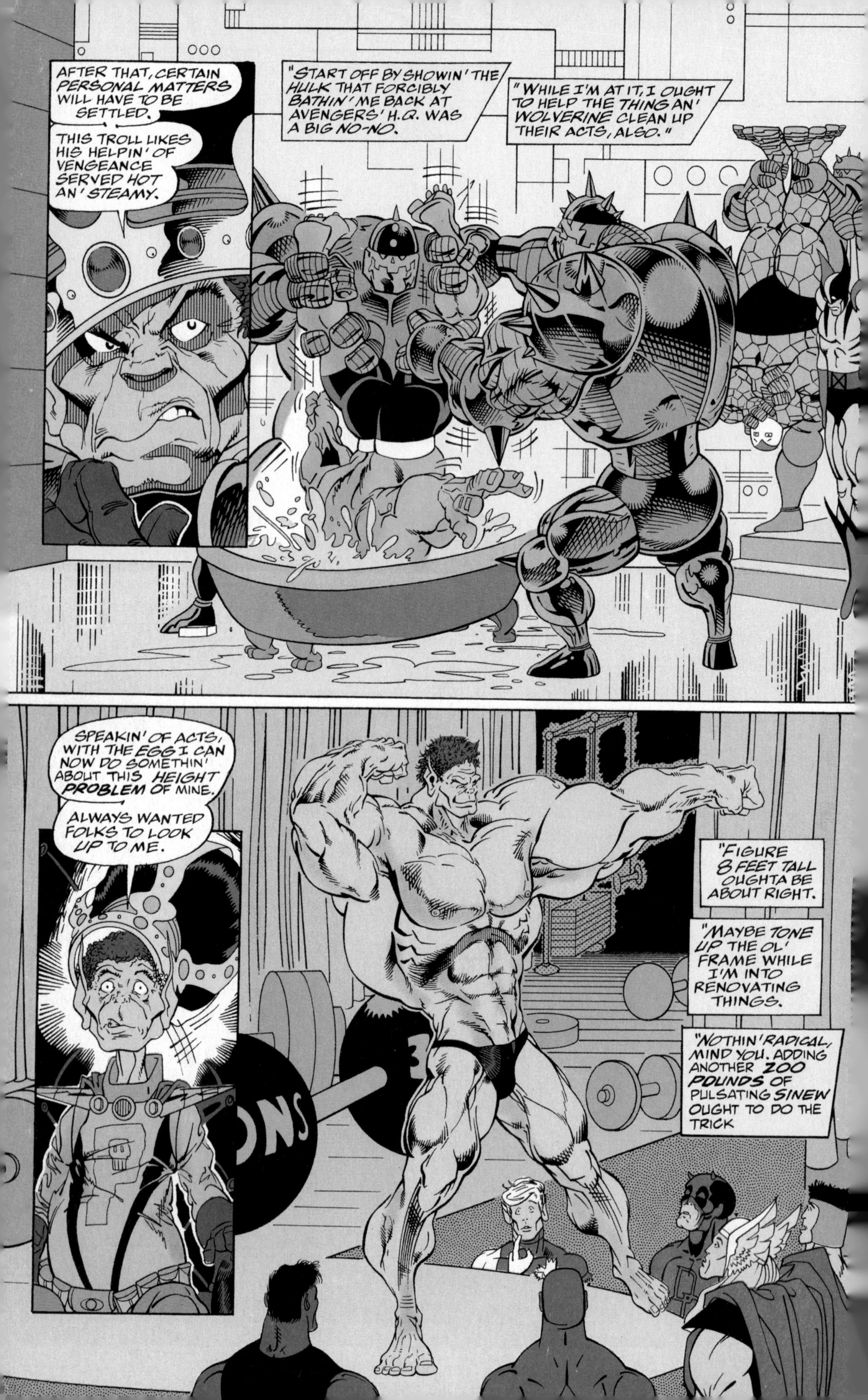
AFTER THAT, CERTAIN PERSONAL MATTERS WILL HAVE TO BE SETTLED.
THIS TROLL LIKES HIS HELPIN' OF VENGEANCE SERVED HOT AN' STEAMY.
"START OFF BY SHOWIN' THE HULK THAT FORCIBLY BATHIN' ME BACK AT AVENGERS' H.Q. WAS A BIG NO-NO.
"WHILE I'M AT IT, I OUGHT TO HELP THE THING AN' WOLVERINE CLEAN UP THEIR ACTS, ALSO."
SPEAKIN' OF ACTS, WITH THE EGG I CAN NOW DO SOMETHIN' ABOUT THIS HEIGHT PROBLEM OF MINE.
ALWAYS WANTED FOLKS TO LOOK UP TO ME.
"FIGURE 8 FEET TALL OUGHTA BE ABOUT RIGHT.
"MAYBE TONE UP THE OL' FRAME WHILE I'M INTO RENOVATING THINGS.
"NOTHIN' RADICAL, MIND YOU. ADDING ANOTHER 200 POUNDS OF PULSATING SINEW OUGHT TO DO THE TRICK

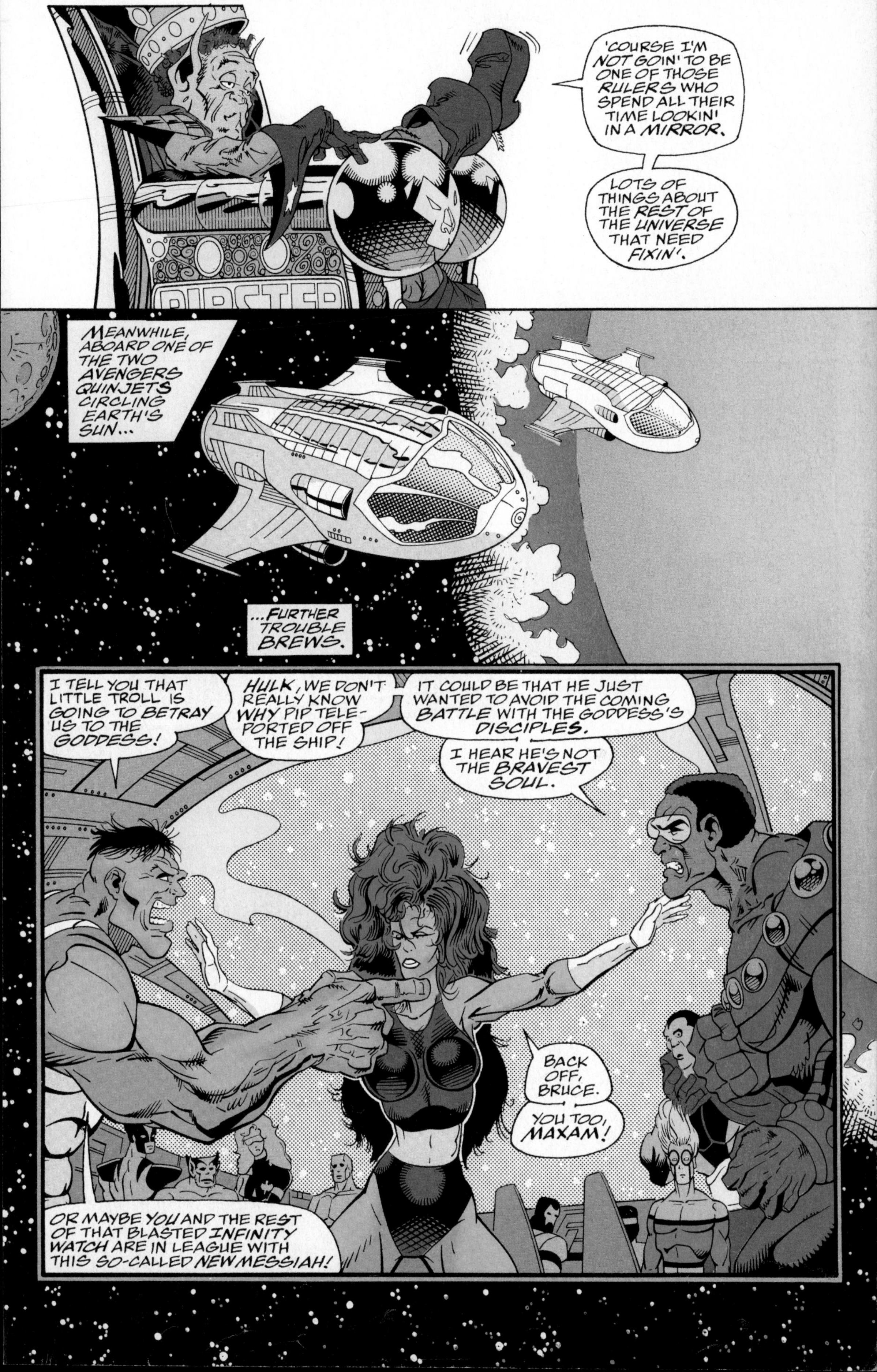
'COURSE I'M NOT GOIN' TO BE ONE OF THOSE RULERS WHO SPEND ALL THEIR TIME LOOKIN' IN A MIRROR.
LOTS OF THINGS ABOUT THE REST OF THE UNIVERSE THAT NEED FIXIN'.
MEANWHILE, ABOARD ONE OF THE TWO AVENGERS QUINJETS CIRCLING EARTH'S SUN...
...FURTHER TROUBLE BREWS.
I TELL YOU THAT LITTLE TROLL IS GOING TO BETRAY US TO THE GODDESS!
HULK, WE DON'T REALLY KNOW WHY PIP TELE-PORTED OFF THE SHIP!
IT COULD BE THAT HE JUST WANTED TO AVOID THE COMING BATTLE WITH THE GODDESS'S DISCIPLES.
I HEAR HE'S NOT THE BRAVEST SOUL.
BACK OFF, BRUCE.
YOU TOO, MAXAM!
OR MAYBE YOU AND THE REST OF THAT BLASTED INFINITY WATCH ARE IN LEAGUE WITH THIS SO-CALLED NEW MESSIAH!

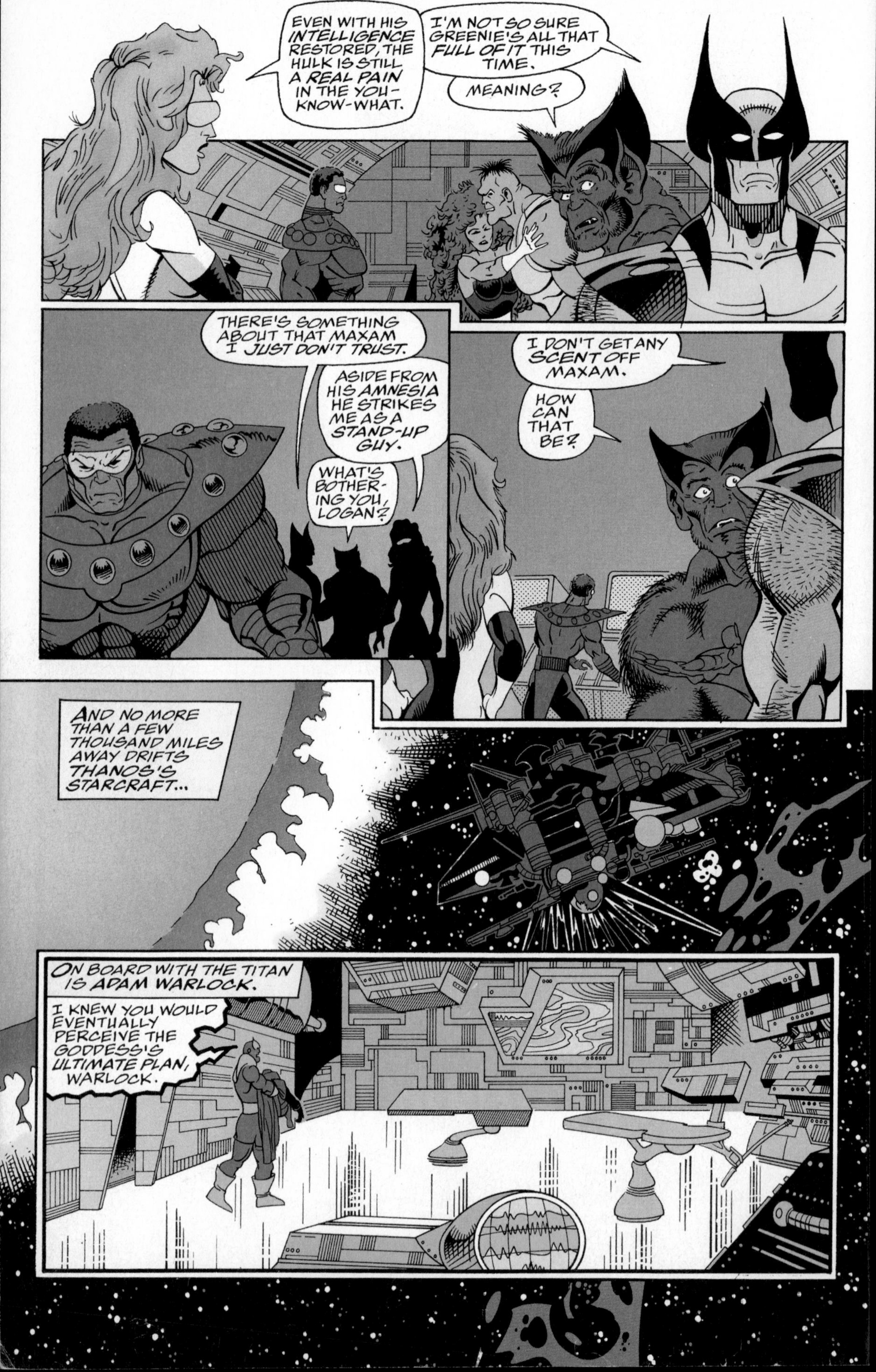

EVEN WITH HIS INTELLIGENCE RESTORED, THE HULK IS STILL A REAL PAIN IN THE YOU-KNOW-WHAT.
I'M NOT SO SURE GREENIE'S ALL THAT FULL OF IT THIS TIME.
MEANING?
THERE'S SOMETHING ABOUT THAT MAXAM I JUST DON'T TRUST.
ASIDE FROM HIS AMNESIA HE STRIKES ME AS A STAND-UP GUY.
WHAT'S BOTHERING YOU, LOGAN?
I DON'T GET ANY SCENT OFF MAXAM.
HOW CAN THAT BE?
AND NO MORE THAN A FEW THOUSAND MILES AWAY DRIFTS THANOS'S STARCRAFT...
ON BOARD WITH THE TITAN IS ADAM WARLOCK.
I KNEW YOU WOULD EVENTUALLY PERCEIVE THE GODDESS'S ULTIMATE PLAN, WARLOCK.

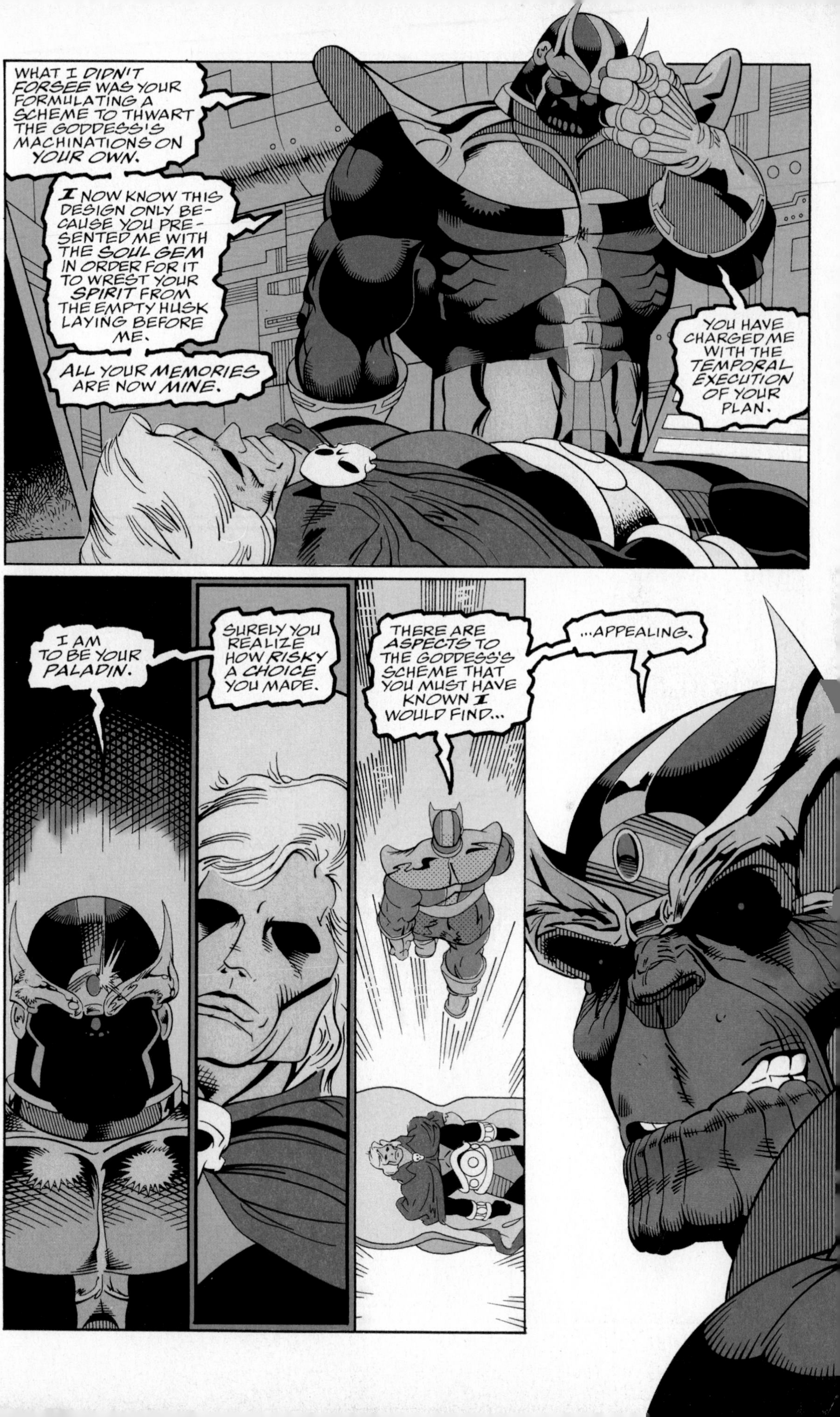
WHAT I DIDN'T FORSEE WAS YOUR FORMULATING A SCHEME TO THWART THE GODDESS'S MACHINATIONS ON YOUR OWN.
I NOW KNOW THIS DESIGN ONLY BE-CAUSE YOU PRE-SENTED ME WITH THE SOUL GEM IN ORDER FOR IT TO WREST YOUR SPIRIT FROM THE EMPTY HUSK LAYING BEFORE ME.
ALL YOUR MEMORIES ARE NOW MINE.
YOU HAVE CHARGED ME WITH THE TEMPORAL EXECUTION OF YOUR PLAN.
I AM TO BE YOUR PALADIN.
SURELY YOU REALIZE HOW RISKY A CHOICE YOU MADE.
THERE ARE ASPECTS TO THE GODDESS'S SCHEME THAT YOU MUST HAVE KNOWN I WOULD FIND...
...APPEALING.

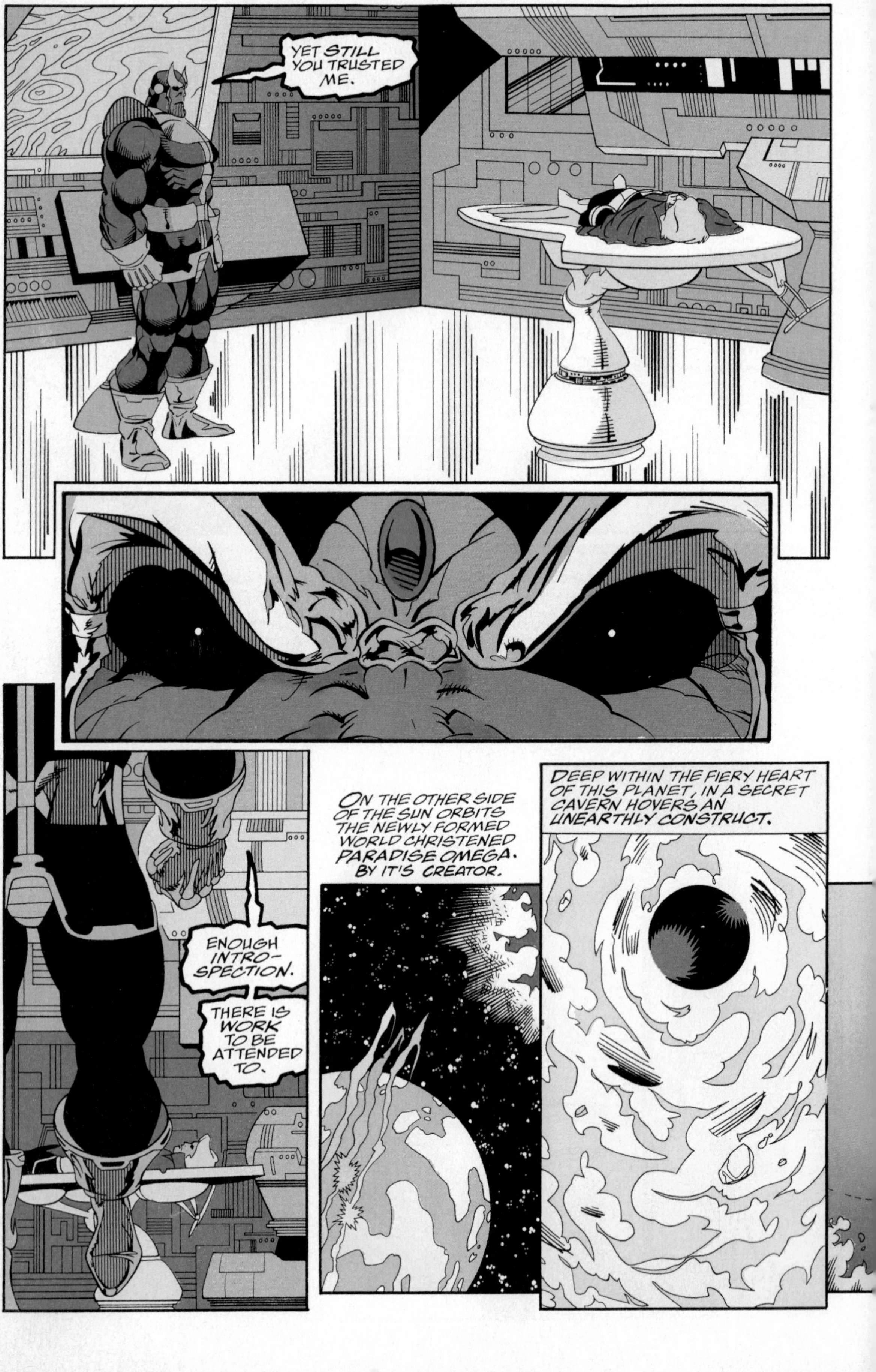
YET STILL YOU TRUSTED ME.
ENOUGH INTRO-SPECTION.
THERE IS WORK TO BE ATTENDED TO.
ON THE OTHER SIDE OF THE SUN ORBITS THE NEWLY FORMED WORLD CHRISTENED PARADISE OMEGA. BY IT'S CREATOR.
DEEP WITHIN THE FIERY HEART OF THIS PLANET, IN A SECRET CAVERN HOVERS AN UNEARTHLY CONSTRUCT.

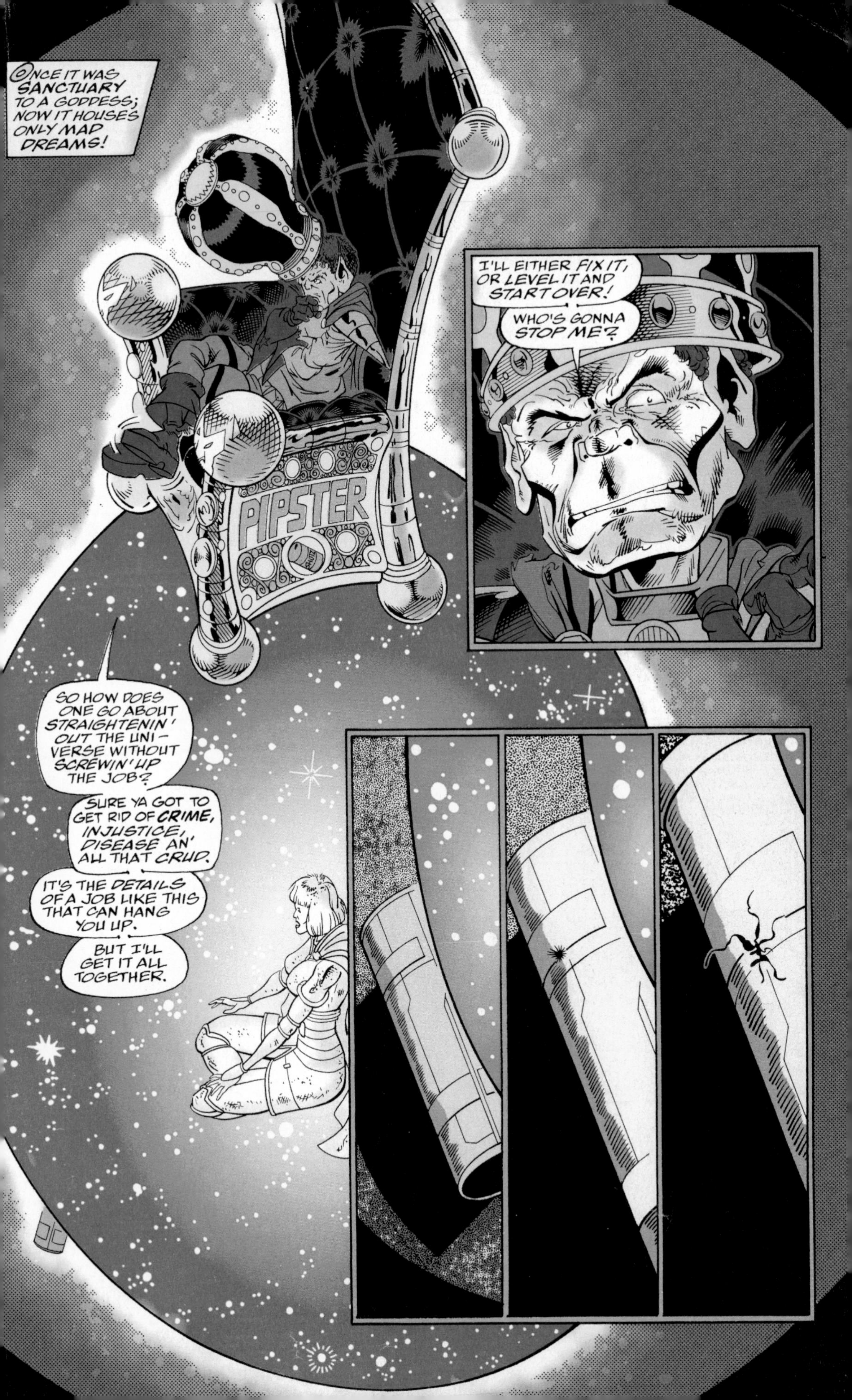

ONCE IT WAS SANCTUARY TO A GODDESS; NOW IT HOUSES ONLY MAD DREAMS!
PIPSTER
I'LL EITHER FIX IT, OR LEVEL IT AND START OVER!
WHO'S GONNA STOP ME?
SO HOW DOES ONE GO ABOUT STRAIGHTENIN' OUT THE UNI-VERSE WITHOUT SCREWIN' UP THE JOB?
SURE YA GOT TO GET RID OF CRIME, INJUSTICE, DISEASE AN' ALL THAT CRUD.
IT'S THE DETAILS OF A JOB LIKE THIS THAT CAN HANG YOU UP.
BUT I'LL GET IT ALL TOGETHER.

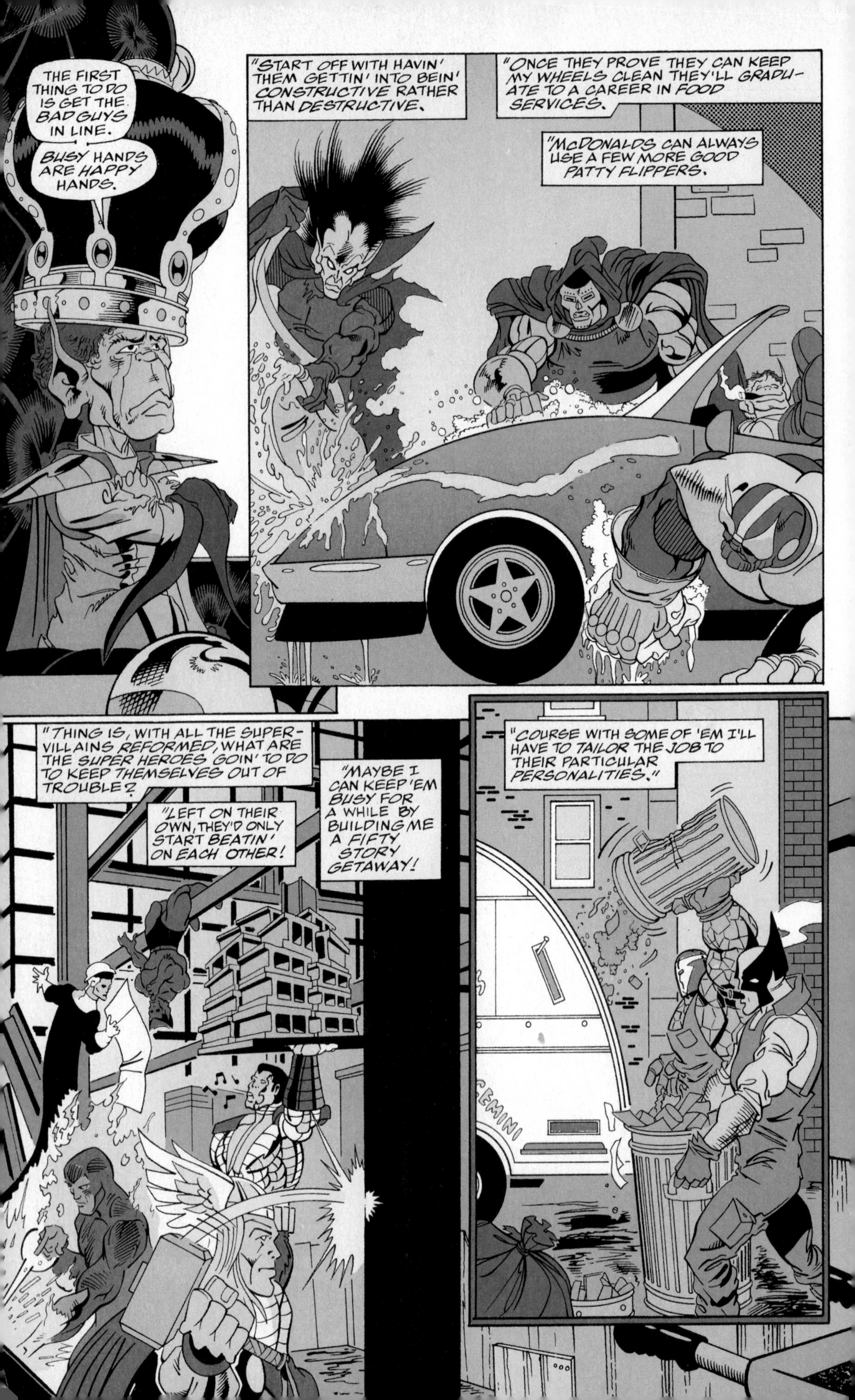

THE FIRST THING TO DO IS GET THE BAD GUYS IN LINE.
BUSY HANDS ARE HAPPY HANDS.
"START OFF WITH HAVIN' THEM GETTIN' INTO BEIN' CONSTRUCTIVE RATHER THAN DESTRUCTIVE.
"ONCE THEY PROVE THEY CAN KEEP MY WHEELS CLEAN THEY'LL GRADUATE TO A CAREER IN FOOD SERVICES.
"McDONALDS CAN ALWAYS USE A FEW MORE GOOD PATTY FLIPPERS.
"THING IS, WITH ALL THE SUPER-VILLAINS REFORMED, WHAT ARE THE SUPER HEROES GOIN' TO DO TO KEEP THEMSELVES OUT OF TROUBLE?
"LEFT ON THEIR OWN, THEY'D ONLY START BEATIN' ON EACH OTHER!
"MAYBE I CAN KEEP 'EM BUSY FOR A WHILE BY BUILDING ME A FIFTY STORY GETAWAY!
"COURSE WITH SOME OF 'EM I'LL HAVE TO TAILOR THE JOB TO THEIR PARTICULAR PERSONALITIES."
GEMINI

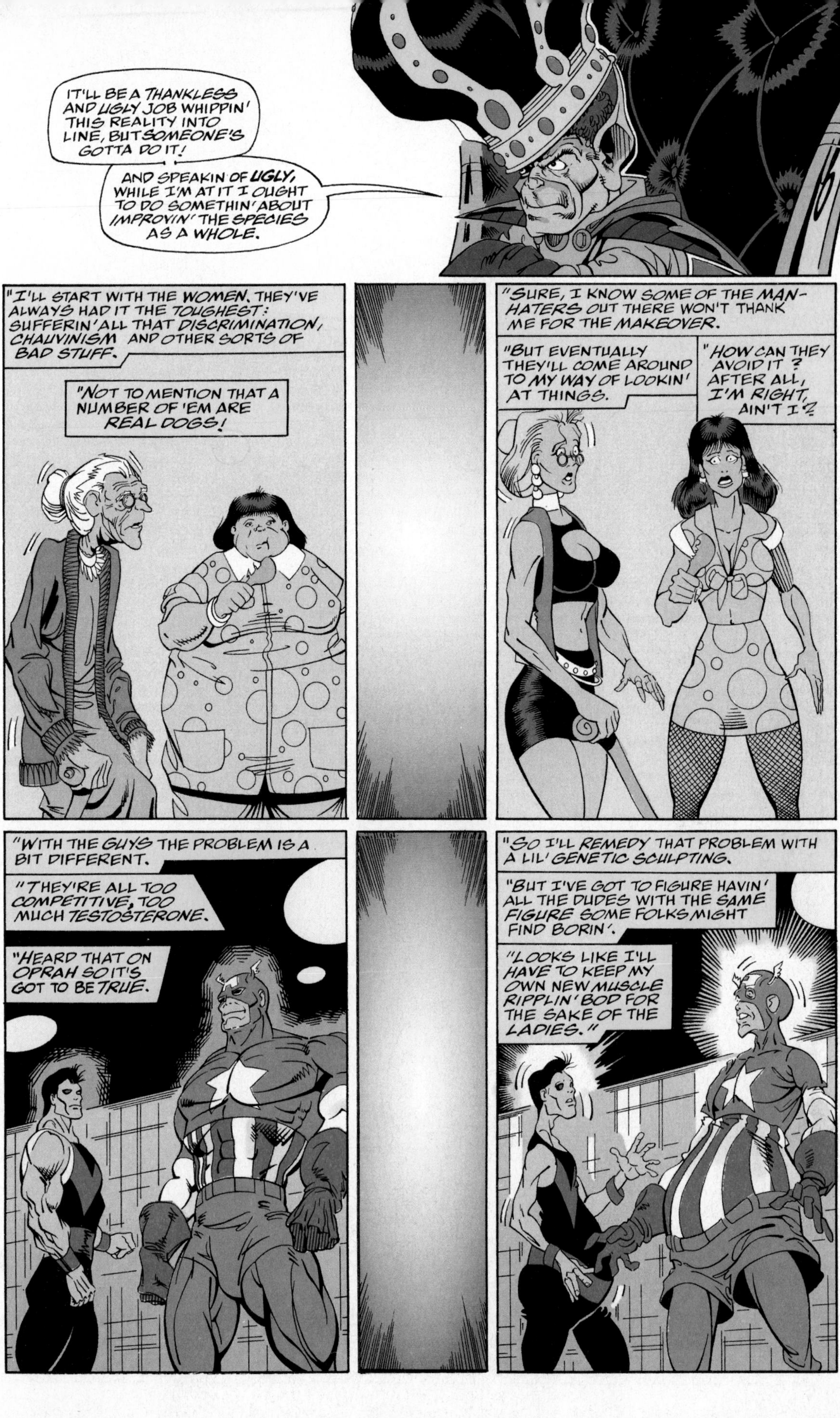
IT'LL BE A THANKLESS AND UGLY JOB WHIPPIN' THIS REALITY INTO LINE, BUT SOMEONE'S GOTTA DO IT!
AND SPEAKIN' OF UGLY, WHILE I'M AT IT I OUGHT TO DO SOMETHIN' ABOUT IMPROVIN' THE SPECIES AS A WHOLE.
"I'LL START WITH THE WOMEN. THEY'VE ALWAYS HAD IT THE TOUGHEST: SUFFERIN' ALL THAT DISCRIMINATION, CHAUVINISM AND OTHER SORTS OF BAD STUFF.
"NOT TO MENTION THAT A NUMBER OF 'EM ARE REAL DOGS!
"SURE, I KNOW SOME OF THE MAN-HATERS OUT THERE WON'T THANK ME FOR THE MAKEOVER.
"BUT EVENTUALLY THEY'LL COME AROUND TO MY WAY OF LOOKIN' AT THINGS.
"HOW CAN THEY AVOID IT? AFTER ALL, I'M RIGHT, AIN'T I?
"WITH THE GUYS THE PROBLEM IS A BIT DIFFERENT.
"THEY'RE ALL TOO COMPETITIVE, TOO MUCH TESTOSTERONE.
"HEARD THAT ON OPRAH SO IT'S GOT TO BE TRUE.
"SO I'LL REMEDY THAT PROBLEM WITH A LIL' GENETIC SCULPTING.
"BUT I'VE GOT TO FIGURE HAVIN' ALL THE DUDES WITH THE SAME FIGURE SOME FOLKS MIGHT FIND BORIN'.
"LOOKS LIKE I'LL HAVE TO KEEP MY OWN NEW MUSCLE RIPPLIN' BOD FOR THE SAKE OF THE LADIES."

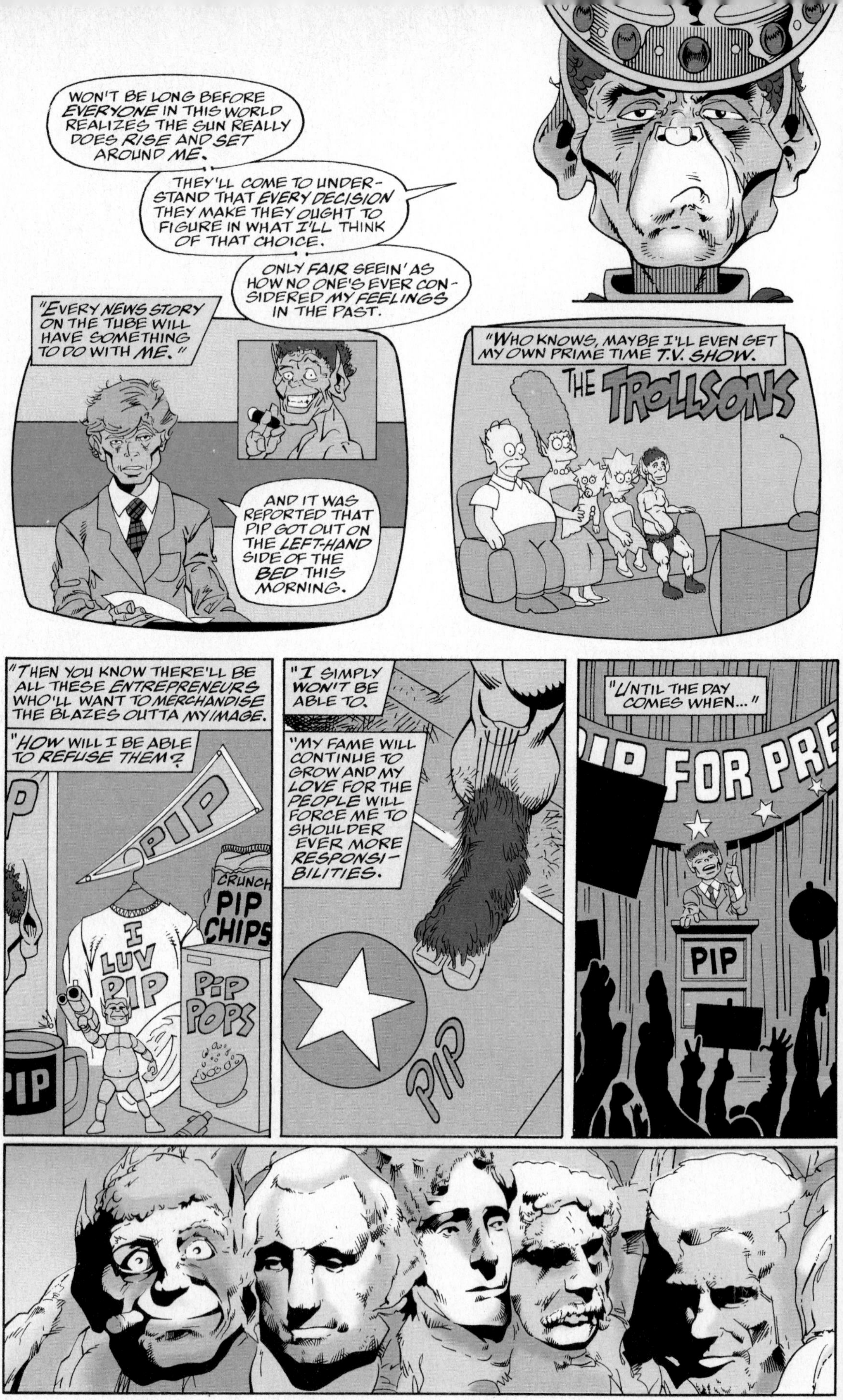

WON'T BE LONG BEFORE EVERYONE IN THIS WORLD REALIZES THE SUN REALLY DOES RISE AND SET AROUND ME.
THEY'LL COME TO UNDER-STAND THAT EVERY DECISION THEY MAKE THEY OUGHT TO FIGURE IN WHAT I'LL THINK OF THAT CHOICE.
ONLY FAIR SEEIN' AS HOW NO ONE'S EVER CON-SIDERED MY FEELINGS IN THE PAST.
"EVERY NEWS STORY ON THE TUBE WILL HAVE SOMETHING TO DO WITH ME."
AND IT WAS REPORTED THAT PIP GOT OUT ON THE LEFT-HAND SIDE OF THE BED THIS MORNING.
"WHO KNOWS, MAYBE I'LL EVEN GET MY OWN PRIME TIME T.V. SHOW.
THE TROLLSONS
"THEN YOU KNOW THERE'LL BE ALL THESE ENTREPRENEURS WHO'LL WANT TO MERCHANDISE THE BLAZES OUTTA MY IMAGE.
"HOW WILL I BE ABLE TO REFUSE THEM?
PIP
CRUNCH PIP CHIPS
I LUV PIP
PIP POPS
PIP
"I SIMPLY WON'T BE ABLE TO.
"MY FAME WILL CONTINUE TO GROW AND MY LOVE FOR THE PEOPLE WILL FORCE ME TO SHOULDER EVER MORE RESPONSI-BILITIES.
PIP
"UNTIL THE DAY COMES WHEN..."
FOR PRE
PIP

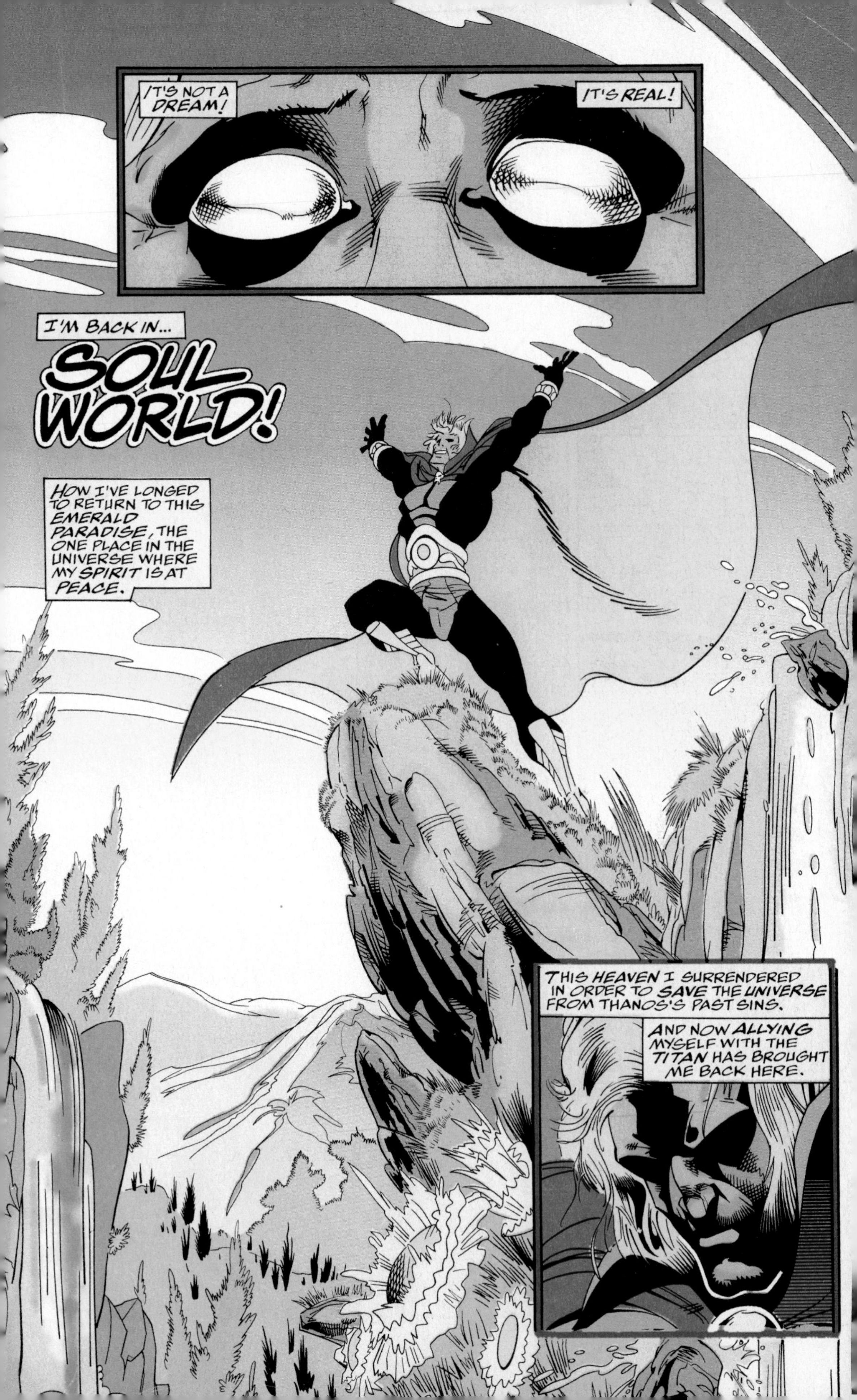
IT'S NOT A DREAM!
IT'S REAL!
I'M BACK IN...
SOUL WORLD!
HOW I'VE LONGED TO RETURN TO THIS EMERALD PARADISE, THE ONE PLACE IN THE UNIVERSE WHERE MY SPIRIT IS AT PEACE.
THIS HEAVEN I SURRENDERED IN ORDER TO SAVE THE UNIVERSE FROM THANOS'S PAST SINS.
AND NOW ALLYING MYSELF WITH THE TITAN HAS BROUGHT ME BACK HERE.

BUT NONE OF THAT IS OF ANY *REAL* IMPORT NOW, FOR THE MOMENT ITSELF IS ALL THAT MATTERS.

I'M *HOME* AND IT FEELS *GRAND!*

IF ONLY I *COULD* STAY....

ALL MY *DREAMS* ARE COMIN' TRUE AND THAT'S *THAT!*

FOR THE FIRST TIME EVER I'M GOING TO HAVE *CONTROL* OVER MY *OWN* LIFE!

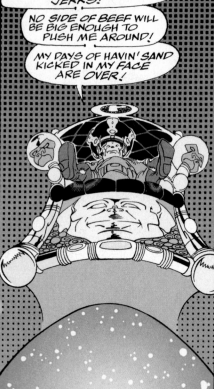

THERE'LL BE NO MORE BEIN' *PUT DOWN* BY LOUDMOUTHED *JERKS!*

NO SIDE OF BEEF WILL BE BIG ENOUGH TO PUSH ME AROUND!

MY DAYS OF HAVIN' SAND KICKED IN MY FACE ARE *OVER!*

'CAUSE NOW *I* GOT THE *POWER* AND I KNOW HOW TA *USE* IT!

NATURALLY, THERE WILL BE THOSE WHO'LL *ENVY* MY MIGHT.

IT'S *TRUE!*

EVEN *PARANOIDS* HAVE *ENEMIES!*

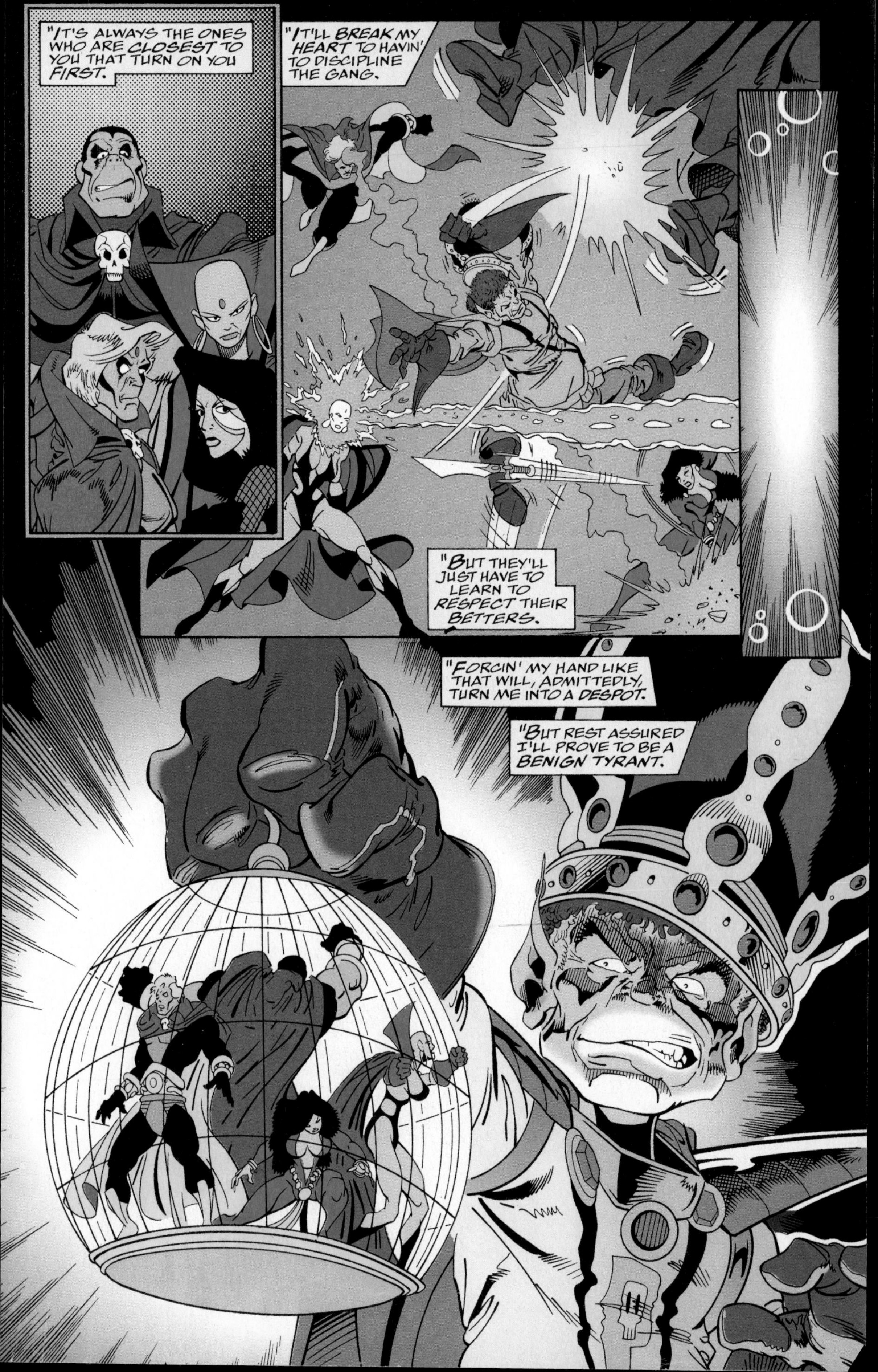
"IT'S ALWAYS THE ONES WHO ARE CLOSEST TO YOU THAT TURN ON YOU FIRST.
"IT'LL BREAK MY HEART TO HAVIN' TO DISCIPLINE THE GANG.
"BUT THEY'LL JUST HAVE TO LEARN TO RESPECT THEIR BETTERS.
"FORCIN' MY HAND LIKE THAT WILL, ADMITTEDLY, TURN ME INTO A DESPOT.
"BUT REST ASSURED I'LL PROVE TO BE A BENIGN TYRANT.

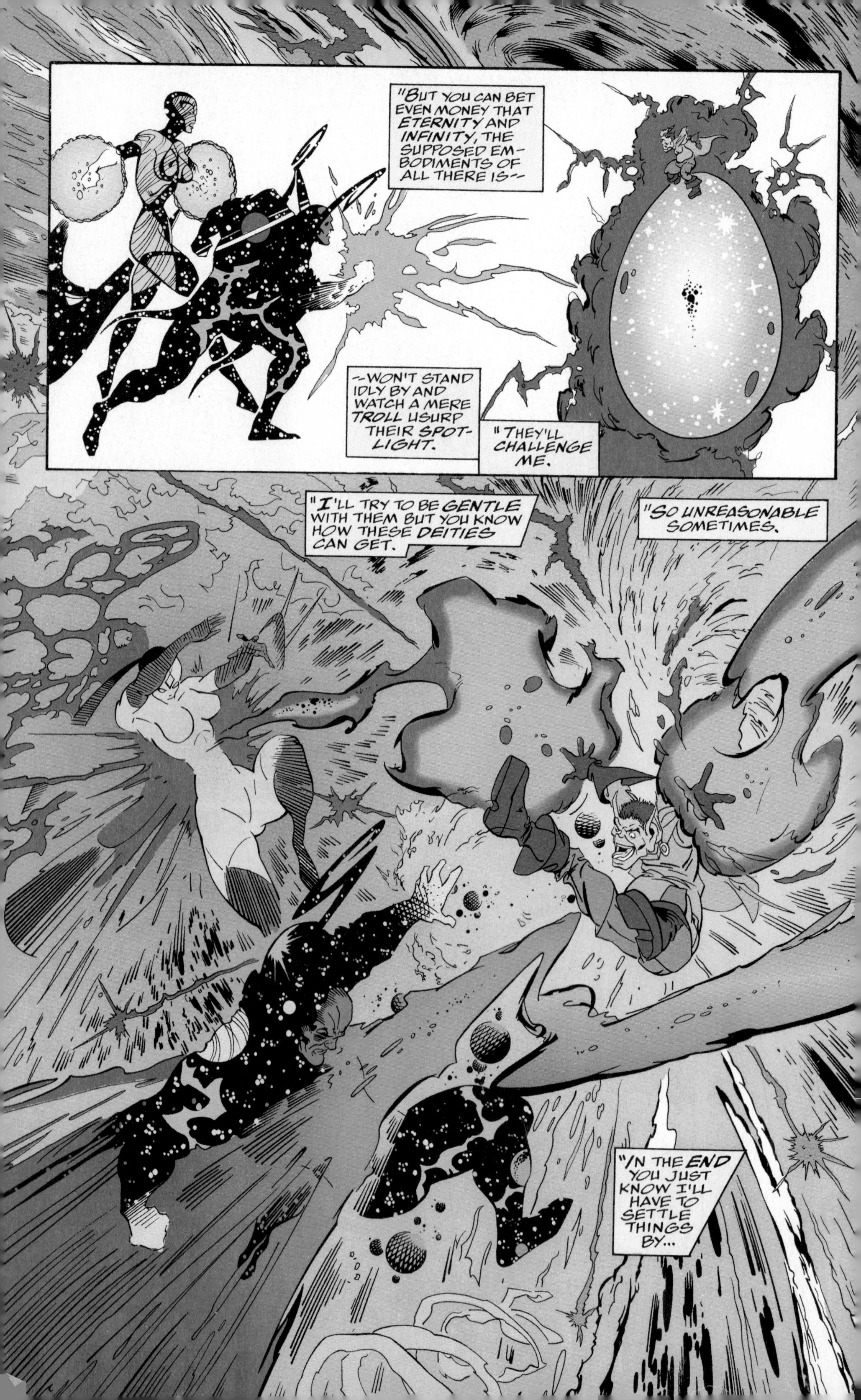
"BUT YOU CAN BET EVEN MONEY THAT ETERNITY AND INFINITY, THE SUPPOSED EM-BODIMENTS OF ALL THERE IS--
--WON'T STAND IDLY BY AND WATCH A MERE TROLL USURP THEIR SPOT-LIGHT.
"THEY'LL CHALLENGE ME.
"I'LL TRY TO BE GENTLE WITH THEM BUT YOU KNOW HOW THESE DEITIES CAN GET.
"SO UNREASONABLE SOMETIMES.
"IN THE END YOU JUST KNOW I'LL HAVE TO SETTLE THINGS BY...

...BECOMING **PIP** THE

GOD!

"BUT IS THAT *REALLY* WHAT I WANT?"

NAW!

AS GOD I'D HAVE TO PAY ATTENTION TO STUFF LIKE *GRASS GROWIN'!*

ALWAYS HATED *MINUTIAE.*

TRUTH IS THIS TROLL DON'T REALLY WANT NO MAJOR OVER-HAULING OF HIS LIFE!

ALL I REALLY NEED TO DO IS *TINKER* A BIT WITH MY PRESENT REALITY.

MAKE IT A TOUCH MORE *COMFY,* MORE PALAT-ABLE.

NO NEED OR HANKER TO BE KING, GOD OR ANYTHIN' FANCY.

ALL I EVER *REALLY* WANTED WAS TO BE LIKED.

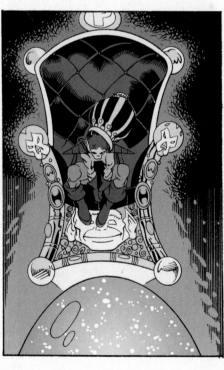

THAT'S IT!

NOW I KNOW WHAT I WANT OUT OF THIS *DEAL!*

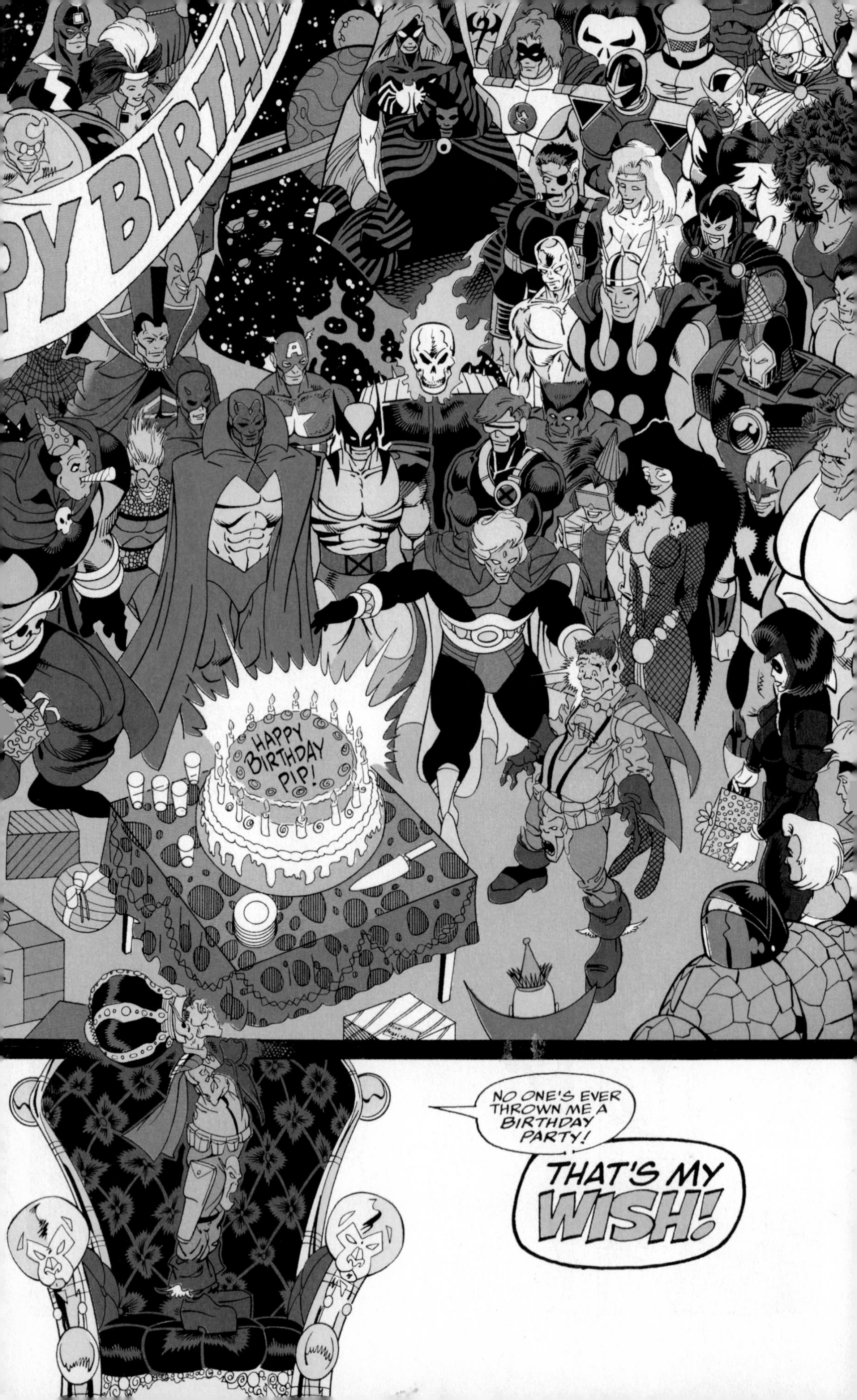
HAPPY BIRTHDAY PIP!
NO ONE'S EVER THROWN ME A BIRTHDAY PARTY!
THAT'S MY WISH!

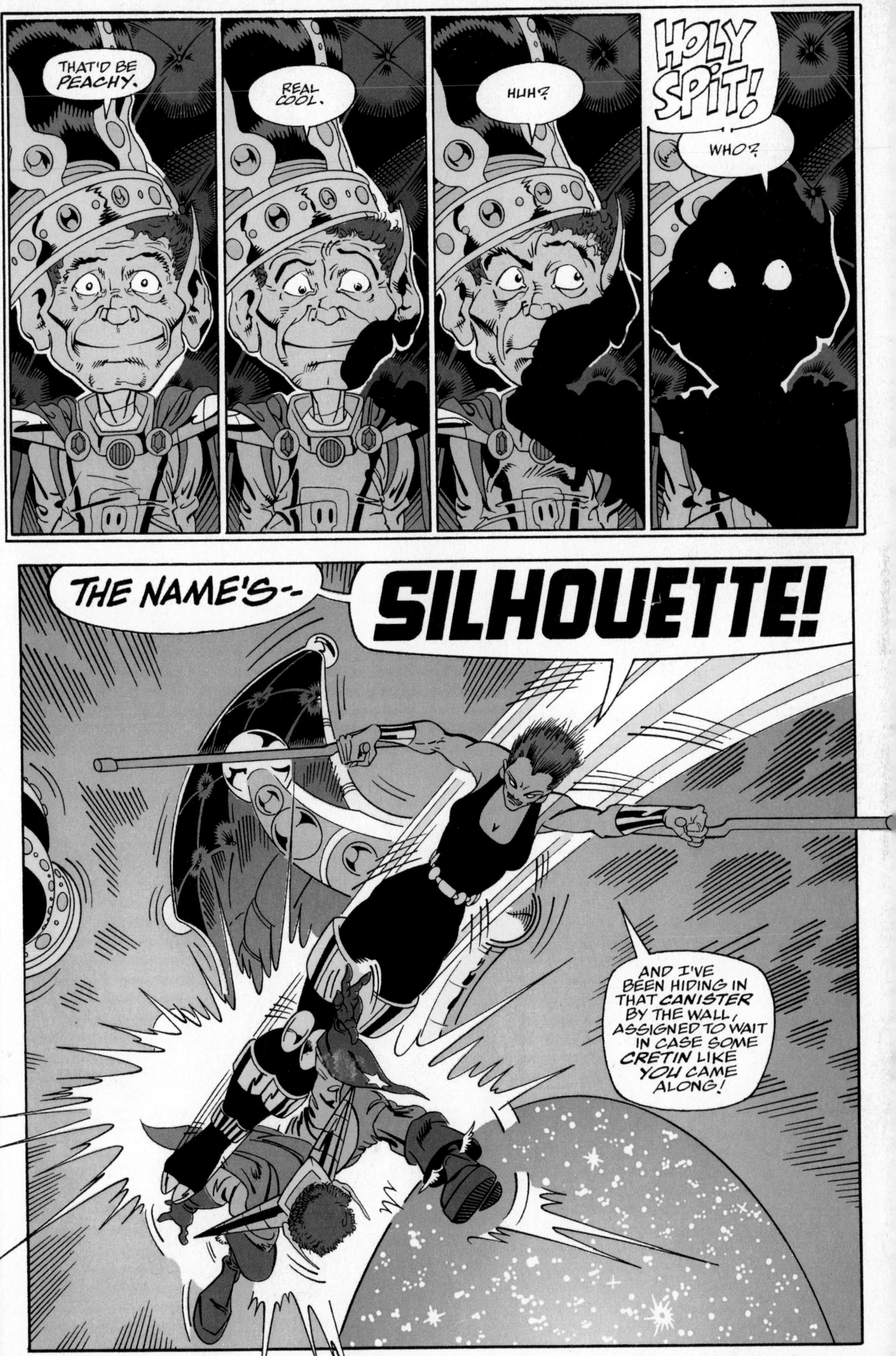
THAT'D BE PEACHY.
REAL COOL.
HUH?
HOLY SPIT!
WHO?
THE NAME'S--
SILHOUETTE!
AND I'VE BEEN HIDING IN THAT CANISTER BY THE WALL, ASSIGNED TO WAIT IN CASE SOME CRETIN LIKE YOU CAME ALONG!

I WOULD HAVE *DISPATCHED* YOU LONG AGO, BUT I COULDN'T *BELIEVE* ALL THE *NONSENSE* YOU KEPT *BABBLING* ON ABOUT.

YOU ARE ONE *TWISTED* INDIVIDUAL, MR. PIP.

THE *UNIVERSE* WILL BE A *BETTER* PLACE WITHOUT YOU.

LET MY *GODDESS* BE AS SHE *WAS.*

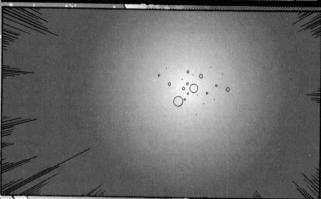

MISTRESS?

I THANK YOU, MY CHILD. THAT WAS INDEED A *NARROW* ESCAPE.

NOTHING FURTHER MUST BE ALLOWED TO IMPEDE OUR *SACRED LABORS.*

LET THE UNIVERSE KNOW THAT IT STANDS ON THE EDGE OF...
...EPIPHANY!
THE COSMIC MYSTERY OF THE GODDESS CONTINUES TO UNFOLD NEXT WEEK IN THE INFINITY CRUSADE #4! THEN THE FOLLOWING WEEK DISCOVER FURTHER ASTRAL SECRETS IN THE WARLOCK CHRONICLES #4! AND THEN RETURN TO THE PAGES OF WARLOCK AND THE INFINITY WATCH #21 TWO WEEKS LATER FOR--
DRAX
VERSUS
THOR

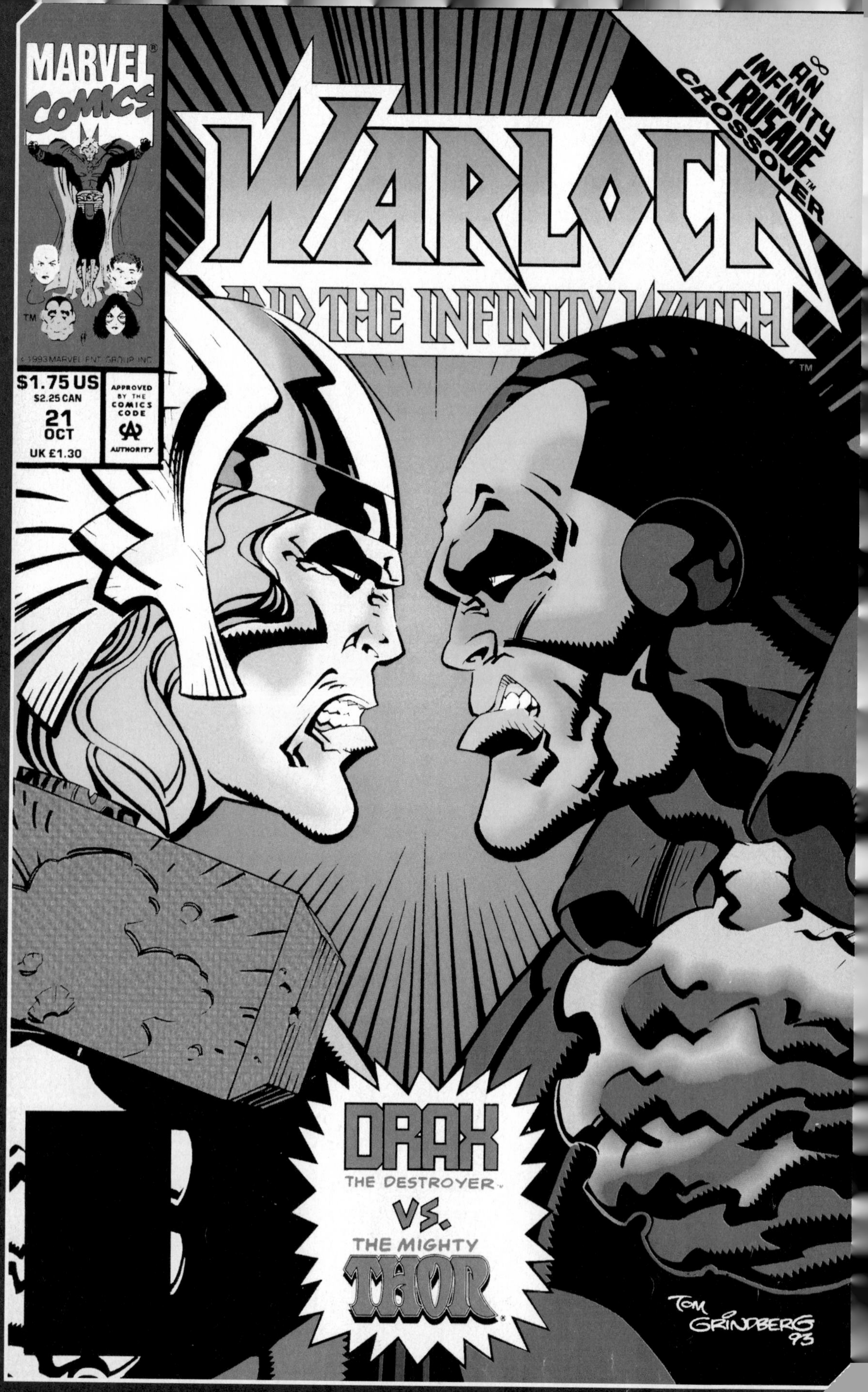

MARVEL COMICS
AN INFINITY CRUSADE CROSSOVER
WARLOCK AND THE INFINITY WATCH
© 1993 MARVEL ENT. GROUP, INC.
$1.75 US
$2.25 CAN
21
OCT
UK £1.30
APPROVED BY THE COMICS CODE AUTHORITY
DRAX THE DESTROYER
VS.
THE MIGHTY THOR
TOM GRINDBERG '93

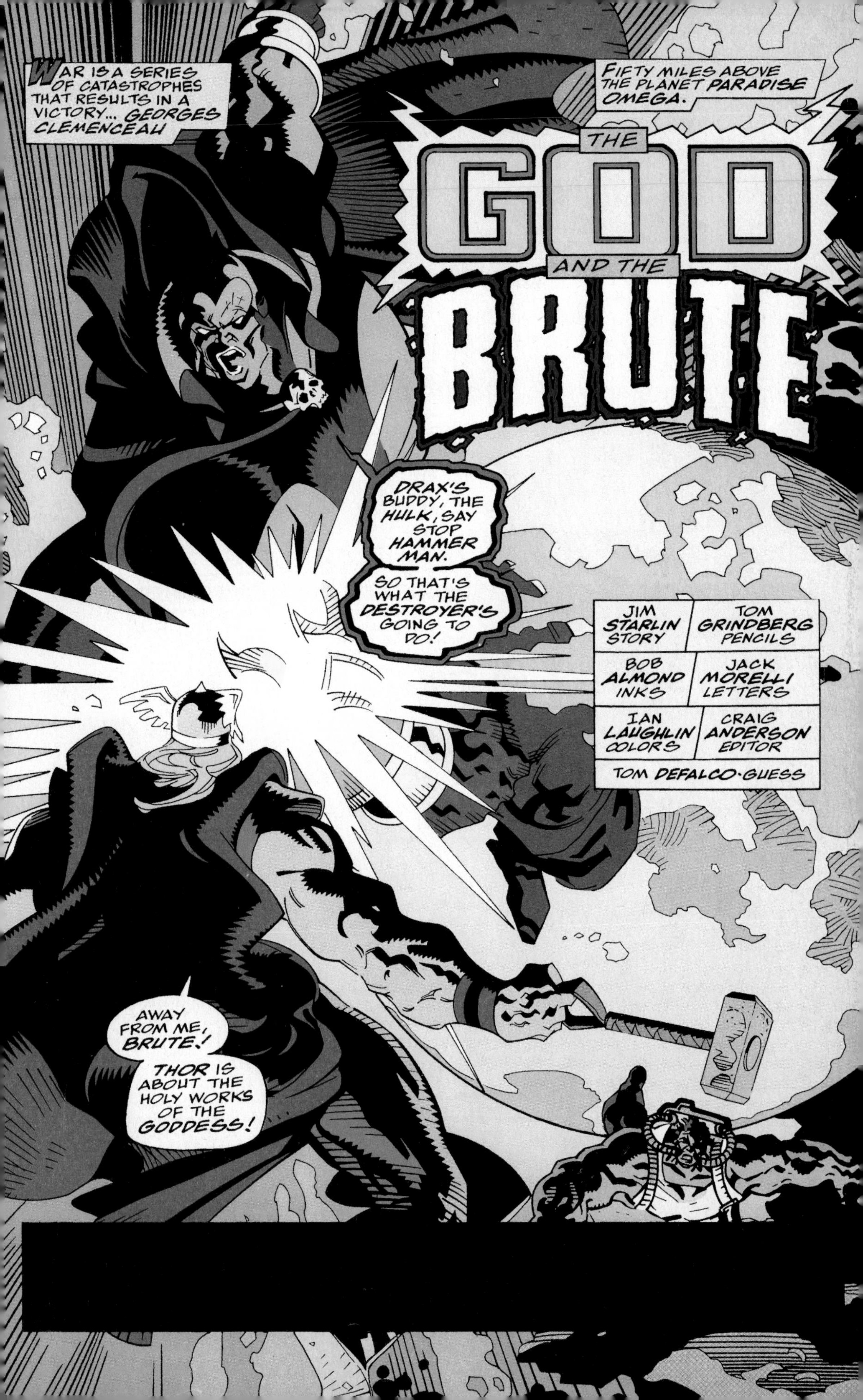

WAR IS A SERIES OF CATASTROPHES THAT RESULTS IN A VICTORY... GEORGES CLEMENCEAU
FIFTY MILES ABOVE THE PLANET PARADISE OMEGA.
THE GOD AND THE BRUTE
DRAX'S BUDDY, THE HULK, SAY STOP HAMMER MAN.
SO THAT'S WHAT THE DESTROYER'S GOING TO DO!
JIM STARLIN STORY
TOM GRINDBERG PENCILS
BOB ALMOND INKS
JACK MORELLI LETTERS
IAN LAUGHLIN COLORS
CRAIG ANDERSON EDITOR
TOM DEFALCO-GUESS
AWAY FROM ME, BRUTE!
THOR IS ABOUT THE HOLY WORKS OF THE GODDESS!

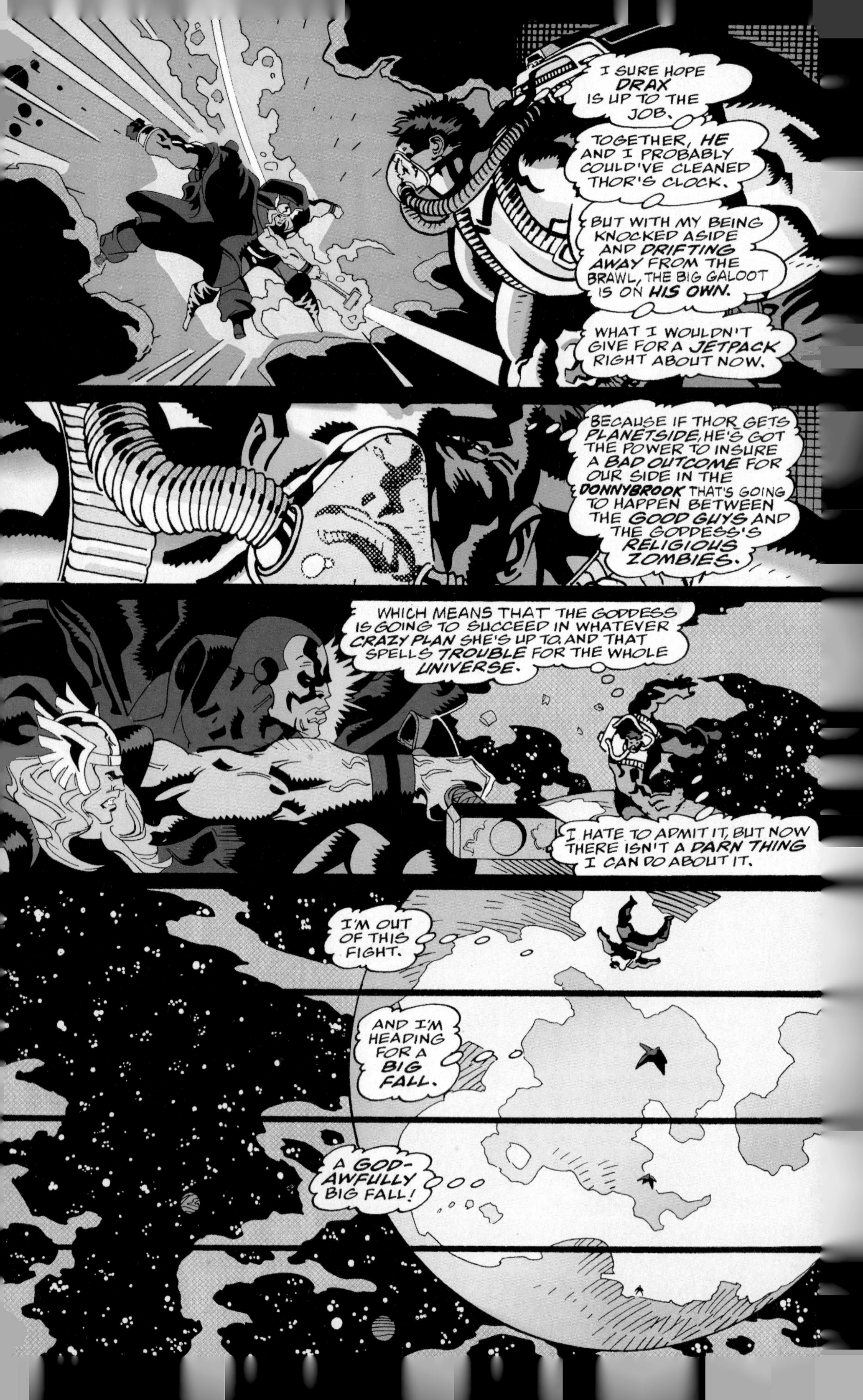

I SURE HOPE DRAX IS UP TO THE JOB.
TOGETHER, HE AND I PROBABLY COULD'VE CLEANED THOR'S CLOCK.
BUT WITH MY BEING KNOCKED ASIDE AND DRIFTING AWAY FROM THE BRAWL, THE BIG GALOOT IS ON HIS OWN.
WHAT I WOULDN'T GIVE FOR A JETPACK RIGHT ABOUT NOW.
BECAUSE IF THOR GETS PLANETSIDE, HE'S GOT THE POWER TO INSURE A BAD OUTCOME FOR OUR SIDE IN THE DONNYBROOK THAT'S GOING TO HAPPEN BETWEEN THE GOOD GUYS AND THE GODDESS'S RELIGIOUS ZOMBIES.
WHICH MEANS THAT THE GODDESS IS GOING TO SUCCEED IN WHATEVER CRAZY PLAN SHE'S UP TO, AND THAT SPELLS TROUBLE FOR THE WHOLE UNIVERSE.
I HATE TO ADMIT IT, BUT NOW THERE ISN'T A DARN THING I CAN DO ABOUT IT.
I'M OUT OF THIS FIGHT.
AND I'M HEADING FOR A BIG FALL.
A GOD-AWFULLY BIG FALL!

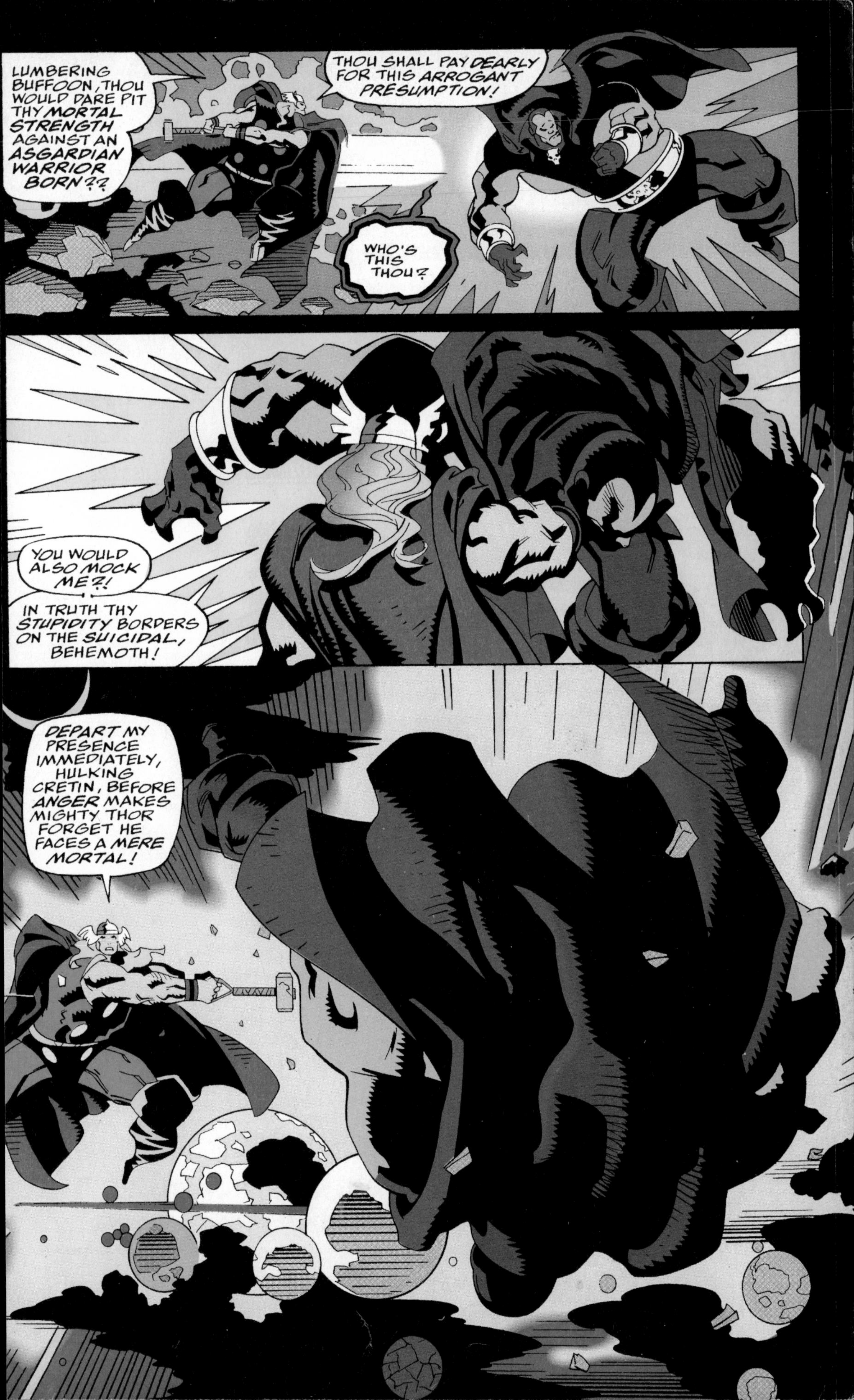
LUMBERING BUFFOON, THOU WOULD DARE PIT THY MORTAL STRENGTH AGAINST AN ASGARDIAN WARRIOR BORN??
THOU SHALL PAY DEARLY FOR THIS ARROGANT PRESUMPTION!
WHO'S THIS THOU?
YOU WOULD ALSO MOCK ME?!
IN TRUTH THY STUPIDITY BORDERS ON THE SUICIDAL, BEHEMOTH!
DEPART MY PRESENCE IMMEDIATELY, HULKING CRETIN, BEFORE ANGER MAKES MIGHTY THOR FORGET HE FACES A MERE MORTAL!

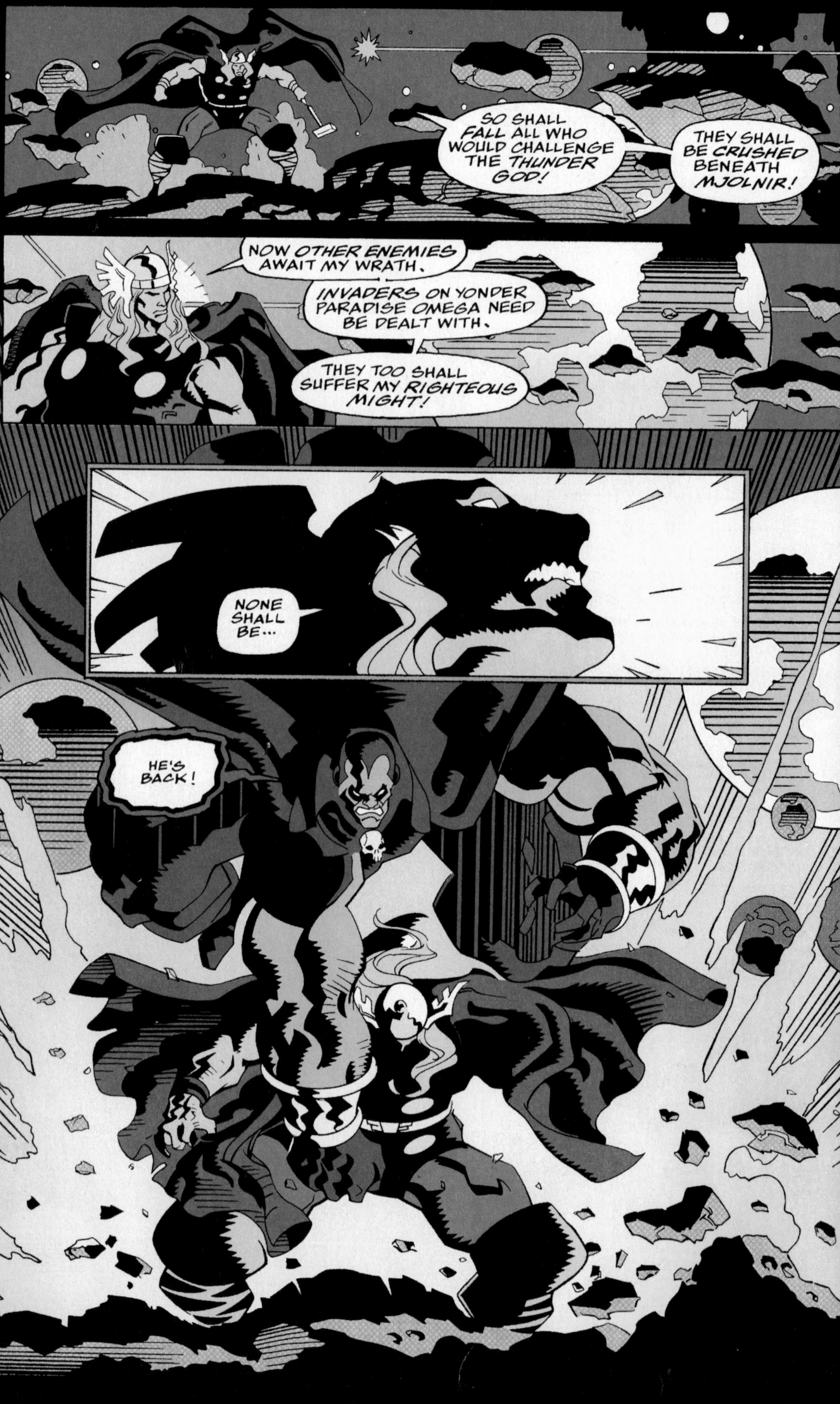
SO SHALL FALL ALL WHO WOULD CHALLENGE THE THUNDER GOD!
THEY SHALL BE CRUSHED BENEATH MJOLNIR!
NOW OTHER ENEMIES AWAIT MY WRATH.
INVADERS ON YONDER PARADISE OMEGA NEED BE DEALT WITH.
THEY TOO SHALL SUFFER MY RIGHTEOUS MIGHT!
NONE SHALL BE...
HE'S BACK!

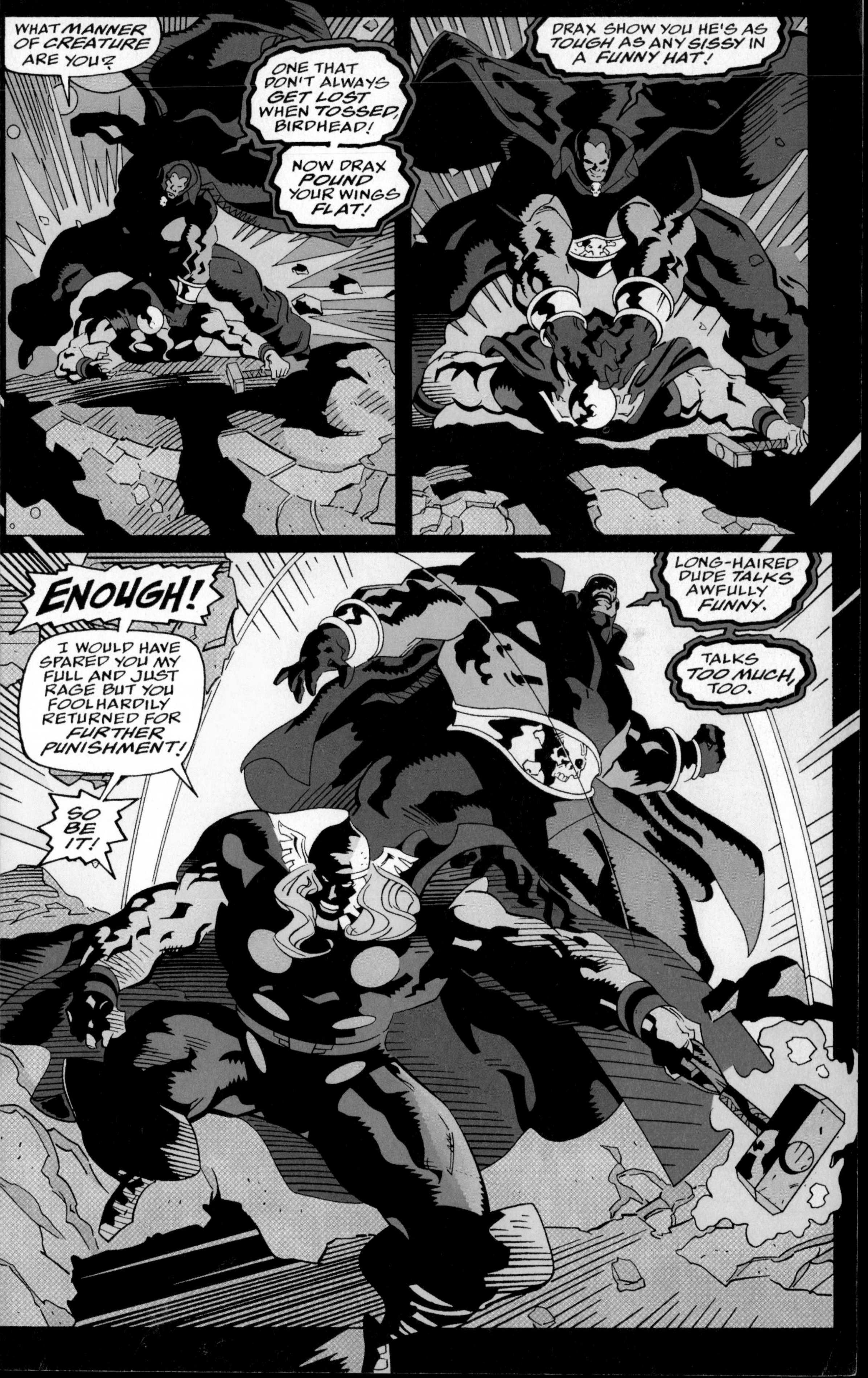
WHAT MANNER OF CREATURE ARE YOU?
ONE THAT DON'T ALWAYS GET LOST WHEN TOSSED, BIRDHEAD!
NOW DRAX POUND YOUR WINGS FLAT!
DRAX SHOW YOU HE'S AS TOUGH AS ANY SISSY IN A FUNNY HAT!
ENOUGH!
I WOULD HAVE SPARED YOU MY FULL AND JUST RAGE BUT YOU FOOLHARDILY RETURNED FOR FURTHER PUNISHMENT!
SO BE IT!
LONG-HAIRED DUDE TALKS AWFULLY FUNNY.
TALKS TOO MUCH, TOO.

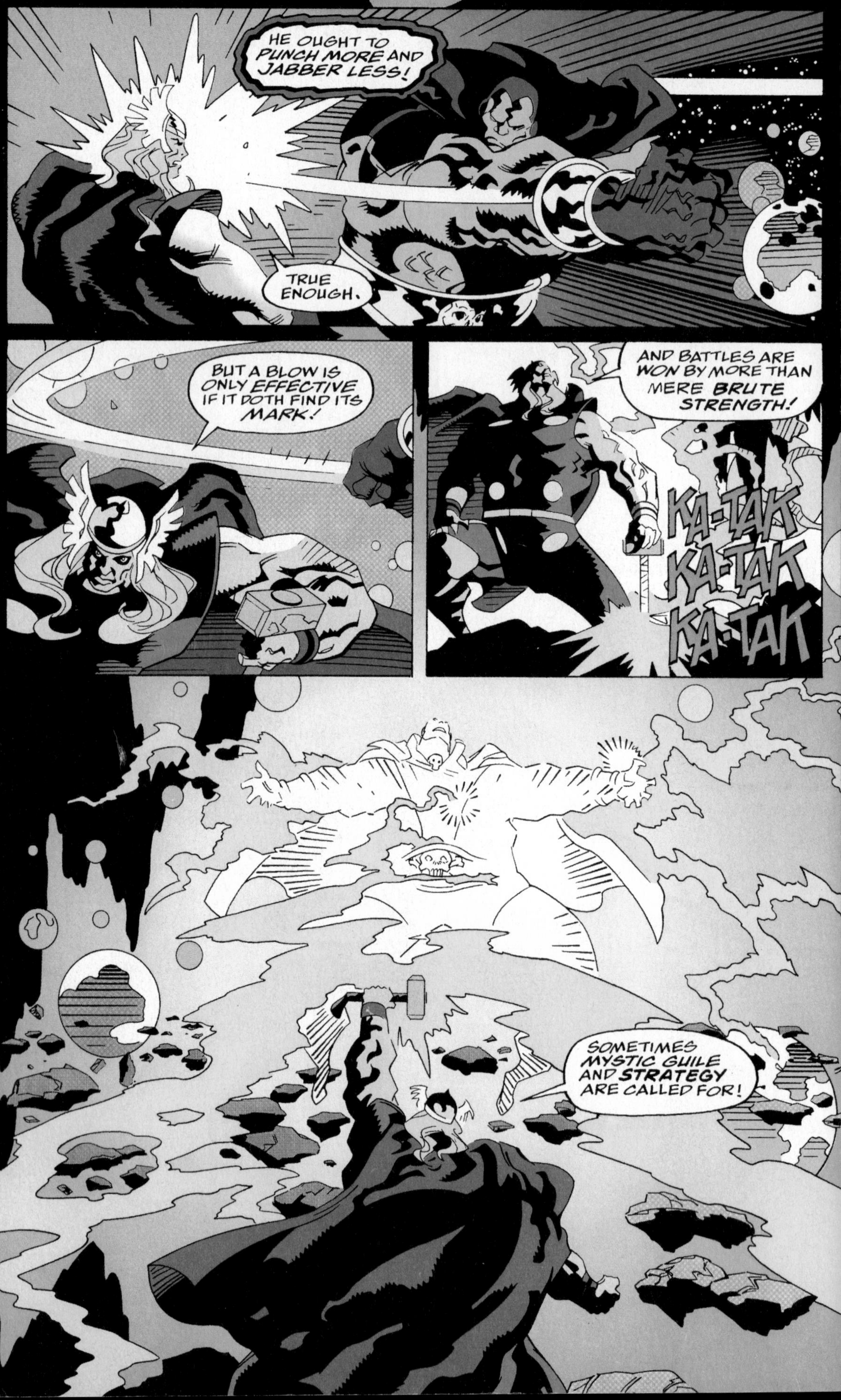

HE OUGHT TO PUNCH MORE AND JABBER LESS!
TRUE ENOUGH.
BUT A BLOW IS ONLY EFFECTIVE IF IT DOTH FIND ITS MARK!
AND BATTLES ARE WON BY MORE THAN MERE BRUTE STRENGTH!
KA-TAK
KA-TAK
KA-TAK
SOMETIMES MYSTIC GUILE AND STRATEGY ARE CALLED FOR!

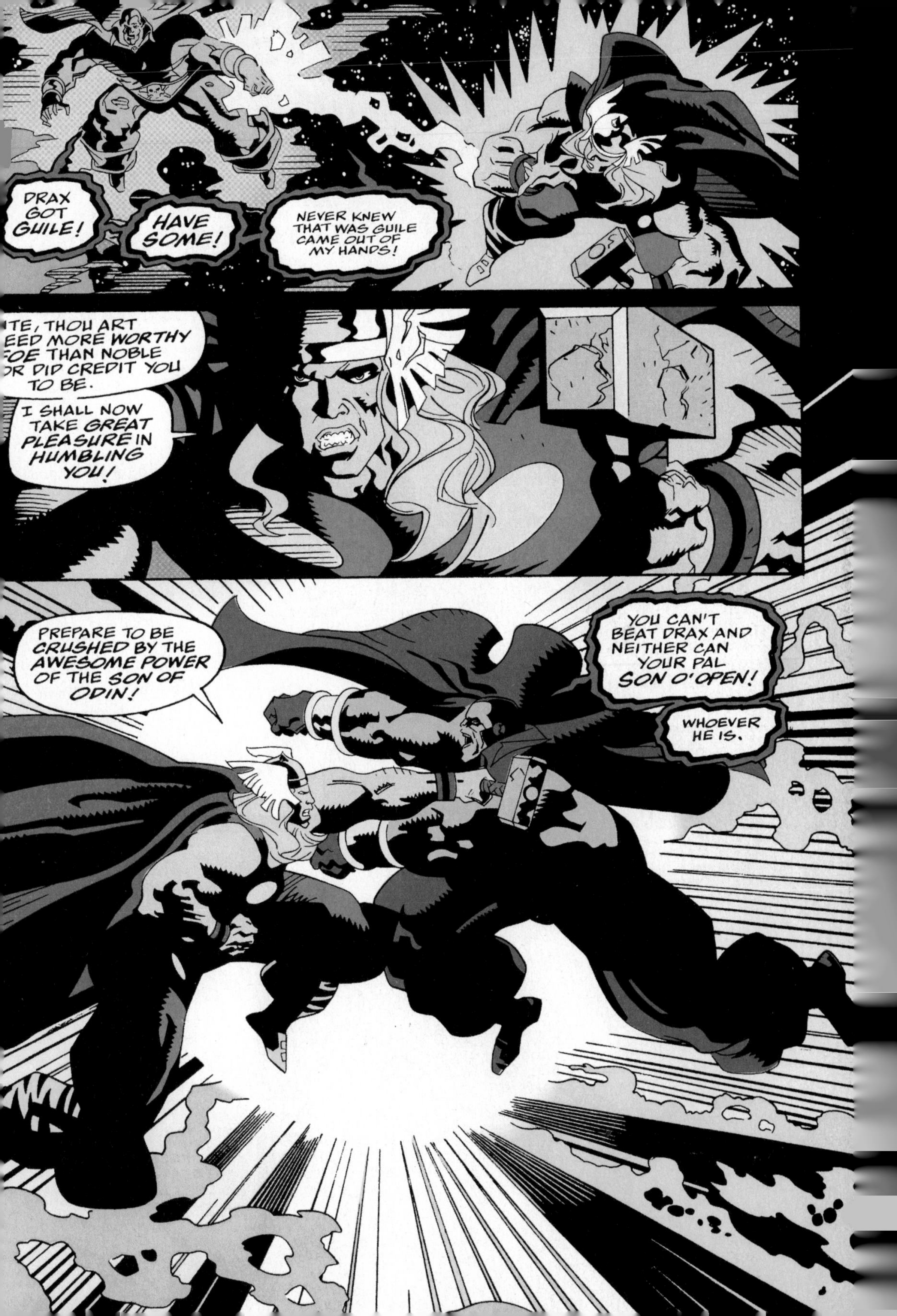

DRAX GOT GUILE!
HAVE SOME!
NEVER KNEW THAT WAS GUILE CAME OUT OF MY HANDS!
TE, THOU ART
EED MORE WORTHY
FOE THAN NOBLE
OR DID CREDIT YOU
TO BE.
I SHALL NOW TAKE GREAT PLEASURE IN HUMBLING YOU!
PREPARE TO BE CRUSHED BY THE AWESOME POWER OF THE SON OF ODIN!
YOU CAN'T BEAT DRAX AND NEITHER CAN YOUR PAL SON O'OPEN!
WHOEVER HE IS.

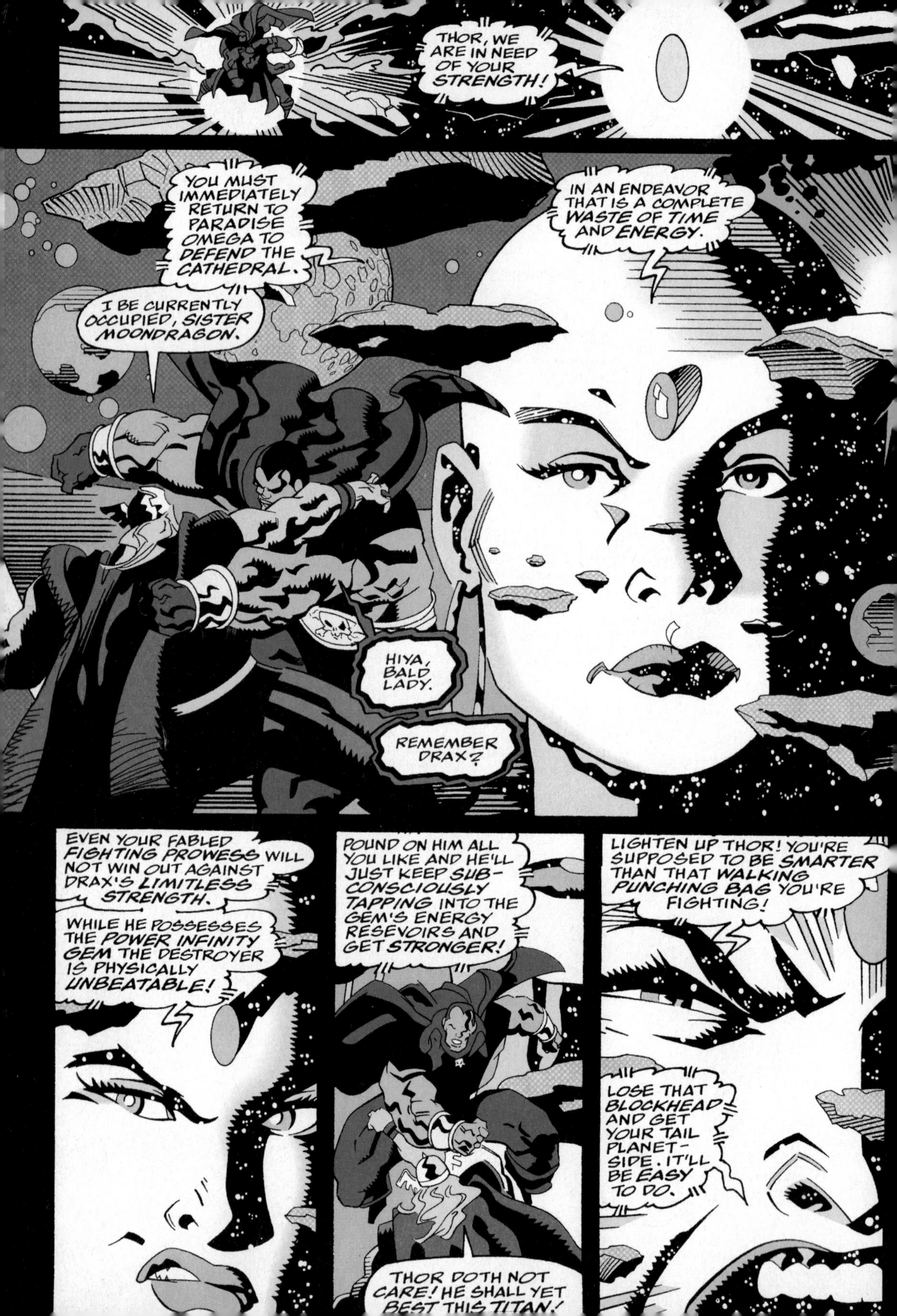

THOR, WE ARE IN NEED OF YOUR STRENGTH!
YOU MUST IMMEDIATELY RETURN TO PARADISE OMEGA TO DEFEND THE CATHEDRAL.
IN AN ENDEAVOR THAT IS A COMPLETE WASTE OF TIME AND ENERGY.
I BE CURRENTLY OCCUPIED, SISTER MOONDRAGON.
HIYA, BALD LADY.
REMEMBER DRAX?
EVEN YOUR FABLED FIGHTING PROWESS WILL NOT WIN OUT AGAINST DRAX'S LIMITLESS STRENGTH.
WHILE HE POSSESSES THE POWER INFINITY GEM THE DESTROYER IS PHYSICALLY UNBEATABLE!
POUND ON HIM ALL YOU LIKE AND HE'LL JUST KEEP SUB-CONSCIOUSLY TAPPING INTO THE GEM'S ENERGY RESEVOIRS AND GET STRONGER!
THOR DOTH NOT CARE! HE SHALL YET BEST THIS TITAN!
LIGHTEN UP THOR! YOU'RE SUPPOSED TO BE SMARTER THAN THAT WALKING PUNCHING BAG YOU'RE FIGHTING!
LOSE THAT BLOCKHEAD AND GET YOUR TAIL PLANET-SIDE. IT'LL BE EASY TO DO.

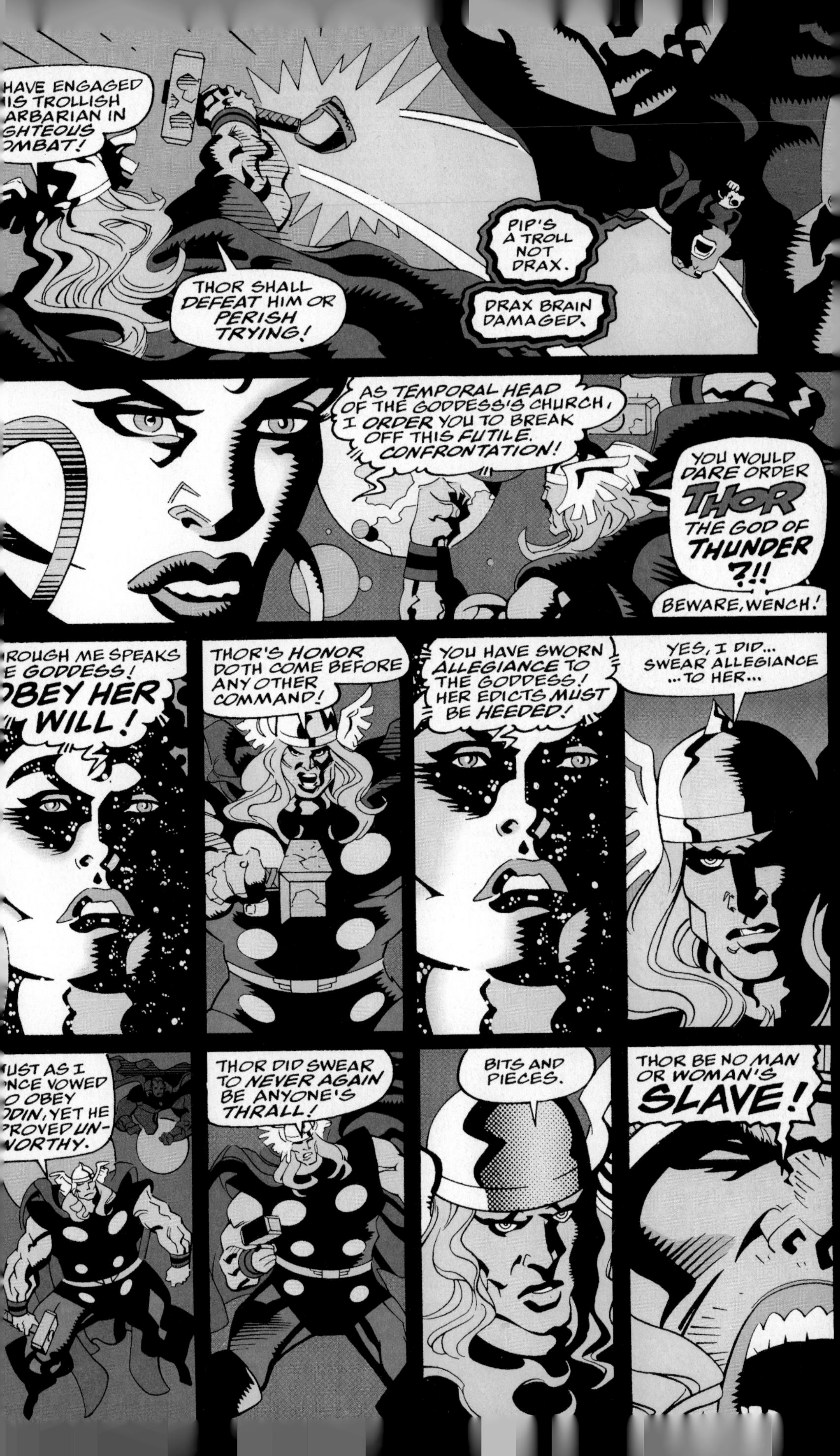

HAVE ENGAGED
IS TROLLISH
ARBARIAN IN
GHTEOUS
OMBAT!
THOR SHALL DEFEAT HIM OR PERISH TRYING!
PIP'S A TROLL NOT DRAX.
DRAX BRAIN DAMAGED.
AS TEMPORAL HEAD OF THE GODDESS'S CHURCH, I ORDER YOU TO BREAK OFF THIS FUTILE CONFRONTATION!
YOU WOULD DARE ORDER THOR THE GOD OF THUNDER ?!!
BEWARE, WENCH!
ROUGH ME SPEAKS
E GODDESS!
OBEY HER
WILL!
THOR'S HONOR DOTH COME BEFORE ANY OTHER COMMAND!
YOU HAVE SWORN ALLEGIANCE TO THE GODDESS! HER EDICTS MUST BE HEEDED!
YES, I DID... SWEAR ALLEGIANCE ...TO HER...
UST AS I
NCE VOWED
O OBEY
DIN, YET HE
ROVED UN-
WORTHY.
THOR DID SWEAR TO NEVER AGAIN BE ANYONE'S THRALL!
BITS AND PIECES.
THOR BE NO MAN OR WOMAN'S SLAVE!

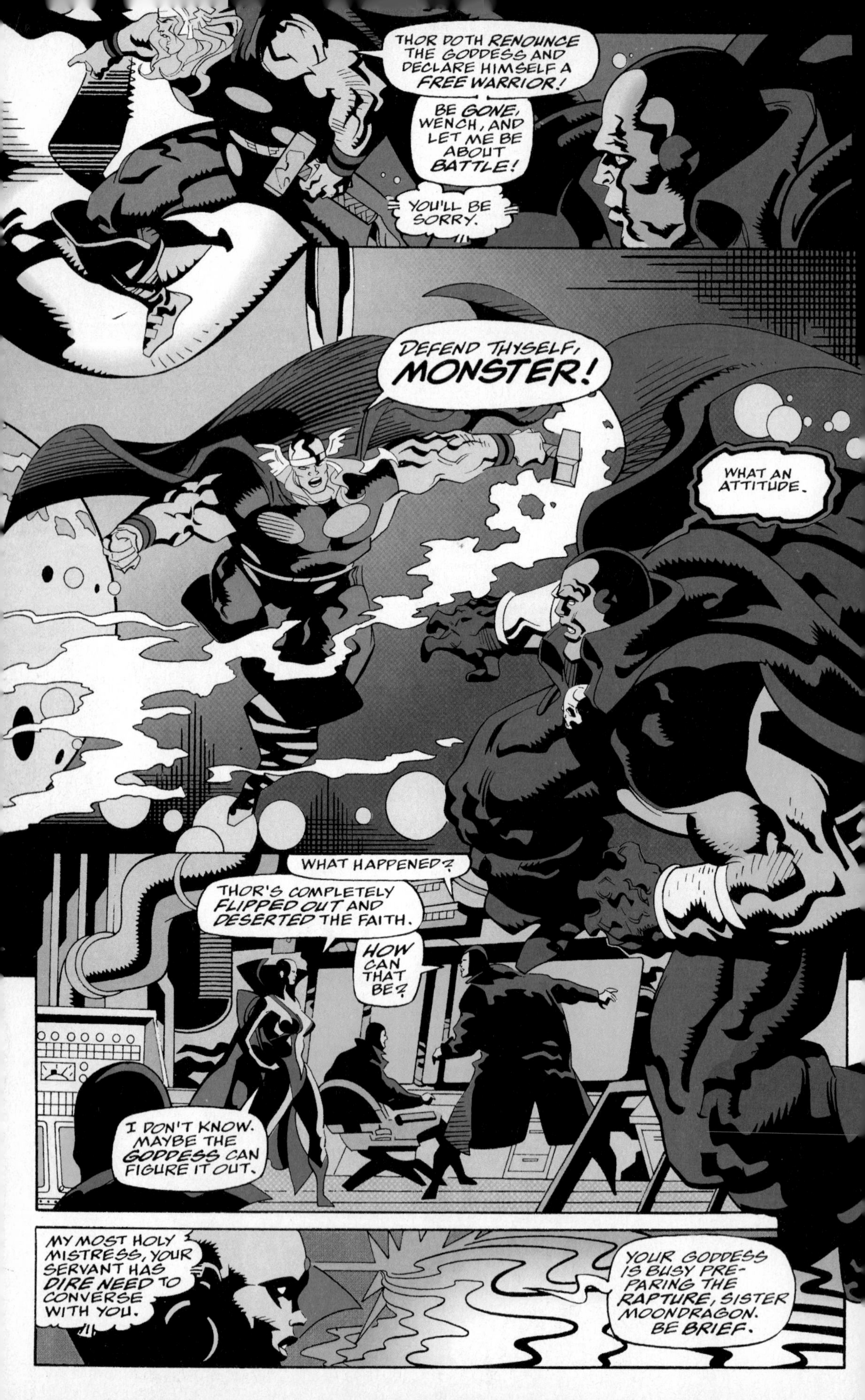
THOR DOTH RENOUNCE THE GODDESS AND DECLARE HIMSELF A FREE WARRIOR!
BE GONE, WENCH, AND LET ME BE ABOUT BATTLE!
YOU'LL BE SORRY.
DEFEND THYSELF, MONSTER!
WHAT AN ATTITUDE.
WHAT HAPPENED?
THOR'S COMPLETELY FLIPPED OUT AND DESERTED THE FAITH.
HOW CAN THAT BE?
I DON'T KNOW. MAYBE THE GODDESS CAN FIGURE IT OUT.
MY MOST HOLY MISTRESS, YOUR SERVANT HAS DIRE NEED TO CONVERSE WITH YOU.
YOUR GODDESS IS BUSY PREPARING THE RAPTURE, SISTER MOONDRAGON. BE BRIEF.

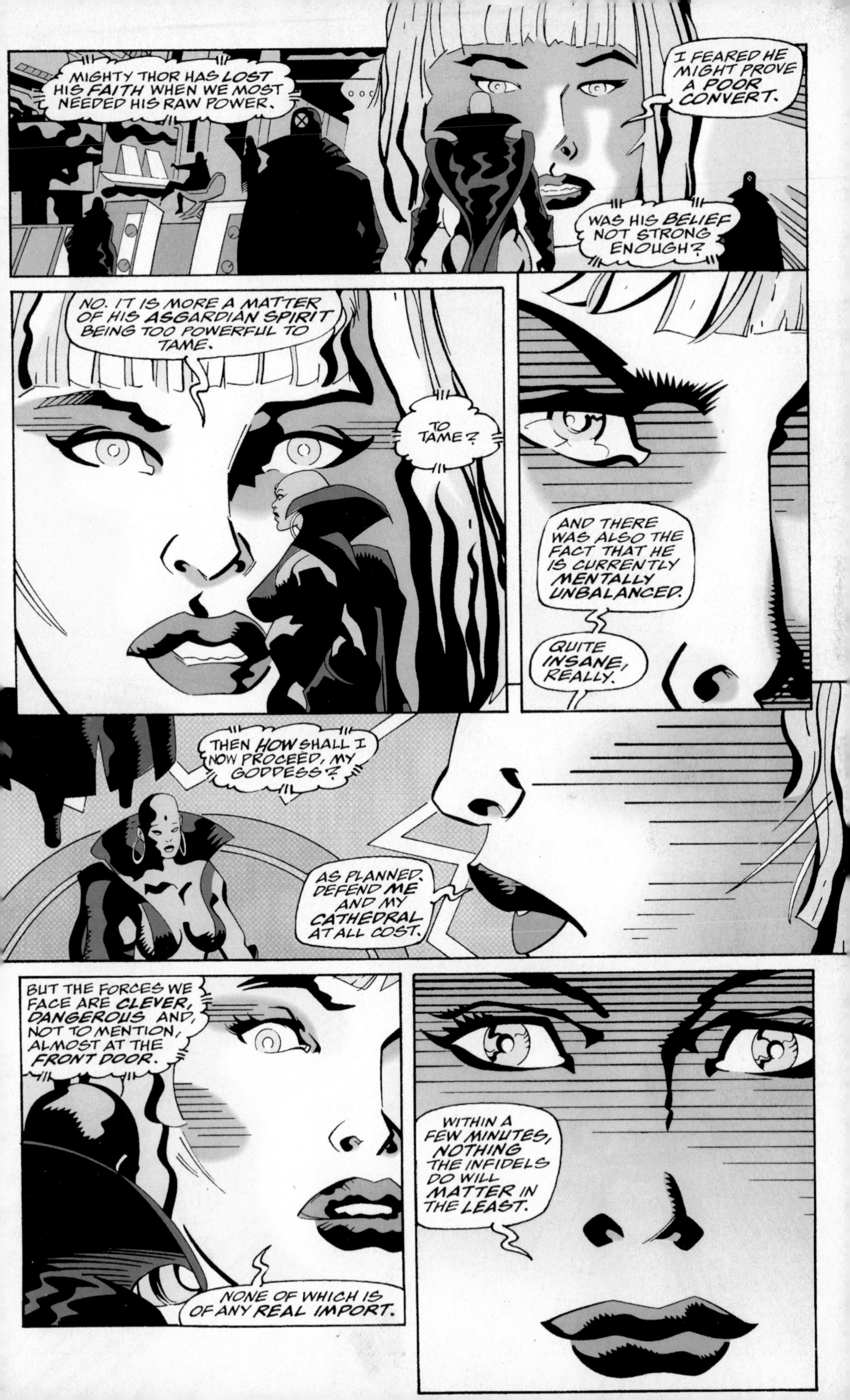
MIGHTY THOR HAS LOST HIS FAITH WHEN WE MOST NEEDED HIS RAW POWER.
I FEARED HE MIGHT PROVE A POOR CONVERT.
WAS HIS BELIEF NOT STRONG ENOUGH?
NO. IT IS MORE A MATTER OF HIS ASGARDIAN SPIRIT BEING TOO POWERFUL TO TAME.
TO TAME?
AND THERE WAS ALSO THE FACT THAT HE IS CURRENTLY MENTALLY UNBALANCED.
QUITE INSANE, REALLY.
THEN HOW SHALL I NOW PROCEED, MY GODDESS?
AS PLANNED. DEFEND ME AND MY CATHEDRAL AT ALL COST.
BUT THE FORCES WE FACE ARE CLEVER, DANGEROUS AND, NOT TO MENTION, ALMOST AT THE FRONT DOOR.
NONE OF WHICH IS OF ANY REAL IMPORT.
WITHIN A FEW MINUTES, NOTHING THE INFIDELS DO WILL MATTER IN THE LEAST.

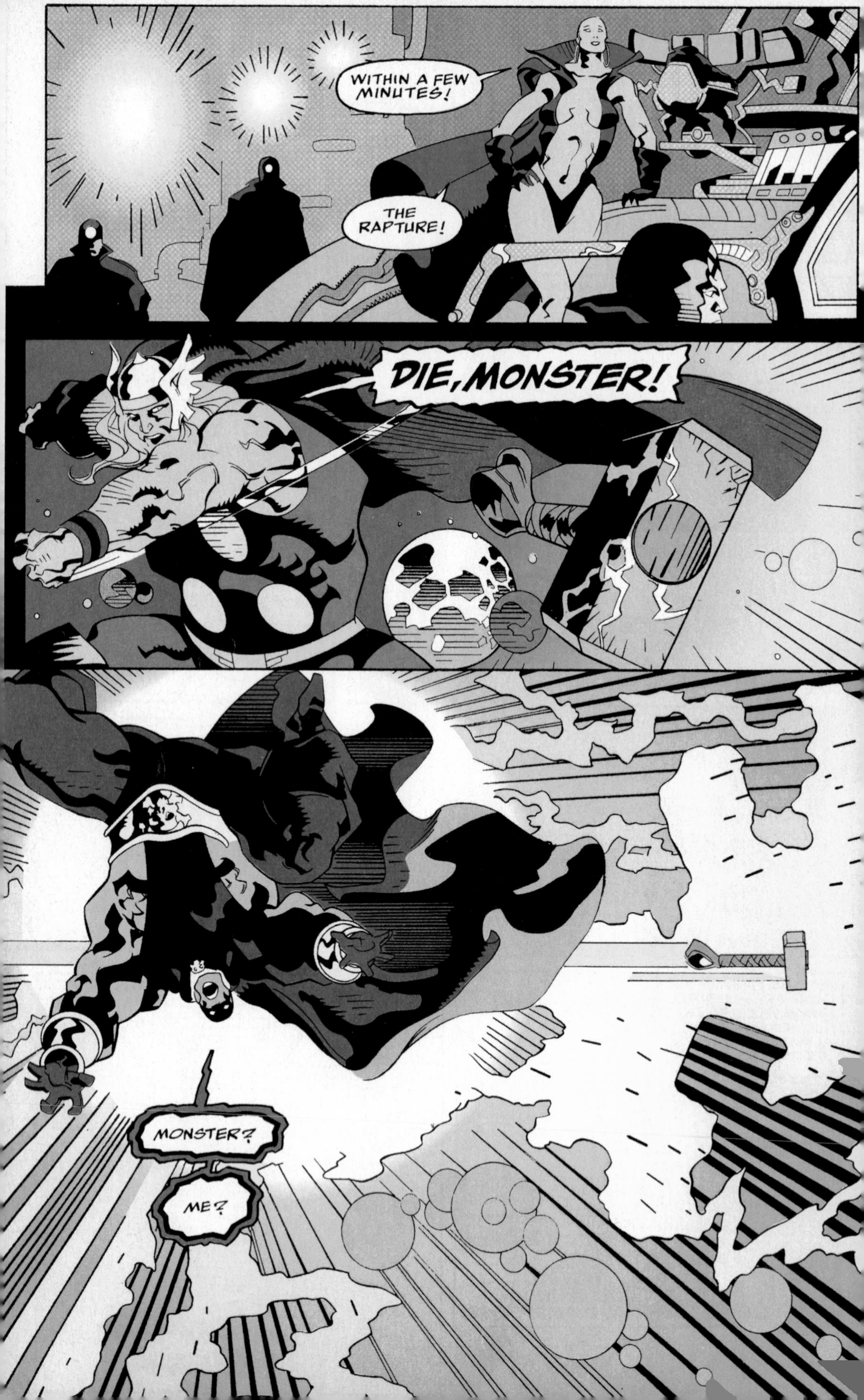
WITHIN A FEW MINUTES!
THE RAPTURE!
DIE, MONSTER!
MONSTER?
ME?

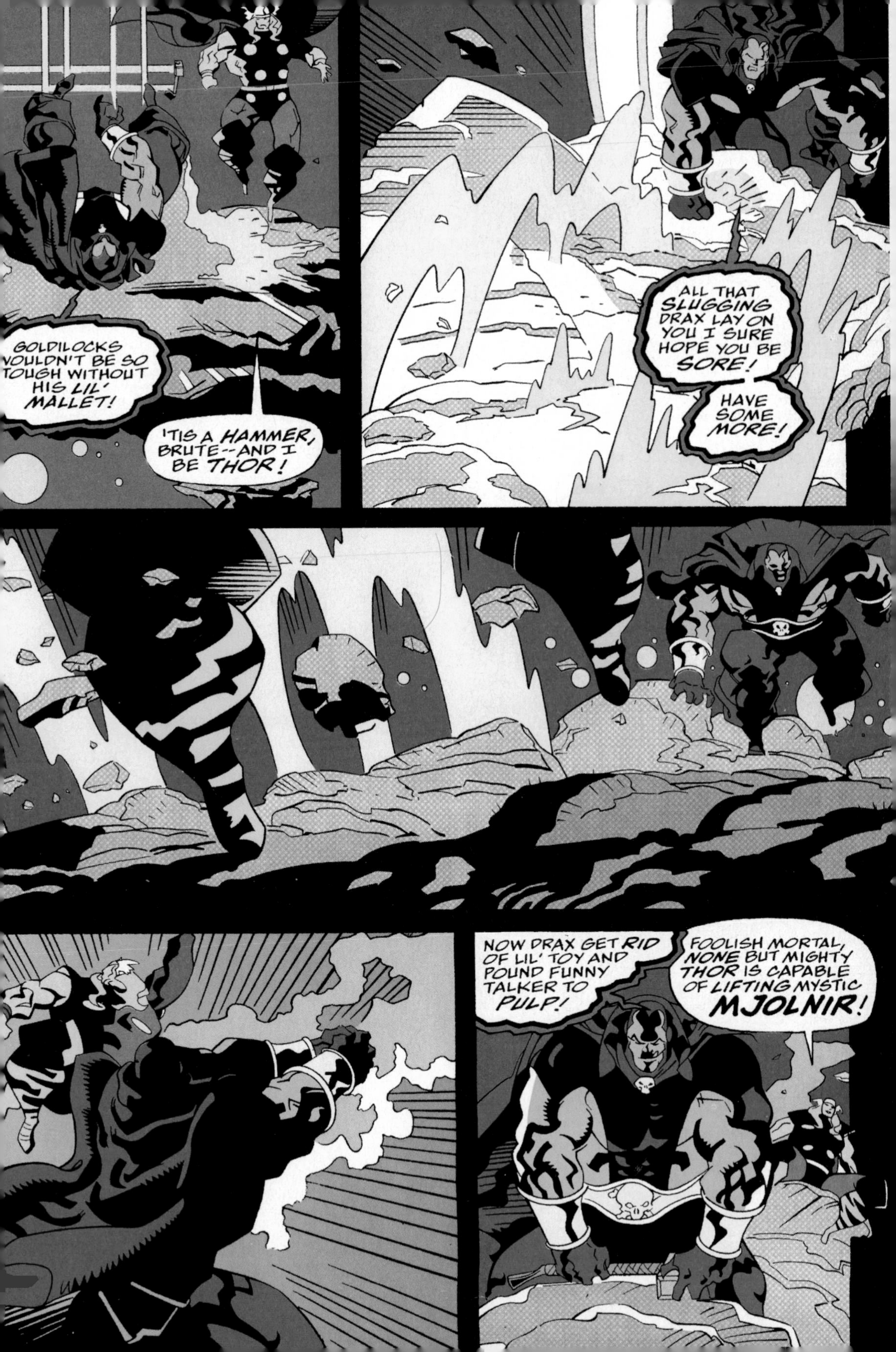
GOLDILOCKS WOULDN'T BE SO TOUGH WITHOUT HIS LIL' MALLET!
'TIS A HAMMER, BRUTE--AND I BE THOR!
ALL THAT SLUGGING DRAX LAY ON YOU I SURE HOPE YOU BE SORE!
HAVE SOME MORE!
NOW DRAX GET RID OF LIL' TOY AND POUND FUNNY TALKER TO PULP!
FOOLISH MORTAL, NONE BUT MIGHTY THOR IS CAPABLE OF LIFTING MYSTIC MJOLNIR!

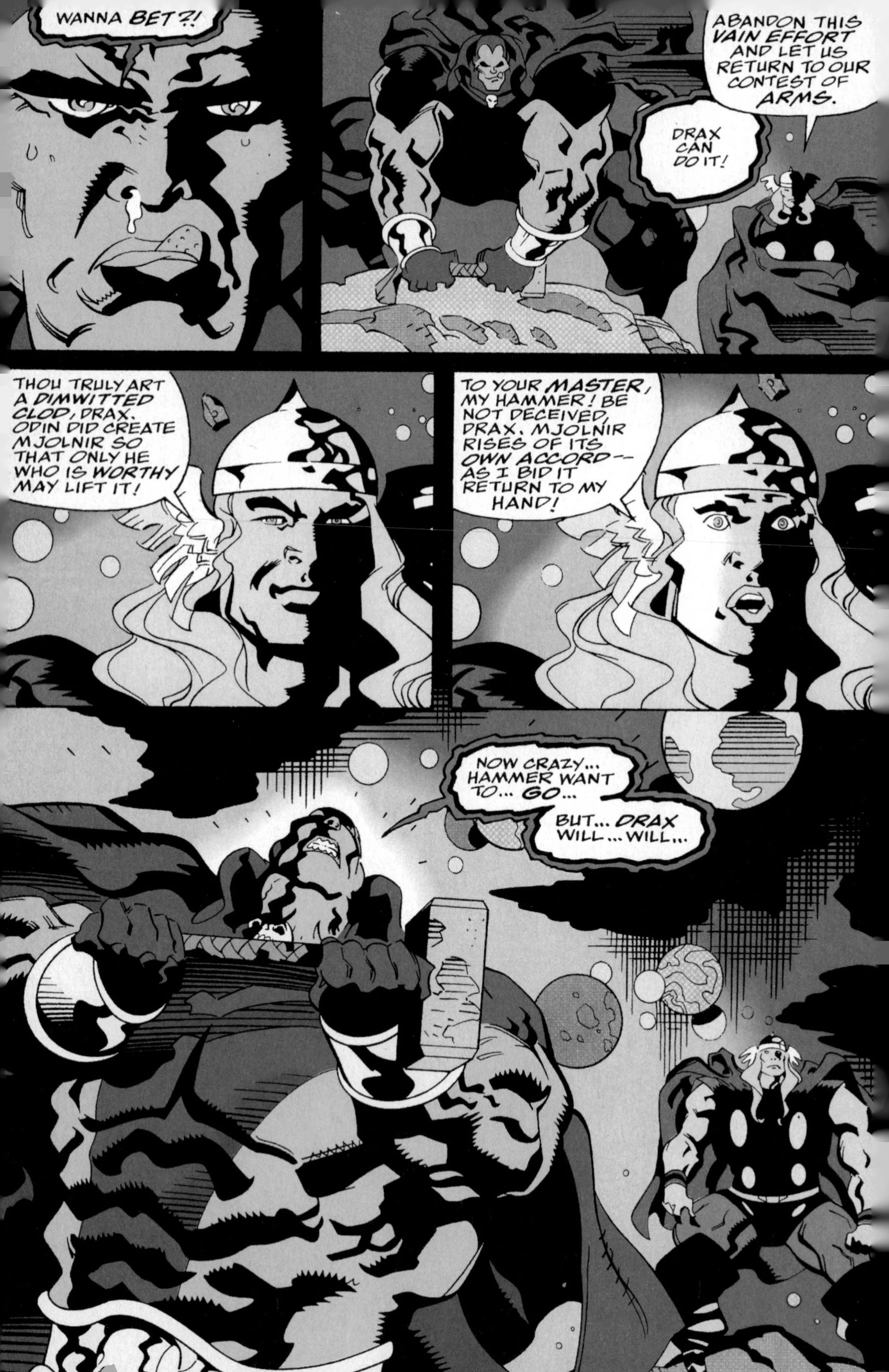
WANNA BET?!
ABANDON THIS VAIN EFFORT AND LET US RETURN TO OUR CONTEST OF ARMS.
DRAX CAN DO IT!
THOU TRULY ART A DIMWITTED CLOD, DRAX. ODIN DID CREATE MJOLNIR SO THAT ONLY HE WHO IS WORTHY MAY LIFT IT!
TO YOUR MASTER, MY HAMMER! BE NOT DECEIVED, DRAX. MJOLNIR RISES OF ITS OWN ACCORD-- AS I BID IT RETURN TO MY HAND!
NOW CRAZY... HAMMER WANT TO... GO...
BUT... DRAX WILL... WILL...

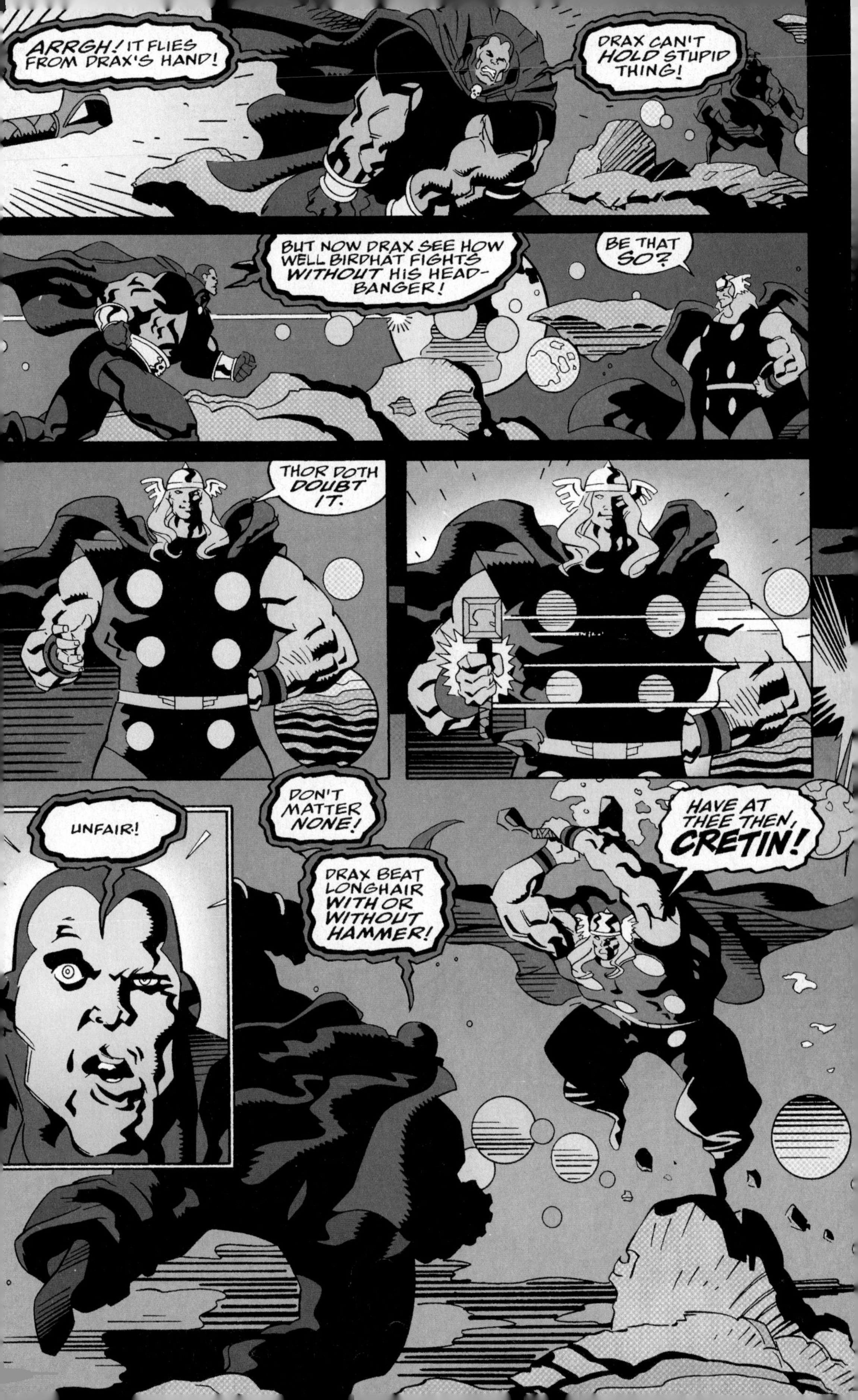
ARRGH! IT FLIES FROM DRAX'S HAND!
DRAX CAN'T HOLD STUPID THING!
BUT NOW DRAX SEE HOW WELL BIRDHAT FIGHTS WITHOUT HIS HEAD-BANGER!
BE THAT SO?
THOR DOTH DOUBT IT.
UNFAIR!
DON'T MATTER NONE!
DRAX BEAT LONGHAIR WITH OR WITHOUT HAMMER!
HAVE AT THEE THEN, CRETIN!

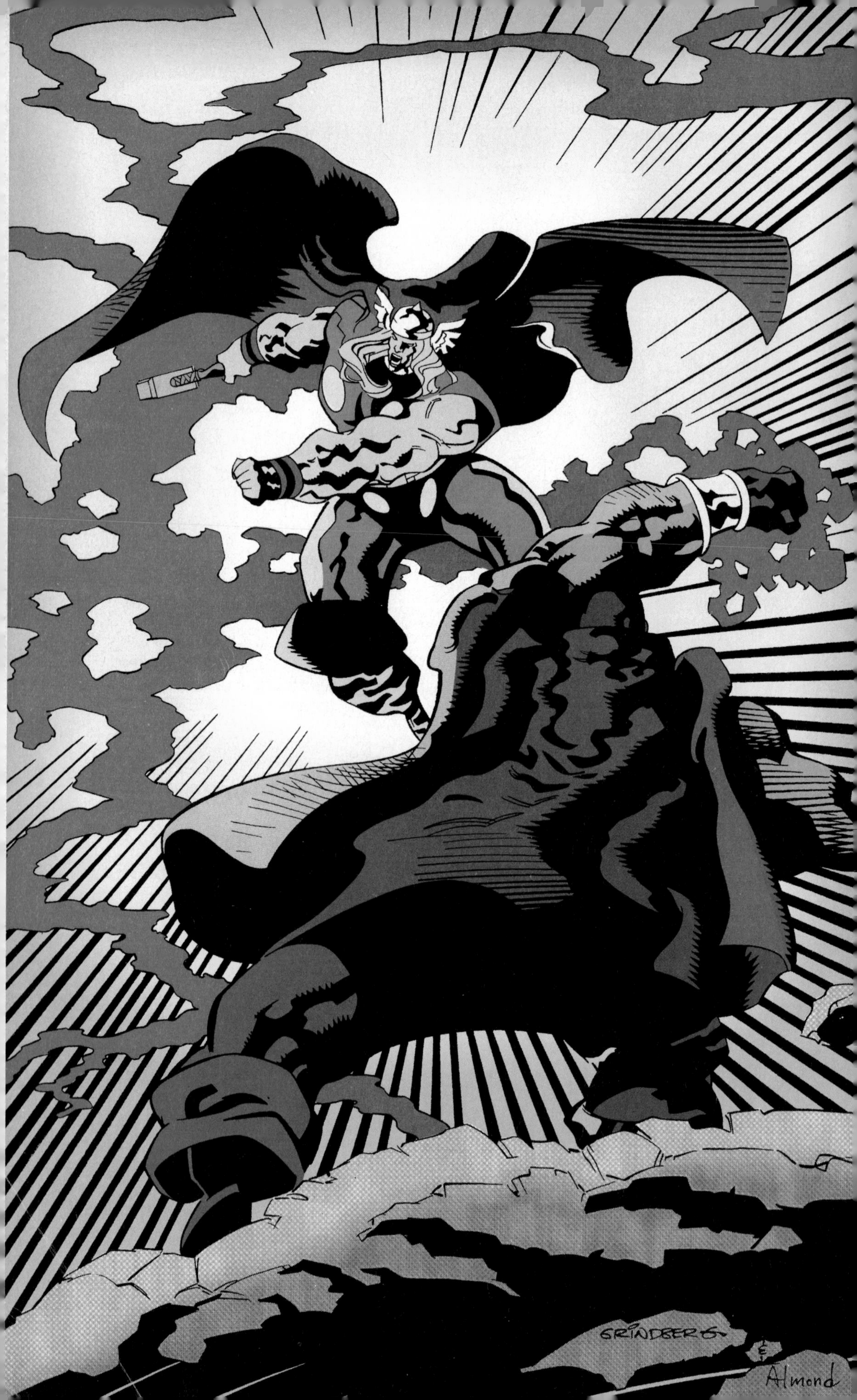
GRINDBERG
&
Almond

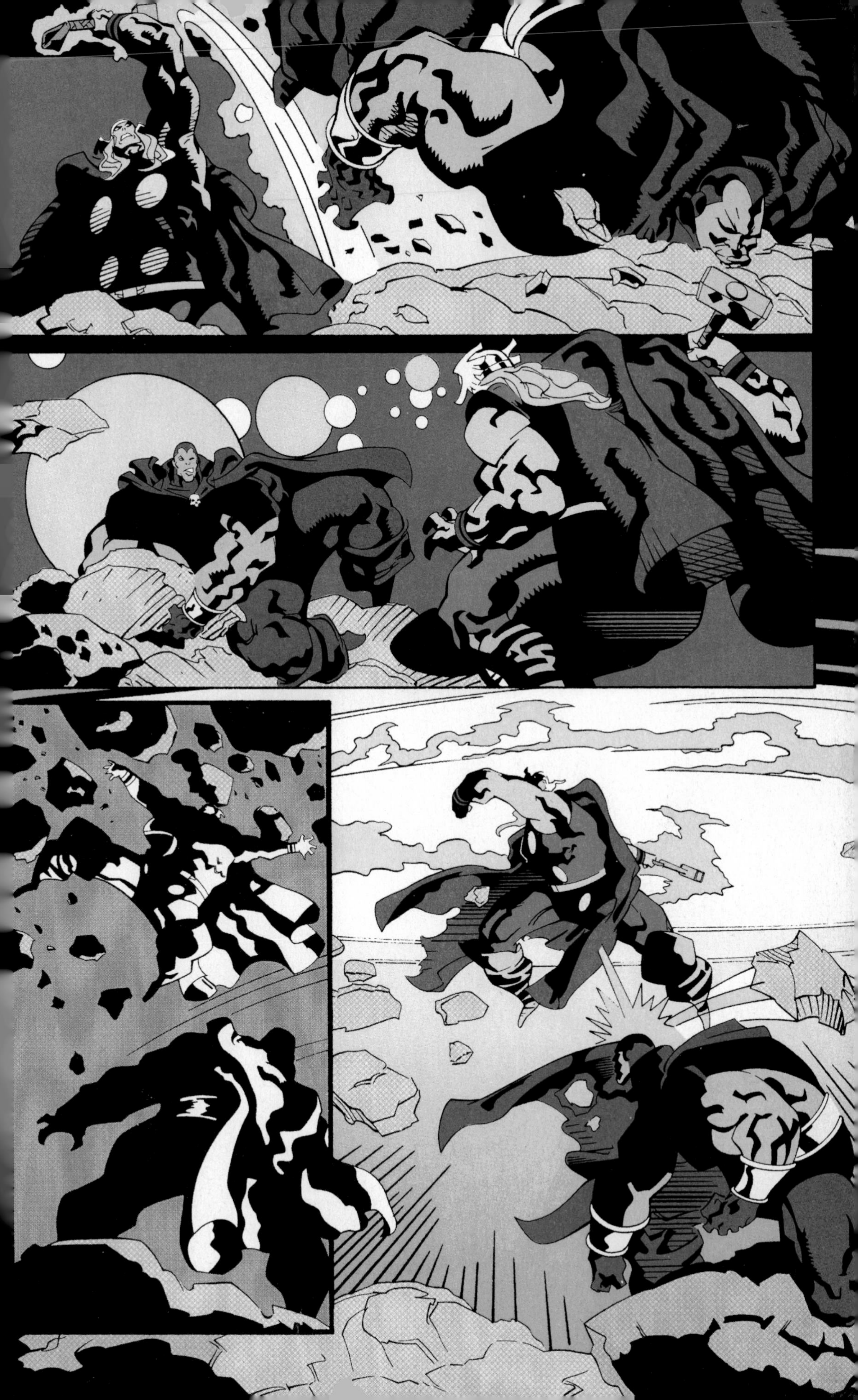

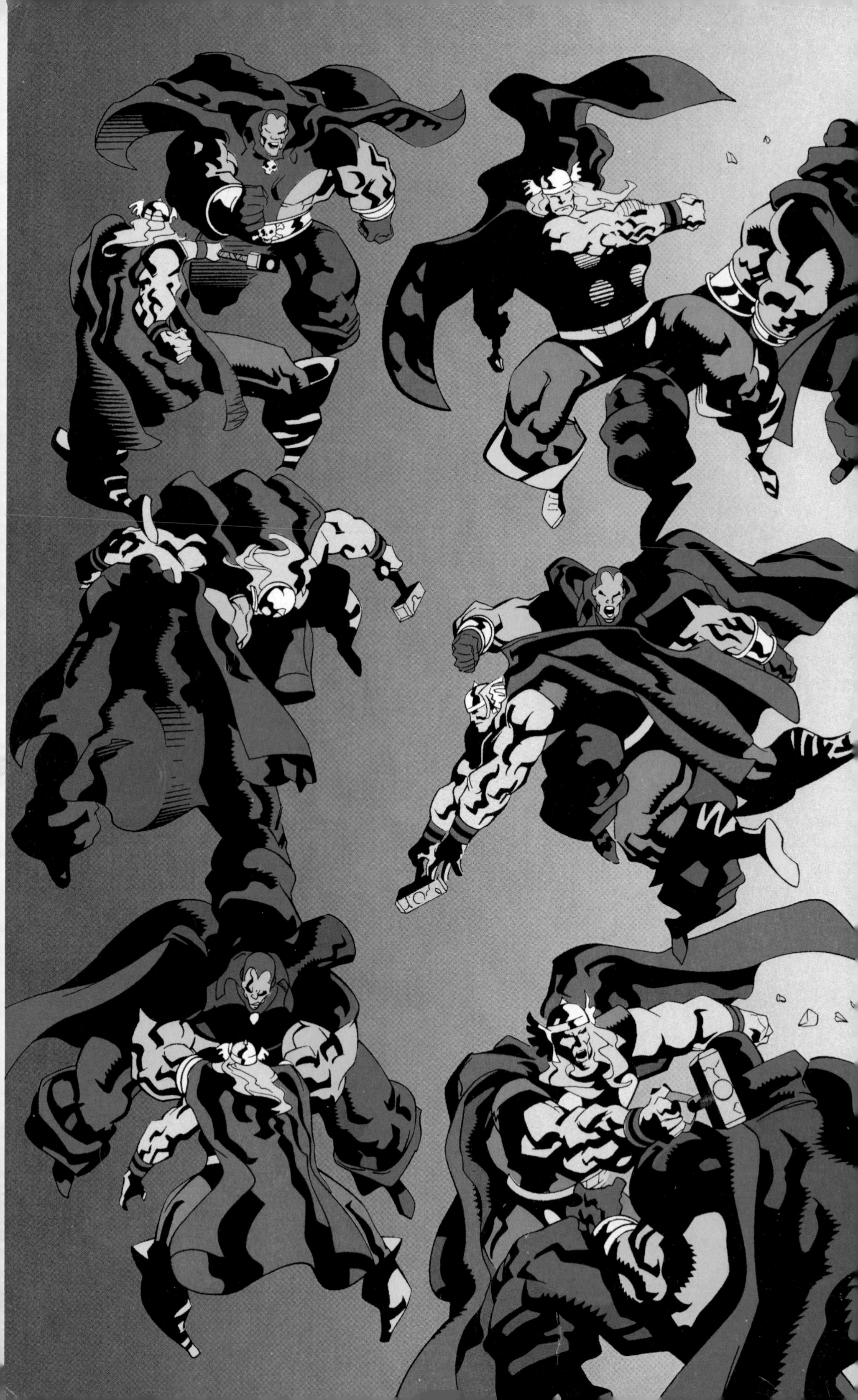

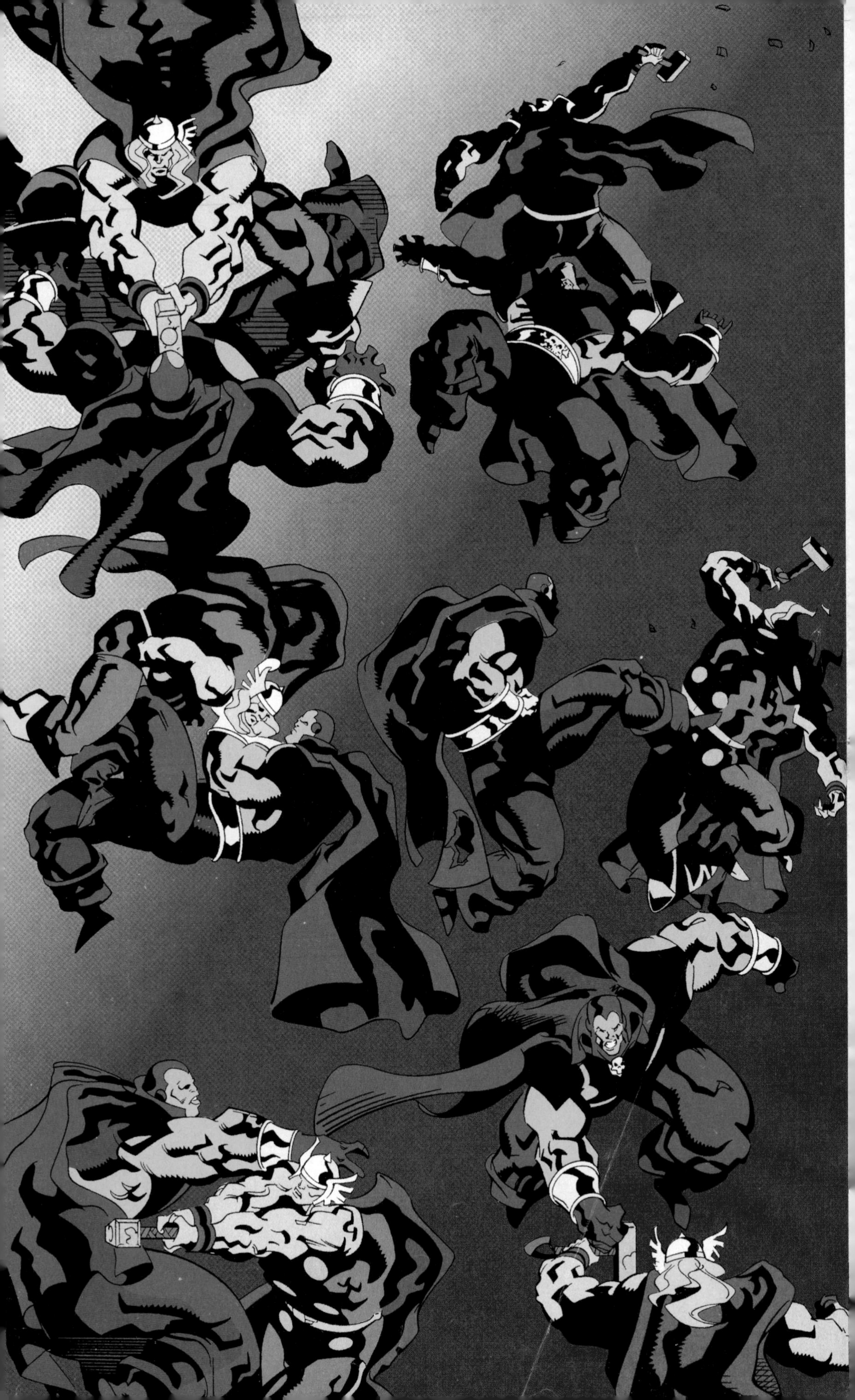

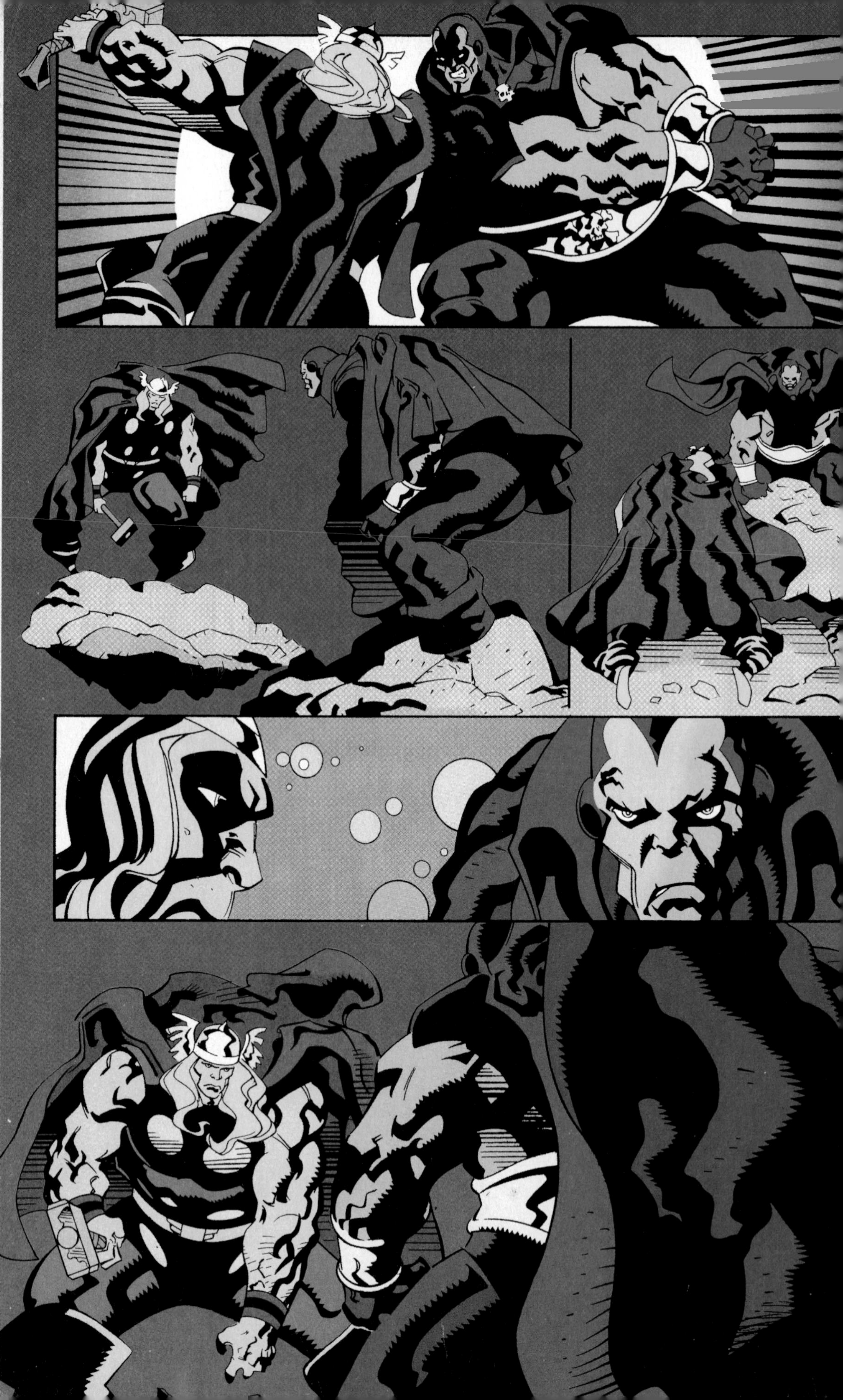

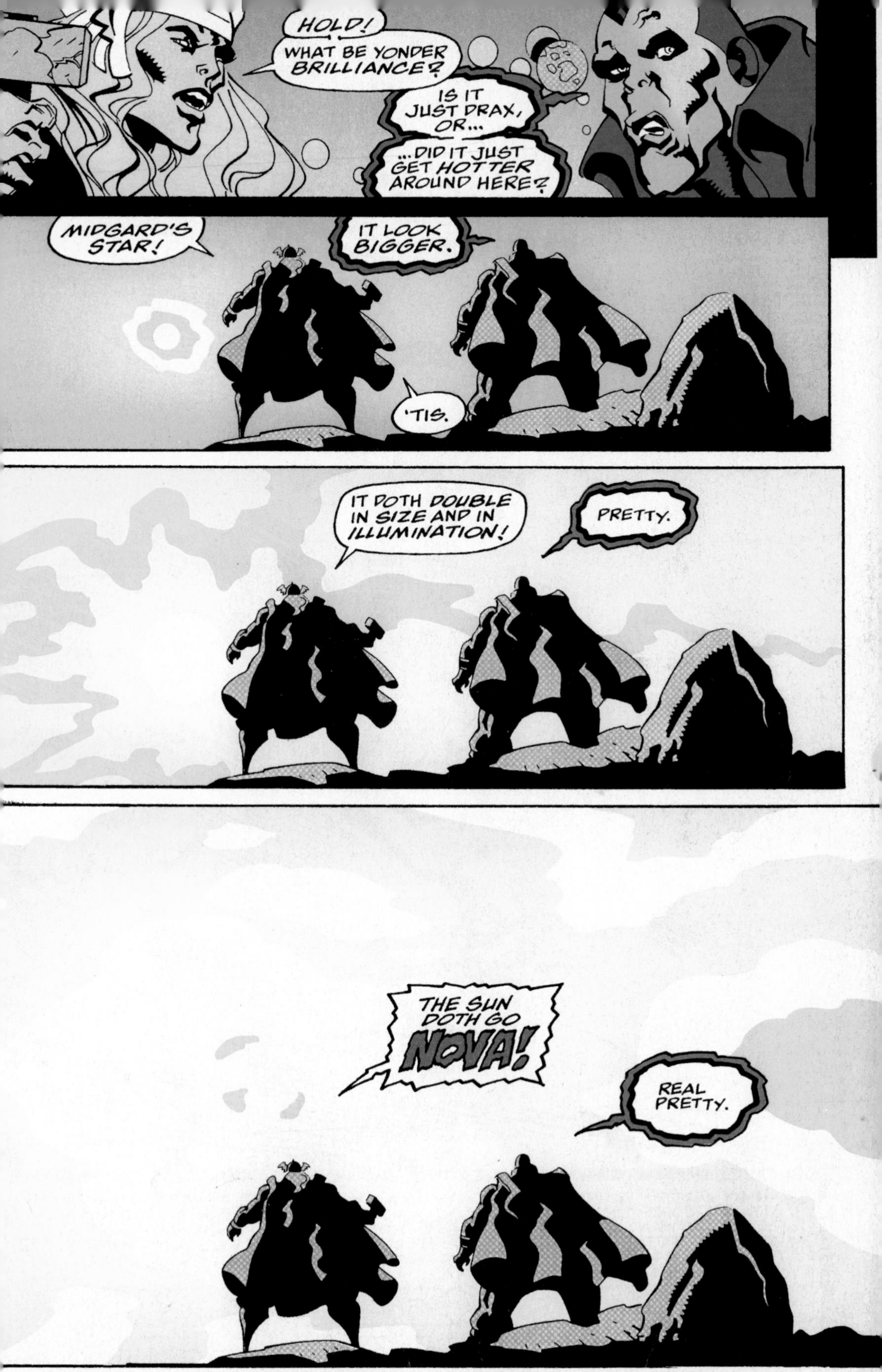
HOLD!
WHAT BE YONDER BRILLIANCE?
IS IT JUST DRAX, OR...
...DID IT JUST GET HOTTER AROUND HERE?
MIDGARD'S STAR!
IT LOOK BIGGER.
'TIS.
IT DOTH DOUBLE IN SIZE AND IN ILLUMINATION!
PRETTY.
THE SUN DOTH GO NOVA!
REAL PRETTY.

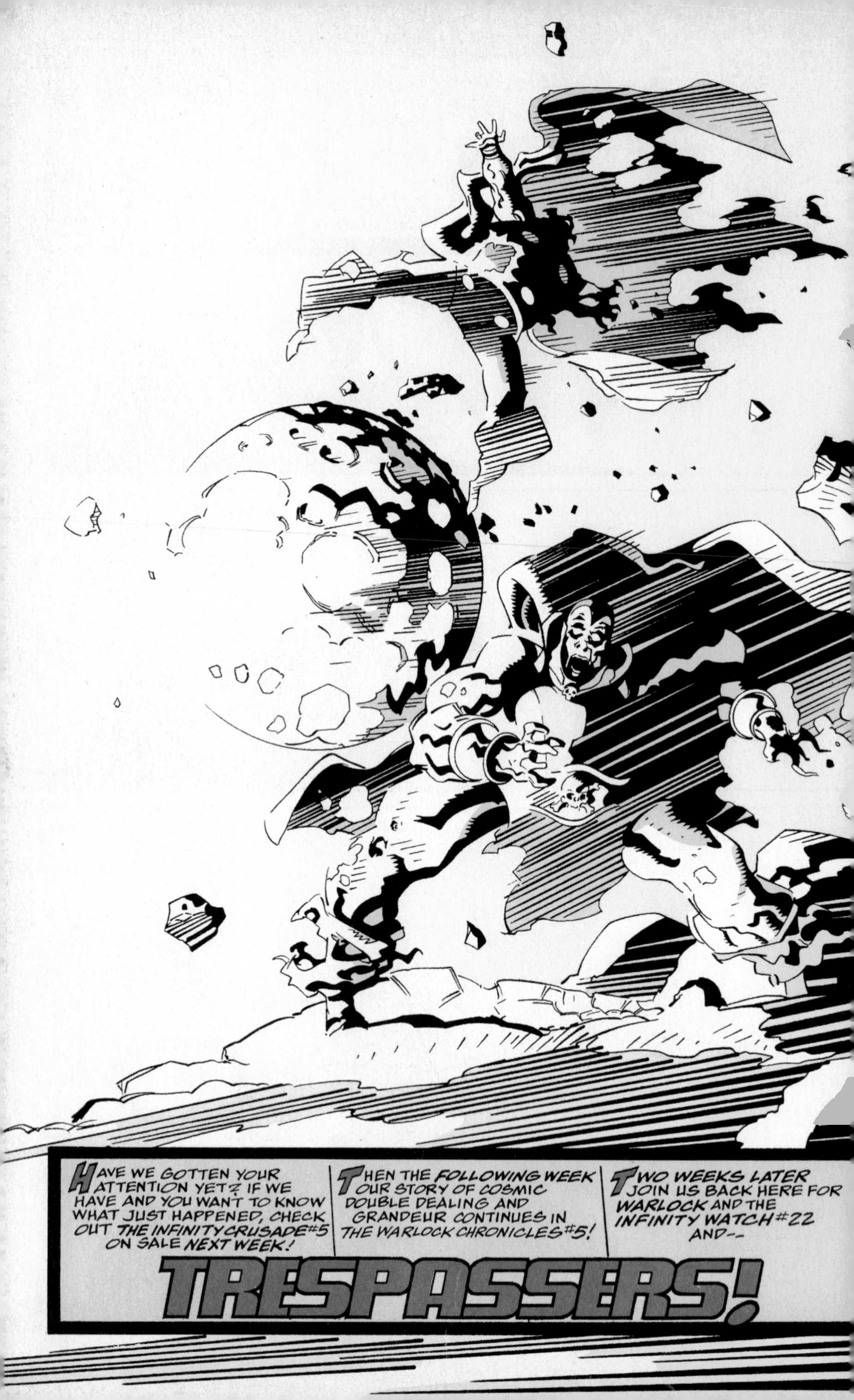
HAVE WE GOTTEN YOUR ATTENTION YET? IF WE HAVE AND YOU WANT TO KNOW WHAT JUST HAPPENED, CHECK OUT THE INFINITY CRUSADE #5 ON SALE NEXT WEEK!
THEN THE FOLLOWING WEEK OUR STORY OF COSMIC DOUBLE DEALING AND GRANDEUR CONTINUES IN THE WARLOCK CHRONICLES #5!
TWO WEEKS LATER JOIN US BACK HERE FOR WARLOCK AND THE INFINITY WATCH #22 AND--
TRESPASSERS!

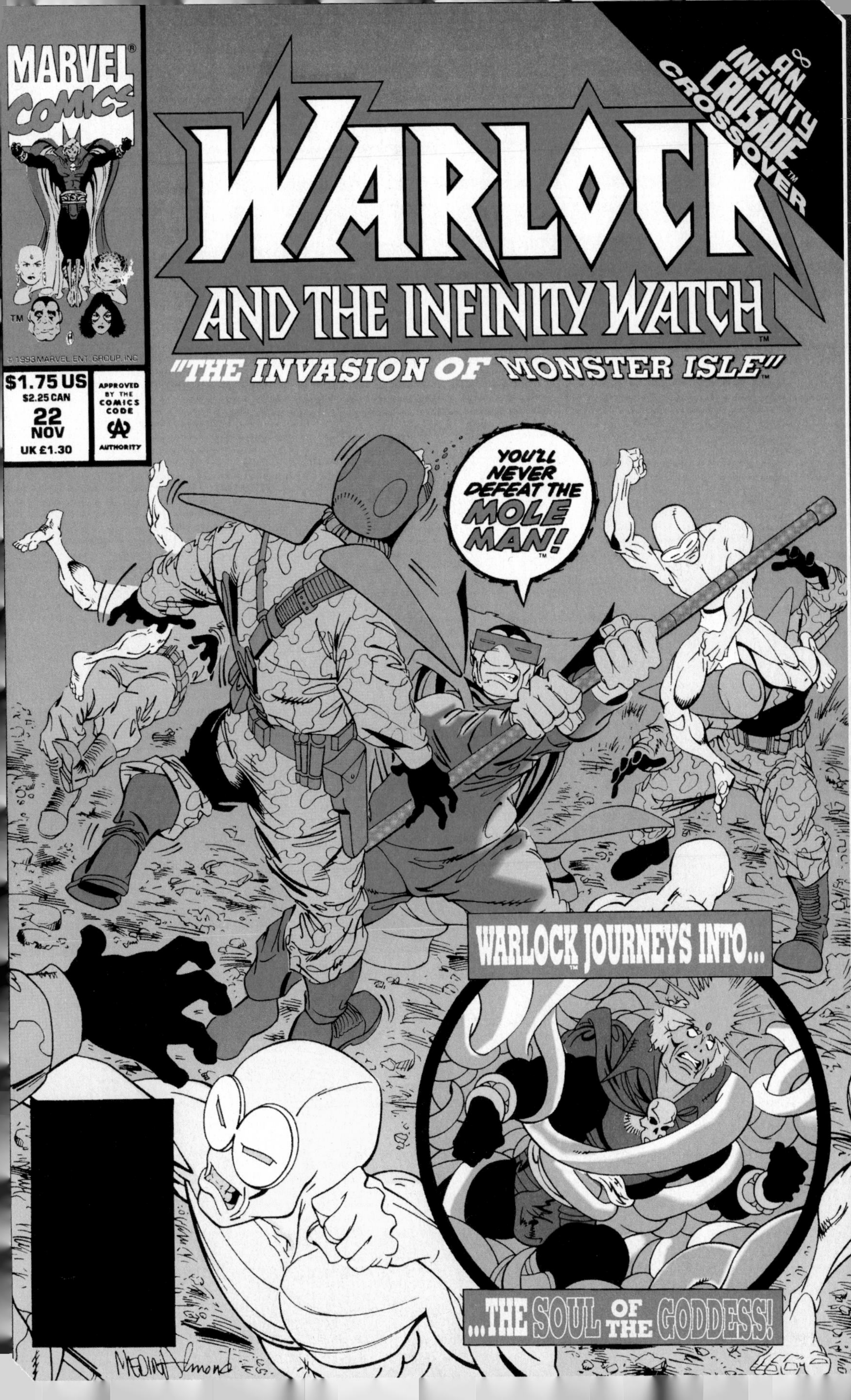
MARVEL® COMICS
AN ∞ INFINITY CRUSADE™ CROSSOVER
WARLOCK
AND THE INFINITY WATCH™
"THE INVASION OF MONSTER ISLE"™
© 1993 MARVEL ENT. GROUP, INC.
$1.75 US
$2.25 CAN
22
NOV
UK £1.30
APPROVED BY THE COMICS CODE AUTHORITY
YOU'LL NEVER DEFEAT THE MOLE MAN!™
WARLOCK™ JOURNEYS INTO...
...THE SOUL OF THE GODDESS!

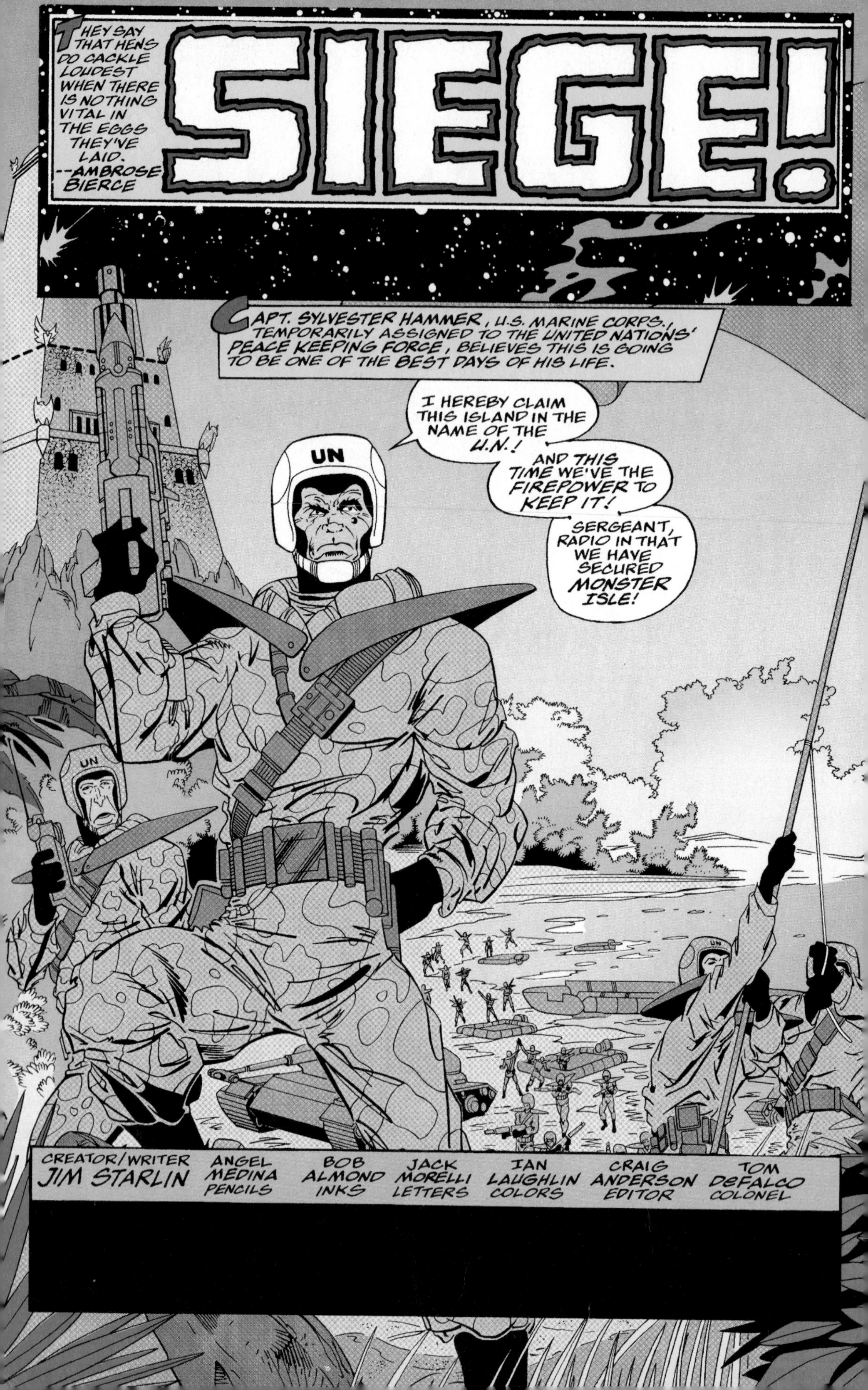
THEY SAY THAT HENS DO CACKLE LOUDEST WHEN THERE IS NOTHING VITAL IN THE EGGS THEY'VE LAID. --AMBROSE BIERCE
SIEGE!
CAPT. SYLVESTER HAMMER, U.S. MARINE CORPS., TEMPORARILY ASSIGNED TO THE UNITED NATIONS' PEACE KEEPING FORCE, BELIEVES THIS IS GOING TO BE ONE OF THE BEST DAYS OF HIS LIFE.
I HEREBY CLAIM THIS ISLAND IN THE NAME OF THE U.N.!
AND THIS TIME WE'VE THE FIREPOWER TO KEEP IT!
SERGEANT, RADIO IN THAT WE HAVE SECURED MONSTER ISLE!
UN
CREATOR/WRITER JIM STARLIN
ANGEL MEDINA PENCILS
BOB ALMOND INKS
JACK MORELLI LETTERS
IAN LAUGHLIN COLORS
CRAIG ANDERSON EDITOR
TOM DEFALCO COLONEL

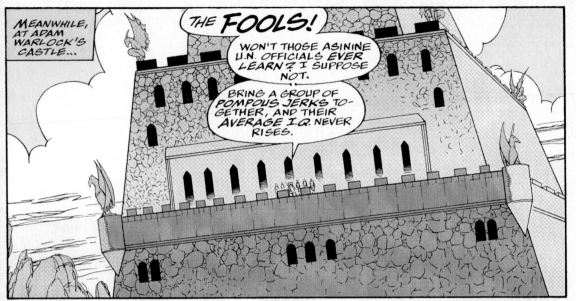

MEANWHILE, AT ADAM WARLOCK'S CASTLE...

THE **FOOLS!**

WON'T THOSE ASININE U.N. OFFICIALS *EVER* LEARN? I SUPPOSE NOT.

BRING A GROUP OF POMPOUS JERKS TOGETHER, AND THEIR AVERAGE I.Q. NEVER RISES.

JUST BECAUSE MONSTER ISLAND IS ON THE PLANET'S *SURFACE* THEY THINK THE MOLE MAN SHOULD HAVE NO CLAIM TO IT.

THEY WOULD DENY ME EVEN THIS LITTLE *SUNSHINE!*

SUCH ARROGANCE!

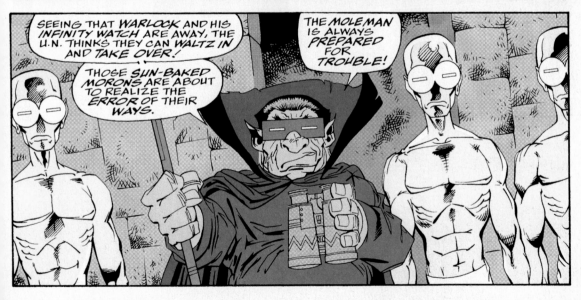

SEEING THAT *WARLOCK* AND HIS *INFINITY WATCH* ARE AWAY, THE U.N. THINKS THEY CAN *WALTZ IN* AND *TAKE OVER!*

THOSE *SUN-BAKED MORONS* ARE ABOUT TO REALIZE THE *ERROR* OF THEIR WAYS.

THE MOLE MAN IS ALWAYS *PREPARED* FOR *TROUBLE!*

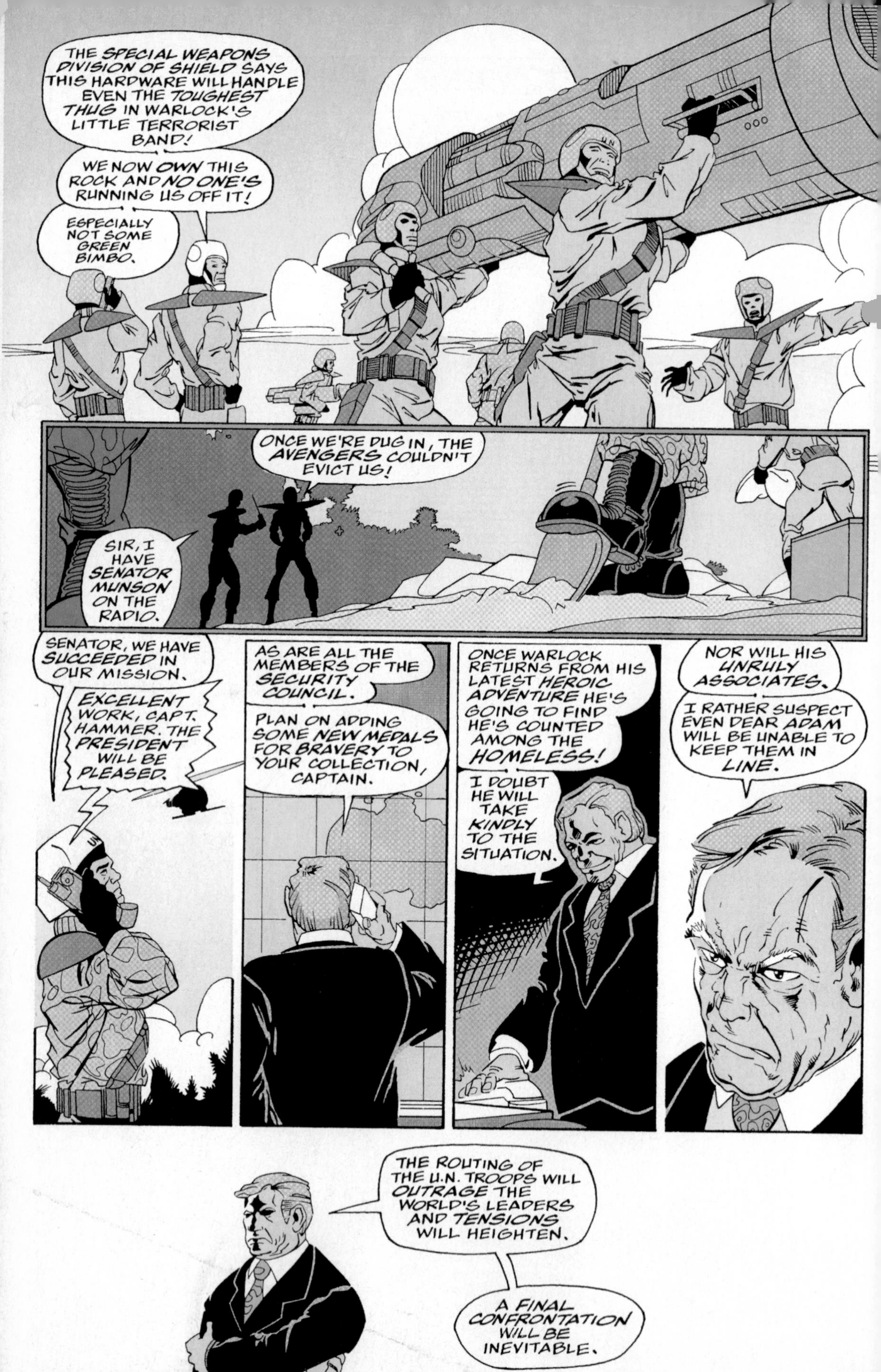
THE SPECIAL WEAPONS DIVISION OF SHIELD SAYS THIS HARDWARE WILL HANDLE EVEN THE TOUGHEST THUG IN WARLOCK'S LITTLE TERRORIST BAND!
WE NOW OWN THIS ROCK AND NO ONE'S RUNNING US OFF IT!
ESPECIALLY NOT SOME GREEN BIMBO.
ONCE WE'RE DUG IN, THE AVENGERS COULDN'T EVICT US!
SIR, I HAVE SENATOR MUNSON ON THE RADIO.
SENATOR, WE HAVE SUCCEEDED IN OUR MISSION.
EXCELLENT WORK, CAPT. HAMMER. THE PRESIDENT WILL BE PLEASED.
AS ARE ALL THE MEMBERS OF THE SECURITY COUNCIL.
PLAN ON ADDING SOME NEW MEDALS FOR BRAVERY TO YOUR COLLECTION, CAPTAIN.
ONCE WARLOCK RETURNS FROM HIS LATEST HEROIC ADVENTURE HE'S GOING TO FIND HE'S COUNTED AMONG THE HOMELESS!
I DOUBT HE WILL TAKE KINDLY TO THE SITUATION.
NOR WILL HIS UNRULY ASSOCIATES.
I RATHER SUSPECT EVEN DEAR ADAM WILL BE UNABLE TO KEEP THEM IN LINE.
THE ROUTING OF THE U.N. TROOPS WILL OUTRAGE THE WORLD'S LEADERS AND TENSIONS WILL HEIGHTEN.
A FINAL CONFRONTATION WILL BE INEVITABLE.

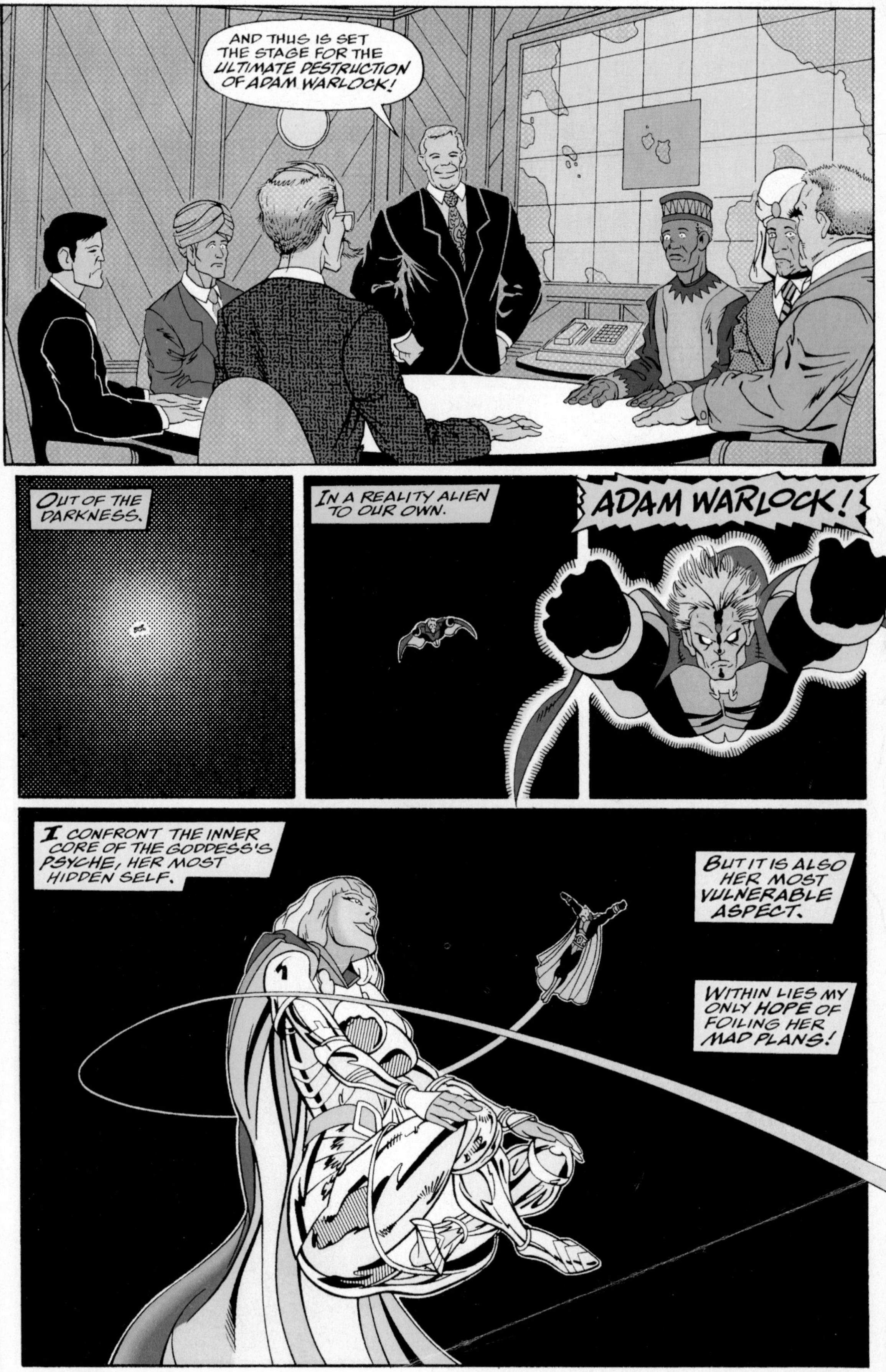
AND THUS IS SET THE STAGE FOR THE ULTIMATE DESTRUCTION OF ADAM WARLOCK!
OUT OF THE DARKNESS.
IN A REALITY ALIEN TO OUR OWN.
ADAM WARLOCK!
I CONFRONT THE INNER CORE OF THE GODDESS'S PSYCHE, HER MOST HIDDEN SELF.
BUT IT IS ALSO HER MOST VULNERABLE ASPECT.
WITHIN LIES MY ONLY HOPE OF FOILING HER MAD PLANS!

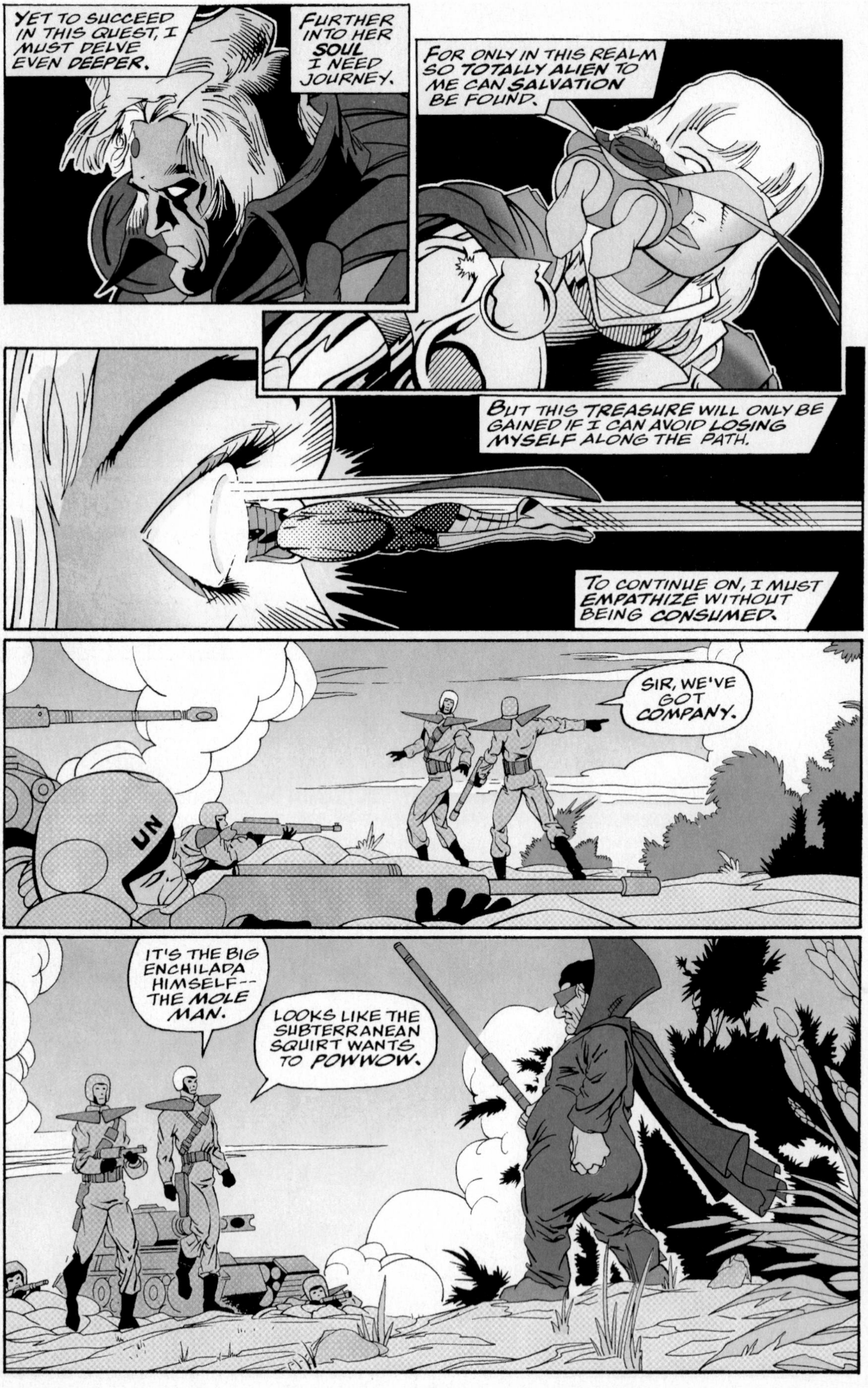

YET TO SUCCEED IN THIS QUEST, I MUST DELVE EVEN DEEPER.
FURTHER INTO HER SOUL I NEED JOURNEY.
FOR ONLY IN THIS REALM SO TOTALLY ALIEN TO ME CAN SALVATION BE FOUND.
BUT THIS TREASURE WILL ONLY BE GAINED IF I CAN AVOID LOSING MYSELF ALONG THE PATH.
TO CONTINUE ON, I MUST EMPATHIZE WITHOUT BEING CONSUMED.
SIR, WE'VE GOT COMPANY.
UN
IT'S THE BIG ENCHILADA HIMSELF-- THE MOLE MAN.
LOOKS LIKE THE SUBTERRANEAN SQUIRT WANTS TO POWWOW.

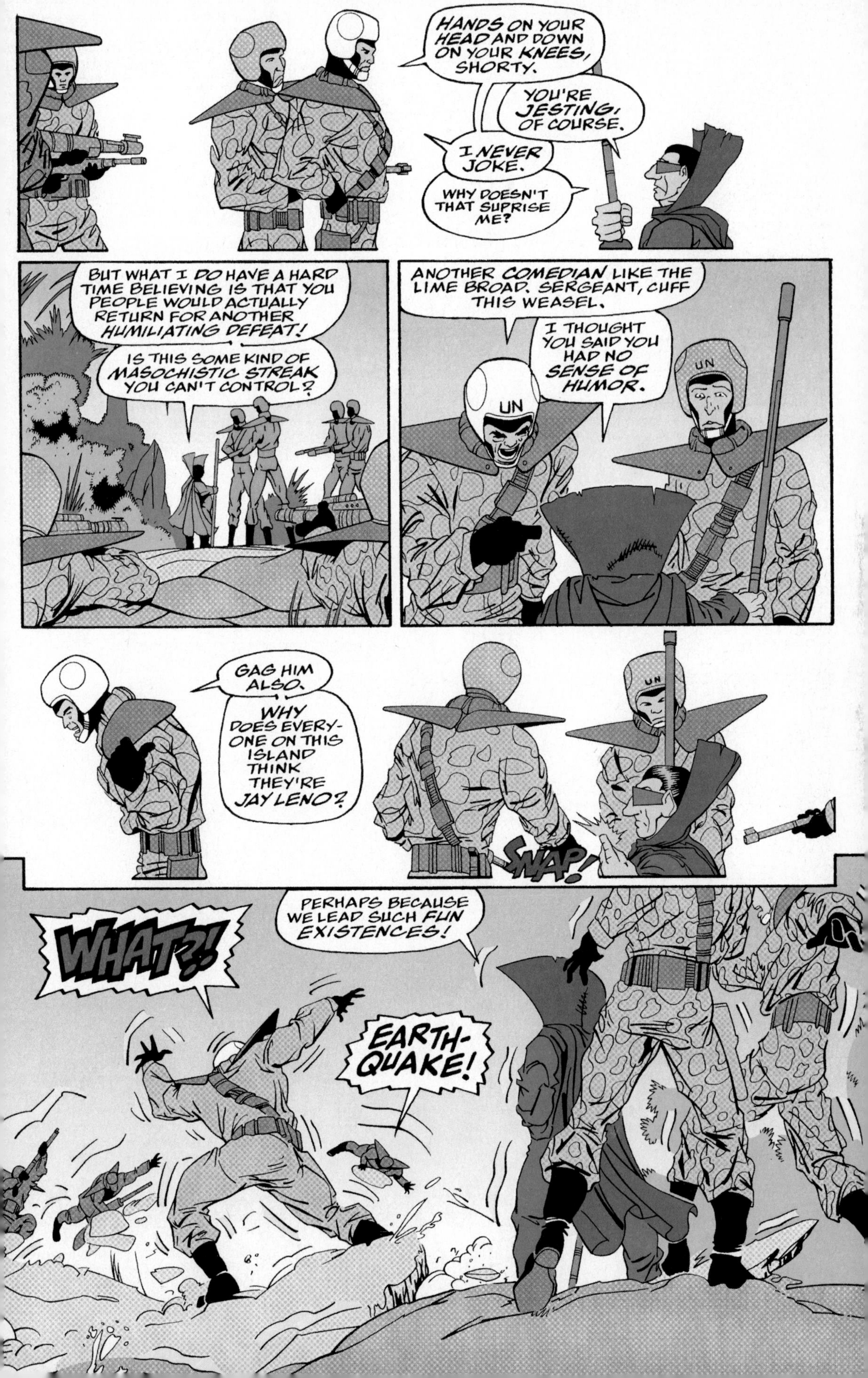

HANDS ON YOUR HEAD AND DOWN ON YOUR KNEES, SHORTY.
YOU'RE JESTING, OF COURSE.
I NEVER JOKE.
WHY DOESN'T THAT SUPRISE ME?
BUT WHAT I DO HAVE A HARD TIME BELIEVING IS THAT YOU PEOPLE WOULD ACTUALLY RETURN FOR ANOTHER HUMILIATING DEFEAT!
IS THIS SOME KIND OF MASOCHISTIC STREAK YOU CAN'T CONTROL?
ANOTHER COMEDIAN LIKE THE LIME BROAD. SERGEANT, CUFF THIS WEASEL.
I THOUGHT YOU SAID YOU HAD NO SENSE OF HUMOR.
UN
UN
GAG HIM ALSO.
WHY DOES EVERY-ONE ON THIS ISLAND THINK THEY'RE JAY LENO?
UN
SNAP!
WHAT?!
PERHAPS BECAUSE WE LEAD SUCH FUN EXISTENCES!
EARTH-QUAKE!

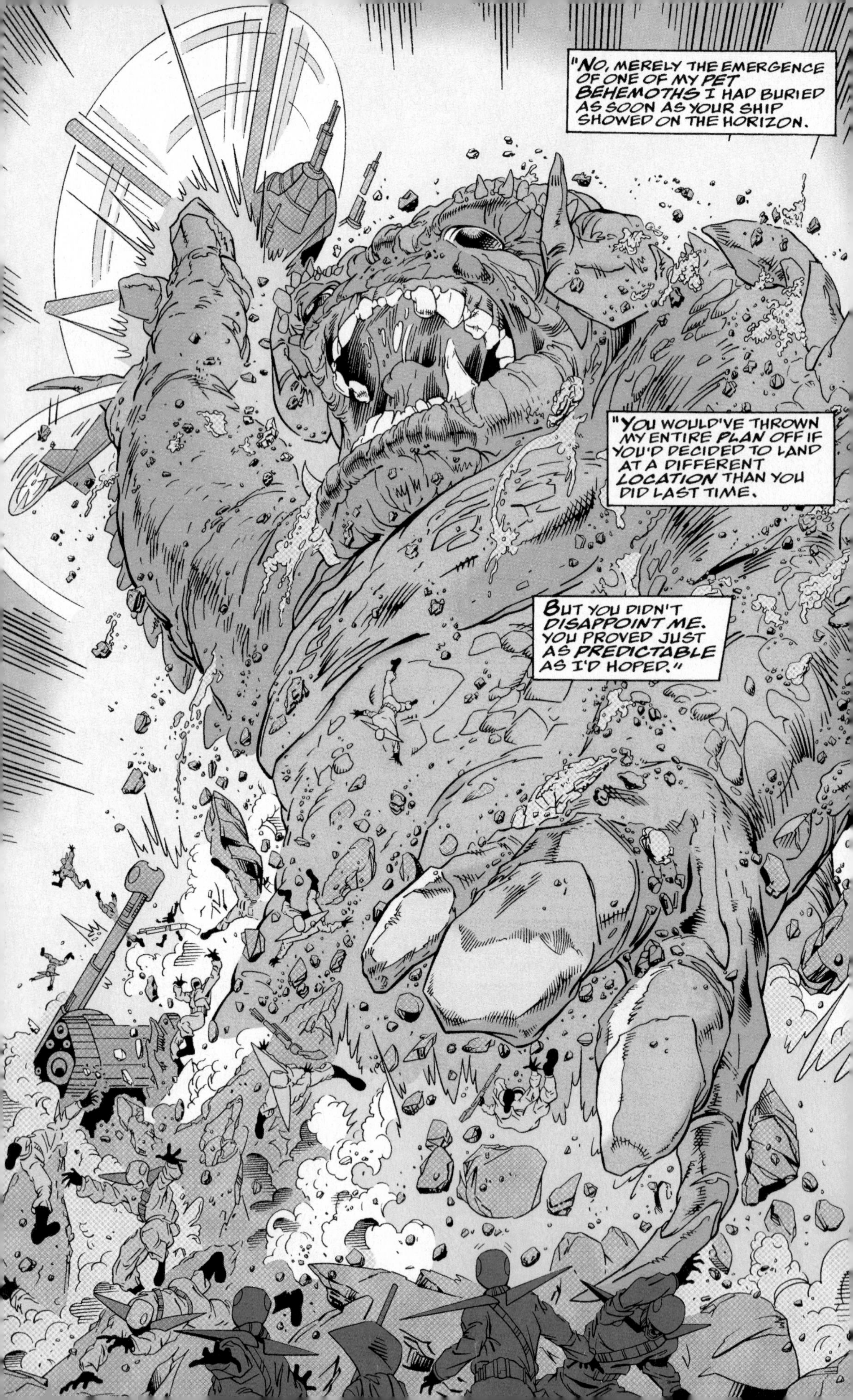
"NO, MERELY THE EMERGENCE OF ONE OF MY PET BEHEMOTHS I HAD BURIED AS SOON AS YOUR SHIP SHOWED ON THE HORIZON.
"YOU WOULD'VE THROWN MY ENTIRE PLAN OFF IF YOU'D DECIDED TO LAND AT A DIFFERENT LOCATION THAN YOU DID LAST TIME.
BUT YOU DIDN'T DISAPPOINT ME. YOU PROVED JUST AS PREDICTABLE AS I'D HOPED."

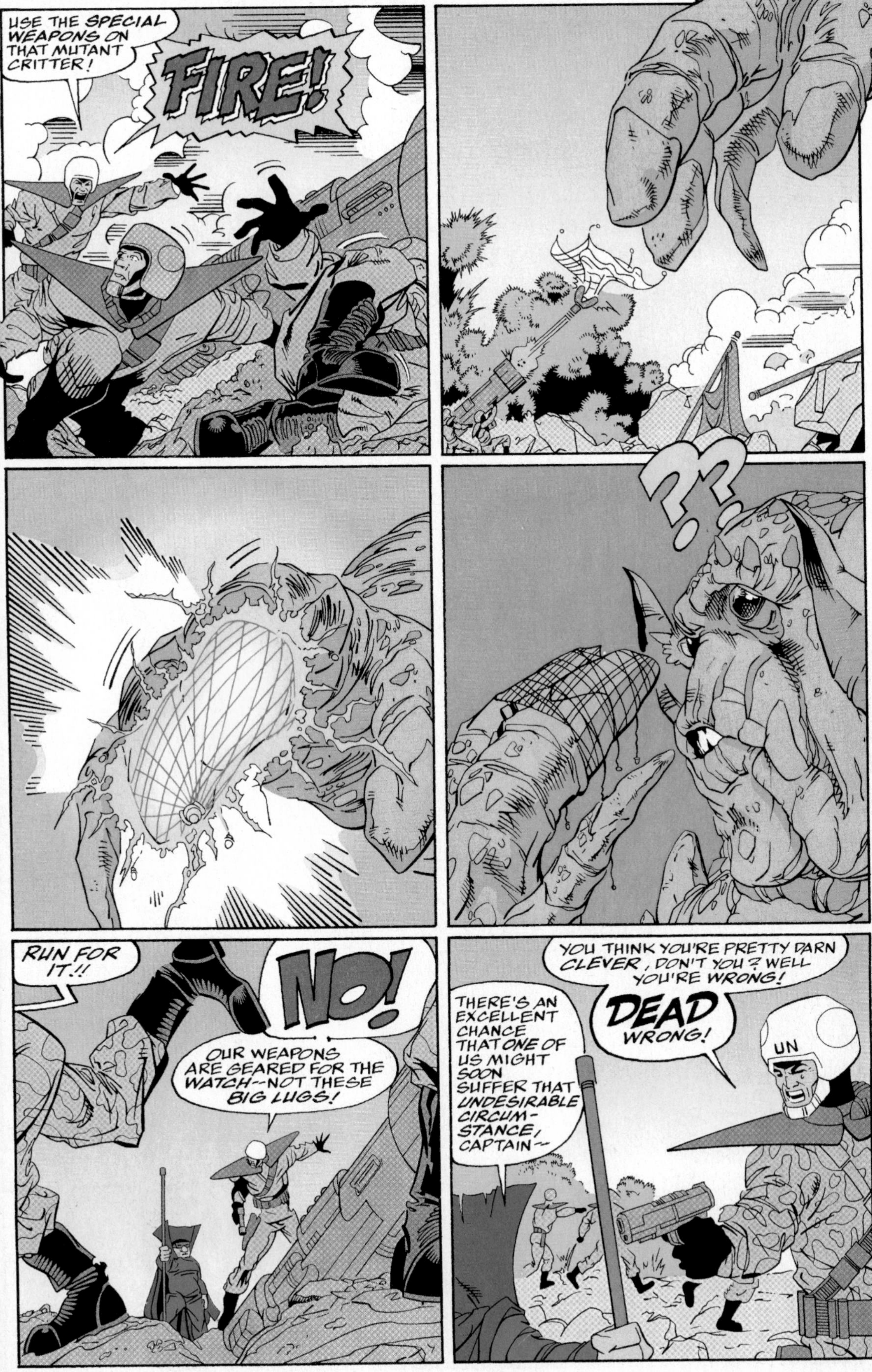
USE THE SPECIAL WEAPONS ON THAT MUTANT CRITTER!
FIRE!
RUN FOR IT!!
NO!
OUR WEAPONS ARE GEARED FOR THE WATCH--NOT THESE BIG LUGS!
YOU THINK YOU'RE PRETTY DARN CLEVER, DON'T YOU? WELL YOU'RE WRONG!
DEAD WRONG!
THERE'S AN EXCELLENT CHANCE THAT ONE OF US MIGHT SOON SUFFER THAT UNDESIRABLE CIRCUM-STANCE, CAPTAIN--
UN

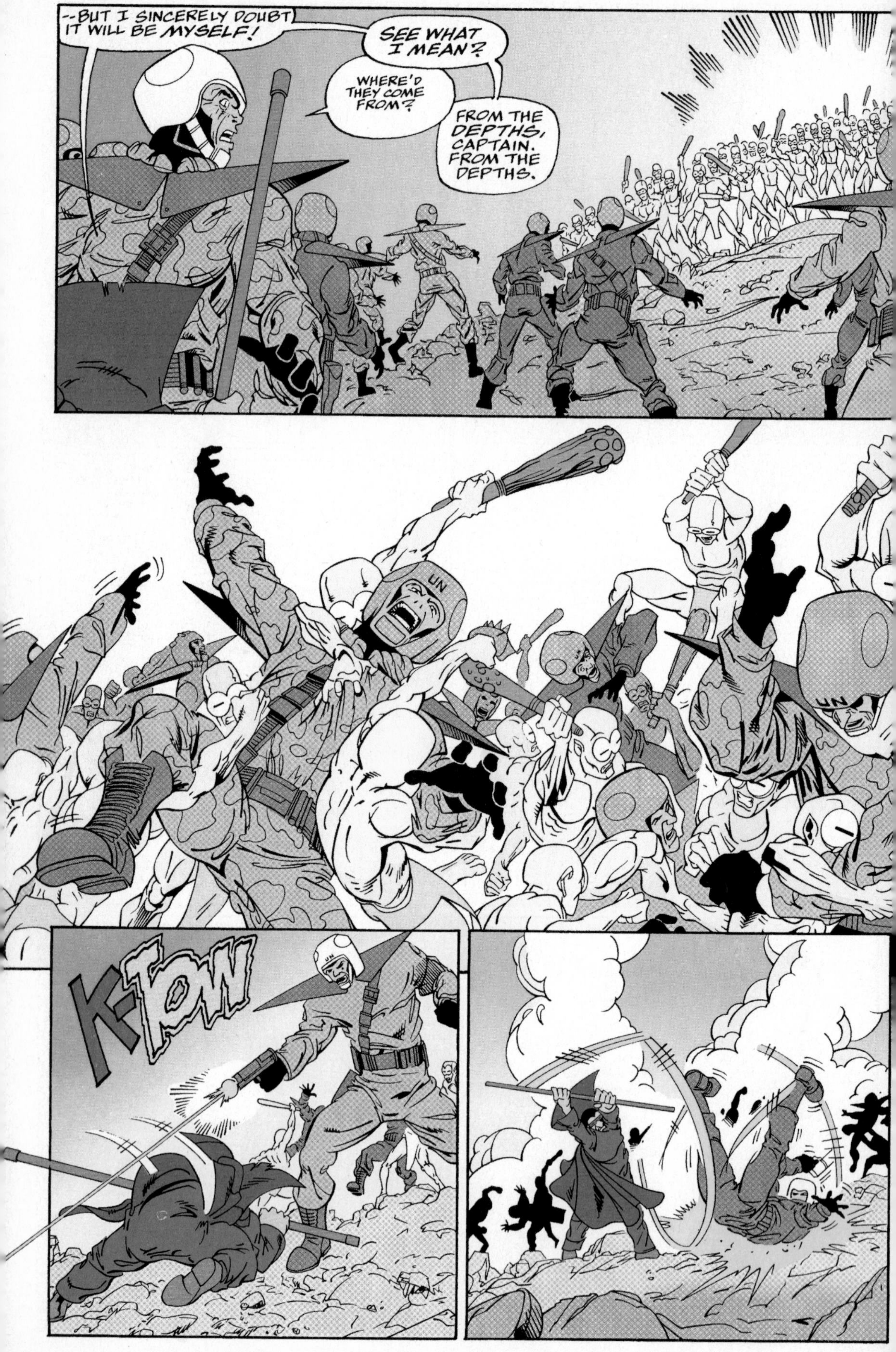
--BUT I SINCERELY DOUBT IT WILL BE MYSELF!
SEE WHAT I MEAN?
WHERE'D THEY COME FROM?
FROM THE DEPTHS, CAPTAIN. FROM THE DEPTHS.
K-TOW

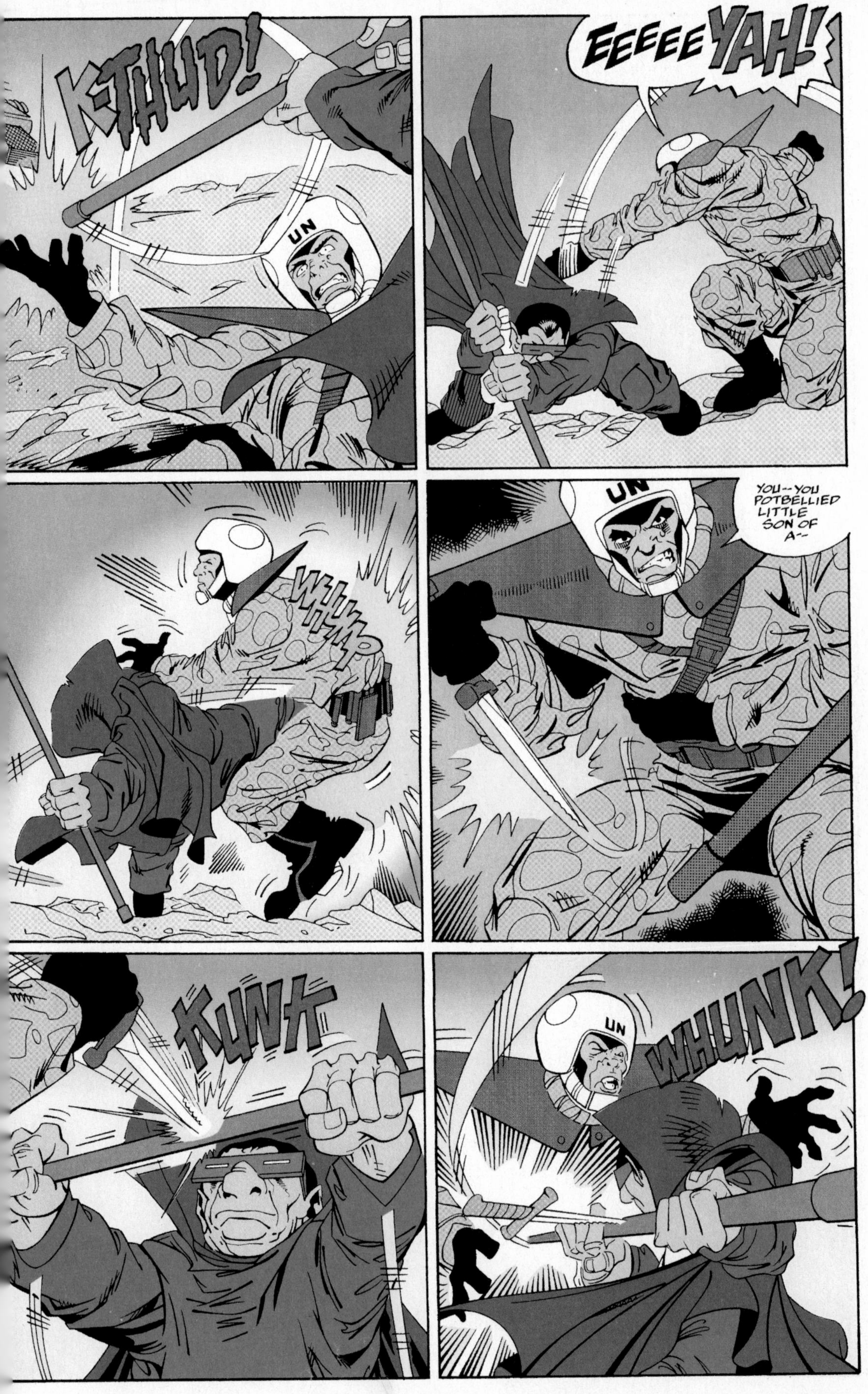
K-THUD!
EEEEEYAH!
WHUMP
YOU--YOU POTBELLIED LITTLE SON OF A--
KUNK
WHUNK!

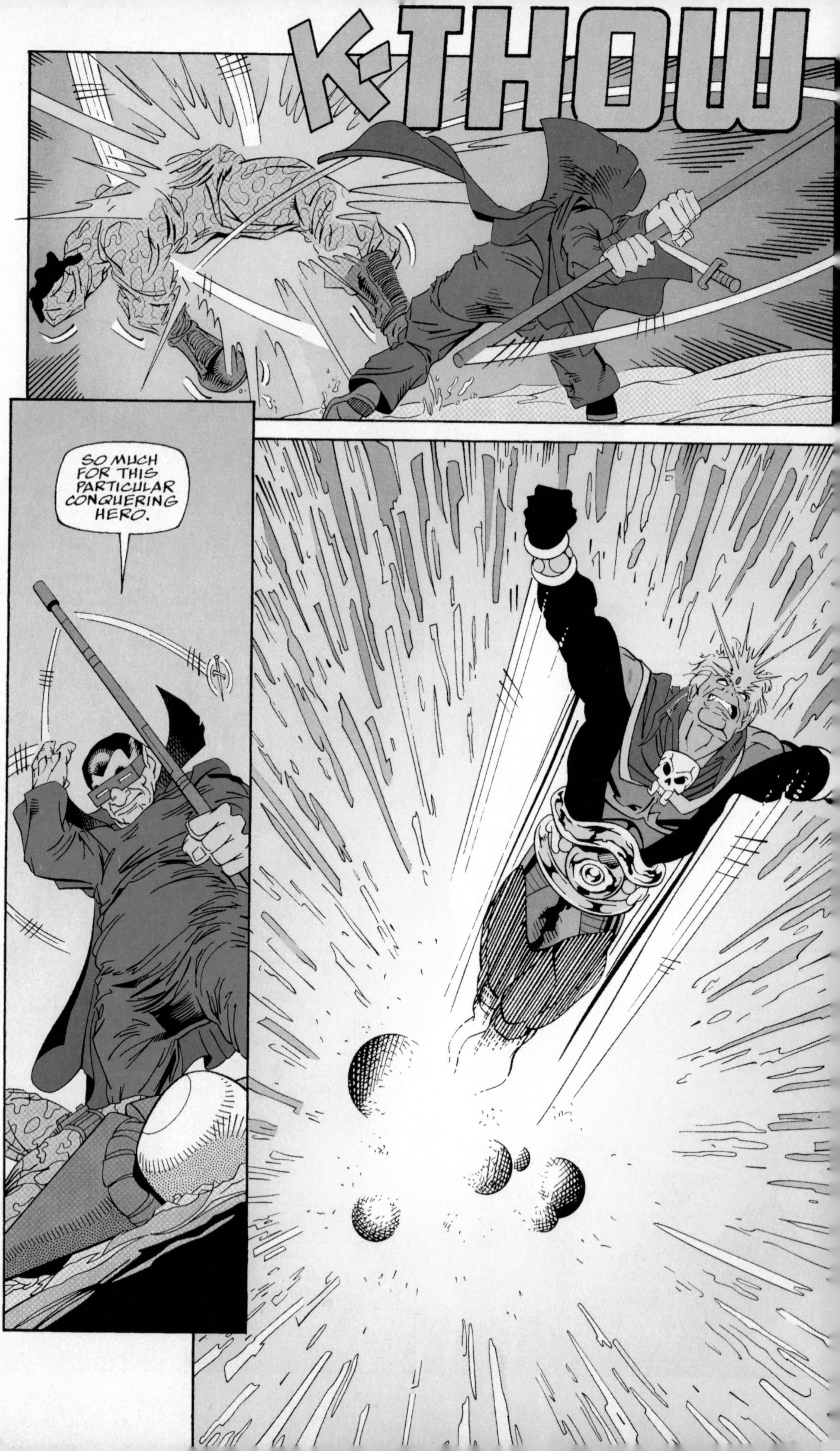
K-THOW
SO MUCH FOR THIS PARTICULAR CONQUERING HERO.

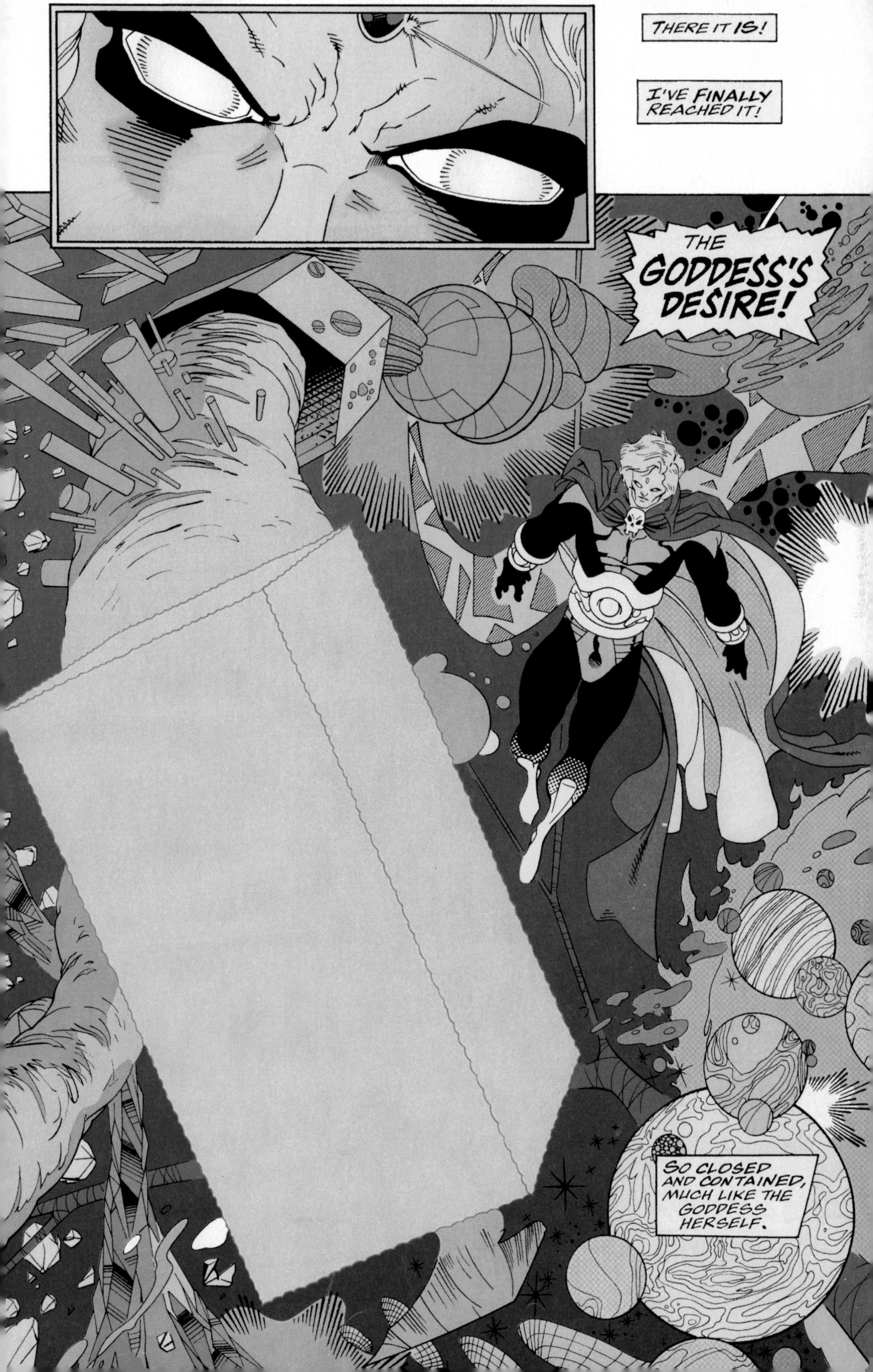
THERE IT IS!
I'VE FINALLY REACHED IT!
THE GODDESS'S DESIRE!
SO CLOSED AND CONTAINED, MUCH LIKE THE GODDESS HERSELF.

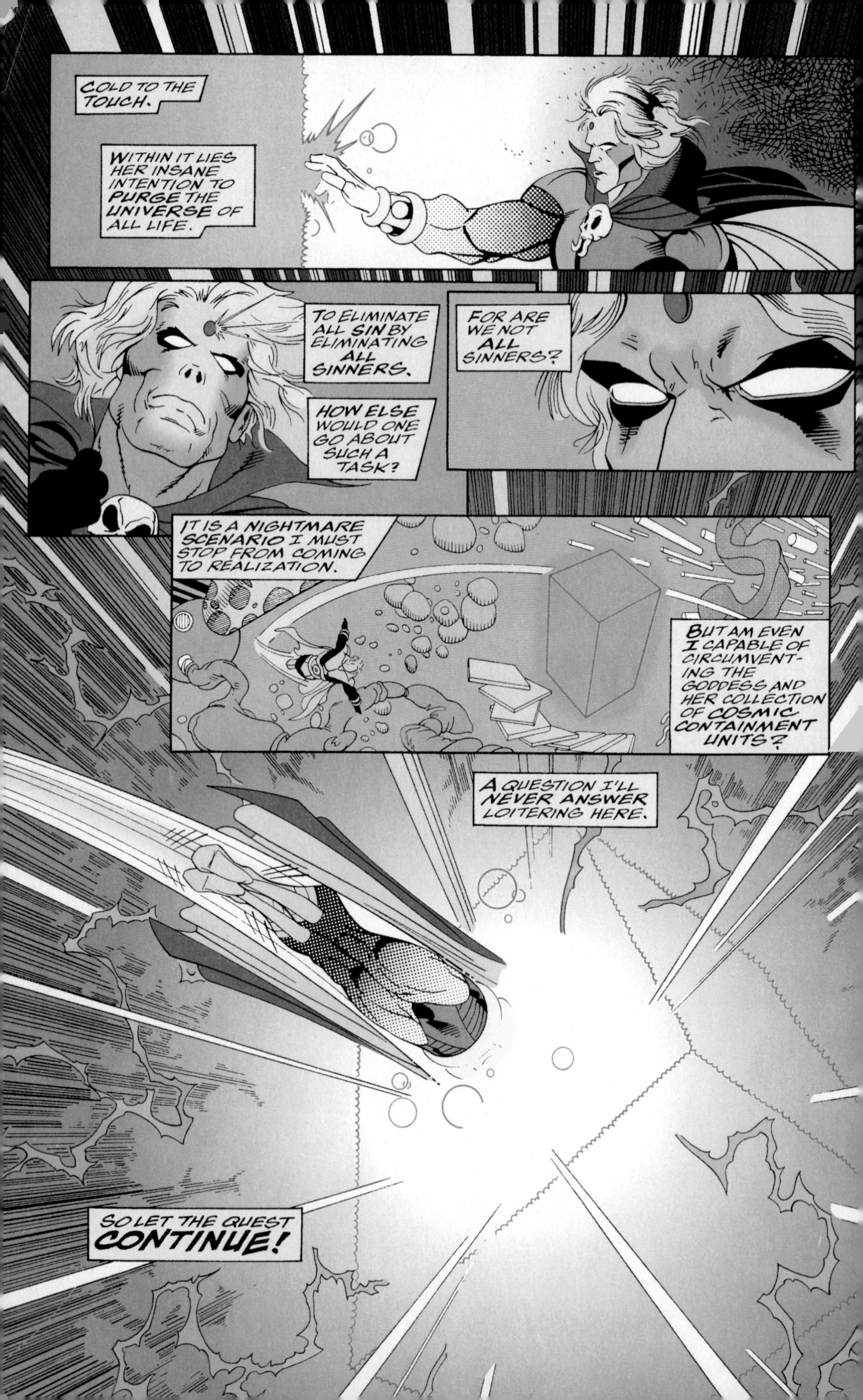
COLD TO THE TOUCH.
WITHIN IT LIES HER INSANE INTENTION TO PURGE THE UNIVERSE OF ALL LIFE.
TO ELIMINATE ALL SIN BY ELIMINATING ALL SINNERS.
HOW ELSE WOULD ONE GO ABOUT SUCH A TASK?
FOR ARE WE NOT ALL SINNERS?
IT IS A NIGHTMARE SCENARIO I MUST STOP FROM COMING TO REALIZATION.
BUT AM EVEN I CAPABLE OF CIRCUMVENTING THE GODDESS AND HER COLLECTION OF COSMIC CONTAINMENT UNITS?
A QUESTION I'LL NEVER ANSWER LOITERING HERE.
SO LET THE QUEST CONTINUE!

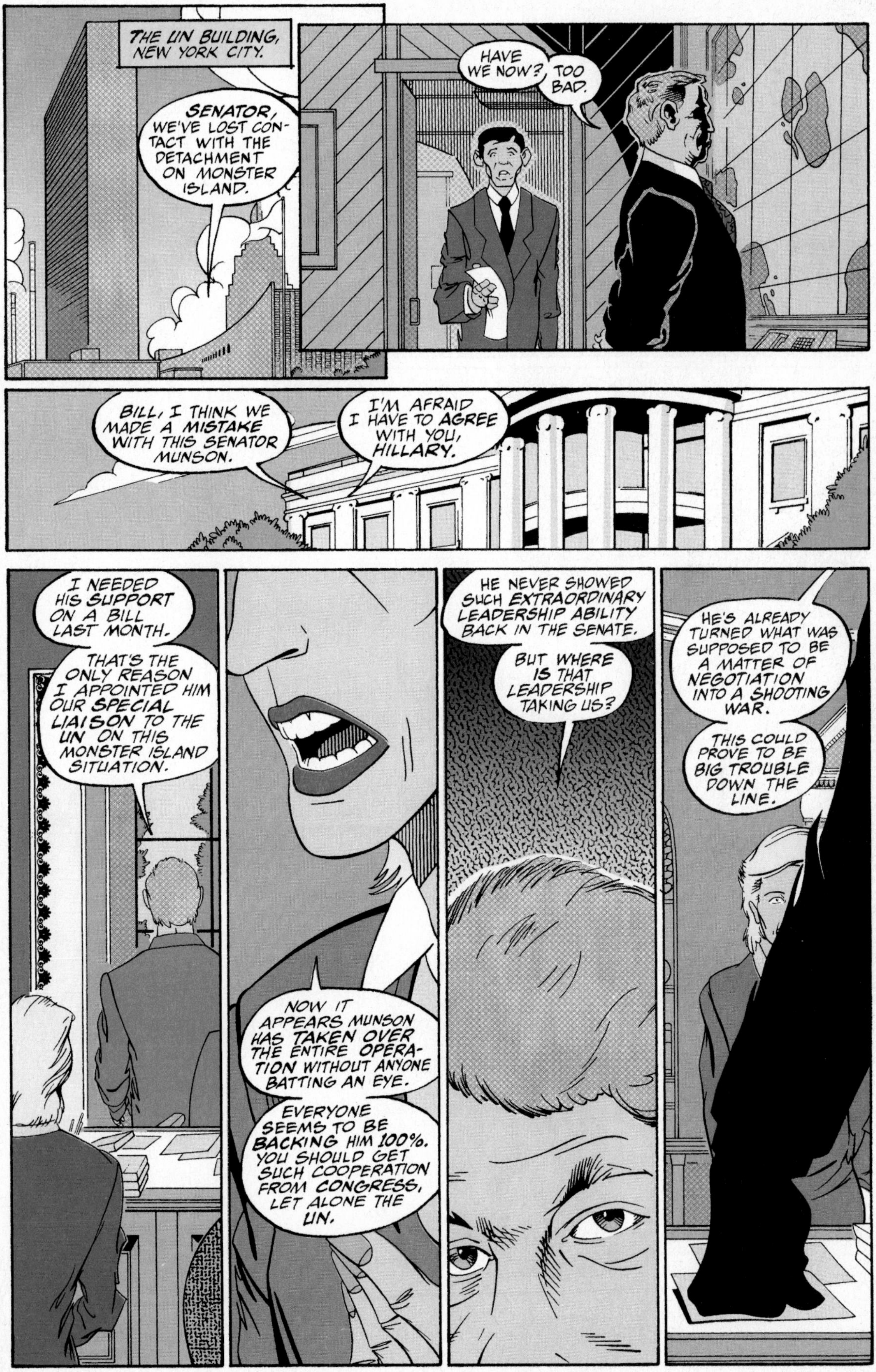
THE UN BUILDING, NEW YORK CITY.
SENATOR, WE'VE LOST CONTACT WITH THE DETACHMENT ON MONSTER ISLAND.
HAVE WE NOW?
TOO BAD.
BILL, I THINK WE MADE A MISTAKE WITH THIS SENATOR MUNSON.
I'M AFRAID I HAVE TO AGREE WITH YOU, HILLARY.
I NEEDED HIS SUPPORT ON A BILL LAST MONTH.
THAT'S THE ONLY REASON I APPOINTED HIM OUR SPECIAL LIAISON TO THE UN ON THIS MONSTER ISLAND SITUATION.
NOW IT APPEARS MUNSON HAS TAKEN OVER THE ENTIRE OPERATION WITHOUT ANYONE BATTING AN EYE.
EVERYONE SEEMS TO BE BACKING HIM 100%. YOU SHOULD GET SUCH COOPERATION FROM CONGRESS, LET ALONE THE UN.
HE NEVER SHOWED SUCH EXTRAORDINARY LEADERSHIP ABILITY BACK IN THE SENATE.
BUT WHERE IS THAT LEADERSHIP TAKING US?
HE'S ALREADY TURNED WHAT WAS SUPPOSED TO BE A MATTER OF NEGOTIATION INTO A SHOOTING WAR.
THIS COULD PROVE TO BE BIG TROUBLE DOWN THE LINE.

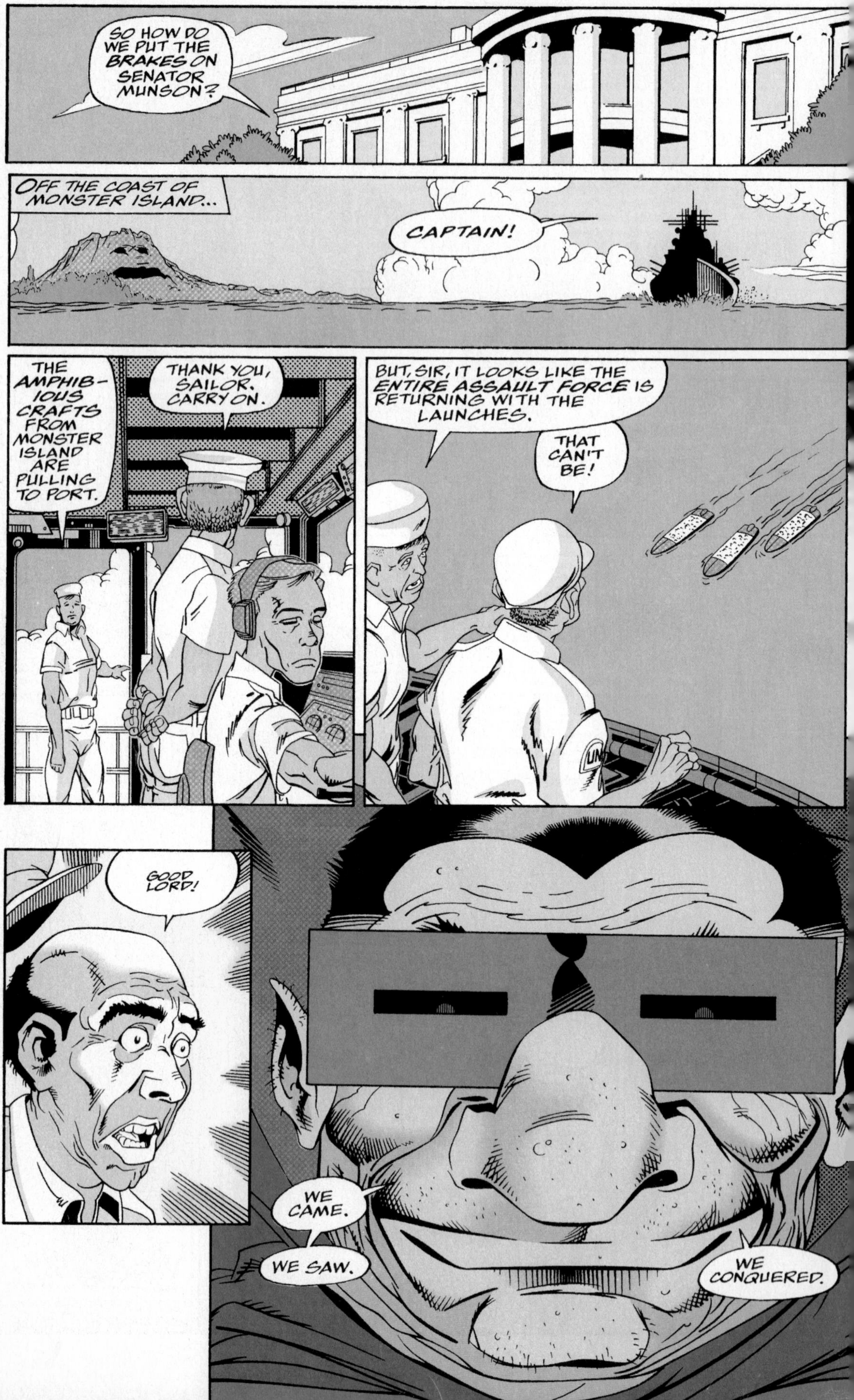

SO HOW DO WE PUT THE BRAKES ON SENATOR MUNSON?
OFF THE COAST OF MONSTER ISLAND...
CAPTAIN!
THE AMPHIBIOUS CRAFTS FROM MONSTER ISLAND ARE PULLING TO PORT.
THANK YOU, SAILOR. CARRY ON.
BUT, SIR, IT LOOKS LIKE THE ENTIRE ASSAULT FORCE IS RETURNING WITH THE LAUNCHES.
THAT CAN'T BE!
GOOD LORD!
WE CAME.
WE SAW.
WE CONQUERED.

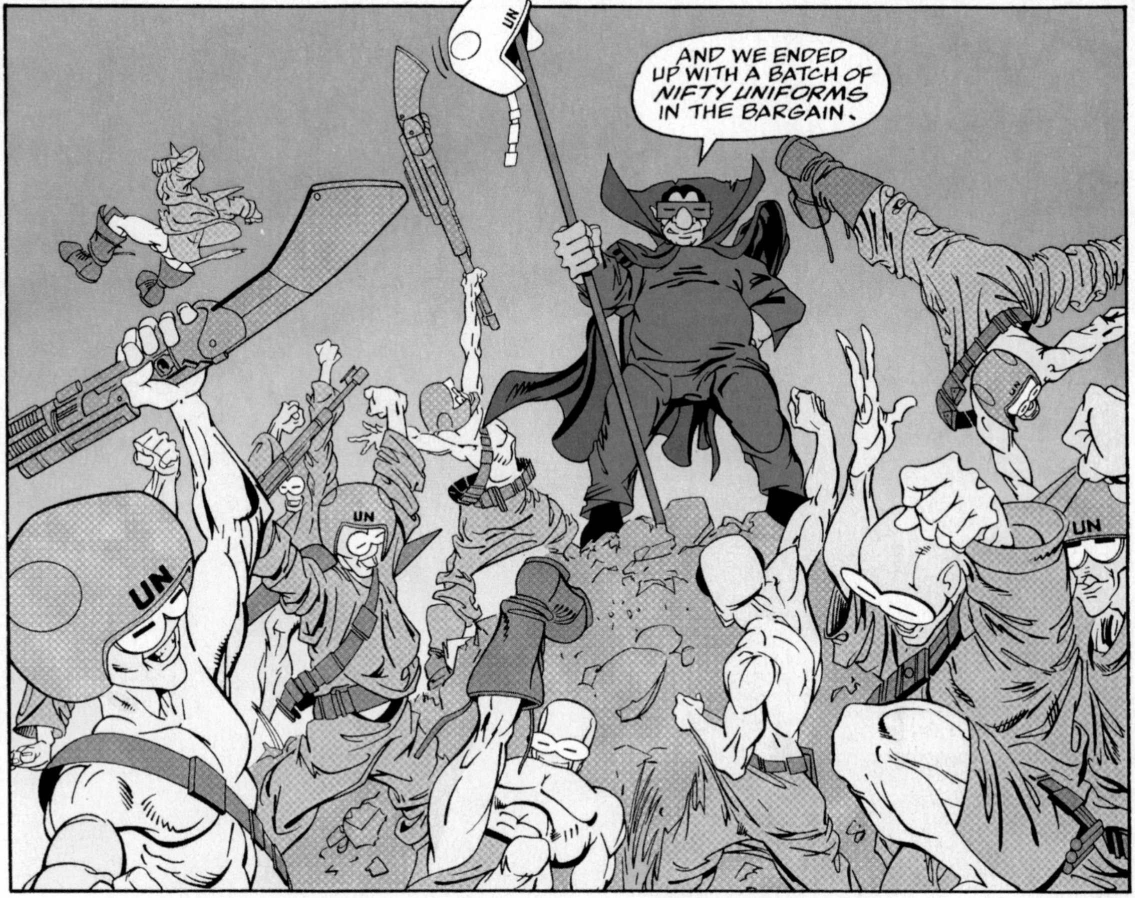
AND WE ENDED UP WITH A BATCH OF NIFTY UNIFORMS IN THE BARGAIN.

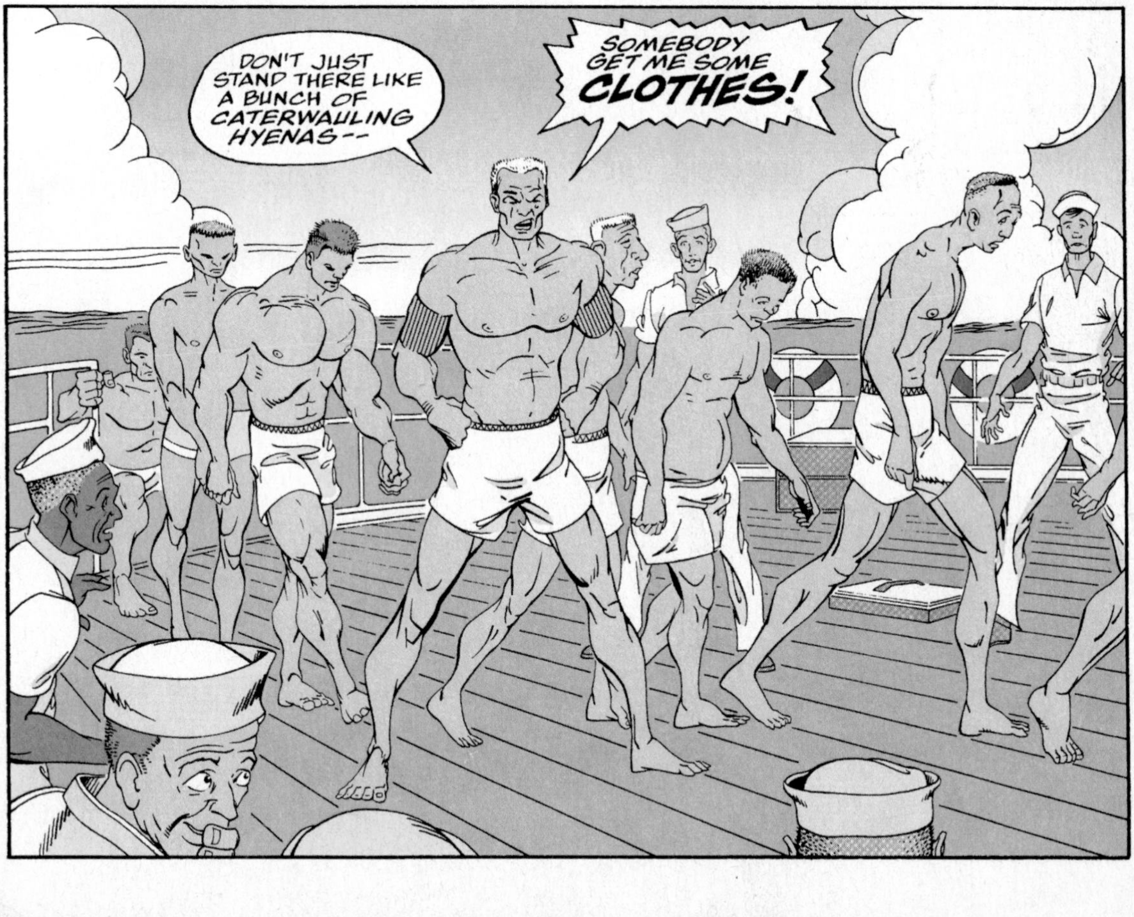
DON'T JUST STAND THERE LIKE A BUNCH OF CATERWAULING HYENAS--
SOMEBODY GET ME SOME CLOTHES!

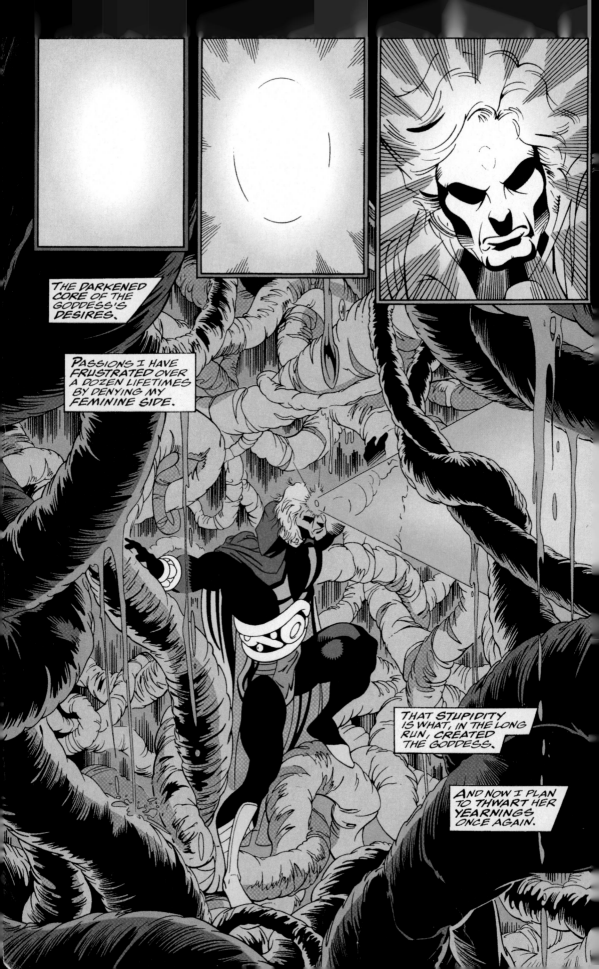

THE DARKENED CORE OF THE GODDESS'S DESIRES.

PASSIONS I HAVE FRUSTRATED OVER A DOZEN LIFETIMES BY DENYING MY FEMININE SIDE.

THAT STUPIDITY IS WHAT, IN THE LONG RUN, CREATED THE GODDESS.

AND NOW I PLAN TO THWART HER YEARNINGS ONCE AGAIN.

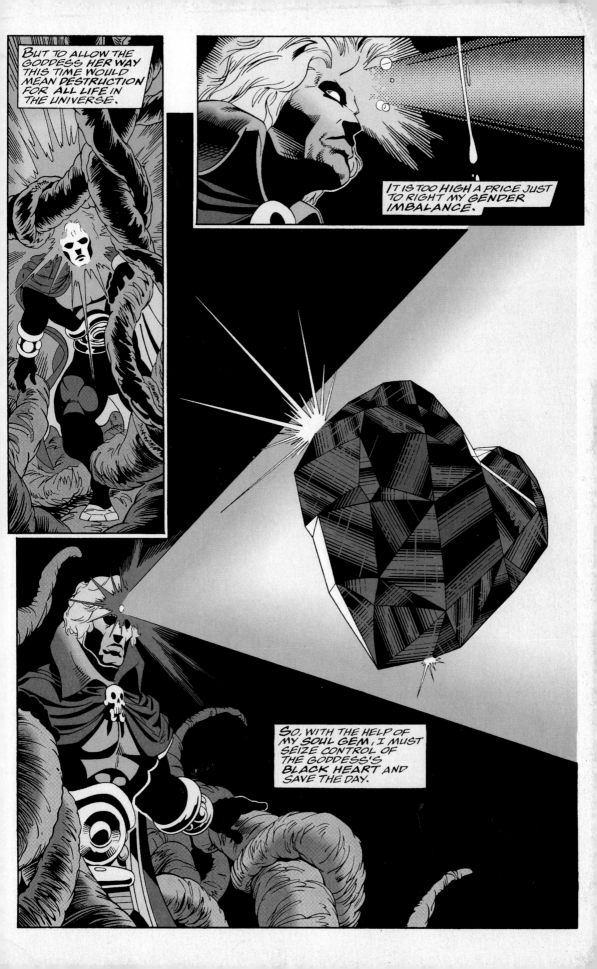

BUT TO ALLOW THE GODDESS HER WAY THIS TIME WOULD MEAN DESTRUCTION FOR ALL LIFE IN THE UNIVERSE.

IT IS TOO HIGH A PRICE JUST TO RIGHT MY GENDER IMBALANCE.

SO, WITH THE HELP OF MY SOUL GEM, I MUST SEIZE CONTROL OF THE GODDESS'S BLACK HEART AND SAVE THE DAY.

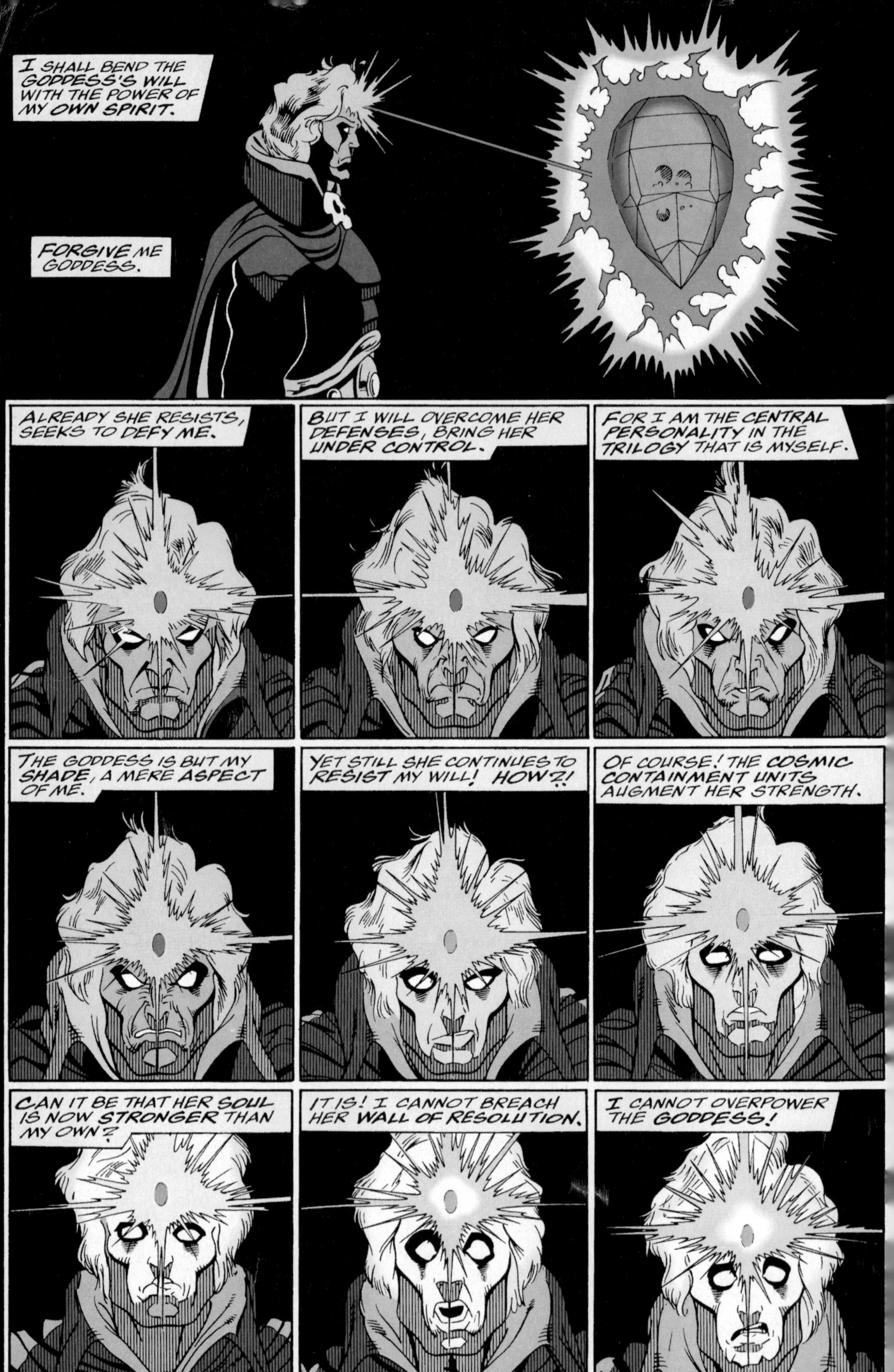
I SHALL BEND THE GODDESS'S WILL WITH THE POWER OF MY OWN SPIRIT.
FORGIVE ME GODDESS.
ALREADY SHE RESISTS, SEEKS TO DEFY ME.
BUT I WILL OVERCOME HER DEFENSES, BRING HER UNDER CONTROL.
FOR I AM THE CENTRAL PERSONALITY IN THE TRILOGY THAT IS MYSELF.
THE GODDESS IS BUT MY SHADE, A MERE ASPECT OF ME.
YET STILL SHE CONTINUES TO RESIST MY WILL! HOW?!
OF COURSE! THE COSMIC CONTAINMENT UNITS AUGMENT HER STRENGTH.
CAN IT BE THAT HER SOUL IS NOW STRONGER THAN MY OWN?
IT IS! I CANNOT BREACH HER WALL OF RESOLUTION.
I CANNOT OVERPOWER THE GODDESS!

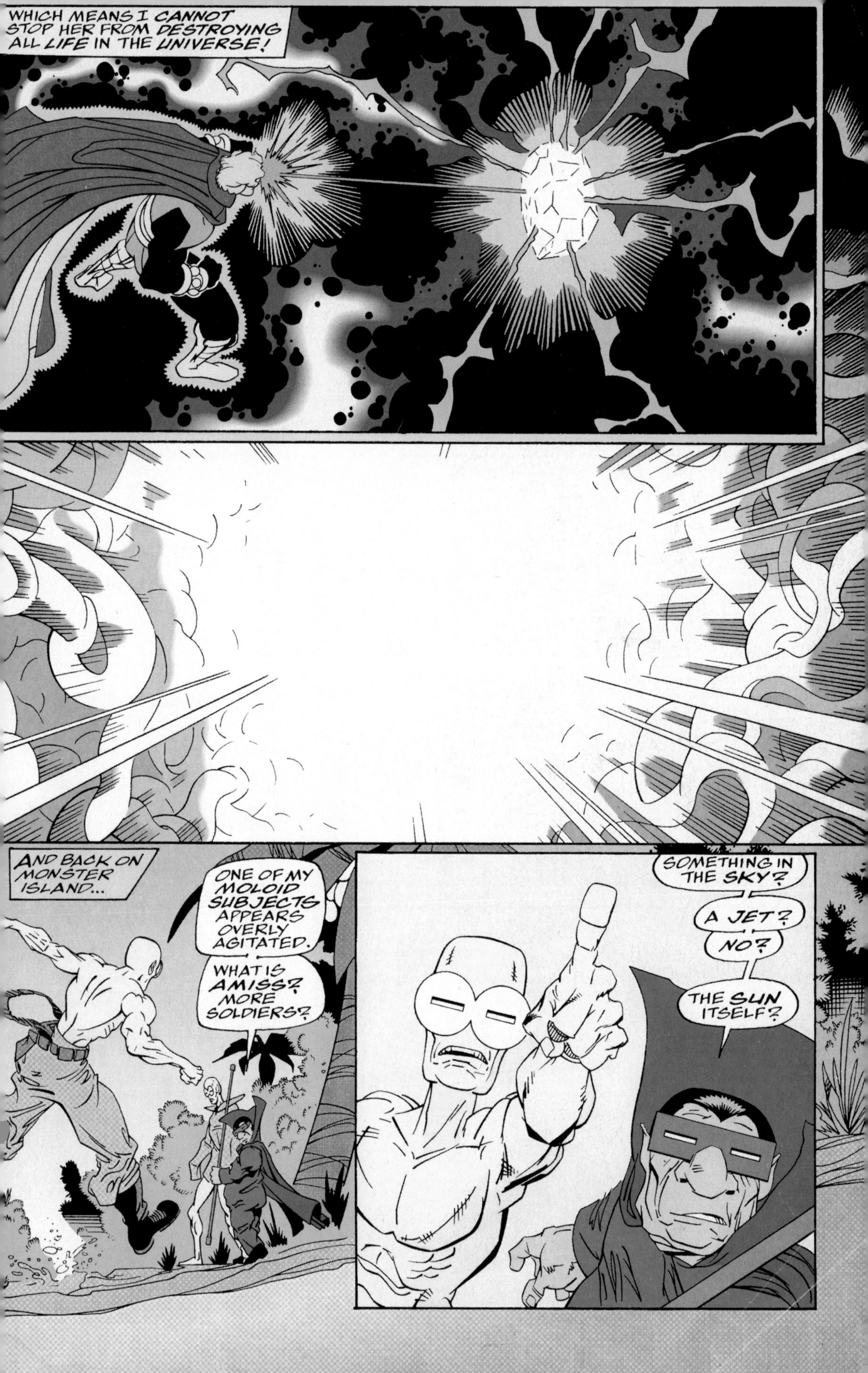
WHICH MEANS I CANNOT STOP HER FROM DESTROYING ALL LIFE IN THE UNIVERSE!
AND BACK ON MONSTER ISLAND...
ONE OF MY MOLOID SUBJECTS APPEARS OVERLY AGITATED.
WHAT IS AMISS? MORE SOLDIERS?
SOMETHING IN THE SKY?
A JET?
NO?
THE SUN ITSELF?

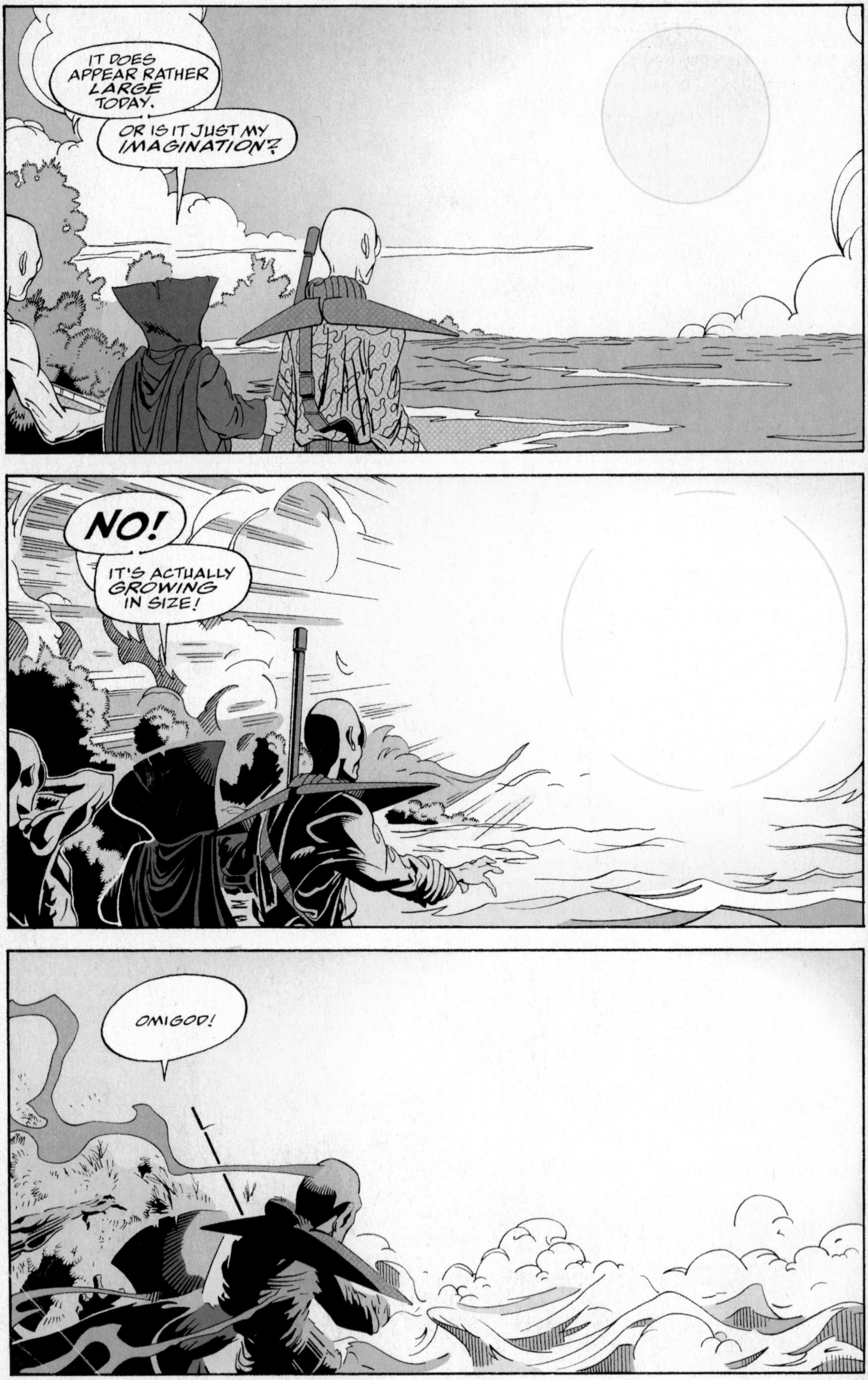
IT DOES APPEAR RATHER LARGE TODAY.
OR IS IT JUST MY IMAGINATION?
NO!
IT'S ACTUALLY GROWING IN SIZE!
OMIGOD!

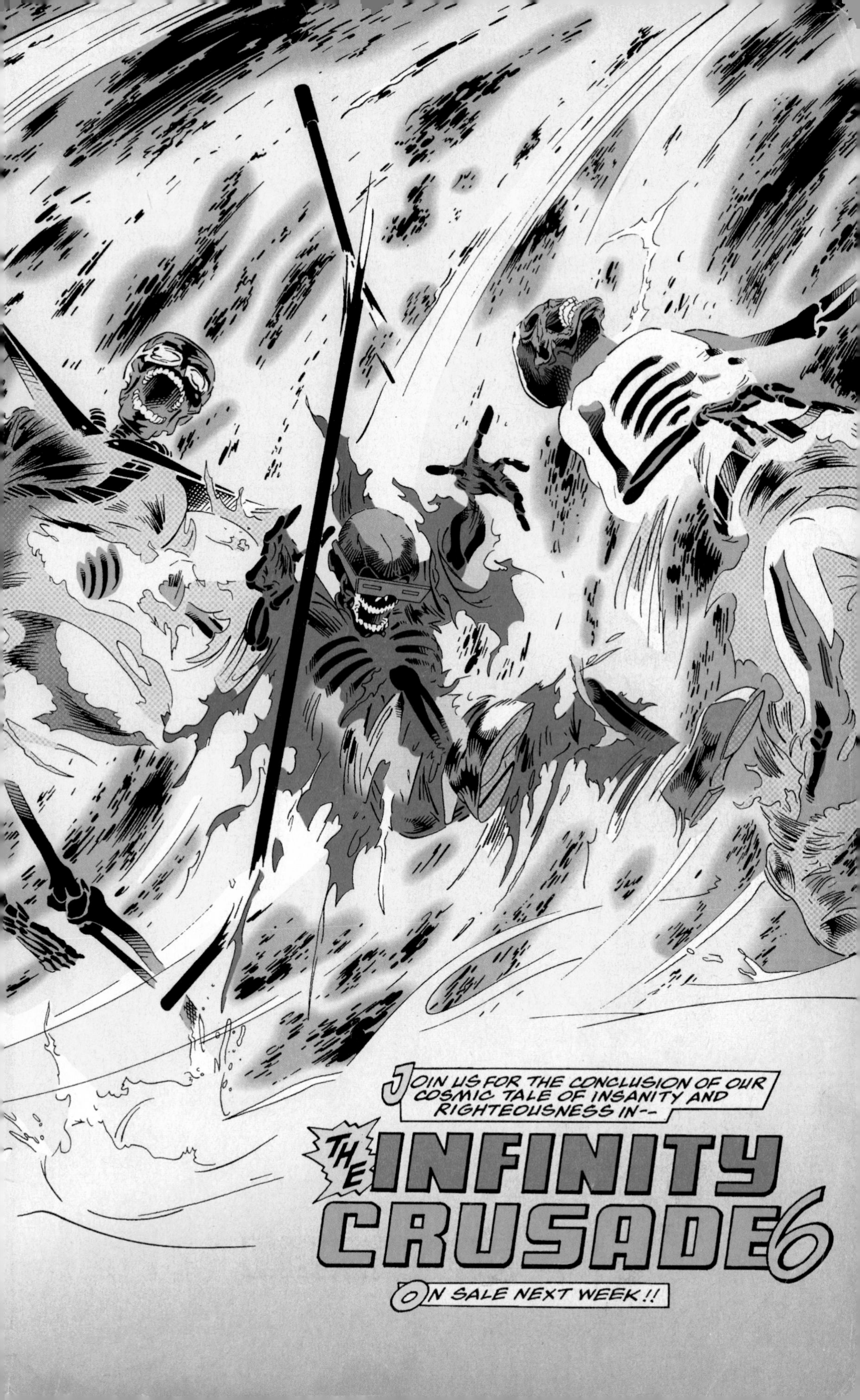
JOIN US FOR THE CONCLUSION OF OUR COSMIC TALE OF INSANITY AND RIGHTEOUSNESS IN--
THE INFINITY CRUSADE 6
ON SALE NEXT WEEK!!

REALIZING THAT THE GODDESS

was about to use the Cosmic Egg to destroy all life in the universe, Adam Warlock took advantage of his location within her psyche — and through her, he had the Egg cast a universe-wide illusion of Armageddon a split second before she would have ordered the actual event.

Once the illusion wore off, the Goddess' followers realized her genocidal intent and lost their faith, weakening her control over the Egg. Warlock battled the Goddess spiritually until Thanos, wielding the Soul Gem, absorbed her into its metaphysical realm. There the Goddess was imprisoned alongside the Magus, and Warlock regained the good and evil aspects that he had previously cast out of himself.

Thanos then commanded the Cosmic Egg to destroy itself so no one else could misuse its power. In the battle's aftermath, Warlock commented that Thanos had carried himself with uncharacteristic honor throughout the entire affair. In fact, it was this long-buried honor that Warlock had detected months before in his omnipotent state, and why he trusted Thanos to carry the most tempting of burdens. For all along, Thanos of Titan had been the secret caretaker of the Reality Gem...

MARVEL
THE INFINITY CRUSADE

MARVEL
THE INFINITY CRUSADE

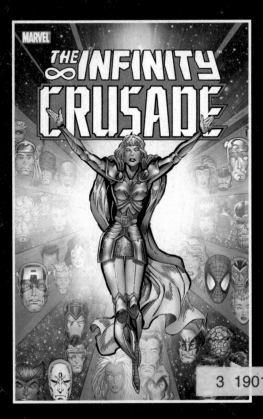

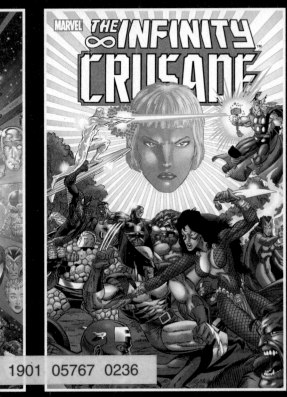